INDEX OF FAMILY AND GROUP NAMES

Roberts' Birds of Southern Africa

by

GORDON LINDSAY MACLEAN

Illustrated by

Kenneth Newman and Geoff Lockwood

Sixth Edition

Published by

The Trustees of the John Voelcker Bird Book Fund

Cape Town

1993

The John Voelcker Bird Book Fund
5 Church Square Cape Town 8001

First published 1940
Second to Fourth editions (1957-1978)
revised by G. R. McLachlan, Ph.D. (Cantab).
and R. Liversidge, Ph.D. (Cape).

Fifth edition 1985
revised by G. L. Maclean, Ph.D (Rhodes) D.Sc. (Natal)
Sixth edition 1993
Second impression 1996

ISBN 0 620 17583 4

Printed by CTP Book Printers, Cape

Dedication

To Cecily Niven

The Trustees of the John Voelcker Bird Book Fund dedicate this Sixth Edition of *Roberts' Birds of Southern Africa* to the memory of the late **Cecily Niven**, D.Sc. (*honoris causa*) (Cape Town), in recognition of her outstanding contributions to the ornithology of southern Africa. Cecily Niven, the daughter of Sir Percy FitzPatrick, was born in London on 19 November 1899 and died at her home, "Amanzi", near Uitenhage in the eastern Cape on 31 May 1992. She joined the South (later Southern) African Ornithological Society in 1935 and served two terms as the Society's President. She became a Trustee of the John Voelcker Bird Book Fund, resigning in 1987 in the belief that she should be replaced by a younger person.

Cecily Niven's interest in professional ornithology led to the establishment of the Percy FitzPatrick Institute of African Ornithology at the University of Cape Town, funded initially by the Percy FitzPatrick Memorial Trust. A further brainchild of hers was the Pan-African Ornithological Congress, which has become a more or less regular event, starting in Livingstone (Zambia) in 1957; the most recent (8th) Pan-African Ornithological Congress was held in October 1992 in Bujumbura (Burundi).

It is a pleasure for us to honour Cecily Niven by dedicating this edition of *Roberts* to her memory.

CONTENTS

CONTENTS

LIST OF COLOUR PLATES

LIST OF COLOUR PLATES (Continued)

LIST OF TEXT FIGURES

LIST OF TABLES

viii

Historical Background to this Book

On 8 June 1940 the now famous book, *The Birds of South Africa*, was published simultaneously in Johannesburg and London. The author was Austin Roberts whose name the book itself has acquired, and which has become a household word in southern Africa. Hardly a home is without its copy of *Roberts*. The book was instantly a bestseller and has been a standard handbook ever since its first appearance.

J. Austin Roberts was born on 3 January 1883 in Pretoria. He received his early schooling at the hands of his father, Archdeacon Alfred Roberts who emigrated to South Africa in 1878. The Roberts family moved to Potchefstroom when Austin Roberts was a teenager, and here he acquired his love of natural history. After working as bank clerk, civil servant and soldier, Austin Roberts went on an expedition to Boror in northern Mozambique with the well known hunter, F.V. Kirby, in 1909. Roberts gave most of his time to collecting birds and small mammals, and on his return to Pretoria in 1910 he obtained a job at the Transvaal Museum, then under the directorship of Dr J.W.B. Gunning, the ornithologist after whom Gunning's Robin was named.

During his 38 years at the Transvaal Museum, Austin Roberts amassed an impressive collection of over 30 000 birds and 13 000 mammals, undertaking many field trips for the purpose. The observations and experience gained on these trips and in his museum work culminated in the publication not only of *The Birds of South Africa*, but also of *The Mammals of South Africa*, published posthumously in 1951, as well as of many papers in scientific journals.

In recognition of his achievements, Roberts received honours from his colleagues. A Carnegie grant in 1934 enabled him to visit Britain and the United States of America. He was awarded an honorary doctorate by the University of Pretoria in 1935, the Captain Scott Medal of the South African Biological Society in 1938 and the Gold Medal and grant of the South African Association for the Advancement of Science in 1940. The Austin Roberts Bird Sanctuary in Pretoria was officially opened by the Mayor of the city on 27 October 1956. It is therefore most fitting that the name of a man whose formal education was not extensive, but whose dedication and enthusiasm were boundless, should be perpetuated in the title of the most important single ornithological book to appear in Africa and one of the most comprehensive for a single region anywhere in the world.

Austin Roberts was killed in a motor accident near Lusikisiki in the Transkei on 5 May 1948; in his time he probably contributed more to the study of birds and mammals in southern Africa than any single person before or since.

In 1957 the first revision of Austin Roberts's *The Birds of South Africa* appeared under the new title of *Roberts Birds of South Africa*. Except for much of the introduction and the accounts of the families of birds, the text was completely rewritten by Drs G.R. McLachlan and R. Liversidge. To Geoff McLachlan and Richard Liversidge southern Africa owes a great debt of gratitude for the way in which they thoroughly reworked the book, making the text easier to read, putting in distribution maps, updating information and producing an outstanding work of ornithology that has remained a model for regional handbooks ever since.

McLachlan and Liversidge drew on their own rich experience of southern African birdlife, as well as on the ever-increasing amount of published ornithological literature, to produce an up-to-date work that could be used by both layperson and professional alike. They prepared two further minor revisions, the first appearing in 1970 and the second in 1978.

With the exception of the 4th Edition for which 31 new colour plates were prepared by Kenneth Newman, all previous editions used the original illustrations by Norman C.K. Lighton, an accomplished draughtsman who was seconded to the Transvaal Museum for the express purpose of painting the birds for Austin Roberts's book. In the

HISTORICAL BACKGROUND

light of present-day knowledge, changing tastes and sophisticated printing techniques, Lighton's paintings have been found to be inadequate; some of them have also been lost or damaged. Kenneth Newman and Geoff Lockwood were therefore selected to illustrate the 5th Edition which appeared in 1985, the text for which was written by Professor Gordon Maclean of the Department of Zoology & Entomology at the University of Natal in Pietermaritzburg.

From its inception publication of *Roberts* has been undertaken by a fund known originally as the South African Bird Book Fund, started by John Voelcker. In 1967 this fund was renamed in memory of its founder and became the John Voelcker Bird Book Fund which is administered by a Board of Trustees, the names of whom are listed after the Dedication on page iii.

Preface to the Sixth Edition

Seven years have passed from the time the Fifth Edition of *Roberts' Birds of Southern Africa* appeared in March 1985 to the time when the text for the Sixth Edition was sent to the printers. Eight years have elapsed between publication of the the Fifth and Sixth Editions. During this period southern African ornithology has made huge strides. Much new information has been accumulated and some of the existing information has been found to be incorrect or at least inadequate for many species of birds. Additions and changes to the text have therefore been necessary, some of them substantial, all of them important.

Under the careful attention of Professor Gordon Maclean, this Sixth Edition of *Roberts* now makes its appearance as the most up-to-date and comprehensive handbook for the subcontinent within the framework of a single volume.

The text for 12 species has undergone a major overhaul: Jackass Penguin, African Crake, Spotted Crake, Ludwig's Bustard, Lesser Jacana, Rock Pratincole, Dune Lark, South African Cliff Swallow, Swynnerton's Robin, Namaqua Warbler (formerly Namaqua Prinia), Paradise Whydah and Broadtailed Paradise Whydah. Sixty percent of all the species have acquired augmented data on measurements, sometimes considerable, especially with regard to sample sizes. Sixteen new species have been added to the southern African avifauna, most of them vagrants, but a few, because of changes in their systematic status, have been upgraded from subspecies to full species. These new species, numbered from 901 upwards are now placed at the end of the book, and are illustrated in the augmented colour Plates 74–77.

The information on identification has been improved for 68 species. Many new sonagrams have been added to the texts of species for which none were available before. Data on distribution have been much improved because of greater awareness among birders and ornithologists, heightened by the Southern African Bird Atlas Project (SABAP) under the auspices of the Southern African Ornithological Society: about half of the existing distribution maps have been updated as a consequence. This has resulted also in a better understanding of the status of many species. About a tenth of the species have augmented sections on habits, reflecting the increasing emphasis on biological observation of birds in southern Africa. For similar reasons, new breeding data have been incorporated into nearly a quarter of the birds in *Roberts*.

Several colour plates have been completely replaced with new plates by Geoff Lockwood, mainly in order to improve some of the illustrations of warblers and flycatchers.

The identification keys are now grouped together before the colour plates, greatly facilitating their use in the field.

German names have been added for the benefit of the many German tourists who visit southern Africa.

The Trustees are proud once again to present the public with a book that is as thoroughly contemporary, accurate and user-friendly as it can be, without departing too far from the admirable tradition established by J. Austin Roberts over 50 years ago. There is still no comparable regional handbook anywhere else in the world.

Everard Read   *4 August 1992*

(Chairman, John Voelcker Bird Book Fund)

List of Sponsors

1 Lorraine Taylor
2 Lorna Roberts
3 Rex M Hilligan
4 Real Estate & Property Services (G Crous)
5 Rian and Les Pauw
6 Francois J van der Merwe
7 Dr and Mrs D G C Presbury
8 I M McK Drummond
9 Rob Armstrong
10 Jörg Blum
11 Anonymous
12 Lynn Hurry
13 Dr Gavin Spowart
14 Edward B L Lightbody
15 Henri and Maureen Viljoen
16 Indian Ocean Export Company (Pty) Ltd
17 William Smith
18 John and Lorraine Larsen
19 Dave and Margie Hidden and Family
20 Johan Marais
21 Peter, Jennifer, Simon and Karen Greaves
22 R M W (Mike) Orchard
23 Dr Jettie-Chipps Webb
24 Derrick Glen Palterman
25 Brian and Lynne McDonogh
26 Herman Meyer
27 Brian and Dawn Livingstone
28 Bruce and Inge Shaw
29 R Bruce Sutherland
30 Darryl L Baxter
31 W A Orrock
32 R J Davies
33 Peter Becker
34 Mike Frampton
35 J D Hepburn
36 Anonymous
37 John S Bentley
38 John and Louise More
39 Val and Tony Jones
40 M J Linnell
41 Rosemarie Breuer
42 Marene and Ron Coote
43 Jack and Robert Koen
44 James McLuskie
45 Trish and Pete Swanepoel
46 Dick and Elize Duncan
47 Robin Yates
48 R D Mattheys
49 Peter and Gaynor Louw
50 Peter J McCulloch
51 Robert B Smith
52 R W Charlton
53 R J Clinton
54 Ian and Karin MacLarty
55 P A Becker
56 Dr Jerzy Przybojewski
57 Graham and Jillian Cox
58 David M Jenkins
59 Jim Gordon
60 Southern African Ornithological Society
61 Aat and Ther van der Dussen
62 Dudley Saville
63 Brian Stott
64 Pat and Mike Buchel
65 Elna and Robert Bachmann
66 Meets, Joe and Colleen
67 John Fellowes
68 Allen, Carol and Andrew Miller
69 Derric H Wilson
70 Dick and Liz van der Jagt
71 Ian, Sue and Kerry Bishop
72 Anonymous
73 Danie, Daniel & Christian Olivier
74 Sally Horne
75 Lenie Franken
76 André Claassen
77 Flanagan, J P D
78 Dawie and Margot Chamberlain
79 Rob Berry
80 Mnr & Mev L B Botha
81 F P Holford Trust
82 Ashmead
83 Dr Eric Horsten and Family
84 Mr and Mrs J J Turner
85 Southern African Ornithological Society
86 Dennis and Ansie Slotow
87 Macintosh, Bruce, Cynthia, Deanne & Gareth
88 Michael Weder
89 Dusan Babich
90 Pat and Karin Goss
91 John S R Edge
92 Jean and Charles du Sautoy
93 Lederle Laboratories
94 Dr D J Gordon-Smith
95 Geoff and Joan Robin
96 Walter Schmid
97 Volker Konrad
98 John and Jill Tresfon
99 Jill and Alan Whyte
100 Fran de Klerk and Vincent Lusted
101 Stegmann, David and Isolde and Family
102 Kathleen Satchwell
103 J J Harris
104 A A Barrell
105 M F Keeley
106 Francioso Family
107 Siegfried J Gross
108 E S C Garner
109 David and Lesley Unite
110 Mr and Mrs Nigel Fernsby

111 K M Peacocke
112 Royden Roche
113 J Willem van der Merwe
114 Grace N Thompson
115 Mrs S J Heyl
116 Harry Freaker
117 Robert W B Hodgson
118 Mr & Mrs R M Pickering
119 Di and Mike Anderson
120 Lowveld Lumber & Pallet CC
121 W Naudé
122 Bob and Elenore Crosbie
123 Luca and Beniamino Pellegrini
124 John and Candy Fraser
125 J S Kirkpatrick
126 Stuart and Clarice Bromfield
127 Bill Adams, Safari Consultants, U K
128 Mr & Mrs Mike Groch
129 Mercedes Rosterg-Eissler
130 D J Elphick
131 G W M van Dusseldorp
132 Eugene Brock
133 Mrs Juditc C E Gottsmann
134 Christine Konz
135 J D Marais
136 Francois van der Merwe
137 Arthian Jones
138 F W Hosken
139 Kevin and Kay Holden
140 Mr G R Allison
141 Ronald S Hart
142 David J Bristow
143 Jerome O'Regan & Alison Dyer
144 M A Traill
145 Michael Weerts
146 Ann Sheard
147 Peter B Ferrett
148 John H Moshal
149 Dr Heimo and Anita Mikkola
150 Chris and Sheila Bester
151 The Hidden Family
152 Nolly and Molly Zaloumis
153 Jimi Mouyis — Happy 40th
154 George and Liz Zaloumis
155 Taeuber, E
156 Sydney and Margaret Reid
157 John and Wendy Milton
158 John Beam Plumbers
159 Cranston F Withers
160 Steve Bales
161 Dr R J Giles
162 Miss C M Potgieter
163 Robert Stein
164 Chris and Estelle Neethling
165 Bob and Elma May
166 John Swinney
167 Mrs Bernadette Peter
168 Sharon Kings
169 Prof. P D Potgieter
170 Dr Walter J Lawson
171 Barry and Janet Sweet
172 Paul and Elaine Magennis
173 Francois and Sharon Malan
174 Leicester Dicey
175 John and June Fannin
176 Geoff Paxton
177 Jopie Müller
178 Dr John B Davies
179 J S Joubert (Jnr)
180 Chris and Liz Hathorn
181 Maj. J E Bishop
182 Don Barrell
183 Mechthild Geiger
184 van Vught, Johan and Lex
185 Peter George Johnson
186 Rob and Chloe Crosbie
187 Mike and Janine Egan
188 Giaco Angelini

List of Subscribers

SUBSCRIBERS

Aubert, Neil
Austen, H E
Austin, John and Margie Phipps
Avery, Graham
Avicultural Research Unit

Badenhorst, F P
Badenhorst, Philip
Baker, Jimmy
Baldwin, Audrey and Roger
Balson, D N and Si
Bamber, Winifred
Banfield, George and Mary
Bantjes, T H (Hein)
Barlow, Pamela
Barnes, B
Barnes, M L
Barnett, Michael J
Barrell, Don
Barry, T J
Basson, M M
Bates, Terry, Sally, Christopher & Jonathan
Bath, David and Cathy
Bebington, Mr & Mrs E R
Beck, N L
Beckbessinger, Lesley
Bednall, D K
Beeton, Frank and Di
Behrens, G W Theo
Behrens, Reinher H
Behrmann, Professor H J
Benfield, Graham and Heather
Beningfield, Diana
Anonymous
Bennett, David and Salomé
Berman, C H
Bernitz, Drs H and Z
Berrisford, M R
Bertram, T H
Bester, D J P
Beukes, Gerard and Joléne
Beumer, Wally
Beyleveldt, Jakobus Arnoldus
Bezuidenhout, Abel
Black, David and Dee
Black, Justin Montgomery
Blaine, Mr & Mrs D A
Bleksley, Cecil and Marian
Bloomer, Anthony G
Blum, Jörg
Boast, Trevor
Boeyens, Jan
Bok, L B
Booth, Richard and Glenda
Boshoff, Willem en Elfriede
Botha, Piet and Petro
Botha, Robert M
Botha, Rudolph
Böttger, H A
Böttger, Walter A

Bourhill, Stephen
Bouwman, Beatrix, Charl en Henk
Bowey, Frank and Hazel
Boy Scouts of South Africa — Northern Rovers
Braatvedt, Mr & Mrs K J
Bramwell-Jones, Mr & Mrs T H
Brandt, Dieter and Susan
Breedt, T F
Brian Musto Attorneys
Brink, P A
Britten, Stephen
Britton, T
Brittz, J du P
Brodie, Gordon and Penny
Bronkhorst, Hannes, Magda and Jean
Brook, Hilton
Broom, Dave and Lynne
Brown, Ian
Brown, Roy and Maureen
Brunner, Waldi and Jutta
Anonymous
Bryant, John
Buchanan, Buck and Diana
Buckle, M G
Buckmaster, Paddy
Bullen, Gerald and Karen
Burman, B W
Burnett, N R
Burton, Grant and Marie Holstenson
Butler, Rhett
Byron, Charles A

Cabaco, Maria
Cadman, Ann and Radclyffe
Cadman, M C and L J Levetan
Cain, Anthony C
Cain, Alan and Marylynne
Calder, D R
Cameron, Virginia
Camp, Kelson
Campbell, Mr & Mrs A M A
Campbell, Duncan and Annette
Campbell, D E F
Candiotes, George
Cannon, Sean, Marta, Sergio & Marco
Cantle, Bruce, Clare and Dustin
Capell, R L
Carman, Edward
Carolin, Ellmine
Carolin-Fiorotto, Charmain
Caulton, Jean and Mark
Chambers, John and Dorothy
Claassen, Japie en Ralie
Clark, Alan and Julia
Clarke, Mary and Brian
Clayson, Mr & Mrs Ted
Anonymous
Cleugh, Marian
Cloete, Bruce

xiv

Cloete, Ruth Elsie
Cloete, Sue and Johnno
Cochrane-Murray, Grant Campbell
Cochrane-Murray, Douglas Charles
Cockbain, General T G E
Cockburn, Kevin
Coetzee, Deon
Coetzee, Johann and Steph
Anonymous
Anonymous
Coetzee, Kurtis
Cohen, Michelle F
Cole, Desmond T
Cole, Pam
Collins, Luke and Tania
Colquhoun, Alister
Colquhoun, Okkie
Connor, M L
Conradie, H D
Constable, Neville I
Cook, Peter and Carol
Cooper, Mark
Cooper, The late Robert Lloyd Stuart
Cordell, Ian and Glenis
Corder, D A
Coy, Anton
Craig, A J F K
Crane, Dr A J
Craven, Dan and Pat
Crawford, Cavin
Crawford, J L
Crewe, Robin
Crisford, Rodney Charles
Croft, Raymond B
Cronjé, Pieter
Crookes, Mrs D
Crosbie, Mr C D
Crosbie, Mike and Shane
Cross, Robert and Lucille
Crossley, Barry
Crouse, David and Bernice & Family
Cruikshank, R B A
Currell, Andrew
Cyrus, Digby and Rose

Dabbs, Simon, Lynne, Andrew, Catherine
  & Lucinda
Daneel, Garth
Davies, Professor Bryan
Davies, Dr David
Davis, Patricia
Davis, Stephen B
Davis, Timothy Oliver
Davison, Andrea and Candice
Davison, G
de Beer, Sam en Ralda
de Figueiredo, Florinda e Amandio
de Figueiredo, Ivone Marina T
Anonymous
de Jager, Dr J L W

de Jong, P F
De Klerk, Louis W
de Klerk, Riann
de Lange, C A
de Munnik, Evert and Annemarie
de Villiers, J C (Kay)
de Viliers, Jake
de Villiers, Jake
de Villiers, Reenen
de Wit, Jan
Deacon, Dr C
Dearmer, G
Dedekind, Hartwig
Deetlefs, Guy
Dench, John and Vee
Denman, E B
Dennill, Michael
Descroizilles, Noel
Dicey, Leicester
Dinkelmann, Patricia and Peter
Ditz, Peter and Carol
Dixon, R A and S A
Doherty, J S
Donaldson, Claude and Grant
Donn Products (Pty) Ltd
Donn Products (Pty) Ltd
Dott, Andy
Dott, Nigel and Sandra
Douglas, Dr Robert E
Dow, P B
Driver, M W
Driver, M W
Drummond, I M McK
du Plessis, N L
du Plessis, René and Joyce
du Toit, André
du Toit, C J H
du Toit, Fanus and Dalene
du Toit, Rean F
Duck, Peter R
Drumbrill, Graham
Dunlop, G R
Dunnill Jones, Colleen
Dunscombe, P C
Dusterhoft, Andre and Nanetie
Dutton, Alan
Dykhouse, Joan

Eastern Cape Wild Bird Society
Edwards, Miss Margaret I
Eksteen, A O
Ellmer, Arno
Ellway, Mr J
Emberton, Barry
Engelbrecht, J C (Koot)
Eustace, Michael
Evans, David
Evans, F Neil
Evans, F Neil
Evans, F Neil

SUBSCRIBERS

Evans, W G A
Everard, Charles H B
Evitts, Andrew

F P Holford Trust
F B Holford Trust
Faber, Ina
Faber, J
Farina, T D W
Farquhar, Pauline
Farrant, John and Wendy
Farrant, John and Wendy
Featherstone, J G
Fenn, Laurence
Fergusson, Mr & Mrs A J F
Fernandes-Costa, F J
Ferrett, Peter B
Ffoulkes, Sharon and Mike
Fincati, G L
Findlay, A
Fisher, Alan and Yvonne
Fisher, N M A
Fletcher, P W
Foggo, S
Forder, P A
Forsberg, Kevin John
Forsyth, Anthony
Fourie, T
Fourways High School
Fowler, L R
Fowler, R L
Francioso Family
Francis, Tony
Frankish, Timothy
Fraser, Kim, Anne, Megan and David
Fredericksz, Nick
Friederich, Mrs M G
Frizelle, H W
Froneman, Albert
Frylinck, John P
Frylinck, Ronelle and Franz Werndle
Fulton, Derek and Liz
Fussell, A H and Mrs A Fussell

Gage, Bryce W
Gamble, Frances
Gamsu, Robert
Gani, Dr Mahomed Iqbal
Ganis, Mervyn
Gant, Jack
Garbutt, Jack
Gernot, E L
Geyer, Hendrik en Jane
Gibson, Barrie and Pam
Gibson, Maaike
Giese, Dave, Carol, Caron and Mark
Gillatt, Joe
Ginn, Peter J
Glaefke, S
Glenday, B S

Glenton, Jon
Glenton, Louise
Glynn, Claudia
Glynn, W E R
Goerbert, F R
Goetsch, Diana
Good, Yvonne
Goott, Mel
Gordon, Neale
Gosnell, Jerry
Goss, Pat and Karin
Goulding, Dr and Mrs K C
Gourley, J E
Gouws, Harald
Grabandt, Maarten and Sheryl
Gradwell, Dudley, Annemarie, Lynnmarie, Andor
Graham, Joan and Alastair
Graham, J A C
Granat, Claude
Grant, Mike and Kathy
Grant, Neil
Greene, S W
Greene, S W
Greyling, J
Greyling, P
Grieve, G K A and J
Griffin, R E and M
Griffioen, M
Griffith, Gertie and Ken
Griffiths, Nicky
Grobbelaar, Johann
Grobbelaar, Michal
Grobler, D C
Grobler, Gerhardus P J
Groch, Kate
Groenewoud, Maggie
Group Five Ltd
Group Five Ltd
Group Five Ltd
Guerin, Brian
Guthrie, Iain Andrew

H L & H Timber Products
Haasbroek, F T and C M
Hadfield, Janet
Haggie, Dawn
Hall, Anthony and Bernie
Hall, Dorothy G
Halton, R G
Hammond, Dr Christopher A
Hampton, R F
Hanaczeck, Helmut and Family
Hapelt, E I
Harding, Mrs Roz
Hardy, Charles and Lois
Harris, Andrew
Harris, Eddie, Liz and Ansel
Harrison, Colin and Margaret
Hartshorne, Keith and Penny

Hattingh, Ray and Julie
Hattingh, Trevor
Hawarden, Judith
Hay, Gordon and Susan
Hearn, Mr P
Hedge, Tessa
Henderson, E A
Henning, Alta
Herd, Jenny
Heritage, Mike, Kathy, Bernard & Tracy
Heritage, Mike, Kathy, Bernard & Tracy
Hes, A D
Hydenrych, G
Heyns, Helena
Heyns, Juan and Errie
Hicks, Julian
Hill, Diane and David
Hinrichsen, Etienne
Hirst, Brian
Hitchins, Peter
Hodes, P B
Hodgkinson, E A
Hoets, Dilys
Hoets, N v R
Hoffman, Hannes
Hofland, Willem
Hofmeyr, Mr & Mrs A H
Hoile, Margaret
Holley, M N H
Holliday, Andrew C
Holmes, D C G
Holtshausen, Gordon and Corinne
Home, John F and Family
Hope, Duncan
Hope, W L
Hoppe, Mr & Mrs G E
Hörne, Mrs T
Horton, Jim and Anne
Howie, Craig and Claerwen
Huggett, Richard
Hughes, John and Margaret
Hughes, Laurence
Hulett, Neil
Hulley, E J
Humphreys, Clive W
Huntley, Ian B
Huskisson, Lynn
Hutton Truck Hire
Hutton Truck Hire

Indian Ocean Export Company (Pty) Ltd
Indian Ocean Export Company (Pty) Ltd
Indian Ocean Export Company
Irving, T J
Isherwood, H B
Anonymous

Jaeger, H–G A
Jagger, Diana and Richard
James, June

Japp, R G
Jardine, C L and R A
Jardine, D H and E E
Jarvis, K G
Jarvis, Mrs S
Jarvis, Mr & Mrs V F
Jearey, Dave (In lasting memory)
Jelk, Arnold and C
Jenner, V S
Jones, C D
Jones, Ron and Mandy
Jones Ayre, H C A R F
Anonymous
Jordan, Inez
Jørgensen, G
Josi, Marco and Michelle
Joubert, Prof. D M
Joubert, Ryk
Junod, S M

Kahn, Hillel M
Kahn, Sidney H
Käsner, Paul and Vicki
Kasselt, R — Th
Kay, Mike and Leigh
Keet, J H
Kemsley, Deane
Kendall, R J
Kerr, Gordon Hugh
Key, Charles G
Kidson, Mrs S C
Kimmince, E S
King, D L
Kip, S and H
Kirchmann, Gail and Brian
Kirkwood, Craig
Kloppers, Johan
Klugman, Leon and Pauline
Klussmann, H–D
Knott, David G
Knowles, D J
Koegelenberg, D E
Koen, Julius H
Kohler, N G
Korten, J B A
Kotze, At and Elna
Kreher, Nora
Krige, J D
Kristal, Errol and Denise
Krone, Franci and Mariaan
Krsic, Mrs S M
Kwa Maritane Game Lodge

Laidler, Dennis and Gigi
Laing, June and John
Lamont, Gavin
Langford, B G
Lanham, C A
Lardner-Burke, John and Di
Laubscher, Dries

SUBSCRIBERS

Laubscher, Julia
Lavery, Barry
Lawrence, R
Lawrie, R M
le Grange, Graham and Marie
le Grange, Graham and Marie
le Grange, Graham and Marie
le Quartier Francais
le Roux, Danie and Irene
le Roux, Eugene M D
Leach, Charles and Bev
Ledgard, Sylvia
Lee, A W
Lee, Dr C A
Leggat, Neil and Anne
Leimer, Rob and Janine
Lewis, I D
Lex Hollmann Trust
Lianshulu Lodge
Lindsay, Lionel
Livesey, Johan and Liz
Lloyd, Anne and Ieuan
Lockwood, Geoff
Lohrke, Dr B
Lombard, Dr & Mrs J
Lorimer, Gill and Rupert
Lötter, Joan
Louw, David and Patsy
Louw, David and Patsy
LPM Chemicals (Pty) Ltd
Luck, H
Ludeke, Nicole
Ludeke, Rick
Lupton, James
Luyt, David, Lesley, Warren and Jessica
Lyall, David

Maakal, Christo
MacDonald, Ann and Peter
MacDonald, Ian and Susan
MacDonald, Scott and Karen
Machin, H R
Mackinlay, Patricia M
Maclean, Cherie
Madden, Stan
Mair, Mrs Lyn
Mair, Dr Mike
Maker, Alan
Malherbe, Dr André P
Maltby, Charles
Marais, Andre and Ann
Marais, Mr J J
Maree, C S M
Marinus, V
Marsch, D R and Family
Marshall, Dr P R
Martin, Rowan
Martin, Saxon and Felicity
Martin, Saxon and Felicity
Marx, André

Matterson, Mrs N V H
Matthis, T J C
Maxwell, Dan
Maynier, L C
McBurnie, Heather
McCann, L G
McCarthy, P M
McCormick, Brian
McCormick, N S R
McCracken, Professor and Mrs D P
McDermid, Rona B
McDonald, B
McDonald, Ron
McGill, Mrs E A (Libby)
McIlleron, Geoff
McIntyre, Bob and Ena
McKendrick, Malcolm and Sheila
McKenna, Kerry Ann
McKersie, J W
McLachlan, Dave
McLeod, David
McLeod, D F S
McLoughlin, Mark
Meaker, Louis and Johanna
Melck, C A
Meredith, Margaret
Mettam, N H
Mettler CMM, Luke A
Meyer, Janette and Willie
Meyrick, Vaughan and Jenny
Michaux, André
Mike Bailes Associates
Millar, G A
Miller, I J
Millet, Geoff and Rosalyn
Milliken, Trisha and Colin
Millin, Peter
Mills, Richard
Milton, Eileen and Ian
Mitchell, Brian
Mitchell, Charles Robert
Mitchell, Duncan
Mizon, Rupert — Bredasdorp
Moerdyk, Alida
Moffett, Rob
Moffett, Rod and Di
Monfoort, K and B L
Moore, Mr & Mrs Ian
Moore, Rory, Ann, Penny & Phillipa
Moore, Rev Robert H
Moran, Mr Chris N
Morris, M N
Morrison, Vere C
Mortimer, Jill
Morton, M G
Moshal, John H
Moss, Sharon Lynda
Mostert, Pieter K N
Mourant Family
Mouton, Bunty

Mudd, R A
Muller, Charles
Müller, Peter
Muller, W O A
Mullinder, B
Mun-Gavin, Mr & Mrs C I
Munn, A C O
Munro, Neil
Murrell, Clive
Mylrea, W J
Mylrea, W J

Nabarro, David
Nathoo, Dr J C
Naudé, Paul and Moira
Needle, M R Q
Neethling, Chris en Estelle
Nel, Andries
Nel, Chris and Ann
Nel, Elias and Liza
Nel, Hans and Leonie
Nelson, Gwyneth
Neser, Walter
Nevill, Mr & Mrs H
Nicholls, J T W
Nicol, Bill and Pam
Nightingale, M E
Nightingale, M E
Nilsson, Mr P
Noakes, Stephen
North East Cape Forests
Notten, Gilly and Bambi
Nourse, Timothy
Noyce, Michael
Nusser, Conrad Georg Ernst
Nutt, Dr D J
Nutt, Eric Eugene
Nyenes, Peter and Lyn

O'Reilly, David and Margaret
O'Reilly, Stephen and Donna
Ochse, James H
Oertel, B
Ogilvie, Adrian
Olivier, Herman, Alta, Marnus en Anna-
  Marie
Olivier, H L
Olivier, Willie and Sandra
Oppenheimer, N F
Oppenheimer, N F
Orpen, John and Molly
Orpen, Mr T J
Osborne, Dave and Margie

Palmer, Geoff and Ann
Parfitt, Otto and Sheila
Parr, Rosemary
Patterson, Miss Claire
Patz, Dr and Mrs I M
Pauw, Rian and Les

Payne, Robert B
Pearce, John Edward
Pearse, John and Jeannine
Penning, Peter
Penzhorn, Banie en Naomie
Penzhorn, Manfred
Peplow, Paul and Della
Pereira, Johnny
Perkins, Neville
Persse, Dave ·
Pet, Mr & Mrs J M
Pfister, H P
Pickering, Avonne
Piek, P Clifton
Pienaar, Herbert and Cynthia
Pienaar, Herbert and Cynthia
Platt, Ann L
Podmore, Kevin and Glynis & Family
Pogulis, E A
Powell, Ronnie
Powell, S R
Prentice, George and Sally
Prince, J W
Pringle, V L
Prinsloo, Dr Fransie R
Prinzinger, Prof. Dr Roland
Proudman, H
Prozesky, Prof. O W

Quinton Smith, O

Raats, W P J
Raijmakers, Kobie and Edith
Raijmakers, Shonie, Ria and Johan
Raikes, A R
Rall, Heather and Tony
Randell, John and Moira
Ranger, Pamela, Bryan and Peter
Raubenheimer, Dr & Mrs H J
Raubenheimer, W J
Rauch, Dr & Mrs R N L
Rautenbach, D F and L
Redtenbacher, Miss N
Reed, Graham and Joan
Reed, Dallas
Rees, D H F H
Reeves-Moore, P
Reichholf, Josef H
Reid, Mr & Mrs J F
Reid, Sydney and Margaret
Reinartz, H and R
Reniers, W A C
Renwick, L A
Repsold, Hetta en Reppies
Reus, Erica (Ms)
Revell, Scott Keith
Richardson, Bruce
Richardson, Geoff
Richardson, Howard
Richter, Muriel B

SUBSCRIBERS

Rickards, Bob and Morelle
Ridley, Allan
Riley, Adam
Riley, Dr John
Ritchie, Derek Christian
Ritz, Tilmann and Mara — Nigel
Robb, Roswitha and Derek
Roberts, Charles
Roberts, Dr Des
Roberts, Vincent Paul
Robertson, David
Robinson, Bridget and Richard
Robinson, Charles V N
Robinson, G B
Robinson, John
Roche, Christopher
Rodel, K G
Rogers, Neville John
Rollo, Ken and Marie
Romeyn, Philip and Leonie
Rookmaaker, L C
Roos, Prof. C J
Roosendaal, Alan and Dera
Rösch, T W
Ross-Munro, Mr & Mrs A D
Rossiter, Dr & Mrs J B
Rossouw, Dr Z A
Roth, Mr K J
Roux, Johan
Rowan, Gary K
Rowley, Joeleen
Rushworth, Paul D
Russell, Thembi
Ryan, Sean and Carol and Family

Safari Consultants, U K
Safari Consultants, U K
Safari Consultants, U K
Safari Consultants, U K
Safari Consultants, U K
Sales, W
Salkow, G W
Salzwedel, Muriel
Samways, Michael J
Sanders, Michael
Sanderson-Smith, Ian
Sandler, Atholl and Maureen
Satchel, Robert and Christine
Sauer, E H
Saunders, Dr Colin R
Saville, Dudley
Saville, Noel R
Schijf, Hazel and Rick
Schneider, Carl F
Schneier, S M
Scholtz, G D and M A
Schroeder, Jannie
Schroeder, Ruth A
Schutte, M
Schutz, Hans and Ute

Schwegler, W
Scott, Mrs F A
Scott, Mr J G
Scott, Jennifer P
Scott-Ronaldson, G E
Scott-Ronaldson, Keith and Karin
Seal, M R
Seaton, A St. Leger
Segal, N C
Segal, N C
Selikowitz, Gary
Selikowitz, Glen
Selikowitz, Selwyn and Wendy
Sellmann, Roy
Semple, Rob and Andrew
Senger, Hildred
Serezro, Susan R
Shall, Jacqueline
Shand, Cyril
Sharp, Alan
Sheehan, Dave and Pam and Family
Siebert, Henry, Jane, Erin, Burghen
Sievers, J F K
Silbernagl, Peter and Suzette
Slavik, Dalibor, Sharon and Lauren
Slotow, Leon and Rochie
Smailes, D M
Smale, G H
Smith, I A
Smith, Mark Derek
Smith, P A
Smith, Mrs S G
Smuts, Michiel and Morag
Smuts, Michiel and Morag
Smuts, Peter
Snyman, J J
Soames, Carol and Chris
Soames, Carol and Chris
Sobey, Maureen and John
Sowry, Lorna
Sowry, Richard
Soyka, Joachim
Spence, W I
Spencer, Derek William
Sprenger de Rover, R L
Springett, Margaret and Derek
Sprott, Archie
Squelch, Andrew and Joan
St. John-Ward, Carey
Stack, Wald and Lilla
Stainthorpe, A L
Stammer, Uschi and Günther
Stanton, Craig Douglas and Eurydice
Stark, John
Stark, W A
Starr, Angela
Stathoulis, Basil
Stathoulis, John Peter
Steenkamp, Johan
Steer, Rob and Glynis

Stegmann, Andrew
Stegmann, David and Isolde and Family
Stegmann, Heidi
Stegmann, Nicolas
Stekhoven, Jan and Ann
Stenvert, Menno and Krysia
Sterk, Uli
Stewart, Hugo
Stewart, Robert Guy
Stewart, Robert Murray
Steyn, Alteny
Steyn, Charl
Steyn, G J and N M
Steytler, Dr J C S
Stiglingh, Johan and Olga
Stipinovich, Joe
Stone, Mrs N M
Storm, Dr A
Stott, Christopher and Carolle
Stowe, John G
Stowell, Catherine
Strachan, M G W
Stratten, Nancy
Stratten, Nancy
Street, B and C
Stricker, W A
Strobos, Johannes and Leonore
Strydom, Casper and Avril
Strydom, Dr H N
Stuart, Marie
Stuart, Pauline
Styles, Christopher and Marielle
Styles, Tom and Lorna
Sülter, D
Summersgill, Colin
Summersgill, Dennis
Summersgill, Peter
Sussman, Quentin
Sutherland, Andrew C
Swanepoel, Wessel
Swart, S P
Swift, P J
Sykes, Peter Michael
Szabo, Peter
Szecsei, Lajos and Margie

Taeuber, E
Takis Family
Takis Family
Takis Family
Tarr, Grant
Taylor, A J P
Taylor, D H
Taylor, Vincent and Pam
Tedder, Colin and Ann
Tennant, John
Thackray, Eddie and Stella
The Image Bank
The Otters
The Wildlife Conservation Co (Pty) Ltd

The Wildlife Conservation Co (Pty) Ltd
Theron, Annettie
Anonymous
Thomas, Bill and Peggy
Thomas, I G
Thompson, A O
Thompson, Hugh
Thompson, Lu and Peter
Thomson, Jim and Iris
Thomson, Capt. M St. J
Tindall, Caroline S
Tindall, Mark A
Todd, M
Traill, Michael D
Triegaardt, Stefan
Tsampiras, Tino and Denise
Tucker, Colin Kidger
Tucker, Mark Kidger
Twaddle, I G
"Twiddie"
"Twiddie"
"Twiddie"
"Twiddie"
"Twiddie"
Twine, Doug and Guntie
Tyrrell, Dr & Mrs J C

Uys, Prof. C J

van Beuningen, Janine
van Bruggen, Dr A C
van de Vyver, H E
van den Berg, Prof. A D P
van den Berg, H D
van den Bogaerde, Jennifer
v d Helm, Anthony and Marianna
v d Helm, Jack and Mavis (Witbank)
    Pieter F
van der Merwe, Hanneke
van der Merwe, J J
van der Merwe, M J R
van der Sandt, Johan and Annatjie
van der Spuy, Ian and Shauna
van der Walt, Dr & Mrs A P
van der Walt, Charl
van der Walt, Lynette
Fam. G van Dijk — Durbanville
van Dyk, Alison
van Dyk, Jacobus
van Heerden, Diana
van Huyssteen, N F C
van Pletsen, E G
van Rensburg, Frik
van Rensburg, Dr Niek and Carien
van Rhyn, Mej A M
van Rijswijck, M and M A
van Staden, Stéphan
van Steenderen-Zeeman, Mrs J
van Vuuren, John
van Wulven, Mr E

SUBSCRIBERS

van Wyk, Attie
van Wyk, Marius and Lenette
van Wyk, Peter A
van Zijl, Helm and Gill
van Zwieten, Axel
van Zyl, Gigi
Vance, A v d M
Venter, Freek and Rinza
Vercoe, Howard G
Verstraete, F J M
Vervoort, Pieter and Nadine
Vickery, Mrs H J
Vigar, J M
Viljoen, Henri and Maureen
Viljoen, Henri and Maureen
Visser Diedrich
Vlok, Etienne and Susann
Volkmann, M J and W E
Volkmann, M J and W E
von Glehn, Eric
von Ludwiger, Ute
Vorster, Marlene

Wacker, Karl and Yankee
Wagner, G W
Wakely-Smith, Rex and Ethne
Walker, Lindsay and Gail
Wallace, Fiona Jean
Walter, Brian C
Walters, Errol and Marge
Walters, Pauline and Wally
Ward, Denzil
Ward, Sue and Martin
Warnes, Bill and Moira
Waterson, Rory Q
Watson, Derek, Tina
Watson, G
Webb, Trevor
Webster, Dave
Webster, J V
Weeds, Frederick D

Weldrick, June
Wessels, Dudley and Aletta
Wessels, Frank (Boetie)
West, D A
Weyers, Joan
Wheeler, Gill
Whitehouse, Paul
Whyte, I J
Wiese, Frik and Marlene
Wilken, Albert
Wilkins, Les and Yvonne
Williams, Geraldine and Alastair
Williams, Jumbo
Williams, M D
Willies, A P
Wilson, Andy and Daphne
Wilson, Derric H
Wilson, Hardy E
Wilson, John and Carol
Wilson, Nick and Carol
Wimble, D C S
Winch, Graham
Winkler, B C
Winkler, Gunter
Winkler, M A
Winkler, Ruth
Withinshaw, Dr G S
Wolhuter, H B
Wood, Patrick, Clare, Graham & Anne
Wood, V H
Woodcock, E J
Woodroffe, Brian

Yaldwyn, R S
York, Rowland
Young, Ross
Yule, Jake and Heather

Zaayman, J
Zamparini, Giordano and Delmarie
Zinn, Dr Albert

xxii

INTRODUCTION

GEOGRAPHICAL COVERAGE

Roberts' birds of southern Africa covers the entire geographical region south of the Kunene, Okavango and Zambezi Rivers, that is to say the political entities of South Africa (including the Black homelands), Lesotho, Swaziland, Botswana, Zimbabwe, Namibia and the Mozambique districts of Sul do Save, Manica e Sofala and the part of Tete south of the Zambezi River. The region is ecologically diverse, but detailed treatment of the major habitats in southern Africa is dealt with under a separate heading.

AVIAN SYSTEMATICS AND NOMENCLATURE

Birds are vertebrate animals belonging to the Class Aves, characterized by the possession of feathers. Along with the mammals, reptiles, amphibians and fishes they share the characteristics of a bony or cartilaginous skeleton, a skull, and two pairs of limbs or appendages (unless, as in the case of the snakes and some lizards, these have been secondarily lost); these classes together form the subphylum Vertebrata or Craniata. This subphylum in turn belongs to the phylum Chordata, with which are grouped various animals like the seasquirts, salps and larvaceans whose larvae, at least, have some features in common with primitive or embryonic vertebrates, such as gill slits, a tail, a dorsal nerve cord and most notably the notochord, a semi-rigid dorsal rod that foreshadows the backbone or vertebral column of the Vertebrata. Inasmuch as the birds can be grouped with other animals into larger groups, so can they be subdivided within the Class Aves into subgroups, the smallest workable unit of which is the species.

A species is a group of organisms sharing a great many genetic features, and interbreeding with each other under normal conditions, but not normally interbreeding with other species. Thus one finds among sparrows the House Sparrow, the Cape Sparrow, the Greyheaded Sparrow and a number of others, clearly different from one another and seldom if ever interbreeding. Yet these sparrows are just as clearly similar to one another and are all placed in the genus *Passer*: their scientific names are, respectively, *Passer domesticus, Passer melanurus* and *Passer griseus*. These scientific names, mostly of Latin or Greek origin, or else latinized versions of some other origin, are used internationally, no matter what language the speaker or publication is using at the time; they are therefore an extremely practical kind of label for use between scientists of different language groups. The first part of the name, *Passer*, is the generic name, the second part, *melanurus*, is the specific name. *Passer melanurus* is called a binomial, a system first proposed by Carl Linnaeus in 1758. Where a species can be divided into two or more geographical races, separable by size, coloration, voice or some other measurable characteristic, each race can be given a third name (a trinomial) to indicate its distinctiveness, such as *Passer melanurus damarensis* for the Cape Sparrow population in the dry western parts of southern Africa. In this case the first population to be described becomes the "nominate" race, *Passer melanurus melanurus*. These races are also called subspecies, but they will not usually be dealt with in the text of this revision, unless races are easily distinguishable in the field (or in the hand in the case of some Palaearctic migrants). Subspecies do not form full species, since they intergrade and interbreed at the edges of their ranges. By definition, a species should not interbreed with any other good species with which it normally comes into contact.

The genus *Passer* is clearly related to other genera, such as *Petronia, Ploceus, Plocepasser* and so on. Related genera are grouped into families, in this case the family Ploceidae. Some families have well defined groups of genera within them, sometimes deserving of the rank of subfamily; thus the true weavers belong to the subfamily Ploceinae, the sparrows to the subfamily Passerinae, and so on. Related families in turn may be grouped into or ders. All the orders of birds form the Class Aves. To summarize then, a Cape Sparrow from the southwestern Cape would be classified into the following series of systematic groupings (or taxa, singular taxon):

CLASS Aves
  ORDER Passeriformes
    SUBORDER Oscines
      FAMILY Ploceidae
        SUBFAMILY Passerinae
          GENUS *Passer*
            SPECIES *melanurus*
              SUBSPECIES *melanurus*

Since most subspecies are seldom identifiably different in the field, they have been omitted from this edition of *Roberts*. The whole range of southern African subspecies and their geographical ranges can be found in the *S.A.O.S. Checklist of southern African birds* (P.A. Clancey, 1980, Southern African Ornithological Society) and in its two Updating Reports (1987 and 1992).

In the text, each order and family is introduced by a paragraph giving its technical diagnosis in broad terms. The sizes of birds in the family and order accounts are given in four categories: small (less than 20 cm total body length), medium (20–40 cm), large (40–70 cm) and very large (more than 70 cm total length). In the species accounts, however, terms like large, medium and small are used relative to other members of the same family, and do not apply to the size ranges in the family accounts. Sometimes suborders and subfamilies are also diagnosed where this has been considered necessary or helpful. These major taxa are numbered serially by orders (1., 2., etc.), then by families within orders (1.1., 1.2., etc.) and, where relevant, by subfamilies within families (1.1.1., 1.1.2., etc.). This gives the reader some idea of the number of orders in the southern African avifauna, and the number of families in a given order. These diagnoses are printed across the page in single-column width to distinguish them from the species accounts which are printed in double columns.

The classification of the Cape Sparrow above, shows that it is a member of the order Passeriformes, the largest order of birds including over half the known species in the world, and commonly known as the *passerines*. For a diagnosis of the Passeriformes see page 421. Increasing familiarity with the groups of birds within the different orders will help one to get a feel of which are passerines and which are non-passerines. It is convenient to divide the non-passerines into non-passerines in the narrowest sense, and the near-passerines which form a sort of shadow-group between them and the passerines. These three major subdivisions are shown in Table 1, from which it is clear that

Table 1. Southern African birds families and their main habitats
Part A: NON-PASSERINES (Plates 1-33, 74, 75, 76)

Family	Main habitat
Ostrich (Struthionidae)	ground
Penguins (Spheniscidae)	aquatic (marine)
Grebes, Dabchick (Podicipedidae)	aquatic (inland, marine)
Albatrosses (Diomedeidae)	aquatic (marine)
Petrels, prions, shearwaters (Procellariidae)	aquatic (marine)
Storm petrels (Oceanitidae)	aquatic (marine)
Tropicbirds (Phaethontidae)	aquatic (marine)
Pelicans (Pelecanidae)	aquatic (inland, marine)
Gannets, boobies (Sulidae)	aquatic (marine)
Cormorants (Phalacrocoracidae)	aquatic (inland, marine)

Table 1
Part A: NON-PASSERINES (Cont.)

Family	Main habitat
Darter (Anhingidae)	aquatic (inland)
Frigatebirds (Fregatidae)	aquatic, aerial (marine)
Herons, egrets, bitterns (Ardeidae)	aquatic (inland, marine), ground
Hamerkop (Scopidae)	aquatic (inland)
Shoebill (Balaenicipitidae)	aquatic (inland)
Storks (Ciconiidae)	aquatic (inland), ground
Ibises, spoonbill (Plataleidae)	aquatic (inland), ground
Flamingos (Phoenicopteridae)	aquatic (inland, marine)
Ducks, geese (Anatidae)	aquatic (inland)
Secretarybird (Sagittariidae)	ground
***Vultures, kites, eagles, buzzards, harriers, hawks** (Accipitridae)	arboreal, cliff
***Osprey** (Pandionidae)	aquatic (inland, marine)
***Falcons, kestrels** (Falconidae)	arboreal, cliff
Francolins, quails (Phasianidae)	ground
Guineafowl (Numididae)	ground
Buttonquails (Turnicidae)	ground
Cranes (Gruidae)	aquatic (inland), ground
Rails, crakes, moorhens, flufftails, coot (Rallidae)	aquatic (inland), ground
Finfoots (Heliornithidae)	aquatic (inland)
Bustards, korhaans (Otididae)	ground
†**Jacanas** (Jacanidae)	aquatic (inland)
†**Painted snipes** (Rostratulidae)	aquatic (inland)
†**Oystercatchers** (Haematopodidae)	aquatic (marine)
†**Plovers** (Charadriidae)	aquatic (inland, marine), ground
†**Sandpipers, curlews, snipes, phalaropes, etc. (="waders")** (Scolopacidae)	aquatic (inland, marine)
†**Avocets, stilts** (Recurvirostridae)	aquatic (inland, marine)
†**Crab Plover** (Dromadidae)	aquatic (marine)
†**Dikkops** (Burhinidae)	aquatic (inland, marine), ground
†**Coursers, pratincoles** (Glareolidae)	ground
†**Sheathbills** (Chionididae)	aquatic (marine), ground
Skuas, gulls, terns (Laridae)	aquatic (marine, inland)
Skimmers (Rynchopidae)	aquatic (inland)
Sandgrouse (Pteroclidae)	ground
Pigeons, doves (Columbidae)	arboreal, ground

*Diurnal raptors (day-hunting birds of prey: see key on page liv)
†These 10 families comprise the systematic group called the WADERS (as distinct from other longlegged wading birds). The term WADERS may also be confined to the family Scolopacidae (sandpipers, snipes, curlews, phalaropes, etc.), most of which are nonbreeding Palaearctic migrants to southern Africa (see key on page lxii)

Table 1
Part B: NEAR-PASSERINES (Plates 34-43)

Family	Main habitat
Parrots, lovebirds (Psittacidae)	arboreal
Louries (Musophagidae)	arboreal
Cuckoos, coucals (Cuculidae)	arboreal, marsh
Barn and Grass Owls (Tytonidae)	ground, marsh, cave, building
Typical owls (Strigidae)	arboreal
Nightjars (Caprimulgidae)	ground, aerial
Swifts, spinetails (Apodidae)	aerial, cliff, building, arboreal
Mousebirds (Coliidae)	arboreal
Trogons (Trogonidae)	arboreal
Kingfishers (Alcedinidae)	arboreal, aquatic (inland, marine)
Bee-eaters (Meropidae)	arboreal, river bank
Rollers (Coraciidae)	arboreal
Hoopoe (Upupidae)	arboreal, ground
Woodhoopoes (Phoeniculidae)	arboreal
Hornbills (Bucerotidae)	arboreal, ground
African barbets (Lybiidae)	arboreal
Honeyguides (Indicatoridae)	arboreal
Woodpeckers (Picidae)	arboreal, ground
Wrynecks (Jyngidae)	arboreal

Table 1
Part C: SLENDERBILLED PASSERINES (Plates 36, 44-65, 77)

Family	Main habitat
Broadbills (Eurylaimidae)	arboreal
Pittas (Pittidae)	ground, arboreal
Larks (Alaudidae)	ground
Swallows, martins (Hirundinidae)	aerial, cliff, bank, building
Cuckooshrikes (Campephagidae)	arboreal
Drongos (Dicruridae)	arboreal
Orioles (Oriolidae)	arboreal
Crows, ravens (Corvidae)	arboreal, ground, cliff
Tits (Paridae)	arboreal
Penduline tits (Remizidae)	arboreal
Spotted Creeper (Salpornithidae)	arboreal
Babblers (Timaliidae)	arboreal, ground
Bulbuls (Pycnonotidae)	arboreal, ground
Thrushes, robins, chats (Turdidae)	arboreal, ground
Warblers, crombecs, cisticolas, prinias, etc. (Sylviidae)	arboreal, grassland, marsh
Flycatchers, batises (Muscicapidae)	arboreal

Family	Main habitat
Wagtails, pipits, longclaws (Motacillidae)	aquatic (inland), ground
Shrikes (Laniidae)	arboreal
Bush shrikes (Malaconotidae)	arboreal, ground
Helmetshrikes (Prionopidae)	arboreal
Starlings (Sturnidae)	arboreal, ground, cliff
Oxpeckers (Buphagidae)	arboreal, large mammal
Sugarbirds (Promeropidae)	arboreal
Sunbirds (Nectariniidae)	arboreal
White-eyes (Zosteropidae)	arboreal

Table 1
Part D: Conical-billed passerines (Plates 66-73)

Family	Main habitat
Weavers, sparrows, queleas, bishops, widows (Ploceidae)	arboreal, grassland, marsh
Waxbills, firefinches, mannikins, etc. (Estrildidae)	arboreal, grassland, ground
Whydahs, widowfinches (Viduidae)	arboreal, ground
Canaries, siskins, buntings (Fringillidae)	arboreal, ground, cliff

about 75% of non-passerine families are mainly aquatic, about 80% of near-passerine families are arboreal (tree-dwelling), and about 80% of passerine families are largely arboreal. This is very helpful in that each major subdivision of birds is associated with a major habitat type; most of the birds near the beginning of *Roberts* are waterbirds, while most of those in the latter two-thirds of the book are arboreal (found therefore in forest, bush or woodland of various types).

Since the non-passerines are mostly large and relatively easy to identify, and since waterbirds often provide an observer with a clear view, a beginner is advised to start with waterbirds, in order to gain practice in bird identification. The waterbird key is a helpful guide and can be found on page li. The use of an identification key is explained on page xxxix.

NAMES

The scientific names of birds in this book are based on those of the 1980 *S.A.O.S. Checklist of southern African birds* with a few minor changes, made where more recent information made such changes seem advisable, or in some cases where colleagues felt sufficiently strongly about some of the *Checklist* usages to urge changes to be made. The order of species, however, has remained substantially unchanged; exceptions have been made in the positions of the Whitebacked Duck *Thalassornis leuconotus*, the Lizard Buzzard *Kaupifalco monogrammicus* and the Greyrumped Swallow *Pseudhirundo griseopyga*.

English names are mostly those in common use in South Africa. Vernacular names are an eternally vexed question. The task of settling on a standard set for southern Africa was bedevilled by the variety of local names, the changes that have been made by previous writers in various books, including the various editions of *Roberts* and by a recent trend in Zimbabwe to lean towards English names originating from East Africa. East African bird names have never been in current use in southern Africa, and there seems to be no good reason to change now, especially since more English-speakers in South Africa use the southern names than all the English-speaking residents or tourists in East Africa combined.

The English names in this edition of *Roberts* are based on the consensus of about 100 ornithologists to whom lists of names (including some alternatives) were circulated with a request for their preferences and to provide reasons for any proposals differing from the names on the list. Where there was sufficient strong difference of opinion falling more or less equally between two names, a first choice had to be made, but the second choice has been included in parentheses as an alternative. It is not intended that the present names shall be fossilized in the literature of South Africa forever; language is too vital a force to allow itself to be rigidly channelled. People will use their own names anyway, no matter what the bird books say, but the present list is probably as good a compromise as any.

Afrikaans names have likewise been drawn up by consensus, but between only a few experts in the fields of ornithology and Afrikaans language. Once again, the idea has been to produce a list of names acceptable to the greatest majority of Afrikaans-speaking people. Most of the names are well established in South African usage anyway. Some of the innovations will stay, others will change. That is as it should be.

Bird names in the African languages present far more problems than in the European-derived languages. Many of them are generic (i.e. all species of sparrow may have the same name), others are regionally limited in application, one name may be applied to two or more different birds, some well known birds may have more than one name in a single language, and so on. Most bird species have no African names at all. It was therefore decided to scrap all the existing African bird names in past editions of *Roberts* (many of which were obviously incorrect, or could not be traced to any known language) and to start afresh by soliciting help from experts in the different language groups. They were asked simply to submit as complete and authoritative a list as could be managed in the time available, to make no guesses, and to ensure that the spelling was correct and up-to-date. Considering the number of African languages in southern Africa, it is gratifying that so many experts could be found to deal with so many of them.

The African languages for which lists of bird names were drawn up included the following: (K) Kwangali, (NS) North Sotho, (SS) South Sotho, (Sh) Shona, (Ts) Tsonga, (Tw) Tswana, (X) Xhosa and (Z) Zulu. In most cases I accepted the linguistic experts' opinions without question, but in others I was able to discuss certain points with them, or at least to query a few individual names that did not seem appropriate. Only time will tell with what degree of cooperative accuracy we have succeeded.

NUMBERS

The decision to change the numbers of the birds from the old "Roberts Numbers" was not taken lightly. Changes in ornithological systematics necessitated moving several species from one position to another (the Yellowspotted Nicator *Nicator gularis* ceased to be a shrike and became a bulbul; *Pinarornis plumosus* changed from the Sooty Babbler to the Boulder Chat; *Namibornis herero* was removed from the flycatchers and turned into the Herero Chat). Some new species were added to the southern African list, others were removed because their presence was considered to be based on doubtful evidence. New species were given letter-suffixes X, Y or Z, tacked onto the number of the previous existing species. This was unsatisfactory, firstly because it allowed only three additional species to be added into any one space, and secondly because subspecies in previous editions of *Roberts* have had letter-suffixes A, B, C, etc. It was therefore considered timely to revise the numbering system completely, based on the 1982 total of 887 species on the southern African list. Any new species would then be numbered as they were incorporated into the list, consecutively from 901 onwards. Anyone currently using the old "Roberts Numbers" for filing purposes can adapt his system to the new numbers, or simply continue to use the old numbers with a cross-reference to the new (or *vice versa*).

SPECIES ACCOUNTS AND HOW TO USE THEM

The species accounts include information on identification and biology, with additional data on measurements. These accounts are laid out in a standard way and are divided into subheadings for ease of reference.

1. Numbers and names

Every species is numbered from 1–887 followed by the old "Roberts Number" in brackets; numbers from 901 onwards are allocated to new species added to the list since it was compiled in 1982. Then follows the English name, the scientific name (in italics) and the Afrikaans name. African names are provided where they exist, which is not by any means for every species. The African-language abbreviations are shown in the section headed **NAMES** above.

2. Plates

The number of the colour plate on which the species is illustrated is given to the right of the names. The plates are grouped at the front of the book and are numbered boldly on the outside corners for quick reference. It is a good idea to use the text in combination with the colour plate when identifying a new bird.

3. Measurements

The most important measurements for the layperson are the total length of the bird and its weight. The length (in centimetres) is measured from billtip to tailtip with the bird stretched out, so will be longer than that of the bird in life; this is where the weight (in grams) is useful as a guide to the bulk of the bird, especially if it has a long bill or tail. The remaining measurements are given for the benefit of ringers and museum workers; they are in millimetres and set out in a standard way, giving the sex and sample size in paren-

theses, the minimum measurement, the mean measurement and the maximum measurement. For example "wing (10 ♂) 14,5–16,2–20" means that the wings of 10 male birds were measured and ranged from 14,5–20 mm, with a mean of 16,2 mm. The symbols ♂ for male and ♀ for female have been used. Where possible the measurements of separate sexes have been given for southern African populations of all species but where the sexes are not separated or where a sample size is omitted, these facts were not known; where a sample size is given for wing measurements, but not for the rest, it means that the same sample size applies to the measurements of tail, tarsus and culmen. Where regional size variations are marked, these have also been shown separately in some cases. Otherwise measurements for as large a sample size as possible have been pooled.

4. Bare parts

The bare parts are any unfeathered areas on a bird, usually the eyes (iris), bill, legs and feet. Where other bare areas exist, such as facial skin, eyerings, wattles, throat patches and so on, these have also been included. Bare parts are also known as "soft parts" by some authors.

5. Identification (See Fig. 7 page xlvii)

This is one of the most important sections in the species accounts, and probably the one that will initially be most useful to the majority of users of *Roberts*. For unfamiliar terms, please see the **Glossary**. The sections on identification in the species accounts are sometimes augmented by dichotomous keys or tables identifying various ecological or systematic groups which present special problems; these are grouped together on pages l–lxxx. The first criterion for identifying any bird is size; in this section the size is given in a general statement relative to other birds in the same family, or in a closely similar family, but the length and weight (given under **Measurements**) must be used for an impression of absolute size. Then follows a series of statements of key characters for use in the field; these are to be read in conjunction with the colour plates and, where necessary, augmented by other information, such as **Voice.** Check especially the information on immature plumages, since the immature may not be illustrated in the plate.

For purposes of this book an *immature* bird is a fully feathered young one between a fledgling (usually called a juvenile) and one that is not yet in full adult plumage (i.e. not usually able to breed). In some cases first and second immature plumages are described. A *chick* is a bird that is still unfeathered, or is covered with down only, whether or not it is still in the nest (see **Glossary** for definitions of altricial and precocial chicks).

It is also important to read the section on identification in conjunction with the descriptions of **Bare Parts**, in case some of these are diagnostic. In some cases identification is made simpler by the use of keys, most of which are taken from my booklet *Aids to bird identification in southern Africa* (Second Edition, 1988, University of Natal Press). Some of the keys have been made especially for this edition of *Roberts*. The nightjar key was kindly drawn up and supplied to me by Mr Des Jackson, formerly of Bulawayo, Zimbabwe.

The question of colour is sometimes difficult for two main reasons; firstly the light may affect colour quite drastically, and secondly everyone sees colours slightly differently from anyone else (not to mention colourblindness which is a great handicap in bird identification).

Even so, most bright colours present few problems. Red, green, yellow, blue, black, brown and white are often straightforward. Problems arise with the use of words like buff, rufous, umber and others with imprecise meanings. Rufous is a particularly overworked word and covers such colour tones as reddish brown, rust, russet, mahogany, chestnut, auburn, ginger, cinnamon, pinkish orange and even "red". Buff on the other hand tends more towards the yellowish side of the spectrum and may include light shades of biscuit, cream, *café au lait*, certain shades of dull pink and yellow, and even paler tones of rufous! Only usage and comparison with the colour plates will familiarize you with particular applications of these words.

Markings are of six main kinds (Fig. 1): streaked (or striped), spotted, barred, blotched, mottled and scaled (or scalloped). Streaks become stripes when they run together longitudinally. The distinction between large spots and small blotches is arbitrary, but usually a look at the illustration will help to clarify a description involving markings.

6. Voice

Sounds are extremely difficult to portray in words. A vocalization has several components which need to be conveyed to the reader if he or she is to be expected to "hear" even an approximation from a verbal description on paper—frequency (pitch), amplitude (loudness), tone (also called timbre or sound quality such as

Figure 1. Markings of birds: a = streaked, b = spotted, c = barred, d = blotched, e = mottled, f = scaled or scalloped. (Drawn by Linda Davis)

purity, sweetness, harshness, "nasal" tone, and so on) and rhythm (speed and duration of notes per unit time). Words cannot adequately do all these things by themselves, so the verbal descriptions are accompanied in most instances by one or more sonagrams which serve as a kind of musical notation, but in some ways tell the reader more than a musical score can do and in a much simpler way.

Sonagrams show three sound characteristics: (a) frequency (pitch) on the vertical axis, (b) duration (time) on the horizontal axis, and (c) amplitude (loudness) by the density of the tracing from grey (quiet) to black (loud). These parameters are illustrated in Fig. 2, taken from a typical vocalization of a familiar bird, the Cape Turtle Dove. Interpretation of the sonagram is aided

Figure 2. Sonagram of call of Cape Turtle Dove.

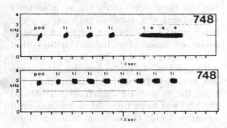

Figure 3. Sonagram of song of Orange-breasted Bush Shrike.

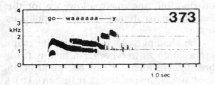

Figure 4. Songram of *g'way* call of Grey Lourie.

by the use of syllables or words of the type commonly given in bird books, such as the *kuk koorrrr ru* of the Cape Turtle Dove. This call may also be rendered as *where's FAther*, which gives some idea of the relative amplitudes of the syllables, as well as of the rhythm of the call as a whole. Frequency is measured in kilo-Hertz (kHz)—the higher the frequency, the higher the pitch of the call and the further above the horizontal baseline will be the tracing of that call. KiloHertz do not correspond exactly to musical notation, but are related as follows: 1–2 kHz = 1 octave, 2–4 kHz = 1 octave, and 4–8 kHz = 1 octave. The octave scale expands on the graph, while the kHz scale remains linear with equal subdivisions. The very low sounds from 0–1 kHz cover about 5 octaves in the lowest division of the sonagram where the human ear discriminates poorly, although the sounds are perfectly audible (such calls as those of the larger owls, the Ostrich and the Ground Hornbill).

Most bird vocalizations fall in the range of 1–8 kHz, which is well within the normal range of human hearing. Sounds covering a narrow range of frequencies have a pure tone, those covering a wide range of frequencies have a harsh, tinny or nasal tone. Compare the pure whistle of the Orangebreasted Bush Shrike (Fig. 3) with the harsh *g'way* of the Grey Lourie (Fig. 4), the somewhat nasal mewing call with lots of harmonics of the Orange-throated Longclaw (Fig. 5) or the hissing of Redbilled Oxpeckers (Fig. 6). These qualities of the call are described in the text, and the syllables used in the text are added to the relevant places on the sonagram tracings to help the reader interpret the actual sound and its rhythm. A sound of short duration makes a short tracing, a drawn-out sound makes a long tracing. A sharp sound, like a harsh note, covers a wide range of frequencies, but is of short duration, so will look like an almost vertical line: most sharp noises are loud, so the tracing will appear densely black.

Changes in pitch are clearly indicated in a sonagram. A downslurred note (i.e. one falling in pitch) makes a tracing descend-

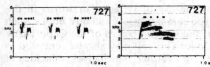

Figure 5. Sonagram of *meew* call of Orangethroated Longclaw.

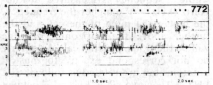

Figure 6. Sonagram of hissing calls of Redbilled Oxpecker.

ing from left to right, an upslurred note rises from left to right; these might be written *wheeeu* and *whooeee* respectively. Compare the voices of the Longbilled Lark and the Clapper Lark for a clear illustration of this. Trilled calls show up as a closely-packed row of almost vertical narrow lines in the case of a harsh trill, or smallish blobs in the case of a melodious trill; the trill itself may rise or fall in pitch, so that the tracings may go up or down the sonagram accordingly. The song of the Melba Finch illustrates this beautifully, having first a rising trill, then a falling one.

The best way in which to learn how to interpret sonagrams is to look at the sonagrams of a number of birdcalls familiar to you, and then try to work out the sounds from some unfamiliar ones *before* reading the descriptions of the sounds in the text. Only in this way will the reader be able to understand clearly what is meant by clicks, rattles, whistles, bell-like notes, trills, hoots, and all the other onomatopaeic terms used for bird sounds. Most of the words are carefully chosen to convey an idea of the sound as the English speaker would probably say it, but they are necessarily rather arbitrary and cannot be interpreted adequately without the aid of sonagrams.

A single sonagram sheet is usually just over 2 seconds long, so only fairly short calls can be illustrated on a single trace, that is to say on a single line. Prolonged and highly characteristic songs, such as that of the Tambourine Dove, are shown

as a composite of up to six traces, one above the other; the nature of the call can be inferred by reading the traces from left to right and from top to bottom. The duration of such a call can be calculated by simply adding the times of the traces; in the case of the Tambourine Dove, the whole song extends over a period of a little more than 14 seconds. The smallest subdivisions of the horizontal axis are 10ths of a second.

Since the majority of the sonagrams produced in *Roberts* are taken from the tapes of Len Gillard and Guy Gibbon, or the more recently issued set by Len Gillard, it is recommended that interested birders buy whichever of these tapes are still available and compare the sonagram directly with the actual call on the tape. Even if a recording is not the very same one as in the sonagram, a good approximation can be obtained from almost any recording, especially of a species with a highly stereotyped vocalization.

7. Distribution

The distribution maps are designed as a rough guide to the area over which a particular species can most likely be found. Birds are dynamic organisms and not confined to rigid boundaries as a rule; nor do they necessarily occur uniformly throughout the shaded map area, since there must inevitably be larger or smaller areas of unsuitable habitat within that shaded area. So the maps must be treated with caution. As far as possible, the maps and text have been prepared together, but since the maps were drawn up in 1990 and the text has been brought up to date until January 1992, there may well be slight differences here and there. The reader must regard these discrepancies as reflecting progress in our knowledge of bird distribution, and make allowance for the fact that maps are not as easy to update as text is.

The shading colours used in the maps are a guide as to whether a bird is (a) a breeding resident or can be found in an area at any time of the year (green), (b) a nonbreeding migrant, such as a Palaearctic wader or the European Swallow (yellow), or (c) a breeding migrant, such as many of the breeding species of swallows and cuckoos (blue) (see the map in Fig. 10). Generally speaking the yellow and blue areas cover occurrence during the summer months (from about September to April). Again the user is urged to use the maps in close conjunction with the text which usually gives the world range of a species, its southern African range and, in the case of migrants, the times of year during which the species may reasonably be expected to occur in its southern African range.

In the text the capital letters N, S, E and W stand for north, south, east and west respectively, while the lower-case letters n, s, e and w stand for northern, southern, eastern and western.

8. Status

The status of a species is concerned with how plentifully it occurs within its range, whether or not it is migratory (and, if so, when it is likely to occur in southern Africa), and in some instances what its taxonomic relations are. Terms relating to abundance are necessarily somewhat arbitrary, but they have been chosen as carefully as possible. A species that is very plentiful in an area, and likely to be seen every day in considerable numbers will fall into the category "abundant" or "very common"; these two terms are usually almost synonymous. Decreasing degrees of abundance are described by expressions like common, fairly common, uncommon, scarce (or sparse), rare or very rare. They do not necessarily correspond with any accurately measurable numerical value, though they could often be made to do so; such a situation, however, is rather artificial and expressions of abundance are intended only to give a reasonable subjective idea of how readily one may see a species in a given area. Naturally, too, a secretive species in a dense habitat will appear less abundant than one which is more active in an open habitat, even if the latter is numerically inferior, so the secretive one may be termed "uncommon", and the more obvious one may be described as "fairly common". Such are

the pitfalls of a subjective approach, but in this instance it seems both appropriate and adequate for the purpose.

Abundance may also be related to whether or not a species is of regular occurrence (even though rare) or of irregular or accidental occurrence. In the latter event a species would be called a vagrant or a straggler, since it has strayed beyond the boundaries of its normal distribution.

Some species of birds breeding in the Republic of South Africa are rare or threatened and in need of urgent conservation measures. These species have been dealt with in detail by Brooke (1984) in the *South African Red Data Book — Birds*. Each such species is listed as Endangered, Vulnerable or Rare. Endangered means that a species is in danger of extinction and that its numbers have been reduced to a critical level, or that its habitat has been drastically diminished or degraded. Vulnerable species are those likely to become Endangered in the near future unless something is done to improve their chances of survival. A Rare species is one with a small population which is at risk, but not yet Vulnerable. The red-data status of these species is indicated under the heading Status, followed by the letters RDB for Red Data Book.

The migratory status of a species is usually self-explanatory. A migrant from Europe or northern Asia is Palaearctic and usually does not breed in the southern hemisphere. Intra-African migrants, whether breeding or nonbreeding in southern Africa, mostly move to southern Africa for the austral summer, and move northwards again (sometimes as far as Sudan or Nigeria) for the austral winter.

The taxonomic status of a bird has to do with its relationships to other closely related species, or relationships within the species at the subspecific level. For example the Greybacked and Wailing Cisticolas, very similar to each other in voice and plumage, are something of an identification problem, and it could well be that they merely represent geographical races of a single species (in other words, they may be conspecific); this is stated in the text, but resolution of the controversy will have to await further research. On the other hand, it is sometimes useful to remark that two substantially different subspecies, such as those of the Black-headed Canary, sometimes overlap seasonally in distribution.

9. Habitat

A habitat is a definable place in which an organism lives. Animal habitats may be defined broadly (as ecological zones or biomes) or narrowly (as habitats in the usual sense, or even more narrowly as subhabitats or microhabitats), usually in terms of elevation, topography, climate, soil types and dominant vegetation type. Although habitats are described as if they were discrete entities, this is seldom the case, since few have sharply defined boundaries; habitats tend to intergrade over zones called ecotones, such as a forest-savanna ecotone and a grassland-karoo ecotone. Exceptions are found in the case of aquatic habitats and some forest patches which do have sharp boundaries. In any case, most habitats are easily recognizable and definable and are strongly influenced by rainfall (Fig. 11), topography and soil types. The main ecological zones and their habitats (Fig. 12) in southern Africa are:

A. *Coastal bush*: A dense evergreen vegetation type ranging in height from that of large bushes (2–3 m) to that of tall trees (up to about 20 m), usually with fairly dense undergrowth and an almost continuous canopy. It usually grows on sandy soil formed from ancient beach deposits, and is confined to regions of fairly high rainfall, mainly therefore along the southern and eastern coasts of southern Africa. As its names implies it is a coastal or littoral vegetation type from the edge of marine dunes to a maximum of perhaps 2–3 km inland. It often merges imperceptibly with lowland evergreen or coastal forest. It is characterized by bird species typical of forests, such as doves, louries, barbets, bulbuls, robins, flycatchers, shrikes, sunbirds and waxbills.

B. *Evergreen forest*: All true forest in southern Africa is evergreen. Forest is a woodland habitat distinguished by a continuous canopy and a tree height of about 5 m and upwards. It may be lowland, mid-altitude (or mistbelt), or montane, but the altitude at which forest becomes montane varies with latitude: the further south the forest, the lower the elevation at which it can be called montane. Forest may or may not have undergrowth in the form of shrubs or climbers, including climbing grasses; the denser the forest, the less undergrowth will there be, because of poor light. Forest occurring along the banks of rivers or in the floor of river valleys in relatively narrow strips is called riverine (or gallery) forest. The birdlife is similar in composition to that of coastal bush.

C. *Woodland*: Any growth of trees with crowns not touching (i.e. a discontinuous canopy) is a woodland. It will be denser in moist regions than in dry, and the varying faces of woodland have been given different names, often rather loosely. There are three main types: (a) broadleaved woodland (or simply woodland), (b) bushveld and (c) savanna.

Woodland in the strict sense has broad-leaved trees, often deciduous. It may have different local names according to the dominant tree species. In Zimbabwe, Zambia and Mozambique occurs a widespread genus of tree, *Brachystegia*, known as miombo woodland (or just miombo). *Baikiaea* is locally called gusu. *Colophospermum* is commonly known as mopane. And so on. These are the main types of woodland in southern Africa; in the text the generic name of the dominant tree will be used in all cases, except for the widespread and well known mopane.

Woodland with relatively dense and scrubby mixed broadleaved and small-leaved, often thorny, trees and bushes growing at lower elevations is known as "bushveld" in South Africa. It is typical of such areas as the greater part of the Kruger National Park and extreme northern Zululand.

Savanna is an open type of woodland characterized by thorntrees (mainly of the genus *Acacia*) and with a more or less continuous ground cover of grass. It covers about 65% of the African continent. There is no sharp line between woodland and savanna. For example in central Natal one may find savanna grading into a dense woodland type known as Valley Bushveld along watercourses in valley bottoms; this has a bird-species composition tending towards that of forest. Savanna is usually drier than other woodland types and intergrades in the west with semidesert, as in the Kalahari in southwestern Botswana and the northern Cape. *Acacia* savanna is known also as thornveld in South Africa.

Birds typical of woodlands generally include a great variety of arboreal passerines like drongos, cuckooshrikes, warblers, flycatchers, shrikes and sunbirds and many arboreal nonpasserines like doves, parrots, cuckoos, louries, woodhoopoes, kingfishers, bee-eaters, hornbills and woodpeckers. Ground birds include francolins, korhaans, buttonquails and some coursers.

D. *Grassland*: Usually treeless, without indigenous woody growth of any significance, grassland (or grassveld) is found mostly at higher elevations in southern Africa, more especially in the region known as the highveld. It intergrades with savanna on the one hand and with mid-altitude grasslands (middleveld) and bush on the other. Typical middleveld is found in the Natal midlands, characterized by rather tall coarse grass, at least in moister localities. Grassland is characterized by francolins, korhaans, larks, cisticolas, longclaws, pipits and species of *Euplectes* (bishops and widows).

E. *Montane*: Montane habitats, always associated with mountains, usually occur at high elevations, but the further south one goes, the nearer are montane habitats to sea level. They are characterized by extreme temperatures, especially low winter temperatures with nightly frosts and often with snow in the more southerly parts (Orange Free State, Natal, Lesotho, Cape Province). The vegetation is low and hardy with plants like *Helichrysum*, *Passerina*, *Stoebe* and characteristically resistant grasses; in the more sheltered valleys taller woody growth like *Leucosidea* is common, especially along watercourses. Well protected valleys may support patches of true evergreen forest. Birdlife in montane habitats is characterized by some interesting endemics like rockjum-

pers, sugarbirds (where proteaceous plants grow), some rockthrushes, chats, pipits and cisticolas. There are also a few large scavengers of restricted distribution such as the Bearded and Cape Vultures.

F. *Semidesert*: A large area of southern Africa falling between the 250-mm and 125-mm rainfall boundaries (isohyets) can be classed as semidesert. It stretches from the eastern Karoo (around Cradock and Middelburg, Cape) across the extreme southern Kalahari in the northern Cape, to southern and central Namibia and peters out in coastal Angola. (In the main text I have used Karoo to denote the geographical region known by that name, and karoo to mean the habitat by which it is defined.) It is mostly stony, with flat-topped hills or low mountains and a low scrubby vegetation with little grass; this vegetation becomes increasingly sparse with decreasing rainfall westwards. The avifauna is characterized by a predominance of ground-living birds like larks, chats, sandgrouse, bustards, korhaans, coursers and some specialized warblers and flycatchers. There are a few endemic species, especially in Namaqualand, such as the Cinnamonbreasted Warbler and the Red Lark.

Along semidesert watercourses or dry washes where a gallery of trees and bushes usually grows, most of them thorny, one finds many kinds of birds in common with those of savanna and the scrubbier parts of woodland. The Damaraland Plateau falls partly within the semidesert region and is the centre of evolution of several endemic birds, such as the Herero Chat, Rockrunner, Hartlaub's Francolin, Monteiro's Hornbill, Whitetailed Shrike and (in the better wooded parts) Rüppell's Parrot.

G. *Desert*: Merging with semidesert along its eastern edge and ending at the west coast is a fairly narrow strip of very dry country with a rainfall of under 125 mm a year, and mostly much less than this. The terrain varies greatly from flat to mountainous and the soils from stony to sandy. The vegetation is very sparse, especially in the west. The coastal belt up to about 100 km inland receives frequent fogs from the Atlantic Ocean, generated by the cold Benguela Current which cools the air moving over it from the west towards the land, causing the moisture in it to condense as fog. The birdlife of the desert is also naturally sparse, but makes up in interest for what it lacks in numbers, being adapted to extreme ecological conditions; its composition is similar to that of semidesert, but with several Namib endemics like the Dune Lark, Gray's Lark, Rüppell's Korhaan and the Tractrac Chat.

H. *Fynbos*: The fynbos is also known as the Cape Flora or macchia. It is a winter-rainfall region dominated by plants of the families Proteaceae, Ericaceae and Restionaceae and is confined to the south-western corner of southern Africa from southern Namaqualand eastwards to about Port Elizabeth. Some montane habitats have fynbos elements in them, even as far north as the eastern highlands of Zimbabwe, but they are mixed with grasslands, montane floras or forest edges. Fynbos proper is usually a low scrubby growth of small-leaved rather woody plants, interspersed with large bushes or even small trees of large leathery-leaved proteaceous species. It has several endemics—Cape Sugarbird, Orange-breasted Sunbird, Protea Canary, Victorin's Warbler, Cape Bulbul and Cape Francolin—along with many characteristic small passerines.

I. *Aquatic habitats*: These are water-associated habitats and may be divided into (a) marine and (b) inland waters. Since aquatic birds are a good group with which to begin birdwatching, because many of them are easy to see and identify, a key to all waterbirds is provided on page li. Marine birds (or seabirds) can be grouped according to whether they are pelagic (occurring in the open ocean), inshore, or shoreline. Typical pelagic seabirds, like albatrosses, petrels, shearwaters, penguins, some gulls and skuas, may sometimes be found inshore, but usually spend the greater part of their lives at sea, coming to land only to breed. Inshore species like gannets, cormorants, most gulls and terns are more familiar to most people, since they can be seen from land and even in harbours at times. Shoreline marine birds include plovers, sandpipers, oystercatchers and other waders, as well as the occasional egret or wagtail.

Inland waters (or fresh waters as they are sometimes called) are highly varied in character, ranging from estuaries near the coast, to rivers, lakes, dams, pans, marshes, vleis and sewage ponds. They are among the easiest habitats at which to watch birds from the shoreline or from a boat. The birdlife at an inland water will vary according to its size, the nature of its shoreline (steep, shelving, bare, densely vegetated, etc.), the composition of its water (fresh, saline, brackish, tidal, etc.) and whether or not it has emergent or floating vegetation (reeds, rushes, water-lilies, etc.). Typical of more open stretches of water are ducks, coots, cormorants and darters. Bare shorelines are used by plovers, many sandpipers, herons and loafing waterfowl. Reedbeds and marshes are the home of bishops, rails, crakes, moorhens, reed and marsh warblers and some waxbills. Floating vegetation in the subtropical parts usually supports jacanas and various crakes.

J. *Cultivated land*: Though not usually qualifying as an ecological zone, cultivated land forms a distinctive habitat created by man who has modified the existing habitat types in order to grow crops. Many kinds of birds have capitalized on these modifications, and on the resulting secondary growth that often springs up at the edges of disturbed ground. Characteristic of this secondary growth are waxbills, canaries, buntings, prinias, robins and some other small skulking passerines. The more open cultivated areas attract guineafowls, korhaans, cranes, larks and pipits, especially when the land is fallow. Young crops also attract many gamebirds, especially guineafowls, quails, and grazing waterfowl like Egyptian Geese.

Within any habitat there will be smaller subhabitats, such as rocky hills or outcrops, patches of denser scrub, watercourses lined with trees, moist areas or vleis, and so on. The finer habitat preferences of any bird will be found in the species accounts in the main text. Further terminology is defined in the **Glossary** (*q.v.*).

10. Habits

The section on habits has been organized along more or less consistent lines. It includes information on social organization (gregarious, solitary, seasonal changes), foraging techniques and foraging substrates, and general behavioural characteristics like flight patterns, gait, and so on. There is obviously more information for some species than for others; in several cases information that is typical of the family and therefore given in the family account is not repeated in each species account. It is suggested that the reader check the family account as well as the species accounts when trying to identify a species, or to find out more about its biology.

11. Food

Detailed information about food is lacking for most bird species in southern Africa, although the usual type of food is known in general terms for nearly all of them. Even where food has been analyzed in great detail, it has been listed fairly generally, since *Roberts* is not the place in which to find anything more than a gross indication of what kinds of food are eaten and, where possible, in what sort of proportions. Unusual food items may be taken from time to time by most birds, but these have generally been omitted.

12. Breeding

Information on breeding has been taken from a wide variety of sources, most of which are listed in the general references in the Introduction or at the end of each species account; the main sources are Dean (1971), Irwin (1981), James (1970), computer printouts of the egg collection of the Transvaal Museum prepared by Richard Dean, and the *Distribution and status of Transvaal birds* by M.I. Kemp, A.C. Kemp and W.R. Tarboton. This last work was kindly supplied to me in manuscript form by Alan Kemp. The section on breeding is presented under standard subheadings. In the case of polygamous species in which each male bird often has two or more females, this is stated at the beginning. In those species whose breeding is rare or unusual for some reason, the localities at which breeding has been recorded are sometimes given.

A. *Season*: This usually includes those months in which egglaying has been recorded, with a statement about the main or peak breeding months in most cases. Where seasons differ somewhat from one region to another, this is given as far as possible, in most cases on a provincial or national basis with subdivisions where necessary. If breeding is dependent on or affected by rainfall, as in the arid zones, this is indicated. Where known, it is also stated whether or not a bird makes more than one breeding attempt in a single season.

B. *Nest*: The nest architecture and materials are described, followed by the site where it is built, the type of nesting habitat and whether nesting is colonial (i.e. grouped together in more or less dense colonies, as opposed to solitary nests in the case of territorial bird species). Nest dimensions and heights above ground are given where available, listing the sample size, minimum, mean and maximum where possible.

C. *Clutch*: Clutch size has been presented like other measurements, with the sample size in parentheses, followed by the minimum, mean and maximum from actual counts, sometimes with a statement as to whether smaller or larger clutches may exceptionally be found; thus "(53) 2–3,6–5 eggs (usually 4, rarely 6)" means that, of 53 complete clutches, the range is 2–5 eggs and 4 is the usual number, but that 6 may occasionally be found. Obviously a bird cannot lay a fraction of an egg, so the "3,6" in the example given indicates that most clutches are between 3 and 4 eggs, but a clutch of 4 eggs is somewhat commoner than a clutch of 3 for that species in the 53 clutches counted.

D. *Eggs*: The eggs are described in terms of shape (where they are markedly different from a normal egg shape), texture and coloration (ground colour followed by type and colour of markings). Since eggs are so variable both between and within a species, or even within a single clutch, it is of small value to distinguish every time between shades of brown or shades of grey unless these are highly characteristic of a particular egg, so these colours have been given only in the most general way. Measurements of eggs are given in millimetres thus: sample size (in parentheses), mean length × mean width at widest part, and (in parentheses) range of length × range of width. Egg weight has also been given if available; egg weights are useful in calculating such things as the total output of a single female per clutch or per season, the ratio of egg weight to adult body weight, or the ratio of egg weight to weight of newly hatched chick. Unless regional variations in coloration or measurements are marked, these data have been pooled from all sources throughout southern Africa. Only the most reliable sources of information have been used in order to eliminate errors as far as possible. Where any doubt existed as to the authenticity of information about eggs, it has been omitted.

E. *Incubation*: Firstly the incubation period is given, then the roles of the sexes in incubation. This information is lacking for a surprising number of southern African birds. The standard method of measuring incubation period is the time between laying of the last egg of the clutch and hatching of the last chick of the brood; where incubation periods of individual eggs have been published, these have been used in preference to periods measured for clutches. Incubation periods recorded in captivity have been identified as such, unless measurements under natural conditions match the captive figures.

F. *Nestling or fledging*: The differential use of these two terms depends on whether the young are altricial or precocial. Altricial or nidicolous chicks (see **Glossary**) stay in the nest until they can fly, or at least until they can clamber around near the nest; they are cared for by one or both parents until they leave the nest, so they have a *nestling period*. Fledging, or the acquisition of true feathers, therefore occurs well before they leave the nest. The nestling period is the time between hatching and nest-departure (sometimes miscalled "fledging"), although the young may be dependent on their parents for a further few days, weeks or months.

Precocial or nidifugous chicks leave the nest almost as soon as they are dry, or at least within the first day or two after hatching. They are downy at first (this is their neonatal plumage), and acquire their true feathers and powers of flight only several days or weeks after nest-departure; in the meantime they are cared for by one or both parents until fully fledged and able to fly, hence the use of the term *fledging period* to cover the time between hatching and flying, although they may not become independent of the parents for a further period of time, usually 2 or more weeks, depending on the species.

FIELD EQUIPMENT

The three most basic pieces of equipment for use in the field are a pair of binoculars, a small notebook (about 10 × 7,5 cm) and a ballpen or pencil. Binoculars come in a great range of makes, models, magnifications and prices. For birding the best sizes are 8 × 32 and 10 × 40 roof-prism binoculars; they are slender, lightweight and easy to hold. Compact folding binoculars are also very useful for keeping in briefcase or handbag while travelling, but have a smaller field of view because of the smaller lens diameter; they come in various sizes: 6 × 16, 8 × 20, 10 × 22, as well as wide-angle and somewhat bulkier 8 × 24 or 8 × 30. Roof-prism binoculars are more expensive than conventional kinds, however, so it is as well to shop around.

For watching waterbirds at sea or inland it is often useful to have a telescope mounted on a tripod so as to get really close looks at relatively hard-to-identify groups like petrels and waders. Good quality lightweight telescopes of several makes that can be easily carried in the field are available, but one is then usually obliged to carry a tripod as well. It is simply a matter of tailoring one's equipment to the circumstances. The most popular sizes are 20 × 60 wideangle or 20–60 × 60 zoom telescopes. The kind with the eyepiece angled at 45 degrees is probably the most useful and comfortable to use in all situations, but especially when looking at a bird high in a tree, when the upward-angled telescope will not necessitate one having to crouch down to look through the eyepiece, as would be the case if it were in line with the objective as in the conventional types.

When buying binoculars, check price, magnification, weight, bulk and lens quality. When testing a lens system don't look through window glass, but through an open door. Make sure that there is no colour aberration—all colours must be true, without any suggestion of rainbow effects or reddish tinges at the edges of objects. Check also that the images are clear to the very edge of the field of view, and that outlines of objects are sharp, without the slightest distortion. If you are likely to watch birds in wet conditions (rainy climate, on board ship, in marshy places) ask for a waterproof pair ("mariner" binoculars). If you do a lot of rock climbing or other rough-country work, or if you are likely to leave your binoculars on the front ledge of a bakkie while bashing through the bundu, try to get a pair of heavy-duty binoculars encased in rubber reinforcing.

IDENTIFICATION KEYS

Before referring to a key get a good look at the bird (with your binoculars). Write down every feature that you think may be useful, and make a simple sketch if you can (in your small field notebook). Note down also the habitat and then decide which key seems to be the most appropriate one. Start at number 1 at the top left margin of the key, make a choice and run your eye along the line to the right margin where you'll find another number which refers to your next choice in the left margin again. Find that number, make your next choice and repeat the process until you arrive at an answer (the correct one, you hope). The technique becomes clearer when one actually uses a key. If one comes up with what seems to be the wrong answer, it is necessary to start again at the beginning and work one's way through the key, trying to decide where one might have made a wrong choice the first time.

Acknowledgments for the Fifth Edition

No book is ever entirely the work of one person. Always there is some kind of exchange of ideas and information between the author and the world around him, and this is especially true of a work like *Roberts' Birds of Southern Africa* which is not the author's book, but southern Africa's book. Every word of the main text has been carefully checked by an independent referee for accuracy and relevance. My debt of gratitude to these colleagues is enormous; some of them spent many days editing text and incorporating new information gleaned from their expert knowledge of the literature, or from their own field notes or personal experience. This service has been unstintingly given at all times—indeed I had to limit the amount of material each referee received from me, so willing were they to help. Most sections of the text were refereed by one ornithologist, but others (like the birds of prey, the swallows, the seabirds, the coraciiforms, the larks and the cisticolas) were seen by up to five different experts in that field. I would not have believed the generosity and helpfulness of my colleagues had I not experienced them myself.

The following colleagues refereed parts of the text: G.M. Bennett, A.F. Boshoff, A.E. Bowland, R.K. Brooke, C.J. Brown, P.A. Clancey, J. Cooper, A.J.F.K. Craig, T.M. Crowe, D.P. Cyrus, R.A. Earlé, P.G.H. Frost, S.K. Frost, C.H. Fry, J.H. Grobler, P.A.R. Hockey, H.D. Jackson, A.C. Kemp, N.F. Kure, H.T. Laycock, R. Liversidge, Geoff Lockwood, G.R. McLachlan, J.M. Mendelsohn, P.J. Mundy, K.B. Newman, T.B. Oatley, K.H. Rogers, Peter Ryan, W.R. Siegfried, J.C. Sinclair, D.M. Skead, Peter Steyn, W.R. Tarboton, C.J. Vernon and E.A. Zaloumis.

Without their help this work would have been fraught with far more errors than is now the case. Any errors that remain are largely my responsibility, at least as far as I have been able to judge while sifting through the enormous literature on southern African ornithology.

Sound reproductions (sonagrams) for the Fifth Edition were made largely from recordings kindly provided by Len Gillard and Guy Gibbon from their tapes *Bird calls of southern Africa* (Tapes 1 & 2) and from Len Gillard's 3-volume cassette tape series *Southern African bird calls*; the rest were made from recordings in the collection of the Fitzpatrick Bird Communication Library. Most sonagrams were made from commercially available tapes or records including the following: *Sonore des Oiseaux d'Europe* (J.C. Roché), *Voices of African Birds* (M.E.W. North), *More Voices of African Birds* (M.E.W. North & D.S. McChesney), *The Peterson Field Guide to Bird Songs of Britain and Europe* (S. Palmér & J. Boswall), *Witherby's Sound Guide to British Birds* (M.E.W. North & E.A. Simms), *The Birds of West Africa, Alauda* (C. Chappuis), *Birds of the African Rain Forest* (S. Keith & W.W.H. Gunn), *Oiseaux d'Afrique du Sud* (J.C. Roché), *Birds of the Soviet Union—A Sound Guide* (T. Pavlova & M. Akatova), *A Field Guide to Western Bird Songs* (Laboratory of Ornithology, Cornell), and *Birds of the Drakensberg* (T. Henley & T. Pooley). The following individuals provided taped vocalizations of birds: D.A. Aspinwall, A. Baker, A. Berruti, J. Burchmore, A.E. Bowland, R. Cassidy, J. Cooke, A.J.F.K. Craig, J. Culverwell, J. Dunning, P.G.H. Frost, G. Gibbon, P. Ginn, G. Goldschagg, C. Haagner, T. Harris, M. Haupt, L. Hurry, K. Hustler, R. Jensen, P. Johnson, J. Jones, W.D. Keibel, A.C. Kemp, R. Kettle (BLOWS), J. Komen, R. Liversidge, A. Manson, R.B. Martin, J.M. Mendelsohn, E. Meyer, R. Meyer, G. Nichols, P.N.F. Niven, M.E.W. North, W.J. Onderstall, O.P.M. Prozesky, N.F. Robson, T. Salinger, J. Shaw, J.C. Sinclair, J. Stannard, R. Stjernstedt, W.R. Tarboton, C.J. Vernon, A. Walker, P. Ward, H. Wilson and D. Wolhuter. I am most grateful to them for their generosity. Sonagrams were produced by Tony Harris of the Fitzpatrick Bird Communication Library of the Transvaal Museum; he spent many weeks on this work, and made some of the best sonagrams that it has ever been my pleasure to work with. Without them this book would have been much the poorer and I thank him for his expertise and thoroughness. I am very grateful to Mrs Joan Hall-Craggs of the Sub-Department of Animal behaviour, University of Cambridge, for allowing me to plagiarize liberally her excellent account on **Voice** in the *Introduction to Birds of the western Palearctic*, Volume 1, by Cramp & Simmons (see **GENERAL REFERENCE WORKS FOR FURTHER READING** for full details). Dr Stanley Cramp, Chief Editor of *Birds of the western Palearctic* also kindly expressed no objection to my using some of the explanatory material for *Roberts*.

The final versions of these sonagrams were prepared by Tony Bruton and Nils Kure of the University of Natal.

Richard Dean provided me with complete computer printouts of all the egg measurements from the Transvaal Museum; this was a monumental task which he undertook voluntarily and he gave me the results as if it were the most natural thing in the world, despite the fact that he had planned to publish them himself. My wife Cherie Maclean calculated thousands of sample sizes, ranges and means from these egg measurements, and helped in many other ways. The late Mrs M.K. ("Bunty") Rowan of Cape Town spent many days of her valuable time sorting ornithological cuttings and notes from her personal files in order to provide me with a great volume of otherwise inaccessible information from which to draw, much of it unique, all of it valuable. Dr D.F. Marais and his daughter, Miss Karin Marais, of Klein Afrika, Louis Trichardt, unselfishly sent me many new data on incubation, fledging and nestling periods for numerous francolins, bustards and other birds, obtained from observations both in captivity and in the wild.

Much of my literature research was done in the magnificent Africana library of Mr Sandy Stretton of "Buffelsfontein" in the Molteno District of the northeastern Cape; I am most grateful to him for his kindness, hospitality and friendship over the years, and for allowing me access to this superb collection of books and journals. Numerous colleagues supplied me with information, literature and reference material from other libraries, especially those of the FitzPatrick Institute and the Durban Museum. For access to these collections I want to thank Richard Brooke, Tim Crowe, John Mendelsohn and Ian Sinclair. An enormous fund of information on the francolins and hornbills was supplied to me in manuscript form by Tim Crowe and Alan Kemp respectively, from their texts for the second volume of *The birds of Africa* (Academic Press)— another entirely voluntary and unselfish gesture for which I am most thankful. Richard Brooke sent me the whole typescript for the second edition of *The South African Red Data Book* and kindly kept me continually up-to-date in this regard.

The Afrikaans bird names were compiled by R.A. Earlé with the help of Dr Banie Penzhorn and Mrs Celia Mendelsohn. Names of birds in the African languages were compiled by various experts who freely spent many hours of their time making their lists as accurate and authoritative as possible: J.K. Kloppers (Kwangali), A.N.B. Masterson (Shona), Dr Amy Jacot-Guillarmod (South Sotho), E.S. Mingard (Tsonga), Prof. D.T. Cole (Tswana and Tsonga), Dr H.W. Pahl (Xhosa), H. Nevill (Xhosa), Adrian Koopman (Zulu), and Philippe la Hausse de la Louvière (Zulu). Their friendly cooperation is acknowledged with thanks.

The artists, Ken Newman and Geoff Lockwood, have been most rewarding to work with. At all times they have shown patience and goodwill. They have gracefully submitted to my nitpicking criticisms of their paintings and have made changes whenever I asked them to do so. It has been a most pleasurable association throughout and I must thank them most warmly for their helpfulness. Geoff Lockwood also drew the coloured rainfall and vegetation maps of southern Africa, and the labelled diagram of "Parts of a Bird" on page xlvii. Nils Kure drew the outline locality map of southern Africa on facing page lxxx.

The distribution maps were painstakingly prepared by Mrs Meg Perrin from

ACKNOWLEDGMENTS

rough tracings derived largely from maps drawn by Kenneth Newman for his field-guide, *Newman's birds of southern Africa*; these maps were thoroughly checked by Charles Clinning, Digby Cyrus, Rob Martin, Warwick Tarboton, Carl Vernon and the late Dr J.M. Winterbottom before being finally reviewed by me. I am much indebted to all these people for their time and hard work.

Help in many forms was provided also by the following people who will know the nature of their contributions, every one of which has added to the completeness of the information provided: Aldo Berruti, Kurt Bonde, O. Bourquin, Neville Brickell, L. John Bunning, Ms Lydia Burger, Mrs Dora Campion, Hugh Chittenden, Arnold Clark, Ashley R. Clark, Charles Clinning, B.D. Colahan, Peter R. Colston; Digby P. Cyrus, A.B.C. Daneel, R.J. Dowsett, Françoise Dowsett-Lemaire, Mrs Kathleen Elwell, Norman Elwell, Mike Fagan, Grahame Fopl, Mrs M.R. Forrest, Mrs Valerie Gargett, Ian Garland, J.N. Geldenhuys, Peter Ginn, C. Grabandt, Brian Graham, Mrs Dorothy Hall, Mrs Dale Hanmer, Tony Harris, R.M. Harwin, Duncan Hay, C. Hilton-Taylor, R.F. Horner, J.H. Hosken, E. Hurd, M.P.S. Irwin, David Johnson, I.A.W. Macdonald, Athol Marchant, John Martin, A.N.B. Masterson, M.T. Mentis, P.N.F. Niven, Mrs E. Olivier, J.N. Perryer, E.O. Pike, S.E. Piper, R.M. Randall, Rank-Xerox (Pty) Ltd, N.F. Robson, D.V. Rockingham-Gill, Mrs Anita Rudolf, Miss T. Salinger, L. Saul & Co. (Pty) Ltd, R.K. Schmidt, M.B. Schmitt, D.M. Schultz, C.J. Skead, David H. Thomas, A.J. Tree, L.G. Underhill, François van der Merwe, Col. Jack Vincent, John Vincent, T.G. Watkins, O. West, Wild + Leitz RSA (Pty) Ltd, A.J. Williams, Mrs J.E. Williamson, E.J. Willoughby and J.M. Winterbottom.

One of my greatest debts of gratitude is owed to Professor M.R. Perrin of the Department of Zoology, University of Natal, Pietermaritzburg, who very kindly agreed to my taking two years off from my university teaching in order to prepare this revision; it was no small sacrifice for him to do without the services of one of his staff members at the very start of his career as Head of Department, and I must thank him warmly for this big-hearted gesture. My sincerest thanks also go to the University of Natal for unselfishly granting me two years unpaid leave shortly after I had returned from six months of study leave abroad; at no time did any of the University authorities put even the smallest obstacle in the way of my application, and I have enjoyed their encouragement throughout.

From time to time when I had to be away from home in order to check artwork, attend meetings or do some library research, friends always offered me the hospitality of their homes and I want particularly to thank Nell Hosken, Cynthia Lockwood, Ursula Newman and Non Stretton for their kindness, and for putting up with a lot of "shop-talk" during my visits.

The Trustees of the John Voelcker Bird Book Fund also gave me their constant support during the preparation of the book. The Chairman, Mr Everard Read, directed our affairs with calm firmness and admirable rationality at all times. The Secretary, Mr Richard Knight, patiently handled financial and other practical matters with Capetonian serenity which at times, I think, belied more anxiety than he cared to reveal. To these gentlemen and to the remaining Trustees, Mrs Cecily Niven, Mr Patrick Niven and Dr Hamish Campbell, I owe two memorable years of ornithological indulgence while I prepared the text for the new *Roberts* (or "*Roberts Five*", as we fondly knew it); they unhesitatingly supported me in every way possible, including providing me with a word-processor, several trips to Johannesburg to consult with the artists, a number of happy Trustees' meetings, and all the encouragement in the world. Words cannot do justice to their magnanimity, and the public can be glad that such dedicated and unselfish people are at the helm of much of the most significant publishing in the ornithology of today's southern Africa.

It is also my pleasure to acknowledge the unstinting helpfulness of Len Clout, Jack Kassen, Sam Weller and the rest of the staff of CTP Book Printers. It has been a most cordial and fruitful association from which I have learned a lot about printing and they may have picked up something about birds. To my late mother, Mary Maclean Corbett, goes the credit for setting my feet firmly upon the path of ornithology when, back in November 1952, she gave me my first copy of *Birds of South Africa* by Dr J Austin Roberts. She sowed the seeds of natural history in my mind from my earliest childhood and supported and encouraged me in my career ever since.

In the final analysis there is one source of vital sustenance and approval that the world may not often see, but that has kept me going from day to day and week to week—that of my wife, Cherie, and of my children, Anne and David. Many an evening and many a weekend did they put up with my absence, and I am sure they wondered more than once whether my loyalties to the computer were perhaps greater than the strength of my family ties. I will never forget, nor take for granted, the tolerance and interest they showed throughout the project. I appreciate them.

ACKNOWLEDGMENTS FOR THE SIXTH EDITION

Since the previous edition of *Roberts* appeared in 1985, much new information has become available through the published literature, through personal observations by colleagues and by members of the public and through my own research and experiences in the field. So many people have given freely of their expertise, that it would take up too much space to name them all. They will know who they are, and my sincerest thanks go to them. Several new colour plates have been prepared by Geoff Lockwood in order to improve and update some of those which were less satisfactory in the Fifth Edition. As always, he and I have worked well together and the results will make this edition a better book to use.

New distributional information has necessitated the revision of 438 (49%) of the distribution maps. These have been updated from all available sources, but have not used data from the Southern African Bird Atlas Project (SABAP) which was in progress at the time, since these data are being processed for the forthcoming *Atlas* and are not yet available for general use. The revised maps were prepared under my guidance by Mr R.J. Nuttall, presently Ornithologist at the National Museum in Bloemfontein. We hope that the end products make *Roberts* a more relevant work; any errors remain my own. I am grateful to him and to Dr C.J. Brown of Namibia (who provided many distributional data) for all their time and trouble.

I made new sonagrams for nearly 90 species on a Multigon Sonagraph from tapes produced by Mr Guy Gibbon in a magnificent set entitled *Southern African Bird Sounds* published late in 1991 and distributed by Southern African Birding CC, P.O. Box 24106, Hilary, 4024. I am deeply indebted to Guy Gibbon for permission to use this material. The finished sonagrams were prepared for publication by Mr Hylton Adie of Pietermaritzburg who also helped to reformat the text for the printers; my thanks go to him for many hours of work. Once again I must thank the Trustees of the John Voelcker Bird Book Fund for their support during the preparation of *Roberts Six*. Mrs Cecily Niven had in the meantime stepped down from the Trusteeship, and her place has been taken by Mr W.S. Stretton of "Buffelsfontein".

My warmest thanks go to all those people who bought copies of the Fifth Edition, used it, criticized it and rewarded me with their comments, both negative and positive. As a result of these responses I have made some changes which make the text more "user-friendly". For example, I have put all the identification keys together and included in them the Plate numbers on which the birds referred to are to be found and together we have made many corrections. I have had a lot of fun using the Fifth Edition in adult-education courses and my gratitude goes out to all those who participated. The greatest support in this, as in all my other ventures, has again come from my wife, Cherie Maclean. She will know what this support means to me.

GLOSSARY OF ORNITHOLOGICAL AND ZOOLOGICAL TERMS

alarm: indicative of the presence of danger (e.g. alarm call).

alate: winged and able to fly.

allopreening: preening of one bird by another; if both preen each other simultaneously, it is called mutual preening.

altricial: type of young bird that is more or less helpless at hatching and has to be fed in the nest by the parents until able to fly (synonymous with nidicolous: see **precocial**).

apterium (pl. **apteria**): the unfeathered parts of a bird's body.

aquatic: living in or on water.

arboreal: living in trees.

arthropod: jointed-legged animal with hard exoskeleton, subdivided into insects (Hexapoda), millipedes (Diplopoda), centipedes (Chilopoda), crustaceans (Crustacea), spiders, scorpions and related animals (Arachnida), sun-spiders or solifugids (Solpugae), ticks and mites (Acari), and some other minor groups.

barred: see Fig. 1, p. xxx.

breeding season: months in which egg-laying has been recorded.

brood parasite: species of bird that lays its eggs in the nests of other (foster or host) species; the host rears the brood parasite's young. Examples of brood parasites are cuckoos, honeyguides, whydahs and widowfinches.

Cainism: process in which older (first-hatched) chick kills younger sibling, commonly found in eagles, boobies and a few other birds.

call: any vocalization, but usually restricted to those that are not definable as **song** (*q.v.*).

casque: horny ridge on top of bill of hornbills.

colonial: usually describes gregarious breeding habits in which nests are built together in more or less dense groups or colonies.

commensal: living together with another animal or plant from which benefit (food, protection) is derived.

conspecific: belonging to the same species.

culmen: ridge along top of bird's bill from tip to base of feathers at forehead.

decurved: curved downwards (e.g. bill of sunbird or ibis).

dentate: toothed or serrated.

dihedral: wings held up at angle above horizontal.

discontinuous (distribution): usually applied to a species with gaps between populations where it does not occur.

disruptive (coloration): patterned so as to break up the outline of an object to enhance camouflage (e.g. stripes or patches in downy plumage of precocial chicks).

distal: away from the body (as opposed to **proximal** which is towards the body; thus the hand is distal to the elbow).

donga: an erosion gully, usually with vertical sides, often used by burrow-nesting birds, such as starlings, chats and the Ground Woodpecker.

dorsal: on the back or upperside.

dorsoventrally: from top to bottom, or from back to belly.

eclipse (plumage): nonbreeding plumage, usually duller-coloured than nuptial or breeding plumage.

endemic: living in, and usually originating in, one geographical area only, and found nowhere else.

eutrophic: rich in nutrients.

exotic: introduced from another part of the world (i.e. not indigenous).

extralimital: beyond the borders of the geographical area under review.

forked: divided into two prongs or points (e.g. tail of many swallows, some swifts and terns).

fynbos: vegetation type characteristic of winter-rainfall region from western Cape to about Port Elizabeth, characterized by plants of families Proteaceae, Ericaceae and Restionaceae; also called macchia or Cape Flora.

gape: angle at base of bill where upper and lower parts of mouth meet.

graduated: decreasing stepwise from long to short.

gregarious: living together in groups or flocks.

helpers: nonbreeding immatures or adults of the same species, which help a breeding pair with the care of their eggs and/or young; helpers are often young of a previous brood, either of the same season or a previous season.

heronry: colonial breeding site of herons or egrets; sometimes also applied to other colonially-breeding wading birds such as ibises and spoonbills.

indigenous: native to a geographical area (i.e. not exotic or introduced).

inselberg: isolated, usually fairly sheer hill or mountain rising from a plain.

karoo: a semi-arid habitat of central and western South Africa consisting of low woody shrubs and little grass, on a largely stony substratum.

kloof: a gully or ravine (often densely wooded), usually on a mountainside.

krill: marine plankton consisting of minute crustaceans of the order Euphausiacea, occuring in vast numbers in colder oceans.

lamellae (sing. **lamella**): comblike teeth or projections along the borders of the bill, designed for filtering out minute food organisms from water or soft mud; found in ducks, flamingoes and some procellariiforms.

lanceolate: pointed like the head of a spear.

lateral (laterally): on the side of head or body.

malar (moustache): line from base of bill down sides of throat, often forming distinctive stripe in birds.

melanistic: tending to be black or blackish, resulting from an excess of the dark feather pigment melanin.

nonpasserine: not belonging to the order Passeriformes (see page 421).

notched: having central tail feathers slightly shorter than outer ones, forming a notch or shallow fork.

omnivorous: eating both plant and animal foods of many kinds.

Palaearctic: pertaining to the zoogeographical region which includes Europe, northern Asia and North Africa.

passage (migration): concerning birds passing through on migration from one point to another, but not stopping over.

passerine: birds of the order Passeriformes (see page 421).

pectinate: provided with comblike teeth.

pelagic: having to do with the open ocean.

pessulus: bony central structure in syrinx (voicebox) of some birds.

plumage: the feather covering of a bird.

polyandrous: having more than a single male to each female.

polygamous: having more than one mate (usually refers to more than one female to each male).

polygynous: having more than one female to each male.

precocial: type of chick able to leave the nest within minutes or hours of hatching; it is covered with down and able to thermoregulate and often able to feed by itself (synonymous with nidifugous: see **altricial**).

primaries (primary remex): outer flight feathers of the wing, attached to the bones of the hand.

proximal: towards the body (as opposed to **distal** which is away from the body; e.g. the elbow is proximal to the hand).

rectrix (pl. **rectrices**): tail feathers.

recurved: curved upwards, like the bill of an Avocet.

remex (pl. **remiges**): flight feathers of the wing.

rounded: descriptive of the tip of the tail or wing in which the feathers decrease evenly and slightly in length from the centre outwards to form a rounded outline.

rouse (plumage): to fluff and shake the body plumage.

rudimentary: describes a structure or behaviour pattern reduced in size or elaborateness, having lost its original function; if very reduced the structure is vestigial.

rufous: reddish.

secondaries (secondary remex): flight feathers of the wing attached to the forearm (specifically the ulna).

serrate: finely toothed.

song: vocalization used to advertise territory, as well as availability as a mate; usually employed by male birds, and not necessarily melodious to the human ear.

speculum: distinctively coloured area on wing (usually on secondaries) of bird, mostly visible only in flight; especially well developed in ducks.

spish (spishing; to spish up): sound made through the teeth by loud *pssshh, pssshh*, which often attracts small birds, especially passerines.

spotted: (see Fig. 1, p. xxx).

square: tail tip with feathers of equal length forming straight border.

streaked: (see Fig. 1, p. xxx).

subterminal: not right at the end or tip of a structure.

sympatric (distribution): occurring together in the same area.

syndactyl: having the toes joined or partly joined.

syrinx: the voicebox of a bird, responsible for vocal sound production.

tarsometatarsus ("tarsus"): the lower part of the leg of a bird, usually bare of feathers.

terminal: at the end or tip of a structure.

terrestrial: living on land (not aquatic).

tibiotarsus ("tibia"): the upper part of the leg of a bird, usually feathered and often referred to as the "thigh".

tomium: length of bill from angle of gape to tip of culmen.

veld: any open country in South Africa (e.g. grassveld, thornveld, sandveld).

ventral: below or on the underside.

vestigial: describes a structure or behaviour pattern that is so reduced through long disuse as to be almost absent.

vlei: seasonally flooded moist or marshy depression in grassland or savanna.

wattle (wattled): bare fleshy structure around eye, base of bill, throat or elsewhere on head of bird.

zygodactyl: having two toes (2nd and 3rd) pointing forwards, and two toes (1st and 4th) pointing backwards.

PARTS OF A BIRD

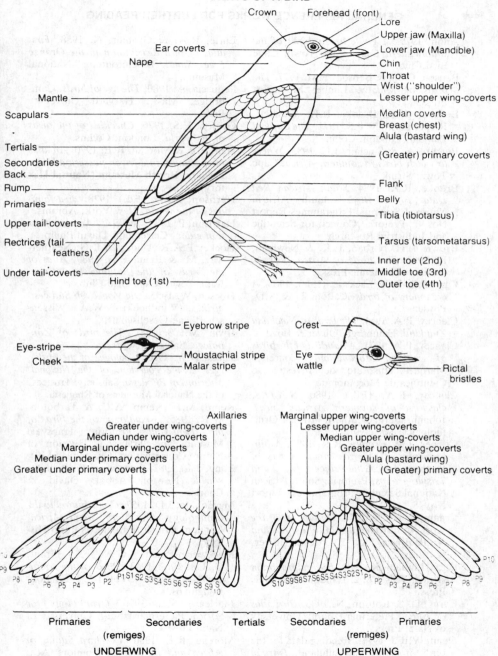

Figure 7. Parts of bird

REFERENCES

GENERAL REFERENCE WORKS FOR FURTHER READING

Anon. 1979. *A guide to the birds of the southwestern Cape*. Cape Town: Cape Bird Club.

Benson, C.W. & Benson, F.M. 1977. *The birds of Malawi*. Limbe: Mountfort Press.

Benson, C.W., Brooke, R.K., Dowsett, R.J. & Irwin, M.P.S. 1971. *The birds of Zambia*. London: Collins.

Berruti, A. & Sinclair, J.C. 1983. *Where to watch birds in southern Africa*. Cape Town: Struik.

Brooke, R.K. 1984. *South African Red Data Book—Birds*. South African National Scientific Programmes Report No. 97. Pretoria: Council for Scientific and Industrial Research.

Brown, L.H., Urban, E.K. & Newman, K. 1982. *The birds of Africa*, Vol. 1. London: Academic Press.

Campbell, B. & Lack, E. (Eds). 1985. *A dictionary of birds*. Calton: T. & A.D. Poyser.

Clancey, P.A. 1964. *The birds of Natal and Zululand*. Edinburgh: Oliver & Boyd.

Clancey, P.A. 1971. *A handlist of the birds of southern Moçambique*. Lourenço Marques: Instituto de Investigação Científica de Moçambique.

Clancey, P.A. (Ed.). 1980. *S.A.O.S. checklist of southern African birds*. Johannesburg: Southern African Ornithological Society.

Cooper, J. & Brooke, R.K. 1981. *A bibliography of seabirds in the waters of southern Africa, the Prince Edward and Tristan groups*. Pretoria: South African National Scientific Programmes, Report No. 48.

Cramp, S. (Ed.). 1977. *Handbook of the birds of Europe, the Middle East and North Africa*. Vol. 1. Oxford: University Press.

Curry-Lindahl, K. 1981. *Bird migration in Africa*. Vols 1 & 2. London: Academic Press.

Cyrus, D. & Robson, N. 1980. *Bird atlas of Natal*. Pietermaritzburg: University of Natal Press.

Dean, W.R.J. 1971. Breeding data for the birds of Natal and Zululand. *Durban Mus. Novit.* 9:59–91.

Earlé, R.A. & Grobler, N. 1988. *First atlas of bird distribution in the Orange Free State*. Bloemfontein: National Museum.

Feduccia, A. 1980. *The age of birds*. Cambridge, Mass.: Harvard University Press.

Gruson, E.S. 1976. *Checklist of the birds of the world*. London: Collins.

Hall, B.P. & Moreau, R.E. 1970. *An atlas of speciation in African passerine birds*. London: British Museum (Natural History).

Harrison, C.J.O. (Ed.). 1978. *Bird families of the world*. New York: Abrams.

Harrison, P. 1983. *Seabirds. An identification guide*. Claremont: David Philip.

Hockey,P.A.R.,Underhill,L.G.,Neatherway, M. & Ryan, P.G. 1989. *Atlas of the birds of the Southwestern Cape*. Cape Town: Cape Bird Club.

Hoesch, W. 1955. *Die Vogelwelt Südwestafrikas*. Windhoek: S.W.A. Wissenschaftliche Gesellschaft.

Irwin, M.P.S. 1981. *The birds of Zimbabwe*. Salisbury: Quest.

James, H.W. 1970. *Catalogue of the birds' eggs in the collection of the National Museums of Rhodesia*. Salisbury: Trustees of the National Museums of Rhodesia.

Kemp, M.I., Kemp, A.C. & Tarboton, W.R. 1985. *A catalogue of the birds of the Transvaal*. Pretoria: Transvaal Museum and Transvaal Division of Nature Conservation (Cyclostyled MS).

Long, J.L. 1981. *Introduced birds of the world*. Newton Abbot: David & Charles.

Macdonald, J.D. 1957. *Contribution to the ornithology of western South Africa*. London: British Museum (Natural History).

Mackworth-Praed, C.W. & Grant, C.H.B. 1962–1963. *Birds of the southern third of Africa*. Vols 1 & 2. London: Longmans.

Maclean, G.L. 1990. *Ornithology for Africa*. Pietermaritzburg: University of Natal Press.

Moreau, R.E. 1966. *The bird faunas of Africa and its islands*. London: Academic Press.

Moreau, R.E. 1972. *The Palaearctic-African bird migration systems*. London: Academic Press.

Nelson, B. 1980. *Seabirds: their biology and ecology*. London: Hamlyn.

Newman, K. (Ed.) 1978. *Birdlife in southern Africa*. (2nd edition). Johannesburg: Macmillan.

Newman, K. 1983. *Newman's birds of southern Africa*. Johannesburg: Macmillan.

Rowan, M.K. 1983. *The doves, parrots, louries and cuckoos of southern Africa*. Cape Town: David Philip.

Smithers, R.H.N. 1964. *A check list of the birds of the Bechuanaland Protectorate*. Trustees of the National Museums of Southern Rhodesia.

Snow, D.W. (Ed.) 1978. *An atlas of speciation in African non-passerine birds*. London: British Museum (Natural History).

Steyn, P. 1982. *The birds of prey of southern Africa*. Cape Town: David Philip.

Thomson, A.L. (Ed.). 1964. *A new dictionary of birds*. London: Nelson.

Traylor, M.A. 1963. *Check-list of Angolan birds*. Lisboa: Diamang.

Tuck, G.S. & Heinzel, H. 1978. *A field guide to the seabirds of southern Africa and the world*. London: Collins.

Urban, E.K., Fry, C.H. & Keith, S. (Eds). 1986. *The birds of Africa*, Vol. 2. London: Academic Press.

Van Someren, V.G.L. 1956. Days with birds. *Fieldiana: Zoology* 38:1–520. Chicago Natural History Museum.

Van Tyne, J. & Berger, A.J. 1959. *Fundamentals of ornithology*. New York: John Wiley & Sons.

List of Identification Keys

IDENTIFICATION KEYS

KEY TO THE WATERBIRDS
(Groups marked * have a separate key)

1   Inland waters (lakes, dams, pans, rivers, streams).....   2
    Marine waters (sea and seashore)...................   12

2   Swimming (or diving from surface of water)..........   3
    Wading on or near shoreline (mostly longlegged)......   6
    Flying, or diving from air (mostly longwinged).......
    ....terns (Pl 32), African Skimmer (Pl 31)

3   About size of turkey, or larger......................   4
    Smaller than turkey................................   5

4   Mainly white..............................pelicans (Pl 4)
    Mainly black.....................Spurwinged Goose (Pl 8)

5   Bill pointed (not hooked at tip)....................
    ....grebes (Pl 6), Darter (Pl 4),
        Redknobbed Coot, Moorhen, African Finfoot (Pl 22)
    Bill blunt or hooked at tip.........................
    ....cormorants* (Pl 4), ducks (Pls 8–9), gulls (Pl 31)

6   Larger than domestic fowl..........................   7
    Smaller than domestic fowl (or about same size).......   10

7   Bill straight.......................................   8
    Bill curved..   9

8   Plumage entirely white.............................
    ....Great White Egret (Pl 5), African Spoonbill (Pl 7)
    Plumage not entirely white.........................
    ....larger herons* (Pl 5), storks* (Pl 7)

9   Bill short, sharply decurved; legs and neck very long...
    ....flamingos* (Pl 7)
    Bill long, slender, gently decurved..................
    ....ibises (Pl 7), Curlew (Pl 25)

10   Plumage boldly black and white....................
    ....Blacksmith Plover (Pl 26),
        Avocet, Blackwinged Stilt (Pl 25),
        Pied Wagtail (Pl 59)
    Plumage not boldly black and white.................   11

11   Uniform dark brown (faintly barred in good light).....
    ....Hamerkop (Pl 7)
    Not uniform dark brown...........................   16

12   Swimming (or diving from surface of water)..........   13

Wading on or near shoreline (mostly longlegged)...... 14
Flying, or diving from air (mostly longwinged).......
.......................**albatrosses (Pl 2), petrels (Pl 3),
gannets, frigatebirds, tropicbirds (Pl 4), terns (Pl 32)**

13 Open sea ....**penguins (Pl 4), albatrosses (Pl 2),
petrels (Pl 3), phalaropes (Pl 29)**
Inshore (within about 4 km of land)..................
........................**Blacknecked Grebe (Pl 6),
pelicans, gannets, cormorants* (Pl 4), gulls (Pl 31)**

14 Mainly black (belly may be white); bill red...........
....................................**oystercatchers (Pl 25)**
Not mainly black.................................. 15

15 Larger than domestic fowl. . .**flamingos* (Pl 7), Curlew (Pl 25)**
Smaller than domestic fowl (or about same size).......
. . .**Turnstone, plovers (Pl 26) 'waders'* (scolopacids) (Pl 29),
Avocet, Crab Plover (Pl 25), gulls (Pl 31), wagtails (Pl 60)**

16 Bill markedly longer than head.....................
....................**some small herons and egrets* (Pl 6),
African Rail (Pl 22),
Painted Snipe, 'waders'* (scolopacids) (Pl 29)**
Bill as long as, or shorter than, head................
....................**some small herons and egrets* (Pl 6),
rails, crakes (Pl 22), jacanas (Pl 23),
plovers (Pl 26), smaller 'waders'* (scolopacids) (Pl 29)
Water Dikkop (Pl 25), wagtails (Pl 60)**

Figure 8. Three goshawks showing different types of barring: a = barred grey on white (bars of equal widths); b = barred white on grey (white bars narrower than grey bars); c = barred grey on white (grey bars narrower than white bars).

KEY TO THE DIURNAL BIRDS OF PREY (RAPTORS)

1   Belly generally pale (white, buff, light brown, pale grey)..   2
    Belly generally dark (rufous, dark grey, dark brown, black).......................................   33

2   Belly unmarked (plain)...........................   3
    Belly barred, streaked, spotted or mottled............   11

3   Belly white..   4
    Belly buff or light brown...........................   70
    Belly grey...   81

4   Chest white like belly..............................   5
    Chest darker than belly............................   9

5   Size very small; wings and tail spotted with white; rump white; back grey in male, dark brown in female.....
    ....**Pygmy Falcon (Pl 19)**
    Size medium to large...............................   6

6   Back plain dove grey...............................   7
    Back dark slate grey, brown, black or mottled........   8

7   Bend of wing black; hovers often....................
    ....**Blackshouldered Kite (Pl 15)**
    No black on bend of wing; sails low over ground......
    ....**male Pallid Harrier (Pl 15)**

8   Size very large; legs feathered to toes...............
    ....**immature Martial Eagle (Pl 13)**
    Size medium to large; legs not feathered.............   16

9   Chest black or brown; legs not feathered to toes.......   10
    Chest dull pinkish; legs feathered to toes............
    ....**immature Crowned Eagle (Pl 13)**

10   Chest and head black.....**Blackbreasted Snake Eagle (Pl 14)**
    Chest brown; head pale; dark line through eye........
    ....**Osprey (Pl 15)**

11   Falcon head pattern (see diagram)...................   12
    No falcon head pattern.............................   17

12   Falcon head pattern rufous; belly finely barred........
    ....**Rednecked Falcon (Pl 19)**
    Falcon head pattern blackish........................   13

13   Finely barred above and below......................
    ....**immature Rednecked Falcon (Pl 19)**
    Spotted and/or streaked below......................   14

14　Crown dark...................................　15
　　Crown rufous or paler.........................　82

15　Build robust; inhabits cliffs and mountains...........
　　..............................**Peregrine Falcon (Pl 19)**
　　Build slender; inhabit open or wooded country.......
　　....................**female Eastern Redfooted Kestrel,**
　　European Hobby Falcon,
　　immature Eastern and Western Redfooted Kestrels
　　(all very similar in the field) (Pl 19)

16　Sides of belly black; shape slender..................
　　.................**Black Sparrowhawk (whitebreasted form)**
　　Underparts all white (throat may be black); shape robust;
　　tail chestnut......................**Augur Buzzard (Pl 15)**

17　Chest colour contrasts with belly colour.............　18
　　Chest and belly colour the same...................　26

18　Chest grey; belly barred or streaked................　19
　　Chest black or brown...........................　60

19　Belly streaked..............**male Montagu's Harrier (Pl 15)**
　　Belly barred....................................　20

20　Legs orange to reddish..........................　21
　　Legs yellow or paler............................　24

21　Rump boldly white..............................　22
　　Rump pale, but not pure white....................
　　.........................**Dark Chanting Goshawk (Pl 16)**

22　Size larger; legs long; primaries black, contrasting with
　　white secondaries; flight slow....................
　　.....................**Pale Chanting Goshawk (Pl 16)**
　　Size smaller; legs relatively short; underwing all white,
　　finely banded..................................　23

23　Vertical black line on white throat; one broad white
　　tailband.........................**Lizard Buzzard (Pl 15)**
　　No black line on throat; four narrow white tailbands...
　　..............................**Gabar Goshawk (Pl 16)**

24　Face bare, bright yellow to reddish.......**Gymnogene (Pl 15)**
　　Face feathered.................................　25

25　Belly finely barred with grey; size fairly large; no rusty
　　patch on nape.................................　64
　　Belly coarsely barred rufous; size medium; rusty patch on
　　nape; head slightly crested..........**Cuckoo Hawk (Pl 19)**

26　Belly markings bold ....　27
　　Belly markings fine or pale......................　28

27　Size large....................................　67
　　Size small....................................　72

28 Streaked or spotted.................................. 29
Barred or obscurely mottled........................ 30

29 Back plain rufous; head bluegrey. .**male Lesser Kestrel (Pl 19)**
Back buffy rufous like belly, boldly barred with black
    chevrons......................**Greater Kestrel (Pl 19)**
Back dark, mottled with whitish.................... 32

30 Rump white.. 31
Rump not white.................................... 45

31 Barring grey; rump narrowly white...................
..........................**Ovambo Sparrowhawk (Pl 16)**
Barring rufous; rump more boldly white.............
..........................**Little Sparrowhawk (Pl 16)**

32 Size large; throat dark; legs feathered to toes........
.............................**Booted Eagle (Pl 14)**
Size small; throat pale; legs bare...................
...................**immature Little Sparrowhawk (Pl 16)**

33 Belly black....................................... 34
Belly brown, grey or rufous......................... 35

34 Belly unmarked (plain)............................. 61
Belly spotted or barred with white.................. 73

35 Belly grey.. 36
Belly brown or rufous............................. 37

36 Undertail coverts rufous, contrasting with belly colour
.... 78
Undertail coverts grey like belly.................... 79

37 Belly brown....................................... 43
Belly rufous, or dark mahogany red................. 38

38 Size large; head chest and tail white................
.............................**African Fish Eagle (Pl 13)**
Size small or medium; head not white............... 39

39 Head bluegrey; chest marked with black; size small.... 71
Head not bluegrey; crown dark or rufous............. 40

40 Falcon head pattern (see diagram).................. 83
No falcon head pattern............................ 41

41 Chest black; lower breast rufous; lower belly barred black
    and white; tail rufous; broad white wingbar in flight
.................................**Jackal Buzzard (Pl 15)**
Chest rufous like belly............................. 42
Chest white, streaked brown; head slender...........
.........................**immature Gymnogene (Pl 15)**

42 Size very large; tail wedge-shaped; wings long.........
.................................**Bearded Vulture (Pl 10)**
Size small to medium; tail rounded.................. 65

43 Whole bird appears uniform dark brown............ 44
Whole bird is dark or light brown and variously marked 53

44 Underwing white; crest long; white windows in wings. .
.................................**Longcrested Eagle (Pl 14)**
Underwing dark; crest short or absent; no white in wings
.... 47

45 Back medium brown; belly mottled and/or barred with
light or dark brown...............................
.....**immature Pale and Dark Chanting Goshawks (Pl 16)**
Back dark brown or slaty; belly finely barred.......... 46

46 Tail with 6–7 narrow dark bands....................
.........................**Little Banded Goshawk (Pl 16)**
Tail with 3–4 broad dark bands.....**African Goshawk (Pl 16)**

47 Tail forked....................................... 48
Tail rounded or square............................ 49

48 Bill yellow; head and body uniform. .**Yellowbilled Kite (Pl 15)**
Bill black; head paler than body..........**Black Kite (Pl 15)**

49 Tail very short; head large; face bluish or orange......
.................................**immature Bateleur (Pl 13)**
Tail not very short............................... 50

50 Pale throat contrasts with dark underparts...**Bat Hawk (Pl 15)**
Throat and rest of underparts uniformly dark......... 51

51 Legs naked; whitish or yellow...................... 76
Legs feathered to toes, dark brown like belly......... 52

52 Pale windows in wingtips....**Booted Eagle (dark form) (Pl 14)**
No distinct pale windows in wings..................
.................................**Wahlberg's Eagle (Pl 14),**
Lesser Spotted Eagle, Steppe Eagle,
Tawny Eagle (dark form) (Pl 13)

53 Heavily marked below with mottling, spots or streaks of
dark and light brown............................ 54
Not heavily marked below, or marked with light brown
only.. 56

54 Heavily mottled or spotted below; pale spots on nape. .
.....................**immature African Goshawk (Pl 16)**
Heavily streaked below............................ 55

55 Shape slender; black line down centre of throat; streaks
on belly rather narrow...........................
.................**immature Black Sparrowhawk (Pl 16)**
Shape robust; streaks on belly broad................. 74

56 Shape slender; wings long, held above horizontal in flight;
     sails low over ground...........................   57
    Shape robust; wings broad, held horizontally in flight. .   58

57 Leading edge of wing pale; sometimes pale band across
     dark chest; no white on rump.....................
    ....**African Marsh Harrier (Pl 15)**
    Leading edge of wing not markedly paler; general colour-
     ing pale brown; rump distinctly white.............
    ....**female Pallid and Montagu's Harriers (Pl 15)**

58 Tail clearly barred or banded; legs partly or wholly
     naked, yellow...................................   59
    Tail obscurely barred; legs feathered to toes; untidy
     tawny brown or pale tawny, sometimes irregularly
     mottled............................**Tawny Eagle (Pl 13)**

59 Two or three dark bands on pale tail; below brown,
     obscurely streaked or barred; legs partly feathered...
    ....**Honey Buzzard (Pl 15)**
    Several fine bars on tail; brown-mottled underparts usu-
     ally divided by obscure pale chest band; often perches
     on poles..   75

60 Chest plain unmarked brown.......................   77
    Chest streaky light brown; belly mottled brown and
     white; obscure paler band on lower chest; legs bare;
     often perches on poles...........................   75

61 Underwing white with black trailing edge; tail very short;
     mantle brown; bare face and legs red.....**Bateleur (Pl 13)**
    Underwing dark; tail not very short.................   62

62 Pale windows in wingtips; size medium to large........   63
    No pale windows in wings; size small; tail faintly barred
    ....**Gabar Goshawk (black form) (Pl 16)**

63 Size large; white V on upper back; lower back white; legs
     feathered to toes; usually in mountain habitat.......
    ....**Black Eagle (Pl 13)**
    Size medium; rump white; tail clearly banded; wings held
     above horizontal in flight; usually over open grassland
     or fynbos; legs bare.................**Black Harrier (Pl 15)**

64 Barring on belly distinct; underwing barred; two white
     bands on tail........**Southern Banded Snake Eagle (Pl 14)**
    Barring on belly indistinct; underwing white; one white
     bar on tail...........**Western Banded Snake Eagle (Pl 14)**

65 Back barred; wings long...........................   66
    Back plain; wings relatively short...................
    ....**Redbreasted Sparrowhawk (Pl 16)**

66 Belly boldly streaked black on light rufous............
....**Greater Kestrel (Pl 19)**
Belly finely streaked brown on amber...............
.................**female Eastern Redfooted Kestrel (Pl 19)**

67 Streaked below.................................   68
Spotted or barred below..........................   69

68 Tail white with narrow black tip; underwing white; legs
bare..................**immature African Fish Eagle (Pl 13)**
Tail dark, banded; underwing dark; legs feathered to
toes, usually plain white........**African Hawk Eagle (Pl 14)**

69 Spotted below; underwing blackish; feathered legs usually spotted.........................**Ayres' Eagle (Pl 14)**
Barred below; underwing deep chestnut in front, with
checkerboard pattern behind........**Crowned Eagle (Pl 13)**

70 Falcon head pattern (see diagram); legs bare..........
..................................**Lanner Falcon (Pl 19)**
No falcon pattern; legs feathered to toes.............
.....................................**Tawny Eagle (Pl 13)**

71 Belly pale rufous, spotted (rarely barred) with black;
back rich chestnut; head, wings and tail blue; often
gregarious...................**male Lesser Kestrel (Pl 19)**
Belly deeper rufous, streaked black; head blue; wings
blackish; usually solitary..............**Rock Kestrel (Pl 19)**

72 Buffy rufous all over; streaked below; bold black chevron
bars on back; underwing white......**Greater Kestrel (Pl 19)**
White below; back slaty; chest streaked; belly barred. .
......................**immature Gabar Goshawk (Pl 16)**

73 Breast chestnut; broad white wingbar in flight.........
..................................**Jackal Buzzard (Pl 15)**
Breast black, spotted with white.....................
............**Black Sparrowhawk (blackbellied form) (Pl 16)**

74 Legs bare, yellow.........**immature Steppe Buzzard (Pl 15)**
Legs feathered to toes........**immature Tawny Eagle (Pl 13)**

75 Belly mainly barred.................**Steppe Buzzard (Pl 15)**
Belly mainly streaked................**Forest Buzzard (Pl 15)**
(These two species are variable in plumage, similar in
general appearance and can be told apart mainly by
habitat preference)

76 Legs yellow; bill bluish at base; head slender; eyes dark
.............................**immature Gymnogene (Pl 15)**
Legs whitish; bill yellowish at base; head large; eyes
yellow, rather owl-like...........................
...................................**Brown Snake Eagle,
immature Blackbreasted Snake Eagle (Pl 14)**

77   Chest dark brown; belly spotted; size large; legs feathered to toes........................**Martial Eagle (Pl 15)**
Chest light brown; belly barred (or mottled); size medium; legs bare, light orange...................
..............**immature Dark Chanting Goshawk (Pl 16)**

78   Underwing white in front...........................
.................**male Eastern Redfooted Kestrel (Pl 19)**
Underwing dark in front............................
.................**male Western Redfooted Kestrel (Pl 19)**

79   Whole body looks uniform grey..................... 80
Body grey; head paler (whitish)....**Dickinson's Kestrel (Pl 19)**

80   Primaries dark; wings extend beyond tail when perched; tail not barred; dark mark under eye...**Sooty Falcon (Pl 19)**
Primaries and tail lightly barred; wings shorter than tail when perched.......................**Grey Kestrel (Pl 19)**

81   Body all grey; head whitish; legs yellow..............
.............................**Dickinson's Kestrel (Pl 19)**
Undertail coverts rufous; legs orange to orange-red....
...................**male Eastern Redfooted Kestrel (Pl 19)**

82   Back dark slate grey or brown.........**Lanner Falcon (Pl 19)**
Back rufous, barred with black. .**female Lesser Kestrel (Pl 19)**

83   Streaked below................................... 84
Not streaked below............................... 85

84   Crown all dark.......**immature African Hobby Falcon (Pl 19)**
Crown rufous....**immature Western Redfooted Kestrel (Pl 19)**

85   Rufous patches on dark hindcrown; build robust.......
....................................**Taita Falcon (Pl 19)**
No rufous patches on dark hindcrown; build slender...
..........................**African Hobby Falcon (Pl 19)**

KEY TO THE FRANCOLINS (Pages 165–175; Plates 20–21)

1   Bill partly or wholly red........................... 2
     No red on bill...................................... 6

2   Throat and eyepatch red........................... 3
     No red on throat or eyepatch....................... 4

3   Belly streaked white on black; legs red. **.Rednecked Francolin**
     Belly streaked black on brown; legs black............
     ....**Swainson's Francolin**

4   Eyepatch yellow; belly finely barred......**Redbilled Francolin**
     No eyepatch; belly streaked or scaled............... 5

5   Belly boldly streaked white on black........**Cape Francolin**
     Belly scaled (and barred) white on black.....**Natal Francolin**

6   Whole body looks lightly mottled rufous brown.......
     ....**female Hartlaub's Francolin**
     Variously and distinctively marked above and below... 7

7   Belly boldly streaked with brown and white...........
     ....**male Hartlaub's Francolin**
     Belly not as above................................. 8

8   Head plain yellowish with reddish crown; underparts
       boldy barred black and white.......**male Coqui Francolin**
     Head variously marked............................. 9

9   Throat looks grey at a distance.........**Greywing Francolin**
     Throat white...................................... 10

10   White throat bordered by black necklace............. 11
     No black necklace around throat; legs red; eyebrow clear
       white; neck spotted with chestnut........**Crested Francolin**

11   Chest reddish cinnamon; belly boldly barred black and
       white...........................**female Coqui Francolin**
     Chest and upper belly streaked chestnut.............. 12

12   Centre of belly barred black and white....**Shelley's Francolin**
     Belly not barred................................... 13

13   Necklace broad, extends to upper breast...**Redwing Francolin**
     Necklace narrow, confined to throat. **.Orange River Francolin**

KEY TO THE SCOLOPACID WADERS
(SANDPIPERS AND ALLIES)
(Pages 232–253; Plates 25, 28, 29, 76)

1 Size large (over 40 cm); bill much longer than head..................... 2
. Size medium to small (under 40 cm); bill length variable................ 6

2 Bill decurved.. 3
Bill straight or slightly upcurved, basal half pink or orange............. 4

3 Eyebrow pale; crown boldly striped; white on rump only; bill about twice
length of head..**Whimbrel (Pl 25)**
Head finely streaked; rump and lower back conspicuously white in flight; bill
about three times length of head..........................**Curlew (Pl 25)**

4 Tail black; rump white; back plain grey............................... 5
Tail barred; back streaked..........................**Bartailed Godwit (Pl 25)**

5 Underwing white; bold white wingstripe............**Blacktailed Godwit (Pl 25)**
Underwing black; narrow white wingstripe...........**Hudsonian Godwit (Pl 76)**

6 Bill noticeably longer than head, straight or slightly upcurved............ 7
Bill as long as, or shorter than head, or markedly decurved.............. 13

7 Bill orange or red at base; legs orange-red........................... 8
Bill uniformly dark throughout, or dull yellowish orange at base; legs dark or
yellow... 9

8 Back faintly streaked; trailing edge of wing broadly white; call loud,
multisyllabled piping......................................**Redshank (Pl 28)**
Back almost plain; dark wings contrast with grey back; trailing edge of wing
darkly mottled; call 2-syllabled *tew-it*...............**Spotted Redshank (Pl 76)**

9 Head and back heavily streaked buff on dark brown; legs shortish; skulks in
dense marshy habitat... 10
Head and back look plain greyish or only faintly patterned; legs long,
greenish or yellowish; wades in open water......................... 11

10 Belly buff with black chevrons; silent when flushed.........**Great Snipe (Pl 25)**
Belly white with black bars; calls when flushed.........**Ethiopian Snipe (Pl 25)**

11 Bill markedly upcurved, orange at base; legs yellow, rather short; dark patch
at bend of wing; trailing edge of wing white; rump and tail grey........
....**Terek Sandpiper (Pl 29)**
Bill all dark, straight or only slight upcurved; legs greenish, long; no white in
wing; rump and lower back white in flight............................ 12

12 Bill thin and tapering to tip; build slender (length about 23 cm); callnote
single *chuk*......................................**Marsh Sandpiper (Pl 29)**
Bill relatively robust, not tapering to tip, sometimes slightly upcurved; build
robust (length about 32 cm); call loud 3-note whistled *tew-tew-tew*......
....**Greenshank (Pl 29)**

KEY TO THE SCOLOPACID WADERS

13 Bill straight or nearly straight.. 16
    Bill decurved at tip... 14

14 Bold white eyebrow forks behind eye; dark patch at bend of wing; sides of
       chest streaky; legs rather short.................**Broadbilled Sandpiper (Pl 29)**
    Eyebrow pale, but not bold, nor forking behind eye; wings and back uniform
       grey; sides of chest washed grey.................................... 15

15 Rump plain white in flight.........................**Curlew Sandpiper (Pl 29)**
    Rump white with black centre line............................**Dunlin (Pl 29)**

16 Back boldly scaled buff; no pale eyebrow; legs usually orange or yellowish   24
    Back plain or variously patterned; eyebrow pale; bill short and straight. . . 17

17 Back looks plain dark brown (faintly barred in good light); chest brownish;
       white of belly extends up around bend of wing; bobs body frequently. . .
       ....**Common Sandpiper (Pl 29)**
    Back spotted or mottled, never plain.................................... 18

18 Chest plain white like belly... 19
    Chest brownish or greyish, contrasting with white belly.................. 21

19 Overall appearance pale; back pale grey, faintly mottled; bill and legs black;
       dark patch at bend of wing; broad white wingbar in flight; mostly marine;
       runs fast..**Sanderling (Pl 29)**
    Back grey or brownish; size small; narrow white wingbar in flight; mostly
       inland waters.. 20

20 Back brownish, heavily mottled; common; gregarious.........**Little Stint (Pl 29)**
    Back greyish, lightly mottled; rare vagrant in small flocks...............
    ....**Rednecked Stint (Pl 29)**

21 Back greyish brown or buffy brown; no white wingbar in flight............ 22
    Back grey, mottled or scaled; bold white wingbar in flight; rump pale,
       mottled; bill and legs black; build chunky.......................**Knot (Pl 29)**

22 Back buffy brown, mottled; brownish streaked chest ends abruptly at white
       belly; rump pale with dark centre line; tail plain brown................
       ....**Pectoral Sandpiper (Pl 29)**
    Back dark greyish brown, spotted or speckled with white; rump white
       without dark centre line; chest coloration merges into white of belly; tail
       barred black and white.. 23

23 Back spotted with white; chest greyish brown merging into white of belly;
       legs yellowish green; underwing pale.................**Wood Sandpiper (Pl 29)**
    Back finely speckled with white; chest brownish, contrasting more with
       white of belly; legs dark; underwing blackish.........**Green Sandpiper (Pl 29)**

24 Pale ring around base of bill; narrow white wingbar in flight; belly white;
       rump white with dark centre line; legs usually dull orange (reddish to
       yellowish); usually silent...**Ruff (Pl 29)**
    Eyering white; underparts uniform deep buff; no wingbar in flight; rump
       mottled like back; underwing pure white; legs dull yellow.............
       ....**Buffbreasted Sandpiper (Pl 76)**

KEY TO THE NEAR-PASSERINES
(Pages 311–421; Plates 34–43, 75, 77)

1 Bill large, decurved, sometimes topped by casque.....
....................................**hornbills (Pl 41)**
Bill relatively smaller, or large and straight........... 2

2 Bill large, long, straight, pointed.........**kingfishers (Pl 40)**
Bill slender or relatively short....................... 3

3 Bill relatively long, slender, decurved................
..........**hoopoes, woodhoopoes (Pl 34), bee-eaters (Pl 40)**
Bill relatively short and/or stout.................... 4

4 Head markedly crested............................ 5
Head not markedly crested........................ 6

5 Size small; tail long, stiff, pointed.........**mousebirds (Pl 42)**
Size medium to large.........**louries (Pl 34), Crested Barbet
(Pl 42) some larger cuckoos (Pl 35)**

6 Bill very short, stout, hooked.....**parrots (Pl 34), owls (Pl 37)**
Bill not as above.................................. 7

7 Bill straight, pointed..........**woodpeckers, wryneck (Pl 43)**
Bill strongly or slightly curved on culmen, or very small   8

8 Outer rectrices strikingly white in flight...............
....................**honeyguides, Klaas's Cuckoo (Pl 36)
some nightjars (Pl 38)**
Outer rectrices not white, or with white spots only..... 9

9 Camouflaged, small-billed, longwinged; usually sit on
ground; nocturnal........................**nightjars (Pl 38)**
Not as above..................................... 10

10 Back green; belly red, orange or dull yellow.......... 16
Not as above..................................... 11

11 Wings bright rufous; tail heavy, dark; bill stout........
....**coucals (Pl 35)**
Not as above..................................... 12

12 Bill bright yellow; body drab greenish. . .**Green Coucal (Pl 35)**
Bill black, or yellow at base only.................... 13

13 Size medium to large; wings blue; perch conspicuously;
bill robust...............................**rollers (Pl 41)**
Size smaller; not as above......................... 14

14 Size small to very small; bill heavy or stubby; head may
be striped black and white................**barbets (Pl 42)**
Not as above...................................... 15

15 Aerial feeders; longwinged; mainly black or grey......
....**swifts (Pl 39)**
Arboreal; size medium to smallish; bill arched; shy and
tend to shelter in foliage of trees......**cuckoos (Pls 35–36)**

16 Back bright dark green; belly brilliant crimson; bill
yellowish.........................**Narina Trogon (Pl 34)**
Back light green; belly orange or dull yellow; bill and
collar on throat black.............**Little Bee-eater (Pl 40)**

IN-HAND KEY TO THE NIGHTJARS (Pages 350–355; Plate 38)

1 Primary 9 more than 176 mm long.................................... 2
   Primary 9 less than 176 mm long..................................... 4

2 Emargination on primary 9 more than 65 mm long............**Freckled Nightjar**
   Emargination on primary 9 less than 65 mm long...................... 3

3 Primary 6 more than 155 mm long; rectrix 1 shorter than rectrix 5; tomium
      21–29 mm; tarsus 20–28 mm.......................**Pennantwinged Nightjar**
   Primary 6 less than 155 mm long; rectrix 1 longer than rectrix 5; tomium
      28–34 mm; tarsus 14–20 mm...........................**European Nightjar**

4 Apical patch on rectrix 5 less than 55 mm long........................ 5
   Apical patch on rectrix 5 more than 55 mm long....................... 6

5 Primary 9 emarginated for less than 38% of its length. . .**Rufouscheeked Nightjar**
   Primary 9 emarginated for more than 38% of its length. . . .**Fierynecked Nightjar**

6 Apical patch on rectrix 5 only (not on rectrix 4); centre of bar on inner web
      of primary 9 well above (proximal to) flexure point of emargination; tarsus
      and middle toe less than 45 mm......................**Mozambique Nightjar**
   Apical patches on rectrices 4 and 5; centre of bar on inner web of primary 9
      below (distal to) or opposite flexure point of emargination; tarsus and
      middle toe more than 45 mm...............................**Natal Nightjar**

Figure 9. A selection of different passerine birds to show the two basic bill shapes:
a–e=conical-billed passerines; f–j=slender-billed passerines.

KEY TO THE WOODPECKERS (Pages 414–420; Plate 43)

1 Crown (or hindcrown) bright red...................................... 5
   Crown black or grey.. 2

2 Crown black... 3
   Crown grey... 4

3 Forecrown brown; belly streaked.................**female Cardinal Woodpecker**
   Forecrown speckled with white; belly barred.......**female Bearded Woodpecker**

4 Belly and back plain green; arboreal.................**female Olive Woodpecker**
   Belly red; back spotted with yellowish white; terrestrial.....**Ground Woodpecker**

5 Belly and back plain green; face grey; rump red.........**male Olive Woodpecker**
   Belly and back patterned.. 6

6 Belly barred; hindcrown, earpatch and heavy malar stripe black..........
   ....**male Bearded Woodpecker**
   Belly streaked, spotted or heavily mottled; hindcrown red............... 7

7 Forecrown spotted white on black.................................... 13
   Forecrown plain (red or brown), or spotted black on red................ 8

8 Forecrown brown; belly streaked..................**male Cardinal Woodpecker**
   Forecrown red, plain or spotted with black........................... 9

9 Belly streaked; malar stripe red................**male Goldentailed Woodpecker**
   Belly spotted or heavily mottled.................................... 10

10 Belly heavily mottled; ear coverts dark; forecrown spotted with black.....
   ....**male Knysna Woodpecker**
   Belly spotted; ear coverts pale.................................... 11

11 Forecrown plain red; belly lightly spotted........................... 12
   Forecrown spotted with black; belly heavily spotted...................
   ....**male Little Spotted Woodpecker**

12 Throat plain white..............................**male Bennett's Woodpecker**
   Throat spotted black on white..............**male Specklethroated Woodpecker**

13 Belly streaked..............................**female Goldentailed Woodpecker**
   Belly spotted or heavily mottled................................... 14

14 Belly heavily mottled; ear coverts dark.............**female Knysna Woodpecker**
   Belly clearly spotted; ear coverts pale.............................. 15

15 Throat and earpatch dark brown................**female Bennett's Woodpecker**
   Throat speckled black on whitish................................... 16

16 Belly heavily spotted; no clear malar stripe....**female Little Spotted Woodpecker**
   Belly lightly spotted; malar stripe formed of black speckles.............
   ....**female Specklethroated Woodpecker**

KEY TO THE SLENDERBILLED ARBOREAL PASSERINES
(Pages 421–705; Plates 36, 47–59, 61–65)
(See diagram, Fig. 9, on page lxvi)

1 Size very small (less than 13 cm; smaller than sparrow). .   2
   Size small to medium (more than 13 cm).   4

2 Bill long, slender, decurved. . . . .**sunbirds (Pl 64–65)**
   Bill not as above.   3

3 Body yellow or greenish above (and often below); eye-
    ring white. . . . .**white-eyes (Pl 65)**
   Not as above, though may be yellow below. . . . .
          . . . . .warblers (Pl 52–57), some flycatchers (Pl 58–59),
                            penduline tits (Pl 54)

4 Body all black, sometimes with blue or green gloss. . . .
        . . . . .male Black Cuckooshrike (Pl 47), drongos (Pl 47),
              Black Flycatcher (Pl 58), most starlings (Pl 63)
   Body not all black.   5

5 Belly bright yellow; bill deep pink; wings with black or
    grey. . . . .**orioles (Pl 47)**
   Not as above (though belly may be bright yellow).   6

6 Bill long, slender, decurved. . . . .
     . . . . .creeper (Pl 48), sugarbirds (Pl 63), sunbirds (Pl 64–65)
   Bill relatively short.   7

7 Tail orange with black centre. . . . .
      . . . . . .some thrushes (Pl 49), robins (Pl 51) and chats (Pl 50)
   Tail not as above.   8

8 Heavily streaked or spotted below. . . . .
           . . . . .African Broadbill (Pl 36), some thrushes (Pl 49),
              Whitebrowed Robin (Pl 51), Striped Pipit (Pl 60),
                female Plumcoloured Starling (Pl 63)
   Not heavily streaked or spotted below.   9

9 Tail about twice body length. . . . .
      . . . . . .Longtailed Shrike (Pl 61), Paradise Flycatcher (Pl 59)
   Tail not very long.   10

10 Belly bright yellow. . . . .
           . . . . .Yellowbellied and Stripecheeked Bulbuls (Pl 48),
               Starred Robin (Pl 51), Yellow Warbler (Pl 52),
                some bush shrikes (Pl 62)
   Belly not bright yellow.   11

11　Plain dove grey all over..........**Grey Cuckooshrike (Pl 47)**
　　Not as above, or dull olive grey all over.............　12

12　Bill yellow, orange or red............................
　　..........**some thrushes (Pl 49) some helmetshrikes (Pl 61),**
　　　　　　　　some starlings (Pl 63), oxpeckers (Pl 63)
　　Bill black, dull coloured or pale....................　13

13　Bill pale pinkish ....**Bush Blackcap (Pl 48),**
　　　　　　　　　　　Wattled Starling (Pl 63)
　　Bill not pale pinkish................................　14

14　Belly pure white ......**Whitebreasted Cuckooshrike (Pl 47),**
　　　　　　Pied Babbler (Pl 49), some flycatchers (Pl 58–59),
　　　　some shrikes (Pl 61), male Plumcoloured Starling (Pl 63)
　　Belly black, coloured or off-white....................　15

15　Belly black............**black tits (Pl 48), Arnot's Chat (Pl 50),**
　　Belly not black....................................　16

16　Head black (with or without eyestripe)..............
　　.......................**tits (Pl 48), some bulbuls (Pl 48),**
　　　　Swynnerton's Robin (Pl 51), some flycatchers (Pl 58, 59,)
　　　　　　　　some shrikes (Pl 61–62)
　　Head not black....................................　17

17　Finely barred below ....**female Black Cuckooshrike (Pl 47),**
　　　　　　female Redbacked Shrike (Pl 61),
　　　　some immature shrikes and bush shrikes (Pl 61–62)
　　Not finely barred below...........................　18

18　Wings chestnut.........................**tchagras (Pl 62)**
　　Wings not chestnut...............................　19

19　Usually in small flocks; often noisy, voices usually harsh
　　....................**some bulbuls (Pl 48), starlings (Pl 63),**
　　　　　　babblers (Pl 49), helmetshrikes (Pl 61)
　　Solitary or in pairs; usually quiet or with mellow
　　song............................. **some bulbuls (Pl 48),**
　　　　　　　thrushes (Pl 49), robins (Pl 51),
　　　　flycatchers (Pl 58–59), bush shrikes (Pl 61–62)

KEY TO THE LARKS (Pages 425–447; Plates 44–45)

1 Belly rufous, buff or white.......................... 6
  Belly black, or with black central patch.............. 2

2 Head black with conspicuous white ear patches and collar
  3
  Head black or streaky; no white ear patches or collar. . 4

3 Back grey or sandy; white patch in centre of crown....
  ....**male Greybacked Finchlark**
  Back chestnut; no white patch on crown..............
  ....**male Chestnutbacked Finchlark**

4 Back grey or sandy...........**female Greybacked Finchlark**
  Back rufous or marked with rufous................. 5

5 Head and belly all black without white markings......
  ....**male Blackeared Finchlark**
  Chest mottled greyish; black patch in centre of belly; pale
  collar on hindneck........**female Chestnutbacked Finchlark**

6 Belly white or off-white.......................... 7
  Belly rufous or buff.............................. 20

7 Crown and pectoral patches plain bright rufous; bill black
  ....**Redcapped Lark**
  Crown mottled, streaked or dark brown............. 8

8 Chest plain white; back pale pinkish...........**Gray's Lark**
  Chest streaked or spotted........................ 9

9 Tail short and narrow (looks almost tailless).....**Rudd's Lark**
  Tail not as above................................ 10

10 Crown and back dark brown, lightly scaled buff; breast
   and head boldly marked dark brown on white. .**Dusky Lark**
   Crown and back light brown, buff or rufous, streaked or
   spotted...................................... 11

11 Bill fairly heavy, yellow at base; breast boldly streaked;
   head may appear crested...............**Thickbilled Lark**
   Bill not as above (if yellowish at base, then breast
   markings not bold)............................ 12

12 Eyebrow clear white............................ 13
   Eyebrow absent or indistinct; whitish ring around eye;
   bill pale whitish............................. 29

13 Bill nearly as long as head, decurved.......**Longbilled Lark**
   Bill shorter than head; usually fairly robust........... 14

14 White above and below eye........................ 16
   White above eye only............................ 15

15 White eyebrow does not extend to base of bill; primaries
    edged rufous; ear coverts heavily streaked . . . .
    . . . .**Monotonous Lark**
    White eyebrow extends to base of bill; primaries edged
    grey or buffy; ear coverts lightly streaked . . . . . .**Sabota Lark**

16 Dark line from gape to ear coverts 17
    No dark line from gape to ear coverts. . . .**Fawncoloured Lark**

17 Back boldly streaked or mottled; not usually rufous. . . . 18
    Back rufous, plain or only lightly streaked 19

18 Outer tail feathers white; breast markings do not extend
    to belly . . . .**Sabota Lark**
    Tail all dark; breast markings extend to belly . . . . .**Karoo Lark**

19 Back deep rufous; head markings bold; confined to red
    Kalahari sand in Bushmanland . . . .**Red Lark**
    Back light rufous; head not boldly marked; confined to
    pale reddish sands of Namib dunes . . . .**Dune Lark**

20 Bill pink 21
    Bill not pink 22

21 Belly uniform light rufous; flanks not streaked . . . .
    . . . .**Pinkbilled Lark**
    Belly shades to whitish towards tail; flanks streaked
    blackish; confined to upper Vaal River catchment
    region . . . .**Botha's Lark**

22 Tail very short and narrow (looks almost tailless) . . . . . .
    . . . .**Rudd's Lark**
    Tail not markedly short and narrow 23

23 Bill rather slender and decurved 24
    Bill rather stouter and more conical 25

24 White of throat contrasts sharply with rufous of breast;
    eyebrow rufous or buff; tail relatively short, tipped
    white . . . .**Spikeheeled Lark**
    White of throat merges with rufous of breast; eyebrow
    white; tail not noticeably short, all dark. .**Shortclawed Lark**

25 Dark vertical mark below eye ("teardrop"); no rufous in
    wing . . . .**Sclater's Lark**
    No dark vertical mark below eye; primaries edged bright
    rufous 26

26 Back lightly and obscurely mottled; rattling or clapping
    display flight 27
    Back boldly mottled or streaked; no rattling flight
    display 28

27   Rattling display flight followed by clear drawn-out rising
whistle; mainly highveld and arid western distribution
....**Clapper Lark**
Rattling display flight in short bursts followed by barely
audible chippering song; mainly subtropical northeastern distribution...........................**Flappet Lark**

28   Size large; shape robust; bill heavy and longish; throat
not clearly white.....................**Rufousnaped Lark**
Size smallish; bill relatively short; throat and outer rectrices clear white......................**Melodious Lark**

29   Back rufous; head does not appear crested............
..........................**female Blackeared Finchlark**
Back sandy buff; crown feathers elongated, often forming
crest.....................................**Stark's Lark**

KEY TO THE SWALLOWS AND MARTINS (Pages 448–465; Plate 46, 77)

1 Size small; body mostly jet black without blue sheen...................... 2
  Body brown or metallic blueblack above; below white, buff, rufous, brown or black... 3

2 All jet black...**Black Sawwing Swallow**
  Underwing white..............................**East African Sawwing Swallow**

3 Body all blueblack; outer tail streamers very long...............**Blue Swallow**
  Body not all blueblack.. 4

4 Upperparts brown... 5
  Upperparts blueblack (look black from distance)........................ 8

5 Belly pale buffy brown; tail square with white windows............**Rock Martin**
  Belly white; tail square or notched without white windows.............. 6

6 Throat white; collar brown.. 7
  Throat brown; tail notched...........................**Brownthroated Martin**

7 Tail square; white patch in front of eye.......................**Banded Martin**
  Tail notched; no white in front of eye...........................**Sand Martin**

8 Underparts streaked black on white................................. 9
  Underparts plain white, buff or rufous.............................. 10

9 Underparts heavily streaked; rump dark orange; ear coverts deep red like crown.......................................**Lesser Striped Swallow**
  Underparts lightly streaked; rump pale orange; ear coverts white with black streaks, like underparts...........................**Greater Striped Swallow**

10 Belly rufous or rufous-buff.. 11
  Belly white or buffy.. 13

11 Throat pure white..**Mosque Swallow**
  Throat rufous, though may be paler than belly........................ 12

12 Hindneck rufous; no white in tail; underparts pale rufous; rare vagrant...**Redrumped Swallow**
  Hindneck blueblack like crown; white windows in tail; underparts deep rufous...**Redbreasted Swallow**

13 Crown deep rufous....................................**Wiretailed Swallow**
  Crown not deep rufous... 14

14 Throat rufous or deep buff... 15
  Throat white like belly.. 17

15 Tail forked, with white windows.................................... 16
  Tail square, without white windows...........................**Cliff Swallow**

16 Rufous or buff on throat only, bordered below by broad dark collar; tail
    deeply forked..**European Swallow**
    Rufous extends from throat to upper breast; collar narrow and incomplete;
    tail less deeply forked.......................................**Angola Swallow**

17 Rump blueblack like back... 18
    Rump grey or white.. 19

18 White windows in tail; forehead chestnut; collar complete...............
    ....**Whitethroated Swallow**
    No white windows in tail; forehead blueblack like crown; collar absent or
    incomplete.......................................**Pearlbreasted Swallow**

19 Rump and crown grey..................................**Greyrumped Swallow**
    Rump white; crown blueblack like back........................**House Martin**

KEY TO THE CISTICOLAS (Pages 574–593; Plates 56–57)

1 Tail relatively short; habitat open grassland, usually without
    trees, or with scattered small trees only............................... 2
    Tail medium to relatively long; habitat rank grassland, vlei or marsh, grassy
    understory of woodland, fynbos or karoo............................ 8

2 Back plain grey; no pattern on tail; habitat with some bushes or trees..... 3
    Back buff, streaked blackish; tail boldly patterned at tip; habitat open
    grassland without bushes or trees.................................. 4

3 Crown plain grey or dull rufous (streaked blackish in winter); below whitish;
    tail very short (29–35 mm) in summer; song feeble *see see see*..........
    ....**Shortwinged Cisticola**
    Crown plain dull rufous; tail longer than 37 mm, frequently flicked from side
    to side; below bluish grey; song penetrating *weep weep weep* from high
    perch..**Neddicky**

4 Back lightly streaked; rump buff or greyish; song high-pitched, variable,
    quick *ting-ting-ting*, 1 note/half second......................**Desert Cisticola**
    Back boldly streaked; rump bright tawny rufous........................ 5

5 Display flight low (up to 10 m), bouncing; song monotonous unmusical *zit zit
    zit*, 1 note/second.....................................**Fantailed Cisticola**
    Display flight very high (bird usually out of sight); song in set phrase of 2 or
    3 different sets of notes... 6

6 Song rapid *see-see-see-chik-chik-chik-chik*......................**Cloud Cisticola**
    Song slower, more deliberate.. 7

7 Song short (fewer than 7 notes), repeated frequently for long period: *chitik
    chitik tsi tsi tsi*..**Ayres' Cisticola**
    Song long (10–20 notes or more), repeated infrequently. . .**Palecrowned Cisticola**

8 Crown plain rufous, or only lightly streaked; size smallish.............. 9

Crown grey, boldly streaked; tail grey, boldly patterned at tip with black and white; bill heavy, decurved; voice loud croaking...........**Croaking Cisticola**

9 Back grey, streaked darker, or back black, scaled with buff or grey....... 12
   Back plain grey (washed rusty in winter)............................... 10

10 Tail plain, often held cocked up; call notes loud and petulant; song jumbled phrases; habitat rank vegetation, often with rocks.............**Lazy Cisticola**
   Tail boldly patterned at tip, not held cocked up....................... 11

11 Rufous crown contrasts with brown back; tail greyish brown; habitat bracken-briar or streamside bush, mostly above 1000 m above sea level
   ....**Singing Cisticola**
   Crown and back both rufous; tail russet; habitat rank marshy vegetation, mostly in lowlands....................................**Redfaced Cisticola**

12 Habitat marshy.. 13
   Habitat not marshy.. 15

13 Back black, scaled buff or grey (or heavily striped black).............. 14
   Back grey, streaked black; tail dusky brown, looks heavy in flight; below rusty buff; northern Botswana (Okavango system) only; song *chip chipchip zeeeee*..**Chirping Cisticola**

14 Rump dull olive-buff, streaked black; tail rusty brown; mainly highveld and southern distribution................................**Levaillant's Cisticola**
   Rump plain grey; tail grey, tipped black; mainly lowland and northern distribution.......................................**Blackbacked Cisticola**

15 Habitat sloping grassland with bracken, or shrubby fynbos and karoo..... 16
   Habitat woodland, bushveld or savanna.............................. 17

16 Breast and flanks greyish white; back lightly streaked; habitat fynbos, karoo and semidesert; distribution mainly western.............**Greybacked Cisticola**
   Breast and flanks buffy white; back boldly streaked; habitat sloping grassland with bracken and herbs; distribution mainly eastern..........**Wailing Cisticola**

17 Tail bright rufous; lores and eyebrow buff; habitat scrub; song bell-like *twee twee twee*; behaviour secretive............................**Tinkling Cisticola**
   Tail dusky brown; lores and eyebrow greyish white; habitat thornveld, bushveld, coastal scrub; song set phrase of 2–4 piping notes followed by trill or rattle; behaviour bold.............................**Rattling Cisticola**

KEY TO THE "BROWNS" OF WIDOWS, BISHOPS AND QUELEAS
(females and eclipse males) (Pages 729–741; Plates 68–69)

1 Bill red or yellow.......................................**adult Redbilled Quelea**
   Bill not red or yellow.. 2

2 Throat and breast plain, faintly mottled or faintly streaked.............. 3
   Throat and breast clearly streaked.................................. 7

3 Wrist patch yellow...............................**male Yellowbacked Widow**
   Wrist patch not yellow.. 4

4 Crown boldly streaked... 5
   Crown faintly streaked.. 6

5 Breast faintly streaked..........................**female Yellowbacked Widow**
   Breast plain, pale tawny..............................**Redcollared Widow**

6 Crown greyish brown............................**immature Redbilled Quelea**
   Crown yellowish brown................................**Redheaded Quelea**

7 Wrist patch rusty or yellowish; tail longish (more than one quarter of body
      length).. 10
   Wrist patch coloured like rest of body; tail short (less than one qurter of body
      length).. 8

8 Build robust; back dull olive brown; belly pale buff................... 9
   Build slender; back dull rufous brown; belly almost white........**Golden Bishop**

9 Wings and tail brown..**Red Bishop**
   Wings and tail black.............................**male Firecrowned Bishop**

10 Wrist patch rusty.. 11
   Wrist patch yellow... 12

11 Size large (more than 18 cm); whole breast streaked.........**Longtailed Widow**
   Size medium to smallish (less than 18 cm); breast streaked at sides only...
   ....**Redshouldered Widow**

12 Wrist patch dull yellow; rump brown....................**Whitewinged Widow**
   Wrist patch and rump bright yellow...............**male Yellowrumped Widow**

KEY TO THE SMALL CORMORANTS (Plate 4)

1 Tail relatively short; eye green or brown; marine...................... 2
   Tail relatively long; eye red (in adult)............................... 3

2 'Face' yellow; bill long and slender.........................**Cape Cormorant**
   'Face' black; bill short and stubby..........................**Bank Cormorant**

3 Freshwater; head not crested.............................**Reed Cormorant**
   Marine; head lightly crested when breeding..............**Crowned Cormorant**

KEY TO THE LARGE GREY HERONS (Plate 5)

1 Bill yellow; hindneck white; black line through eye; underwing uniform grey
      in flight...**Grey Heron**
   Bill blackish; hindneck and crown black or slaty; underwing sharply two-
      toned black-and-white in flight........................**Blackheaded Heron**

KEY TO THE WHITE EGRETS (Plate 5)

1   Legs and feet all black; bill black or yellow; black line under eye extends well
behind eye..**Great White Egret**
    Legs or feet with touch of yellow; line under eye faint or absent, not
extending to behind eye.. 2

2   Bill black, slender; legs black; toes yellow.........................**Little Egret**
    Bill yellow or orange.. 3

3   Legs and toes black; thighs yellowish; bill yellow; neck longish...........
....**Yellowbilled Egret**
    Legs and toes dull yellow or greenish; head, back and chest tinged buff in
summer; neck short; bill orange in summer....................**Cattle Egret**

KEY TO THE STORKS (Plate 7)

1   Plumage mainly white... 2
    Plumage mainly black or very dark brown........................... 3

2   Bill red, pointed; face feathered; tail white......................**White Stork**
    Bill yellow, decurved at tip; face naked, red; tail black.......**Yellowbilled Stork**

3   Neck white...**Woollynecked Stork**
    Neck black... 4

4   Belly black or very dark brown...........................**Openbilled Stork**
    Belly white... 5

5   Bill and legs red; face mostly feathered.........................**Black Stork**
    Bill black; legs blackish with red toes and ankles; face naked, blue.......
....**Abdim's Stork**

KEY TO THE FLAMINGOS (Plate 7)

1   Body looks white at a distance; bill pale (pink) with black tip; flocks loosely
aggregated..**Greater Flamingo**
    Body looks pink at a distance; bill dark (red), looks black from far; flocks
tightly packed...**Lesser Flamingo**

KEY TO THE LARGE BUSTARDS (Plate 24)

1   Hindneck rufous.. 2
    Hindneck not rufous; whole neck barred......................**Kori Bustard**

2   Folded wing shows bold black-and-white pattern...................... 3
    Folded wing shows hardly any black-and-white pattern..............
....**female Ludwig's Bustard**

3 Crown black with white median streak; foreneck grey or lightly barred with
   brown..**Stanley's Bustard**
   Crown and foreneck solid dark brown...................**male Ludwig's Bustard**

KEY TO THE SMALL, UNCOLLARED PLOVERS (Plate 26)

1 Black band behind white front does not meet eye..........**Whitefronted Plover**
   Black band behind white front meets eye; broad black stripe from behind eye
   down side of neck.......................................**Kittlitz's Plover**

KEY TO THE BLACKWINGED PLOVERS (Plate 26)

1 White of front extends to above eye; eyering scarlet; legs dull red; secondaries tipped black (in flight)............................**Blackwinged Plover**
   White of front stops in front of eye; eyering and legs brown; secondaries all
   white (in flight)................................**Lesser Blackwinged Plover**

KEY TO THE DIKKOPS (Plate 25)

1 Back streaked; dark and light bar on folded wing................**Water Dikkop**
   Back spotted; no bars on folded wing........................**Spotted Dikkop**

KEY TO THE PLAIN RUFOUS COURSERS (Plate 30)

1 Black chestband extends between legs onto belly; hindcrown rufous......
   ....**Temminck's Courser**
   Black chestband does not extend between legs; hindcrown bluegrey......
   ....**Burchell's Courser**

KEY TO THE "WHITE-RUMPED" SWIFTS (Pages 358–360, 363; Plate 39)

1 Tail square; rump broadly white.. 3
   Tail forked.. 2

2 Tail deeply forked; white on rump narrow, V-shaped........**Whiterumped Swift**
   Tail slightly forked; white on rump broad and straight.............**Horus Swift**

3 Throat plain white; no white under tail; habitat buildings and cliffs...**Little Swift**
   Throat mottled with white; white line under tail; habitat woodland with
   baobabs...**Mottled Spinetail**

KEY TO THE SMALL BLUE KINGFISHERS (Pages 372–373; Plate 40)

1 Bill black; eyebrow white...........................**Halfcollared Kingfisher**
   Bill red; eyebrow rufous or absent.................................... 2

2 Crown turquoise blue; no chestnut eyebrow; waterside habitat............
....**Malachite Kingfisher**
Crown violet blue; eyebrow chestnut; woodland habitat.......**Pygmy Kingfisher**

KEY TO THE PIPITS
(excluding Yellowbreasted, Golden and Redthroated) (Pages 625–633, 798; Plate 60, 77)

1 Upperparts streaked; malar stripe present or absent.................... 2
Upperparts not streaked; malar stripe absent.......................... 8

2 Dorsal streaks clear, dark, usually bold............................... 3
Dorsal streaks brown, not clearly defined; breast streaks and malar stripe
dark brown.. 6

3 Wing and tail feathers edged yellow; breast and flanks heavily streaked;
malar stripe absent; habitat rocky woodland....................**Striped Pipit**
Wing and tail feathers not edged yellow.............................. 4

4 Back boldly streaked; breast and flanks heavily streaked or spotted....... 5
Back finely streaked; throat pure white; heavy black malar stripe; habitat
savanna and woodland...**Tree Pipit**

5 Throat buffy; walks with crouched gait; habitat savanna and woodland....
....**Bushveld Pipit**
Throat white; size small; habitat open (montane) grassland.....**Shorttailed Pipit**

6 Outer rectrices white; display flight in rising loops, ending in vertical dive;
habitat open grassland....................................**Grassveld Pipit**
Outer rectrices buff or greyish; habitat rocky or montane............... 7

7 Back fairly distinctly streaked; display flight as for Grassveld Pipit; summer
habitat exclusively montane...............................**Mountain Pipit**
Back indistinctly streaked; display flight fluttering; habitat rocky, hilly or
woodland.. 10

8 Outer rectrices white; breast faintly streaked; habitat rocky hills and mountains; song diagnostic......................................**Rock Pipit**
Outer rectrices buff or greyish; breast plain or barely streaked.......... 9

9 Row of dark spots on wing coverts; base of lower jaw yellowish; back fairly
dark brown...**Plainbacked Pipit**
Wing coverts almost plain buffy brown; base of lower jaw pinkish; back buffy
brown...**Buffy Pipit**

10 Eyebrow and underparts white; habitat subtropical woodland........**Wood Pipit**
Eyebrow and underparts buff; habitat rocky and stony hillsides. .**Longbilled Pipit**

KEY TO THE TCHAGRAS (Pages 649–653; Plate 62)

1 Pale eyebrow present; underparts greyish white or yellowish buff......... 2
No pale eyebrow; crown all black; underparts yellowish buff...♂ **Marsh Tchagra**

2 Crown black.. **4**
Crown brown.. 3

3 Crown rusty brown; no black line above pale eyebrow........**Southern Tchagra**
  Crown earth brown; black line above and below pale eyebrow...........
  ....**Threestreaked Tchagra**

4 Back and central rectrices brown; underparts greyish white.............
  ....**Blackcrowned Tchagra**
  Back rufous; tail black; underparts yellowish buff............♀ **Marsh Tchagra**

KEY TO THE GREEN-AND-YELLOW BUSH SHRIKES
(Pages 653–658; Plate 62)

1 Black collar across breast.. 2
  No black collar across breast... 3

2 Throat red; crown and nape green.....................**Gorgeous Bush Shrike**
  Throat yellow; crown and nape grey...........................**Bokmakierie**

3 Underparts pinkish white......................**Olive Bush Shrike (ruddy form)**
  Underparts orange and/or yellow..................................... 4

4 Crown and nape green.......................**Olive Bush Shrike (olive form)**
  Crown and nape grey... 5

5 Face grey; eye yellow; bill very heavy................**Greyheaded Bush Shrike**
  Face black; eye dark.. 6

6 Yellow eyebrow separates black face from grey crown..................
  ....**Orangebreasted Bush Shrike**
  No yellow eyebrow..............................**Blackfronted Bush Shrike**

KEY TO THE ADULT BREEDING MALE YELLOW WEAVERS
(Pages 717–726; Plate 67)

1 Back and crown plain black; underparts golden yellow...........**Forest Weaver**
  Back greenish or yellowish, plain or variously marked................... 2

2 Face mask black.. 3
  Face mask brown, green or absent.................................... 6

3 Black of face mask extends to front and/or crown.................... 4
  Black of face mask does not extend to front (front orange or yellow)..... 5

4 Mask extends onto chest in narrow point; iris red...................... 10
  Mask rounded below; crown mostly black; iris cream.....**Lesser Masked Weaver**

5 Mask extends across whole face, throat and upper breast; crown yellow; back
   boldly spotted..........**southern forms of Spottedbacked Weaver** (*spilonotus*)
  Mask forms narrow bib and eyestripe only; crown orange-yellow; back plain
   green..**Spectacled Weaver**

KEY TO THE YELLOW CANARIES (MALES ONLY)

6   Face mask distinct, brown or green...................................... 7
    Face mask indistinct or absent.. 8

7   Face mask brown..................................**Brownthroated Weaver**
    Face mask green; breast chestnut.........................**Oliveheaded Weaver**

8   Face deep chestnut-orange merging into yellow of head and body; iris cream
        to yellow..**Cape Weaver**
    Head all yellow (no mask); iris red or yellow.......................... 9

9   Iris red; underparts daffodil yellow............................**Yellow Weaver**
    Iris yellow; underparts golden yellow.........................**Golden Weaver**

10 Crown yellow; back greenish with faint streaks...............**Masked Weaver**
    Crown black; back heavily spotted or mottled........................
    ....**northern form of Spottedbacked Weaver (*nigriceps*)**

KEY TO THE YELLOW CANARIES (MALES ONLY)
(Pages 774–783; Plate 73)

1   Back greenish; habitat not rocky..................................... 3
    Back brown; habitat rocky.. 2

2   Tail and wings tipped white; distribution largely winter-rainfall region of
        southern and western Cape....................................**Cape Siskin**
    Only outer rectrices white; distribution largely Drakensberg massif and
        adjacent mountain ranges...........................**Drakensberg Siskin**

3   Nape and mantle blue-grey....................................**Cape Canary**
    Nape and mantle greenish like back................................. 4

4   Chin black; underparts streaked dark green....................**Forest Canary**
    Chin yellow; belly not streaked...................................... 5

5   Size large; bill very heavy; underparts rich sulphur yellow; facial markings
        green, not well defined; breast washed greenish...............**Bully Canary**
    Size smallish; underparts clear yellow; facial markings distinct............ 6

6   Size medium; underparts deep yellow, including flanks; rump dull greenish
        yellow; (female dull streaky grey)..........................**Yellow Canary**
    Size small; underparts light yellow, fading to greyish on flanks; rump bright
        yellow; rectrices tipped white; (sexes alike)..............**Yelloweyed Canary**

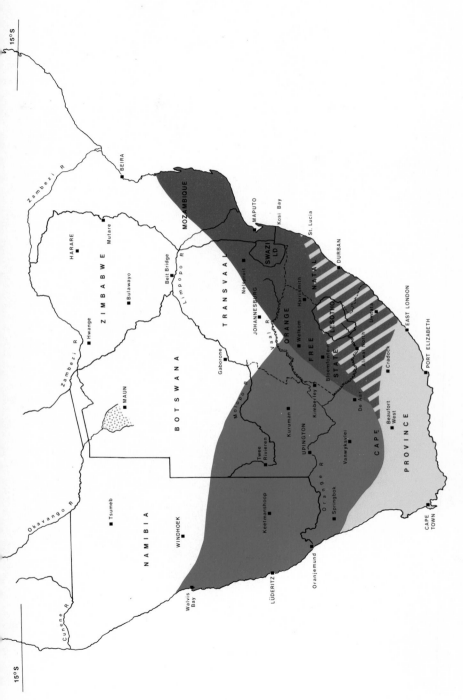

Figure 10. Map of southern Africa with some important place names, showing the types of bird distribution: green = resident species, blue = breeding migrant, yellow = nonbreeding migrant. Striped combinations of colour indicate that different populations of a species may occupy an area at any given time; for example a resident population and a nonbreeding population occurring together will show as green-and-yellow striped.

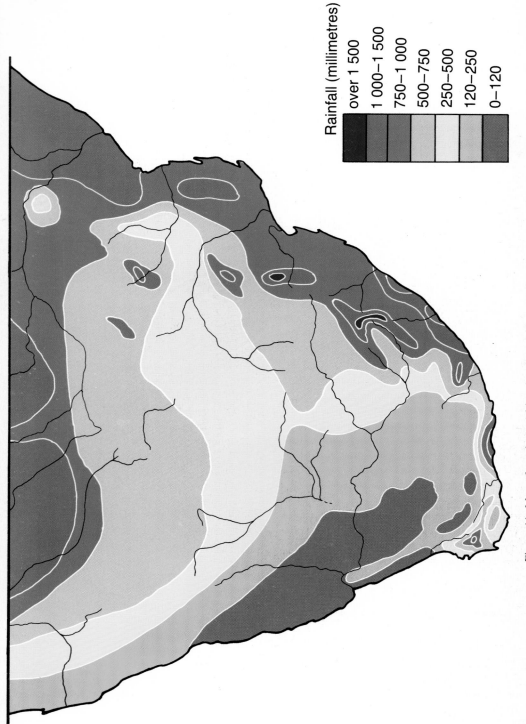

Figure 11. Map of southern Africa showing major rainfall regions

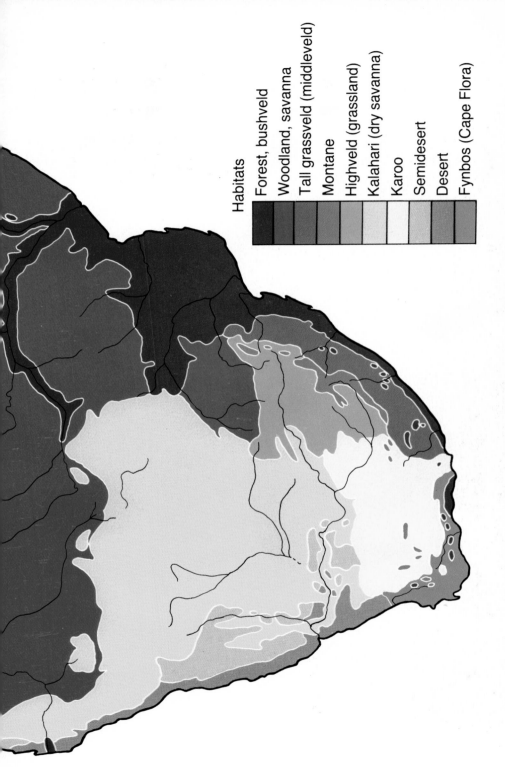

Habitats

Forest, bushveld
Woodland, savanna
Tall grassveld (middleveld)
Montane
Highveld (grassland)
Kalahari (dry savanna)
Karoo
Semidesert
Desert
Fynbos (Cape Flora)

Figure 12. Map of southern Africa showing main vegetation types (habitats).

1

♂ ♀ Imm.

463
Southern Ground Hornbill
p.399

♂ ♀

1
Ostrich
p.1

2

10
Wandering Albatross
p.8

♀

♂

Imm.

12
Blackbrowed Albatross
p.10

Imm.

Imm.

14
Yellownosed Albatross
p.11

Imm.

13
Greyheaded Albatross
p.10

11
Shy Albatross
p.9

16
Lightmantled Sooty Albatross
p.12

18
Northern Giant Petrel
p.14

17
Southern Giant Petrel (White form)
p.13

Imm.

15
Darkmantled Sooty Albatross
p.12

K. NEWMAN '76

3

20
Antarctic Petrel
p.15

21
Pintado Petrel
p.15

19
Antarctic Fulmar
p.14

24
Softplumaged Petrel
p.17

23
Greatwinged Petrel
p.16

28
Blue Petrel
p.19

26
Atlantic Petrel
p.18

29
Broadbilled Prion
p.20

31
Fairy Prion
p.22

33
Grey Petrel
p.23

32
Whitechinned Petrel
p.22

35
Great Shear-water
p.24

34
Cory's Shearwater
p.24

41
Wedge-tailed Shearwater
p.28

37
Sooty Shearwater
p.26

36
Fleshfooted Shearwater
p.25

40
Audubon's Shearwater
p.28

39
Little Shearwater
p.27

38
Manx Shearwater
p.26

K. NEWMAN '76

4

48
*Whitetailed
Tropicbird*
p.33

47
*Redtailed
Tropicbird*
p.32

Imm.

53
Cape Gannet
p.37

♂

61
Greater Frigatebird
p.44

52
Brown Booby
p.36

55
*Whitebreasted
Cormorant*
p.38

N-Br.

Imm.

Br.

57
*Bank
Cormorant*
p.40

54
*Australian
Gannet*
p.38

Imm.

56
Cape Cormorant
p.39

59
Crowned Cormorant
p.42

58
Reed Cormorant
p.41

Br. ♀

N-Br.

Br. ♂

Br. ♂

60
Darter
p.43

N-Br.

2
*King
Penguin*
p.2

Br. ♂

50
*Pinkbacked
Pelican*
p.35

Br.

5
*Rock-
hopper
Penguin*
p.4

49
*White
Pelican*
p.34

3
*Jackass
Penguin*
p.3

4
*Macaroni
Penguin*
p.4

K. NEWMAN '74

5

80
Bittern
p.61

76
*Blackcrowned
Night Heron*
p.57

Imm.

77
Whitebacked Night Heron
p.58

Br.

66
*Great White
Egret*
p.48

N-Br.

Br.

71
Cattle Egret
p.53

N-Br.

68
*Yellowbilled
Egret*
p.50

67
*Little
Egret*
p.49

Imm.

65
Purple Heron
p.47

64
Goliath Heron
p.47

63
*Blackheaded
Heron*
p.46

Imm.

62
Grey Heron
p.45

K B NEWMAN 73

78
Little Bittern
p.59

Imm.

74
Greenbacked Heron
p.55

Imm.

6

73
Madagascar Squacco Heron
p.55

Br.

72
Squacco Heron
p.54

79
Dwarf Bittern
p.60

Imm.

N-Br.

70
Slaty Egret
p.52

69
Black Egret
p.51

75
Rufousbellied Heron
p.56

8
Dabchick
p.6

N-Br.

7
Blacknecked Grebe
p.6

Br.

6
Great Crested Grebe
p.5

K B NEWMAN '73

7

96
Greater Flamingo
p.77

97
Lesser Flamingo
p.78

81
Hamerkop
p.62

91
Sacred Ibis
p.72

94
Hadeda Ibis
p.75

93
Glossy Ibis
p.74

92
Bald Ibis
p.73

84
Black Stork
p.66

87
Openbilled Stork
p.68

86
Woollynecked Stork
p.67

83
White Stork
p.65

85
Abdim's Stork
p.67

88
Saddlebilled Stork
p.69

89
Marabou Stork
p.70

95
African Spoonbill
p.76

90
Yellowbilled Stork
p.71

K B NEWMAN '72

8

99
Whitefaced Duck
p.81

100
Fulvous Duck
p.82

101
Whitebacked Duck
p.82

♂

115
Knobbilled Duck
p.95

♀

114
Pygmy Goose
p.94

♂ ♀

102
Egyptian Goose
p.83

103
South African Shelduck
p.84

♂

♀

116
Spurwinged Goose
p.96

98
Mute Swan
p.80

K B NEWMAN 1972

9

112
Cape Shoveller
p.92
♂
♀
♂
♀
♂

111
Northern Shoveller
p.91
♀
♂
♂
♀

108
Redbilled Teal
p.89

104
Yellowbilled Duck
p.85

110
Garganey
p.91
♂
♀

105
African Black Duck
p.86

106
Cape Teal
p.87

109
Pintail
p.90
♂
♀
♂
♀

107
Hottentot Teal
p.88

117
Maccoa Duck
p.97
♂
♀
♂
♀

113
Southern Pochard
p.93
♂
♀
♀
♂

K B NEWMAN 1972

10

147
Palmnut Vulture
p.127

Imm.

120
Egyptian Vulture
p.102

Imm.

Imm.

121
Hooded Vulture
p.103

125
Whiteheaded Vulture
p.107

♀

Imm.

123
Whitebacked Vulture
p.105

Imm.

Imm.

122
Cape Vulture
p.104

Imm.

119
Bearded Vulture
p.101

Imm.

124
Lappetfaced Vulture
p.106

118
Secretarybird
p.100

K. NEWMAN '84

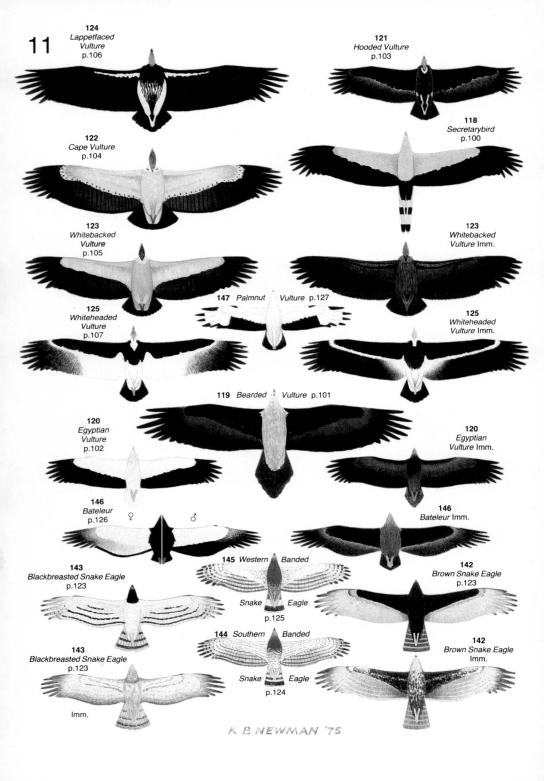

11

124
*Lappetfaced
Vulture*
p.106

121
Hooded Vulture
p.103

122
Cape Vulture
p.104

118
Secretarybird
p.100

123
*Whitebacked
Vulture*
p.105

123
*Whitebacked
Vulture Imm.*

125
*Whiteheaded
Vulture*
p.107

147 *Palmnut   Vulture* p.127

125
*Whiteheaded
Vulture Imm.*

120
*Egyptian
Vulture*
p.102

119 *Bearded   Vulture* p.101

120
*Egyptian
Vulture Imm.*

146
Bateleur
p.126 ♀   ♂

146
Bateleur Imm.

143
Blackbreasted Snake Eagle
p.123

145 *Western   Banded*

Snake   Eagle
p.125

142
Brown Snake Eagle
p.123

143
Blackbreasted Snake Eagle
p.123

144 *Southern   Banded*

Snake   Eagle
p.124

142
*Brown Snake Eagle
Imm.*

Imm.

K B NEWMAN '75

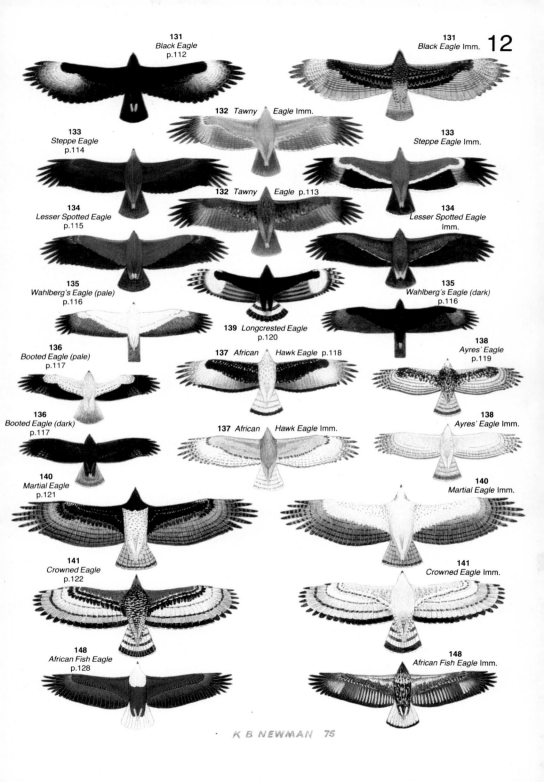

131
Black Eagle
p.112

131
Black Eagle Imm.

12

132 *Tawny Eagle* Imm.

133
Steppe Eagle
p.114

133
Steppe Eagle Imm.

134
Lesser Spotted Eagle
p.115

132 *Tawny Eagle* p.113

134
Lesser Spotted Eagle
Imm.

135
Wahlberg's Eagle (pale)
p.116

139 *Longcrested Eagle*
p.120

135
Wahlberg's Eagle (dark)
p.116

136
Booted Eagle (pale)
p.117

137 *African Hawk Eagle* p.118

138
Ayres' Eagle
p.119

136
Booted Eagle (dark)
p.117

137 *African Hawk Eagle* Imm.

138
Ayres' Eagle Imm.

140
Martial Eagle
p.121

140
Martial Eagle Imm.

141
Crowned Eagle
p.122

141
Crowned Eagle Imm.

148
African Fish Eagle
p.128

148
African Fish Eagle Imm.

K B NEWMAN 75

13

131
Black Eagle
p.112

Imm.

132
Tawny Eagle
p.113

Imm.

140
Martial Eagle
p.121

Imm.

133
Steppe Eagle
p.114

Imm.

134
Lesser Spotted Eagle
p.115

148
African Fish Eagle
p.128

Imm.

146
Bateleur
p.126

Imm.

♂

♀

Imm.

141
Crowned Eagle
p.122

K. D. NEWMAN

14

139
Longcrested Eagle
p.120

(pale form)

(dark form)

(intermediate)

135
Wahlberg's Eagle
p.116

136
Booted Eagle
p.117

(pale)

(dark)

(pale)

Imm.

Imm.

137
African Hawk Eagle
p.118

143
Blackbreasted Snake Eagle
p.123

Imm.

Imm.

Imm.

Imm.

138
Ayres' Eagle
p.119

Imm.

Imm.

145
Western Banded Snake Eagle
p.125

Imm.

Imm.

144
Southern Banded Snake Eagle
p.124

142
Brown Snake Eagle
p.123

K B NEWMAN '78

15

Imm. A

149
Steppe Buzzard
p.129

Imm. B

Imm.

150
Forest Buzzard
p.130

130
Honey Buzzard
p.111

154
Lizard Buzzard
p.134

170
Osprey
p.149

153
Augur Buzzard
p.133

Imm.

152
Jackal Buzzard
p.132

Imm.

Imm.

126 A
Yellowbilled Kite
p.107

126 B
Black Kite
p.107

Imm.

127
Blackshouldered Kite
p.109

Imm.

129
Bat Hawk
p.110

♂

164
Eurasian Marsh Harrier
p.144

♂

♀

Imm.
A

169
Gymnogene
p.148

Imm. B

♀

Imm.

165
African Marsh Harrier
p.144

♂

167
Pallid Harrier
p.146

♀

♂

166
Montagu's Harrier
p.145

♀

Imm.

168
Black Harrier
p.147

K B NEWMAN 76

159
Little Banded Goshawk
p.139

♂
♀
Imm. ♂

157
Little Sparrowhawk
p.137

16

♂
♀
Imm. ♀

♀
Imm. ♀

161
Gabar Goshawk
p.141

♀

♂
♀

156
Ovambo Sparrowhawk
p.136

Imm. ♀

Imm. ♂
(rufous form)

♂

160
African Goshawk
p.140

Imm.

155
Redbreasted Sparrowhawk
p.135

Imm.

♀

158
Black Sparrowhawk
p.138

A ♀ Imm.

Melanistic

♂

Imm.

162
Pale Chanting Goshawk
p.142

m. ♀ B

163
Dark Chanting Goshawk
p.143

Imm.

K. NEWMAN '83

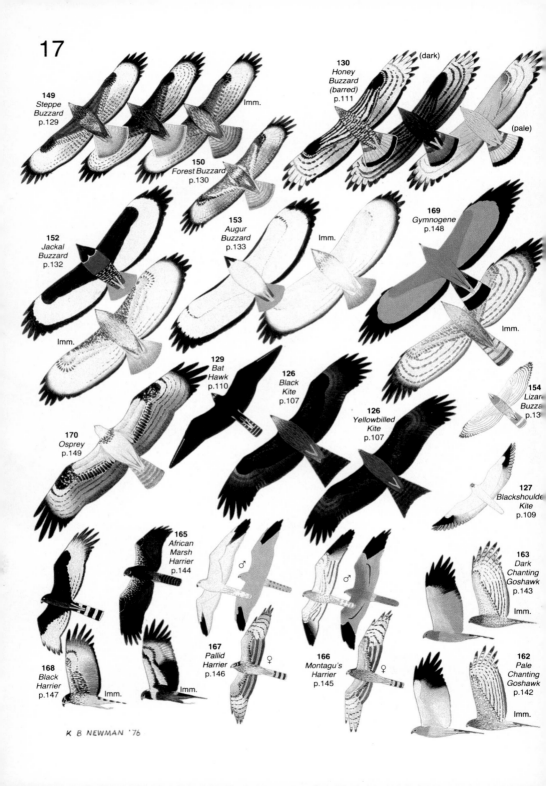

17

149
Steppe Buzzard
p.129

Imm.

150
Forest Buzzard
p.130

130
Honey Buzzard (barred)
p.111

(dark)

(pale)

152
Jackal Buzzard
p.132

Imm.

153
Augur Buzzard
p.133

Imm.

169
Gymnogene
p.148

Imm.

129
Bat Hawk
p.110

126
Black Kite
p.107

126
Yellowbilled Kite
p.107

154
Lizard Buzzard
p.13

170
Osprey
p.149

127
Blackshoulder Kite
p.109

165
African Marsh Harrier
p.144

♂

♂

163
Dark Chanting Goshawk
p.143

Imm.

168
Black Harrier
p.147

Imm.

Imm.

167
Pallid Harrier
p.146

♀

166
Montagu's Harrier
p.145

♀

162
Pale Chanting Goshawk
p.142

Imm.

K B NEWMAN '76

18

175
Sooty
Falcon
p.154

174
African
Hobby
Falcon
p.153

173
Northern
Hobby
Falcon
p.152

172
Lanner
Falcon
p.151

171
Peregrine
Falcon
p.150

185
kinson's
erstrel
.162

184
Grey
Kestrel
p.161

128
Cuckoo
Hawk
p.110

178
Red-
necked
Falcon
p.156

176
Taita
Falcon
p.155

182
Greater
Kestrel
p.160 ♂

179
Western
Redfooted
Kestrel
p.157

180
Eastern
Redfooted
Kestrel
p.158

183
Lesser
Kestrel
p.161 ♂

♂

♀

♀

181
Rock
Kestrel
p.159

♀

61
bar
hawk
141

158
Black
Sparrowhawk
p.138

159
Little
Banded
Goshawk
p.139

156
Ovambo
Sparrowhawk
p.136

(dark
form)

155
Redbreasted
Sparrowhawk
p.135

157
Little
Sparrowhawk
p.137

160
African Goshawk
p.140

K. NEWMAN '75

19
(F. p. minor)

171
Peregrine Falcon
p.150

Imm.

(F. p. calidus)

172
Lanner Falcon
p.151

Imm.

173
Northern Hobby Falcon
p.152

Imm.

174
African Hobby Falcon
p.153

Imm.

176
Taita
Falcon
p.155

Imm.

♀

186
Pygmy Falcon
p.163

♂

178
Rednecked Falcon
p.156

Imm.

128
Cuckoo Hawk
p.110

Imm.

175
Sooty
Falcon
p.154

Imm.

184
Grey
Kestrel
p.161

185
Dickinson's
Kestrel
p.162

182
Greater
Kestrel
p.160

♂

179
Western Redfooted Kestrel
p.157

♀

Imm.

181
Rock Kestrel
p.159

Imm.

♀

♂

180
Eastern Redfooted
Kestrel
p.158

♀

Imm.

♂

♀

183
Lesser
Kestrel
p.161

K. NEWMAN '74

♂
200
Common Quail
p.175
♀

♂
201
Harlequin Quail
p.176
♀

202
Blue Quail
p.177
♀

♂
188
Coqui Francolin
p.165
♀

(sephaena)
189
Crested Francolin
p.166
(rovuma)

193
*Orange River
Francolin*
p.169
(levaillantoides)

(levaillantoides)

(langi)

191
*Shelley's
Francolin*
p.168

(pallidior)

190
*Greywing
Francolin*
p.167

192
*Redwing
Francolin*
p.168

187
Chukar Partridge
p.164

K. NEWMAN '83

21

195
Cape Francolin
p.171

194
Redbilled
Francolin
p.170

♂

♀

197
Hartlau
Franco
p.17

(lehmanni)

196
Natal
Francolin
p.172

(cunenensis)

(castaneiventer)

(swynnertoni)

199
Swainso
Francol
p.174

198
Rednecked
Francolin
p.173

(notatus)

(coronata)

(mitrata)

204
Crested
Guineafowl
p.179

203
Helmeted
Guineafowl
p.178

K. NEWMAN '76

22

206
Blackrumped Buttonquail
p.182

221
Striped Flufftail
p.195

♂

220
Longtoed Flufftail
p.194

205
urrichane
uttonquail
p.181

♀

♂

♀

219
*Streakybreasted
Flufftail*
p.194

♂

217
Redchested Flufftail
p.192

218
*Buffspotted
Flufftail*
p.193

♀

♂

215
Baillon's Crake
p.190

♀

♂

♀

216
Striped Crake
p.191

♂

♀

222
Whitewinged Flufftail
p.196

214
Spotted Crake
p.189

♂

212
African Crake
p.187

213
Black Crake
p.188

♂

211
Corncrake
p.186

210
African Rail
p.186

K. NEWMAN 83

23

223
Purple Gallinule
p.196

224
Lesser Gallinule
p.197

225
American Purple Gallinule
p.198

227
Lesser Moorhen
p.199

226
Common Moorhen
p.198

228
Redknobbed Coot
p.200

♀

♂

229
African Finfoot
p.201

240
African Jacana
p.212

241
Lesser Jacar
p.213

Geoff Lockwood '83

24

233
Whitebellied Korhaan
p.205

234
Blue Korhaan
p.206

237
Redcrested Korhaan
p.208

235
Karoo Korhaan
p.207

238
Blackbellied Korhaan
p.209

239A
Black Korhaan
p.210

236
Rüppell's Korhaan
p.208

232
Ludwig's Bustard
p.204

231
Stanley's Bustard
p.204

230
Kori Bustard
p.203

207
Wattled Crane
p.183

209
Crowned Crane
p.184

208
Blue Crane
p.184

Geoff Lockwood 84

25

297
Spotted Dikkop
p.258

244
African Black
Oystercatcher
p.216

243
Eurasian Oystercatcher
p.215

298
Water Dikkop
p.259

290
Whimbrel
p.253

289
Curlew
p.252

288
Bartailed
Godwit
p.251

287
Blacktailed Godwit
p.250

296
Crab Plover
p.258

295
Blackwinged Stilt
p.257

294
Old World Avocet
p.256

♂   ♀

285
Great Snipe
p.249

286
Ethiopian
Snipe
p.249

242
Old World
Painted Snipe
p.214

K B NEWMAN '73

249
Threebanded Plover
p.221

246
Whitefronted Plover
p.218

Imm.

247
Chestnutbanded Plover
p.219

26

262
Ruddy Turnstone
p.232

248
Kittlitz's Plover
p.220

N-Br.

252
Caspian Plover
p.224

250
Mongolian Plover
p.222

253
Asiatic Golden Plover
p.224

245
Ringed Plover
p.217

251
Sand Plover
p.223

254
Grey Plover
p.225

255
Crowned Plover
p.226

257
Blackwinged Plover
p.228

256
Lesser Blackwinged Plover
p.227

258
Blacksmith Plover
p.229

259
Whitecrowned Plover
p.230

260
Wattled Plover
p.231

261
Longtoed Plover
p.231

K B NEWMAN '73

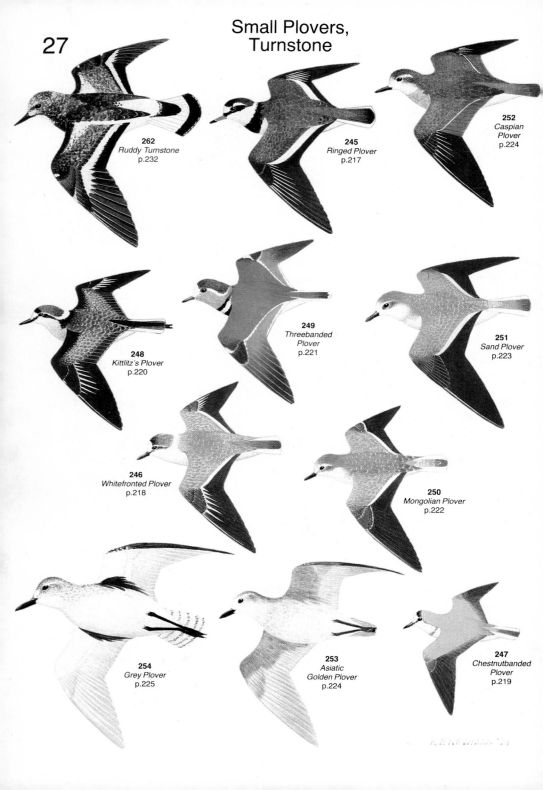

27

262
Ruddy Turnstone
p.232

245
Ringed Plover
p.217

252
Caspian Plover
p.224

248
Kittlitz's Plover
p.220

249
Threebanded Plover
p.221

251
Sand Plover
p.223

246
Whitefronted Plover
p.218

250
Mongolian Plover
p.222

254
Grey Plover
p.225

253
Asiatic Golden Plover
p.224

247
Chestnutbanded Plover
p.219

Scolopacids

273
Dunlin
p.241

274
*Little
Stint*
p.242

279
*Pectoral
Sandpiper*
p.244

283
*Broadbilled
Sandpiper*
p.247

276
*Rednecked
Stint*
p.243

291
*Grey
Phalarope*
p.253

272
*Curlew
Sandpiper*
p.240

292
Rednecked Phalarope
p.254

266
*Wood
andpiper*
p.236

265
*Green
Sandpiper*
p.235

264
*Common
Sandpiper*
p.234

281
Sanderling
p.246

271
*Common
Knot*
p.239

284
Ruff
p.248

263
*Terek
Sandpiper*
p.233

268
*Common
Redshank*
p.237

269
*Marsh
Sandpiper*
p.238

270
Greenshank
p.239

K B NEWMAN '73

29

272
Curlew Sandpiper
p.240
Br.

274
Little Stint
p.242
Br.

276
Rednecke
Stint
p.243

273
Dunlin
p.241

283
Broadbilled
Sandpiper
p.247

263
Terek
Sandpiper
p.233

279
Pectoral
Sandpiper
p.244

266
Wood Sandpiper
p.236

265
Green Sandpiper
p.235

Br.

271
Common
Knot
p.239

Br.

281
Sanderling
p.246

264
Common
Sandpiper
p.234

292
Rednecked Phalarope
p.254

291
Grey Phalarope
p.253

269
Marsh
Sandpiper
p.238

♂

268
Common
Redshank
p.237

270
Greenshank
p.239

♂

284
Ruff
p.248

♀

K.B.NEWMAN '73

299
Burchell's Courser
p.261

300
Temminck's Courser
p.261

Imm.

301
Doublebanded Courser
p.262

302
Threebanded Courser
p.264

303
Bronzewinged Courser
p.265

304
Redwinged Pratincole
p.265

306
Rock Pratincole
p.267

305
Blackwinged Pratincole
p.266

♂

♀

345
Burchell's Sandgrouse
p.295

♀

344
Namaqua Sandgrouse
p.294

346
Yellowthroated Sandgrouse
p.296

347
Doublebanded Sandgrouse
p.297

Geoff Lockwood '82

31

307
Arctic Skua
p.268

308
Longtailed Skua
p.269

309
Pomarine Skua
p.270

Imm. A

Imm. B

312
Kelp Gull
p.272

310
Subantarctic Skua
p.270

311
South Polar Skua
p.271

312
Kelp Gull
p.272

313
Lesser Blackbacked Gull
p.273

N-Br.

Br.

317
Franklin's Gull
p.276

N-Br.

316
Hartlaub's Gull
p.275

315
Greyheaded Gull
p.274

Imm.

Imm.

318
Sabine's Gull
p.276

343
African Skimmer
p.293

K B NEWMAN 76

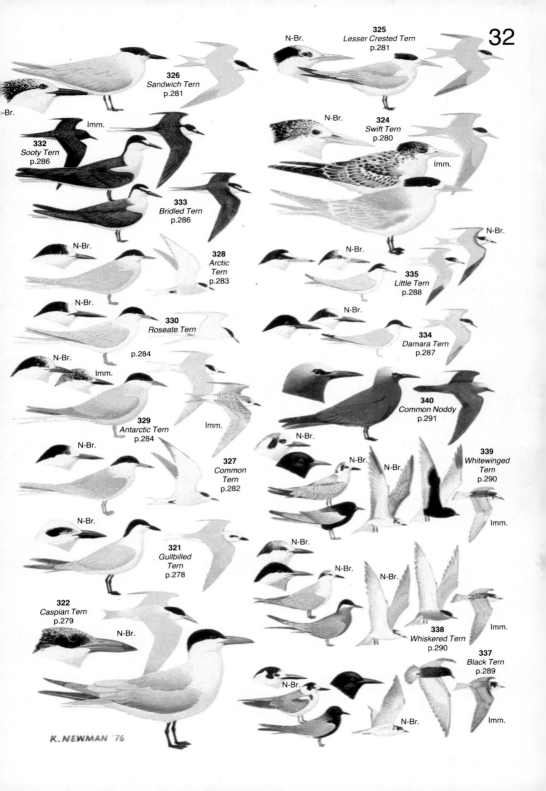

-Br.

326
Sandwich Tern
p.281

Imm.

332
Sooty Tern
p.286

333
Bridled Tern
p.286

N-Br.

328
*Arctic
Tern*
p.283

N-Br.

330
Roseate Tern

p.284

N-Br.

Imm.

329
Antarctic Tern
p.284

N-Br.

327
*Common
Tern*
p.282

N-Br.

321
*Gullbilled
Tern*
p.278

322
Caspian Tern
p.279

N-Br.

K. NEWMAN '76

N-Br.

325
Lesser Crested Tern
p.281

N-Br.

324
Swift Tern
p.280

Imm.

N-Br.

N-Br.

335
Little Tern
p.288

N-Br.

334
Damara Tern
p.287

340
Common Noddy
p.291

N-Br.

N-Br.

N-Br.

339
*Whitewinged
Tern*
p.290

Imm.

N-Br.

N-Br.

N-Br.

338
Whiskered Tern
p.290

Imm.

337
Black Tern
p.289

N-Br.

N-Br.

Imm.

33

350
Rameron Pigeon
p.300

349
Rock Pigeon
p.299

348
Feral Pigeon
p.298

352
Redeyed Dove
p.302

353
African Mourning Dove
p.303

♀

♂

351
Delegorgue's Pigeon
p.301

354
Cape Turtle Dove
p.304

355
Laughing Dove
p.305

360
Cinnamon Dove
p.309

♀

♂

356
Namaqua Dove
p.306

♂

♀

359
Tambourine Dove
p.308

358
Greenspotted Dove
p.307

357
Bluespotted Dove
p.307

361
*African
Green Pigeon*
p.310

(delalandii)

(schalowi)

Geoff Lockwood '82

452
Redbilled Woodhoopoe
p.389

Imm.

454
Scimitarbilled Woodhoopoe
p.391

451
African
Hoopoe
p.388

453
Violet Woodhoopoe
p.390

(schalowi)
p.319

373
Grey Lourie
p.320

372
Ross's Lourie
p.320

371
Purplecrested Lourie
p.319

(corythaix) **370**
Knysna Lourie
p.318

366
Roseringed Parakeet
p.315

369
Blackcheeked Lovebird
p.317

368
Lilian's Lovebird
p.316

367
Rosyfaced Lovebird
p.315

364
Meyer's Parrot
p.313

♀

427
Narina Trogon
p.368

♂

365
Rüppell's Parrot
p.314

♀

363
Brownheaded Parrot
p.312

362A
Cape Parrot
p.311

Geoff Lockwood '83

35

374
Eurasian Cuckoo
p.322

375
African Cuckoo
p.322

Imm.

377
Redchested Cuckoo
p.324

383
Thickbilled Cuckoo
p.329

379
Barred Cuckoo
p.326

376
Lesser Cuckoo
p.323

378
Black Cuckoo
p.325

Imm.

380
Great Spotted Cuckoo
p.326

(black form)

(whitebreasted form)

382
Jacobin Cuckoo
p.328

381
Striped Cuckoo
p.327

387
Green Coucal
p.333

N-Br.

388
Black Coucal
p.334

389
Coppertailed Coucal
p.335

390
Senegal Coucal
p.336

391B
Whitebrowed Coucal
p.337

(loandae)

391A
Burchell's Coucal
p.337

(burchellii)

Geoff Lockwood '83

384
Emerald Cuckoo
p.330

♂

♀

Imm. ♂

Imm.

386
Diederik Cuckoo
p.332

♂

♀

385
Klaas's Cuckoo
p.331

♂

♀

Imm.

474
Greater Honeyguide
p.408

475
Scalythroated Honeyguide
p.410

476
Lesser Honeyguide
p.410

477
Eastern Honeyguide
p.411

479
Slenderbilled Honeyguide
p.413

478
Sharpbilled Honeyguide
p.412

490
African Broadbill
p.422

491
Angola Pitta
p.423

Geoff Lockwood '82

37

392
Barn Owl
p.338

393
Grass Owl
p.339

398
Pearlspotted Owl
p.344

399
Barred Owl
p.345

403
Pel's Fishing Owl
p.349

396
Scops Owl
p.342

397
Whitefaced Owl
p.343

394
Wood Owl
p.340

395
Marsh Owl
p.341

401
Spotted Eagle Owl
p.347

400
Cape Eagle Owl
p.346

Geoff Lockwood '82

402
Giant Eagle Owl
p.348

38

407
Natal Nightjar
p.352

♂   ♀

409
Mozambique Nightjar
p.354

♂   ♀

406
Rufouscheeked Nightjar
p.352

♂   ♀

405
Fierynecked Nightjar
p.351

♂   ♀

408
Freckled Nightjar
p.353

♂   ♀

404
Eurasian Nightjar
p.350

♂   ♀

♂ Br.

♀

410
Pennantwinged Nightjar
p.355

♂   ♀

Geoff Lockwood '82

39

421
Palm Swift
p.363

422
Mottled Spinetail
p.363

411
Eurasian Swift
p.356

412
Black Swift
p.356

418
Alpine Swift
p.361

413
Bradfield's Swift
p.357

420
Scarce Swift
p.362

423
Böhm's Spinetail
p.364

419
Mottled Swift
p.361

414
Pallid Swift
p.358

417
Little Swift
p.360

415
Whiterumped Swift
p.358

416
Horus Swift
p.359

K.B.NEWMAN '75

443
Whitefronted Bee-eater
p.381

442
Böhm's Bee-eater
p.381

439
Olive Bee-eater
p.379

440
Bluecheeked Bee-eater
p.379

40

441
Carmine Bee-eater
p.380

444
Little Bee-eater
p.382

445
Swallowtailed Bee-eater
p.383

438
Eurasian Bee-eater
p.378

♂

428
Pied Kingfisher
p.369

♀

♀

♂

430
Halfcollared Kingfisher
p.371

429
Giant Kingfisher
p.370

431
Malachite Kingfisher
p.372

432
Pygmy Kingfisher
p.373

433
Woodland Kingfisher
p.374

434
Mangrove Kingfisher
p.374

435
Brownhooded Kingfisher
p.375

437
Striped Kingfisher
p.377

436
Greyhooded Kingfisher
p.376

K. NEWMAN '83

41

446
Eurasian Roller
p.384

448
Rackettailed Roller
p.386

447
Lilacbreasted Roller
p.385

449
Purple Roller
p.386

450
Broadbilled Roller
p.387

460
Crowned Hornbill
p.396

♀

♂

457
Grey Hornbill
p.394

459
Southern Yellowbilled Hornbill
p.395

458
Redbilled Hornbill
p.395

♂

455
Trumpeter Hornbill
p.392

♂

456
Silverycheeked Hornbill
p.393

461
Bradfield's Hornbill
p.397

462
Monteiro's Hornbill
p.398

Geoff Lockwood '91

426
Redfaced Mousebird
p.367

425
Whitebacked Mousebird
p.366

424
Speckled Mousebird
p.365

(yellow headed form)
(rare)

464
Blackcollared Barbet
p.400

473
Crested Barbet
p.407

466
White-eared Barbet
p.402

467
Whyte's Barbet
p.403

Imm.

465
Pied Barbet
p.401

468
Green Barbet
p.403

469
Redfronted Tinker Barbet
p.404

470
Yellowfronted Tinker Barbet
p.405

472
Green Tinker Barbet
p.407

471
Goldenrumped Tinker Barbet
p.406

Geoff Lockwood '82

43

480
Ground Woodpecker
p.414

481
Bennett's Woodpecker
p.415

482
Specklethroated Woodpecker
p.415

483
Goldentailed Woodpecker
p.416

484
Knysna Woodpecker
p.417

485
Little Spotted Woodpecker
p.417

486
Cardinal Woodpecker
p.418

487
Bearded Woodpecker
p.419

488
Olive Woodpecker
p.420

489
Redthroated Wryneck
p.420

Geoff Lockwood 82

44

492
*Melodious
Lark*
p.425

493
*Monotonous
Lark*
p.426

(grisescens)

497
*Fawncoloured
Lark*
p.429

(africanoides)

494
*Rufousnaped
Lark*
p.427

(sabota)

(transvaalensis)

(sarwensis)

498
*Sabota
Lark*
p.430

512
*Thickbilled
Lark*
p.443

502
*Karoo
Lark*
p.434

(waibeli)

505
*Dusky
Lark*
p.437

503
*Dune
Lark*
p.434

(apiata)

(adendorffi)
Imm.

501
*Shortclawed
Lark*
p.433

495
*Clapper
Lark*
p.428

(hewitti)

(pintoi)

496
*Flappet
Lark*
p.429

(mababiensis)

(kalaharica)

K B NEWMAN
77

45

509
Botha's Lark
p.440

499
Rudd's Lark
p.431

(boweni)

(alticola)

506
Spikeheeled Lark
p.437

(kaokensis)

500
Longbilled Lark
p.432

(curvirostris)

(damarensis)

514
Gray's Lark
p.444

504
Red Lark
p.436

515
Chestnutbacked Finchlark
p.445

♀

♂

516
Greybacked Finchlark
p.446

♂

♀

517
Blackeared Finchlark
p.447

♀

♂

Imm.

507
Redcapped Lark
p.438

(spleniata)

(niveni)

510
Sclater's Lark
p.441

508
Pinkbilled Lark
p.439

511
Stark's Lark
p.442

K B NEWMAN '77

525
Mosque Swallow
p.454

524
Redbreasted
Swallow
p.453

526
Greater
Striped Swallow
p.455

527
Lesser
Striped Swallow
p.456

518
Eurasian
Swallow
p.448

520
Whitethroated
Swallow
p.449

531
Greyrumped
Swallow
p.460

523
Pearlbreasted Swallow
p.452

522
Wiretailed Swallow
p.451

521
Blue Swallow
p.450

528
South African
Cliff Swallow
p.457

536
Black
Sawwing
Swallow
p.464

530
House
Martin
p.459

534
Banded Martin
p.462

529
Rock Martin
p.458

535
Mascarene
Martin
p.463

532
Sand Martin
p.460

533
Brownthroated
Martin
p.461

537
Eastern Sawwing
Swallow
p.464

K B NEWMAN 1970

47

538
Black Cuckooshrike
p.465

539
Whitebreasted Cuckooshrike
p.466

540
Grey Cuckooshrike
p.467

541
Forktailed Drongo
p.468

542
Squaretailed Drongo
p.469

Imm.

544
African Golden
Oriole
p.471

Imm.

543
Eurasian Golden Oriole
p.470

Imm.

545
Blackheaded Oriole
p.472

546
Greenheaded Oriole
p.473

548
Pied Crow
p.474

547
Black Crow
p.474

550
Whitenecked Raven
p.476

549
House Crow
p.475

Geoff Lockwood 84

551
Southern Grey Tit
p.477

552
Ashy Tit
p.478

555
Carp's Black Tit
p.481

553
Northern Grey Tit
p.479

556
Rufousbellied Tit
p.482

554
Southern Black Tit
p.480

567
Redeyed Bulbul
p.492

565
Bush Blackcap
p.490

566
Cape Bulbul
p.491

559
Spotted Creeper
p.485

568
Blackeyed Bulbul
p.493

569
Terrestrial Bulbul
p.494

570
Yellowstreaked Bulbul
p.494

571
Slender Bulbul
p.495

572
Sombre Bulbul
p.496

573
Stripecheeked Bulbul
p.497

574
Yellowbellied Bulbul
p.498

575
Yellowspotted Nicator
p.499

Geoff Lockwood '83

49

560
Arrowmarked Babbler
p.486

563
Pied Babbler
p.489

564
Barecheeked Babbler
p.489

562
Hartlaub's Babbler
p.488

561
Blackfaced Babbler
p.487

611
Cape Rockjumper
p.529

612
Orangebreasted Rockjumper
p.530

578
Spotted Thrush
p.502

580
Groundscraper Thrush
p.503

581
Cape Rockthrush
p.504

576
Kurrichane Thrush
p.500

577
Olive Thrush
p.501

579
Orange Thrush
p.502

582
Sentinel Rockthrush
p.505

584
Miombo Rockthrush
p.507

583
Shorttoed Rockthrush
p.506

Geoff Lockwood 83

585
Eurasian Wheatear
p.508

Imm.

586
Mountain Chat
p.508

♂ ♂ ♀

587
Capped Wheatear
p.509

Imm.

588
Buffstreaked Chat
p.510

♂ ♀

589
Familiar Chat
p.511

590
Tractrac Chat
p.512

591
Sicklewinged Chat
p.513

618
Herero Chat
p.536

♀

593
Mocking Chat
p.515

♂

595
Anteating Chat
p.516

592
Karoo Chat
p.514

♂

596
Stonechat
p.517

♀

610
Boulder Chat
p.529

♂

♀

594
Arnot's Chat
p.516

♀ ♂

597
Whinchat
p.518

Geoff Lockwood '83

51

614
Karoo Robin
p.532

609
Thrush Nightingale
p.528

613
Whitebrowed Robin
p.531

607
Swynnerton's Robin
p.526

Imm.

606
Starred Robin
p.525

608
Gunning's Robin
p.527

601
Cape Robin
p.522

602
Whitethroated Robin
p.523

615
Kalahari Robin
p.533

600
Natal Robin
p.521

616
Brown Robin
p.534

599
Heuglin's Robin
p.520

617
Bearded Robin
p.535

598
Chorister Robin
p.519

603
Collared Palmthrush
p.523

605
Whitebreasted Alethe
p.525

604
Rufoustailed Palmthrush
p.524

K. NEWMAN '83

52

628
Great Reed Warbler
p.544

636
Greater Swamp Warbler
p.549

635
Cape Reed Warbler
p.549

637
African Yellow Warbler
p.550

629
Basra Reed Warbler
p.544

631
African Marsh Warbler
p.546

632
Cinnamon Reed Warbler
p.547

633
Eurasian Marsh Warbler
p.547

630
Eurasian Reed Warbler
p.545

638
African Sedge Warbler
p.551

639
Barratt's Warbler
p.552

640
Knysna Warbler
p.553

627
River Warbler
p.543

641
Victorin's Warbler
p.554

634
Eurasian Sedge Warbler
p.548

Geoff Lockwood '92

53

661
Grassbird
p.571

663
Moustached Warbler
p.573

642
Broadtailed Warbler
p.555

662
Rockrunner
p.572

N-Br.

♂

N-Br.

Br.

682
Redwinged Warbler
p.593

688
Rufouseared Warbler
p.599

657
Greybacked Camaroptera
p.568
(brevicaudata)

Br.

657
Bleating Warbler
p.567
(brachyura)

660
Cinnamonbreasted Wart
p.570

650
Redfaced Crombec
p.561

651
*Longbilled
Crombec*
p.562

N-Br.

652
*Redcapped
Crombec*
p.563

659
Stierling's Barred Warbler
p.569

Br.

658
*Desert
Barred Warble*
p.568

Geoff Lockwood '92

54

♀

♂

620
Whitethroat
p.538

625
Icterine Warbler
p.542

(trochilus)

(yakutensis)

643
Willow Warbler
p.556

911
Eurasian Blackcap
p.799

626
Olivetree Warbler
p.542

557
Cape Penduline Tit
p.483

558
Grey Penduline Tit
p.484

619
Garden Warbler
p.537

Imm.

656
Burntnecked Eremomela
p.567

654
Karoo Eremomela
p.565

653
Yellowbellied Eremomela
p.564

655
*Greencapped
Eremomela*
p.566

Geoff Lockwood '92

55

646
Chirinda Apalis
p.558

(neglecta)

♀

♂

(flavida) ♂

648
Yellowbreasted Apalis
p.560

647
Blackheaded Apalis
p.559

(capensis)

♀

♂

(spelonkensis)

♂

♀

649
Rudd's Apalis
p.561

N-Br.

645
Barthroated Apalis
p.557

♀

(rhodesiae)

♀

687
Namaqua Warbler
p.598

Br.

685
*Blackchested
Prinia*
p.596

684
Brier Warbler
p.595

683
*Tawnyflanked
Prinia*
p.594

621
Titbabbler
p.538

686B
Karoo Prinia
p.597

686A
Spotted Prinia
p.597

622
Layard's Titbabbler
p.539

Geoff Lockwood '92

♂ N-Br.

664
*Fantailed
Cisticola*
p.575

♂ Br.

♂ N-Br.

665
Desert Cisticola
p.576

♂ Br.

(textrix)

♂ Br.

666
Cloud Cisticola
p.577

(textrix)

♂ N-Br.

♂ Br.

667
Ayres' Cisticola
p.578

(major)

♂ Br.

♂ N-Br.

680
*Shortwinged
Cisticola*
p.591

(fulvicapilla)

668
*Palecrowned
Cisticola*
p.579

681
Neddicky
p.592

(ruficapilla)

K B NEWMAN '77

57

Br.

671
*Tinkling
Cisticola*
p.582

Br.

670
*Wailing
Cisticola*
p.581

Br.

669
*Greybacked
Cisticola*
p.581

(subruficapilla)

N-Br.

676
*Chirping
Cisticola*
p.587

N-Br.

N-Br.

(karasensis)

Br.

674
*Redfaced
Cisticola*
p.585

Br.

673
*Singing
Cisticola*
p.584

Br.
(chiniana)

675
*Blackbacked
Cisticola*
p.586

Br.

672
*Rattling
Cisticola*
p.583

N-Br.

N-Br.

N-Br.
frater

N-Br.

Br.

677
*Levaillant's
Cisticola*
p.588

N-Br. ♂

678
*Croaking
Cisticola*
p.589

679
*Lazy
Cisticola*
p.590

N-Br.

Br. ♂

♀ Br.

K. NEWMAN '83

689
Spotted Flycatcher
p.600

690
Dusky Flycatcher
p.601

692
Collared Flycatcher
p.602
♂

♀

707
Livingstone's Flycatcher
p.616

♂

624
Mashona Hyliota
p.541

♀

♂

♀

644
Yellowthroated Warbler
p.557

623
Yellowbreasted Hyliota
p.540

693
Fantailed Flycatcher
p.603

Imm.

691
Bluegrey Flycatcher
p.601

696
Pallid Flycatcher
p.605

695
Marico Flycatcher
p.605

Imm.

697
Chat Flycatcher
p.606

♂

♀

♂

698
Fiscal Flycatcher
p.607

699
Vanga Flycatcher
p.608

694
Black Flycatcher
p.604

Geoff Lockwood '92

59

700
Cape Batis
p.609

701
Chinspot Batis
p.610

703
Pririt Batis
p.612

704
Woodwards' Batis
p.613

(granti)

702
Mozambique Batis
p.611

(violacea)

705
Wattle-eyed Flycatcher
p.614

710
Paradise Flycatcher
p.618

706
Fairy Flycatcher
p.615

708
Bluemantled Flycatcher
p.616

709
Whitetailed Flycatcher
p.617

Geoff Lockwood '83

711
*African Pied
Wagtail*
p.620

712
*Longtailed
Wagtail*
p.621

713
*Cape
Wagtail*
p.622

714 ♂
*Yellow
Wagtail*
p.623

♂ *(thunbergi)*

♂ *(lutea)*

♀

(flava)

716
*Grassveld
Pipit*
p.625

717
*Longbilled
Pipit*
p.626

718
Plainbacked Pipit
p.627

♂

♀

715
Grey Wagtail
p.624

721
Rock Pipit
p.630

723
*Bushveld
Pipit*
p.631

720
Striped Pipit
p.629

719
Buffy Pipit
p.628

725
*Yellowbreasted
Pipit*
p.633

♂

♀

726
*Golden
Pipit*
p.634

722
*Tree
Pipit*
p.630

724
Shorttailed Pipit
p.632

727
*ngethroated
Longclaw*
p.635

728
*Yellowthroated
Longclaw*
p.636

729
*Fülleborn's
Longclaw*
p.637

730
*Pinkthroated
Longclaw*
p.637

Geoff Lockwood '83

61

Imm.

(collaris)

731
Lesser Grey Shrike
p.639

732
Fiscal Shrike
p.639

♂

♀

(subcoronatus)

733
Redbacked Shrike
p.641

♂

♀

735
Longtailed Shrike
p.642

736
Southern Boubou
p.643

737
Tropical Boubou
p.644

734
Sousa's Shrike
p.641

738
Swamp Boubou
p.645

756
Whitecrowned
Shrike
p.663

754
Redbilled
Helmetshrike
p.661

755
Chestnutfronted Helmetshrike
p.662

(miomben

♂

740
Puffback
p.647

♀

753
White Helmetshrike
p.660

752
Whitetailed Shrike
p.659

(solivagus)

741
Brubru
p.648

Geoff Lockwood '83

62

(yellow form (rare))

739
Crimsonbreasted Shrike
p.646

742
Southern Tchagra
p.649

743
Threestreaked Tchagra
p.650

744
Blackcrowned Tchagra
p.651

♂

745
Marsh Tchagra
p.652

(olive form)

♀

750
Olive Bush Shrike
p.657

♂

♂

(ruddy form)

♀

749
Blackfronted Bush Shrike
p.656

Imm.

♀

747
...eous Bush Shrike
p.654

Imm.

748
*...ngebreasted Bush
Shrike*
p.655

746
Bokmakierie
p.653

751
Greyheaded Bush Shrike
p.658

Geoff Lockwood '83

63

760
Wattled Starling
p.667

♂

♀ ♂

758
Indian Myna
p.665

761
Plumcoloured Starling
p.668

♀

♂

759
Pied Starling
p.666

757
Eurasian Starling
p.664

N-Br.

Br.

♂ **769**
Redwinged Starling
p.675

♀

771
Yellowbilled Oxpecker
p.677

773
Cape Sugarbird
p.679

774
Gurney's Sugarbird
p.681

♂

770
Palewinged Starling
p.676

768
Blackbellied Starling
p.674

772
Redbilled Oxpecker
p.678

Imm.

766
Lesser Blue-eared Starling
p.672

765
Greater Blue-eared Starling
p.672

767
Sharptailed Starling
p.673

762
Burchell's Starling
p.669

764
Glossy Starling
p.671

763
Longtailed Starling
p.670

K NEWMAN 84

787
Whitebellied Sunbird
p.694 ♂

♀

788
Dusky Sunbird
p.695 ♂

778
Coppery Sunbird
p.685 ♀

♂

N-Br. ♂

775
Malachite
Sunbird
p.682

795
Violetbacked
Sunbird
p.702 ♂

♀

776
Bronze
Sunbird
p.683

♀

784
Miombo
Doublecollared
Sunbird
p.691

775
Malachite Sunbird
p.682

♂

♀

782
Neergaard's Sunbird
p.689

♂

♀

777
Orangebreasted
Sunbird
p.684

♀

♂

♂

♀

780
Purplebanded
Sunbird
p.687 ♂

♂

783
Lesser
Doublecollared
Sunbird
p.690

779
Marico Sunbird
p.686 ♀

♀

785
Greater
Doublecollared
Sunbird
p.692

K. B. NEWMAN '75

65

786
*Yellowbellied
Sunbird*
p.693
♀
♂

789
Grey Sunbird
p.696

792
Black Sunbird
p.699
♂
Imm. ♂
♀

790
*Olive
Sunbird*
p.697

♂ Br.

♂ N-Br.

791
*Scarletchested
Sunbird*
p.698

793
Collared Sunbird
p.700
♀
♂

794
*Bluethroated
Sunbird*
p.701

797
Yellow White-eye
p.704

(capensis)

796
Cape White-eye
p.703

(caniviridis)

(atmorei)

K NEWMAN 83

66

Imm.

800
Sociable Weaver
p.707

♂

♀

♂

798
Redbilled Buffalo Weaver
p.705

♀

799
Whitebrowed Sparrowweaver
p.706

♂

803
Cape Sparrow
p.710

♀

♂

801
House Sparrow
p.709

♀

♂

♀

802
Great Sparrow
p.710

804
Greyheaded Sparrow
p.711

805
Yellowthroated Sparrow
p.712

♂

♂

♀

819
Redheaded Weaver
p.727

♂ N-Br.

807
Thickbilled Weaver
p.714

Geoff Lockwood '84

67

(bicolor)

(stictifrons)

808
Forest Weaver
p.717

809
Oliveheaded Weaver
p.717

810
Spectacled Weaver
p.718

813
Cape Weaver
p.721

816
Golden Weaver
p.724

817
Yellow Weaver
p.725

814
Masked Weaver
p.722

815
Lesser Masked Weaver
p.723

818
Brownthroated Weaver
p.726

(nigriceps)

(spilonotus)

811
Spottedbacked Weaver
p.719

812
Chestnut Weaver
p.720

Geoff Lockwood '84

824
Red Bishop
p.732

825
Firecrowned Bishop
p.733

♂ N-Br.

832
Longtailed Widow
p.740

♂ N-Br.

828
Redshouldered Widow
p.736

♂

831
Redcollared Widow
p.739

♂ N-Br.

830
Yellowbacked Widow
p.738

♂ N-Br.

829
Whitewinged Widow
p.737

♂

♂ N-Br.

827
Yellowrumped Widow
p.735

♀

826
Golden Bishop
p.734

Geoff Lockwood '84

♂ ♂ ♂ N-Br. ♀ Br.

821
Redbilled Quelea
p.729

♂ ♀

822
Redheaded Quelea
p.730

♂ ♀

833
Goldenbacked Pytilia
p.742

♂ ♀

834
Melba Finch
p.742

♀ ♂

823
Cardinal Quelea
p.731

♀ ♂

855
Cutthroat Finch
p.761

♂ ♀

856
Redheaded Finch
p.762

Imm.

857
Bronze Mannikin
p.763

Imm.

859
Pied Mannikin
p.765

Imm.

858
Redbacked Mannikin
p.764

806
Scalyfeathered Finch
p.713

70

837
Nyasa Seedcracker
p.745

836
Redfaced Crimsonwing
p.744

835
Green Twinspot
p.743

♂ ♀

838
Pinkthroated Twinspot
p.746

♂ ♀

♂ ♀

839
Redthroated Twinspot
p.747

843
Brown Firefinch
p.751

♀ ♂

♂

842
Redbilled Firefinch
p.750

♀

(rubricata)

♀ ♂

♂

♀

(haematocephala)

840
Bluebilled Firefinch
p.748

♀ ♂

841
Jameson's Firefinch
p.749

Geoff Lockwood '83

71

850
Swee Waxbill
p.757

♂
♀

851
East African Swee
p.758

854
Orangebreasted Waxbill
p.760
♀
♂

852
Quail Finch
p.759
♂
♀

844
Blue Waxbill
p.752
♂
♀

845
Violeteared Waxbill
p.753
♂
♀

853
Locust Finch
p.760
♂
♀

847
Blackcheeked Waxbill
p.755

846
Common Waxbill
p.754

848
Grey Waxbill
p.755

849
Cinderella Waxbill
p.756

864
Black Widowfinch
p.770
♂
♀

865
Purple Widowfinch
p.771
♂
♀

867
Steelblue Widowfinch
p.772
♂
♀

Geoff Lockwood '83

♂

♀

♂

♀

887
Larklike Bunting
p.791

860
Pintailed Whydah
p.766

861
Shafttailed Whydah
p.767

885
Cape Bunting
p.789

♂

♀

886
Rock Bunting
p.790

♂

♀

♂

♂

N-Br.

862
Paradise Whydah
p.768

884
Goldenbreasted Bunting
p.788

♀

863
Broadtailed Paradise Whydah
p.769

♂

♀

883
Cabanis's Bunting
p.787

868
Chaffinch
p.774

Geoff Lockwood '83

73

820
Cuckoofinch
p.728

Imm.

♂
874
Cape Siskin
p.779
♀

♂
875
Drakensberg Siskin
p.780
♀

872
Cape Canary
p.777

873
Forest Canary
p.778

869
Yelloweyed Canary
p.774

♂
(flaviventris)

♂
878
Yellow Canary
p.783
♀
(marshalli)

870
Blackthroated Canary
p.775

♂
(leucolaema)

♂
(alario)

871
Lemonbreasted Canary
p.776
♀

876
Blackheaded Canary
p.781
♀

877
Bully Canary
p.782

879
Whitethroated Canary
p.784

881
Streakyheaded Canary
p.785

882
Blackeared Canary
p.786

880
Protea Canary
p.784

Geoff Lockwood '83

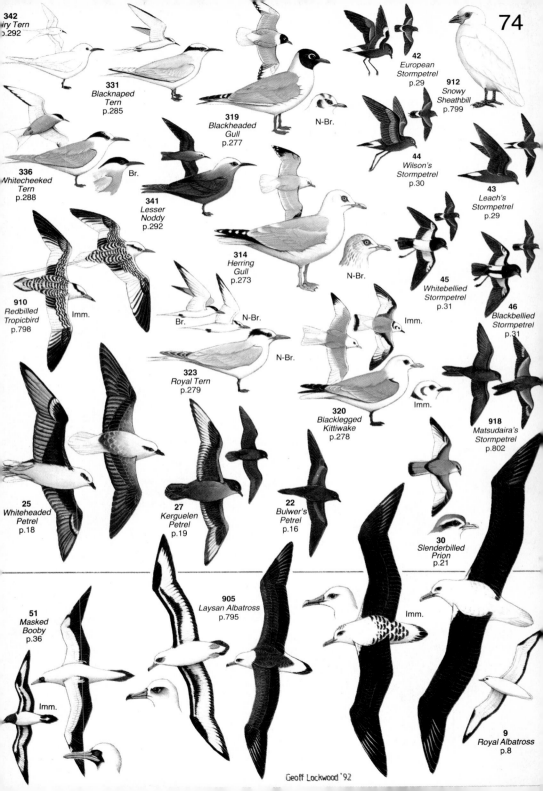

342
Fairy Tern
p.292

331
Blacknaped Tern
p.285

336
Whitecheeked Tern
p.288

Br.

319
Blackheaded Gull
p.277

N-Br.

42
European Stormpetrel
p.29

912
Snowy Sheathbill
p.799

44
Wilson's Stormpetrel
p.30

43
Leach's Stormpetrel
p.29

341
Lesser Noddy
p.292

314
Herring Gull
p.273

N-Br.

45
Whitebellied Stormpetrel
p.31

46
Blackbellied Stormpetrel
p.31

910
Redbilled Tropicbird
p.798

Imm.

Br.

N-Br.

N-Br.

Imm.

323
Royal Tern
p.279

Imm.

320
Blacklegged Kittiwake
p.278

918
Matsudaira's Stormpetrel
p.802

25
Whiteheaded Petrel
p.18

27
Kerguelen Petrel
p.19

22
Bulwer's Petrel
p.16

30
Slenderbilled Prion
p.21

51
Masked Booby
p.36

905
Laysan Albatross
p.795

Imm.

Imm.

9
Royal Albatross
p.8

Imm.

Geoff Lockwood '92

75

919
Eurasian Turtle Dove
p.803

362B
Greyheaded Parrot
p.312

♂

♀

♂

362A
Cape Parrot
p.311

(dark form)

151
Longlegged Buzzard
p.131

(dark form)

(dark form)

177
Eleonora's Falcon
p.155

239B
Whitequilted Korhaan
p.211

♂

239A
Black Korhaan
p.210

♂

♂

82
Shoebill
p.63

239B
Whitequilled Korhaan
p.211

♀

Geoff Lockwood '92

280
Temminck's Stint
p.245

275
Longtoed
Stint
p.242

277
Whiterumped Sandpiper
p.243

278
Baird's Sandpiper
p.244

282
Buffbreasted Sandpiper
p.246

293
Wilson's Phalarope
p.255

♀ Br.

908
Kentish Plover
p. 797

920
Spurwinged Plover
p.803

902 + 906

914
Hudsonian Godwit
p.800

267
Spotted Redshank
p.236

902
Lesser Yellowlegs
p.794

906
Greater Yellowlegs
p.796

Geoff Lockwood '92

77

913
Whiteheaded Sawwing Swallow
p.800

♂

♀

519
Angola Swallow
p.449

904
Redrumped Swallow
p.795

♂

♀

916
Eurasian Redstart
p.801

917
Whitethroated Bee-eater
p.802

♀

♂

907
Pied Wheatear
p.796

513
Bimaculated Lark
p.444

915
Isabelline Wheatear
p.801

♂

♀

866
Violet Widowfinch
p.772

♂

♀

781
Shelley's Sunbir
p.689

901
Mountain Pipit
p.793

909
Wood Pipit
p.797

903
Redthroated Pipit
p.794

Geoff Lockwood '92

1. Order STRUTHIONIFORMES (One family)

1:1. Family 1 STRUTHIONIDAE—OSTRICH

Very large – the largest living bird. Flightless; feathers soft and drooping; no keel on sternum; coracoid and scapula fused; no oil gland; only two toes (3rd and 4th); neck and legs very long; neck and head covered with very fine bristles; legs bare to top of tibiotarsus; males black with white and buff in wings and tail; females largely grey; gregarious; males polygynous; nest a scrape on ground; eggs 15–20 (several females may contribute), plain glossy yellowish cream; parental care by both sexes; young downy, precocial. Distribution Africa and (formerly) Syria and Arabia; one species.

1 (1)

Ostrich
Volstruis
Struthio camelus

Plate 1

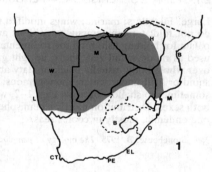

Mpšhe (NS, SS), Mpshoe (SS), Mhou, Mhowani (Sh), Bulume, Nyimbu (Ts), Ntšhe, Mpshe (Tw), Inciniba (X), iNtshe (Z), [Strauß]

Measurements: Height of male up to 2 m; wing about 900; tail about 490; tarsus: ♂ 450, ♀ 370; culmen 130–140. Weight (25) 59,5–68,7–81,3 kg (up to 157 kg recorded).

Bare Parts: Iris hazel; bill horn; legs lead grey, front scales red in breeding male.

Identification: Very large size; male mostly black with white wings and white, buff or rufous tail; female brownish grey; neck and legs very long; neck nearly naked, bristly. *Chick:* Striped buff and black on head and neck; body with black and white bristles overlying buff down; below off-white.

Voice: Male has deep booming 4-syllabled *boo boo booooh hoo*, sounding like roar of lion far away.

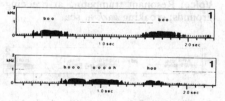

Distribution: See family account. Mainly in western parts of southern Africa N of Orange River; also across to Zimbabwe, e Transvaal and extreme s Mozambique; scarce in settled areas.

Status: Common resident; somewhat nomadic at times. In farming areas *S. c. australis* of s Africa much interbred with subspecies *camelus* and *syriacus* to improve stock for feather trade.

Habitat: Bushveld to desert.

Habits: Occurs in flocks of 30–40 birds when not breeding; up to 600 birds may gather at waterholes in desert regions. Adults and young of 1 month old or more can run at speeds of at least 50–60 km/h, sometimes with wings held out for balance. Males may perform elaborate displays in courtship and distraction when breeding.

Food: Grass, berries, seeds, succulent plants, small reptiles, insects.

Breeding: *Season:* All months, may depend on rainfall in arid zones; peak in Zimbabwe July-September, not related to rainfall. *Nest:* Scrape about 3 m diameter in sandy soil. *Breeding unit*: Average is 1 male to 3 females in drier years, otherwise more nearly monogamous. Male guards eggs until clutch complete. *Clutch*: (44) 4–13–26 eggs; laid about 48 hours apart; up to 43 eggs recorded (each female lays 3–8 eggs, depending on age and rank). *Eggs*: Deep creamy yellow, glossy, deeply pitted; measure (130) 145 × 121,2 (122–158 × 110–130); weigh, fresh (51) 1221–1346–1 752 g; volume (91) 742–998,5–1420 m (about 24 chicken eggs); laid afternoon or evening of every second day. *Incubation*: 39–53 days, usually by male from late afternoon to after sunrise next day, and by major female for rest of day.

Ref. Bertram, B.C.R. 1980. *Proc. 17th Int. Orn. Congr.*:890–894.
Sauer, E.G.F. & Sauer, E.M. 1966. *Ostrich Suppl.* 6:183–191; 1966. *Living Bird* 5:45–75.

2. Order SPHENISCIFORMES (One family)

2:1. Family 2 SPHENISCIDAE—PENGUINS

Large. Flightless; marine; wings modifed to form flattened flippers for swimming, and do not fold; tarsometatarsus very short and broad; neck short; spines on tongue and palate for holding fish; hind toe rudimentary; three front toes stout and joined by webs used as rudders; tail very short; upright gait on land; plumage of dense small feathers over whole body; usually black or slaty above and white below; sexes alike; hunt fish, squid or krill under water; monogamous; colonial; nest on ground of stones or grass, sometimes in shallow burrow; eggs 1–2, white; chick downy, altricial; parental care by both sexes. Distribution mostly s hemisphere; about 16 species; four species in s Africa, one endemic, mostly in cooler seas.

Ref. Stonehouse, B. 1975. *The biology of penguins*. London: Macmillan.

2 (–)   **King Penguin**   **Plate 4**
Koningspikkewyn
Aptenodytes patagonicus

[Königspinguin]

Measurements: Length about 94 cm; overall length of flipper ♂ 325–332–352, ♀ 317–329–340; tail ♂ 55–76–95, ♀ 40–56–75; culmen ♂ 100–104–105, ♀ 97–102–107; Weight (38 ♂) 10,5–12,1 –13,9 kg, (38 ♀) 8,8–10,9–13,4 kg, (26 unsexed) 10,8–13–15,3 kg.
Bare Parts: Iris dark brown; bill black with orange-red line at base; legs and feet black.
Identification: Size very large; top of head, cheeks and throat black; patch behind ear bright orange; rest of upperparts blue-grey; below white, merging to deep yellow-orange on upper chest; bill long. *Immature*: Paler than adult.
Voice: Resonant trumpeting at breeding grounds; croaking *aark* at sea.

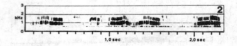

Distribution: Subantarctic islands, including Falklands, South Georgia, Prince Edward, Marion, Crozet, Kerguelen, Heard and Macquarie. Vagrant to s African waters.
Status: Rare vagrant (1 record only).

3 (2)

Jackass Penguin
Brilpikkewyn
Spheniscus demersus

Plate 4

Inguza, Unombombiya (X), [Brillenpinguin]

Measurements: Length about 60 cm; total length of flipper (72) 173–186–206; tarsus 25; whole foot (76) 102–116–128; culmen (41 ♂) 57–60,5–65, (25 ♀) 51,5–55,5–58,5. Weight (103) 2125–2946–3675 g.
Bare Parts: Iris hazel; skin above eye pink; bill black with pale horn band behind tip; legs and feet black, variably blotched pink.
Identification: Size smallish; black above, white below; chin and face patch black, separated from crown by broad white band; narrow black band across chest and down flanks toward legs; sometimes narrower partial or complete black neck band present. *Immature*: Sooty black with white chest and belly.
Voice: Loud donkey-like braying at breeding grounds, mainly at night; also honks and growls; usually silent at sea, but calls in fog or at night.

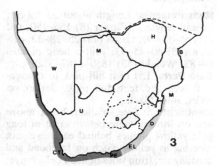

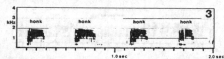

Distribution: Sw coastal regions and islands of s Africa, especially W coast; vagrant to Natal and Mozambique. Breeds from Sylvia Hill, Namibia, to Bird Island, Algoa Bay; nonbreeding birds move as far N as Gabon on W coast and Inhaca Island on E coast. Half of breeding population on few offshore islands: Ichaboe, Mercury, Possession, Dassen, Dyer and St Croix.
Status: Common but severely reduced in numbers by commercial overfishing and oil pollution; in need of conservation; estimated breeding population 1978–1979 was 133 600 birds. Resident. Vulnerable (RDB).
Habitat: Marine.
Habits: Typical penguin, foraging underwater at sea; usually departs at dawn, returns at dusk; forages mainly around midday, seldom late afternoon, mostly within 12 km of land. Comes to land to roost and breed. Occasionally washed up on mainland beaches. Walks with waddling gait on land.
Food: Fish (mainly Anchovy and Pelagic Goby), squid, octopus.
Breeding: *Season*: Almost throughout year, but mainly in summer; peaks in November-December; second peak in June on Dassen Island. Colonial on offshore islands. Breeds about every 10,5 months. *Nest*: Pad of feathers and plant material in burrow, between boulders or against bank of earth; sometimes hollow in guano or debris with little or no lining. *Clutch*: (70) 2 eggs; laying interval (11) 2–3–4 days. *Eggs*: White, rather rounded; measure (219) 68,1 × 52,1 (43–81 × 34,2–56,3); weigh (136) 75–105,8–132 g. *Incubation*: (19) 36–37,7–41 days by both sexes; changeover every 24 hours. *Nestling*: (112) 64–78,7–105 days; weighs (32) 54–71,7–81 g at hatching.

Ref. Eggleton, P. & Siegfried, W.R. 1979. *Ostrich* 50:139–167.
Frost, P.G.H., Siegfried, W.R. & Burger, A.E. 1976. *J. Zool., Lond.* 179:165–187.
Shelton, P.A., Crawford, R.J.M., Cooper, J. & Brooke, R.K. 1984. *S. Afr. J. mar. Sci.* 2:217–257.
Williams, A.J. & Cooper, J. 1984. *Proc. 5th Pan-Afr. Orn. Congr.*:841–853.

4 (3)   Rockhopper Penguin   Plate 4
Geelkuifpikkewyn
Eudyptes chrysocome

[Felsenpinguin]

Measurements: Length about 55–60 cm; overall length of flipper (8) 155–190; tail (15) 65–81–90; tarsus (15) 25–28–30; culmen (15) 40–45–53; yellow head plumes 68–83. Weight (83) 1850–2482–3520 g.

Bare Parts: Iris red; bill pink to orange-red; legs and feet dull pink, darker on webs, soles black.

Identification: Size smallish; black above and on throat; white below; crest of long pale yellow plumes behind each eye, not meeting as yellow patch on forehead and bristling out from sides of head behind eye; bill reddish and heavy. *Immature*: Lacks head plumes (line of creamy feathers over eyes only); chin and throat mottled grey.

Voice: Loud trumpeting *kaa kaa* and *karaa karaa* at breeding grounds; usually silent at sea.

Distribution: Antarctic and subantarctic seas, breeding on many subantarctic islands, including Marion and Prince Edward; vagrant to s Africa shores from Cape Town to Port Shepstone, mostly moulting juveniles in January and February. Birds of n subspecies, *E. c. moseleyi* (breeding Tristan da Cunha, Gough, St Paul and Amsterdam Islands), and s subspecies, *E. c. chrysocome* (breeding Prince Edward Islands and elsewhere), both recorded in s Africa.

Status: Rare but regular vagrant in s Africa.

Habitat: Marine.

Habits: Typical penguin, foraging underwater at sea. On land progresses mostly by hopping with both feet together. Tame.

Food: Crustaceans and squid.

Breeding: Extralimital.

5 (–)   Macaroni Penguin   Plate 4
Macaronipikkewyn
Eudyptes chrysolophus

[Goldschopfpinguin]

Measurements: Length 66–76 cm; overall length of flipper 170–190–210; tail 88–93–98; tarsus 38; culmen 63–69–75. Weight (55) 3300–4766–6150 g.

Bare Parts: Iris red; bill reddish brown to black; legs and feet dull pink, soles black.

Identification: Black above and on throat; white below; crest of long orange-yellow feathers behind each eye, meeting on forehead as orange band, drooping behind eyes at sides of head (not standing out as in Rockhopper Penguin); top of feet whiter than in Rockhopper Penguin.

Voice: Loud trumpeting at breeding grounds; harsh barking at sea.

Distribution: Antarctic and subantarctic seas.

Status: Very rare vagrant to s African coast (only 4 records, Natal 1974, Cape Agulhas 1978, Bakoven 1980, Ryspunt 1982), mostly autumn.

Habitat: Marine.

Habits: Noisy, aggressive. Waddles on land (does not hop like Rockhopper Penguin).

Food: Crustaceans and squid.

Breeding: Extralimital.

3. Order PODICIPEDIFORMES (One family)

3:1. Family 3 PODICIPEDIDAE—GREBES

Medium to large. Aquatic; walk with difficulty on land; bill pointed; neck longish; legs set far back on body; tarsometatarsus laterally flattened; toes lobed for swimming; hind toe rudimentary; claws flattened like nails; no rectrices (appear tailless); plumage soft and silky, mostly black, white and rufous; nuptial head plumes in some; sexes alike; wings short; flight fast with rapid wingbeats; moult of remiges simultaneous, so birds flightless for a time; swim and dive well; land on belly (not on feet like ducks); feed on aquatic animals and some plants; monogamous, usually solitary nesters; nest a built-up mound of decaying plant material; eggs 3–9, white, becoming nest-stained to yellow or brown; parental care by both sexes; chick precocial, downy, head and neck boldly striped; chicks often ride on parents' backs. Distribution worldwide; 19–20 species; three species in s Africa.

6 (4)   Great Crested Grebe   Plate 6
Kuifkopdobbertjie (-duikertjie)
Podiceps cristatus

Nyakupetana, Ripetani (Ts), [Haubentaucher]

Measurements: Length about 50 cm; wing (8) 173–176,3–182; tarsus 56,5–59,6–64; culmen 43–47,9–51,6. Weight (3) 492–595–775 g.

Bare Parts: Iris crimson; bill reddish brown; legs blackish brown.

Identification: Size large; brown above, silky white below; neck relatively longer and thinner than in ducks; head looks big, with conspicuous rufous-and-black crest; white wingbar in flight. *Immature*: Head and neck striped dark and light. *Chick*: Longitudinally striped dark and light with bare red patches between eye and bill and on crown; bill white with two narrow vertical black bands.

Voice: Various trumpeting, groaning and cackling sounds; ringing *karr-arr* and shrill *or-whick*. Generally rather silent.

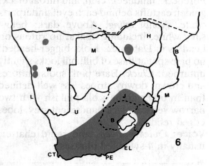

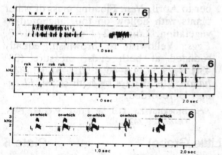

Distribution: Most of Old World; absent from drier w parts of s Africa.

Status: Sparse over most of s Africa, but can be locally common; resident or nomadic.

Habitat: Larger pans, vleis and dams, usually with emergent aquatic vegetation around shoreline; rarely at sea.

Habits: Solitary, usually in pairs, or in small groups, either among water plants or on open water; groups of 50–100 birds common. Elaborate courtship involves members of pair swimming towards each other with lowered heads, then heads raised with crests erect and flagged from side to side. Feeds by diving from surface of water.

Food: Fish, insects, crustaceans, molluscs and water plants.

Breeding: *Season*: Most months, but mainly in autumn and winter (March to August). *Nest*: Floating heap of water plants anchored to aquatic vegetation, often among reeds or rushes in water from 35–150 cm deep; usually solitary, but nests may be only 10 m apart. *Clutch*: (232) 2–3,4–4 eggs. *Eggs*: Chalky white, tinged greenish at first, becoming nest-stained to brownish; measure (154) 53 × 35,7 (47–58,9 × 33–39,5); weigh (73) 35–38–43 g. Eggs covered with nesting material when sitting bird departs. *Incubation*: 25–28 days. *Fledging*: Unrecorded.

Ref. Dean, W.R.J. 1977. *Ostrich Suppl.* 12:43–48.

7 (5) Blacknecked Grebe Plate 6
Swartnekdobbertjie (Swartnekduikertjie)
Podiceps nigricollis

[Schwarzhalstaucher]

Measurements: Length about 28 cm; wing (12) 117–125,4–137; tarsus 35,5–38,7–44; culmen 19,1–21,7–25,7. Weight (1) 298 g.

Bare Parts: Iris crimson with inner white circle; bill, legs and feet blackish.

Identification: Size medium. *Breeding*: Foreneck, hindneck, chin, and throat black; golden eartufts behind each eye; underparts white. *Nonbreeding*: Above dark; below silky white, including flanks; no rufous on head as in Dabchick; looks bigger-headed; no pale spot at base of bill; bill looks slightly upturned. *Chick*: Bare pink spots on lores and crown; downy stripes less well defined than in other grebes; bill pinkish with two narrow vertical black bands; feet grey, lobes edged reddish.

Voice: Quiet *pooeep*, and rapid chatter, usually in 4-syllabled phrases.

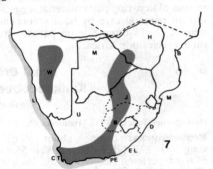

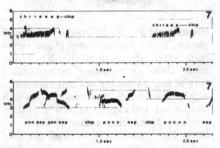

Distribution: Eurasia, Africa, N America; in s Africa mainly in highveld, sw Cape and drier w areas; nonbreeding birds also offshore along W coast. Absent from Kalahari; vagrant to Hardap Dam, Windhoek and Bushmanland.

Status: Uncommon; nomadic in arid areas, breeding sporadically when conditions right; vagrant to Zimbabwe and Natal. Many migrate to coastal areas when not breeding.

Habitat: Larger pans and vleis inland; often marine on W coast when not breeding.

Habits: Occurs in pairs or small groups when breeding; nonbreeders occur in large rafts of 250–1 300 birds which swim and dive in unison. Often preens floating on its side, exposing white belly.

Food: Small aquatic animals.

Breeding: *Season*: Irregular, mostly October to April. *Nest*: Floating mass of water plants with hollow on top, anchored to vegetation. *Clutch*: 2–4 eggs, usually 3. *Eggs*: Yellowish to brownish, equally rounded at both ends, measure (23) 43,1 × 29,5 (39,8–46 × 27,7–31,3). *Incubation*: 20–21 days by both sexes. *Fledging*: Unrecorded.

Ref. Broekhuysen, G.J. & Frost, P.G.H. 1968. *Ostrich* 39:242–252.

8 (6) Dabchick (Little Grebe) Plate 6
Kleindobbertjie (-duikertjie)
Tachybaptus ruficollis

Thoboloko (SS), Unolwilwilwi, Unoyamembi (X), [Zwergtaucher]

Measurements: Length about 20 cm; wing (19) 93–102; tarsus 29–35; culmen 18–23. Weight (2 ♂) 186–197,1 g, (1 ♀) 163 g, (14 unsexed) 119–147–188 g.

Bare Parts: Iris brown; bill black, greenish at base; legs and feet black; swelling at gape creamy white.

Identification: Size small; above blackish; below pale rufous; neck rufous (breeding) or smoky grey (nonbreeding); white secondaries conspicuous in flight. *Chick*: Lacks bare patches on head; bill pale with vertical black band near base of lower jaw.

Voice: Shrill ascending then descending trill; alarm note loud, sharp *chik*.

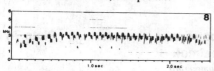

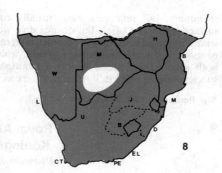

Distribution: Most of Eurasia and Africa; in s Africa absent from most of dry central Kalahari, otherwise widespread.

Status: Common resident or nomad.

Habitat: Dams, lakes, slow-flowing streams, usually with some emergent aquatic vegetation, or overhanging plants; rarely marine on W coast.

Habits: Usually in pairs or family groups of 5–6 birds when breeding. Nonbreeders may occur in flocks of up to 600 birds. Raises body to vertical position on water while vigorously flapping wings, and shaking body as it settles back. When disturbed or when chasing conspecifics often runs pattering across surface of water with wings flapping; chases often end in calling between two or more birds. May follow moving hippopotamuses to feed on disturbed aquatic animals. Dives either silently or with splash of feet; remains submerged for up to 50 seconds; can travel up to 30 m under water.

Food: Small aquatic animals (mainly frogs, tadpoles and arthropods).

Breeding: *Season*: All months; mainly August to February in s Cape, February to June in Transvaal, January and February in Zimbabwe. *Nest*: Floating heap of water plants, either in open or concealed in vegetation, anchored to stems or branches; often low in water so that eggs at water level. Bowl about 110–115 mm diameter, 25–40 mm deep. *Clutch*: (20) 1–3,2–5 eggs (rarely 6 eggs). *Eggs*: White or bluish at first, becoming nest-stained to yellowish or dark brown; measure (81) 35,6 × 25,2 (33–40 × 22–27). Covered with nesting material by departing parent. *Incubation*: 18–25 days by both sexes. Young leave nest at hatching and often ride on parents' backs, remaining there even when parent dives. *Fledging*: About 50 days; fed by both parents.

Ref. Broekhuysen, G.J. 1973. *Ostrich* 44:111–117.

4. Order PROCELLARIIFORMES (Tubenoses) (Four families; three in s Africa)

Small to very large. All marine; long-winged, good fliers; nostrils open into one or two tubes on top of bill; bill strong, hooked and covered by horny plates; well developed salt gland over eye for excreting excess salt from seawater; hind toe rudimentary or absent; front toes webbed for swimming (sometimes also used as rudders in flight); tongue spiny for holding slippery prey; sense of smell well developed, at least in some species; plumage white, grey, black or brown, plain or in combinations of these; sexes usually alike; feed on fish, squid, krill, offal, etc.; monogamous; egg one, white; chick downy, altricial.

4:1. Family 4 DIOMEDEIDAE—ALBATROSSES

Very large (70–130 cm). Wings very long and narrow, designed for gliding in wind; tail relatively short; large webbed feet may be used as rudders or air-brakes in flight, or for swimming; bill relatively long, usually characteristically coloured; feed largely on surface squid and offal, but do not dive well; glide for long periods without flapping wings; monogamous; nest in colonies on remote oceanic islands; nest a scrape on ground or mound of earth and grass; egg one, white; chick downy, altricial; parental care by both sexes. Distribution mostly s hemisphere, but four species in n Pacific; 13–14 species; nine species in s African waters as nonbreeding visitors.

Ref. Berruti, A. 1982. *Bokmakierie* 34:58–62.

9 (–)   Royal Albatross   Plate 74
Koningmalmok
Diomedea epomophora

[Königsalbatroß]

Measurements: Length 107–122 cm; wingspan 305–351 cm; wing (17) 590–616–639; tail 182–189–197; tarsus 111–115–120; culmen 156–161–170. Weight (7 ♂) 8165–9703–13 154 g, (7 ♀) 6576–7710–9072 g.

Bare Parts: Iris brown; eyelids black; bill pale pinkish yellow with dark cutting edges; legs bluish white.

Identification: Size very large; large pinkish bill; *D. e. epomophora* white except for black primaries and broad black trailing edge to upperwing (much more black on upper wing than fully adult Wandering Albatross), narrow black trailing edge to underwing; *D. e. sanfordi* has whole upperwing black; black cutting edge of bill visible at close range; does not have dark markings on back like Wandering Albatross. *Immature*: Body white; wings black, whitening progressively from leading edge backwards with age; tail narrowly tipped black (broadly tipped in Wandering Albatross).

Voice: Silent at sea; at breeding grounds rattle, *kruk-kr-kr-kr...*, followed by moaning *mooaaaooo*.

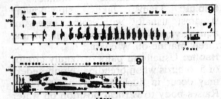

Distribution: Mainly seas around New Zealand; vagrant elsewhere.

Status: Uncommon and localized; very rare vagrant to s African waters – July 1970 about 70 km W of Cape Columbine, w Cape 1979 and 1982; may be commoner than records show because of confusion with similar Wandering Albatross.

Habitat: Open seas.

Habits and Food: Similar to those of Wandering Albatross.

Breeding: Extralimital.

Ref. Harrison, P. 1979. *Cormorant* 6:13–20.

10 (7)   Wandering Albatross   Plate 2
Grootmalmok
Diomedea exulans

[Wanderalbatroß]

Measurements: Length about 120–130 cm; wingspan 280–324–350 cm; wing (24) 585–645–679; tail 117–194,5–205; tarsus 111–120–128; culmen 156–168–177. Weight (14 ♂) 8200–9260–11 300 g, (21 ♀) 6400–7780–9000 g.

Bare Parts: Iris brown; eyelids pale grey or pink; bill pale flesh-pink; legs and feet pale bluish to pinkish.

Identification: Very large, with large pale pink bill; mostly white, except for black primaries and narrow dark trailing edge to wing above and below; some black markings on back sometimes visible at close range; subadult with more black above, upper wing often mostly black. *Immature*: Mostly dark brown with white face and underwing with dark trailing edge (later immature has white belly and white underwing with dark trailing edge); upperwing whitens progressively from central white patch with age. Adult plumage attained in not less than five years, so intermediate plumages common.

Voice: Harsh croaking when fighting for food at sea; at breeding islands a variety of braying, squealing and gobbling calls accompanied by bill clappering.

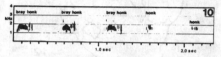

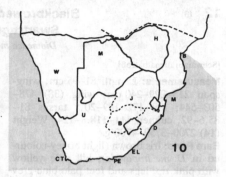

Distribution: Southern oceans. Breeds on many subantarctic islands.
Status: Nonbreeding visitor to s African waters, especially in winter; most common off continental shelf.
Habitat: Open ocean.

Habits: In flight bill usually angled slightly downwards, and back looks somewhat humped. Flies in long sweeping glides, seldom flapping wings. Settles on water to feed, taking off into wind.
Food: Squid, fish, offal.
Breeding: Extralimital.

Ref. Harrison, P. 1979. *Cormorant* 6:13–20.

11 (11) Shy Albatross (Whitecapped Albatross) Plate 2
Bloubekmalmok
Diomedea cauta

[Scheuer Albatroß]

Measurements: Length 89–99 cm; wingspan 243 cm; wing (32) 523–556–585; tail 188–205–220; tarsus 86–88–95; culmen 117–128–135. Weight (2) 3300–4100 g.
Bare Parts: Iris brown; bill bluish, yellowish, or greenish grey with orange tip (some races have yellow bill), dark horseshoe stripe behind nostrils, vertical orange stripe at base of lower jaw; legs and feet bluish pink.
Identification: Size large; sides of head and back greyish; crown white, giving capped effect; upperwing and tail greyish brown; rump and rest of body white; underwing white, narrowly edged black, with small black patch where wing joins body (diagnostic, even at distance); eyebrow dark; bill greenish to bluish in local birds. *Immature*: Bill grey with darker tip; head and underwing similar to those of adult.
Voice: At sea loud drawn-out *waak*.
Distribution: Breeds on islands around Tasmania and New Zealand; ranges

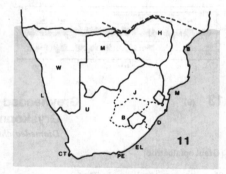

widely in s oceans, including around s Africa.
Status: Fairly common nonbreeding visitor, especially in winter to s African seas.
Habitat: Open ocean.
Habits: Flight and foraging behaviour similar to that of other large albatrosses.
Food: As for other large albatrosses.
Breeding: Extralimital.

Ref. Johnstone, G.W., Milledge, D. & Dorward, D.F. 1975. *Emu* 75:1–11.

9

12 (8)

Blackbrowed Albatross
Swartrugmalmok
Diomedea melanophris

Plate 2

[Schwarzbrauenalbatroß]

Measurements: Length 81–95 cm; wing-span 215–229–240 cm; wing (38) 478–503–544; tail 172–189–201; tarsus 81–85,6–92; culmen 111–118,8–124. Weight (14) 2700–3750–4700 g.

Bare Parts: Iris brown (light honey-coloured in *D. m. impavida*); bill pale yellow with pink tip; legs and feet pale blue-grey to pinkish or yellowish with bluish webs.

Identification: Size medium; back, upper-wing and broad leading and trailing edges of underwing sooty black; tail grey with blackish tip; rest of plumage white, except for black eyebrow and small area around eye; bill yellow. Underwing white surrounded by broad black border. *Immature*: Bill dark with blackish tip; nape greyish; underwing similar to that of adult, but with less white in centre.

Voice: Croaking when fighting for food, but usually silent; loud braying at breeding islands.

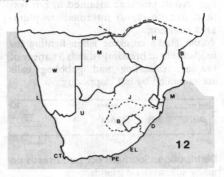

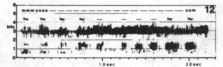

Distribution: Southern oceans. Breeds on many subantarctic islands.

Status: Common nonbreeding visitor, especially in winter; commonest albatross off sw Cape.

Habitat: Open ocean.

Habits: Solitary or gregarious. May come close inshore, even into coastal bays. In flight may touch water with wingtips; flaps more than larger albatrosses. Gathers in large numbers (1 000 or more birds) to feed on fish offal from trawlers.

Food: Krill, fish, squid, salps, offal.

Breeding: Extralimital.

Ref. Prince, P.A. 1980. *Ibis* 122:476–488.

13 (9)

Greyheaded Albatross
Gryskopmalmok
Diomedea chrysostoma

Plate 2

[Graukopfalbatroß]

Measurements: Length 71–82 cm; wing-span 203–216 cm; wing (19) 473–508,4–555; tail 175–193,4–205; tarsus 79–85,3–91; culmen 106–114,4–122. Weight (13) 2680–3665–4350 g.

Bare Parts: Iris brown; bill black with yellow line along top of culmen and along bottom of lower jaw; legs and feet bluish flesh.

Identification: Size medium; whole head and neck light dusky or slaty grey; upper-wing and back blackish; tail dark grey;

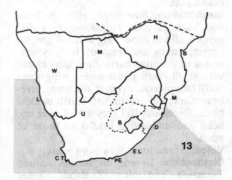

10

underwing white bordered blackish along leading and trailing edges; characteristic bill coloration visible in good light at sea; darkish patch in front of and through eye. *Immature*: Similar to adult but with less white under wing; bill greyish black, tip yellow.
Voice: Similar to voice of Blackbrowed Albatross; usually silent at sea.

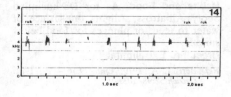

Distribution: Southern oceans, usually between 60 and 40 °S. Breeds on islands of Diego Ramirez, Prince Edward, Marion, Crozet, Kerguelen, Macquarie and Campbell.
Status: Rare vagrant to coasts of Namibia and Natal.
Habitat: Open ocean.
Habits: Similar to Blackbrowed Albatross, but not so readily attracted to ships.
Food: Lampreys (fed to young in large numbers); also krill, squid, fish, offal.
Breeding: Extralimital.

14 (10) Yellownosed Albatross Plate 2
Geelneusmalmok
Diomedea chlororhynchos

[Gelbnasenalbatroß]

Measurements: Length 74–86 cm; wingspan 175–200–205 cm. *D. c. chlororhynchos*: wing (37) 456–496,4–520; tail (37) 178–194,3–214; tarsus (36) 74–81,7–86; culmen (36) 107–115–125; weight (39) 1650–2157–2840 g. *D. c. bassi*: wing (55) 453–481,8–505; tail (23) 172–193,9–210; tarsus (56) 74–81,9–86,6; culmen (56) 106–116,4–124,2; weight (15) 2490–2640–2930 g.
Bare Parts: Iris brown; bill black, yellow along top of culmen, pinkish tip; legs and feet pale chalky blue with pink webs.
Identification: Size medium to smallish; build slender; bill looks dark and slender, pink tip conspicuous; head mainly grey (*D. c. chlororhynchos*) or white with grey sides (*D. c. bassi*); dark area around eye; otherwise similar to Greyheaded Albatross, but underwing largely white, with broad dark leading edge and narrow dark trailing edge. *Immature*: Bill dark; head and neck white.
Voice: Silent at sea; at breeding islands utters high-pitched clattering calls.

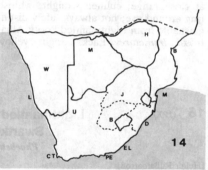

Distribution: Mainly S Atlantic and Indian Oceans; in S Pacific only between Australia and New Zealand; breeds Tristan da Cunha group, Gough, Prince Edward, Saint-Paul and Amsterdam Islands.
Status: Common nonbreeding visitor, especially in winter.
Habitat: Open ocean.
Habits: Similar to Blackbrowed Albatross. Attracted to trawling grounds for fish offal.
Food: Mostly cephalopods; also fish, large shrimps, offal.
Breeding: Extralimital.

Ref. Brooke, R.K., Sinclair, J.C. & Berruti, A. 1980. *Durban Mus. Novit.* 12:171–180.
Rowan, M.K. 1951. *Ostrich* 22:139–155.

15 (12)   Darkmantled Sooty Albatross   Plate 2
Bruinmalmok
Phoebetria fusca

[Dunkler Rußalbatroß]

Measurements: Length 81–86 cm; wingspan 180–198–240 cm; wing (101) 490–516,5–551; tail (118) 245–265,5–294; tarsus (212) 77,5–82,7–90; culmen (212) 99,9–112,1–120,2. Weight (176) 2,1–2,5–3,4 kg.

Bare Parts: Iris brown; bill black with yellow or orange groove (sulcus) along lower jaw; legs and feet pale grey to pinkish.

Identification: Size medium; build slender; body all dark; wings long, slender; tail wedge-shaped; head somewhat darker than body, but not contrasting sharply with it; yellow groove on dark bill visible at close range; culmen straight; whitish ring around eye; not always safely distinguishable from Lightmantled Sooty Albatross. *Immature*: Lacks bright yellow sulcus on lower jaw; otherwise similar to adult.

Voice: Silent at sea; on breeding islands, loud two-syllabled call of higher pitched note followed by lower note, *pee-oo*.

Distribution: Southern Atlantic and Indian Oceans; breeds on islands of Prince Edward, Marion, Crozet, Tristan da Cunha group, Gough, Amsterdam and St Paul.

Status: Rare vagrant to all s African coastal waters.

Habitat: Open ocean.

Habits: Flight graceful, with effortless gliding. Inquisitive, follows ships closely.

Food: Squid, fish, crustaceans, carrion.

Breeding: Extralimital.

Ref. Berruti, A. 1979. *Emu* 79:161–175; 1981. *Ostrich* 52:98–103.

16 (12X)   Lightmantled Sooty Albatross   Plate 2
Swartkopmalmok
Phoebetria palpebrata

[Heller Rußalbatroß]

Measurements: Length 71–90 cm; wingspan 208–213 cm; wing (17) 507–533,7–559; tail (13) 236–265,9–282; tarsus (20) 75,5–82,4–88,7; culmen (20) 99–104,8–111,1. Weight (6) 2390–2823–3250 g.

Bare Parts: Iris brown; bill black with narrow blue groove (sulcus) on lower jaw; legs and feet light bluish grey to pinkish.

Identification: Similar in shape and flight to Darkmantled Sooty Albatross, but back and underparts ashy grey, so that dark head contrasts markedly with light body; dark remiges and rectrices show pale yellowish or white shafts; no yellow on bill; culmen slightly concave. *Immature*: Similar to adult, but less contrast and hard to tell apart from immature Darkmantled Sooty Albatross; sulcus may be pale yellow.

Voice: Silent at sea; on breeding islands a 2-syllabled *pee-ow*.

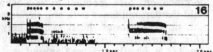

Distribution: Southern oceans; breeds on islands of South Georgia, Prince Edward, Marion, Crozet, Kerguelen, Heard, Macquarie, Auckland, Campbell and Antipodes.

Status: Very rare vagrant to Cape coastal waters.

Habitat: Open ocean.

Habits and Food: As for Darkmantled Sooty Albatross. Alights on surface of water to feed, or plunges for food below surface.

Breeding: Extralimital.

Ref. Berruti, A. 1979. *Emu* 79:161–175; 1981. *Ostrich* 52:98–103.

12

4:2. Family 5 PROCELLARIIDAE—PETRELS, SHEARWATERS, PRIONS, ETC.

Mostly medium, a few large. Adapted for gliding over open ocean; legs and feet relatively weak, except in giant petrels; leg bones shorter than wing bones; most nest in burrows or in scrape on ground or cliff ledge; egg one, white; chick downy, altricial; parental care by both sexes; some species nocturnal on breeding grounds. Distribution worldwide, mostly s oceans; about 55 species; 25 species in s African waters as nonbreeding visitors.

17 (13)   Southern Giant Petrel   Plate 2
Reuse Nellie
Macronectes giganteus

[Riesensturmvogel]

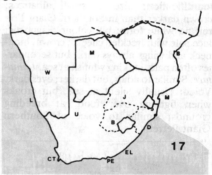

Measurements: Length 86–99 cm; wingspan 185–205 cm; wing (16 ♂) 500–528–565; tail 166–180–189; tarsus 92–95,8–103; culmen 90–99,1–105; wing (19 ♀) 462–498–526; tail 162–171–183; tarsus 80–87,6–99; culmen 78–87,5–101. Weight (6 ♂) 4510–5109–5710 g, (14 ♀) 3420–3860–4020 g.

Bare Parts: Iris dark brown, less often pale grey; bill greenish yellow to pale horn, greener near tip; legs and feet brown to sooty black or pinkish.

Identification: About size of smaller albatrosses. *Dark form*: Dusky grey-brown, paler below; head and neck much paler, even whitish; sometimes looks mottled; bill greenish yellow with elongated nasal tube; eyes pale. *Light form*: Mostly white with few dark feathers. *Immature*: Uniform rich chocolate brown with dark eyes.

Voice: Usually silent at sea, but croaks when fighting over food; at breeding grounds various neighing, mewing, retching, hissing sounds, and bill-snapping.

Distribution: Southern oceans; breeds mainly S of Antarctic convergence to Ant-

arctica, somewhat later than Northern Giant Petrel. Both giant petrels breed on Prince Edward and Marion Islands.

Status: Nonbreeding visitor to s African waters, but less common than Northern Giant Petrel; immatures migrate to temperate seas.

Habitat: Open ocean and inshore near harbours.

Habits: Solitary or gregarious. Alights on water for food; also gathers at seal harvests and seabird breeding colonies to scavenge offal, or prey on chicks. Flight somewhat stiff, less graceful than that of albatrosses; looks somewhat hunched in flight, with smaller wings than albatross of comparable size. Not much attracted to ships.

Food: In summer mainly carrion and seabird chicks; at sea cephalopods, fish, crustaceans, offal.

Breeding: Extralimital.

18 (–)   Northern Giant Petrel   Plate 2
Grootnellie
Macronectes halli

[Nördlicher Riesensturmvogel]

Measurements: Length 81–94 cm; wingspan 180–200 cm; wing (5 ♂) 505–522–542; tail 170–175–184; tarsus 89–95–101; culmen 93–98–106; wing (3 ♀) 485–509–512; tail 171–177–185; tarsus 85–92–97; culmen 85–98–108. Weight (14 ♂) 3930–4546–5690 g, (21 ♀) 2900–3360–3860 g.

Bare Parts: Iris pale grey to whitish; bill yellowish brown to brown with darker markings, dull pink to reddish near tip; legs and feet dusky grey or brown.

Identification: Size of small albatross; crown darker than in Southern Giant Petrel; no white form; bill colour diagnostic; face pale with freckled cheeks; crown, hindneck and wings always dark, but secondaries often pale, looking whitish at sea. *Immature*: Similar to adult, but darker; eyes dark.

Voice: Usually silent at sea, but croaks when fighting over food; at breeding grounds, similar to voice of Southern Giant Petrel.

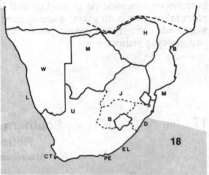

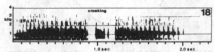

Distribution: Southern oceans; breeds mainly N of Antarctic convergence, some-

what earlier than Southern Giant Petrel. Both giant petrels breed on Prince Edward and Marion Islands.

Status: Nonbreeding visitor to all s African waters; commoner than Southern Giant Petrel, especially in Benguela Current.

Habitat: Open ocean, sometimes inshore around harbours.

Habits: Solitary at sea, except when congregating at food supply. Strongly attracted to ships. Flight as for Southern Giant Petrel.

Food: As for Southern Giant Petrel.

Breeding: Extralimital.

Ref. Bourne, W.R.P. & Warham, J. 1966. *Ardea* 54:45–67.

19 (15)   Antarctic Fulmar (Southern Fulmar)   Plate 3
Silwerstormvoël
Fulmarus glacialoides

[Silbermöwen-Sturmvogel]

Measurements: Length 46–50 cm; wingspan 107–127 cm; wing (20) 325–340–351; tail 114–123–136; tarsus 46–49–52; culmen 39–43–47. Weight (41) 640–775–1030 g

Bare Parts: Iris brown; bill pink with blue markings on nasal tubes and on lower jaw, tip black; legs and feet flesh.

Identification: Size medium; gull-like, pale grey above, white below washed grey on flanks; dark spot in front of eye; dark primaries show white flashes on inner webs; legs and bill pale, bill with dark markings.

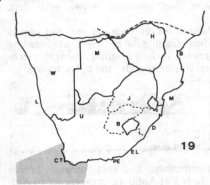

Voice: Usually silent at sea, but cackles when squabbling over food; on breeding grounds, soft droning and guttural croaks.

Distribution: Extreme southern oceans and up cold ocean currents, mainly on w side of continents, but also E to Algoa Bay; breeds on islands of South Sandwich, South Orkney, South Shetland, Bouvet, Peter I, and on Antarctica.

Status: Scarce nonbreeding winter visitor to all s African waters, August to January (mainly September); occasionally wrecked in larger numbers.

Habitat: Cold Antarctic waters in summer; otherwise up cold currents as far as sub-tropics, but rarely N of 40 °S. Highly pelagic.

Habits: Agile in flight, alighting and taking off with ease; alternates fast wingbeats with long glides on stiff wings, with light rocking motion. Wings look long and narrow. Gregarious at sea, resting or feeding in small flocks.

Food: Mainly shrimps and other crustaceans; some cephalopods, fish and offal from ships.

Breeding: Extralimital.

20 (15X) Antarctic Petrel   Plate 3
Antarktiese Stormvoël
Thalassoica antarctica

[Grauweißer Sturmvogel]

Measurements: Length 43–45 cm; wingspan 92–104 cm; wing (12) 305–315–338; tail 101–112–125; tarsus 41,6–44,5 46,5; culmen 33–36,4–40. Weight (87) 530–680–750 g.

Bare Parts: Iris brown; bill brown to black; legs and feet pale bluish, yellowish or pinkish.

Identification: Size medium; boldly pied; above brown with broad white trailing edge to wing, tipped dark brown; rump and tail white, tipped dark brown; below white, with brownish wash on chin and throat and very narrow brown border to underwing; bill dark; legs pale; nape sometimes mottled with whitish. *Immature*: Somewhat darker brown than adult; bill black.

Voice: Silent at sea; on breeding grounds has variety of churring, cackling and more resonant calls.

Distribution: Extreme southern oceans; breeds on several subantarctic islands and on Antarctica.

Status: Very rare vagrant to s Africa; collected once at Bird Island, Algoa Bay, September 1965.

Habitat: Open ocean, often among pack-ice.

Habits: Flight similar to that of Antarctic Fulmar, but wingbeats shorter, stronger and faster; usually flies high over water. Gregarious, gathering on ice floes in large flocks. Follows ships for food.

Food: Krill, some cephalopods, fish and offal from ships.

Breeding: Extralimital.

21 (14) Pintado Petrel   Plate 3
Seeduifstormvoël
Daption capense

[Kapsturmvogel]

Measurements: Length 36–40 cm; wingspan 89–91 cm; wing (35) 249–261,7–273; tail 89–95–103; tarsus 34–44–47; culmen 28–30,8–34. Weight (21) 310–390–610 g.

Bare Parts: Iris brown; bill black; legs black; feet black with some white mottling.

Identification: Size medium to smallish; build chunky; upperparts chequered black and white; wings mainly dark with two white patches in each; head, throat and tail tip black; belly and underwing white with narrow black leading and trailing edges.

Voice: Chattering *kak-kak, kak-kak*; highly vocal at sea and on breeding grounds.

Distribution: Southern oceans to Tropic of Capricorn; breeds on many subantarctic islands and on Antarctica.

Status: Common nonbreeding visitor to all s African seas, especially in winter; may be completely absent in summer.

Habitat: Open ocean; nonbreeding birds mainly follow cooler ocean currents. Seldom seen inshore.

Habits: Flight stiff-winged, alternating flapping with gliding. Follows ships.

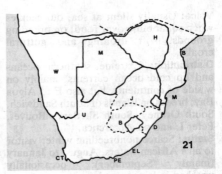

Usually gregarious, flocks settling on water to feed. Makes shallow dives for food, or paddles with feet to bring food to surface.

Food: Krill, fish, carrion, offal.

Breeding: Extralimital.

22 (–) Bulwer's Petrel Plate 74
Bulwerse Stormvoël
Bulweria bulwerii

[Bulwersturmvogel]

Measurements: Length 26–28 cm; wingspan 61–73 cm; wing (29) 191–200–209; tail 102–109–116; tarsus 24–27,5–30; culmen 19–21,4–23. Weight 87–93–98 g.

Bare Parts: Iris brown; bill black; legs and feet flesh, dusky on outer webs.

Identification: Size small; usually dark all over, slightly paler below, with faint paler diagonal band on upperwing; wings long, narrow; tail long, wedge-shaped, looks pointed; bill dark; legs pale.

Voice: Silent at sea; at breeding grounds deep croak like barking dog.

Distribution: N Atlantic and Pacific Oceans; breeds on islands of Hawaiian group, Bonin, Volcano, Phoenix and Marquesas, and on Chinese coast.

Status: Very rare vagrant to s African waters (sight records only).

Habitat: Open ocean.

Habits: Flies low over water in shallow swooping arcs, or with deep irregular wingbeats.

Food: Probably krill and squid.

Breeding: Extralimital.

23 (16) Greatwinged Petrel Plate 3
Langvlerkstormvoël
Pterodroma macroptera

[Langflügel-Sturmvogel]

Measurements: Length 38–42 cm; wingspan 97–107 cm; wing (6) 300–306–312; tail 116–123–129; tarsus 40–41–44; culmen 34–37–39. Weight (71) 435–588–745 g.

Bare Parts: Iris brown; bill, legs and feet black.

Identification: Large, long-winged petrel; sooty brown sometimes with paler greyish area around face at base of bill; bill stubby and hooked; wings held somewhat bent in flight. *Immature*: Face always pale.

Voice: Silent at sea; on breeding grounds whistles, screams, grunts and brays.

Distribution: More northerly parts of s oceans.
Status: Nonbreeding visitor to all s African seas. Vulnerable (RDB).
Habitat: Open ocean.
Habits: Flight swift with swoops and soaring, usually rather high in broad arcs, with

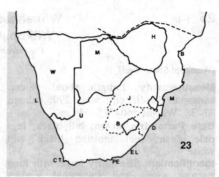

characteristically long, narrow, bent wings.
Food: Mainly cephalopods; some fish.
Breeding: Extralimital.

24 (19) Softplumaged Petrel Plate 3
Donsveerstormvoël
Pterodroma mollis

[Weichfeder-Sturmvogel]

Measurements: Length 32–37 cm; wingspan 83–95 cm; wing (39) 239–251,6–268; tail 102,5–109,3–117; tarsus 32,5–34,5–36; culmen 26,5–28,2–30,5. Weight (86) 250–312–380 g.
Bare Parts: Iris brown; bill black; legs and webs pinkish; toes dark brown to black.
Identification: Size medium; bill dark; legs pale. *Light form*: Upperparts slaty grey, darker around eyes and on leading half of wing, showing as dark W in flight; below white with greyish chest band; underwing grey, darker in front, contrasting with white belly. *Dark form* (very rare): Sooty grey all over with darker coverts on upper and underwing; dark patch around eye.
Voice: Silent at sea; on breeding grounds moans and whistles.

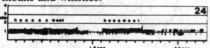

Distribution: Atlantic and s Indian Oceans; breeds on islands of Madeira, Cape Verde, Tristan da Cunha group,

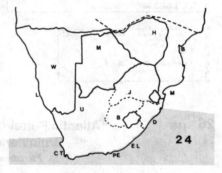

Gough, Marion, Crozet, and possibly elsewhere.
Status: Common nonbreeding visitor to s African seas, especially in winter. Vulnerable (RDB).
Habitat: Mainly subtropical and subantarctic seas.
Habits: Flight fast with zigzagging and rapid wingbeats, interspersed with gliding in arcs low over water and then high. Shy and solitary. Does not follow ships.
Food: Cephalopods and fish.
Breeding: Extralimital.

25 (–)   Whiteheaded Petrel   Plate 74
Witkopstormvoël
Pterodroma lessonii

[Weißkopf-Sturmvogel]

Measurements: Length about 46 cm; wingspan 92–107 cm; wing 290; culmen 37–38. Weight 560–595–630 g.

Bare Parts: Iris brown; bill black; legs pale flesh; feet mottled black and white.

Identification: Size fairly large with long narrow wings and somewhat wedge-shaped tail; upperparts pale grey with contrasting sooty brown wings; forehead, lower half of head and underparts white with contrasting dark grey underwing; black patch around and in front of eye; bill short and black; legs pale.

Voice: Silent at sea; on breeding grounds a variety of slurred, throaty calls.

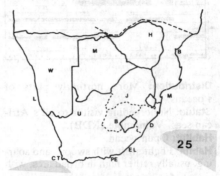

Distribution: Southern oceans; breeds on islands of Kerguelen, Macquarie, Auckland, Antipodes, and possibly elsewhere.
Status: Very rare vagrant to s African waters; recorded only twice.
Habitat: Open ocean.
Habits: Solitary or gregarious. Flight fast with much banking and swooping on sharply arched wings which look M-shaped. Usually solitary, sometimes in small groups. Does not usually follow ships.
Food: Mainly cephalopods; occasionally fish.
Breeding: Extralimital.

26 (18)   Atlantic Petrel (Schlegel's Petrel)   Plate 3
Bruinvlerkstormvoël
Pterodroma incerta

[Schlegels Sturmvogel]

Measurements: Length 45–46 cm; wingspan 104 cm; wing (12) 313–323–335; tail 121–131–138; tarsus 43–45–47; culmen 35–37–39. Weight (54) 440–522–595 g.

Bare Parts: Iris brown; bill black; legs and feet pinkish, brown on outer toes and webs.

Identification: Size medium; stoutly built; dark brown above, paler on hindneck; foreneck brown (throat sometimes paler, whitish) sharply divided from white belly; underwing, flanks and undertail brown; bill dark; legs pale. Distinguished from

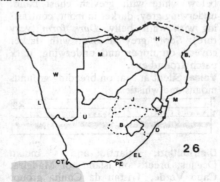

Softplumaged Petrel by dark undertail and greater size.
Voice: Silent at sea; on breeding grounds, similar to calls of Whiteheaded Petrel, but more mellow.
Distribution: S Atlantic and w Indian Oceans as far N as 50 °S.

Status: Rare nonbreeding visitor to Cape waters; one record Natal.
Habitat: Warmer subantarctic waters.
Habits: Similar to those of Whiteheaded Petrel, but tends to follow ships.
Food: Probably mainly squid.
Breeding: Extralimital.

27 (–)   Kerguelen Petrel   Plate 74
Kerguelense Stormvoël
Lugensa brevirostris

[Kerguelensturmvogel]

Measurements: Length 33 cm; wingspan 66–69 cm; wing (16) 242–257–265; tail 104–107–114; tarsus 34–38–40; culmen 25,5–26,7–28,5. Weight (126) 255–357–451 g.
Bare Parts: Iris brown; bill black; legs and feet blackish to greyish with purple tinge.
Identification: Size smallish; almost uniformly dark grey (bright silver-grey in sunlight), slightly darker on wings and tail; base of primaries paler grey below; leading edge of wing paler grey (to whitish), clear when seen head-on; faint mottling on forehead and face; looks bigheaded with high forehead; bill dark, stubby and narrow; legs dark.
Voice: Silent at sea; on breeding grounds, hoarse screeching alarm notes.

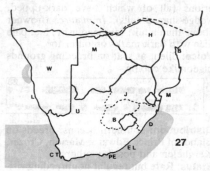

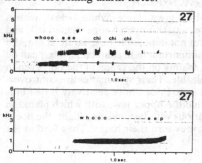

Distribution: Southern oceans; breeds on islands of Marion, Crozet, Kerguelen, Gough and possibly Tristan da Cunha group.
Status: Rare vagrant to sw Cape and Natal.
Habitat: Open ocean.
Habits: Usually solitary, but sometimes in small flocks. Flies with rapid wingbeats to gain altitude, hangs in high wind, then swoops low into wave trough with fast wing-flicking. Attracted to ships, but does not follow them. Dives from surface.
Food: Mainly cephalopods; some crustaceans.
Breeding: Extralimital.

28 (20)   Blue Petrel   Plate 3
Bloustormvoël
Halobaena caerulea

[Blausturmvogel]

Measurements: Length 28–30 cm; wingspan 58–66 cm; wing (40) 200–215–224;

tail 83–89–95; tarsus 28–32–36; culmen 24–26–28. Weight (107) 171–201–235 g.
Bare Parts: Iris brown; bill blue with black culmen and nasal tubes, or black with

bluish line on lower jaw; legs and feet pale blue with pinkish webs.

Identification: Size small; looks very prion-like (genus *Pachyptila*). Crown and nape blackish; forehead white (grey or blackish in prions) with black mottling; rest of upperparts blue-grey with dark line along wings, forming W-pattern; square tail tipped white; face and underparts white, including underwing; dark patches at sides of chest form incomplete collar. Square white-tipped tail distinguishes it from prions (all of which have dark-tipped, wedge-shaped tails). *Immature*: Browner above than adult; forehead ashy; feet pale lilac with dark marks on outer toe.

Voice: Silent at sea; on breeding grounds pigeonlike cooing.

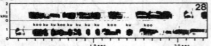

Distribution: Southern oceans; breeds on islands of Prince Edward, Marion, Crozet, Kerguelen and possibly others.

Status: Rare but regular nonbreeding visitor to s African waters from w Cape to Natal, mainly May to October.

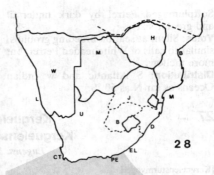

28

Habitat: Colder antarctic and subantarctic seas; open ocean.

Habits: Solitary at sea. Rather steady flier, less erratic than prions, usually low over water with much gliding. Swims and dives; patters over water on take-off. Follows ships and whales, sometimes in company with prions.

Food: Mainly krill and small cephalopods; some fish.

Breeding: Extralimital.

Ref. Every, B., Hosten, L.W. & Brooke, R.K. 1981. *Cormorant* 9:19–22.

THE PRIONS, GENUS *PACHYPTILA*

The three species of prion are small petrels, blue-grey above, white below, with a characteristic dark W-shaped line along the wings, a dark-tipped wedge-shaped tail, and a dark patch around the eye. They are difficult but not impossible to separate at sea; the bill shape and undertail patterns are particularly important field characters. They can be identified with reasonable certainty in the hand, mainly on the shape of the bill, even in beached birds whose plumage may be unrecognizable. Their systematics are controversial and the number of species has varied from 2–6. Prions have relatively broad bills with two rows of fine lamellae on the palate inside the upper jaw, with which plankton is filtered out of seawater. They are largely gregarious with fast, twisting flight, the flocks flashing white and then seeming to disappear as they turn their backs. They feed at the surface, or by diving.

Ref. Cox, J.B. 1980. *Rec. S. Austr. Mus.* 18:91–121.

29 (21, 21X, 22)   **Broadbilled Prion**   Plate 3
Breëbekwalvisvoël
Pachyptila vittata

[Entensturmvogel und Taubensturmvogel]

Measurements: (This species here includes also Salvin's Prion *P. salvini* and the Dove Prion *P. desolata*) Length 25–30 cm; wingspan 57–66 cm; wing (167) 171–189,8–214; tail (140) 72–89,3–113; tarsus (168) 28–32,4–38,4; culmen (168) 23,7–28,2–37; width of bill

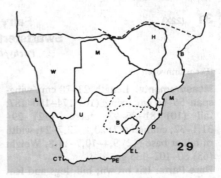

at base (140) 11–15,1–22,6. Weight (590) 106–162–238 g.

Bare Parts: Iris brown; bill blackish; legs and feet blue, webs pinkish.

Identification: Size small; crown dark blue-grey (pale in other prions); eye-stripe black (no eyestripe in Fairy Prion); eyebrow white; rest of upper-parts blue-grey with dark W across wings and back; tail narrowly tipped black (broadly tipped black in Fairy Prion; outer rectrices white in Slenderbilled Prion); below white; incomplete grey collar in *P. v. desolata*; undertail white with dark centre and tip, forming black T (no black tip on undertail of Slenderbilled Prion; no dark centre to undertail of Fairy Prion); bill black, broad, heavy.

Voice: Silent at sea; on breeding grounds various cooing and cackling calls.

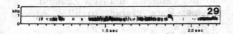

Distribution: Southern oceans; breeds on most subantarctic islands and on Antarctica.

Status: Fairly common nonbreeding visitor (mostly *P. v. desolata*), mainly in winter to all s African waters; often found beached after storms.

Habitat: Open ocean.

Habits: See account for prions.

Food: See account for prions.

Breeding: Extralimital.

---

30 (22Y) **Slenderbilled Prion** **Plate 74**
Dunbekwalvisvoël
Pachyptila belcheri

[Dünnschnabel-Sturmvogel]

Measurements: Length 26–28 cm; wing-span 56 cm; wing (13) 169–184–191; tail (10) 86,2–92,1–96,5; tarsus (13) 31–32,5–34; culmen (13) 20,1–25,1–28,3; width of bill at base (13) 9,6–10,4–11,4. Weight (126) mean 133 g.

Bare Parts: Iris brown; bill, legs and feet blue.

Identification: Size small; above blue-grey, forehead darker; dark W across wings and back; tail grey, outer rectrices white, tip narrowly black; broad dark stripe from eye to sides of neck (no dark marks in Fairy Prion); eyebrow white; below white; undertail white with black central stripe (no black tip as in other prions); bill blue, slender (black, heavy in Broadbilled Prion).

Voice: As for Broadbilled Prion.

Distribution: Southern oceans; breeds on Falklands, Crozet and Kerguelen Islands,

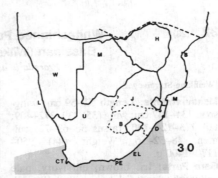

and possibly other islands S of Tierra del Fuego, and elsewhere.

Status: Very rare vagrant to s African waters from False Bay to Zululand.

Habitat: Open ocean.

Habits: See prion account.

Food: See prion account.

Breeding: Extralimital.

31 (22X) Fairy Prion Plate 3
Swartstertwalvisvoël
Pachyptila turtur

[Feensturmvogel]

Measurements: Length 23–28 cm; wing-span 56–60 cm; wing (10) 174–180–187; tail (10) 81–86–93; tarsus (12) 29–31,1–32; culmen (12) 20,1–22,7–24; width of bill at base (12) 9,4–10,7–11,8. Weight (63) 80–102–135 g.

Bare Parts: Iris brown; bill, legs and feet blue.

Identification: Size small; above light blue-grey with dark W across wings and back; eyebrow white; no dark head markings as in other prions; tail broadly tipped black (narrowly tipped in other prions); below white; undertail white, tipped black (no black centre line as in other prions).

Voice: As for Broadbilled Prion.

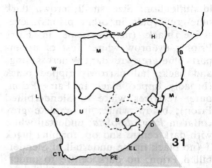

Distribution: Southern oceans; breeds on Marion Island; probably also on islands of Crozet, Macquarie, Falklands, and around Tasmania and New Zealand.

Status: Rare vagrant to all s African waters.

Habitat: Open ocean.

Habits: As for other prions.

Food: As for other prions.

Breeding: Extralimital.

32 (23) Whitechinned Petrel (Cape Hen) Plate 3
Bassiaan (Witkenpylstormvoël)
Procellaria aequinoctialis

[Weißkinn-Sturmvogel]

Measurements: Length 51–59 cm; wing-span 134–147 cm; wing (35) 339–372–409; tail 113–124–140; tarsus 56–63–72; culmen 48–52–56. Weight (44) 950–1170–1400 g.

Bare Parts: Iris brown; bill ivory, pale yellowish to greenish horn with dark patch on culmen, blackish groove on lower jaw; legs and feet black.

Identification: Size large; build heavy; blackish brown all over except for white chin; amount of white variable; crown sometimes flecked white; bill long, massive and pale (dark ridge on culmen sometimes visible at sea); legs dark; wings long,

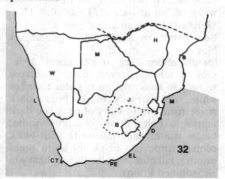

broad; tail rounded to wedge-shaped. (Also known to fishermen as Tunny Duck and Shoemaker.)

Voice: Silent at sea; on breeding grounds deep croaking and trilling.

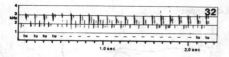

Distribution: Southern oceans; breeds on islands of South Georgia, Prince Edward, Marion, Crozet, Kerguelen, Macquarie, Falklands, Tristan da Cunha group, Campbell, Antipodes and Auckland; possibly on some other islands.

Status: Common nonbreeding visitor to all s African waters.

Habitat: Open ocean and offshore waters.

Habits: Solitary or gregarious at food supply, sometimes in flocks of hundreds of birds. Tame; follows boats and ships; scavenges around trawlers. Sometimes enters harbours. Flies gracefully with slow, deliberate wingbeats like albatross, usually low over water. Dives from surface.

Food: Mainly cephalopods; also fish, krill, other crustaceans and offal.

Breeding: Extralimital.

---

33 (24)   Grey Petrel (Grey Shearwater)   Plate 3
Pediunker (Gryspylstormvoël)
Procellaria cinerea

[Grausturmvogel]

Measurements: Length 48–50 cm; wingspan 117–127 cm; wing (17) 340–347–355; tail 110–116–124; tarsus 57–59–64; culmen 45–47–49. Weight (11) 960–1093–1360 g.

Bare Parts: Iris brown; bill pea green laterally, tip horn, nostrils and culmen black; legs and feet pinkish grey, blackish on joints and laterally, webs yellow.

Identification: Size large; build heavy; wings long and broad; brownish grey above, white below with dark greyish underwing (mostly white in Cory's Shearwater) and dusky undertail (light in Whiteheaded Petrel); bill pale and relatively massive. Looks brownish in worn plumage. Lacks white on head of Whiteheaded Petrel.

Voice: Silent at sea; on breeding grounds loud melodious braying and cheerful *pe-di-unker*.

Distribution: Southern oceans; breeds on islands of Tristan da Cunha group,

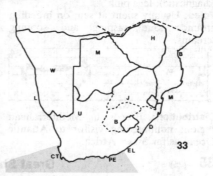

Gough, Prince Edward, Marion, Crozet, Kerguelen, Campbell, Antipodes, and possibly elsewhere.

Status: Rare nonbreeding visitor to Cape seas in summer; vagrant to Natal. Vulnerable (RDB).

Habitat: Open ocean, seldom less than 65 km from land.

Habits: Usually solitary, but gathers in groups at fishing boats and around whales; dives for food from the air from heights of up to 10 m, or picks up offal from surface. Flies like albatross with gliding and quick ducklike wingbeats.

Food: Cephalopods, fish, offal.

Breeding: Extralimital.

34 (26)   Cory's Shearwater   Plate 3
Geelbekpylstormvoël
Calonectris diomedea

[Gelbschnabel-Sturmtaucher]

Measurements: Length 45–56 cm; wing-span 112 cm; wing (9 ♂) 339–346–351; (5 ♀) 330–339–347; tail (4) 118–131–140; tarsus 50–53,8–57; culmen 45–50,3–55. Weight (12) 560–654–730.

Bare Parts: Iris brown; bill pale yellow, tip dusky; legs and feet pale reddish pink, lateral surfaces of legs, outer toes and webs dusky.

Identification: Size fairly large; wings broad; build heavy; similar to Great Shear-water, but cheeks and sides of neck mottled grey; crown paler with less marked capped effect; upperparts medium to light brown; underparts white, including under-wing which has darker borders; sometimes pale line at base of dark tail; bill yellow (diagnostic); legs pink.

Voice: Usually silent at sea; on breeding grounds loud rasping and sobbing screams.

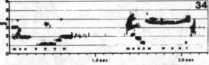

Distribution: Breeds in Mediterranean region; nonbreeding visitor to Atlantic Ocean as far S as s Africa.

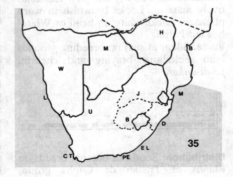

Status: Fairly common summer visitor off W and S coasts, rarer further E to Natal, mainly January.

Habitat: Open ocean.

Habits: Solitary or gregarious. Flight rather slow and effortless, gliding low; sometimes makes shallow wingbeats; wings seem to droop slightly and tips point forward and below belly. Follows whales, predatory fishes and ships for food scraps; feeds by surface-skimming in flight, or by shallow dives from up to about 10 m.

Food: Fish, plankton, cephalopods, krill, offal.

Breeding: Extralimital.

Ref. Harrison, P. 1978. *Cormorant* 5:19–20.

35 (25)   Great Shearwater   Plate 3
Grootpylstormvoël
Puffinus gravis

[Großer Sturmtaucher]

Measurements: Length 45–53 cm; wing-span 100–118 cm; wing (39) 318–325–348; tail 105–112,8–126; tarsus 53–58,7–63; culmen 41,8–45,3–50. Weight 715–834–950 g.

Bare Parts: Iris brown; bill blackish horn; legs and feet pinkish, brown on outer edge.

Identification: Size large; above brown, dark cap on crown, distinct white band at base of tail; below white, dark mottling in centre of belly; underwing white with dark edges and broken dark line; bill dark, long and slender; legs pale. Separable from

Cory's Shearwater by dark bill and cap, and mottled belly, and from Grey Petrel by white underwing, dark bill, pale legs and mottling on belly.

Voice: Harsh screams when squabbling over food at sea; on breeding grounds strident braying calls.

Distribution: Atlantic Ocean; breeds on islands of Tristan da Cunha group, Gough and Falklands; migrates from May to October to N Atlantic.

Status: Common nonbreeding visitor to cooler s African waters, especially in summer; vagrant to Natal.
Habitat: Cool oceanic waters near subtropical convergence (around 40 °S).
Habits: Gregarious; often rests on water in large rafts. Flight stiff-winged and rather slow, low over water; wingbeats faster than those of Cory's Shearwater, interspersed with gliding. Feeds by diving from air or surface, or by picking off surface. Follows whales, porpoises and ships; scavenges around trawlers.
Food: Fish, squid, crustaceans; also offal from fishing boats.
Breeding: Extralimital.

36 (26X)   Fleshfooted Shearwater   Plate 3
Bruinpylstormvoël
Puffinus carneipes

[Blaßfuß-Sturmtaucher]

Measurements: Length 41–45 cm; wingspan 99–106 cm; wing (12) 294–309–317; tail 102–107–112; tarsus 49–51–54; culmen 39–42–44. Weight 696–768 g, (6) mean 619 g.
Bare Parts: Iris brown; bill pinkish with black tip; legs and feet reddish pink.
Identification: Size large; build heavy; all dark brown; bill and feet pale (bill with dark tip); tail short and rounded.
Voice: Usually silent at sea, but squabbles over food with high-pitched notes; on breeding grounds various mewing, gagging, crooning and screaming sounds.

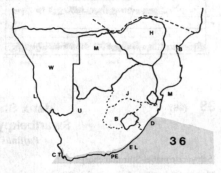

Distribution: S Indian and s Pacific Oceans; breeds on islands of Saint-Paul, Lord Howe, and off sw Australia and n New Zealand.

Status: Rare but regular summer visitor to Agulhas Current.
Habitat: Mostly offshore waters around subtropical convergence (around 40 °S).
Habits: Somewhat gregarious when feeding, otherwise solitary. Flight deliberate with alternating slow flapping and gliding low over water. May dive at angle into water from air; also feeds from surface. Accompanies sardine run off Natal coast.
Food: Crustaceans, squid, fish.
Breeding: Extralimital.

37 (29)

Sooty Shearwater
Malbaatjie (Grysvlerkpylstormvoël)
Puffinus griseus

Plate 3

[Dunkler Sturmtaucher]

Measurements: Length 41–56 cm; wing-span 104–109 cm; wing (50) 280–293,6–309; tail 80–88,8–99; tarsus 52–55–60; culmen 38–42–45. Weight (6) 700–807–900 g.

Bare Parts: Iris brown; bill black; legs slate grey, webs tinged purple, outer toe blackish.

Identification: Medium size; all dark, rather paler below, especially under chin; contrasting silvery greyish-white under-wing coverts conspicuous in flight; bill black, slender; wings long, narrow, set well back on body. Pale silvery underwing distinguishes it from other all-brown shearwaters.

Voice: Silent at sea; on breeding grounds raucous screaming, howling and coughing.

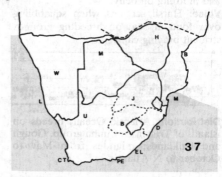

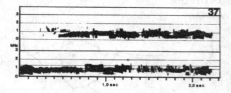

Distribution: Worldwide; breeds islands of Macquarie, Falklands, off s S America, New Zealand and se Australia.

Status: Most abundant procellariid in s African waters; nonbreeding visitor, mainly in winter; less common on E coast than W coast.

Habitat: Colder temperate oceanic waters; further S into Antarctic waters in summer.

Habits: Flight distinctively stiff-winged, fast and graceful, rising and falling; wings flapped rapidly to gain height before banking; soars and glides low over water.

Food: Squid, crustaceans, fish.

Breeding: Extralimital.

38 (26Y)

Manx Shearwater
Swartbekpylstormvoël
Puffinus puffinus

Plate 3

[Schwarzschnabel-Sturmtaucher]

Measurements: Length 30–38 cm; wing-span 76–89 cm; wing (31) 232–243,3–256; tail 70–75–79; tarsus (36) 44–47,4–51; culmen (37) 34,2–37,6–42. Weight (117 ♂) mean 461,3 g, (70 ♀) mean 435,4 g.

Bare Parts: Iris blackish brown; bill black-ish, paler below, cutting edge tinged green; legs and feet pale pink with black markings.

Identification: Size smallish; above dark; below white; dark crown extends below eye; bill dark, long and slender; legs pale; wings long and narrow.

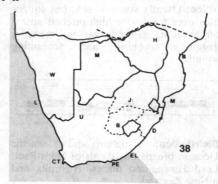

Voice: Silent at sea; on breeding grounds a great variety of howls, screams, croons and harsh notes.

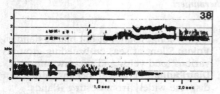

Distribution: Temperate and tropical Atlantic and Pacific Oceans; breeds on islands in Mediterranean, Hawaiian group, off N American W coast and off NW coast of New Zealand.

Status: Uncommon to rare summer visitor to S and W coasts as far E as Algoa Bay.

Habitat: Open ocean and inshore waters.

Habits: Gregarious, especially at food source. Flight stiff-winged with wheeling and gliding; feet protrude beyond tail in flight. Swims buoyantly. Forages by diving, plunging or surface-picking.

Food: Small fish; also cephalopods, crustaceans and offal.

Breeding: Extralimital.

39 (27)   Little Shearwater   Plate 3
Kleinpylstormvoël
Puffinus assimilis

[Kleiner Sturmtaucher]

Measurements: Length 25–30 cm; wingspan 58–67 cm. *P. a. elegans:* (10) wing 180–188,5–199; tail 53–60,5–65; tarsus 40–41,8–44; culmen 25–26,7–29. *P. a. tunneyi:* wing (32) 162–174,3–184; tail (36) 60–65,6–69; tarsus (37) 34–36,5–40,3; culmen (30) 23,7–24–26. Weight (91 *P. a. elegans*) 170–226–275 g.

Bare Parts: Iris brown; bill dull blue-grey to blackish; legs and feet blue with pinkish webs.

Identification: Both subspecies occur in s African waters. Size small; black and white with short, dark bill; black above, but black on head extends only to eye in *P. a. tunneyi*, not below it as in Manx Shearwater; in *P. a. elegans* black extends to below eye, so hard to distinguish from Manx Shearwater in field (legs blue not pink; flutter-and-glide flight distinctive); below white, including underwing; dark legs visible against white undertail coverts; tail short.

Voice: Silent at sea; on breeding grounds screams, trills and coos.

Distribution: Temperate s oceans and N Atlantic; breeds on islands of Tristan, Gough, Saint-Paul and many offshore islands around s Australia and New Zea-

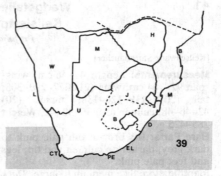

land; also Lord Howe, Norfolk, Kermadec, Austral, Madeira, Azores, Canaries and Cape Verde Islands.

Status: Rare nonbreeding visitor along W, S and E coasts of s Africa.

Habitat: Offshore temperate waters, usually not far from land.

Habits: Gregarious when feeding. Flies fast with stiff wings alternating with bursts of rapid wingbeats, low over water. Swims and dives well. Follows ships.

Food: Cephalopods; also fish and crustaceans.

Breeding: Extralimital.

Ref. Sinclair, J.C., Brooke, R.K. & Randall, R.M. 1982. *Cormorant* 10:19–26.

40 (28)   Audubon's Shearwater   Plate 3
Swartkroonpylstormvoël
Puffinus lherminieri

[Audubonsturmtaucher]

Measurements: Length 30–31 cm; wingspan 69 cm; wing (26) 200–208–216; tail 82–87–92; tarsus 39–40–43; culmen 26–30–32.

Bare Parts: Iris brown; bill slate-grey, culmen and tip black; legs pink; feet pinkish to yellowish white, lateral surface of tarsus and outer toe black, webs pale yellow.

Identification: Size small; build stocky; above dark (but not jet black); below white (including underwing) with black undertail; dark crown extends to just below eye; feet pale pinkish, (bluish in very similar Manx Shearwater); tail moderately long, rounded; bill black, slender.

Voice: Silent at sea; on breeding grounds various loud yelps and see-saw cries.

Distribution: Tropical oceans; does not disperse widely from nesting islands.

Status: Rare nonbreeding visitor along Natal coast to East London.

Habitat: Offshore waters.

Habits: Usually solitary, but gregarious at good food supply. Flies with 6–7 quick wingbeats and short glides low over water. Swims and dives well; may catch food at surface.

Food: Cephalopods and fish.

Breeding: Extralimital.

41 (–)   Wedgetailed Shearwater   Plate 3
Keilstertpylstormvoël
Puffinus pacificus

[Keilschwanz-Sturmtaucher]

Measurements: Length 41–46 cm; wingspan 97–104 cm; wing (21) 277–290–308; tail (20) 119–126–138; tarsus (20) 42–46–48; culmen (20) 36–38–41. Weight 285–425 g.

Bare Parts: Iris brown; bill pale pink to dark grey, darker on culmen and tip; legs and feet pale pink.

Identification: Size medium to large. *Dark form*: Plain dark brown, wings and tail darker; tail markedly long, wedge-shaped; bill dark, slender (pale in Fleshfooted Shearwater); legs pale. *Pale form*: Somewhat paler above, white below, including underwing which has dark margins; undertail dark; dark wedge-shaped tail.

Voice: Silent at sea; on breeding grounds crooning wailing notes and catlike *ooo-ow*.

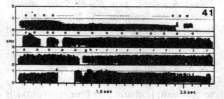

Distribution: Tropical Indian and Pacific Oceans.

Status: Rare nonbreeding visitor mainly to E coast of s Africa, S to Algoa Bay.

Habitat: Open ocean and offshore waters.

Habits: Usually solitary unless feeding. May follow ships. Flies low over water, often banking from side to side, touching water with wingtip; flight fast and graceful. Forages in flight, picking up food by dipping head under water without stopping, but often with foot-paddling. Also feeds on surface.

Food: Cephalopods, crustaceans and fish.

Breeding: Extralimital.

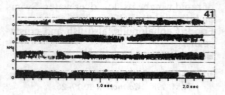

Ref. Batchelor, A.L. 1980. *Cormorant* 8:11–14.

4:3. Family 6 OCEANITIDAE—STORMPETRELS

Small. Southern hemisphere species (subfamily Oceanitinae) have shorter wings, square tails, long legs and short toes; adapted for fluttering flight while pattering over water with their feet (the name petrel derives from St Peter, reputed to have walked on water); n hemisphere species (subfamily Hydrobatinae) have forked tails, longer wings, short legs and long toes; adapted for skimming flight over water rather like terns; may feed on floating oil from mammal carcases at sea; nest in burrows on oceanic islands. About 20 species; six species in s African waters as nonbreeding visitors.

42 (30)
European Stormpetrel
Swartpootstormswael
Hydrobates pelagicus

Plate 74

[Sturmschwalbe]

Measurements: Length 14–19 cm; wing-span 36–39 cm; wing (20 ♂) 116–120–127; tail (20 ♂) 47–52,6–56, (25 ♀) 46–54,5–61; tarsus (20 ♂) 19,6–21,5–22,3, (25 ♀) 20,2–22,1–24,3; culmen (20 ♂) 9,5–10,8–11,5. Weight (62, St Kilda) 22–24,5–29 g.

Bare Parts: Iris dark brown; bill, legs and feet black.

Identification: Size small; dark, with paler line on upperwing; rump white; distinctive whitish patch at base of underwing; some white under tail; tail black, square; legs and feet dark.

Voice: Silent at sea; on breeding grounds harsh buzzing calls.

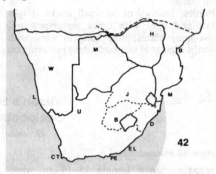

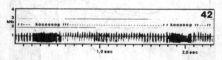

Distribution: E Atlantic Ocean and Mediterranean; breeds islands off Britain, France and in Mediterranean; migrates S to W coast of Africa.

Status: Common nonbreeding visitor to all s African waters, mainly in summer.

Habitat: Offshore and inshore waters.

Habits: Gregarious in small flocks. Flight weak and dainty, rather swallowlike when gliding, batlike when fluttering with feet pattering on surface of water. Follows ships.

Food: Krill, fish, cephalopods, small jelly-fishes, animal fat.

Breeding: Extralimital.

43 (31)
Leach's Stormpetrel
Swaelstertstormswael
Oceanodroma leucorhoa

Plate 74

[Wellenläufer]

Measurements: Length 19–23 cm; wing-span 45–48 cm; wing (60) 148–157,8–165; tail 74–80,1–91; tarsus 22,9–24,1–26; culmen 14,2–16–17,8. Weight 29,9 g.

Bare Parts: Iris dark brown; bill, legs and feet black.

Identification: Size medium; sooty black-ish brown; rump white with dark centre; tail forked, tips broad (not pointed); some white under tail; wings long, pointed.

Voice: Chattering musical notes with descending pitch sometimes heard at sea.

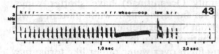

Distribution: Tropical and temperate Atlantic and Pacific Oceans; recorded St Croix Island, Algoa Bay; breeds both sides of N Atlantic and N Pacific.

Status: Rare but regular vagrant to s Africa, especially in summer, October to January.

Habitat: Offshore waters around continental shelf.

Habits: Solitary or in small flocks. Flight fast and light with quick wingbeats and swooping glides; may hang in wind with wings slightly above body, feet pattering on

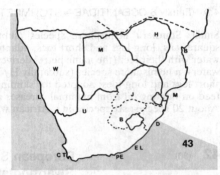

water. Sometimes follows ships. Often settles on water with wings and tail held up.

Food: Crustaceans, molluscs, fish, animal fat.

Breeding: Extralimital.

---

44 (33)   Wilson's Stormpetrel   Plate 74
Geelpootstormswael
Oceanites oceanicus

[Buntfuß-Sturmschwalbe]

Measurements: Length 15–19 cm; wingspan 38–42 cm; wing (118) 133–144,4–155,5; tail 52–63,1–73; tarsus 31–34,6–37; culmen 10–12,4–13,2. Weight (140) mean 40 g.

Bare Parts: Iris dark brown; bill black; legs and feet black with yellow webs.

Identification: Size small; sooty black with white rump; slightly paler band on upperwing; some white under tail; tail square, but looks rounded at corners; yellow webs rarely visible at sea; legs very long, sometimes protruding beyond tail in flight. *Immature:* Similar to adult, with pale spots on lores; secondary, scapular and belly feathers tipped white.

Voice: At sea barely audible rapid squeaking; on breeding grounds monotonous nasal cries of 2–3 syllables.

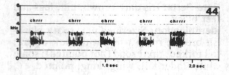

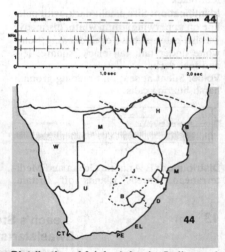

Distribution: Mainly Atlantic, Indian and Southern Oceans; breeds many islands in subantarctic and on Antarctica; migrates to n hemisphere March to November.

Status: Commonest stormpetrel in s African waters all year round, but especially in winter. Nonbreeding visitor.

Habitat: Open ocean and offshore waters.
Habits: Gregarious. Flight somewhat loose and zigzagging, swallowlike with gliding and fluttering with wings held high; often trails or patters feet on sur-

face of water. Often follows ships for scraps.
Food: Krill, cephalopods, animal fat, offal.
Breeding: Extralimital.

45 (37)   Whitebellied Stormpetrel   Plate 74
Witpensstormswael
Fregetta grallaria

[Weißbauch-Meeresläufer]

Measurements: Length 20 cm; wingspan 46–48 cm; wing (63) 146–156–163; tail 71–74–77; tarsus 33–35–37; culmen 12,6–13,2–14. Weight (29) mean 50 g.
Bare Parts: Iris brown; bill, legs and feet black.
Identification: Size medium; sometimes difficult to separate at sea from Black-bellied Stormpetrel; head, neck and upperparts sooty black; uppertail coverts white; underparts and underwing white; wing broadly bordered below with black; tail square. In hand, nasal tubes low and straight on top (raised in Blackbellied Stormpetrel); claws flattened, naillike.
Voice: Silent at sea; on breeding grounds high-pitched piping whistles.

Distribution: Temperate and tropical southern oceans; breeds on islands of Tristan da Cunha group, Gough, Lord Howe, Austral and Mas a Tierra (Juan Fernandez group).

Status: Rare vagrant to s African waters, mainly on E coast.

Habitat: Open ocean.

Habits: Usually solitary; rarely gregarious with conspecifics or other stormpetrels. Flight weak and fluttering, rather butter-flylike, but agile, bouncing with feet from side to side on surface of water and splashing into water breast first every few seconds; wings held horizontally. Flies in front of ships, but seldom follows. Feeds on surface of sea.

Food: Cephalopods, crustaceans, fish.

Breeding: Extralimital.

46 (36)   Blackbellied Stormpetrel   Plate 74
Swartpensstormswael
Fregetta tropica

[Schwarzbauch-Meeresläufer]

Measurements: Length 19–22 cm; wing-span 48 cm; wing (26) 154–160,7–167; tail 72–74–76; tarsus 40–41,5–44; culmen 14–15,1–15,8. Weight (11) mean 48 g.
Bare Parts: Iris brown; bill, legs and feet black.
Identification: Size medium; sometimes difficult to distinguish from Whitebellied Stormpetrel at sea; similar except for black line down centre of white belly. In hand, nasal tubes raised to form bump on top of bill (low and straight in Whitebellied Stormpetrel); claws narrow (not flattened).

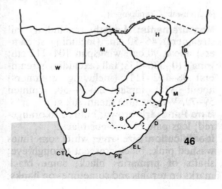

BLACKBELLIED STORM PETREL

Voice: As for Whitebellied Stormpetrel.

Distribution: Southern oceans, including subantarctic; breeds on islands of Prince Edward, S Shetlands, S Orkneys, S Sandwiches, S Georgia, Crozet, Kerguelen, Auckland, Bounty and Antipodes; migrates northwards to subtropics in austral winter.

Status: Very rare vagrant to S and W coasts of s Africa.

Habitat: Open ocean.

Habits: As for Whitebellied Stormpetrel.

Food: Cephalopods, crustaceans, fish.

Breeding: Extralimital.

5. Order PELECANIFORMES (Six families)

Large to very large. Bill longish to very long, often hooked at tip; neck rather long except in Phaethontidae; legs short; toes long; all four toes joined by webs (totipalmate condition), adapted for swimming; subcutaneous air sacs present except in Fregatidae; mostly adapted for diving from air or from surface of water; nostrils sealed off by bone and not functional except in Phaethontidae; throat pouch present except in Phaethontidae, especially well developed in Pelecanidae; sexes usually alike; mostly feed on fish and other aquatic vertebrates; most species breed colonially on ground or in stick nests on cliffs or in trees; eggs bluish or white. Distribution worldwide.

5:1. Family 7 PHAETHONTIDAE—TROPICBIRDS

Large. Marine; bill pointed, yellow, red or orange; nostrils slit-like at base of bill; legs very short, relatively weak; hind toe reduced; head large; neck short; wings long and pointed; tail wedge-shaped, two central rectrices longer than total body length; plumage mainly white with black markings, immatures heavily barred black on white; sexes alike; dive from air into sea for squid, fishes, crustaceans; somewhat gregarious; nest colonially on oceanic islands; no nest; one egg, buff with darker markings, laid on ground in caves, crevices, or among tree roots; chick downy, altricial; parental care by both sexes. Three species in tropical oceans; three species vagrant in s African waters.

Ref. Diamond, A.W. 1975. *Auk* 92:16–39.
  Prŷs-Jones, R.P. & Peet, C. 1980. *Ibis* 122:76–81.
  Stonehouse, B. 1962. *Ibis* 103b:124–161.
  Batchelor, A.L. 1979. *Cormorant* 7:21–23.

47 (39)   Redtailed Tropicbird   Plate 4
Rooipylstert
Phaethon rubricauda

[Rotschwanz-Tropikvogel]

Measurements: Length (excluding tail streamers) 46–50 cm, (including streamers) about 90 cm; wingspan 104–112 cm; wing 310–336–358; tail (excluding streamers) 98–102–111, (including streamers) about 370; tarsus 28–29–30; culmen 59–70. Weight (18) mean 762 g.

Bare Parts: Iris brown; bill red to orange-red; legs pale blue, webs black.

Identification: Size large; white sometimes washed pink; black crescent through eye; shafts of primaries black; some black marks on tertials and sometimes on flanks;

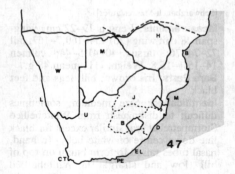

32

tail white, wedge-shaped with two long red central streamers (absent in moult); bill red or orange. In hand has 16 rectrices. *Immature*: White, heavily barred above with black; bill black; no long tail streamers.

Voice: Silent at sea; at breeding grounds harsh 2-syllabled *kelek*.

Distribution: Tropical Indian and Pacific Oceans (not usually Atlantic, but one bird at Milnerton Lagoon, sw Cape in June 1985); breeds on oceanic islands.

Status: Very rare vagrant, usually to S coast of s Africa; occasional windblown birds inland (Pretoria, Orange Free State).

Habitat: Open ocean, seldom coming into offshore waters.

Habits: Solitary or gregarious. Most pelagic of tropicbirds. Flies with relatively slow laboured wingbeats, interspersed with gliding. Dives or swoops to catch food. Seldom attracted to ships.

Food: Fish (especially flying fish), squid.

Breeding: Extralimital.

Ref. Batchelor, A.L. 1979. *Cormorant* 7:21–23.

48 (40)　　　Whitetailed Tropicbird　　　Plate 4
Witpylstert
Phaethon lepturus

[Weißschwanz-Tropikvogel]

Measurements: Length (excluding tail streamers) 38–43 cm, (including tail streamers) about 81 cm; wingspan 89–96 cm; wing (9) 273–285; tail (excluding streamers) about 180, (including streamers) 355–524; tarsus 23–25; culmen 46–50,6. Weight (59) mean 334 g.

Bare Parts: Iris blackish; bill yellow; legs yellowish to greyish white; feet black.

Identification: Size medium to large; mainly white, seldom tinged pink; black crescent through eye; wingtips, band across upperwing, and some flank feathers black; bill yellow, slightly decurved; tail wedge-shaped with very long white streamers with black shafts. In hand, has 12 rectrices. *Immature*: White, heavily barred above with black; bill yellow; no central tail streamers.

Voice: Silent at sea; at breeding grounds harsh chatter.

Distribution: All tropical oceans; subspecies *P. l. lepturus* (described above) confined to Indian Ocean and is the only one likely to occur in s Africa.

Status: Very rare vagrant on E and S coast; sightings at Cape Recife, Double Mouth Estuary, Port Alfred, Umgeni River and Onrusrivier.

Habitat: Tropical seas around breeding islands; seldom far out to sea.

Habits: Solitary or in small groups, plunging or swooping for food. Flight buoyant with much gliding. Attracted to ships, hovering and perching in rigging.

Food: Fish and cephalopods.

Breeding: Extralimital.

Ref. Batchelor, A.L. 1979. *Cormorant* 7:21–23.

5:2.　Family 8 PELECANIDAE—PELICANS

Very large. Marine and inland waters; bill very long, straight with hooked nail at tip; throat pouch highly distensible; nostrils obsolete; neck long; wings long and broad; legs short and stout; feet large and fully webbed; plumage predominantly white, pinkish, grey or brown; head sometimes slightly crested; sexes alike; gregarious; swim and soar well; some American species dive from air into sea for food; feed largely on fish; breed colonially; nest of sticks on ground or in trees (sometimes hardly any nest at all); eggs 1–4, white; young naked at hatching, altricial; parental care by both sexes. Distribution worldwide; 6–7 species; two species in s Africa.

Ref. Din, N.A. & Eltringham, S.K. 1974. *Ibis* 116:28–43.

49 (42)   White Pelican   Plate 4
Witpelikaan
Pelecanus onocrotalus

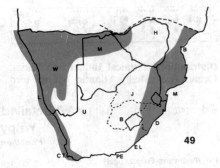

49

Gumbula, Khungulu, Xilandzaminonga, Manawavembe (Ts), Ingcwanguba (X), iVubu, iFuba, iKhungula (Z), [Rosapelikan]

Measurements: Length 140–178 cm; wingspan ♂ 272–286–305 cm, ♀ 226–264–266 cm; wing ♂ 650–702–735, ♀ 605–618; tail ♂ 150–181–210, ♀ 135–190; tarsus ♂ 130–142–150, ♀ 115–135; culmen 413–450. Weight ♂ 9–11,5–15 kg, ♀ 5,4–7,6–9 kg.
Bare Parts: Iris red to red-brown; bill greyish to yellowish, edges pink, pouch yellow; facial skin pink or purplish (♂) or orange (♀); legs and feet pink or yellow.
Identification: Size huge; generally white, tinged pinkish when breeding; remiges black; small crest at back of head; forehead feathers converge to point at base of bill; yellowish tinge on breast; tail white, legs pink. *Immature:* Buff or brownish with some white on back, rump and belly, soon becoming white like adult. *Chick:* Naked red, turning black, then with dark brown down.
Voice: Usually silent; at breeding colonies grunts and moos.

49

Distribution: Coastal areas and larger inland waters of Namibia, Botswana, Transvaal, and Mozambique; also Africa S of Sahara, s Europe, central Asia; migrates to tropical Asia.
Status: Common resident in breeding areas; nomadic elsewhere. Rare (RDB).
Habitat: Coastal bays, estuaries, lakes, larger pans and dams.
Habits: Solitary or gregarious; forages in coordinated groups. Flies in V-formation; soars effortlessly. Flies up to 200 km from nesting colony to forage.

Food: Fish of 0,1–2818 g (usually less than 100 g); some crustaceans; eats larger fish than does Pinkbacked Pelican, occasionally up to 4 kg (possibly caught dead).
Breeding: *Localities:* Dassen Island, sw Cape, Walvis Bay, Etosha Pan, Hardap Dam, Makgadikgadi Pan, Lake Ngami, Lake St Lucia. *Season:* Usually April to August in E and N, October to January in sw Cape. *Nest:* Scrape in ground lined with grass, sticks, feathers collected by ♂ and built by both sexes; diameter 35–60 cm; in dense colonies of hundreds or thousands, usually on islands. *Clutch:* (13) 1–1,8–3 eggs (usually 2). *Eggs:* Chalky white over pale bluish shell, usually stained brownish; measure (245) 92,8 × 60,8   (82–107,5 × 52,7–67,9); weigh (178) 140–188–250 g. *Incubation:* 37–41 days by both sexes. *Nestling:* 65–70 days, fed by both parents; only one chick/brood survives because older kills younger; eggs and young may be deserted by parents if disturbed.

Ref. Berry, H.H., Stark, H.P. & van Vuuren, A.S. 1973. *Madoqua, Ser I.* 7:17–31.
Brown, L.H. & Urban, E.K. 1969. *Ibis* 111:199–237.
Whitfield, A.K. & Blaber, S.J.M. 1979. *Ostrich* 50:10–20.

50 (41)

Pinkbacked Pelican
Kleinpelikaan

Pelecanus rufescens

Plate 4

Gumbula, Khungulu, Xilandzaminonga, Manawa-vembe (Ts), Ingcwanguba (X), iFuba, iVubu (Z), [Rötelpelikan]

Measurements: Length 135–152 cm; wing-span ♂ 226–234–242 cm, ♀ 216–224–236 cm; wing ♂ 595–605–615, ♀ 545–560–580; tail ♂ 160–172–185, ♀ 140–166–180; tarsus ♂ 90–96–100, ♀ 75–87–100; culmen 300–360. Weight ♂ 4,5–6–7 kg, ♀ 3,9–4,9–6,2 kg.

Bare Parts: Iris dark brown; bill greyish, yellowish or pinkish with pink or orange tip and pinkish pouch with yellowish stripes; facial skin greyish pink, black in front of eye; legs and feet orange or yellow.

Identification: Size large; greyish with pink tinge on back, rump, belly and undertail coverts; crest on head fairly distinct; breast feathers long, pointed and somewhat shaggy; remiges darker than rest of plumage, but not black as in White Pelican; tail grey; legs yellow. *Immature*: Brownish; head and neck greyish white; belly, rump and back white. *Chick*: Naked pink, later covered with white down.

Voice: Usually silent; on breeding grounds various guttural notes.

Distribution: Mainly E coast; occasional at Walvis Bay, Okavango delta system, Barberspan (w Transvaal) and s Cape.

Status: Uncommon resident Zululand northwards; vagrant elsewhere (Zimbabwe, e Transvaal, Namibia). Rare (RDB).

Habitat: Coastal bays and estuaries, sel-

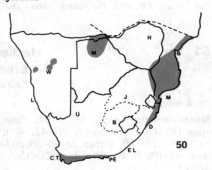

dom inland on larger rivers, marshes and floodplains.

Habits: Gregarious, sometimes in company with White Pelicans. Forages singly, not in coordinated groups.

Food: Fish of up to 400 g, especially family Cichlidae; overall size of prey usually smaller than that of White Pelican.

Breeding: *Localities*: Northern Botswana, Zululand. *Season*: June to January. *Nest*: Platform of sticks 50–60 cm diameter, in dense colonies (up to several hundred nests) in tall trees, from 10–50 m up. *Clutch*: (48) 1–2,8–4 eggs (usually 3). *Eggs*: Pale bluish with chalky white covering, measure (8) 92,2 × 60,3 (89–95,6 × 53,6–64,5). *Incubation*: 30 days by both sexes. *Nestling*: about 84 days, cared for by both parents; only one chick survives in each brood because older kills younger.

Ref. Burke, V.E.M. & Brown, L.H. 1970. *Ibis* 112:499–512.

5:3. Family 9 SULIDAE—GANNETS AND BOOBIES

Large to very large. All marine; bill moderately long, stout, conical, pointed, slightly decurved at tip; nostrils obsolete; neck moderately long; body robust; tail longish and wedge-shaped; wings long and pointed; legs short and stout; feet large, fully webbed; large air spaces under skin as shock-absorbers for diving; plumage dense and soft or somewhat scale-like, white, or brown,usually with black in wings and tail; bill, bare skin around face and feet often brightly coloured; sexes similar; plunge for fish and squid from the air; gregarious; breed colonially on islands or cliffs; nest a hollow on ground, or built of seaweed or sticks on ground or in tree; eggs 1–3, pale blue with white chalky overlay; chick naked at hatching, later downy, altricial; parental care by both sexes. Distribution mostly tropical oceans, but gannets also temperate seas; 8–9 species; four species in s African waters.

Ref. Nelson, J.B. 1978. *The Sulidae: gannets and boobies.* Oxford: University Press.

51 (45)   Masked Booby   Plate 74
Brilmalgas
Sula dactylatra

[Maskentölpel]

Measurements: Length 81–92 cm; wingspan 152–170 cm; wing (6) 407–421–430; tail 169–176–180; tarsus 51–56–58; culmen 97–100,7–104. Weight 1480–1565–1660 g.

Bare Parts: Iris yellow; bill orange-yellow to yellow-green, blackish at base; skin on face and throat dark blue-grey; legs and feet grey.

Identification: Size large; mainly white with blackish tail and largely blackish wings (white on leading edge); bill usually yellowish. Similar to Cape Gannet, but lacks yellow on head; legs pale (black in gannets). *Immature*: Head and neck brown, rest of upperparts greyish brown; bill pale horn.

Voice: Bugle-like double honk at start of feeding dive.

Distribution: Tropical oceans; breeds on oceanic and offshore islands.

Status: Very rare vagrant to s African waters.

Habitat: Mainly open ocean.

Habits: Pairs or small groups forage at sea, flying high with downward-pointing bills, then diving almost vertically into water for food.

Food: Fish and squid.

Breeding: Extralimital.

52 (46)   Brown Booby   Plate 4
Bruinmalgas
Sula leucogaster

[Brauntölpel]

Measurements: Length 64–70 cm; wingspan 132–150 cm; wing (13 ♂) 372–381–391, (10 ♀) 384–400–415; tail (4 ♂) 196–203–209, (3 ♀) 190–194–200; tarsus (7) 40–45–47; culmen (4 ♂) 97–97,7–99, (3 ♀) 100–104,6–110. Weight (20 ♂) mean 962 g, (29 ♀) mean 1260 g.

Bare Parts: (Indian and Pacific Ocean, *S. l. plotus*): iris dark; bill yellow to greenish grey, pinkish or bluish at tip; skin on face and throat yellow or greenish; legs and feet bright yellow to greenish; (Atlantic Ocean, *S. l. leucogaster*): iris silvery to grey; bill pale pinkish to blue-grey, yellow at base; skin on face and throat bright yellow; eyering blue; legs and feet yellow or green.

Identification: Size medium; upperparts, head, neck and breast sooty brown; belly and front of underwing white; bill and legs yellow to greenish. *Immature*: Underparts washed brownish; bill and face grey.

Voice: ♂ has high-pitched wheezy whistle; ♀ has loud, strident honk.

Distribution: Tropical oceans.

Status: Rare vagrant off Mozambique coast; 1 at Durban, August 1985.

Habitat: Shallow waters around oceanic islands.

Habits: Solitary or in small groups. Forages by plunging from few metres into water, with tail spread and partly open wings. Perches on rocks and buoys.

Food: Fish, squid, crustaceans.

Breeding: Extralimital.

53 (44)

Cape Gannet
Witmalgas
Morus capensis

Plate 4

Umkholonjane (X), [Kaptölpel]

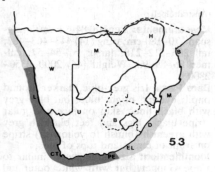

53

Measurements: Length 84–94 cm; wingspan 171–185 cm; wing (20 ♂) 450–480–510, (16 ♀) 477–487–510; tail (16 ♂) 180–189–205, (30 ♀) 191–198–206; tarsus (8) 56–62,8–73; culmen (53 ♂) 88–92,4–100, (61 ♀) 85–93,5–100. Weight (116 ♂) 2296–2640–3005 g, (114 ♀) 2240–2636–3291 g.

Bare Parts: Iris silver-white; eyering cobalt blue; bill pale blue-grey with black lines; skin on lores, around eyes and on malar and gular stripes black; legs and feet black with greenish blue line down front of tarsus and along top of each toe.

Identification: Size large; mainly white (whitest large seabird around s African coasts); tail, wingtips and broad trailing edge black (outer 2 pairs of rectrices rarely white); head yellow; bill pale; legs black; gular stripe long. Australian Gannet always has white outer tail feathers; gular stripe short. *Immature*: Brown with white spots. *Chick*: Black-skinned, covered with white down.

Voice: Usually silent at sea, but feeding flocks may call harsh *warra warra*; on breeding grounds rasping *kara-kara-kara*.

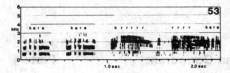

Distribution: Coastal waters to Spanish Sahara on W coast and Mozambique on E coast (rarely to Kenya); vagrant to Australia and Scotland.

Status: Very common resident, breeding on 6 offshore islands; numbers much reduced by human factors; in need of conservation. Immatures migrate up E and W coasts.

Habitat: Offshore coastal waters, especially in Benguela and Agulhas Currents, seldom beyond continental shelf.

Habits: Gregarious, plunging for fish in large flocks usually within sight of land. Hundreds of birds follow "sardine run" up Natal coast in June and July each year. Roosts at sea or on breeding islands at night.

Food: Fish (mainly pilchards, horse mackerel, anchovies and mackerel); some cephalopods. Each bird eats about 300 g of food/day.

Breeding: *Season*: August to December (mainly October to December); occasionally as late as March. *Nest*: Hollow-topped mound of guano, sticks and seaweed collected from ground by both sexes; in dense colonies on ground. *Clutch*: 1 egg (very rarely 2). *Eggs*: bluish white to white with chalky overlay, becoming stained brownish; measure (500) 82,5 × 47,6 (73–84 × 45,6–49). *Incubation*: 40–43 days by both sexes; egg covered with webs of feet instead of brood patch. *Nestling*: 93–97–105 days, cared for by both parents.

Ref. Crawford, R.J.M., Shelton, P.A., Cooper, J. & Brooke, R.K. 1983. *Fish. Bull. S. Afr.* 17:1–40.
Jarvis, M.J.F. 1971. *Ostrich Suppl.* 8:497–513; 1972. *Ostrich* 43:211–216.
Randall, R. & Ross, G.J.B. 1979. *Ostrich* 50:168–175.

54 (–)   Australian Gannet   Plate 4
Australiese Malgas
Morus serrator

[Australtölpel]

Measurements: Length 84–91 cm; wingspan 170–180 cm; wing (14) 443–463–482; tail 206–212–218; tarsus 51–54–57; culmen 85–89–93. Weight (44) 2000–2350–2800 g.

Bare Parts: Iris grey-blue, darker around pupil; eyering bright blue; bill blue-grey with black lines; skin on face and gular stripe black; legs and feet blackish grey with greenish (bluish to yellowish) stripe on front of tarsus and tops of toes.

Identification: Size large; very similar to Cape Gannet, but with white outer tail feathers (tail usually all dark in Cape Gannet, all white in Northern or North Atlantic Gannet *Morus bassana*); gular stripe much shorter (about third of length); secondaries black (white in Cape Gannet).

Immature: Upperparts brown spotted with white; chin to chest brownish mottled with white; belly white, contrasting with dark chest (more uniform in Cape Gannet).

Voice: Similar to that of Cape Gannet, but higher pitched.

Distribution: S coast of Australia and coasts of Tasmania and New Zealand.

Status: Very rare vagrant; 1 bird ringed Bird Island, Lambert's Bay, 25 January 1982; 1 bird ringed Crozets, vagrant to Marion Island 1981–1983; 1 bird at Bird Island, Algoa Bay, 15 March 1990.

Habitat: As for Cape Gannet.

Habits: As for Cape Gannet.

Food: As for Cape Gannet.

Breeding: Extralimital.

Ref. Cassidy, R.J. 1983. *Ostrich* 54:182.

5:4. Family 10 PHALACROCORACIDAE—CORMORANTS

Medium to large. Marine and inland waters; bill straight, hooked at tip; nostrils obsolete; neck longish; body robust, but elongate; legs short and stout; feet large, fully webbed; eyes, facial skin and bill often brightly coloured; tail longish, stiff and rounded; wings rather short, often held outstretched when perched after swimming; plumage mainly black, brownish or grey, sometimes with white areas; sexes alike; head may be slightly crested; mostly gregarious; dive from surface of water for fishes, frogs and crustaceans; breed colonially; nest of seaweed or sticks on ground, rocks, cliffs or trees; eggs 2–4, white or pale bluish green; chick naked at hatching, later downy, altricial; parental care by both sexes. Distribution worldwide; 30 species; five species in s Africa (three endemic).

Ref. Bowmaker, A.P. 1963. *Ostrich* 34:2–26.

55 (47)   Whitebreasted Cormorant   Plate 4
Witborsduiker
Phalacrocorax carbo

Nkororo (K), Ngulukwani (Ts), Timêlêtsane (Tw), Ugwidi (X), iWonde (Z), [Weißbrustkormoran]

Measurements: Length about 90 cm; wingspan about 150 cm; wing (10) 304–325–350; tail 125–139,4–148; tarsus 48–53,3–61; culmen 60–65,5–70. Weight (6) 1039–1616–2229 g.

Bare Parts: Iris green; bill black above, tan below shading to black at tip; skin on lores yellow; gular pouch dark green; legs and feet black.

Identification: Size large; above black with greenish gloss; white from chin to upper belly (extent of white somewhat variable); rest of underparts black; breeding birds usually have white thigh patches; nonbreeding adults browner, and lack white thigh patches. *Immature*: Dark brown above, off-white below. *Chick*: Naked black, then with sooty black down. **Voice:** Usually silent; at breeding colony guttural grunts, growls and hisses.

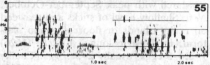

Distribution: Throughout s Africa; also most of Africa s of Sahara, Europe, c and s Asia, Australasia, e N America.
Status: Common resident.
Habitat: Marine and inland waters, usually larger dams and pans.
Habits: Solitary or gregarious. Sits erect when perched. Often flies low over water at speeds of up to 60 km/h. Swims with body partly submerged when alarmed.
Food: Mainly fish; also frogs, crustaceans and molluscs.
Breeding: *Season*: Variable, April to October in Natal, May to June in Transvaal, February to October in Zimbabwe; may breed throughout year. *Nest*: Coarse stick platform in tree, on cliffs or on

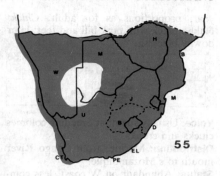

55

ground or rocky islands, in more or less dense colonies of a few to hundreds of nests; becomes covered with guano; often re-used year after year. *Clutch*: (60) 2–3,1–4 eggs. *Eggs*: Pale greenish blue overlain with chalky white, somewhat elongate; measure (134) 63 × 39,7 (52–70,7 × 32,4–42,2); weigh (81) 36–54–64 g. *Incubation*: 27–28 days by both sexes. *Nestling*: about 53 days, cared for by both parents. If disturbed, young may leave nest at 28 days. Chicks weigh at hatching (32) 32–38–47 g.

Ref. Brooke, R.K., Cooper, J., Shelton, P.A. & Crawford, R.J.M. 1982. *Gerfaut* 72:188–220. Olver, M.D. & Kuyper, M.A. 1978. *Ostrich* 49:25–30.

56 (48)   Cape Cormorant   Plate 4
Trekduiker
Phalacrocorax capensis

Ugwidi (X), [Kapkormoran]

Measurements: Length 61–64 cm; wingspan 109 cm; wing (10) 245–253,5–275; tail 86–95,3–100; tarsus 56–58,7–63; culmen 50,4–53,8–56,4. Weight ♂ mean 1306 g, ♀ mean 1155 g.
Bare Parts: Iris turquoise; eyelids with bright blue beads; face and gular skin bright orange-yellow; bill, legs and feet black.
Identification: Size medium; all black with markedly short tail; throat yellow; bill relatively slender and long. *Immature*: Brown; no yellow on throat until 2nd

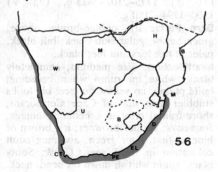

56

year; proportions as for adult. *Chick*: Naked black with pink bill and feet; later downy blackish.

Voice: Usually silent; at breeding colonies clucks and croaks.

Distribution: Marine, from Congo River mouth to s Mozambique.

Status: Abundant on W coast, less common on E coast; highly nomadic, but some present all year round off SW Cape.

Habitat: Coastal waters usually within 10 km of shore; also brackish estuaries.

Habits: Highly gregarious. Flies in long undulating lines low over sea; flight speed up to 75 km/h. Settles in large flocks to feed, diving from surface and submerging for up to 30 seconds. Roosts in large numbers on islands or guano platforms.

Food: Fish (mainly anchovies, pilchards, maasbankers); off Namibia mostly Pelagic Goby *Sufflogobius bibarbatus* 45–50 mm long, 1,7 g mean weight; also occasionally crustaceans, mussels, cephalopods.

Breeding: *Localities*: Offshore islands from Namibia to Algoa Bay, or guano platforms off Namibian coast. *Season*: Throughout year, but mainly September to March with peak September-October. *Nest*: Shallow bowl of sticks and seaweed on rocky islands or floor of guano platform, in dense colonies. *Clutch*: (1626) 1–2,4–5 eggs, usually 2–3. *Eggs*: Chalky white, long ovals, measure (210) 54,5 × 35,5 (47–61 × 32–38), weigh (14) 31–37–42 g. *Incubation*: 22–23 days, by both sexes. *Nestling*: About 9 weeks to flying age, but still dependent on parents for food for several weeks; chick weighs 24–31 g at hatching.

Ref. Berry, H.H. 1976. *Madoqua* 9(4):5–55.
Cooper, J., Brooke, R.K., Shelton, P.A. & Crawford, R.J.M. 1982. *Fish. Bull. S. Afr.* 16:121–143.

57 (49)   Bank Cormorant   Plate 4
Bankduiker
Phalacrocorax neglectus

[Küstenscharbe]

Measurements: Length 75–76 cm; wingspan about 132 cm; wing (37 ♂) 277–292–309, (44 ♀) 262–276–291; tail (37 ♂) 113–129–137, (44 ♀) 107–117–132; tarsus (37 ♂) 62–66,6–70,5, (40 ♀) 61–63,7–66; culmen (39 ♂) 56–60,3–64,5, (44 ♀) 50–56,9–62,5. Weight (77 ♂) 1775–2107–2425 g, (92 ♀) 1500–1794–2150 g.

Bare Parts: Iris orange-brown above, green below; gular skin black; bill black, paler at tip; legs and feet black.

Identification: Size medium; completely black, white on rump when breeding; build plump; no yellow on face; bill looks stubbier than that of Cape Cormorant; short frontal crest in breeding plumage. *Immature*: Rather browner; iris brown or blue at first, later green, attaining adult coloration in third year. *Chick*: Sooty black, some whitish down on head, neck, wings and rump.

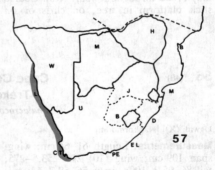

Voice: Usually silent; guttural calls at nest.

Distribution: Coastal, from Walvis Bay to Cape Agulhas.

Status: Common resident; total population about 18 000 birds. In need of conservation.

Habitat: Cold-water W coast with beds of Kelp *Ecklonia maxima* and *Laminaria* sp., usually within 10 km of land; seldom

found more than 10 km from breeding islands.
Habits: Gregarious at roosting and breeding grounds. Usually feeds solitarily among Kelp beds inshore; sometimes in small groups; forages by diving as deep as 28 m; dive duration (157) 25–45–64 seconds; food swallowed under water. Forages throughout daylight hours, but each bird for only about 4 hours/day. Roosts in groups on offshore islands, and some rocky mainland localities.
Food: Fish, crustaceans, cephalopods, molluscs.
Breeding: *Localities*: Offshore islands on W coast of Cape and Namibia. *Season*: Most months, peak May-July. *Nest*: Large bowl of red, green and brown algae, sticks, some feathers and some artificial material; external diameter (61) 36–47–58 cm, external depth (61) 6,5–14,5–33,5 cm, bowl diameter (61) 19–21–27 cm, bowl depth (61) 4–6,4–9 cm; in more or less dense colonies on rocky islands. *Clutch*: (252) 1–2–3 eggs, usually 2. *Eggs*: Chalky white, long ovals, measure (674) 59,1 × 38,4 (50–67,1 × 31,3–42,1); weigh (87) 44–50,4–69 g; 1st and 2nd eggs laid 3 days apart, 2nd and 3rd eggs laid 4 days apart. *Incubation*: (25) 25–29,6–32 days by both sexes. *Nestling*: Unrecorded.

Ref. Cooper, J. 1981. *Ostrich* 52:208–215; 1985. *Ostrich* 56:79–85; 86–95; 1986. *Ostrich* 57:170–179; 1987. *Ostrich* 58:1–8.

---

58 (50) Reed Cormorant Plate 4
Rietduiker
Phalacrocorax africanus

Nkororo (K), Ngulukwani, Nyakolwa (Ts), Ugwide (X) iPhishamanzi, uLondo (Z), [Riedscharbe]

Measurements: Length 60 cm; wingspan about 89 cm; wing (71) 200–210,9–234; tail 142–155,3–174; tarsus 33–35,6–38; culmen 28–31–35. Weight (40 ♂) mean 568,5 g, (7 ♂) 590–651–685 g, (10 ♀) mean 513 g, (13 ♀) 425–503,6–570 g.
Bare Parts: Iris ruby red; bill yellow with black culmen, dark stripes on lower jaw; bare skin of face yellow to red; legs and feet black.
Identification: Size small; all dark; tail longish; bill and neck short; crest short (not as long or conspicuous as that of Crowned Cormorant); in good light broad black tips to scapulars and upperwing coverts visible (much narrower in Crowned Cormorant); eye red; inland habitats. *Immature*: Below off-white; long tail, short bill and small size distinguish it from Whitebreasted Cormorant. *Chick*: Naked at first, then covered with jet black down.
Voice: Usually silent; bleating *hahahaha* at roost; also hissing and cackling at nest.
Distribution: Africa S of Sahara; throughout s Africa.

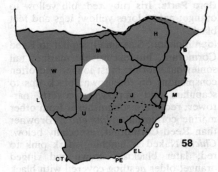

Status: Common resident.
Habitat: Inland waters of any size, down to tiny dams and ponds.
Habits: Usually solitary when fishing; roosts gregariously, usually in trees or reedbeds in water. Flies high between feeding waters. May perch for long periods on low rocks, stumps or on shoreline. Swims low in water. Flies when alarmed, seldom diving.
Food: Frogs and fish of 1–15 g (mostly 3–4 g); also insects, crustaceans; rarely small birds.
Breeding: *Season*: July to April in Cape, November-February in Natal (rarely to

April), January-March in Transvaal, all months in Zimbabwe; most months throughout s Africa. *Nest*: Platform of sticks or reeds about 25 cm diameter; on reeds, branch of tree, ledge of cliff, at almost any height; colonial, adjacent nests sometimes touching; built by both sexes in about 7 days. *Clutch*: (117) 2–3,4–6 eggs (usually 3–4). *Eggs*: Pale

bluish or greenish with chalky overlay; measure (400) 44 × 29,1 (38–54 × 26–42), weigh (58) 17–20,9–25 g. *Incubation*: 23–25 days by both sexes. *Nestling*: 23–25 days by both sexes; weighs (32) mean 14,9 g at hatching; fed by both parents.

Ref. Olver, M.D. 1984. *Ostrich* 55:133–140.

59 (51) Crowned Cormorant Plate 4
Kuifkopduiker
Phalacrocorax coronatus

[Wahlbergscharbe]

Measurements: Length 54 cm; wingspan about 85 cm; wing (11 ♂) 206–213,7–220, (6 ♀) 203–207–213; tail (8 ♂) 123–130,9–141, (3 ♀) 136–138,3–142; tarsus (12 ♂) 37–45,8–52, (8 ♀) 41–45,1–49; culmen (11 ♂) 28–29,6–31, (8 ♀) 27–28,4–30. Weight (6 ♂) 710–791,7–880 g, (5 ♀) 670–728–780 g.

Bare Parts: Iris ruby red; bill yellow to orange; naked lores yellow; legs and feet black.

Identification: Size small; similar to Reed Cormorant, but exclusively marine; tail somewhat shorter; crest longer and often conspicuous on forecrown; black tips to scapulars and upperwing coverts narrower; red eye distinguishes it from other marine cormorants. *Immature*: Browner than Reed Cormorant, especially below. *Chick*: Naked at hatching, dark pink to red, later blackish; crown red ringed orange; older nestling covered with black down, except for bare light yellow crown; legs and feet black; weighs (46) 13–16,8–22 g at hatching.

Voice: High-pitched croak.

Distribution: W coast of s Africa from Swakopmund to Cape Infanta.

Status: Uncommon resident; total population about 5500–6 000 birds.

Habitat: Cold coastal marine waters; rocky shores of mainland and offshore islands.

Habits: Occurs singly or in small flocks. Never found inland, but occasional in estuaries. Usually forages on bottom-dwelling animals close inshore, often between breakers and among Kelp beds;

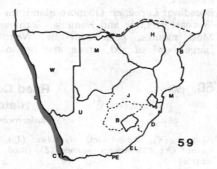

dives last (142) 7–24–59 seconds.

Food: Bottom-dwelling klipfish (Cliniidae) of 0,6–1,6 g, pipefish *Syngnathus* species; also polychaetes, cephalopods, crustaceans.

Breeding: *Season*: All months, peak August-December in S Africa, October-February in Namibia; 70% of all nests in September-January. *Nest*: Platform of algae, sticks, bones and debris about 12 cm diameter, 2–3 cm deep; on ground, rock, ledge or bush; colonial in groups of up to 150, on mainland cliffs or offshore islands. *Clutch*: (91) 2–2,8–4 eggs (rarely 5). *Eggs*: Pale blue with chalky white overlay; measure (498) 46,9 × 30,8 (41–58 × 27,6–35); weigh (119) 19–24–28,6 g. *Incubation*: (44) 22–23–25 days. *Nestling*: Leaves nest by 15 days when disturbed; leaves permanently at about 22 days to form creche; flies at 35 days; independent at about 45–60 days.

Ref. Crawford, R.J.M., Shelton, P.A., Brooke, R.K. & Cooper, J. 1982. *Gerfaut* 72:3–30. Williams, A.J. & Cooper, J. 1983. *Ostrich* 54:213–219.

5:5. Family 11 ANHINGIDAE—DARTERS

Large. Inland waters; bill longish, slender and pointed; nostrils obsolete; head small; neck long; body long and slender; tail long and stiff; legs short and stout; feet large, fully webbed; wings long and pointed, often held outstretched while perched after swimming; plumage mainly dark with rufous on neck and white streaks on back; sexes alike when not breeding; breeding males differ from females in coloration; swim low in water; dive from surface for fish, frogs, etc.; often solitary when feeding, otherwise gregarious; breed colonially; nest of sticks in trees; eggs 3–6, white or bluish; chick naked at hatching, later downy, altricial; parental care by both sexes. Distribution mainly tropical, all continents; two species; one species in s Africa.

60 (52)   Darter   Plate 4
Slanghalsvoël
Anhinga melanogaster

Endeda (K), Gororo, Nyakolwa (Ts), Ivuzi (X), iVuzi (Z), [Schlangenhalsvogel]

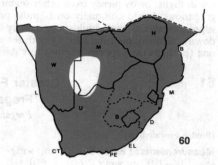

60

Measurements: Length 79 cm; wing (8 ♂) 328–349–364, (7 ♀) 331–344–360; tail (8 ♂) 229–238–253, (4 ♀) 233–239–248; tarsus (11 ♂) 41–44–46; (7 ♀) 41–42–45; culmen (12 ♂) 75–81–89, (6 ♀) 71–76–78. Weight (11 ♂) mean 1485,5 g, (10 ♀) mean 1530,3 g; range both sexes 948–1815 g.

Bare Parts: Iris golden yellow, ringed brownish; bill greenish horn to yellowish brown; naked face brown to yellowish brown; legs and feet brown to grey.

Identification: Medium (rather bigger than Reed Cormorant); build slender; long neck, long tail and pointed bill diagnostic; dark above and below with white streaks on wings; foreneck chestnut with white lateral stripe. *Female, nonbreeding ♂ and immature:* Above browner; below light brown. *Chick:* Naked at hatching, then covered with white down; later light reddish brown.

Voice: Usually silent; harsh croak at nest.

60

Distribution: Africa S of Sahara; also Middle East, India, Sri Lanka, se Asia to Australia; all s Africa except most of Kalahari sandveld.

Status: Common resident.

Habitat: Almost any inland water of any size; preferably quiet lakes, pans and slow-flowing rivers. Occasional on estuaries and lagoons.

Habits: Solitary or gregarious when feeding. Swims low in water, often with only head and neck showing (hence called "snakebird"). Dives well; spears fish under water with bill. Often perches on rock or post with outspread wings. When disturbed, slips away quietly and dives, so often overlooked. Flies well with characteristically kinked neck; may soar. Roosts gregariously, often with cormorants in reedbeds or on partly submerged trees.

Food: Mainly fish; also frogs and arthropods.

Breeding: *Season:* All months in Zimbabwe, peak March-April; January to March in Transvaal; September to January in Cape; mainly summer breeder in s Africa. *Nest:* Platform of sticks and reeds, up to 46 cm diameter, built in about a day;

colonial nester in trees, reeds or bushes, usually over water, often with cormorants and herons. *Clutch*: (848) 2–3,2–7 eggs (usually 3–5). *Eggs*: Elongate, greenish or bluish with chalky overlay; occasionally with brown spots; measure (213) 53,4 × 35,2 (46–61,4 × 31–40). *Incubation*: About 21–28 days by both sexes. *Nestling*: About 3 weeks, flies at about 6 weeks; fed by both parents.

5:6. Family 12 FREGATIDAE—FRIGATEBIRDS

Large. All marine; bill long, straight, sharply hooked at tip; nostrils obsolete; legs very short, feathered; feet small, webs rudimentary; claws strong; middle claw pectinate; body long and slender; neck moderately long; female larger than male; wings very long and pointed, with largest area/weight ratio of any bird; tail long and deeply forked; throat bare, red and inflatable in male; plumage mostly black or brown, somewhat iridescent, sometimes with white patches; buoyant fliers, catching food from surface of sea in flight, or by piracy from other seabirds; do not swim or settle on surface of sea; gregarious; breed colonially on islands; nest of sticks in trees or on ground; female supplies material, male builds; egg usually one, white; chick naked when hatched, later downy, altricial; parental care by both sexes. Distribution tropical oceans; five species; one (perhaps two) species vagrant to s African waters.

61 (53) Greater Frigatebird Plate 4
Fregatvoël
Fregata minor

[Binden-Fregattvogel]

Measurements: Length 86–100 cm; wingspan 206–230 cm; wing ♂ 600, ♀ 610; tail ♂ 427, ♀ 386; tarsus (1) 17,5; culmen ♂ 104, ♀ 117. Weight ♂ 1–1,2–1,5 kg, ♀ 1,2–1,4–1,6 kg.

Bare Parts: Iris dark brown; eyering black (♂), red or pink (♀); throat pouch of ♂ scarlet; bill blue-grey; legs and feet red, pink or black.

Identification: Size large; wings extremely long, somewhat angled; tail long, forked. *Male:* All black with red throat pouch (not always easy to see when deflated). *Female:* Similar but with greyish throat merging with white breast and upper belly. *Immature:* Head and throat white, separated from white breast by dark bar.

Voice: Silent at sea.

Distribution: S Atlantic, Indian and Pacific Oceans. Breeds oceanic islands, including Aldabra.

Status: Very rare vagrant to Cape and Natal seas (most recently Durban, November 1985); one or two inland records.

Habitat: Mostly open ocean when not breeding.

Habits: Usually solitary, but may gather in large numbers at offal. Flies higher than most seabirds, with motionless wings and scissoring action of tail for steering; may flap with deep, slow wingbeats. Roosts in trees on islands at night.

Food: Mostly stomach contents of other seabirds, obtained by harrying them to regurgitate; also seabird nestlings, floating scraps and marine animals.

Breeding: Extralimital.

6. Order CICONIIFORMES – WADING BIRDS (Five families)

Medium to very large. Mostly wading birds of freshwater or marine shores; bill long, straight, curved or spatulate; neck long; legs long, tibiotarsus mostly unfeathered; all four toes present, but hind toe sometimes slightly raised, front toes long; wings fairly long and broad; most breed colonially; nest usually of sticks in trees, on cliffs, or on ground; eggs bluish, greenish or white, sometimes marked. Distribution worldwide.

6:1. Family 14 ARDEIDAE—HERONS, EGRETS, BITTERNS

Medium to very large. Mostly inland waters; a few marine; bill long, straight and pointed; legs and toes long, middle claw pectinate; neck long, held folded in flight; wings broad, bowed downwards in flight; plumage lax, usually white, black, grey or rufous, plain or patterned; long plumes on head, back and chest usually in breeding plumage only; powder down well developed; sexes usually similar; most feed by wading in shallows; food any aquatic animals; voice harsh croaks and squawks; most breed colonially; nest of sticks or reeds in trees, reedbeds, or on cliffs or islands; eggs 3–6, usually light bluish green, sometimes white; chick sparsely downy, altricial; parental care by both sexes. Distribution worldwide; about 60 species; 19 species in s Africa.

Ref. Fraser, W. 1971. *Ostrich* 42:123–127.
Hancock, J. & Elliott, H. 1978. *The herons of the world.* London: London Editions.
Payne, R.B. & Risley, C.J. 1976. *Misc. Publns Mus. Zool. Univ. Mich.* 150:1–115.
Whitfield, A.K. & Blaber, S.J.M. 1979. *Ostrich* 50:1–9.

62 (54)   Grey Heron   Plate 5
Bloureier
Ardea cinerea

Samunkoma (K), Kokolofitoe (SS), Kôkôlôhutwê (Tw), Isikhwalimanzi (X), umKholwa, uNokilonki (Z), [Graureiher]

Measurements: Length about 100 cm; wing (20 ♂) 440–457–485, (12 ♀) 428–443–463; tail (20 ♂) 161–174–187, (12 ♀) 157–166–174; tarsus (23 ♂) 136–151–172, (16 ♀) 132–141–153; culmen (26 ♂) 110–120–131, (19 ♀) 101–112–123. Weight (17 ♂) 1,1–1,5–2,1 kg, (13 ♀) 1,0–1,4–1,8 kg.

Bare Parts: Iris, bill and lores yellow (orange to vermilion at start of breeding); legs and feet brown with yellow at back (red at start of breeding).

Identification: Size large; neck white; bill yellow; black stripe above eye, ends in lax black crest; black streaks on foreneck only; black patch at shoulder; underwing uniform grey (markedly black-and-white in Blackheaded Heron). *Immature:* Paler grey than adult; crown and hindneck grey; no black above eye or on shoulder; bill brown above, yellow below; differs from immature Blackheaded Heron by lack of black on head.

Voice: Loud, strident croak, *frrank* or *kraak*, especially on take-off.

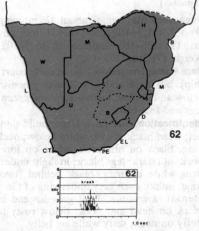

62

Distribution: Eurasia (including Japan and Taiwan), Africa and Madagascar; throughout s Africa.

Status: Relatively uncommon (less common than Blackheaded Heron in S Africa); resident.

Habitat: Mostly shallow inland waters; also coastal pans or lagoons; sometimes open grassland near water.

Habits: Commonly seen wading in shallow water; may swim in deeper water; stands for long periods waiting for food; rarely dives for fish from perch up to 2 metres above water, submerging completely; may feed at night. Usually solitary. Roosts communally on trees, cliffs or islands with much noisy vocalization and crest-raising displays. Flight ponderous, about 142 wingbeats/min.

Food: Fish (1–110 g in weight, mostly 10–20 g), frogs, crabs, insects, spiders, centipedes, reptiles, small mammals and birds, molluscs and worms; rarely plant material.

Breeding: *Season*: All months except June in Natal, all months except April-May in Zimbabwe, August to March in Transvaal; mainly summer months throughout s Africa. *Nest*: Large platform of sticks, lined with grass, usually colonial (sometimes solitary) in trees or reedbeds, or on cliffs. *Clutch*: (559) 2–2,7–4 eggs (usually 2–3). *Eggs*: Somewhat pointed at each end, blue or greenish blue; measure (231) 60,4 × 43,2 (53–72 × 34–48,8), weigh about 61 g. *Incubation*: 23–26–28 days by both sexes. *Nestling*: 20–30 days; flies at 50 days, independent at 60–70 days; fed by both parents.

63 (55)   Blackheaded Heron (Blacknecked Heron)   Plate 5
Swartkopreier
Ardea melanocephala

Ebo (K), Kokolofitoe (SS), Kôkôlôhutwê (Tw), Isikhwalimanzi (X), uNokilonki (Z), [Schwarzkopfreiher]

Measurements: Length about 97 cm; wing (9) 387–401,3–410; tail 142–157–160; tarsus 118–136–180; culmen 85–99,9–105. Weight (7) 710–1135–1505 g.

Bare Parts: Iris yellow (red in early courtship); bill black above, yellow to greenish below and at base; lores yellow and green; legs and feet black.

Identification: Size fairly large; build slender; head black above, white below; neck long, black on hindneck, white on foreneck; bill dark; legs black; in flight underwing white in front, black behind (two-tone, unlike even grey underwing of Grey Heron). *Immature*: Dull grey instead of black on head and neck; below rusty to buffy on neck, dirty white on belly.

Voice: Various croaks, squawks, growls and gurgles.

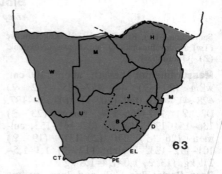

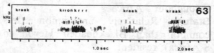

Distribution: Africa S of Sahara, and Madagascar; throughout s Africa.
Status: Common resident.

Habitat: Open grassland, fallow fields, edges of inland waters, forest clearings.
Habits: Solitary when feeding, either standing and waiting for prey, or stalking slowly. Roosts colonially in trees, reedbeds and on islands up to 30 km from feeding grounds. Flight slow, about 143 wingbeats/minute.
Food: Frogs, fish, crabs, insects, rodents, birds (up to size of Laughing Dove), small reptiles, worms, spiders, scorpions, snails, golden moles.
Breeding: *Season*: July to January in Cape, all months in Transvaal; all months except April-May in Zimbabwe; mainly summer months throughout s Africa.

Nest: Large platform of sticks, lined with finer plant material, wool and hair, in tree, reeds and on cliff ledges; colonial, often in company with other waterbirds. *Clutch*: (370) 2–2,8–6 eggs (usually 2–4).

Eggs: Oval, pale blue; measure (220) 61,3 × 43,7 (52–73 × 39–46,1). *Incubation*: 23–27 days by both sexes. *Nestling*: Flies at about 40–55 days, independent at 60 days; fed by both parents.

64 (56)   Goliath Heron   Plate 5
Reuse-reier
Ardea goliath

Ebo (K), Kokolofitoe (SS), Kôkôlôhutwê (Tw), umKholwa, uNozalizingwenyana (Z), [Goliathreiher]

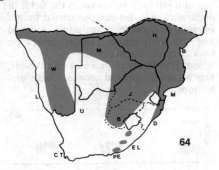

64

Measurements: Length about 140 cm; wing (7 ♂) 570–591–630, (8 ♀) 560–575–599; tail (5) 200–226–235; tarsus (5) 225–231–238; culmen (9 ♂) 183–193–208, (10 ♀) 156–177–196. Weight (2 ♂) 4310–4345 g.
Bare Parts: Iris yellow; bill black above, horn below; lores and eyering greenish yellow; legs and feet black.
Identification: Size very large; mainly slate and chestnut; bill very large; legs tend to sag below horizontal in flight. *Immature*: Browner above, more buffy rufous below, mottled.
Voice: Deep raucous *kowoorrk-kowoorrk-woorrk-work-work*; hippopotamus-like *mmmmm-haw-haw-haw-haw*; other harsh grunts and organlike notes.

Distribution: Africa S of Sahara, and Madagascar; vagrant to India. Mainly e and n parts of s Africa.
Status: Uncommon resident.
Habitat: Larger shallow inland waters and estuaries.
Habits: Solitary. Stands in water for long periods waiting for prey. Flies slowly, about 98 wingbeats/minute, with down-curved wings. Rather shy.
Food: Fish (90–980 g, mostly 500–600 g); also frogs, small reptiles and mammals, crustaceans, carrion.
Breeding: *Season*: All months in Zimbabwe, mainly June to January in S Africa. *Nest*: Platform of sticks up to 1,5 m diameter, in tree or bush, on rock, ground, island, cliff or flattened water plants; usually solitary; sometimes colonial or in mixed heronry. *Clutch*: (126) 2–2,7–5 eggs (usually 3–4). *Eggs*: Pale blue or greenish blue; measure (23) 72,1 × 52,1 (65,7–77,5 × 47,6–54,9). *Incubation*: About 24–30 days by both sexes. *Nestling*: 8–11 weeks, fed by both parents.

Ref. Mock, D.W. & Mock, K.C. 1980. *Auk* 97:433–448.

65 (57)   Purple Heron   Plate 5
Rooireier
Ardea purpurea

Samunkoma Gomugeha (K), Rikolwa (Ts), Kôkôlôhutwê (Tw), Undofu, Ucofuza (X), [Purpurreiher]

Measurements: Length about 89 cm; wing (13 ♂) 357–371–383, (9 ♀) 337–355–372; tail (13 ♂) 118–125–136, (8 ♀) 112–119–127; tarsus (13 ♂) 113–122–131, (8 ♀) 112–118–125; culmen (13 ♂) 120–126–131. Weight (17) 525–920,2–1218 g.

Bare Parts: Iris yellow; bill buffy brown above with yellow base, buffy horn below with yellow tip; legs and feet dark brown with yellow behind tarsus and on soles of feet.

Identification: Medium-sized, slender build; bill very slim; above brownish grey with black crown and rufous neck, striped black at sides; below rufous and black; legs and bill look yellowish in the field; in flight neck has distinct downward bulge. *Immature*: Browner than adult, mottled and streaked; crown rufous; stripes on neck faint or absent.

Voice: Harsh *kwaak* or *kreek* on take-off; various other guttural croaks, clacks and whoops.

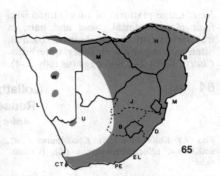

65

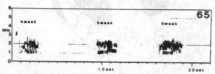

Distribution: Africa, Madagascar, Eurasia; most of s Africa, except dry west; vagrant to Windhoek and Hardap Dam.

Status: Mostly uncommon; may be common locally; resident.

Habitat: Inland and estuarine waters with dense reedbeds and other aquatic vegetation.

Habits: Solitary feeder, wading or standing in marshy places, often with bill and neck held horizontally. Shy and seldom seen until it takes off, usually with squawk. In flight legs look very long; about 114 wingbeats/minute. When alarmed may adopt upright "bittern posture" with bill pointing vertically and neck

stripes giving excellent camouflage in reeds. Feeds by day or night. Roosts communally in reedbeds.

Food: Mostly fish; also frogs, small reptiles, birds (weavers, ducklings) and small mammals.

Breeding: *Season*: August to March in Transvaal (peak December), August to April in Zimbabwe; mainly spring and summer months in s Africa. *Nest*: Loosely made platform (about 35 cm diameter, 18 cm thick) of reeds and rushes on base of stems pulled down from surrounding vegetation; sometimes in small bush, mangrove or other tree up to 4 m above water; solitary or in small colonies, sometimes in mixed heronries. *Clutch*: (192) 2–2,3–5 eggs. *Eggs*: Pointed ovals, pale blue or greenish blue; measure (171) 55,8 × 40,1 (49,7–67,5 × 37–45); weigh (35) 39–47,4–59 g. *Incubation*: (31) 25–25,7–27 days by both sexes, starting with first egg. *Nestling*: About 24 days; flies at 30–35 days; fed by both parents.

Ref. Tomlinson, D.N.S. 1974. *Ostrich* 45:175–181; 209–223; 1975. *Ostrich* 46:157–165.

66 (58)   **Great White Egret**   **Plate 5**
Grootwitreier
Egretta alba

Samunkoma Gomuzera (K), Svorechena (Sh), umThotshane, iLanda (Z), [Silberreiher]

Measurements: Length about 95 cm; wing (8) 343–383–396; tail 131–147–163; tarsus 134–149–170; culmen 104–108–115. Weight (1) 1110 g.

Bare Parts: Iris pale yellow (bright red when breeding); bill yellow (black when breeding); lores and eyering olive green (emerald green when breeding); narrow line from gape to below and behind eye black; legs and feet black. Breeding coloration kept for only short period at start of breeding season.

Identification: Size large; all white; neck very long, curved, bulged distinctively below in flight; dark line below eye extends to at least 1 cm behind eye (in Yellowbilled Egret, dark line ends at level of eye); yellow bill of nonbreeding adult much longer and slimmer than that of Yellowbilled Egret; legs all black (yellow at top of tibiotarsus in Yellowbilled Egret). *Immature*: Like nonbreeding adult.

Voice: Raucous croaks, deeper than those of other egrets.

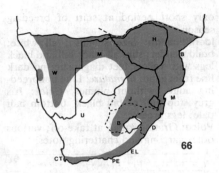

Distribution: Worldwide; s Africa, except most of dry west.

Status: Uncommon, especially in extreme S of range; mostly resident, but with some local movements; vagrant in Cape Province.

Habitat: Shores of inland (rarely marine) waters.

Habits: Usually shy and solitary. When foraging, holds neck stretched forward at angle; feeds in fairly deep water, standing still for long periods or stalking slowly. Roosts communally, usually in trees.

Food: Mostly fish (1–45 g weight, mostly 5–10 g) and frogs; also insects and small mammals.

Breeding: *Season*: August to March in Transvaal (peak January), January to March (also September) in Zimbabwe and Natal; mostly in midsummer months in s Africa. *Nest*: Platform of sticks and twigs, lined with finer plant material, about 34 cm diameter, 12 cm thick; colonial in trees near or away from water, or in reedbeds, sometimes in mixed heronries. *Clutch*: (106) 2–3,2–5 eggs. *Eggs*: Pale blue, coarse-textured; measure (77) 56 × 39,8 (51,1–65,6 × 30,9–45,5). *Incubation*: 24–26,4–27 days by both sexes. *Nestling*: Flies at 40 days, but dependent on parents until 60 days; fed by both parents.

Ref. Tomlinson, D.N.S. 1976. *Ostrich* 47:161–178.

67 (59)   Little Egret   Plate 5
Kleinwitreier
Egretta garzetta

Samunkoma (K), Leholosiane (SS), iNgekle (Z), [Seidenreiher]

Measurements: Length about 64 cm; wing (17 ♂) 245–280–303, (17 ♀) 251–272–297; tail (16 ♂) 84–98–113, (14 ♀) 81–94–101; tarsus (17 ♂) 78–101–112, (17 ♀) 88–97–110; culmen (17 ♂) 67–84–93, (17 ♀) 68–80–89. Weight (Europe) 280–614 g.

Bare Parts: Iris yellow (orange to red when breeding); bill black; lores greyish green (orange to purplish when breeding); legs black (orange to red when breeding); feet yellow. Breeding coloration kept for

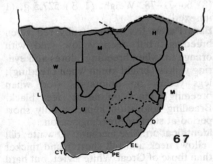

49

only short period at start of breeding season.

Identification: Size smallish; all white; build slender; slim all-black bill and black legs with yellow feet diagnostic; no dark line from gape. *Immature*: Like nonbreeding adult, without plumes. *Chick*: Iris grey; top half of bill black, bottom half pale; legs green.

Voice: Grating *kraak* at take-off; various other gargling and chattering notes.

Distribution: Africa, Madagascar, s Eurasia to Australia; most of s Africa.

Status: Fairly common; mostly resident, but some birds move about locally; one ringed bird found 1 840 km NE of Rondevlei.

Habitat: Shores of inland and marine waters.

Habits: Usually solitary when feeding, but may gather in hundreds at good food supply. Roosts gregariously. Active hunter, darting, twisting and turning to catch prey; sometimes stands and waits for prey. High-stepping gait when wading shows off yellow feet. May disturb prey by shuffling one foot in pool bottom. May fish cooperatively in groups of up to 14 birds.

Food: Fish (of up to 14 g weight, mostly less than 1 g); also frogs, insects, crustaceans, molluscs, small lizards.

Breeding: *Season*: August to January in sw Cape (peak December), September to March in Transvaal, May-June in Botswana, January-February in Zimbabwe; mostly October to December throughout s Africa. *Nest*: Platform of sticks or reeds, 30–35 cm diameter, 10–15 cm thick, in trees, bushes or reedbeds, or on rocks or cliff ledges; colonial, often in mixed heronries. *Clutch*: (125) 2–2,6–4 eggs. *Eggs*: Pale greenish blue; measure (311) 46,5 × 34,2 (41–58,1 × 31–43,4); weigh 28 g. *Incubation*: 21–27 days by both sexes. *Nestling*: About 30 days; flies at only 40–50 days; fed by both parents.

Ref. Blaker, D. 1969. *Ostrich* 40:150–155.

---

68 (60)   **Yellowbilled Egret**   **Plate 5**
Geelbekwitreier
Egretta intermedia

Esingangombe (K), Leholosiane (SS), iNgekle (Z), [Edelreiher, Mittelreiher]

Measurements: Length about 69 cm; wing (5) 305–311–318; tail (5) 118–125–132; tarsus (7) 104–107–110; culmen (8) 66–71–78. Weight (1 ♂) 527,5 g, (1 unsexed) 314 g.

Bare Parts: Iris yellow (ruby red when breeding); bill deep yellow (red with orange tip when breeding); lores and eye-ring yellow (bright green when breeding); legs yellow on tibiotarsus (red when breeding), black on tarsus; feet black. Breeding coloration kept for only short period at start of breeding season.

Identification: Size medium; all white; bill yellow; neck and bill shorter and thicker than those of Great White Egret, but hard to distinguish in field; black line from gape

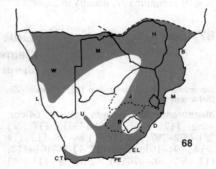

ends at posterior level of eye (does not extend beyond it as in Great White Egret); legs greenish yellow above tarsal joint (all black in Great White Egret), but hard to see in field. Distinguished from Cattle Egret by black lower legs, lack of buff in plumage, and longer neck. *Imma-ture*: Like nonbreeding adult. *Chick*: Bill yellow; iris buff; legs greenish grey.

Voice: Hoarse buzzing notes, staccato chatter and reedy *whooee-whooee*; usually silent away from nest.

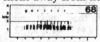

Distribution: Africa S of Sahara, s Asia to Australia; most of s Africa except central Kalahari and dry west.

Status: Uncommon to locally common, subject to local movements and fluctuations in numbers, but possibly migratory in part; one ringed Rondevlei recovered Zambia (2 180 km NNE).

Habitat: Edges of inland waters, estuaries and lagoons; also grassland near water.

Habits: Often solitary, sometimes in loose flocks of 15–20 birds. Roosts communally at night in trees. Shy and wary. Feeds by wading slowly in water or walking over grassy pasture.

Food: Mainly fish and amphibians; also other small vertebrates.

Breeding: *Season*: July to March in Transvaal, August to January in Zimbabwe; mainly September to February throughout s Africa. *Nest*: Platform of reeds or sticks, usually lined with grass; in trees or reed-beds over water; colonial, usually in mixed heronry. *Clutch*: (119) 2–2,3–3 eggs (rarely up to 5). *Eggs*: Pale greenish blue; measure (31) 48,7 × 35,2 (43,8–53,5 × 33,2–37); weigh about 31 g. *Incubation*: 24–27 days by both sexes. *Nestling*: About 21 days; flies at only about 35 days.

Ref. Blaker, D. 1969. *Ostrich* 40:150–155.

---

69 (64)   Black Egret   Plate 6
Swartreier
Egretta ardesiaca

Samunkoma Gomusovagani (K), iKuwela (Z), [Glockenreiher]

Measurements: Length about 66 cm; wing (18 ♂) 244–266–273, (9 ♀) 235–249–263; tail (?) 90–95,5–101; tarsus (15 ♂) 78–85–89, (7 ♀) 78–85–89; culmen (17 ♂) 58–65–69, (8 ♀) 56–62–66. Weight (9) 270–313–390 g.

Bare Parts: Iris bright yellow; bill black; lores black; legs black; feet yellow (orange to red at start of breeding season).

Identification: Size medium; all black or slaty black; bill thin, black; head rather heavily crested at back; throat black (never rufous as in Slaty Egret); slightly larger than Slaty Egret; yellow eyes and feet conspicuous; flight swift with quick wingbeats.

Voice: Low cluck; harsh scream when defending nest.

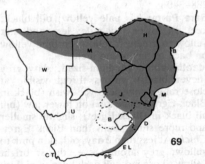

Distribution: Africa S of Sahara, except Congo Basin, and dry w parts of s Africa.

Status: Common in tropical parts of s Africa; rare in Cape and Orange Free State; resident.

Habitat: Edges of inland and estuarine waters, mainly in higher-rainfall regions.

Habits: Solitary or gregarious, sometimes feeding cooperatively in groups of up to 50 birds (even up to 70 further N in Africa). When feeding forms canopy over head by

quickly spreading wings forwards to overlap in front of bird; foot then stirs bottom while bill jabbed into water to catch prey. Holds canopy pose for about 2–3 seconds, then returns to normal before repeating performance. Flocks may canopy in unison. Canopying done in any weather, day or night, possibly to improve visibility by eliminating reflection, or to attract food to dark shelter formed by wings. Often rouses, shakes plumage and slowly subsides. Roosts communally in trees.

Food: Fish, crustaceans and insects.

Breeding: *Season*: December to January in Natal, August and January in Zimbabwe, February to April in Botswana and Transvaal; mainly summer months throughout s African range. *Nest*: Platform of sticks and twigs in trees or reedbeds, up to 6 m above water. *Clutch*: (12) 2–2,6–4 eggs. *Eggs*: Blue to greenish blue, somewhat darker than most small heron eggs; measure (41) 44,8 × 32,4 (41,9–48 × 30,2–33,5). *Incubation*: Unrecorded. *Nestling*: Unrecorded.

Ref. Lawson, W.J. 1964. *Ostrich* 35:58–59.
Vandewalle, F.J. 1985. *Bokmakierie* 37:73–75.

---

70 (64X)   Slaty Egret   Plate 6
Rooikeelreier
Egretta vinaceigula

Samunkoma (K), [Braunkehlreiher, Schieferreiher]

Measurements: Length about 60 cm; wing (4 ♂) 229–237–242, (1 ♀) 226; tarsus (4 ♂) 82–94–86, (1 ♀) 76; culmen (4 ♂) 53–57–60, (1 ♀) 56. Weight (5) 250–288–340 g.

Bare Parts: Iris pale yellow; bill black, keel on lower jaw pale; legs and feet yellow to greenish yellow, chrome yellow on back of tarsus and feet.

Identification: Medium-sized, slaty grey (never black); rufous throat visible at close range only; legs yellowish (black in Black Egret); pale keel on lower jaw (bill all black in Black Egret); slightly smaller and more slimly built than Black Egret. *Chick*: At less than 2 days old, skin pink to yellow, grey around eye, throat bright yellow to orange; bill dark horn to pinkish at base, merging to dark brown at tip; iris dark brown; legs and feet pink to orange-yellow; down dull purplish black.

Voice: Heronlike squawk; triple harsh *kraak kraak kraak* in aggression.

Distribution: N Botswana, nw Zimbabwe (vagrant to Harare) to s Zambia (and possible extreme se Angola); formerly w Transvaal, but now absent from S Africa.

Status: Uncommon resident; undergoes local movements.

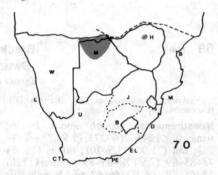

Habitat: Shallower marshes, pans, and pools on floodplains with tallish grass and preferably falling water levels.

Habits: Forages singly or in small groups of up to 8 birds, rarely in parties of up to 30, sometimes with other species of wading birds. Forages by walking quickly about, stirring with feet and darting at prey; does not form canopy with wings like Black Heron, but may spread wings partly when stabbing at prey. Main foraging time about 14:30. Seldom in open water. May perch in trees. About 190 wingbeats/minute in flight.

Food: Mostly fish 5–10 cm long; also insects and molluscs.

Breeding: *Season*: February to June. *Nest*: Platform of twigs (no reed lining) 30–40 cm diameter, 10–15 cm thick, with shallow centre depression; in reedbeds or under canopy of *Ficus verruculosa* trees 1–2,5 m above water, mainly in shade; colonial, 8–50 nests together, sometimes in company with Rufousbellied Herons

and Little Egrets. *Clutch*: (16) 2 eggs. *Eggs*: Pale blue; measure (1) 42 × 31 mm. *Incubation*: Unrecorded. *Nestling*: Unrecorded.

Ref. Fry, C.H. Hosken, J.H. & Skinner, D. 1986. *Ostrich* 57:61–64.
Mathews, N. & McQuaid, C.D. 1983. *Afr. J. Ecol.* 21:235–240.

71 (61) Cattle Egret Plate 5
Veereier (Bosluisvoël)
Bubulcus ibis

Esingangombe (K), Madišadipere (NS), Leholosiane, Leholotsiane (SS), Kafudzamombe (Sh), Dzandza, Munyangana, Muthecana, Nyonimahlopi (Ts), Mmamoleane, Manawane, Modisane (Tw), Ilanda (X), umTho, inGevu, iLanda, umLindankomo (Z), [Kuhreiher]

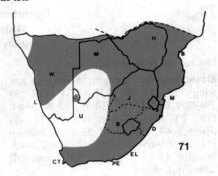

Measurements: Length about 54 cm; wing (20 ♂) 241–253–266, (20 ♀) 240–248–258; tail (20 ♂) 79–88–93, (20 ♀) 74–86–93; tarsus (20 ♂) 70–77–85, (20 ♀) 70–76–81; culmen (12 ♂) 52–56–60, (? ♀) 52–54–58. Weight (1 ♂) 372 g, (1 ♀) 360 g, (4 unsexed) 324,9–344,7–387,1 g.

Bare Parts: Iris yellow (red when breeding); bill yellow (red-orange when breeding); lores yellow (purplish pink when breeding); legs and feet olive brown (dull yellow to red when breeding).

Identification: Small, stocky, all white when not breeding; white with pinkish buff plumes on crown, back and breast when breeding; bill stout; neck shortish, not curved into S-shape as in larger white egrets; bill yellow or orange; legs dull brownish or yellow. *Immature*: Bill, legs and feet black (Little Egret has yellow feet, more slender build and thin bill). *Chick*: Bill blackish with light tip; iris buff; legs greenish grey.

Voice: Harsh croaks of 1–2 syllables, *rik-rak, kraa*; deep staccato *thonk*; various chattering calls.

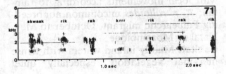

Distribution: Africa, Madagascar, Mediterranean region, s Asia, n Australia, N and S America; most of s Africa except Kalahari basin; vagrant to Kalahari Gemsbok National Park and Hardap Dam.

Status: Very common resident; sparser in dry west; may disperse widely through Africa, but not true migrant; s African birds recovered Uganda and Central African Republic (3 400–3 500 km N).

Habitat: By day grasslands, pastures, semi-arid steppes, open savanna, usually with large game mammals or domestic stock; also cultivated fields; in evening usually around shorelines of inland waters.

Habits: Highly gregarious. Feeds on insects disturbed by grazing mammals in grassland; may perch on mammals' backs; also follows ploughs to pick up soil invertebrates. Sometimes fishes in shallow water. Large flocks gather in evenings around shorelines of dams and pans to drink before roosting. Flies in V-formation to and from roosts; roosts in great numbers in trees or reedbeds. May fly low in high wind.

Food: Mainly grasshoppers, caterpillars and earthworms; many other kinds of insects, spiders, scorpions, frogs, lizards, nestling birds; few ticks.

Breeding: *Season:* August to April in Zimbabwe; August to February in S Africa (peak November-December); mainly summer months throughout s Africa. *Nest:* Rather small platform of sticks or reeds in tree or reedbed, taking

up to 11 days to build; highly colonial, often in mixed heronries. *Clutch:* (3167) 1–2,6–7 eggs (usually 2–4). *Eggs:* Pale blue or greenish blue; measure (205) 44,9 × 33,8 (40–52,1 × 29,8–35,5). *Incubation:* 22–23,7–26 days by both sexes. *Nestling:* Leaves nest at 20 days, flies at about 30 days, independent at 45 days; fed by both parents.

Ref. Blaker, D. 1969. *Ostrich* 40:75–129.
Siegfried, W.R. 1966. *Ostrich* 37:157–169; 1971. *J. appl. Ecol.* 8:447–468; 1972. *Ostrich* 43:43–55; 1972. *Living Bird* 11:193–206.
Skead, C.J. 1966. *Ostrich Suppl.* 6:109–139.

72 (62)   Squacco Heron   Plate 6
Ralreier
Ardeola ralloides

Hakaruu (K), [Rallenreiher]

Measurements: Length about 43 cm; wing (15 ♂) 201–221,8–234, (19 ♀) 194–209,4–228; tail (14 ♂) 67–80,3–84, (19 ♀) 66–72,7–84; tarsus (15 ♂) 51–58,2–63, (19 ♀) 50–55,2–59; culmen (14 ♂) 62–65–70, (19 ♀) 58–62,7–65. Weight (1 ♀) 241 g, (31 unsexed) 230–299,1–370 g.

Bare Parts: Iris yellow (deeper when breeding); bill greenish yellow (slate blue when breeding) with black tip; lores yellowish green (blue to green when breeding); legs and feet yellowish green (bright red when breeding). Breeding coloration kept for short period at start of breeding season only.

Identification: Smallish (about two-thirds size of Cattle Egret); short-necked. *Breeding:* Above buffy brown; dark streaky drooping crest; bill darkish yellow or blue with black tip; legs yellow; wings, rump and tail startlingly white in flight, contrasting with brown body. *Nonbreeding:* Darker brown; streaky on foreneck; crest shorter; otherwise similar to breeding adult. *Immature:* Similar to nonbreeding adult, but duller brown and more streaked below; belly greyish; wings lightly mottled brown. *Chick:* downy white, shoulders and crown buff; iris olive-yellow; bill yellow with dark tip; legs olive in front, yellow behind.

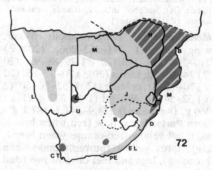

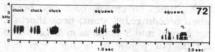

Voice: Usually silent; harsh squawks and clucks.

Distribution: Africa, Madagascar, s Europe, w Asia; in s Africa mainly in E and N; vagrant to Kalahari Gemsbok National Park, Windhoek, Fish River (Namibia).

Status: Two populations: *A. r. paludivaga* uncommon to locally common resident with local movements according to rainfall; *A. r. ralloides* uncommon nonbreeding Palaearctic migrant, October to May, Natal to Mozambique.

Habitat: Mainly inland waters with dense marginal vegetation, especially quiet

backwaters, sluggish rivers and streams; more rarely estuaries.
Habits: Solitary, shy and skulking; very well camouflaged and easily overlooked. Roosts communally, sometimes with other waterbirds. Forages by stalking slowly in shallow water, but stands still for long periods. Flies with quick shallow wingbeats, little gliding.
Food: Mainly insects; also spiders, crabs, molluscs, fish, frogs and rarely small birds.
Breeding: *Season*: August to March in Transvaal, December to January in Zim-babwe, May to June in Namibia and Botswana; most months in s Africa, mainly after rains. *Nest*: Platform of sticks, reeds and grass in tree, bush or reedbed, usually less than 1 m above water; colonial, often in mixed heronries; built in 1–3 days. *Clutch*: (108) 2–2,7–4 eggs. *Eggs*: Greenish blue; measure (45) 38,2 × 28,9 (35,8–42,6 × 27–31,1). *Incubation*: 18 days (Madagascar), 22–24 days (Europe), by both sexes. *Nestling*: May leave nest at 14 days when alarmed; usually leaves nest at 35 days; flies at only 45 days; fed by both parents.

73 (62X)   Madagascar Squacco Heron   Plate 6
Malgassiese Ralreier
Ardeola idae

[Madagaskar-Rallenreiher]

Measurements: Length about 47 cm; wing (26) 210–232,5–262; tail 77–89–101.
Bare Parts: Iris yellow; bill greenish grey with black tip (blue with black tip when breeding); lores green when breeding; legs greenish yellow (pink when breeding); feet greenish yellow (green when breeding).
Identification: Size smallish; stockier and slightly larger than Squacco Heron (but very similar in appearance). *Nonbreeding*: Dull brown above with heavy streaking on breast; wings, rump and tail white; bill heavier than that of Squacco Heron; toes brighter yellow; lacks buffy appearance of Squacco Heron, more dull brown. *Breeding*: Entirely white; bare parts as above. *Immature*: Like nonbreeding adult, with dark streaks in secondaries.

Voice: Raucous croak; rattling *burr* threat note.
Distribution: Breeds Madagascar; E and C Africa when not breeding.
Status: Uncommon nonbreeding migrant to African mainland May to October; may be commoner than records suggest, because of confusion with Squacco Heron; rare vagrant to Zimbabwe; possibly frequent in Mozambique on passage migration. Immatures may be present on African mainland at all times.
Habitat: Wooded streams, lakes, ponds; also marine reefs at low tide.
Habits: Similar to those of Squacco Heron, but perches more readily in trees when disturbed. Solitary, foraging along shorelines.
Food: Fish, frogs, small lizards, insects.
Breeding: Extralimital.

74 (63)   Greenbacked Heron   Plate 6
Groenrugreier
Butorides striatus

Hakaruu (K), [Mangrovereiher]

Measurements: Length about 41 cm; wing (40) 167–178,4–190; tail (40) 56–62,9–70; tarsus (34) 42–46,9–53; culmen (39) 54–64,1–66. Weight 193–235 g.

Bare Parts: Iris yellow (deep orange when breeding); bill black above, yellow-green below, dark tip (glossy black when breeding); lores dark blue to greenish (yellow when breeding); legs and feet grey-brown in front, yellow behind (bright yellowish to reddish orange when breeding). Breeding coloration kept for only brief period at start of breeding season.

Identification: Size small; short-necked; above mostly blackish green (looks black at distance); below grey, white on throat, buff line down foreneck (not heavily streaked black as in Dwarf Bittern); legs and lower half of bill yellow. *Immature*: Above dark brown spotted white; below heavily streaked buff and dark brown.

Voice: Usually silent; sharp *kyah* when flushed; staccato *ka-ka-ka-ka* when coming in to land; various croaks and harsh sneezing calls.

Distribution: Africa S of Sahara, except dry SW; also Asia to Australia, islands in Indian and Pacific Oceans, and S America.

Status: Usually uncommon; sometimes locally abundant; resident.

Habitat: Densely vegetated rivers, streams, ponds, lakes and mangrove swamps.

Habits: Solitary, shy and skulking; partly nocturnal. Runs with ease over branches and reeds. Stands motionless for long periods, often with neck and head held horizontally or pointing downward at angle. Posture typically hunched with

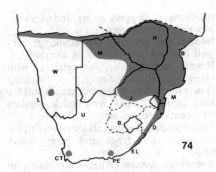

neck drawn into shoulders. Strikes at prey from perch or shoreline, sometimes submerging part or all of body. May adopt upright "bittern posture".

Food: Fish, frogs, small reptiles, insects, crustaceans, spiders, molluscs.

Breeding: *Season*: September to February in Natal, August to June in Transvaal, all months in Zimbabwe; almost any month in s Africa, usually after good rains. *Nest*: Flimsy platform of sticks, twigs and reeds about 30 cm diameter, 2–7 m above ground or water, near ends of branches of trees; as low as 30 cm above water in small bush; singly or in small colonies. *Clutch*: (142) 2–2,7–5 eggs (usually 2–3). *Eggs*: Pale bluish green; measure (107) 37,6 × 28,3 (33–41,5 × 26,1–30); weigh (1) 17 g. *Incubation*: 21–25 days by both sexes. *Nestling*: About 21 days; flies at 34–35 days; fed by both parents.

75 (65)   Rufousbellied Heron   Plate 6
Rooipensreier
Butorides rufiventris

Hakaruu (K), [Rotbauchreiher]

Measurements: Length about 38 cm; wing (17) 198–216–231; tail 70–74,7–83; tarsus 51–57,4–66; culmen 56–61,5–75.

Bare Parts: Iris yellow with orange outer ring; bill yellow with black tip (brown above, yellow below when breeding); lores yellow (very pale when breeding); legs and feet bright orange-yellow, sometimes reddish on toes.

Identification: Size small; very dark. *Male*: Mostly black with dark rufous to maroon wings, belly, rump and tail; much smaller than Black or Slaty Egrets, and

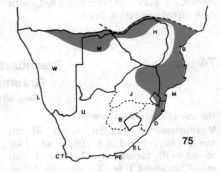

distinguishable by yellow bill with black tip; appears all black in flight. *Female*: Sooty brown where male is black; wings maroon, belly, rump and tail as in male. *Immature*: Like female, but streaked buffy brown on sides of head, neck and upper chest. *Chick*: Skin yellowish pink, becoming grey; pinker on crown, yellower on nape and wings; bill pinkish yellow at base, merging to brownish yellow and brown at tip (becomes orange to yellow with age); legs and feet grey, merging to yellow on toes; down dull blackish grey.
Voice: Muffled crowlike *kar*; rasping *kraak*; other harsh churring sounds.
Distribution: S Africa to Kenya and Congo; in s Africa mainly in E and N, but vagrant as far S as e Cape.
Status: Uncommon to rare resident. Rare (RDB).
Habitat: Larger rivers with marshy shallows, floodplains, lagoons, reedbeds.
Habits: Solitary; rarely in groups of up to 5 birds. Partly nocturnal. Adopts horizon-

tal posture while feeding; remains motionless for long periods, usually well hidden. When disturbed may land in tree or drop back into cover after short flight. Roosts in small groups.
Food: Fish, frogs, insects, worms.
Breeding: *Season*: December to May in Transvaal, all months in Zimbabwe; most months in s Africa, mainly summer. *Nest*: Small platform of reed stems, twigs and leaves 25–35 cm diameter, 10–12 cm thick; 0,5–4 m above water in reedbeds, trees and thickets in water (often lower than nest of Slaty Egret); colonial, sometimes in mixed heronries. *Clutch*: (122) 1–2,9–4 eggs. *Eggs*: Pale blue to uniform deep turquoise; measure (91) 37,7 × 28,6 (29–42,6 × 25–30,7). *Incubation*: Unrecorded. *Nestling*: Leaves nest for short periods at 7–14 days; flies weakly at 24 days, strongly at 32 days.

Ref. Tarboton, W.R. 1967. *Ostrich* 38:207.
　　Uys, J.M. & Clutton-Brock, T.H. 1966. *Puku* 4:171–180.

76 (69) Blackcrowned Night Heron　　Plate 5
Gewone Nagreier
Nycticorax nycticorax

Hakaruu Gomasiku (K), uSiba (Z), [Nachtreiher]

Measurements: Length 56 cm; wing (43) 276–289,5–308; tail (32) 103–111–119; tarsus (26) 68–74,1–84; culmen (43) 64–70,7–78. Weight (2 immatures) 432,5–595 g, (125 unsexed, Europe) 339–535–780 g.
Bare Parts: Iris crimson; bill greenish black (black when breeding); skin around eye greenish (blue-black when breeding); legs and feet pale yellow (red during courtship).
Identification: Size medium; build chunky; relatively short-legged; head looks large; crown and back black; wings grey; below white; eye large, red; long white plumes on crown when breeding. *Immature*: Above brown spotted with white; below broadly streaked brown on buff; bill yellow; eyes orange-yellow to red. Similar to Bittern, but smaller (eye colour distinctive; spotted above; ventral streaks broad).

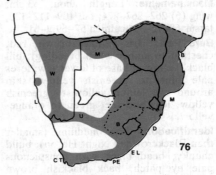

Voice: Generally silent; when flushed may call *quock*; also various clicking, twanging and rasping (*wik-kraak*) sounds at breeding colony.

Distribution: Africa, Madagascar, Eurasia, N and S America; in s Africa absent from most of dry w regions, but recorded Sandwich Harbour, Namib-Naukluft Park, Mariental (Namibia).

Status: Common; mostly resident, but subject to much local dispersal; bird ringed Rondevlei (w Cape) recovered Mozambique; some nonbreeding Palaearctic migrants reach s Africa, bird ringed Romania recovered Mozambique.

Habitat: Marshes, swamps, lakes, rivers, streams with good vegetation cover; also mangroves.

Habits: Solitary or gregarious. Largely nocturnal. Roosts singly or communally in groups of up to 200 birds. Remains motionless for long periods while hunting from shoreline or perch above water. Flies with fast wingbeats on rounded wings, feet projecting slightly beyond tail.

Food: Fish, frogs, reptiles, young and eggs of birds (including those of other herons), crustaceans, insects, molluscs, small mammals; rarely adult birds up to size of Laughing Dove.

Breeding: *Season*: August to March in Transvaal, September to April in Zimbabwe; in s Africa mainly August to January. *Nest*: Flimsy platform of sticks in low tree, bush or reedbed, often over water; ♂ collects material, ♀ builds. *Clutch*: (212) 2–2,5–4 eggs. *Eggs*: Pale green to bluish green; measure (45) 48,7 × 34,6 (44,6–54 × 32–36,7). *Incubation*: 22–26 days, by both sexes. *Nestling*: Can leave nest at 20–25 days; flies at 40–50 days.

77 (70)   Whitebacked Night Heron   Plate 5
Witrugnagreier
Gorsachius leuconotus

Hakaruu (K), [Weißrücken-Nachtreiher]

Measurements: Length about 53 cm; wing (6) 262–267–274; tail 109–112–120; tarsus 68–72–79; culmen 57–59,9–61.

Bare Parts: Iris yellow (brown, red, chestnut to amber when breeding); bill black, yellow at base of lower jaw; lores pale blue to greenish yellow; skin around eye lemon yellow to greenish yellow; legs and feet green to orange-yellow.

Identification: Size medium (smaller than Blackcrowned Night Heron); build chunky; head black with conspicuous pale eye-patch; back blackish brown with white patch in centre (conspicuous in flight); rest of plumage rufous brown fading to whitish on throat and belly; legs bright yellowish. *Immature*: Similar to immature Blackcrowned Night Heron, but with plain dark forehead and crown; white back plumes distinctive.

Voice: Usually silent; clashing *taash-taash-taash* at night; toadlike *kraak*.

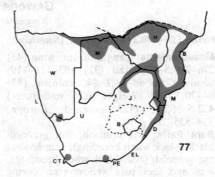

77

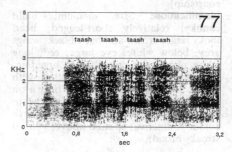

77

taash taash taash taash

58

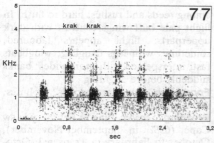

Distribution: Africa S of Sahara; in s Africa from Caprivi and Okavango, down Zambezi Valley, coastal Mozambique to Keurbooms River (s Cape); also e Transvaal and Swaziland, and up Limpopo River to s Zimbabwe. Vagrant to lower Orange River (Aussenkehr).
Status: Uncommon to rare in s Africa; resident. Vagrant to C Transvaal (Mosdene, Nylsvley). Probably Rare (RDB).
Habitat: Quiet tree-lined rivers and streams, mangroves; less commonly in

reedbeds along rivers and in marshes.
Habits: Solitary or in pairs; largely nocturnal. Roosts by day in densely foliaged trees or marshy vegetation. Hunts by standing still on waterplants or floating islands.
Food: Fish, frogs, insects, molluscs.
Breeding: *Season:* July, September, March in Transvaal, November and January in Natal, all months except May-June in Zimbabwe; mainly September to January in s Africa. *Nest:* Platform of sticks and reeds, 25–30 cm diameter; solitary in low trees or euphorbias about 30–60 cm above water; also on shrubs or rocks near water level. *Clutch:* (33) 2–2,6–3 eggs (rarely up to 5). *Eggs:* Pale greenish white to bluish; measure (28) 45,5 × 34,9 (43,3–48,1 × 33–37,2); weigh (1) 28 g. *Incubation:* 23–26 days, probably by both sexes. *Nestling:* 40–41 days (captivity); 42–56 days (in wild).

78 (67) Little Bittern Plate 6
Woudapie (Kleinrietreier)
Ixobrychus minutus

Hakaruu Mwene-mwene (K), Ihashe (X), [Zwergrohrdommel]

Measurements: Length about 36 cm. Two subspecies. *I. m. minutus*: wing (38) 142–150,3–157 (more than 40 mm between 1st and longest primary remex); tail (11) 41–44,9–49; tarsus (11) 41–43,2–46; culmen (11) 46–47,5–51; weight (11 ♂) 145–149–150 g, (7 ♀) 140–146–150 g. *I. m. payesii*: wing (40) 130–142,6–150 (less than 40 mm between 1st and longest primary remex); tail (28) 36–45,3–46; tarsus (28) 40–43–46; culmen (28) 43–47,9–54,5. Weight (1 ♂) 108 g, (2 ♀) 110–124 g, (4 unsexed) 87–96,3–114,5 g.
Bare Parts: Iris yellow, orange or reddish brown; bill yellow to greenish yellow, darker on culmen; lores yellow (dull red in courtship); legs and feet greenish, yellow on back of tarsus and soles of feet.
Identification: Size small; neck long and thick. *Male:* Blackish green on crown and back; buff on wings; neck and sides of wings ashy buff (*I. m. minutus*) or

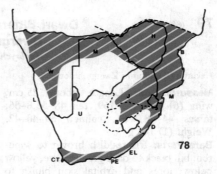

deep russet brown (*I. m. payesii*); foreneck and chest streaked with light brown. *Female (both subspecies):* Back dull brown with paler edges to feathers; otherwise similar to male. *Immature:* Mottled above, streaked below with brown on reddish buff (two subspecies separable only on wing formula). *Chick:* Reddish buff; bill and legs pinkish; lores, skin around eyes and base of bill bluish.

LITTLE BITTERN

Voice: Soft, far-carrying *gogh*; loud *gak*, rapid *gak-gak-gak-gak* or gurgling *ghrrrrr* when nesting; alarm *squawk*.

Distribution: Africa, Madagascar, Eurasia, Australia, New Zealand; throughout s Africa, except Namib and most of Kalahari sandveld.

Status: *I. m. minutus* nonbreeding Palaearctic migrant to Zimbabwe, Transvaal, Orange Free State, Natal, coastal Transkei and e Cape, December to March; common. *I. m. payesii* breeding resident from sw Cape to Natal and Zambezi Valley; also n Botswana, Caprivi and most of Namibia; uncommon, but locally common in sw Cape. Rare (RDB).

Habitat: Reedbeds, wooded streams and rivers, rank vegetation around sewage ponds.

Habits: Solitary; partly nocturnal; shy and skulking. When alarmed adopts "bittern posture" with bill pointing vertically; stripes on neck provide good camouflage

among reeds and rushes; hard to flush. In flight pale buff wings contrast with dark upperparts; flight appears laboured, sometimes with legs dangling; wingbeats fast, interspersed with short glides; banks suddenly before alighting.

Food: Fish, frogs, arthropods, molluscs, small reptiles.

Breeding: *Season*: June to February in sw Cape (63% in September-November), October to February in Transvaal, October to February in Zimbabwe (also May); 2–3 broods/season. *Nest*: Fairly substantial platform of dead reedstems, sometimes lined with green grass, about 20–35 cm diameter, 14–25 cm thick (20 nests in sw Cape); solitary or in loose groups, 23–135 cm above water in reeds or rushes, usually near clearing or channel. *Clutch*: (25) 2–3,3–5 eggs (usually 3–4). *Eggs*: Chalky white; measure (59) 34,5 × 26,3 (32–37,5 × 24,4–27,9); weigh about 13 g. *Incubation*: 19–20 days by both sexes. *Nestling*: Clambers about in rushes from 8th day, leaves nest at 14–16 days, flies at 23 days; fed by both parents.

Ref. Langley, C.H. 1983. *Ostrich* 54:83–94.

---

79 (66)   Dwarf Bittern (Rail Heron)   Plate 6
Dwergrietreier
Ixobrychus sturmii

Hakaruu (K), [Sturms Zwergrohrdommel]

Measurements: Length about 25 cm; wing (6) 154–162–169; tail 48–52,8–56; tarsus 44–48,7–51; culmen 39–40–42. Weight (1) 142 g.

Bare Parts: Iris reddish brown to wine-red; bill black to dark green above, yellow below; lores and orbital skin bluish to yellowish green; legs and feet greenish to yellowish brown in front, yellow behind and on toes (sometimes bright orange in courtship).

Identification: Size small; above blackish; below pale with heavy black streaks and black line down centre of foreneck (foreneck pale without streaks in Greenbacked Heron); underwing slaty black with narrow buff leading edge; bright yellow legs. Distinguished from Little Bittern by lack

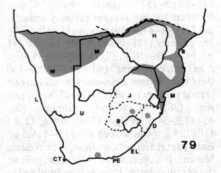

of pale area on wing and by heavy dark streaks on underparts. *Immature*: Paler and duller than adult, with dorsal feathers tipped buff, giving barred appearance; underparts more russet; legs paler yellow. *Chick*: Downy ginger.

Voice: Loud croak when flushed; deep *hoot-hoot-hoot.*

Distribution: Africa S of Sahara; in s Africa mainly in N and E, but occasional also to sw Cape and C Namibia.
Status: Uncommon to rare, but locally common when breeding; breeding migrant to s Africa from equatorial Africa, October to April (juveniles may leave only by early June). Probably Rare (RDB).
Habitat: Reedbeds on rivers, streams and ponds; also marshes, floodplains with scattered trees and bushes, and mangroves; dense grassland near flooded pans; ephemeral pans when breeding.
Habits: Solitary or in pairs; partly nocturnal; skulking, but not shy. Adopts "bittern posture" when alarmed. Flight slow and laboured, sometimes with legs dangling and neck outstretched.
Food: Fish, frogs, arthropods.
Breeding: *Season:* December to March in Transvaal, November to April in Zimbabwe. *Nest:* Flimsy platform of twigs and coarse grass stems, 23–28 cm diameter; solitary or in loose small groups of up to 17 nests; from near water level to 3,7 m up (mean height of 44 nests = about 1 m) in trees or bushes over water (usually thorntrees), on horizontal or sloping branch. *Clutch:* (114) 2–3,5–5 eggs. *Eggs:* White or pale bluish or greenish white, fading to white, smooth-shelled; measure (65) 37,1 × 27,8 (33,2–40 × 25,8–31); weigh (5) 19–19,5–20,2 g. *Incubation:* (4) 18–20–26 days. *Nestling:* Leaves nest for short periods at 7 days; remiges appear by 11th day; full nestling period unrecorded; fed by both parents.

Ref. Hustler, K. & Williamson, C. 1985. *Honey-guide* 31:145–147.

80 (71) Bittern Plate 5
Grootrietreier (Roerdomp)
Botaurus stellaris

Shivo (K), Khoiti-mohlaka (SS), Kgapu (Tw), uMabu (Z), [Große Rohrdommel]

Measurements: Length about 64 cm; wing (6) 280–310; tail 92–95; tarsus 80–90; culmen 57–60,2–64,6. Weight (Europe) ♂ 966–1940, ♀ 867–1150 g.
Bare Parts: Iris yellow to brownish yellow; bill greenish yellow, brown to black on culmen; lores and orbital skin greyish yellow; legs and feet green.
Identification: Size medium; stocky and thick-necked; rich golden brown with black markings; crown, eyepatch and malar stripe black; bigger than immature Blackcrowned Night Heron and lacks white spots. *Immature:* Like adult. *Chick:* Covered with long rufous down; legs and feet pale green to pink; bill pale green to pinkish yellow; iris dark brown.
Voice: Harsh *squark* in flight; deep booming by male in breeding season, slow *up-rumb* or *rumb rumb rumb*, repeated 3–4 times every 1–2 seconds and audible up to 5 km in still air; female may respond with softer booming *wumph.* Calls day and night.

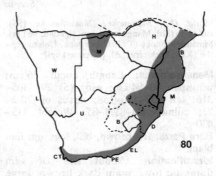

Distribution: Much of Africa S of 8 °S, Eurasia; in s Africa absent from dry w areas.
Status: Uncommon to rare resident; some populations may have local movements; extinct in s Cape. Vulnerable (RDB).
Habitat: Reedbeds, marshes, papyrus swamps.

Habits: Solitary, shy and secretive. Adopts upright posture ("bittern posture") with vertical bill when disturbed; markings confer excellent camouflage in reedbeds. More heard than seen, but active by day and night. When flushed flies short distance before landing in reeds; flight owllike with rounded, downcurved wings; sometimes soars, circling high. Walks slowly while feeding, stopping for long periods. Roosts solitarily, usually in reeds.

Food: Fish, frogs, insects, crustaceans, spiders.

Breeding: *Season*: September to January throughout s Africa. *Nest*: Platform of reeds or rushes, 30–40 cm diameter, 10–15 cm thick, low down in reedbed over water at least 30 cm deep; solitary (neighbouring nests usually more than 50 m apart); built by ♀ alone. *Clutch*: 3–4 eggs (rarely 5). *Eggs*: Pale olive green, with somewhat greasy feel; measure (12) 50,5 × 38,8 (49,5–52,5 × 37,9–40,3). *Incubation*: 25–26 days by female only. *Nestling*: Leaves nest for short periods at 15–16 days; flies at 50–55 days.

6:2. Family 15 SCOPIDAE—HAMERKOP

Large. Inland waters; bill straight, slightly hooked at tip, rather deep, strongly compressed laterally; head large, crested; neck short; legs moderately long; toes long; wings longish and broad; plumage dark brown all over with purplish sheen; sexes alike; nest a huge oven-shaped mass of sticks with small front entrance, in tree or on cliff; eggs 3–6, white; chick downy, altricial; parental care by both sexes. Distribution Africa, sw Arabia, Madagascar; one species.

81 (72) Hamerkop Plate 7
Hamerkop
Scopus umbretta

Mfune (K), Masianoke, 'Mamasianoke (SS), vaKondo (Sh), Manghondzwana, Nghondzwe (Ts), Mmamasiloanokê (Tw), Uthekwane, Uqhimngqoshe (X), uThekwane (Z), [Hammerkopf]

Measurements: Length about 56 cm; wingspan 90–94 cm; wing (5) 297–305–316; tail 152–156–158; tarsus 69–70,2–73; culmen 80–81,8–85. Weight 415–430 g.

Bare Parts: Iris brown; bill, legs and feet black.

Identification: About size of slim domestic fowl; plain dark brown; large bill and crest give hammerhead effect (hence Hamerkop); legs moderately long; flight buoyant on large wings, somewhat jerky with flaps and glides. *Chick*: Covered with pale grey down; iris light grey; legs pinkish at first, later brown.

Voice: Usually silent when solitary, vocal in groups; loud, somewhat nasal yelping and trumpeting of varying tempo; *yip-purrr, yik-yik-yik-purrr-purr-yik-yik*, sometimes in chorus.

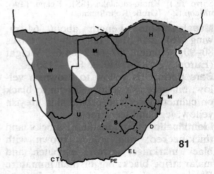

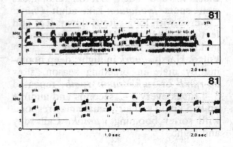

Distribution: Africa S of Sahara, Madagascar, sw Arabia; throughout s Africa.
Status: Common resident in most areas; nomadic in more arid zones according to rainfall.
Habitat: Most inland waters, even small temporary roadside pools filled with rainwater; occasional on seashore.
Habits: Usually solitary, sometimes in pairs or small groups of 4–5 birds; rarely in larger groups of up to 50. Diurnal. Forages by wading in or around shallow water, sometimes stirring mud with foot; may probe in mud with bill; may forage by flying slowly over water and snatching food from surface with bill. Birds in groups display to each other with bowing and wingspreading, sometimes standing on each other's backs.
Food: Mainly adults and tadpoles of Platannas *Xenopus laevis*; also fish and some invertebrates; rarely small mammals.
Breeding: *Season:* July to January in S Africa, all months in Zimbabwe. *Nest:* Huge oven-shaped mass of sticks, reeds, weeds and debris, including manmade artefacts; in stout fork of tree, cliff ledge, rock in river, rarely on ground or sandbank, at any height up to 20 m; may be built cooperatively by 4 or more birds; measures up to 2 m in diameter, with roof 1 m or more thick; chamber 30–50 cm diameter roughly plastered with mud; entrance tunnel 13–18 cm diameter, 40–60 cm long, smoothly plastered with mud, faces outward and downward to least accessible part of site; nest weighs 25–50 kg; takes 3 weeks to 6 months to complete, material added continually; built by both sexes; started as bowl shape, then sides and roof added; roof withstands weight of fullgrown man; nest sometimes taken over by bees, owls or other birds. *Clutch:* (17) 1–3,3–5 eggs (rarely up to 7). *Eggs:* White; measure (110) 45,7 × 34,8 (41,3–52,5 × 32–36,8); weigh (41) 25,2–27,7–31,3 g. *Incubation:* 28–32 days by both sexes. *Nestling:* 44–50 days; fed by both parents.

Ref. Kahl, M.P. 1967. *Ibis* 109:25–32.
Liversidge, R. 1963. *Ostrich* 34:55–62.
Nel, J.E. 1966. *Bokmakierie* 18:70–72.
Wilson, R.T. & Wilson, M.P. 1984. *Proc. 5th Pan-Afr. Orn. Congr.*:855–865.

6:3 Family 13 BALAENICIPITIDAE – SHOEBILL

Very large. Inland marshy waters with papyrus and other tall aquatic vegetation; bill very large, broad and deep, somewhat shoe-shaped, hooked at tip; head large with short crest; neck moderately long; legs long; toes long; wings large and broad; soar well; plumage dull grey with slight greenish gloss above; sexes alike; solitary; feed mostly on lungfishes caught by lunging into shallow water; usually silent, but have shrill call and bill-rattling; nest a large platform of rushes or sedges on ground in marsh; eggs 2, white with bluish tinge; chick downy, altricial; parental care by both sexes. Distribution tropical Africa; one species.

82 (–) Shoebill / Skoenbekooievaar Plate 75
Balaeniceps rex

[Schuhschnabel]
Measurements: Length about 117 cm; stands about 105 cm tall; wing 655–707–780; tail 258; tarsus 245; culmen 191.
Bare Parts: Iris grey, bluish white or pale yellow; bill pinkish or yellowish with darker streaks; legs and feet blackish.

Identification: Size huge; wholly dark grey with faint greenish gloss; bill enormous, bulbous, hooked at tip; long-legged. *Immature:* Browner than adult; bill smaller. *Chick:* Downy, white or silvery grey; gape wide; bill relatively small.

Voice: Usually silent; shrill kitelike whistle or whine, *beeeeeh*; laughing notes; clappers bill like stork.

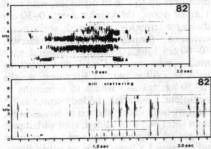

Distribution: Eastern tropical Africa from s Sudan to e Zaire and Zambia; also recorded once Okavango Swamps near South Gate, Moremi Wildlife Reserve, Botswana.

Status: Rare in s Africa, probably vagrant; elsewhere fairly common, but threatened by human interference; resident.

Habitat: Large swamps with papyrus and open channels; also marshes, lakes, slow-flowing rivers.

Habits: Solitary or in pairs; rarely in small groups, but does not fish cooperatively. Moves slowly, about one step every 5 seconds; or stands still for long periods with head resting on chest; lunges suddenly for food, plunging whole head and forepart of body into water; uses wings to help in standing upright again; only about 54% of plunges successful. Prey may be swallowed, regurgitated, bitten several times and swallowed again; turtles and snakes may be worked for up to 10 minutes before being swallowed; bill then usually rinsed in water. Forages in shallow waters or at edge of floating islands. Flight slow and direct, usually low, but soars well

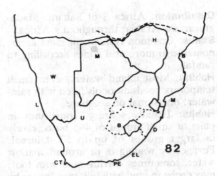

to great heights; legs extend out behind, neck drawn into shoulders. Roosts on ground, on nest or in trees, and may land in trees if disturbed.

Food: Mostly African lungfish *Protopterus* species in tropical Africa; also other fish (up to 50 cm long), frogs, molluscs, snakes, young crocodiles, turtles, small mammals, floating carrion.

Breeding: Probably extralimital, but could breed Okavango Swamps. *Season:* April to July in Zambia. *Nest:* Bulky platform of rushes, leaves and grass up to 2,5 m diameter; solitary in thick vegetation in swamp or on island; lined with finer material; shallow central bowl 55–65 cm diameter; built by both sexes. *Clutch:* 1–3 eggs (usually 2). *Eggs:* Dull white, becoming nest-stained; measure (4) 85,7 × 59,4 (80,1–90 × 56,9–63); weigh about 164 g. *Incubation:* About 30 days by both sexes; water regurgitated over eggs (and chicks) in hot midday hours. *Nestling:* 95 days, fed by both parents; flies at about 105 days.

Ref. Buxton, L. Slater, J. & Brown, L.H. 1978. *E. Afr. Wildl. J.* 16:201–220.
Guillet, A. 1979. *Ostrich* 50:252–255; 1984. *Proc. 5th Pan-Afr. Orn. Congr.*:231–236.
Mathews, N.J.C. 1979. *Ostrich* 50:185.
Möller, W. 1982. *J. Orn.* 123:19–28.

6:4. Family 16 CICONIIDAE – STORKS

Very large. Bill large, long, straight, pointed, sometimes decurved at tip, often red or yellow; legs long; toes long, webbed at base; neck long; wings long and broad; plumage usually black and white; often gregarious; soar well; fly with neck extended; most species nearly voiceless, clap or rattle jaws together; diet variable, aquatic or terrestrial animals; breed colonially; nest a large stick platform on trees, cliffs or buildings; eggs

3–5, white; chick naked at hatching, later downy, altricial; parental care by both sexes. Distribution worldwide, mainly tropical; 17 species; eight species in s Africa.

Ref. Kahl, M.P. 1971. *Living Bird* 10:151–170.

83 (80)   White Stork   Plate 7
Witooievaar
Ciconia ciconia

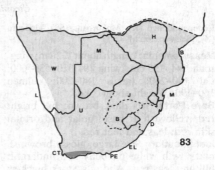

Nkumbinkumbi (K), Leakaboswana le Lešweu (NS), Mokotatsie, Mokoroane (SS), Gumba, Ntsavila, Xaxari (Ts), Lekôlôlwane, Mokôtatsiê (Tw), Ingwamza, Unowanga (X), uNogolantethe, uNowanga (Z), [Weißstorch]

Measurements: Length about 120 cm; wingspan 155–165 cm; wing 530–580–630; tail 218–227–251; tarsus 213–220–225; culmen 140–163–190. Weight ♂ 2,6–3,6–4,4 kg, ♀ 2,3–3,3–3,9 kg, (1 unsexed) 2,4 kg.

Bare Parts: Iris brown; bill bright red; gular skin black; legs and feet bright red (see **Habits**).

Identification: Size large; body and tail white; wings black; bill and legs red; bill straight and pointed at tip. Yellowbilled Stork has yellow bill downcurved at tip, bare red face, black tail and pink tinge to body plumage. *Immature*: Bill and legs dull red; wings dark brown. *Chick*: Downy white; bar on wing black; iris grey; bill black; legs and feet greyish yellow.

Voice: Weak hiss; bill-clattering at nest.

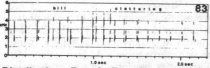

Distribution: Breeds Eurasia, nw Africa and (rarely) S Africa; nonbreeding birds occur over most of Africa S of Sahara; in s Africa absent only from dry w regions; s African populations mainly from central and e Europe.

Status: Mostly nonbreeding Palaearctic migrant; a few pairs breed extreme s Cape; common to abundant, November to March; numbers declining; most common causes of death probably collisions with powerlines, hunting and hailstorms, possibly also because of pesticide use in locust and other insect control. Few birds over-winter in S Africa. S African breeding populations Rare (RDB).

Habitat: Highveld grasslands, mountain meadows, cultivated lands, marshes, karoo.

Habits: Usually gregarious in loose flocks of a few birds to several hundred; larger numbers concentrate at good food supplies, such as locust plagues. Forages by walking slowly across veld or wading in shallow grassy marshland. Soars well, spiralling high on thermals, especially when flocks gather in late summer before northward migration. Roosts communally in trees. May gather in groups near water around midday. In hot weather defaecates on legs for cooling, so that legs may be whitish or pink rather than red.

Food: Mostly large insects like locusts; also other arthropods, small reptiles, mammals, young of ground-nesting birds, frogs, tadpoles, molluscs.

Breeding: Mainly extralimital. Also in small numbers in extreme s Cape (Bredasdorp and Mossel Bay regions). *Season*: September to November. *Nest*: Large platform of sticks, reeds, clods and grass, 80–150 cm diameter, 1–2 m deep; in trees in open veld. *Clutch*: (22) 2–3–4 eggs.

Eggs: Dull chalky white; measure (150) 73 × 52 (65–82 × 47–56); weigh 96–111– 119 g. *Incubation*: 33–34 days by both sexes. *Nestling*: 58–64 days, fed by both parents; young dependent on parents for up to 20 days after leaving nest.

Ref. Oatley, T.B. & Rammesmayer, M.A.M. 1988. Ostrich 59:97–104.

84 (79) Black Stork Plate 7
Grootswartooievaar
Ciconia nigra

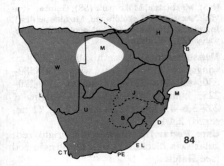

Endongondongo (K), Mokoroane (SS), Unocofu (X), [Schwarzstorch]

Measurements: Length about 122 cm; wing-span 144–155 cm; wing (9) 520–539–600; tail 190–240; tarsus 180–200; culmen 160–190. Weight about 3 kg.

Bare Parts: Iris dark brown; bill bright red, yellowish at base; gular and orbital skin red; legs and feet red.

Identification: Size large; glossy brownish black with white on belly and undertail; bill and legs red. Abdim's Stork blacker; bill and legs greyish; facial skin blue; rump and lower back white. *Immature*: More sooty brown than adult; bill yellowish with orange tip; legs yellowish green. *Chick*: Downy white with yellow bill; legs pinkish.

Voice: Generally silent. Various tremulous whistles and croaks; also bill clattering.

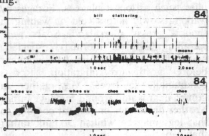

Distribution: Throughout s Africa, mostly along Drakensberg and Transvaal escarpments, and in Zimbabwe; also northward to s Kenya; separate populations in N and E Africa and Eurasia, but Palaearctic migrants reach only as far S as Tanzania.

Status: Uncommon to rare; occasionally locally common; resident or locally nomadic, dispersing from nesting areas after breeding. Probably Rare (RDB).

Habitat: Feeds in or around marshes, dams, rivers and estuaries; breeds in mountainous regions.

Habits: Solitary or in pairs or small groups (rarely as many as 15 birds together); gregarious only when not breeding. Forages by walking slowly, usually in shallow water, and stabbing at prey. Soars well. Roosts in trees or on cliffs or power pylons.

Food: Mainly fish; also frogs, tadpoles, arthropods, small mammals, nestling birds and tortoises.

Breeding: *Season*: May to September in Zimbabwe, May to July (over 75 % in June) in Transvaal; generally winter months throughout s African range. *Nest*: Large stick platform up to 2 m diameter; on cliff ledge, in cave or pothole, rarely on nest of Hamerkop or Black Eagle; solitary, but sometimes in colonies of nesting Cape Vultures or Bald Ibises. *Clutch*: (24) 2–3,2–5 eggs (usually 3). *Eggs*: Dull chalky white, rather elongate; measure (47) 69 × 48,7 (60–74 × 45–56); weigh about 86 g. *Incubation*: 35–36 days by both sexes. *Nestling*: 63–71 days, fed by both parents; mean of 2,3 young reared per pair (1–4 young in 22 nests).

Ref. Siegfried, W.R. 1967. *Ostrich* 38:179–185.
    Tarboton, W. 1982. *Ostrich* 53:151–156.

85 (78)   Abdim's Stork (Whitebellied Stork)   Plate 7
Kleinswartooievaar (Blouwangooievaar)
Ciconia abdimii

Endongondongo (K), Mokoroane, Lekololoane, Roba-re-bese (SS), Shuramurove (Sh), Xaxari (Ts), Lekôlôlwane, Mokôtatsiê (Tw), [Abdimsstorch, Regenstorch]

Measurements: Length about 76 cm; wing 400–475; tail 167–205; tarsus 117–136; culmen 103–127. Weight (1 ♀) 1517 g.

Bare Parts: Iris brown; bill dull greyish green, dull red at tip; bare facial skin blue, red in front of eye and on chin; legs dull greenish grey, red on tarsal joint; feet red.

Identification: Size large; smaller than Black Stork; highly gregarious; mainly black with purplish gloss; belly, rump and lower back white; bill and legs greyish. Black Stork has brownish cast to black plumage; bill and legs bright red; no white on back; not usually gregarious. *Immature*: Less glossy than adult, rather browner; bill reddish; legs darker.

Voice: Usually silent in s Africa; weak double whistle *heep-heep* at roost; also bill-clattering.

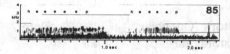

Distribution: Most of Africa S of Sahara; also sw Arabia; in s Africa widespread N of Orange River, except extreme dry W and most of Natal.

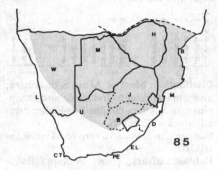

Status: Nonbreeding intra-African migrant, October to April; breeds E and W Africa; very common.

Habitat: Mainly highveld grassland; also semi-arid Kalahari (especially after rain), cultivated lands, inland waters.

Habits: Highly gregarious, flocks often numbering hundreds of birds. Forages by day in open veld, walking slowly; may gather around water when not feeding. Roosts in huge numbers in trees (especially *Eucalyptus*), or on cliffs at night. Soars well, often to great heights, sometimes descending swiftly with swerving flight and half-closed wings to suitable feeding grounds.

Food: Mainly larger insects; also frogs, lizards, mice, fish, crabs, molluscs.

Breeding: Extralimital.

Ref. Kahl, M.P. 1971. *Ostrich* 42:233–241.

86 (77)   Woollynecked Stork   Plate 7
Wolnekooievaar
Ciconia episcopus

Endongondongo (K), isiThandamanzi (Z), [Wollhalsstorch]

Measurements: Length about 86 cm; wing 440–485; tail 180–214; tarsus 140–171; culmen 135–168.

Bare Parts: Iris dark red; bill black, tip and culmen red; legs and feet blackish red, darker on tarsal joints and feet.

Identification: Size large; mainly black with white neck, hindcrown, forehead,

belly and undertail; forecrown blackish blue; thighs black. White neck distinguishes it from other large blackish storks. In flight long white undertail coverts project beyond black forked tail. *Immature*: Above blackish brown; neck and breast pale sooty brownish; belly and crown dull white; bill and face black; legs dark grey, tibiotarsal joint whitish. *Chick*: Pale grey; neck buff; iris dark green; lores and eyering black; bill black, tip reddish brown; legs and feet grey.

Voice: Usually silent; raucous calls at nest; also bill-clattering.

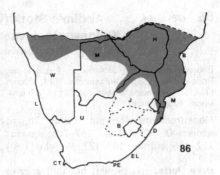

Distribution: Most of Africa S of Sahara; also tropical Asia to Indonesia and Philippines; in s Africa confined to higher rainfall areas in E and N.

Status: Uncommon to rare resident. Rare (RDB).

Habitat: Rivers, pans, swamps, floodplains, dams, lagoons, tidal mudflats; also grassland; mainly in wooded regions.

Habits: Usually solitary or in pairs. Feeds at edge of water, walking slowly, or standing still for long periods; sometimes forages on grassland. Attracted to grass fires for food. Roosts in trees at night.

Food: Mainly large insects; also molluscs, crabs, fish, frogs, lizards; rarely oil palm fibres.

Breeding: *Season*: August to November in Zimbabwe, Kruger National Park and Zululand. *Nest*: Platform of sticks, lined with finer twigs and grass; about 1 m diameter, 30 cm thick, usually on horizontal fork of lateral branch of leafy tree in swamp forest, 30–50 m above ground; solitary. *Clutch*: 2–4 eggs (usually 3–4). *Eggs*: Dull white, often mudstained; measure (7) 62 × 44,4 (59,3–67 × 43–45,4); weigh (7) 53–59,3–70 g. *Incubation*: 30–31 days by both sexes. *Nestling*: 40 days; flies at 55–65 days; fed by both parents; young dependent on adults for about 21 days after leaving nest.

Ref. Scott, J.A. 1975. *Ostrich* 46:201–207.

87 (74)   Openbilled Stork (Openbill)   Plate 7
Oopbekooievaar
Anastomus lamelligerus

Etongorokofu (K), Mukyindlopfu (Ts), isiQhophamnenke (Z), [Klaffschnabel]

Measurements: Length about 94 cm; wing 370–435; tail 165–206; tarsus 133–165; culmen 153–200; greatest width of gap between jaws 5,5–6. Weight (1 ♂) 1250 g, (3 ♀) 1000–1052–1140 g.

Bare Parts: Iris brown with yellow inner ring; bill brownish, paler at base; lores and skin around eye blue to blackish; legs and feet black.

Identification: Size large; brownish black all over; feathers on mantle, neck and chest glossed greenish; bill large with distinct gap between upper and lower jaw. *Immature*: Bill almost straight with little or no gap. *Chick*: Sooty black; iris brown; bill black; gular skin pink.

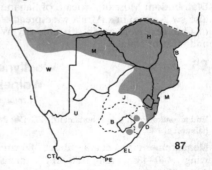

Voice: Loud raucous croaks or honks, *horrrh-horrrh*.

Distribution: Africa S of Sahara, Madagascar; in s Africa absent from S and W; mainly tropical.

Status: Uncommon, to locally common; intra-African migrant, but movements not mapped; some birds resident. Rare (RDB).
Habitat: Larger inland waters; marshes, swamps, floodplains, river shallows, pools, lakes.
Habits: Feeds solitarily; otherwise gregarious. Roosts in trees. Forages by wading in quiet water and among floating plants. Spends much of day standing still on shoreline. Gap in bill for structural strength at tip while prey extracted from shell. Forages by jabbing slightly open bill into mud; when prey contacted, bill is quickly closed and withdrawn; may also hunt by sight. Snails extracted from shell under water with tip of lower jaw while holding shell with tip of upper jaw, then shell shaken free before body swallowed; *Achatina* shells may be crushed for prey extraction. Extraction of mussels may take 10 minutes. May leave bivalve molluscs in sun to open before eating them, sometimes collecting 50–60 mussels on shore until they open.

Food: Snails (especially *Pila* (= *Ampullaria*) species and *Lanistes ovum*) and mussels (probably *Caelatura* and *Aspatharia* species).
Breeding: *Localities*: Eastern Zimbabwe lowveld; near Harare, Zimbabwe; Makgadikgadi Pan, Botswana; n Zululand; n Kruger National Park; near Tsumeb, Namibia. *Season*: September to May in Zimbabwe; mainly summer months in s Africa. *Nest*: Platform of sticks and twigs, lined with grasses and sedges; 45–56 cm diameter (about 20 cm across bowl); built by both sexes in about 1 week; bowl lined with fresh waterplants; colonial in trees or reedbeds. *Clutch*: (28) 3–3,9–5 eggs (usually 3–4, sometimes only 2). *Eggs*: Dull white, usually much stained; measure (39) 55,4 × 40 (51–61,4 × 36,7–43,2); weigh 35–50 g. *Incubation*: About 25 days by both sexes. *Nestling*: About 80 days, fed by both parents.

Ref. Anthony, A.J. & Sherry, B.Y. 1980. *Ostrich* 51:1–6.
Kahl, M.P. 1971. *J. Orn.* 112:21–35.

88 (75) Saddlebilled Stork (Saddlebill)   Plate 7
Saalbekooievaar
Ephippiorhynchus senegalensis

Kandjendje (K), Hukumihlanga, Kokwasabi (Ts), [Sattelstorch]

Measurements: Length about 145 cm; wingspan up to 270 cm; wing 600–670; tail 250–288; tarsus 311–365; culmen 273–334. ♀ about 10% smaller than ♂.
Bare Parts: Iris brown in ♂, yellow in ♀; bill bright red on distal half and at base, broad black band on proximal half; skin around eye red; wattles below chin red or yellow; frontal shield ("saddle") on bill yellow; legs black with red tarsal joint; feet red.
Identification: Size huge; black-and-white; bill enormous, slightly upturned, red and black with yellow saddle; neck and head all black; legs very long; naked red patch on breast. *Immature*: Dull grey where adult black; white areas mottled with sooty black; legs greenish. *Chick*: Downy white; bill grey or black.
Voice: Adults silent; young beg weakly; no bill-clattering recorded.

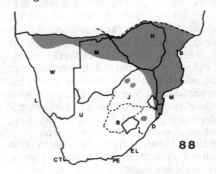

Distribution: Africa S of Sahara; in s Africa absent from S and W; mainly tropical.
Status: Fairly common resident, but local. Rare (RDB).
Habitat: Larger inland waters; rivers, dams, pans, floodplains, swamps usually in open or lightly wooded country.
Habits: Solitary or in pairs; usually shy

and wary. Forages in shallow water by walking slowly and jabbing at prey with bill; sometimes stands and waits for prey; may stir mud with foot like Yellowbilled Stork; may toss prey into air before catching and swallowing it; nips spines off larger fish before swallowing them. Roosts in trees; not gregarious. Flies and soars well.

Food: Mainly fish up to 500 g; also frogs, small mammals and birds, crustaceans, reptiles, molluscs.

Breeding: *Season*: January to July in Zimbabwe (mainly February-March), March to July in n Transvaal, March to July in Zululand. *Nest*: Platform of sticks up to 2 m diameter, 50 cm thick, lined with reeds, sedges and earth; bowl deep enough to hide sitting bird; solitary on top of bush or tree near water, up to 30 m above ground; built by both sexes. *Clutch*: (54) 1–2,8–5 eggs (usually 2–3). *Eggs*: Dull white, faintly glossy and pitted; measure (9) 79,1 × 56,7 (75,6–81,3 × 56–58); weigh about 146 g. *Incubation*: About 30–35 days by both sexes. *Nestling*: About 70–100 days (not accurately assessed), fed by both parents.

89 (73)   Marabou Stork   Plate 7
Maraboe
Leptoptilos crumeniferus

Nyumbu (K), Mmakaitšimeletša (NS), Svorenyama (Sh), Qandlopfu, Tsewane (Ts), [Marabu]

Measurements: Length 152 cm; wingspan ♂ mean 263 cm, max. 287 cm, ♀ mean 247 cm; wing ♂ 70,5–74,5–79,4, ♀ 63,1–67,8–70,9; tail ♂ 27,8–32,3–35,8, ♀ 24–28,2–30,2; tarsus ♂ 26,6–29,3–31,9, ♀ 24,5–26,6–28,3; culmen ♂ 27,9–34,6, ♀ 24,1–31,4.

Bare Parts: Iris brown; bill and face greenish to yellowish horn or pinkish, mottled with black; head and neck pink or reddish, mottled with black; gular air sac pinkish red; air sac on hindneck (usually hidden) orange-red when inflated; legs black, usually covered with white powder.

Identification: Size huge; blackish above, white below; head naked, pinkish; bill very large, dirty greyish; legs very long, white. *Immature*: Duller than adult.

Voice: Usually silent; bill-clattering in threat; at nest various squeals, whines, whistles and moos.

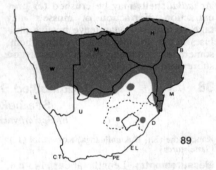

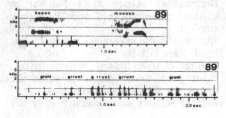

Distribution: Africa S of Sahara; in s Africa mainly tropical to subtropical in E and N; vagrant elsewhere (s Namibia, e Cape, Orange Free State, Natal).

Status: Rare vagrant over most of S Africa; elsewhere locally common. Rare (RDB).

Habitat: Open to semi-arid woodland, bushveld, fishing villages, rubbish tips, lake shores.

Habits: Usually gregarious, especially around carcasses of large mammals and at offal dumps near abattoirs, often in company with vultures. Spends most of day standing still, sometimes squatting on tarsal joints; usually docile and will give way even to smaller vultures at carcass. Largely scavenger, but may forage in grassveld or freshly ploughed fields for

insects, sometimes with other stork species, or wades in shallow water, sometimes foot-stirring to disturb fish; detects prey by sight or touch. Takes off running with lowered head; 5–8 wingbeats between short glides in flapping flight, about 145 wingbeats/min; may do aerobatics when descending from great height; soars well, sometimes for hours. Inflates throat sac and neck balloon in threat and courtship. Urinates on legs for cooling in hot weather, so that legs often look white. **Food:** Carrion, refuse, rodents, insects, birds (including queleas and even adult flamingos), fish up to 450 g, young crocodiles, lizards, snakes, frogs. May wash offal in water before swallowing.
Breeding: *Season*: May in Transvaal,

August to September in Botswana and Caprivi, May to July in Zimbabwe. *Nest*: Stick platform about 1 m diameter, 20–30 cm thick, lined with smaller sticks and green leaves; 3–40 m above ground, in trees, villages or on cliffs; built in 7–10 days, male collecting sticks and female building; colonial. *Clutch*: (108) 1–2,4–4 eggs (usually 2–3). *Eggs*: Dull chalky white, usually stained; measure (40) 79,1 × 55,9 (71–86,2 × 50–62); weigh about 138 g. *Incubation*: (6) 29–30,3–31 days by both sexes. *Nestling*: 95–115 days, fed by both parents; postnestling dependence up to 130 days.

Ref. Fraser, W. 1971. *Ostrich* 42:123–127.
Kahl, M.P. 1966. *Behaviour* 27:76–106.

90 (76) Yellowbilled Stork Plate 7
Nimmersat (Geelbekooievaar)
Mycteria ibis

Nepando (K), [Nimmersatt]

Measurements: Length about 97 cm; wingspan 150–165 cm; wing 455–517; tail 168–190; tarsus 195–229; culmen 203–243.
Bare Parts: Iris greyish brown; bill golden yellow; face red, narrowly bordered orange; legs red to pinkish, waxy orange proximally.
Identification: Size large; mainly pinkish white with black wings and tail; bill yellow, blunt and decurved at tip; bare face red. White Stork has pure white body, white tail, straight red bill and feathered face. *Immature*: Greyish brown with dull greyish yellow bill, dull orange face and brownish legs (adult plumage attained only at 3 years). *Chick*: Downy white.
Voice: Usually silent; at nest squeaky whines and screams; also bill-clattering.
Distribution: Africa S of Sahara, Madagascar; in s Africa mainly absent from dry W, but widespread at times after rains as far S as Eastern Cape.
Status: Mainly nonbreeding intra-African migrant in S Africa, October to April; uncommon to locally common. Breeding resident in Zimbabwe and probably n Botswana; common. Rare (RDB).

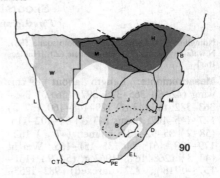

90

Habitat: Mainly inland waters; rivers, dams, pans, floodplains, marshes; less often estuaries.
Habits: Usually gregarious in small parties; rarely solitary. Forages by walking slowly in shallow water with bill immersed and held slightly open, foot-stirring to disturb prey which is caught by feel, even in turbid water. Spends much of daytime standing quietly on shoreline. Roosts communally on sandbanks or in trees, often in company with other wading birds.
Food: Fish, frogs, insects, worms, crustaceans, small mammals.
Breeding: *Season*: August to September

in Botswana, June to August in Zululand. *Nest*: Platform of sticks, lined with finer material, about 1 m diameter, 20–30 cm thick; colonial, in trees; built in 7–10 days by both sexes. *Clutch*: (51) 2–2,6–4 eggs (usually 2–3). *Eggs*: Dull white, nest-stained; measure (51) 66,2 × 44,4 (59–72,3 × 42–47,6); weigh mean 77 g. *Incubation*: About 30 days by both sexes. *Nestling*: At least 55 days, fed by both parents.

Ref. Fraser, W. 1971. *Ostrich* 42:123–127.

6:5. Family 17 PLATALEIDAE (= THRESKIORNITHIDAE)—IBISES AND SPOONBILLS

Large to very large. Bill long and decurved in ibises, straight and spatulate in spoonbills; face often naked, head and neck sometimes naked; head sometimes crested; neck long; wings long and fairly broad; tail short; legs and toes long to moderately long; toes partly webbed at base; plumage largely white in most species, sometimes dark with iridescence; sexes similar; fly with neck extended; gregarious; feed by wading in shallows or probing in grassland; food fish, frogs, insects, and other animals, also carrion and detritus; most breed colonially; nest a platform of sticks on trees, cliffs or in reeds; eggs 2–5, white or green, plain or marked; chick downy, altricial; parental care by both sexes. Distribution worldwide, mostly tropical; about 30 species; five species in s Africa.

91 (81)   **Sacred Ibis**   **Plate 7**
Skoorsteenveër
Threskiornis aethiopicus

Ndingilira (K), Lehalanyane, Leholotsoane (SS), N'wafayaswitlangi (Ts), umXwagele (Z), [Heiliger Ibis]

Measurements: Length about 89 cm; wing (42 ♂) 365–378–397, (56 ♀) 345–363–382; tail (43 ♂) 129–148–160, (57 ♀) 127–145–167; tarsus (43 ♂) 94–102–116, (58 ♀) 85–92–103; culmen (47 ♂) 162–179–198, (61 ♀) 135–151–165. Weight (40 ♂) 1268–1618–1963 g, (54 ♀) 1131–1378–1718 g, (22 unsexed) 982–1253–1530 g.

Bare Parts: Iris brown (ringed with red when breeding); head and neck naked, black; bill black, tip horn; legs and feet black with red tinge.

Identification: Size large; mainly white with black head, neck and plumelike feathers on back when wings folded; bill long, decurved; in flight wings white with black trailing edge; line of red skin on underwing. *Immature*: Similar to adult, but with some whitish feathering on neck. *Chick*: Downy white with downy black head and neck; white spot on crown; iris pale grey; bill, legs and feet pinkish white.

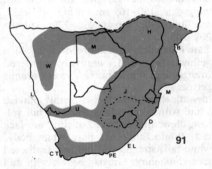

Voice: Usually silent; at nest harsh croaks, moans, squeals and wheezing sounds.

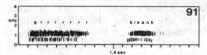

Distribution: Africa S of Sahara, Madagascar, Middle East; Australian White Ibis *T. molucca* now usually considered conspecific; in s Africa widespread, but absent from most of Namibia and Kalahari sandveld.

Status: Common to very common resident; some birds nomadic or migratory within s Africa as far as Namibia, Botswana, Angola and Zambia.
Habitat: Very varied; inland waters, cultivated lands, sewage works, playing fields, open grassveld, rubbish dumps, coastal lagoons, tidal flats, offshore islands.
Habits: Gregarious; flocks may number hundreds of birds. Scavenges around farmyards, dairies, piggeries, abattoirs, seabird breeding colonies; forages also in other habitats, taking live prey, often by probing in mud, walking slowly with deliberate steps. Roosts in trees, reedbeds or on islands. In flight wingbeats shallow, alternating with short glides; flies to and from roosting and feeding sites in V-formation.
Food: Very varied; arthropods, small mammals, nestling birds, eggs of birds and crocodiles, molluscs, frogs, small reptiles, offal, carrion, seeds.
Breeding: *Season*: August to May in Transvaal (mainly September-October), April to August in Namibia, February-March and August-September in Zimbabwe; mainly winter in W and summer in E. *Nest*: Platform of sticks lined with leaves and grass; 28–43 cm diameter, about 20 cm thick; colonial, sometimes in hundreds, in trees, bushes or on ground. *Clutch*: (690) 2–2,3–5 eggs (usually 2–3). *Eggs*: Dull white, sometimes tinged bluish green, usually with some spots of reddish brown; measure (108) 66,2 × 43,6 (59–73,8 × 39,7–51,2); weigh about 62 g. *Incubation*: 28–29 days by both sexes. *Nestling*: Leaves nest at 14–21 days; flies at 35–40 days; leaves colony at 44–48 days; fed by both parents.

Ref. Clark, R.A. 1979. *Ostrich* 50:104–111; 129–133; 134–138.
Clark, R.A. & Clark, A. 1979. *Ostrich* 50:94–103.
Lowe, K.W., Clark, A. & Clark, R.A. 1985. *Ostrich* 56:111–116.

92 (82)   Bald Ibis   Plate 7
Kalkoenibis (Wilde Kalkoen)
Geronticus calvus

Lesuhla-ngeto, Mokhotlo (SS), Umcwangele (X), uNkondlo, umXwagele (Z), [Glattnackenrapp]

Measurements: Length about 79 cm; wing (7) 369–386–403; tail 175–191–200; tarsus 66–70,4–73; culmen 140–146–151.
Bare Parts: Iris red to orange-red; bill and naked domed crown bright red; rest of head and upper neck whitish beige; legs and feet dull red.
Identification: Size medium; dark glossy green with conspicuous red head and bill; neck whitish; legs relatively short, red; metallic coppery wingpatch visible at close quarters. *Immature*: Feathered greyish on head and neck; red on forecrown only; no coppery wingpatch. *Chick*: Downy grey; iris dark blue; bill black with grey tip; legs and feet dark grey.
Voice: Usually silent; at nest 2-syllabled, somewhat resonant *whee-ohh*, mainly in flight; also piping *ek-ek-ek-ek*; other growls and moans.

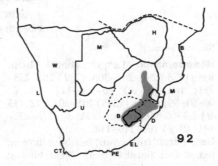

Distribution: Lesotho, Transkei, e Orange Free State, inland Natal, se Transvaal, Swaziland.

Status: Uncommon resident; formerly more widespread, but present population stable. Total population around 5 000 birds. Out of Danger (RDB).

Habitat: High grassveld (especially after burning), heavily grazed pastures, cultivated lands; breeds in mountainous or highly dissected country.

Habits: Gregarious in flocks of up to 100 birds. Forages by probing and turning over leaves and dung; collects fire-killed arthropods on winter-burnt grassland. Roosts communally on cliffs; also in trees, sometimes in company with herons and other ibises. Disperses from nesting cliffs after breeding. Flies buoyantly with much gliding; soars well. Rather shy.

Food: Insects, snails, worms, frogs, small mammals and birds; also carrion; swallows buttons, possibly mistaking them for beetles. Up to 33% of stomach contents of young may be maize-stalk borer.

Breeding: *Season*: July to October, rarely March. *Nest*: Platform of sticks about 50 cm diameter, 15 cm thick, on cliff ledge or in pothole on mountainside or in riverine gorge or waterfall face; colonial (mean of 13 nests/colony), nests often touching. *Clutch*: (529) 1–2–3 eggs. *Eggs*: Pale blue, spotted with reddish brown; measure (24) 64,2 × 42,8 (57–71 × 38–49). *Incubation*: 27–31 days by both sexes. *Nestling*: 40–45 days, fed by both parents; dependent on parents for about 2 months after leaving nest.

Ref. Cooper, K.H. & Edwards, K.Z. 1969. *Bokmakierie* 21:4–9.
Manry, D.E. 1982. *S. Afr. J. Wildl. Res.* 12:85–93; 1984. *S. Afr. J. Zool.* 19:12–15; 1985a. *Ibis* 127:159–173; 1985b. *Biol. Conserv.* 33:351–362.
Milstein, P. le S. & Siegfried, W.R. 1970. *Bokmakierie* 22:36–39.
Siegfried, W.R. 1966. *Ostrich* 37:216–218; 1971. *Biol. Conserv.* 3:88–91.

93 (83) Glossy Ibis Plate 7
Glansibis
Plegadis falcinellus

[Brauner Sichler]

Measurements: Length about 71 cm; wing (7 ♂) 280–297–306, (7 ♀) 267–273–281; tail (6 ♂) 96–106–111, (7 ♀) 90–94–99; tarsus (18 ♂) 101–107–113, (13 ♀) 82–86–90; culmen (11 ♂) 126–132–141, (8 ♀) 106–110–114.

Bare Parts: Iris brown; bill olive brown; naked face purplish black (light blue at start of breeding) bordered by narrow white line along forehead and cheeks; legs and feet olive brown.

Identification: Size smallish; all dark with slender decurved bill (rather like very dark Curlew); at close range looks chestnut with purplish gloss; back and wings metallic green; nonbreeding plumage greener, but greyish below. *Imma-*

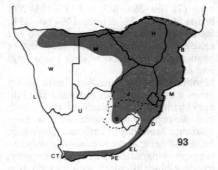

ture: Like sooty nonbreeding adult; brown below. *Chick*: Downy black with pinkish white patch on back of crown; iris greyish brown; bill black with two vertical pink stripes; face and feet pink.

Voice: Usually silent; croaking *graa-graa-graa* in flight; gull-like *keeauw-klaup-klaup*; guttural *kwuk-kwuk-kwuk* at nest.

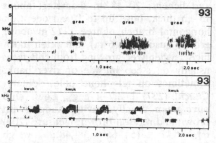

Distribution: Almost worldwide; in s Africa absent from dry W.

Status: Locally common to rare; increasing in numbers and distribution in S Africa; scarce and irregular in Zimbabwe; some resident, others disperse at least as far as Zambia from Witwatersrand after breeding.

Habitat: Shallow inland waters and neighbouring wet grasslands.

Habits: Solitary or gregarious in flocks of up to over 40 birds. Roosts communally in trees or on ground, sometimes in company with other wading birds. Forages by probing in mud while walking slowly. Flight buoyant and graceful, sometimes in V-formation.

Food: Insects, crustaceans, worms, molluscs, fish, frogs and small reptiles.

Breeding: *Season*: September to March in Transvaal (peak November), September to November in sw Cape, January in Zimbabwe, August in Namibia. *Nest*: Compact platform of twigs or reeds, about 30 cm diameter; colonial in trees, bushes or reedbeds, often in mixed heronries. *Clutch*: (97) 2–2,3–4 eggs (usually 2–3). *Eggs*: Bright blue to blue-green, slightly glossy; measure (133) 52 × 37 (45–59 × 33–40); weigh about 38 g. *Incubation*: 20–21–23 days, by both sexes. *Nestling*: Leaves nest for short periods at about 21 days; flies at about 42 days.

94 (84)　　　Hadeda Ibis　　　Plate 7
Hadeda
Bostrychia hagedash

Ngoromuduva (K), Lengangane (SS), Man'an'ani, Nangane (Ts), Ing'ang'ane (X), iNkankane (Z), [Hagedasch-Ibis]

Measurements: Length about 76 cm; wing (17) 334–353–370; tail 137–154–170; tarsus 63–67,9–73; culmen 117–134–153. Weight (1) 1262 g.

Bare Parts: Iris dark brown with narrow white outer ring (sometimes red); bill black, culmen crimson; lores black; legs and feet greyish black, top of toes dull red.

Identification: Size large; plain dark greyish, rather short-legged (legs do not extend beyond tail in flight); metallic purple or green on wing seen in good light; whitish malar stripe; voice highly characteristic (see below); in flight bill points downward; wings broad and rounded. *Chick*: Rufous brown; bill straight, black; legs and feet pale pink.

Voice: Very loud, rather raucous *haaa* or *ha-ha-hadeda*, usually given in flight, especially at take-off.

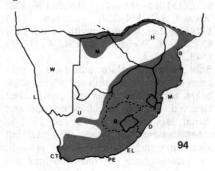

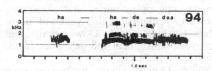

Distribution: Africa S of Sahara; in s Africa largely absent from dry W but extending range; recorded Clanwilliam, Nieuwoudtville, Aughrabies Falls.

Status: Very common resident; range expanding into highveld and dry W.

Habitat: Grasslands, savannas, bushveld, forest edges, large gardens, playing fields, airfields; less often also marshes and shores of inland waters; confined to large rivers in Zimbabwe lowveld.

Habits: Usually gregarious in groups of 5–20 birds; flocks of up to 100 or more when not breeding. When disturbed takes off with loud calls; flight somewhat jerky with irregular wingbeats. Roosts in trees or on power pylons, usually in small groups; highly vocal when leaving roost in morning. Forages on ground by probing with long bill, or picking from surface.

Food: Mainly insects; also crustaceans, myriapods, spiders, snails, small reptiles, earthworms.

Breeding: *Season*: November to January in e Cape, July to January in Transvaal and Natal (mainly October-November), September to March in Zimbabwe. *Nest*: Flimsy platform of sticks, lined with grass and lichens; 20–45 cm diameter, about 15 cm thick, bowl up to 10 cm deep; on horizontal branch of tree 1–12 m above ground (usually 3–6 m), but often much higher when tree growing from cliff face; usually on steep hillside or river bank; sometimes on telephone pole; solitary. *Clutch*: (237) 2–2,7–4 eggs. *Eggs*: Dull olive green, usually heavily smudged with brown and reddish brown; measure (200) 60,3 × 42 (54–66 × 38–48); weigh 55–62 g. *Incubation*: 25–28 days by both sexes. *Nestling*: 35–37 days, fed by both parents; independent at 49 days.

Ref. Raseroka, B.H. 1975. *Ostrich* 46:51–54; 208–212.
Skead, C.J. 1950. *Ibis* 93:360–382.

95 (85) African Spoonbill Plate 7
Lepelaar
Platalea alba

iNkenkane, isiXulamasele (Z), [Afrikanischer Löffler]

Measurements: Length about 91 cm; wing (15) 365–384–414; tail 105–124–152; tarsus 131–144–157; culmen (11) 172–193–230; greatest width of bill (11) 45–50,6–56. Weight (1 ♂) 1542,4 g, (2 ♀) 1543,3–1790 g.

Bare Parts: Iris white, pale blue or pale grey; bill grey above with red edges, black below with yellow edges and spots; naked face red, shading to yellow on chin and throat; legs and feet pink or red.

Identification: Size large; all white; bill long, straight, spoon-shaped, reddish; conspicuous bare red face and long red legs. *Immature*: Streaked blackish on head; tips of primaries and underwing coverts blackish; bill dull yellowish horn; legs blackish. *Chick*: Downy white; bill narrow, light green with pale pink edges; iris and legs black.

Voice: Usually silent; various guttural croaks, grunts and quacks, sometimes in flight; 2 birds may duet with alternating moans at about 2-second intervals; may clatter bill softly.

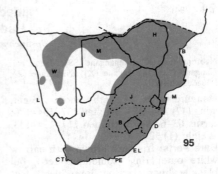

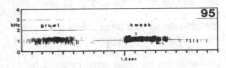

Distribution: Africa S of Sahara, Madagascar; in s Africa absent from dry W; vagrant to Sandwich Harbour and Naute Dam, Namibia.

Status: Locally common; nomadic, possibly migratory; Transvaal bird recovered Zambia.

Habitat: Shallow inland waters (dams,

marshes); less often coastal lagoons and estuaries.

Habits: Solitary or gregarious. Forages by wading slowly, bill partly or wholly submerged and sweeping from side to side; also probes in mud. Roosts communally in trees or reedbeds. Flight graceful with quick, shallow wingbeats, often in flocks in V-formation. Rather shy. Spends long periods standing still on one leg with head tucked into back feathers.

Food: Small fish and aquatic invertebrates.

Breeding: *Season*: March to September in Transvaal, May to September in Zimbabwe, August to November in sw Cape,

July to October in Natal; mainly winter to early spring in s Africa. *Nest*: Flattish platform of sticks or reeds, elliptical, about 38 × 47 cm diameter; bowl up to 11 cm deep; colonial in partly submerged trees, reeds or on rocky islets, often in mixed heronries. *Clutch*: (303) 2–2,6–4 eggs. *Eggs*: White to pale buff, blotched and spotted with brown, reddish brown and some grey undermarkings; measure (205) 68 × 45 (57–82 × 39,7–48); weigh about 69 g. *Incubation*: 25–26–29 days by both sexes. *Nestling*: 21–28 days, fed by both parents; independent at about 46 days.

Ref. Whitelaw, D. 1968. *Ostrich* 39:236–241.

7. Order PHOENICOPTERIFORMES (One family)

7:1. Family 18 PHOENICOPTERIDAE—FLAMINGOS

Very large. Ordinal relationships still unsettled, formerly believed to be related either to Ciconiiformes and Anseriformes on the one hand, or to the avocets and stilts (family Recurvirostridae) on the other. Marine and inland waters; bill large, sharply decurved from middle, with filtering lamellae along sides; neck extremely long; legs extremely long; toes rather short, three front toes webbed, hind toe rudimentary; wings long; tail short; plumage white or pink, remiges black, upperwing coverts scarlet, vermilion or magenta (more intensely coloured when breeding); face bare; fly with neck extended; highly gregarious and nomadic after breeding; filter-feed in shallow water on small animals or microscopic algae, usually while wading, but sometimes while swimming; breed colonially; nest a low cone of mud with hollow on top, on exposed mud or in shallow water; sometimes no nest – eggs laid on scanty pad of grass and feathers on bare rock; eggs 1–2, white; chick downy, altricial for few days, then precocial; parental care by both sexes. Distribution Caribbean, S America, Africa, s Europe to India; 4–5 species; two species in s Africa.

Ref. Brown, L. 1959. *The mystery of the flamingos*. London: Country Life.
Kear, J. & Duplaix-Hall, N. 1975. *Flamingos*. Berkhamstead: Poyser.
Olson, S.L. & Feduccia, A. 1980. *Smithson. Contrib. Zool.* 316:1–73.

96 (86) **Greater Flamingo** **Plate 7**
Grootflamink
Phoenicopterus ruber

uKholwase, uNondwebu (Z), [Flamingo]

Measurements: Length (4 ♂) 161–166–172 cm, (3 ♀) 136–146–158 cm; wingspan (3 ♂) 164–169,2–175 cm, (3 ♀) 149–150,4–151 cm; wing (4 ♂) 405–419,8–435, (3 ♀) 382–395–405; tail (4 ♂) 145–157,5–170, (3 ♀) 135–140–145; tarsus (4 ♂) 289–303,8–318, (3 ♀) 255–270–280; culmen (4 ♂) 123–125,3–127, (3 ♀) 117–121,3–126. Weight (4 ♂) 2630–2855–3000 g, (3 ♀) 2300–2573,3–2720 g.

Bare Parts: Iris pale yellow; bill pink, distal third black; lores and ring around eye pink; legs and feet bright coral pink.

Identification: Size large; very tall, long-legged and long-necked; generally white (Lesser Flamingo looks pinker); bill bent in middle, pink with black tip (bill of Lesser Flamingo looks all dark at distance); very conspicuous flame red wing in flight (trace of red visible on folded wing); flight feathers black. *Immature*: Greyish where adult pink; lacks red on wings; bill grey with black tip. *Chick*: Downy grey; iris blackish; bill grey; legs swollen, bright pink.

Voice: Gooselike double *honk-honk*, often in chorus; alarm nasal *kngaaa*; chuckling *kuk-kuk* and grunts when feeding.

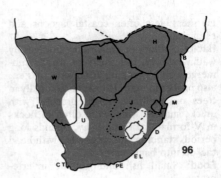

Distribution: Whole of s Africa; also E Africa to Red Sea, Mediterranean and coast of W Africa; s Eurasia; S and C America, se N America.

Status: Locally abundant; highly nomadic; partly migratory, moving N in winter.

Habitat: Large bodies of shallow water, both inland and coastal; saline and brackish waters preferred.

Habits: Highly gregarious, flocks often numbering hundreds of birds (in E Africa thousands or millions), often mixed with Lesser Flamingos. Feeds by wading with bill upside down in water, filtering out small organisms; may stir mud with foot; swims well in deeper water. Flocks fly in long skeins or V-formation about 50–60 km/h.

Food: Small aquatic invertebrates, detritus, microscopic algae.

Breeding: Irregular in s Africa. *Localities*: Bredasdorp (1960–61), Vanwyksvlei (1978), Etosha Pan, Lake St Lucia (1972), Makgadikgadi Pan, Orange Free State Goldfields. *Season*: Any month, depending on water conditions and food supply. *Nest*: Usually cone of mud with hollow top, on mudflat; 15–45 cm tall, 40–55 cm diameter at base; bowl 30–40 cm diameter; sometimes slight collection of debris on rocky islet; in dense colonies of hundreds or thousands of pairs. *Clutch*: 1 egg (rarely 2). *Eggs*: Pale blue with thick chalky white coating, measure (135) 88,8 × 54 (79–103 × 48,3–58,6); weigh about 140 g. *Incubation*: 27–28–31 days by both sexes. *Nestling*: Leaves nest at about 5 days to join creche of hundreds of young; feeds independently at 70–75 days; flies at 75–80 days.

Ref. Berry, H.H. 1972. *Madoqua Ser. I*, 5:5–27.
Uys, C.J., Broekhuysen, G.J., Martin, J. & MacLeod, J.G. 1963. *Ostrich* 34:129–154.

97 (87)   Lesser Flamingo   Plate 7
Kleinflamink
Phoeniconaias minor

uNondwebu (Z), [Zwergflamingo]

Measurements: Length (2 ♂) 121–122 cm, (6 ♀) 104–112,8–126; wingspan (2 ♂) 138–140 cm, (6 ♀) 102–116,7–126 cm; wing (2 ♂) 349–357, (6 ♀) 313–327–345; tail (2 ♂) 106–114, (6 ♀) 93–101,2–107; tarsus (2 ♂) 210–224, (6 ♀) 173–182,8–185; culmen (2 ♂) 90–95, (6 ♀) 93–94,3–108. Weight (2 ♂) 1600–1780 g, (6 ♀) 1440–1560–1750 g, (3 unsexed) 1590–1721–1930 g.

Bare Parts: Iris red, orange or yellow; bill dark red, tip black; lores and eyering dark red; legs and feet bright red.

Identification: Size large (smaller and pinker than Greater Flamingo); bill dark

red (pink in Greater Flamingo), looks
almost black at distance; wings red-and-
black in flight. *Immature*: Grey with dark
streaks and no red on wings; bill and legs
grey. *Chick*: Downy grey, often darker
than chick of Greater Flamingo, otherwise
similar; bill and iris blackish.
Voice: High-pitched *kwirrik*; bleating
murmur, *murr-err, murr-err* at rest; shrill
quie-ow.

Distribution: Throughout s Africa, except
Kalahari; also up Rift Valley to E Africa
and Red Sea, coastal W Africa, Madagascar, India.
Status: Locally abundant; highly nomadic.
Habitat: Larger brackish or saline inland
and coastal waters.
Habits: Highly gregarious in flocks of hundreds or thousands; often mixed with
Greater Flamingos. Forages in calm
water, walking or swimming with head
swinging from side to side, filtering food
from surface of water with bill upside-
down (air-filled lower jaw acts as float);
rarely feeds on bottom like Greater Flamingo; commonly forages at night. Flies
in long skeins or V-formation, sometimes
very high.

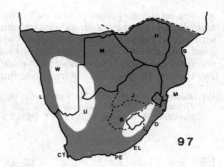

Food: Mainly microscopic blue-green
algae and diatoms.
Breeding: *Localities*: Etosha Pan (most
years); unsuccessful attempts Welkom,
Port Elizabeth, w Transvaal. *Season*:
June-July. *Nest*: Low mud cone with hollow top, 15–40 cm tall, 35–56 cm diameter at base; bowl 14–19 cm diameter
inside; densely colonial on mudflats of
saline lakes. *Clutch*: 1 egg (very rarely 2).
Eggs: Pale bluish with chalky white
coating, stained; measure (120) 82,3 ×
49,9 (72–94 × 44–56); weigh (100)
61–97–118 g. *Incubation*: About 28 days
by both sexes. *Nestling*: Leaves nest at
about 6 days to join creche of thousands of
young; flies at 70–90 days; fed by both
parents.

Ref. Berry, H.H. 1972. *Madoqua Ser. I*, 5:5–27.
Brown, L.H. & Root, A. 1971. *Ibis*
113:147–172.

8. Order ANSERIFORMES (Two families; one in s Africa)

Medium to very large. Mainly aquatic, marine or inland waters; swim well; front toes
webbed, hind toe reduced (family Anatidae), or toes partly webbed, hind toe well
developed (family Anhimidae); bill flattened (Anatidae) or arched (Anhimidae) with
hooked or rounded tip; legs robust, usually short; spur sometimes present on wrist;
often gregarious; nest mostly on or near ground near water; clutch fairly large; chick
downy, precocial. Distribution of Anatidae worldwide, of Anhimidae S America only.

8:1. Family 19 ANATIDAE—DUCKS, GEESE AND SWANS

Medium to very large. Bill flattened with curved nail at tip of upper jaw; lamellae inside
bill for filter-feeding; neck moderately to very long; body robust; wings rather short,
narrow and pointed (a few species flightless); tail short; legs short, robust; front toes
webbed, hind toe rudimentary; plumage variable in colour, smooth with dense
underdown; sexes usually alike in s African species, but often different in n hemisphere

species; mostly gregarious; swim well; dive or dabble for aquatic food (both plant and animal); some graze; moult all remiges simultaneously, so flightless for 4–8 weeks; nest solitarily on ground, in holes (in ground or tree), or in old nests of other birds; nest often lined with female's down; eggs 2–16, plain cream, white or greenish; chick downy, precocial; parental care variable, but usually by female only. Distribution worldwide; 146 species; 20 species in s Africa (one introduced; now probably extinct in the wild).

Ref. Delacour, J. 1954–1964. *The waterfowl of the world.* 4 vols. London: Country Life.
Geldenhuys, J.N. 1975. *Ostrich* 46:219–235.
Skead, D.M. & Dean, W.R.J. 1977. *Ostrich Suppl.* 12:49–64.

98 (87X)   Mute Swan   Plate 8
Swaan
Cygnus olor

[Höckerschwan]

Measurements: Length 130–160 cm; wingspan 208–238 cm; wing (12 ♂) 580–606–623, (10 ♀) 533–562–589; tail (6 ♂) 205–224–246, (10 ♀) 190–211–232; tarsus (12 ♂) 107–114–118, (10 ♀) 99–104–114; culmen from knob (12 ♂) 74–80,6–88, (13 ♀) 69–74,2–79. Weight (59 ♂) 9,2–11,8–14,3 kg, (35 ♀) 7,6–9,7–10,6 kg (maximum weight 22,5 kg).

Bare Parts: Iris brown; bill orange with black tip, cutting edge, base, nostrils and frontal knob; legs and feet black.

Identification: Size very large; all white; neck long and gracefully curved; bill black-and-orange. *Immature*: Dingy brown above, paler below; no frontal knob; bill greyish; attains white plumage after 2 years. *Chick*: Pale grey above, white below; bill black; legs and feet grey.

Voice: Usually silent; *hiss* in threat; rarely snorting *whrrk*.

Distribution: Introduced (probably escaped from captivity) to s Cape; formerly Gamtoos, Kromme, Bitou, Seekoei River mouths and Groenvlei, near Knysna. Original range C Europe and C Asia; introduced also to e Europe, N America, Australia and New Zealand.

Status: Feral, resident; probably extinct.

Habitat: Estuaries.

Habits: In pairs; flocks of up 60 birds when not breeding (January-February). Swims with bill pointing downward, and wings arched over back. Takes off with

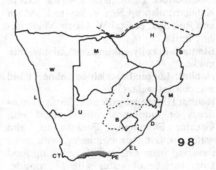

heavy pattering over water until airborne; flies strongly with outstretched neck; wings produce whining sound. Feeds by immersing head and neck in water up to 1 m deep; also grazes and dabbles in shallow water. Usually roosts on ground on island.

Food: Mainly aquatic plants; also frogs, tadpoles, molluscs, worms, insects.

Breeding: *Season*: September-October. *Nest*: Large mound of plant material on islet, shoreline, or in reeds; 1–2 m diameter, 60–80 cm thick; bowl on top up to 15 cm deep; solitary, male highly territorial. *Clutch*: 5–8 eggs (rarely up to 11). *Eggs*: Pale green with chalky coating, stained yellow to brown; measure (88) 113 × 74 (100–122 × 70–80); weigh (80) 294–354–385 g. *Incubation*: 35–36–41 days, by ♀; eggs covered with nest material when ♀ absent. *Fledging*: 120–150 days, young attended by both parents.

99 (100)

Whitefaced Duck
Nonnetjie-eend
Dendrocygna viduata

Plate 8

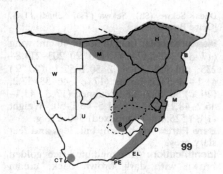

Ehilili (K), Dada, Sekwe (Sh), Sekwa (Ts), Sehudi (Tw), iVevenyane (Z), [Witwenente]

Measurements: Length about 48 cm; wing (29) 216–225,9–240; tail 52–60,8–71; tarsus 47–52–56; culmen 45–49,1–53. Weight (42 ♂) 611–739–980 g, (33 ♀) 600–738–933 g, (10 unsexed) 635–690,5–760 g.

Bare Parts: Iris brown; bill black with transverse blue-grey bar near tip; legs and feet bluish grey.

Identification: Size medium; mainly brown with longish dark neck and conspicuous white face (usually stained brownish in dirty water); no white in wing; feet extend beyond tail in flight; barring on flanks visible at close range. Female South African Shelduck also has white face, but body rich golden brown and has large white area on wing. *Immature*: Similar, but face light brown. *Chick*: Above olive brown; below pale creamy yellow; cream patches at base of wing and sides of rump; crown dark with pale eyebrow; pale line from under eye to back of head.

Voice: Both sexes have characteristic 3-syllabled whistle *swee-swee-sweeu* falling slightly in pitch, usually in flight; alarm note single *sweee*.

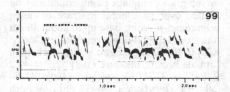

Distribution: Africa S of Sahara, Madagascar, Comoros, tropical S America; in s Africa mainly absent from dry W (vagrant to Orange River mouth, Port Nolloth, Fish River Canyon and Windhoek); spreading southwards.

Status: Common resident, mainly in subtropical areas; disperses to sw Cape in very wet years; nomadic, but with seasonal movements to warmer areas; numbers probably increasing.

Habitat: Larger inland waters; rivers, lakes, dams, pans, sewage ponds, flood-plains, usually with some aquatic vegetation.

Habits: Gregarious, sometimes in flocks of hundreds or thousands (up to 24 000 in Zambezi Valley); usually in pairs or family parties when breeding. On land stands upright on longish legs; often allopreens. Swims high in water with neck erect. Dabbles or up-ends for food; often dives, sometimes in dense rafts of up to 500 birds; often forages at night.

Food: Buds, seeds, grain, rhizomes, tubers; some insect larvae; incidentally also grass, algae, fruit, molluscs, crustaceans.

Breeding: *Season*: October to April in Natal, December to May in Transvaal, January in Orange Free State, September to May in Zimbabwe; mainly summer months in s Africa. *Nest*: Grass-lined hollow in tall grass or aquatic vegetation; surrounding plants pulled down to conceal nest; seldom any down. *Clutch*: (72) 4–7,5–16 eggs. *Eggs*: Creamy white; measure (123) 49,3 × 37,7 (44,4–57,6 × 35–40,1); weigh (100) 27,5–35–52,5 g. *Incubation*: 26–30 days by both sexes. *Fledging*: About 60 days; young attended by both parents.

Ref. Clark, A. 1974. *Ostrich* 45:1–4; 1976. *Ostrich* 47:59–64; 1978. *Ostrich* 49:31–39.
Rogers, K.H. 1980. *Studies on the ecology of Maputaland*. Grahamstown: Rhodes Univ. Press:69–77.
Siegfried, W.R. 1973. *Auk* 90:198–201.

100 (101)   Fulvous Duck   Plate 8
Fluiteend
Dendrocygna bicolor

Dada, Sekwe (Sh), Sekwa (Ts), Sehudi (Tw), [Gelbe Baumente]

Measurements: Length about 46 cm; wing (17 ♂) 202–217–242, (20 ♀) 203–214,8–235; tail (17 ♂) 44,2–50,1–57,1, (20 ♀) 41,1–44–53,3; tarsus (17 ♂) 46–53–57,2, (20 ♀) 50–53,6–58,9; culmen (17 ♂) 43,1–46,2–48,1, (20 ♀) 41,5–46,1–50. Weight (1 ♂) 525,4 g, (6 unsexed) 540–916 g.

Bare Parts: Iris brown; bill, legs and feet slaty grey.

Identification: Size medium; rich golden brown with dark brown back; cream stripes on flanks; no white on face; black stripe down back of neck; rump black; uppertail coverts obvious in flight as white V; wings all dark; feet extend beyond tail in flight. *Chick:* Pale grey above; white below; crown dark grey, eyebrow pale; bill dark grey; feet olive green.

Voice: Both sexes have harsh 2-syllabled wheezy whistle *tsu-ee*, usually in flight; alarm note resonant *zeee*.

Distribution: Africa S of Sahara, Madagascar, India to Burma, s N America to n tropical S America; in s Africa mainly absent from dry W; spreads into sw Cape in very wet years.

Status: Common in subtropical areas and Witwatersrand; uncommon elsewhere; resident, but with some local movements.

Habitat: Larger inland waters; pans, floodplains, sewage ponds, dams, preferably with surface vegetation.

Habits: Gregarious, sometimes flocking with Whitefaced Ducks. Spends much of day loafing in large groups on shoreline or water. Shy and wary. Feeds mainly by diving; also dabbles or up-ends in shallow marshy water.

Food: Seeds and fruits of aquatic plants; very little animal material.

Breeding: *Season:* July in sw Cape, December to March in Orange Free State, November to March in Natal, August to April in Transvaal, January to February and May to September in Zimbabwe; mainly summer months in S Africa, also in winter further N. *Nest:* Bowl of grass or rushes in marshy ground near water's edge, in tall grass or aquatic plants which may be pulled over to conceal it; trace of down sometimes present; base up to about 30 cm thick on tramped-down vegetation. *Clutch:* (22) 6–10–13 eggs. *Eggs:* White, darkening to pale brown; measure (107) 52,7 × 40,2 (48–55 × 37–41,9); weigh (100) 41,5–50–59 g. *Incubation:* 30–32 days by both sexes. *Fledging:* About 52–63 days; young attended by both parents.

Ref. Clark, A. 1976. *Ostrich* 47:59–64; 1978. *Ostrich* 49:31–39.
Siegfried, W.R. 1973. *Auk* 90:198–201.

101 (104)   Whitebacked Duck   Plate 8
Witrugeend
Thalassornis leuconotus

Letata (SS), Dada, Sekwe (Sh), Sekwa (Ts), Sehudi (Ts), [Weißrückenente]

Measurements: Length 38–43 cm; wing (11) 163–168,2–171; tail 43–48,3–53; tarsus 34–37,5–39; culmen 36–37,2–39. Weight (5) 558–677,6–790 g.

Bare Parts: Iris dark brown; bill slaty black, speckled green and yellow, much of lower jaw and cutting edge of upper jaw dull yellow; legs and feet grey to brown.

Identification: Size medium to smallish; generally mottled brown; conspicuous white patch near base of bill; in flight back shows white, feet extend beyond tail; swims low in water with hump-backed appearance; wings all dark. *Chick*: Top of head blackish; back olive-buff; lower half of head and neck tawny olive; chest pale pinkish ochre; belly blackish grey with pale lateral stripe.

Voice: Rather silent; quiet musical 2-syllabled whistle *curwee curwee*; at nest soft trilling flutelike whistle.

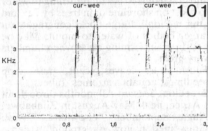

Distribution: Most of Africa S of Sahara, Madagascar; in s Africa mainly absent from dry W.

Status: Uncommon resident; somewhat nomadic.

Habitat: Quiet inland waters, usually clear and deep, with emergent marginal vegetation and floating rafts of waterlilies and other aquatic plants.

Habits: Usually in pairs or small groups of up to 10 birds. Highly aquatic; spends most of its time on water; quiet, unobtrusive and often hard to see as it floats low among water plants. Flies reluctantly, taking off with long pattering run; once air-

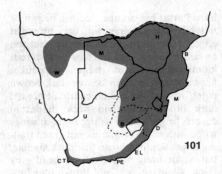

101

borne flies strongly with large feet trailing behind. Dives well, foraging under water.

Food: Waterlily seeds, other parts of water plants, aquatic animals; young feed largely on insect (chironomid) larvae and seeds.

Breeding: *Season*: All months in Transvaal and Zimbabwe, peak March-June; all months in Natal, peak December-March; November to September in Botswana, peak April. *Nest*: Pile of plant material about 30 cm diameter, 25 cm thick; bowl 15–20 cm diameter, up to 10 cm deep; surrounding plants pulled over for concealment; solitary or loosely colonial (neighbouring nests only a few metres apart) in grass tuft, floating island, reedbed, close to water; no down. *Clutch*: (74) 4–6,8–9 eggs (usually 6). *Eggs*: Rich yellowish to chocolate brown; measure (85) 61,9 × 48,7 (55–68,8 × 44,9–51,7); weigh (31) 77–81–94 g. *Incubation*: 29–33 days by both sexes. *Fledging*: About 55 days; fully grown about 90 days.

Ref. Clark, A. 1979. *Ostrich* 50:59–60.
Kear, J. 1967. *Ostrich* 38:227–229.
Rogers, K.H. 1980. Chapter 7 in *Studies on the ecology of Maputaland*. Grahamstown: Rhodes University.
Wintle, C.C. 1981. *Honeyguide* 105:13–20.

---

102 (89)   **Egyptian Goose**   **Plate 8**
                           Kolgans
                        Alopochen aegyptiacus

Lefaloa (NS, SS), Dada, Sekwe, Hanzi (Sh), Sekwa, Sekwamhala (Ts), Legôu (Tw), Ilowe (X) iLongwe (Z), [Nilgans]

Measurements: Length 63–73 cm; wing (11 ♂) 378–396,1–407, (12 ♀) 340–369,8– 390; tail (11 ♂) 116–131,6–150, (11 ♀) 111–127,4–145; tarsus (12 ♂) 74,5– 82,4–95, (15 ♀) 67–76,7–85; culmen (12 ♂) 45–49,1–55, (15 ♀) 43–49–54. Weight (41 ♂) mean 2348 g, (98 ♀) mean 1872 g.

Bare Parts: Iris orange, reddish brown or red; bill pink margined with dark brown at edges, base and around nostrils, maroon on cutting edge; legs and feet pinkish red.
Identification: Size large; gooselike; brown above, greyish below; dark brown patch around eye and on centre of breast; dark brown collar on neck; undertail coverts bright yellow ochre; in flight wings white with black primaries and green trailing edge. South African Shelduck similar, but whole body bright rufous, head grey (face white in ♀), no brown patches. *Immature*: Duller than adult; eyepatch small; usually no breast patch. *Chick*: Above brown; eyebrow, wingspots and underparts whitish.
Voice: Hoarse *haaa* by ♀, hissing by ♂ (like airbrakes of bus); rapid honking *ka-ka-ka-ka-ka* just before take-off, ♀ more resonant than ♂. Calls with neck stretched forwards.

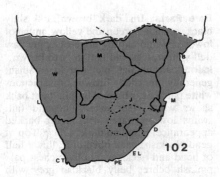

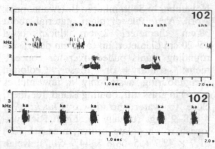

Distribution: Africa S of Sahara, Egypt, Middle East, se Europe; in s Africa widespread, but absent from Namib Desert.
Status: Very common resident; regular moult migrations occur; nomadic in drier areas.
Habitat: Most inland waters: rivers, dams, floodplains, pans, marshes; also estuaries, coastal lakes, cultivated fields.
Habits: Highly gregarious when not breeding; otherwise mainly in pairs.

Swims high in water; spends much of day loafing on shoreline or sandbank. Flies early morning and evening to farmlands and grasslands to graze, returning to water to roost on shoreline or in trees by day and after nightfall. Large flocks congregate on larger bodies of water to moult. May be pest in grain farming areas when numbers very great.
Food: Grass, leaves, seeds, grain, crop seedlings; aquatic rhizomes, tubers.
Breeding: *Season*: All months throughout s Africa; peak May-August in Zimbabwe, August-September elsewhere. *Nest*: Grass-lined hollow on ground in dense vegetation; also holes in cliffs, caves, trees, buildings, up to 60 m above ground; often uses old nests of crows, raptors and Hamerkops in tree or on cliff; nest hollow lined thickly with grey down, used for covering eggs when parent absent; near water or over 1 km away. *Clutch*: (654) 5–6,7–11 eggs. *Eggs*: Cream coloured; measure (277) 68,4 × 51,3 (57,9–75,8 × 46–57,7); weigh (100) 78,5–98–110 g. *Incubation*: 28–30 days by ♀ only. *Fledging*: About 55 days; young attended by both parents; newly hatched young leave nest after about 6 hours by jumping in response to call of ♀.

Ref. Maclean, G.L. 1988. *Pelea* 7:30–39.
Milstein, P. le S. 1975. *Bokmakierie* 27:49–51.

103 (90) South African Shelduck Plate 8
Kopereend (Bergeend)
Tadorna cana

Lefaloa (SS), [Graukopf-Rostgans]

Measurements: Length 61–64 cm; wing (5 ♂) 345–355,8–365, (5 ♀) 315–326,2– 335; tail (5 ♂) 120–125,9–136, (5 ♀) 120–124,5–129; tarsus (5 ♂) 56–58–60, (5 ♀) 52–56–58; culmen (5 ♂) 42–45,2–

48, (5 ♀) 39,5–42,4–45. Weight (1 171 ♂) 910–1357–2200 g, (1 092 ♀) 700–1115–1835 g.

Bare Parts: Iris dark brown; bill, legs and feet black.

Identification: Size large; bright chestnut (brighter when breeding, with fine vermiculations in ♂); head and upper neck all grey in ♂, grey with white face in ♀; in flight wings white with black primaries and green trailing edge; breast of nonbreeding ♂ dull buff, becoming bright creamy yellow before breeding. Egyptian Goose similar but with dark brown patches around eye, neck and on centre of breast; greyish (not chestnut) below. Whitefaced Duck dark brown with all-dark wings; stands upright on land. *Chick:* Dusky brown above; wingbar, patches on back, and underparts white.

Voice: ♀ has loud resonant *honk*; call of ♂ is hoarser, more wheezy *hoogh*; hissing threat note by both sexes.

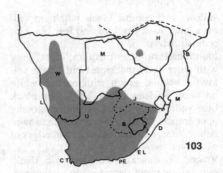

Distribution: Southern Africa S of 19 °S, mainly in highveld and semi-arid regions; most birds in Orange Free State; vagrant to Sandwich Harbour and Namib-Naukluft Park, Namibia.

Status: Common; migrates to larger bodies of water for wing moult in November-December, then disperses again; some birds probably resident.

Habitat: Most inland waters, especially temporary brackish pans; also dams, coastal lakes, rivers, estuaries, vleis; rarely at sea off W coast; breeds only near freshwater bodies, mostly farm dams.

Habits: Highly gregarious when not breed-ing; otherwise in pairs. Moulting flocks may number thousands of birds; males flightless for about 32 days, females for 26 days. Feeds by dabbling in shallows or on mud-flats, or by grazing in grasslands; feeds on dry land mainly around sunrise and sunset. Spends much of day loafing on shoreline. Courtship by ♀ (not by ♂ as in most ducks), hence white head; ♂ selects mate.

Food: In winter mainly crop seeds and algae; in summer also insects and crustaceans.

Breeding: *Season:* May to September (90% of eggs laid July-August). *Nest:* Scrape thickly lined with light grey down; in underground chamber at end of mammal burrow (Aardvark, Springhare, Porcupine) up to 9 m from entrance; up to 1,7 km from water. *Clutch:* Up to 15 eggs (probably usually about 8–10). *Eggs:* Cream coloured; measure (12) 68,5 × 50,3 (64,5–72 × 48–52); weigh (50) 74,5–89–99,5 g. *Incubation:* About 30 days by ♀ only; ♂ guards nest site during incubation. *Fledging:* About 56 days; flying at 70 days; young attended by both parents.

Ref. Geldenhuys, J.N. 1980. *S. Afr. J. Wildl. Res.* 10:94–111; 1981. *Ostrich* 52:129–134.

104 (96)   **Yellowbilled Duck**   **Plate 9**
Geelbekeend
Anas undulata

Siwoyo (K), Letata (SS), Dada, Sekwe (Sh), Sekwa (Ts), Sehudi (Tw), Idada (X), iDada (Z), [Gelbschnabelente]

Measurements: Length 51–63 cm; wing (10 ♂) 251–260,6–271, (5 ♀) 235–242,7–249; tail (100 ♂) 90–100–109, (100 ♀) 86–97–108; tarsus (100 ♂) 39–45–51, (100 ♀) 39–43–48; culmen (100 ♂) 46–52–56, (100 ♀) 44–49–54. Weight (7 839 ♂) 533–965–1310 g, (6 080 ♀) 600–823–1123 g, (42 unsexed) 660–1007,7–1220 g.

Bare Parts: Iris reddish brown; bill bright

85

yellow with central black patch on culmen, and black tip; legs and feet black or reddish brown.

Identification: Size medium; dark grey with paler scaly markings; bill bright yellow; speculum green with narrow white borders. African Black Duck has black bill, yellow legs and feet; more blotchy appearance. *Chick*: Above greyish brown; below, face, patches on back, and edges of wings yellow.

Voice: ♀ quacks like domestic duck; descending rapid decrescendo *quagagagagagag*; ♂ usually silent, but sometimes has soft hoarse *hwee*.

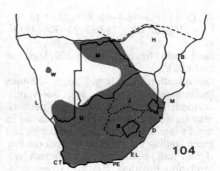

104

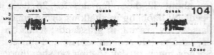

Distribution: Throughout s Africa except parts of dry W, through C and E Africa to Ethiopia.

Status: Very common; commonest duck in agricultural areas of most of s Africa; resident with local movements.

Habitat: Dams, pans, marshes, floodplains, pools, sewage works, slow rivers; more rarely estuaries.

Habits: Gregarious when not breeding; otherwise in pairs or family groups. Flight fast and high; often calls in flight, especially on take-off. Feeds by dabbling in shallows or up-ending in deeper water (rarely dives); grazes on land; gleans grain

from fields after reaping. Loafs for much of day on shoreline in groups.

Food: Plant material; seeds, stems, tubers and leaves of water plants, grain, sunflower seeds, grass; also insects and their larvae.

Breeding: *Season*: All months; mainly September to April in Transvaal, July to January in e Cape, March, April and October in Zimbabwe. *Nest*: Grass-lined hollow in bunch of grass, reeds, matted tree roots, or other vegetation, usually within 20 m of water; 18–21 cm diameter, up to 11 cm deep; thickly lined with down, dark brown with pale centre; built by ♀. *Clutch*: (40) 4–7,7–12 eggs. *Eggs*: Creamy to yellowish buff; measure (268) 54,7 × 41,5 (51–60,6 × 37–46); weigh (64) 44–54,9–62 g. *Incubation*: 28–30 days by ♀ only. *Fledging*: About 68 days, attended by ♀ only; dependent on ♀ for up to 6 weeks after flying.

Ref. Rowan, M.K. 1963. *Ostrich Suppl.* 5:1–56.

105 (95)   African Black Duck   Plate 9
Swarteend
Anas sparsa

Letata, Letata-la-noka (SS), Idada (X), iDada (Z), [Schwarzente]

Measurements: Length (22 ♂) 510–570, (20 ♀) 480–530; wing (8 ♂) 245–261–275, (5 ♀) 232–241–248; tail (28 ♂) 100–115,3–125, (23 ♀) 90–95–114; tarsus (28 ♂) 38–42,3–45, (23 ♀) 29–39,6–42; culmen (28 ♂) 40,5–46,7–51, (23 ♀) 40,5–43,8–46. Weight (4 ♀) 760–1077 g.

Bare Parts: Iris dark brown; bill slate-grey, culmen and tip black, base of lower jaw pink; legs and feet yellow-orange.

Identification: Size medium; body shape elongate; black with conspicuous white blotches on back; bill blackish; legs and feet yellow; tail relatively long; speculum green or blue-green, narrowly edged white. Yellowbilled Duck has bright yellow bill, dark legs and scaly appearance. *Immature*: Barred white on belly. *Chick*:

Above black; below buffy white; black collar on chest; face patterned with black and yellow lines; bill black; legs dusky, yellowish in front.

Voice: ♀ has loud *quack*, sometimes persistent; ♂ has barely audible wheezy whistled *peep* or *peep-peep-peep-peep*.

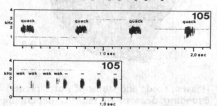

Distribution: Southern Africa except Kalahari sandveld and most of arid W, N to Nigeria and Sudan; vagrant to Daan Viljoen Game Park and Namib-Naukluft Park, Namibia.

Status: Uncommon localized resident.

Habitat: Rivers, usually shallow with stony bottoms and wooded banks; also wooded mountain streams; more rarely dams and sewage ponds.

Habits: Highly territorial year-round, occurring in pairs (less often in groups of up to 4 birds) on rivers by day; may roost on larger dams at night in large loose flocks made up of smaller groups of up to 6 birds. Shy and easily overlooked when hidden by waterside vegetation, sitting quite still until too closely approached. Jumps up from water into low fast flight, 1–2 m above water, following course of river. Feeds by dabbling, head-dipping or

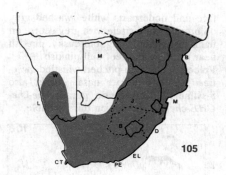

up-ending, usually within territory of less than 1 km long.

Food: Mainly chironomid larvae and pupae gleaned from under stones in rapids; also other aquatic insects, plant material, grain, fruit, seeds, acorns, small fish and crabs.

Breeding: *Season*: July to December in sw Cape, March to January in Zimbabwe; probably most months in s Africa. *Nest*: Hollow in driftwood, or in matted grass on ground above flood level, usually near water; thickly lined with dark down. *Clutch*: (46) 4–5,9–8 eggs. *Eggs*: Pale cream or buffy yellow; measure (39) 62,7 × 45   (56,4–65,5 × 40,2–49,1); weigh (5) 66,5–68–71 g. *Incubation*: 28–32 days by ♀ only. *Fledging*: About 86 days; young attended by ♀ only.

Ref. Frost, P.G.H., Ball, I.J., Siegfried, W.R. & McKinney, F. 1979. *Ostrich* 50:220–233.
McKinney, D.F., Siegfried, W.R., Ball, I.J. & Frost, P.G.H. 1978. *Z. Tierpsychol.* 48:349–400.
Siegfried, W.R., Frost, P.G.H., Ball, I.J. & McKinney, D.F. 1977. *Ostrich* 48:5–16.

106 (98)   **Cape Teal**   **Plate 9**
                              Teeleend
                             Anas capensis

Siwoyo (K), Sehudi (Tw), iDada (Z), [Kapente]

Measurements: Length about 46 cm; wingspan 78–82 cm; wing (52) 168–193,8–206; tail 53–64,3–74; tarsus 32–37–40; culmen 36–39,6–44. Weight (31 ♂) 352–419–502 g, (25 ♀) 316–380–451 g.

Bare Parts: Iris light hazel, scarlet to

orange; bill rose pink, bluish white at tip, edged black laterally and around nostrils; legs and feet dull yellow, webs dusky.

Identification: Size smallish; very pale grey, almost whitish; bill pink, somewhat upturned; speculum mainly white with metallic green rectangle in centre (diagnostic in flight). *Chick*: Above ash grey;

face and underparts white, washed grey on breast; white circle with grey centre on flank just behind wing; bill dusky, pinkish near tip; legs and feet dull pinkish.

Voice: ♂ has high-pitched whistled *swee-tseeu*; ♀ has deeper nasal *querk*; also 5-syllabled decrescendo phrase *che-che-CHE-che-che*, accent on third syllable.

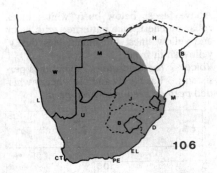

106

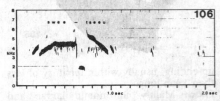

Distribution: Throughout s Africa northward to Angola, E Africa, Ethiopia, Sudan, Chad and s Libya.

Status: Common in drier w regions; uncommon in Natal; rare in s Mozambique; resident, but nomadic, especially in W.

Habitat: Mostly shallow brackish inland waters; pans, vleis, sewage ponds, lagoons, estuaries, tidal flats.

Habits: Usually in pairs or small groups; less often in larger flocks of a few hundred birds. Takes off in shallow climb, circles and lands nearby. Forages by head-dipping or up-ending; less often by dabbling in shallow water; also dives for food.

Food: 99% animal material (insects, crustaceans, tadpoles); 1% plant material

(leaves, seeds and stems of water plants).

Breeding: *Season*: All months, depending on rainfall and food supply; mainly November to July in w Transvaal, August in Zimbabwe, March to September in Karoo, April to September in Natal, January to October in C Transvaal, January to August in Namibia. *Nest*: Grass-lined hollow well concealed in dense vegetation near water, often on island; 10–15 cm diameter; thickly lined with pale grey down with which eggs covered when ♀ leaves nest. *Clutch*: (356) 5–8,2–11 eggs. *Eggs*: Pale to deep cream; measure (798) 49,6 × 36,1 (43–56,8 × 31–45,5); weigh (46) 25,5–30,5–39 g. *Incubation*: 26–30 days by ♀ only. *Fledging*: 6–8 weeks; young attended by ♀; ♂ often accompanies family.

Ref. Winterbottom, J.M. 1974. *Ostrich* 45:110–132.

107 (99)   Hottentot Teal   Plate 9
Gevlekte Eend
Anas hottentota

Siwoyo (K), Letata (SS), Dada, Sekwe (Sh), Sekwa (Ts), Sehudi (Tw), iDada (Z), [Hottentottenente, Pünktchenente]

Measurements: Length 33–36 cm; wing (37) 147–151,4–157; tail 55–59,5–66; tarsus 22–26,1–29; culmen 32–36,8–42. Weight (1 ♂) 288 g, (1 ♀) 294 g, (3 unsexed) 216–243–283 g.

Bare Parts: Iris blackish brown; bill light blue-grey, blackish on culmen and tip, darker on lower jaw; legs and feet blue-grey.

Identification: Size small; head dark above, light below; bill blue; breast and

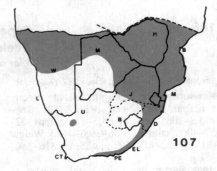

107

back spotted; speculum green with broad white trailing edge. Redbilled Teal head pattern similar, but larger size, buffier (less yellowish) plumage and red bill diagnostic. *Chick*: Above brown; underparts, eyebrow, 3 stripes on sides of body yellow; bill grey with pink tip.

Voice: Resonant *tze-tze-tze* alarm and take-off call; ticking notes by courting ♂.

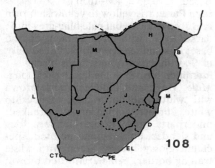

Distribution: E to s Africa; also n Nigeria and Madagascar; in s Africa absent from dry W; along S coast as far W as Plettenberg Bay.

Status: Uncommon to locally common resident; usually sedentary, but undergoes some movements.

Habitat: Quiet inland waters with emergent and surface vegetation; vleis, marshes, sewage ponds, floodplains.

Habits: Quiet and unobtrusive, in pairs or small groups. Often sits quietly on water near overhanging plants, or loafs on shoreline. Takes off reluctantly; flies with body at slightly upward angle and head characteristically raised until fully airborne. Forages by filter-feeding with bill or head immersed and by up-ending.

Food: Seeds, fruits, crustaceans, insects, detritus in mud; in Natal about 95% molluscs in winter.

Breeding: *Season*: All months; peak January to April in Transvaal, April, May and August in Zimbabwe. *Nest*: Hollow in clump of emergent vegetation near or in water, concealed by pulling down surrounding stems and leaves; thickly lined with black down; 15–18 cm diameter. *Clutch*: (9) 6–7,2–9 eggs. *Eggs*: Cream or yellowish buff; measure (45) 44 × 32,4 (41–48 × 31–35,5); weigh (7) 26–28–30 g. *Incubation*: 24 days in captivity; 25–27 days in wild; by ♀ only. *Fledging*: 60–65 days; young usually attended by ♀ only; rarely also by ♂.

Ref. Clark, A. 1971. *Ostrich* 42:131–136.

108 (97)   Redbilled Teal   Plate 9
Rooibekeend
Anas erythrorhyncha

Siwoyo (K), Letata, Sefuli (SS), Dada, Sekwe (Sh), Sekwa (Ts), Sehudi (Tw), iDada (Z), [Rotschnabelente]

Measurements: Length 43–48 cm; wing (6 ♂) 218,5–223,8–228, (6 ♀) 207–211,5–216,5; tail (6 ♂) 81,5–85,1–90, (6 ♀) 74–76,3–80; tarsus (6 ♂) 35–36–37, (6 ♀) 30–33,4–37; culmen (6 ♂) 42–44,3–46,5, (6 ♀) 41,5–43,5–47. Weight (1 366 ♂) 345–591–954 g, (1 177 ♀) 338–544–955 g.

Bare Parts: Iris hazel; bill carmine pink with brown culmen and tip; legs and feet slate-grey.

Identification: Size medium; head dark above, pale below; bill bright pink; upperparts brown; underparts buff, mottled or barred; speculum light creamy beige. Hottentot Teal has similar head pattern, but bill blue, size much smaller, plumage more yellowish. *Immature*: Spotted below; rectrices notched. *Chick*: Above brown with yellow patches on sides of

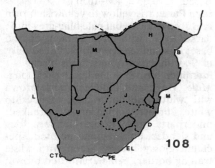

back; below buffy yellow with dark ear coverts.

Voice: ♂ has soft swizzling *whizzzt*; ♀ guttural *krraak*.

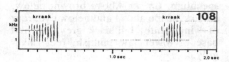

Distribution: Ethiopia and Sudan to throughout s Africa; also Madagascar.
Status: Common over most of range; less common in E; resident but nomadic, ranging as far N as Zambia and Angola.
Habitat: Most inland waters; dams, pans, sewage ponds, floodplains.
Habits: In pairs when breeding; otherwise in flocks of hundreds or thousands of birds, especially towards end of dry season (winter). Feeds by immersing head or bill, or by up-ending; grazes aquatic plants.
Food: About 24% water plants (seeds, fruits, stems, rhizomes); about 76%

aquatic invertebrates (molluscs, crustaceans, insects, worms, arachnids).
Breeding: *Season*: November to May in Transvaal, June to November in sw Cape, all months (except June) in Zimbabwe. *Nest*: Grass-lined hollow in dense waterside vegetation; 15–18 cm diameter; lined with down, brown with pale centre. *Clutch*: (12) 5–10–12 eggs. *Eggs*: Buff or cream, measure (124) 50 × 37,5 (44,2–54,6 × 32–41,7), weigh (20) 36–38–40. *Incubation*: 25–28 days by ♀ only. *Fledging*: About 8 weeks; young usually attended by ♀ only, rarely also by ♂.

---

109 (99X)   **Pintail**   **Plate 9**
Pylsterteend
Anas acuta

[Spießente]

Measurements: Length 51–66 cm (to 76 cm including long rectrices); wingspan 80–95 cm; wing (20 ♂) 267–275–282, (12 ♀) 254–260–267; tail (8 ♂) 172–179–189, (7 ♀) 95–104–113; tarsus (40 ♂) 40–42,6–45, (30 ♀) 39–41–43; culmen (55 ♂) 47–50,9–56, (31 ♀) 44–46,7–51. Weight ♂ 550–1300 g, ♀ 400–1050 g.
Bare Parts: Iris yellow to yellowish brown in ♂, brown in ♀; bill pale blue-grey in ♂, darker in ♀, with black culmen, tip and base; legs and feet grey in ♂, tinged olive in ♀, with darker joints, webs black.
Identification: Size medium; neck long. *Male*: Head and hindneck dark brown with white line down sides of neck to white breast; upperparts streaked; underparts grey; neck relatively long and slender; tail long and pointed; speculum glossy bronzy green with white trailing border. *Female*: Mottled brown; tail shorter, but more pointed than in most *Anas* species; speculum browner; head looks plain greyish; generally paler than all s African *Anas* species except Cape Teal and Garganey; Garganey ♀ smaller with pale eyebrow and green speculum. *Chick*: Above brown; below, cheeks, stripe above and below eye, rear of wing white; bill dark grey, tip and base of lower jaw pinkish; feet olive-grey.

Voice: ♂ has drawn-out, rising and falling *geeee*; ♀ quacks loudly and also makes various rattles and chuckles.

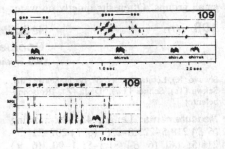

Distribution: Breeds Holarctic region; Palaearctic breeders migrate to N, W and E Africa (except Sahara); rare straggler to Zimbabwe and Transvaal.
Status: Nonbreeding Palaearctic migrant to Africa, breeding recently in N Africa; straggler to Transvaal.
Habitat: Dams and other inland waters.
Habits: Gregarious when not breeding, otherwise in pairs. Flocks roost on water or shoreline. Feeds in water 10–30 cm deep by submerging head, or up-ending; rarely dives, or digs for food on dry land.
Food: Seeds, tubers and rhizomes of water plants, grass, algae, grain, insects, molluscs, crustaceans and amphibians.
Breeding: Extralimital.

110 (97X)   **Garganey**   **Plate 9**
Somereend
Anas querquedula

[Knäkente]

Measurements: Length 37–41 cm; wing-span 60–63 cm; wing (34 ♂) 190–198–211, (16 ♀) 184–189–196; tail (28 ♂) 60–66,1–70, (17 ♀) 58–62,6–69; tarsus (38 ♂) 29–31,3–33, (20 ♀) 28–30,1–32; culmen (70 ♂) 38–39,6–43, (34 ♀) 36–38–40. Weight (22 ♂) 320–348,5–440 g, (14 ♀) 290–337,7–420 g.

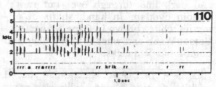

Bare Parts: Iris umber brown; bill black or grey, tinged greenish in ♀; legs and feet dull grey, tinged olive in ♀.

Identification: Size small. *Breeding ♂*: Head dark brown with conspicuous white eyebrow curving back down sides of nape; breast brown; belly white; flanks pale grey (finely vermiculated); back dark, streaked; wing blue-grey above and below with dark border below, dark primaries, green speculum and white trailing edge above. *Female and eclipse ♂*: Speckled brown; eyebrow pale; green speculum and blue-grey forewing diagnostic and separate them from other white-browed s African ducks (♀ Southern Pochard and ♀ Maccoa Duck).

Voice: ♂ calls *krik* or *krik-et*; also strident *rrar-rrar-rrar* like stick drawn across railings; ♀ has harsh *gack; krrrt* alarm note.

Distribution: Palaearctic region, migrating to Africa, s Asia and New Guinea; in s Africa to Zimbabwe, Botswana and Transvaal.

Status: Rare nonbreeding Palaearctic migrant November to April; occurrence in s Africa coincides with droughts in Sahel; also reported unseasonally in Botswana and Zimbabwe in May.

Habitat: Sheltered shallow inland waters with emergent aquatic vegetation; also sewage ponds.

Habits: Usually in small flocks; larger numbers gather during migration. Feeds with head submerged, or by up-ending. Flight fast and agile; takes off easily from water with quick wingbeats.

Food: Insects, crustaceans, molluscs, worms, frog spawn, tadpoles, fish; also aquatic plant material (buds, leaves, roots, tubers and seeds).

Breeding: Extralimital.

---

111 (93)   **Northern Shoveller** (European Shoveller)   **Plate 9**
Europese Slopeend
Anas clypeata

[Löffelente]

Measurements: Length 44–52 cm; wing-span 70–84 cm; wing (27 ♂) 239–244–249, (18 ♀) 222–230–237; tail (26 ♂) 76–81,7–86, (15 ♀) 72–75,8–80; tarsus (48 ♂) 35–37,2–40, (39 ♀) 35–36–38; culmen (61 ♂) 62–66,1–72, (47 ♀) 56–60,7–64. Weight ♂ 300–1000 g, ♀ 300–800 g.

Bare Parts: Iris yellow or orange in ♂,

brown to yellow in ♀; bill leaden black with paler spots on lower jaw in ♂, olive grey to brown with yellowish sides and orange lower jaw in ♀; legs and feet orange-red.

Identification: Size medium. *Breeding ♂*: Head metallic green; breast white; belly chestnut; bill broad, black; forewing light blue separated from green speculum by narrow white band; primaries dark.

91

Female and eclipse ♂: Mottled brown; broad bill and wing pattern (described above) diagnostic; separable from Cape Shoveller at close range by pale eyebrow and dark line through eye, but ranges seldom overlap. In hand, shafts of primaries white (brown in Cape Shoveller).
Voice: Weak and wheezy in ♂, *whey* and quiet *took*; ♀ quacks.

Distribution: Holarctic; migrates to s hemisphere; recorded Cape, Transvaal, Namibia, Botswana, Zimbabwe.
Status: Very rare irregular nonbreeding straggler to s Africa, July to February; normal nonbreeding range only as far S as Tanzania.
Habitat: Shallow inland waters with muddy bottoms.
Habits: Occurs singly or in small groups. Filter-feeds by sweeping surface of water with side-to-side movments of bill, sometimes also with head immersed, and by up-ending; rarely dives.
Food: Mainly aquatic invertebrates; also some plant material, tadpoles and frog eggs.
Breeding: Extralimital.

---

112 (94)   **Cape Shoveller**   Plate 9
                      Kaapse Slopeend
                       Anas smithii

Siwoyo (K), Letata (SS), Dada, Sekwe (Sh), Sekwa (Ts), Sehudi (Tw), iDada (Z), [Kaplöffelente]

Measurements: Length about 53 cm; wing (42 ♂) 222–238,6–253, (32 ♀) 208–227,4–248; tail (42 ♂) 63–76,4–98, (32 ♀) 61–71,7–83; tarsus (42 ♂) 34–40,4–43, (32 ♀) 33–37,8–41; culmen (42 ♂) 54,5–57,7–65, (32 ♀) 52–56,8–64; width of bill (4 ♂) 25,5–27,8–30, (3 ♀) 24–26–27,5. Weight, w Transvaal (27 ♂) 522–603–680 g, (24 ♀) 492–572–665 g; sw Cape (32 ♂) 548–688,3–830 g, (26 ♀) 476–597,8–691 g.
Bare Parts: Iris light yellow in ♂, dark brown in ♀; bill black in ♂, horn in ♀; legs and feet yellow (tinged orange when breeding) in ♂, brownish olive with dusky webs in ♀.
Identification: Size medium; dull greyish brown with contrasting pale grey head and broad black bill in ♂; head of ♀ less contrasting, bill dark grey; in flight blue forewing separated from green speculum by white bar diagnostic (though similar to eclipse and ♀ Northern Shoveller); long

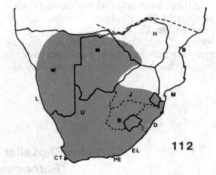

112

heavy dark bill distinguishes Cape Shoveller from other dull brown ducks; uniformly coloured head distinguishes it from Northern Shoveller which has eye stripes (ranges unlikely to overlap). Wings make characteristic whistling sound, especially during courtship. *Chick*: Above olive brown; below, lines on back near wing and tail, sides of face pale yellowish; bill black with reddish tip.
Voice: ♂ has loud *rrarr* and rapid *rararararra*; ♀ has descending series of

quacks, starting with one long note, followed by up to 14 short notes; also more simple series of quacks like Yellowbilled Duck.

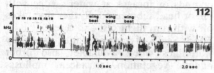

Distribution: Southern Africa and se Angola; absent from e Zimbabwe and all except extreme s Mozambique.
Status: Common sw Cape and highveld; uncommon elsewhere; resident but with some dispersive movements, e.g. from sw Cape to Ondangua, Namibia (1 680 km).
Habitat: Mainly shallow temporary pans and vleis; also sewage ponds, estuaries, lagoons.
Habits: In pairs or small groups; rarely in flocks of up to 600 birds; seldom with other species; if so, in discrete conspecific groups. Takes off steeply with fast flight and wings well set back on body; wings make distinctive rapid whooping sound,

exaggerated when male makes jump-flight in front of female during courtship. Loafs on shorelines or islands; feeds day or night, surface-dabbling with bill immersed and almost horizontal while swimming quickly forwards with forepart of body low in water; may immerse head but rarely up-ends.
Food: Planktonic invertebrates, molluscs, insects, crustaceans, tadpoles; very rarely water plants and seeds.
Breeding: *Season*: All months, peak August to October. *Nest*: Grass-lined hollow in ground in dense vegetation, usually within 20 m of water; ringed with down (dark grey-brown with light centre) with which ♀ covers eggs when absent. *Clutch*: 5–9,4–12 eggs. *Eggs*: Cream, sometimes with green tinge; measure (350) 53,4 × 38,7 (48,4–59,5 × 36,6–41,1); weigh (85) 34–38–43,5 g. *Incubation*: 27–28 days by ♀ only. *Fledging*: about 8 weeks; young attended by ♀ only.

Ref. Siegfried, W.R. 1965. *Ostrich* 36:155–198.

---

113 (102)   **Southern Pochard** (Redeyed Pochard)   **Plate 9**
Bruineend
Netta erythrophthalma

Letata (SS), Dada, Sekwe (Sh), Xinyankakeni (Ts), Sehudi (Tw), [Rotaugenente]

Measurements: Length about 51 cm; wing (38 ♂) 202–217,1–225, (38 ♀) 201–210–221; tail (38 ♂) 52–58,7–66, (38 ♀) 52–56,6–68; tarsus (38 ♂) 35–39,3–44, (38 ♀) 35–39,3–44; culmen (38 ♂) 40–44–48, (38 ♀) 38–43,3–49. Weight (577 ♂) 592–799–1010 g, (463 ♀) 484–763–1018 g.
Bare Parts: Iris vermilion (red-brown in ♀); bill pale blue-grey with black tip (dark slate grey with blackish tip in ♀); legs and feet dull grey with black webs.
Identification: Size medium. *Male*: Glossy brown, paler below, blackish on head and neck, eye red, bill bluish. *Female*: Paler brown with white crescent behind eye to

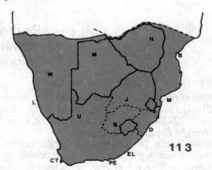

sides of neck, and white patch around base of bill; white bar along upperwing in flight in both sexes; high forehead and thin neck characteristic in flight. ♀ and eclipse

♂ Maccoa Duck have horizontal white lines on face (not vertical crescent); no white bar on upperwing; different body shape. *Immature*: Like adult ♀, but paler. *Chick*: Mostly pale yellow; brown markings on back and thighs.

Voice: Usually silent; ♂ calls soft purring *prerr...prerr...* in flight; also ratchetlike *whreeoooorrr*; ♀ has nasal *krrrrow* in flight, falling in pitch; threat is growling *quarrrk*.

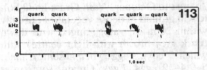

Distribution: Southern Africa to Ethiopia; also tropical S America.

Status: Common to very common; undergoes seasonal movements from S Africa to Zimbabwe, Mozambique and possibly further N to Malawi; largely absent from parts of S Africa March to August; some birds resident.

Habitat: Deeper inland waters; flooded vleis, dams, sewage ponds; prefers clear water, with or without emergent vegetation.

Habits: Gregarious in flocks of up to several hundreds or thousands of birds. Highly aquatic, seldom seen on land. Feeds day or night, usually by diving; also up-ends or forages at water's edge with bill or head submerged. Rather shy; takes off with run; flight fast and direct.

Food: Seeds of aquatic plants, especially waterlilies when available; also other aquatic vegetation, crustacea, molluscs and insects.

Breeding: *Season*: July to December in sw Cape, February to June in Orange Free State, November to May in Transvaal, almost all months in Zimbabwe (not recorded August, October or November). *Nest*: Bowl of grass, sedge and waterplants, 18 cm diameter, 8 cm deep, sometimes sparsely lined with grey down; in dense waterside vegetation or in reeds over water; built by ♀. *Clutch*: (23) 6–8,9–15 eggs. *Eggs*: Smooth, slightly glossy, pale brown or light fawn darkening to brownish yellow; measure (87) 56,5 × 43,8 (53,2–62,4 × 41–45,9); weigh about 59 g. *Incubation*: 26–28 days by ♀ only. *Fledging*: 56–65 days; young attended by ♀; ♂ sometimes accompanies ♀ and brood.

Ref. Middlemiss, E. 1958. *Ostrich Suppl.* 2:1–34.

---

114 (92)   **Pygmy Goose**   **Plate 8**
Dwerggans
Nettapus auritus

Kamugcara (K), [Afrikanische Zwerggans]

Measurements: Length 31–36 cm; wing (18) 152–157,4–165; tail 52–64,9–73; tarsus 22–24,3–26; culmen 23–24,9–26. Weight (3) 260–277–290 g.

Bare Parts: Iris brown; bill bright yellow with black tip (duller in ♀, greenish at sides, buff on lower jaw, no black on tip); legs and feet grey.

Identification: Small size; dark green above, rusty orange below; head green and white with large green patches on sides of neck in ♂; bill of ♂ bright yellow;

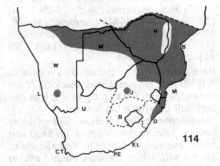

114

94

speculum pure white. *Immature*: Like adult ♀. *Chick*: Above black; below white; streak through eye, spots below eye and on cheeks black; bill and legs black; tail long, stiff.

Voice: ♂ has soft whistled *choo-choo-pee-wee*; also repeated 2-syllabled whistled *tsu-tswi*. ♀ has weak *quack*; also rather sharp twittering whistle.

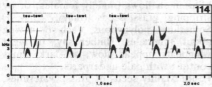

Distribution: Africa S of Sahara; Madagascar; in s Africa mainly subtropical in E and N.

Status: Uncommon to rare; resident but nomadic. Rare (RDB).

Habitat: Clear tropical to subtropical waters with emergent and floating vegetation; floodplains, pans, pools, quieter river backwaters; also estuaries.

Habits: Usually in pairs or small groups; less often in flocks of up to 500 birds. Highly aquatic, but may perch on logs and trees. Easily overlooked when sitting quietly in water among emergent plants or overhanging branches. Flies short distance when disturbed, usually fast and low over water. Forages by diving or at surface of water.

Food: Mainly ripe seeds of waterlilies *Nymphaea*; also other water plants, insects and fish fry.

Breeding: *Season*: November to May in Natal, January to February in Transvaal, October to May in Zimbabwe. *Nest*: Usually in hole in tree (up to 20 m above ground), termite mound, cliff, Hamerkop nest or nest box; usually lined with white down. *Clutch*: 6–12 eggs (usually 9). *Eggs*: Ivory white; measure (39) 43,5 × 32,8 (40,8–46,5 × 30,6–35,8); weigh about 27 g. *Incubation*: 23–24 days, probably by ♀ only. *Fledging*: 56–63 days; young leave nest by jumping.

115 (91)   Knobbilled Duck   Plate 8
Knobbeleend
Sarkidiornis melanotos

Nkuva (K), Pura (Sh), Xikuvikuvi (Ts), Legóu, Sefalabogôgô (Tw), [Höckerente]

Measurements: Length ♂ 70–79 cm, ♀ 55–64 cm; wing (10 ♂) 347–360–380, (6 ♀) 279–286,6–300; tail (10 ♂) 117–136–150, (6 ♀) 100–109–120; tarsus (10 ♂) 56–63,9–67,5, (6 ♀) 42–48,2–50; culmen (10 ♂, from behind knob to tip) 57–62–66, (6 ♀) 42,5–46,6–52. Weight (17 ♂) 1300–1915–2610 g, (4 ♀) 1025–1407–2325 g.

Bare Parts: Iris brown; bill (and knob in ♂) black to slaty; legs and feet lead grey to greyish brown.

Identification: Size fairly large. *Male*: Much larger than ♀; back and wings black with purplish iridescence; below white;

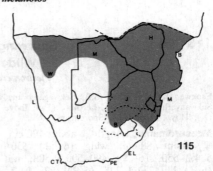

undertail yellow; head yellowish when breeding, otherwise white, speckled black; underwing black; large laterally

95

compressed black knob on top of bill (reduced when not breeding). *Female*: Head and undertail white; otherwise similar to ♂, but smaller; lacks knob on bill. *Immature*: More speckled on sides of chest and flanks. *Chick*: Above brown; face and underparts yellow ochre; dark patch above thigh; bill slate-grey with yellow tip; legs and feet grey with yellowish webs.

Voice: Usually silent; in display ♂ makes weak hissing and wheezing sounds; harsh *guk-guk* threat notes; ♀ calls *chuk-chuk* and soft melodious *karoo-oo* to ♂; short *krruk krruk krruk*.

Distribution: Africa S of Sahara, Madagascar, tropical Asia, tropical S America; in s Africa largely absent from S and W.
Status: Locally common with some long-distance seasonal movements from Zimbabwe to Mozambique and N to Chad (3 879 km) and Sudan; movements elsewhere not mapped; straggler to highveld and more arid parts.

Habitat: Floodplains, pans, shallow marshes with clear water and emergent and surface vegetation.
Habits: Highly gregarious when not breeding, sometimes in flocks of separate sexes; otherwise in pairs of groups of about 5 birds. Loafs for much of day on shorelines and islets; often perches in trees; feeds early and later hours by dabbling in shallows (mainly females) or by stripping grass seeds (mainly males). Sometimes polygynous, each ♂ having about 3 females. Rather shy. In flight wingbeats appear slow; all-dark wings contrast with pale underparts.
Food: Mainly seeds of grass, waterlilies, grain crops; also locusts and aquatic insect larvae and plant propagules.
Breeding: *Season*: November to March (mostly November-December) in S Africa, September to April in Zimbabwe. *Nest*: In hole in tree near water or up to 1 km away; usually lined with white down. *Clutch*: 6–20 eggs (usually about 8). *Eggs*: Glossy yellowish; measure (32) 58,6 × 43 (53–71 × 38,6–46,5); weigh about 46–56 g. *Incubation*: 28–30 days by ♀ only. *Fledging*: About 9–10 weeks; young jump from nest hole; attended by ♀ only.

Ref. Siegfried, W.R. 1978. *Living Bird* 17:85–104.

---

116 (88)   **Spurwinged Goose**   **Plate 8**
                           Wildemakou
                        Plectropterus gambensis

Esokwe (K), Letsikhui (SS), Sekwagongwana, Sekwanyarhi (Ts), Legôu, Letsikwe (Tw), Ihoye (X), iHoye, iHophe (Z), [Sporengans]

Measurements: Length ♂ about 100 cm, ♀ about 88 cm; wing (6 ♂) 530–534,3–550, (6 ♀) 490–500,6–508; tail (6 ♂) 230–232,4–235, (6 ♀) 182–194,7–207; tarsus (4 ♂) 105–112,5–120, (4 ♀) 90,5–100–107,5; culmen (4♂, from nostrils) 59–61–63, (4 ♀) 52–55,5–59; spur on wing ♂ 20, ♀ 16–18. Weight ♂ 5,4–10 kg, ♀ 4,1–5,4 kg.
Bare Parts: Iris dark brown; bill and bare facial skin deep pinkish red, tip white; legs and feet pinkish red.
Identification: Size very large; boldly pied; mainly black with variable amount of white on face and belly; forehead, bill and legs red; ♂ larger than ♀, bare facial skin extends to behind eye (con-

fined to base of bill and forecheek in ♀).
Immature: Feathered on face; body
feathers browner; white areas less extensive. *Chick*: Above and through eye
yellowish brown; two pale yellow bands
on sides of body at base of wing and at
sides of rump; face and underparts buffy
yellow.
Voice: Quiet, high-pitched, rather wheezy
cherwit in flight and when alarmed; ♀
usually silent, but has high-pitched, rapid
chi-chi-chi-chi when alarmed.

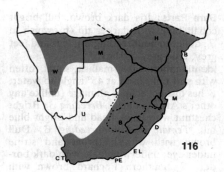

116

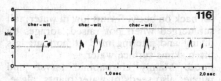

116

Distribution: Africa S of Sahara; in s
Africa mainly absent from dry W; vagrant
to Maltahöhe, Namibia.
Status: Common to very common; resident, or with seasonal movements of up to
a few hundred km, not yet mapped.
Habitat: Mainly larger inland waters;
floodplains, pans, dams, sewage ponds.
Habits: Highly gregarious when not
breeding, especially during moult; flocks
number up to 2 000 birds. Usually in pairs
on smaller bodies of water when breeding.
Shy and wary. Rests on shorelines and
sandbanks; forages in flooded grasslands,
pastures, cultivated fields in early morning, evening or at night. Flocks fly in
staggered lines, sometimes in V-
formation; wings make swishing sound in
flight. When disturbed, flies to nearest
water, settling far from shore.

Food: Grass shoots and seed, grain,
lucerne, tubers (like potatoes), fruit,
aquatic plants. Sometimes damages crops
if numbers large enough.
Breeding: *Season*: September to April in
Orange Free State, Transvaal and Natal;
August to October in Cape Province;
December to May in Zimbabwe; generally
breeds during rains. *Nest*: Grass-lined hollow on ground, 40–45 cm diameter,
8–9 cm deep; usually in dense grass near
water; also in reed clumps, on termite
mounds, on top of Sociable Weaver,
Hamerkop or African Fish Eagle n~sts;
very rarely on cliffs, in tree holes or in
Aardvark burrows; some white down
present. *Clutch*: (64) 6–7,8–23 eggs (usually 6–12; rarely up to 27; clutches of more
than 14 probably laid by more than 1 ♀).
Eggs: Glossy ivory to pale brown; measure (93) 75,2 × 55,4 (68–86,2 × 49,2–
59,2); weigh about 127 g. *Incubation*:
32–36 days by ♀ only. *Fledging*: About 12
weeks; 75% of broods attended by ♀
only, rest by both parents.

Ref. Clark, A. 1980. *Ostrich* 51:179–182.

117 (103)　　　**Maccoa Duck**　　　**Plate 9**
Bloubekeend (Makou-eend)
Oxyura maccoa

Letata (SS), [Maccoa-Ente]

Measurements: Length about 46 cm;
wing (6 ♂) 165–170–165, (6 ♀) 155–
160–165; tail (6 ♂) 72–73,6–76, (6 ♀)
63,5–67,1–71; tarsus (6 ♂) 34–34,4–36,
(6 ♀) 31–31,9–33,5; culmen (6 ♂) 38,5–
40,7–42, (6 ♀) 35,5–37,4–40. Weight
(1 ♂) 820 g, (3 ♀) 516–554–580 g.

Bare Parts: Iris dark brown; bill bright cobalt blue with darker tip (brownish in ♀, duller in nonbreeding ♂); legs and feet grey, blue-grey or slaty.

Identification: Size smallish; squat, often with stiff tail raised at 45° angle to water; ♂ has distinct eclipse plumage (unlike any other s African duck). *Breeding* ♂: Bright chestnut with black head and bright blue bill. *Female and nonbreeding* ♂: Dull brown with whitish throat and stripe under eye; underwing pale with dark border. ♀ Southern Pochard brown with white vertical crescent behind eye; size larger. *Immature*: Like adult ♀. *Chick*: Brownish black except for white belly; side of head white bordered below by brown stripe from bill to nape.

Voice: Usually silent; in display ♂ has loud guttural *prrrr* and soft whistle; both sexes give quiet grunts in threat.

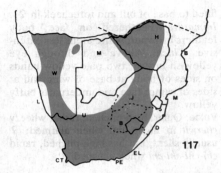

Distribution: Southern Africa and E Africa to Ethiopia; in s Africa absent from C Kalahari and extreme dry W, but recorded Walvis Bay and Bushmanland, Namibia.

Status: Uncommon resident; sometimes locally common; local movements in Transvaal and probably elsewhere.

Habitat: Deep, highly eutrophic inland waters with emergent vegetation; small dams, lakes, sewage ponds.

Habits: Usually in pairs or small groups. Highly aquatic, diving rather than flying when disturbed; can almost completely submerge body when alarmed. Patters along water on take-off; flies strongly when fully airborne, wings appearing well set back on body. Swims low in water; tail submerged when not raised; forages by diving and filtering mud at bottom; less often skims surface water.

Food: Mainly chironomid larvae and pupae; also seeds of water plants, algae, roots, insects, crustaceans, molluscs.

Breeding: Male polygamous. *Season*: All months except May in S Africa; January to March, June and August in Zimbabwe; probably all months throughout s Africa. *Nest*: Built by ♀ only of reed, sedge and rush leaves forming bowl about 20 cm diameter, 8 cm deep; placed in trampled reeds and rushes, sometimes floating; also uses nests of coots and grebes as base; usually no down; ♀ sometimes lays in nests of Redknobbed Coot, Southern Pochard or other Maccoa Duck, where eggs incubated by host; young survive with little or no parental care. *Clutch*: 4–12 eggs (usually 5–6). *Eggs*: Dull blueish white, matt and pitted; measure (119) 67,3 × 50,4 (63–72,8 × 45,8–52,7); weigh (5) 73–88–98 g. *Incubation*: 25–27 days by ♀ only. *Fledging*: About 8 weeks; young attended by ♀ only.

Ref. Clark, A. 1964. *Ostrich* 35:264–276.
Siegfried, W.R. 1976. *Auk* 93:560–570.
Siegfried, W.R., Burger, A.E. & Caldwell, P.J. 1976. *Condor* 78:512–517.

9. Order FALCONIFORMES (Five families; four in s Africa)

Mostly large to very large, a few small to medium. Bill strong and sharply hooked; eyes relatively large, often red, yellow or orange; feet strong with stout, sharply curved claws, mostly adapted to grasping live prey; wings well developed, mostly broad and long for soaring, some short for manoeuvrability, others pointed for speed; carnivorous, catching prey actively, or scavenging on carrion; nest normally a stick platform in a tree or on a cliff; eggs 1–4, white or yellowish, plain or marked; chick downy, altricial. Distribution worldwide.

Ref. Brown, L. & Amadon, D. 1968. *Eagles, hawks and falcons of the world*. 2 vols. London: Country Life.
Davidson, I. 1978. *Bokmakierie* 30:43–48.
Grossman, M.L. & Hamlet, J. 1965. *Birds of prey of the world*. London: Cassell.
Steyn, P. 1982. *Birds of prey of southern Africa*. Cape Town: David Philip.
Tarboton, W.R. & Allan, D.G. 1984. The status and conservation of birds of prey in the Transvaal. *Tvl Mus. Monogr.* 3. Pretoria: Transvaal Museum.
Weick, F. & Brown, L.H. 1980. *Birds of prey of the world*. London: Collins.

IDENTIFICATION OF SOUTHERN AFRICAN RAPTORS

Because many of the raptors are among the most difficult birds to identify a key (page liv) has been provided to assist in identifying the Accipitridae (except the vultures) and the Falconidae. This key attempts to key out every major plumage variation in southern African raptors, whether based on species, sex, form, age or distribution, sometimes even allowing for the more important individual variations. Since most raptors are first seen from below, belly coloration has been selected as a starting point, mainly between paler colours and darker colours. If in doubt, try first one then the other. In the case of some variable species, the same correct answer may be obtained starting from either choice.

Several raptors, especially the goshawks and sparrowhawks (genus *Accipiter*) have a plain grey or brown chest and a barred belly. The barring may be white-and-grey, grey-and-brown or white-and-brown. In the key a decision needs sometimes to be made as to whether the chest and belly colours are the same or contrasting. The rule for purposes of this key is: if the belly is barred with equal widths of two colours, the lighter colour is the background colour, but if the barring is of unequal widths, the colour of the broader bars is the background colour (Fig. 8, page liii).

The length of the raptor key, and therefore the time it may take to key out a bird makes it imperative to write down as many features as possible before the bird flies away, and before you attempt to use the key. One should work on the principle that one is unlikely to get a second look at any bird.

9:1. Family 20 SAGITTARIIDAE—SECRETARYBIRD

Very large. Typical falconiform bill; neck moderately long; legs long, tibiotarsus feathered; toes short, webbed at base, claws strong; wings long and broad; plumage mostly pale grey with black remiges, tail pattern and tibiotarsus; face bare, orange; crest of long drooping feathers; central rectrices very long. Distribution Africa S of Sahara (but fossils found in Oligocene and Miocene of France); one species. (Name "Secretarybird" said to derive from crest's resemblance to old-time secretary's quill pens, but is also said to be Anglicized corruption of Arabic *saqr-et-tair*, meaning hunter-bird.)

118 (105)   **Secretarybird**   **Plates 10 & 11**
Sekretarisvoël
Sagittarius serpentarius

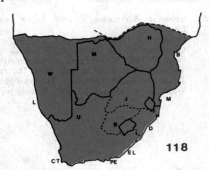

Mukongo (K), Thlame (NS), 'Mamolangoane, Koto-li-peli, Lekheloha (SS), Hwata, Munditi (Sh), Mampfana (Ts), Tlhamê, Mmamolangwane (Tw), Ingxangxosi (X), iNtungunono (Z), [Sekretär]

Measurements: Length about 125–150 cm; wing (5 ♂) 630–670, (5 ♀) 610–660; tail (5 ♂) 670–854, (5 ♀) 570–705; tarsus (2) 295–320; culmen (10) 45–54. Weight (8) 3405–3941–4270 g.

Bare Parts: Iris hazel (grey in young); bill and cere pale blue-grey; facial skin orange or yellow; legs and feet greyish pink.

Identification: Size very large; about 1,3 m tall, with long legs and tail; body mainly pale grey; belly, tibial feathering, remiges, subterminal tail bands, rump and crest feathers black; crest long and drooping at nape (erectile); face bright orange. *Immature*: Face yellow; central rectrices shorter than in adult. *Chick*: Downy white, becoming pale grey; legs and face yellow.

Voice: Usually silent; croaking *korr-orr-orr*; mewing calls at roost.

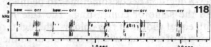

Distribution: Africa S of Sahara, except forested areas; throughout s Africa.

Status: Mostly uncommon to fairly common resident; sedentary or nomadic; very conspicuous, so not easily overlooked.

Habitat: Semidesert, grassland, savanna, open woodland, farmland, mountain slopes.

Habits: Usually in pairs; sometimes in groups of 3–4 birds; at waterholes in arid areas in groups of up to 50. Strides slowly across veld with measured tread of about 120 paces/minute at about 2,5–3 km/h; catches all prey on ground, usually with bill, sometimes by stamping on it with feet, as when killing rodent or snake; stamping also used to disturb prey; wings sometimes held open when killing or pursuing prey; prey swallowed whole. Flies seldom but well, soaring like vulture on broad wings until very high; takes off usually with run, but can do so from standing position; when landing runs several paces with open wings. Performs soaring and undulating courtship flights. Roosts on top of bush or tree (often nesting tree) at night, usually pair together.

Food: Insects, small amphibians, lizards, snakes, rodents, young hares, birds' young and eggs; insects (87%, very largely grasshoppers), rodents (4%), lizards (3%), birds (2%) most important items; snakes and other items form less than 1% of food.

Breeding: *Season*: All months in s Africa, peak August-December. *Nest*: Flat platform of sticks, 1–1,5 m diameter at first, up to 2,5 m after prolonged use; about 50 cm thick; central depression lined with grass, dung and regurgitated pellets; on top of dense thorny bush or tree, height (20) 2–4–9 m, mainly in indigenous *Acacia* species, but commonly also in exotic pines; rarely on ground. *Clutch*: (154) 1–1,9–3 eggs (usually 2), laid up to 8 days apart. *Eggs*: Elongate ovals, white or pale bluish green, chalky, sometimes bloodstained; measure (162) 77,5 × 56,4 (68–92 × 51,2–65); weigh about 130 g. *Incubation*: 40–46 days, mostly by ♀; fed by ♂ on nest. *Nestling*: 65–106 days (usually 75–85 days); fed by both parents.

9:2. Family 21 ACCIPITRIDAE—EAGLES, HAWKS, BUZZARDS, KITES, VULTURES, ETC. (RAPTORS OR DIURNAL BIRDS OF PREY)

Mostly large to very large, some medium; female usually larger than male. Bill short and strongly hooked, somewhat longer in vultures; neck short, but moderately long in vultures; legs strong, short to moderately long, feathered to toes in eagles; toes and claws strong and used for grasping, except in vultures; plumage variable; sexes alike or different; cere and orbital skin naked, often brightly coloured; whole head and neck in vultures covered only with short, sparse, downy feathers; strong fliers, larger species tend to soar, especially vultures; usually solitary (vultures and some kites gregarious). Distribution worldwide; about 210 species; 52 species in s Africa.

Ref. (Vultures): Attwell, R.I.G. 1963. *Ostrich* 34: 235–247.
 Mundy, P.J. 1982. *The comparative biology of southern African vultures.* Johannesburg: Vulture Study Group.
 (Eagles): Boshoff, A.F. & Vernon, C.J. 1980. *Ann. Cape Prov. Mus. (Nat. Hist.)* 13:107–132.
 Steyn, P. 1973. *Eagle days.* Johannesburg: Purnell.
 (General): Mendelsohn, J. M., Kemp, A. C., Biggs, H. C., Biggs, R. & Brown, C. J. 1989. *Ostrich* 60:35–42.

119 (150)   Bearded Vulture (Lammergeier)   Plates 10 & 11
Baardaasvoël (Lammergier)
Gypaetus barbatus

Ntsu, Ntsu-kobokobo (SS), uKhozilwentshebe (Z), [Bartgeier]

Measurements: Length about 110 cm; wingspan 263–282 cm; wing (16 ♂) 720–752,5–787, (33 ♀) 715–766,8–810; tail (26 ♂) 427–443–460, (26 ♀) 437–453–469; tarsus 88–101; culmen 49. Weight (6) 5200–5760–6250 g.

Bare Parts: Iris pale yellow ringed broadly with opaque red; bill brownish horn; legs and feet slaty grey.

Identification: Size very large; wings long, pointed; tail longish, wedge-shaped; above dark with whitish head; below rusty, yellowish or whitish (highly variable); black face mask and bristly beard diagnostic. *Immature*: Above dark brown; head blackish brown, whitening with age from face backwards; underparts brown, mottled white, becoming more uniform rufous brown with age; iris brown; eyering brown, becoming red with age; feet yellowish white; adult plumage acquired in about 7 years. *Chick*: Downy greyish brown; iris brown; legs and feet grey.

Voice: Usually silent; in display has wheezy *feeee* or shrill *cheek-acheek-acheek-acheek*, weak and querulous.

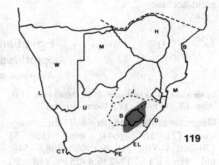

Distribution: Mountainous regions of s Europe and Asia, ne and s Africa; isolated population in s Africa confined to highlands of Lesotho, Natal, Orange Free State and ne Cape; formerly also Karoo, s and sw Cape, and e Transvaal; sporadically in highlands of Zimbabwe on Mozambique border.

Status: Rare and endangered; only about 200 pairs in s Africa; resident. Rare (RDB).

Habitat: Drakensberg massif and foothills down to about 2 000 m.

Habits: Solitary, but small groups may gather at carrion, often in company with vultures and other birds of prey. Glides fast with wings held slightly below horizontal; seldom flaps; searches ground below for food, usually within home range of up to 40 km diameter, but immatures range further afield. Roosts on cliffs, often on or near nest site. Rusty colour of underparts from iron oxide obtained by dusting or bathing (method not determined); otherwise underparts white; colour paler after rain.

Food: Carrion and bones, mainly of sheep and goats (70% bone and marrow, 25% meat, 5% skin); bones dropped on flat rocky ossuaries to break them into pieces small enough to swallow (up to 25 cm long); ossuaries used for many years; glides in with bone in feet, releasing it from height of 50–150 m, hitting rock with great accuracy.

Breeding: *Season*: May to July. *Nest*: Large flat platform of sticks up to 2 m diameter; central depression lined with grass, hair, skin, bones, rags and dung; most material brought by ♂; all building done by ♀; in cave or ledge under overhang high on sheer cliff face. *Clutch*: (26) 1–1,8–2 eggs, laid at interval of 3–5 days. *Eggs*: Broad oval; white at first, becoming stained buff, cream or brownish, usually mottled and clouded with purplish grey and brownish yellow, and sparsely dotted with dark brown; measure (7) 85,5 × 64,8 (82,8–90,4 × 62,3–67,8); weigh 224–235 g. *Incubation*: 55–58 days by both sexes, mostly by ♀; ♀ incubates at night. *Nestling*: 124–128 days, fed by both parents; only one chick survives, second dying of starvation; dependent on parents about 60 days after first flight; may accompany parents until following breeding attempt, after which forms groups with 1–2 other immature Bearded Vultures.

Ref. Brown, C.J. 1990. *Ostrich* 61: 24–49.

120 (111)   Egyptian Vulture   Plates 10 & 11
Egiptiese Aasvoël
Neophron percnopterus

Lehonyane, Tlakatsooana (SS), Mpenyani (Ts), Inkqo (X), uPhalane (Z), [Schmutzgeier]

Measurements: Length 64–71 cm; wingspan (2) 1642–1644; wing (15 ♂) 470–501,3–536, (16 ♀) 460–508,6–545; tail (15 ♂) 232–239,4–251, (16 ♀) 240–252,4–267; tarsus (15 ♂) 78,5–81,6–84,5, (16 ♀) 78–83,1–87; culmen (14) 31–34. Weight 1584–2200 g.

Bare Parts: Iris red; bill pale brown, tip black; facial skin orange-yellow; legs and feet yellow to pinkish.

Identification: Size large; mainly white or buffy with bare yellow face and black remiges, including all primaries; tail white, wedge-shaped. Palmnut Vulture has primaries mainly white with black tips; tail black, square. *Immature*: All dark brown; face bluish or buffy; iris brown; legs and feet greyish or buffy; head appears untidily crested (immature Hooded Vulture downy blackish brown

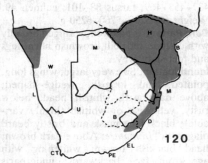

on head and neck; immature Palmnut Vulture has heavier bill; immature Gymnogene longer-legged, smaller-billed, slender shape). *Chick*: Downy white.

Voice: Usually silent; rarely heard mews, hisses, grunts and whistles.

Distribution: Arid parts of N to E Africa, s Europe, Middle East and C Asia; sw Angola to n Namibia; e Cape and Transkei.

Status: Very rare; sight record Transkei as recently as 1983; possibly also Zimbabwe (1971) and Natal (1975); several sight records n Namibia (1973–1979), Limpopo River (1974), Levubu River (1979) and Phalaborwa (1977); most recent sighting January 1989, Langjan Nature Reserve, northern Transvaal; reports of nesting in Hluhluwe Game Reserve (May 1971) probably erroneous. Endangered (RDB).

Habitat: Semidesert and open plains; abattoirs, refuse dumps, seashore; absent from woodland.

Habits: Scavenger; usually solitary, rarely in small groups. Roosts gregariously at night on cliff or tree. Subordinate to other vultures at kill, eating scraps. Slim and graceful in flight, soaring to great heights.

Hurls stones held in bill onto Ostrich eggs to break them, then eats contents.

Food: Carrion, birds' eggs, offal, refuse, insects.

Breeding: *Season*: December (one record only, but no recent records in s Africa). *Nest*: Large platform of sticks, thickly lined with skin, hair and dung; outside diameter 70–150 cm, bowl 30–40 cm diameter; on cliff. *Clutch*: 1–3 eggs (usually 2). *Eggs*: Dull white, blotched and mottled with reddish brown and grey; measure (200, Europe) 66 × 50,4 (58,2–76,4 × 43–56,1); weigh 81,5–97 g. *Incubation*: About 42 days by both sexes. *Nestling*: 77 days, fed by both parents.

Ref. Mundy, P.J. 1978. *Biol. Conserv.* 14:307–315.

---

121 (110)   Hooded Vulture   Plates 10 & 11
Monnikaasvoël
Necrosyrtes monachus

Ekuvi (K), Gora (Sh), Khoti, Mavalanga (Ts), [Kappengeier]

Measurements: Length 65–75 cm; wingspan 170–176 cm; wing (19) 503–522,7–550; tail (15) 235–262–285; tarsus (15) 78–83–90; culmen (15) 29,5–31–33,5. Weight (39) 1,8–2,1–2,6 kg.

Bare Parts: Iris dark brown; bill greenish black, brown at tip; facial skin pink, flushing red or purplish when excited; legs and feet bluish grey.

Identification: Size medium; body all dark brown; head pink with sparse white down; bill slender; in flight wings broad; tail shortish, almost square (immature Egyptian Vulture has wedge-shaped tail; neck and hindcrown feathered; face bluish). *Immature*: Head paler pink with blackish brown down (immature Egyptian Vulture has feathered neck). *Chick*: Downy greyish brown, paler on head and neck.

Voice: Usually silent; thin squealing calls at nest and carcasses.

Distribution: Africa S of Sahara, except forested and arid regions; in s Africa absent from S and W.

Status: Common resident. Rare (RDB).

Habitat: Open woodland and savanna; not

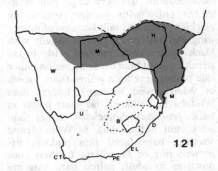

commensal with man in s Africa as in N Africa.

Habits: Solitary. Cannot compete with larger vultures at carcass; picks up scraps that bigger birds leave or drop. Not only scavenges, but feeds also on insects dug from dung and soil with slim bill. Roosts in trees at night. Soars less than larger vultures, so can start to forage earlier in morning; may be attracted to food by watching other vultures.

Food: Carrion, offal, insects, bones.

Breeding: *Season*: June to October in Zimbabwe, June to August in Transvaal. *Nest*: Platform of sticks 60–100 cm diameter, lined with leaves, grass, hair, skin, rags; mostly in *Diospyros* and *Xanthocercis* trees in main fork below canopy. *Clutch*: 1 egg. *Eggs*: White, plain or blotched with brown and grey, mainly at larger end; measure (12) 75,3 × 56,3 (68,7–78,6 × 54–58,8); weigh 94–130 g. *Incubation*: 46–51 days by both sexes. *Nestling*: 89–130 days (usually 95–120); fed by both sexes; young dependent on parents about 4 months after first flight.

122 (106)   Cape Vulture   Plates 10 & 11
Kransaasvoël
Gyps coprotheres

Ekuvi (K), Lenong, Letlaka (SS), Khoti, Mavalanga (Ts), Lenông, Diswaane (Tw), Ixhalanga (X), iNqe (Z), [Kapgeier]

Measurements: Length (9) 101–111–120 cm; wing (19) 650–713–760; tail (12) 280–314–350; tarsus (12) 105–115–122; culmen (4) 51–54,6–60. Weight (29) 7,3–8,6–10,9 kg.

Bare Parts: Iris pale straw; bill and cere black; bare facial skin bluish; legs and feet greyish black.

Identification: Size very large; pale whitish to buffy with strongly contrasting blackish wings and tail; last row of upperwing and underwing coverts usually with black spots; back mottled with broad streaks; paired blue bare patches on either side of crop; eye light yellow (dark brown in Whitebacked Vulture). Larger than Whitebacked Vulture; no white patch on back. *Immature*: Somewhat darker than adult, but not as dark as Whitebacked Vulture; bare facial skin pinkish; iris brown; ruff of lanceolate feathers, not down as in adult; paired bare magenta patches on either side of crop; first breeding at 4–6 years old. *Chick*: Dull downy white; iris black; bill and feet blackish.

Voice: Fairly vocal at nesting colonies and carcasses; grunts, squeals, cackles and hisses.

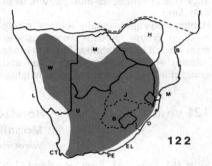

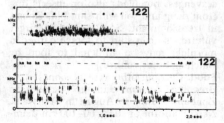

Distribution: Most of s Africa, except Mozambique.

Status: Locally common, but numbers declining; numbers have fluctuated in the past; rare in Namibia and n Botswana, common in s and w Zimbabwe; present decline probably result of reduced herds of game, improved stock-farming practices, indiscriminate use of poisons (mainly strychnine), electrocution on power lines, and reduced breeding success through juvenile mortality (mainly because of inadequate supply of bone fragments); formerly very common; probably mainly sedentary, but some birds disperse more widely; 1 bird from Transkei to Gonarezhou, Zimbabwe (1 230 km). Vulnerable (RDB).

Habitat: Mostly mountainous country, or open country with inselbergs and escarpments; less commonly in savanna or desert.

Habits: Highly gregarious at all times; roosts and nests on precipitous cliffs which are white from droppings. Soars out 2–3 hours after sunrise (rarely earlier) to forage over wide area, often well away from mountains; cruises at 26–69 km/h. Aggressive at carcasses.

Food: Carrion, bone fragments; grooves and serrations on tongue enable rapid feeding on soft tissues of carcass.

Breeding: *Season*: April to July. *Nest*: Sparse platform of sticks, brush and stems, lined with grass and leaves; sometimes hardly any nest; on cliff ledge. *Clutch*: 1 egg, very rarely 2. *Eggs*: White; measure (239) 91,7 × 68,3

(83,2–103 × 62,5–73,8), weigh (2) 220–259 g. *Incubation*: 55–58 days by both sexes. *Nestling*: 140 days, fed by both parents; dependent on parents for up to 221 days after leaving nest.

Ref. Boshoff, A.F. & Currie, M.H. 1981. *Ostrich* 52:1–8.

Boshoff, A.F. & Vernon, C.J. 1980. *Ostrich* 51:230–250.

Mundy, P., Ledger, J. & Friedman, R. 1980. *Bokmakierie* 32:2–8.

123 (107) Whitebacked Vulture Witrugaasvoël

Gyps africanus

Plates 10 & 11

Ekuvi (K), Gora (Sh), Lenông, Kopajammutla (Tw), [Weißrückengeier]

Measurements: Length 90–98 cm; wingspan 212–220–228 cm; wing (12) 550–615,1–640; tail 240–260,4–275; tarsus 86–95,7–118; culmen (10) 46–48–50. Weight (261) 4,4–5,4–6,6 kg.

Bare Parts: Iris dark brown; bill and cere black; bare skin of head dark grey; skin of lower neck blackish; legs and feet black.

Identification: Large size; body plumage generally brown, faintly streaky; iris dark; face blackish, neck pink; white lower back conspicuous when flying away; buffy white underwing contrasts with dark remiges. Cape Vulture has pale yellowish iris; no white on back; paler coloration overall; larger size. *Immature*: Darker than adult; lower back streaked brown and white; underparts streaked light and dark; underwing mottled brown and white. *Chick*: Greyish brown; iris dark brown; cere and legs greyish black.

Voice: Fairly vocal at carcass; hisses and squeals.

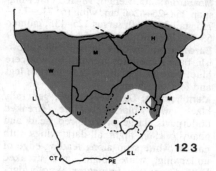

123

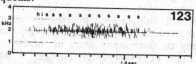

Distribution: Much of Africa S of Sahara, except forests and extreme desert; in s Africa absent from most of Cape Province (except n Cape), Natal, Lesotho and Orange Free State.

Status: Common; most abundant vulture in n parts of s Africa; mostly confined to game reserves; sedentary or locally nomadic.

Habitat: Savanna and bushveld.

Habits: Gregarious; less so when breeding. Roosts in trees at night, soaring out soon after sunrise to forage; gliding speed about 58–65 km/h, but can dive at up to 120 km/h; follows other vultures, crows, kites, Bateleur and hyaenas or lions to locate food. Often rests on ground by day; drinks and bathes regularly at waterholes. Aggressive at carcass, new arrivals bounding in with wings and neck outstretched; may loaf on ground near carcass for hours after feeding.

Food: Carrion and bone fragments; mainly softer parts of large game mammals.

Breeding: *Season*: May to June in S Africa, April to July in Zimbabwe. *Nest*: Platform of sticks 40–100 cm diameter, 15–90 cm deep; bowl 18–20 cm diameter, lined with grass and sometimes with green leaves; solitary or in small loose groups;

usually on very top of *Acacia* tree, 8–50 m above ground (usually 15–25 m); nest used several years in succession. *Clutch*: 1 egg. *Eggs*: White, rarely marked with reddish brown; measure (110) 88,2 × 66,4 (79,5–96,5 × 59,2–71,5); weigh about 214 g. *Incubation*: 56–58 days by both sexes. *Nestling*: 120–130 days, fed by both parents; dependent on parents for about 4 months after first flight.

Ref. Kemp, A.C. & Kemp, M.I. 1975. *Koedoe*: 18:51–68.

124 (108)   Lappetfaced Vulture   Plates 10 & 11
Swartaasvoël
Torgos tracheliotus

Ekuvi (K), Lenong le Leso (NS), Letlakapipi (SS), Gora (Sh), Nkotimpfumu, Mpfumo (Ts), Lenông, Bibing (Tw), Isilwangangubo (X), iNqe (Z), [Ohrengeier]

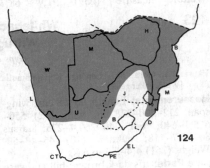

Measurements: Length 98–105 cm; wingspan 258–264–266 cm; wing (6) 715–733–755; tail 340–380; tarsus 125–135; culmen 68–71. Weight (23) 5,9–6,6–7,9 kg.

Bare Parts: Iris dark brown; bill yellowish, base sometimes greenish brown; cere blue; bare skin of head pink to red; legs and feet bluish grey.

Identification: Size very large; generally black with black-and-white streaked underparts, large pinkish red head and heavy bill; in flight all-dark wings with narrow white strip along leading edge of underwing, white thighs, and streaked belly diagnostic. *Immature*: Wholly dark brown; white feathering acquired gradually over 5–6 years; bill horn in 1st year, later yellow; head dull pinkish. *Chick*: Downy white, later grey; iris brown; cere whitish; legs and feet grey.

Voice: Usually silent, even at carcass; rarely heard shrill whistle.

Distribution: Much of Africa S of Sahara; parts of NW Africa, Arabia and Israel; in s Africa largely absent from S of Orange, Vaal and Tugela Rivers; mainly confined to game reserves.

Status: Uncommon, except in Namib and s Zimbabwe where common; resident; young may disperse up to 700 km from nest area (e.g. from Namib to Kalahari Gemsbok National Park). Vulnerable (RDB).

Habitat: Savanna to desert.

Habits: Solitary or in pairs; sometimes several birds at a carcass in company with other vulture species. Roosts in trees (usually pair together) at night; flies with difficulty in absence of thermals; soars out well after sunrise to forage over wide area.

Tears into tough carcasses by ripping with stout bill; rarely steals carrion from smaller vultures; dominant over all other species at carcass, feeding until satisfied and retiring to periphery of group. May loaf for hours near carcass after feeding.

Food: Carrion; can eat tougher material (skin, ligaments) than other vulture species; also kills small mammals down to size of hare; kills barbel *Clarias* and nestling flamingoes and eats flamingo eggs.

Breeding: *Season*: May to September in Namibia, April to July in Zimbabwe; mainly winter months throughout s Africa. *Nest*: Huge platform of sticks, up to 3 m diameter, 50–100 cm deep, lined with grass, hair and skin; on top of flat-topped tree or bush, 3–15 m above ground; solitary, but in loose groups in adjacent trees where trees scarce; nest may be used many years in succession. *Clutch*: 1 egg (very rarely 2). *Eggs*: White, spotted and blotched with brown and underlying grey; measure (56) 92,7 × 71,1 (85,6–102 × 66,9–78,6); weigh (8) 235–266–318 g. *Incubation*: 56 days by both sexes. *Nestling*: 125–130 days, fed by both parents; dependent on parents for up to 6 months after first flight.

125 (109)   Whiteheaded Vulture   Plates 10 & 11
Witkopaasvoël
Trigonoceps occipitalis

Ekuvi (K), Gora (Sh), Nkotimpenyana, Ridya-mangwa, Mawalangi (Ts), [Wollkopfgeier]

Measurements: Length 78–82 cm; wingspan 202–220 cm; wing (9) 610–626–670; tail 265–295; tarsus 95–110; culmen 48–54. Weight (22) 3,3–4–5,3 kg.

Bare Parts: Iris amber; bill red, tip black; cere bluish green; bare skin of head whitish to pink, blushing red; legs and feet pinkish to red.

Identification: Size medium; mainly black with white belly; secondaries white in ♀, dark grey in ♂, conspicuous both at rest and in flight; head whitish, triangular in shape; bill red with blue cere; in flight white line on underwing between coverts and remiges. *Immature:* Browner on head than adult, but triangular head, red bill and blue cere diagnostic; secondaries brown; line on underwing whitish. *Chick:* Downy white with black crop patch.

Voice: Usually silent; shrill chittering at carcass.

Distribution: Most of Africa S of Sahara, except forests and desert; in s Africa absent from S of about latitude 29 °S.

Status: Uncommon resident. Rare (RDB).

Habitat: Woodland to semidesert scrub.

Habits: Solitary or in pairs. Roosts in trees at night, solitarily or a pair together; flies out early to forage within restricted area. Usually arrives first at carcass, but cannot compete with larger vultures as they

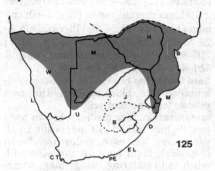

arrive; later pirates chunks from them.

Food: Carrion; also smaller prey down to size of hares (possibly kills for itself at times), flying termites, lizards, guineafowls; kills nestling flamingos and eats flamingo eggs.

Breeding: *Season:* May to August (peak in June, 40% of nests). *Nest:* Large platform of sticks, 1,5–1,7 m diameter, 50 cm thick; lined with grass; on top of Baobab, *Terminalia, Acacia* or other flat-topped tree; (52) 6–13–19 m above ground; solitary. *Clutch:* (19) 1 egg. *Eggs:* White, sometimes marked with brown and grey; measure (20) 86,6 × 66,6 (79–94,5 × 62,4–70,9); weigh (1) 181 g. *Incubation:* About 55 days by both sexes. *Nestling:* About 110 days.

Ref. Hustler, K. & Howells, W.W. 1988. *Ostrich* 59:21–24.

126 (128, 129)   Yellowbilled Kite and Black Kite   Plates 15 & 17
Geelbekwou en Swartwou
Milvus migrans

Siimbi (K), Mmankgodi (NS), 'Mankholi-kholi, Kholokholo (SS), Njerere (Sh), Mangatlu (Ts), Segôdi, Mmankgôdi (Tw), Untloyiya, Untloyila (X), uNhloyile, uKholwe (Z), [Schmarotzermilan und Schwarzer Milan]

Measurements: Yellowbilled Kite *M. m. parasitus:* Length about 55 cm; wingspan 133–140 cm; wing (47 ♂) 385–422–460, (43 ♀) 380–427–455; outer rectrices (14) 240–272; central rectrices 30–46 mm shorter; tarsus 41–60; culmen (46 ♂) 22–24,3–26, (41 ♀) 22–25–27. Weight (4 ♂) 567–637–760 g, (5 ♀) 617–696–750 g, (5 unsexed) 619–660–765 g. Black Kite

M. m. migrans: Length about 55 cm; wingspan 160–180 cm; wing (103 ♂) 410–444–500, (95 ♀) 430–461–505; outer rectrices (12) 230–260; central rectrices 20–30 mm shorter; tarsus (12) 53–60; culmen (13 ♂) 24–25,5–29, (18 ♀) 23–26,4–28. Weight (34 ♂) 450–754–850 g, (22 ♀) 750–857–1076 g. *M. m. lineatus*: wing ♂ 420–435–455, ♀ 430–456–480.

Bare Parts: Iris brown; bill yellow in Yellowbilled Kite, black in Black Kite; cere yellow; legs and feet yellow.

Identification: Size medium; brown body and slightly forked tail diagnostic in all subspecies; legs bare, yellow (feathered in eagles); flight buoyant and agile with much tail-ruddering; wings long, somewhat angled. Black Kite has head markedly paler than body (not so contrasty in Yellowbilled Kite); bill black at all ages; *M. m. lineatus* larger, duller brown with white inner secondaries and last row of secondary coverts. Yellowbilled Kite adult has yellow bill (black in immature). *Chick*: Above greyish white; below white.

Voice: Usually silent; quavering *quillll-errrr*, lower pitched on second trill; high pitched *keeee-kik-kik-kik*.

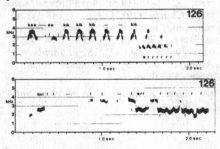

Distribution: Africa, Madagascar, Eurasia, Australia; Black Kite widespread in s Africa, but uncommon S of Orange River in Cape Province.

Status: Yellowbilled Kite *M. m. parasitus* breeding migrant from equatorial Africa, July to March; very common, mainly in E. Black Kite (2 subspecies): *M. m. migrans* nonbreeding Palaearctic migrant (from Europe, N Africa, Middle East), October to March; common throughout, abundant in dry W; *M.*

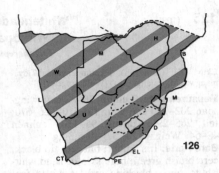

m. lineatus nonbreeding Palaearctic migrant (C Asia), October to March; recorded Zimbabwe and Transvaal; probably uncommon, but status uncertain. Yellowbilled and Black Kites now generally considered to be separate species, *M. parasitus* and *M. migrans* respectively.

Habitat: Woodland, human habitations, semi-arid savanna.

Habits: Highly gregarious when not breeding; otherwise solitary or in pairs. Frequents roads for road-killed animals; highly manoeuvrable in flight, swooping down to pick up prey, even between moving motor vehicles. Scavenges in towns and villages; may rob other raptors of prey. May gather in large numbers at carrion.

Food: Almost any animal material; insects, small vertebrates, molluscs, crustaceans, carrion; also oil-palm husks.

Breeding: *Season*: September to November in S Africa, August to December in Zimbabwe. *Nest*: Bowl of sticks about 50–80 cm diameter, 30–50 cm deep, lined with rags, wool, dung, skin and other rubbish; in canopy of tree, usually 5–15 m above ground. *Clutch*: (36) 1–2–4 eggs (usually 2–3). *Eggs*: White, usually marked with brown and underlying grey; measure (104) 53,5 × 40,1 (49,8–58,5 × 38–45); weigh about 53,5 g. *Incubation*: 31–38 days by both sexes, but mainly by ♀. *Nestling*: 42–45 days, fed by ♀ only, but ♂ brings food.

Ref. Brooke, R.K. 1974. *Durban Mus. Novit.* 10:53–66.

127 (130)   Blackshouldered Kite   Plates 15 & 17
Blouvalk
Elanus caeruleus

Tuyu (K), Phakoana-tšoana, Phakoana-mafieloana (SS), Rukodzi (Sh), N'watavangani, Xikhava-khwani (Ts), Phakalane, Segôôtsane (Tw), Umdla-mpuku, Unongwevana (X), [Gleitaar]

Measurements: Length about 30 cm; wingspan (27) 84,4 cm; wing (23 ♂) 246–268,7–280, (24 ♀) 248–267,9–276; tail (26 ♂) 110–117,6–129, (27 ♀) 106–115,9–122; tarsus 35–38; culmen (26 ♂) 15,4–16,6–18,7, (27 ♀) 16,1–17,3–18,4. Weight (88 ♂) 197–235,8–277 g, (65 ♀) 219–257,3–343 g, (5 unsexed) 230–251,8–275 g.

Bare Parts: Iris ruby red to orange-red; bill black; cere, legs and feet yellow.

Identification: Size smallish; above pale grey; below white; black patches on upperwing at wrist; gull-like appearance and flight. *Immature:* Washed rusty on neck and breast; above brownish with pale edges to feathers; iris grey-brown to yellow-orange; black "shoulders" spotted white. *Chick:* Buff; gape and legs pink; cere yellow.

Voice: Wheezy whistles and screams; high-pitched *peeeu*; rasping *wee-ah* and *weep-weep*.

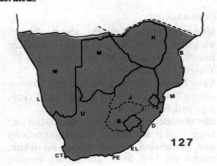

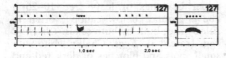

Distribution: Africa (except Sahara), Madagascar, Iberia, tropical Asia to New Guinea; throughout s Africa.

Status: Probably commonest raptor in most parts of s Africa, except dry W; resident, but highly nomadic.

Habitat: Varied; mainly grassland and farmland; also woodland, savanna, semi-arid scrub.

Habits: Usually solitary or in pairs by day; roosts communally at night when not breeding, sometimes in flocks of over 100 birds, from 10–35 minutes after sunset. Hunts from perch (tree or tele-phone pole), or by hovering over open grassland; drops onto prey with legs extended, sometimes in stages before final strike. Wags tail exaggeratedly up and down in threat. Flight graceful and buoyant.

Food: Rodents (up to 98% of diet: mainly *Otomys, Praomys* and *Rhabdomys*), shrews, small birds, reptiles and insects.

Breeding: *Season:* All months in s Africa, mainly July-October in sw Cape, peak in November in e Cape, peak in March in Transvaal and Orange Free State, peak in March-April in Zimbabwe. *Nest:* Small platform of sticks, about 30 cm diameter and 10 cm thick, lined with grass; in fork 2–20 m (usually (54) 2–3,2–8 m) above ground, near top of tree (usually thorn tree if available), accessible from above; built by both sexes; may add to old nest of another species. *Clutch:* (124) 2–3,5–6 eggs (usually 3–4). *Eggs:* Cream to buff, more or less heavily blotched with brown and rust; measure (123) 39,8 × 30,8 (35,6–46,1 × 27,5–34,8); weigh about 21 g. *Incubation:* 30–31–33 days, all or mostly by ♀. *Nestling:* 30–35 days, fed by ♀ only; prey brought by ♂; fledgling cared for only by ♂ for 80–90 days.

Ref. Mendelsohn, J.M. 1982. *Durban Mus. Novit.* 13:75–116; 1983. *Ostrich* 54:1–18; 1984. *Proc. 5th Pan-Afr. Orn. Congr.*:799–808.

128 (127) Cuckoo Hawk   Plates 19 & 17
Koekoekvalk
Aviceda cuculoides

[Kuckucksweih]

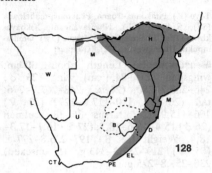

Measurements: Length about 40 cm; wingspan 90 cm; wing (17) 293–305–328; tail 190–208; tarsus 31–38; culmen 18–22. Weight (2) 220–296 g.

Bare Parts: Iris dark brown (♂), brown ringed bright yellow (♀); bill black; cere, legs and feet yellow.

Identification: Size medium; somewhat like large Eurasian Cuckoo; breast grey; belly and underwing barred rufous on white, rufous on buff in ♀ (buff bars broad); slightly crested head and back blackish grey with rufous patch at nape (diagnostic from behind); throat and neck lightly streaked buff in ♀; longish wings almost reach tail tip when folded; tail dark above with three broad black bars; double tooth on bill seen at close range only. *Immature*: Above dark brown with buff feather edges; below whitish with heavy brown blotches (including underwing); eye brown. Similar to immature African Goshawk, but shorter legs, longer wings and short crest at back of head diagnostic. *Chick*: Downy white; bill black, tipped yellow.

Voice: Loud *pee-oo*; soft *tu-yuua* or *tu-tu-ooo-yuua* when perched; quick whistled *choo-titti-too* or *wiki-tu-yoo*.

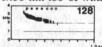

Distribution: Africa S of Sahara, except for arid zones; in s Africa in E, NE and N only.

Status: Uncommon to fairly common resident. Probably Rare (RDB).

Habitat: Forest and dense woodland, indigenous or exotic.

Habits: Solitary, skulking, but not usually shy. Flies low from tree to tree in short glides, with wings held high so that chestnut underwing markings visible, swooping up to perch at end of glide; flight buoyant. Hunts in grass and undergrowth. Easily overlooked when sitting still, but does not sit in one place for very long.

Food: 95% insects (especially grasshoppers), 1,4% small lizards and snakes, 1,9% birds, 1,4% rodents.

Breeding: *Season*: September to December in S Africa; as late as February in Zimbabwe. *Nest*: Flimsy platform of leafy branches, 25–42 cm diameter, bowl 10–15 cm diameter, 15–20 cm deep, lined with green sprigs during incubation; in upper branches of leafy tree 10–25 m above ground, below canopy; often in *Eucalyptus*; built by both sexes. *Clutch*: 2 eggs (rarely 3). *Eggs*: Chalky white with small spots and blotches of dark red and brown, with grey undermarkings; measure (31) 43,4 × 35,4 (41–48,5 × 33,4–37,8); weigh about 28 g. *Incubation*: About 32–33 days by both sexes or by ♀ only. *Nestling*: 28–36 days, fed by both parents.

Ref. Chittenden, H. 1984. *Proc. 2nd Symp. Afr. Pred. Birds*:47–56.

Jones, J.M.B. 1985. *Honeyguide* 31:196–202.

129 (131) Bat Hawk   Plates 15 & 17
Vlermuisvalk
Macheiramphus alcinus

[Fledermausaar]

Measurements: Length about 45 cm; wing (4 ♂) 324–333–338, (5 ♀) 336–347–360; tail (9) 154–188; tarsus (9) 57–64; culmen (9) 16–17. Weight (3) 600–623–650 g.

Bare Parts: Iris yellow; bill black; cere and gape bluish grey; legs bluish white.

Identification: Size medium; blackish brown (black at distance) with white streak above and below eye; variable amount of white on throat, with dark centre line; two white nape spots resemble eyes; head and bill slender; eye large, yellow; legs and feet whitish; long wings reach almost to tail tip when folded; in flight resembles large dark falcon; wings long, broad, pointed; tail longish. *Immature*: White on belly. *Chick*: Downy white.

Voice: High-pitched *kwik-kwik-kwik-kwik*; mellow *woot-woot-woot*; whistles like man calling dog; also falconlike *kek-kek-kek* and whimpering notes.

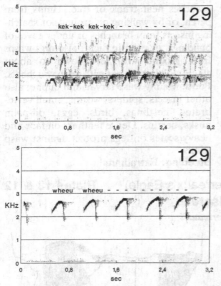

Distribution: Africa S of Sahara, Madagascar, SE Asia to New Guinea; in s Africa absent from s and w regions.

Status: Uncommon to rare resident. Rare (RDB).

Habitat: Dense woodland and riverine forest.

Habits: By day sits still in shady parts of leafy tree. Hunts before and during dusk for only about half an hour each day, over open areas (pools, rivers, estuaries, beaches, railway yards, large lawns). May hunt also just after dawn. Catches prey in feet and swallows it whole in flight; flight leisurely except in pursuit; wingbeats silent.

Food: Mainly smaller bats 20–75 g in weight (mostly less than 30 g); each bird may catch several bats in an evening; also small birds, especially swifts and swallows, sometimes as large as Cape Turtle Dove; rarely insects.

Breeding: *Season*: August to January (mostly September-November) in Zimbabwe, November to December in Transvaal. *Nest*: Stick platform like inverted basin, about 56 cm diameter, 40 cm deep; built of sticks about 1 cm thick; bowl about 14 cm diameter lined with finer twigs and some leaves; on lateral branch of large tree 10–60 m above ground. *Clutch*: 1 egg. *Eggs*: White, plain or sparingly blotched with reddish brown; measure (18) 61,6 × 46,2 (57,7–67,2 × 43–49,3). *Incubation*: About 30 days by both sexes. *Nestling*: 35–40 days, fed by both parents.

Ref. Hustler, K. 1983. *Ostrich* 54:156–160.
Milstein, P. le S., Olwagan, C.D. & Stein, D.J. 1975. *Bokmakierie* 27:12–14.

130 (132) **Honey Buzzard** **Plates 15 & 17**
Wespedief
Pernis apivorus

[Wespenbussard]

Measurements: Length 54–60 cm; wingspan 135–150 cm; wing ♂ 370–402–425, ♀ 372–409–447; tail 210–275; tarsus (12) 53–60; culmen (12) 21–23. Weight (10 ♂) 510–684–800 g, (8 ♀) 625–832–1050 g.

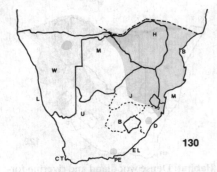

130

Bare Parts: Iris bright yellow in ♀, orange in ♂; bill black; cere dark grey; legs and feet yellow.

Identification: Size medium to largish; coloration variable; light to dark brown all over (except for greyish head), sometimes pale below with streaking or barring; looks like Steppe Buzzard, but has very slender bill and head (somewhat pigeon-like appearance); tail-barring diagnostic (two broad dark bars near base and one broad dark bar at tip). In flight head protrudes forward more than that of Steppe Buzzard; soars on flat wings (Steppe Buzzard has slight dihedral); flight feathers and underwing distinctively barred. *Immature*: Four evenly spaced bars on tail; eye brown.

Voice: Usually silent in Africa; squeaky *kee-er* and rapid *kikikiki*.

130

Distribution: Breeds Holarctic to Indonesia; some races migrate to Africa and s Asia; in s Africa found mainly in E and N; scattered records from e Cape and Windhoek.

Status: Scarce but regular nonbreeding Palaearctic visitor, November to April.

Habitat: Woodland and forest edge.

Habits: Solitary; somewhat sluggish; perches inside leafy canopy on thick branches near trunk of tree. Hunts from perch, or by walking on ground, or snatching insects from branches or under eaves of buildings, or even in flight; also digs wasps from ground with feet down to about 40 cm. Flight buoyant with deep wingbeats.

Food: Mainly wasp larvae and pupae; also other insects, spiders, worms, small vertebrates, nestlings, birds' eggs, oil-palm husks, berries. Dense feathers on face and heavy scales on legs protect against wasp stings.

Breeding: Extralimital.

131 (133)   Black Eagle (Verreaux's Eagle)   Plates 13 & 12
Witkruisarend
Aquila verreauxii

Ngongo Zonsovagani (K), Seoli, Moja-lipela (SS), Rovambira (Sh), Gama (Ts), Ntswi, Ntsu (Tw), Untsho, Ukhozi (X), uKhozi (Z), [Felsenadler, Kaffernadler]

Measurements: Length about 84 cm; wingspan (5) 199,4 cm; wing (4 ♂) 565–580,3–595, (6 ♀) 590–624–640; tail (9) 315–360; tarsus (9) 105–110; culmen (9) 42–47,5. Weight (6 ♂) 3000–3700–4150 g, (8 ♀) 3100–4453–5800 g, (1 unsexed) 3300 g.

Bare Parts: Iris light brown; bill leaden horn; cere, eyelids and feet yellow.

Identification: Size very large; legs feathered to toes; jet black except for white lower back and white V on upper back (only narrow white V visible at rest); in flight wing characteristically narrow at

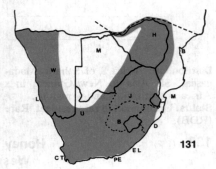

131

base, broad at tip, with whitish windows in primaries; broad white Y-pattern on back visible from above. *Immature*: Rich rufous on crown and mantle; rest of upperparts streaked brown and white; base of tail black; below light brown with black chest and cheeks; fully mature at 5 years. *Chick*: Downy white; iris dark brown; cere and feet yellow.

Voice: Usually silent; staccato *chuck* or barking *chyow*; ringing *keee-oo* or *wha-ee*; various mewing and whistling calls.

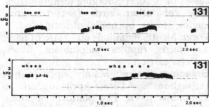

Distribution: S to E Africa and Sinai; in s Africa absent from most of Botswana and Mozambique.

Status: Locally fairly common in suitable habitat; resident; vagrant to n Botswana.

Habitat: Rocky hills, mountains and gorges, especially where Rock Dassie (Hyrax) *Procavia capensis* and Yellow-spotted Dassie *Heterohyrax brucei* plentiful.

Habits: Usually seen gliding swiftly along rock faces, or soaring on thermals, sometimes to great heights; may spend hours perched on crag or shady ledge. Almost invariably in pairs, or pair with juvenile; pair occupies home range of about 65 km²

in Drakensberg, 35 km² in Magaliesberg, 9 km² in Matobo. Hunts by surprise attack on prey as it swoops around corner of cliff; less often by stoop from perch; may (incidentally ?) knock prey over cliff and retrieve it below. Pair may hunt cooperatively; rarely pirates food from larger eagles and Bearded Vulture.

Food: About 90% dassies (Rock and Yellowspotted Dassies in equal proportions in Zimbabwe); also hares, monkeys, small antelopes, squirrels and other mammals, guineafowls, francolins, korhaans, doves and other birds; less often reptiles and carrion; rarely domestic stock like lambs, kids and chickens.

Breeding: *Season*: April to June (sometimes to August in Zimbabwe). *Nest*: Huge platform of sticks 1,5–2 m diameter; depth varies with usage and may reach 4 m; bowl 30–40 cm diameter lined with green leaves; on cliff ledge or in pothole (very rarely in tree). *Clutch*: (206) 1–1,8–2 eggs (usually 2; rarely 3 in sw Cape). *Eggs*: White, plain or marked with reddish and mauve; measure (82) 75 × 58,3 (66,7–86 × 52–62); weigh 115–158 g. *Incubation*: 43–46 days by both sexes (mainly by ♀). *Nestling*: 90–98 days, fed by ♀ on food caught by ♂; older chick kills younger within about 3 days; post-nestling dependence 13–19 weeks.

Ref. Gargett, V. 1990. *The Black Eagle*. Johannesburg: Acorn Books & Russel Friedman.

---

132 (134) **Tawny Eagle** **Plates 13 & 12**
Roofarend
Aquila rapax

Ngongo (K), Ntshukôbôkôbô (NS), Gondo (Sh), Gama (Ts), Ntswi, Ntsu (Tw), Ukhozi (X), [Raubadler]

Measurements: Length 65–72 cm; wingspan (15) 182,3 cm; wing (33 ♂) 485–512–542, (40 ♀) 518–541,5–565; tail (8 ♂) 248–260–275, (15 ♀) 242–264–290; tarsus 73–92; culmen (9 ♂) 37–38,2–40, (18 ♀) 37–39,7–44. Weight (2 ♂) 1849–1954 g, (2 ♀) 1572–2378 g, (27 unsexed) 1696–2352–3100 g.

Bare Parts: Iris dull yellow to pale brownish; bill brown, tip black; cere and feet yellow.

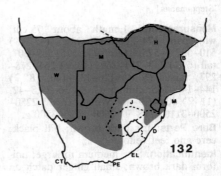

Identification: Size medium to large; scruffy or shaggy appearance; generally light brown, but colour variable from dark brown to blond; darker birds usually mottled with tawny (no tawny coloration in Steppe or Wahlberg's Eagles); feathering on legs like baggy trousers (legs of Lesser Spotted Eagles much neater-looking); tail rounded (square in darker-coloured Wahlberg's Eagle), usually slightly spread in flight; gape extends only to below eye (to rear border of eye in Steppe Eagle). Very difficult to tell apart from Steppe Eagle, but much commoner; Steppe Eagle absent in winter (see text for that species). *Immature:* As variable as adult. *Chick:* Downy white; iris brown; cere and feet pale yellow.

Voice: Barking *kah*; guttural *kwork*; ♀ calls sibilant *shreep-shreep* at nest.

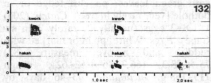

132

Distribution: Africa except forests and deserts; also se Europe, Middle East, India and Burma; in s Africa widespread except in s, C and w Cape.

Status: Common in game reserves; rare and declining elsewhere, especially in Cape Province; resident.

Habitat: Woodland and savanna to semi-arid savanna or grassland with scattered Acacia trees.

Habits: Solitary or somewhat gregarious, especially at good food supply. Usually perches on top of tree (Steppe Eagle often perches on ground). Hunts by stooping from perch or in flight; gathers at carcasses or around emerging termite alates; may rob other birds (Secretarybirds, eagles, storks, hornbills) of their food.

Food: Mostly mammals up to size of hare; also birds, reptiles, amphibians, fishes, insects, carrion.

Breeding: *Season:* Mainly April to July throughout s Africa; April to June in Zimbabwe. *Nest:* Flat platform of sticks, about 1 m diameter, 30–50 cm thick; bowl 25–40 cm diameter lined with grass and green leaves; 4,5–30 m (usually 6–15 m) above ground in top of thorn tree; rarely on power pylon. *Clutch:* 1–1,7–3 eggs (usually 2). *Eggs:* White, plain or blotched with rusty red and grey; measure (90) 70,5 × 55,3 (62,5–77,7 × 50–60); weigh (10 fresh eggs) 106–119,2–132 g. *Incubation:* 39–44 days by both sexes; mainly by ♀. *Nestling:* 11–12 weeks, fed by both parents but mainly by ♀; ♂ brings most prey; older chick kills younger within first few days; post-nestling dependence at least 6 weeks.

Ref. Boshoff, A.F., Rous, R.C. & Vernon, C.J. 1981. *Ostrich* 52:187–188.
Steyn, P. 1973. *Ostrich* 44:1–22.

133 (135) **Steppe Eagle** **Plates 13 & 12**
Steppe-arend
Aquila nipalensis

[Steppenadler]

Measurements: Length about 75 cm; wingspan 174–260 cm; wing (42 ♂) 510–537,1–575, (46 ♀) 525–569–607; tail (6 ♂) 240–254–260, (10 ♀) 264–278–297; tarsus (6 ♂) 126–135–140, (8 ♀) 144–148–155; culmen (7 ♂) 36–39,3–42, (11 ♀) 40–41,9–45. Weight (6 ♂) 2250–2500–3110 g, (8 ♀) 2600–3030–3800 g.

Bare Parts: Iris dark brown; bill black; cere and feet yellow.

Identification: Size medium to large; uniform dark brown; small ginger patch on

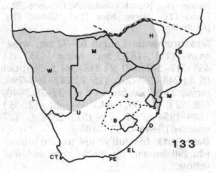

133

nape; gape yellow, extending to back margin of dark brown eye (Tawny Eagle has yellow eye and gape ends in line with middle of eye); no tawny coloration; trailing edge of wing shallow S-shape. Bigger than either Wahlberg's or Lesser Spotted Eagles; flight pattern different. *Immature*: Clay-brown; tail tipped pale; uppertail coverts and underwing white; pale bands on upperwing in flight (shows as double bar at rest), and pale window in primaries; adult plumage attained in 5–7 years.

Voice: Usually silent in Africa; some throaty croaks.

Distribution: Breeds e Europe to Kazakhstan; migrates to s Asia and Africa; in s Africa seldom S of Orange, Vaal and Tugela Rivers.

Status: Common but unpredictable nonbreeding Palaearctic migrant, October to February; most birds move westward to Namibia from Zimbabwe from December.

Habitat: Woodland and open savanna, including semi-arid savanna.

Habits: Highly gregarious, sometimes in flocks of hundreds of birds, especially in association with rain fronts and resulting emergence of termite alates. Frequently feeds on ground, running clumsily after termites as they emerge. Perches in trees after feeding. Does not stay long in one area. Mostly immatures seen in Africa.

Food: Largely termites; also queleas taken in nesting colonies, small mammals; carrion.

Breeding: Extralimital.

Ref. Brooke, R.K., Grobler, J.H., Irwin, M.P.S. & Steyn, P. 1972. *Occ. Pap. Natn. Mus. Rhod.* 1972, B5:61–114.

---

134 (136)   **Lesser Spotted Eagle**   **Plates 13 & 12**
Gevlekte Arend
Aquila pomarina

Ngongo (K), [Schreiadler]

Measurements: Length about 65 cm; wingspan 134–159 cm; wing (8 ♂) 460–473,5–495, (14 ♀) 458–489,7–525; tail (7 ♂) 220–232–255, (12 ♀) 217–236,3–265; tarsus ♂ 82–90,6–97, ♀ 81–91,1–99; culmen (8 ♂) 28–30,3–33, (13 ♀) 28–31,3–34. Weight (16 ♂) 1053–1197–1509 g, (21 ♀) 1195–1499–2160 g.

Bare Parts: Iris yellow; bill black; cere and feet yellow.

Identification: Size large; uniform brown, easily confused with Steppe and Wahlberg's Eagles, but iris yellow (not brown); smaller than Steppe Eagle; feathering on tarsus narrow (not baggy as in Tawny Eagle); in flight looks long-winged; tail short and rounded (longish and square in Wahlberg's Eagle), usually spread slightly in flight; small white windows in primaries seen on upperwing; trailing edge of wing almost straight; body plumage rarely pale yellowish (less than 5% of population). *Immature*: Warm brown all over; narrow white line on upperwing and white patch

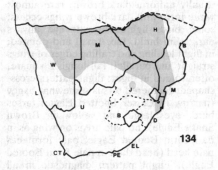

134

at base of tail; wing coverts boldly spotted white; underparts streaked pale; ginger patch on nape in first-year birds; iris brown; tail barred (plain brown in adult); undertail coverts white in first-year birds.

Voice: Usually silent in Africa; shrill yapping like that of small dog.

Distribution: Breeds e Europe, Russia and India; migrates to Africa; in s Africa mainly confined to n parts.

Status: Uncommon but regular nonbreeding Palaearctic migrant, October to

March; may be commoner than supposed, because of confusion with other brown eagles.
Habitat: Woodland and savanna.
Habits: Less gregarious than Steppe Eagle; prefers more heavily wooded country; often solitary. May occur in flocks with Steppe Eagle. Almost entirely imma-

tures in s Africa; few adults S of E Africa. Moves about with weather fronts; feeds on emerging termite alates on ground.
Food: Mainly small mammals; also termites, quelea nestlings, birds and frogs.
Breeding: Extralimital.

Ref. As for Steppe Eagle.

135 (137)   Wahlberg's Eagle   Plates 14 & 12
Bruinarend (Wahlbergse Arend)
Aquila wahlbergi

Ekangakodi (K), Gondo (Sh), Gama (Ts), Ntswi, Ntsu (Tw), [Wahlbergs Adler]

Measurements: Length 55–60 cm; wingspan (15) 140,7 cm; wing (27 ♂) 376–416–445, (14 ♀) 397–427–450; tail (27 ♂) 203–216–232, (14 ♀) 207–223–234; tarsus ♂ 71–76, ♀ 79–82; culmen (27 ♂) 24–25,9–29, (14 ♀) 24–27,1–29. Weight ♂ 437–845 g, (42 unsexed) 670–1147–1400 g.
Bare Parts: Iris dark brown; bill black; cere and feet yellow.
Identification: Size medium to largish; usually uniform dark brown; rare almost white form with dark brown wings occurs; some birds lighter brown; eye always dark; slim build; face small and pointed; in flight leading and trailing edges of wings straight and parallel; tail longish, square, often folded in flight; flight pattern cross-shaped; feathered tarsus somewhat baggy (narrow in Lesser Spotted Eagle; tarsus bare, eyes large and yellow in Brown Snake Eagle); no pale areas on wing as in dark-form Booted Eagle; pale form has pale head (head dark in pale-form Booted Eagle). Flight pattern diagnostic in all plumages. *Immature*: Resembles adult. *Chick*: Downy dark chocolate brown.
Voice: Fluty *kleeeeu* while soaring; contact call rapid *kyip-kyip-kyip*; other squealing and yelping notes.

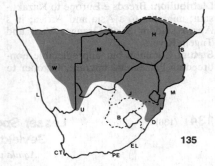

135

Distribution: Africa S of Sahara; in s Africa mainly in E and N.
Status: Common intra-African breeding migrant, August to April; absent in winter, migrating to tropical Africa.
Habitat: Woodland and savanna; also in cultivated areas if enough woodland available.
Habits: Usually solitary, unobtrusive and easily overlooked. Perches in leafy trees. Soars often to great heights. Hunts by stooping in flight, or by parachuting vertically with extended legs. Attracted to veld fires.
Food: Reptiles, birds (up to size of francolin or guineafowl), mammals (up to size of hare), insects.
Breeding: *Season*: Mainly September to October; rarely earlier or later. *Nest*: Smallish platform of sticks, 60–70 cm diameter, 30–40 cm thick with leaf-lined bowl 20–27 cm diameter; in tree, below canopy, usually in shade; height (407) 5–11–22 m above ground. *Clutch*: Usually 1 egg (only 4% of 127 clutches

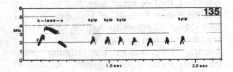

had 2 eggs). *Eggs*: White, almost plain or heavily marked with reddish brown; measure (167) 61,5 × 49 (57–66 × 44–52,9); weigh (3) 67–82 g. *Incubation*: 44–46 days, mostly by ♀, seldom by ♂. *Nestling*: 70–75 days, fed usually by ♀ only on food brought by ♂ (later ♀ brings food too); dependent on adults for several weeks after first flight.

Ref. Steyn, P. 1980. *Ostrich* 51:56–59.
Tarboton, W. 1977. *Bokmakierie* 29:46–50.

136 (139)   Booted Eagle   Plates 14 & 12
Dwergarend
Hieraaetus pennatus

Ekangakodi (K), [Zwergadler]

Measurements: Length 48–52 cm; wingspan 110–132 cm; wing ♂ 353–369,1–390, ♀ 380–409,3–428; tail ♂ 187–195,3–202, ♀ 196–211,2–218; tarsus ♂ 59–61,7–64, ♀ 65–68,8–71; culmen 21,5–23,5. Weight (10 ♂) 510–712–770 g, (10 ♀) 840–975–1250 g.

Bare Parts: Iris light brown; bill black; cere and feet yellow.

Identification: Size medium; tarsus heavily feathered (booted appearance); tail square or slightly rounded, often flexed from side to side when soaring (Black Kite has slightly forked tail); white patches ("landing lights") on leading edge of wing near body diagnostic in all plumages; white band at base of tail; pale wedge at bend of wing. Two forms, pale and dark (80% and 20% of population respectively). *Pale form*: Above brown; below white; streaked on breast; throat dark, often divided by pale line; broad buff band on upperwing. *Dark form*: Uniform dark brown, except for buff band on upperwing, white patches on front of wing and white at base of tail. *Immature*: Pale form washed below with rufous; dark form same as adult; wing pattern as in adults. *Chick*: Downy white or grey; iris grey; bill bluish with black tip; cere and feet yellow.

Voice: Usually silent when not breeding; in display high-pitched staccato *pi-pi-pi-pi*, almost trilled; drawn out *peeee-peee*; loud rapid *kyip-kyip-kyip*; squealing and chattering notes.

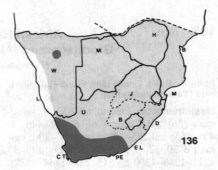

136

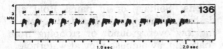

136

Distribution: Africa, Europe and Asia; throughout s Africa.

Status: Two populations. Intra-African migrants breed s, w and e Cape and Waterberg Plateau, Namibia; migrate mostly to nw Cape, Kalahari, Namibia and Angola; common, but some breeding birds present all year; most birds in Namibia March-August. Nonbreeding Palaearctic migrants present October to March; probably common, but indistinguishable from breeding birds.

Habitat: Breeding birds occur in semi-arid hilly country and edges of karoo; nonbreeding birds occur in wide variety of habitats from woodland to semi-desert.

Habits: Solitary or in pairs; rarely 6-8 birds together. Inconspicuous when perched; usually seen when flying. Hunts in flight, stooping from about 200 m or more; chases prey through woodland; also hunts from perch, swooping at prey on ground. Soars often. Has undulating courtship flight.

Food: Mostly birds (54% of prey), up to size of Redbilled Francolin; also lizards, rodents, insects.

BOOTED EAGLE

Breeding: *Season*: September in Cape, June in Namibia. *Nest*: Rather small platform of sticks, 45–65 cm diameter, up to 1 m thick, with bowl 28 cm diameter, 7 cm deep, lined with green leaves; on cliff ledge, at base of tree on cliff, in *Euphorbia*, or 3–10 m above ground in isolated leafy *Eucalyptus* in flat country. *Clutch*: (9) 2 eggs. *Eggs*: White, sometimes with faint reddish speckles; measure (10) 54,6 × 44 (51,5–58 × 42,2–45,8);

weigh 56–58,6 g. *Incubation*: 40 days, 92% by ♀, 8% by ♂. *Nestling*: 50–54 days, fed mostly by ♀, less often by ♂; both chicks may be reared (Cainism recorded once); dependent on parents up to 60 days after leaving nest.

Ref. Brown, C.J. 1985. *Madoqua* 14:189–191.
Martin, J.E. & Martin, R. 1974. *Bokmakierie* 26:21–22.
Steyn, P. & Grobler, J.H. 1981. *Ostrich* 52:108–118; 1985. *Ostrich* 56:151–156.

137 (141)   African Hawk Eagle   Plates 14 & 12
Grootjagarend (Afrikaanse Jagarend)
Hieraaetus spilogaster

Ekangakodi (K), Gondo (Sh), Gama (Ts), Ntswi, Ntsu (Tw), [Habichtsadler]

Measurements: Length 60–65 cm; wingspan (36) 141,7 cm; wing ♂ 412–446, ♀ 435–465; tail 255–290; tarsus 90–100; culmen ♂ 30–32, ♀ 32,5–34,5. Weight (3 ♂) 1221–1248–1300 g, (3 ♀) 1444–1582–1640 g, (56 unsexed) 1150–1421–1750 g.

Bare Parts: Iris yellow; bill black; cere and legs greenish yellow.

Identification: Size medium to large; above blackish; below white, heavily streaked with black, except on legs (leg feathering of Ayres' Eagle spotted); much larger than Ayres' Eagle and less heavily streaked; in flight shafts of primaries white (black in Ayres' Eagle); large white windows in primaries (none in Ayres' Eagle); trailing edge of underwing broadly black; underwing coverts mostly black with broad band of white spots (more spotted in Ayres' Eagle); pale grey wrist patch above and below diagnostic; blackish cap less extensive than in Ayres' Eagle; tail pale, narrowly barred, with broad black terminal bar (tail tends to be grey and more coarsely and evenly barred in Ayres' Eagle); head not crested (slightly so in Ayres' Eagle). *Immature*: Above brown; below bright rufous; narrowly streaked on breast; iris brown; underwing rufous; remiges whitish, barred black. *Chick*: Dark grey; whitish on belly and legs; at 14–21 days white except on head and back; cere and feet dull yellow.

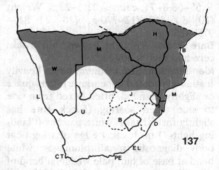

137

Voice: Musical *klu-klu-klu-kluee*; loud *kwee-oo kwee-oo* or *ko-ko-ko-kwee-le-oo*; ♀ calls *skwee-ya skwee-ya* to ♂ at nest; also other harsh calls.

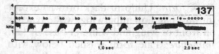

Distribution: Southern Eurasia and Africa S of Sahara; in s Africa absent from about 25 °S.

Status: Uncommon to fairly common resident.

Habitat: Woodland, often hilly; avoids open savanna and forest, but occurs at forest edge or on isolated forested mountains.

Habits: Solitary or in pairs. Bold and dashing, hunting from perch, or quartering low over ground, or stooping from soaring; may ambush prey at waterhole.

Flight silent. Inconspicuous when perched; usually seen soaring, sometimes very high.
Food: About 75% birds (mainly francolins and guineafowls); also mammals (dassies, rodents, mongooses), reptiles.
Breeding: *Season*: May to July, peak in June (rarely April to September). *Nest*: Platform of sticks about 1 m diameter; bowl 25–50 cm diameter, lined with green leaves; in fork of large tree, (134 nests) 4–13–36 m above ground; mainly in riverine trees. *Clutch*: (85) 1–1,6–2 eggs (usu-

ally 2; very rarely 3). *Eggs*: Chalky white with rusty red markings, evenly distributed or forming cap at one end; measure (123) 64,5 × 51,3 (59,5–75,2 × 46–55,7); weigh (10) 75–87–100 g. *Incubation*: 42–44 days by both sexes, about 90% by ♀. *Nestling*: (7) 61–68–71 days, fed mostly by ♀; only one chick reared; older chick kills younger; dependent on adults for up to 2 months after first flight.

Ref. Hustler, K. & Howells, W.W. 1988. *Condor* 90:583–587.
Steyn, P. 1975. *Ostrich* 46:87–105.

138 (140) Ayres' Eagle Kleinjagarend
Hieraaetus ayresii
Plates 14 & 12

[Fleckenadler]

Measurements: Length 46–55 cm; wingspan (2) 123,3–124 cm; wing ♂ 326–345, ♀ 360–420; tail ♂ 175, ♀ 205–233; tarsus 56–78; culmen 20,5–26. Weight (1 ♂) 714 g, (2 ♀) 879–940 g, (2 unsexed) 900–1000 g.
Bare Parts: Iris deep yellow to yellow-orange; bill black; cere and feet lime yellow.
Identification: Size medium (smaller than African Hawk Eagle); above blackish; below white, heavily blotched with black (highly variable); forehead and spot at base of each wing ("landing lights") usually white; underwing heavily spotted; tail heavily barred (more so than that of Booted Eagle); see African Hawk Eagle species account for further comparison. *Immature*: Above grey-brown, crown rufous; upperwing feathers tipped white to give scaly effect; rufous below (paler than immature African Hawk Eagle), some dark streaking on breast; heavily barred on remiges and rectrices (immature Booted Eagle less heavily barred); iris yellow (brown in immature African Hawk Eagle). *Chick*: Dull white with dark patch in front of eye; iris pale greyish brown; cere and feet yellow.
Voice: High-pitched melodious *wheeep-hip-hip-hip-wheeep*; rapid piping *hip-hip-hip*; threat *kak-kak-kak*.
Distribution: Africa S of Sahara; in s

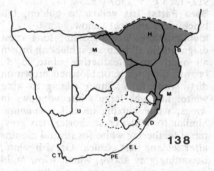

138

Africa only in ne parts and w Caprivi.
Status: Scarce intra-African migrant in s parts of range, recorded January to May in Johannesburg area, September to April around Bulawayo; no records June to August in s Africa.
Habitat: Dense woodland, forest edge, *Eucalyptus* groves in towns; avoids arid zones.
Habits: Solitary; unobtrusive; usually seen flying over treetops or forest edge. Spends hours perched in leafy tree, easily overlooked. Fast and dashing; hunts by stooping with wingtips folded to tail tip in heart-shaped silhouette; pursues prey through trees, twisting fast among branches; dives into tree canopy, emerging with prey without stopping.
Food: Mainly birds of 40–200 g; doves preferred, but wide variety taken, including small goshawks.

Breeding: *Season*: April to May (rarely to September) in Zimbabwe. *Nest*: Platform of smallish sticks, 70–90 cm diameter, 45–90 cm thick; bowl 20–25 cm diameter lined with green sprigs; in leafy tree in dense woodland, 8–20 m above ground. *Clutch*: 1 egg. *Eggs*: White, variably marked with reddish brown; measure (3) 63 × 50,6 (61,8–64,6 × 49,7–52). *Incubation*: (3) 45 days by ♀ only. *Nestling*: 75 days, fed by ♀ only; food provided mostly by ♂; young accompanies parents up to 3 months after first flight.

139 (138)   Longcrested Eagle   Plates 14 & 12
Langkuifarend
Lophaetus occipitalis

Pfinye, Kondokondo (Sh), Masworhimasworhi (Ts), Uphungu-phungu, Isiphungu-phungu (X), isiPhungumangathi (Z), [Schopfadler]

Measurements: Length 53–58 cm; wing ♂ 350–376, ♀ 370–408; tail ♂ 192–200, ♀ 205–215; tarsus ♂ 92–97, ♀ 95–100; culmen ♂ 27–28, ♀ 29–30. Weight ♂ 912–1363 g, ♀ 1367–1523 g.

Bare Parts: Iris yellow to golden; bill black; cere and feet yellow.

Identification: Size medium; long crest diagnostic in all plumages; blackish brown all over, tarsal feathering white in ♂, brown, dirty white or blotched brown on dirty white in ♀; inner edging to wing white; in flight large white windows in wings, white barring on tail. *Immature*: Similar to adult; crest shorter; iris grey; tarsal feathering white for several months after leaving nest. *Chick*: Greyish white, becoming grey above, white below at 14 days; iris grey; cere and feet yellow.

Voice: Screaming *keeee-eh*; sharp high-pitched *kik-kik-kik-kee-eh*.

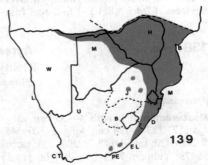

Distribution: Africa S of Sahara, except arid zones; in s Africa from e Cape to Zimbabwe, n Botswana and Caprivi.

Status: Fairly common, but much reduced in s parts of range; resident.

Habitat: Woodland, exotic plantations, forest edge, cultivated land with orchards, grassland and vlei.

Habits: Usually solitary. Often perches conspicuously on top of tree or telephone pole; flies frequently from perch to perch with shallow wingbeats; soars seldom, usually not high, often calling in flight. Hunts from perch, stooping to ground; prey swallowed whole.

Food: Mainly rodents and shrews; some birds, arthropods and reptiles; rarely fruit (mulberries and figs).

Breeding: *Season*: July to November in Transvaal, April to January in Zimbabwe. *Nest*: Smallish platform of sticks, about 50–60 cm diameter, 15–30 cm thick; bowl 25–30 cm diameter, lined with green leaves. *Clutch*: (21) 1–1,6–2 eggs (usually 2). *Eggs*: Dull white, marked with red-brown blotches and smears and some underlying purplish spots; measure (37) 59,4 × 48,4 (54,1–67 × 45–51,1); weigh about 75 g. *Incubation*: 42 days mostly by ♀ (82% of time), seldom by ♂. *Nestling*: (5) 53–58 days, fed by ♀, rarely also by ♂; food brought mostly by ♂; dependent on adults for 3–4 months after first flight.

Ref. Hall, D. 1979. *Ostrich* 50:256–257; 1979. *Bokmakierie* 31:65–72.

Steyn, P. 1978. *Bokmakierie* 30:3–10.

140 (142)

Martial Eagle
Breëkoparend
Polemaetus bellicosus

Plates 13 & 12

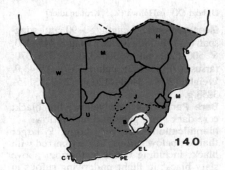

Ngongo Gepampa (K), Gondo (Sh), Man'ole, Xatobola (Ts), Ntswi, Ntsu (Tw), Ukhozi (X), uKhozi, isiHuhwa (Z), [Kampfadler]

Measurements: Length 78–83 cm; wingspan 195–260 cm; wing ♂ 560–610, ♀ 605–675; tail ♂ 273–280, ♀ 280–320; tarsus ♂ 97–118, ♀ 114–130; culmen (11) 40,5–49. Weight (1 ♂) 5100 g, (2 ♀) 5924–6200 g, (17 unsexed) 3012–3965–5657 g.

Bare Parts: Iris yellow; bill black; cere and feet pale greenish or bluish white.

Identification: Size very large; head, upperparts and breast dark brown; belly white with dark brown spots (spots may not be easily visible at distance); head broad and flat-crowned; underwing mostly dark brown, faintly barred (underwing of Blackbreasted Snake Eagle white, boldly barred on remiges); wings long and broad; tail relatively short. *Immature*: Above grey, below white; overall pale appearance; iris dark brown; cere and feet pale greenish white (feet yellow in immature Crowned Eagle); in flight mainly white below; fine barring on wings and tail visible at close range (immature Crowned Eagle washed rufous on underwing and sometimes on breast; boldly barred on wings and tail; much shorter-winged than Martial Eagle). *Chick*: Dark grey above, white below; iris brown; cere grey; feet pale grey.

Voice: Usually silent; musical ringing *ko-wee-o ko-wee-o*; rapid trilling *kwi-kwi-kwi-kluee-kluee*; soft gulping *kwolp* at nest.

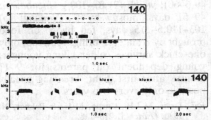

Distribution: Africa S of Sahara; throughout s Africa, except Lesotho and sw Cape.

Status: Fairly common in game reserves; uncommon to rare in farming areas; resident. Vulnerable (RDB).

Habitat: Woodland, savanna or grassland with clumps of large trees or power pylons for nest sites.

Habits: Shy, avoids man. Solitary or in pairs. Soars to great heights; sometimes perches on top of dead tree or power pylon. Hunts by scanning ground while in flight or from perch, stooping in shallow dive; rarely hovers.

Food: Birds (gamebirds, waterfowl, storks, owls), mammals (goats, smaller antelopes up to size of Grey Duiker *Sylvicapra grimmia*, mongooses, hares, dassies), reptiles (up to size of monitor lizards *Varanus* spp.).

Breeding: *Season*: February to August (mainly April to June), rarely to November. *Nest*: Large basin of thick sticks, up to 2 m diameter and 2 m deep; leaf-lined bowl 40–50 cm diameter; in fork of large tree, 5–30 m above ground (usually 10–20 m, rarely as high as 70 m), sometimes on power pylon. *Clutch*: 1 egg. *Eggs*: Chalky white to pale greenish blue, plain or variously marked with brown, reddish and mauve blotches; measure (57) 79,9 × 63,4 (72–87,5 × 60–69); weigh about 182 g. *Incubation*: 47–51 days by ♀ only. *Nestling*: 96–99 days, fed by ♀ only; food provided mostly by ♂; dependent on parents for 3–8 months after first flight.

121

141 (143)

Crowned Eagle
Kroonarend

Plates 13 & 12

Stephanoaetus coronatus

Ukhozi (X), isiHuhwa (Z), [Kronenadler]

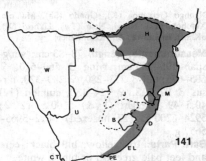

Measurements: Length 80–90 cm; wingspan (3) 152–190–209 cm; wing ♂ 445–490, ♀ 500–525; tail ♂ 300–330, ♀ 325–370; tarsus (9) 85–103; culmen (9) 37–43,9. Weight (2 ♂) 3400–4120 g, (2 ♀) 3175–3853 g.

Bare Parts: Iris pale yellow; bill black; cere dark grey; gape and feet yellow.

Identification: Size very large, ♀ larger than ♂; below rufous, heavily barred with black, including tarsal feathering; above slaty black; in flight underwing rufous in front, white behind, heavily barred black; tail boldy barred black and white; looks very broad-winged with checkerboard pattern when light shines through wings. *Immature:* Above grey; below white, sometimes with rufous wash on breast; underwing light rufous in front (white in immature Martial Eagle), boldly barred black and white behind (finely barred in immature Martial Eagle); tail boldly barred black and white; iris grey; feet yellow (whitish in immature Martial Eagle). *Chick:* Downy white; iris and cere grey; feet pale yellow.

Voice: Melodious *kewee-kewee-kewee* by ♂ in display; deeper *koi-koi-koi* by ♀; at nest various *kwee* and *kew* calls.

Distribution: Tropical Africa; in s Africa only in E and S to about Knysna; discontinuously distributed because of fragmented habitat.

Status: Common resident in suitable habitat, but numbers declining through deforestation.

Habitat: Dense indigenous forest, including riverine gallery forest; may range far from forest to hunt.

Habits: Usually solitary or in pairs. Unobtrusive when perched in leafy tree, but conspicuous when flying above forest, especially in undulating flight display with vocalizations (see **Voice**); sometimes to great heights; pair may display together. May soar quietly on thermals, sometimes plunging into forest canopy; can fly almost vertically from forest floor. Hunts from perch, less often in flight; drops onto prey, sometimes subduing animals of up to 20 kg weight. Prey may be dismembered and cached.

Food: Mainly mammals (monkeys, baboons, antelopes, dassies, mongooses, cats); also birds (gamebirds, pigeons) and monitor lizards; rarely takes goats and sheep.

Breeding: *Season:* February to November (mainly August-September) in Zimbabwe, August to October in S Africa. *Nest:* Huge pile of sticks, up to 2,5 m diameter and 3 m deep, depending on length of use; bowl lined with green leaves; in stout fork of large forest tree (16 nests) 8–16,6–28 m above ground (sometimes up to 40 m). *Clutch:* (43) 1–1,7–2 eggs (usually 2). *Eggs:* Dull white, sometimes sparingly spotted with reddish brown and purplish grey; measure (49) 68,8 × 55,3 (56,4–74,8 × 49,6-60); weigh (2) 87–100 g. *Incubation:* 49–51 days, mostly by ♀. *Nestling:* (5) 103–110,5–115 days, fed by ♀ on food brought by ♂; later ♀ brings food too; only one chick survives, older killing younger; young dependent on parents for 9–11 months after first flight; breeding usually possible only every two years.

Ref. Jarvis, M.J.F., Currie, M.H. & Palmer, N. 1980. *Ostrich* 51:215–218.
Tuer, V. & Tuer, J. 1974. *Honeyguide* 80:33–41.

142 (145)

Brown Snake Eagle
Bruinslangarend
Circaetus cinereus
Plates 14 & 11

Ekangakodi (K), [Brauner Schlangenadler]

Measurements: Length 71–76 cm; wingspan (3) 164 cm; wing ♂ 490–508, ♀ 490–567; tail (19) 245–295; tarsus (19) 92–108; culmen (19) 42–45. Weight (26) 1540–2048–2465 g.

Bare Parts: Iris bright yellow; bill black; cere and legs greyish white.

Identification: Size medium; dark brown (faint purple gloss on upperparts in good light); eyes large, yellow; face owl-like; legs white (but often dirty), naked; in flight brown forepart of underwing contrasts with white remiges; 3 narrow white bars and narrow white tip to dark brown tail (immature Blackbreasted Snake Eagle barred with black on remiges; tail whitish with indistinct dark barring). *Immature*: Similar to adult or with white mottling on belly; sometimes white streaks on crown. *Chick*: Downy white; iris dark brown; cere and legs greyish white.

Voice: Guttural *hok-hok-hok*; drawn-out *kwee-oo*.

Distribution: Most of Africa S of Sahara; in s Africa mainly in N and NE.

Status: Mostly uncommon resident; fairly common in sw Zimbabwe; vagrant to s Natal and e Cape.

Habitat: Woodland, savanna, drier bushveld; mopane and granite koppie country of Zimbabwe.

Habits: Usually solitary. Perches prominently for long periods on tree or hilltop, watching for prey; rarely hovers or hunts in flight low over ground. Flies at intervals from one hunting perch to another. Kills

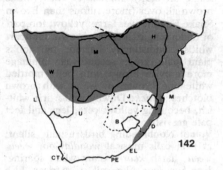

and swallows prey on ground. Soars in display flight with *hok-hok* calls.

Food: Snakes up to 3 m long, including cobras, adders and mambas; also Nile Monitor *Varanus niloticus* and smaller lizards.

Breeding: *Season*: July to March in Zimbabwe, December to March in Botswana and Transvaal (peak in January). *Nest*: Small flat platform of pencil-thin sticks, 60–70 cm diameter, 15–25 cm thick; leaf-lined bowl about 25 cm diameter; usually in flat-topped tree or euphorbia, 3,5–12 m (usually 9–10 m) above ground. *Clutch*: 1 egg. *Eggs*: Chalky white, sometimes bloodstained; measure (12) 75,5 × 60,9 (69,5–78,6 × 58,2–66); weigh 140–170 g. *Incubation*: 48–50 days by ♀ only. *Nestling*: 97–113 days (usually about 109 days); fed by ♀ on prey brought by ♂; later both parents bring prey for chick to eat by itself; dependent on parents for up to 2 months after first flight.

Ref. Steyn, P. 1964. *Ostrich* 35:22–31; 1972. *Ostrich* 43:149–164.

143 (146)

Blackbreasted Snake Eagle
Swartborsslangarend
Circaetus pectoralis
Plates 14 & 11

uKhozi (Z), [Schwarzbrust-Schlangenadler]

Measurements: Length 63–68 cm; wingspan (23) 177,6 cm; wing (6) 490–530; tail 255–290; tarsus 85–90; culmen 32–37. Weight (46) 1178–1502–2260 g.

Bare Parts: Iris yellow; bill black; cere blue-grey; legs and feet white.

Identification: Size medium; upperparts, head and breast black; rest of underparts white; eyes large, yellow; face owl-like;

legs white, bare; in flight underwing white, remiges and rectrices boldly barred with black (underwing of adult Martial Eagle all dark). *Immature*: Rich rufous brown all over (more rufous than Brown Snake Eagle); eyes large, yellow; forepart of underwing rich rufous brown, hindpart whitish, indistinctly barred; tail looks plain pale grey; second-year plumage more greyish brown with belly mottled white and brown, or white with brown blotches. *Chick*: Downy white; iris whitish, becoming yellow; cere, legs and feet pale greyish.

Voice: Nonbreeding birds usually silent; at nest calls musical *woodlay-oo, weeu, weeu*; harsh *kaarr, kaarr* when soaring; *kwo-kwo-kwo* like call of African Fish Eagle; various other fluting and yapping calls.

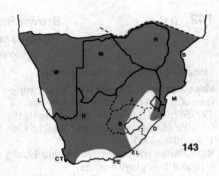

143

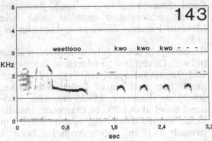

Distribution: S Africa (except sw Cape) to Zaire and Ethiopia.

Status: Uncommon, especially S of Orange River; some birds resident throughout s Africa, others intra-African migrants, present Transvaal November to May, Zimbabwe May to September.

Habitat: Highly variable; mostly lightly wooded open plains to semidesert with scattered trees; avoids forest and denser woodland.

Habits: Usually solitary; nonbreeding birds may roost communally in dry season, in flocks of up to 200. Hunts mostly while soaring, less often from perch on tree or telephone pole; often hovers. Drops like parachute onto prey, sometimes in stages; smaller prey swallowed in flight, larger prey torn up and eaten on ground. May hunt gregariously.

Food: Mainly snakes of all kinds, up to about 2 m long; also lizards, rodents, frogs, insects, fish (caught with the feet in flight from near surface of water); rarely birds and bats.

Breeding: *Season*: July to August in Transvaal, March to October in Zimbabwe; mainly winter months throughout s Africa. *Nest*: Smallish platform of thin sticks, 60–70 cm (up to 1 m) diameter, 20–25 cm thick; bowl lined with leaves; in top of tree or euphorbia, 4–9 m above ground. *Clutch*: 1 egg. *Eggs*: Chalky white, becoming nest-stained; measure (32) 72,5 × 57 (69,6–78,7 × 52–62,1); weigh about 136 g. *Incubation*: 51–52 days mostly by ♀, rarely by ♂. *Nestling*: 89–90 days, fed by both parents; still fed by parents up to 6 months after first flight.

Ref. Steyn, P. 1966. *Ostrich Suppl.* 6:141–154.

144 (147) Southern Banded Snake Eagle Plates 14 & 11
Dubbelbandslangarend
Circaetus fasciolatus

[Graubrust-Schlangenadler]

Measurements: Length 55–60 cm; wing ♂ 363–380, ♀ 371–390; tail 245–270; tarsus 76–87; culmen (3) 27–32,5. Weight (2 ♂) 908–960 g, (1 ♀) 1100 g, (2 unsexed) 950–1110 g.

Bare Parts: Iris pale yellow to cream; bill black; cere yellow; legs pale yellow.

Identification: Size medium; greyish brown with white barring from lower breast to belly and thighs (Western Banded Snake Eagle indistinctly barred on lower belly and thighs only; barring may be absent); tail longish, extending well beyond wingtips at rest (wingtips reach almost to end of shortish tail in Western Banded Snake Eagle); eyes pale yellow; face owl-like; in flight tail shows 3 dark bars and 2 white bars, hence Afrikaans name (Western Banded Snake Eagle shows single broad white band on black tail); underwing whitish, barred with blackish, and with dark trailing edge. *Immature*: Above dark brown, marked with white on wings, crown and nape; chin and throat white, streaked black; breast pale buff, narrowly streaked black; belly, flanks and thighs barred brown and white; in flight underwing and tail grey, barred with black like adult; iris pale yellow. *Chick*: Undescribed.

Voice: Rapid high-pitched *ko-ko-ko-kaau*; sonorous *kowaa*; crowing *kurrkurr*.

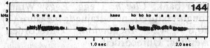

Distribution: Eastern coastal woodlands from Natal to s Somalia; also se lowlands and Chipinga Uplands of Zimbabwe.
Status: Rare and localized resident. Rare (RDB).
Habitat: Forest, riverine woodland; rarely in savanna.

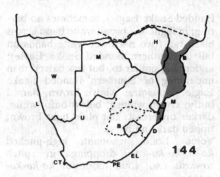

Habits: Shy and secretive; usually perches quietly in leafy cover, but sometimes conspicuously in open, scanning ground for prey. Seldom soars above forest. Flies from perch to perch with quick shallow wingbeats. Betrays presence by calling from cover.
Food: Mainly snakes and lizards; also small rodents, birds, insects.
Breeding: *Season*: September. *Nest*: Platform of twigs, about 60 cm diameter; bowl lined with green leaves; in fork of forest tree, well hidden below canopy, 7–8 m above ground; sometimes in canopy among creepers. *Clutch*: 1 egg. *Eggs*: White to greenish white; no measurements available. *Incubation*: Unrecorded. *Nestling*: Unrecorded.

Ref. Brown, L.H. 1969. *Ibis* 111:390–391.

145 (148) Western Banded Snake Eagle Plates 14 & 11
Enkelbandslangarend
Circaetus cinerascens

[Band-Schlangenadler]

Measurements: Length 55–60 cm; wingspan (1) 113,5 cm; wing (15) 367–408; tail 220–231; tarsus 80–84; culmen 31–33. Weight (1) 1126 g.
Bare Parts: Iris pale lemon yellow; bill orange-yellow at base, black at tip; cere orange-yellow; legs yellow.
Identification: Size medium; mainly ashy brown; at rest wingtips reach almost to tail tip (tail longer in Southern Banded Snake Eagle), giving stocky appearance; faint whitish barring on lower belly and flanks only (whole belly barred in Southern

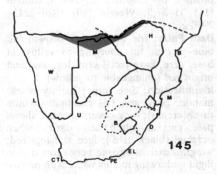

Banded Snake Eagle), sometimes no barring; in flight one broad white band across black tail (two narrower white bands on tail in Southern Banded Snake Eagle); underwing similar to, but less barred than underwing of Southern Banded Snake Eagle. *Immature*: Above brown, barred buffy; crown whitish; below buffy white, darker on breast; tail plain light brown, tipped dark (no bars).

Voice: Loud, resonant, high-pitched *ko-ko-ko-ko-ko*, dropping in pitch towards end; loud mournful *ko-ko-ko-waaa*.

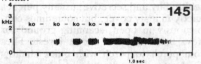

Distribution: Tropical Africa from Senegal to Ethiopia and S to Caprivi, n Botswana and n Zimbabwe (does not appear to overlap with Southern Banded Snake Eagle).

Status: Fairly common locally; mostly uncommon; resident.

Habitat: Riverine woodland along Okavango, Chobe and Zambezi river systems.

Habits: Usually solitary. Perches for long periods in tree, surveying ground for prey, swooping down to catch it, then carrying it to perch to eat it; also catches prey in trees. Flight fast and direct with quick shallow wingbeats; seldom flies far. Usually silent and secretive, but not shy.

Food: Mainly snakes of all kinds; also tortoise hatchlings, rodents, frogs, fish and insects.

Breeding: *Season*: Probably February to September (no definite breeding records for s Africa). *Nest*: Substantial bowl of sticks (may use old nest of other raptor); one Malawian nest 60 cm diameter, 15 cm thick, lined with green leaves; 9–18 m above ground in canopy of large tree near river bank. *Clutch*: 1 egg. *Eggs*: White, rough-textured, nest-stained; measure (1) 70,6 × 54,9. *Incubation*: Unrecorded. *Nestling*: Unrecorded.

146 (151)   Bateleur   Plates 13 & 11
Berghaan (Stompstertarend)
Terathopius ecaudatus

Sipupa (K), Chapungu (Sh), Ximhungu (Ts), Pêtlêkê, Ntsu (Tw), Ingqanga (X), iNgqungqulu (Z), [Gaukler]

Measurements: Length 55–70 cm; wingspan 172,7–186,2 cm; wing ♂ 482–515–553, ♀ 530–539–559; tail ♂ 98–109–124; tarsus ♂ 67–73–75, ♀ 72–74–75; culmen (11) 35–37,5. Weight (10) 1820–2242–2950 g.

Bare Parts: Iris deep honey-brown; bill blue-grey at tip, merging to yellow at base; cere, bare facial skin, legs and feet bright red (changeable to yellow).

Identification: Size large; mainly black; mantle, back and tail chestnut (mantle rarely cream); wing coverts grey; ♀ shows pale greyish white secondaries when perched (black in ♂); face and legs red; wingtips extend beyond very short tail; in flight underwing mainly white with narrow

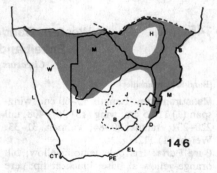

(in ♀) or broad (in ♂) black trailing edge; flight pattern characteristic, with upswept wingtips; feet extend slightly beyond very short tail (looks almost tailless in flight). *Immature*: Light brown lightly flecked with white; bill black; cere and face pale greenish blue; legs and feet whitish; tail longer than feet in flight; later plumages mainly plain dark brown; progressively more black feathering with age, face becoming orange, then reddish; adult plumage attained at about 7–8 years. *Chick*: Downy chocolate brown with cream coloured head and flanks; iris dark brown; bill black; cere and legs pale greenish.

Voice: Usually silent; barking *kow-ow*; chattering *ka-ka-ka*.

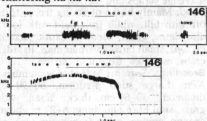

Distribution: Most of Africa S of Sahara; also Arabia and Iraq; in s Africa mostly absent from S of Auob, Malopo, Limpopo and Tugela Rivers, but present in Transvaal lowveld.

Status: Common resident; numbers declining rapidly in settled areas, but probably stable in game reserves; absent from much of former range (e Cape, most of Natal, Orange Free State and Transvaal). Vulnerable (RDB).

Habitat: Woodland and savanna on open plains, including Kalahari thornveld.

Habits: Solitary or somewhat gregarious in flocks of up to 40 birds, sometimes in company with Tawny Eagles. Spends much of each day in direct or circling flight (at 60–80 km/h), seldom flapping wings; takes off with rapid shallow wingbeats. Seldom flies in wet weather. Hunts live prey by stooping in flight or parachuting gently with wings held up and legs extended; may rob larger eagles and vultures of food; also scavenges, especially in immature stages, often along roads for traffic kills. Roosts in trees; by day may sunbathe with wings spread.

Food: Birds, mammals, reptiles, fish; mostly mammals by weight, birds by number; also carrion, eggs of ground-nesting birds, crabs and insects.

Breeding: *Season*: All months in Zimbabwe (peak December-March); mostly December to June elsewhere in s Africa (peak January-March). *Nest*: Platform of sticks, about 60 cm diameter, 30 cm thick; leaf-lined bowl about 25 cm diameter; (42 nests) 8–12–16 m above ground, usually in canopy or on horizontal fork of large tree; may use old nests of other raptors. *Clutch*: 1 egg. *Eggs*: Plain white (rarely with few red marks), becoming nest-stained; measure (50) 79,1 × 62,7 (74,2–87 × 57–68,1); weigh about 168 g. *Incubation*: 52–55–59 days mostly by ♀, but also by ♂. *Nestling*: (6) 93–115 days (1 exact measurement 111–112 days); fed by both parents; young dependent on parents 90–120 days after first flight.

Ref. Watson, R.T. 1990. *Ostrich* 61: 13–23.

147 (112)   Palmnut Vulture   Plates 10 & 11
Witaasvoël
Gypohierax angolensis

Gungwa, Ngungwamawala (Ts), [Palmengeier]

Measurements: Length about 60 cm; wingspan about 130–140 cm; wing (123) 397–426,6–446; tail (120) 182–206,8–252; tarsus (15) 75–85; culmen (15) 40–45. Weight (3 ♂) 1361–1505–1710 g, (1 ♀) 1712 g.

Bare Parts: Iris yellow; bill pale yellowish grey; cere pale blue; bare facial and malar skin red to orange; legs and feet dull orange, yellow or pinkish.

Identification: Size large; mostly white with black on scapulars, wings and tail;

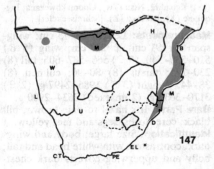

head mostly feathered, white, with bare red patches around eye and below bill; in flight tail short, rounded, black with white tip; wings white except for black inner secondaries, black tips to primaries and small black patches on leading edge. African Fish Eagle has brown belly and all-dark underwing; tail all white, square to rounded; Egyptian Vulture has all-white diamond-shaped tail; all remiges black; naked yellow face. *Immature*: Brown; bare facial skin yellowish; iris brown; legs whitish; bill much stouter than those of immature Hooded or Egyptian Vultures; much larger than immature Gymnogene. *Chick*: Downy brown; iris brown; facial skin and legs whitish.

Voice: Usually silent; guttural *prak-karr* in display and threat; cawing *kwuk-kwuk-kwuk*.

Distribution: Most of Africa S of Sahara; in s Africa confined to e littoral, S to Zululand; stragglers recorded e and n Cape, Orange Free State, Lesotho, n Transvaal, Etosha National Park (Namibia), n Botswana and w Zimbabwe.

Status: Rare and localized resident in E; vagrant (mainly immatures) elsewhere in s Africa. Rare (RDB).

Habitat: Forest, mangroves, marine shores; always in association with Raffia Palms *Raphia australis* (and elsewhere with Oil Palm *Elaeis guineensis*), even

where planted outside of normal range (as in Zululand).

Habits: Solitary or gregarious; highly sedentary when adult, spending most of each day resting near palms. Roosts communally in palms or baobabs. Soars well; takes off with quick wingbeats. Hunts live prey by stooping from flight; may catch fish from near water surface, or may completely submerge; walks about on shorelines to catch invertebrates and to scavenge scraps and carrion.

Food: Mainly husks of Raffia fruits, torn off with bill, while fruit held with foot; also dates, grain, seeds of exotic *Acacia cyclops*, small birds and mammals, lizards, crabs, molluscs, frogs and carrion.

Breeding: *Season*: May to September. *Nest*: Large stick platform, 60–90 cm diameter, 30–60 cm thick; lined with grass, sisal fibre and dung; 6–27 m above ground among palm fronds, in fork of baobab or top of euphorbia. *Clutch*: 1 egg. *Eggs*: White, often washed with buff or rusty, freckled and blotched with reddish brown, chocolate and lilac; measure (19) 71,2 × 53,6   (66,1–78,3 × 50,2–56,8); weigh about 107 g. *Incubation*: About 44 days, probably by ♀ only. *Nestling*: At least 90 days.

Ref. Austen, W.M. 1953. *Ostrich* 24:98–102.
Brooke, R.K. & Jeffery, R.D. 1972. *Bull. Brit. Orn. Club* 92:15–21.
Donnelly, B.G. & Irwin, M.P.S. 1972. *Bull. Brit. Orn. Club* 92:11–15.

148 (149) African Fish Eagle Plates 13 & 12
Visarend
Haliaeetus vocifer

Mpungu (K), Hungwe (Sh), N'hwati, Ngungwa (Ts), Kgoadirê, Ntsu (Tw), Unomakhwezana, Ingqolane (X), iNkwazi (Z), [Schreiseeadler]

Measurements: Length 63–73 cm; wingspan ♂ 191 cm, ♀ 237 cm; wing (5 ♂) 510–530–540, (3 ♀) 565–587–605; tail (8) 230–275; tarsus (8) 80–90; culmen (8) 38–44. Weight (3 ♂) 1986–2497 g, (2 ♀) 3170–3630 g, (2 unsexed) 2634–2900 g.

Bare Parts: Iris hazel to pale brown; bill black; cere, lores, legs and feet yellow.

Identification: Size large; body and wings dark, contrasting with white head and tail; belly and upperwing coverts dark chest-

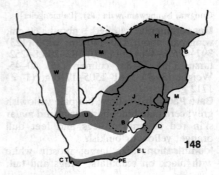

nut; wings and back black; in flight underwing chestnut, remiges black; tail short, square, white; head white. Palmnut Vulture has black tail with white tip; underwing mostly white; belly white. Egyptian Vulture has wedge-shaped tail; underwing white in front, black behind; belly white. *Immature*: Above dull mottled brown; below mostly whitish with heavy blackish blotching on belly, streaking on chest; tail white, broadly tipped black; underwing white in front, mostly black on remiges with whitish windows; adult plumage attained in more than 5 years. *Chick*: Downy white; bill horn; cere pale yellow; legs pink.

Voice: Highly vocal; loud ringing *WHOW-kayow-kwow*, dropping slightly in pitch and loudness towards end of phrase; pitch of ♂ higher than that of ♀; duetting common, starting with loud *weee*, followed by alternating high and low *kow-kow-kow-kow*.

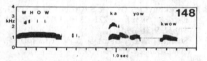

Distribution: Africa S of Sahara; throughout s Africa, except most of Little Namaqualand, nw Cape and s Namibia.
Status: Common in E and N; uncommon elsewhere; resident, sometimes nomadic.
Habitat: Larger rivers, lakes, pans and dams, usually with large trees; also coastal lagoons and estuaries.
Habits: Usually in pairs. Perches for hours (85–95% of daylight) on tall trees near water; also soars; often calls in flight. Most vocal at dawn. Hunts from perch, stooping at fish, catching them with feet, usually within 15 cm of surface, without checking flight; may submerge at times; more rarely hunts while soaring; robs other fish-eating birds of their prey; raids colonies of nesting waterbirds for young and eggs.
Food: Mainly fish up to 1 kg weight, less often up to 3 kg; maximum weight of live fish caught about 3,7 kg, but fish of over 2,5 kg not carried in flight, but planed along surface of water to shore. Also eats carrion, nestlings and eggs of waterbirds and queleas, some adult waterbirds (up to size of flamingo); rarely dassies, monkeys, monitor lizards, frogs, terrapins, insects.
Breeding: *Season*: March to September in S Africa (peak June-August), January to October in Zimbabwe (mainly April-July). *Nest*: Large pile of sticks, 120–180 cm diameter, 30–60 cm thick (up to 120 cm after long use); bowl lined with grass, green leaves and reeds; (37 nests) 4–13–22 m above gound in fork of tree near water; less often on cliff ledge, or low bush on steep slope. *Clutch*: (117) 1–2–3 eggs (usually 2). *Eggs*: Plain white, rarely with reddish markings, usually neststained; measure (74) 70,3 × 53,7 (63,5–76,8 × 48,2–57,9); weigh about 120 g. *Incubation*: About 42–45 days by both sexes. *Nestling*: 70–75 days, fed mostly by ♀; ♂ feeds small nestlings only; usually only 1 or 2 young survive; dependent on parents up to 60 days after first flight.

Ref. Brown, L. 1980. *The African Fish Eagle*. Folkestone: Bailey Bros & Swinfen.

149 (154) Steppe Buzzard Plates 15 & 17
Bruinjakkalsvoël
Buteo buteo

Siimbi (K), Khajoane (SS), Segôdi, Phakwê (Tw), Isangxa (X), [Mäusebussard]

Measurements: Length 45–50 cm; wingspan ♂ 102–120 cm, ♀ 118–128 cm; wing (67) 341–368,9–394; tail ♂ 170–185–207, ♀ 175–191–209; tarsus 69–82; culmen (22) 18,9–21,5–23,7. Weight (3 ♀) 712,8–754,6–783,4 g, (144 unsexed) 453–714,2–925 g.

Bare Parts: Iris brown; bill black; cere, legs and feet yellow.
Identification: Size medium; highly variable in plumage; above brown, slightly more rufous on tail; below generally brown barred white, or white barred and blotched brown; paler band across chest usually visible in most plumages; in flight mostly brown with pale chest band and

whitish remiges, tipped blackish; tail looks paler brown. Similar to Forest Buzzard, but usually browner and usually inhabits open country. *Immature*: Similar to adult, but usually more blotchy on belly, streaked on chest (not finely barred); iris pale yellow or biscuit-coloured; very similar to Forest Buzzard; age classes not easily separable in field.

Voice: Usually silent in s Africa; high mewing *kee-oo* (not separable from call of Forest Buzzard).

Distribution: Breeds Eurasia and N Africa; migrates to coastal W Africa, Mediterranean Africa, and Egypt to S Africa; in s Africa absent from dry W.

Status: Common nonbreeding Palaearctic migrant, October to April; ringed birds recovered Russia (12 000 km NNE).

Habitat: Open country; grassveld, farmland, savanna.

Habits: Solitary or gregarious; flocks occur at good food source and on migra-

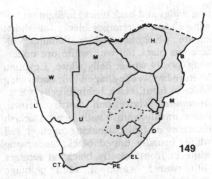

tion; usually seen perched on telephone pole, fence post or leafless branch. Hunts by dropping onto prey from perch; rarely also by hovering or by walking on ground. Often soars; dive-bombing display flights occur towards March.

Food: Mainly insects in s Africa; also small birds (weavers, quails), small mammals, lizards, frogs.

Breeding: Extralimital.

Ref. Broekhuysen, G.J. & Siegfried, W.R. 1971. *Ostrich Suppl.* 8:221–237; 1971. *Ostrich Suppl.* 9:31–39.
Schmitt, M.B., Baur, S. & Von Maltitz, F. 1980. *Ostrich* 51:151–159.

150 (155)   Forest Buzzard   Plates 15 & 17
Bosjakkalsvoël
Buteo trizonatus

[Bergbussard]

Measurements: Length about 45 cm; wing ♂ 318–335–352, ♀ 330–349–362, (12 unsexed) 330–344,2–365; tail (E African birds) ♂ 174–183, ♀ 180–196; tarsus 60; culmen (12) 20–21,6–23. Weight (1) 700 g.

Bare Parts: Iris dark brown; bill blackish; cere, legs and feet yellow.

Identification: Size medium; plumage variable; above brown; below white, heavily streaked or blotched with drop-shaped dark brown markings on belly and breast, leaving broad white chest band; very similar to Steppe Buzzard, but generally whiter below; easily confused with immature Steppe Buzzard, but usually

occurs at forest edges and in forest (not open veld); flight pattern like that of Steppe Buzzard; wide dark band at tip of tail. *Immature*: More streaky below than adult; iris yellow or biscuit-coloured; no wide band at tip of tail. *Chick*: Downy white; iris brown; cere and feet pale yellow.

Voice: Clear, mewing, drawn-out *keee-oo* or *keee-he-he-he*; whistled *tzeee*.

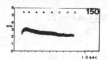

Distribution: Discontinuously in forest patches from sw Cape to Ethiopia (more in montane forests from Natal northward); in s Africa confined to s Cape, Natal uplands and e Transvaal escarpment.

Status: Uncommon localized resident; possibly threatened species.

Habitat: Edge of indigenous and exotic forest, especially pine plantations; not in high mountains in s Africa.

Habits: Solitary or in pairs; unobtrusive, except when soaring over forest or nearby

cliffs, or when calling. Hunts usually from perch inside forest tree (also on telephone pole, rock or leafless branch), dropping onto prey. Hunts both in open at forest edge, or inside forest.

Food: Mainly small rodents; also golden moles, lizards, snakes, small birds, frogs, insects and scorpions.

Breeding: *Season*: September-October. *Nest*: Stick platform 60–70 cm diameter, 30–35 cm thick; bowl 18–20 cm diameter, 8 cm deep, lined with green leaves, lichens and pine needles until nestling 4 weeks old; in fork of tree (7) 9–16–20 m above ground (commonly in pine tree, about 18 m up). *Clutch*: 2–3 eggs (probably usually 2). *Eggs*: Pale green with scattered spots and blotches of rust and grey-brown; measure (10) 55,6 × 42,6 (52,5–58,2 × 39,8–45). *Incubation*: Unrecorded. *Nestling*: About 50 days; independent at 80–130 days.

Ref. Palmer, N.G., Norton, P.M. & Robertson, A.S. 1985. *Ostrich* 56:67–73.

151 (–)   Longlegged Buzzard   Plate 75
Langbeenjakkalsvoël
Buteo rufinus

[Adlerbussard]

Measurements: Length 51–66 cm; wingspan ♂ 126–143 cm, ♀ 141–148 cm; wing (19 ♂) 425–437–459, (18 ♀) 448–466–496; tail (20 ♂) 207–227–244, (20 ♀) 223–241–262; tarsus (22 ♂) 85–89–93, (23 ♀) 87–90,5–94; culmen (20 ♂) 23,6–26,1–29,2, (20 ♀) 25,9–27,8–31,9. Weight (8 ♂) 590–1035–1281 g, (11 ♀) 945–1314–1760 g.

Bare Parts: Iris light sepia to dark brown; bill blackish horn; cere yellow to greenish yellow; legs and feet bright yellow.

Identification: Larger than other s African buzzards; long yellow legs characteristic when perched; plumage variable, similar to Steppe Buzzard, but head markedly pale, and underparts usually more rufous; tail usually plain pale rufous; in flight whitish patch at base of primaries; underwing pale behind, darker in front with dark wrist patches at

bend of wing; wings almost uniformly broad; hovers often; underparts pale; tail pale, unmarked. *Immature*: Probably indistinguishable in field from immature Steppe Buzzard; eyes yellow; tail barred; legs somewhat longer than those of Steppe Buzzard.

Voice: Silent in s Africa; sharp mewing calls.

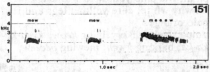

Distribution: *B. r. rufinus* breeds se Europe, Asia, N Africa; migrates to tropical Africa when not breeding; in s Africa recorded only Namibia, Natal (specimen in Transvaal Museum) and 100 km N of Nata, Botswana (April 1985).

Status: Very rare nonbreeding Palaearctic

migrant; vagrant to s Africa. All claims S of Tanzania now considered unsubstantiated (1988).

Habitat: Open woodland, savanna, semi-desert.

Habits: Solitary. Sluggish; usually perches on tree or post, scanning ground below for prey.

Food: Mainly small mammals up to size of hares; also small reptiles; possibly some birds and carrion.

Breeding: Extralimital.

Ref. Brooke, R.K. 1974. *Bull. Brit. Orn. Club* 94:59–62.
Davidson, I. 1976. *Bokmakierie* 28:74.

152 (152) Jackal Buzzard Plates 15 & 17
Rooiborsjakkalsvoël
Buteo rufofuscus

Khajoane, Tlatloatšoana (SS), Indlandlokazi (X), iNhladlokazi, isiKhobotho (Z), [Felsenbussard]

Measurements: Length 44–53 cm; wing (15 ♂) 393–407–430, (22 ♀) 423–439–467; tail (19) 180–220; tarsus (19) 76–85; culmen (19) 24–30. Weight (7 ♂) 865–951–1080 g, (11 ♀) 1150–1308–1695 g, (55 unsexed) 790–1064–1370 g.

Bare Parts: Iris dark brown; bill black; cere, legs and feet yellow.

Identification: Size medium; upperparts, head and throat slate grey (blackish at distance); breast dark rufous to chestnut (very rarely black or white) bordered above by irregular white band; belly black, lightly barred or blotched with white; tail plain rufous; in flight wing blackish with broad white band; short, light rufous tail conspicuous. *Immature*: Above brown, with some buff markings; below plain light rufous; underwing as in adult, but rufous (not black) in front; tail greyish with darker barring, then with terminal bar, finally plain; iris pale yellow to whitish. *Chick*: Downy white; cere yellow; legs and feet pale orange.

Voice: Jackal-like yelping *keow, kyaa-ka-ka-ka*; barking *kweh*; mewing *peeeew*.

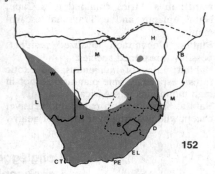

152

Distribution: S Africa and s Namibia.

Status: Locally common in mountainous country; less common elsewhere.

Habitat: Mostly mountainous and hilly country, including high Drakensberg; also arid coastal regions of Namibia.

Habits: Solitary or in pairs. Usually seen in flight, characteristically broad-winged (sometimes mistaken for Bateleur, but much smaller and longer-tailed), soaring over valleys and along mountainsides; inconspicuous when perched on rock. Perches also on telephone poles along roads. Often hovers on updraught. Hunts by stooping in flight or gliding from perch.

Food: Small mammals (up to size of dassie), birds (up to size of francolin), reptiles (including poisonous snakes like Puffadder); also insects, road-kills, carrion.

Breeding: *Season*: May to October (peak August-September). *Nest*: Bulky pile of sticks, 60–70 cm diameter, up to 35 cm deep; leaf-lined bowl about 20 cm diameter; usually (80%) on ledge (18 nests) 9–27–62 m above foot of cliff; also in trees, especially pines (6 nests) 6–10,5–12 m above ground. *Clutch*: (56)

1–1,9–3 eggs (usually 2). *Eggs*: Chalky white, spotted and blotched with red-brown; measure (44) 60,2 × 47,3 (56,3–64,9 × 43,3–49,9). *Incubation*: About 40 days by both sexes. *Nestling*: 50–53 days, fed mostly by ♀; ♂ provides all food

initially, later both parents hunt; older chick may kill younger, but not always.

Ref. Brooke, R.K. 1975. *Bull. Brit. Orn. Club* 95:152–154.
   Norgarb, C. & Lasbrey, J. 1953. *Ostrich* 24:33–36.

153 (152B)   Augur Buzzard   Plates 15 & 17
Witborsjakkalsvoël
Buteo augur

[Augurbussard]

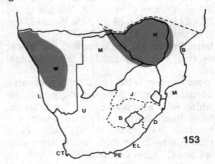

153

Measurements: Length about 55–60 cm; wing (15 ♂) 395–420–450, (7 ♀) 430–439–450; tail ♂ 218, ♀ 235; tarsus ♂ 86, ♀ 93; culmen (15 ♂) 25–26,3–28, (6 ♀) 28–29,2–30. Weight (5 ♂) 880–998–1160 g, (7 ♀) 1097–1130–1303 g, (6 unsexed) 853–994–1130 g.

Bare Parts: Iris dark brown; bill black; cere, legs and feet yellow.

Identification: Size medium; above blackish slate; below white (sometimes with black throat or bib in ♀) with rufous undertail coverts; tail deep rufous (distinguishes it from somewhat similar Blackbreasted Snake Eagle); in flight underwing white with narrow black trailing edge and black comma-shaped mark at each wrist. *Immature*: Above brown, marked with buff; below buff, lightly streaked brown on throat and sides of breast; in flight underwing buff in front, otherwise as in adult; tail greyish below, lightly barred darker. *Chick*: Downy greyish white; iris and bill grey; cere, legs and feet yellow.

Voice: Yelping *kow-kow-kow* in courtship, sometimes preceded by whistling note.

Distribution: Northern parts of s Africa to Ethiopia; in s Africa restricted to nw Namibia, e Zimbabwe and w border of Mozambique.

Status: Fairly common resident; straggler to Transvaal.

Habitat: Mountainous country, rocky koppies; usually at higher elevations, but also to sea level in arid coastal Namibia.

Habits: Solitary or in pairs. Spends much time perched on rock or tree; scans ground below, either from perch or in flight, stooping or parachuting onto prey. Sometimes hovers in wind, or walks on ground to catch insects. Courtship includes spectacular aerobatic displays.

Food: Mainly snakes and lizards; also small mammals, a few birds and insects; not known to eat carrion.

Breeding: *Season*: July to October (peak August-September). *Nest*: Pile of sticks, 56–64 cm diameter, 15–19 cm thick; bowl lined with finer sticks and green leaves; usually on cliff ledge, sometimes in tree or at base of tree growing from cliff. *Clutch*: 2 eggs (rarely 3). *Eggs*: Plain bluish white, or pale blue with chocolate and mauve spots; measure (53) 57,1 × 46,3 (55,1–59,3 × 43,5–47,2); weigh 65–74 g. *Incubation*: 39–40 days by both sexes, mostly by ♀ (66%). *Nestling*: 48–55 days, fed by both parents, mainly by ♀; ♂ provides all food at first; older chick kills younger within first week; young dependent on parents for up to 6 weeks after first flight.

Ref. Brooke, R.K. 1975. *Bull. Brit. Orn. Club* 95:152–154.
   Lendrum, A.L. 1979. *Ostrich* 50:203–214.

154 (144)

Lizard Buzzard
Akkedisvalk

Plates 15 & 17

Kaupifalco monogrammicus

Rukodzi (Sh), Rikhozi (Ts), Segôôtsane, Phakalane (Tw), uKlebe (Z), [Sperberbussard]

Measurements: Length 35–37 cm; wingspan (9) 78,5 cm; wing (9 ♂) 210–
218–225, (12 ♀) 222–233–248; tail ♂
130–136, ♀ 141–155; tarsus ♂ 50–54, ♀
53–55; culmen (21) 16–18. Weight (6 ♂)
220–245,5–275 g, (8 ♀) 248–304,3–374 g,
(119 unsexed) 223–297,3–410 g.

Bare Parts: Iris dark brown; bill black;
eyering, cere, legs and feet red to orange-
red.

Identification: Size smallish; upperparts,
head and breast plain light grey; throat
white with median vertical black stripe;
belly finely barred grey and white; tail
blackish with one broad white band
(sometimes 2); in flight white rump conspicuous. Gabar Goshawk lacks black line
on white throat and has several white tail
bands; otherwise somewhat similar; Lizard Buzzard dumpier-looking than any
Accipiter species. *Immature*: Similar to
adult, but with buff edges to dorsal plumage. *Chick*: Downy white; iris brown; bill
black; cere, legs and feet yellow.

Voice: Melodious whistling *klioo-klu-klu-
klu*; loud sharp *pee-oo pee-oo*.

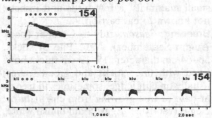

Distribution: Most of Africa S of Sahara;
in s Africa confined to N and NE.
Status: Fairly common resident; somewhat nomadic.
Habitat: Savanna and woodland, espe-

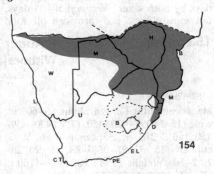

cially mature broadleaved deciduous
woodland.
Habits: Usually solitary. Perches for quite
long periods on conspicuous tree or post,
scanning ground for prey; makes quick
dash when prey sighted. Flies low, swooping up to perch; soars occasionally.
Food: Mostly insects; also lizards, small
snakes, some frogs, small mammals and
birds.
Breeding: *Season*: May to December in
Transvaal, August to January in Zimbabwe (peak September-November).
Nest: Compact platform of sticks, about
40 cm diameter; bowl about 15 cm diameter lined with *Usnea* lichen, dry grass and
green leaves; in fork of tree, usually
6–10 m above ground. *Clutch*: (44)
1–1,9–3 eggs (usually 2). *Eggs*: White,
greenish white or pale blue, plain or
sparsely marked with brown and reddish
brown; measure (108) 44,7 × 35,5
(41,5–49,6 × 32–38,2); weigh about
28–29 g. *Incubation*: 33–34 days by ♀
only. *Nestling*: 40 days, fed by ♀ only, at
least at first; dependent on parents for
about 30–40 days after first flight.

Ref. Chittenden, H.N. 1979. *Ostrich* 50:186–187.

SPARROWHAWKS AND GOSHAWKS (GENUS *ACCIPITER*)

The sparrowhawks and goshawks belong to the genus *Accipiter*, the largest genus of
diurnal birds of prey, containing nearly 50 species. They are mostly relatively small to
medium-sized, though a few are large. They are slender-bodied, with short rounded
wings, a longish tail (over half total body length), a small sharp bill for eating birds and

small reptiles, and rather long slender legs and toes with sharp claws. They inhabit woodlands from savanna to forest. Their flight is dashing, with much twisting and turning as they pursue prey through trees and branches. Their identification is sometimes confusing, many species having similar colour patterns of grey back and barred belly; immatures tend to be heavily blotched below.

Ref. Black, R.A.R. & Ross, G.J.B. 1970. *Ann. Cape Prov. Mus. (Nat. Hist.)* 8:57–65.
Irwin, M.P.S., Benson, C.W. & Steyn, P. 1982. *Honeyguide* 111/112:28–44.

155 (156)   Redbreasted Sparrowhawk   Plates 16 & 18
Rooiborssperwer
Accipiter rufiventris

Kakodi (K), Rukodzi (Sh), Segôôtsane, Phakalane (Tw), Ukhetshana (X), [Rotbauchsperber]

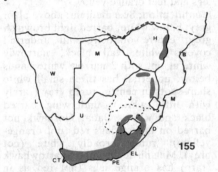

Measurements: Length 33–40 cm; wing-span (1) 72 cm; wing ♂ 200–214–225, ♀ 230–235–245; tail (6 ♂) 155–162, (8 ♀) 180–195; tarsus (14) 49–57; culmen (14) 11–14. Weight (3) 180–191,7–210 g.

Bare Parts: Iris yellow; bill black; cere, legs and feet yellow.

Identification: Size medium; above slate; below plain rufous; head dark to below eye (rufous-breasted immature of Ovambo Sparrowhawk has broad pale eyebrow; dark ear patches only; iris brown); in flight wings and tail boldly barred black and white. *Immature*: Variable; mostly rufous below with dark streaks and sometimes pale edging to feathers, giving barred effect; throat white; iris pale grey to yellow. *Chick*: Downy white; iris dark brown; bill black; cere, legs and feet yellow.

Voice: Staccato *kew-kew-kew-kew*; ♀ has plaintive drawn-out *kieeeu* when soliciting food from ♂.

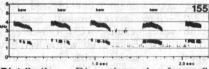

Distribution: Discontinuously from S Africa to Ethiopia; also w Angola; in s Africa mainly in S and E.

Status: Uncommon, but regular resident; probably increasing range and numbers because able to exploit exotic plantations.

Habitat: Montane forest-grassland mosaic, wooded kloofs, exotic plantations; hunts over open grassland and fynbos near forest.

Habits: Solitary or in pairs; shy and unobtrusive. Swift bold hunter, dashing out fast and low from tree to take prey on ground or in flight; makes surprise attacks from cover; less often hunts by soaring and stooping. During courtship ♂ flies high over forest, calling.

Food: Birds up to size of larger doves; rarely mice, bats, insects.

Breeding: *Season*: September to December; mainly October in sw Cape. *Nest*: Platform of small sticks, 40–45 cm diameter, 20–30 cm thick; bowl lined with bark, moss, grass or finer twigs; built by both sexes; in fork of tree (12 nests) 8–13–20 m above ground. *Clutch*: (14) 2–2,9–4 eggs (usually 3). *Eggs*: White to greenish white, blotched with reddish brown, usually forming cap at one end; measure (45) 41 × 32,2 (36,7–44,5 × 30–35,1); weigh about 23 g. *Incubation*: 34 days, almost all by ♀. *Nestling*: 35 days, fed by ♀ on food brought by ♂; young dependent on parents for up to 73 days after first flight.

Ref. Steyn, P. 1988. *Bokmakierie* 40:66–73.

156 (157) Ovambo Sparrowhawk **Plates 16 & 18**
Ovambosperwer
Accipiter ovampensis

Kakodi (K), Rukodzi (Sh), Segôôtsane, Phakalane (Tw), [Ovambosperber]

Measurements: Length 31–40 cm; wing ♂ 210–255, ♀ 245–253; tail ♂ 145–150, ♀ 160–190; tarsus (16) 43–52; culmen (16) 11–15. Weight (18) 119–196,4–305 g.

Bare Parts: Iris dark red; bill black; cere, legs and feet orange-yellow.

Identification: Size medium; above plain grey; below white, barred light brownish grey; centre of belly and undertail coverts white; tail black, narrowly white at tip, with 3 narrow white bands below; uppertail has three small white shaft-spots in centre; rump grey (rarely with little white); underwing barred black and white. Gabar Goshawk not barred on breast; legs red (not orange-yellow); rump broadly white (not grey). Melanistic Ovambo Sparrowhawk (rare) has orange legs (not red as in melanistic Gabar Goshawk). *Immature (2 forms)*: (a) above brown, no white on rump; below whitish, streaked brown; flanks barred; broad white eyebrow; dark patch behind eye (head of Rufous-breasted Sparrowhawk all dark to below eye); iris brown; cere, legs and feet yellow; (b) similar, but barred grey and white below. *Chick*: Downy white; iris dark brown; cere and legs pinkish orange.

Voice: Usually silent; in breeding season sustained *keep-keep-keep*; threat *krrr-krrr* to conspecific; alarm call high-pitched *ki-ki-ki-ki*.

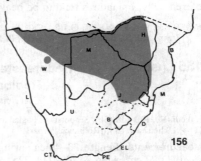

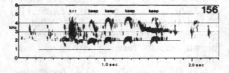

Distribution: Africa S of Sahara, mainly in tropics; in s Africa mainly in N and NE, as far S as Windhoek in W.

Status: Generally uncommon, though common locally; resident; numbers probably increasing through adaptation to exotic plantations. In s Transvaal about 1 pair/27 km².

Habitat: Any woodland, savanna and exotic plantations.

Habits: Shy and unobtrusive when not breeding; when breeding soars above trees in pairs, calling loudly. Agile and graceful in flight; hunts from perch or from soaring position, either in woodland or in adjacent open country.

Food: Birds up to size of Redeyed Dove.

Breeding: *Season*: September to November in Transvaal, August to November in Zimbabwe. *Nest*: Platform of thin sticks, 35–50 cm diameter (mean of 15 nests 30 cm), 24 cm thick (mean of 11 nests); bowl, about 15 cm diameter, 5–7 cm deep, lined with finer sticks, bark flakes or green leaves; usually in fork against main trunk of tree, (60) 12–17–26 m above ground; built by both sexes. *Clutch*: (63) 1–3–5 eggs (usually 3). *Eggs*: Dull white, variably spotted or marbled with chestnut and purplish; measure (123) 41,3 × 32,6 (38,5–46,2 × 28,7–34,7). *Incubation*: 33–35 days, almost entirely by ♀. *Nestling*: About 33 days, fed by ♀ only, on food brought by ♂ (♂ rarely feeds); postnestling period (3) about 30 days.

Ref. Allan, D.G. & Hustler, C.W. 1984. *Proc. 2nd Symp. Afr. Pred. Birds*:57–58.
Kemp, A.C. & Kemp, M.I. 1975. *Ann. Tvl Mus.* 29:185–190.

157 (158)

Little Sparrowhawk
Kleinsperwer
Accipiter minullus

Plates 16 & 18

Kakodi Gomununu (K), Rukodzi (Sh), Ukhe-tshana (X), uMqwayini (Z), [Zwergsperber]

Measurements: Length 23–27 cm; wing (21 ♂) 136–141,4–145, (11 ♀) 156–160,2–165; tail (21) 105–130; tarsus (21) 38–46; culmen (21) 8–12. Weight (6 ♂) 74,3–78,1–85 g, (1 ♀) 101,2 g, (4 unsexed) 68–82,7–105 g.

Bare Parts: Iris yellow to orange-yellow; bill black; cere, legs and feet yellow.

Identification: Size small; above grey; below white, finely barred rufous brown; flanks washed rufous; upper tail blackish with two central white eyespots, one above the other, and narrow white tip; rump broadly white in flight; eyespots conspicuous; undertail white with three dark bars. *Immature*: Above brown (no white eyebrow); narrowly white at base of tail; tail dark with white eyespots as in adult; below whitish, plain on throat (dark centre line absent or less well developed than in much larger immature African Goshawk), with heavy dark brown drop-shaped spots on breast and belly; underwing pale rufous, spotted blackish. *Chick*: Downy buff; iris dark brown; cere pale yellow; legs and feet pale orange.

Voice: Noisy when breeding; rapid high-pitched *kik-kik-kik* (♀) or mellower *kew-kew-kew* (♂); slow *kiak...kiak...kiak* by ♂ to ♀.

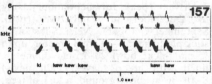

157

Distribution: Africa, from Cape to Zaire and Ethiopia; in s Africa absent from most of Lesotho, Orange Free State, Cape Province, s Botswana and s Namibia.

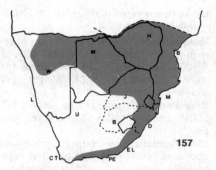

157

Status: Generally uncommon resident. Habitat: Woodland, forest (montane and riverine), exotic plantations.

Habits: Usually solitary; easily over-looked when perched within canopy of tree, but bold and quite tame. Seldom flies in open; usually dashes quickly from tree to tree. Hunts from perch, from ground or in flight from dense cover, seizing prey on ground or as it flies past.

Food: Mainly small birds, 10–40 g weight, rarely up to 80 g (own body weight); occasionally insects and lizards.

Breeding: *Season*: September to December. *Nest*: Platform of coarse sticks, lined with finer sticks and sometimes green leaves; 18–30 cm diameter, 10–15 cm thick; bowl 7–9 cm diameter; (28 nests) 5–13,4–23 m above ground in upper branches or main fork of tree; built by both sexes, but mostly by ♀; material carried usually in feet. *Clutch*: (33) 1–2–4 eggs (usually 2). *Eggs*: Plain white or greenish white; measure (43) 34,8 × 28,1 (32,6–37,8 × 27–31,6); weigh about 18 g. *Incubation*: 31–32 days by both sexes (75% by ♀). *Nestling*: 25–27 days, fed almost entirely by ♀, on food brought by ♂; usually only 1 chick reared per brood, so Cainism possible.

Ref. Liversidge, R. 1962. *Ibis* 104:399–406.
    Steyn, P. 1972. *Bokmakierie* 24:13–16.

158 (159)   **Black Sparrowhawk**   **Plates 16 & 18**
Swartsperwer
Accipiter melanoleucus

Kakodi Gomusovagani (K), Rukodzi (Sh), [Mohrenhabicht, Trauerhabicht]

Measurements: Length 46–58 cm; wingspan (3) 101,7 cm; wing (5 ♂) 287–295, (3 ♀) 333–342; tail (8) 210–267; tarsus (8) 73–90; culmen (8) 18–24. Weight (19) 476–699,3–980 g.

Bare Parts: Iris wine-red to amber; bill black; cere lime-yellow; legs and feet yellow.

Identification: Size large; upperparts and head black, with pale patch at nape (usually concealed); underparts white, flanks black with white blotching or barring; tail silver-grey below with 4–5 black bars; rarely all black below with white throat (no barring on black tail); legs yellow (not orange as in melanistic Ovambo Sparrowhawk which lacks white throat); in flight underwing white, barred black on remiges. *Immature*: Above dark brown; below buff or rufous, · heavily marked with drop-shaped blackish streaks; iris greyish brown; legs yellow, naked (immature African Hawk Eagle has feathered legs and different flight pattern). *Chick*: Downy white; iris grey; cere and legs pinkish.

Voice: Usually silent, except when breeding; drawn out *wheeeow*; sharp musical *kyip* (♂); deeper *chep* (♀); may duet *kyip-chep-kyip-chep*; loud ringing alarm call, *kow-kow-kow*.

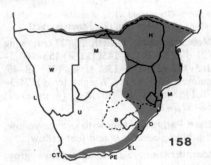

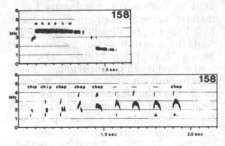

Distribution: Much of Africa S of Sahara; in s Africa mostly confined to E and extreme S; also isolated population in n Namibia.

Status: Uncommon to fairly common resident; numbers increasing through adaptation to exotic plantations.

Habitat: Forest, wooded kloofs and gorges, exotic plantations (especially *Eucalyptus*) in grassveld.

Habits: Unobtrusive when not breeding; stays inside cover of trees, seldom soaring. Retiring, but not shy; bold in presence of man, but sits quietly when approached. Flight silent and dashing; can overtake a dove on the wing; may pursue prey over open veld.

Food: Mainly birds up to size of Helmeted Guineafowl (nearly twice own maximum body weight), mostly doves (70–80%) and francolins (12–13%); also small mammals, birds' eggs, snakes.

Breeding: *Season*: May to October in Transvaal (peak July-September), July to December in Zimbabwe (peak September-October). *Nest*: Substantial stick platform, 50–70 cm diameter, up to 75 cm thick; bowl 20–25 cm diameter, lined with green leaves; (120 nests) 8–16–36 m above ground in fork of tree, preferably *Eucalyptus* when available; about 95% of Transvaal nests in exotic trees; sometimes builds on top of old nest of other raptor species; may use same nest for up to 22 years. *Clutch*: (71) 1–2,6–4 eggs (usually 3). *Eggs*: Usually plain white to greenish white, rarely

138

sparsely spotted with brown and lilac; measure (79) 56,3 × 43,9 (52–61,1 × 40,1–47,8). *Incubation*: 36–38 days by both sexes. *Nestling*: 37–47 days, fed mostly by ♀; ♂ brings food; young dependent on parents up to 55 days after first flight.

Ref. Brown, L.H. & Brown, B.E. 1979. *Ardea* 67:77–95.
Hartley, R. 1976. *Bokmakierie* 28:61–63.

159 (161)   Little Banded Goshawk (Shikra)   Plates 16 & 18
Gebande Sperwer
Accipiter badius

Rukodzi (Sh), [Schikra]

Measurements: Length 28–30 cm; wingspan (34) 57,8 cm; wing (9 ♂) 165–172–184, (11 ♀) 185–191–200; tail (20) 120–155; tarsus (20) 40–48; culmen (20) 10–12. Weight (2 ♀) 122–124 g, (57 unsexed) 75–123,1–158 g.

Bare Parts: Iris red in ♂, orange in ♀; bill blackish; cere, legs and feet yellow.

Identification: Size small; above blue-grey (no white rump as in Gabar Goshawk and Little Sparrowhawk); below white, finely barred russet; uppertail plain grey at rest, barred when spread (no white eyespots as in Ovambo and Little Sparrowhawks); undertail whitish with four black bars; underwing coverts white barred with russet; legs yellow (orange in Ovambo Sparrowhawk, red in Gabar Goshawk). *Immature*: Above brown, marked with buff on wings; below white, breast heavily blotched with rufous brown, belly barred with rufous brown; throat white with dark vertical centre line; five blackish bars on tail (no white eyespots as in immature Little Sparrowhawk). Immature Gabar Goshawk has streaked (not blotched) breast, and white on rump. *Chick*: Pale buff; whitish patch on nape; iris dark brown; bill black; cere, legs and feet yellow.

Voice: ♂ calls *kli-vit*; ♀ calls *tee-uu* to ♂; alarm call *tu-wi* and rapid *wit-wit-wit*....

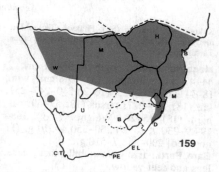

Distribution: Africa S of Sahara, Middle East, s and se Asia; in s Africa mostly absent from dry W, but vagrant to Aus, Namibia.

Status: Common resident.

Habitat: Savanna, woodland, exotic plantations, riverine bush.

Habits: Usually solitary. Perches within canopy of tree; less often overlooked than other *Accipiter* species because more vocal. Usually hunts from perch, dropping to prey on ground; seldom catches birds in flight. Flight undulating with flap-and-glide pattern. Bold and dashing; not shy.

Food: Mostly lizards (about 70%) and small birds (about 25%); also nestlings, birds' eggs and bats.

Breeding: *Season*: September to November in S Africa (mainly October), August to December in Zimbabwe (mainly September-November). *Nest*: Platform of twigs, 20–30 cm diameter, 8–15 cm thick; bowl lined with leaf petioles and bark chips (only ♀ brings bark chips); in multiple fork or on horizontal branch, (18 nests) 6–11–16 m above ground. *Clutch*: (52) 2–2,5–3 eggs (rarely 1 or 4). *Eggs*: Dull white, variably marked with reddish brown, some-

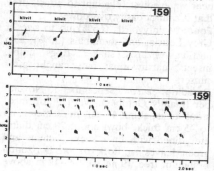

times over almost whole egg; measure (192) 36,9 × 29,7 (33,2–43,2 × 27,3–34,2); weigh 16–17 g. *Incubation*: 30 days, mostly by ♀, only 4% by ♂.

Nestling: About 32 days, fed by ♀ only; food provided by ♂; independent at 4–5 weeks.

Ref. Tarboton, W.R. 1978. *Ostrich* 49:132–143.

160 (160)   African Goshawk   Plates 16 & 18
Afrikaanse Sperwer
Accipiter tachiro

Kakodi (K), Rukodzi (Sh), Phakwê (Tw), iMvumvuyane, iKlebe (Z), [Afrikanischer Sperber, Tachirosperber]

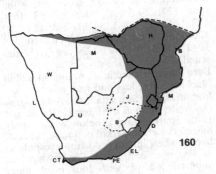

Measurements: Length ♂ 36–41 cm, ♀ 44–47 cm; wingspan (3) 69,8 cm; wing (8 ♂) 200–212–225, (10 ♀) 240–247–257; tail (18) 168–227; tarsus (18) 57–69; culmen (18) 15–20. Weight (7 ♂) 168–199,9–230 g, (6 ♀) 230–350,4–510 g, (19 unsexed) 230–341,7–510 g.

Bare Parts: Iris yellow; bill black; cere, legs and feet yellow.

Identification: Large size; ♀ much larger than ♂; above dark slate-blue (no white on rump); below white, barred brown in ♀, rufous in ♂; 4 dark bars in tail of ♀; tail of ♂ indistinctly barred, with small white eyespots above; underwing barred like underparts; legs yellow (orange in Ovambo Sparrowhawk). *Immature*: Above brown with some buff markings on wings; below white, boldly marked with brown drop-shaped blotches, broadly barred on flanks; throat white with vertical black streak; iris brown; legs yellow, long (short in immature Cuckoo Hawk, which has crest and much longer wings). *Chick*: Downy white; iris brown; cere and legs coral red (turning yellow at about 2 weeks).

Voice: Sharp high-pitched *krit* or *whit* at intervals of 2–3 seconds, usually while flying high over forest for up to half an hour, especially early morning or evening, hard to locate; also softer *wheet* at nest; musical scream *keeeeu*.

Distribution: Africa S of Sahara, except arid zones; in s Africa confined to N, E and S.

Status: Common resident; usually commonest *Accipiter* species in forested areas.

Habitat: Mainly indigenous forest; also dense riverine woodland and exotic plantations.

Habits: Usually solitary or in pairs; most easily noticed when giving characteristic flight calls (see **Voice**). Unobtrusive, keeping to dense forest canopy. Captures prey in flight or on ground by quick dash from cover; usually hunts inside forest, often near waterholes; reluctant to attack prey that it cannot easily overpower.

Food: Mainly birds (66%) up to size of Grey Lourie, and mammals (30%); also nestlings, lizards, snakes, frogs, crabs, insects, earthworms; bats caught after sunset.

Breeding: *Season*: September to November (mainly October). *Nest*: Platform of stout sticks; about 45–60 cm diameter, up to 45 cm thick; bowl about 20 cm diameter, lined with finer sticks, lichens and green leaves; in fork or on horizontal branch of tree, (9 nests) 4–9–12 m above

ground (sometimes up to 20 m), usually well concealed in foliage. *Clutch*: (37) 2–2,5–3 eggs (rarely only 1). *Eggs*: Plain white, becoming nest-stained; measure (56) 44,6 × 36,1 (41,8–48,7 × 33,8–

39,5); weigh about 34 g. *Incubation*: About 35 days by ♀ only. *Nestling*: 32–35 days, fed by ♀; food brought by ♂; young dependent on parents for up to 2 months after first flight.

161 (162) Gabar Goshawk Plates 16 & 18
Witkruissperwer (Kleinsingvalk)
Micronisus gabar

Mamphoko (SS), Rukodzi (Sh), Segôôtsane, Phakalane (Tw), [Gabarhabicht]

Measurements: Length 28–36 cm; wingspan (7) 59,8 cm; wing (15 ♂) 183–189–198, (10 ♀) 197–202–206; tail (20) 150–177; tarsus (20) 42–48; culmen (20) 11,5–14,5. Weight (11 ♂) 110–141,5–173 g, (9 ♀) 180–199–221 g, (30 unsexed) 95–154,2–217 g.

Bare Parts: Iris dark red-brown; bill black; cere, legs and feet red to orangered.

Identification: Size small (very like small *Accipiter*). *Typical form*: Above grey with broad white rump; breast grey (not barred as in Ovambo and Little Sparrowhawks and Little Banded Goshawk); throat grey like breast (not white with black vertical bar as in Lizard Buzzard); belly barred grey and white; 4 black bars on white tail (Lizard Buzzard has single white bar on black tail); underwing barred grey and white. *Melanistic (black) form*: (up to 15% of population) wholly black with faint paler barring on tail, and white barring on remiges; cere and legs red (legs orange in melanistic Ovambo Sparrowhawk, yellow in melanistic Black Sparrowhawk, which also has white throat and plain black tail). *Immature (grey form)*: Above brown, marked with buff; rump white (no white rump in immature Little Banded Goshawk); pale buff below, streaked on breast (blotched in immature Little Banded Goshawk) and barred on belly with rufous; iris grey, turning yellow; cere grey; legs and feet yellow. *Immature (black form)*: Like adult but with yellow legs. *Chick*: Downy white in grey form, smoky grey in black form; iris dark brown; bill black; cere, legs and feet orange-red.

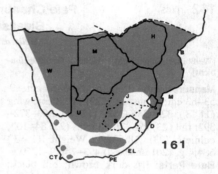

161

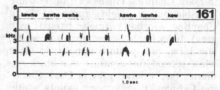

161

Voice: Usually silent; in display high-pitched reedy *kew-he-kew-he-kew-he* and chanting *sweee-pee-pee-pee*; rapid *ki-ki-ki-ki* near nest.

Distribution: Africa S of Sahara, s Arabia; in s Africa absent only from sw Cape.
Status: Common resident.
Habitat: Any woodland from riverine forest to arid savanna; in Zimbabwe also urban areas.
Habits: Usually in pairs. Like *Accipiter*; perches unobtrusively in canopy of tree; flies quickly from one tree to the next; seldom soars. Hunts in flight and from perch, catching prey on the wing or on ground; also tears open weavers' nests for contents. Bold, adapts to human settlement.
Food: Mostly small birds up to size of thrush; rarely up to size of francolin (over twice own body weight); also small mammals, reptiles and insects.

Breeding: *Season*: August to March in Transvaal (mainly September-October), August to December in Zimbabwe (mainly September-October). *Nest*: Small platform of little sticks, 25–30 cm diameter, about 15 cm thick, usually covered with spider web; bowl about 12 cm diameter, lined with earth, rags and spider web (not green leaves); in vertical fork of upper branches of tree, (10 nests) 6–10–15 m above ground. *Clutch*: (28) 2–2,3–3 eggs (rarely 4). *Eggs*: Plain bluish white, measure (92) 39,6 × 31,1 (37–43,8 × 28–33). *Incubation*: About 33–35 days by both sexes. *Nestling*: 30–35 days, fed by ♀ on food brought by ♂.

Ref. Kemp, A.C. & Snelling, J.C. 1973. *Ostrich* 44:154–162.

---

162 (165)   **Pale Chanting Goshawk**   **Plates 16 & 17**
Bleeksingvalk

Melierax canorus

[Weißbürzel-Singhabicht, Heller Grauflügelhabicht]

Measurements: Length ♂ 46–54 cm, ♀ 53–63 cm; wingspan (229) 110,8 cm; wing (11 ♂) 328–346–362, (12 ♀) 360–372–392; tail (23) 228–268; tarsus (23) 84–100; culmen (23) 18,5–22. Weight (1 ♂) 684,4 g, (261 unsexed) 493–746,9–1250 g.

Bare Parts: Iris dark brown; bill black; cere, legs and feet red to orange-red.

Identification: Size largish; upperparts, head and breast light grey, paler on wing coverts (coverts uniform with upperparts in Dark Chanting Goshawk); rump white (conspicuous in flight; rump of Dark Chanting Goshawk finely barred with grey); belly finely barred grey and white; legs long, red; posture upright; in flight white secondaries contrast with black primaries (secondaries grey in Dark Chanting Goshawk); underwing mainly white, tipped black. *Immature*: Above brown; rump broadly white; below streakily mottled brown and whitish on breast (more uniform darker brown in immature Dark Chanting Goshawk), indistinctly barred brown and whitish on belly; legs orange, long; iris pale yellow; cere dull orange. *Chick*: Above grey; below white; long hairlike plumes on head; iris greyish (yellow when fledged); bill black; cere grey; legs and feet yellow.

Voice: Melodious piping *WIP-pi-pi-pi-pi-pip* speeding up towards end, repeated several times, increasing in pitch and loudness, then dying away (somewhat like call of Fierynecked Nightjar in quality); sings in flight or from perch, usually at first light

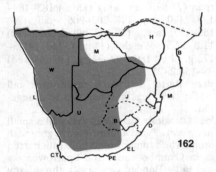

162

during breeding season; also musical *chee-it, chee-it* in display flight; alarm call is quavering *ee-e-e-e-e-e*.

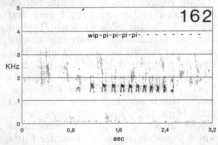

Distribution: Sw Angola, Namibia, Botswana, sw Zimbabwe, w Transvaal, w Orange Free State and most of drier Cape Province.

Status: Common to very common resident.

Habitat: Arid savanna, tree-lined watercourses, semidesert.

Habits: Solitary or in pairs; usually perches on treetop or telephone pole for long periods. Flies low from perch to perch, swooping up to alight; flight looks slow with shallow wingbeats alternating with gliding, but can fly fast after prey. Hunts mainly from perch, swooping to ground; also walks about on ground to catch prey, sometimes running after insects or rodents; rarely catches birds in flight; up to 6 goshawks may follow Honey Badger or Slender Mongoose for disturbed animals (mainly rodents).

Food: Lizards, insects, small birds (up to size of korhaan) and mammals (up to size of hare), carrion (road kills), snakes.

Breeding: *Season*: June to December (mainly September-October); no breeding in drought years in Namibia. *Nest*: Stick platform, about 40 cm diameter; bowl lined with rags, hair, dung, clods, grass and skin; in vertical fork of thorntree below canopy, 3–9 m above ground; also on telephone poles in treeless areas. *Clutch*: 1–2 eggs. *Eggs*: Plain greenish white to white, measure (25) 57,1 × 43,8 (53,6–60 × 41,5–46,6); weigh 52–57 g. *Incubation*: 36–38 days, mostly by ♀. *Nestling*: 7–8 weeks, fed mostly by ♀, but also by ♂; young dependent on parents for at least 7 weeks.

Ref. Biggs, H.C., Biggs, R. & Freyer, E. 1984. *Proc. 2nd Symp. Afr. Pred. Birds*:61–70.

163 (163)   Dark Chanting Goshawk   Plates 16 & 17
Donkersingvalk
Melierax metabates

Kakodi (K), [Graubürzel-Singhabicht, Dunkler Grauflügelhabicht]

Measurements: Length ♂ 43–51 cm, ♀ 50–56 cm; wingspan (1 ♂) 104 cm, (17 unsexed) 101,2 cm; wing ♂ 295–321, ♀ 305–325; tail ♂ 200–220, ♀ 202–230; tarsus 76–89; culmen 20–21. Weight (2 ♂) 646–695 g, (2 ♀) 841–852 g, (69 unsexed) 468–658,2–815 g.

Bare Parts: Iris dark brown; bill black; cere, legs and feet red to orange-red.

Identification: Size largish; very like Pale Chanting Goshawk, but rather darker; wing coverts not paler than upperparts; rump pale grey (not white); in flight wing looks grey (not white) with black tip; secondaries grey (not white). *Immature*: Similar to immature Pale Chanting Goshawk, but breast plainer, darker brown (not streaky), more clearly separated from barred belly; rump barred greyish brown (not white). *Chick*: Above greyish; below white; long hairlike plumes on head; iris brown, then grey, then yellow by fledging; bill black; cere grey; legs pale orange-ochre.

Voice: Similar to that of Pale Chanting Goshawk; usually silent when not breeding.

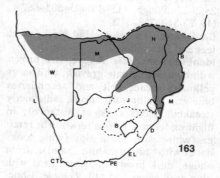

163

163

Distribution: Tropical Africa, sw Morocco and sw Arabia; in s Africa confined to N and NE; in Namibia S to Waterberg Plateau and Grootfontein.

Status: Common resident.

Habitat: Woodland and savanna (not forest or arid savanna).

Habits: Solitary or in pairs. Usually perches on top of tree, scanning ground for prey; hunts less on foot than Pale Chanting Goshawk, otherwise habits similar. May catch prey in flight. Soars in breeding display.

Food: Lizards, snakes, birds (up to size of guineafowl), mammals (up to size of squirrel), insects, carrion.

Breeding: *Season*: July to November (peak September-October). *Nest*: Platform of sticks, sometimes mixed with mud, often festooned with spider web, 35–60 cm diameter; bowl 20–25 cm diameter, lined with dung, grass, spiders' nests, birds' nests (sunbirds, penduline tits), hair and rags; 4,5–9 m above ground in vertical fork of tree, within canopy. *Clutch*: 1–2 eggs.

Eggs: Plain bluish white to white, becoming nest-stained; measure (45) 52,5 × 41,6 (47–57,8 × 39–45,5); weigh about 48–52 g. *Incubation*: Unrecorded; probably by ♀ only. *Nestling*: About 50 days; usually only one chick reared.

164 (–) Eurasian Marsh Harrier — Plate 15
Europese Paddavreter
Circus aeruginosus

[Europäische Rohrweihe]

Measurements: Length 48–56 cm; wingspan 115–130 cm; wing (16 ♂) 372–393–418, (17 ♀) 404–413–426; tail (21 ♂) 213–224–237, (17 ♀) 225–239–252; tarsus (21 ♂) 79–84,7–92, (17 ♀) 86–88,4–93; culmen (19 ♂) 20,2–21,6–23, (13 ♀) 23,8–25,2–27. Weight (15 ♂) 405–505–667 g, (19 ♀) 540–728–1100 g.
Bare Parts: Iris yellow; bill black; cere, legs and feet yellow.
Identification: *Male*: Above dark brown with contrasting pale greyish, whitish or yellowish head; tail and secondaries blue-grey; below dull rufous, indistinctly streaked (looks dark at distance); in flight underwing rufous to whitish; remiges white with black tips (wing looks dark with broad white band); from above, dark brown body contrasts with blue-grey wings and tail. *Female*: Chocolate brown with creamy white crown, nape, throat and leading edge of wing; primaries paler brown; yellowish patch on breast (may be indistinct); no barring on wings and tail (as in African Marsh Harrier). *Immature*: Like adult ♀, but

darker and lacks yellowish breast patch; iris dark brown.
Voice: Usually silent in s Africa; feeble *kik-kik*; various chatters and screams.

Distribution: Breeds Europe, N Africa and C Asia; migrates to rest of Africa and India; in s Africa recorded only Zimbabwe (Hwange, Harare), Botswana, Transvaal, Natal and Mozambique.
Status: Rare nonbreeding Palaearctic migrant, seldom further S than Zaire and Zambia; straggler to s Africa, November to February.
Habitat: Marsh, swamp and adjacent open grassland.
Habits: Usually solitary; quarters low over grass or reeds, checking in flight to drop with outstretched legs onto prey. May occur together with African Marsh Harrier.
Food: Mainly frogs; also other small vertebrates, birds' eggs and insects.
Breeding: Extralimital.

165 (167) African Marsh Harrier — Plates 15 & 17
Afrikaanse Paddavreter
Circus ranivorus

'Mankholi-kholi (SS), Nghotsana (Ts), Mmankgôdi, Phakwê (Tw), uMamhlangeni (Z), [Afrikanische Rohrweihe, Froschweihe]

Measurements: Length 44–49 cm; wing (10 ♂) 340–353–368, (8 ♀) 365–375–395; tail (18) 210–248; tarsus (18) 72–82; cul-

men (18) 19–22. Weight (14) 382–518–590 g.
Bare Parts: Iris yellow; bill black; cere, legs and feet yellow.
Identification: Very variable; sexes similar, but ♀ often darker and more rufous

than ♂; above brown with whitish leading edges to wings; facial disc paler brown, outlined with white; breast brown, merging with deep rufous belly and thighs; tail brown, boldly barred black; in flight boldly barred black-and-white remiges diagnostic (different from all other s African harriers); underwing coverts buff, streaked brown. *Immature*: Chocolate brown, uniform or with variable white band across chest; throat and nape whitish; underwing coverts dark rufous; remiges barred grey and black (♀ Eurasian Marsh Harrier lacks barring in wings); iris brown. *Chick*: Downy white; iris dark brown; bill black; cere yellow; legs and feet pinkish.

Voice: Usually silent; during courtship soft *woot* (♂) or *chip* (♀); *churruk, churruk* at nest; whistled *keeeu*; alarm loud ringing *kekekekek*.

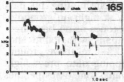

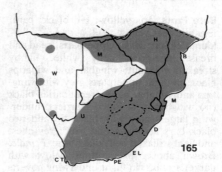

Distribution: From S Africa to Sudan; in s Africa absent from dry W, except as straggler.

Status: Common resident.

Habitat: Marsh, vlei, grassland (usually near water); may hunt over grassland, cultivated lands and open savanna.

Habits: Solitary or in pairs. Sails low over grass and reedbeds, wings held at slight dihedral (typical of harriers), checking in flight as prey sighted or heard, then drops into vegetation. Sometimes perches on fence post to rest, but hunts in flight; soars well, sometimes high. Roosts in dense grass or reeds, sometimes communally when not breeding.

Food: Mainly small rodents and birds (up to size of Redbilled Teal); also frogs, reptiles, insects, nestlings, birds' eggs, carrion.

Breeding: *Season*: All months throughout s Africa, mainly June to November in sw Cape, December to June in Zimbabwe. *Nest*: Platform of sticks and dry grass; 45–60 cm diameter, thickness varying with site (thicker in wetter sites); bowl about 23 cm diameter; in marsh among reeds over water, on ground in grassveld or cropland; rarely on low bushy tree. *Clutch*: (132) 3–3,6–6 eggs (usually 3–4). *Eggs*: Rounded, plain white or bluish white, sometimes with some reddish markings, usually nest-stained; measure (121) 46,6 × 37,1 (41–54,5 × 32,4–40,3); weigh 36,5–39 g. *Incubation*: 31–34 days by ♀ alone. *Nestling*: 38–41 days, fed by ♀ on food brought by ♂.

Ref. Nichol, W. 1963. *Bokmakierie* 14:32–34.

166 (170)   **Montagu's Harrier**   **Plates 15 & 17**
Bloupaddavreter

Circus pygargus

[Wiesenweihe]

Measurements: Length 40–47 cm; wingspan 105–120 cm; wing (31 ♂) 346–365–393, (22 ♀) 355–372–391; tail (34 ♂) 204–218–237, (16 ♀) 209–225–236; tarsus (33 ♂) 52–58,1–62, (22 ♀) 56–60,5–65; culmen (30 ♂) 13,2–15,2–16,3, (21 ♀) 15,2–16,4–17,6. Weight (13 ♂) 227–261–305 g, (6 ♀) 310–370–445 g.

Bare Parts: Iris yellow; bill black; cere, legs and feet yellow.

Identification: *Male*: Upperparts, head and breast blue-grey; belly white, lightly streaked chestnut; wingbar and wingtips black; in flight upperparts grey with wingtips and wingbar across secondaries black (no wingbar in ♂ Pallid Harrier); underwing largely grey with black tip and two black bars across secondaries; grey chest and light streaked belly diagnostic. *Female*: Brown above, pale rufous below with darker streaks; in flight underwing coverts pale rufous; remiges and tail blue-grey barred with black; upperwing uniformly dark (not barred as in African Marsh Harrier); rump white (brown in African Marsh Harrier). Cannot safely be separated in field from ♀ Pallid Harrier. *Immature*: Similar to ♀, but deeper rufous below, without streaks; no distinct whitish collar behind ear coverts (as in immature Pallid Harrier); iris dark brown.

Voice: Usually silent in s Africa; shrill *kek-kek-kek*.

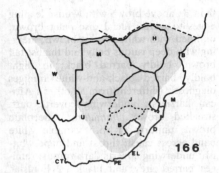

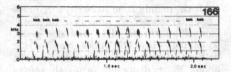

Distribution: Breeds Europe to C Asia; migrates to s Asia and Africa; in s Africa mainly in N and E.

Status: Scarce nonbreeding Palaearctic migrant, October to April (rarely as early as August in Natal); numbers declining.

Habitat: Open grassland, vleis; less often semi-arid scrub.

Habits: Solitary when hunting by day; roosts communally at night on ground in grassveld, among stones or on bare area, sometimes in company with Pallid Harriers. Flies upwind 3–5 m above ground, swerving and dropping onto prey; flight graceful and buoyant; sometimes perches on ground or low post to rest.

Food: Small mammals, birds, reptiles, amphibians, and insects.

Breeding: Extralimital.

167 (168)   Pallid Harrier   Plates 15 & 17
Witborspaddavreter
Circus macrourus

Seitlhoaeleli (SS), Nghotsana (Ts), Ulubisi, Umphungeni (X), [Steppenweihe]

Measurements: Length 40–48 cm; wingspan 95–120 cm; wing (26 ♂) 327–340–355, (21 ♀) 350–371–393; tail (25 ♂) 199–208–222, (19 ♀) 222–236–251; tarsus (24 ♂) 61–66,5–73, (19 ♀) 63–71,8–76; culmen (23 ♂) 14,8–15,8–17, (17 ♀) 17,3–18,6–20,2. Weight (17) 235–312–416 g, (7 ♀) 255–404–454 g.

Bare Parts: Iris yellow; bill black; cere, legs and feet yellow.

Identification: *Male*: Pale grey above, white below; wingtips black (no black bars on wing as in ♂ Montagu's Harrier). *Female*: Indistinguishable from ♀ Mon-

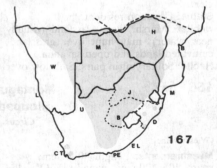

tagu's Harrier in field, but collar behind ear coverts sometimes paler. *Immature*:

Like that of Montagu's Harrier, but with paler collar behind ear coverts; not separable in field with certainty.

Voice: Usually silent in s Africa; sometimes chattering calls near roost.

Distribution: Breeds e Europe to C Asia; migrates to s Asia and Africa; in s Africa absent from dry W and SW.

Status: Nonbreeding Palaearctic migrant, October to April; formerly common, now uncommon to rare.

Habitat: Open grassveld, cultivated fields; less commonly in open to semi-arid savanna (but more likely in arid areas than Montagu's Harrier).

Habits: Similar to those of Montagu's Harrier, both species sometimes occurring together. Usually solitary by day, roosting communally at night on ground. Flight buoyant low over ground, tilting lightly from side to side; sometimes perches on ground or low mound or post to rest. Attracted to grass fires.

Food: Small mammals, birds, lizards, insects.

Breeding: Extralimital.

168 (169)   Black Harrier   Plates 15 & 17
Witkruispaddavreter
Circus maurus

[Mohrenweihe]

Measurements: Length 48–53 cm; wing ♂ 331–347, ♀ 363–370; tail 230–265; tarsus 63–71; culmen 18–20.

Bare Parts: Iris yellow; bill black; cere, legs and feet rich yellow.

Identification: Sexes alike; mostly black with conspicuous white rump; tail boldly barred black-and-white; in flight wing coverts black, remiges white below, grey above, black at tips and on trailing edge. *Immature*: Above brown, marked with buff on wings; below buff, heavily mottled with brown on breast; rump white; broad white area on remiges diagnostic (remiges grey with black barring in ♀ Pallid and Montagu's Harriers); iris yellow (brown in other immature harriers). *Chick*: Downy white; iris dark brown; skin around eye greyish; bill black; cere pinkish yellow; legs pale yellow.

Voice: Usually silent except near nest; shrill whistled *seeeeu*; mellow *pi-pi-pi-pi*; chattering *chek-ek-ek-ek*.

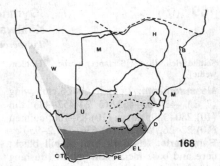

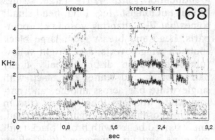

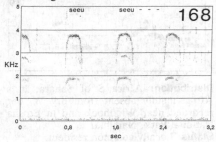

Distribution: Breeds in Cape Province S of 31 °S, N to Oliviershoek Pass, Natal; nonbreeding birds migrate N to n Cape, s Namibia, Botswana, Orange Free State, s Transvaal, Lesotho and s Natal; vagrant to Klein Fei-as Fountain, Damaraland and to e Caprivi.

Status: Uncommon local migrant, mostly absent from breeding distribution January to July.

Habitat: Grassveld, karoo scrub, mountain fynbos, cultivated lands, subalpine vegetation, semidesert.

Habits: Usually solitary. Quarters low over ground, sometimes making quick short stoops to disturb prey; occasionally soars or hovers; seldom hunts from perch; rarely catches birds in flight. Perches on ground or termite mound to rest, less often on fence post. Has undulating courtship flight over breeding territory.

Food: Birds (up to 350 g weight), nestlings, birds' eggs, small rodents (especially *Otomys*), frogs, insects, carrion.

Breeding: *Season*: July to September (1 November record). *Nest*: Pad of dry grass, sometimes on foundation of sticks or reeds, 35–45 cm diameter; on ground or up to 50 cm above ground, well concealed by surrounding vegetation; in wheatfield, fynbos or vlei. *Clutch*: (16) 3–3,5–4 eggs (sometimes 2–5). *Eggs*: Chalky white, sometimes blotched with red-brown; measure (20) 47,1 × 37,3 (43,6–50,4 × 33,5–40,9); weigh about 33 g. *Incubation*: 34 days by ♀ only. *Nestling*: 36–41 days, fed by ♀ on food brought by ♂; young dependent on parents for at least 3 weeks after first flight.

Ref. Van der Merwe, F. 1981. *Ostrich* 52:193–207.

---

169 (171)   Gymnogene   Plates 15 & 17
Kaalwangvalk
Polyboroides typus

Seitlhoaeleli (SS), [Schlangensperber, Höhlenweihe]

Measurements: Length 60–66 cm; wing (7 ♂) 443–453–463, (3 ♀) 457–483; tail (10) 280–320; tarsus (10) 83–100; culmen (10) 22–26. Weight (6) 636–725,2–950 g.

Bare Parts: Iris dark brown; bill black; cere and bare facial skin yellow (flushing red in display); legs and feet yellow.

Identification: Size fairly large; wings broad, tail longish, legs long, head small; somewhat like chanting goshawk; upperparts, head and breast grey; large black spots on wing coverts; face bright yellow (blushing red in display); belly finely barred black and white; tail black with single white bar across middle, and narrow white tip; legs long, yellow (red in chanting goshawks); in flight wings broad, finely barred below with broad black trailing edge and tip. *Immature (first plumage)*: Uniform dark brown; bill black; cere and legs yellow; facial skin bluish; small head diagnostic. *Immature (second plumage)*: Above mainly brown, marked with buff; ruff on hindneck mottled buff and brown; below whitish, washed rufous, blotched on neck and flanks with brown; bare parts as in first plumage; shape of head and flight pattern diagnostic. *Chick*: Downy buff to orange-brown; at about 10

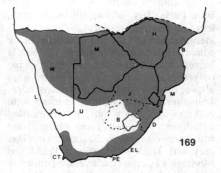

days above greyish, below white; iris dark brown; cere and face pale olive-grey; legs and feet greenish yellow.

Voice: Usually silent; plaintive whistled *su-eeeee-oo*; high-pitched *wheep-wheep* near nest; rapid chattering *ki-ki-ki-ki*.

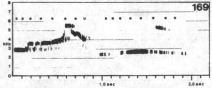

Distribution: Africa S of Sahara; in s Africa mainly absent from dry W, but recorded near Windhoek and in Etosha National Park, Namibia.

Status: Locally common resident.

Habitat: Forest, denser woodland, wooded kloofs; rarely open savanna and karoo.
Habits: Usually solitary. Unobtrusive when perched; usually seen flying high over forest; flight slow and buoyant. Hunts by soaring, watching from perch, walking on ground, clambering over tree trunks with loosely flapping wings; robs nests of weavers, swallows and swifts, and invades nesting colonies of waterbirds; may locate nests of small birds by their mobbing behaviour. Tarsal joint bends forwards, backwards and sideways, allowing bird to reach into holes with foot; small head can extract prey from narrow crevices. In courtship flight ♀ rolls over in air and touches talons with ♂.
Food: Reptiles and amphibians (40%), birds and nestlings (33%), small mammals (15%), insects (11%), birds' eggs, oil-palm husks (when available).

Breeding: *Season*: June to November (peak September-October). *Nest*: Stick platform, about 75 cm diameter, 20 cm thick; bowl 20–30 cm diameter, lined with green sprigs; in canopy of tree, in bush on cliff ledge, in small rock niche, (15 nests) 5–13–25 m above ground. *Clutch*: (86) 1–1,7–2 eggs (usually 2). *Eggs*: Buff or cream, washed reddish, heavily blotched with mahogany red; measure (88) 55,8 × 44 (51–63 × 40,6–47,3); weigh about 57–60 g. *Incubation*: 35 days by both sexes, mainly by ♀. *Nestling*: 45–55 days, fed by ♀ on food brought by ♂; Cainism sometimes occurs in broods of 2 chicks.

Ref. Brown, L. 1972. *Ostrich* 43:169–175.
 Thurow, T.L. & Black, H.L. 1981. *Ostrich* 52:25–35.

9:3. Family 22 PANDIONIDAE—OSPREY

Large. Similar to Accipitridae, but specialized for diet of fish; wings long and pointed; outer toe reversible; claws large; soles of feet spiny; catches fish by diving into water. Distribution mostly n hemisphere, but almost worldwide; nonbreeding migrant to S America, India and s Africa; one species.

170 (172)   **Osprey**   **Plates 15 & 17**
      Visvalk
     Pandion haliaetus

[Fischadler]
Measurements: Length 55–58 cm; wingspan 145–170 cm; wing (19 ♂) 448–469–494, (14 ♀) 476–495–518; tail (8 ♂) 187–201–210, (6 ♀) 194–216–232; tarsus (14 ♂) 52–56–58, (10 ♀) 54–56–57; culmen (9 ♂) 29,9–31,5–33, (7 ♀) 31,8–34,4–36,1. Weight (10 ♂) 1220–1403–1600 g, (14 ♀) 1250–1568–1900 g.
Bare Parts: Iris yellow; bill black; cere, legs and feet pale blue-grey.
Identification: Size medium to large; above dark brown; crown white; below white, faintly streaked on breast; broad mask of dark brown from base of bill through eye to nape; in flight underwing coverts white with dark patches at bend of wing; rest of underwing and undertail barred dark and light.
Voice: Usually silent in s Africa; melodious whistle *chewk-chewk-chewk.*

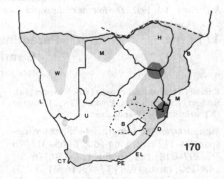

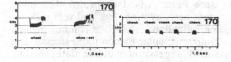

Distribution: Breeds n hemisphere and Australia; migrates to S America and Africa S of Sahara; in s Africa mostly absent from dry W.

Status: Mostly uncommon nonbreeding Palaearctic migrant, mainly August to May, but recorded all months; 1st-year birds overwinter, but hard to distinguish from adults. Some birds may breed.

Habitat: Inland and coastal waters (rarely at sea).

Habits: Usually solitary. Hunts by soaring over water; when fish seen, checks and may hover briefly before plunging into water at up to 60 km/h, feet first, wings raised and head close to feet, often submerging completely for up to 1 second; rises, shakes plumage and takes off, carrying fish head first in both feet to perch; if prey large, bird waits on water, wings spread for several seconds before take-off; sometimes robbed by African Fish Eagle.

About 33% of dives successful. Perches conspicuously on post or dead tree.

Food: Fish, mostly up to 300 g weight, but rarely as much as 3000 g.

Breeding: *Season:* Only 2 possible records, Limpopo River near Messina, December 1933, and Ndumu Game Reserve, October 1963. *Nest:* Large untidy stick platform in fork of *Ficus sycomorus* on river bank (1 record). *Clutch:* (1) 2 eggs. *Eggs:* Dull white, heavily blotched with brown; measure (1) 61,2 × 43,7; weigh about 72 g. *Incubation:* (13, Europe) 34–37–40 days by both sexes, mostly by ♀. *Nestling:* (35, Europe) 49–53–57 days; fed by ♀ on food brought by ♂.

Ref. Boshoff, A.F. & Palmer, N.G. 1983. *Ostrich* 54:189–204.
Dean, W.R.J. & Tarboton, W.R. *Ostrich* 54:241–242.
Rüppell, G. 1981. *J. Orn.* 122:285–305.

9:4. Family 23 FALCONIDAE—FALCONS AND KESTRELS

Mostly medium, a few small. Bill strongly hooked and notched (or toothed) behind tip; wings long and pointed; tail medium to longish; legs strong, medium to longish; toes rather long with strong sharp claws; females usually larger than males; plumage grey, white, buff, black or rufous, often spotted or barred; usually solitary, some species gregarious; hunt by stooping or hovering; food small animals; usually build no nest, laying in holes, on cliff ledges or in old nests of other birds. Distribution worldwide; about 60 species; 16 species in s Africa.

Ref. Cade, T.J. 1982. *The falcons of the world.* London: Collins.

171 (113)   **Peregrine Falcon**   **Plates 19 & 18**
Swerfvalk
Falco peregrinus

Kakodi (K), Phakoe, Leubane (SS), Rukodzi (Sh), Rikhozi, Rigamani (Ts), Phakwê (Tw), Ukhetshe (X), uHeshe (Z), [Wanderfalke]

Measurements: Length 34–38 cm; wingspan 80–117 cm; wing (6 ♂) 265–311, (6 ♀) 297–318; tail (6 ♂) 127–150, (6 ♀) 148–160; tarsus (6 ♂) 17–23, (6 ♀) 21–23; culmen (6 ♂) 35–43, (6 ♀) 39–42. Weight ♂ about 500 g, (3 ♀) 610–687–750 g.

Bare Parts: Iris dark brown; bill blue-grey; cere, eyering, legs and feet yellow.

Identification: Size medium; shape chunky (Lanner Falcon more slender and slightly bigger); above dark slate, shading

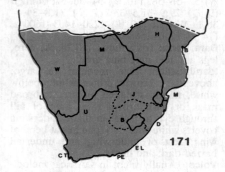

to blue-grey on rump; crown, nape and broad malar streak black (Lanner Falcon has pale rufous crown in all plumages); below creamy buff, spotted and barred on belly and undertail; at rest wingtips extend beyond end of tail; in flight underwing finely barred (coverts almost plain buff in Lanner Falcon). *Immature*: Above dark brown, feathers edged rufous; head like that of adult; underparts buff, heavily streaked blackish. *Chick*: Downy white; iris black; cere and legs pale grey.

Voice: Raucous *kak-kak-kak-kak* alarm call; threat call *chik-ik, chik-ik*; creaking *wi-chew* at nest; whining *waaik, waaik*.

Distribution: Worldwide; *F. p. calidus* breeds tundra of Russia, migrates to Africa; *F. p. minor* resident in Africa S of Sahara; throughout s Africa.

Status: *F. p. calidus* rare nonbreeding Palaearctic migrant, summer months; *F. p. minor* rare resident. Rare (RDB).

Habitat: Cliffs, mountains, steep gorges; may hunt over open grassland, farmland and forests; rarely enters cities to hunt pigeons.

Habits: Usually solitary or in pairs. Perches for long periods on favourite ledge or crag; hunts from perch or in flight, flapping fast to accelerate, then stooping with wingtips folded to tail (may reach 250–380 km/h); strikes with hind-claws, usually killing prey instantly; otherwise kills by biting through neck. May catch birds in level flight with talons ("binding to" prey).

Food: Mostly birds 25–300 g in weight (mostly doves), up to size of Rufous-bellied Heron; also termite alates.

Breeding: *Season*: June to September (mainly July-August). *Nest*: Scrape in soil on cliff ledge, (14) 40–187–300 m high, usually overlooking water; may use base of old nest of Black Stork. *Clutch*: 3–4 eggs (usually 3). *Eggs*: Buff or yellowish, heavily marked with dark red-brown smears, speckles and blotches; measure (51) 50,5 × 40 (44,2–56,1 × 33–42); weigh about 40 g. *Incubation*: 29–32 days, 65% by ♀, 35% by ♂ by day; by ♀ only at night. *Nestling*: 35–42 days, fed by ♀ only at first, later by both parents; independent at about 8 weeks.

Ref. Hickey, J.J. (ed.) 1969. *Peregrine Falcon populations.* Madison: University of Wisconsin Press.
Hustler, K. 1983. *Ostrich* 54:161–171.
Tarboton, W. 1984. *Raptor Res.* 18:131–136.

172 (114) Lanner Falcon Plates 19 & 18
Edelvalk
Falco biarmicus

Kakodi (K), Pekwa (NS), Phakoe (SS), Rukodzi (Sh), Rikhozi, Rigamani (Ts), Phakwê (Tw), Ukhetshe (X), uHeshe (Z), [Lannerfalke]

Measurements: Length ♂ 35–40 cm, ♀ 40–45 cm; wingspan 95–115 cm; wing (9 ♂) 308–317–332, (7 ♀) 340–350–360; tail (9 ♂) 160–178, (7 ♀) 185–210; tarsus (9 ♂) 46–55, (7 ♀) 45–53; culmen (9 ♂) 18–20, (7 ♀) 20–23. Weight (1 ♂) 528 g, (1 ♀) 756 g, (48 unsexed) 430–587–910 g.

Bare Parts: Iris dark brown; bill horn, bluish at tip; cere, eyering, legs and feet rich yellow.

Identification: Similar to Peregrine Falcon, but larger, and with pale rufous crown in all plumages; upperparts bluish grey, paler on rump and tail; face, fore-

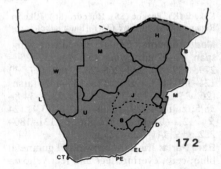

crown, sides of crown and malar stripe black; underparts pinkish buff to whitish, sparsely spotted brown on sides of belly;

in flight underwing coverts unmarked buff; remiges and tail barred. *Immature*: Above brown, feathers edged buff; underparts buff, heavily streaked brown or blackish; cere and eyering grey; head marked like that of adult, but paler. *Chick*: Greyish white; cere and eyering pale grey; legs yellow.

Voice: Harsh *kak-kak-kak*; piercing *kirree, kirree*; trilling *kirrr-kirrr*.

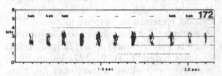

Distribution: Africa, Middle East, s Europe; throughout s Africa.

Status: Fairly common resident; some evidence for migration (n Cape to Malawi, 2 090 km NE).

Habitat: Mountains or open country from semidesert to woodland and agricultural land; also cities (Durban, Harare).

Habits: Solitary, in pairs or locally gregarious in flocks of 20 or more birds, such as around waterhole. Perches in dead trees and on telephone poles, but may roost on cliffs. Hunts in flight or from perch, sometimes 2 or more birds cooperatively, one flushing birds, the other catching them by sudden dash from perch. May accompany hunters to snatch dead or wounded quarry.

Food: Birds up to size of francolin, small mammals, reptiles, and insects.

Breeding: *Season*: June to November (peak July-August). *Nest*: None built; scrape on ledge of cliff or building, or in old nest of crow, raptor or heron in tree, on cliff or on power pylon; (35 cliff nests) 20–56–220 m above ground; usually 5–20 m up in tree. *Clutch*: (61) 2–3,6–5 eggs (usually 3–4). *Eggs*: Creamy white, heavily washed brick red, spotted dark rusty red; measure (93) 51,8 × 40,5 (47,7–56,5 × 38,5–44,6); weigh (16) 38,7–44,4–48,1 g. *Incubation*: About 32 days by both sexes. *Nestling*: 38–47 days (usually 42–45); fed mostly by ♀, rarely by ♂; ♂ provides food; young remain in nest area for about 1 month.

Ref. Barbour, D.Y. 1971. *Bokmakierie* 23:2–5.
Osborne, T.O. & Colebrook-Robjent, J.F.R. 1984. *Proc. 2nd Symp. Afr. Pred. Birds*:19–22.

173 (115)   **Northern Hobby Falcon**   **Plates 19 & 18**
Europese Boomvalk
Falco subbuteo

Kakodi (K), Phakoe (SS), Rukodzi (Sh), Rikhozi, Rigamani (Ts), Phakwê (Tw), [Baumfalke]

Measurements: Length 30–36 cm; wingspan 82–92 cm; wing (53 ♂) 237–256–279, (37 ♀) 248–268–282; tail (27 ♂) 124–130–143, (28 ♀) 128–135–145; tarsus (26 ♂) 32–33,2–35, (21 ♀) 33,5–34,8–36,5; culmen (29 ♂) 11,7–12,6–13,4, (24 ♀) 12,2–14–15,1. Weight ♂ 131–180–222 g, ♀ 141–225–325 g.

Bare Parts: Iris dark brown; bill gunmetal blue; cere, eyering, legs and feet yellow.

Identification: Size smallish; slim build; upperparts dark slate; narrow eyebrow and forehead white; crown, nape and malar stripe black; pale patch on either

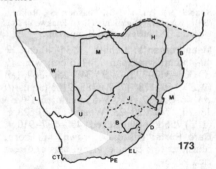

side of nape (hard to see); underparts buff, heavily streaked black; undertail coverts and thighs rufous; flight leisurely, like large swift; underwing heavily streaked and barred. *Immature*: Browner than adult above, feathers edged rufous; no rufous on underparts; much slimmer than immature Peregrine Falcon.

Voice: Usually silent in s Africa, but rarely a repeated *kew-kew-kew-kew*.

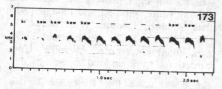

Distribution: Breeds Palaearctic region; migrates to Africa and s Asia; in s Africa absent from dry W; in Cape as far sw as Stellenbosch

Status: Uncommon (commoner in n parts of s Africa) nonbreeding migrant, October to March.

Habitat: Mostly lightly wooded country; avoids arid zones and forests.

Habits: Solitary or gregarious, depending on food supply; movements in s Africa erratic, birds appearing and disappearing in association with rainstorms and concentrated food supply. Hunts insects in leisurely flight, flapping and gliding alternately on narrow wings, grasping insects in foot and passing them to mouth; also pursues birds and bats with great burst of speed stooping from air or from perch; much hunting done crepuscularly at dawn and dusk. Roosts singly or in small groups in trees.

Food: Mainly insects, including crickets caught at dusk; also swallows, swifts, other small birds, and bats (caught after sunset).

Breeding: Extralimital.

---

174 (116)

African Hobby Falcon
Afrikaanse Boomvalk

Plates 19 & 18

Falco cuvierii

Kakodi (K), [Afrikanischer Baumfalke]

Measurements: Length 28–30 cm; wing ♂ 208–243, ♀ 230–254; tail (14) 108–125; tarsus (14) 30–35; culmen (14) 12–14. Weight ♂ 150–166–178 g, ♀ 186–200–224 g.

Bare Parts: Iris dark brown; bill gunmetal blue; cere, eyering, legs and feet yellow to orange.

Identification: Size smallish; build slender; above slaty black with typical falcon head pattern; below rich rufous, finely streaked black (streaks not visible at distance); looks very dark. (Taita Falcon bigger, more stoutly built, with rufous patches on nape; throat white.) *Immature*: Like adult, but upperparts edged lightly with rufous; underparts more broadly streaked black. *Chick*: Downy white, becoming grey at about 2 weeks; cere grey; legs greenish yellow.

Voice: High-pitched *keeeee-ee* or *kiki-keee*; shrieking *kik-kik-kik-kik*.

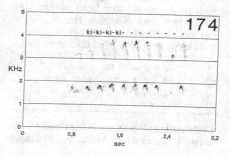

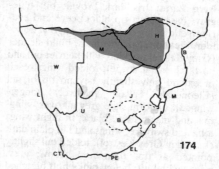

Distribution: Tropical Africa, except w forests and arid regions; in s Africa confined to NE, but reported from Kalahari Gemsbok National Park, January 1989.
Status: Rare breeding migrant to s Africa, September to March; some birds may be resident; vagrant to Natal and e Cape.
Habitat: Moist savanna and woodland.
Habits: Solitary or in pairs (somewhat gregarious elsewhere in Africa). Flight highly manoeuvrable, fast and long-winged; hunts mainly in late afternoon until almost dusk, perching quietly for most of day in tops of tall trees.
Food: Mainly insects when not breeding; otherwise mainly small birds, rarely as big as doves.
Breeding: *Season*: September to December. *Nest*: Old nest of larger raptor or crow; in trees, 9–30 m above ground; may usurp active nests, discarding owner's eggs. *Clutch*: 2–4 eggs (usually 3). *Eggs*: Dull creamy white, mottled and blotched with dark reddish; measure (22) 39,3 × 31,3 (36–40,8 × 29–33,2); weigh about 20,5 g. *Incubation*: Unrecorded. *Nestling*: Unrecorded; fed by ♀ on food brought by ♂.

Ref. Pitman, C.R.S. 1966. *Ostrich* 37:6–7.
Steyn, P. 1965. *Ostrich* 36:29–31.

175 (116Y) Sooty Falcon Plates 19 & 18
Roetvalk (Woestynvalk)
Falco concolor

[Schieferfalke, Blaufalke]
Measurements: 33–36 cm; wingspan 71–110 cm; wing (12 ♂) 264–274–283, (7 ♀) 273–285–297; tail (15 ♂) 127–131–135, (8 ♀) 130–136–141; tarsus (16 ♂) 32–34–35,5, (8 ♀) 34–34,8–36,5; culmen (13 ♂) 13–13,7–14,7, (6 ♀) 14,4–15,4–15,8. Weight (1 ♀) 210 g.
Bare Parts: Iris dark brown; bill blue-grey, base paler, tip black; cere and eye-ring yellow; legs and feet orange-yellow.
Identification: Size medium; build slender (Grey Kestrel stockier, with heavier bill and no black malar stripe); folded wings reach or extend only slightly beyond tip of tail (Eleonora's Falcon relatively longer-winged); uniform slate grey all over; wing-tips and malar stripe black; in flight wings long and swiftlike; wings and tail plain dark (barred in Grey Kestrel); folded tail slightly pointed at tip. *Immature*: Above grey, edged with buff; below pinky buff blotched with grey; typical falcon head pattern; similar to immature Northern Hobby Falcon, but more diffusely marked below.
Voice: Shrill *kilik* or *ki-kilik* alarm call.

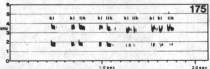

Distribution: Breeds ne Africa and Middle East; migrates to se Africa and Madagas-

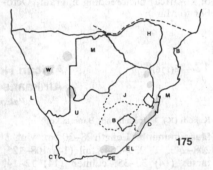

175

car; in s Africa mostly confined to e and se littoral, to Port Elizabeth in e Cape, but recorded sporadically in Namibia.
Status: Uncommon nonbreeding migrant, December to May (mainly January-March); more frequent in coastal Natal since 1980; vagrant to Kruger and Kalahari Gemsbok National Parks.
Habitat: Large trees, usually near water (breeding habitat is arid).
Habits: Solitary when hunting; roosts in small groups in trees. Mainly crepuscular; hunts in flight on flying prey, stooping with rapid wingbeats; also hunts from perch on top of tall tree, hawking insects in daylight. May enter larger towns, but often overlooked.
Food: Insects, birds and bats.
Breeding: Extralimital.

Ref. Clancey,P.A. 1969. *Bokmakierie* 21:50–51.

176 (116X)   Taita Falcon   Plates 19 & 18
Taitavalk
Falco fasciinucha

[Kurzschwanzfalke]

Measurements: Length about 28 cm; wing (9 ♂) 202–205,3–210, (9 ♀) 224–233,4–240; tail about 80. Weight (5 ♂) 212–217,4–233,2 g, (6 ♀) 297,2–319,7–346,2 g.

Bare Parts: Iris brown; bill gunmetal blue, tip black; cere, eyering, legs and feet yellow.

Identification: Size smallish; looks like little Peregrine Falcon; above slate grey, paler on rump, with distinctive patches of rufous on nape; typical falcon head pattern; below rufous (whitish on throat), finely streaked black; in flight rufous underparts (including underwing) and white throat diagnostic. (African Hobby Falcon has slimmer build, longer wings and deeper wingbeats; rufous to chin.) *Immature*: Like adult, but with buff feather edges above; lower flanks spotted; nape patches pale cinnamon; rump dark slate like back; breast less evenly rufous. *Chick*: Greyish white; cere and legs light grey.

Voice: Squealing *kreee-kreee*; loud *kek-kek-kek-kek* alarm call.

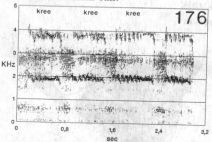

Distribution: From n Zimbabwe and adjacent Mozambique to Zambia and Malawi;

separate population in E Africa; in Zimbabwe from Victoria Falls down Zambezi Valley, Mount Darwin, Inyanga, Sabi Valley; in October 1990 found breeding on Eastern Transvaal escarpment.

Status: Rare resident.

Habitat: Cliffs and gorges when breeding; otherwise in nearby woodland.

Habits: Like small Peregrine Falcon; solitary or in pairs. Perches for hours on crag or tree. Flies with quick shallow wingbeats (parrotlike); hunts by stooping from perch or from flight. Roosts on cliffs, usually in pairs.

Food: Small birds (mostly 80–120 g), up to size of Purplecrested Lourie; also insects.

Breeding: *Season*: July to October. *Nest*: Scrape in soil at back of hole in cliff, up to 140 m from base. *Clutch*: 3–4 eggs. *Eggs*: Yellowish buff, variably marked with yellowish brown and some ashy grey; measure (7) 43,2 × 34,6 (41,9–45,2 × 34,1–34,7). *Incubation*: 26 days by both sexes (80% by ♀). *Nestling*: About 30–35 days; postnestling period at least 3 weeks.

177 (–)   Eleonora's Falcon   Plate 75
Eleonoravalk
Falco eleonorae

[Eleonorenfalke]

Measurements: Length 36–40 cm; wingspan 110–130 cm; wing (18 ♂) 300–312–323, (29 ♀) 312–327–347; tail (21 ♂) 156–169–178, (31 ♀) 164–178–190; tarsus (20 ♂) 34–35,2–36, (23 ♀) 35–36,4–38; culmen (17 ♂) 15,1–16,5–17,4, (26 ♀)

16,4–18,2–19,4. Weight (1 ♂) 350 g, (11 ♀) 340–388–450 g.

Bare Parts: Iris dark brown; bill horn-grey, tip black; cere and eyering pale blue (♂), pale yellow, tinged blue (♀); legs and feet yellow.

Identification: Size large; slim build; wingtips extend beyond tail tip when folded. *Normal form*: Above dark slaty or sooty brown; brown malar stripe contrasts with white throat and cheek; rest of underparts rufous, streaked black; in flight dark underwing coverts contrast with pale remiges; wings not barred (as in Northern Hobby Falcon). *Dark form*: Plain slaty or sooty brown all over; larger than Sooty Falcon, but hard to distinguish in field; lacks rufous thighs of ♂ Western Redfooted Kestrel. *Immature*: Similar to adult in each phase, but with barred tail and some rufous edges to feathers.

Voice: Largely silent in nonbreeding quarters; typically falconlike *ki-ki-ki-ki*.

Distribution: Breeds islands in Mediterranean and off NW Africa to Canaries; migrates through N and E Africa to Madagascar; in s Africa reported only from Inhaca Island, Mozambique and Victoria Falls, Zimbabwe (April 1985).

Status: Nonbreeding vagrant, summer 1977, April 1985.

Habitat: Woodland.

Habits: Little known in nonbreeding quarters. Hunts insects in flight, eating them on the wing. Seems to migrate at great height, because seldom seen *en route*.

Food: Insects in nonbreeding quarters; migratory birds on breeding islands.

Breeding: Extralimital.

Ref. Walter, H. 1979. *Eleonora's Falcon*. Chicago: University of Chicago Press.

---

178 (117)   Rednecked Falcon   Plates 19 & 18
Rooinekvalk
Falco chicquera

Kakodi (K), Rukodzi (Sh), Rikhozi, Rigamani (Ts), [Rothalsfalke]

Measurements: Length 30–36 cm; wingspan (10) 68,7 cm; wing ♂ 185–227, ♀ 212–241; tail ♂ 116–125, ♀ 136–140; tarsus (20 ♂) 33–39, (11 ♀) 38–40; culmen 13,5–15,5. Weight (8 ♂) 139–163,3–176 g, (4 ♀) 225–251–305 g, (6 unsexed) 178–212–255 g.

Bare Parts: Iris dark brown; bill slaty blue, base yellow; cere, eyering, legs and feet yellow.

Identification: Size smallish; build slender; above blue-grey, finely barred black; head mostly rich chestnut (diagnostic) down to neck and mantle; blackish malar stripe and line behind eye; underparts white, washed rufous across upper breast, barred black from lower breast to belly; tail blue-grey, barred black, with broad black subterminal band and white tip.

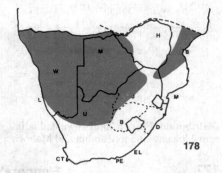

Immature: Browner than adult; tail as in adult; head and mantle brown (not chestnut); below dull rufous, barred and streaked lightly with blackish; throat white. *Chick*: Creamy white; cere and eyering greenish yellow; legs and feet pinkish.

Voice: Usually silent; shrill *ki-ki-ki-ki* and *tirrirri tirrirreee*.

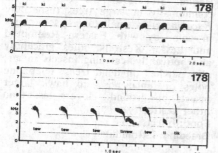

Distribution: Africa S of Sahara; also peninsular India; in s Africa mainly in dry W and extreme NE.

Status: Uncommon to rare resident. Probably Rare (RDB).

Habitat: Savanna, riverine woodland, especially in arid zones; in Botswana and Mozambique usually around Northern Ilala Palms *Hyphaene benguellensis*.

Habits: Solitary, less often in pairs. Swift, long-winged flier; wingbeats rapid; hunts mainly in flight, less often from perch. Perches in canopy of trees, seldom in open, so often overlooked.

Food: Mainly birds (98%); also small mammals (including bats), reptiles, and insects.

Breeding: *Season*: July to December (peak August-September). *Nest*: None built; lays in old nest of crow or raptor, or at base of Northern Ilala Palm frond; 4–20 m above ground, depending on site. *Clutch*: 2–4 eggs (usually 3). *Eggs*: Creamy white, thickly smeared and speckled with red-brown; measure (29) 44 × 32,9 (41,4–47 × 30,8–34,5); weigh (15) 21,2–23,3–25,3 g. *Incubation*: (11) 32–34–35 days, 80% by ♀, 15–20% by ♂. *Nestling*: (5) 34–36–37 days, fed by ♀ on food brought by ♂; later ♀ also hunts; chick weighs (13) 18,3–19,7–21,1 g at hatching.

Ref. Olwagen, C.D. & Olwagen, K. 1984. *Koedoe* 27:45–59.

Osborne, T.O. 1981. *Ibis* 123:289–297.

179 (120) Western Redfooted Kestrel   Plates 19 & 18
Westelike Rooipootvalk
Falco vespertinus

Kakodi (K), Phakwê (Tw), [Rotfußfalke]

Measurements: Length 29–31 cm; wingspan 66–78 cm; wing (29 ♂) 237–244–252, (16 ♀) 240–246–264; tail (35 ♂) 121–128–135, (17 ♀) 126–132–142; tarsus (22 ♂) 28–29,8–32, (9 ♀) 28–29,5–33; culmen (35 ♂) 11,3–12,5–14,3, (17 ♀) 12,4–13,1–13,9. Weight (20 ♂) 115–154–190 g, (16 ♀) 130–170–197 g.

Bare Parts: Iris dark brown; bill horn-grey, tip darker, base orange-red; cere, eyering, legs and feet orange (♀) to orange-red (♂).

Identification: *Male*: Size small; build slender; above dark slate grey; below paler blue-grey; lower belly and thighs chestnut (diagnostic); underwing and tail slaty like back (underwing of Eastern Redfooted Kestrel white in front). *Female*: Above blue-grey, barred black; crown, mantle and underparts bright rufous to orange-buff, lightly streaked

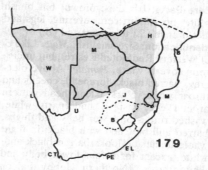

black; sides of head and throat white; blackish falconlike head markings behind and below eye; underwing and tail boldly barred black and white (7–8 dark bars on tail). *Immature*: Similar to adult ♀, but browner; black malar stripe, pale cheeks and streaked pale rufous underparts diagnostic (hard to identify with certainty from immatures of some other Falco species; presence of adults helpful).

Voice: Usually silent by day; at roost shrill babble of *kee-kee-kee* calls.

Distribution: Breeds e Europe to Mongolia; migrates to southern third of Africa; in s Africa mainly confined to NW, but also occurs in E to Transvaal and Natal, where overlaps with Eastern Redfooted Kestrel; rarely to e Cape.

Status: Common in n Namibia and nw Botswana; otherwise uncommon to rare; nonbreeding Palaearctic migrant, November to March.

Habitat: Open grassveld to semi-arid savanna; also cultivated lands.

Habits: Gregarious in s Africa; roosts communally in large trees (especially *Eucalyptus*) in small towns, sometimes in company with Eastern Redfooted and Lesser Kestrels. Flies gracefully and buoyantly, catching insects in air; also perches on dead trees, telephone poles or fence posts to hawk larger insects on ground. Hovers less than other kestrels.

Food: Insects.

Breeding: Extralimital.

---

180 (119) Eastern Redfooted Kestrel Plates 19 & 18
Oostelike Rooipootvalk
Falco amurensis

Rukodzi (Sh), Xikavakava, Kavakavana (Ts), [Amur-Rotfußfalke]

Measurements: Length about 30 cm; wingspan 58–70 cm; wing ♂ 218–232–235, ♀ 225–234,3–242; tail ♂ 110–119,8–132, ♀ 111–123,1–132; tarsus and culmen about same as for Western Redfooted Kestrel. Weight ♂ 97–136–155 g, ♀ 111–148–188 g.

Bare Parts: Iris dark brown; bill bluish white, tip darker; cere, eyering, legs and feet orange (♀) to orange-red (♂).

Identification: Size smallish. *Male*: Like ♂ of Western Redfooted Kestrel, but underwing coverts white. *Female*: Above bluegrey, barred black; forehead, cheeks and throat white; black falcon head pattern around eye; rest of underparts white, washed rufous on lower belly and thighs, barred and blotched with black; in flight whole underside looks barred black-and-white, except for rufous lower belly and white throat. (Northern Hobby Falcon very similar, but more heavily streaked below, deeper chestnut on undertail, and not barred on slaty upperparts.) *Immature*: Similar to adult ♀, but browner above with buff feather edges; more streaked below; head pale with distinct falcon head pattern.

Voice: Mainly silent except at communal roost; high-pitched *kiwee-kiwee*.

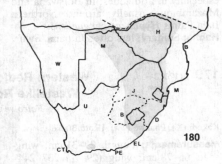

Distribution: Breeds e Siberia, Machuria and n China; migrates to s Africa *via* India, E Africa and possibly Indian Ocean; in s Africa mainly confined to E and NE, straggling to Plettenberg Bay in S, and to n Namibia in N (Etosha and Caprivi).

Status: Very common nonbreeding Palaearctic migrant, November to March; numbers declining; rarely overwinters in s Africa.

Habitat: Open grassland, cultivation, grassy foothills, lightly wooded country.
Habits: Very similar to those of Western Redfooted Kestrel which may overlap in range; gregarious, roosting communally (up to 5 000 birds) in tall *Eucalyptus* trees, often in towns, in company with Lesser Kestrel; leaves roosts before sunrise and returns at dusk. Flight fast and swallow-like; often glides and hovers low over ground. Perches commonly on telephone wires.
Food: Insects.
Breeding: Extralimital.

181 (123)   Rock Kestrel (Common Kestrel)   Plates 19 & 18
Rooivalk (Kransvalk)
Falco tinnunculus

Kakodi (K), Seotsanyana (SS), Rukodzi (Sh), Xikavakava, Kavakavana (Ts), Phakalane (Tw), Intambanane, Uthebe-thebana (X), uTebetebana, uMathebeni (Z), [Turmfalke]

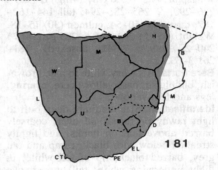

Measurements: Length 30–33 cm; wing-span about 70–80 cm; wing (21 ♂) 217–236–248, (17 ♀) 240–247–258; tail (38) 147–164; tarsus (38) 34–37; culmen (38) 13,5–15. Weight (37 ♂) 113–180–230 g, (29 ♀) 170–223–271 g, (99 un-sexed) 145–192,3–247 g.
Bare Parts: Iris dark brown; bill black; cere, eyering, legs and feet yellow.
Identification: Size small; sexes similar, but ♀ duller; deep rufous above and below, spotted lightly with black; head and tail blue-grey; broad subterminal black tailband and white tip to tail (tail usually more barred in ♀); in flight under-wing white, barred black; undertail silvery (black tailband visible from above and below). (♂ Lesser Kestrel similar, but paler and clearer in coloration; much paler below; no black spots dorsally; broad blue-grey bar on upperwing.) *Immature:* Lacks blue-grey on head and tail; streaked black above; barred black on tail; otherwise similar to adult. *Chick:* Downy white, becoming greyish; cere pale green; legs and feet pale yellow.
Voice: Shrill *kee-kee-kee* or *kik-kik-kik*; trilled *krreee*.

Distribution: Africa, Eurasia to Philippines; throughout s Africa.
Status: Generally common; uncommon in e lowveld; resident, but may have local migrations in Transvaal highveld.
Habitat: Mainly montane grassland with rocky outcrops, but highly variable, including arid savanna and desert.
Habits: Solitary or in pairs (never gregarious like Lesser Kestrel); Sometimes resident in small towns. Perches on roadside telephone poles, dead trees, or fence posts; also on ground or termite mounds. Flies with rapid wingbeats, white under-wing conspicuous; hovers frequently, hanging motionless in wind, wings winnowing and tail spread; drops onto prey by parachuting in stages; may catch small birds in flight by fast stoop.
Food: Mostly small mammals (rarely bats); also lizards, snakes, insects and small birds.
Breeding: *Season:* August to December (peak September-October). *Nest:* None built; scrape on cliff ledge or in pothole; also old nests of larger birds in trees; sometimes ledge or hole in building or bridge. *Clutch:* (34) 3–3,6–5 eggs (usually 4). *Eggs:* Creamy white, heavily smeared

and blotched with red-brown; measure (67) 39,2 × 32,6 (36,6–43 × 30,3–34,3); weigh about 20 g. *Incubation*: About 30 days by both sexes (mostly by ♀). *Nestling*: About 34 days, fed by both parents; postnestling period about 1 month.

182 (122)   Greater Kestrel   Plates 19 & 18
Grootrooivalk
Falco rupicoloides

Kakodi (K), Seotsanyana (SS), Phakalane (Tw), [Steppenfalke]

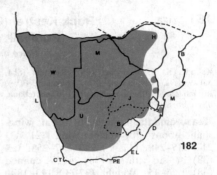

Measurements: Length about 36 cm; wingspan (72) 83,6 cm; wing ♂ 259–276–290, ♀ 265–281–294; tail 144–162–187; tarsus 44–50–54; culmen (30) 15–18. Weight (15 ♂) 209–260,5–285 g, (14 ♀) 240–274–299 g, (341 unsexed) 181–261,3–333 g.

Bare Parts: Iris ivory white to pale brownish; bill bluish, base yellow; cere, eyering, legs and feet yellow.

Identification: Size medium; deep buff to light tawny or rufous all over, coarsely barred above and on flanks, and lightly streaked below with black; rump and tail grey, barred black; tip of tail white; in flight underwing white, tail barred; eye white (diagnostic). *Immature*: Streaked on flanks and belly (Immature Rock Kestrel spotted); rump and tail rufous; iris dark brown; cere and eyering bluish white; more rufous than ♀ Lesser Kestrel. *Chick*: Downy white, tinged brownish, moulting into grey down at 12 days; iris brown; cere and bill greyish pink; legs and feet salmon-orange.

Voice: Usually silent; *kwirrr* courtship call; *kweek-kweek* threat call; sharp *chuk* and *kwit* calls between sexes.

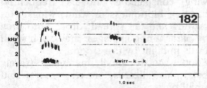

Distribution: S Africa to Somalia; in s Africa mainly confined to highveld and dry W.

Status: Common resident; sometimes nomadic.

Habitat: Drier grassveld, cultivated lands, arid savanna, desert.

Habits: Usually solitary or in pairs, sometimes in loose groups of several birds. Perches on telephone poles, fences, dead trees, termite mounds or low rocks; hunts from perch, dropping by stages to ground; sometimes hovers, rarely soars; may catch small birds in flight. May cache prey under grasstuft or stone.

Food: Mainly arthropods (insects, centipedes, scorpions, spiders, etc.); also small mammals, birds and reptiles.

Breeding: *Season*: July to January (peak in October). *Nest*: Usually old nest of crow or raptor in tall tree, telephone pole or power pylon; rarely in hole in tree; 2–20 m above ground (mostly 4–8 m). *Clutch*: (55) 1–3,3–5 eggs (usually 3–4). *Eggs*: Cream or buff, variably speckled, spotted and blotched with red-brown; measure (119) 41,9 × 33,6 (38,4–45 × 31–36,5); weigh 21–27 g. *Incubation*: 32–33 days by both sexes (70% by ♀). *Nestling*: 30–32 days, fed by ♀ on food brought by ♂; ♀ may also hunt when young above 5 days old; young dependent on parents for at least 30 days after first flight.

Ref. Brown, C.J., Paxton, M.W. & Henrichsen, I. 1987. *Madoqua* 15: 147–156.
Hustler, K. 1983. *Ostrich* 54:129–140.

183 (125)

Lesser Kestrel
Kleinrooivalk
Falco naumanni

Plates 19 & 18

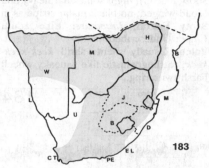

183

Kakodi (K), Seotsanyana (SS), [Rötelfalke]

Measurements: Length 29–32 cm; wing-span 58–74 cm; wing (25 ♂) 229–239–246, (20 ♀) 225–240–251; tail (26 ♂) 133–144–154, (20 ♀) 138–148–158; tarsus (21 ♂) 29–30,8–32, (16 ♀) 30–31,2–33; culmen (19 ♂) 12,3–13,3–14,4, (18 ♀) 12,2–13,3–14,5. Weight (18 ♂) 92–136–176 g, (7 ♀) 101,5–131–148 g.
Bare Parts: Iris dark brown; bill blue-grey, tip black, base yellow; cere, eyering, legs and feet yellow; claws white.
Identification: Size small; build slender. *Male*: Back bright rufous (not spotted as in Rock Kestrel); head, wingbar (diagnostic) and tail blue-grey; broad black subterminal band on white-tipped tail; below creamy buff (rufous in Rock Kestrel), sparsely spotted black; in flight underwing white. *Female*: Above light sandy rufous, spotted dark brown; below buff, narrowly streaked brown (immature Rock Kestrel spotted on deeper rufous); tail barred black; small black malar stripe; in flight underwing buff, spotted black. *Immature*: Like adult ♀.
Voice: Usually silent except at communal roost; high-pitched *ki-ki-ki-ki* or rasping *kirrri-kirrri*.

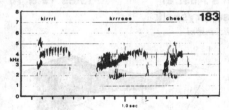

Distribution: Breeds s Europe to C Asia and China; migrates to Africa and India; in s Africa absent from dry W.
Status: Abundant nonbreeding Palaearctic migrant, October to March (rarely to April); numbers declining in recent years.
Habitat: Open grassveld, mainly on high-veld, usually near towns or farms.
Habits: Highly gregarious; roosts communally in thousands in tall trees, usually around human habitations, especially in towns. Disperses in early morning to surrounding grasslands; perches on telephone poles and wires, and fences. Flight light and graceful, long-winged; hunts in flight or from perch, catching insects in air or on ground; attracted to grass fires; hovers in wind.
Food: Mainly insects (locusts, termites, beetles, crickets); less often small birds, lizards and rodents.
Breeding: Extralimital.

Ref. Siegfried, W.R. & Skead, D.M. 1971. *Ostrich* 42:1–4.

184 (121X)

Grey Kestrel
Donker Grysvalk
Falco ardosiaceus

Plates 19 & 18

[Graufalke]

Measurements: Length 30–33 cm; wing ♂ 205–232, ♀ 235–251; tail ♂ 128–152, ♀ 150–164; tarsus ♂ 38–45, ♀ 40–47. Weight (5 ♂) 215–232–250 g, (5 ♀) 195–248,4–300 g.

Bare Parts: Iris brown; bill lead-grey; cere, eyering, legs and feet yellow.
Identification: About size of Rock Kestrel, but much more stockily built; uniform slate-grey; head and bill relatively heavy (lighter in Sooty Falcon); at rest,

wingtips do not reach tail tip (wingtips reach tail tip in Sooty Falcon); in flight wings and tail faintly barred (plain in Sooty Falcon); flight somewhat heavy and broad-winged; no black malar stripe as in Sooty Falcon. *Immature*: Like adult. *Chick*: Undescribed.

Voice: Usually silent; shrill *keek-keek-keek*; rattling whistle like squeaky wheel; harsh twittering.

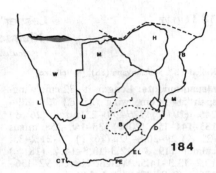

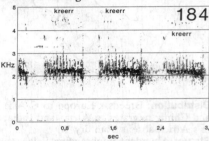

Usually seen perched about 15 m in tree, or flying slowly low over ground; sometimes hovers. Hunts from perch or in swift flight; most prey taken on ground, but some in flight by fast pursuit. Not attracted to grass fires.

Food: Insects, lizards, frogs, small mammals, worms; rarely oil-palm husks; not proven to catch bats.

Distribution: Tropical Africa from Senegal to Ethiopia and S to n Namibia and Zambia; in s Africa confined to Ovamboland W of Rundu.

Status: Rare resident; at very edge of range.

Habitat: Savanna, woodland, forest clearings.

Habits: Solitary or in pairs; shy and silent.

Breeding: Not yet recorded in s Africa. *Season*: August to September in Angola. *Nest*: None built; lays mainly in Hamerkop nest or hole in tree. *Clutch*: 3–5 eggs. *Eggs*: Whitish, heavily spotted, streaked and blotched with brown; measure (9) 41 × 33,3 (40,4–43 × 31,6–34). *Incubation*: Unrecorded. *Nestling*: About 30 days, fed by ♀.

---

185 (121)

Dickinson's Kestrel

Dickinsonse Grysvalk

Falco dickinsoni

Plates 19 & 18

Tuyu (K), [Schwarzrückenfalke]

Measurements: Length 28–30 cm; wingspan (11) 66,9 cm; wing (8) 210–236; tail 130–150; tarsus 35–38; culmen 16–17. Weight (3 ♂) 169–192–207 g, (2 ♀) 207–235 g, (37 unsexed) 167–210–246 g.

Bare Parts: Iris dark brown; bill slate-grey; cere, eyering, legs and feet yellow.

Identification: About size of Rock Kestrel, but more stockily built; above slate-grey with contrasting pale whitish grey head; below light grey (darker than head); tail barred; in flight wings look uniformly dark; conspicuously white rump and barred tail distinctive. *Immature* : Like adult, but flanks barred white. *Chick*:

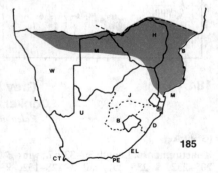

Greyish white; bill pale pinkish to yellowish mauve; legs and feet yellow.

Voice: Usually silent; high-pitched *keee-keee*; mewing *ki-ki-ki-ki*.

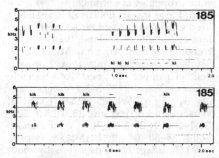

Distribution: Southern tropical Africa from Tanzania and Zaire to Angola, Zimbabwe, s Mozambique and ne Transvaal; in s Africa confined to N and NE.
Status: Rare resident; possibly moves about locally after breeding. Rare (RDB).
Habitat: Lowland savanna, woodland, swamp (often with *Borassus* or *Hyphaene*

palms); also open country near water.
Habits: Usually solitary. Perches upright on prominent dead trees in open, scanning ground for prey; hunts from perch, gliding slowly to ground; also catches birds in fast flight; hovers occasionally. Tame and easy to approach. Attracted to grass fires, catching disturbed birds by stooping from air above smoke.
Food: Small birds, bats, rodents, lizards, frogs, insects, crabs.
Breeding: *Season*: September to November. *Nest*: Hole in tree, hollow top of palm stump, old Hamerkop nest. *Clutch*: 3–4 eggs. *Eggs*: Dull creamy white, heavily blotched and smeared with brick-red; measure (50) 39,2 × 31,4 (35,3–42,1 × 28,4–33,8). *Incubation*: Unrecorded. *Nestling*: About 35 days, fed initially by ♀ only, on food brought by ♂; later ♀ hunts too.

Ref. Cook, G. 1971. *Honeyguide* 68:33–34.

186 (126)   Pygmy Falcon   Plate 19
Dwergvalk
Polihierax semitorquatus

[Zwergfalke]

Measurements: Length 19,5 cm; wingspan (9) 37,2 cm; wing (11 ♂) 110–115–119, (13 ♀) 110–116–119; tail (9) 69–74; tarsus (9) 24–28; culmen (9) 10–10,5. Weight (2 ♂) 59–64 g, (12 ♀) 54–59,6–67 g.
Bare Parts: Iris brown; bill blue-grey, tip black; cere and eyering red-orange; legs and feet pinkish orange.
Identification: Small, shrikelike in ́ size and appearance; grey above, white below; ♀ has deep chestnut upper back; wings and tail blackish, spotted white (diagnostic); rump white, conspicuous in flight. *Immature*: Similar to adult, but washed with rufous on back and breast. *Chick*: Downy white; skin and bare parts pink; iris brown.
Voice: High-pitched, penetrating; *kiki-KIK* or *kiKIK-kikiki*, often repeated; squeaky *tsip-tsip* or *twee-twee-twip*; *ki-ki-ki-ki* threat call.

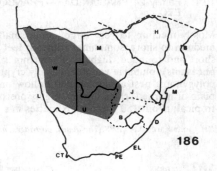

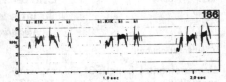

Distribution: Namibia, sw Botswana, n Cape, sw Transvaal and extreme w Orange Free State (coincides with range

PYGMY FALCON

of Sociable Weaver); possibly also s Mozambique, n Kruger National Park; separate population in E Africa.
Status: Fairly common resident; somewhat nomadic.
Habitat: Arid to semi-arid *Acacia* savanna; also arid scrub with *Aloe dichotoma*.
Habits: Solitary or in pairs; sometimes 3–4 together. Perches on top of dead tree or telephone pole, scanning ground; drops in quick stoop to catch prey; may catch insects in flight. Flight fast and undulating, woodpeckerlike. Quite vocal, especially between members of pair; has mutual head-bobbing and tail-wagging displays. Nearly always found near nests of Sociable Weavers, less often of Whitebrowed

Sparrowweavers, in which it roosts; occupied chambers recognizable by coating of white droppings at entrance.
Food: Large insects and small lizards; less often small rodents and birds; rarely nestlings and adults of Sociable Weaver.
Breeding: *Season*: August to March (peak October-November); may raise 2 broods. *Nest*: Chamber in nest of Sociable Weaver. *Clutch*: (17) 2–3,1–4 eggs (usually 3). *Eggs*: White, rather rounded, coarse-textured; measure (33) 28 × 22,5 (26,1–29,8 × 21,3–23,7). *Incubation*: About 28–30 days by both sexes (mostly by ♀). *Nestling*: 27–40 days (usually about 30); fed by both parents; postnestling period up to 2 months.

Ref. Maclean, G.L. 1970. *Koedoe* 13:1–21.

10.   Order GALLIFORMES (Six families; two in s Africa)

Small to very large. Bill short, strongly arched; legs medium to fairly long, strong; feet large and strong; hind toe usually reduced and raised; males (and sometimes females) may have spurs on tarsometatarsus; wings short and rounded for rapid take-off; largely terrestrial, but may roost in trees; plumage and habits variable; sexes alike or different; nest usually on ground; eggs 2–20, cream or brown, plain or spotted; chick downy, precocial; parental care variable. Distribution worldwide.

10:1.   Family 24 PHASIANIDAE—FRANCOLINS, QUAIL, PHEASANTS, PARTRIDGES, ETC.

Mostly medium to very large, some small. Bill short, arched and chicken-like; legs medium to short, sometimes spurred; feet strong, hind toe reduced and raised; wings short and rounded; flight rapid but not sustained; tail short (but very long in some pheasants); plumage variable, usually cryptic, but often highly ornate; monogamous or polygynous; nest a simple lined hollow on ground; eggs 4–9, yellowish to brownish, plain or marked; chick downy, highly precocial. Distribution almost worldwide, mainly tropical; about 180 species; 16 species in s Africa (one introduced).

Ref. Johnsgard, P.A. 1988. *The quails, partridges, and francolins of the world.* Oxford: Oxford University Press.

187 (188X)   **Chukar Partridge**   **Plate 20**
                            Asiatiese Patrys
                              Alectoris chukar

[Chukar Steinhuhn]

Measurements: Length 31–38 cm; wingspan 47–52 cm; wing (5 ♂) 162–168–172, (12 ♀) 148–154–160; tail (5 ♂) 76–82,3–87, (12 ♀) 74–78,9–86; tarsus (5 ♂) 45–46,8–48, (12 ♀) 42–44,1–46; culmen (5 ♂) 14–15,2–16, (12 ♀) 13–14,3–15. Weight (14 ♂) 460–509–595 g, (8 ♀) 365–446–545 g.
Bare Parts: Iris brown or hazel; bill, legs and feet red.
Identification: About size of francolin; brownish grey above, buffy grey below;

black collar around throat, extending through eye to bill; heavy black-and-chestnut bars on flanks; bright red bill and legs. *Immature*: Lacks black collar; flank markings faint; bill and legs dull pinkish. *Chick*: Rich buff with darker stripes dorsally.
Voice: Loud crowing *chuk . . . chuk . . . chuk . . per-chuk per-chuk chukar chukar chukara chukara*; harsh *chak-chak* lasting up to 5 minutes.
Distribution: Southern Europe, C Asia to China; introduced to sw Cape (Table Mountain, Villiersdorp, Robben Island), Natal and Zimbabwe (Umvukwes in 1969, but since died out); apparently successful only on Robben Island; also introduced to other parts of the world.

Status: About 500 birds on Robben Island in 1971.
Habitat: Semi-arid stony scrub.
Habits: In pairs when breeding; otherwise gregarious. Runs well over rough ground; flies strongly, usually low.
Food: Seeds and leaves; some insects.
Breeding: *Season*: Unrecorded for s Africa. *Nest*: Sparsely lined shallow scrape on ground, usually next to rock or bush. *Clutch*: 8–15 eggs (in Europe). *Eggs*: Cream or buff, spotted with brown; measure (17) 39 × 30 (37–41 × 29–31); weigh about 19 g. *Incubation*: 22–24 days by ♀ only. *Fledging*: About 50 days, young can fly at 7–10 days; cared for by both parents.

188 (173)   Coqui Francolin   Plate 20
Swempie
Francolinus coqui

Sitentu (K), Lebudiane (NS), Chimutowatsva, Horgwe, Gokwe (Sh), Mantantana (Ts), Lesogo, Letsiakarana (Tw), iNswempe (Z), [Coquifrankolin]

Measurements: Length about 28 cm; wing (221 ♂) 123–134,2–147, (139 ♀) 123–134,2–147; tail (10 ♂) 63–68,5–70, (8 ♀) 58–65,5–72; tarsus (12 ♂) 31–35,1–40,5, (8 ♀) 30–33,8–35; culmen (10 ♂) 9,5–11,4–13,5, (8 ♀) 9–10,3–11,5. Weight (3 ♂) 227–243,2–255 g, (1 ♀) 218 g, (5 unsexed) 153,9–255,4–350 g.
Bare Parts: Iris light reddish brown; bill blackish, base yellow; cere, legs and feet yellow.
Identification: Size smallish; yellowish head and heavily black-and-white barred belly diagnostic in both sexes; ♀ has white eyebrow and throat outlined narrowly in black. *Immature*: Like adult but browner above, mottled with rufous; more buffy below.
Voice: Tinny grating rasp *kraank-kraank-rank-rank-rank* falling in pitch and volume, and speeding up towards end; also 2-syllabled *kwee-kit, kwee-kit* or *coqui, coqui* much repeated (from which name derived).

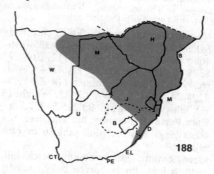

188

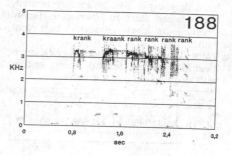

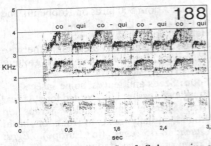

Distribution: Africa S of Sahara; in s Africa mainly in E and N.
Status: Common resident.
Habitat: Savanna and woodland with grass; sometimes open grassland with few trees.
Habits: Usually in pairs or coveys of up to 12 birds. Crouches when dis

turbed; flies reluctantly, but once flushed flies far and fast. Roosts on ground, sometimes in small groups. Males call from termite mounds, stumps or large stones.

Food: Seeds, shoots, insects and other invertebrates; gleans ticks from grass stems.

Breeding: *Season*: August to June in Zimbabwe (peak December-February), October to March in S Africa. *Nest*: Hollow in ground, 10–12 cm diameter, lined with grass and leaves; under shrub or grasstuft. *Clutch*: 3–8 eggs (usually 5). *Eggs*: White, cream or pinkish buff; measure (74) 32,5 × 27,3 (30,3–34,6 × 25,5–28,6). *Incubation*: Unrecorded. *Fledging*: Unrecorded.

---

189 (174) **Crested Francolin** **Plate 20**
Bospatrys
Francolinus sephaena

Sitjindakarare (K), Hwerekwere (Sh), Cecerekungwa, N'hwarikungwa, N'hwarimampfimba (Ts), isiKhwehle (Z), [Schopffrankolin]

Measurements: Length 30–35 cm; wing (61 ♂) 137,5–155,9–170, (65 ♀) 135–146–166; tail (54 ♂) 85–96,2–112, (65 ♀) 83–94,1–113; tarsus (58 ♂) 42–45,7–51, (65 ♀) 37–42,4–52; culmen (14 ♂) 19,5–21,9–24,5, (10 ♀) 20–21,7–23. Weight (8 ♂) 308–387–482 g, (3 ♀) 225,5–352,7 g.
Bare Parts: Iris brown; bill and cere dull black; legs and feet dull pinkish or purplish red.
Identification: Size medium; black bill, reddish legs, finely barred belly, heavily streaked chest and dark-and-light striped head diagnostic. Not noticeably crested, except when alarmed. *Immature*: Finely streaked on chest; eyebrow buff (not white).
Voice: Loud, lilting crow *chak*, *KIKwerri-kwetchi* repeated several times, ending with single *chak*; harsh *krraarr*.

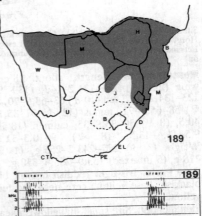

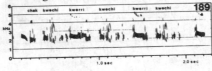

Distribution: S Africa to Ethiopia; in s Africa confined to N and E.
Status: Very common resident.
Habitat: Bushveld, riverine forest, dense woodland, especially around rocky koppies; also cultivated lands near woodland.
Habits: Usually in pairs or family groups. Very noisy at dusk and dawn. Often runs with tail cocked like bantam; keeps to

matted vegetation; escapes by running into dense grass rather than flying; does not fly far when flushed; roosts in trees. Often feeds at roadsides.
Food: Bulbs, seeds, berries, insects, molluscs.
Breeding: *Season*: October to May. *Nest*: Sparsely lined scrape on ground, in rank grass or under thorny shrub. *Clutch*: 4–9 eggs. *Eggs*: White, cream or pinky buff; thick-shelled and hard; measure (64) 39,7 × 30,4 (36,3–43,7 × 26,7–32,2). *Incubation*: (2) 21 days in captivity. *Fledging*: Flies short distances at 6 weeks; fully fledged at 8 weeks.

190 (176) Greywing Francolin Plate 20
Bergpatrys
Francolinus africanus

Khoale (SS), Isakhwatsha (X), iNtendele (Z), [Grauflügelfrankolin]

Measurements: Length 30–33 cm; wing (47 ♂) 144–159–173, (37 ♀) 142–156–167; tail (10 ♂) 69,5–76–79, (8 ♀) 63,5–67,8–74; tarsus (18 ♂) 36,5–40,2–44, (8 ♀) 35–36,5–38; culmen (10 ♂) 23–24,5–26, (8 ♀) 23–24,2–26. Weight (14 ♂) 354–424,3–539 g, (3 ♀) 354–359–369 g.

Bare Parts: Iris dark brown; bill blackish; legs and feet dull yellowish brown.

Identification: Belly finely barred; throat grey (other black-billed francolins have white throats), circled with broad black-spotted collar; bill heavy; in flight wings grey (no rufous); voice diagnostic.

Voice: Loud, lilting, almost musical, ringing call, starting with 2–7 quick staccato notes rising in pitch, followed by strident 4-note phrase, last note drawn out, first rising then falling in pitch, *ki-ki-ki-ki kiWIP, kiWEEoo*; squealing notes when flushed.

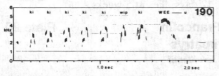

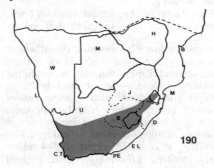

Distribution: S Africa to Ethiopia and Somalia; in s Africa confined to s and e Cape, e Orange Free State, Lesotho, Natal highlands and se Transvaal.
Status: Common resident; numbers apparently reduced in Natal.
Habitat: Montane scrub and grassland, karoo, stunted fynbos.
Habits: Coveys number up to 18 birds, usually 5–8 (2 adults and previous brood); flushes with loud squealing as covey scatters then crouches tightly; difficult to flush again; flies strongly, ending with stiff-winged glide over rise. Roosts on ground; calls from top of rock or stone wall, dawn and late evening.

Food: Monocotyledonous bulbs (75%), insects (20%), other plant food like potatoes and fallen grain (5%).

Breeding: *Season*: August to October in Cape, October to January in Natal; may be double-brooded. *Nest*: Deep scrape in ground under grasstuft or shrub, lined with dry grass and roots. *Clutch*: 4–10 eggs (usually 5; clutches of up to 15 eggs probably laid by 2 females). *Eggs*: Dull yellowish brown, sometimes speckled with brown and slate; measure (81) 38,9 × 29,8 (36–41,8 × 27,3–32,5). *Incubation*: About 22 days; 20 days in captivity. *Fledging*: Flutters at 2 weeks; fully fledged at 5–6 weeks.

Ref. Mentis, M.T. & Bigalke, R.C. 1981. *Ostrich* 52:84–97.

191 (177)   Shelley's Francolin   Plate 20
Laeveldpatrys
Francolinus shelleyi

Njenjele (Ts), iNtendele (Z), [Shelleyfrankolin]

Measurements: Length about 33 cm; wing (89 ♂) 152–163,6–178, (73 ♀) 145–159–172; tail (6 ♂) 79–81,5–83, (6 ♀) 67–75,8–80; tarsus (11 ♂) 39,5–42,2–46, (14 ♀) 36–40,8–45,5; culmen (12 ♂) 21–25,5–30, (11 ♀) 20,5–24–27. Weight (7 ♂) 397–497–600 g, (10 ♀) 411–482,4–600 g.

Bare Parts: Iris brown; bill blackish horn, base yellow; legs and feet dull yellow ochre.

Identification: Size medium; throat white, narrowly bordered with black collar; breast and flanks chestnut, surrounding boldly black-and-white barred belly; in flight small rufous patch in wing. *Immature*: Tawny where adult chestnut, streaked white and barred sepia.

Voice: Lilting musical whistle, *tel-el-keBIR*, *tel-el-keBIR*, repeated 3–4 times; also written *I'll-drink-yer-BEER*; shrill alarm call when flushed.

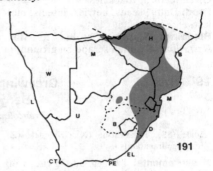

191

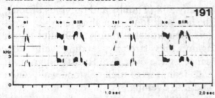

191

Distribution: From S Africa to Kenya and Uganda; in s Africa confined to E.

Status: Fairly common resident.

Habitat: *Acacia* savanna with good grass cover, edges of cultivated lands, often on stony ground.

Habits: In pairs or small coveys of 6–8 birds; shy and elusive. Sits very tight when alarmed; runs fast, or takes off with shrill calls; does not fly far. Calls briefly early and late in day, one bird often answered by others. Roosts in groups on ground in thick grass.

Food: Seeds, grain, fruit, shoots, bulbs, roots, insects; digs for food, making cone-shaped hole 3–5 cm deep, 2–3 cm across top.

Breeding: *Season*: August to June in Zimbabwe, August to December in Natal. *Nest*: Shallow scrape under shrub or grass-tuft, lined with grass and roots. *Clutch*: (15) 3–4,8–8 eggs. *Eggs*: White, pinkish, or pale beige; measure (71) 38,7 × 31,2 (26,9–43,8 × 29,2–35,4). *Incubation*: (1) 20 days in captivity. *Fledging*: Flutters at 12 days; flies at 5 weeks.

192 (178)   Redwing Francolin   Plate 20
Rooivlerkpatrys
Francolinus levaillantii

Khoale (SS), Isakhwatsha, Intendele (X), iNtendele (Z), [Rotflügelfrankolin]

Measurements: Length about 33 cm; wing (29 ♂) 149–164,2–179,5, (20 ♀) 140–159,2–172; tail (6 ♂) 67,5–70,4–73, (3 ♀) 60–66,5–73; tarsus (9 ♂) 42,5–46,9–50,5, (7 ♀) 40–43,8–46,5; culmen (6 ♂) 30–31,7–33, (3 ♀) 31–31,8–33. Weight (3 ♂) 369–463–567 g, (4 ♀) 354–401–454 g.

Bare Parts: Iris brown; bill blackish horn, base yellow; legs and feet yellowish brown.

Identification: Throat white in centre, tawny around edge, with broad black-and-white collar (collar narrow in Orange River Francolin); belly buff, heavily streaked chestnut, becoming almost solid chestnut on breast; hindneck bright tawny-rufous (visible at distance); conspicuous white streaks on back; in flight wings mostly rufous (much less rufous in wing of Orange River and Shelley's Francolins); habitat different from that of Orange River Francolin; mainly e distribution. *Immature*: Similar to but paler than adult.

Voice: High-pitched phrase, starting with 1–9 staccato notes, followed by 3-note phrase at higher pitch, accented on middle note, *chip-chip-chip-chip chiREEcheu*, less musical than voice of Greywing Francolin, repeated several times.

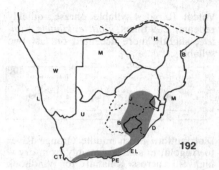

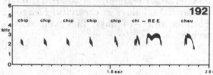

Distribution: S Africa to E Africa; in s Africa confined to SE, from s Cape to Transvaal.

Status: Fairly common resident.

Habitat: Moister montane grassland, usually at somewhat lower elevations than Greywing Francolin, though overlapping; low-lying grasslands in s Cape.

Habits: In pairs or coveys numbering up to 10 birds (usually 3–5). Sits tight when alarmed, flushing suddenly with whistling wings, flying quite far, then gliding stiff-winged before landing; seldom flushes a second time. Calls early morning and late evening. Roosts on ground in coveys.

Food: Monocotyledonous bulbs (80%), insects (20%); also grain, shoots, berries, molluscs.

Breeding: *Season*: August to February in Natal, March to July in e Cape; probably most months, but mainly summer. *Nest*: Shallow scrape on ground, in rank grass or sedge, sparsely lined with grass and roots. *Clutch*: 3–8 eggs (rarely up to 10). *Eggs*: Buff to brownish yellow, spotted with darker brown; measure (57) 40 × 32,1 (35,8–44 × 29–34). *Incubation*: Unrecorded. *Fledging*: Unrecorded.

193 (179)   Orange River Francolin   Plate 20
Kalaharipatrys
Francolinus levaillantoides

Khoale (SS), Lesogo (Tw), [Rebhuhnfrankolin]

Measurements: Length 33–35 cm; wing (62 ♂) 142–163–173, (42 ♀) 146–160,3–175; tail (10 ♂) 74–77–80, (3 ♀) 71–74–76; tarsus (10 ♂) 39–40–41, (3 ♀) 34–36,7–39; culmen (10 ♂) 26–26,2–27, (3 ♀) 25–26,7–28. Weight (3 ♂) 370–440,7–538 g, (6 ♀) 379–450 g.

Bare Parts: Iris brown; bill blackish horn, base yellow or pinkish; legs and feet pale yellowish brown.

Identification: Size medium; throat all white, bordered by narrow black band (broad in Redwing Francolin); in flight large rufous patch in wing; voice and habitat different from those of Redwing

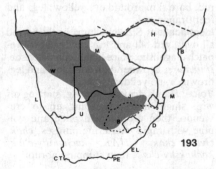

Francolin; mainly w distribution; w birds much paler than e birds. *Immature*: Lacks black collar; barred below.

Voice: Rapid 4-syllable phrase, quickly repeated 2–9 times, *kibitele, kibitele, kibitele*; slightly more accented on last two syllables.

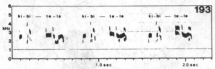

Distribution: From middle Orange River to Angola; in s Africa mainly from dry w highveld, across Kalahari to Windhoek and Ovamboland.

Status: Fairly common resident.

Habitat: Open grassland, dry savanna, grassy mountain slopes with low scrub, croplands, edges of pans.

Habits: Usually in pairs or coveys of up to 12 birds; sits very close; difficult to flush, even with dogs; flies rather higher than most francolins when flushed; shy and elusive. Calls morning and evening, often several birds together.

Food: Bulbs, corms, seeds, shoots, berries, insects.

Breeding: *Season*: September to May (probably varies with rainfall). *Nest*: Scrape on ground, under grasstuft or shrub, lined with some dry grass. *Clutch*: 4–8 eggs. *Eggs*: Pale yellowish brown, speckled with darker brown; measure (25) 36,6 × 28,8 (34,3–40,7 × 26,2–32). *Incubation*: 20–21 days in captivity. *Fledging*: Flutters at 12–14 days; flies well at 5–6 weeks.

---

194 (182)   Redbilled Francolin   Plate 21
Rooibekfisant
Francolinus adspersus

Siswagaragwali (K), [Rotschnabelfrankolin, Sandhuhn]

Measurements: Length ♂ about 38 cm, ♀ about 33 cm; wing (147 ♂) 157–179,4–201, (148 ♀) 150–164,3–178; tail (115 ♂) 93–103,2–119, (117 ♀) 83–94,5–104; tarsus (116 ♂) 48–54,3–60, (117 ♀) 44–46,7–53; culmen (10 ♂) 20,5–21,1–22, (6 ♀) 17–18,8–20,5. Weight (12 ♂) 340–465–635 g, (24 ♀) 340–394–549 g.

Bare Parts: Iris brown; bill red or orange-red; bare skin around eye yellow; legs and feet orange-red.

Identification: Size medium; finely barred all over; red bill and legs, and yellow eye-patch diagnostic; voice highly characteristic. *Immature*: Browner than adult; bill and legs brownish; no yellow eyepatch.

Voice: Harsh strident crowing, starting off with single notes, speeding up to crescendo, then dropping in pitch and volume with rapid chattering phrases, *chak, chak, chak, CHAK, kachakitty-chak, kachakitty-chak*, then stopping abruptly.

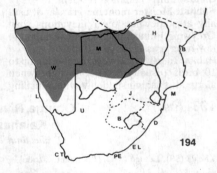

Distribution: Western parts of s third of Africa; Namibia, Botswana, w Transvaal and w Zimbabwe.

Status: Common resident.

Habitat: Dry scrub thickets, edges of Kalahari woodland, riverine thornbush; usually near water.

Habits: In pairs or coveys of up to 20 birds. Runs into cover when disturbed; flies reluctantly but well, sometimes perching in trees or bushes; may be quite tame, feeding in clearings and old cultivated lands. Very noisy morning and evening and on moonlit nights. Drinks late afternoon.

Food: Seeds, fallen grain, shoots, leaves, aquatic plants, bulbs, berries, insects, molluscs.

Breeding: *Season:* All months in Botswana and Namibia (peak March-April), January to August in Zimbabwe. *Nest:* Sparsely lined scrape in ground under bush or in tangled vegetation. *Clutch:* (14) 4–5,9–10 eggs. *Eggs:* Dull yellowish, cream or pinkish buff, hard and thick-shelled, finely pitted with pores; measure (65) 42,2 × 33,4 (38,9–46,5 × 31,9–35,2). *Incubation:* Unrecorded. *Fledging:* Unrecorded.

195 (181)   Cape Francolin   Plate 21
Kaapse Fisant
Francolinus capensis

[Kapfrankolin]

Measurements: Length 40–42 cm; wing (18 ♂) 203–215,7–230,5, (27 ♀) 185–198,1–220; tail (18 ♂) 94,5–115,2–128, (27 ♀) 97–108,2–125; tarsus (18 ♂) 61,5–66,8–72, (27 ♀) 55–60,3–76; culmen (6 ♂) 18,5–21,8–24,5, (7 ♀) 19–20,5–22. Weight (11 ♂) 600–855,5–966 g, (28 ♀) 435–679–837 g.

Bare Parts: Iris reddish brown; bill dark horn, base and lower jaw dull orange to red; legs dark yellow, orange or red.

Identification: Size large; looks uniformly dark at distance; base of bill and legs dull orange to red (not always easy to see); belly broadly streaked white (Natal Francolin has barred scaly pattern on belly, but ranges do not overlap).

Voice: Loud harsh crowing cackle, *kak-keek, kak-keek, kak-keek*, accented on 2nd syllable; spluttering cries when flushed.

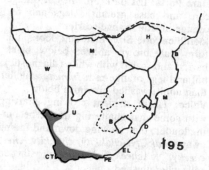

Distribution: Winter rainfall area: sw Cape, N to lower Orange River, E to about lower Fish River.

Status: Common resident.

Habitat: Dense riverine scrub in drier areas, coastal and montane fynbos, exotic *Acacia* thickets.

Habits: Usually in pairs or in coveys of up to 20 birds. Very noisy morning and evening. Often tame, feeding in clearings at edge of bush and in farmyards. Flies reluctantly but well; prefers to run into cover; may land in trees when flushed. Roosts in trees on lateral branch.

Food: Seeds, shoots, leaves, bulbs, corms, berries, insects, molluscs.

Breeding: *Season:* August to January. *Nest:* Thinly lined scrape on ground under dense bush, brushwood or rushes. *Clutch:* 6–8 eggs (clutches of up to 14 eggs probably laid by two females). *Eggs:* Pinkish stone to buff, sometimes with few small white spots; measure (32) 47 × 37 (42–55,7 × 35,2–38,8). *Incubation:* (377 eggs) 22–23,4–25 days (captivity). *Fledging:* Newly hatched chick weighs (45) 19–21,8–27 g; can fly short distances on 12th day; remiges fully grown at (11) 7–12–14 weeks.

196 (183) Natal Francolin   Plate 21
Natalse Fisant
Francolinus natalensis

Renge (Sh), Mangokwe, N'hwari, N'hwarimabvimba (Ts), Kgwalê, Sogonokê (Tw), isiKhwehle (Z), [Natalfrankolin]

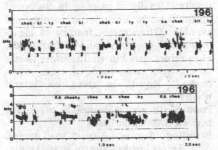

196

Measurements: Length ♂ about 38 cm, ♀ about 30 cm; wing (78 ♂) 150–173,4–189, (47 ♀) 149–158,4–170; tail (48 ♂) 88–99–120, (38 ♀) 82–92,9–102; tarsus (56 ♂) 42–50,5–58,6, (13 ♀) 42–44,9–53; culmen (16 ♂) 17,5–21,4–27,1, (13 ♀) 15,5–18,4–24. Weight (11 ♂) 415,1–588,6–723 g, (5 ♀) 370–425,8–482 g.

Bare Parts: Iris dark brown; bill orange, cere and base greenish; legs and feet orange or dull orange-scarlet.

Identification: Size medium; looks uniform dull brown above; below black, barred and scaled with white (diagnostic); bill and legs orange-red. *Immature*: Paler than adult; washed brownish below.

Voice: Harsh strident crowing, starting with somewhat chattering notes, becoming louder, then slowing down and fading away; *chakkity, chakkity, chakkity, chee, cheeky, KAcheeky, KAcheeky*; startled calls when flushed.

Distribution: Se Africa from S Africa to Zambia; in s Africa mainly in E, but also to n Cape, Orange Free State and e Botswana.

Status: Common resident.

Habitat: Dense thickets along watercourses, on hillsides and mountains, and in *Acacia* bushveld; coastal dune forest, edge of evergreen forest; often in rocky terrain.

Habits: In pairs or coveys of up to 10 birds. When flushed, covey separates; does not fly far; runs into dense cover on landing; may settle in tree. Calls at dawn and dusk. Roosts on branches up to 4 m above ground.

Food: Molluscs, insects, roots, bulbs, fruit, seeds.

Breeding: *Season*: All months (peak March-May in Zimbabwe); mainly midsummer in S Africa. *Nest*: Scrape on ground, lined with roots, grass and stalks; well hidden under thorny tangles or shrubs. *Clutch*: 5–8 eggs (larger clutches, 10 or more, probably laid by 2 females). *Eggs*: Creamy or yellowish white; measure (60) 41,9 × 34,2 (36,1–46,8 × 28,4–37,8). *Incubation*: 21–22 days in captivity. *Fledging*: Flutters at 10–14 days; flies well at 7–8 weeks.

197 (184) Hartlaub's Francolin   Plate 21
Klipfisant (Hartlaubse Fisant)
Francolinus hartlaubi

[Hartlaubfrankolin]

Measurements: Length ♂ about 28 cm, ♀ about 25 cm; wing (42 ♂) 131–144,2–172, (35 ♀) 131–136,2–148; tail (32 ♂) 75–87,5–94, (23 ♀) 73–83,7–94; tarsus (32 ♂) 32–37,4–57, (23 ♀) 30–34,3–40; culmen (5 ♂) 21,5–23,3–25, (4 ♀)

19,5–21–22. Weight (4 ♂) 245–290 g, (4 ♀) 210–240 g.

Bare Parts: Iris hazel; bill yellowish brown; legs and feet dull yellow or yellow ochre.

Identification: Size small; build stocky; head small; bill looks disproportionately large. *Male*: Above mottled dark brown and buff; below buffy white, heavily streaked dark brown; pale underparts contrast strongly with dark upperparts; forehead and eyestripe black; eyebrow and line over forecrown white; black-and-white undertail coverts conspicuous in flight and in display. *Female*: Above like ♂; below almost uniform light cinnamon brown, faintly mottled whitish; eyebrow orange-brown. *Immature* ♂: Paler above than adult; shaft streaks narrower below; ♀ similar to adult ♀.

Voice: Antiphonal duet by ♂ and ♀; low grating *cackle cackle* by ♂, similar to calls of Natal Francolin; ♀ responds similarly or with *eeha-eeha*; cackling *kok-kok-kok* alarm notes when flushed; plaintive whistled *keeooo* distress call; *chirrup-churr* contact call.

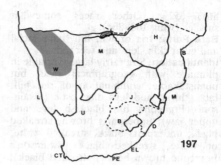

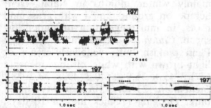

Distribution: Namibia from Windhoek, N to Angola.

Status: Uncommon and localized resident.

Habitat: Dense mixed grass-shrub cover with undergrowth and sandy soil on rocky koppies, mountain slopes and escarpments in arid country.

Habits: Usually in pairs; strongly territorial; pair bond maintained year-round. Vocal about 10 minutes before sunrise, calling from top of koppie. ♀ forages by digging with bill for up to 45 minutes; ♂ turns over leaf litter; does not drink water; sometimes in company with Redbilled Francolin. Seeks shade of rocks in heat of day. Flies readily when disturbed, alternating bursts of rapid wingbeats with gliding on downcurved wings, uttering ventriloquial alarm calls; runs fast along ledges and through fissures. Roosts on ground among rocks or under bushes.

Food: Seeds, fruit, shoots, bulbs (especially of *Cyperus edulis*), insects, snails.

Breeding: Monogamous. *Season*: About April to August; also November and February; possibly varies with rainfall. *Nest*: Only one known; scrape on ledge of precipice. *Clutch*: Only known clutch had 3 eggs. *Eggs*: Plain cream coloured; measure (5) 41,6 × 30,2 (40–43,5 × 29–32,1). *Incubation*: Unrecorded. *Fledging*: Unrecorded.

Ref. Komen, J. 1987. *S. Afr. J. Wildl. Res. Suppl.* 1: 82–86.
Komen, J. & Myer, E. 1984. *S.W.A. Annual*: 39–43.

198 (188)   Rednecked Francolin   Plate 21
Rooikeelfisant
Francolinus afer

Sigwali (K), Gorwe, Hwari (Sh), Makokwe, N'warimakokwe (Ts), Inkwali (X), iNkwali (Z), [Nacktkehlfrankolin, Rotkehlfrankolin]

Measurements (*F. a. notatus*, s Cape, and *F. a. castaneiventer*, e Cape to e Transvaal): Length ♂ about 38 cm, ♀ about 33 cm; wing (26 ♂) 171–200,3–215, (13 ♀) 170–186,5–198; tail (21 ♂) 90–100–110, (12 ♀) 79–92–105; tarsus (22 ♂) 53–58,5–64, (14 ♀) 51–55,6–64; culmen (9 ♂) 20–22,1–23,5, (6 ♀) 18,5–20,8–22. Weight (1 ♂) 907 g, (3 ♀) 465–

563,7–652 g. Other races somewhat smaller (wing 160–204).

Bare Parts: Iris brown; bill, bare facial and gular skin, legs and feet red.

Identification: Size fairly large; variable in plumage with geographical race, but unmistakable; combination of red bill, face, throat and legs diagnostic (Swainson's Francolin has blackish legs and upper jaw); upperparts brown, streaked black; underparts black, streaked white, or white, streaked black (Swainson's Francolin brown below, streaked black); sides of head black or white. *Immature*: Lacks red throat; underparts edged chestnut; bill dusky; legs and feet yellowish.

Voice: Loud harsh crowing, *krrr krrr krrr, korWA, korWA, korWA*, or *koraaki, koraaki koraaki*, increasing in volume then fading away at end; *chuka chuka* on take-off; clucking alarm notes when treed.

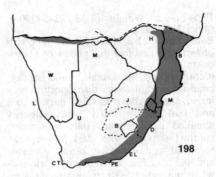

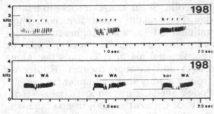

Distribution: S Africa to Kenya; in s Africa from George E to Natal, e Transvaal, Mozambique and e Zimbabwe.

Status: Locally common resident; numbers declining because of habitat destruction.

Habitat: Wooded gorges, edges of upland evergreen forests, riverine scrub; feeds in clearings and cultivated lands.

Habits: In pairs or small coveys. Calls at dawn and dusk. Flies reluctantly, taking refuge in dense trees; shy and wary; runs fast into dense cover when disturbed. Roosts in trees or dense bushes.

Food: Seeds, fruit, shoots, roots, bulbs, snails and insects.

Breeding: *Season*: November to July in Zimbabwe, April to August in e Cape, mainly winter months in Natal. *Nest*: Scrape on ground, lined with grass and roots, in rank vegetation or under low shrub. *Clutch* : 4–7 eggs (rarely 9). *Eggs*: Plain pinkish buff, yellowish cream or light brown with white pitting; measure (77)　45 × 35,9　(40,3–49 × 30,2–38). *Incubation*: 23 days (in captivity) by ♀ only. *Fledging* : Chick flies at 10 days; fully fledged at about 130 days.

199 (185)　Swainson's Francolin　Plate 21
Bosveldfisant
Francolinus swainsonii

Gwarimutondo, Gwari, Horwe (Sh), Makwekwe, N'hwarimakokwe (Ts), Kgwalê, Sogonokê (Tw), [Swainsonfrankolin]

Measurements: Length ♂ about 38 cm, ♀ about 33 cm; wing (81 ♂) 172–192,3–208, (46 ♀) 158–175,2–190; tail (68 ♂) 70–89,1–100, (36 ♀) 66–78,9–92; tarsus (85 ♂) 50–61,4–77, (40 ♀) 47–51,8–58; culmen (22 ♂) 20,5–22,4–25, (14 ♀) 18–20,4–23. Weight (90 ♂) 400–706–875 g, (100 ♀) 340–505–750 g.

Bare Parts: Iris brown; bill blackish brown above, red below; bare facial and gular skin red; legs and feet black.

Identification: Size medium; brown above and below, streaked with black; bill dark above, red below (all red in Rednecked Francolin); face and throat red; legs black (red in Rednecked Francolin). *Immature*: Feathered buffy white on throat and face; brown, streaked and spotted white above and below; no red on bill; legs and feet yellowish brown.

Voice: Very loud, harsh crowing, *krrraa krrraa krrraa*, repeated 6–7 times, dropping in pitch and volume towards end (similar to call of Rednecked Francolin, but lower-pitched); also trilling *chirr chirr* in group; mewing contact call.

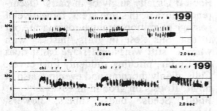

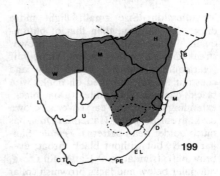

199

Distribution: S Africa to Mozambique, Zambia, Angola and Malawi; in s Africa mainly in N and NE, and Namibian highlands.

Status: Very common resident; range expanding through adaptation to cultivation.

Habitat: Bushveld, edges of woodland in grass and thickets, cultivated lands, savanna, grassveld with scattered woody vegetation, riverine bush, rank vegetation around vleis; generally in more open country than Rednecked Francolin.

Habits: Singly, in pairs or in coveys of up to 8 birds, sometimes in company with Rednecked or Redbilled Francolin. Feeds in clearing and open fields, seeking cover in dense vegetation when disturbed; shy and wary; runs with head well down, body sleeked, weaving through grass. Flight fast and manoeuvrable. Calls from tree or termite mound at dawn and dusk. Roosts in trees at night. Drinks morning and evening.

Food: Seeds, berries, shoots, roots, bulbs, insects, molluscs.

Breeding: *Season*: November to August in Zimbabwe (peak January-June), February to May elsewhere; possibly varies with rainfall. *Nest*: Hollow in ground, about 18 cm diameter, lined with dry grass; in grass or among brushwood. *Clutch*: (24) 4–6,2–12 eggs. *Eggs*: Pinkish or buffy cream with white pores; measure (113) 43,9 × 35,7 (41,4–48,6 × 32,4–38,2). *Incubation*: 21–22 days in captivity. *Fledging*: Flutters at 10–14 days; flies well at 12 weeks.

200 (189) Common Quail Plate 20
Afrikaanse Kwartel
Coturnix coturnix

Erurumbe (K), Sekhwiri (NS), Koekoe, Sekoenqe (SS), Huta (Sh), Mavolwane, Khevezi (Ts), Tshosabannê (Tw), Isagwityi (X), isiGwaca (Z), [Wachtel]

Measurements: Length 16–18 cm; wing (113 ♂) 96–101,6–108, (110 ♀) 96–103,2–111; tail (10 ♂) 34–35,9–38,5, (10 ♀) 31–35,8–40; tarsus (53 ♂) 23–26,4–29,5, (67 ♀) 22–26,6–29,5; culmen (54 ♂) 10–12,6–13,8, (67 ♀) 9–12,8–14,5. Weight (184 ♂) 75,6–92–115,2 g, (175 ♀) 80,7–102,5–131,6 g.

Bare Parts: Iris light brown to yellowish brown; bill blackish; legs and feet yellowish pink.

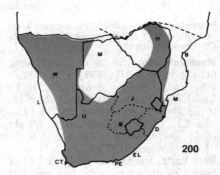

200

Identification: Size small; flight more direct, less fluttery, than that of button-quails. *Male*: Above mottled brown, streaked with white; below stone-buff (Harlequin Quail has black belly and chestnut flanks), streaked on flanks with black, chestnut and white; throat black, extending in line to ear coverts; crown dark; eyebrow white (Harlequin Quail has much bolder head pattern). *Female*: Similar to ♂, but without black throat; eyebrow buff; (similar to ♀ Harlequin Quail, but paler below and lacks brownish collar on foreneck). *Immature*: Similar to adult ♀. *Chick*: Longitudinally striped orange-buff and black.

Voice: Penetrating high-pitched *whit-WHITtit*, *whit-WHITtit*, repeated 4–8 times; squeaky *skree, skree* when flushed.

Distribution: Africa and Eurasia to Japan;

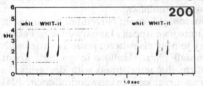

in s Africa breeds mainly in S and E (sw Cape, e Cape, Natal, Lesotho, Orange Free State, s and e Transvaal, Zimbabwe); some nonbreeding birds migrate to n Cape, Namibia, Angola and Zaire.

Status: Common; some populations resident, others migratory, occurring se S Africa mainly August to April.

Habitat: Open grassland, lightly wooded savanna, cultivated fields; nonbreeding birds occur also in karoo, Kalahari sandveld and semi-desert.

Habits: Usually singly or in pairs. Occurrence sporadic in some areas, indicative of passage migration; many birds migrate out to sea. Sits close in grass, flushing with whirr of stiff wings and *skree* calls; does not fly far, pitching suddenly into cover. Calls mainly morning and evening; also at night. Roosts on ground in coveys.

Food: Seeds, buds, tubers, flowers, leaves, arthropods, worms, snails.

Breeding: *Season*: October to April in Natal (mainly November-January), September to October in sw Cape. *Nest*: Scrape on ground, lined with grass and rootlets; well hidden in dense grass, weeds, standing crops, or thorny shrubs. *Clutch*: (79) 2–6,6–14 eggs (usually 5–7). *Eggs*: Yellowish white or buff to brownish, variably spotted, blotched or speckled with dark brown; measure (286) 30 × 23 (25,8–33,1 × 20–27,3); weigh 6,5–9 g. *Incubation*: 17–20 days by ♀ only (sometimes up to 24 days). *Fledging*: About 21 days, cared for by ♀ only; chicks can fly short distances at 9–10 days; fully grown at 30 days.

Ref. Clancey, P.A. 1976. *Durban Mus. Novit.* 11:163–176.

---

201 (190)   Harlequin Quail   Plate 20
Bontkwartel
Coturnix delegorguei

Erurumbe (K), Huta (Sh), N'hwarixigwaqa, Dzurhini, Xigwatla (Ts), Tshosabannê (Tw), isiGwaca (Z), [Harlekinwachtel]

Measurements: Length 16–18 cm; wing (45 ♂) 91–95,8–100, (36 ♀) 93–100,1–105; tail (10 ♂) 30–31,5–33, (6 ♀) 32–33,7–34; tarsus (10 ♂) 24–24,9–26, (6 ♀) 24–24,5–26; culmen (10 ♂) 10,5–11,2–12, (6 ♀) 10,5–11,2–12. Weight (6 ♂) 49–74,7–90,6 g, (10 ♀) 63–81,1–93,3 g, (1 unsexed) 83 g.

Bare Parts: Iris brown; bill black (♂) or horn (♀), base yellowish; legs and feet pink or yellowish pink.

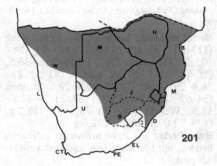

Identification: Size of Common Quail; ♀ very similar to that of Common Quail, but has collar of blackish on throat; ♂ has bold black-and-white facial pattern, black breast, and bright chestnut flanks, heavily streaked black; underparts look dark in flight.

Voice: Somewhat similar to call of Common Quail, but more deliberate, higher-pitched and less rhythmic; sounds rather like reedfrog; *wit, wit, wit, wit-wit* repeated 5–6 times; squeaky *kree* when flushed.

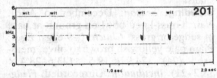

Distribution: Africa S of Sahara, except forested areas; also s Arabia; in s Africa mainly absent from dry W and SW.

Status: Locally common breeding migrant, September to early May; many overwinter in Zimbabwe at times, most probably further N; numbers vary greatly from year to year because of local nomadic movements.

Habitat: Rank grass in moist grasslands, borders of vleis, fallow lands.

Habits: Usually gregarious in coveys of 6–20 birds when not breeding. Flushes reluctantly especially when grass wet; when flushed, flies low and not far, then drops and runs; tame, often killed by traffic. Migrates in large flocks. Breeding males fight vigorously; vocal morning and evening, often several males together.

Food: Seeds, shoots, leaves, insects, snails.

Breeding: *Season*: October to June in Zimbabwe (peak January-February), July to September in Namibia; varies with rainfall. *Nest*: Sparsely lined scrape on ground; in grass, crops or weeds, often among scattered tufts of shortish grass with runways between; eggs may be moved to new site if disturbed; sometimes in loose colonies. *Clutch*: (16) 3–4,5–8 eggs (up to 15, possibly from 2 females). *Eggs*: Creamy-buff to yellowish, speckled, spotted and blotched with dark brown; measure (109) 29,3 × 22,2 (26,8–32 × 20,1–24,4). *Incubation*: 17–20 days by ♀ only. *Fledging*: Flutters at 9 days; flies well at 3–4 weeks.

---

202 (191) **Blue Quail** **Plate 20**

Bloukwartel

Coturnix adansonii

Huta (Sh), Xitshatshana, Xindogo (Ts), [Zwergwachtel]

Measurements: Length about 15 cm; wing (9 ♂) 78–80–82, (5 ♀) 80–81,6–84,5; tail (9 ♂) 26–29,1–32, (5♀) 29–30,3–31; tarsus (9 ♂) 18–18,9–19,5, (5 ♀) 18–19–20; culmen (9 ♂) 8–8,8–10, (5 ♀) 8,5–9,8–10. Weight (2 ♂) 43–46,6 g, (1 ♀) 44 g.

Bare Parts: Iris red-brown to ruby red; bill (♂) black, base tinged blue, (♀) dark horn, base tinged pinkish; legs and feet yellow to orange-yellow.

Identification: Somewhat smaller than other quails. *Male*: Above dark slate; below slate blue; flanks and wings chestnut, streaked blue-grey; bold black-and-

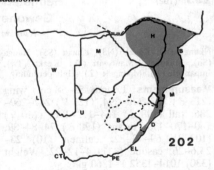

white facial pattern. *Female*: Similar to other quails, but distinctively barred below (not streaked). *Immature*: Similar to adult ♀ but streaked pale on wing.

BLUE QUAIL

Voice: Nasal buzzing 3-note song, first note loud and shrill, second two dropping in pitch by semi-tones, and softer, *ZI-zi-zi*; piping notes somewhat like call of Little Bee-eater; squeaky little triple note when flushed.

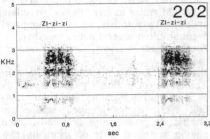

Distribution: Africa S of Sahara; in s Africa confined to extreme E.

Status: Rare breeding migrant, mostly November to April, from tropical Africa; some birds present all year. Probably Rare (RDB).

Habitat: Seasonally moist grassland, vleis, edges of fallow lands, grassy plains, rice fields.

Habits: Usually in pairs or small groups, never in large coveys. Flight fast and direct for 20–40 m; flushes reluctantly. Moves about according to rainfall.

Food: Mainly seeds; also insects and snails.

Breeding: *Season*: December to April. *Nest*: Grass-lined bowl on ground at base of sedge or grass. *Clutch*: 6–9 eggs. *Eggs*: Plain pale yellowish brown to olive; measure (24) 24,9 × 19,5 (23,6–28,4 × 18,2–21). *Incubation*: Unrecorded. *Fledging*: Unrecorded.

10:2. Family 25 NUMIDIDAE—GUINEAFOWL

Large. Bill strong and arched; legs fairly long, spurred in a few species; feet strong; hind toe reduced and raised; wings short and rounded; neck longish, partly bare; head small, usually with wattles, comb or crest, and brightly coloured; tail medium, drooping and heavily overlain with coverts; plumage usually dark slaty or blackish, finely spotted, streaked or barred with white or blue; sexes alike; gregarious; terrestrial, but roost in trees; food variable, plant and animal; nest on ground in lined hollow, well concealed; eggs 6–22, plain cream to light brownish; chick downy, precocial. Distribution Africa and Madagascar; seven or eight species; two species in s Africa.

203 (192)   **Helmeted Guineafowl**   **Plate 21**
                                 Gewone Tarentaal
                                 Numida meleagris

Nkanga (K), Kgaka (NS), Khaka (SS), Hanga (Sh), Mhangela, Mantswiri (Ts), Kgaka (Tw), Impangele (X), iMpangele (Z), [Helmperlhuhn]

Measurements: Length 53–58 cm; wing (213 ♂) 253–270–294, (123 ♀) 247–260–286; tail (198 ♂) 164–172–176, (110 ♀) 160–170–179; tarsus (198 ♂) 74–84–89, (103 ♀) 69–79–82; culmen (10) 23–24,6–26; casque (311) 4–12–22. Weight (330) 1014–1352,1–1860 g.

Bare Parts: Iris brown; bill and casque yellowish horn; face and upper neck blue, washed green around eyes; wattles blue, tipped red; cere and crown red; legs and feet blackish.

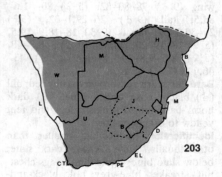

203

Identification: About size of domestic chicken; slate grey, finely spotted white; head small, naked, blue-and-red; conspicuous horny casque on top of head; shape of casque variable with age and locality. *Immature:* Browner with downy neck; casque small or absent.

Voice: Raucous grating *cherrrrr* or *kek-kek-kek-krrrrrr* alarm call; breeding ♀ has repeated 2-syllabled whistle, second note higher and louder than first, *pittoo, pittoo*; ♂ calls *check* or *cheng*.

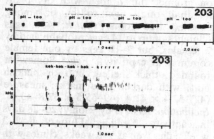

Distribution: Africa S of Sahara, nw Africa, s Arabia; widespread in s Africa, scarcer in dry W, but into Namib Desert at Rössing and Namib-Naukluft Park.

Status: Very common resident.

Habitat: Open grassland, vleis, savanna, cultivated lands, edge of karoo scrub, bushveld.

Habits: Highly gregarious, especially when not breeding; flocks may number several hundred birds; usually in pairs when breeding. Forages in flocks in open ground, scratching for food with feet or bill; males often chase each other, especially at start of breeding season. Runs fast when disturbed; flies well, taking to trees when hard pressed, uttering cackling alarm notes; roosts communally in trees at night. Tame when not persecuted, otherwise very wary. Walks in single file to waterhole.

Food: Seeds, bulbs, tubers, berries, insects, snails, ticks (may be gleaned from warthogs), millipedes; fallen grain in winter where available.

Breeding: *Season:* October to April (mainly November-January). *Nest:* Scrape on ground, lined with dry grass; 25–30 cm diameter, up to 6 cm deep; usually in dense cover of grass or bush. *Clutch:* 6–19 eggs (larger clutches, up to 50 eggs, probably laid by 2 females). *Eggs:* Deep creamy white to light yellowish brown, with large brownish pore marks; sometimes finely speckled; flattened at thick end, pointed at thin end; shell very hard; measure (218) 52,6 × 40,2 (46,4–57,6 × 34,7–42,5); weigh about 45 g. *Incubation:* 24–26–30 days by ♀ only. *Fledging:* Flies weakly at 14 days; fully fledged at about 4 weeks; young brooded by both parents.

Ref. Grafton, R.N. 1971. *Ostrich Suppl.* 8:475–485.
Skead, C.J. 1962. *Ostrich* 33(2):51–65.
Van Niekerk, J.H. 1979. *Ostrich* 50:188–189.

204 (193)

Crested Guineafowl
Kuifkoptarentaal

Plate 21

Guttera pucherani

Hangatoni (Sh), Mangoko, Xiganki (Ts), iMpangele-yehlathi, iNgekle, umQanki (Z), [Kräuselhauben-Perlhuhn]

Measurements: Length about 50 cm; wing (55 ♂) 253–268–280, (34 ♀) 245–260,9–279; tail (40 ♂) 130–151–160, (21 ♀) 136–144–154; tarsus (38 ♂) 87–93–97, (20 ♀) 83–86–90; culmen (10) 24,5–25,7–26,5. Weight 1130–1500 g.

Bare Parts: Iris crimson; bill grey-green to yellowish horn, base darker; bare skin on face and upper neck slate-grey; fold of skin from gape to nape whitish; legs and feet olive-black.

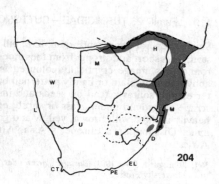

Identification: Similar to Helmeted Guineafowl, but head topped by curly black crest; no red on head. *Immature*: Above barred chestnut, black and grey; below blackish with buff feather edges.

Voice: Rattling alarm call, deeper and more resonant than that of Helmeted Guineafowl, *gruk, gruk, grraang*; in breeding season gives challenging *ticktack ticktack tirr tirr tirr*.

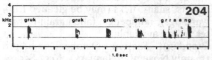

Distribution: Most of Africa S of Sahara; in s Africa confined to NE, as far S as Durban.

Status: Locally common resident; possibly introduced in s part of range.

Habitat: Matted thickets and tangles at edge of lowland evergreen forest, gallery forest, bushveld.

Habits: In pairs when breeding; otherwise gregarious in flocks of 10–30 birds (rarely up to 50). May come out onto roads and other open places to feed; follows troops of monkeys to feed on fallen fruit; forages by scratching in leaf litter and debris; also gleans fruit in trees. Shy and wary; flies readily when disturbed, landing in tall trees. Roosts communally in trees.

Food: Fruit, berries, leaves, stems, seeds, roots, corms, insects, spiders, millipedes, snails.

Breeding: *Season*: November to February (peak November-December). *Nest*: Scrape on ground, thinly lined with dry plant material; often next to log or among exposed tree roots. *Clutch*: 4–6 eggs (clutches of up to 14 eggs probably laid by 2 females, but 9–12 eggs by one female common in captivity). *Eggs*: Somewhat rounded, thick-shelled, buff or pinkish buff, with darker pore marks; measure (42) 52,4 × 41,4 (49–55,5 × 37,8–43,4). *Incubation*: 23 days by ♀ only; 26–28 days in captivity. *Fledging*: Flutters at 2–3 weeks; flies well at 5–6 weeks; climbs with aid of bill as hook before able to fly properly.

11. Order GRUIFORMES (11 families; five in s Africa)

Small to very large. A heterogeneous order, possibly artificial, difficult to define because of diversity between families (see family accounts for Turnicidae, Gruidae, Rallidae, Heliornithidae and Otididae). Most terrestrial, a few arboreal in woodland; many inhabit inland waters, others grassland or semidesert.

Ref. Cracraft, J. 1973. *Bull. Amer. Mus. Nat. Hist.* 151(1):1–127.

11:1. Family 26 TURNICIDAE—BUTTONQUAILS

Small. General appearance quail-like; bill short, slender and arched; neck short; body stout; legs short and strong; front toes moderately long; hind toe absent; wings short and rounded; plumage cryptically coloured in patterns of white, buff, rufous and black above; usually plain or lightly patterned below; males smaller and duller than females; terrestrial; solitary; feed on seeds and insects in grassland and savanna; nest a lined scrape on ground under grass or shrub; eggs usually four (sometimes only two), pale, heavily marked with brown, yellow and grey; chick downy, precocial; parental care by male. Distribution s Europe, s Asia, Africa, Australia; 15 species; two species in s Africa.

Ref. Johnsgard, P.A. 1991. *Bustards, hemipodes, and sandgrouse: birds of dry places.* Oxford: Oxford University Press.

205 (196)   Kurrichane Buttonquail   Plate 22
Bosveldkwarteltjie
Turnix sylvatica

Mauaneng, Mabuaneng (SS), Huta (Sh), Xitsatsana (Ts), Lephurrwane (Tw), Ingolwane (X),
uNgoqo (Z), [Laufhühnchen, Rostkehl-Kampf-
wachtel]

Measurements: Length ♂ 14–15,7 cm, ♀
15,4–16,2 cm; wing (4 ♂) 70–76,5–82,
(4 ♀) 78–85,4–90; tail (3 ♂) 32–35, (3 ♀)
35–38; tarsus (3 ♂) 20–23, (3 ♀) 21–24;
culmen (3 ♂) 11–13, (3 ♀) 13–15. Weight
(3 ♂) 28–36,5–47,5 g, (3 ♀) 32,8–49,9–
62,9 g, (3 unsexed) 37–42–48 g.

Bare Parts: Iris cream; bill blue-grey; legs
and feet pink.

Identification: Smaller than Common
Quail; iris pale (dark in Common Quail
and Blackrumped Buttonquail); ♀ larger
and more brightly coloured than ♂; flight
somewhat fluttering, but stiff-winged,
sometimes with dangling legs; wing shows
pale buff panel on secondaries in flight;
sides of head whitish (rufous in Blackrumped Buttonquail); large brown heart-
shaped marks on flanks (marks smaller in
Blackrumped Buttonquail); no black on
rump. *Chick*: Above pale chestnut, with 2
tawny-white stripes down back; head with
central pale stripe, margined dark brown;
lores and eyebrow whitish; below pale
brownish white.

Voice: ♀ calls deep hooting *hoom hoom
hoom* at about 2-second intervals (similar
to hooting of Redchested Flufftail, but
deeper and slower), or double *oo-oo*,
rather ventriloquial; ♀ calls with bill
closed and neck inflated; ♂ calls like sparrowhawk; soft peeping contact call
between sexes.

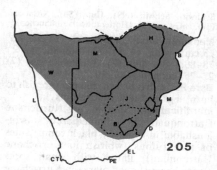

2 0 5

Distribution: Africa, sw Europe, s Asia; in
s Africa mainly absent from SW.

Status: Usually uncommon (possibly commoner than sightings show); resident, but
somewhat nomadic.

Habitat: Drier grasslands, fallow lands,
light savanna or woodland.

Habits: In pairs or small groups. Flushes
reluctantly; does not usually fly far before
landing, then walking slowly on tiptoe
with jerky steps, body rocking back and
forth; flies lower than Common Quail. ♀
feeds ♂ during courtship; ♀ polyandrous
when breeding.

Food: Seeds, insects, other invertebrates;
chick insectivorous for first 10 days, then
eats seeds too.

Breeding: *Season*: All months, peak
October to March. *Nest*: Shallow scrape,
lined with dry grass; placed under tuft of
grass or herb, or at base of shrub or
sapling. *Clutch*: (42) 2–3,2–4 eggs. *Eggs*:
Pale cream, pinkish buff or greyish white,
thickly spotted with brown, yellowish and
grey; broad at thick end, pointed at narrow end; measure (109) 23,7 × 17,5
(19,6–26,2 × 16,9–20); weigh 2,8–5,1 g.
Incubation : 12–14–15 days by ♂ only.
Fledging: First flight at 7–9 days; flies well
at 30–35 days; independent by 37–39
days; mature at 120 days; newly hatched
chick weighs 2,2–2,7–3,1 g; fed for first 4
days by ♂.

Ref. Flieg, G.M. 1973. *Avicult. Mag.* 79:55–59.
    Wintle, C.C. 1975. *Honeyguide* 82:27–30.

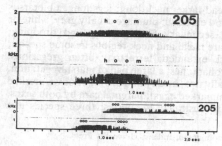

206 (194) Blackrumped Buttonquail (Hottentot Buttonquail) Plate 22
Kaapse Kwarteltjie
Turnix hottentotta

Sekhwiri, Sehwiri (NS), Huta (Sh), Xitsatsana (Ts), isiGwaca (Z), [Hottentottenlaufhühnchen]

Measurements: Length ♂ 14 cm, ♀ 15 cm; wing (4 ♂) 73–76,8–80, (7 ♀) 78–80,9–86; tail (7) 32–36; tarsus (7) 22–25; culmen (7) 9–10.

Bare Parts: Iris brown; bill pale greyish to horn; legs and feet whitish pink.

Identification: Similar to Kurrichane Buttonquail, but immediately distinguishable in flight by black rump; sides of face rufous (whitish in Kurrichane Buttonquail); flanks with small spots (large heart-shaped marks in Kurrichane Buttonquail); eye dark (pale in Kurrichane Buttonquail). *Immature*: Spotted across chest.

Voice: Similar to that of Kurrichane Buttonquail, but lower-pitched.

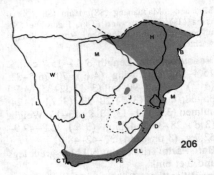

Distribution: Africa S of Sahara; in s Africa confined to S and E.

Status: Fairly common locally, but mostly uncommon resident, or partial migrant; commonest December to April. Endangered (RDB).

Habitat: Open grassland 25–50 cm tall, montane grassland, edges of vleis, scrubland with thin grass cover, fallow lands.

Habits: Hard to flush; flies straight and fast, but not far; on landing, runs into cover; seldom flushes a second time.

Food: Seeds, insects, other invertebrates.

Breeding: *Season*: September to March. *Nest*: Scanty pad of dry grass, about 50 mm diameter, on ground under tuft of grass drawn down to form canopy about 75 mm above eggs. *Clutch*: (8) 3 eggs (2–5 recorded). *Eggs*: Top-shaped, yellowish grey, evenly freckled with tiny marks of dark grey (not brown as in Kurrichane Buttonquail); measure (13) 23 × 18,5 (21,3–24,5 × 17,3–20). *Incubation*: 12–14 days by ♂ only. *Fledging*: Unrecorded.

Ref. Masterson, A.N.B. 1973. *Honeyguide* 74:12–16.

11:2. Family 27 GRUIDAE—CRANES

Very large. Bill rather long and straight; head large; neck long; legs long, tibiotarsus mostly naked; toes short, hind toe reduced and elevated; plumage usually grey, white or brown with modified scapular and inner secondary feathers long and drooping; ornamental head plumes in some species; bare facial and neck regions in some species, sometimes brightly coloured; fly with neck extended; terrestrial; often gregarious; perform dancing displays; voice loud and resonant; nest a large pad of marsh vegetation, sometimes no nest on bare ground; eggs usually two, mostly dull brown or olive, marked brown and grey (one species has pale blue unmarked eggs); parental care by both sexes. Distribution N America, Eurasia, Africa, n Australia; 14 species; three species in s Africa.

Ref. Johnsgard, P.A. 1983. *Cranes of the world*. Bloomington: Indiana University Press.

207 (215)   Wattled Crane   Plate 24
Lelkraanvoël
Grus carunculatus

Epanda (K), Motlathomo (SS), Jowori (Sh), Nya-
kukolwe (Ts), Mogôlôdi (Tw), Iqaqolo, Igwampi
(X), uBhamukwe (Z), [Klunkerkranich]

Measurements: Length about 120 cm;
wing (7 ♂) 613–669,7–717, (7 ♀) 619–
634,1–687; tail (7 ♂) 233–257–270, (7 ♀)
227–261,3–295; tarsus (7 ♂) 298–321,6–
342, (7 ♀) 232–309,8–330; culmen (7 ♂)
150–174–185, (7 ♀) 124–161,4–183.
Weight (1 ♂) 8966 g, (1 ♀) 8285 g.

Bare Parts: Iris orange to orange-yellow;
bill light reddish brown; bare warty facial
skin red; legs and feet black.

Identification: Size very large; neck
white; back grey; belly black; two whitish wattles below chin. *Immature*: Has
smaller wattles and white crown (crown
grey in adult). *Chick*: Greyish buff;
crown ginger; brown stripe on back,
wings and thighs; bill horn; legs and feet
blue-black.

Voice: Usually silent; ringing *kronk*; various low-toned jabbering calls while feeding; alarm *screech*.

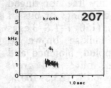

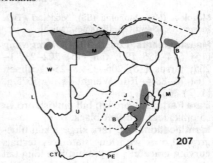

Distribution: S Africa to Somalia; in s
Africa discontinuously from Transkei to
Transvaal, n Zimbabwe and Okavango
Delta.

Status: Uncommon, but conspicuous, resident; straggler to e Cape. Endangered
(RDB); only 20–30 breeding pairs in
Transvaal; threatened by loss of sponge
habitats.

Habitat: Midland to highland marshes,
vleis and moist grasslands; seasonal
floodplains in tropics; breeding habitat of 18–40 ha of wetland, with up to
150 ha of surrounding undisturbed grassland.

Habits: Usually in pairs or small flocks
(up to 40 birds; elsewhere in Africa up
to 400 birds); shy and wary, but reluctant to fly, usually walking slowly
away from danger. Forages by wading in
shallow water or walking through adjacent grassveld or cultivated land, sometimes in company with other crane
species.

Food: Small reptiles, frogs, insects, grain,
tubers, rhizomes, small mammals.

Breeding: *Season*: All months (peak
May-August); successive clutches of one
pair 10–22 months apart. *Nest*: Large
flattened heap of plant material,
1–1,8 m diameter, 20 cm high, in small
pond 3–6 m diameter, 40–80 cm
deep; in marsh; sometimes in grassland or on small islet. *Clutch*: (107) 1–
1,6–2 eggs. *Eggs*: Pale pinkish buff or
biscuit, dappled and blotched with elongate marks of red-brown, brown, slate,
olive and purple; measure (74)
101,2 × 65,6 (91–117,2 × 55,9–71,5);
weigh (3) 215,8–244,1–265,3 g. *Incubation*: 39–40 days by both sexes. *Fledging*:
16–18 weeks, cared for by both parents;
full flight at 21 weeks; only 1 young
reared.

Ref. Cooper, J. 1969. *Honeyguide* 60:17–20.
Tarboton, W.R. 1984. *Proc. 5th Pan-Afr.
Orn. Congr.*:665–678.
Walkinshaw, L.H. 1965. *Ostrich* 36:73–81.
West, O. 1963. *Ostrich* 34:63–77; 1982. *Nat-
uralist* 26 (2):2–9.

208 (216)   Blue Crane   Plate 24
Bloukraanvoël
Anthropoides paradiseus

Mogolodi (NS), Mohololi (SS), Mogôlôri (Tw), Indwe (X), iNdwa (Z), [Paradieskranich]

Measurements: Length 102–107 cm; wing (15) 514–556–590; tail (15) 202–237,1–265; tarsus (16) 205–234,8–254; culmen (16) 76–88,4–101. Weight (1 ♂) 5675 g, (1 ♀) 3632 g.

Bare Parts: Iris brown; bill pinkish brown to pink; legs and feet black.

Identification: Size very large; plain blue-grey all over with long slate-grey tertials curving gracefully to ground like long tail streamers. *Immature*: Paler grey than adult, without long plumes; crown pale chestnut. *Chick*: Grey with light rufous head.

Voice: Distinctive guttural rattling croak, *kraaaarrrk*, fairly high-pitched and very loud.

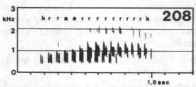

Distribution: Cape Province (except NW) to Natal, Orange Free State, Transvaal highveld, w Lesotho and Swaziland; isolated population at Etosha and in Bushmanland, n Namibia; occasional in nw Botswana.

Status: Common resident with local movements.

Habitat: Midland and highland grassveld, edge of karoo, cultivated land, edges of vleis.

Habits: Highly gregarious when not breeding; otherwise in pairs or family groups; flocks usually 30–40 birds, some

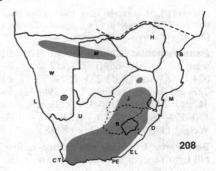

times up to 300. Flies strongly and soars well, often calling from great heights; roosts on ground or in shallow water. Often performs display dances in groups or pairs. Wary when breeding, otherwise fairly tame.

Food: Frogs, reptiles, insects, fish, grain, green shoots; strips grass seeds from standing inflorescences.

Breeding: *Season*: October to February. *Nest*: Scrape on bare ground or rock (*klipplaat*) in open grassveld, often in moist places; sometimes thinly lined or ringed with pebbles, sheep droppings or bits of plant material. *Clutch*: (150) 1–1,8–3 eggs (usually 2). *Eggs*: Pinkish brown to brownish yellow, dappled, blotched and clouded with brown, olive and grey; measure (79) 94,2 × 60,2 (83,8–100 × 52–64,6); weigh (6 fresh eggs) 168–185–202 g. *Incubation*: (5) 30 days by both sexes, mainly by ♀. *Fledging*: 12–13 weeks, fed by ♀ only for at least 6 weeks on insect larvae and worms; chick weighs (5) 97,1–103,1–109,2 g at hatching.

Ref. Van Ee, C.A. 1966. *Ostrich* 37:23–29.

209 (214)   Crowned Crane   Plate 24
Mahem
Balearica regulorum

Engwangali (K), Lehehemu (SS), Sekwarhandzana (Ts), Leowang (Tw), Ihem (X), uNohemu (Z), [Kronenkranich]

Measurements: Length about 105 cm; wing (33) 523–561,4–642; tail (31) 212–239,4–256; tarsus (31) 183–207,5–234; culmen (31) 57–62,3–68. Weight about 3600 g.

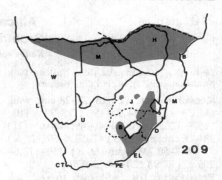

Bare Parts: Iris whitish or pale grey; bill, legs and feet black; cheek patch white; gular wattles red.

Identification: Size very large; spiky straw-coloured crest, grey body and large white wing patch distinctive, especially in flight; head mainly velvety black with white cheeks and red wattles. *Immature*: Has shorter crest; head flecked buff; upperparts tipped rusty; cheeks feathered buff; no gular wattles. *Chick*: Greyish rufous with pale pinkish legs.

Voice: Highly characteristic 2-syllabled trumpeting *maHEM*, second note higher and louder than first; often calls in flight; also deep booming call when breeding.

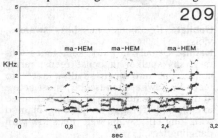

Distribution: S Africa to Kenya and Uganda; in s Africa confined to N, NE and SE.

Status: Common resident.

Habitat: Marshes, vleis, moist grasslands, cultivated fields.

Habits: Gregarious unless breeding; flocks may number 30–150 birds. Tame when not molested. Often performs dancing displays in pairs or groups. Roosts on ground or in trees.

Food: Frogs, reptiles, insects, fallen grain.

Breeding: *Season*: November to May in Zimbabwe, December to February in Natal and Transvaal; mainly summer months throughout s Africa. *Nest*: Large flattened mound of reeds, rushes and grass, well screened by vegetation in marsh; rarely on top of small tree (possibly on old nest of Secretarybird). *Clutch*: (51) 1–2,6–4 eggs (usually 2–3). *Eggs*: Pale bluish with chalky white coating; measure (72) 85 × 57 (75,9–93,9 × 50,4–61,5); weigh (13) 126,1–149,7–182 g. *Incubation*: 29–31 days by both sexes. *Fledging*: About 4 months; young remain with parents about 10 months.

11:3. Family 28 RALLIDAE—RAILS, CRAKES, GALLINULES, MOORHENS, COOTS, ETC.

Small to large. Highly diverse family. Bill medium to long, stout or slender, usually arched or decurved and laterally compressed; neck medium to longish; body usually laterally compressed; wings short and rounded (some species flightless); legs and toes long; tibiotarsus partly naked; hind toe reduced and elevated; toes lobed for swimming in coots (though many species swim without lobed toes); plumage variable; sexes usually alike; most inhabit dense aquatic vegetation; secretive but vocal; appear weak fliers; most solitary; a few gregarious (especially coots); nest on ground or low over water, a bowl of plant material, sometimes roofed over (in terrestrial flufftails), sometimes floating; eggs 2–16, white, buff or olive, usually speckled (plain white in flufftails); chick downy, usually black, precocial; parental care by both sexes. Distribution worldwide; about 130 species; 19 species in s Africa.

Ref. Keith, S., Benson, C.W. & Irwin, M.P.S. 1970. *Bull. Amer. Mus. Nat. Hist.* 143(1):1–84.
Ripley, S.D. 1977. *Rails of the world*. Toronto: Feheley.

210 (197)

African Rail
Grootriethaan
Rallus caerulescens

Plate 22

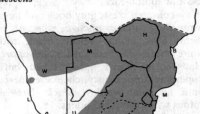

210

Sipika (K), Mopaka-paka (SS), Nhapata (Sh), Nwatsekutseku (Ts), isiZinzi (Z), [Kapralle]

Measurements: Length 27–28 cm; wing (35 ♂) 115–124,5–135, (28 ♀) 110–116,8–126; tail (12) 40–49; tarsus (12) 38–43; culmen (35 ♂) 47–53,1–59, (28 ♀) 42–46,9–50. Weight (66 ♂) 150–178,6–205 g, (50 ♀) 120–149,3–170 g.

Bare Parts: Iris red-brown to red; bill vermilion; legs and feet red.

Identification: Size medium; long bright red bill and red legs diagnostic; above brown; below slate-grey on chest, barred black-and-white on belly. *Immature*: Throat whitish; flanks brown, barred buff and white; bill, legs and iris brown. *Chick*: Downy black; iris grey; bill pink with black tip; legs and feet slate; weighs about 9,5 g at hatching.

Voice: Low growling purr threat note; loud high-pitched *preeee* followed by rapid *pi-pi-pi-pi-* ..... slowing down and dropping in pitch towards end; wheezy *skreee* about every 2–3 seconds.

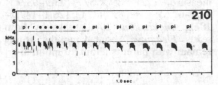

Distribution: S Africa to Ethiopia; also islands in Gulf of Guinea; in s Africa mainly absent from dry W and Kalahari basin.

Status: Fairly common resident; more often heard than seen.

Habitat: Reedbeds, marshes, swamps, vleis.

Habits: Usually in pairs; sometimes solitary; shy skulker in dense reeds; rarely comes out into open shallow water to feed. Somewhat crepuscular, most active at dusk. Movements jerky, with tail raised and flicked; forages by probing in mud with long bill; swims well. Flies low with dangling legs.

Food: Crabs, insects, worms, small frogs.

Breeding: *Season*: July to February in Transvaal, January to May in Zimbabwe; probably most months throughout s Africa. *Nest*: Bowl of reed and rush blades; about 15–20 cm diameter, 5–10 cm thick; central cup 2–5 cm deep; placed inside border of reedbed, 10–40 cm above water level. *Clutch*: 2–6 eggs. *Eggs*: Creamy white, spotted and speckled with brown and grey, more densely at broad end; measure (56) 38,1 × 27,5 (32,5–40,3 × 25,8–29,1). *Incubation*: 20 days by both sexes. *Fledging*: 6–7 weeks.

Ref. Schmitt, M.B. 1976. *Ostrich* 47:16–26.

211 (198)

Corncrake
Kwartelkoning
Crex crex

Plate 22

Katukutuku (K), [Wachtelkönig]

Measurements: Length 27–30 cm; wingspan 46–53 cm; wing (15 ♂) 139–144–150, (6 ♀) 130–136–145; tail (38 ♂) 41–47,1–52, (24 ♀) 40–44,4–49; tarsus (36 ♂) 37–40–43, (23 ♀) 35–38,1–40; culmen (37 ♂) 20–21,4–25, (25 ♀) 19–20,5–23. Weight (Europe) (36 ♂) 135–169,4–210 g, (16 ♀) 119–145–197 g.

Bare Parts: Iris pale brown to hazel; bill pale pinkish brown, tip darker brown; legs and feet pale pinkish grey.

Identification: Size smallish to medium; rusty wings diagnostic, especially in flight; above streaked brown and buff; below buff, rufous on flanks; bill short and stout.
Voice: Usually silent in s Africa; toneless tearing or rasping call of 2 parts, *kzz-kzzz, kzz-kzzz*.

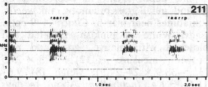

Distribution: Breeds Eurasia; migrates to Africa; in s Africa mainly confined to E.
Status: Uncommon to fairly common nonbreeding Palaearctic migrant, November to April; about 30% of specimens are *C. c. similis* from Asia, rest are *C. c. crex* from Europe.
Habitat: Rank grasslands, fallow fields, grassy edges of streams and vleis, growing crops.

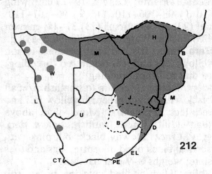

Habits: Usually solitary; skulks in dense grass, running fast with head down, weaving between tufts; flushes reluctantly, flight heavy with dangling legs; does not fly far before dropping into vegetation.
Food: Insects, arachnids, molluscs, millipedes, earthworms, young frogs, leaves, shoots, seeds (mostly animal material).
Breeding: Extralimital.

212 (199) African Crake Plate 22
Afrikaanse Riethaan
Crex egregia

Katukutuku (K), Nhapata (Sh), [Steppenralle]

Measurements: Length 20–23 cm; wing (8) 123–126–129; tail 37–47; tarsus 39–43; culmen 22–25. Weight (1 ♂) 121 g.
Bare Parts: Iris orange to red; bill grey, culmen blackish, base purplish; legs and feet brown.
Identification: Size medium to small; somewhat similar to African Rail with grey chest and black-and-white barred belly, but bill short (long and bright red in African Rail); back heavily mottled black on brown (plain dark brown in African Rail); short white eyebrow distinctive; no white spotting as in Spotted Crake. *Immature*: Similar to adult, but browner below; barring less distinct; crown black; bill and legs dusky; iris dark brown. *Chick*: Downy black; bill purplish grey.
Voice: Series of 8–9 high-pitched rapid whistling notes, somewhat trilled; nonbreeding birds give single loud sharp *kup*, sometimes in series, *kup-kup-kup*; short harsh *krrr*.

Distribution: Africa S of Sahara; in s Africa mainly confined to E of 300-mm isohyet, but many stragglers to W coast and n Namibia, usually after strong e winds.

187

Status: Uncommon breeding migrant from tropical Africa, November to April.
Habitat: Marshes, edges of vleis, seasonally flooded grassland, rank vegetation fringing streams, edges of neglected cultivation, lightly bushed grassland; mainly tussock grassland 0,3–1 m tall.
Habits: Usually solitary. Active mostly 06:00–07:30 and again 17:30–18:30. Crouches when disturbed, though often tame and approachable on foot; difficult to flush, except with dogs; flies usually less than 50 m before dropping into vegetation, often on far side of thicket. May forage by probing into base of grasstuft, often along tracks in grassland. Roosts in depression at base of tussock.
Food: Insects, molluscs, earthworms, small frogs, shoots and leaves of plants, seeds.
Breeding: *Season*: November to March (peak January-February in Zimbabwe). *Nest*: Shallow cup of grass, 22 cm diameter, 4 cm thick overall; internal diameter 11 cm, depth 2 cm; in depression on ground, in tall grass or among rank weeds, sometimes near marsh. *Clutch*: 4–9 eggs. *Eggs*: White or pinkish, freckled and blotched with mauve, grey and red-brown; measure (112) 34,5 × 25,5 (31,5–38,9 × 24–27,9); weigh (8) 9,6–11,6–13,1 g. *Incubation*: About 14 days by both sexes. *Fledging*: 4–5 weeks.

Ref. Avery, G., Brooke, R.K. & Komen, J. 1988. *Ostrich* 59:25–29.
Taylor, P.B. 1985. *Ostrich* 56:170–185.

213 (203)   Black Crake   Plate 22
Swartriethaan
Amaurornis flavirostris

Katukutuku (K), Nhapata (Sh), Hukunambu, Nkukumezane (Ts), umJengejenge, umJekejeke (Z), [Mohrenralle, Negerralle]

Measurements: Length 19–23 cm; wing (10 ♂) 98–106–110, (13 ♀) 96–101–110; tail (23) 36–49; tarsus (23) 37–44; culmen (23) 23–28. Weight (133) 70–90,6–118 g.
Bare Parts: Iris red; bill greenish lemon yellow; legs and feet bright red (breeding) to dull red (nonbreeding).
Identification: Medium to smallish size; all black with bright greenish yellow bill and red legs. *Immature*: More olive above than adult; throat whitish; below dark grey. *Chick*: Downy black; bill pink with vertical black band in centre; legs and toes slate; weighs 8–9 g at hatching.
Voice: High-pitched clucking notes, followed by deep growling bullfroglike note, *k-k-k-k-rrrung*, sometimes in duet or several birds together, repeating phrase 2–3 times; also *rru-rru-rru-rru*, speeding up as call progresses; clucks while foraging; high-pitched metallic *chuk* alarm note.

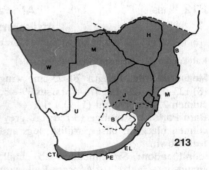

Distribution: Africa S of Sahara; in s Africa absent from dry W and Kalahari.
Status: Common resident.
Habitat: Marshes, reedy watercourses and lake fringes, weedy ponds, river backwaters.
Habits: Solitary, in pairs or small groups; less shy than other rallids, often coming out into open, walking over floating water plants, jerking head and flicking tail. Flies reluctantly but strongly, low over water; swims well; often perches in reeds, or on low bushes. Very active after rain; sometimes vocal at night.
Food: Insects, crustaceans, molluscs,

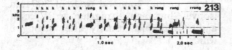

worms, small fish, nestlings, small birds caught in mistnets, herons' eggs, seeds, water plants.

Breeding: *Season*: October to March in Transvaal, October to February in sw Cape, August to April and June in Zimbabwe; double-brooded. *Nest*: Bulky bowl of rushes, grass and other water plants, 20–50 cm above water at rim; also on ground or rarely in bush up to 3 m above ground; cup 5–9 cm deep; in reeds, rushes or sedges. *Clutch*: 2–6 eggs (usually 3). *Eggs*: Cream to pinkish buff, speckled or blotched with red-brown and pale purplish grey, especially at thick end; measure (48) 33,5 × 24 (30,1–35,7 × 21,5–26). *Incubation*: 14–19 days. *Fledging*: About 5 weeks; young fed by both parents for 10 days; earlier broods help build nest and care for later broods.

Ref. Schmitt, M.B. 1975. *Ostrich* 46:129–138.

214 (201) Spotted Crake Plate 22
Gevlekte Riethaan
Porzana porzana

Katukutuku (K), [Tüpfelsumpfhuhn]

Measurements: Length about 22–24 cm; wingspan 37–42 cm; wing (46 ♂) 117–122–128, (27 ♀) 111–118–123; tail (45 ♂) 42–47,5–54, (26 ♀) 44–47,3–52; tarsus (45 ♂) 32–34,1–37, (27 ♀) 30–33–35; culmen (45 ♂) 18–19,7–22, (27 ♀) 17–18,4–20. Weight (1 ♀) 84 g, (8, s Africa) 59–71–83 g, (142, Europe) 61–87,6–147 g.

Bare Parts: Iris yellow-brown to red-brown; bill yellow, orange or red, tip yellow to greenish yellow; legs and feet light olive green.

Identification: Size medium (noticeably smaller than African Crake); white spots on brown back and chest diagnostic; belly less distinctly barred than that of African Crake; undertail coverts buff; bill short, bright orange with yellowish tip; legs green; white margin along leading edge of wing conspicuous in flight (in Striped Crake white does not extend to dorsal surface of wing); flight looks weak. *Immature*: Buffy on breast, less spotted than adult.

Voice: Usually silent in Africa; ♂ rarely calls loud short high-pitched ascending whistled *kwit* about once a second (sounds like water dropping into full barrel); repeated *week-week-week* up to more than 20 notes.

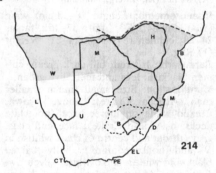

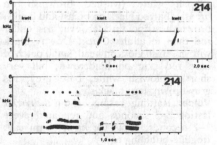

Distribution: Breeds Eurasia; migrates to s Europe, Africa and India; in s Africa as far S as Walvis Bay in W and Lesotho in E.

Status: Uncommon nonbreeding Palaearctic migrant, December to April (rarely May); numbers fluctuate from year to year.

Habitat: Marshes, vleis, flooded grass-lands.

Habits: Solitary. Forages at edge of water on surface of mud or by probing into mud; may submerge head to reach bottom mud in belly-deep water; skulks in marginal vegetation, seldom emerging into open, but tame if undisturbed; moves quickly between cover, flicking erect tail and jerking head when nervous; tail rarely somewhat drooped; runs with bent legs into cover when alarmed; walks and pecks erratically at vegetation or water surface; may swim. Flushes reluctantly; flies low, even on migration. Crepuscular, roosting by day on ground, in shrubbery or in dense overhanging grass at water's edge.

Food: Aquatic invertebrates and plants, insects, spiders, earthworms, grass seeds; rarely small fish.

Breeding: Extralimital.

Ref. Brooke, R.K. 1974. *Durban Mus. Novit.* 10:43–52.
Taylor, P.B. 1987. *Ostrich* 58:107–117.

215 (202) Baillon's Crake   Plate 22
Kleinriethaan
Porzana pusilla

Katukutuku (K), Nhapata (Sh), Isizinzi, Isazenza (X), isiZinzi (Z), [Zwergsumpfhuhn]

Measurements: Length 16–18 cm; wing (104) 76–84,2–93; tail 37–46; tarsus 24–28; culmen (84) 16–18,4–21. Weight (1) 30 g.

Bare Parts: Iris red; bill dark green, culmen blackish; legs and feet olive green.

Identification: Size small (much smaller than African Crake); above brown, flecked white on upper back (no white flecks in African Crake); face and chest grey (throat and centre of chest whitish in ♀ and nonbreeding ♂); belly barred black-and-white; no white eyebrow. *Immature:* Above similar to adult; below greyish white (washed brownish on breast), barred black on breast and flanks; brownish stripe through eye; iris duller red than in adult. *Chick:* Downy black with greenish gloss on head; small patch of bare red skin on hindcrown; bill very short, yellowish white, base grey; iris grey-brown; legs blackish.

Voice: Rattling rasping *ti-ti-ti-ti-tirrrrrrr* lasting 2–3 seconds and repeated every 1–2 seconds; explosive *krrik* alarm call; froglike bubbling call.

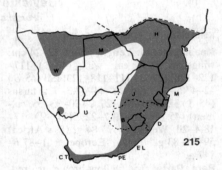

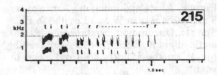

Distribution: Eurasia, N Africa, S Africa to E Africa, Madagascar, Australasia; in s Africa absent from dry W and Kalahari.

Status: Fairly common resident, though mostly absent in winter in Zimbabwe and Transvaal, so possibly some populations regularly migratory. Probably Rare (RDB).

Habitat: Reedbeds, marshes, vleis.

Habits: Usually solitary. Shy skulker in dense marginal vegetation, making rodentlike runs and tunnels; seldom seen in open; flies low and fast, but not far; walks with jerking tail and back-and-forth head movements. May swim or walk on floating plants while foraging.

Food: Mainly aquatic insects; also molluscs, worms, crustaceans, green plants, seeds.

Breeding: *Season:* November in Natal, December to March in Transvaal, January to March in Zimbabwe; mainly summer months in s Africa. *Nest*: Cup of dead plant material, 9–10 cm diameter, 8–10 cm thick; internal diameter 7 cm, depth 3 cm; on ground in dense grass, or on tussock in marsh; surrounding plants pulled down to form canopy over nest. *Clutch*: 4–6 eggs. *Eggs*: Olive-buff, brown or yellowish, clouded with darker olive, more densely at thick end; measure (25) 28,2 × 20,3 (26,1–31 × 19,4–21,3). *Incubation*: 14–16 days by both sexes. *Fledging*: About 35 days; fed by both parents for few days; young independent of parents before flying age.

Ref. Benson, C.W. 1964. *Bull. Brit. Orn. Club* 84:2–5.

216 (200)   Striped Crake   Plate 22
Gestreepte Riethaan
Aenigmatolimnas marginalis

[Graukehl-Sumpfhuhn]

Measurements: Length 18–21 cm; wingspan 36–39 cm; wing (3 ♂) 104–107–109, (6 ♀) 104–106–109; tail (3 ♂) 44–46,5–49, (6 ♀) 42–43,5–47; tarsus (3 ♂) 35–36–37, (6 ♀) 33–35–37; culmen (3 ♂) 17–18–19, (6 ♀) 15–17,5–19. Weight (1 ♀) 61 g.

Bare Parts: Iris golden brown; eyering orange; bill apple green above, bluish white below, culmen black; legs and feet jade green, marked yellow on anterior scales.

Identification: Size small; bill short and heavy (diagnostic). *Male*: Above dark brown, streaked white on upper back and wings; rump and tail blackish; face, sides of neck and chest deep rufous buff; flanks buff, faintly mottled brown; undertail deep buff (all other small crakes barred under tail). *Female*: Above similar to ♂; below mostly grey, faintly streaked whitish. *Immature*: Like ♂, but more rufous below. *Chick*: Undescribed.

Voice: *Tak-tak-tak* repeated about once a second; unmusical wooden rattle; grunts and growls in alarm; *chup* contact call between members of family group.

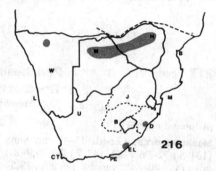

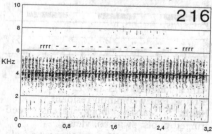

Distribution: Africa and Aldabra; in s Africa from e Cape to Natal, Zimbabwe, Ovamboland; vagrant to s Namibia.

Status: Breeding migrant from tropical Africa, December to February; common around Harare, Zimbabwe; uncommon elsewhere.

Habitat: Marshes, small vleis, flooded grasslands with pools, edges of drainage ditches.

Habits: Solitary or in small family groups. Highly secretive; flies reluctantly; may freeze and can sometimes be picked up by hand. Probably partly nocturnal. Migrates at night; some birds fly into lighted windows.

Food: Snails; probably also insects and worms.

Breeding: *Season*: December to February in Zimbabwe (peak January). *Nest*: Bowl of grass on soggy ground, or 10–15 cm over water. *Clutch*: (6) 5 eggs. *Eggs*: Pinkish yellow, heavily marked with reddish brown; slightly glossy; measure (24) 26–33 × 20–23,5. *Incubation*: Unrecorded. *Fledging*: Unrecorded.

Ref. Hopkinson, G. & Masterson, A.N. 1975. *Honeyguide* 84:12–21.

FLUFFTAILS (GENUS *SAROTHRURA*)

The flufftails are smallish rallids of marsh or forest edge. The males are characterized by brick red heads, necks and (sometimes) chests, with blackish bodies variously marked with spots or streaks of white or buff. The tail is fluffy in most species, and either dark or rufous. The combination of tail colour, head colour and body markings is usually diagnostic for males. The females are all drab and usually barred with whitish; a few are striped or spotted, but they are all hard to identify in the field, except for the Whitewinged Flufftail whose white secondaries are diagnostic in both sexes. Their vocalizations are highly characteristic, mostly loud and far-carrying hooting sounds.

Ref. Keith, S., Benson, C.W. & Irwin, M.P.S. 1970. *Bull. Amer. Mus. Nat. Hist.* 143:1–84.

217 (205)   Redchested Flufftail   Plate 22
Rooiborsvleikuiken
Sarothrura rufa

[Rotbrust-Zwergralle]

Measurements: Length 15–17 cm; wing (104 ♂) 71–76,1–82, (47 ♀) 71–76,9–81; tail (4) 40–55; tarsus (79 ♂) 19,5–22,2–23, (37 ♀) 19,5–20,5–23; culmen (80 ♂) 13–14,3–15, (38 ♀) 13–13,8–15. Weight (4 ♂) 30–34,6–42 g, (1 ♀) 29,4 g.
Bare Parts: Iris brown; bill grey, culmen darker; legs and feet greyish olive.
Identification: *Male*: Bright rufous on head, neck and well down breast and upper belly (rufous extends just to chest in Buffspotted Flufftail); tail not red (barred black and rufous in Buffspotted Flufftail); spots and streaks fine and white (coarser and buff in Buffspotted Flufftail). *Female*: Finely barred above and below (♀ of Buffspotted Flufftail spotted above, coarsely barred below). Inhabits marshy ground (Buffspotted Flufftail inhabits forest). *Chick*: Downy black; iris black; bill black, base pink, tip white; legs purplish black.
Voice: Series of loud ascending notes in quick succession *tuwi-tuwi-tuwi-tuwi*; repeated hoot-grunt call, *wooah-boo* (grunt sometimes inaudible), *woo, woo*; deep drumming *wuk-wuk-wuk-wuk*; rapid double *tudu, tudu, tudu*; ♂ and ♀ may call in duet; also growling, wheezing and chirping sounds.

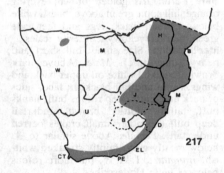

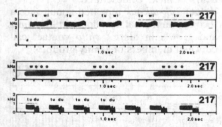

Distribution: Africa S of Sahara; in s Africa confined to S and E.
Status: Fairly common resident.
Habitat: Marshy, boggy areas, reed-fringed pools, swamps, vleis.
Habits: Solitary or in pairs; shy and elusive. Active only by day, but often calls at night also. Flies reluctantly for few metres

when flushed; runs fast through grass with tail depressed.

Food: Seeds, insects, snails, spiders.

Breeding: *Season*: August to January in sw Cape, December to March in Zimbabwe. Up to 5 broods per season. *Nest*: Bowl of dry reedlike leaves, grass and rootlets; on ground among grass or reeds; inside diameter 9,5 cm, depth 3 cm. *Clutch*: 3–5 eggs. *Eggs*: White; measure

(16) 27,9 × 20,9 (27–28,7 × 19,2–22,2). *Incubation*: About 14 days by both sexes. *Fledging*: About 6 weeks; fed and brooded by both parents; chicks may be carried under parent's wing.

Ref. Broekhuysen, G.J., Lestrange, G.K. & Myburgh, N. 1964. *Ostrich* 35:117–120.
Steyn, P. & Myburgh, N. 1986. *Afr. Wildl.* 40:22–27.

218 (206)   Buffspotted Flufftail   Plate 22
Gevlekte Vleikuiken
Sarothrura elegans

[Schmuckzwerggralle]

Measurements: Length 15–17 cm; wing (43 ♂) 83–92,9–94, (22 ♀) 85–89,6–93; tail (7) 33–44; tarsus (20 ♂) 22–24–26, (11 ♀) 23–24–25; culmen (18 ♂) 15,5–16,2–17,5, (11 ♀) 14–15–17. Weight (1 ♂) 45,2 g, (8 unsexed) 32–43,6–50 g.

Bare Parts: Iris brown; bill (♂) black, grey at base, (♀) dark horn; legs and feet olive grey.

Identification: *Male*: Rufous on head and neck extends only to upper breast (much more extensive in Redchested Flufftail); tail barred rufous and black; no white secondaries; boldly spotted buff above and below. *Female*: Coarsely barred dark and light below (barring fine in ♀ Redchested Flufftail, looks paler there)); above spotted with buff. Inhabits forest (not marshy ground). *Immature*: Lacks rufous on head in ♂; both sexes have plain sepia-brown mantle; lacks chestnut tone of adults. *Chick*: Downy black; bill black (no pale markings as in chick of Redchested Flufftail).

Voice: Mournful wailing foghornlike hoot or whistle, with resonance of tuning fork, lasting 2–4 seconds, usually starting low and increasing in pitch towards end, *whoooooo-eeeeeeeeee*; repeated every 5–10 seconds, usually at night in misty or drizzly weather; low repeated *whoo-whoo* in rapid succession by ♂; ♀ replies with low croaks *wak wak wak*; both sexes give 2-note *whoo-whoo*; also whining, mewing and growling notes; alarm call sounds like spitting cat.

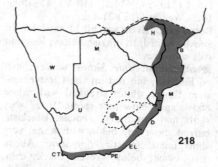

Distribution: Africa S of Sahara; in s Africa mainly confined to S and E; also Bloemfontein.

Status: Fairly common resident.

Habitat: Evergreen forest and adjoining thickets, overgrown gardens.

Habits: Usually solitary; very seldom seen; hard to locate, even when calling. ♂ calls from inside tangled growth up to several metres above ground; by day may forage on forest floor, walking with quick steps; when disturbed darts mouselike into undergrowth, but sometimes confiding; flight heavy and fluttering.

Food: Insects, snails, seeds.

Breeding: *Season*: September to March. *Nest*: Ball-shaped, 21–23 cm outside diameter, 16–17 cm inside diameter, about 9 cm inside height, with side entrance 7–8 cm long, 7 cm high, 9 cm wide; built of dry grass, dead leaves and roots, lined with rootlets; roof camouflaged with moss and lichen; placed on sloping, well drained ground among leaf and twig litter near undergrowth; sur-

rounding vegetation pulled down to form canopy. *Clutch*: 3–5 eggs. *Eggs*: Glossy white; measure (17) 27,8 × 21,1 (25–31,3 × 19–22). *Incubation*: 15–18 days by both sexes. *Fledging*: Unrecorded; chicks remain in or near nest for about 48 hours after hatching.

Ref. Manson, A.J. 1986. *Honeyguide* 32:137–142.

219 (207X) Streakybreasted Flufftail Plate 22
Streepborsvleikuiken

Sarothrura boehmi

[Boehmzwergralle]

Measurements: Length about 15 cm; wing (21 ♂) 80–84,3–88, (14 ♀) 83–85,6–89; tail 32–35; tarsus (15 ♂) 18,5–19,5–21,5, (10 ♀) 18–19,4–20; culmen (15 ♂) 13–13,9–14,5, (10 ♀) 13–13,8–14,5. Weight (1 ♀) 21,4 g.

Bare Parts: Iris brown; bill blackish brown above, whitish to pinkish below; legs and feet slate-grey.

Identification: *Male*: Similar to Redchested Flufftail, but red on chest less extensive; throat white; streaked with white above and below (not spotted); tail very short and not fluffy. *Female*: Blackish, barred above and below with white; very short tail diagnostic. *Immature*: Above matt black; below greyish black; chin, throat and centre of belly white. *Chick*: Downy black; bill black, tip paler.

Voice: Repeated hoot *hooo hooo*; higher-pitched pumping tooting, preceded by barely audible grunt, *t'oo t'oo*, given at just over half-second intervals, up to 25 times with varying tempo; this call sometimes trails off into softer agitated *wu-wu-wu-wu-wu* notes.

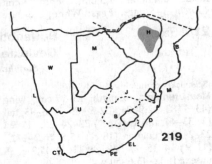

219

Distribution: Africa S of Sahara to e Zimbabwe only.
Status: Fairly common breeding migrant from tropical Africa, November to April.
Habitat: Drier open grasslands subjected to seasonal flooding.
Habits: Usually solitary or in pairs. Flies strongly; runs swiftly through grass.
Food: Mostly small seeds; also some insects.
Breeding: *Season*: November to March in Zimbabwe (peak January). *Nest*: Saucer of dry grass and weed stems; on ground at base of grasstuft, or 2–7 cm up inside tuft on moist ground; tops of surrounding grass pulled down to form canopy. *Clutch*: (34) 2–3,8–5 eggs (usually 3–4). *Eggs*: Creamy white with pinpoint spots of brown; measure (22) 27 × 19,3 (24,8–28,1 × 18,3–20,3). *Incubation*: Unrecorded; by both sexes. *Fledging*: Unrecorded; young cared for by both parents.

220 (206X) Longtoed Flufftail (Chestnutheaded Flufftail) Plate 22
Langtoonvleikuiken (Bronskopvleikuiken)

Sarothrura lugens

[Trauerschmuckralle]
Measurements: Length about 15 cm; wing (32 ♂) 75–78–82, (22 ♀) 70–76,7–82; tail (6 ♀) 40–55; tarsus (30 ♂) 19–20,5–22,5, (20 ♀) 17–20–22; culmen (30 ♂) 13–14,3–15, (20 ♀) 12,5–13,8–15.

Bare Parts: Iris dark greyish brown; bill dusky brown, lower jaw whitish; legs and feet brown to dark slate.

Identification: *Male*: Rufous on head only (not onto breast); throat white; rest of body blackish with fine white streaks; tail fluffy (tail very short in Streakybreasted Flufftail), all black (tail rufous in Striped Flufftail). *Female*: Very similar to ♀ Streakybreasted Flufftail, but less barred above; below finely streaked on belly, spotted on breast (not barred); tail fluffy, all black with scarcely visible white spots. *Chick*: Downy black; bill black, base and tip white.

Voice: Hooting, similar to that of Buffspotted Flufftail, but less prolonged, more guttural, *whoo-whoo-whoo*, repeated with hardly a pause; loud high-pitched pumping, quickly repeated crescendo, *kyoo-kyoo-kyoo*; may call in duet.

Distribution: Tropical Africa.

Status: Southern African specimen from e

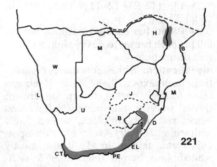

Zimbabwe is in fact misidentified ♀ Redchested Flufftail *S. rufa*, so Longtoed Flufftail must be removed from s African list.

Habitat: Marshes and vleis (occurs together with Redchested and Streakybreasted Flufftails).

Habits: Unrecorded.

Food: Insects and seeds.

Breeding: Not recorded in s Africa. *Season*: November to March in Zambia. *Nest, Clutch, Eggs, Incubation, Fledging*: Unrecorded.

221 (207)   Striped Flufftail (Redtailed Flufftail)   Plate 22
Gestreepte Vleikuiken
Sarothrura affinis

[Streifenzwergralle]

Measurements: Length 14–15 cm; wing (20 ♂) 70–76,8–85, (16 ♀) 68–76,5–85; tail 35–40; tarsus (21 ♂) 15,5–17,3–19,5, (16 ♀) 15–17–20; culmen (21 ♂) 12,5–13,1–14, (16 ♀) 12–13–14. Weight (1 ♂) 28,8 g.

Bare Parts: Iris dark brown; bill black above, whitish to pinkish below; legs and feet grey to pinkish brown.

Identification: *Male*: Rufous head and plain rufous tail (no barring) diagnostic; throat white; body striped black-and-white. *Female*: Very similar to other ♀ flufftails, barred and spotted dark and light; not safely separable in the field; in the hand, tail barred black and rusty; upperparts mottled buff and brown.

Voice: Hooting note lasting about 1 second, repeated at about 2-second intervals,

whooop ...whooop ...whooop; each note starts softly, increases in volume and drops away; various rattles, grunts and growls; rapid *ti-ti-ti-ti-ti*, slowing down to *tee-tee-tee*; harsh brief barks *zrrk zrrk zrrk* at intervals of 1 second or more, heard at dusk.

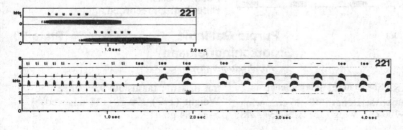

Distribution: Cape Town to e Cape, Natal, highlands of Zimbabwe (also old records from Transvaal highveld); also montane habitats in Malawi, Kenya and Sudan.
Status: Uncommon resident. Rare (RDB).
Habitat: Rank vegetation at forest edges, tall grass and sedge in upland marshes and forests, short montane grassland, brackenbrier, croplands; not confined to marshy places.
Habits: Usually solitary or in pairs. Shy skulker; flies reluctantly; can sometimes be picked up by hand; flies weakly for short distance when flushed; hard to flush again.
Food: Insects, seeds and some green plant material.
Breeding: *Season*: December to February. *Nest*: Bowl of grass and rootlets, built into dense grasstuft; grass pulled down to form canopy over nest. *Clutch*: 4–5 eggs. *Eggs*: White; measure (8) 25,8 × 19,4 (23,8–28,3 × 17,7–21,6). *Incubation*: Unrecorded; by both sexes. *Fledging*: Unrecorded.

222 (204)   Whitewinged Flufftail   Plate 22
Witvlerkvleikuiken
Sarothrura ayresi

[Weißflügel-Zwerggralle]

Measurements: Length 14–16 cm; wing (13 ♂) 73–76–79, (12 ♀) 67–76,1–80; tail 34–44; tarsus (13 ♂) 17–18,3–19,5, (12 ♀) 16–18,8–21,5; culmen (13 ♂) 12–12,3–13, (12 ♀) 12–12,5–13,5. Weight (1 ♀) 37 g.
Bare Parts: Iris hazel to purplish brown; bill purplish brown to dusky pink; legs and feet dusky pink.
Identification: White secondaries diagnostic in both sexes in flight. *Male*: Head and chest rufous, darker brown on crown; throat whitish; tail barred rufous and black; rest of body black, striped finely with white. *Female*: Above blackish, spotted white; tail as in ♂; below mostly whitish (less barred than other ♀ flufftails). *Immature*: Brownish black above and below; throat and centre of belly white; chest barred white.
Voice: Repeated deep hooting *oop-oop, oop-oop, oop-oop*.

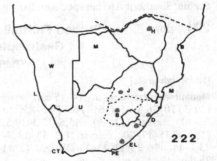

222

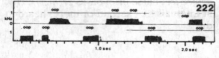

Distribution: Eastern S Africa and Ethiopian highlands; in S Africa recorded from King William's Town (e Cape), Bloemfontein (Orange Free State), Potchefstroom, Heidelberg, Dullstroom (Transvaal) and Franklin (Natal).
Status: Rarest and least known flufftail. Possibly breeding migrant; occurrence sporadic. Rare (RDB).
Habitat: Large marshes; similar habitat to that of Wattled Crane.
Habits: Usually solitary. Hard to flush; flies low and not far. Poorly known.
Food: Insects.
Breeding: Unrecorded.

223 (208)   Purple Gallinule   Plate 23
Grootkoningriethaan
Porphyrio porphyrio

Edenene (K), Nhapata (Sh), [Purpurhuhn]

Measurements: Length 40–46 cm; wingspan 90–100 cm; wing (15) 225–237–248; tail 82–101; tarsus 70–92; culmen 56–71. Weight (1 ♀) 390 g, (134 unsexed) 325–543–784 g.

Bare Parts: Iris red; bill and frontal shield bright red; legs and feet pinkish red.

Identification: Size large; mainly deep blue, greenish on back; huge bright red bill and frontal shield diagnostic; white undertail conspicuous. (Lesser Gallinule much smaller, frontal shield green; American Purple Gallinule has yellow legs.) *Immature*: Brownish, face and underparts buffy; bill and frontal shield blackish. *Chick*: Downy black, tipped silver-grey on head, back and wings; small red frontal shield; bill white, base red, tip black; legs and feet pink; eyelids red.

Voice: Various loud shrieks, groans, cackles, grunts, cackles and explosive bubbling calls.

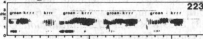

Distribution: Africa S of Sahara, N Africa, Madagascar, extreme s Europe, tropical Asia, Australasia; in s Africa absent from most of dry W and Kalahari; vagrant to Hardap Dam, Namibia.

Status: Fairly common resident.

Habitat: Reedy swamps and marshes; prefers rushes (*Typha*) and sedges (*Cyperus*) to reeds (*Phragmites*) but occurs in all three.

Habits: Solitary or in small groups. Usually shy, keeping to dense vegetation; sometimes forages in open shallows; may hold food in foot while feeding; walks with high-stepping gait, tail raised and flicking;

clambers about vegetation with large red feet. Flies reluctantly and heavily, legs dangling; swims well, but rarely; flightless in wing moult, October to December.

Food: Roots, tubers, stems, flowers, grain, insects, nestlings, birds' eggs, young ducklings, carrion.

Breeding: *Season*: September to January in sw Cape, August to April in Natal, July to February in Transvaal, all months (except November and December) in Zimbabwe; mainly summer months in s Africa, but probably throughout year. *Nest*: Large bowl of rushes, reeds and grass, built on floating island, or up to 1 m above water among tall vegetation. *Clutch*: 2–6 eggs. *Eggs*: Pinky buff to creamy white, sparsely spotted with brown and grey; measure (62) 53,9 × 36,6 (45,3–59,9 × 32,3–40); weigh about 42 g. *Incubation*: 23–25 days by both sexes (mostly by ♀). *Fledging*: About 8 weeks; young fed and brooded by both parents.

224 (209) Lesser Gallinule
Kleinkoningriethaan
Porphyrula alleni

Plate 23

Edenene (K), Nhapata (Sh), [Afrikanisches Sultanshuhn]

Measurements: Length 25–26 cm; wing ♂ 150–170, ♀ 144–160; tail 60–73; tarsus 45–56; culmen (including shield) 35–45. Weight (2 ♂) 132–134 g, (1 ♀) 117 g.

Bare Parts: Iris coral red (breeding) or brown (nonbreeding); bill dark red; frontal shield brown (nonbreeding), bright blue (breeding ♂) or apple green (breeding ♀); legs and feet red (brighter when breeding).

Identification: Size medium (much smaller than Purple Gallinule); above dark bluish green; below dark blue; undertail white;

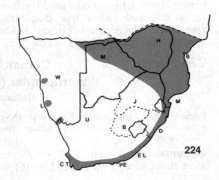

iris, bill and legs red; frontal shield green, blue or brown (red in Purple Gallinule). *Immature*: Above brown, edged with buff; below buff. *Chick*: Above downy black; below buff; bill greyish black, base pink, vertical white stripe near tip; legs pale brown; iris grey-brown.
Voice: Most frequent call 6–8 rapid clicks, *dik-dik-dik-dik* ....; froglike rolling *gurrr*.

Distribution: Africa S of Sahara; in s Africa absent from dry W; vagrant to Cape Peninsula and coastal Namibia.
Status: Breeding migrant from tropical Africa, mostly December to April; some birds overwinter; locally common in tropics and subtropics, otherwise uncommon.

Habitat: Marshes, especially seasonal floodplains and pans.
Habits: Usually solitary; shy skulker. Clambers about in reeds, feeding on flowers; may hold food in foot while feeding; forages also on floating water plants in open. Swims reluctantly.
Food: Seeds, flowers, bulbs and stems of water plants, insects, spiders, worms, fish eggs.
Breeding: *Season*: December to March in Zimbabwe and Transvaal (possibly also April); also recorded September, and February-May. *Nest*: Loosely built cup of dry reeds low down over water, hidden in reeds or floating water plants. *Clutch*: 3–6 eggs. *Eggs*: Dull pinkish white, blotched and speckled with reddish brown and purplish; measure (58) 36,6 × 26,2 (31,8–39,8 × 23,6–27,5). *Incubation*: Unrecorded. *Fledging*: Unrecorded.

225 (208X) American Purple Gallinule   Plate 23
Amerikaanse Koningriethaan
Porphyrula martinica

[Amerikanisches Sultanshuhn]
Measurements: Length about 33 cm; wing ♂ 168–192, ♀ 161–184; tail ♂ 60–82, ♀ 60–78; tarsus ♂ 56–67, ♀ 52–65; culmen (including shield) ♂ 45–52, ♀ 41–50. Weight (America) ♂ 203–269 g, ♀ 213–291 g; (S Africa, 4 emaciated birds) 119–141,5–160 g.
Bare Parts: Iris brown; bill red, tip greenish yellow; frontal shield dull blue to bluish white; legs and feet yellow.
Identification: Coloration similar to that of Purple Gallinule, but size smaller; above brownish green; below deep blue; undertail white; blue frontal shield, yellow tip to bill and yellow legs diagnostic. *Immature*: Above olive brown; below light rufous brown; bill greenish, base

orange; legs and feet greenish yellow.
Voice: Silent in s Africa; in America shrill, laughing, rapid *hiddy-hiddy-hiddy, hit-up, hit-up, hit-up*.
Distribution: Southern USA to n Argentina and Chile; in s Africa only in sw Cape.
Status: Windblown vagrant from S America, mostly April to July; mostly immature birds.
Habitat: Vegetated margins of ponds, lagoons, marshes, estuaries.
Habits: Birds arriving in S Africa all exhausted and starving; attempts to keep them alive usually unsuccessful. Unlikely to establish viable local population.
Food: Insects, spiders, frogs, grass seeds.
Breeding: Extralimital.

Ref. Silbernagl, H.P. 1982. *Ostrich* 53:236–240.

226 (210) Common Moorhen   Plate 23
Waterhoender (Grootwaterhoender)
Gallinula chloropus

Edenene (K), Kgogomeetse, Kgogonoka (NS), Khohonoka (SS), Nhapata (Sh), Kukumezane (Ts), [Teichhuhn]

Measurements: Length 30–36 cm; wingspan about 45 cm; wing (52) 139–161,4–

177; tail (26) 65–77; tarsus (23) 36–42,6–47; culmen (27) 36–40,4–46. Weight (1 ♂) 332 g, (1 ♀) 239 g, (143 unsexed) 173–247–347 g.
Bare Parts: Iris red; bill red, tip greenish

yellow; frontal shield red; legs and feet yellowish green, garter above tarsal joint red.

Identification: Size medium; slaty black all over, except for white undertail and white streaks on flanks; red shield and bill with yellow tip diagnostic (Lesser Moorhen smaller; bill yellow with red on culmen and frontal shield only). *Immature*: Above dark brown; below buffy, paler in centre of belly; iris greyish brown; bill and frontal shield greenish brown; legs and feet greenish, garter yellow. *Chick*: Downy black, tipped white around neck; skin above eye blue; bill red, tip yellow; small frontal shield red; legs and feet blackish brown.

Voice: High-pitched croaking *krrruk*, falling in tone; staccato *killik* or rapid *kik-kik-kik*; murmuring *kook*.

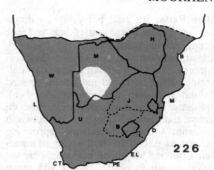

226

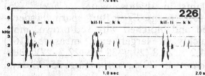

Distribution: Worldwide, except Arctic, s S America, Australasia; throughout s Africa, except parts of dry W and Kalahari.
Status: Common resident.
Habitat: Reedbeds, marshes, marginal vegetation of lakes, rivers, pans and sewage ponds.
Habits: Solitary or in small family groups; nonbreeding birds loosely gregarious. Spends most of day swimming in open water, wading in shallows or walking over nearby wet grasslands; flicks tail when alarmed; less secretive than most rallids,

but swims or runs for cover if disturbed, sometimes fluttering and pattering over water; flies heavily with dangling legs for short distances; in sustained flight, legs extend beyond tail; flightless when in wing moult. Clambers about reeds; roosts in reeds or low bushes.
Food: Water plants, seeds, berries, molluscs, worms, arachnids, insects, tadpoles, offal, carrion.
Breeding: *Season*: All months in Zimbabwe and sw Cape, August to February (also June) in Transvaal; most months throughout s Africa, but probably little breeding in highveld winter; may rear up to 8 broods/year. *Nest*: Neat bowl of rushes and reeds, concealed in dense aquatic vegetation well above water level; sometimes in fork of flooded tree; built by both sexes. *Clutch*: (102) 4–6,6–9 eggs (sometimes up to 11, possibly laid by 2 females). *Eggs*: Dark buff to greyish white, spotted, freckled and blotched with red-brown and slate; measure (126) 42,3 × 30,5 (38–46,3 × 28,3–35); weigh about 25 g. *Incubation*: 21–22 days by both sexes (72% by ♂, 28% by ♀); ♀ incubates only by day; ♂ incubates at night. *Fledging*: 40–50 days, cared for by both parents; young dependent on parents for 1–6 weeks after first flight.

Ref. Siegfried, W.R. & Frost, P.G.H. 1975. *Ibis* 117:102–109.

227 (211)   **Lesser Moorhen**   **Plate 23**
Kleinwaterhoender
Gallinula angulata

Edenene (K), Nhapata (Sh), Kukumezani (Ts), [Zwergteichhuhn]
Measurements: Length 22–23 cm; wing (15) 132–146; tail 56–60; tarsus 38–40; culmen 18–21. Weight (1 ♀) 92,4 g, (1 unsexed) 149 g.

Bare Parts: Iris red; bill yellow, culmen scarlet; frontal shield scarlet; legs and feet orange to yellowish green.

Identification: Like small Common Moorhen, but bill nearly all yellow; only culmen and frontal shield red; shield pointed behind (rounded in Common Moorhen). *Immature:* Above dark brown, more russet on crown and hindneck (greyish olive brown in immature Common Moorhen); upperwing coverts edged buff (no buff edging in immature Common Moorhen); below light brown, paler greyish in centre; cheeks and throat white; frontal shield orange-red. *Chick:* Downy black; bill white, cutting edges and base black; small orange frontal shield.

Voice: Muted *dodo do* like muffled pump.

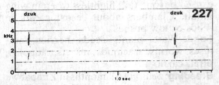

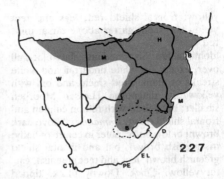

227

Distribution: Africa S of Sahara; in s Africa absent from sw parts, dry W and Kalahari; mainly subtropical to tropical.

Status: Uncommon to locally common breeding migrant from tropical Africa, October to May (mainly December-April).

Habitat: Vleis, seasonally flooded grassland, reedbeds, waterside vegetation.

Habits: Solitary and secretive, seldom venturing into open. Otherwise similar to habits of Common Moorhen.

Food: Seeds, reed flowers, insects, molluscs.

Breeding: *Season*: December to April in Zimbabwe and Transvaal (mainly January-February); breeds during rainy season. *Nest*: Bowl of grass and rush blades, about 15 cm diameter, 2,5 cm deep; domed by pulling down surrounding plants to form canopy; hidden among plants in shallow water. *Clutch*: (25) 4–6,2–9 eggs. *Eggs*: Buff, sparingly speckled and blotched with red-brown, more thickly at larger end; measure (161) 34,2 × 24,8 (29,9–38,5 × 22,7–27). *Incubation*: 19–20 days. *Fledging*: 35–38 days.

---

228 (212)   **Redknobbed Coot**   **Plate 23**
Bleshoender
Fulica cristata

Mohetle, Mohoetle (SS), Nhapata (Sh), Kukumezani (Ts), Kgogonoka (Tw), Unomkqayi, Unompemvana (X), [Kammbleβhuhn]

Measurements: Length about 43 cm; wingspan 75–85 cm; wing (15 ♂) 219–227–239, (13 ♀) 208–217–224; tail (15 ♂) 56–59,4–66, (17 ♀) 54–58,7–65; tarsus (14 ♂) 68–71,8–75, (19 ♀) 61–66–70; culmen (16 ♂) 30–32,9–36, (20 ♀) 29–31–33. Weight (4 ♂) 620–758,2–910 g, (10 ♀) 455–790 g, (4 053 unsexed) 363–737,8–1236 g.

Bare Parts: Iris red (breeding) to red-brown (nonbreeding); bill and frontal shield white, tinged greyish at sides; knobs above shield deep red to maroon; legs and

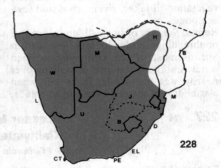

228

feet olive to dark green (breeding) to dull slate (nonbreeding).

Identification: About size of domestic chicken; all black with white bill and frontal shield, backed by two dark red knobs (knobs often hard to see in field, especially in nonbreeding birds). *Immature*: Above ashy brown to greyish; below whitish grey; frontal shield smaller than that of adult. *Chick*: Slaty black, paler below; neck, mantle and back golden yellow; bare skin above eye blue; bare skin on head bright pink; bill red, tipped white and black; legs and feet greyish green.

Voice: Resonant *klukuk* or *kluk*; breathy *vvvvm*; snorting *cholf* alarm call.

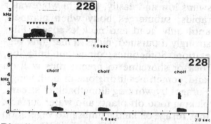

Distribution: Africa S of Sahara, Madagascar, nw Africa, s Iberia; throughout s Africa where water available.

Status: Abundant resident; highly nomadic, but no regular migrations.

Habitat: Almost any inland waters, especially with floating water plants like *Potamogeton*; less commonly on rivers and coastal lagoons.

Habits: Usually in pairs or large flocks of over 1 000 birds; highly gregarious when not breeding. Spends most of time swimming in open water; floats higher than duck; birds often chase each other, pattering across water; also patter when disturbed, seldom taking full flight, pitching onto belly (ducks pitch onto feet when landing); once airborne flies strongly, feet extending well beyond tail. Forages in water from surface or by diving; also grazes on shoreline, running to water when disturbed. May stand on shoreline to preen.

Food: Mainly water plants and grass; also insects and seeds.

Breeding: *Season*: All months; two peaks in July-September and January-March in Transvaal; peak March-August in Zimbabwe. *Nest*: Large heap of water plants with bowl-shaped hollow on top; in shallow open water or in deeper water anchored to vegetation; usually exposed. *Clutch*: (33) 3–5,2–9 eggs (sometimes up to 11). *Eggs*: Pinkish buff or stone, with small round dots of purplish brown; measure (243) 53,6 × 37,7 (49–61,1 × 32,8–42); weigh about 40 g. *Incubation*: 18–25 days by both sexes. *Fledging*: About 55–60 days; young cared for by both parents; brood divided between ♂ and ♀.

Ref. Dean, W.R.J. & Skead, D.M. 1979. *Ostrich* 50:199–202.

11:4. Family 29 HELIORNITHIDAE—FINFOOTS

Medium to large. Bill fairly long, strong and tapered, red, green or yellow; legs short and stout; toes long and lobed for swimming; hind toe reduced and elevated; legs and feet red, green or yellow; neck longish; body robust and elongate; wings short and rounded; tail fairly long and broad; sexes similar, but female smaller and duller; solitary; aquatic on wooded rivers; flutter along surface of water when alarmed; nest a platform of reeds or sticks on branch over water; eggs 2–6, pale cream, reddish or greenish, blotched with brown and grey; chick downy, altricial or semi-precocial (altricial chick carried in flank pouches of male parent in American Finfoot, even in flight); parental care by both sexes. Distribution tropical America, Africa S of Sahara, tropical Asia; three species; one species in s Africa.

229 (213)   **African Finfoot**   **Plate 23**
Watertrapper
Podica senegalensis

[Afrikanische Binsenralle]
Measurements: Length ♂ 51–65 cm, ♀ 45–56 cm; wing (13 ♂) 219–237–255, (15♀) 185–202–220; tail (12 ♂) 148–180–228, (13 ♀) 132–151–182; tarsus (5 ♂) 44,5–49,3–55, (9 ♀) 35–42–48; cul-

men (12 ♂) 49–51,2–55,5, (14 ♀) 41,5–45,4–48.

Bare Parts: Iris brown; bill bright red, darker on culmen; legs and feet orange-red, brown at back.

Identification: About size and shape of large cormorant; head greyish (more blue-grey in ♂) with white stripe from behind eye down side of neck; back dark brown, spotted white; bill, legs and feet bright red; lobed toes large, visible if bird out of water; tail long, held flat on water when swimming. *Immature*: Similar to ♀, but browner; less white spotting; buff on throat. *Chick*: Above chocolate brown; forehead rufous; black line on lores, centre of back, side of rump and top of wing; cheeks and throat pale brown; breast dull cinnamon; belly white; iris brown; bill black above, horn below; mouth pale pink; legs bright orange.

Voice: Sharp *skwak* like two blocks of wood knocked together; bull-like roaring alarm note; flutelike *pay-pay*; ducklike barking *kwark*; loud bill-snapping by ♀ during display.

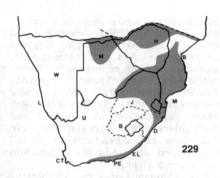

229

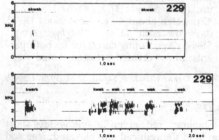

Distribution: Africa S of Sahara; in s Africa confined to higher-rainfall areas in E, NE and N.

Status: Uncommon resident. Probably Rare (RDB).

Habitat: Quiet reaches of streams, rivers, pans and lakes, fringed with dense trees and bush drooping into water.

Habits: Usually solitary or in pairs; shy and retiring; when disturbed splashes into water and flutters pattering along surface; dives only when wounded or chased; swims low and easily, even in whitewater rapids; submerges body when alarmed, until only head and neck exposed. Flies strongly if pursued; hides in marginal vegetation. Sometimes comes out onto log, rock or shoreline to preen; runs well on land, sometimes lifting one or both wings. Forages by working along bank of stream, picking food off plants and water surface; may forage on land; climbs into vegetation by clawed toes and wing digit. Roosts at night on branch overhanging water. Female displays by raising alternate wings and snapping bill.

Food: Insects, spiders, crabs, snails, frogs, fish, snakes.

Breeding: *Season*: August to April (mainly September to March). *Nest*: Bowl of sticks, lined with reeds, coarse grass and shiny leaves; internal diameter 15–16,5 cm, depth 5–8 cm; outside diameter about 32 cm, depth 9 cm; on horizontal or sloping branch overhanging water; often in driftwood caught on branches; from ground level to about 60 cm above water in rushes, or up to 1,5 m over water on branch. *Clutch*: 1–2 eggs. *Eggs*: Pale buffy green, streaked and blotched with brown, reddish and purplish; measure (9) 55,5 × 40 (51,3–59 × 34–42,1). *Incubation*: Unrecorded. *Fledging*: Unrecorded.

Ref. Percy, W. & Pitman, C.R.S. 1963. *Bull. Brit. Orn. Club* 83:127–132.
   Skead, C.J. 1962. *Ostrich* 33(2):31–33.

11:5. Family 30 OTIDIDAE—BUSTARDS AND KORHAANS

Medium to very large. Bill short to medium, straight, rather flattened at base; body robust; neck long; head large; legs long; toes short, hind toe absent; dorsal plumage finely patterned in brown, black, grey and white, cryptic; ventral plumage often boldly coloured black, white, blue or buff; sexes usually different; wings long and broad, downcurved in flight; tail short to medium; solitary or in small parties, seldom gregarious; terrestrial in open country or savanna; nest a scrape on ground in open; eggs usually 1–2, buff, brown or olive, marked with brown and grey; chick downy, precocial; parental care by female. Distribution Africa, s Europe, s Asia, Australia; 21 species; 10 or 11 species in s Africa.

Ref. Clancey, P.A. 1972. *Bokmakierie* 24:74–79; 25:10–14.

Johnsgard, P.A. 1991. *Bustards, hemipodes, and sandgrouse: birds of dry places.* Oxford: Oxford University Press.

Kemp, A. & Tarboton, W. 1976. *Bokmakierie* 28:40–43.

Osborne, P., Collar, N. & Goriup, P. 1984. *Bustards.* Dubai: Dubai Wildlife Research Centre.

230 (217) Kori Bustard Plate 24
Gompou
Ardeotis kori

Epwezampundu (K), Kgori (NS), Ngomanyuni (Sh), Manthensi, Mthisi (Ts), Kgôri, Thulakomê (Tw), Iseme (X), umNgqithi (Z), [Riesentrappe]

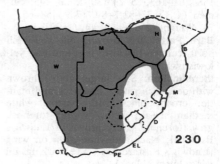

Measurements: Length ♂ 120–150 cm, ♀ 105–120 cm; wing (9 ♂) 717-747-798, (12 ♀) 575-608-685; tail (21) 310–430; tarsus (21) 177–235; culmen (21) 72–124. Weight ♂ 13,5–19 kg.

Bare Parts: Iris pale yellow; bill light greenish horn; legs and feet dull greyish yellow.

Identification: Size very large; above greyish brown (no rufous on hindneck as in Ludwig's and Stanley's Bustards); neck and breast finely barred (look grey at distance); belly white; head slightly crested; bill longish; walks with bill angled slightly upwards. *Immature*: More spotted on mantle.

Voice: Usually silent; deep *vum* on take-off; breeding ♂ calls drumming *wum-wum-wum-wum*.

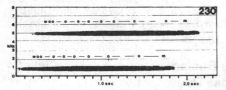

Distribution: S Africa to E Africa; in s Africa absent only from coastal lowlands of sw Cape and Natal and from high mountains; exterminated from much of former range.

Status: Rare to uncommon resident (some populations locally migratory, but movements not mapped); common only in game reserves. Vulnerable (RDB).

Habitat: Open plains of karoo, highveld grassland, Kalahari sandveld, arid scrub, Namib Desert, lightly wooded savanna, bushveld.

Habits: Solitary or in pairs when breeding; otherwise somewhat gregarious in flocks of up to 40 or more birds. Walks slowly and sedately when foraging. When disturbed walks quickly; flies reluctantly, but powerfully; normally runs before take-off, but can take off from standing position. Male displays with neck inflated, tail raised over back, and undertail coverts fanned.

Food: Insects, small vertebrates, seeds, carrion, *Acacia* gum (hence Afrikaans name).

Breeding: *Season*: October to February. *Nest*: None; eggs laid on bare ground, sometimes in slight scrape. *Clutch*: 2 eggs (sometimes only 1). *Eggs*: Pale olive green or olive brown, faintly clouded and streaked with darker green, brown and grey; measure (31) 82,5 × 59,1 (71,9–90,2 × 54,2–64,6). *Incubation*: (4) 27–30 days in captivity. *Fledging*: Flies weakly at 4–5 weeks; flies several hundred metres at 3–4 months; mature at 3 years.

231 (219) Stanley's Bustard (Denham's Bustard) Plate 24
Veldpou
Neotis denhami

Epwezampundu Lyomomusitu (K), Khupa (SS), Kgôri, Kgôrithamaga (Tw), Iseme (X), iSeme (Z), [Stanleytrappe]

Measurements: Length ♂ 100–110 cm; ♀ 80–87 cm; wing (4 ♂) 554–559,7–570, (5 ♀) 444–464,8–492; tail (4 ♂) 282–302,5–324, (4 ♀) 220–248,2–279; tarsus (4 ♂) 158–161–163, (5 ♀) 130–138,8–145; culmen (4 ♂) 77–82,7–89, (7 ♀) 58–65,7–73. Weight (2 ♂) 9–10 kg, (1 ♀) 3 kg.

Bare Parts: Iris brown; bill yellowish horn, culmen blackish; legs and feet yellowish white.

Identification: Size large; above brown with deep rich rufous hindneck and mantle; crown black with narrow white median streak; below white, foreneck grey (foreneck sooty brown in Ludwig's Bustard); black-and-white area on wing (Ludwig's Bustard has white markings on wing, but no black).

Voice: Usually silent; barking *kaa kaa*; on take-off low clucking *chook*, repeated about every second as bird flies away.

Distribution: Africa S of Sahara; in s Africa mainly in S, SE and highveld; vagrant to nw Zimbabwe, Botswana and n Namibia.

Status: Mostly uncommon resident; undergoes local movements, mostly altitudinal. Vulnerable (RDB).

Habitat: Montane and highland grassveld, savanna, karoo scrub.

Habits: Solitary or in pairs when breeding;

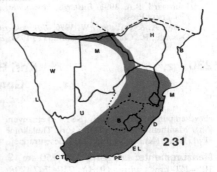

otherwise in groups of up to 10 birds. Shy and wary, walking away quickly when disturbed; flies strongly, usually at some height. In courtship ♂ inflates neck, raises tail and fans undertail coverts, forming white balloonlike shape visible from 2 km or more.

Food: Mainly insects; also millipedes, grass, seeds, flowers, lizards, small rodents.

Breeding: Male polygamous. *Season*: September to April (peak in November). *Nest*: None; eggs laid on bare ground in slight scrape; often among rocks or screening vegetation. *Clutch*: (41) 1–1,5–2 eggs. *Eggs*: Pale olive brown or greenish, clouded with streaks of brown, olive and grey; measure (41) 76,8 × 55,3 (63,5–88 × 50–60). *Incubation*: Unrecorded; by ♀ only. *Fledging*: About 5 weeks.

Ref. Herholdt, J.J. 1988. *Ostrich* 59:8–13.

232 (218) Ludwig's Bustard Plate 24
Ludwigse Pou
Neotis ludwigii

Khupa (SS), Iseme (X), iSeme (Z), [Ludwigstrappe]

Measurements: Length ♂ 78–95 cm, ♀ 76–85 cm; wing (7 ♂) 500–548,6–587, (14 ♀) 433–461,8–490; tail (4 ♂) 235–255,3–274, (8 ♀) 215–223,5–232; tarsus (4 ♂) 131–144,4–150, (8 ♀) 115,9–122,6–132,8; culmen (4 ♂) 58,9–62,9–71,5, (8 ♀) 43,4–51,7–57,4. Weight (5 ♂) 3,9–4,4–4,7 kg, (4 ♀) 2,2–2,4–2,5 kg.

Bare Parts: Iris greyish brown; bill dark

horn, pale at base; legs and feet greyish to greenish white.

Identification: Very similar to Stanley's Bustard, but slightly smaller; crown, face and foreneck sooty brown, paler in ♀ (foreneck grey in Stanley's Bustard); hindneck bright chestnut, paler in ♀; wing coverts brown-and-white (black-and-white in Stanley's Bustard); white on folded wing of ♂ covers nearly half wing area, only just visible in ♀; white markings show conspicuously in flight; sides of neck and whole belly white.

Voice: Deep resonant croak, *woomp* or *joompf*, by displaying ♂, like brief low drumbeat.

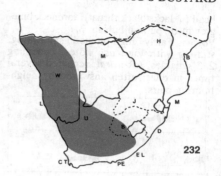

232

Distribution: Drier parts of s Africa to extreme sw Angola; also to e Cape; formerly vagrant to upland Natal.

Status: Uncommon resident. Vulnerable (RDB).

Habitat: Dry open plains, from grassland to desert.

Habits: Solitary or in groups of up to 36 birds; shy and wary. Flies readily when disturbed, usually until out of sight; takes off by running with lowered head and wings raised before starting to flap and becoming airborne; sometimes squats to avoid detection. Group may forage by walking slowly abreast to drive insects ahead. ♂ displays with inflated neck, raised tail and fanned undertail coverts.

Food: Insects (mostly locusts), arachnids, small vertebrates; little plant material.

Breeding: *Season:* August to December. *Nest:* None; eggs laid on bare ground in open, often among stones. *Clutch:* (11) 1–1,6–2 eggs. *Eggs:* Light brown, dull salmon pink to yellowish olive, clouded or blotched with reddish brown and slate; measure (28) 74,2 × 54,7 (63–81 × 44,6–62,1). *Incubation:* Unrecorded; by ♀ only. *Fledging:* Unrecorded.

Ref. Earlé, R.A., Louw, S. & Herholdt, J.J. 1988. *Ostrich* 59: 178–179.
Herholdt, J.J. 1987. *Mirafra* 4:34–35; 1988. *Ostrich* 59:8–13.

---

233 (222) **Whitebellied Korhaan** **Plate 24**
Witpenskorhaan (Natalse Korhaan)
Eupodotis cafra

Mokagatwê (Tw), iNgangalu (Z), [Weißbauchtrappe]

Measurements: Length ♂ 50–53 cm, ♀ 48 cm; wing (9 ♂) 290–294–302, (3 ♀) 270–278; tail (12) 130–145; tarsus (12) 85–93; culmen 28–35. Weight about 1,4 kg.

Bare Parts: Iris brown; bill dusky, base yellow; legs and feet yellowish.

Identification: Smallish (about size of domestic rooster); belly white in both sexes; hindneck golden tawny (diagnostic); black line around crown and on throat, forming incomplete border around white sides of

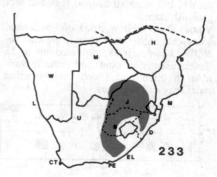

233

head (♀ lacks black throat); foreneck blue-grey in ♂, pinkish buff in ♀.
Voice: Fairly high-pitched squawking, starting with loud *aaa* notes, becoming 2–3 syllables, *tak-warat*, repeated several times in duet; often answered by neighbouring pairs.

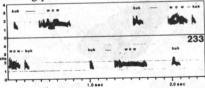

Distribution: Africa S of Sahara; in s Africa confined to e Cape, nw Natal, Orange Free State, Transvaal highveld, w Swaziland and se Botswana.
Status: Uncommon resident; may have local movements, but details not known.

Habitat: Open grassland; sometimes in sparse *Acacia* thornveld.
Habits: Usually in pairs or small family groups. Shy and wary; keeps to cover of taller grass; may become reasonably tame on outskirts of towns on lawns and golf courses. Male displays by raising crown and throat feathers, and extending neck horizontally (does not pump head like Blue Korhaan).
Food: Insects and other invertebrates; possibly plant material also.
Breeding: *Season*: November to February. *Nest*: None; eggs laid on bare ground. *Clutch*: (9) 1–1,8–2 eggs (usually 2). *Eggs*: Dark olive brown, streaked and clouded with dark brown; measure (17) 50,9 × 40,1 (46,4–56,8 × 38,3–42,4). *Incubation*: Unrecorded. *Fledging*: Unrecorded.

234 (223) Blue Korhaan Bloukorhaan Plate 24

Eupodotis caerulescens

Tlatlaoe (SS), uMbukwane (Z), [Blautrappe]

Measurements: Length 50–58 cm; wing 325–353; tail (3 ♂) 160–173; tarsus (3 ♂) 86–95; culmen (3 ♂) 30–32. Weight (2) 1120–1612 g.
Bare Parts: Iris brown, outer ring tawny; bill blackish, base yellow; legs and feet yellow.
Identification: Size medium; entirely blue below and on neck; above brown; sides of head white surrounded by black; ear coverts grey in ♂, rusty in ♀. *Immature*: Paler than adult; ear coverts brownish. *Chick*: Striped ginger-buff and olive brown; bill blackish brown; legs and feet greenish slate.
Voice: Deep mellow croak of 3 syllables, somewhat higher in ♀ than in ♂, *kuk-ka-ROW, kuk-ka-ROW*, repeated up to 15 times, usually in duet; individually variable in pitch and speed; neighbouring pairs may call together.

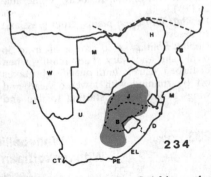

Distribution: Confined to S Africa and w Swaziland; e Cape, Orange Free State, nw Natal, Transvaal highveld E of Potchefstroom.
Status: Fairly common to uncommon resident.
Habitat: Open grassveld, karoo scrub, cultivated lands.
Habits: Usually in pairs or family groups of 3–4 (mean size of 361 groups = 3,3 birds); sometimes up to 6 or 7 birds together, rarely flocks of up to 11 at water or on burnt veld; breeding groups usually 3 birds (1 ♀ and 2 ♂, or 1 ♂ and 2 ♀). Male displays with neck held horizontally,

head feathers puffed up and head rapidly pumped up and down; drives large mammals from nest with spread wings; when disturbed usually crouches flat; if closely approached creeps or runs away with head lowered; flies quite far when flushed. Calls mostly morning and evening.

Food: Insects, small lizards, seeds and other plant material.

Breeding: *Season*: November to February (also August). *Nest*: Scrape on bare ground, 23–30 cm diameter; usually in open, less often in standing cropland. *Clutch*: (15) 1–1,7–3 eggs (usually 2). *Eggs*: Rounded to oval; olive green to brownish green, clouded and streaked with brown and grey; measure (42) 56,2 × 42,5 (49,5–62 × 40–46). *Incubation*: 24–28 days usually by ♀ only; rarely also by ♂. *Fledging*: About 5 weeks.

235 (220)   Karoo Korhaan   Plate 24
Vaalkorhaan
Eupodotis vigorsii

[Namatrappe]

Measurements: Length 56–60 cm; wing (9 ♂) 334–354–360, (4 ♀) 317–326–330; tail (13) 155–180; tarsus (13) 80–90; culmen (13) 34–41.

Bare Parts: Iris greyish brown; bill dark horn, base pale pinkish; legs and feet yellowish.

Identification: Size medium (about same as Blue Korhaan); plain greyish brown to sandy (individually variable) with sparse black and pearly grey blotching above; throat black, outlined with white when puffed out during vocal display; small black patch at nape joining black lines at sides of crown. *Immature*: Similar to adult, but spotted whitish on crown and back; faintly barred below.

Voice: Loud mellow 2-syllabled croaking, varying individually in pitch and usually given as duet, *kraak-rak, kraak-rak* (likened to the phrase *hotnot, platvoet*); slightly accented on first syllable; sometimes 3 syllables, *kraak-rak-rak*; neighbouring pairs often call together; ♀ answers ♂ from nest; usually silent in flight.

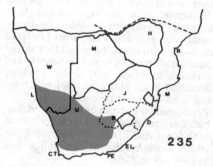

Distribution: South Africa and Namibia; Karoo, sw Orange Free State, Namaqualand, n Cape, s Namibia.

Status: Fairly common resident.

Habitat: Karoo, semidesert, desert edge, usually on stony ground with scattered shrubs and grass stubble.

Habits: Usually in pairs, threes or small groups, even when breeding. Walks slowly over veld while foraging; not as shy as other korhaans, but prefers thin cover of shrubs or grass, just high enough to look over; drinks at pools morning and evening. When disturbed, squats rather than runs away; easily overlooked unless calling. Flies reluctantly but fast, usually some distance before landing, sometimes jinking or rolling from side to side in flight. Most vocal early morning and late evening; voice carries far.

Food: Insects, other invertebrates, small reptiles, seeds and other plant material.

Breeding: *Season*: August to March. *Nest*: Slight scrape, about 23 cm diameter, on bare ground. *Clutch*: (16) 1–1,4–2 eggs. *Eggs*: Variable; buffy or yellowish olive, lightly streaked and clouded with redbrown and grey; measure (21) 53,8 × 41,7 (48,4–65,7 × 38,9–43,3). *Incubation*: Unrecorded; by ♀ only. *Fledging*: Unrecorded.

236 (221) Rüppell's Korhaan Plate 24
Woestynkorhaan (Damara Korhaan)
Eupodotis rueppellii

[Rüppelltrappe]

Measurements: Length 50–55 cm; wing (8 ♂) 320–330–340, (7 ♀) 293–308–323; tail (15) 145–165; tarsus (15) 78–86; culmen (15) 37–45.

Bare Parts: Iris grey-brown; bill yellowish pink, grading to black at tip; legs and feet dull pale yellowish grey.

Identification: Similar to Karoo Korhaan in size and coloration, but body paler and more sandy pink; head and neck pattern distinctive; neck and sides of face light blue-grey, separated by white on upper neck; blue-grey and white areas bordered narrowly with black, forming black throat patch and running down hindneck and foreneck as black line; eyebrow white, bordered black above and below; crown and sides of breast blue-grey.

Voice: Similar to voice of Karoo Korhaan, but distinguishable with practice, *krak-raak, krak-raak*, in duet; may be 3 syllables *kraak-kraak-rak*; sometimes calls *kwak kwak* in flight.

Distribution: Namib desert from Maltahöhe and Mariental to Kaokoveld and sw Angola.

Status: Fairly common resident; sometimes considered to be subspecies of Karoo Korhaan, but plumage, voice and habitat somewhat different.

Habitat: Barren stony and gravelly semi-desert to desert; usually associated with pale pinkish gravel flats of true Namib Desert.

Habits: Usually in pairs or threes; after breeding groups may join to form parties of up to 7 birds (5 adults and 2 young). Runs when disturbed, but flies readily when hard pressed; flight rather goose-like, wings beating quickly below shoulder height; usually flies far before landing. Very hard to see, even on open desert plains.

Food: Insects, seeds, succulent leaves.

Breeding: *Season:* September to February. *Nest:* Scrape in gravelly soil, ringed with small stones. *Clutch:* 1 egg. *Eggs:* Pale pinkish cream or buff, streaked and blotched with greyish brown and lilac; measure (7) 57,4 × 41,1 (54,6–61,3 × 38,6–43). *Incubation:* Unrecorded. *Fledging:* Unrecorded.

237 (224) Redcrested Korhaan Plate 24
Boskorhaan
Eupodotis ruficrista

Epampa (K), Gaundya (Sh), Muchukwana, Ntsukwani (Ts), Mokgwêba (Tw), [Rotschopftrappe]

Measurements: Length about 50 cm; wing (30 ♂) 255–268,8–290, (24 ♀) 238–253,4–268,5; tail (9 ♂) 134,5–142,2–148, (8 ♀) 129–135,9–142; tarsus (9 ♂) 74–84,5–92, (8 ♀) 73–78,5–86,5; culmen (9 ♂) 41–44,3–47,5, (8 ♀) 39,5–43,1–49; crest (3 ♂) 39,5–41,5–43, (4 ♀) 13,5–14,4–15. Weight (3 ♂) 550–680–770 g.

Bare Parts: Iris pale yellowish; bill dark horn, base yellow; legs and feet creamy white.

Identification: Size medium (smaller than Blackbellied Korhaan, similar coloration, but not so long-necked and long-legged); back finely mottled black and buff with bold buff chevrons (back barred in ♂ Black Korhaan, heavily blotched and barred with black in Blackbellied Korhaan); neck uniform greyish (no black line up foreneck as in Blackbellied Korhaan); throat blackish in ♂; crown bluish grey; broad pale eyebrow; belly black, contrasting with white border of folded wing (much more white on wing of Blackbellied Korhaan); large white half-crescent patch on either side of chest; reddish crest not visible, except in display (Blackbellied Korhaan has black-and-white patch at nape); breast grey in ♂, mottled in ♀.

Voice: Song starts off with 7–15 tongue clicks (sounding like Zulu *Q*), becoming loud single, double or triple piping calls, usually falling in pitch and volume towards end; *Q, Q, Q, Q, peep, peep, peep*, etc.; or *pipi, pipi, pipity, pipity pipity*, etc.; in presence of ♀ during breeding season, ♂ calls croaking *wak wak wak*, increasing in volume and speed to become 2-note *wuka wuka wuka*, with thin piping croak between each phrase; *krok* alarm note; also deep *wop, wop, wop*, rising in pitch; often vocal on moonlit nights.

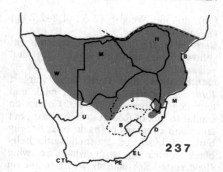

237

Distribution: More northerly parts of s Africa to Angola and Zambia.
Status: Common resident.
Habitat: Savanna, semidesert grassland (Kalahari), bushveld.
Habits: Usually solitary or in in pairs. Not shy, but easily overlooked in tall grass or scrub; stands quite still, relying on camouflage for concealment. When flushed, flies fast, weaving through bush until out of sight. After giving song (see **Voice**), ♂ performs spectacular flight display, running fast for few metres, taking off and flying vertically upward to 10–30 m, tumbling over with plumage fluffed, dropping straight down, opening wings just before hitting ground, and gliding or fluttering short distance before landing; only in courtship display to ♀ does ♂ show brick red crest on nape, standing upright and puffing throat and neck plumage. Silent in normal flight. Calls with bill wide open, head drawn back and tongue showing.
Food: Arthropods, seeds, fruit, gum.
Breeding: *Season*: September to February. *Nest*: None; eggs laid on bare ground. *Clutch*: 2 eggs (sometimes only 1). *Eggs*: Rounded, pinkish buff, olive buff or olive yellow, spotted and smudged with brown and grey; measure (19) 49,4 × 42,1 (46,2–54 × 37–45,2). *Incubation*: About 22 days by ♀ only. *Fledging*: About 6 weeks, but flies poorly up to 3 months.

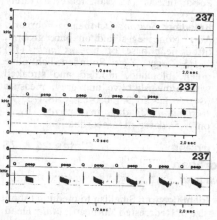

238 (227)   Blackbellied Korhaan   Plate 24
Langbeenkorhaan
Eupodotis melanogaster

Epampa (K), Guhwi (Sh), Cocololwani, Nkololwane (Ts), uFumba, uNofunjwa (Z), [Schwarzbauchtrappe]

Measurements: Length 58–65 cm; wing (8 ♂) 360–364–375, (2 ♀) 335–350; tail (10) 170–203; tarsus (10) 123–140; culmen

(10) 40–48. Weight (2 ♂) 1,8–2,7 kg, (1 ♀) 1,4 kg.

Bare Parts: Iris brown; bill blackish horn, yellow at sides and base; legs and feet dull yellowish.

Identification: Size fairly large (largest *Eupodotis* species); long thin neck and long legs diagnostic. *Male:* Coloration similar to that of Redcrested Korhaan, but lacks buff chevrons on back; back heavily blotched black on mottled buff; belly black contrasting with white on wing (Redcrested Korhaan shows white line on wing only); black-and-white patch at nape; black line down foreneck, edged white onto breast; no pale eyebrow; iris brown (yellowish in Redcrested Korhaan). *Female:* Inconspicuous and secretive; above similar to ♂; belly white; no black-and-white nape patch or neck stripes; wings buff (not white as in ♂). *Immature:* Like adult ♀.

Voice: In breeding season song of ♂ hoarse *k-woik* with neck and body stretched upward, neck then folded onto back, followed after about 2–4 seconds by *zzz-WIK* with neck slightly raised and stretched forwards; second part like cork drawn from bottle (squeak-pop effect); phrase repeated every 7–10 seconds.

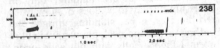

Distribution: Africa S of Sahara; in s Africa confined to NE.

Status: Uncommon resident; some local southward movement in winter.

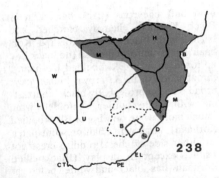

Habitat: Bushveld, savanna, grassland, vleis, cultivated lands.

Habits: Usually singly or in pairs. Relatively tame, standing still and relying on camouflage. Walks with exaggerated sinuous neck movements and cautious small steps; may crouch to avoid detection, neck stretched out on ground. In display flight ♂ flies for several hundred metres with slow exaggerated wingbeats showing conspicuous white wings, then glides to ground with wings held at dihedral, neck extended and raised, feet drawn up and black chest puffed out.

Food: Insects and plant material (rarely seeds).

Breeding: *Season:* October to February. *Nest:* None; eggs laid on bare ground, often near base of tree. *Clutch:* (19) 1–1,5–2 eggs. *Eggs:* Rounded; light olive green, blotched, mottled and streaked with brownish olive and grey; measure (84) 58,1 × 51,9 (50,1–65 × 48,4–55,7). *Incubation:* 23 days in captivity; by ♀ only. *Fledging* : Unrecorded.

---

239 (225) **Black Korhaan** **Plates 24 & 75**
Swartkorhaan
Eupodotis afra

Epampa (K), Lekakarane (SS), Tlatlagwê, Motlatlawê (Tw), Ikhalu-khalu (X), [Gackeltrappe]

Measurements: Length 50–53 cm; wing (10 ♂) 263–276–299, (4 ♀) 260–270–282; tail (14) 115–150; tarsus (14) 74–92; culmen (14) 30–37. Weight (39 ♂) 536–732,7–851 g, (83 ♀) 500–677,1–878 g.

Bare Parts: Iris light brown; eyering yellow; bill orange-red to coral red, tip greyish; legs and feet yellow.

Identification: Smallish to medium (about size of Redcrested Korhaan). *Male:* Head, neck and belly black; large white patches on sides of head; orange bill and yellow legs conspicuous in field; back finely barred buff-and-black (back of Redcrested Korhaan mottled with buff chevrons, back of Blackbellied Korhaan mottled with black blotches); very noisy and conspicuous; birds in summer-rainfall regions have white in remiges (see **Status**). *Female*: Very inconspicuous and secretive; head, neck and breast buff, paler on breast (no black); belly black; no white on breast or wing as in Redcrested Korhaan; no black line on foreneck as in Blackbellied Korhaan; legs bright yellow (dull yellowish in Redcrested and Blackbellied Korhaans). *Immature*: Striped on head and neck.

Voice: ♂ very noisy; loud harsh crowing *kraaak, kraaak*, falling in volume towards end; in flight display *krak krak krraka krraka kraka, kraka.*

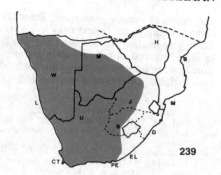

239

Distribution: Western S Africa, most of Botswana, and Namibia.

Status: Very common resident. Populations outside of sw Cape winter-rainfall area have white in remiges; may be separate species, 239B Whitequilled (or Whitewinged) Korhaan *Eupodotis afraoides* (Plate 75).

Habitat: Open dry grassland, karoo, Kalahari sandveld, arid scrub, semidesert, fallow lands, coastal dunes in sw Cape.

Habits: Usually solitary; sometimes in pairs; ♀ seldom seen. ♂ conspicuous, often standing on termite mound or hummock; in display, flies up calling, cruises around, then slowly descends with rapidly flapping wings and dangling yellow legs, tempo of call increasing; on landing stands still or runs into grass; up to 5 males may display to ♀; bold plumage and habits associated with unpalatable flesh. Runs with head down; usually stands with back towards observer.

Food: 70% animal matter (mostly insects; also ticks, spiders, myriapods and solifugids); 30% plant material (mostly seeds).

Breeding: *Season*: July to March (mainly October-December). *Nest*: Slight scrape on ground among grasstufts, or completely exposed in ploughed field. *Clutch*: 1 egg (85%) or 2 eggs (15%). *Eggs*: Rounded; khaki, olive green or olive brown, usually dark; clouded, spotted and streaked with brown and dull purple; measure (71) 52,2 × 42,6 (46–59,3 × 38,3–47,5). *Incubation*: (3) 21 days in captivity; by ♀ only. *Fledging*: About 75 days; fed by ♀ only for about 25 days (captivity).

12. Order CHARADRIIFORMES—WADERS, GULLS, AUKS (Three suborders; 16 families; 12 in s Africa)

Small to large. One of the largest avian orders with over 300 species in three suborders: Charadrii (waders), Lari (skuas, gulls, terns, skimmers), and Alcae (auks, found in n hemisphere only). These groups are linked on technical similarities of feathers, skeletal structure, internal anatomy, egg-white proteins, egg colour and structure, chick morphology and other features; but the diversity of the order makes it hard to define. Only Charadrii and Lari represented in s Africa and will be defined separately.

12:1. Suborder CHARADRII (WADERS) (12 families; ten in s Africa)

Small to large. Bill variable in shape; body robust; legs medium to long, tibiotarsus largely naked; toes short to very long; hind toe present, or reduced and elevated, or absent; wings mostly long and pointed (not in jacanas and painted snipe); tertials long and pointed; usually gregarious, especially when not breeding; anxiety indicated by head-bobbing display; nest usually a sparsely lined scrape on ground (sometimes on floating vegetation; Crab Plover nests in burrow); eggs 1–4, whitish, yellowish, brown or olive, marked with dark brown and grey (plain white in Crab Plover); chick downy, precocial, usually elaborately patterned (altricial, plain grey in Crab Plover); parental care variable. Distribution worldwide.

Ref. Hayman, P., Marchant, J. & Prater, T. 1986. *Shorebirds: an identification guide to the waders of the world*. London: Croom Helm.
Jehl, J.R. 1968. *San Diego Soc. Nat. Hist. Mem.* 3:1–54.
Johnsgard, P.A. 1981. *The plovers, sandpipers, and snipes of the world*. Lincoln: Univ. of Nebraska Press.
Maclean, G.L. 1972. *Zool. afr.* 7:57–74; 1972. *Auk* 89:299–324.
Makatsch, W. 1981. *Die Limikolen Europas*. Melsungen: Neumann-Neudamm.
Prater, T., Marchant, J. & Vuorinen, J. 1977. *Guide to the identification and ageing of Holarctic waders*. Tring: British Trust for Ornithology.
Strauch, J.G. 1978. *Trans. Zool. Soc. Lond.* 34:263–345.
Summers, R.W. & Waltner, M. 1979. *Ostrich* 50:21–37.

12:1:1. Family 31 JACANIDAE—JACANAS

Small to medium. Bill medium, straight, arched on culmen; bare frontal shield brightly coloured in most species; legs long; toes very long with long, almost straight claws, especially on hind toe, to distribute weight over floating vegetation; wings rounded, with spur or knob on wrist; tail usually short (long in one species); plumage usually brown with white areas and yellow on neck or wings; sexes similar but female larger; inhabit inland waters with floating vegetation; swim and dive; moult of remiges simultaneous, so birds flightless for a time; food aquatic animals and seeds; polyandrous; often gregarious; nest a small pad of vegetation on floating leaves; eggs usually four, brownish with scrawls of black, very glossy; chick downy, precocial; parental care mostly or entirely by male. Distribution mostly tropical America, Africa, Madagascar, Asia, Australasia; seven species; two species in s Africa.

240 (228)   African Jacana   Plate 23
Grootlangtoon
Actophilornis africanus

Nkongoro (K), Mogatsakwena (Tw), uNondwa-yiza, iThandaluzibo (Z), [Jacana, Blaustirn-Blatthühnchen]

Measurements: Length 25–30 cm; wing (19) 143–156–180; tail 38–56; tarsus 56–68; culmen 47–58 (variable in size; ♀ usually bigger than ♂). Weight (17 ♂) 115–132,8–162 g, (12 ♀) 176–238,3–274 g.

Bare Parts: Iris dark brown; bill and frontal shield pale grey-blue; legs and toes slate grey.

Identification: About size of bantam; long-legged, with very long toes; body rich chestnut; hindneck black; foreneck white (conspicuous at distance) grading into golden yellow on breast; bill and frontal shield pale bluish. *Immature*: Similar to

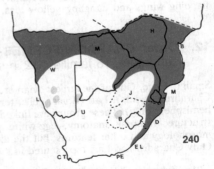

adult Lesser Jacana, but much bigger; above light brown (dark brown in adult Lesser Jacana), below white; breast washed golden (no gold in adult Lesser

Jacana); flanks brown; frontal shield small (not visible in field); crown and hindneck blackish brown (crown rufous in adult Lesser Jacana); black line through eye; buff eyebrow (eyebrow of adult Lesser Jacana white, forehead buff).

Voice: Husky whirling screech, *kyowrrr*, or shorter grating *kreep-kreep-kreep*; loud high-pitched trumpeting *weep-weep-weep-weep* repeated quickly.

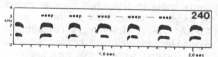

Distribution: Africa S of Sahara; in s Africa mainly absent from dry W and highveld, except as vagrant (Bloemfontein, Mariental, Keetmanshoop, Okahandja, Kalahari Gemsbok National Park).

Status: Common to abundant resident; local movements apparent, but not mapped.

Habitat: Lagoons, lakes, pans, vleis, river backwaters; usually with fringing vegetation and floating waterlilies, *Polygonum* and other water plants.

Habits: Usually in small loose groups; sometimes solitary or in pairs; less often in flocks of up to 100 or more birds. Walks or runs quickly over floating plants (hence name of lilytrotter), pecking at surface, or turning up edges of leaves for food. Highly vocal. Flies low over water with quick irregular wingbeats and long toes trailing behind; raises wings briefly on landing; swims and dives well, especially when in flightless wing-moult.

Food: Insects, molluscs, crustaceans, seeds, waterlily bulbs.

Breeding: Often polyandrous. *Season*: All months in tropics; mainly October to April in S Africa. *Nest*: Small pad of plant stems on floating vegetation at water level. *Clutch*: (28) 2–3,6–4 eggs (usually 4, rarely 5). *Eggs*: Pointed at narrow end; deep tan-yellow to brown, heavily streaked, scrolled and dotted with black; measure (200) 32,9 × 23,2 (29,9–37,4 × 21–24,8). *Incubation*: (5) 22–23–26 days by ♂; when sitting, ♂ holds eggs off wet nest by folding wings under body. *Fledging*: 35–40 days; chicks highly precocial; cared for by ♂ which may carry small chicks under wings when threatened; chicks swim and dive well.

Ref. Wilson, G. 1974. *Ostrich* 45:185–188.

241 (229)   Lesser Jacana   Plate 23
Dwerglangtoon
Microparra capensis

Nkongoro Gwakambatu (K), [Zwergblatthühnchen]

Measurements: Length about 15 cm; wing (5 ♂) 82–86,8–90, (5 ♀) 88–90,6–94; tail (5 ♂) 26–28,4–31, (5 ♀) 27–29,2–31; tarsus (5 ♂) 33–34,4–36, (5 ♀) 33–34,8–36; middle toe (5 ♂) 48–49,3–50, (5 ♀) 50–52,2–55; culmen (5 ♂) 14–15,6–17, (5 ♀) 15–16,2–17. Weight (1 ♀) 41,3 g.

Bare Parts: Iris hazel; bill dull greenish to brown; legs and feet olive green to greenish brown.

Identification: About size of small thrush; similar to immature African Jacana but smaller; above dark brown, mantle and crown rufous, crown sometimes edged

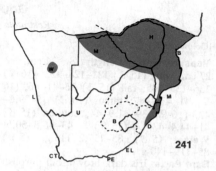

black, especially in males; eyebrow white; forehead buff; black line through eye; below white (no golden wash on breast as in immature African Jacana); in flight white band on wing conspicuous (no white in wing of African Jacana); underwing black, conspicuous when wings held open on landing. *Immature*: Like adult, but crown blackish; nape golden brown; upperparts fringed buff; rump and upper-tail coverts black, fringed buff; tail dark brown, marked with buff and rufous.

Voice: Mellow rapid *poop-poop-poop*; quiet peevish *ksh ksh*; chattering *ti-ti-ti-*; rapid *hwi-hwi-hwi* alarm call.

Distribution: Africa S of Sahara; in s Africa confined to N and E.

Status: Uncommon and localized resident. Rare (RDB).

Habitat: Shallow lagoons, vleis, dams, lakes, with emergent and floating vegetation.

Habits: Solitary or in small loose groups; shy and retiring; easily overlooked. When alarmed bobs head; flies strongly on short rounded wings; raises wings after landing. Forages by walking on emergent plants or by swimming like phalarope as it pecks at water surface; may climb plant stems to reach prey. Sometimes flicks tail downward while foraging.

Food: Insects, crustaceans, molluscs, plant material.

Breeding: *Season*: February to October. *Nest*: Small pad of plant stems on floating vegetation at or near water level; 10–25 cm diameter; raises eggs 5–10 mm above water level; usually close to clump of sedge or grass; built by both sexes. *Clutch*: (18) 2–3,2–4 eggs (usually 3). *Eggs*: Deep tan-yellow, scribbled, scrolled and blotched with black; measure (44) 24,8 × 18 (23–26,9 × 16,9–18,8). *Incubation*: Unrecorded; by both sexes almost equally; eggs held against body on inner surface of wings. *Fledging*: Unrecorded; chicks may be carried under parent's wing.

Ref. Tarboton, W.R. & Fry, C.H. 1986. *Ostrich* 57:233–243.

12:1:2. Family 32 ROSTRATULIDAE—PAINTED SNIPE

Small to medium. Bill long, decurved at tip; legs longish; front toes long; hind toe reduced and elevated; neck short; wings rounded; tail short; dorsal plumage elaborately patterned in brown, green and buff; breast dark, belly white; female brighter and larger than male; solitary; partly crepuscular; inhabit marshes; food aquatic animals and seeds; polyandrous; nest a pad of grass in a tussock or on mud; eggs 2–4, buff, heavily spotted with brown and black; chick downy, precocial; parental care by male. Distribution mainly tropical, S America, Africa, Asia, Australia; two species; one species in s Africa.

242 (230)   **Old World Painted Snipe**   **Plate 25**

Goudsnip

Rostratula benghalensis

[Goldschnepfe]

Measurements: Length ♂ 24 cm, ♀ 27 cm; wing (15 ♂) 121–128–132, (16 ♀) 136–139–145; tail (15 ♂) 36–41–46, (16 ♀) 41–43,9–47; tarsus (15 ♂) 35–39,6–42, (16 ♀) 39–41,9–44; culmen (15 ♂) 41–44,4–47, (16 ♀) 43–46,8–50,5. Weight (5 ♂) 85–117,2–118 g, (5 ♀) 85–119–140 g.

Bare Parts: Iris dark brown; bill purplish brown to horn, base pinkish; legs and feet greenish grey to dull slate blue.

Identification: Snipelike in size and appearance, but bill shorter, somewhat

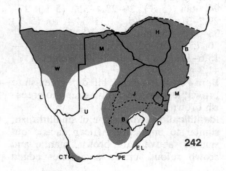

242

decurved at tip (snipes have long straight bills); head, back and chest greenish brown or greyish (more richly coloured, almost russet, in ♀); mask around eye white, extending behind eye in ♀; below white, extending up around bend of folded wing; legs longish; in flight 4 golden stripes conspicuous down back; wings dark, spotted golden buff. *Immature*: Like adult ♂.

Voice: ♀ has metallic drawn-out whistle, *wh-ooook* or *wuk-oo*, like sound of air blown across large-mouthed bottle; about 1 note/second in runs of 20–80 notes, usually at night; ♀ also calls single notes while flying 3–4 m above marsh; ♂ has squeaky note.

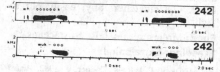

Distribution: Africa, Madagascar, s Asia to Philippines, Australia; in s Africa mainly absent from dry W, except as rare vagrant; otherwise widespread.

Status: Uncommon resident; somewhat nomadic according to rainfall.

Habitat: Marshes, swamps, edges of lakes, dams, ponds and streams, with marginal vegetation.

Habits: Solitary or in pairs. Shy and skulking, somewhat rail-like; freezes when disturbed; easily overlooked. When flushed flies short distance with dangling legs, then pitches into vegetation; wings rounded; bobs head and tail on landing.

Food: Insects, crustaceans, worms, molluscs, seeds.

Breeding: *Season*: August to November in w Cape, August to March in Transvaal, July to March in Zimbabwe. *Nest*: Shallow scrape in damp soil, sparsely lined with bits of plant material; either exposed or among waterside plants; sometimes built-up pad of stems in tussock in marsh. *Clutch*: 2–5 eggs (usually 4). *Eggs*: Pointed at thin end; yellow-ochre to buff, heavily blotched and mottled with dark brown, black and purplish slate; rather glossy; measure (61) 35,5 × 25 (31–37,3 × 23,6–26,5). *Incubation*: 19 days by ♂ only. *Fledging*: Unrecorded.

12:1:3. Family 33 HAEMATOPODIDAE—OYSTERCATCHERS

Large. Bill long, straight, laterally compressed and blade-like at tip, bright red; legs moderatly long and robust, pink, red or white; toes strong, slightly webbed at base; hind toe absent; plumage black, or black and white; sexes alike; wings long and pointed; tail short; calls loud and piping; gregarious; inhabit marine and inland shores and grasslands; food molluscs and other aquatic animals; nest on shorelines or grasslands, a scrape on ground lined with debris; eggs 2–3, buff to greenish, spotted with black and grey; chick downy, precocial, grey above with black lines; fed by parents; parental care by both sexes. Distribution almost worldwide; about seven species; two species in s Africa (one endemic).

243 (231X)   **Eurasian Oystercatcher**   **Plate 25**
Bonttobie

Haematopus ostralegus

[Austernfischer]

Measurements: Length about 43 cm; wing (34 ♂) 245–259–272, (30 ♀) 249–259,8–277; tail 99–114; tarsus (14) 47–50,3–55; culmen (14) 84–89,5–97. Weight mean about 500 g.

Bare Parts: Iris red; eyering and bill orange-red; legs and feet pink.

Identification: Slightly smaller than domestic chicken; boldly pied, black above and on chest; white below; eyes and bill red; legs pink; in flight wingbar and tail white, tail broadly tipped black; nonbreeding bird has white collar on fore-neck. *Immature*: Above brownish with buffy tips; white collar on foreneck; bill brown, base orange; legs greyish.

Voice: Loud plaintive piping *kleep, kleep, kleep*; loud *pik-pik-pik trrrr kwip-kwip-kwip, k-wip k-wip*, etc.

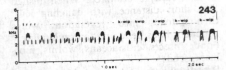

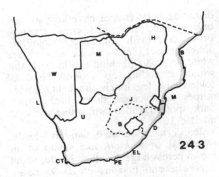

Distribution: Breeds Europe to e Siberia; migrates to Africa and s Asia; in s Africa along Namibian, Cape, Natal and Mozambique coasts.

Status: Rare but regular straggler to s Africa between about October and February; seldom migrates further S than C Africa; rarely overwinters.

Habitat: Marine shores; mainly sandy beaches and lagoons.

Habits: Usually solitary in s Africa, but sometimes in groups of up to 8 birds; may associate loosely with flocks of African Black Oystercatcher. Shy; easily put to flight.

Food: Molluscs, annelids, crustaceans.

Breeding: Extralimital.

Ref. Hockey, P.A.R. & Cooper, J. 1982. *Ardea* 70:55–58.

244 (231) African Black Oystercatcher — Plate 25
Swarttobie
Haematopus moquini

[Schwarzer Austernfischer]

Measurements: Length 41 cm; wing (64 ♂) 265–275,5–286, (64 ♀) 265–279,2–289; tail (13 ♂) 104–107,2–112, (8 ♀) 101–107,1–111; tarsus (64 ♂) 50,6–56,1–60,8, (64 ♀) 52–57,8–62; culmen (64 ♂) 57,7–63,2–69,5, (64 ♀) 63,6–71,6–79,1. Weight (64 ♂) 582–668–735 g, (64♀) 646–730–835 g.

Bare Parts: Iris red; eyering orange-red; bill red, tip orange; legs and feet purplish pink.

Identification: Slightly larger than Eurasian Oystercatcher; plumage all black; red eye, bill and legs. *Immature*: Browner than adult; iris brown; eyering dark orange; bill orange, tip brownish; legs and feet grey to greyish pink.

Voice: Loud piping, varying with context; *klee-weep, klee-weep*; *kik-kik-kik* alarm call; *tsa-pee, tsa-pee*; several birds may call together in piping party.

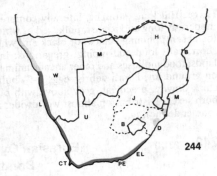

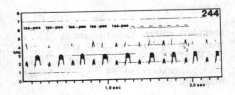

Distribution: Coasts and offshore islands of s and sw Africa; in s Africa from Namibia (breeds from Hoanib River) to Transkei; rarely to Natal.

Status: Locally common resident, especially on offshore islands; numbers threatened by development and disturbance; total population fewer than 5 000 birds.

Habitat: Rocky and sandy shores of mainland and coastal islands; less often coastal vleis and lagoons.

Habits: In pairs or small groups; roosting flocks of up to 120 birds when not breeding. Forages along waterline, probing in sand or rock crevices, prising molluscs from rocks, or picking food from surface; rests in flocks on rocks or beach at high tide. Flies with quick shallow wingbeats; often calls in flight.

Food: Mainly mussels and limpets; also whelks, periwinkles, crustaceans, annelids, sea anemones, sea cucumbers and tunicates (seasquirts).

Breeding: *Season*: October to March (mainly December-February, peak early January). *Nest*: Scrape in sand, 21 cm diameter, 4 cm deep (mean of 95 nests); on exposed beach or rocky area, often next to dried black kelp or among stones; adjacent nests 3–29–90 m apart (rarely only 1,5 m apart). *Clutch*: (185) 1–1,7–3 eggs (80% of 2 eggs, laid at 2-day interval). *Eggs*: Greenish or buffy stone colour, spotted and scrolled with blackish brown and purplish grey; measure (200) 60,7 × 40,5 (55,8–65,2 × 37,9–43,7); weigh (237) 45–56,3–65 g. *Incubation*: 27–32–39 days by both sexes. *Fledging*: About 40 days; young cared for by both parents.

Ref. Hall, K.R.L. 1959. *Ostrich* 30:143–154.
Hockey, P.A.R. 1981a. *Ostrich* 52:244–247; 1981b. *Proc. Symp. Birds Sea Shore* (U.C.T., 1979): 99–115; 1983. *Ostrich* 54:26–35.
Summers, R.W. & Cooper, J. 1977. *Ostrich* 48:28–40.

12:1:4. Family 34 CHARADRIIDAE—PLOVERS

Small to medium. Bill short, straight, slightly swollen at tip; legs long; toes short; hind toe reduced or absent; wings long and pointed in smaller species, somewhat rounded in larger species; tail shortish; dorsal plumage usually plain brown or grey, rarely patterned; breast bands often present; sexes similar; inhabit shorelines, grasslands, deserts, mountains, tundra; nest on ground in open habitats, a scrape, usually lined with stones or other debris; eggs 2–4, buff, greenish or brownish, spotted with brown, black and grey; chick downy, precocial, not fed by parents; parental care by both sexes. Distribution worldwide; about 60 species; 19 species in s Africa.

Ref. Blaker, D. 1966. *Ostrich* 37:95–102.
Bock, W.J. 1958. *Bull. Mus. Comp. Zool.* 118:28–97.
Nielsen, B.P. 1971. *Ornis Scand.* 2:137–142; *Ornis Scand.* 6:65–82.

245 (233) Ringed Plover · Plates 26 & 27
Ringnekstrandkiewiet
Charadrius hiaticula

Unokrekre (X), [Sandregenpfeifer]

Measurements: Length 18–19 cm; wing (76) 118–127,7–135; tail (22) 48–55,6–60; tarsus (122) 22,5–25,1–27; culmen (100) 13–14–16. Weight October to February (13) 45–54,5–65 g, April (9) 65–72,4–78 g.

Bare Parts: Iris brown; bill orange-yellow, tip black; legs and feet bright orange-yellow.

Identification: Size small; orange-yellow legs diagnostic; crown and back greyish brown; forehead white, broadly outlined black, joining black line through eye and around nape; broad black breastband runs around back of neck; rest of underparts and collar around neck white; in flight conspicuous white bar on secondaries; tail dark with white outer feathers and tip. *Immature*: Dark brown where adult black; breastband sometimes incomplete in cen-

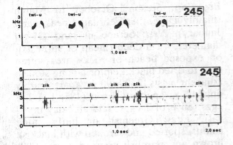

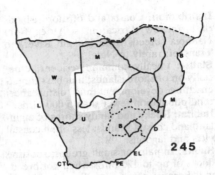

tre; bill blackish, faintly yellow at base; legs dull orange-yellow.

Voice: 2-syllabled liquid piping *twi-u* or single *kwik*; raspy *zik-zik-zik*.

Distribution: Breeds Greenland, Europe, Asia; migrates to Africa, s Asia and (rarely) Australia; in s Africa absent only from parts of Kalahari sandveld.

Status: Common nonbreeding Palaearctic migrant, September to April; birds ringed Rondevlei (sw Cape) recovered France (9 600 km N) and Russia (12 000 km NNE); some birds overwinter.

Habitat: Sandy, muddy and rocky shores of marine, estuarine and inland waters; also dry pans and airfields.

Habits: Solitary or in small loose groups. Forages on mud or sandbanks, seldom wades; runs fast on almost invisible legs, stopping suddenly to peck or probe at substrate; bobs head when alarmed. Migrates down African E coast and Rift Valley.

Food: Molluscs, crustaceans, insects.

Breeding: Extralimital.

Ref. Laven, H. 1940. *J. Orn.* 88:183–287.

---

246 (235)   **Whitefronted Plover**   **Plates 26 & 27**

Vaalstrandkiewiet

Charadrius marginatus

Unocegceya, Unotelela (X), [Weißstirn-Regenpfeifer]

Measurements: Length about 18 cm; wing (24) 103–109,5–115; tail 45–50,3–54; tarsus 23–25,3–29; culmen 15,5–16,9–18. Weight (72) 38–48,7–59 g.

Bare Parts: Iris dark brown; bill black; legs and feet black or grey.

Identification: Size small; above light sandy grey; below white, sometimes washed pale pinkish buff on breast, especially in more easterly parts of range (Kittlitz's Plover usually distinctly yellowish on breast); forehead and eyebrow white; forecrown blackish; collar on hindneck white; black line through eye stops at ear coverts (extends down sides of neck in Kittlitz's Plover); in flight conspicuous white bar on secondaries (no wingbar in Kittlitz's Plover); tail

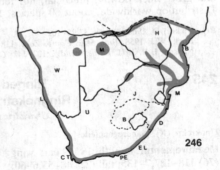

dark with white outer feathers; feet do not extend beyond tail as in Kittlitz's Plover. *Immature*: Lacks blackish forecrown; pure white below. *Chick*: Above very pale grey with broken pattern of black down midline of crown and back; below white.

Voice: Gentle piping *wit* or *twirit* on take-off and in flight; sharp *kittup* alarm note; drawn-out *churrr* threat note.

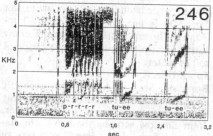

Distribution: Africa S of Sahara, and Madagascar; in s Africa mainly coastal, but also on bigger rivers—Zambezi and larger tributaries (not Kariba), Kunene (Rundu), Limpopo to Tuli Circle, Sabi, Nuanetsi and Lundi Rivers; also Lake McIlwaine (Zimbabwe), n Botswana, Caprivi, Etosha Pan, Bushmanland (Namibia).

Status: Common resident; may have local movements.

Habitat: Sandy shores of marine and larger inland waters (lakes, pans, rivers).

Habits: Usually in pairs; pair bonds and territories maintained year-round; flocks of up to 100 birds when not breeding. Runs very fast, sometimes slightly sideways; usually tucks head into shoulders; forages along waterline, among kelp and other debris, and away from water into dunes. Flies fast and low when disturbed, settles a little way off, bobs and runs.

Food: Mainly insects; also crustaceans, arachnids, worms, molluscs.

Breeding: *Season*: All months; peaks in Namibia December-January, sw Cape September-November, Natal July-August, Zimbabwe August-September; mostly after rains in sw Cape, before rains elsewhere. *Nest*: Scrape in sand, gravel or shingle, sometimes lined with small pieces of shell; usually just above high water, sometimes well up from beach or on inland side of coastal dunes; usually next to driftwood, seaweed or other object. *Clutch*: (238) 1–2–3 eggs (usually 2). *Eggs*: Pale putty colour or creamy buff, sparsely marked with fine spots and lines of blackish brown; measure (171) 32,7 × 23,3 (29,5–37 × 21–25). *Incubation*: 26–33 days by both sexes; eggs partly covered with sand by parent when disturbed at nest. *Fledging*: 35–38 days; young cared for by both parents.

Ref. Liversidge, R. 1965. *Ostrich* 36:59–61.
Maclean, G.L. & Moran, V.C. 1965. *Ostrich* 36:63–72.
Summers, R.W. & Hockey, P.A.R. 1980. *J. nat. Hist.* 14:433–445; 1981. *Ornis Scand.* 12:240–243.

247 (236) Chestnutbanded Plover
Rooibandstrandkiewiet
Charadrius pallidus

Plates 26 & 27

[Fahlregenpfeifer]

Measurements: Length 15 cm; wing (13) 100–102,3–105; tail 39–41,4–44; tarsus 26–27,6–29; culmen 12,5–13,3–14. Weight (27) 28–35,1–39 g.

Bare Parts: Iris brown; bill black; legs and feet grey, joints blackish.

Identification: Size small (smallest *Charadrius* species); above very pale grey; below white with narrow chestnut band on breast (band lightly scaled with black in ♂); forehead and eyebrow white; black line through eye to ear coverts in ♂; forecrown narrowly black in ♂; distin-

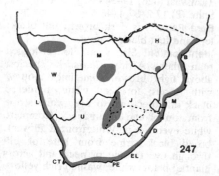

guished from Whitefronted Plover by smaller size, chubbier build, hunched posture, paler back, chestnut breastband, and no white wingbar in flight. *Immature*: Lacks black head markings; breastband greyish; often incomplete or absent. *Chick*: Above pale grey, mottled lightly with black, forming irregular lines down crown and back; below white.

Voice: Quiet *chuk* in flight; rather thin *peep* alarm note.

Distribution: S Africa to E Africa; in s Africa mainly on W and S coast and brackish inland pans of Botswana, w Transvaal, w Orange Free State, nw Cape and Etosha; less commonly on Sabi River, Shashi-Limpopo confluence, Bulawayo, Victoria Falls and E coast.

Status: Locally common resident; some populations necessarily nomadic on temporary inland pans. Rare (RDB).

Habitat: Saline lagoons, saline and brackish pans, saltworks; occasionally estuaries and sandy lagoons.

Habits: Usually singly or in pairs; flocks of up to 50 birds when not breeding. Similar to Whitefronted Plover, but shy and wary, especially when nesting; flies low over ground when disturbed. Easily overlooked when standing still on white salt flats. May forage in company with Whitefronted Plovers, Little Stints and Curlew Sandpipers, picking food from surface of soil or water.

Food: Insects.

Breeding: *Season*: All months; probably varies with local conditions, but mainly winter months, March to September. *Nest*: Shallow scrape, about 6–7 cm diameter, 1,5 cm deep, lined with bits of shell, small stones, feathers or dry plant debris; on exposed salt flats or bare shoreline. *Clutch*: (11) 2 eggs. *Eggs*: Pale putty colour, finely spotted and scrawled with blackish brown and grey; measure (32) 30,6 × 22,6   (28,6–33,2 × 20,7–24,4). *Incubation*: Unrecorded; by both sexes. *Fledging*: Unrecorded; young cared for by both parents.

Ref. Jefferey, R.G. & Liversidge, R. 1951. *Ostrich* 22:68–76.

---

248 (237) **Kittlitz's Plover** **Plates 26 & 27**
Geelborsstrandkiewiet
Charadrius pecuarius

[Hirtenregenpfeifer]

Measurements: Length 16 cm; wing (89) 98–106,6–113; tail (19) 42–44,6–49; tarsus 27–29,5–31; culmen 15–16,4–18. Weight sw Cape (91) 33–42,6–54 g, w Transvaal (426) 19–34–49 g, Orange Free State (8) 17,2–37,4–46,6 g.

Bare Parts: Iris dark brown; bill black; legs and feet black to grey.

Identification: Size small; longer-legged than other s African *Charadrius* species; above light brown, sometimes mottled with rufous; forehead white, bordered black on forecrown to eye; white stripe from top of eye to hindneck (complete white eyebrow in Whitefronted Plover); broad black stripe from base of bill through eye to side of neck and across mantle; below white, washed rich yellow-

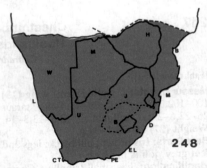

ish buff across breast; in flight no white wingbar as in Whitefronted Plover. *Immature*: Lacks black forecrown and bold lines on face; upperparts finely speckled dusky; underparts whiter; has complete pale band around hindneck like adult. *Chick*:

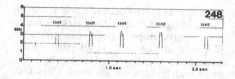

248

Similar to that of Whitefronted Plover, but less boldly marked; back somewhat darker.

Voice: Rich piping *tip-peep* in flight; trilling *trrr-rit-rit-rit-rit*; alarm *chrrrt*.

Distribution: Africa and Madagascar; throughout s Africa, except parts of Kalahari sandveld.

Status: Common resident; largely nomadic on temporary inland pans; largely migratory in Zimbabwe, April to December, possibly moving to n Botswana after breeding.

Habitat: Wide open shorelines of inland waters, especially shallow saline waters; also short grass on airfields, playing fields, dry pans; less commonly on seashore.

Habits: Solitary, in pairs, or in loose groups; usually somewhat gregarious even when breeding; flocks of up to 100 birds when not breeding. Similar to Whitefronted Plover, but looks longer-legged when running. Flies fast with characteristic call. Easily overlooked unless running.

Food: Insects, crustaceans, molluscs, worms.

Breeding: *Season*: March to November in Zimbabwe (mainly September), all months, except January, May and June in Transvaal (mainly July-October), May to October in Natal (mainly July-September); variable according to water levels, but mainly winter months. *Nest*: Deep scrape or hoofprint, filled with bits of soil, small stones and dry plant fragments; usually fully exposed on open shoreline or stubbly field; often loosely colonial, adjacent nests only few metres apart. *Clutch*: (250) 1–1,8–2 eggs (usually 2). *Eggs*: Creamy to greenish yellow, fairly thickly covered with thin black wavy lines and speckles; measure (152) 31,9 × 22,2 (28,6–35,5 × 19–23,5); weigh (5) 5,3–6,4–6,9 g. *Incubation*: 23–27 days by both sexes; ♂ incubates mostly at night, ♀ by day; eggs covered with nest material by quick foot movements whenever parent leaves nest by day (not at night); eggs uncovered before incubation. *Fledging*: About 30 days; at hatching chick weighs (14) 4–5,5–6 g; cared for by both parents.

Ref. Clark, A. 1982. *Ostrich* 53:120–122.
Conway, W.G. & Bell, J. 1968. *Living Bird* 7:57–70.
Hall, K.R.L. 1958. *Ostrich* 29:113–125; 1959. *Ostrich* 30:33–38.

249 (238)   Threebanded Plover   Plates 26 & 27
Driebandstrandkiewiet
Charadrius tricollaris

N'wantshekutsheku, Xitsekutseku (Ts), Unokrekre, Inqatha (X), [Dreiband-Regenpfeifer]

Measurements: Length 18 cm; wing (198) 104–111,1–119; tail (199) 55–62–69; tarsus (48) 21–22,8–24; culmen (48) 14–15,7–17,5. Weight sw Cape (55) 25–34–43 g, w Transvaal (92) 25–31,2–37,8 g, Orange Free State (10) 32–36,9–45,2 g.

Bare Parts: Iris hazel to light yellowish brown; eyering red; bill red, tip black; legs and feet pinkish grey.

Identification: Size small; two black breast bands, separated by white band, diagnostic; above brownish grey; face grey, sepa-

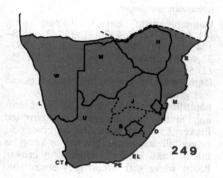

249

rated from dark crown by white stripe from forehead to hindneck; rest of underparts white; very narrow white wingbar in flight; tail bordered with white. *Chick*: Above mottled smoky grey and buff, bordered black along sides of back; large black blotches down centre of back; crown grey, outlined black; nape white; long black tail plumes characteristic.

Voice: Penetrating piping *pi-peep* or *peep* in flight and when alarmed; churring *chizzle-chizzle* in intraspecific display.

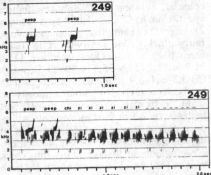

Distribution: S Africa to E Africa, Madagascar; throughout s Africa.

Status: Common resident; nomadic on temporary inland waters.

Habitat: Firm or gravelly shorelines of lakes, dams, pans, rivers, sewage ponds, marshes; less commonly on rocky seashore.

Habits: Usually in pairs when breeding; otherwise in loose flocks of up to about 40 birds. Movements quick and jerky; runs in short spurts, stops to peck at substrate or to probe in mud with rapid jabs; stands with body slightly tilted forward; bobs head and body when alarmed. Flies fast with quick jerky wingbeats, calling *peep* at take-off. Groups of birds run together or towards each other, white flank feathers fluffed, giving chizzling display calls. Easily overlooked when standing still.

Food: Insects, crustaceans, molluscs, worms.

Breeding: *Season*: All months in Zimbabwe (mainly June-October), April to January in S Africa (mainly July-September); variable according to water levels and food supply; may be induced to breed by partially draining dams or ponds. *Nest*: Shallow scrape, lined or ringed with small stones, bits of soil or dry plant fragments; on exposed gravel or mudflat near water. *Clutch*: (212) 1–1,9–2 eggs (usually 2). *Eggs*: Pale cream or yellowish, densely covered with fine short lines and scribbles of blackish brown and grey, usually forming cap or 1–2 bands around thick end; measure (155) 30 × 22 (27–32,7 × 20–24,1). *Incubation*: About 26–30 days by both sexes. *Fledging*: 30–32 days; young cared for by both parents; dependent on parents until 40–42 days.

Ref. Clark, A. 1982. *Ostrich* 53:222–227.
Maclean, G.L. 1982. *Ostrich* 53:52–54.
Tyler, S. 1978. *Scopus* 2:39–41.

250 (234) Mongolian Plover (Lesser Sandplover) Plates 26 & 27
Mongoolse Strandkiewiet

Charadrius mongolus

[Mongolenregenpfeifer]

Measurements: Length 19 cm; wing (41 ♂) 119–127,8–132, (31 ♀) 123–128,8–134; tail (2) 46,7–48; tarsus (81) 30–32,4–35; culmen (80) 15–17,4–20. Weight (2) 54–58,5 g.

Bare Parts: Iris brown; bill black; legs and feet greyish olive-brown.

Identification: Size smallish. *Nonbreeding*: Similar to immature Whitefronted Plover, but lacks white bar on hindneck; heavy bill diagnostic (but not as heavy as bill of Sand Plover); above grey-brown; below white with broad grey breastband

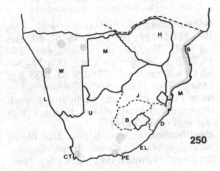

or lateral patches; eyebrow and forehead white; face and ear coverts darker grey-brown; smaller body and bill size than those of Sand Plover, but looks very similar; in flight faint narrow white wingbar. *Breeding*: Above brown; crown and nape rufous; face black with small white forehead patch; broad rufous breastband; rest of underparts white. *Immature*: Like nonbreeding adult, but dorsal feathers edged buff.

Voice: Usually silent in s Africa; *trrip* take-off call; trilling *drit , drit, dirrit*; frog-like *kurrup* alarm note.

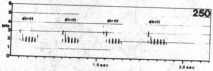

Distribution: Breeds C Asian plateau,

China and ne Siberia; migrates to s Asia, Africa and Australia.

Status: Uncommon nonbreeding Palaearctic migrant, September to March; 1 recorded Fish River estuary, e Cape, 4 August 1985, so may rarely overwinter.

Habitat: Tidal mudflats, sandy beaches, estuaries; rarely on inland waters.

Habits: Gregarious in small flocks, often in company with other wader species. Runs in short spurts with hunched neck; pecks at surface of mud for food. When disturbed, flocks fly tightly bunched, moving in unison. Roosts in hollows on ground.

Food: Small crabs, sandhoppers, marine worms.

Breeding: Extralimital.

Ref. Nielsen, B.P. 1971. *Ornis Scand.* 2:137–142; 1975. *Ornis Scand.* 6:65–82.
Sinclair, J.C. & Nicholls, G.H. 1980. *Brit. Birds* 73:206–213.

---

251 (239)   Sand Plover (Greater Sandplover)   Plates 26 & 27
Grootstrandkiewiet
Charadrius leschenaultii

[Wüstenregenpfeifer]

Measurements: Length 22 cm; wing (25 ♂) 139–144,8–150, (39 ♀) 135–145–153; tail 55–65; tarsus (75) 34–36,7–40; culmen (80) 20–24,5–28. Weight (8) 73–105,7–130 g.

Bare Parts: Iris dark brown; bill black; legs and feet grey, tinged pink, green or yellow.

Identification: Size medium to smallish; similar to Mongolian Plover, but larger, with longer heavier bill (diagnostic). *Nonbreeding*: Above grey-brown; below white with incomplete broad greyish breastband; no white collar on hindneck; forehead and eyebrow white; in flight narrow white wingbar (fainter in Mongolian Plover). *Breeding*: Above brown; nape rufous; face black with large white forehead patch outlined in black; underparts white with narrow chestnut breastband; this plumage rarely seen in s Africa, but easily distinguished from Chestnutbanded Plover by black-and-white face pattern, larger size, heavy bill and darker upper-

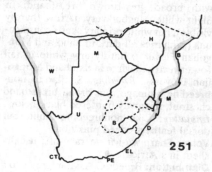

parts. *Immature*: Like nonbreeding adult, but dorsal feathers fringed buff.

Voice: Usually silent in s Africa; low musical *trrrt* on take-off; clear mellow *tweep, tweep*.

Distribution: Breeds C Asia to Korea, S to Jordan and Iran; migrates to s Asia, s Africa and Australia; in s Africa on all coasts.

Status: Uncommon nonbreeding Palaearctic migrant, October to May.

Habitat: Tidal flats, salt pans, estuaries.

Habits: Gregarious in small flocks, often with other wader species. Similar to Mongolian Plover, but not so shy; does not fly far when flushed. At high tide flocks rest among stunted plants.

Food: Crustaceans, insects, worms.
Breeding: Extralimital.

Ref. Sinclair, J.C. & Nicholls, G.H. 1980. *Brit. Birds* 73:206–213.

---

252 (240) **Caspian Plover** **Plates 26 & 27**
Asiatiese Strandkiewiet
Charadrius asiaticus

[Wermutregenpfeifer]

Measurements: Length 22 cm; wing (20 ♂) 141–149,8–157, (12 ♀) 140–146,7–154; tail 50–60; tarsus (44) 37–39,7–42; culmen (41) 18–20,2–22. Weight ♂ 63–88 g, ♀ 65–91 g.
Bare Parts: Iris dark brown; bill black; legs and feet dull greenish or greenish yellow.
Identification: Size medium (larger than Mongolian Plover, with heavier bill, but not as heavy-billed as Sand Plover); habitat not normally waterside like Sand and Mongolian Plovers. *Nonbreeding*: Above brown; forehead and broad eyebrow whitish; dark patch behind eye; below white with broad grey-brown breastband; in flight white wingbar very narrow (hardly visible), but white primary shafts conspicuous (primaries all dark in Sand and Mongolian Plovers); hardly any white in tail (outer rectrices white in Sand and Mongolian Plovers). *Breeding*: Similar to nonbreeding plumage, but broad breastband chestnut, narrowly bordered black below. *Immature*: Like nonbreeding adult, but dorsal feathers edged pinky buff.
Voice: Sharp *ku-wit* on take-off; usually silent in s Africa.
Distribution: Breeds C Asia; migrates to s Asia and Africa; in s Africa fairly general, except in S; mainly in dry interior, especially n Namibia and Botswana.

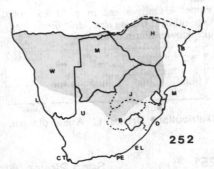

252

Status: Common nonbreeding Palaearctic migrant in dry W; uncommon elsewhere; August to March.
Habitat: Mostly arid plains, open grassveld, sportsfields, airfields; not usually near water.
Habits: Gregarious, sometimes in flocks of 30–40 birds. Difficult to see unless moving; rather courserlike in habits and habitat. Prefers to run than fly when disturbed; when flushed flocks fly in unison, circling about and landing together; often runs to plant or behind mound of earth for concealment. Undergoes local movements, so numbers fluctuate markedly. Active at night. Moults into breeding plumage shortly before departure.
Food: Mainly insects (especially harvester termites); also grass seeds.
Breeding: Extralimital.

---

253 (240X) **Asiatic Golden Plover** **Plates 26 & 27**
Goue Strandkiewiet
Pluvialis fulva

[Wanderregenpfeifer]

Measurements: Length 24 cm; wing (32 ♂) 157–163,7–173, (28 ♀) 152–162,1–168; tail (12) 59–65; tarsus (68) 39–41,6–46; culmen (70) 20–22,5–25. Weight 106–134 g.
Bare Parts: Iris brown; bill black; legs and feet slate grey.

Identification: Size medium; slightly smaller than Grey Plover, but back spotted golden, not white or buff; more slender and longer-legged. *Nonbreeding*: Above greyish, lightly mottled golden, including rump white in Grey Plover); below whitish, lightly mottled yellowish on chest; forehead and eyebrow broadly whitish or buff (more conspicuous than that of Grey Plover); in flight underwing and axillaries greyish (axillaries black in Grey Plover); wingbar faint (conspicuous in Grey Plover). *Breeding*: Above mottled gold and black; below including face and undertail solid black (undertail white in Grey Plover); broad white area between dorsal and ventral coloration. *Immature*: Similar to nonbreeding adult, but with brown spots on flanks.

Voice: Usually silent in s Africa; clear single whistle *teeh*; also high-pitched 2-syllabled *tew-tewee* (richer in tone than similar call of Greenshank); scratchy *kree, kree*.

Distribution: Breeds n Siberia to Alaska;

migrates to se Asia, Australasia and Pacific islands; regular straggler to Africa.

Status: Very rare nonbreeding straggler from Palaearctic (and possibly Nearctic), December to March. Sometimes regarded as subspecies of Lesser Golden Plover *Pluvialis dominica fulva*.

Habitat: Marine shores and estuaries; also sportsfields, airfields and ploughed lands.

Habits: Singly or in small groups. Tamer than Grey Plover when solitary; flocks shy and wary, taking off in unison, wheeling and flying low and fast, turning and banking; on landing, closes wings suddenly and stands erect.

Food: Insects, molluscs, crustaceans, worms.

Breeding: Extralimital.

Ref. Kieser, J.A. 1981. *Bokmakierie* 33:62–64.

---

254 (241)   **Grey Plover**   **Plates 26 & 27**
Grysstrandkiewiet
Pluvialis squatarola

[Kiebitzregenpfeifer]

Measurements: Length 28–30 cm; wing (35 ♂) 190–198,2–215, (53 ♀) 186–199,5–207; tail (6) 67–74–82; tarsus (113) 42–46,3–52; culmen (112) 25–29–34. Weight September to January (22) 178–216,4–246 g, February to April (23) 209–286,2–345 g.

Bare Parts: Iris dark brown; bill black; legs and feet grey.

Identification: Size medium to largish; build chunky; legs look shortish. *Nonbreeding*: Above brownish grey mottled with whitish or buff; rump white (no white on rump of Lesser Golden Plover); below white, mottled grey and buff on chest; ear coverts dark; in flight underwing white with black axillaries (best field character);

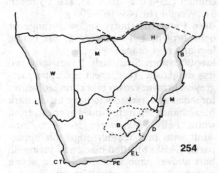

tail barred. *Breeding*: Above spangled black and white; below black, bordered above broadly with white; undertail white (black in Lesser Golden Plover); when moulting into breeding plumage, black of

underparts appears first on chest. *Immature*: Mottled above with pale gold, but always distinguishable from Asiatic Golden Plover in flight by black axillaries.
Voice: Far-carrying melodious whistle *tlooo, tlui-tlui*, or 3-syllabled *too-ee-u*, lower in tone on middle syllable.

Distribution: Breeds extreme n Russia and N America; migrates to s Europe, Africa, s Asia, Australasia; in s Africa mainly coastal, but occasional inland.
Status: Fairly common to common non-breeding Palaearctic migrant, August to May; some birds overwinter on S and W coasts.
Habitat: Tidal flats on coast and estuaries, open sandy beaches, rocky shores; less commonly on larger shallow inland waters.
Habits: Usually solitary or in small flocks of 10–20 birds often in company with other waders; sometimes in large flocks of hundreds or thousands when concentrated at high tide. Runs in bursts, stopping here and there to peck for food; usually keeps body horizontal and head somewhat hunched; partly nocturnal. Flight swift and twisting; flocks manoeuvre in unison; wary and hard to approach.
Food: Crustaceans, molluscs, worms; rarely seeds.
Breeding: Extralimital.

255 (242)   Crowned Plover   Plate 26
Kroonkiewiet
Vanellus coronatus

Runkerenkere (K), Mororwane (NS), Letletleruane, Lekekeruane (SS), Hurekure (Sh), Nghelekele (Ts), Lethêêtsane, Lethêjane, Lerweerwee (Tw), Igxiya (X), [Kronenkiebitz]

Measurements: Length 30 cm; wing (23 ♂) 192–204–216, (10 ♀) mean 200,5; tail (23 ♂) 85–93–101, (10 ♀) mean 90,4; tarsus (23 ♂) 61–69,5–73, (10 ♀) mean 66,8; culmen (23 ♂) 28–30,6–33, (10 ♀) mean 31. Weight (6) 148–167–200 g.
Bare Parts: Iris buffy yellow, orange or light brown; bill orange-red, tip black; legs and feet orange-red.
Identification: Size fairly large; long red legs diagnostic; face, chest and upperparts greyish brown; crown black, ringed white; forehead and eyebrow to nape black; dark breastband separates brown chest from white belly. *Immature*: Browner than adult with buff feather edges on upperparts. *Chick*: Mottled black and yellowish buff above; nape white, bordered above with black; underparts white with mottled buffy chest.
Voice: Very noisy, especially when breeding; strident *kreeep*; excited *kree-kree-kreeip-kreeip* in flight; chattering *tri-tri-tri-tri* in display.

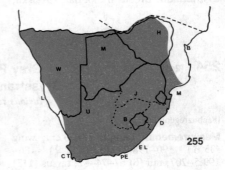

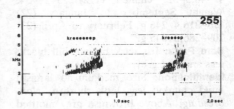

Distribution: S Africa to E Africa; throughout s Africa.
Status: Common resident; nomadic in drier areas and in summer.
Habitat: Short dry grassland, burnt veld,

lightly wooded savanna; semidesert, airfields, playing fields, city parks with large lawns.

Habits: Gregarious, especially when not breeding; flocks number up to 40 birds. Rather wary; runs in short bursts, stopping to peck at food with short jabs of bill; digs for food in soft soil; often active and vocal at night. Flight buoyant with deep wingbeats; commutes in flocks between feeding areas. Birds with young or hatching eggs attack intruders by divebombing with noisy screams; neighbouring pairs often join in such attacks.

Food: Insects, earthworms.

Breeding: *Season*: March to December in Zimbabwe (mainly August-October), July to March in w Transvaal (mainly October-December), June to September in Natal; mainly late winter and spring in most parts of s Africa. *Nest*: Shallow scrape on ground, lined with bits of soil, small stones and dry plant fragments; usually exposed in very short or burnt grassveld. *Clutch*: (348) 1–2,3–4 eggs (usually 2–3); clutches tend to be larger in E than in W. *Eggs*: Dark yellowish buff to deep khaki or olive-brown, boldly spotted with black and grey; measure (274) 40 × 28,9 (32–45,9 × 26–31,5). *Incubation*: 28–32 days by both sexes. *Fledging*: Unrecorded; young cared for by both parents for up to 3 months.

Ref. Ade, B. 1979. *Bokmakierie* 31:9–16.
Skead, C.J. 1955. *Ostrich* 26:88–98.

256 (244) Lesser Blackwinged Plover   Plate 26
Kleinswartvlerkkiewiet
Vanellus lugubris

[Trauerkiebitz]

Measurements: Length about 23 cm; wing ♂ 178–184, ♀ 174; tail 66–77; tarsus 54–60; culmen 20–23. Weight 107–117 g.

Bare Parts: Iris orange-yellow; bill black; legs and feet blackish brown.

Identification: Size medium; very similar to Blackwinged Plover, but slightly smaller; white patch on forehead does not meet eye; back greyish brown with slight greenish tinge; narrow black breast band separates brownish grey breast from white belly; eyering black (not red); legs blackish (not dark reddish), look proportionately longer than in Blackwinged Plover; in flight secondaries all white (black-tipped in Blackwinged Plover); underwing brown and white (all white in Blackwinged Plover). *Immature*: Similar to adult, but dorsal feathers edged buff. *Chick*: Mottled buff and black above (no dark lines or patches on back).

Voice: Mellow clarinetlike *ti-whoo* or *ti-hi-whoo*, lower-pitched on last note; considerably lower-toned and less screechy than calls of Blackwinged Plover.

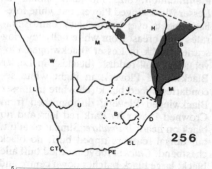

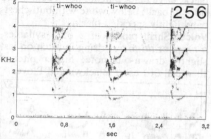

Distribution: Africa S of Sahara; in s Africa confined to extreme E.

Status: Uncommon breeding migrant, July to November in Zimbabwe; present most months in Zululand, but usually absent December-January; movements not mapped. Rare (RDB).

Habitat: Lightly wooded savanna, clearings in bushveld, scrubby grassland, especially where heavily grazed by large mammals.

Habits: Gregarious in small groups. Easily overlooked unless moving; not very shy, but runs away if disturbed; flight leisurely. Highly vocal when with eggs or young.

Food: Insects, spiders, millipedes and other invertebrates; some grass seed.

Breeding: *Season*: August to November. *Nest*: Shallow scrape on exposed ground among grass stubble. *Clutch*: (25) 1–3,2–4 eggs (usually 3). *Eggs*: Khaki to yellowish buff, boldly spotted with black and grey; measure (7) 34,2 × 26,3 (33–35,6 × 25,3–27). *Incubation*: 18–20 days (probably longer, up to 27 days). *Fledging*: Unrecorded; young remain with parents for up to 2 months.

257 (243) Blackwinged Plover   Plate 26
Grootswartvlerkkiewiet
Vanellus melanopterus

Igxiya (X), iHoye, iTitihoye (Z), [Schwarzflügelkiebitz]

Measurements: Length about 27 cm; wing ♂ 211–216, ♀ 198–203; tail 68–76; tarsus 53–59; culmen 25–28. Weight (3) 163–167,7–170 g.

Bare Parts: Iris pale yellow; eyering scarlet; bill black, base tinged red; legs and feet deep purplish red.

Identification: Size medium; similar to Lesser Blackwinged Plover, but white forehead meets eye; broad black band separates grey breast from white belly; eyering scarlet (black in Lesser Blackwinged Plover); legs dull reddish (blackish in Lesser Blackwinged Plover); in flight white secondaries tipped black (all white in Lesser Blackwinged Plover); distinguished from Crowned Plover by dark red legs and no black on head. *Immature*: Similar to adult, but dorsal feathers tipped buff; no black chestband. *Chick*: Above mottled buff and black; large black patches down centre and sides of back; below white with buff chestband lightly speckled black.

Voice: Shrill piping of 2 or 3 syllables, *ti-tirree* or *titi-tirree*, rising in pitch on last slightly drawn-out note; higher pitched than call of Lesser Blackwinged Plover.

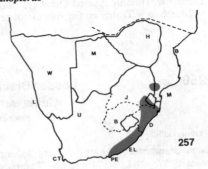

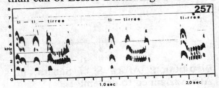

Distribution: S Africa to E Africa; in s Africa confined to SE and E.

Status: Locally fairly common breeding migrant to inland e Cape, Natal, w Swaziland and e Transvaal, mostly May to November; postbreeding migration to coastal flats of e Cape, Natal and Mozambique; movements often irregular, sometimes temporarily resident in one area; recently found breeding coastal Zululand (Lake St Lucia).

Habitat: Open short grassland, fallow lands, pastures, airfields, playing fields, race courses.

Habits: Gregarious even when breeding, usually in groups of 4–20 birds; often in company with Crowned Plover; larger flocks of up to 50 birds when not breeding. Shyer and less obtrusive than Crowned Plover, but noisy when breeding; divebombs intruders near nest or young. Easily overlooked unless moving or calling; favours burnt

grassland when available. Forages by running in short spurts, stopping to peck at ground; bobs when alarmed.
Food: Insects, molluscs, earthworms, other invertebrates.
Breeding: *Season*: July to October. *Nest*: Scrape in soil, usually thickly lined with bits of earth, dry plant fragments or dry grass

blades; in exposed site among grass stubble. *Clutch*: (69) 1–3,1–4 eggs (usually 3). *Eggs*: Deep khaki or greenish khaki, heavily spotted with black and grey; measure (82) 41,8 × 29,4 (36,5–46,5 × 26,7–31,3). *Incubation*: 24–25 days by both sexes. *Fledging*: Unrecorded; young attended by both parents for about 2 months.

258 (245)   Blacksmith Plover   Plate 26
Bontkiewiet
Vanellus armatus

Runkerenkere (K), Mo-otla-tšepe (SS), Comela-khwatsi (Ts), Lethulatshipi (Tw), iNdudumela (Z), [Waffenkiebitz, Schmiedekiebitz]

Measurements: Length 30 cm; wing 202–221,5; tail 84–92; tarsus 70–76; culmen 25–31. Weight (300) 110–158–226 g.
Bare Parts: Iris ruby red; bill, legs and feet black.
Identification: Size medium; boldly pied black-and-white with greyish back and wings; underparts black from chin to upper belly (face white in Longtoed Plover). *Immature*: Brownish with less white on forehead than in adult; chin and throat white; chest buff, speckled brown. *Chick*: Above mottled buff and blackish; irregular black lines down midline and sides of head and back; nape black-and-white; below white with speckled breastband.
Voice: Characteristic *klink, klink, klink*, like hammer on anvil (hence name); klinking becomes screaming when agitated near nest or young.

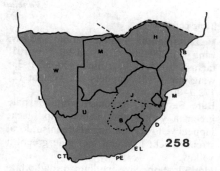

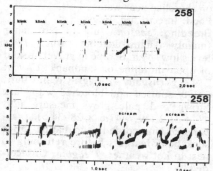

Distribution: S Africa to E Africa; throughout s Africa, but patchy in dry W; range expanding.
Status: Common resident; somewhat nomadic; numbers increasing in W.
Habitat: Shorelines of dams, pans, vleis, sewage ponds; also wet pastures, large lawns, playing fields, short grassy verges of inland waters; less often tidal flats in bays and lagoons.
Habits: Often solitary or in pairs; non-breeding birds may gather in loose flocks of 20–30, sometimes more. Silent when foraging or resting, usually calling only in flight and when alarmed; forages in short grass or on shorelines, stepping quickly in short bursts, stopping to peck suddenly at food. Rather wary; flight buoyant with slow heavy wingbeats. At rest stands with head hunched into shoulders.
Food: Insects, worms, molluscs.
Breeding: *Season*: All months in Zimbabwe (mainly March-September), all

months in Transvaal (peak September); all months, but mainly July to October in most of s Africa, seldom in summer months. *Nest*: Scrape in soil, usually lined with dry plant fragments, bits of earth or small stones; in exposed site, usually within 100 m of water on bare shoreline or short sward. *Clutch*: (74) 2–3,4–6 eggs (usually 3–4). *Eggs*: Deep yellow-ochre to

khaki-yellow, boldly blotched and spotted with black and grey; measure (117) 39,7 × 29 (35–45,2 × 27–31,3). *Incubation*: 26–31 days by both sexes; may wet belly feathers at intervals on hot days, in order to moisten eggs. *Fledging*: About 41 days; young attended by both parents.

Ref. Hall, K.R.L. 1959. *Ostrich* 30:117–126; 1964. *Ostrich* 35:3–16.

259 (246) Whitecrowned Plover Witkopkiewiet — Plate 26

Vanellus albiceps

[Langspornkiebitz]

Measurements: Length about 30 cm; wing (7) 200–209–218; tail 90–100–105; tarsus 71–74,4–77; culmen 30–32,1–33; wingspur 17–23; lappets 25. Weight (2) 172,7–201 g.
Bare Parts: Iris greenish white or pale greenish yellow; bill yellow, tip black; lappets yellow, base tinged greenish, loral streak black; legs and feet pale greenish yellow.
Identification: Size medium; broad white stripe between brownish back and black wing diagnostic at rest; head grey with broad white crown stripe (bordered narrowly with black in ♂); underparts white; large yellow lappets hang from base of bill; wings look mostly white in flight. *Chick*: Above mottled black and buff; narrow black-and-white collar on hindneck; below white; bill horn, tip black; wattles buff, about 25 mm long.
Voice: Sharp high-pitched *kyip, kyip, kyip*.

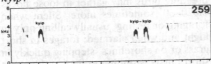

Distribution: S Africa to E Africa; in s Africa confined to larger tropical rivers— Limpopo, Sabi, Lundi, Nuanetsi, Zambezi and larger tributaries.
Status: Fairly common resident. Rare (RDB).

Habitat: Mud and sandbanks on large rivers; also shores and gravel bars of Lake Kariba.
Habits: Usually singly or in pairs; nonbreeding birds in small groups. Shy and wary, readily flying up calling when alarmed. Flight slow and buoyant. Forages like typical *Vanellus* species, mainly on shoreline near water.
Food: Insects, fish, frogs.
Breeding: *Season*: July to November (mainly August-October) when river levels low. *Nest*: Scrape in gravel or sand of open shoreline or sandbank. *Clutch*: 2–4 eggs (usually 4). *Eggs*: Creamy buff, boldly spotted and blotched with dark brown and pale grey; measure (29) 43 × 31,2 (39,7–47,6 × 28–34,3). *Incubation*: Unrecorded; incubating birds soak belly feathers before returning to nest in hot weather. *Fledging*: Unrecorded.

260 (247)   **Wattled Plover**   **Plate 26**
                             Lelkiewiet
                          Vanellus senegallus

Hurekure (Sh), Nghelekele (Ts), [Senegalkiebitz]

Measurements: Length 35 cm; wing (22) 221–234–247; tail (15) 96–99–107; tarsus 80–85,3–91; culmen 31–34,1–37,5. Weight 197–277 g.

Bare Parts: Iris lemon yellow; bill yellow, tip black; lappets and eyering yellow; forehead wattle red to orange; legs and feet greenish yellow.

Identification: Size fairly large; long-legged; white forecrown, red-and-yellow wattles and streaked neck diagnostic; rest of body greyish brown, darker on belly; undertail white. *Immature*: Has smaller white forecrown and smaller wattles than adult; chin and throat streaked black and white. *Chick*: Similar to that of other *Vanellus* species, with black patches on midline of crown and back.

Voice: Sharp high-pitched *kip-kip-kip*, sometimes rising in pitch, *kip-kip-kip-kipKEEP-KEEP*; alarm *ke-weep*, *ke-weep* on take-off; more intense *kee-up, kee-up*.

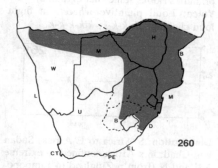

Distribution: Africa S of Sahara; in s Africa from inland Natal, ne Orange Free State, C and e Transvaal to Mozambique, Zimbabwe, n Botswana and n Namibia.

Status: Locally common resident at lower elevations; otherwise breeding migrant, September to about January, but movements somewhat irregular and unmapped.

Habitat: Upland grassveld along streams and vleis; also rocky slopes and burnt grassveld; on coastal plain mainly on exposed areas around lakes and pans.

Habits: Solitary or in pairs; nonbreeding birds in larger groups or flocks. Walks slowly and deliberately while foraging. Squats on ground if danger threatens, then flies up calling; on landing holds wings vertically open for brief moment before folding them. Active at night.

Food: Insects; some grass seed.

Breeding: *Season*: July to January. *Nest*: Scrape in soil, lined with bits of soil, dry plants or small stones; in open grassland, often on low bank or ridge. *Clutch*: (28) 2–3,6–4 eggs (usually 4), laid 24–48 hours apart. *Eggs*: Dull buff, blotched and spotted with black, brown and grey; measure (96) 48,8 × 34,3 (43,8–53,8 × 31–36). *Incubation*: 30–32 days by both sexes. *Fledging*: About 40 days; young attended by both parents.

Ref. Little, J. de V. 1967. *Ostrich* 38:259–280.

261 (248)   **Longtoed Plover** (Whitewinged Plover)   **Plate 26**
                 Witvlerkkiewiet
                      Vanellus crassirostris

[Langzehenkiebitz]

Measurements: Length about 30 cm; wing (♂) 204–210, (2 ♀) 187–188; tail (8) 90–95–100; tarsus (8) 71–74–77; culmen (8) 32–32,6–34,5. Weight (4) 162–191,3–225 g.

Bare Parts: Iris red; eyering purplish pink; bill purplish pink, tip black; legs and feet dull red, blackish in front.

Identification: Size medium; forecrown, face and throat white; hindcrown, hindneck and broad chest band black; rest of

underparts white; rest of upperparts brown; broad white leading edge to wing; in flight wing all white except for 3 black outer primaries (looks somewhat egretlike).
Voice: Loud plaintive *wheeet*; in flight loud clicking *kik-k-k-k, kik-k-k-k.*

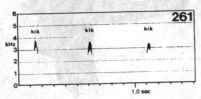

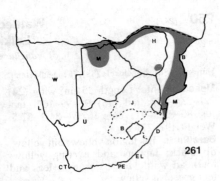

Distribution: S Africa to E Africa, Sudan and Chad; in s Africa confined to extreme NE and N (from n Zululand to Limpopo, lowland Mozambique, se Zimbabwe, Zambezi Valley, n Botswana and Caprivi).
Status: Rare in S Africa; otherwise uncommon resident; colonizing Lake Kariba.
Habitat: Permanent water with floating vegetation, especially waterlilies.
Habits: Solitary or in pairs or small family groups. Shy and wary except when breeding. Walks jacanalike on floating water plants, hence long toes to distribute weight.

Food: Insects, molluscs.
Breeding: *Season:* July to October. *Nest:* Pad of water plants, built up in shallow water, or on floating water plants; also scrape in soil or mud, lined with bits of plant material, within 100 m of water. *Clutch:* 2–4 eggs (usually 4 in Botswana). *Eggs:* Dark olive-khaki to greyish green, heavily blotched with black, brown and underlying grey; measure (14) 44 × 30,6 (40–47,8 × 27,3–33,5). *Incubation:* Unrecorded. *Fledging:* Unrecorded.

Ref. Saunders, C.R. 1970. *Honeyguide* 62:27–29.

12:1:5. Family 35 SCOLOPACIDAE—SANDPIPERS, SNIPE, ETC. (see page lxii)

Small to large. Bill short or long, usually slender, straight, decurved, or slightly recurved; legs moderately long to long; toes longish, lobed in phalaropes for swimming; hind toe reduced and elevated (absent in Sanderling); wings long and pointed; tail short to medium; dorsal plumage usually patterned in brown, buff, white and rufous; ventral plumage usually plain white, buff or rufous, breast sometimes streaked darker; sexes usually similar, female sometimes more brightly coloured; often gregarious, especially when not breeding; nest a lined scrape on ground in tundra, grassland or marsh; eggs 2–4, greenish to yellowish, spotted with brown, black and grey; chick downy, precocial, not usually fed by parents; parental care by both sexes, or by male, or by female. Distribution worldwide, most species breeding in n hemisphere, migrating to s hemisphere in nonbreeding season; 80–85 species; 35 species in s Africa (only one breeding).

Ref. Hockey, P.A.R., Brooke, R.K., Cooper, J., Sinclair, J.C. & Tree, A.J. 1986. *Ostrich* 57:37–55.
Kieser, J.A. & Tree, A.J. 1981. *Bokmakierie* 33:89–92.
Pringle, J.S. & Cooper, J. 1975. *Ostrich* 46:213–218; 1977. *Ostrich* 48:98–105.
Summers, R.W., Cooper, J. & Pringle, J.S. 1977. *Ostrich* 48:85–97.

262 (232)   **Ruddy Turnstone**   **Plates 26 & 27**
                  Steenloper
                  Arenaria interpres

[Steinwälzer]
Measurements: Length 23 cm; wing (23 ♂) 147–155–163, (13 ♀) 150–158–164; tail (7) 57–61–64; tarsus (30 ♂) 25–25,7–27, (22 ♀) 24–25,6–27; culmen (31 ♂) 20–22–25, (24 ♀) 20–22–25.

Weight November to February (115) 86–99–116 g, April (9) 92–103,4–113 g.

Bare Parts: Iris brown; bill black; legs and feet orange, joints blackish.

Identification: Size smallish; somewhat ploverlike, but looks shorter-legged; bill slightly upturned; bold black-and-white head pattern and orange legs diagnostic; upperparts mottled dull brown and black (plain in Ringed Plover); underparts white except for black-and-white breastband. Breeding plumage similar, but brighter rufous-and-black above and more boldly patterned on head and chest; looks pied in flight.

Voice: Sharp staccato *kit-it-it-it-it* in flight; deep husky wavering rattle *quitta-a-a*; ringing *keeoo*.

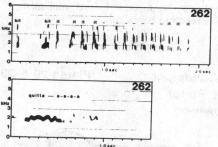

Distribution: Breeds Holarctic at higher latitudes; migrates to s parts of n hemisphere, and to s hemisphere; in s Africa

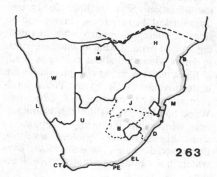

262

confined to seacoast; vagrant at few inland localities.

Status: Common nonbreeding Palaearctic migrant, September to April; many birds overwinter, probably immatures.

Habitat: Mostly rocky marine shores, tidal reefs and mudflats; less often sandy shores.

Habits: Usually in smallish flocks of up to 20 birds. Forages on shore and wave-washed rocks, turning over stones, seaweed, shells and other objects, and probing into crevices for food; walks with quick short steps, turning busily from side to side. When flushed flies low and strongly, calling. Some late-season birds moult into partial breeding plumage before departure.

Food: Crustaceans, molluscs, worms, insects.

Breeding: Extralimital.

263 (257)   Terek Sandpiper   Plates 29 & 28
Terekruiter
Xenus cinereus

[Terekwasserläufer]

Measurements: Length about 23 cm; wing (33 ♂) 129–133,5–142, (21 ♀) 131–135,9–140; tail (12) 47–56; tarsus (65) 26–28,3–32; culmen (34 ♂) 43–46,2–52, (19 ♀) 42–48–52. Weight May to March (97) 58–73,7–100 g, April (8) 88–101,5–120 g.

Bare Parts: Iris brown; bill blackish horn, base tinged yellow-orange; legs and partially webbed feet light orange-yellow.

Identification: Size smallish; rather short-legged; bill long, noticeably upturned; back plain grey; bend of wing blackish;

263

legs orange-yellow; below white, tinged greyish at sides of breast; in flight shows white trailing edge to wing, contrasting with dark remiges. Breeding plumage browner above with broad dark streaks on upper back. *Immature*: More brownish above than adult, streaked darker; pale rufous edges to upperwing and uppertail coverts.

Voice: Rapid high-pitched musical whistle *tee-tee-tee*; fluty *tu-tu-tu* ; musical trill *too-trrr-weee*; hooting *wutpeeu*.

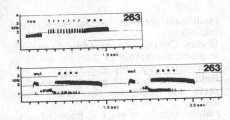

Distribution: Breeds Palaearctic tundra; migrates to Africa, s Asia and Australia; in s Africa mainly coastal, especially E coast; vagrant inland.

Status: Uncommon nonbreeding Palaearctic migrant; rarely overwinters; bird ringed Langebaan recovered Russia, 12 640 km NNE.

Habitat: Estuaries, lagoons, mangrove swamps, tidal mudflats.

Habits: Singly or in flocks, sometimes of several hundred birds. Runs after small crabs in crouched posture; also probes in mud with long bill; bobs head and tail while moving about. Hunched when standing, but long-necked when alert. Flight strong and direct, often high. Usually roosts with flocks of other wader species.

Food: Crustaceans, insects, molluscs.

Breeding: Extralimital.

264 (258)   Common Sandpiper   Plates 29 & 28
Gewone Ruiter
Actitis hypoleucos

Koe-koe-lemao (SS), N'wantshekutsheku (Ts), Uthuthula (X), [Flußuferläufer]

Measurements: Length about 19 cm; wing (15 ♂) 107–111,5–115, (12 ♀) 109–112,5–116; tail (10 ♂) 52–55,6–58, (10 ♀) 54–55,5–56; tarsus (36) 22–23,6–25; culmen (33) 22–24,8–27. Weight (24) 34–44–56 g.

Bare Parts: Iris brown; bill brown, base greenish; legs and feet greenish grey.

Identification: Size smallish; looks uniform darkish bronzy brown above and on sides of chest; underparts white, extending around bend of wing as white crescent; eyebrow white; bill about as long as head; in flight white wingbar conspicuous (wing uniformly dark in Green and Wood Sandpipers); no white on rump as in Green and Wood Sandpipers; flight highly characteristic with rapid flickering wingbeats in short bursts below shoulder level on downcurved wings, usually low over water; bobs body constantly while feeding.

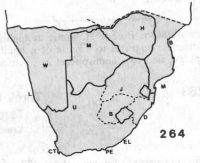

Voice: High-pitched whistled *tsee-see-see*, usually on take-off.

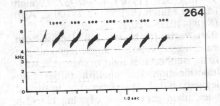

Distribution: Breeds Europe to Asia and Japan; migrates to Africa, s Asia and Australasia; throughout s Africa.

Status: Fairly common nonbreeding Palaearctic migrant, July to May (mostly August to April); some birds overwinter.

Habitat: Almost any shoreline, from seacoast to estuaries, dams, pans, rivers, streams, lakes, sewage ponds, marshes.

Habits: Usually solitary, but roosts in small groups of up to 30 birds on coast; roosts on ground near water, usually in small depression. Flight and movements quick and jerky; body usually tilted forward at angle when walking. Forages by pecking at surface of mud or water, and by probing in mud or mammal dung with bill; may take leeches off hippos.

Food: Insects, molluscs, crustaceans, leeches, fish fry.

Breeding: Extralimital.

---

265 (259)

Green Sandpiper
Witgatruiter
Tringa ochropus

Plates 29 & 28

[Waldwasserläufer]

Measurements: Length 23–24 cm; wing (23 ♂) 137–142,6–147, (27 ♀) 140–146,7–155; tail (3) 54–59; tarsus (26 ♂) 32–33,9–37, (31 ♀) 31–33,9–36; culmen (25 ♂) 31–34,3–38, (29 ♀) 31–34,5–37. Weight ♂ 73–104 g, ♀ 67–119 g.

Bare Parts: Iris brown, bill dark horn, base paler; legs and feet olive green.

Identification: Size smallish; similar to Wood Sandpiper, but less boldly spotted with buff (not white) above; back darker, more greenish brown than in Wood Sandpiper; looks almost blackish in field; eyebrow and underparts white, neck slightly streaked brownish; bill longish; in flight white rump conspicuous; no wingbar; underwing coverts blackish (greyish in Wood Sandpiper); tail mainly white with few dark bars near tip (more finely and extensively barred in Wood Sandpiper).

Voice: Loud high-pitched triple note *weet-EEE-weet* or *tler-REEE-wee*; sharp *wit-wit-wit*.

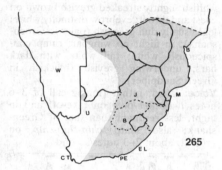

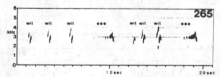

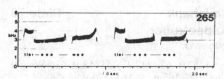

Distribution: Breeds European and Asian taiga and woodland zones; migrates to s Asia and Africa, usually as far S as Zambezi River; in s Africa widespread in e half; vagrant to Kalahari Gemsbok National Park.

Status: Rare nonbreeding Palaearctic migrant, September to April; vagrant to s Africa.

Habitat: Short swampy vegetation, woodland streams and shaded ponds.

Habits: Solitary. Forages at water's edge, running about probing into mud; bobs excessively when disturbed, before rising sharply with snipelike flight, giving 3-note call.

Food: Insects, crustaceans, molluscs, worms.

Breeding: Extralimital.

266 (264)   Wood Sandpiper   Plates 29 & 28
Bosruiter
Tringa glareola

Koe-koe-lemao (SS), N'wantshekutsheku, Xitshe-kutsheku (Ts), Uthuthula (X), [Bruchwasserläufer]

Measurements: Length 20–21 cm; wing (23 ♂) 120–125,6–131, (12 ♀) 123–127,2–131; tail (21) 46–50,3–56; tarsus (62) 32–36,8–40; culmen (62) 27–28,6–31. Weight (142) 34–59,8–89 g.

Bare Parts: Iris brown; bill dark horn, base greenish; legs and feet greenish grey, olive green or yellowish green.

Identification: Size smallish; above olive brown, clearly spotted with white (diagnostic); bill about as long as head; below whitish, lightly streaked greyish brown on chest and throat; eyebrow distinctly white; legs usually dull greenish (paler in Greenshank); in flight no wingbar; rump conspicuously white; tail white with dark bars; underwing greyish (blackish in Green Sandpiper).

Voice: Loud, rather ringing call of 3–6 notes *twee-twee-twee* on take-off and in flight, less resonant than that of Greenshank; also sharp *chip-chip-chip* on ground, about 2–3 notes/second.

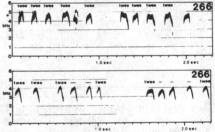

Distribution: Breeds n Europe and Asia; migrates to s Asia, Australia and Africa S of Sahara; throughout s Africa.

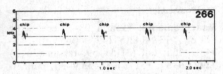

Status: Common nonbreeding Palaearctic migrant, July to May (mostly August to March); some birds overwinter.

Habitat: Pools, streams, rivers, flooded grasslands, sewage ponds, estuaries; prefers slightly marshy shorelines.

Habits: Solitary or in small loose groups, rarely up to 50 birds. Stands still to avoid detection; easily overlooked; sometimes hides under drooping vegetation; when flushed rises suddenly with 3-note whistle, not always flying far before settling and bobbing body briefly. Forages on floating vegetation, on shoreline or in flooded grassy meadows, pecking food from surface; less often wades up to belly in deeper water, probing in bottom ooze.

Food: Molluscs, crustaceans, insects, worms, fish fry.

Breeding: Extralimital.

267 (–)   Spotted Redshank   Plate 76
Gevlekte Rooipootruiter
Tringa erythropus

[Dunkler Wasserläufer]

Measurements: Length 30–33 cm; wing (19 ♂) 158–167–173, (16 ♀) 162–170,1–178; tail 63; tarsus (20 ♂) 52–58,6–61, (18 ♀) 54–56,9–60; culmen (17 ♂) 54–57,4–62, (17 ♀) 55–58,9–62. Weight ♂ 106–183 g, ♀ 164–176 g.

Bare Parts: Iris brown; bill blackish brown, base orange-salmon; legs and feet orange-red.

Identification: Size medium; larger and more elegant than Common Redshank; legs extend well beyond tail in flight. *Nonbreeding:* Paler and more uniformly grey above (Common Redshank dark, slightly mottled); bill long and slender, red at base only (Common Redshank has most of bill orange-red, black at tip only); in flight white secondaries barred with black (plain white in Common Redshank); rump and lower back white. *Breeding:* Sooty black; back spotted white; rump white.

Voice: 2-syllabled liquid whistle *tew-it*, somewhat drawn out.

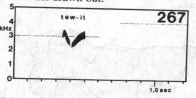

Distribution: Breeds n Scandinavia and Russia; migrates to s Asia, Mediterranean and W Africa; straggler to s Africa, recorded Marondera, Harare (Zimbabwe, 1979), Inhaca Island (Mozambique), Serondela (Botswana, 1987), Rondebult and Benoni (S Africa, 1988).

Status: Very rare nonbreeding Palaearctic vagrant, November to February.

Habitat: Edges of dams, pans, tidal mudflats and estuaries.

Habits: Solitary in s Africa; sometimes in small flocks elsewhere. Similar to Common Redshank.

Food: Small aquatic invertebrates, and small fish.

Breeding: Extralimital.

Ref. Worsley-Worswick, P.V. 1980. *Ostrich* 51:251–252.

268 (261) Common Redshank
Rooipootruiter
Tringa totanus

Plates 29 & 28

[Rotschenkel]

Measurements: Length 25–28 cm; wing ♂ 150–160,4–170, ♀ 154–162–174; tail (11 ♂) 57–65; tarsus ♂ 41–49,1–54,9, ♀ 43,5–48,8–55; culmen ♂ 34–43,1–54,9, ♀ 38,5–43,4–50; all measurements, except tail, combined for *T. t. totanus*, *T. t. eurhinus* and *T. t. ussuriensis*. Weight (100 ♂) 107–123,3–142 g, (100 ♀) 121–134,9–152 g.

Bare Parts: Iris brown; bill red basally, black towards tip; legs and feet orange-red.

Identification: Size medium; above mottled greyish brown, looks uniform brownish at distance (Spotted Redshank plain pale grey above); whitish below, mottled greyish brown on neck and chest; no pale eyebrow; red legs and base of bill diagnostic; bill shorter and stouter than that of Spotted Redshank; in flight rump, tail and trailing edge of wing broadly white (trailing edge of secondaries barred in Spotted Redshank); tail barred blackish (barring only at tip of tail in Spotted Redshank); feet do not extend beyond tail in flight.

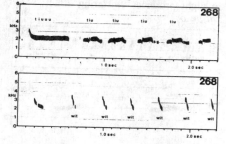

Voice: Shrill piping *tiu-tiu-tiu* in flight; call very similar to that of Greenshank, though slightly higher-pitched.

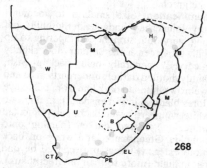

237

Distribution: Most of Europe, C Asia to China; in s Africa from various coastal and scattered inland localities.
Status: Rare nonbreeding Palaearctic migrant, September to March.
Habitat: Tidal mudflats, estuaries, lagoons; inland on shallow pans.
Habits: Solitary or in small flocks, often in company with other wader species. Shy

and restless; bobs body when alarmed; flies fast and directly; on landing holds wings momentarily raised. Runs briskly about when foraging, pecking at mud, or wading in deeper water and immersing head; rarely swims.
Food: Molluscs, worms, crustaceans, insects.
Breeding: Extralimital.

269 (262)   Marsh Sandpiper   Plates 29 & 28
Moerasruiter
Tringa stagnatilis

[Teichwasserläufer]

Measurements: Length 23–25 cm; wing (28 ♂) 134–139,8–145, (24 ♀) 135–141,7–148; tail (17) 55–57,6–62; tarsus (29 ♂) 47–51,7–56, (23 ♀) 48–51,9–57; culmen (22 ♂) 38–39,6–42, (20 ♀) 36–40,8–45. Weight sw Cape (77) 55–75,1–94 g, w Transvaal (21) 36–58–67 g.
Bare Parts: Iris brown; bill black; legs and feet light greenish grey, olive green or dull sage green.
Identification: Size smallish to medium; very longlegged and slenderly built; bill long, very thin, straight and tapering to tip (bill of Greenshank stouter and slightly upcurved); generally pale; back greyish, faintly mottled darker; underparts, face and eyebrow white, no dark line from bill to eye (lores blackish in Greenshank); in flight no white wingbar; lower back, rump and tail white, tail barred darker (barring onto rump in Greenshank, and white on back more extensive); legs project well beyond tail in flight (more so than in Greenshank).
Voice: Loud whistled *tew-tew-tew-tew* or shrill piping *che-weep* on take-off, quieter and faster than call of Greenshank; flock in flight produces twittering effect; song *wit-peeo*.

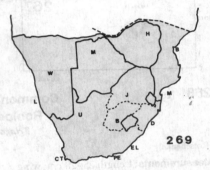

Distribution: Breeds se Europe, C and s Russia and n Mongolia; migrates to Africa, s Asia, Australia; widespread in s Africa.
Status: Fairly common nonbreeding Palaearctic migrant, August to April.
Habitat: Shallow inland waters with muddy substrate, sewage ponds, tidal mudflats, estuaries, saltpans.
Habits: Usually solitary; sometimes in small flocks; rarely larger flocks of up to 100 birds. Fairly tame (Greenshank very wary); movements quick and lively; pecks at surface of soft mud for food, turning quickly from side to side in semicircles as it moves forward; also wades in slightly deeper water and feeds with head submerged.
Food: Molluscs, crustaceans, insects, worms.
Breeding: Extralimital.

Ref. Tree, A.J. 1979. *Ostrich* 50:240–251.

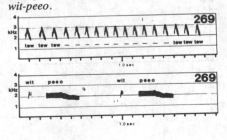

270 (263)

Greenshank
Groenpootruiter
Tringa nebularia

Plates 29 & 28

Koe-koe-lemao (SS), N'wantshekutsheku, Xitshe-kutsheku (Ts), Uphendu (X), [Grünschenkel]

Measurements: Length 32–36 cm; wing (13 ♂) 174–186–204, (48 ♀) mean 190,8; tail (13 ♂) 68–74,4–82, (47 ♀) mean 77,3; tarsus (13 ♂) 57–60–66, (47 ♀) mean 60,8; culmen (13 ♂) 50–54,3–60, (47 ♀) mean 55,4. Weight October to February (16) 168–191,1–243 g, March to April (9) 213–258,9–290 g.

Bare Parts: Iris brown; bill black, base paler; legs and feet greenish grey to yellowish green.

Identification: Size medium; longlegged and longbilled; bill stouter than that of Marsh Sandpiper, often 2-toned dark and light, and slightly upturned (especially lower jaw); above mottled grey; face whitish, with dark line from bill to eye (no dark line in Marsh Sandpiper); below white, slightly streaked at sides of chest; legs greenish; in flight no wingbar; lower back and rump extensively white; barring on tail and lower rump; almost always calls on take-off.

Voice: Loud ringing *tew-tew-tew* (3–5 notes) on take-off; clearer and more penetrating than take-off calls of most *Tringa* species.

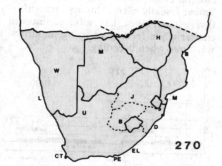

Distribution: Breeds n Europe to Kamchatka Peninsula; migrates to s Europe, s Asia, Africa and Australasia; widespread in s Africa.

Status: Common nonbreeding Palaearctic migrant, late July to early May; many birds overwinter.

Habitat: Dams, pans, swamps, sewage ponds, vleis, seashores (both rocky and sandy), estuaries.

Habits: Usually solitary; sometimes in small loose groups; occasionally in flocks of up to 150 birds. Roosts communally in flocks of 20–400 birds in shallow water of quiet bays and lagoons. Forages in water 40–120 mm deep, gathering into groups where fish fry abundant; wades quickly, darting bill forward to catch prey or to probe substrate. Bobs when alarmed; shy and wary, taking flight readily.

Food: Insects, molluscs, crustaceans, worms, tadpoles, fish fry up to 70 mm long.

Breeding: Extralimital.

271 (254)

Common Knot
Knoet
Calidris canutus

Plates 29 & 28

[Knutt]

Measurements: Length about 25 cm; wing (29 ♂) 160–167,9–176, (17 ♀) 167–170,5–177; tail (12) 50,5–66,5; tarsus (34) 29–31,7–33; culmen (28 ♂) 29–32,6–36, (18 ♀) 31–34,2–37. Weight September to March (496) 108–133–159 g, April (211) 116–169–216 g.

Bare Parts: Iris brown; bill black; legs and feet olive green.

Identification: Size smallish to medium; build chunky, with relatively short legs and heavy straight or slightly downcurved bill diagnostic; bill about as long as head or slightly longer. *Nonbreeding*: Above fairly uniform grey; below white, slightly mottled grey on chest; in flight white wingbar; rump whitish, mottled grey; tail all dark. *Breeding*: Above mottled chestnut and black; below bright rufous.

Voice: Usually silent; throaty *knut*; whistled *wit-wit*; flock has subdued musical chatter while feeding or flying; mournful *whoo-zee* when breeding.

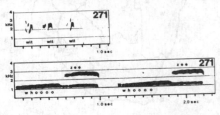

Distribution: Breeds Holarctic; in s Africa mainly on W coast; occasional from Cape Point to Richards Bay; rare inland (Botswana, Barberspan).

Status: Uncommon to locally common nonbreeding Palaearctic migrant, November to April; few birds overwinter; *C. c. canutus* breeds n Russia.

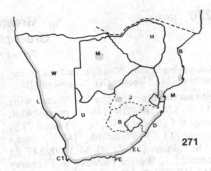

Habitat: Seashore and tidal flats.

Habits: Sometimes solitary; often in small groups or larger flocks of up to 150 birds; flocks densely packed, whether feeding or flying. Forages by probing bill several times into sand at each pause, while walking forward. Flight swift and strong; flocks perform aerial manoeuvres; solitary birds may join flocks of other species.

Food: Aquatic invertebrates.

Breeding: Extralimital.

---

272 (251)   **Curlew Sandpiper**   **Plates 29 & 28**
Krombekstrandloper
Calidris ferruginea

[Sichelstrandläufer]

Measurements: Length 20 cm; wing (37 ♂) 125–131–136, (20 ♀) 125–131,1–136; tail (8) 44–48,5–51; tarsus (31 ♂) 27–29,3–32, (15 ♀) 29–29,7–31; culmen (138 ♂) 32–36,6–42, (139 ♀) 35–40,7–45. Weight (3 ♀) 53,9–58,8–65,3 g, summer (1 779 unsexed) mean 57 g, March-April (257 unsexed) mean 75,4 g.

Bare Parts: Iris dark brown; bill black; legs and feet greyish to olive brown.

Identification: Size small; bill longish, decurved at tip; posture somewhat hunched. *Nonbreeding*: Above mottled brownish grey; eyebrow white; below white, sparsely streaked grey on breast; in flight white wingbar conspicuous; rump white (no dark centre line as in most other

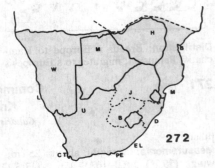

Calidris species); tail dark. *Breeding*: Above dark brown, mottled with chestnut and buff; below deep reddish chestnut; white around bill and over eye; some birds acquire this plumage in late summer.

Voice: Whistled *chirrip*; sharp *chit-chit* when in flocks; wheezy *choo-eeee* when breeding.

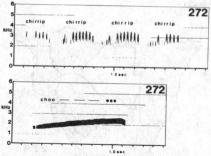

Distribution: Breeds extreme n Siberia; migrates to Africa, Madagascar, s Asia, Australasia; widespread in s Africa.

Status: Very common nonbreeding Palaearctic migrant, August to April; first-year birds overwinter, numbers fluctuating on 3-year cycle, dependent on lemming and fox populations on Siberian breeding grounds; birds ringed sw Cape recovered Russia, 10 000–14 000 km NNE; passage migrant through Zimbabwe.

Habitat: Seashore, inland pans, dams and vleis.

Habits: Highly gregarious; flocks may number 2 000 birds, but usually 10–200. Forages on mud or sand around open water, or among weed and mussel beds on rocky shores, walking quickly and probing with bill into substrate. Resting and flying flocks usually compact, manoeuvring in unison; when disturbed, resting birds often stretch wings over back before walking away, or hopping away on one leg.

Food: Polychaete worms, molluscs, crustaceans, fly larvae.

Breeding: Extralimital.

Ref. Elliott, C.C.H., Waltner, M., Underhill, L.G., Pringle, J.S. & Dick, W.J.A. 1976. *Ostrich* 47:191–213.
Puttick, G.M. 1978. *Ostrich* 49:158–167.

273 (251Y)   Dunlin   Plates 29 & 28
Bontstrandloper
Calidris alpina

[Alpenstrandläufer]

Measurements: Length 18–19 cm; wing (20 ♂) 105–113,3–125, (20 ♀) 107–116,6–128; tail 36; tarsus mean 23,4; culmen (20 ♂) 23,2–29,9–35,5, (20 ♀) 26–32,3–43. Weight (9 ♂) 38–43,9–50 g, (13 ♀) 35–50–61 g.

Bare Parts: Iris hazel to dark brown; bill, legs and feet black.

Identification: Size small; similar to Curlew Sandpiper, but bill less downcurved near tip; posture similarly hunched. *Nonbreeding*: Above greyish brown; below white, lightly mottled brownish at sides of breast; in flight narrow white wingbar; rump white with dark centre line (no dark centre line in Curlew Sandpiper). *Breeding*: Above black scalloped with chestnut; below white with black patch in centre of belly.

Voice: Prolonged shrill *we-weep* or *we-we-weep* on take-off; raspy *zz-zz-zz-zz* in display; various trills and clucks.

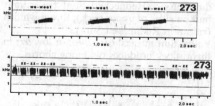

Distribution: Breeds Holarctic, but origin of s African birds probably Palaearctic only; migrates to s Europe, Africa, s Asia, Australasia (rarely); vagrant to scattered localities in s Africa.

Status: Very rare nonbreeding Palaearctic straggler to s Africa; seldom migrates further S than E Africa.

Habitat: Tidal mudflats, inland pans, marshes.

Habits: Usually solitary in s Africa; gregarious elsewhere in closely coordinated flocks. Runs about probing in mud with bill. When flushed flies fast with much twisting and turning.

Food: Molluscs, crustaceans, worms, insects; also seeds.

Breeding: Extralimital.

274 (253)   Little Stint   Plates 29 & 28
Kleinstrandloper
Calidris minuta

[Zwergstrandläufer]

Measurements: Length 14–15 cm; wing (36 ♂) 91,5–95,1–99, (36 ♀) 95–99–103; tail (12) 39–41,6–44; tarsus (9 ♂) 19–20,5–22, (13 ♀) 21–21,3–22; culmen (30 ♂) 16,8–17,8–19, (36 ♀) 17–18,9–20. Weight (6 ♂) 18,3–21,8–24,5 g, (32 unsexed) 20,1–24,1–29 g.

Bare Parts: Iris dark brown; bill, legs and feet black.

Identification: Size very small (smallest wader in s Africa); bill rather short, stout and straight; very similar to rare Rednecked Stint. *Nonbreeding*: Above mottled greyish brown or dusky (Rednecked Stint greyer above, less mottled), with pale V on brownish-washed mantle; below white; trace of greyish shading at sides of breast; eyebrow white; in flight narrow white wingbar; rump narrowly white at sides, broadly blackish in centre. *Breeding*: Dorsal feathers edged rufous; foreneck and upper breast indistinctly spotted brown, and washed with dull rufous (Rednecked Stint has rufous buff on sides of upper neck); throat whitish (rufous in Rednecked Stint).

Voice: Soft musical *tsit-tsit-tsit* or low *trrr* in flight; flock produces twittering chorus.

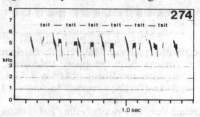

Distribution: Breeds extreme n Europe and Asia; migrates to s Asia and Africa; widespread in s Africa.

Status: Common nonbreeding Palaearctic migrant, September to April; many birds overwinter; birds ringed sw Cape recovered Russia, up to 11 000 km NNE.

Habitat: Open muddy shores of estuaries, tidal flats, lakes, pans, dams and sewage ponds.

Habits: Gregarious, usually foraging in flocks of few to several hundred birds, probing rapidly with bill into soft mud and running actively about; often associates with other wader species. Flies in closely packed, well coordinated flocks, twisting and banking, showing first grey backs then white bellies, twittering incessantly.

Food: Molluscs, crustaceans, insects, worms.

Breeding: Extralimital.

275 (–)   Longtoed Stint   Plate 76
Langtoonstrandloper
Calidris subminuta

[Langzehen-Strandläufer]

Measurements: Length 14,5–16,5 cm; wing (22 ♂) 90–93,5–97, (30 ♀) 91–95,4–100; tail 34–36; tarsus (26) 20–21,4–23; culmen (10 ♂) 17–17,6–19, (14 ♀) 17–18,3–19. Weight (12 ♂) 23–29–33 g, (8 ♀) 28–32–37 g.

Bare Parts: Iris brown; bill blackish; legs and feet pale brown to olive yellow.

Identification: Small (about size of Little Stint); similar to Little Stint, but legs yellowish (not black) with long toes (middle toe 20–23 mm). *Nonbreeding*: Above mottled grey; eyebrow white; below white, smudged and streaked on breast with greyish brown, forming fairly distinct breastband; in flight similar to Little Stint, but wingbar not obvious; rump dark with white edges. *Breeding*: Crown chestnut; head neck and upper breast cinnamon; eyebrow white; dark line through eye; upperparts mottled black and chestnut; below whitish. **Voice:** Loud trilled *chrree-chrree* or *chrring* like sound of bicycle bell; also rapidly repeated *chee*.

Distribution: Breeds s Siberia from Ural Mountains to n Pacific; migrates to s Asia and n Australasia; straggler to Africa and Australia.

Status: Very rare nonbreeding Palaearctic vagrant to s Africa; Maputo (December 1976).

Habitat: Shores of coastal and inland waters.

Habits: Usually solitary in s Africa, but possibly in mixed flocks of other sandpiper species. Forages slowly or with quick little runs. Flight fast and zigzagging.

Food: Aquatic invertebrates.

Breeding: Extralimital.

276 (253X)   Rednecked Stint   Plates 29 & 28
Rooinekstrandloper
Calidris ruficollis

[Rotkehl-Strandläufer]

Measurements: Length 14–16 cm; wing (21 ♂) 96–102,5–108, (25 ♀) 96–105,2–111; tail 44–47; tarsus (11) 19–19,2–20; culmen (14) 16–17,5–19. Weight (62 ♂) 21–32–47 g, (29 ♀) 27–36–51 g.

Bare Parts: Iris dark brown; bill, legs and feet black.

Identification: Small (about size of Little Stint). *Nonbreeding*: Similar to Little Stint, but plainer grey above, less mottled (feathers finely streaked with dusky, not blotched); no brown wash or pale V on mantle; below white, greyish at sides of breast; in flight like Little Stint. *Breeding*: Above heavily spangled chestnut and black; narrow pale eyebrow; below bright chestnut on throat, foreneck and breast; rest of underparts white with brown and russet arrowmarks on flanks, sides of breast mottled.

Voice: Squeaky *pit-pit-pit*; nasal *whoo-oop, whoo-oop* when breeding.

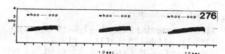

Distribution: Breeds extreme ne Siberia and Alaska; migrates to Japan, se Asia, Australasia; vagrant to s Africa (Berg River, Durban, Port Elizabeth, Maputo).

Status: Very rare nonbreeding Palaearctic straggler, September to December (mainly October-November).

Habitat: Tidal mudflats, lagoons, saltpans.

Habits: Gregarious in small groups of up to about 10 birds. Forages by pecking and probing in soft mud or sand with sewing-machine movements of head, very similar to Little Stint, but tends to frequent slightly drier areas.

Food: Worms, arthropods, molluscs, seeds.

Breeding: Extralimital.

Ref. Sinclair, J.C. & Nicholls, G.H. 1976. *Bokmakierie* 28:59–60.

277 (–)   Whiterumped Sandpiper   Plate 76
Witrugstrandloper
Calidris fuscicollis

[Weißbürzel-Strandläufer]

Measurements: Length 17–18 cm; wing (51 ♂) 117–122–129, (41 ♀) 116,5–124,4–127; tail (22 ♂) 48–51–54, (12 ♀) 47–50,9–53; tarsus (49) 22–23,9–25; culmen (37 ♂) 22–26,7–38, (31 ♀) 23–26,4–33. Weight (7 ♂) 31–39,7–45 g, (6 ♀) 31,7–45,8–51 g.

WHITERUMPED SANDPIPER

Bare Parts: Iris brown; bill black, base brownish; legs and feet yellowish brown.
Identification: Size smallish (larger than Little Stint, smaller than Curlew Sandpiper); bill slightly decurved, about as long as head (bill much longer in Curlew Sandpiper); legs yellowish (not black). *Nonbreeding*: Upperparts faintly mottled grey; eyebrow white; below white, lightly streaked on breast; in flight rump white (no dark centre line as in other small *Calidris* species); wingbar white. *Breeding*: Above rufous, blotched with blackish; below white, speckled brownish on breast.
Voice: Thin *jeet*.
Distribution: Breeds tundra of n Canada;

migrates to S America; vagrant to s Africa (Strandfontein Sewage Works, Cape Town; Hoanib River, Namibia; Port Alfred, e Cape).
Status: Very rare straggler to s Africa, collected once, December 1979.
Habitat: Coastal beaches, tidal flats, inland pools.
Habits: Solitary, but accompanies other sandpiper species. Feeds by probing in soft sand or mud. Similar to other *Calidris* species.
Food: Aquatic invertebrates.
Breeding: Extralimital.

Ref. Ryan, P.G. & Abernethy, D.A. 1981. *Ostrich* 52:225.

278 (252) Baird's Sandpiper   Plate 76
Bairdse Strandloper
Calidris bairdii

[Bairds Strandläufer]

Measurements: Length 17,5–19 cm; wing (21 ♂) 119–125,8–131, (17 ♀) 123–128,3–135; tail (9 ♂) 48–51,1–53, (9 ♀) 49–51,7–54; tarsus (43) 20–22–24; culmen (22 ♂) 20,5–22,1–24, (19 ♀) 21,5–22,5–24. Weight (30 ♂) 32–39–48 g, (12 ♀) 34–39–45 g.
Bare Parts: Iris brown; bill, legs and feet black or greenish black.
Identification: Size smallish to medium (larger than Little Stint); above distinctively scaled with dark feather centres and buff edges; clear buffy rufous breastband, lightly speckled darker; face and eyebrow whitish; in flight short narrow white wingbar; white rump has dark centre line; looks longer and slimmer than most *Calidris* species; holds body horizontally with long wingtips protruding beyond tail; breeding and nonbreeding plumages similar.
Voice: Short *kwirrt* or *kreep* in flight; various piping and trilling calls.

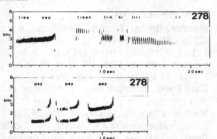

Distribution: Breeds tundra of n Canada; migrates to S America; vagrant to s Africa.
Status: Very rare nonbreeding straggler to s Africa.
Habitat: Grassy marshes, shores and mudflats.
Habits: Similar to those of other *Calidris* species; fairly tame; usually solitary. Forages by pecking at surface rather than by probing.
Food: Aquatic invertebrates.
Breeding: Extralimital.

279 (251X) Pectoral Sandpiper   Plates 29 & 28
Geelpootstrandloper
Calidris melanotos

[Graubrust-Strandläufer]

Measurements: Length 17–22 cm; wing (30 ♂) 138–144,2–149, (20 ♀) 126–129,6–135; tail (8 ♂) 59–62,4–65, (15 ♀) 51–55,3–60; tarsus (31 ♂) 27–28,8–31, (20 ♀) 25–26,6–28; culmen (29 ♂) 27–29,3–32, (22 ♀) 24–27,4–29. Weight (9 ♂) 96–110–126 g, (6 ♀) 47,4–78,1–97 g.

Bare Parts: Iris brown; bill black, base yellowish; legs and feet greenish yellow.

Identification: Size medium (considerably larger than Little Stint); bill short and slightly decurved at tip (markedly decurved in Curlew Sandpiper); above mottled buff and dark brown; speckling on chest forms abrupt line against white belly; legs greenish yellow (not black as in most *Calidris* species); in flight white rump has dark centre line; faint buffy wingbar; looks dark, snipelike.

Voice: Low *prrrp, kreek-kreek* or *treek*; deep *whoop-whoop-whoop* when breeding.

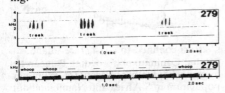

Distribution: Breeds N America and ne Palaearctic tundra; migrates to S America, Japan, Korea and Pacific islands; straggles to Europe, Africa and Australia; recorded several coastal and inland localities in s Africa.

Status: Nonbreeding Nearctic vagrant, August to April.

Habitat: Flooded grassland, marshy pans, vleis, sewage ponds.

Habits: Solitary or in company with other wader species (Curlew Sandpiper, Little Stint, Ruff). Shy; when disturbed stretches up on tiptoe, or crouches flat; flight zigzagging, snipelike, with characteristic call.

Food: Aquatic invertebrates.

Breeding: Extralimital.

Ref. Ginn, P.J. & Brooke, R.K. 1971. *Bull. Brit. Orn. Club* 91:125–126.
Myers, J.P. 1982. *Amer. Birds* 36:119–122.

280 (–)   **Temminck's Stint**   **Plate 76**

Temminckse Strandloper

Calidris temminckii

[Temminckstrandläufer]

Measurements: Length about 15 cm; wing (31 ♂) 94–97,6–103, (14 ♀) 95–98,1–102; tail 38–49; tarsus (34) 17–17,5–18; culmen (30) 16–16,9–18. Weight (50) 15–19–25 g.

Bare Parts: Iris brown; bill black; legs and feet olive green to yellowish olive.

Identification: Size small (about same as Little Stint); plainer grey-brown above (less mottled); below whitish, breast pale brownish grey; plumage and leg colour similar to small version of Common Sandpiper (legs greenish or yellowish, not black as in most *Calidris* species); in flight outer tail feathers pure white (brownish or all dark in other small sandpipers); narrow white wingbar; rump white with dark centre line.

Voice: High-pitched trilling twitter *tirrrrrrrrr*, rising and falling in pitch, different from call of Little Stint.

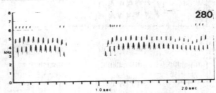

Distribution: Breeds n Europe and n Asia; migrates to s Asia, Mediterranean; straggler to s Africa, recorded Leeupan (near Johannesburg), Swakopmund (also Zambia and Malawi).

Status: Very rare nonbreeding Palaearctic vagrant, February.

Habitat: Inland and marine shores.

Habits: Similar to those of Little Stint with which it associates. When flushed flies straight up, rather snipelike.

Food: Molluscs, crustaceans, worms, insects.

Breeding: Extralimital.

281 (255)   **Sanderling**   **Plates 29 & 28**
                          Drietoonstrandloper
                              Calidris alba

[Sanderling]

Measurements: Length 19–20 cm; wing
(30 ♂) 120–125,1–131, (34 ♀) 119–
127,2–131, (1 242 unsexed) 116–126,9–
136; tail (12) 46–55; tarsus (17 ♂)
22–24,2–27, (19 ♀) 24–24,9–27; culmen
(18 ♂) 21–24–26, (19 ♀) 22–25,2–27,
(1 400 unsexed) 21–25,2–29. Weight September to March (1 889) 43–56,1–75 g,
April-May (701) 46–76,4–102 g.
Bare Parts: Iris brown; bill, legs and feet
black.
Identification: Size smallish to medium;
bill short, stout and black (as long as head
or slightly shorter); legs black, hind toe
absent. *Nonbreeding*: Generally pale;
above pale mottled grey; below white;
dark wrist patches contrast with white on
either side of chest; in flight white wingbar
very broad; rump white with dark centre
line; tail pale greyish. *Breeding*: Head,
back and breast rufous, mottled darker.
Voice: Usually silent; shrill liquid *twick-
twick* in flight; harsh *krrr krrr*; repeated
wik-wik-wik.

Distribution: Breeds extreme n Siberia, n
Canada, Greenland and Arctic islands;
migrates to s N America, C and S America, Europe, Africa, s Asia, Australasia; in
s Africa confined to coast; rare inland.
Status: Common nonbreeding Palaearctic
migrant, September to May; total summer
population in S Africa and Namibia about
80 000 birds; some birds overwinter; bird
ringed Langebaan (w Cape) recovered
Russia, 12 700 km NNE.
Habitat: Sandy marine shores; less often
tidal mudflats, weed-covered rocky
shores.
Habits: Gregarious in flocks of 10–200
birds. Forages on wave-washed beach,
running after receding wave, ploughing
bill through sand; as next wave breaks,
flock turns and runs upshore; movements
quick and lively. When flushed flies fast;
flocks manoeuvre in unison, banking and
wheeling.
Food: Crustaceans, insects, molluscs,
beach-washed scraps of fish and other
animal fragments.
Breeding: Extralimital.

Ref. Summers, R.W., Underhill, L.G., Waltner,
  M. & Whitelaw, D.A. 1987. *Ostrich*
  58:24–39.

282 (–)   **Buffbreasted Sandpiper**   **Plate 76**
                        Taanborsstrandloper
                            Tryngites subruficollis

[Grasläufer]

Measurements: Length about 20 cm;
wing (20 ♂) 133–136,6–140, (19 ♀)
124–128,3–132; tail (7 ♂) 58–60,6–63,
(4 ♀) 54–57–62; tarsus (28 ♂) 30–32–37,
(23 ♀) 27–29,5–37; culmen (23 ♂)
19–20–21. (23 ♀) 17,5–18,6–20. Weight
(4 ♂) 64–71–80,5 g, (6 ♀) 50–53–58 g.
Bare Parts: Iris dark brown; bill black,

base olive grey; legs and feet dull orange-yellow.

Identification: Size small to medium; above scaled rich buff and dark brown; below uniform rich buff; eyering white; in flight underwing white; no white in upperwing, rump or tail; bill short and straight; legs yellow.

Voice: Low trilled *prrreet*; sharp tik; piping *q-wi-weet-q-wi-weet*, the *q* like a short click.

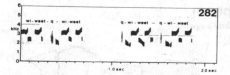

Distribution: Breeds extreme n Canada and Alaska; migrates to tropical S America; accidental visitor to s Africa, recorded Richards Bay and Pretoria.

Status: Very rare Nearctic vagrant, December.

Habitat: Tidal mudflats; usually short grassland, golfcourses, airfields.

Habits: Usually solitary; rather ploverlike. When disturbed freezes and can be approached closely; sometimes very tame. Flight zigzagging, snipelike, showing white underwing clearly.

Food: Insects, spiders, seeds.

Breeding: Extralimital.

Ref. Robson, N.F. & Robson, J.H. 1979. *Ostrich* 50:116–117.
Kieser, J.A. 1982. *Bokmakierie* 34:14–17.

283 (251Z) Broadbilled Sandpiper Plates 29 & 28
Breëbekstrandloper
Limicola falcinellus

[Sumpfläufer]

Measurements: Length about 17 cm; wing (13 ♂) 102–104,8–109, (17 ♀) 103–109,6–114; tail 35–42; tarsus (13 ♂) 20–20,9–22, (17 ♀) 20–21,5–22; culmen (11 ♂) 28–30,4–33, (15 ♀) 29–33,2–35. Weight (2 ♂) 26–37,5 g, (unsexed) 25–40–50 g.

Bare Parts: Iris dark brown; bill blackish or brownish horn, tinged olive green; legs and feet dark grey (yellowish olive in immature).

Identification: Size smallish (slightly larger than Little Stint); looks short-legged; above mottled light and dark grey (very pale in nonbreeding plumage, paler than other waders; much darker in breeding plumage with creamy white lines on crown and back); crown shows as dark centre line bordered by white; below white, lightly streaked grey on sides of chest; eyebrow broadly white, in breeding plumage forked behind eye; bill mostly straight, kinked downward near tip; dark wrist patch on folded wing; in flight tail and rump white with well defined dark centre line; no wingbar.

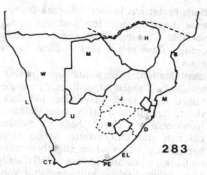

Voice: Twittering *chrr-tik* when flushed; *chitter-chitter* in flight; rasping *srr-ee, srr-ee*.

Distribution: Breeds n Europe and n Asia; migrates to Africa, s Asia and Australia; in s Africa recorded from Lake McIlwaine, Inhaca Island, Richards Bay, Durban, Port Elizabeth, Velddrif, Walvis Bay, Swakopmund, Hoanib River.

Status: Rare nonbreeding Palaearctic migrant, September to January; mostly first-year birds on passage in Zimbabwe.

Habitat: Marine beaches, sewage ponds,

brackish river pools up to 6 km from the coast.

Habits: Solitary or in small groups; often associates with Curlew Sandpiper and Little Stint. Less lively in movements than most small sandpipers, but runs fast; forages deliberately with sewing-machine movements of bill, often with head immersed.

Food: Molluscs, worms, insects, seeds.

Breeding: Extralimital.

Ref. Becker, P., Jensen, R.A.C. & Berry, H.H. 1974. *Madoqua Ser. I*, 8:67–71.

---

284 (256)   **Ruff (♂), Reeve (♀)**   **Plates 29 & 28**
Kemphaan

Philomachus pugnax

Koe-koe-lemao (SS), [Kampfläufer]

Measurements: Length ♂ 30–31 cm, ♀ 24–25 cm; wing (177 ♂) 170–185,8–203, (937 ♀) 132–154,4–170; tail (6 ♂) 66–67,1–68, (12 ♀) 51–57,2–61; tarsus (65 ♂) 45–50,4–54, (36 ♀) 38–40,7–44; culmen (174 ♂) 30–34,6–39, (937 ♀) 26,5–30,2–34. Weight (119 ♂) 140–180,3–220 g, (1 241 ♀) 61,5–103,8–147 g.

Bare Parts: Iris brown; bill dark brown, base tinged orange; legs and feet highly variable (orange, salmon, greenish orange, olive green, pinkish olive, rarely black).

Identification: Size medium; posture hunched; ♂ much larger than ♀; orange-tinged legs usually diagnostic; bill dark, short, straight and fairly stout at base. *Nonbreeding*: Above heavily mottled blackish and buffy white, giving scaly appearance; below white, slightly mottled on flanks; white area at base of bill usually highly characteristic but somewhat variable; in flight rump white with dark centre line; tail dark; narrow white wingbar not always visible; usually silent. *Breeding*: ♀ darker above, otherwise similar to nonbreeding; ♂ very variable with black, white, chestnut or barred erectile ruff around neck and onto lower breast; ♂ may have traces of breeding coloration on chest on arrival.

Voice: Usually silent; rarely heard *tu-wit* in flight.

Distribution: Breeds n Europe and n Asia; migrates to Africa, s Asia, Australia; widespread in s Africa.

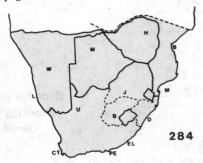

284

Status: Very common nonbreeding Palaearctic migrant, August to April.

Habitat: Estuaries and most inland waters, moist grasslands; occasionally seashore.

Habits: Gregarious in flocks of 5–25 birds, rarely as many as 1000; flocks may be all of one sex or mixed; females outnumber males about 7:1; most males may spend summer further N. Forages both night and day by wading quickly in shallow water, or walking through short grass, picking up food from surface or probing into mud with bill; may submerge head in water; feeds with body horizontal, shoulders hunched and long tertials curving upward over tail, sometimes blowing about in wind. Flies strongly and fast, landing with body almost vertical; stands upright when alarmed.

Food: Molluscs, crustaceans, insects, worms, seeds, berries, fallen grain.

Breeding: Extralimital.

Ref. Kieser, J.A. 1982. *Bokmakierie* 34:14–17. Schmitt, M.B. & Whitehouse, P.J. 1976. *Ostrich* 47:179–190.

285 (249)

Great Snipe
Dubbelsnip
Gallinago media

Plate 25

[Doppelschnepfe]

Measurements: Length about 28 cm; wing (49 ♂) 142–147,3–154, (23 ♀) 145–149,155; tail 50,5–58; tarsus (52 ♂) 35–36,9–39, (27 ♀) 36–38,3–40; culmen (43 ♂) 58–62,1–67, (24 ♀) 59–66,7–72. Weight (3 ♂) 126–168–225 g, both sexes mean 199 g.

Bare Parts: Iris dark brown; bill horn brown; legs and feet greyish or yellowish green.

Identification: Size medium; bill straight, about twice length of head (shorter than that of Ethiopian Snipe); above mottled brown and white; whitish spots on wing conspicuous; underparts buff marked with dark chevrons, including centre of belly (underparts of Ethiopian Snipe white with dark barring on chest and sides of belly only); head striped buff and brown; in flight much white in outer tail feathers (less white in Ethiopian Snipe); seldom calls on take-off like Ethiopian Snipe and flight not zigzagging.

Voice: Rarely low guttural croak when flushed.

Distribution: Breeds n Europe and w Rus-

sia; migrates to Africa, Arabia and India; in s Africa widespread in n Zimbabwe, s Mozambique, Transvaal; also Ovamboland; no recent records Natal to e Cape; numbers apparently declining.

Status: Scarce nonbreeding Palaearctic migrant, October to April; few birds may overwinter.

Habitat: Vleis, moist grassland, streams.

Habits: Usually solitary or in pairs. Usually rises silently when flushed, flying straight without zigzagging. Somewhat crepuscular.

Food: Aquatic invertebrates.

Breeding: Extralimital.

Ref. Lemnell, P.A. 1978. *Ornis scand.* 9:146–163.

286 (250)

Ethiopian Snipe
Afrikaanse Snip
Gallinago nigripennis

Plate 25

Nkoko (K), Motjoli-matsana, Koe-koe-lemao (SS) Umnquduluthi (X), uNununde (Z), [Afrikanische Bekassine]

Measurements: Length about 28 cm; wing 120–141; tail 51–59; tarsus 32–35; culmen 73–88. Weight (6) 101–109,5–116 g.

Bare Parts: Iris brown; bill pinkish brown, tip blackish, base pinker; legs and feet yellowish olive to greenish grey.

Identification: Size medium; bill very long (more than twice length of head, longer than bill of Great Snipe); above boldly striped golden buff on dark brown; below

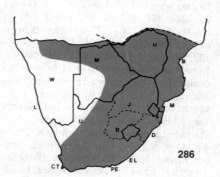

white, barred on chest and sides of belly (belly buff in Great Snipe with markings onto centre of belly); in flight little white in tail; wings rather rounded (more pointed in Great Snipe); almost always calls when flushed. *Chick*: Chestnut brown, above striped black, tipped white; iris dark brown; bill short, black, somewhat expanded at tip; legs dark grey.

Voice: Sucking sound, *hleep*, on take-off, rather like foot being drawn out of mud; on ground calls monotonous *kek-kek-kek-kek*; rapid resonant drumming *wm-wm-wm-wm-wm* lasting 2–5 seconds and rising in pitch at end, produced by fanned outer rectrices in diving display flight over territory.

Distribution: S Africa to Angola and Ethiopia; widespread in s Africa, but absent from large areas of dry W.

Status: Locally common resident; nomadic at temporary waters.

Habitat: Vleis, marshes, flooded grasslands, sewage ponds, marshy dams.

Habits: Usually solitary or in pairs; also in small loose groups. Freezes when disturbed, flushing reluctantly; rises at last moment, with sucking sound, flying away in zigzag course, then straight, dropping suddenly into marsh. In aerial display flight, mostly May to August (but also other months), ♂ rises to 10–40 m, then dives in steep or shallow path to about 3 m, drumming; flight circuit about 30 m diameter; drums on moonlit nights and in cool of day; displays on ground with tail cocked and fanned. Usually secretive, but sometimes forages on open shoreline; probes deeply into mud with bill; walks with short steps; partly nocturnal.

Food: Insects, worms, crustaceans, molluscs.

Breeding: *Season*: March to August in Zimbabwe, mostly July to August in Natal; breeds all months, but mostly midwinter in s Africa. *Nest*: Saucer-shaped pad of dry grass, well concealed in dense grasstuft or clump of rushes, usually in or at edge of marsh. *Clutch*: (23) 1–1,7–3 eggs (usually 2). *Eggs*: Olive green to greenish brown, pointed and fairly glossy; measure (78) 41,2 × 29,6 (36,9–44,8 × 27–32). *Incubation*: Unrecorded. *Fledging*: Unrecorded.

287 (265)   Blacktailed Godwit   Plate 25
Swartstertgriet
Limosa limosa

[Uferschnepfe]

Measurements: Length ♂ 41 cm, ♀ 50 cm; wing (67 ♂) 188–207–228, (41 ♀) 201–219–231; tail 74–89; tarsus (70 ♂) 64–74–96, (41 ♀) 73–81–88; culmen (63 ♂) 79–92,2–123, (41 ♀) 95–107,4–122. Weight ♂ 280–440 g, ♀ 350–500 g.

Bare Parts: Iris hazel to dark brown; bill orange-pink, tip brown to blackish; legs and feet greyish green to blackish.

Identification: Size large; legs and bill very long; bill straight (slightly upcurved in Bartailed Godwit), mostly pinkish, blackish at tip. *Nonbreeding*: Above plain greyish brown (mottled brown in Bartailed Godwit); head, neck and upper breast

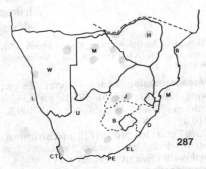

sandy buff, paler over eyebrow, shading to whitish belly; in flight broad white wingbar and rump (no wingbar in Bartailed Godwit); underwing white (barred in Bartailed Godwit); tail with solid black terminal band (barred in Bartailed Godwit). *Breeding*: Above mottled; chest rusty red; flanks barred; belly whitish (Bartailed Godwit wholly rusty red below in breeding plumage).

Voice: Usually silent in s Africa; repeated mellow *wika-wika-wika* on take-off; plaintive *pirree*.

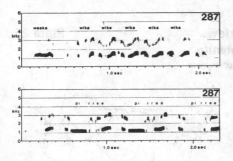

Distribution: Breeds C Europe and C Asia to Kamchatka Peninsula; migrates to Mediterranean, Africa, s Asia, Australia; in s Africa at scattered inland and coastal localities (Botswana, Orange Free State, Transvaal, Natal, Cape, Zimbabwe).

Status: Very rare nonbreeding Palaearctic vagrant, September to May (mostly January-May), not normally migrating further S than Sahel; few birds overwinter.

Habitat: Dams, pans, marshes, tidal mudflats, larger rivers (Zambezi, Olifants).

Habits: Solitary or gregarious, often in company with Bartailed Godwits. Movements deliberate while probing in mud for food; walks fast between probes; may wade in water up to belly, immersing head while foraging. Flight fast, often low; flocks manoeuvre in unison.

Food: Molluscs, crustaceans, worms, seeds.

Breeding: Extralimital.

288 (266) Bartailed Godwit Plate 25
Bandstertgriet
Limosa lapponica

[Pfuhlschnepfe]

Measurements: Length ♂ 36 cm, ♀ 41 cm; wing (64 ♂) 200–211,3–221, (31 ♀) 214–223,3–231; tail 67–77; tarsus (65 ♂) 46–50–53, (28 ♀) 52–55,4–59; culmen (62 ♂) 69–78,5–87, (30 ♀) 86–99,2–108. Weight January (4) mean 291,5 g, March-April (5) 283–398,8–423 g.

Bare Parts: Iris brown; bill basal half orange-pink, apical half blackish; legs and feet greyish green to blackish.

Identification: Size large; bill and legs long; bill pinkish at base, blackish at tip, slightly upcurved (straight in Blacktailed Godwit). *Nonbreeding*: Above mottled brown (plainer in Blacktailed Godwit); below whitish, streaked on neck (no streaks in Blacktailed Godwit); in flight no white wingbar (broad white wingbar in Blacktailed Godwit); rump white; tail barred black-and-white (plain black terminal band in Blacktailed Godwit).

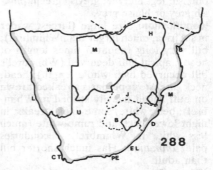

Breeding: Underparts plain rusty red (no barring on flanks as in Blacktailed Godwit).

Voice: Usually silent; sometimes loud whistled *low-eet, low-eet* on take-off.

Distribution: Breeds extreme n Europe and n Asia; migrates to Mediterranean, Africa, s Asia, Australasia; in s Africa mainly coastal (especially W coast), few inland records.

Status: Uncommon to locally common nonbreeding Palaearctic migrant, August to May; bird ringed Swartkops (e Cape) recovered Iran, 8 300 km N.
Habitat: Tidal flats, estuaries, lagoons, shallow inland dams or pans.
Habits: Solitary or gregarious in flocks of 20–100 birds, often with other wader species. Forages in shallow water or on exposed mud, keeping head down while probing with bill; head sometimes immersed when feeding in shallow water. Flight fast, often in V or wavy line low over water.

Food: Molluscs, worms, insects, crustaceans.

Breeding: Extralimital.

---

289 (267)   Curlew   Plate 25
Grootwulp
Numenius arquata

[Großer Brachvogel]

Measurements: Length 53–59 cm; wing (41 ♂) 269–289,6–305, (43 ♀) 286–306,4–324; tail (8 ♂) 100–109–115, (12 ♀) 108–116–125; tarsus (45 ♂) 67–78–85, (45 ♀) 72–84,7–92; culmen, *N. a. arquata* (25 ♂) 95–115,2–141, (17 ♀) 130–151,5–185, *N. a. orientalis* (22 ♂) 118–132,9–155, (28 ♀) 138–163,8–184. Weight ♂ 572–662,4–779 g, (62 ♀) 680–787,7–919 g.
Bare Parts: Iris brown; bill brown, base pinkish; legs and feet greyish green, pinkish grey or bluish grey.
Identification: Size large (largest wader in s Africa, much larger than Whimbrel); bill very long (about 3 times length of head), apical half decurved (Whimbrel's bill decurved over whole length); head, neck, breast, upperparts streaked brown on buff (head heavily striped in Whimbrel); belly white, some flank streaks; in flight lower back and rump white (much less white in Whimbrel); secondaries pale. *Immature:* Has much shorter bill than adult.
Voice: Onomatopaeic *kurlee, kurlee* in flight; mellow rolling trill.

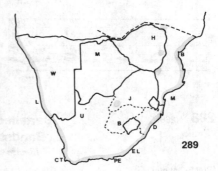

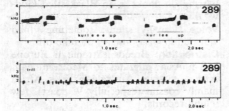

Distribution: Breeds Europe (*N. a. arquata*) and C Asia to China (*N. a. orientalis*); migrates to Mediterranean, Africa, s Asia; in s Africa mainly coastal, less often inland in E; absent from dry W; vagrant Zimbabwe.
Status: Uncommon nonbreeding Palaearctic migrant, August to March; few birds overwinter; most s African birds are longer-billed *N. a. orientalis*.
Habitat: Seashore, tidal mudflats, estuaries, shallow inland waters.
Habits: Solitary inland; solitary or gregarious on coast in flocks of up to about 60 birds. Shy and wary; runs with flapping wings before taking off, usually with characteristic call. Runs or walks about on mud, probing deeply with very long bill.
Food: Molluscs, crustaceans (especially crabs), mudskippers, insects, berries; rarely probes fresh cowdung for insects.
Breeding: Extralimital.

290 (268)

Whimbrel
Kleinwulp
Numenius phaeopus

Plate 25

Ingoyi-ngoyi (X), [Regenbrachvogel]

Measurements: Length 43 cm; wing (16 ♂) 239–245,9–255, (12 ♀) 232–253,4–265; tail (8) 90–94–104; tarsus (16 ♂) 53–58–64, (11 ♀) 56–61,1–65; culmen (16 ♂) 76–82,1–92, (12 ♀) 76–83,7–99. Weight November to December (4) 380–475 g, March (2) 370–627 g.

Bare Parts: Iris hazel to dark brown; bill horn brown, base pinkish; legs and feet greenish grey.

Identification: Size medium; like smallish Curlew; head boldly striped, buff on crown, dark brown at sides (Curlew's head lightly streaked brown and buff); eyebrow buff; rest of upperparts and most of underparts buff streaked dark brown; belly whitish; bill about twice length of head, decurved over whole length; in flight rump boldly white (not as extensively white as in Curlew).

Voice: Drawn-out whistled *foo-eeee*, rising in pitch; prolonged rippling whistle, *prrrr-r-r-r-whetti-whetti-whetti-whetti-whet*, usually in flight.

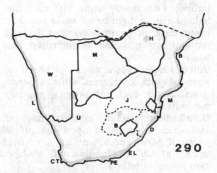

Distribution: Breeds n Europe and n Asia (separate breeding population n N America); migrates to Africa, Madagascar, s Asia, Australasia (American birds migrate to s N America and S America); in s Africa on all marine shores (rarely inland).

Status: Common nonbreeding Palaearctic migrant, September to April; passage migrant inland, mainly September-December.

Habitat: Sandy and rocky shores; inland on larger dams and pans on passage.

Habits: Usually solitary; also in flocks of up to 50 birds (especially on W coast). Not as shy as Curlew, but seldom allows close approach; flight fast and direct. Forages by probing in soft substrate, raising head between probes.

Food: Molluscs and crustaceans.

Breeding: Extralimital.

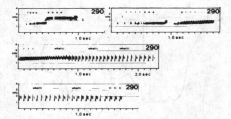

291 (271)

Grey Phalarope
Grysfraiingpoot
Phalaropus fulicaria

Plates 29 & 28

[Thorshühnchen]

Measurements: Length 18–20 cm; wing (53 ♂) 121–128,7–134, (31 ♀) 130–135,7–141; tail (3) 62–64; tarsus (18) 20–21,6–23; culmen (53 ♂) 20–22,1–24, (29 ♀) 22–23,3–25. Weight (69 ♂) 41–50,8–60 g, (51 ♀) 49–61–73 g.

Bare Parts: Iris brown; bill yellow, tip blackish; legs and feet dull yellow.

Identification: Size smallish; sandpiperlike (similar to Sanderling); swims on water; bill fairly stout, yellow, tipped black (slender, all black in other phalaropes); legs yellowish (dark in other phalaropes).

Nonbreeding: Above grey (paler than in Rednecked Phalarope); below white, marked grey on sides of breast (extending further forwards than in Rednecked Phalarope); face mostly white with dark line behind eye; in flight broad white wingbar; rump dark in centre. *Breeding*: Above mottled brown; below bright rusty; face white.

Voice: Usually silent when not breeding; series of quick low slurred whistles, *preep*, sometimes in duet with popping *pup pup pup* notes.

Distribution: Breeds high latitudes of Holarctic; migrates to open sea off W coasts of Africa and S America; in s Africa mainly at sea off Namibia and w Cape; rare straggler inland.

Status: Common at sea; rare inland; non-breeding Holarctic migrant, August to February.

Habitat: Usually open sea when not breeding; less often along marine shores, sewage ponds, pans, dams.

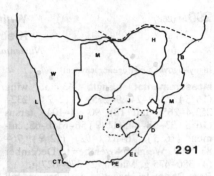

Habits: Usually in flocks at sea, solitary inland. Swims buoyantly on water, neck held straight up; swims in circles to stir up food in water, pecking quickly at surface. Flight fast and erratic. Usually tame.

Food: Plankton, insects, crustaceans, molluscs, worms.

Breeding: Extralimital.

Ref. Sinclair, J.C. 11977. *Bokmakierie* 29:90–91.
Stanford, W.P. 1953. *Ibis* 95:483–491.

---

292 (272)　　　**Rednecked Phalarope**　　　**Plates 29 & 28**
Rooihalsfraiingpoot
Phalaropus lobatus

[Odinshühnchen]

Measurements: Length 16–19 cm; wing (51 ♂) 103–107,8–114, (31 ♀) 109–113,4–118; tail (11 ♂) 46–48,3–50, (11 ♀) 48,5–50,2–52,5; tarsus (18 ♂) 19–20,4–22, (13 ♀) 20–20,8–22; culmen (17 ♂) 19–21,1–22, (11 ♀) 20–21,6–23. Weight (14 ♂) 29–32–35 g, (7 ♀) 29–35–43 g.

Bare Parts: Iris dark brown; bill black; legs and feet brown to bluish grey.

Identification: Size small; bill about length of head, thin, needle-like, black (bill yellow in Grey Phalarope, much longer in Wilson's Phalarope). *Nonbreeding*: Similar to Grey Phalarope, but bill thinner, back darker grey, less grey on upper breast; in flight white wingbar (no wingbar in Wilson's Phalarope); rump dark in centre (all white in Wilson's Phalarope). *Breeding*: Above dark grey with light golden stripes on scapulars; below white with rufous collar on upper chest bordered below by slaty grey.

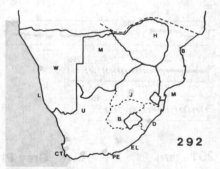

Voice: Usually silent when not breeding; series of low scratchy notes, *chik-chik-cher*; duet of chuckling *pur pur* notes with mellow *hoot*.

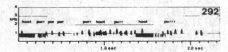

254

Distribution: Breeds high latitudes of Holarctic; migrates to tropical oceans and shores.

Status: Rare nonbreeding Holarctic migrant, mainly October to April.

Habitat: Coastal and inland pans, salt-works, sewage ponds.

Habits: Usually solitary or in groups of up to 5 birds. Similar to Grey Phalarope.

Food: As for Grey Phalarope.

Breeding: Extralimital.

Ref. Sinclair, J.C. 1977. *Bokmakierie* 29:90–91.

293 (–)   Wilson's Phalarope   Plate 76
Bontfraiingpoot
Phalaropus tricolor

[Wilsons Wassertreter, Amerikanisches Odinshühnchen]

Measurements: Length 21–23 cm; wing (32 ♂) 119–124,7–129, (31 ♀) 130–135,4–142; tail (10 ♂) 48–51,2–54, (11 ♀) 52,5–55,9–65; tarsus (42 ♂) 28,5–30,9–34, (42 ♀) 30,5–32,5–35; culmen (38 ♂) 28–30,9–33, (40 ♀) 31–33,4–36. Weight (100 ♂) 30–50,1–64 g, (53 ♀) 55–68–85 g.

Bare Parts: Iris brown; bill black; legs and feet dull yellow to greenish.

Identification: Size smallish to medium; bill longer than head, very thin, black (Marsh Sandpiper has thicker shorter bill). *Nonbreeding*: Above pale grey; below white; grey line through eye; in flight no white wingbar (wingbar present in both other phalaropes); rump all white (dark in centre in other phalaropes); legs long, extend beyond tail in flight (not in other phalaropes). *Breeding*: Similar to nonbreeding plumage, but with broad blackish stripe through eye, down sides of neck, becoming rufous stripe onto back (♂ duller than ♀); rufous wash on fore-neck and sides of chest.

Voice: Usually silent when not breeding; low gallinule-like *wurk* and *chek-chek-chek*.

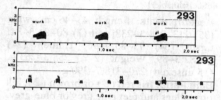

Distribution: Breeds interior N America (sw Canada and nw USA); migrates to s S America; vagrant to Muizenberg, Velddrif, Rietvlei (Cape Province), Umvoti Mouth (Natal) and Swakopmund.

Status: Very rare nonbreeding Nearctic straggler to s Africa, midsummer to May.

Habitat: Ponds, saltpans, shallow lakes, lagoons.

Habits: Swims less than other phalaropes; forages on floating plants or on shoreline, running on flexed legs, stabbing quickly at prey from side to side with bouncy lunging motion, or sweeping from side to side with bill. Flight fast and direct, sometimes erratic.

Food: Aquatic invertebrates.

Breeding: Extralimital.

Ref. Sinclair, J.C. & Hockey, P.A.R. 1980. *Bokmakierie* 32:114–115.

12:1:6. Family 36 RECURVIROSTRIDAE—AVOCETS AND STILTS

Medium to large. Bill long, slender and straight or curved upwards; legs very long; toes moderately long, partly to fully webbed; hind toe reduced or absent; neck fairly long; wings long and pointed; tail short and square; plumage usually black and white, sometimes with rufous on head, neck or chest; sexes alike; inhabit shallow waters, marine or inland; food mostly small aquatic animals; gregarious; nest colonially on shores or islands; nest a scrape lined with plant material, often quite substantial; eggs 3–4, buff to olive, spotted with brown, black and grey, sometimes plain; chick downy, precocial, dorsally grey with black lines in most species, fed by parents; parental care by both sexes. Distribution almost worldwide, especially in subtropics; seven species; two species in s Africa.

Ref. Hamilton, R.B. 1975. *Orn. Monogr.* 17:1–98.

294 (269)   Old World Avocet   Plate 25
Bontelsie
Recurvirostra avosetta

[Säbelschnäbler]

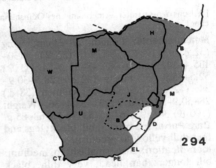

294

Measurements: Length 43–46 cm; wing (35) 213–224,3–238; tail (7) 80–81,3–84; tarsus (34) 75–85,9–96; culmen (24) 75–82,3–89. Weight (2 ♀) 258,3–263 g, (15 unsexed) 270–318,7–390 g.

Bare Parts: Iris red (♂) or brown (♀); bill black; legs and feet pale grey or blue-grey.

Identification: Size medium to large; bill long, upcurved; legs very long and pale grey; general plumage boldly pied; above black and white; crown and hindneck black; below white; in flight black-and-white wing pattern conspicuous. *Immature*: Dark brown where adult black. *Chick*: Above grey with irregular black stripes down centre and sides of back; nape and underside white; bill short, almost straight, black; iris dark brown; legs and feet blue-grey; weighs 20–22 g at hatching.

Voice: Clear liquid *klooit*, usually in flight; alarm call *kleet-kleet-kleet*; twittering noise in flock.

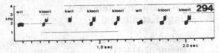

Distribution: Breeds discontinuously in Africa, Europe and C Asia; Palaearctic birds migrate to Africa, India and se Asia; throughout s Africa.

Status: Locally common, especially in w parts of s Africa; some birds resident and nomadic; others possibly nonbreeding Palaearctic migrants, summer months.

Habitat: Shallow water in estuaries, lagoons, marine shores, dams, sewage ponds, pans, coastal lakes.

Habits: Usually gregarious in small flocks, sometimes solitary; nonbreeding birds may form flocks of several hundred. Forages by wading briskly (less often by swimming) in shallow water, sweeping with bill from side to side over surface of water; sometimes submerges entire head and sweeps muddy bottom; when swimming may up-end like duck to reach bottom. Flocks fly in close formation; black-and-white wings give fluttery effect to flight.

Food: Insects, crustaceans, worms, molluscs, small fish; some seeds and other plant material; detritus scooped up from bottom.

Breeding: *Season*: Mainly August to November, but opportunistically in any month after suitable rain. *Nest*: Shallow scrape on damp soil, lined with twigs, grass, mud pellets; usually in small loose colonies, often on islets formed by flooding, or by receding waters after floods. *Clutch*: 3–5 eggs (usually 4). *Eggs*: Light greenish grey or yellowish khaki, boldly spotted with blackish and grey; measure (25) 51,5 × 35,2 (48–53,9 × 34,2–37). *Incubation*: (16) 22–24,3–27 days by both sexes. *Fledging*: (57) 26–26,6–28 days; young cared for by both sexes.

295 (270)   **Blackwinged Stilt**   **Plate 25**
Rooipootelsie
Himantopus himantopus

[Stelzenläufer]

Measurements: Length about 38 cm; wing (14) 215–226–235; tail 74–80,9–91; tarsus 106–115–130; culmen 58–63,5–68. Weight (2 ♂) 153,7–163,7 g, (1 ♀) 163,8 g, (2 unsexed) 160–195 g.

Bare Parts: Iris ruby red; bill black; legs and feet red.

Identification: Size medium; slender build; legs very long, red; bill long, slender, straight; mostly white; back and wings black (♂) or brown (♀). *Immature*: Like ♀ with greyish nape and hindneck. *Chick*: Above yellowish grey, with irregular black stripes; below buffy white; iris dark brown; bill shortish, black; legs and feet pinkish grey; weighs about 17 g at hatching.

Voice: Puppylike yapping *yip-yip-yip-yip*, loud and penetrating; shrill *chek-chek-chek* alarm call.

Distribution: Almost worldwide, except n Holarctic and S America; throughout s Africa.

Status: Locally common resident; highly nomadic.

Habitat: Shallow waters of estuaries, pans, dams, sewage ponds, vleis and marshes.

Habits: Solitary or gregarious; occasionally in large flocks of up to 500 birds. Forages by wading quickly with high-stepping gait in shallow water (rarely by swimming) sweeping bill over surface and pecking at food; may submerge head and neck. Flight somewhat flapping, long legs trailing out behind, often accompanied by loud calls.

Food: Insects, crustaceans, molluscs, worms, seeds.

Breeding: *Season*: April to November in Zimbabwe, October to November in e Cape, April to September in Natal; probably most months in s Africa, depending on rainfall, but usually in dry season in E. *Nest*: Scrape on ground or mud, lined with twigs, grass, and mudpellets; sometimes substantial pile of plant material built up in shallow water or on floating water plants. *Clutch*: 4 eggs (rarely 3 or 5). *Eggs*: Yellowish stone, boldly blotched and spotted with blackish brown and grey; measure (134) 42,9 × 31 (36,8–47,1 × 26,4–33,8). *Incubation*: 24–27 days by both sexes. *Fledging*: About 28 days; young cared for by both parents.

12:1:7. Family 37 DROMADIDAE—CRAB PLOVER

Medium. Bill about as long as head, deep and stout, laterally compressed; legs long; front toes moderately long, webbed at base; middle claw pectinate; hind toe reduced and elevated; wings long and pointed; tail short; plumage mostly white with black on back and wings; sexes similar, female smaller; crepuscular; gregarious; food mostly crustaceans and some molluscs; inhabit marine shores; nest colonially in burrows in sandy beaches; egg one, plain white; chick downy, altricial, plain grey; parental care by both sexes. Distribution Indian Ocean shores—breeds s Red Sea to w peninsular India, migrates to E coast of Africa, Madagascar, Sri Lanka; one species (vagrant to s Africa).

296 (273)

Crab Plover
Krapvreter
Dromas ardeola

Plate 25

[Reiherläufer]

Measurements: Length 38–41 cm; wing (46) 203–213,2–226; tail 64–76; tarsus (51) 87–93,5–102; culmen (50) 51–58,9–64. Weight (1) 325 g.

Bare Parts: Iris red (breeding) or brown (nonbreeding); bill black; legs and feet greyish white to whitish blue.

Identification: Size medium to large (slightly smaller than Old World Avocet); mostly white with black stripe down back and black primaries; heavy black bill diagnostic; legs very long, pale greyish; nonbreeding plumage pale grey on crown. *Immature:* Brownish grey on back, wings and tail; crown and neck pale grey, blackish streaks on crown.

Voice: Harsh ternlike *krook*; shrill *chuk-chuk-chuk*; sharp *cheeruk* on take-off.

Distribution: Breeds n and w shores of Indian Ocean, mainly in tropics; disperses southward when not breeding; in s Africa only on E coast from about Maputo; vagrant to Natal and e Cape as far S as Port Elizabeth.

Status: Very rare nonbreeding straggler, mainly September to April, but recorded all months.

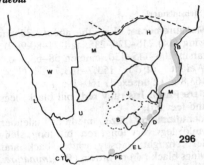

296

Habitat: Sandy marine shores, tidal mudflats, estuaries.

Habits: Usually solitary in s Africa; otherwise gregarious in flocks of up to 70 birds. Shy and wary; largely crepuscular. Forages along shoreline, running with mincing steps, stopping now and then to jab at prey; when disturbed runs with springy action, neck withdrawn, looking like small Ostrich; when flushed, circles around and lands short distance away; flight rather jacana-like, long legs trailing behind.

Food: Mainly crabs.

Breeding: Extralimital.

12:1:8. Family 38 BURHINIDAE—DIKKOPS (THICK-KNEES, STONE-CURLEWS)

Medium to large. Bill plover-like, but longer and stouter, usually yellowish at base; legs long, yellow; toes short, slightly webbed at base, hind toe absent; wings long and pointed, boldly patterned black and white on remiges; tail medium, somewhat wedge-shaped; body plumage cryptically coloured in buff, brown, grey and black, sometimes boldly marked on head and wings; sexes alike; inhabit stony, sandy or semi-arid areas or shorelines, both marine and freshwater; often gregarious; crepuscular and nocturnal; voice loud and melodious; food various animals; nest a scrape in the open; eggs 1–2, buff with brown markings; chick downy, grey above with black lines, precocial, fed by parents; parental care usually by both sexes. Distribution mainly tropical, C and S America, Africa, Europe, Asia, Australia; nine species; two species in s Africa.

297 (275)

Spotted Dikkop
Dikkop
Burhinus capensis

Plate 25

Eswaita (K), Khoho-ea-lira (SS), Gwarimutondo (Sh), Mongwangwa, Tswangtswang, Kgoadirê (Tw), Ingqangqolo (X), umBangaqhwa, umJenjana (Z), [Kaptriel, Bändertriel]

Measurements: Length 43–44 cm; wing (36) 223–231–242; tail 112–123–138; tarsus 87–95–105; culmen 34–36,8–40,5.

Weight (1 ♀) 480 g, (18 unsexed) 375–453,5–610 g.

Bare Parts: Iris bright yellow; bill black, basal third yellow; legs and feet yellow.

Identification: Size large; ploverlike; large yellow eyes conspicuous; above spotted dark brown on buff (streaked in Water Dikkop); no wingbar as in Water Dikkop; below white, faintly washed cinnamon and streaked brown on chest; undertail coverts deep buff; in flight bold black-and-white pattern in wing; lives away from water. *Chick:* Above grey, with black lines down back and head; below white; iris pale yellow.

Voice: Loud piping notes, rising in pitch and volume, then dying away, *pi-pi-pi-pi peo peo peo-pi-pi pi*; more musical than calls of Water Dikkop; growling alarm notes.

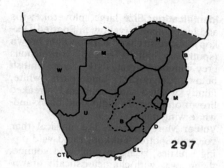

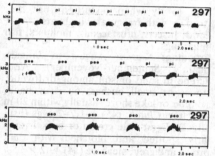

Distribution: Africa S of Sahara, except forested areas of W Africa and Congo basin; throughout s Africa.

Status: Common resident.

Habitat: Open grassland near trees or bushes, savanna, large lawns, playing fields, cemeteries, airfields, agricultural land, stony semidesert with scrub; less often wide marine beaches.

Habits: Solitary or in pairs when breeding; otherwise may be gregarious in flocks of 40–50 birds. Largely crepuscular and nocturnal, but also active on cloudy days; by day stands or crouches in shade of bush or tree; when disturbed runs off with head low; flies strongly with shallow erratic wingbeats, holding wings out briefly as it runs on landing; usually stands still or crouches unless disturbed again. Vocal at night and on heavily overcast days, especially after rain.

Food: Insects, crustaceans, molluscs, grass seeds, frogs.

Breeding: *Season:* Mainly August to December; rarely as late as April. *Nest:* Shallow scrape on ground, sometimes lined or ringed with small stones, clods, dry plant fragments, antelope droppings; usually in open among grasstufts or next to stone or shrub; sometimes under shade of bush or large tree. *Clutch:* (88) 1–2–3 eggs (usually 2). *Eggs:* Pale cream, buff or clay-colour, blotched and spotted with irregular angular marks of dark brown and grey; measure (148) 52 × 38,1 (46,9–58,7 × 34,6–41,8). *Incubation:* 24 days by both sexes. *Fledging:* About 7–8 weeks.

Ref. Maclean, G.L. 1966. *Ostrich Suppl.* 6:155–170.

298 (274)   **Water Dikkop**   **Plate 25**
Waterdikkop

Burhinus vermiculatus

Eswaita (K), Ngelekele (Ts), Ingqangqolo (X), [Wassertriel]

Measurements: Length 38–40 cm; wing (16) 191–205–211; tail 98–109–118; tarsus 72–74,8–77; culmen 41–44–46.

Weight (2 ♂) 293–301 g, (2 ♀) 308–315 g.

Bare Parts: Iris pale green; bill black, base pale greenish yellow; legs and feet pale greenish grey.

WATER DIKKOP

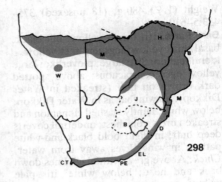

Identification: Size large, ploverlike; iris and legs greenish (yellow in Spotted Dikkop); above streaked dark on light brown (spotted in Spotted Dikkop); conspicuous grey wingbar at rest, dark above, whitish below (diagnostic); underparts white, faintly washed cinnamon and streaked brown on chest; in flight bold black-and-white wing pattern.

Voice: More strident, less musical than voice of Spotted Dikkop; rapid wild piping whistles, rising in pitch and volume, dying away with characteristically drawn-out notes *ti-ti-ti-ti-ti tee-tee-tee ti-teee-teeeee teee-teee*.

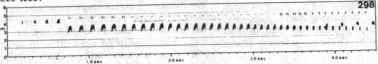

Distribution: Wetter parts of Africa S of Sahara; in s Africa confined mainly to extreme S, E, NE and N; avoids dry W.

Status: Locally common resident.

Habitat: Rivers, dams, lakes, pans, estuaries, mangrove swamps, beaches.

Habits: Solitary or in pairs when breeding; otherwise in loose flocks of 20–30 birds. Mainly crepuscular and nocturnal, but more active by day than Spotted Dikkop; often vocal in full daylight; groups usually stand hunched around edge of water, or squat in cover of bushes and trees by day. Prefers to run than to fly when disturbed, but flies strongly with irregular wingbeats.

Food: Insects, crustaceans, molluscs, fish fingerlings.

Breeding: *Season*: August to January (mainly September-November). *Nest*: Scrape in sand or soil among driftwood, stones or small bushes; on river bank, sandbar or lake shore, usually within 20 m of water. *Clutch*: (45) 1–1,7–2 eggs (usually 2). *Eggs*: Pale cream or buff, irregularly spotted and blotched with dark brown and grey; measure (54) 49,2 × 35,7 (44–54 × 32,7–39). *Incubation*: About 24 days. *Fledging*: Unrecorded.

12:1:9. Family 39 GLAREOLIDAE—COURSERS AND PRATINCOLES

Small to medium. Two subfamilies, coursers (Cursoriinae) and pratincoles (Glareolinae). Bill short to medium, strongly arched on culmen, gape wide and red in pratincoles; legs medium (pratincoles) to long (coursers); toes long (pratincoles) or short (coursers); middle claw pectinate (except in Egyptian Plover *Pluvianus aegyptius* and Australian Pratincole *Stiltia isabella*); hind toe reduced and elevated (pratincoles) or absent (coursers); basal web between middle and outer toe in most species; wings long and pointed, very long in pratincoles; plumage brown, with or without pattern; bands often present on throat, breast or belly; tail square (coursers and Australian Pratincole) or forked (all other pratincoles); sexes alike; solitary, gregarious, or in small flocks; inhabit open places—large rivers, grasslands, deserts, savanna; partly or wholly crepuscular; pratincoles partly aerial feeders; coursers cursorial; food mainly insects, some seeds; nest on ground (pratincoles nest colonially), a scrape, usually unlined; eggs 1–3, buff with dark markings; chick downy, precocial, fed by parents; parental care by both sexes. Distribution Africa, s Europe, Asia, Australia; 18 species; eight species in s Africa.

299 (276)

Burchell's Courser
Bloukopdrawwertjie
Cursorius rufus

Plate 30

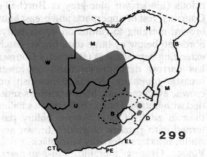

Mokopjoane (SS), Ingegane, Ucelithafa (X), uNobulongwe (Z), [Rostrennvogel]

Measurements: Length about 23 cm; wing (13) 132–135–138; tail 48–51,2–53; tarsus 46,5–48–51; culmen 21–22,9–25,5. Weight (1) 75 g.

Bare Parts: Iris brown; bill blackish; legs and feet greyish white.

Identification: Size smallish (looks like small Crowned Plover at distance); ploverlike, but longer-legged; bill fairly long, decurved; upperparts, foreneck and breast brown; forecrown rufous; hindcrown blue-grey (rufous in Temminck's Courser); line through eye black; eyebrow white; dark brown band separates brown chest from white belly (dark brown does not extend between legs as in Temminck's Courser); in flight shows whitish speculum on wing (wing all dark in Temminck's Courser). *Immature*: Mottled and barred with buff and black; head markings absent; looks similar to Doublebanded Courser at distance, but lacks breastbands and has longer bill.

Voice: Single hoarse *chuk* on take-off; grunting *chuk, chuk* in flight; nasal honking *konk-konk kwink, konk-konk-konk kwink* or double *kwirrt-kwirrt* contact call; more mellow than calls of Temminck's Courser.

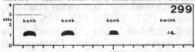

Distribution: Mainly w parts of s Africa; occasional in Natal and e Cape.

Status: Locally fairly common nomadic resident; numbers decreasing in s parts of range.

Habitat: Open short or burnt grassland, overgrazed veld, karoo, stony or gravelly semidesert and desert flats, stubbly sandveld, bare saltpans, ploughed and fallow lands.

Habits: Usually gregarious in groups of 5–15 birds; sometimes in pairs. Stands very upright; when alarmed bobs tail and sways body slowly while holding head still; runs very fast, stopping behind low shrub or tuft; easily overlooked; flies strongly when flushed. Forages in quick runs, stopping to peck at ground; may dig in soft soil with bill.

Food: Insects (especially Harvester Termites) and seeds.

Breeding: *Season*: July to January; possibly most months, but mainly August-December. *Nest*: None; eggs laid on bare ground; site may be ringed with small antelope droppings, stones or pieces of earth; completely exposed among stubble tufts, small stones, antelope dung or low shrubs. *Clutch*: (16) 1–1,9–2 eggs (usually 2). *Eggs*: Creamy white to pale stone or fawn, thickly covered with fine speckles and streaks of dark brown and black over some grey undermarkings; somewhat rounded; measure (42) 30,4 × 24 (27,8–32,9 × 22,8–26,2). *Incubation*: Unrecorded. *Fledging*: Unrecorded.

300 (277)

Temminck's Courser
Trekdrawwertjie
Cursorius temminckii

Plate 30

Ucelithafa (X), uNobulongwe (Z), [Temminckrennvogel]

Measurements: Length about 20 cm; wing (16 ♂) 120–125,8–132, (17 ♀) 119–124,4–132; tail (27) 41–45,9–50; tarsus (27) 37–39,9–43; culmen (27) 19–20,2–22. Weight (5) 67–74,1–80,5 g.

Bare Parts: Iris dark brown; bill greyish

black, base yellowish horn; legs and feet greyish white.

Identification: Size small; very similar to Burchell's Courser, but entire crown rufous (hindcrown blue-grey in Burchell's Courser); rest of upperparts and breast light brown, merging to rufous on upper belly, bordered below by large dark brown patch extending between legs (Burchell's Courser has narrow dark brown band on lower breast). *Immature*: Streaked blackish on crown; eyebrow buff; brown feathers mottled with buff and black; belly patch smaller than in adult. *Chick*: Above boldly patterned with patches of golden brown and white, interlaced broadly with black.

Voice: Grating metallic *pup-pup-prrrr, pup-pup-prrrr* in flight, like sound of rusty hinge.

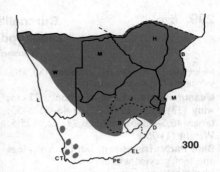

300

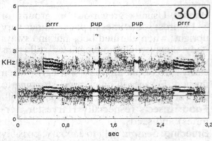

Distribution: Africa S of Sahara; in s Africa mostly absent from dry W.

Status: Uncommon to locally common nomadic resident; w populations largely sedentary; s populations may be migratory, present usually February to August; birds breeding in Sahel migrate to Orange Free State and e Cape, March-July; numbers decreasing in s parts of range.

Habitat: Bare short grassland in savanna or bushveld, edges of vleis, airfields, overgrazed areas, burnt grassveld, ploughed or fallow lands, bare granite whalebacks.

Habits: Usually in pairs or small groups; appears within few days after veld burnt. Forages by alternate runs and pecks at ground. When alarmed raises and lowers body by straightening and bending legs, keeping head still. Similar to habits of Burchell's Courser.

Food: Insects, molluscs, seeds.

Breeding: *Season*: May to January (mainly July-November). *Nest*: None; eggs laid on bare ground; site sometimes ringed with antelope droppings. *Clutch*: (26) 1-1,8-2 eggs (usually 2). *Eggs*: Pale creamy white to yellowish, densely speckled and streaked with blackish brown over grey undermarkings; somewhat rounded; measure (52) 27,7 × 22,8 (25-32,3 × 21,5-24,8). *Incubation*: Unrecorded; by both sexes. *Fledging*: Unrecorded; attended by both parents.

Ref. Clancey, P.A. 1984. *Gerfaut* 74:361-374.

301 (278)   **Doublebanded Courser**   **Plate 30**
               Dubbelbanddrawwertjie

Smutsornis africanus

Segolagola, Segwelegwele (Tw), [Doppelband-Rennvogel]

Measurements: Length 22-25 cm; wing (28) 145-151-159; tail 61-65,4-73; tarsus 49-53,7-59; culmen 13-14,1-15. Weight (1 ♀) 80 g, (27 unsexed) 69-88,7-104 g.

Bare Parts: Iris dark brown; bill black; legs and feet greyish white.

Identification: Size smallish; ploverlike, but longer-legged; above boldly mottled buff, brown and blackish; below buff, streaked on neck; two bold black bands on

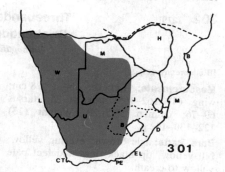

chest, running right around to mantle (diagnostic; 3 breast bands in Threebanded Courser); bill shorter than in other coursers; legs white (yellowish in Threebanded Courser); in flight shows rufous speculum in wings, white rump and black tail. *Immature*: Similar to adult, but lacks breastbands until 3 months old. *Chick*: Above intricately patterned in browns, black and white; white areas surrounded by black; below off-white, washed brownish in centre of breast; iris dark brown; bill black to horn; legs and feet blue-grey or slate grey with whitish bloom.

Voice: Plaintive mellow whistled *peeu-wee*, dropping in pitch, then rising at end; sharp *kikikik* alarm call; piercing *pee pee tititi* anxiety call near nest; musical sharp *wik-wik* on take-off.

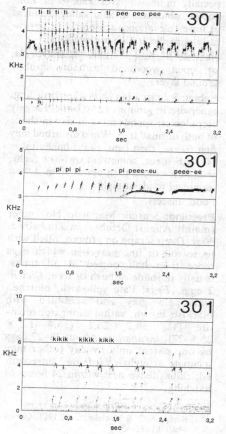

Distribution: 3 separate populations in s Africa, E Africa and NE Africa; confined to w half of s Africa.

Status: Locally common, but sparsely distributed nomadic resident.

Habitat: Stony or gravelly semidesert with stunted shrubs; also eroded and overgrazed grassveld.

Habits: Solitary or in pairs or family groups of 3–4 birds. Shy and wary; easily overlooked when standing still; runs very fast; flies reluctantly but strongly when hard pressed. Partly nocturnal, especially on moonlit nights; by day stands in shade of shrub. Forages by pecking at ground after quick run. When disturbed bobs head back and forth, and raises and lowers hind end of body slowly. May disappear from an area when vegetation gets too dense after rain.

Food: Insects (especially Harvester Termites).

Breeding: *Season*: All months; mainly August to December in sw Transvaal; at least 2 or 3 broods a year. *Nest*: None, or shallow scrape, usually ringed or lined with small stones, dry plant fragments or small antelope droppings; 60% of eggs laid among antelope droppings for camouflage; exposed on stony ground among scattered shrubs. *Clutch*: (86) 1 egg. *Eggs*: Pale creamy buff densely streaked and spotted with dark brown and grey, sometimes concentrated into band; measure (73) 31,4 × 25,5 (27,9–35,6 × 23–28,8). *Incubation*: About 26–27 days by both sexes. *Fledging*: 5–6 weeks; young fed by both parents.

Ref. Maclean, G.L. 1967. *Ibis* 109:556–569.

302 (279)

Threebanded Courser
Driebanddrawwertjie
Rhinoptilus cinctus

Plate 30

[Bindenrennvogel]

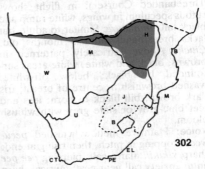

302

Measurements: Length about 28 cm; wing (4) 162–165; tail 81–85; tarsus 69–76; culmen 19,5–20. Weight (13) 122–130–142 g.

Bare Parts: Iris brown; eyering yellow; bill yellow, tip black; legs and feet pale yellow to cream.

Identification: Size smallish; ploverlike, but longer-legged; above boldly marked with elongate blotches of dark brown on buff; below white with 3 bands of brown, black and chestnut across throat and breast (Doublebanded Courser has only 2 black bands); upper breast streaked; face boldly marked with dark and light stripes; ear coverts tawny yellow. *Immature*: Similar to adult, but chestnut chestband faint or absent. *Chick*: Above mottled tan and pale grey, with sparse blackish brown blotches on forehead, centre of head, upper back and smaller patches scattered elsewhere; below whitish; iris dark brown; bill dull blackish; legs and feet grey.

Voice: Piping *wik wicker wicker wik wik wik...ik ik...k-k-k-k* first up scale then down again, accelerating until notes run together, then fading away; when disturbed calls *chuk-a-chuk-a-chuk*; on take-off sandpiperlike *phew-phew phew-phew phew-phew phoo*; also soft rattle.

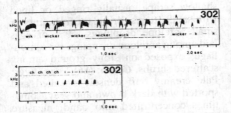

Distribution: Kruger National Park (n of Levubu River), Zimbabwe and n Namibia to s Angola, Zambia, Tanzania to Somalia, Ethiopia and se Sudan.

Status: Sparse but locally common, es-pecially in major river valleys in Zimbabwe; abundant in Sabi valley; resident at lower elevations, seasonally or irregularly nomadic at higher elevations.

Habitat: Mopane, *Acacia, Brachystegia*, or open woodland without shrubby ground layer.

Habits: Solitary or in pairs when breeding; otherwise in groups of 5–6 birds. Largely crepuscular; spends most of day in shade of bush or small tree. When disturbed may first freeze, then runs away; finally takes off with silent, somewhat owl-like flight, seldom for more than about 20 m. Often on gravel roads at night.

Food: Insects.

Breeding: *Season*: March to November (mainly August-October) in Zimbabwe. *Nest*: Deep scrape on ground, filled with loose soil or fine gravel in which eggs more than half buried at all times; usually in shade of bush or tree. *Clutch*: 2 eggs. *Eggs*: Pale yellowish, blotched with pale grey and scribbled with blackish brown; rather elongate; measure (11) 38,2 × 26,1 (36,4–41,2 × 25,5–27). *Incubation*: About 25–27 days by one parent only by day (other may incubate at night). *Fledging*: Unrecorded; chicks leave nest within 24 hours of hatching.

Ref. Hornby, H.E. 1960. *Bokmakierie* 12:19.
Kemp, A.C. & Maclean, G.L. 1973. *Ostrich* 44:80–81; 82–83.

303 (280)   **Bronzewinged Courser**   **Plate 30**
Bronsvlerkdrawwertjie
Rhinoptilus chalcopterus

Tshembyana (Ts), [Bronzeflügel-Rennvogel, Amethystrennvogel]

Measurements: Length about 25 cm; wing (8) 176–180–186; tail 77–80,4–84; tarsus 71–75,8–80; culmen 20–22,5–24. Weight (8 ♂) 117–154,3–172 g, (4 ♀) 135–150,2–160 g.

Bare Parts: Iris brown; eyering purplish red; bill black, base purplish red; legs and feet dull red.

Identification: Size medium; ploverlike, but longer-legged; bold facial pattern of brown and white diagnostic; upperparts and breast dull brown; breastband dark brown; belly white; legs red (pale whitish or yellowish in other coursers); in flight white wingbar, white rump and black tail conspicuous; underwing white. *Immature*: Faintly mottled rufous above.

Voice: Piping *ji-ku-it*, similar to call of Spotted Dikkop; harsh plaintive nasal *kwow-grorrraang* given in flight or from ground.

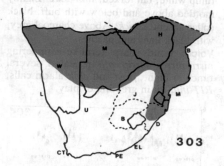

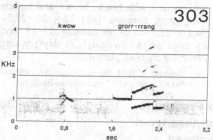

Distribution: Africa S of Sahara; in s Africa confined to E, NE and N.

Status: Uncommon to locally common; resident in N, migratory to SE September to May; migrations not mapped.

Habitat: Woodland with shrub layer, *Acacia* savanna; at night moves to open grassland, roads, tracks, and clearings.

Habits: Solitary, in pairs or small groups. When disturbed may crouch with lowered head and turn to face intruder so that camouflage enhanced by disruptive facial and breast pattern; when flushed flies short distance, lands and runs or freezes. Mainly nocturnal; spends day among small bushes in woodland.

Food: Insects.

Breeding: *Season*: July to December (mainly September-October) in Zimbabwe. *Nest*: None; eggs laid on bare ground. *Clutch*: 2–3 eggs. *Eggs*: Rich buff, boldly spotted with dark brown and lavender-grey; measure (44) 37,4 × 27,1 (32,6–41,4 × 25,2–28,3). *Incubation*: 25–27 days by both sexes. *Fledging*: Unrecorded; cared for by both parents.

304 (281)   **Redwinged Pratincole** (Collared Pratincole)   **Plate 30**
Rooivlerksprinkaanvoël
Glareola pratincola

iWamba (Z), [Brachschwalbe]

Measurements: Length 26–27 cm; wing (4) 176–189–194; tail 107–113–118; tarsus 28–29,3–31; culmen 17–17,8–18,5. Weight (11 ♂) 57–59 g, (7 ♀) 62–85 g.

Bare Parts: Iris dark brown; bill black, base red; legs and feet greyish black.

Identification: Size medium; looks like smallish tern or large swallow; long wings obvious at rest and in flight; above dull brown; below whitish, washed ochre and brown on breast; throat yellow-ochre, narrowly bordered black; thin black line from gape visible at close quarters (absent in Blackwinged Pratincole); in flight dark red axillaries in underwing visible in good light (black in Blackwinged Pratincole); rump white; tail forked. *Immature*: Lightly mottled above and below with buff; black collar absent. *Chick*: Above charcoal grey, with black lines and patches.

Voice: Loud sharp ternlike chippering *pirri pirree pirrip pip* repeated several times in flight; *pree* and *chik* alarm calls; *RIT-ititit-itit* in greeting display.

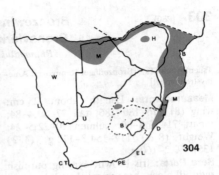

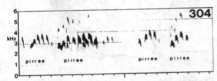

Distribution: Africa, Mediterranean, to India and Sri Lanka; in s Africa confined to extreme E and N.
Status: Locally common breeding migrant from tropical Africa, April to November in Zimbabwe; in Natal mostly absent March-May, but some birds present all months. Rare (RDB).
Habitat: Open ground, burnt grass, overgrazed veld, ploughed fields; usually near estuaries, pans and coastal lakes; also along larger rivers.
Habits: Gregarious at all times, sometimes in flocks of hundreds of birds, sometimes rising in thermal in spiral column. Flight buoyant, ternlike; forages in flight or by

running about on ground. Bobs head in alarm; flies about calling loudly at breeding colony; after landing holds wings briefly open, showing reddish underwing.
Food: Insects (especially locusts, grasshoppers, beetles, dragonflies); also spiders, molluscs.
Breeding: *Season*: August to November in Zimbabwe, November-December in Natal. *Nest*: Shallow scrape on bare ground, sometimes lined with soil fragments; loosely colonial, nests may be only 1 m apart. *Clutch*: (44) 1–1,8–2 eggs (usually 2). *Eggs*: Pale cream to rich buff, heavily blotched and spotted with black, brown and underlying grey; measure (48) 32 × 24 (29,5–34,1 × 22,2–25,6). *Incubation*: 17–18 days by both sexes. *Fledging*: 30 days; young cared for by both parents.

Ref. Sterbetz, I. 1974. *Die Brachschwalbe*. Wittenberg Lutherstadt: Neue Brehm-Bücherei.

305 (282)   Blackwinged Pratincole   Plate 30
Swartvlerksprinkaanvoël
Glareola nordmanni

Lehlakangoato (SS), [Schwarzflügel-Brachschwalbe]
Measurements: Length 26–27 cm; wing (29 ♂) 190–197,2–216, (20 ♀) 177–191,2–206; tail, longest rectrix (4 ♂) 95–102–115, (5 ♀) 84–92–100; tail, difference between longest and shortest rectrices (11 ♂) 42–47,7–52, (11 ♀) 39–44,8–53; tarsus (27) 35–37,3–41; culmen (26) 12–15–19,5. Weight ♂ 91–105 g, (6 ♀) 84,5–91,7–99 g, (5 unsexed) 89,6–93–96,5 g.
Bare Parts: Iris brown; bill black, base red; legs and feet black.

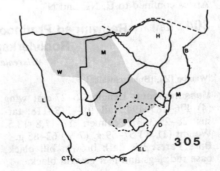

Identification: Very similar to Redwinged Pratincole, distinguishable only at close range; underwing all black; no black line from gape. *Immature*: Mottled above and below; no black collar on throat.
Voice: Mellow *wi-pi-tip weeup*; flocks make low chittering sounds.

Distribution: Breeds se Europe and sw Asia; migrates to s Africa, mainly to high-veld; absent from most of dry W and extreme E and NE; irregularly to sw Cape.
Status: Locally abundant nonbreeding Palaearctic migrant, October to March; uncommon and sporadic in Zimbabwe on passage, usually in March; numbers declining.
Habitat: Open grassland.
Habits: Highly gregarious, flocks often numbering hundreds of birds. Flies in loose formation; may hawk insects in flight; also forages on ground, often among cattle dung. Flocks rest on ground, all birds facing into wind.
Food: Insects (especially locust hoppers).
Breeding: Extralimital.

306 (283) Rock Pratincole (Whitecollared Pratincole)   Plate 30
Withalssprinkaanvoël
Glareola nuchalis

[Halsband-Brachschwalbe,   Weißnacken-Brach-schwalbe]

Measurements: Length about 18 cm; wing (10 ♂) 136–143–158, (12 ♀) 138–150–158; tail (3 ♂) 59–61–63, (3 ♀) 58–60–61; tarsus (10 ♂) 14–16–19, (6 ♀) 15–16,3–18; culmen (5 ♂) 10–10–10, (2 ♀) 10–11. Weight 43–52 g.
Bare Parts: Iris brown; bill black, base coral red; legs and feet coral red.
Identification: Size small; mainly grey; white collar from ear coverts around hindneck diagnostic; no throat collar as in other pratincole species; legs red (black in other pratincoles); in flight rump white, tail black, forked. *Immature*: Crown sooty brown; back paler brown, spotted white; collar absent; rump white; tail blackish; chin and throat whitish, streaked brown; underparts pale brown, streaked darker; belly whitish; bill blackish, base orange; legs and feet orange.
Voice: Repeated *kek-kek-kek-kek*; repeated high-pitched *pi-pi-pi-pi* or *twee-twee*.

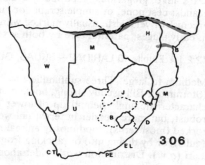

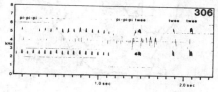

Distribution: Africa S of Sahara to Zambezi and Save Rivers (s Mozambique), and Caprivi (Okavango River).
Status: Fairly common breeding migrant from tropical Africa, July to January; arrives when water levels falling; departs as water levels begin to rise.
Habitat: Larger rivers with midstream rocks and boulders; also lakes.
Habits: Gregarious in flocks of 2–10 birds, rarely up to 200; birds arrive paired. Largely crepuscular, especially during rains. Flits from rock to rock when disturbed; hawks insects in swallowlike flight over water and adjacent forest, often in company with swallows and swifts; foraging flights last 5–8 minutes; may hawk insects around street lights at night. Dis-

plays with collar flared, bill open and head bobbing. Roosts on emergent rocks at low water, otherwise in trees or on fenceposts. **Food:** Insects.

Breeding: *Season*: August to December (mainly September-November) in Zimbabwe. *Nest*: None; eggs laid on ledge (36%), under overhang or in recess (31%), in slight hollow (26%) or flat exposed surface (7%) of bare rock in midstream, surrounded by deep and/or fast-flowing water; usually less than 50 cm above water; solitary or loosely colonial.

Clutch: (135) 1–1,7–2 eggs (rarely 3). *Eggs*: Greyish, brownish green or creamy white, scrawled, spotted and blotched with grey-brown, purplish black, buff and dark grey; measure (66) 29,4 × 21,7 (27,2–32,4 × 20,2–22,8). *Incubation*: 20 days by both sexes; incoming parent soaks belly before nest relief. *Fledging*: 20–30 days; fed by regurgitation by both parents; young swim well at 2–3 days; remain with parents until about 3 months old.

Ref. Williams, G.D., Coppinger, M.P. & Maclean, G.L. 1989. *Ostrich* 60: 55–64.

12:2. Suborder LARI (SKUAS, GULLS, TERNS, SKIMMERS) (Two families, both represented in s Africa)

Medium to large. Mostly marine, some freshwater; bill medium to long, variable in structure according to subfamily or family, usually yellow, orange, red or black; legs short; front toes fully webbed; hind toe rudimentary; plumage mostly grey and white, black and white, or brown; wings long and pointed; tail medium, variable in shape; sexes alike; gregarious; good fliers; usually breed colonially on ground, cliffs, trees or islands; nest none, or simple scrape, or built-up bowl of plant material; eggs 1–4, buff, greenish or yellowish, usually marked with black, brown and grey; chick downy, altricial in early stages; parental care by both sexes. Distribution worldwide.

12:2:1. Family 40 LARIDAE—SKUAS, GULLS, TERNS

Medium to large. Three subfamilies: skuas (Stercorariinae), gulls (Larinae) and terns (Sterninae). Bill usually strong, hooked at tip (skuas and gulls) or pointed (terns), with characteristic angle behind tip of lower jaw; bill black, yellow, red or orange; body robust, but more slender in terns; tail wedge-shaped (skuas), rounded (most gulls) or forked (most terns); food mostly animal matter obtained by piracy (skuas), scavenging (gulls), or by diving into or plucking from water (terns); other features as for suborder Lari (*q.v.*). Distribution worldwide; about 90 species; 36 species in s Africa.

307 (284)   **Arctic Skua**   **Plate 31**
Arktiese Roofmeeu
Stercorarius parasiticus

[Schmarotzerraubmöwe]

Measurements: Length 46–67 cm including tail streamers; wingspan 96–114 cm; wing (16 ♂) 301–320–340, (14 ♀) 317–323,7–341; tail (16 ♂) 164,5–189,9–235, (14 ♀) 164,5–188,9–235; tarsus (16 ♂) 39,5–41,9–45,5, (14 ♀) 39–42,1–45; culmen (16 ♂) 28–31,2–35, (14 ♀) 29–31,8–34,5. Weight (20 ♂) 325–382–448 g, (19 ♀) 325–452–525 g.

Bare Parts: Iris dark brown; bill pinkish brown to greyish black, tip black; cere whitish; legs and feet bluish grey to black.

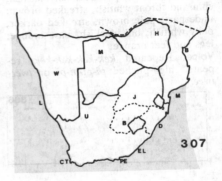

307

Identification: Size medium; gull-like in size and shape, but longer-winged, more falconlike; tail wedge-shaped; 2 central rectrices elongate (not as long as in Longtailed Skua), straight, pointed (rounded and twisted in Pomarine Skua); in flight pale patches in primaries. *Pale form*: Above brown; blackish cap on head (more diffuse than that of Longtailed Skua); below white with brownish wash across breast; sides of neck and head yellowish; undertail brown; upperwing lacks distinct dark trailing edge as in Longtailed Skua. *Dark form*: Sooty brown all over, except for pale wing patches; only length and shape of long central rectrices diagnostic. Intermediate form also occurs. *Immature*: Lacks elongate rectrices; barred above and below.

Voice: Plaintive *kaaau*; yelping *kewow*; low *chuk chuk*.

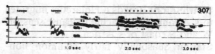

Distribution: Breeds n Holarctic; migrates to tropical and temperate Atlantic, s Indian and Pacific Oceans; all offshore waters of s Africa to about Zululand.

Status: Fairly common nonbreeding Palaearctic migrant, mainly September to April; commoner on W coast than on E coast.

Habitat: Open ocean and inshore waters.

Habits: Usually in pairs or small loose groups. Flies high with much wing flapping; steals food from gulls and terns by attacking singly or in pairs; also gathers around boats at sea for offal.

Food: Fish and offal.

Breeding: Extralimital.

---

308 (–)   **Longtailed Skua**   **Plate 31**
Langstertroofmeeu
Stercorarius longicaudus

[Falkenraubmöwe]

Measurements: Length 41–49 cm (50–58 cm including central rectrices); wingspan 76–84 cm; wing (16 ♂) 295–309,1–327, (6 ♀) 305–313,3–317; longest rectrix (16 ♂) 263–299–350, (6 ♀) 238–295–350; tarsus (16 ♂) 38–41,4–44, (6 ♀) 40–41,8–42,5; culmen (16 ♂) 27–28,6–31,5, (6 ♀) 27,5–28,8–30.

Bare Parts: Iris dark brown; bill pale brown to blackish grey, tip black; cere blue or horn; legs and feet bluish grey, webs and toes distally black.

Identification: Size medium; very similar to Arctic Skua, but smaller and slimmer; wings longer, narrower; central rectrices longer (highly variable and not always certain field distinction). *Pale form*: Above ashy grey, contrasting more with dark hood than in other skuas; dark cap neater than that of Arctic Skua; lacks brownish wash on breast present in other *Stercorarius* species; distinct dark trailing edge to upperwing in flight; very little white in primaries. *Dark form*: Wholly sooty brown; very little white in wings

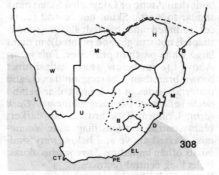

(large white windows in primaries of Arctic Skua). *Immature*: Barred above and below; greyer and paler than immatures of other skuas; lacks tail streamers.

Voice: Usually silent at sea; sharp *kreee*.

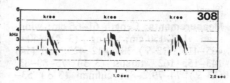

269

Distribution: Breeds n Holarctic; migrates to s Atlantic and Pacific Oceans; seas off W and S coast of s Africa.

Status: Seasonally fairly common non-breeding Palaearctic migrant, summer months.

Habitat: Open ocean, seldom coming inshore.

Habits: Gregarious in small flocks; more pelagic than Arctic Skua. Flight more graceful and ternlike than that of other skuas; less piratical than other skuas.

Food: Fish.

Breeding: Extralimital.

309 (285) Pomarine Skua Plate 31
Knopstertroofmeeu
Stercorarius pomarinus

[Spatelraubmöwe]

Measurements: Length 51–57 cm (65–78 cm including tail streamers); wingspan 122–127 cm; wing (10 ♂) 349–361,9–374, (9 ♀) 351–359,7–370; tail (10 ♂) 172–207,9–243, (9 ♀) 128–181,2–205; tarsus (10 ♂) 48–52–54, (9 ♀) 50–52,1–55; culmen (10 ♂) 38–40,4–43,5, (9 ♀) 38–40,2–44.

Bare Parts: Iris dark brown; bill dull brown, grey or whitish, tip black; legs and feet black, above bluish.

Identification: Size large; more stoutly built than Arctic or Longtailed Skua; most similar to Arctic Skua, but central rectrices rounded and twisted at tip (spoon-shaped, not straight and pointed); in flight large white patch in primaries. *Pale form*: Above brown; below white, with distinct brown breastband, barring on flanks, and undertail; sides of neck and collar behind neck yellow in breeding plumage. *Dark form*: Uniform dark brown, cap darker; blunt central rectrices diagnostic. *Immature*: Barred above and below; very similar to other immature *Stercorarius* skuas; lacks long central rectrices.

Voice: Gull-like *weeu*.

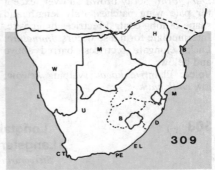

Distribution: Breeds n Holarctic; migrates to s Atlantic, Indian and Pacific Oceans; mainly W coast of s Africa, rarely to Durban.

Status: Uncommon nonbreeding Holarctic migrant, summer months.

Habitat: Mainly open ocean.

Habits: More pelagic than Arctic Skua, seldom coming inshore. Active pirate on other seabirds for food; agile in flight, but less buoyant than smaller skuas; wings held bent at wrist.

Food: Mainly fish.

Breeding: Extralimital.

310 (286) Subantarctic Skua Plate 31
Bruinroofmeeu
Catharacta antarctica

[Skua]

Measurements: Length 61–66 cm; wingspan 147–150 cm; wing (3 ♂) 400–405–415, (13 ♀) 385–412–425; tail (14) 143–153–162; tarsus (3 ♂) 75–80–83, (13 ♀) 74–79,2–82; culmen (3 ♂) 53– 55,7–57, (12 ♀) 51–54,8–58. Weight (61) 1150–1612–2150 g.

Bare Parts: Iris pale to dark brown; bill dark reddish brown to black; legs and feet black.

Identification: Large (about size of Kelp

Gull; larger than South Polar Skua); build stocky; tail rather short, wedge-shaped; bill more massive than that of South Polar Skua; mostly brown (darker than more golden light-form South Polar Skua; more like dark form) with conspicuous white patches in wings in flight; sometimes tinged rufous below; somewhat hoary appearance in worn plumage but always white blotches on back; in breeding season feathers of cheeks and nape tipped golden, forming light collar. *Immature*: More uniform brown than adult, usually tinged rufous below.

Voice: Plaintive *kwee-kek-kek*; harsh *charr charr charr*.

Distribution: Breeds Subantarctic islands in Southern Ocean; migrates northward to temperate and tropical seas; mainly W coast of s Africa, less often as far NE as s Mozambique.

Status: Regular but uncommon nonbreeding migrant from Subantarctic, mainly April to July.

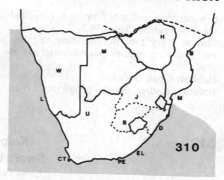

Habitat: Open ocean; less often inshore and into harbours.

Habits: Somewhat solitary, less gregarious than South Polar Skua. Highly aggressive, attacking seabirds up to size of large albatrosses which regurgitate food that skua catches before it reaches water; also scavenges around fishing boats for offal; preys on seabird colonies.

Food: Regurgitated fish, squid, etc. from other seabirds; offal, carrion, fish, crustaceans, cephalopods, eggs and young of colonial seabirds.

Breeding: Extralimital.

Ref. Brooke, R.K. 1978. *Durban Mus. Novit.* 11:295–308.
Devillers, P. 1977. *Auk* 94:417–429.

---

311 (–) South Polar Skua
Suidpoolroofmeeu
Catharacta maccormicki

Plate 31

[Antarktische Raubmöwe]

Measurements: Length 53–61 cm; wingspan 127 cm; wing (80) 373–394–412; tail (2) 145–150; tarsus (80) 58,5–63,8–70; culmen (80) 42,6–46,6–49,6. Weight (80) 968–1156–1370 g.

Bare Parts: Iris brown; bill, legs and feet blackish grey.

Identification: Size medium; smaller than Subantarctic Skua; bill slender and delicate (heavy in Subantarctic Skua); usually much paler overall than Subantarctic Skua, but plumage variable; all plumages have white patch in wing, conspicuous in flight. *Pale form*: Head, neck and underparts pale greyish or pinkish brown to whitish, plain or mottled, contrasting with blackish wings (diagnostic); nape always pale; golden streaks on nape and sides of neck sometimes conspicuous; rest of upperparts uniform blackish brown. *Dark form*: Head, neck and underparts dark blackish brown; upperparts somewhat darker; no pale area on nape; golden streaks on nape and sides of neck conspicuous. *Immature*: Lacks golden streaks on nape; bill and legs light bluish (bill tip black).

Voice: Usually silent at sea; low plaintive quacking at nest; challenging *charr charr charr*.

Distribution: Breeds Antarctic mainland and adjacent islands; migrates northward

to subtropics and n hemisphere; recorded Cape St Francis, May 1963.
Status: Very rare nonbreeding vagrant, but could be regular passage migrant at sea.
Habitat: Open ocean.
Habits: Rather more gregarious than

Subantarctic Skua. Other habits similar to those of Subantarctic Skua.
Food: As for Subantarctic Skua.
Breeding: Extralimital.

Ref. Brooke, R.K. 1978. *Durban Mus. Novit.* 11:295–308.
Devillers, P. 1977. *Auk* 94:417–429.

312 (287)   Kelp Gull   Plate 31
Swartrugmeeu
Larus dominicanus

Ingaba-ngaba (X), [Dominikanermöwe]

Measurements: Length 56–60 cm; wingspan 127–132 cm; wing (13 ♂) 419–429–452, (25 ♀) 395–414–438; tail (9) 152–162–170; tarsus (13 ♂) 66–68,6–75, (25 ♀) 60,5–65,1–70; culmen (13 ♂) 54–57,4–61,5, (25 ♀) 50–52,5–54,5. Weight (3 ♂) 1060–1080–1096 g, (3 ♀) 870–935–970 g, (17 unsexed) 780–924,3–1047 g.
Bare Parts: Iris light grey, straw yellow, hazel or brown; eyering red to orange; bill bright yellow, patch of scarlet near tip of lower jaw; legs and feet greenish grey, joints darker.
Identification: Size large; mostly white; wings and back black; legs greenish or bluish grey, iris grey, rarely yellowish (both yellowish in Lesser Blackbacked Gull). *Immature*: Mottled brownish grey and whitish; rump barred; tail blackish; later plumage progressively whiter; dark terminal band on white tail; bill light greyish, tip black. *Chick*: Mottled blackish on grey; bare parts blackish.
Voice: Plaintive screaming *meew*; staccato *ko-ko-ko-ko-ko*.

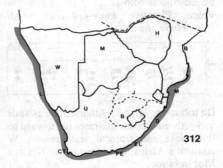

312

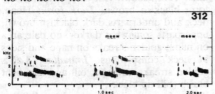

312

Distribution: S America, s Africa, Madagascar, s Australia, New Zealand, Subantarctic islands; in s Africa mainly on W and S coasts, as far NE as Maputo.

Status: Very common resident; some seasonal movements on E coast; numbers increasing.
Habitat: Estuaries, coastal beaches, offshore waters, rubbish dumps; rare inland.
Habits: Solitary or gregarious. Forages on beaches, over water or on dumps, walking or flying; follows ships up to 200 km from land for scraps. Flight slow and leisurely with much gliding. Drops molluscs from air onto rocks to break them.
Food: Fish, offal, sandmussels, limpets, insects, birds' eggs and young.
Breeding: *Season*: September to March (mainly November). *Nest*: Scrape on ground, more or less built up with grass, twigs, feathers and seaweed; usually next to rock or bush; on rocky islets, cliffs, dunes; also rarely on some inland waters (Rondevlei and De Hoop Vlei, sw Cape). *Clutch*: (80) 1–2,1–3 eggs. *Eggs*: Pale olive, green, turquoise or ochre-brown, spotted and blotched with brown, black and grey; measure (412)

70,7 × 48,3 (62,5–80,7 × 42,2–53,8); weigh (88) 74,5–89,5–108,5 g. *Incubation*: 26–28 days by both sexes. *Nestling*: Variable; young semi-precocial, leaving nest when disturbed; only 1–2 young reared, by both parents; fly at 6–7 weeks; independent at 7–8 weeks;

weight at hatching (68) 49,5–63,4–77 g.

Ref. Burger, J. & Gochfeld, M. 1981. *Ibis* 123:298–310.
Crawford, R.J.M., Cooper, J. & Shelton, P.A. 1982. *Ostrich* 53:164–177.
Williams, A.J., Cooper, J. & Hockey, P.A.R. 1984. *Ostrich* 55:147–157.

313 (287X) Lesser Blackbacked Gull Plate 31
Kleinswartrugmeeu
Larus fuscus

[Heringsmöwe]

Measurements: Length 51–61 cm; wingspan 127 cm; wing ♂ 420–450, ♀ 405–420; tail ♂ 145–160; tarsus ♂ 59–66; culmen ♂ 50–55, ♀ 46–49.

Bare Parts: Iris pale cream to white; eyering red to orange; bill yellow with red patch near tip of lower jaw; legs and feet yellow.

Identification: Similar to Kelp Gull, but smaller; mainly white; wings and back black; legs bright yellow or greenish yellow (blue-grey or green-grey in Kelp Gull); in flight white trailing edge of upperwing narrower than in Kelp Gull. *Immature*: Coarsely mottled brown; head paler; tail with broad black band and very narrow white tip; legs pinkish brown; bill blackish at first, later pale greyish with black tip.

Voice: Harsh mewing; deep *kokokokok*.

Distribution: Breeds w Palaearctic; migrates to s Europe, Arabia, Africa; in s Africa regular on middle Zambezi (especially Kariba) and W of Victoria Falls;

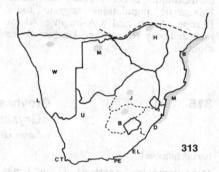

also other waters in Zimbabwe, C Transvaal, Orange Free State Goldfields; regular straggler on E coast as far S as Durban.
Status: Uncommon nonbreeding Palaearctic migrant, October to March; some birds overwinter; rare straggler to S Africa.
Habitat: Inland and coastal waters.
Habits: Usually gregarious; often solitary in s Africa. Scavenges from surface of water in flight, or settles on water to pick up offal; also wades in surf to catch crabs and scraps; may pirate food from other seabirds; rarely swoops down for fish.
Food: Offal, scraps, dead fish, crabs, molluscs, worms.
Breeding: Extralimital.

314 (–) Herring Gull Plate 74
Haringmeeu
Larus argentatus

[Silbermöwe]

Measurements: Length 56–66 cm; wingspan 132 cm; wing 410–450; tail 158–180; tarsus 63–68; culmen 47–53.
Bare Parts: Iris white to yellow; eyering

vermilion; bill yellow with red patch near tip of lower jaw; legs and feet bright yellow (pink or bluish in some subspecies).
Identification: Large (about size of Kelp

Gull); white with silver-grey back and black-tipped wings with white spots; in flight grey upperwing has narrow white leading and trailing edge; bill yellow; legs yellowish.

Voice: Plaintive mewing *kee-ew*; sonorous *ka-ka-ka-ka*.

Distribution: Breeds Holarctic; some Palaearctic populations migrate to s Europe, Africa and s Asia; in s Africa recorded only Umvoti and Umgeni River mouths.

Status: Very rare nonbreeding Palaearctic vagrant, not normally recorded further S than E Africa; Durban, November 1976. Sometimes considered to be race of Lesser Blackbacked Gull.

Habitat: Estuaries and marine shores; rare inland.

Habits: Usually gregarious, but solitary in s Africa. Scavenges around harbours and seashore, settling on water to pick up food; swims buoyantly. Roosts on sheltered sandbars. Flight strong and light, with leisurely wingbeats and effortless gliding.

Food: Fish offal, molluscs, crabs, insects.

Breeding: Extralimital.

---

315 (288)   Greyheaded Gull   Plate 31
Gryskopmeeu
Larus cirrocephalus

[Graukopfmöwe]

Measurements: Length 41–43 cm; wingspan 102 cm; wing (24) 285–311–329; tail 110–118–127; tarsus 44–48,3–51; culmen 35–38,4–41. Weight (50) 211–279,6–377 g.

Bare Parts: Iris yellowish white; eyering, bill, legs and feet crimson (legs and feet dark red when not breeding).

Identification: Smaller than Kelp Gull. *Breeding*: White with grey head, back and upperwing; wingtip black with white spots; bill and legs red. *Nonbreeding*: Similar, but lacks grey on head (except at times as faint grey crescent behind ear); bill much brighter red than that of Hartlaub's Gull, and overall size larger; eye whitish (brown in Hartlaub's Gull). Hybridizes with Hartlaub's Gull. *Immature*: Mottled ashy brown on back and crown; ear coverts brownish; black subterminal bar on tail; underparts white; bill pinkish, tip dark; legs and feet dull red to brown. *Chick*: Light grey, mottled with black; centre of crown almost plain grey; iris blackish brown; bill blackish; legs and feet slate, tinged reddish.

Voice: Harsh raucous *kraaa*; staccato *ka-ka-ka-ka* or *krrup*.

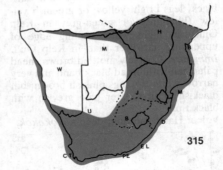

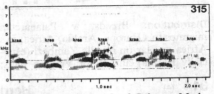

Distribution: Africa S of Sahara, Madagascar, S America; in s Africa both coastal and inland, absent only from waterless parts of Kalahari, Karoo and Namibia.

Status: Common to abundant resident or local migrant; Transvaal birds come from sw Cape, Orange Free State, Harare, Angola and Maputo (probably postbreeding dispersal); dry-season visitor to Zimbabwe, mainly July to October; uncommon in sw Cape.

Habitat: Larger dams, pans, estuaries, coastal lakes, seashore.

Habits: Gregarious; nonbreeding flocks 5–20 birds; breeding flocks may number hundreds; rarely solitary. Forages in loose flocks over water, on shore or on rubbish dumps and in picnic sites; swims and flies gracefully and buoyantly. Very noisy at breeding colonies.

Food: Offal, scraps, fish, insects, birds' eggs and young.

Breeding: *Season*: July to October in Zim-babwe, March to November in Transvaal; mainly June to November throughout s Africa. *Nest*: Shallow bowl of grass, weeds and twigs; on flat ground, often next to grasstuft or other plant; on islands, protected shorelines, old Redknobbed Coot nests; in colonies of several dozen nests. *Clutch*: 2–3 eggs. *Eggs*: Blue-green, olive or rich brown, spotted and blotched with brown and grey; measure (113) 53,8 × 37,3 (48,6–58,6 × 33–40,7). *Incubation*: Unrecorded; by both sexes. *Nestling*: Variable; young leave nest when disturbed; flying age unrecorded.

316 (289) Hartlaub's Gull Plate 31
Hartlaubse Meeu (Sterretjie)
Larus hartlaubii

[Hartlaubsmöwe, Weißkopflachmöwe]

Measurements: Length 36–38 cm; wingspan 92 cm; wing (7) 267–277–295; tail 102–106–112; tarsus 42–44,7–47; culmen 32–35–38,5. Weight (18) 235–292–340 g.

Bare Parts: Iris brown to golden brown; eyering, bill, legs and feet dark red (reddish black when not breeding).

Identification: Size smallish; mostly white; back grey; wingtips black with white spots; bill and legs dark red (brighter red in Greyheaded Gull); iris dark (white in Greyheaded Gull); most breeding birds have pale lavender hood bordered by darker grey line from hindcrown to throat. Hybridizes with Greyheaded Gull. *Immature*: Similar to that of Greyheaded Gull, but seldom has black subterminal tailband; bill and legs dark brown.

Voice: Strident *kwarrr*; staccato *kek-kek-kek-kek* and *krruk*.

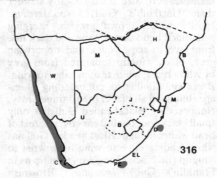

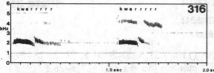

Distribution: Coastal Namibia and w Cape; vagrant to e Cape and Natal.

Status: Very common resident; numbers increasing.

Habitat: Seashore, offshore islands, city centre (Cape Town), rubbish dumps, cultivated farmland, estuaries.

Habits: Highly gregarious. Frequents human habitations, gardens, parks and restaurants for scraps; usually fairly tame, but wary; also follows fishing vessels for offal, but seldom far out to sea; follows ploughs for soil invertebrates; catches insects at streetlights at night; forages by wading in shallow water. Often bathes in urban ponds and fountains. Roosts on rooftops, ledges and islands.

Food: Offal, scraps, dead fish, insects, earthworms.

Breeding: *Season*: April to September. *Nest*: Bowl of roots, grass, twigs, bleached snail shells; on ground, often next to shrub; colonial, usually on offshore islands; also on roofs of tall buildings in Cape Town; in colonies of 10–1 000 pairs. *Clutch*: (1 962) 1–1,8–5 eggs (usually 1–3). *Eggs*: Greenish ochre to pale brown, spotted and blotched with darker brown and grey; measure (100) 52,2 × 37,1 (47,4–56,9 × 34,1–40,3). *Incubation*: About 25 days by both sexes. *Nestling*: About 40 days.

317 (–) Franklin's Gull
Franklinse Meeu
Larus pipixcan

Plate 31

[Franklins Möwe]

Measurements: Length 34–38 cm; wingspan 89 cm; wing (15 ♂) 274–288,7–302, (14 ♀) 270–282,9–293; tail (15 ♂) 90–103,5–115, (14 ♀) 91–98,2–105; tarsus (5 ♂) 38–40,8–42,5, (4 ♀) 39–39,9–41; culmen (15 ♂) 28–31,6–34, (14 ♀) 26,3–29,9–34,5.
Bare Parts: Iris brown; bill, legs and feet deep red.
Identification: Size small (slightly smaller than Hartlaub's Gull). *Nonbreeding*: Mostly white; crown greyish, merging with black band across nape and dark line from eye to nape; back and upperwing grey, black wingtip separated from grey by white band; white trailing edge to wing. *Breeding*: Similar to nonbreeding plumage, but head all black; breast tinged rosy. Nonbreeding Blackheaded Gull has only small black spot behind ear coverts, rest of head white; in flight Blackheaded Gull has white leading edge to wing from wrist to wingtip (no black triangle on wingtip as in Franklin's Gull). *Immature*: Brownish above and on hindcrown; primaries all blackish; secondaries brown with white trailing edge; black subterminal band on white tail; bill dusky; legs and feet dull red.
Voice: High-pitched nasal *kaar, kaar*; shrill *kuk-kuk-kuk*.

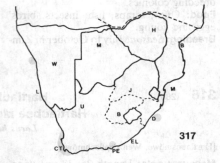

Distribution: Breeds N America; migrates to S America; vagrant to sw Cape, e Cape, Natal.
Status: Very rare nonbreeding vagrant, all months, but mainly late summer.
Habitat: Marine shores and open ocean when not breeding.
Habits: Gregarious in S America; probably solitary in s Africa. Floats high on water; flight light and billowy.
Food: Marine invertebrates; scraps, offal.
Breeding: Extralimital.

318 (289X) Sabine's Gull
Mikstertmeeu
Larus sabini

Plate 31

[Schwalbenmöwe]

Measurements: Length 30–36 cm; wingspan 86 cm; wing (13 ♂) 263–275–286, (9 ♀) 258–266,7–276; tail, outer rectrices (11 ♂) 111–120,9–130, (7 ♀) 111–115,2–126, inner rectrices (3 ♂) 84–90–98; tarsus (11 ♂) 31,5–33,2–34,5, (7 ♀) 28–31–32; culmen (13 ♂) 25,1–27,3–28,5, (9 ♀) 25–26,6–29,8. Weight (2 ♂) 164–174 g, (2 ♀) 168–170 g.
Bare Parts: Iris dark brown; eyering vermilion; bill black, tip yellow; legs and

feet brownish to dusky pink, webs yellow-ish.

Identification: Size small; tail forked, white; in flight primary coverts and primaries mostly black, forming black triangle at wingtip; innermost primaries, trailing edge and secondaries white; coverts mostly grey like back; yellow-tipped black bill diagnostic at close range. *Nonbreeding*: Head white with blackish nape joined to eye by narrow dark line. *Breeding*: Head dark grey, separated from white neck by narrow black border. *Immature*: Similar to adult, but back, hindneck and hindcrown brown; tail tipped black.

Voice: Harsh grating ternlike cry.

Distribution: Breeds n Holarctic; migrates to oceans off S America and Africa; recorded all coasts of Namibia and S Africa.

Status: Locally common nonbreeding Holarctic migrant, November to April; immatures present also throughout winter.

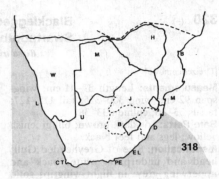

Habitat: Open ocean.

Habits: Gregarious and pelagic, usually in small groups of up to 20 birds; also in larger flocks of up to 60 birds, but up to 4 000 can be seen regularly off sw Cape coast (Mouille Point). Often accompanies Grey Phalaropes. Flight graceful, ternlike; settles on water to feed.

Food: Mainly marine invertebrates.

Breeding: Extralimital.

319 (–) Blackheaded Gull Plate 74
Swartkopmeeu
Larus ridibundus

[Lachmöwe]

Measurements: Length 38–43 cm; wingspan 92 cm; wing ♂ 295–315, ♀ 285–302; tail ♂ 110–125; tarsus ♂ 43–49; culmen ♂ 31–36, ♀ 29–33.

Bare Parts: Iris dark brown or red-brown; bill, legs and feet deep crimson.

Identification: Size smallish (smaller than Greyheaded Gull). *Nonbreeding*: Very like Greyheaded Gull, but with black spot in front of eye and behind ear coverts; in flight wingtip narrowly bordered black; long triangle of white from wrist to outer primaries (Greyheaded Gull has mostly black wingtip with small white spots). *Breeding*: Head dark blackish brown.

Voice: Sharp *kriaa*; various raucous cries.

Distribution: Breeds Palaearctic; migrates to Mediterranean, Red Sea, Persian Gulf, India, China, Japan; vagrant to s Africa (recorded Johannesburg and Beira).

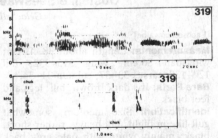

Status: Very rare nonbreeding Palaearctic vagrant, November-December; populations increasing and range expanding in recent years.

Habitat: Inland and coastal waters.

Habits: Usually gregarious; occurs in mixed flocks with Greyheaded Gull, so may be overlooked. Similar to Greyheaded Gull.

Food: Fish, prawns, offal, insects, worms, molluscs; also young shoots of growing grain.

Breeding: Extralimital.

320 (–)   Blacklegged Kittiwake   Plate 74
Swartpootbrandervoël
Rissa tridactyla

[Dreizehenmöwe]

Measurements: Length 39–41 cm; wingspan 92 cm; wing 300–325; tail 112–127; tarsus 33–36; culmen 33–38.

Bare Parts: Iris dark brown; bill greenish yellow: legs and feet black.

Identification: Size of Greyheaded Gull; head and underparts white; back and upperwing grey; in flight wingtips solid black (no white spots as in Greyheaded Gull), contiguous with grey upperwing; narrow white trailing edge (no such trailing edge in Greyheaded and Hartlaub's Gulls); underwing white (underwing grey in Greyheaded Gull). *Immature*: Has black terminal tailband, more extensive black from wingtips across upperwing to back (forms open W pattern in flight), black collar on hindneck, black spot on ear coverts, and blackish mottling on upper secondary coverts; mainly grey above; tail square or very slightly forked; inner primaries and secondaries grey; (immature Sabine's Gull brown above; tail slightly forked; inner primaries and secondaries white).

Voice: 3-syllabled onomatopoeic *kitteewaaak*; mewing moan *aaaaa*.

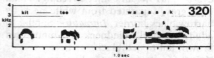

Distribution: Breeds n Holarctic; migrates to United States, Mediterranean, Japan; probably regular at sea off Cape Town.

Status: Rare nonbreeding Palaearctic migrant, December to February.

Habitat: Open ocean.

Habits: Usually gregarious. Flight light and buoyant, usually low over water. Follows ships in small flocks.

Food: Fish and other marine organisms; offal.

Breeding: Extralimital.

321 (290X)   Gullbilled Tern   Plate 32
Oostelike Seeswael (Oostelike Sterretjie)
Gelochelidon nilotica

[Lachseeschwalbe]

Measurements: Length about 38–41 cm; wingspan 86 cm; wing 315–332; tail 120–138; tarsus 33–37; culmen 31–34.

Bare Parts: Iris dark brown; bill, legs and feet black.

Identification: Size medium; somewhat gull-like in flight; bill heavy, rather short, black; mainly white with pale grey back and upperwing; cap black when breeding (crown and nape white, faintly speckled black, when not breeding; thick black stripe behind eye only); tail slightly forked; looks long-legged at rest.

Voice: High-pitched scolding *hik hik-hik-hik-hik*.

Distribution: Breeds s N America, Caribbean, S America, Palaearctic, s Asia, Australasia; migrates to tropics when not breeding; vagrant to s Africa.

Status: Rare nonbreeding Palaearctic migrant, not usually coming further S than E Africa; in s Africa recorded various inland and coastal localities, December, January, June, July.

Habitat: Mainly larger inland lakes and pans; less often on coast.

Habits: Solitary or gregarious, sometimes in company with other terns. Forages over water or land, dipping down to pick food from surface or off plants; may attend grassfires to hawk insects in flight. Rests in flocks on sandbanks and shorelines.

Food: Crustaceans, fish, frogs, lizards, offal.

Breeding: Extralimital.

322 (290) Caspian Tern
Reuseseeswael (Reusesterretjie)
Hydroprogne caspia

Plate 32

[Raubseeschwalbe]

Measurements: Length 48–56 cm; wingspan 135 cm; wing 380–425; tail, outer rectrices 135–150, central rectrices 98–110; tarsus 40–47; culmen 64–72.

Bare Parts: Iris dark brown; bill bright red (breeding) or dull red with blackish tip (nonbreeding); legs and feet black.

Identification: Size large; large red bill diagnostic; underparts white; cap black (streaked black-and-white when not breeding); back and upperwing grey; tail slightly forked; undersurface of primaries black. *Immature*: Mottled brownish on back. *Chick*: Above buffy grey; below off-white; bill light coral, tip black; legs and feet blackish slate.

Voice: Raucous *kraka-kraaa* and *kraaak*; rapid *kak-kak-kak-kak*; long plaintive whistle.

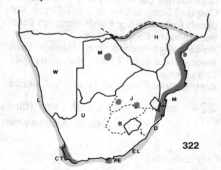

322

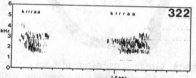

322

Distribution: Africa, Holarctic, Australasia; in s Africa at scattered coastal and inland localities.

Status: Locally common resident on coast; uncommon inland; irregular on Middle Zambezi, probably migrating from S African coasts. Rare (RDB).

Habitat: Estuaries, marine shores, larger inland dams and pans.

Habits: Solitary or in small flocks. Flight leisurely, somewhat gull-like. Hovers with bill pointing downward, then plunges for food; usually submerges completely; swallows food in flight. Rarely alights on water; rests on shoreline, sometimes with other species of terns.

Food: Fish, 5–240 g (mostly 10–20 g).

Breeding: *Localities*: Vaaldam, Barberspan, Lake St Lucia, Robben Island, Bredasdorp, Saldanha Bay, Berg River, Zambezi River. *Season*: Usually July-August; also December-January. *Nest*: Shallow scrape, 22–29 cm diameter, 2,5–5 cm deep; lined with small stones and other loose material; on ground, sometimes next to grasstuft; solitary or in small loose colonies. *Clutch*: (85) 1–2–3 eggs (usually 2). *Eggs*: Sandy to stone or greenish cream, spotted and blotched with dark brown, purplish and mauve; measure (73) 63,8 × 44 (56,8–69,2 × 40,4–47,4); weigh (19) 52–63,3–72 g. *Incubation*: 20–22 days by both sexes. *Nestling*: Unrecorded.

323 (–) Royal Tern
Koningseeswael (Koningsterretjie)
Sterna maxima

Plate 74

[Königsseeschwalbe]

Measurements: Length 48–50 cm; wingspan 109 cm; wing (6) 335–352,8–365; tail 145–163–172; tarsus 30–31,2–33; culmen 62–65–68.

Bare Parts: Iris dark brown; bill orange or yellow-orange; legs and feet black.

Identification: Size large (similar to Swift Tern; much larger than Lesser Crested Tern); slightly smaller, shorter-legged and more slimly built than Caspian Tern; below white; back and upperwing grey (much paler than in Swift Tern); cap black, crested behind (nonbreeding birds have white forehead, streaked crown, black from behind each eye across hindcrown); forehead sometimes white in breeding birds also; large orange bill diagnostic (bill rich red in Caspian Tern, yellow in Swift Tern); tail deeply forked; in flight underwing tips paler than those of Caspian Tern.

Voice: High-pitched *keer* (higher than voice of Caspian Tern); also sharp *kak* and *chirrup*.

Distribution: Coasts of N and S America

from Virginia to Peru and Argentina, Caribbean, W Africa; vagrant to coast of Namibia (Walvis Bay).

Status: Very rare nonbreeding vagrant from W Africa.

Habitat: Sandy seashores and inshore waters.

Habits: Gregarious. Flies with slow wingbeats; dives for food at sea.

Food: Almost entirely fish.

Breeding: Extralimital.

324 (298) Swift Tern (Greater Crested Tern) Plate 32
Geelbekseeswael (Geelbeksterretjie)
Sterna bergii

[Eilseeschwalbe]

Measurements: Length 46–50 cm; wingspan 109 cm; wing (25) 322–345,4–374,5; tail (17) 163,5–173,8–184; tarsus (27) 26–29,2–32; culmen (27) 54,5–58,2–65,5. Weight (3 ♂) 325–340–350 g, (1 ♀) 350 g.

Bare Parts: Iris dark brown; bill yellow or greenish yellow; legs and feet black, soles sometimes yellow.

Identification: Size fairly large, somewhat smaller than Caspian Tern; forehead and underparts white (forehead black in Lesser Crested Tern); cap black (speckled when not breeding), crested behind; back and upperwing grey; bill yellow, drooping (diagnostic; orange in Lesser Crested and Royal Terns); tail deeply forked; in flight wings long and narrow. *Immature*: Heavily blotched and barred black and white above.

Voice: Loud screaming *kreee-kreee*; staccato *rak-rak-rak*; harsh *zeek zeek*.

Distribution: Southern Africa, Madagascar, Indian Ocean islands to Australasia, se China and w Pacific; s African coasts from Swakopmund to Mozambique.

Status: Common resident; wanders widely after breeding.

Habitat: Marine shores, estuaries.

Habits: Gregarious, often in flocks of up to 50 birds; sometimes in company with gulls or other tern species. Flight graceful, wingbeats quick. Feeds by plunge-diving and by dipping to surface of water.

Food: Mainly fish (86%); also cephalopods, crustaceans, insects; prey length 7–138 mm, weight 0,1–30 g.

Breeding: *Season*: February to October. *Nest*: Shallow scrape on flat open ground, sometimes lined with dry grass; colonial; on offshore islands and manmade islands in vleis and pans near coast; sometimes in mixed colony with Hartlaub's Gulls. *Clutch*: (20) 1–1,3–2 eggs. *Eggs*: Cream, buff, pale pink, turquoise or whitish, blotched and streaked with brown and deep mauve; measure (111) 61,8 × 42,9 (55,4–66,8 × 39,3–45,3). *Incubation*: Unrecorded. *Nestling*: 35–40 days.

Ref. Uys, C.J. 1978. *Bokmakierie* 30:64–66.
Walter, C.B., Cooper, J. & Suter, W. 1987. *Ostrich* 58:49–53.

325 (297)
Lesser Crested Tern
Kuifkopseeswael (Kuifkopsterretjie)
Sterna bengalensis
Plate 32

[Rüppell-Seeschwalbe]

Measurements: Length 36–41 cm; wingspan 89 cm; wing (2) 260–275; tail 103–123; tarsus 23–24; culmen 50–53.
Bare Parts: Iris dark brown; bill orange-yellow to orange; legs and feet black, soles yellowish.
Identification: Size medium; bill usually orange (yellow in Swift Tern), fairly heavy; underparts white; crown and forehead black (forehead white in Swift Tern); nonbreeding birds have forecrown white, hindcrown speckled in front with black crest behind, and black spot in front of eye; upperparts grey; in flight wingtips darker than in Swift Tern. *Immature*: Mottled with brown on back and upperwing.
Voice: Various screaming and chattering calls; sharp *chirruk*.
Distribution: Breeds coasts of Mediterranean, Red Sea, s Asia and Australia; migrates to s Africa and Madagascar; mainly confined to E coast as far S as Durban; vagrant to Knysna and sw Cape.

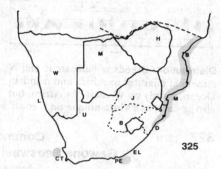

Status: Fairly common nonbreeding Palaearctic and n Indian Ocean migrant, mostly in summer; some birds overwinter.
Habitat: Estuaries and offshore waters.
Habits: Gregarious, often in company with other species of terns. Flies with graceful measured wingbeats. Rests on sandbanks with other terns, often in groups of up to 20 birds; roosts in shallow water at night.
Food: Fish and crustaceans.
Breeding: Extralimital.

326 (296)
Sandwich Tern
Grootseeswael (Grootsterretjie)
Sterna sandvicensis
Plate 32

[Brandseeschwalbe]

Measurements: Length 41–46 cm; wingspan 94 cm; wing (14) 267–311,4–325; tail, outer rectrices (14) 105–126,4–170, central rectrices 72–85; tarsus (14) 24–26,4–30; culmen (14) 46–52,6–58. Weight (30) 215–267–275 g.
Bare Parts: Iris dark brown; bill black, tip light yellow; legs and feet black.
Identification: Size medium to fairly large; slender black bill with yellow tip diagnostic; underparts white; forehead and crown black (forecrown white, hindcrown streaked when not breeding); upperparts pale grey; rump white; looks generally very pale, tinged pink in breeding plum-

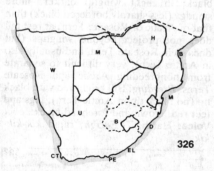

age. *Immature*: Has largely brown forehead, mottled upperparts and slate-grey tail.

Voice: Loud grating *kirrik*, strident and rasping.

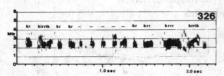

Distribution: Breeds w Palaearctic and N America; migrates to Africa and n Indian Ocean; mainly on W coast of s Africa, but also as far N as s Mozambique on E coast.

Status: Common nonbreeding Palaearctic migrant, August to April; some birds overwinter; ringed birds from France, Denmark, United Kingdom.
Habitat: Marine shores, estuaries.
Habits: Highly gregarious, flocks numbering hundreds of birds. Very noisy, even at night. Gathers in large flocks on coastal rocks and estuarine sandbanks, often in company with other tern species. Plunges or swoops for food; flight rather gull-like.
Food: Fish, worms, crustaceans.
Breeding: Extralimital.

---

327 (291)   **Common Tern**   **Plate 32**
Gewone Seeswael (Gewone Sterretjie)
Sterna hirundo

Unothenteza (X), [Flußseeschwalbe]

Measurements: Length 32–38 cm; wingspan 79 cm; wing (10) 233–288; tail, outer rectrices 135–175, central rectrices 65–87; tarsus (10) 18–20; culmen (10) 33–39,5. Weight (323) 93–124–155 g.
Bare Parts: Iris dark brown; bill (breeding) scarlet, tip black, (nonbreeding) black, base sometimes red; legs and feet (breeding) vermilion, (nonbreeding) red to red-brown.
Identification: Size smallish. *Nonbreeding*: Bill black; legs and feet dull red; bill and leg proportionately longer than in Arctic Tern; underparts white; upperparts pale grey including rump (rump white in Arctic Tern); forehead white; crown black; in flight wingtip darker, more smudgy (less sharply bordered black) than that of Arctic or Roseate Tern; at rest tail does not project beyond wingtips (but does so in Roseate Tern, and usually also in Arctic Tern); very difficult to separate from nonbreeding Arctic and Roseate Terns. *Breeding*: Bill bright red with black tip (no black tip in Arctic Tern); legs and feet red; crown and forehead black.
Voice: Harsh *KEEarrgh*; rapid *kik-kik-kik*.

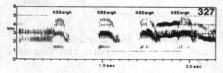

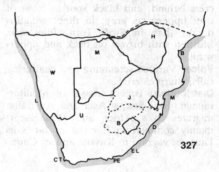

Distribution: Breeds Holarctic; migrates to s hemisphere; coastal s Africa from Namibia to about Bazaruto Island, Mozambique.
Status: Very common nonbreeding Palaearctic migrant, August to April; some birds overwinter; ringed birds from United Kingdom, Finland, Denmark, Germany. Because of difficulty of separating Common and Arctic Terns in field, they are jointly called "Comic" Terns.
Habitat: Marine shores, estuaries.
Habits: Highly gregarious. Plunges for food; flight swallowlike, buoyant. Roosts

on estuarine sandbanks, boats, rocks, often in company with other tern species. Covers 80–110 km/day on migration.

Food: Mainly fish; also crustaceans, molluscs, insects.
Breeding: Extralimital.

328 (294) Arctic Tern Plate 32
Arktiese Seeswael (Arktiese Sterretjie)
Sterna paradisaea

Unothenteza (X), [Küstenseeschwalbe]

Measurements: Length 33–41 cm; wingspan 79 cm; wing (22 ♂) 257–272,5–290, (16 ♀) 238–263,1–277; tail, outer rectrices (22 ♂) 148–176,8–202,5, (16 ♀) 135–165,5–193, central rectrices ♂ 70–80, ♀ 66–75; tarsus (22 ♂) 13,5–14,9–16, (16 ♀) 13,5–14,4–15,5; culmen (22 ♂) 29,5–33,2–42, (16 ♀) 28–31,1–35. Weight (39) 76–94–120 g.
Bare Parts: Iris dark brown; bill (breeding) blood red, (nonbreeding) black; legs and feet (breeding) coral red, (nonbreeding) black.
Identification: Size small to medium; very similar to Common Tern, but bill relatively shorter. *Nonbreeding*: Like Common Tern; bill black (shorter than that of Common Tern); wingtips paler than those of Common Tern, more sharply bordered black above and below (underwing tip of Roseate Tern plain white); tail slightly longer than that of Common Tern, deeply forked; wingtips extend about to end of tail at rest (tail of Roseate Tern extends well beyond folded wingtips); difficult to tell apart from Common Tern. *Breeding*: Pale pearl grey below, separated from black cap by white cheeks; bill usually wholly red (tipped black in Common Tern and mostly black in Roseate Tern); outer rectrices dark grey (tail all white in Antarctic and Roseate Terns).
Voice: Similar to voice of Common Tern, but harsher, more nasal, accented on 2nd syllable *keeAARGH*; staccato *ki-ki-ki-ki*.

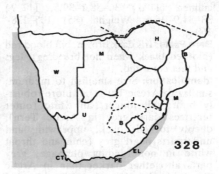

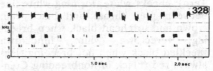

Distribution: Breeds n Holarctic; migrates to southern oceans and Antarctica; around coasts of s Africa as far as Natal.

Status: Very common nonbreeding Holarctic migrant on W coast, rare on E coast, July to November (probably on passage southward); again in May (on passage northward); ringed birds from Labrador and Greenland recovered Margate, Natal, and Doringbaai, Cape, respectively.

Habitat: Open ocean, marine shores (vagrant inland).

Habits: Highly gregarious, flocks numbering hundreds of birds; often in company with other species of terns, especially Common Terns. Flight rather direct.

Food: Krill, small fish.

Breeding: Extralimital.

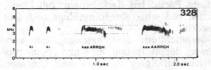

329 (292)   Antarctic Tern   Plate 32
Grysborsseeswael (Grysborssterretjie)
Sterna vittata

[Gabelschwanz-Seeschwalbe]

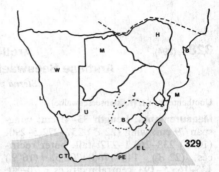

Measurements: Length 38–41 cm; wingspan 79 cm; wing (11 ♂) 245–258–274, (16 ♀) 236–255–272; tail (7 ♂) 166–180–196, (10 ♀) 162–173–189; tarsus (11 ♂) 19–20,2–22, (14 ♀) 18–19,8–21,4; culmen (11 ♂) 36–38,1–39,5, (12 ♀) 33–34,9–36,6. Weight (85) 105–128–160 g.

Bare Parts: Iris dark brown; bill blood red (mottled black when not breeding); legs and feet coral red.

Identification: Size smallish to medium; similar to Arctic Tern, but more robustly built; tail longer, all white (outer rectrices dark grey in Arctic Tern), deeply forked; back, upperwing and underparts pearl grey (chin and throat white in nonbreeding plumage; grey parts altogether darker than in Arctic Tern); cheeks white, forming white line between grey throat and black cap; crown and forehead black when breeding; forecrown white, hindcrown speckled black when not breeding; legs always red (black in nonbreeding Common and Arctic Terns); bill fairly heavy, all red when breeding (mottled with black when not breeding; all-black in nonbreeding Common and Arctic Terns). *Immature*: Above barred dark brown; bill black; tail shorter than that of adult.

Voice: Shrill *trr-trr-kriaa* or *chit-chit-churr*; chattering notes like rattling pebbles.

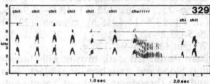

Distribution: Breeds on many Antarctic and Subantarctic islands (breeding record for Stag Island off Algoa Bay is equivocal); disperses northward after breeding; *S. v. vittata* occurs E coast (Mozambique to Durban); *S. v. tristanensis* occurs w and s Cape coasts.

Status: Nonbreeding migrant from southern oceans; common off w Cape, uncommon elsewhere. Rare (RDB).

Habitat: Open sea and offshore waters.

Habits: Gregarious in small flocks. Flight undulating and graceful; usually forages at sea; often hovers over water.

Food: Small fish, crustaceans, scraps, stranded marine animals.

Breeding: Extralimital.

330 (293)   Roseate Tern   Plate 32
Rooiborsseeswael (Rooiborssterretjie)
Sterna dougallii

[Rosenseeschwalbe]

Measurements: Length 37–40 cm; wingspan 76 cm; wing (10 ♂) 222–230–231,5, (10 ♀) 218,5–230–233; tail (10 ♂) 166–187,6–214,5, (10 ♀) 138–187,6–215; tarsus (10 ♂) 18–19–20, (10 ♀) 17,5–17,9–20; culmen (10 ♂) 36–38,1–40,5, (10 ♀) 36–38,1–40. Weight (27) 102,5–112,2–136,5 g.

Bare Parts: Iris dark brown; bill black, base red when breeding; legs and feet scarlet.

Identification: Size medium; tail very long, deeply forked, all white (outer rectrices dark grey in Arctic and Common

Terns); tail extends well beyond wings at rest; legs and feet red at all times; back and wings pale grey (much paler than in other small terns); crown and forehead black (forehead white when not breeding); underparts white, tinged pink; wingtip smudgy black above, plain white below (underwing tip black-edged in Arctic Tern, smudgy black in Common Tern); bill long, slender, mostly black. *Immature*: Above mottled ashy brown; dark band on upperwing coverts. *Chick*: Buffy grey above and on chin and throat, faintly mottled with blackish at base of down; rest of underparts white; weighs (12) 14,4–16,2–18,6 g at hatching.
Voice: Harsh *aar aaar, chirrrik* and *chipik chipik*.

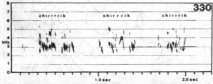

330

Distribution: Worldwide on tropical and temperate coasts; sw and s Cape coasts, rarely to Natal.
Status: Uncommon resident, wandering widely after breeding. Endangered (RDB).
Habitat: Coastal waters and offshore islands.
Habits: Gregarious; flocks may number up to hundreds of birds; similar to Common and Arctic Terns, but poorly known.

Flight fast; feeds by plunge-diving or by dipping to surface of water; rests on offshore banks and reefs.
Food: Mainly fish, especially Beaked Sandfish *Gonorynchus gonorynchus*.
Breeding: *Localities*: St Croix and Bird Islands in Algoa Bay, and Dyer island off sw Cape; formerly also Cape Recife. *Season*: July to October (mainly July). *Nest*: Scrape on ground among stones or on rock; colonial. *Clutch*: (37) 1–1,3–2 eggs (about 70% of 1 egg). *Eggs*: Pale cream, ochre or brown, blotched and spotted with black, brown and purplish; measure (60) 43,1 × 30,2 (37,1–48,5 × 27,2–32,5). *Incubation*: About 25 days by both sexes. *Nestling*: Chicks leave nest and colony at 7–12 days; fed by both parents, first by regurgitation, then on live fish; flies at 23–28 days.

Ref. Randall, R.M. & Randall, B.M. 1980. *Ostrich* 51:14–20; 1981. *Ostrich* 52:17–24.

331 (–)   Blacknaped Tern   Plate 74
Swartkroonseeswael (Swartkroonsterretjie)
Sterna sumatrana

[Schwarznacken-Seeschwalbe]

Measurements: Length 34–37 cm; wingspan 61 cm; wing 199–221; tail 129–150; tarsus 18–19; culmen 37–41.
Bare Parts: Iris brown; bill black, tip usually yellow; legs and feet black, soles pinkish.
Identification: Size smallish to medium; general appearance very pale; distinctive black line from behind eye to nape; crown and underparts white, belly sometimes tinged pinkish; upperparts very pale grey;

tail very long, deeply forked, grey in centre, outer rectrices white; outer web of first primary black, showing as narrow black line on leading edge in flight; legs and bill black (yellow tip not always present). *Immature*: Mottled grey-brown on crown; back barred greyish brown; black patch on nape; bill dusky yellow; legs and feet yellowish brown to blackish.
Voice: High *tsee-chee-tsi-chip; chit-chit-chit-rer* alarm call.
Distribution: Sandy islands, reefs and

285

atolls of tropical Indian and Pacific Oceans; coast of s Mozambique and n Natal.

Status: Very rare vagrant.

Habitat: Marine coasts, islands, offshore waters.

Habits: Gregarious, often with other tern species. Wingbeats fast and shallow; plunges and swoops to pick food from surface of water.

Food: Mainly fish.

Breeding: Extralimital.

Ref. Sinclair, J.C. 1977. *Bokmakierie* 29:18–19.

332 (295) Sooty Tern Plate 32
Roetseeswael (Roetsterretjie)
Sterna fuscata

[Rußseeschwalbe]

Measurements: Length 40–47 cm; wingspan 86 cm; wing ♂ 275–310, ♀ 272–290; tail 157–173; tarsus 22–25; culmen 39–48.

Bare Parts: Iris dark brown; bill, legs and feet black.

Identification: Size medium; above blackish (no contrast between crown and back as in Bridled Tern); forehead white (not extending over eye as in Bridled Tern); below white; tail long, deeply forked, outer rectrices white. *Immature*: Sooty brown all over with white spots on mantle.

Voice: Nasal 3-syllabled *wek-a-wek* or *wideawake*; deep *krrrr*.

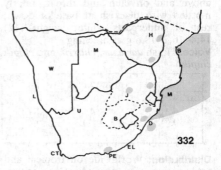

Distribution: All tropical and subtropical oceans; mainly confined to E coast of s Africa; also S coast and rarely inland after storms.

Status: Uncommon vagrant, mainly after strong easterly winds at sea.

Habitat: Open ocean.

Habits: Gregarious, in flocks of up to 60 birds. Highly pelagic; follows ships, even at night; flight buoyant and undulating with steady wingbeats, seeming to pause briefly on downstroke; also soars on motionless wings. Active and vocal even at sea. Fishes by plunging from height.

Food: Fish and squid; flying fish caught in air.

Breeding: Extralimital.

333 (295X) Bridled Tern Plate 32
Brilseeswael (Brilsterretjie)
Sterna anaethetus

[Zügelseeschwalbe]

Measurements: Length 36–42 cm; wingspan 76 cm; wing 268; tail (10) 170–182–201; tarsus (10) 20–22–23; culmen (10) 38–41–43.

Bare Parts: Iris brown; bill, legs and feet black.

Identification: Size medium; very similar to Sooty Tern, but crown black, contrasting with pale greyish brown mantle; back and wings dark greyish brown; forehead white, extending backwards as white eyebrow (Sooty Tern has white on forehead only—no eyebrow); below white; tail brown, deeply forked, outer rectrices white. *Immature*: Heavily scaled cream and grey on back; forecrown white; hindcrown streaked black-and-white, merging to black on nape; below pale greyish white.

Voice: Mainly silent; puppylike *yap* or *kee-yarr*.

Distribution: Islands of tropical Atlantic, Indian and sw Pacific Oceans, w coast of C and S America, Caribbean, W Africa; E coast of s Africa.

Status: Rare vagrant, mainly after easterly storm winds.

Habitat: Open ocean and oceanic islands; seldom coastal.

Habits: Solitary or gregarious. Forages in offshore or pelagic waters, plunging from height; food swallowed at surface before taking off. Roosts on estuarine sandbars, boats, rocks and buoys. Flight looks somewhat stiff-winged with quicker wingbeats than those of Sooty Tern.

Food: Mainly fish.

Breeding: Extralimital.

Ref. Nicholls, G.H. 1977. *Bokmakierie* 29:20–23.

334 (300) Damara Tern — Plate 32
Damaraseeswael (Damarasterretjie)
Sterna balaenarum

[Damaraseeschwalbe]

Measurements: Length 22–23 cm; wingspan 51 cm; wing (4) 160–167–171; tail 62–63,8–65; tarsus 12–12,9–13,5; culmen 27,8–29,9–32.

Bare Parts: Iris dark brown; bill black; legs and feet yellow.

Identification: Size small; below white; forehead and crown black (forecrown white when not breeding; Little Tern has white forehead and yellow bill with black tip when breeding); back and wings pale grey; bill always black (Little Tern has black bill only when not breeding); in flight wingtips dark grey (not blackish as in Little Tern); rump and tail grey (white in Little Tern); yellow feet diagnostic, but hard to see. *Immature*: Similar to adult, but darker grey on wings, with brownish markings. *Chick*: Above buff speckled with black; below white.

Voice: High-pitched repeated *tsit-tsit* or *tit-tit*.

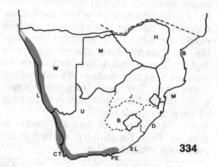

Distribution: Breeds coast of se and sw Cape and Namibia; migrates N to Nigeria.

Status: Uncommon to rare breeding migrant; highly localized and vulnerable to disturbance. Rare (RDB).

Habitat: Sandy marine shores, sheltered bays, lagoons, estuaries.

Habits: Solitary or gregarious in small groups. Flight quick and swallowlike; vocal while foraging; feeds in inshore waters. Roosts in company with other tern species, but usually forages alone.

Food: Mostly small fish and crustaceans.

Breeding: *Season*: November to February. *Nest*: Shallow scrape, sometimes sparsely lined with bits of shell; in sand or gravel on open gravel flats up to 1 km from sea, or in wide dune troughs; in small loose colonies of up to 20 pairs, or in scattered pairs. *Clutch*: 1 egg. *Eggs*: Buff or fawn, spotted with brown and blotched with purplish; measure (70) 33,3 × 23,9 (30,9–35,8 × 23–25,2); weigh (2) 7,8–8,2 g. *Incubation*: 18–22 days by both sexes. *Nestling*: About 20 days; dependent on parents for about another 75 days.

Ref. Clinning, C.F. 1978. *Madoqua* 11:31–39.
Randall, R.A. & McLachlan, A. 1982. *Ostrich* 53:50–51.

335 (299) Little Tern Plate 32
Kleinseeswael (Kleinsterretjie)
Sterna albifrons

[Zwergseeschwalbe]

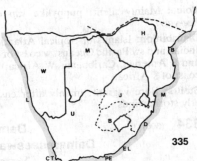

335

Measurements: Length 20–28 cm; wing-span 51 cm; wing (12) 164–180; tail, outer rectrices ♂ 75–95, ♀ 74–85, central rectrices ♂ 43–48, ♀ 42–48; tarsus ♂ 15–18; culmen ♂ 27–32.

Bare Parts: Iris dark brown; bill (breeding) yellow, tip black, (nonbreeding) black; legs and feet orange to brown.

Identification: Size small; underparts white; back and upperwing grey; rump white (grey in Damara Tern); crown black, forehead white (nonbreeding birds have whole forecrown white, hindcrown speckled); bill and legs yellow (tip of bill black; whole bill black when not breeding; bill of Damara Tern always black); in flight wingtips blackish (dark grey in Damara Tern). *Immature:* Whitish buff on crown, with dark patch from eye to nape; above mottled grey and buff; leading edge of wing dark; bill black.

Voice: Sharp *kreek* or *kree-uk* (similar to note of Pied Kingfisher); excited *peep-peep-peep* while hovering.

Distribution: Breeds s Holarctic, s Asia, N Africa, Australasia; migrates N or S after breeding; most of coastal s Africa.

Status: Nonbreeding Palaearctic migrant; rare on W and S coasts as far as Port Elizabeth, fairly common on E coast as far S as Durban.

Habitat: Estuaries, coastal lagoons, saltworks, brackish lakes.

Habits: Solitary or in small flocks. Rests in groups on sandspits or dunes. Flies with quick swallowlike wingbeats back and forth over water, bill pointed downwards; hovers at times; swoops or plunges for food, even into very shallow water.

Food: Small fish, crustaceans, insects.

Breeding: Extralimital.

335

336 (–) Whitecheeked Tern Plate 74
Witwangseeswael (Witwangsterretjie)
Sterna repressa

[Weißwangen-Seeschwalbe]

Measurements: Length 32–37 cm; wing (11 ♂) 232–240–248, (5 ♀) 236–243–249; tail (9 ♂) 131–142–154, (4 ♀) 132–136–140; tarsus (11 ♂) 18–18,6–20, (4 ♀) 18–18,3–19; culmen (11 ♂) 34–35,7–37, (5 ♀) 34–35,1–37. Weight (9 ♂) 78–90–105 g, (3 ♀) 87–90–92 g.

Bare Parts: Iris brown; bill dark blood red at base, black on distal half, tip pale; legs and feet red.

Identification: Size medium to smallish; similar to Arctic Tern, but darker lead-grey on back, upperwing and underparts; white cheeks separate grey throat from black crown and forehead; nonbreeding birds have forecrown white, hindcrown speckled, nape black; in flight wing looks uniform lead grey; underwing paler grey; outer rectrices dark grey; central rectrices whitish. *Immature:* Similar to nonbreeding adult, but has dark band on upperwing coverts; underparts white.

Voice: Loud clear *kee-leek, kee-leek.*
Distribution: Breeds n Indian Ocean from E Africa to India; disperses after breeding; recorded Umvoti Mouth and Richards Bay, n Natal.
Status: Very rare vagrant.
Habitat: Marine shores and open ocean.
Habits: Typical of marine terns. Hunts by dipping at surface of water, less often by plunging from air, usually within 3 km of land; seldom submerges when diving.
Food: Probably mainly small fish.
Breeding: Extralimital.

Ref. Sinclair, J.C. 1976. *Bokmakierie* 28:28.

---

337 (305X)   Black Tern   Plate 32
Swartmeerswael (Swartsterretjie)
Chlidonias niger

[Trauerseeschwalbe]

Measurements: Length 23–24 cm; wing 183–215; tail 69,5–90; tarsus 14–17,5; culmen 25–30. Weight (12) 51–58–73 g.
Bare Parts: Iris dark brown; bill black (tinged red when breeding); legs and feet reddish brown.
Identification: Size small; similar to Whitewinged Tern; tail only slightly forked, grey (white in Whitewinged Tern). *Nonbreeding*: Underparts, forecrown and collar around sides of neck white; hindcrown, and nape black, extending as broad stripe onto ear coverts (hindcrown of Whitewinged Tern speckled black and white); blackish smudge on sides of white chest (diagnostic) and small black spot in front of eye; rest of upperparts grey (darker than in Whitewinged Tern); in flight leading edge of wing markedly darker than rest of upperwing; underwing greyish white. *Breeding*: Body and head jet black; back and upperwing dove grey (upperwing of Whitewinged Tern greyish white); whole underwing white (underwing coverts of Whitewinged Tern black like body); bill blackish (red in Whitewinged Tern). *Immature*: Like nonbreeding adult but upperparts browner.
Voice: Screeching nasal *ski-aa*; squeaky *ki-ki-ki.*

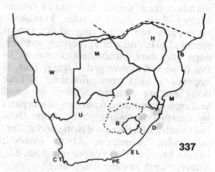

Distribution: Breeds temperate Holarctic; migrates to tropics of s hemisphere; recorded coast of Namibia, Port Elizabeth, Natal and various inland localities.

Status: Common nonbreeding Palaearctic migrant on Namibian coast; uncommon elsewhere; summer months; uncommon vagrant inland.

Habitat: Open ocean, quiet coastal waters; inland lakes, pans and dams.

Habits: Solitary or in small flocks. Forages in flight, taking flying insects, or picking up scraps from water or ground; flight somewhat erratic, with full deep wingbeats. Usually in company with Whitewinged Tern.

Food: Insects, offal.

Breeding: Extralimital.

Ref. Jensen, R.A.C. & Berry, H.H. 1972. *Madoqua, Ser. 1,* 5:53–56.
Schmitt, M.B., Milstein, P. le S., Hunter, H.C. & Hopcroft, C.J. 1973. *Bokmakierie* 25:91–92.

338 (305) **Whiskered Tern** **Plate 32**
Witbaardmeerswael (Witbaardsterretjie)
Chlidonias hybridus

[Weißbart-Seeschwalbe]

Measurements: Length 24–25 cm; wing ♂ 232–250, ♀ 230–242; tail (12) 83–90; tarsus (12) 22–25; culmen (12) 30–34. Weight (2) 61–82 g.

Bare Parts: Iris brown to red-brown; bill red (breeding) or black (nonbreeding); legs and feet red.

Identification: Size smallish; nonbreeding birds similar to nonbreeding Black and Whitewinged Terns; tail squarish or slightly forked, greyer than that of Whitewinged Tern. *Nonbreeding*: Forehead, underparts and underwing white; crown speckled black on white, merging to black nape (no dark patch behind eye as in Black and Whitewinged Terns); rest of upperparts light grey. *Breeding*: Whole body lead grey, except for black forehead and crown separated from grey underparts by conspicuous white cheek stripe from bill to sides of neck; underwing and undertail white. *Immature*: Above mottled; otherwise similar to nonbreeding adult.

Voice: Harsh rasping *kreek kreek*.

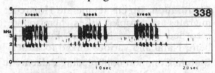

Distribution: Africa, s Palaearctic, s Asia, Australasia; most of s Africa except dry W.

Status: Locally common nomad, moving about according to rainfall.

Habitat: Inland waters; vleis, pans, reedy dams, flooded pastures.

Habits: Usually gregarious in small flocks. Dips to surface of water for food; sometimes plunges into water, or hawks insects in flight; flies fairly low back and forth over water with somewhat slow and laboured wingbeats, flight more direct than that of Whitewinged Tern.

Food: Insects, small frogs.

Breeding: *Season*: September to April. *Nest*: Floating pad of plant material on surface vegetation, old nests of other waterbirds, or among reeds; about 25 cm diameter, with flattish or hollow top; material added during incubation. *Clutch*: (42) 2–2,7–3 eggs (rarely only 1). *Eggs*: Cream or greenish buff, blotched with reddish brown; measure (33) 38,3 × 27,7 (35,6–41,4 × 26,3–29,3). *Incubation*: 22–29 days by both sexes. *Nestling*: 20 days.

Ref. Dean, W.R.J. & Skead, D.M. 1979. *Ostrich* 50:118.
Tarboton, W.R., Clinning, C.F. & Grond, M. 1975. *Ostrich* 46:188.

339 (304) **Whitewinged Tern** **Plate 32**
Witvlerkmeerswael (Witvlerksterretjie)
Chlidonias leucopterus

[Weißflügel-Seeschwalbe]

Measurements: Length 23 cm; wing ♂ 200–218, ♀ 192–210; tail (12) 67–75; tarsus (12) 19–22; culmen (12) 23–24. Weight (144) 42–56,6–80 g.

Bare Parts: Iris dark brown; bill black (nonbreeding) or crimson (breeding); legs and feet vermilion.

Identification: Size smallish; similar to Black and Whiskered Terns in nonbreeding plumage; tail almost square, barely forked. *Nonbreeding*: Forecrown, underparts and sides of neck white; hindcrown speckled with black (solid black in Black Tern); large black patch behind eye (black streak to nape in Whiskered Tern), small black patch in front of eye; no black pectoral patches as in Black Tern; rest of upperparts grey (paler than in Black Tern), slightly mottled on wing coverts; in flight underwing and tail white (grey in Black Tern). *Breeding*: Underparts, head and underwing coverts jet black (whole underwing white in Black Tern); tail, upperwing and remiges white, contrasting with black of body and underwing; rest of upperparts grey. *Immature*: Similar to nonbreeding adult, but back darker brownish grey.

Voice: Raucous buzzing *zrrk-zrrk-zrrk*; rapid *kik-kik-kik*; guttural *kerr*.

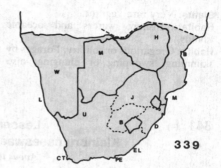

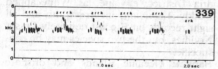

Distribution: Breeds e and se Europe, Asia to Mongolia; migrates to Africa, s Asia, Australasia; in s Africa absent only from most of dry W.

Status: Common to abundant nonbreeding Palaearctic migrant, August to April.

Habitat: Inland and coastal lakes, dams, pans, vleis, marshes, sewage ponds, estuaries.

Habits: Solitary or gregarious, flocks sometimes numbering up to 2 000 birds. Flies slowly into wind over open water, swooping for food; also hawks insects in flight, sometimes over dry land far from water; flight fluttery and buoyant. Rests on mats of floating vegetation, posts or stumps; roosts in dead trees in water. Begins to moult into breeding plumage from about March; many in full breeding dress before departure in April.

Food: Insects and their larvae, small fish (especially *Limnothrissa*), crustaceans, spiders.

Breeding: Extralimital.

Ref. Begg, G.W. 1973. *Ostrich* 44:149–153.

340 (303) Common Noddy Plate 32
Grootbruinseeswael (Grootbruinsterretjie)
Anous stolidus

[Noddiseeschwalbe]

Measurements: Length 37–41 cm; wingspan 84 cm; wing 253–290; tail 138–175; tarsus 22–25; culmen 38–53.

Bare Parts: Iris brown; bill black; legs and feet reddish brown to brownish black.

Identification: Size small to medium; dark sooty brown all over (browner, less blackish, than Lesser Noddy), except for whitish forehead merging with lavender grey crown, grading to brown nape; small white crescent below eye; black lores contrast sharply with white forehead (forehead merges with darker lores in Lesser Noddy); tail longish, wedge-shaped, with V-notch in centre; bill rather robust (heavier than bill of Lesser Noddy).

Voice: Rasping *karrk*; sharp *kwok, kwok* and *eyak*.

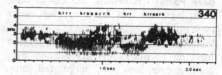

Distribution: Tropical and subtropical oceans; recorded Durban, Cape Peninsula.

Status: Very rare vagrant.
Habitat: Inshore waters and oceanic islands.
Habits: Gregarious or solitary. Forages by skimming, swooping or plunging; also catches fish in flight; flight swift and direct with long glides. Rests on water, flotsam, reefs or buoys.
Food: Mainly small fish.
Breeding: Extralimital.

341 (–) Lesser Noddy Plate 74
Kleinbruinseeswael (Kleinbruinsterretjie)
Anous tenuirostris

[Schlankschnabelnoddi]

Measurements: Length 30–34 cm; wingspan 71 cm; wing 209; tail 106; tarsus 21; culmen 38.
Bare Parts: Iris brown; bill black; legs and feet brownish black.
Identification: Size smallish; very similar to Common Noddy, but slightly smaller; not easily separable at distance. Whole body dark blackish brown (darker than Common Noddy); whitish forehead merges with pale lavender grey crown behind (crown paler than in Common Noddy), and with dark lores in front (not sharply demarcated from lores as in Common Noddy); small white crescent below eye; bill longer and thinner than that of Common Noddy.

Voice: Soft rattling *churr*.
Distribution: Tropical and subtropical Indian Ocean; recorded Durban.
Status: Very rare vagrant, May-June. Identification of specimen from Alexandria District, e Cape, as Whitecapped Noddy *A. minutus* incorrect; this and all sight records on E coast definitely Lesser Noddies, but the two species may be conspecific.
Habitat: Oceanic islands and offshore waters.
Habits: Solitary or gregarious. Flight fluttery (less direct than that of Common Noddy) and erratic.
Food: Probably small fish.
Breeding: Extralimital.

342 (–) Fairy Tern (White Tern) Plate 74
Feeseeswael (Feesterretjie)
Gygis alba

[Feenseeschwalbe]

Measurements: Length 27–33 cm; wingspan 71 cm; wing 246; tail 112; tarsus 14; culmen 38.
Bare Parts: Iris brown; bill black, base blue; legs and feet black to blue, webs pale yellow.
Identification: Size small; all white, except for ring of black feathers around eye, making eyes look very large; tail long, forked.
Voice: Raucous notes like laughter; guttural *heekh*.

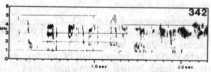

Distribution: Islands of tropical oceans.
Status: Doubtfully recorded from s African waters ("Cape Seas"); should probably be excluded.
Habitat: Tropical oceanic islands.
Habits: Usually gregarious. Flight darting or airy; swoops for food at surface of water.
Food: Small fish.
Breeding: Extralimital.

12:2:2. Family 41 RYNCHOPIDAE—SKIMMERS

Medium to large. Bill long, lower jaw longer than upper jaw, laterally compressed, bright red, yellow or orange; legs very short; toes short, webs somewhat reduced; dark above (black or brown), white below; wings very long and pointed; tail forked; gregarious; feed by flying low over water with blade-like tip of lower jaw cleaving surface of water; food fishes snapped up on contact with bill; inhabit mostly larger rivers, occasional on marine shores; nest colonially on river sandbanks, an unlined scrape in sand; other features as for suborder Lari (*q.v.*). Distribution e N America, S America, tropical Africa, India to SE Asia; three species; one species in s Africa.

343 (306)   **African Skimmer**   **Plate 31**
Waterploeër
Rynchops flavirostris

[Braunmantel-Scherenschnabel]

Measurements: Length 36–40 cm; wing-span 106–107 cm; wing (10 ♂) 311–336–374, (10 ♀) 321–334–361; tail (10 ♂) 105–115–127, (10 ♀) 102–108–120; tarsus (10 ♂) 26–28,2–31, (10 ♀) 25–26,4–31; culmen (10 ♂) 52–62,6–71, (10 ♀) 49–55,3–64; lower jaw (10 ♂) 68–83–96, (10 ♀) 58–73,5–104. Weight (10) 111–164–204 g.

Bare Parts: Iris brown; bill orange-red above, orange below, merging to yellow at tip; legs and feet vermilion.

Identification: Size medium to large; long-winged, ternlike; bill bright orange-red, lower jaw much longer than upper; upper-parts brownish black (whitish collar on hindneck when not breeding); underparts, sides of face, forehead and tips of secondaries white; tail whitish, deeply forked. *Immature*: Streaked on forehead; upperparts mottled with buff; bill yellow, tip black. *Chick*: Ternlike; lower jaw not longer than upper.

Voice: Loud sharp *kik-kik-kik*.

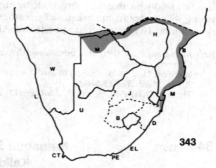

343

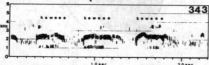

Distribution: Tropical Africa as far S as Zambezi, Lundi and Okavango River systems; rarely further S.

Status: Common intra-African migrant, April to December, when water levels low; rare vagrant to S Africa, but has bred Zululand.

Habitat: Larger rivers, lakes, pans, coastal lagoons.

Habits: Gregarious in flocks of up to 20 or more birds. Usually wary and unapproachable, but may be approached closely by boat. Flocks rest on sandbanks, facing into wind. Flies fast with leisurely wing-beats and lower jaw just dipped below surface of water, cutting narrow wake, then returning along same course; snaps bill closed as food swept up; forages day and night, usually when water calm.

Food: Small fish, mostly 2–5 cm long.

Breeding: *Season*: July to October. *Nest*: Deep unlined scrape on sandbar in river; in loose colonies. *Clutch*: (58) 1–2,3–4 eggs. *Eggs*: Buffy stone, boldly blotched with blackish, purple and slate; measure (104) 39,8 × 28,6 (35,7–44 × 22,4–30,8). *Incubation*: About 21 days by both sexes; eggs wetted by belly-soaking at each nest relief; clutch sometimes abandoned after first chick hatches. *Fledging*: 5–6 weeks; chick carried by parent in bill if disturbed.

Ref. Coppinger, M.P., Williams, G.D. & Maclean, G.L. 1988. *Ostrich* 59:85–96.

13. Order PTEROCLIFORMES (One family)

13:1. Family 42 PTEROCLIDAE—SANDGROUSE

Medium. Bill short, arched, feathered to over nostrils; legs very short, feathered on front of tarsometatarsus, or completely feathered including toes; toes short, hind toe rudimentary or absent; body robust; neck short; head small; appearance pigeon-like; wings long and pointed; tail medium to longish, wedge-shaped; central rectrices elongated in some species; plumage camouflaged, elaborately patterned in dull shades of yellow, green, rufous, brown, black and white; sexes different, females usually more barred or streaked than males; gregarious; inhabit open areas from deserts to dry savanna; food dry seeds; monogamous; nest a scrape on bare ground, sometimes sparsely lined with small stones or bits of plant material; eggs 2–3, buff, pink, cream or greenish, marked with brown and grey; chick downy, precocial, not fed by parents; female usually incubates by day, male by night; both sexes care for young; male provides young with water from soaked belly feathers. Distribution Africa, s Europe, Arabia, c Asia, India; 16 species; four species in s Africa.

Ref. Johnsgard, P.A. 1991. *Bustards, hemipodes, and sandgrouse: birds of dry places.* Oxford: Oxford University Press.
Maclean, G.L. 1976. *Proc. 16th Int. Orn. Congr.*:502–516; 1983. *BioScience* 33:365–369; 1985. *S. Afr. J. Wildl. Res.* 15:1–6.
Thomas, D.H. 1984. *S. Afr. J. Zool.* 19:113–120.

---

344 (307)   **Namaqua Sandgrouse**   **Plate 30**
Kelkiewyn
Pterocles namaqua

Simbote (K), Setlatlawe sa Namakwa (NS), Kokoi (SS), Lekwêtêkwiê, Lekotokobii (Tw), [Namaflughuhn]

Measurements: Length ♂ 26–28 cm, ♀ 24 cm; wing (20 ♂) 167–172,4–180, (20 ♀) 160–166,1–173; tail (10 ♂) 89–112,5–124, (10 ♀) 88–95,6–106; tarsus (10 ♂) 21–22,6–24, (10 ♀) 20–21,8–23; culmen (10 ♂) 11–11,9–13, (10 ♀) 11–12,2–13,5. Weight (13 ♂) 166–180–191 g, (17 ♀) 143–172,8–192 g.

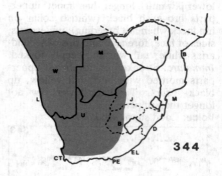

344

Bare Parts: Iris dark brown; eyering yellow; bill light greyish horn; legs and feet pinky grey or buff.

Identification: About size of Cape Turtle Dove; tail wedge-shaped, central rectrices long, pointed (diagnostic). *Male*: Head, mantle and breast yellowish olive, yellower on throat and forehead; double breastband of white and deep maroon; belly dark brown; wing coverts spotted pearly grey on olive. *Female*: Body barred brown and buff; head and breast streaked brown and buff; throat plain yellowish. *Immature*: Similar to adult ♀ but more finely barred; belly plain rufous in ♂. *Chick*: Above yellowish brown, with crossbars of white outlined with black, forming double figure-of-8 on head and back; below pale buff, darker on breast; iris brown; bill black; legs and feet dusky grey.

Voice: Nasal 3-note flight call *ki-ki-keeu* or *kelkiewyn*, accented and higher-pitched on last syllable; *kip-kip-kip* contact call in flock on ground; louder *wip-wip-wip* on take-off; *kikeee* alarm call.

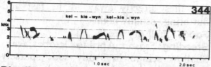

Distribution: Dry w parts of s Africa from sw Cape and Karoo to sw Angola; vagrant to Zimbabwe and Natal.

Status: Common resident; somewhat nomadic; southern populations migratory, but movements unmapped.

Habitat: Open desert and semidesert (rainfall less than 300 mm/year), usually stony, with sparse low shrubs and grass-tufts; less commonly Kalahari sandveld and arid savanna.

Habits: Gregarious or in pairs; flocks number 5–10 or several hundred birds; flies up to 60 km or more to water in flocks of hundreds or thousands daily, 1–3 hours after sunrise; individuals may drink only every 3–5 days; flocks land several metres away from water, then run down to drink;

some birds may drink again in evening. Forages by walking with small steps while pecking at ground. Crouches when disturbed. Takes off rapidly; flies fast and straight, ploverlike, at 60–70 km/h, calling intermittently.

Food: Small hard seeds.

Breeding: *Season*: All months, dependent on rainfall; mainly April to September, peak July–November (73 % of nests). *Nest*: Shallow scrape, 10–12 cm diameter, sparsely lined with small stones, bits of earth or dry plant fragments; on ground, usually near shrub or grasstuft; sometimes exposed among stones or on gravel. *Clutch*: (62) 2–2,9–3 eggs (usually 3). *Eggs*: Pale greenish buff, greyish green, or pinkish stone, blotched, spotted and smeared with brown, red-brown and pale grey; measure (190) 36,3 × 25,2 (31–42,7 × 22,5–27,8); weigh 11–12,5 g. *Incubation*: 21–23 days by ♀ during day, ♂ at night. *Fledging*: About 28 days; young attended by both parents; dependent on parents for at least 2–3 weeks after flying age.

Ref. Maclean, G.L. 1968. *Living Bird* 7:209–235; 1983. *BioScience* 33:365–369.

---

345 (308)

Burchell's Sandgrouse
Gevlekte Sandpatrys

Plate 30

Pterocles burchelli

Simbote (K), [Fleckenflughuhn]

Measurements: Length about 25 cm; wing (10 ♂) 162,5–169,4–175, (10 ♀) 163–167,1–173; tail (10 ♂) 66–70,8–75, (10 ♀) 63–66,7–72; tarsus (10 ♂) 23–27,3–29, (10 ♀) 25–26,7–29; culmen (10 ♂) 11–11,8–12,5, (10 ♀) 9,5–10,9–12. Weight (4 ♂) 180–192–200 g, (4 ♀) 160–171–185 g.

Bare Parts: Iris dark brown; bare skin around eye yellow; bill blackish; legs and feet dull yellowish pink.

Identification: About size of Cape Turtle Dove; build stocky; legs relatively long; tail rounded; body generally pinkish rufous below, yellowish rufous above, spotted with white; throat, face and eye-

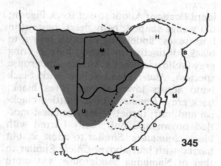

brow light grey in ♂, yellow ochre in ♀; belly lightly barred with white. *Immature*: Like adult ♀, but barred with buff all over. *Chick*: Similar to that of Namaqua Sandgrouse.

Voice: Mellow, staccato *kwok-wok* in flight; rapid *wok-wok-wok* on take-off.

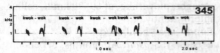

Distribution: Dry interior of s Africa and sw Angola.

Status: Common resident.

Habitat: Red Kalahari sand with grass 30–50 cm tall, mixed with shrub or scrub; also dry savanna.

Habits: Usually in pairs or small groups of 3–6 birds. Shy and wary; crouches when disturbed, or creeps away through grass, so easily overlooked; runs well on long legs, with body almost upright. Flies to drink at waterholes, 2–4 hours after sunrise, in flocks of up to 50 birds, sometimes in company with Namaqua or Yellowthroated Sandgrouse; lands at water's edge or on surface, drinks very quickly and flies directly away; flight fast and fluttering, usually high.

Food: Small dry seeds.

Breeding: *Season*: April to October. *Nest*: Shallow scrape in sandy soil, sparsely lined with dry plant material; usually under grasstuft or shrub. *Clutch*: 3 eggs (rarely 2). *Eggs*: Pale cream, olive buff or buff, with elongate smears of dark olive brown and greyish mauve; measure (15) 36,7 × 25,7 (34,5–38,8 × 23,4–27,3). *Incubation*: Unrecorded. *Fledging*: Unrecorded; young attended by both parents.

Ref. Maclean, G.L. 1968. *Living Bird* 7:209–235.

346 (309) Yellowthroated Sandgrouse Plate 30
Geelkeelsandpatrys
Pterocles gutturalis

Simbote (K), [Gelbkehl-Flughuhn]

Measurements: Length about 30 cm; wing (19 ♂) 205–215,5–228, (17 ♀) 198–211,5–221; tail (10 ♂) 83,5–88,1–94, (10 ♀) 75–81,1–88; tarsus (10 ♂) 28–29,9–32, (10 ♀) 28–29,2–31; culmen (10 ♂) 13,5–14,6–16, (10 ♀) 13,5–14,9–16. Weight (3 ♂) 340–342–345 g, (6 ♀) 285–336–400 g.

Bare Parts: Iris dark brown; eyering grey; bill pale bluish grey; legs and feet pinkish brown.

Identification: About size of Rock Pigeon; tail wedge-shaped; belly deep chestnut in both sexes; underwing blackish brown to black (distinctive in flight); bare eyering grey (yellow in other s African sandgrouse species). *Male*: Head yellow with black band across lower throat; lores black; back grey. *Female*: Above mottled blackish and buff; throat yellowish; chest mottled brown and buff; belly barred with black. *Immature*: Similar to adult ♀, but barred with buff above. *Chick*: Similar to that of Namaqua Sandgrouse, but more rufous brown above.

Voice: Deep *ipi aw aw*; guttural *kik-zzz kwozz-zok* or *zzik-kik zzzok*; harsh *glok-glok-glok* on take-off.

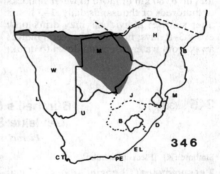

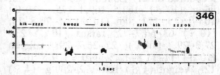

Distribution: Two or three separate populations; part of s population breeds s Zambia, n Botswana and Caprivi, may migrate to s Botswana, nw Transvaal, n Cape and w Zimbabwe (has bred n Cape, but not recently); separate breeding population in Waterberg region of nw Transvaal; n population ranges from n Zambia to Ethiopia.

Status: Fairly common localized resident in w Transvaal; otherwise common intra-African migrant to Zambia, May to October; southward after breeding, mainly October to January, but some birds present all months S of Zambezi River. Probably Rare (RDB).

Habitat: Short-grass plains, usually not far from water; also recently burnt ground, cultivated fields, especially on black clay soils.

Habits: Usually in pairs or small groups; flocks of up to 1 000 birds on migration. Gathers in large flocks at water, usually 1–3 hours after sunrise, sometimes again in afternoon. Forages conspicuously in open, but crouches when disturbed; takes off with noisy wingbeats.

Food: Seeds, fallen grain.

Breeding: *Season*: May to September in Zambia, September in Zimbabwe, April to October in w Transvaal. *Nest*: Scrape or natural hollow, like hoofprint, sometimes sparsely lined with plant fragments; on open ground among grass stubble. *Clutch*: 3 eggs (rarely 2). *Eggs*: Light brown to pale buff, spotted and blotched with brown, red-brown and mauve; measure 42–43 × 27,5–33,3. *Incubation*: 27 days; by ♀ by day, ♂ at night. *Fledging*: Unrecorded; young can fly when only about half size of adults.

Ref. Blane, S. & Tarboton, W. 1990. *Afr. Wildl.* 44:272–274.

Brooke, R.K. 1968. *Ostrich* 39:33–34.

---

347 (310) **Doublebanded Sandgrouse** **Plate 30**
Dubbelbandsandpatrys
Pterocles bicinctus

Simbote (K), Xikwarhakwarha, Byarabyara (Ts), Mokgwarakgwara (Tw), [Nachtflughuhn]

Measurements: Length about 25 cm; wing (25 ♂) 171–179,8–188, (21 ♀) 169–176–185; tail (10 ♂) 73,5–80,6–86,5, (10 ♀) 76–79,1–82,5; tarsus (46) 22–23,8–29; culmen (26) 15–16,1–17. Weight (9 ♂) 215–233–250 g, (19 ♀) 210–239–280 g.

Bare Parts: Iris dark brown; eyering yellow; bill yellow to reddish, tip darker; legs and feet yellowish brown.

Identification: About size of Cape Turtle Dove; tail rather short, rounded (wedge-shaped with long central rectrices in Namaqua Sandgrouse). *Male*: Black-and-white pattern on forehead, and yellow bill distinctive; throat and breast rufous buff; double breastband of white and black; belly barred (belly dark brown in Namaqua Sandgrouse); back mottled brownish, spotted with white. *Female*: Finely barred above and below, including breast (♀ Namaqua Sandgrouse streaked on breast); eyering yellow (grey in ♀ Yellowthroated Sandgrouse). *Immature*: Similar to adult ♀, but more pinkish fawn above and below. *Chick*: Similar to that of

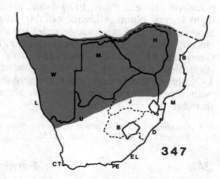

347

Namaqua Sandgrouse, but darker brown; white pattern bolder; bill black, tip paler.

Voice: Soft, slightly raspy, quick conversational *weep-weeu, chuk-chukki, weep-weeu*, much repeated; sometimes up to 9 syllables, set to words *oh NO, he's gone and done it aGAIN*, uttered quickly; harsh *chuk-chuk-chuk on take-off*; churring anxiety note.

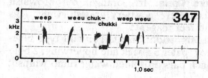

Distribution: Southern Africa from s Namibia, n Cape and Transvaal to s Angola, Zambia and s Malawi.

Status: Common resident.

Habitat: *Acacia* and other savanna, dry bushveld, mopane woodland, stony and eroded areas, rocky desert hills with scrub and tussocky grass.

Habits: Usually in pairs or small groups by day; highly gregarious when flying to water after dusk, often in flocks of hundreds of birds. Mainly crepuscular, lying up by day in shade of rocks or vegetation. Flies low and silently to drinking places; flocks on ground may chatter quietly. May fly at least 30 km to good food source.

Food: Small dry seeds, including those of *Datura innoxia* (over 850 seeds per crop).

Breeding: *Season*: April to October in Zimbabwe; as late as December in Namibia; mainly May-July throughout s Africa. *Nest*: Shallow scrape, usually lined with few bits of dry plant material; on ground between grasstufts or under small shrub, but usually open from above. *Clutch*: (17) 2–2,6–3 eggs (mostly 3). *Eggs*: Light pink to pinkish buff, spotted with purple-brown, red-brown and slate; measure (40) 37,3 × 26,7   (31,1–39,9 × 24,5–27,8); weigh (1) 10,2 g. *Incubation*: 19 days in captivity; ♀ incubates by night and for part of morning, ♂ for rest of daylight hours. *Fledging*: About 4 weeks; young attended by both parents.

14. Order COLUMBIFORMES (One family)

14:1. Family 43 COLUMBIDAE—PIGEONS AND DOVES

Small to very large, mostly medium. Bill usually short, soft at base, swollen at tip, with waxy cere over nostrils; legs short to medium; toes strong for walking and perching; body robust; neck short; head small; wings short to longish, rather rounded in most; flight strong; plumage highly variable, often grey, sometimes with iridescent patches especially on neck and wings; sexes usually alike; voice cooing or whistling with bill closed; often gregarious; habitat variable; mostly arboreal; food mostly plant material (seeds and fruits), also termites and snails; wings usually make characteristic sounds in flight; nest in trees, on cliffs, or on ground, a light platform of twigs and rootlets; eggs 1–2, plain white or buff; chick sparsely downy at hatching, altricial; parental care by both sexes. Distribution worldwide; about 290 species; 15 species in s Africa, one introduced.

Ref. Goodwin, D. 1967. *Pigeons and doves of the world*. London: British Museum (Natural History).
Siegfried, W.R. 1971. *Ostrich* 42:155–157.

348 (–)   **Feral Pigeon**   **Plate 33**
Tuinduif
Columba livia

[Haustaube]

Measurements: Length 32–33 cm; wing ♂ 213–242, ♀ 202–241; tail 97–115; tarsus 30–33; culmen 24–26. Weight (Europe) (41 ♂)   290–393–535 g,   (36 ♀)   304–359–433 g.

Bare Parts: Iris orange; bill brownish black; cere powdery greyish white; legs and feet magenta.

Identification: Size large; wild type blue-grey, paler on back and upperwing; 2 bold black bars on folded wing; rump whitish;

neck and upper breast iridescent purple and green; feral type very variable—brown, grey, white, black; plain or mixed, with or without typical wingbars.

Voice: Moaning *ooorh* or *oh-oo-oor*, somewhat guttural; rapid cooing *oo-roo-coo-t'coo*; deep nasal *goo, goo, goo* at nest site.

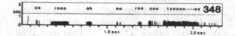

Distribution: Originally se Europe, sw Asia, India, Arabia, N Africa, British Isles; now introduced worldwide, including most s African cities.

Status: Abundant resident; first introduced from the Netherlands, later from elsewhere in Europe.

Habitat: Urban areas, especially centres of larger cities, railway yards; less often farmland.

Habits: Gregarious, often in flocks of hundreds of birds, rarely in company with Rock Pigeon with which it may produce viable hybrids. Feeds in city squares, cultivated fields and on open lawns. Male displays by flying with wingclaps, landing next to ♀, bowing and turning with pouted chest, spread tail and bill pointed down.

Flocks manoeuvre together in flight, often gliding with wings held up in V.

Food: Mostly seeds and fragments of discarded farinaceous foods (bread, biscuits, etc.); also green shoots, leaves, berries, molluscs, earthworms.

Breeding: *Season*: All months. *Nest*: scanty platform of sticks, twigs, wire, feathers, rubbish; on ledge or in crevice of building; rarely on rocky cliff in s Africa. *Clutch*: 2 eggs. *Eggs*: White; measure about 38,4 × 28,5; weigh about 10,2 g. *Incubation*: 17–18 days by both sexes. *Nestling*: 28–35 days; fed by both parents.

Ref. Brooke, R.K. 1981. *Bokmakierie* 33:37–40. Simms, E. 1979. *The public life of the Street Pigeon*. London: Hutchinson.

---

349 (311)   Rock Pigeon (Speckled Pigeon)   Plate 33
Kransduif (Bosduif)
Columba guinea

Haifoko (K), Leeba, Lehoboi (SS), Leeba, Leeba-rope, Letseba (Tw), Ivukuthu (X), iJuba, iVukuthu (Z), [Guineataube]

Measurements: Length about 33 cm; wing (14 ♂) 225–232–241, (13 ♀) 220–227–235; tail (38) 102–125; tarsus (38) 24–30; culmen (38) 20–25. Weight (7 ♂) 326–348,2–375,7 g, (6 ♀) 270–321,1–370 g, (126 unsexed) 217–347,2–405,3 g.

Bare Parts: Iris yellow to cream (pupil keyhole-shaped); skin around eye dull red; bill blackish; cere whitish; legs and feet purplish red.

Identification: About size of Feral Pigeon; neck, breast, back and upperwing deep maroon-brown, speckled with white on neck, spotted with white on wings; head, rump and rest of underparts grey; red eyepatch around yellow eye diagnostic; tail grey, tipped broadly black.

Voice: About 10–20 deep mellow coos, *doo, doo, doo*, increasing in volume, then falling away; in courtship, emphatic *VUkutu-kooo*, accented on first syllable, drawn out on last, repeated several times.

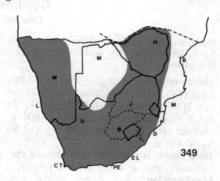

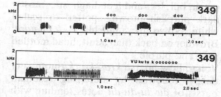

Distribution: Africa S of Sahara; almost throughout s Africa, but absent from much of Kalahari sandveld.

Status: Mostly common to abundant resident; nomadic at times, especially in arid areas; uncommon in Zimbabwe.

Habitat: Mountains, cliffs, gorges, koppies, boulder hills, buildings (rural or urban); feeds in open country, especially cultivated lands.

Habits: Solitary or gregarious, sometimes in company with Feral Pigeon with which it may produce viable hybrids; flocks usually of 10–20 birds, at times several hundred at food concentrations. Usually roosts on cliff ledges, buildings, or in caves; less often in trees; roosting ledges characteristically splashed with white droppings. Flies out to agricultural lands to feed by day. In display flight, ♂ flies out from ledge, clapping wings in bursts below body, interspersed with glides on flat wings (Feral Pigeon glides on V-shaped wings).

Food: Seeds, fallen grain, green shoots.

Breeding: *Season*: All months. *Nest*: More or less flimsy platform of sticks, twigs, weeds and grass; on ledge of cliff, cave, donga or building; also in crown of tall *Phoenix* palms; rarely in stout upright fork of large tree; on ground or in low niches of stone walls on offshore islands without mammalian predators. *Clutch*: 2 eggs. *Eggs*: White; measure (105) 36,5 × 27,5 (33,8–42,7 × 25–31,2); weigh 13,5–14,5 g shortly before hatching, about 20 g fresh. *Incubation*: 14–14,8–16 days; one parent (probably ♂) incubates 10:30–16:40, other parent for rest of day and all night. *Nestling*: 25–26 days; fed by both parents.

Ref. Cooper, J. 1975. *Ostrich* 46:154–156.
   Elliott, C.C.H. & Cooper, J. 1980. *Ostrich* 51:198–203.
   Skead, D.M. 1971. *Ostrich* 42:65–69.

350 (312)   Rameron Pigeon   Plate 33
Geelbekbosduif
Columba arquatrix

Ngalakana (Ts), Leeba, Leebaphêpane (Tw), Izuba, Izubantonga (X), iVukuthu-lehlathi (Z), [Oliventaube]

Measurements: Length about 40 cm; wing (16) 214–226–245; tail 125–147; tarsus 21–27; culmen 18–22. Weight (1 ♀) 406,5 g, (6 unsexed) 324–414,7–500 g; without crop (11 ♂) mean 463 g, (20 ♀) mean 415 g.

Bare Parts: Iris yellow; skin around eye, bill, cere, legs and feet chrome yellow.

Identification: Size large; yellow eyepatch, bill, legs and feet diagnostic; mostly dark purplish brown, spotted or scaled white; crown grey; tail black. *Immature*: Browner on back than adult; head mottled grey and purple.

Voice: Low hoarse *kroo-ku* (*ku*-note very deep), followed by stuttering resonant bursts of *du-du-du-du* notes, ending with mournful drawn-out *wooo*; also 1–3 soft trumpeting *kraaa, kraaa* or *preem, preem* notes while gliding between flapping in circular display flight.

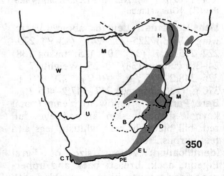

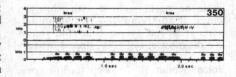

Distribution: Africa from Cameroon and Ethiopia to Cape; in s Africa confined to forested regions of E and S.

Status: Locally common resident; some-what nomadic seasonally, depending on fruiting of trees.

Habitat: Canopy of lowland·and montane evergreen forest; less often also in exotic evergreen plantations (wattles, conifers).

Habits: Usually in small groups of 5–10 birds; sometimes in larger flocks when not breeding. Shy and wary. Flies high from one forest patch to another; flight power-ful and direct; displays with spectacular undulating flight while descending to trees; also over forest in circular flight of 50–100 m while calling at intervals (see **Voice**); vocally silent when feeding, but betrays presence by loud wingflapping while balancing on thin branches to pluck fruit. Flocks often rest on tops of bare trees, less often on fences. Rarely comes to ground, except to drink. Roosts in small groups of up to 15 birds.

Food: Fruit (indigenous *Olea, Ocotea, Celtis, Prunus*; exotic Mulberry *Morus nigra* and Inkberry *Cestrum laevigatum*), seeds; partly responsible for spread of exotic Bugweed *Solanum mauritianum* in Natal and Cape.

Breeding: *Season*: September to April. *Nest*: Platform of twigs and sticks in high fork of tree, usually at forest border. *Clutch*: 1 egg. *Eggs*: White; measure (21) 39 × 29,3 (36,2–42,2 × 26,3–31,5). *Incu-bation*: 16–17 days by both sexes. *Nest-ling*: 20–21 days.

Ref. Uys, C.J. 1967. *Ostrich* 38:200–202.

---

351 (313) Delegorgue's Pigeon (Bronzenaped Pigeon) Plate 33
Withalsbosduif
Columba delegorguei

Indenga (X), iJuba (Z), [Bronzehalstaube, Glanz-nackentaube]

Measurements: Length 28–30 cm; wing (6 ♂) 178–181,5–185, (6 ♀) 163–172,8–179; tail 100–110; tarsus 19–21; culmen (8) 18–20,3–22,5. Weight (2 ♂) 170 g.

Bare Parts: Iris dark brown to reddish; skin around eye dull red; bill slate, tip pale horn; cere powdery grey; legs and feet purplish pink.

Identification: Little larger than Cape Turtle Dove; generally dark, looking almost black at distance; back and wings maroon-brown with white collar on man-tle of ♂; rest of body dark slate; head of ♂ bronzy grey with pink and green high-lights, of ♀ more brownish, except on grey forehead. *Immature*: Similar to adult, but with head grey.

Voice: High-pitched series of 10–20 hoots, 1st 3 evenly pitched, 4th louder and higher-pitched, rest falling in pitch and volume, and speeding up towards end, *koo, koo, koo, KOO, ku-ku-ku-ku-ku-ku-ku*; soft ducklike *kwearg* flight call in breeding season.

Distribution: Eastern and se Africa; dis-continuously distributed in certain forest patches in Transkei, Natal, Transvaal (doubtful), Zimbabwe and Mt Goron-gosa, Mozambique.

Status: Rare resident; fairly common only in Ngoye and Dlinza Forests; some populations have altitudinal migrations. Probably Rare (RDB).

Habitat: Canopy of tall mistbelt, lowland, riverine and coastal forest.

Habits: Shy and elusive; located mostly by call; usually in pairs or small groups; freezes when first approached, then flies off fast and straight. Perches in tops of tall trees; forages morning and evening mainly in upper branches, flapping noisily about while gathering fruit, sometimes in company with Rameron Pigeons; drinks at forest streams.

Food: Fruit *(Trema, Cassipourea, Podocarpus, Macaranga capensis*, occasionally *Ficus)*, larvae of cicadas.

Breeding: *Season*: November to April. *Nest*: Platform of twigs, 5–7 m above ground in fork of forest tree. *Clutch*: 2 eggs. *Eggs*: White; measure (3) 33,1 × 26,9 (31,5–34,5 × 26,9–27). *Incubation*: Unrecorded; by both sexes. *Nestling*: Unrecorded; young fed by both parents.

TURTLE DOVES (GENUS *STREPTOPELIA*)

Doves of the genus *Streptopelia* are generally grey, sometimes tinged with purple, blue or rufous. They range in size from that of a large pigeon (about 36 cm long) down to about 25 cm. Most have a black half-collar on the hindneck. Their tail patterns differ and are good field characters for identification; the presence or absence of white in the tail should be looked for as the tail is spread on take-off. They share the habit of a towering territorial defence display, in which the male bird takes off from a perch, flapping its wings exaggeratedly as it climbs, sometimes with audible wingclaps; at the top of its trajectory it holds the wings stiffly out as it planes back to another perch, often in a wide circle or semicircle. They are all arboreal, but feed on the ground, usually on seeds. They are highly vocal, their calls being among the most characteristic sounds of Africa. They are also highly aggressive toward conspecifics, often fighting with the wings and driving off rivals with threat displays. All but the Laughing Dove have characteristic alighting calls uttered when coming in to land on a branch. These doves may commonly be seen sunbathing on lawns or other open ground.

352 (314)   **Redeyed Dove**   **Plate 33**
Grootringduif
Streptopelia semitorquata

Haikonda (K), Leebamosu, Leebana-khoroane (SS), Bvukutiva (Sh), Khopola, Nyakopo (Ts), Indlasidudu, Umakhulu (X), iHophe (Z), [Halbmondtaube]

Measurements: Length 33–36 cm; wing (16 ♂) 182–192–201, (19 ♀) 181–186–193; tail (35) 119–125–133; tarsus (35) 23–24,6–27; culmen (35) 21,5–21,8–22,5. Weight (44 ♂) 207,8–240,7–326 g, (13 ♀) 211,4–229–260,8 g, (385 unsexed) 162–251,7–310 g.

Bare Parts: Iris orange to red; skin around eye dull purplish red; bill black; cere powdery grey; legs and feet purplish red.

Identification: Large (about size of Rock Pigeon); generally dark purplish slate grey, paler pinkish grey below (other *Streptopelia* doves greyer, less tinged with mauve); black collar on hindneck; head paler grey; no white in tail (other *Strepto-*

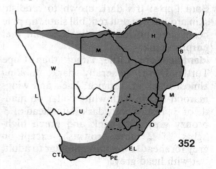

pelia doves all have white in tail, seen in flight); tail blackish, tipped dark grey; red eye and eyering not good field characters except in good light at close quarters. *Immature*: Lacks black collar; edged buffy above and below; eyering dull grey.

Voice: Far-carrying syncopated cooing phrase, *kooROOkuku, KOOku,* or *KOOku, kooROOkuku,* repeated without pause many times, somewhat higher-pitched on the 2 accented notes; in courtship somewhat subdued *ROOkuku or ROOkukuku;* quiet rasping *zzzz, zzzz* when coming in to land in tree.

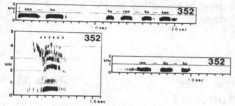

Distribution: Africa S of Sahara; in s Africa confined to S, E and NE.

Status: Common resident; range apparently spreading, probably through planting of exotic trees.

Habitat: Well developed woodland, riverine forest, exotic plantations, suburban and rural gardens with tall trees.

Habits: Solitary or in pairs, except at good food source when flocks of up to 30 birds may gather. Flight heavy but powerful; lands rather heavily compared with other *Streptopelia* species. Feeds on ground, coming to feeding stations, but more wary than other doves; rests high in tree, sometimes on exposed leafless branch.

Food: Seeds (grass, maize, sunflower, peanut, sorghum, castor oil, *Acacia cyclops,* other *Acacia* species), bulbs of *Cyperus esculentus,* fruits of *Lantana camara,* bread, termite alates.

Breeding: *Season:* All months; mainly January to September in w Transvaal. *Nest:* Platform of twigs, collected from ground or broken from tree, in fork of tree or bush; usually 2–3 m above ground, but as high as 15 m. *Clutch:* 2 eggs. *Eggs:* White; measure (58) 31,1 × 23,7 (27,2–34,5 × 21,9–25,6). *Incubation:* 16–17 days by both sexes. *Nestling:* 17–20 days; young fed by both parents.

---

353 (315) African Mourning Dove
Rooioogtortelduif
Streptopelia decipiens

Plate 33

Haikonda (K), Tuba (Ts), [Angolaturteltaube, Angolalachtaube, Brillentaube]

Measurements: Length about 30 cm; wing (13) 160–167–180; tail 107–118; tarsus 22–24; culmen 18–19. Weight (4 ♂) 145–162,2–177,7 g, (1 ♀) 160 g.

Bare Parts: Iris yellow; skin around eye red; bill brown to blackish; legs and feet purplish pink.

Identification: About size of Cape Turtle Dove; red skin around eye conspicuous (distinguishes it from Cape Turtle Dove); coloration similar to that of Redeyed Dove, but belly paler, head greyer, eye yellow, and ends of outer tail feathers white (no white in tail of Redeyed Dove); black collar on hindneck. *Immature:* Browner than adult.

Voice: Resonant 3-syllabled *wuwu-woo,* dropping in pitch on last note; loud growling *krrrowrrr* on landing, sometimes followed by hoot-growl notes, *krrrowrrr, woop-rr.*

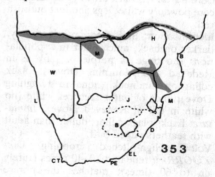

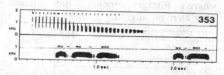

Distribution: Africa S of Sahara; in s Africa confined to subtropical N and NE.

Status: Locally common resident.

303

AFRICAN MOURNING DOVE

Habitat: Lowland riverine *Acacia* and adjacent fringing forest, cultivated lands and African villages.

Habits: Usually in pairs, but flocks gather to drink morning and evening. Feeds on ground among trees, huts and domestic stock; often tame. On landing raises tail and gives alighting call. Often vocal at night.

Food: Seeds and fallen grain.

Breeding: *Season*: September to December in Zimbabwe, June to August in Transvaal lowveld. *Nest*: Platform of twigs in fork of small tree; nesting tree may be in water. *Clutch*: 2 eggs. *Eggs*: White; measure (4) 29,9 × 22,4 (29,6–30,3 × 22–22,7). *Incubation*: 13–14 days in captivity. *Nestling*: 16–19 days; postnestling period at least 5–7 days.

354 (316) Cape Turtle Dove
Gewone Tortelduif
Streptopelia capicola
Plate 33

Haikonda (K), Leaba Kgorwana (NS), Leebanakhoroana, Lekunkunroane (SS), Njiva (Sh), Tuva (Ts), Lephôi, Mhiri, Leeba (Tw), Ihobe, Untamnyama (X), iHophe, uSamdokwe (Z), [Kapturteltaube, Kaplachtaube, Gurrtaube]

Measurements: Length 26–28 cm; wing (38 ♂) 152–160,5–170,5, (34 ♀) 152–163–174, (72 unsexed) 147–155,2–166; tail (30) 95–105,6–113,5; tarsus (7) 18–21,4–24; culmen (6) 14,5–15,7–18. Weight (1 267) 92–152,9–202 g.

Bare Parts: Iris dark brown; bill blackish; cere powdery white; legs and feet purplish red.

Identification: Size medium; clear grey, darker on back, much paler in w populations (no tinge of purple or pink as in Redeyed and Mourning Doves); black collar on hindneck (none in Laughing Dove); ends of outer rectrices white (no white in tail of Redeyed Dove). *Immature*: Lacks black collar; duller than adult with feathers edged buff.

Voice: High-pitched crooning *kuk-KOORR-ru* repeated 10–40 times (rarely up to 60 times); matches the phrase *where's FAther*; repeated high-pitched *kirrr kirrr* on alighting in tree.

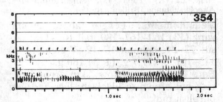

Distribution: S Africa to E Africa; throughout s Africa.

Status: Very common resident, especially in drier parts.

Habitat: Woodland (not forest), savanna, riverine bush, farmland, urban and rural gardens, city parks.

Habits: Solitary, in pairs or in flocks, sometimes of several hundred birds, especially at waterholes or good food supply. Forages on ground, walking with small steps and bobbing head; rests in tops of trees; drinks mainly in morning. Towers often; flight swift and direct. Vocal

throughout day and often at night. Becomes very tame in cities.
Food: Seeds (including those of *Acacia cyclops*, other *Acacia* species and sorghum), insêcts, fallen grain, bread, termite alates.
Breeding: *Season:* All months; mainly September-October and April-May. *Nest:* Flimsy platform of twigs and rootlets in fork of tree or bush; 1–12 m

above ground; nest may be used several times; ♂ brings nest material, ♀ builds. *Clutch:* 2 eggs. *Eggs:* White; measure (173) 28,1 × 21,6 (24,2–32 × 18,7–23,4); weigh mean 7,1 g. *Incubation:* 12–17 days by both sexes, ♂ usually by day, ♀ by night. *Nestling:* 16–20 days; fed by both sexes; dependent on parents for about 2 weeks after leaving nest.

355 (317)   Laughing Dove   Plate 33
Rooiborsduifie (Lemoenduifie)
Streptopelia senegalensis

Katere, Hamanku (K), Leebana-khoroane (SS), Njiva (Sh), Gugurhwana (Ts), Lephôi, Tsôkwane (Tw), Icelekwane, Uvelemaxhoseni (X), uKhonzane (Z), [Senegaltaube, Palmtaube]

Measurements: Length about 25 cm; wing (58 ♂) 127–138,7–149, (46 ♀) 124–134,2–144; tail (29) 104–110–118; tarsus (29) 20–22,5–25; culmen (29) 16–18,7–21. Weight (24 ♂) 83,5–97,4–118,7 g, (24 ♀) 74,4–92,5–110,1 g, (1 909 unsexed) 72–101,5–139 g.
Bare Parts: Iris dark brown; bill blackish; legs and feet purplish red.
Identification: Size smallish; chest deep rufous, spotted with black (diagnostic); head pinkish grey; back cinnamon; wings mixed cinnamon and blue; belly mostly white, merging to pale pinkish towards breast; no black ring on hindneck; ♀ overall paler than ♂; tail tipped white. *Immature:* Paler and greyer than adult; feathers edged buff; breast plain greyish.
Voice: Bubbling phrase of 6–8 notes, *koo koo kuRUkutu-koo*, individually slightly variable, but always with gentle laughing quality, falling somewhat in pitch and loudness towards end; lacks alighting call of most *Streptopelia* doves.

Distribution: Africa, Arabia, C Asia; throughout s Africa.
Status: Very common resident; somewhat nomadic in arid regions; moves from Zambia into Kalahari and Zimbabwe in wet season.
Habitat: Open woodland, savanna, Kalahari sandveld with trees (but not in as arid

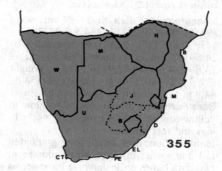

country as Cape Turtle Dove), parks, gardens, city centres.
Habits: Solitary, in pairs or in flocks at water or feeding places. Tame, especially in towns; one of the first birds to appear in new suburbs as trees grow up; comes readily to feeding stations. Forages on ground in hunched posture, walking with small steps and nodding head.
Food: Seeds (up to 8 300 per crop, mainly of grasses, sedges and ruderal weeds), fallen grain, termite alates, other insects and their larvae, small snails (animal food taken especially by ♀).
Breeding: *Season:* All months; mainly March to September (dry season). *Nest:* Frail platform of twigs and rootlets in fork of bush or tree; overall diameter 8–14 cm, thickness 3–4 cm (up to 12 cm with re-use); 1–6 m above ground; same nest used up to 8 times; material collected by ♂, built by ♀ in 2–4 days. *Clutch:* 2 eggs (rarely 1–4). *Eggs:* White; measure (164) 26,1 × 20,1 (23,8–29,5 × 18,1–22,8); weigh (1) 5,2 g. *Incubation:* 12–17 days by

both sexes, ♂ by day, ♀ by night. *Nestling*: 11–14 days; fed by both parents; post-nestling dependence 3–7 days.

Ref. Dean, W.R.J. 1977. *Ostrich Suppl.* 12:102–107; 1979a. *Ostrich* 50:215–219; 234–239; 1980. *Ostrich* 51:80–91.

356 (318)   Namaqua Dove   Plate 33
Namakwaduifie
Oena capensis

Kambowo (K), Mokhoroane, Mokhorane (SS), Kanjivamutondo, Nhondoro (Sh), Xibamba, Xituvana (Ts), Rrankundunyane, Mmalommi, Tsêbêru (Tw), Ihotyazana (X), uNkombose, isiKhombazane-senkangala (Z), [Kaptäubchen]

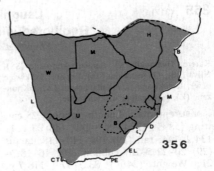

Measurements: Length 24–27 cm; wing (59 ♂) 94–107,7–117, (34 ♀) 97–104,6–111; tail (70) 121–160; tarsus (70) 14,5–15,5–16,5; culmen (10 ♂) 12,6–13,8–14,4, (4 ♀) 13,9–14,2–14,6. Weight (39 ♂) 29–40,2–47 g, (39 ♀) 29–38,8–44,8 g, (101 unsexed) 32–40–48 g.
Bare Parts: Iris brown; bill (♂) yellow to yellow-orange, base purple, (♀) blackish; legs and feet purple.
Identification: Size small; long graduated tail diagnostic; in flight wings cinnamon; two dark bands enclosing pale band across lower back. *Male*: Face and breast black; bill yellow with purple base. *Female*: No black on face and breast; bill black. *Immature*: Heavily spotted with buff and barred with black.
Voice: Quiet 2-syllabled hoot, lower on explosive first note, higher on mournful longer second note, *kuh-whooo*, repeated several times by ♂.

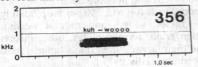

Distribution: Africa, Arabia and Madagascar; almost throughout s Africa, but scarce in E.
Status: Very common in drier areas, common to scarce in other parts; resident, but nomadic, especially in arid zones.
Habitat: Dry bushveld, *Acacia* thornveld, arid scrub, semidesert, riverine bush in desert, rural gardens, farmyards, fallow lands.
Habits: Solitary or in pairs, except at waterholes where large numbers come and go all day, even in midday heat. Flight fast and direct with quick irregular wingbeats, somewhat swallowlike; on landing raises and slowly lowers tail; takes off with rattling burst of wings. Usually perches low down on bush, tree or fence; also on telephone wires; forages on open ground, often on gravel roads; walks hunched with tiny steps.
Food: Small seeds.
Breeding: *Season*: All months (mainly September to December in Cape); in arid areas breeds after rain. *Nest*: Small saucer of twigs, grass stems and rootlets; usually less than 1,5 m above ground in low bush, rarely up to 3 m; sometimes on ground among shrubs or on fallen twigs or grass stems. *Clutch*: 2 eggs (sometimes 3). *Eggs*: Creamy yellow or deep buff; somewhat pointed; measure (137) 21,3 × 15,7 (18,5–24,5 × 14,2–17,8); weigh (2) mean 3,2 g. *Incubation*: 13–16 days by both sexes, ♂ from about 09:30–15:30, ♀ remainder of day and all night. *Nestling*: 15–16 days; fed by both parents.

Ref. Hoffmann, K. 1969. *J. Orn.* 110:448–464.

357 (320)

Bluespotted Dove
Blouvlekduifie
Turtur afer

[Stahlflecktaube]

Measurements: Length 22 cm; wing (5 ♂) 107–108,8–112, (5 ♀) 109–110–112; tail (10) 79–83–87; tarsus (10) 17,5–18,3–19; culmen (10) 15,5–16,3–17. Weight (2) 62,5–68,8 g.

Bare Parts: Iris brown; eyering red; bill yellow, base red; legs and feet purplish red.

Identification: Size small; above brown (Greenspotted Dove greyer above), grey on crown; two dark bands enclosing paler band across lower back; below pinkish grey (white in Tambourine Dove), shading to white on throat and belly; spots on folded wing dark iridescent blue (not green); bill yellow (blackish in Greenspotted Dove); in flight wings cinnamon. *Immature*: Has buff breast (white in Tambourine Dove).

Voice: Hooting phrase, starting off slowly and speeding up only slightly towards end, ending abruptly after only 6–9 quick notes (up to 20 quick notes in Tambourine Dove) *hoo, hoo, hoo, huwoo, huwoo, hu-hu-hu-hu-hu-hu*; altogether slower, lower-pitched, more even-toned, and less prolonged than call of Greenspotted Dove; similar in pitch to call of Tambourine Dove, but much shorter and not speeding up so much at end.

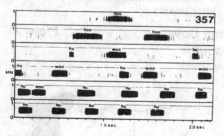

Distribution: Africa S of Sahara; in s Africa confined to e Zimbabwe, adjacent Mozambique, and n Transvaal.

Status: Locally common resident. Probably Rare (RDB).

Habitat: Edges of lowland evergreen forest and riverine woodland; also dense thickets and clearings in montane evergreen forest; in parts of Mozambique replaces Greenspotted Dove in open woodland.

Habits: Solitary or in pairs or small groups. Forages in clearings, on roads and in cultivated lands; when disturbed flies into dense evergreen cover, rising with sharp wingclap. Often tame around villages.

Food: Small seeds.

Breeding: *Season*: August to April in Zimbabwe. *Nest*: Small platform of twigs and rootlets; in fork of tree up to about 3 m; may use old nest as foundation. *Clutch*: 2 eggs. *Eggs*: Creamy buff; measure (9) 23 × 17,2 (22–24,6 × 16,9–17,5). *Incubation*: 15–17 days. *Nestling*: 15–18 days in captivity.

358 (321)

Greenspotted Dove
Groenvlekduifie
Turtur chalcospilos

Njiva Mutondo (Sh), Xivambalana (Ts), Ivukazana (X), isiKhombazane-sehlanze (Z), [Bronzeflecktaube]

Measurements: Length 19–20 cm; wing (7 ♂) 110,5–112,9–116, (6 ♀) 108–109,9–111,5; tail (13) 75–83,5–89; tarsus (13) 17–18–19; culmen (13) 17–18,2–19,5. Weight (6 ♂) 58,5–65,9–77 g, (7 ♀) 50,2–59,7–68,8 g, (45 unsexed) 50,5–61,9–74,8 g.

Bare Parts: Iris dark brown; bill blackish; legs and feet purplish red.

Identification: Size small; similar to Bluespotted Dove, but wingspots green; back grey (brown in Bluespotted Dove); bill black (yellow in Bluespotted Dove); in flight looks greyer than Bluespotted Dove; two darks bands enclosing pale band across lower back; wings cinnamon; below pinkish (Tambourine Dove white below). *Immature*: Similar to adult, but no bars across lower back; secondaries blacker; buffy below; no wingspots; barred buff and blackish above and below.

Voice: Similar to voice of Tambourine and Bluespotted Doves, but higher-pitched than either, and falling in pitch slightly towards end (pitch even in other two *Turtur* species), *hoo, wuhoo, hoo, whoo, tu, tu-tu-tu-tu-tu*, starting off deliberately and speeding up at end.

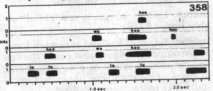

Distribution: S to E Africa; in s Africa absent from sw Cape and dry W; vagrant to Windhoek and Mariental, Namibia.

Status: Common resident.

Habitat: Most woodland, *Acacia* scrub, gardens; not forest (except dry sand forest in Thongaland) or arid savanna.

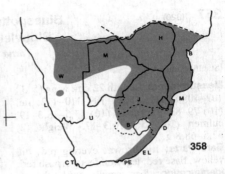

358

Habits: Usually solitary or in pairs. Takes off with loud wingclap when disturbed; flight zigzagging, usually not far; lands abruptly, then raises tail once or twice. Feeds on bare ground under trees or on roads and clearings. ♂ usually perches on low exposed branch while calling.

Food: Seeds, berries, termite alates.

Breeding: *Season*: All months (mainly September to March); little breeding June to August. *Nest*: Small platform of twigs and rootlets; usually less than 3 m above ground, in bush or small tree. *Clutch*: 2 eggs. *Eggs*: Creamy yellow or buff; measure (31) 23,2 × 17,6 (21,8–24,9 × 16,8–19,1); weigh (2) mean 4 g. *Incubation*: 17 days by both sexes, mostly by ♀. *Nestling*: 16–20 days; fed by both parents on seeds, insects and molluscs; young dependent on parents for up to 2 weeks after leaving nest.

---

359 (319) **Tambourine Dove** **Plate 33**
Witborsduifie
Turtur tympanistria

Xiwambalane (Ts), Isavu (X), isiKhombazane-sehlathi, isiBhelu (Z), [Tamburintaube]

Measurements: Length 21–23 cm; wing (118 ♂) 107,5–116,1–123, (63 ♀) 98–113,6–120; tail (64 ♂) 72–89–100, (35 ♀) 70–87,5–95, (52 unsexed) 79–94,2–100; tarsus (153) 16–19,8–22,5; culmen (159) 13–15,6–19. Weight (163 ♂) 60–72,8–88 g, (101 ♀) 57,3–69,4–87 g, (1 unsexed) 82 g.

Bare Parts: Iris brown; eyering purplish; bill blackish to purplish; legs and feet purplish red.

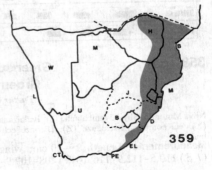

359

Identification: Size small; similar to Greenspotted and Bluespotted Doves, but underparts and face white in ♂; breast grey in ♀; clear white eyebrow in both sexes; wingspots metallic blueblack; in flight wings cinnamon; bands across rump faint (distinct in other *Turtur* species); outer rectrices broadly tipped pale grey (tipped black in other *Turtur* species). *Immature*: Barred with tawny and dark brown above and below.

Voice: Similar to voice of other *Turtur* species, but more prolonged; pitch even throughout call, starting deliberately and ending with up to 20 quick notes (only 6–9 quick notes in Bluespotted Dove) *woo, woohoo, woo, woo, tutoo tu-tu-tu-tu-tu-tu-tu.....*; lower-pitched than call of Greenspotted Dove.

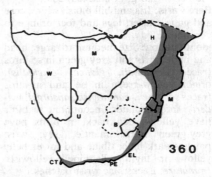

Distribution: Africa S of Sahara; in s Africa confined to S and E.

Status: Common resident.

Habitat: Lowland evergreen forest, riverine woodland, dense thickets; less often on edges of montane forest.

Habits: Usually solitary or in pairs. Forages in clearings and on roads at forest edge; when disturbed rises suddenly; flies zigzagging through trees, seldom far. When calling, wings twitch slightly at each note.

Food: Seeds, berries, molluscs, insects.

Breeding: *Season*: September to May in Zimbabwe, mainly October to March in S Africa. *Nest*: Frail platform of twiglets and rootlets; placed toward end of horizontal branch, or among interlaced creepers; 1–10 m above ground. *Clutch*: 2 eggs. *Eggs*: Creamy white; measure (24) 24,5 × 18 (22,9–26 × 16,6–19). *Incubation*: 17–20 days by both sexes, mainly by ♀. *Nestling*: 19–22 days; fed by both parents; dependent on adults for about a week after leaving nest.

360 (322) Cinnamon Dove Plate 33
Kaneelduifie
Aplopelia larvata

Mhuputi (Sh), Indenge, Isagqukhwe (X), isAgqukwe (Z), [Zimttaube]

Measurements: Length 25–30 cm; wing (26 ♂) 145–152,6–158, (27 ♀) 143–148,6–155; tail (6 ♂) 103–106,8–112, (11 ♀) 92–99,8–110, (10 unsexed) 91–101,8–117; tarsus (36) 23–26,9–30; culmen (10) 20–21,3–22,5. Weight (7 ♂) 133,2–152,5–165,5 g, (15 ♀) 133–149,7–169,3 g, (8 unsexed) 146–165,9–195 g.

Bare Parts: Iris reddish to dusky, outer rim pink; eyering pink; bill black; legs and feet purplish pink.

Identification: Size medium; dark with pale face; above greenish black; below cinnamon; in flight outer rectrices broadly tipped pale grey; wings all dark like body. *Immature*: Barred and scaled with rust and black above; below buff, finely barred greyish brown.

Voice: Usually silent; deep resonant *woo-oop, woo-oop* repeated several times, each note rising slightly at end.

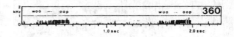

CINNAMON DOVE

Distribution: S and E Africa; in s Africa confined to S and E.
Status: Common resident, but easily overlooked.
Habitat: Understory of evergreen forest and thickets; also exotic plantations (pine, oak).
Habits: Solitary, in pairs, or small groups. Keeps to deep shade of forest undergrowth, foraging among leaf litter on forest floor with restless steps, and tail held high; drinks regularly at forest streams, landing some way off and walking to and from water before taking off again. When disturbed flies up suddenly, but not far, dropping again into thick cover; sometimes perches in small tree. Most

vocal early morning, October to March.
Food: Seeds, berries, insects, molluscs, bulbs, tubers.
Breeding: *Season*: July to March in Zimbabwe, October to April in Natal. *Nest*: Platform of twigs, usually on horizontal branch or among matted creepers; built in just over 7 days; from about 1–20 m above ground in tree at edge of clearing. *Clutch*: 2 eggs. *Eggs*: Creamy to yellowish white; measure (12) 28,1 × 22,2 (26–29,9 × 20,9–23,6). *Incubation*: 14–18 days, mainly or entirely by ♀. *Nestling*: 20–21 days; fed by both parents; young accompany parents for up to 2 more months.

Ref. Uys, C.J. 1973. *Bokmakierie* 25:66–69.

361 (323)   **African Green Pigeon**   **Plate 33**
Papegaaiduif
Treron calva

Huriti (Sh), Mbambawunye, Ngwambani (Ts), Intendekwane (X), iJubantondo (Z), [Grüne Fruchttaube, Grüntaube]

Measurements: Length 28–30 cm; wing (22 ♂) 171–175–179, (15 ♀) 162–168–174; tail (37) 88–110; tarsus (37) 20–25; culmen (from cere) (37) 12–14; cere (37) 7–9. Weight (3 ♂) 234,4–238,9–242,7 g, (3 ♀) 215–243,7–269 g, (1 unsexed) 285,6 g.
Bare Parts: Iris and bill bluish white; cere and gape scarlet; legs and feet orange to vermilion.
Identification: Size medium to large; head and underparts soft grey-green in se birds (races *delalandii, glauca, orientalis*), bright yellow-green in ne and n birds (races *schalowi, damarensis, ansorgei, vylderi*); intermediates uncommon; se birds have yellow-green back, n birds have grey-green back; mantle grey; wrist patches dark lilac; tibiae and lower belly yellow; in flight tail tipped yellowish. *Immature*: Lacks lilac wrist patches.
Voice: Various whistling and growling notes interspersed, *tweeu, tweety, tweety tweety, krrr, krrr, krrup, krrr, krrr,* etc.

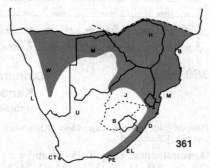

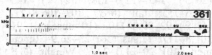

Distribution: Africa S of Sahara; in s Africa in higher-rainfall areas from Humansdorp northwards; absent from arid regions, Kalahari Basin and highveld.
Status: Common resident.
Habitat: Woodland, especially riverine fig forest; also edges of evergreen forest.
Habits: Usually gregarious in small groups. Forages in trees, flapping to keep balance, and often hanging upside down; somewhat parrotlike; green plumage makes effective camouflage; remains still

310

when not feeding and when alarmed. Flight fast and direct.

Food: Fruit (mainly figs).

Breeding: *Season*: May to February in Zimbabwe, August to January in S Africa; probably most months in s Africa. *Nest*: Frail platform of coarse twigs and leaf petioles on sloping or horizontal fork of leafy tree with good visibility from nest site; sometimes in mistletoe clump on branch; 2–5–21 m (97 nests) above ground; built by both sexes; nests may be in loose aggregations, 18–20 m apart. *Clutch*: 1–2 eggs (usually 2). *Eggs*: White; measure (42) 30,5 × 23,7 (28,3–34,3 × 21,6–25,7). *Incubation*: 13–14 days by both sexes. *Nestling*: 11–13 days.

Ref. Tarboton, W.R. & Vernon, C.J. 1971. *Ostrich* 42:190–192.

15. Order PSITTACIFORMES (One family; sometimes considered as three families)

15:1. Family 44 PSITTACIDAE—PARROTS, COCKATOOS, ETC.

Small to very large. Bill short, deep, stout and hooked downwards on upper jaw, upwards on lower jaw; tongue large and rounded or brush-like; head large; neck short; legs short and stout; feet strong, zygodactyl; body robust; wings strong, pointed or rounded (a few species almost flightless); plumage firm and sparse, usually brightly coloured; sexes alike or different; apteria prominent; tail variable; bare areas often present around eye, sometimes brightly coloured; many gregarious; most arboreal; climb with feet and bill; food fruit, nuts, seeds, nectar, etc.; usually monogamous; nest in holes in trees, banks, rocks, termite mounds, natural or excavated by the birds themselves; usually no lining; a few build nests of twigs in holes or among branches; eggs 1–8, plain white, rounded; chick naked, then sparsely downy, altricial; parental care by both sexes (sometimes incubation by female only). Distribution mainly tropical, most of s hemisphere, and tropical to subtropical parts of n hemisphere; about 330 species; eight or nine species in s Africa, one introduced.

Ref. Forshaw, J.M. & Cooper, W.T. 1989. *Parrots of the world*. London: David & Charles (Third Edition).

362 (326)

**Cape Parrot
Grootpapegaai**
Poicephalus robustus

Plates 34 & 75

Hokwe (Ts), Isikhwenene (X), isiKhwenene (Z), [Kappapagei]

Measurements: Length 33–35 cm; wing (11 ♂) 204–213,1–223, (6 ♀) 201–208,5–218; tail (11 ♂) 81–89,3–97, (6 ♀) 83–88,3–93; tarsus (11 ♂) 21–22–25, (6 ♀) 21–22,3–23; culmen (11 ♂) 31–34,1–37, (6 ♀) 32–33,5–35; mandible width (5) 17,5–20; mandible depth (5) 22–25. Weight (2 ♂) 295–326 g, (1 ♀) 320,7 g.

Bare Parts: Iris brown to red-brown; bill whitish horn; legs and feet bluish grey.

Identification: Size large; mainly dull green, brighter on rump and below; head

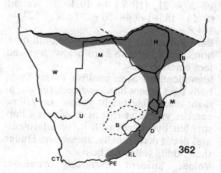

362

311

dull pale brown, darker in front of eye; tibia and bend of wing orange-scarlet; forehead dull rufous (♀) or olive yellow (♂). *Immature*: Lacks orange-scarlet in wings and legs.

Voice: Shrill high-pitched *zzkeek* or *zeek* with variations, harsh and piercing.

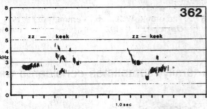

Distribution: Africa S of Sahara; in s Africa confined to E, SE, Caprivi and Kavango (Kaudom).

Status: Locally common to rare nomadic resident; seasonal migrant in n Zimbabwe, August to December. Vulnerable (RDB). Northern subspecies *P. r. suahelicus* has grey head and probably discontinuous distribution, so could be separate species, 362A Greyheaded Parrot *Poicephalus sauhelicus* (Plate 75).

Habitat: Evergreen and riverine forest, well developed woodland.

Habits: Usually in flocks of up to 12 birds. Roosts and nests in montane forests above 900 m in most of S Africa, but in Baobab and riverine woodland in Limpopo Valley; roosts singly, not in flocks. May fly over 100 km to feeding areas, usually lower-lying and coastal forests, using set flight paths; forages by clambering about high in trees. Calls in flight.

Food: Berries, kernels of fruit (*Podocarpus, Olea, Terminalia, Commiphora, Parinari, Uapaca, Pseudolachnostylis, Monotes, Syzygium, Lannea, Diospyros*; soft flesh discarded), nectar of *Erythrina*, figs.

Breeding: *Season*: October to November and March to June in Zimbabwe, September to December and May in S Africa. *Nest*: In hole in tree, usually very high and inaccessible. *Clutch*: (15) 2–3,2–4 eggs. *Eggs*: White, rounded, glossy; measure (27) 34,1 × 27,9 (30,4–39,2 × 26–30,2). *Incubation*: 24–28 days by both sexes. *Nestling*: 67–72 days (average about 69 days).

Ref. Skead, C.J. 1964. *Ostrich* 35:202–223; 1971. *Ostrich Suppl.* 9:165–178.

363 (328)　Brownheaded Parrot　Plate 34
Bruinkoppapegaai
Poicephalus cryptoxanthus

Hokwe (Ts), [Braunkopfpapagei]

Measurements: Length 22–24 cm; wing (28 ♂) 144–154,4–160, (22 ♀) 141–152,4–160; tail (10 ♂) 60–67,7–75, (10 ♀) 61–66,9–73; tarsus (10 ♂) 17–17,3–18, (10 ♀) 16–17–19; culmen (10 ♂) 19–20,4–21, (10 ♀) 18–19,4–21. Weight (5 ♂) 135–149,4–156 g, (2 ♀) 123,4–144,8 g.

Bare Parts: Iris greenish yellow; bill dark horn above, whitish horn below; legs and feet blackish grey.

Identification: Size smallish to medium; body light green; head and neck brown; in flight underwing bright yellow; no yellow patches visible at rest as in Meyer's Parrot, but hybridizes with it, so intermediates occur occasionally. *Immature*: Duller than adult; yellowish below.

Voice: Strident *chree-oo, chree-oo, KREEK*, with variations.

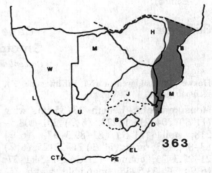

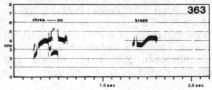

Distribution: S and E Africa; in s Africa confined to extreme E, as far S as Zululand.
Status: Common resident.
Habitat: Woodland and riverine forest.
Habits: Usually gregarious in small groups; flocks of up to 50 birds at good food source. Very noisy but hard to see in leafy trees; clambers about with feet and bill while foraging; holds pods in foot while extracting seeds (e.g. *Erythrina*).

Flight fast and direct. Sometimes perches conspicuously in dead tree.
Food: Fruit (like figs), nuts, grain, flowers, nectar, seeds.
Breeding: *Season*: April to October. *Nest*: In hole in tree; up to 10 m above ground. *Clutch*: (6) 2–2,8–3 eggs (usually 3) eggs. *Eggs*: White, glossy, rounded; measure (3) 32,5 × 26,3 (31–35,5 × 26–27). *Incubation*: 26–30 days by ♀ only; ♂ feeds ♀ on nest. *Nestling*: 84 days in captivity.

364 (327) Meyer's Parrot   Plate 34
Bosveldpapegaai
Poicephalus meyeri

Papalagae (NS), Hwenga, Gwere (Sh), Hokwe (Ts), [Goldbugpapagei]

Measurements: Length 21–23 cm;; wing (10 ♂) 144–151,5–157, (10 ♀) 141–151,7–160; tail (10 ♂) 60–67,7–75, (10 ♀) 61–66,9–73; tarsus (10 ♂) 17–17,3–18, (10 ♀) 16–17–19; culmen (10 ♂) 19–20,4–21, (10 ♀) 18–19,4–21. Weight (1) 118,3 g.
Bare Parts: Iris red-orange; bill greenish horn to blackish; legs and feet blackish grey.
Identification: Size smallish to medium; head, breast, back, wings and tail brown; belly and rump green (blue in Rüppell's Parrot); yellow patch on midcrown (sometimes absent; always absent in Rüppell's Parrot), and on bend of wing and thighs; in flight underwing yellow; hybridizes with Brownheaded Parrot, so intermediates occur in region of overlap. *Immature*: Similar to adult, but lacks yellow on crown, thighs and wing.
Voice: High-pitched *chee-chee-chee*; highly synchronized double *klink-kleep, cheewee, cheewee* duet, each note given by one member of pair; snoring or growling *kraw-her kraw-her* and shrieking alarm calls.

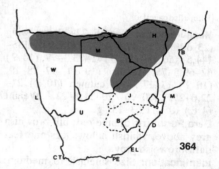

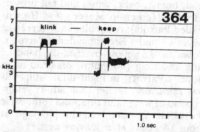

Distribution: Africa S of Sahara, except W Africa; in s Africa from n and w Transvaal to Zimbabwe, n Botswana and n Namibia.
Status: Common and widespread resident.
Habitat: Savanna woodland, riverine forest, secondary growth around cultivation, dry *Acacia* scrub with taller trees (especially Baobabs), usually near water.
Habits: In pairs or small groups. Shy and wary; when disturbed, dives out of tree before flying away low and fast. Roosts in holes in trees. Often perches conspicuously in dead tree.

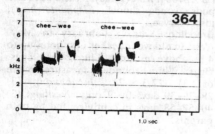

Food: Nuts, fruit kernels, fruit *(Uapaca, Monotes, Combretum, Grewia, Sclerocarya, Pseudolachnostylis, Ziziphus, Melia)*, seeds *(Brachystegia)*, flowers *(Schotia)*, grain.
Breeding: *Season*: January to October in Zimbabwe, March to June and November in Transvaal; probably all months. *Nest*: Hole in vertical tree trunk, often in old barbet's nest hole; sometimes among dense creepers and tangles. *Clutch*: (27)

2–2,7–4 eggs. *Eggs*: White; measure (15) 26,2 × 20,7 (23,6–28,5 × 18,5–23,2). *Incubation*: 29–31 days. *Nestling*: 8–9 weeks (captivity); fed by both parents by regurgitation, about every 3 hours; parent may hang upside down at nest hole while regurgitating, then swing upright to feed young.

Ref. Tarboton, W.R. 1976. *Bokmakierie* 28:44.

---

365 (329)   Rüppell's Parrot   Plate 34
Bloupenspapegaai
Poicephalus rueppellii

[Rüppellpapagei]

Measurements: Length 22–23 cm; wing (23 ♂) 145–147,9–157, (15 ♀) 135–144,5–156; tail (10 ♂) 71–73,3–77, (10 ♀) 62–69,5–75; tarsus (10 ♂) 17–18–19, (10 ♀) 17–17,7–19; culmen (10 ♂) 21–22,6–25, (10 ♀) 20–21,1–22. Weight (4 ♂) 105–115,3–132 g.
Bare Parts: Iris orange-red; bill brownish grey above, whitish below; legs and feet dark brownish grey.
Identification: Size smallish to medium; head, breast, back, wings and tail brown; belly blue (green in Meyer's and Brownheaded Parrots); rump blue in ♀ (green in Meyer's and Brownheaded Parrots), brown in ♂; yellow patches on bend of wing and tibia (no yellow on head as in Meyer's Parrot); in flight underwing yellow. *Immature*: Duller than adult; yellow on bend of wing faint or absent; otherwise like adult ♀; attains adult plumage at about 14 weeks after leaving nest.
Voice: Sharp *quaw*; shrill alarm notes increasing in pitch and volume before take-off.

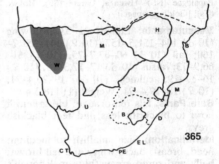

365

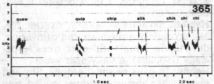

365

Distribution: Namibia from s of Windhoek to Kaokoland and w Caprivi; also coastal Angola to Luanda.

Status: Locally fairly common resident.
Habitat: Dry woodland, mostly along watercourses with tall trees; also dry *Euphorbia* forests.
Habits: Usually in pairs or small groups of up to 20 birds. Often perches in tops of tall trees, but shy and hard to see. When disturbed adopts upright posture and calls loudly before taking off; flight swift and direct. Drinks morning and afternoon.
Food: Seeds *(Acacia, Combretum, Elephantorrhiza,* wild melons), flowers *(Acacia karroo)*, fruit *(Ficus)*, *Acacia* buds and pods, young shoots *(Elephantorrhiza)*, insect larvae.
Breeding: *Season*: February to May. *Nest*: In old woodpecker nest holes up to 4 m above ground. *Clutch*: 3–4 eggs. *Eggs*: White, rounded; measure (mean of 3) 27,3 × 24. *Incubation*: (3) 28–29–30 days by ♀ only. *Nestling*: (3) 40–52–58 days in captivity; fed by both parents.

366 (329X)

Roseringed Parakeet
Ringnekparkiet
Psittacula krameri

Plate 34

[Halsbandsittich]

Measurements: Length about 40 cm; wing (9 ♂) 170–173,9–177, (8 ♀) 170–172,4–175; tail (9 ♂) 226–239,2–253, (8 ♀) 211–220–230; tarsus (9 ♂) 17–17,7–18, (8 ♀) 18–18,3–19; culmen (9 ♂) 22–23,2–25, (8 ♀) 21–23–24. Weight (5 ♂) 116–139 g.

Bare Parts: Iris yellowish white; bill coral red; legs and feet greenish slate.

Identification: Size medium; long tail diagnostic; light green all over, bluer on crown and tail; bill bright red; ♂ has pink and black collar around neck; ♀ has indistinct emerald green ring around neck. *Immature:* Like ♀; adult ♂ plumage attained after 2 years.

Voice: Loud shrill screaming *kee-ak*, sometimes repeated several times, fast or slow; also variety of whistles and chattering notes.

Distribution: Sahelian zone of Africa from Senegal to Somalia; also peninsular India to sw China; introduced to various parts of world; in s Africa established near Sodwana Bay (Zululand) and Durban.

Status: Scarce and local; numbers probably increasing; nature of introduction unknown, but probably from escaped cagebirds; established in Johannesburg since about 1970.

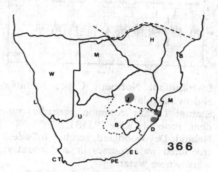

366

Habitat: Woodland and adjacent cultivated lands.

Habits: Gregarious in flocks of up to 60 birds. Noisy flocks raid croplands, doing considerable damage; holds food in foot while nibbling with bill. Roosts communally in tall trees. Flight swift and direct with fast wingbeats.

Food: Fruit, grain, seeds, flowers, nectar.

Breeding: *Season:* September in Johannesburg. *Nest:* In hole in tree, sometimes in old nest of barbet or woodpecker, 8–10 m above ground; entrance 7–11 cm diameter; floor lined with bark chips. *Clutch:* 3–5 eggs. *Eggs:* White, roundish ovals, not glossy; measure (39) 30,7 × 23,8 (29–33 × 23–25). *Incubation:* 26–28 days by ♀ only; ♂ feeds ♀ in nest. *Nestling:* 6–7 weeks in captivity.

367 (330)

Rosyfaced Lovebird
Rooiwangparkiet
Agapornis roseicollis

Plate 34

[Rosenpapagei]

Measurements: Length 15–18 cm; wing (14 ♂) 98–102,7–108, (13 ♀) 98–103,2–110; tail (8 ♂) 44–46,8–50, (8 ♀) 44–46,3–48; tarsus (8 ♂) 15–16–17, (8 ♀) 14–15,1–16; culmen (8 ♂) 17–17,5–18, (8 ♀) 17–17,6–19. Weight (1 ♂) 56,7 g, (14 unsexed) 48–54,8–61 g.

Bare Parts: Iris dark brown; bill green-

ish horn to yellowish; legs and feet grey.

Identification: Size small; bright green, more yellowish below; face, throat and breast rose pink; forecrown and eyebrow bright red; rump bright blue; dumpy shape; tail short. *Immature:* Duller than adult; bill marked with black at base of upper jaw. *Chick:* Has red down at hatching.

ROSYFACED LOVEBIRD

Voice: Shrill metallic *shreek*, singly or in series; often calls in flight.

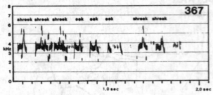

Distribution: Northern Cape, Namibia and sw Angola.
Status: Locally common nomadic resident. Probably Rare (RDB).
Habitat: Dry woodland, scrubby hillsides, tree-lined watercourses in arid country; usually near water.
Habits: Usually gregarious in small flocks of up to 15 birds; sometimes in larger flocks of hundreds at good food source. Flight very fast and direct, but manoeuvres dextrously between trees. Forages by clambering about in branches of trees; drinks regularly at waterholes. May roost in nests of Whitebrowed Sparrowweaver or Sociable Weaver.
Food: Seeds, berries, flowers, grain crops.
Breeding: Pair bonds formed while still

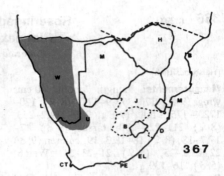

367

in immature plumage, maintained for life. *Season:* February to April. *Nest:* Cup-shaped structure of bark strips, leaves and grass, carried by ♀ in rump feathers (rarely in bill); in hole in rock face or building, or in chamber of Sociable Weaver nest; colonial. *Clutch:* 4–6 eggs. *Eggs:* Dull white; measure (43) 23,7 × 17,5 (20,4–26,3 × 16,3–19). *Incubation:* 23 days by ♀ only. *Nestling:* 42–43 days; fed by both parents, more by ♂ than by ♀; dependent on parents for about 14 days after leaving nest.

Ref. Dilger, W.C. 1962. *Sci. Amer.* 206 (1):89–98; 1964. *Living Bird* 3:135–148.

368 (332) Lilian's Lovebird Plate 34
Niassaparkiet
Agapornis lilianae

Poro (K), [Erdbeerköpfchen]

Measurements: Length 13–14 cm; wing (8 ♂) 90–92,8–95, (8 ♀) 89–91,9–94; tail (8 ♂) 36–38,4–41, (8 ♀) 35–36,8–38; tarsus (8 ♂) 13–14,1–15, (8 ♀) 13–13,9–15; culmen (8 ♂) 14–14,5–15, (8 ♀) 14–14,8–16. Weight (1) 29,2 g.
Bare Parts: Iris dark red-brown; eyering white; bill coral red, base white; legs and feet grey-brown.
Identification: Size small; bright green, yellower below and on rump; face and forecrown orange-red to salmon pink; bill red; broad white eyering. *Immature:*

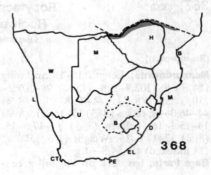

368

Blackish on cheeks; black marks at base of upper jaw.

Voice: Shrill chatter, like rattling of metal chain; also shrill sharp screech.

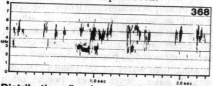

Distribution: Southern Tanzania to Zambezi Valley; does not overlap with Blackcheeked or Rosyfaced Lovebirds.

Status: Very common resident in patches along Zambezi River.

Habitat: Low-altitude river valleys, associated with mopane and *Acacia* woodland.

Habits: Highly gregarious in noisy flocks of 20–300 or more birds. Forages on ground and in trees; flocks of 200–300 birds feed on Wild Rice *Oryza perennis*

and grass seeds; visits water often. Flight fast and direct. Towards sundown flocks break up into smaller groups of 4–20 birds that perch on treetops; about half an hour after sunset they enter holes, 3–8 cm diameter (mainly in Mopane trees), to roost; holes entered tail-first until 4–25 birds together, depending on size of hole.

Food: Seeds, grain, fruit, leaf buds, flowers.

Breeding: *Season:* September, January and February (January to July in Zambia). *Nest:* Bulky domed bowl with tubular entrance, built by ♀ of bark strips, twigs and stalks carried in bill; in hollow tree, under eaves of building, and possibly in nests of Redbilled Buffalo Weaver. *Clutch:* 3–5 eggs. *Eggs:* White; measure (17) 21,3 × 16,4 (19,7–22,8 × 15,6–17). *Incubation:* 22–23 days by ♀ only. *Nestling:* 35–40–44 days; fed by both parents.

369 (331) Blackcheeked Lovebird / Swartwangparkiet

Agapornis nigrigenis

Plate 34

Poro (K), [Rußköpfchen]

Measurements: Length 13–14 cm; wing (8 ♂) 91–94,6–97, (8 ♀) 90–94,5–98; tail (8 ♂) 40–42,3–45, (8 ♀) 40–42,8–45; tarsus (8 ♂) 13–13,5–14, (8 ♀) 13–13,8–14; culmen (8 ♂) 14–14,6–15, (8 ♀) 14–14,9–16.

Bare Parts: Iris brown; eyering white; bill coral red, base white; legs and feet greybrown.

Identification: Size small; bright green, yellower below and on rump; cheeks and throat brownish black (diagnostic); upper breast pale orange-red; forecrown reddish brown; bill red. *Immature:* Has black marks at base of bill; iris pale brown.

Voice: Shrill chatter, somewhat like that of Rosyfaced Lovebird.

Distribution: Victoria Falls, Zimbabwe, to sw Zambia.

Status: Locally common resident; numbers severely reduced by trapping for cagebird trade. Sometimes considered conspecific with Lilian's Lovebird, but ranges do not overlap.

Habitat: Lowland river valleys between

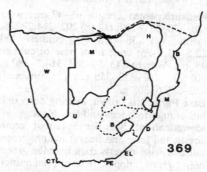

600 and 1 000 m; closely associated with mopane woodland.

Habits: Gregarious, often in large flocks. Similar to Lilian's Lovebird.

Food: Seeds, grain, flowers, buds, fruit.

Breeding: *Season:* November-December in Zambia (possibly September at Victoria Falls). *Nest:* Similar to that of Lilian's Lovebird; material carried in bill; in hole in tree. *Clutch:* 3–6 eggs. *Eggs :* White; measure (33) 21,7 × 16,8 (19,6–24,9 × 15–18). *Incubation:* 23 days by ♀ only. *Nestling:* (7) 30–39 days in captivity; sometimes up to 40 days; fed by both parents.

16. Order MUSOPHAGIFORMES (One family)

16:1. Family 45 MUSOPHAGIDAE—LOURIES OR TOURACOS

Medium to large. Bill short, strong, stout and broad, sometimes brightly coloured, sometimes with nostrils near tip; legs short to medium, strong; feet strong with 4th toe (outermost) reversible—semizygodactyl; tail long and broad; wings short and rounded; plumage usually brightly coloured (mostly red, green, purple and blue), some species grey, or grey and white; red (turacin) and green (turacoverdin) pigments copper-based, unique to the family; red pigment does not wash out in water as sometimes claimed; head conspicuously crested; skin around eye usually naked; sexes alike; arboreal; often gregarious; flight laboured but strong; run well along branches; voice loud and croaking; food mostly fruit, seeds and buds, some insects, molluscs and worms; monogamous; nest a platform of sticks in a tree; eggs 2–3 plain white or bluish; chick downy, altricial; parental care by both sexes. Distribution Africa S of the Sahara (not Madagascar); 22–24 species; four (possibly five or six) species in s Africa.

Ref. Chapin, J.P. 1963. *Living Bird* 2:57–67.
  Dowsett-Lemaire, F. & Dowsett, R.J. 1988. *Tauraco* 1:64–71.
  Moreau, R.E. 1958a. *Ibis* 100:67–112; 1958b. *Ibis* 100:238–270.

370 (336) Knysna Lourie / Knysnaloerie — Plate 34

Tauraco corythaix

Hurukuru (Sh), Ntlume, Tlulutlulu (Ts), Igolomi (X), iGwalagwala (Z), [Helmturako]

Measurements: Length 45–47 cm; wing (28) 170–181–190; tail (8) 202–214,2–228; tarsus (8) 38–41,8–44; culmen (8) 22,5–23,5–25; crest from base of culmen 45–60. Weight (13 ♂) 280–314,1–380 g, (10 ♀) 262–312–350 g, (5 unsexed) 280–296,6–308 g.

Bare Parts: Iris brown; eyering deep red; bill orange-red; legs and feet black.

Identification: Size large (about crow-sized); tail long and heavy; mainly green; tail and wing coverts dark metallic green; crest green, tipped white (diagnostic); length of crest varies geographically, being longer in n birds; bill red (black in Purple-crested Lourie); in flight crimson remiges conspicuous. *Immature*: Duller than adult; less red in wings; crest shorter; bill olive brown. *Chick*: Downy greyish brown.

Voice: Deliberate series, starting with about 3 trumpetlike notes, followed by 7–10 growling notes, rising in volume, then falling again slightly, *woop woop woop korr, korrr, korrr, korrr....*; much slower than call of Purplecrested Lourie; also guttural breathy *khrrr , khrrr* alarm notes with head thrown back onto shoulders.

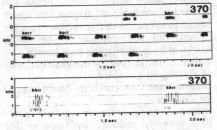

Distribution: S to E Africa; in s Africa confined to extreme SE, E and Caprivi.
Status: Fairly common resident. Probably should be regarded as three separate spe-

cies: Knysna Lourie *T. corythaix* in S Africa, Livingstone's Lourie *T. livingstonii* in Mozambique and e Zimbabwe, and Schalow's Lourie *T. schalowi* along Zambezi Valley, distinguishable on voice and shape of crest.

Habitat: Evergreen and riverine forest, dense thickets; sometimes also well developed adjacent *Brachystegia* or *Uapaca* woodland.

Habits: Solitary or in small groups of up to 14 birds. Flight heavy on rounded red wings; glides and lands in centre of tree; runs with flexed legs along branches, and bounds with agility from branch to branch; raises tail between runs. Often vocal in response to one bird's call, until several birds calling together.

Food: Fruit, insects, earthworms.

Breeding: *Season*: November to January and June-July in s and e Cape, August to November in Natal, September to March in Zimbabwe. *Nest*: Shallow platform of sticks, like large dove's nest; in leafy tree or dense creepers. *Clutch*: (10) 1–1,7–2 eggs (usually 2, sometimes 3). *Eggs*: White and smooth; measure (15) 38,2 × 33,5 (35,6–40,9 × 31,6–35,8); weigh (5) 25,5–26,3–27 g. *Incubation*: 23–28 days by both sexes; parents may incubate together. *Nestling*: About 26 days, but chicks may leave nest briefly at 20 days; fed by both parents by regurgitation; parents also eat faeces of young.

Ref. Jarvis, M.J.F. & Currie, M.H. 1979. *Ostrich* 50:38–44.

371 (337) Purplecrested Lourie
Bloukuifloerie
Tauraco porphyreolophus

Plate 34

Hurukuru, Chikurungadovi (Sh), Ntlume, Tlulutlulu (Ts), iGwalagwala (Z), [Glanzhaubenturako]

Measurements: Length 41–42 cm; wing (6 ♂) 172–179,9–185, (6 ♀) 171–180,8–189; tail (35) 180–210; tarsus (35) 35–40; culmen 24–28. Weight (5 ♂) 224,6–269,2–303,2 g, (11 ♀) 217,8–287,3–328,4 g.

Bare Parts: Iris brown; eyering scarlet; bill, legs and feet black.

Identification: Size large to medium; mainly green; rounded crest and wing coverts metallic purple; tail greenish black; bill black; in flight crimson wings conspicuous. *Immature*: Duller than adult. *Chick*: Downy greyish brown.

Voice: Rapid, rather high-pitched series of 10–15 *ko-ko-ko-ko* notes, rising in volume and pitch and merging into about 20 slower growling *krr-krr-krr-krr* notes, ending abruptly; much faster than call of Knysna Lourie; also wild high-pitched gobbling *kro-kro-kro-kro* and explosive *kok kok*.

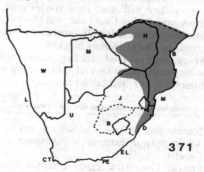

371

Distribution: S to E Africa; in s Africa confined to extreme E.

Status: Fairly common resident.

Habitat: Riverine forest, evergreen thickets, woodland, dense thornveld, savanna, parks and gardens.

Habits: In pairs or small groups. Shy and hard to observe; keeps to canopy of trees. Very agile; runs along branches and leaps through canopy from branch to branch. Flight heavy, interspersed with glides. Calls answered by neighbouring birds until several calling at once. Similar to Knysna Lourie, with which it may overlap, but prefers drier country generally.

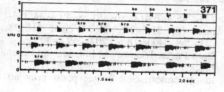

Food: Fruit; young fed insects and slugs.
Breeding: *Season*: August to January.
Nest: Platform of sticks in tree or creeper, up to about 4 m above ground; often in isolated thicket or at edge of forest. *Clutch*: (38) 1–2,4–4 eggs (usually 2–3). *Eggs*: White, glossy; measure (25) 38,1 ×

34,6 (36,2–42,9 × 33,3–37); weigh (6) 26,4 g. *Incubation*: 22–25 days by both sexes; both parents may incubate together. *Nestling*: About 25 days; full flight at 35–38 days; young fed by both parents by regurgitation; parents eat faeces of young.

372 (–) Ross's Lourie Plate 34
Rooikuifloerie
Musophaga rossae

[Rossturako]

Measurements: Length about 51 cm; wing 218–242; tail 230–254; tarsus 39–49; culmen 41–51.
Bare Parts: Iris dark brown; facial skin yellow; bill yellow, tinged red on frontal shield, base of lower jaw brownish; legs and feet black.
Identification: Size large; deep violet-black, except for crimson crest and remiges; yellow bill and face conspicuous. *Immature*: Duller than adult; bill blackish; forehead feathered; only centre of crown crimson. *Chick*: Downy blackish.
Voice: Various loud cackling, cooing and rolling calls, often several birds together, something like orchestra tuning up.

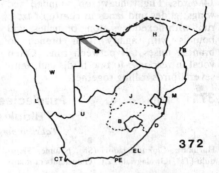

372

372

Distribution: Africa S of Sahara; enters s Africa only in extreme n Botswana and Caprivi.
Status: Uncertain; fairly common elsewhere in Africa; probably resident, but at very edge of range; heard calling frequently near Ikoga, n Botswana, but only 1 specimen collected there.
Habitat: Belts and patches of lowland evergreen and riverine forest; edges of

larger forest tracts, but not forest interior; also *Euphorbia* forest and dense *Brachystegia* woodland, especially thickets on termite mounds.
Habits: Usually in groups of 10–12 birds. Elusive but noisy, mostly June to December; freezes when disturbed. Flies clumsily; runs and hops like squirrel along branches.
Food: Fruit.
Breeding: *Season*: Unknown in s Africa; September to February in Zambia. *Nest*: Platform of sticks and twigs in tree. *Clutch*: 2 eggs. *Eggs*: White or bluish white; measure (2) 40,9–41,2 × 37–37,1. *Incubation*: Unrecorded. *Nestling*: Unrecorded.

373 (339) Grey Lourie Plate 34
Kwêvoël
Corythaixoides concolor

Nkwe (K), Mokowe (NS), Kuwe, Pfunye (Sh), Nkwenyana (Ts), Mokuê (Tw), umKlewu (Z), [Graulärmvogel]

Measurements: Length 47–50 cm; wing (38 unsexed) 198–214,4–228,5, (5 ♂) 214–219,8–228, (4 ♀) 216–219,2–224; tail (9) 233–245,4–264; tarsus (9) 38–40,4–44; culmen (9) 23,5–24,3–25. Weight (16 ♂) 221–268–340 g, (8 ♀) 202–269,8–305 g.
Bare Parts: Iris brown; bill, legs and feet black.
Identification: Size large; plain grey all

over; faint greenish wash on breast hardly visible in field; crest long and slightly shaggy; no red in wings. *Immature*: Tinged buff; crest shorter than that of adult. *Chick*: Downy dusky brown.

Voice: Loud drawn-out nasal *go-'way* (hence called Goaway Bird) or *kwê*; various yowls, grunts and shrieks.

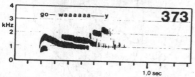

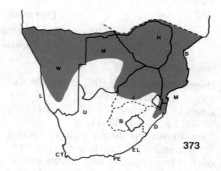

Distribution: Zululand and Angola to Tanzania; in s Africa absent from s parts, drier Kalahari sandveld and extremely arid parts of Namibia.

Status: Common resident.

Habitat: Bushveld, savanna, riverine woodland in arid country.

Habits: In pairs or small groups; larger groups (up to 60 birds) may gather at water to drink. Highly vocal, especially when disturbed; raises and lowers crest when alarmed; alert and inquisitive. Quick and agile in trees, bounding about from branch to branch and weaving through matted creepers. Flight laboured, but often sustained for several hundred metres. Roosts in groups of 3–5 birds at night.

Food: Fruit, flowers, buds, leaves; also insects, nestling birds, seeds.

Breeding: *Season*: All months. *Nest*: Scanty platform of sticks and twigs; in fork of crown of tree (usually thorny); also in clump of mistletoe or matted creeper; 1,5–5–20 m above ground (128 nests; usually 3–10 m). *Clutch*: (174) 1–2,6–4 eggs (usually 2–3). *Eggs*: Pale bluish white, slightly glossy; measure (60) 40,8 × 32,9 (38,0–45,1 × 31–34,8). *Incubation*: 26–28 days by both sexes. *Nestling*: 14–21 days; flies at about 42 days; fed by regurgitation by both parents and sometimes at least 1 helper.

17. Order CUCULIFORMES (One family)

17:1. Family 46 CUCULIDAE—CUCKOOS, COUCALS, ANIS, ROADRUNNERS, COUAS, ETC.

Small to large. Bill arched on culmen, strong and sometimes deep and stout; legs short to medium; feet zygodactyl; claw of 1st toe (inner hind toe) straight in coucals (genus *Centropus*), curved in other genera; wings long and pointed in cuckoos, short and rounded in coucals; tail usually rather heavy and longish; plumage variable, often spotted and barred; sexes usually similar; most arboreal (a few terrestrial); voice usually loud and monotonous; food mostly insects and other invertebrates, also smaller vertebrates like frogs and reptiles; many true cuckoos brood-parasitic, laying their eggs in nests of other bird species; non-parasitic species build stick platforms, bowl-shaped nests, or domed nests (coucals) in trees; eggs 2–6, variable in colour and markings, often matching those of host in cuckoos; young naked or coarsely downy at hatching, altricial; no parental care in brood parasites, otherwise parental care by both sexes. Distribution worldwide, mainly tropical and lower temperate latitudes; 127 species; 18 (possibly 19 or 20) species in s Africa.

Ref. Friedmann, H. 1964. *Smithson. Misc. Coll.* 146(4):1–127; 1968. *U.S. Natn. Mus. Bull.* 265:1–137.
Payne, R.B. & Payne, K. 1967. *Ostrich* 38:135–143.
Skead, C.J. 1951. *Ostrich* 22:163–175; 1952. *Ostrich* 23:2–15.

374 (340) Eurasian Cuckoo
Europese Koekoek
Cuculus canorus

Plate 35

Mukuku (K), [Kuckuck]

Measurements: Length about 38 cm; wing ♂ 216–228, ♀ 200–223; tail 165–180; tarsus 18–24; culmen 24–28. Weight (2 ♂) 103–113 g, (2 ♀) 113–117 g.

Bare Parts: Iris bright yellow; eyering chrome yellow; bill dark horn, grading to olive at base; legs and feet chrome yellow.

Identification: Size medium. *Normal (grey) form*: Very similar to African Cuckoo, hard to distinguish in field; above grey; chest grey; belly barred black-and-white (barring coarser than that of African Cuckoo); bill blackish with pale greenish base (bill of African Cuckoo yellow, tip black); tail black, long and heavy, spotted and barred with white (bars incomplete; complete in African Cuckoo). *Erythristic (red) form*: Very rare (♀ only); above reddish brown, barred black; below off-white, barred black.

Voice: Silent in s Africa (any vocal greyish cuckoo is therefore likely to be African Cuckoo); in breeding area calls *KOOK-koo*, accented on first syllable.

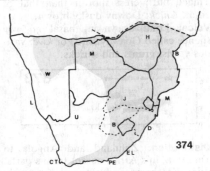

374

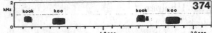

374

Distribution: Breeds Europe, Asia and N Africa; migrates S to rest of Africa; in s Africa absent from most of Cape Province, Kalahari sandveld and more arid parts of Namibia.

Status: Uncommon nonbreeding Palaearctic migrant, September to April. Two populations visit s Africa, *C. c. canorus* from Europe and n Asia (uniform dark grey head and back), and *C. c. subtelephonus* from s Asia (paler grey above; very pale on throat).

Habitat: Woodland, coastal bush, open rolling foothills with scattered trees.

Habits: Solitary. Shy and secretive, usually keeping to leafy trees, but sometimes perches in open on fence or telephone wire. Rather goshawklike in flight; wingbeats quick, but wings more pointed than those of hawk. Forages in trees, or sometimes walks on ground among leaf litter.

Food: Mainly hairy caterpillars; also other insects and their larvae.

Breeding: Extralimital.

375 (341) African Cuckoo
Afrikaanse Koekoek
Cuculus gularis

Plate 35

Mukuku (K), [Afrikanischer Kuckuck]

Measurements: Length 30–33 cm; wing (15 ♂) 201–217,1–230, (11 ♀) 200–205,9–215; tail (10) 115–152,3–169; tarsus (10) 19–20–21; culmen (10) 22–24,9–28. Weight (1 ♀) 104 g, (3 unsexed) 100–107,7–113 g.

Bare Parts: Iris yellow (♂) or light brown (♀); eyering yellow; bill yellow-orange, tip black; gape and inside of mouth red-

dish orange; legs and feet orange-yellow.

Identification: Size medium; very similar to Eurasian Cuckoo, hard to distinguish in field; upperparts dark slate grey, paler on rump; throat and breast pale grey; belly barred black-and-white (more finely than belly of Eurasian Cuckoo); bill mainly yellow, tip black (bill of Eurasian Cuckoo mainly blackish, base pale greenish); orange gape noticeably broad; tail

heavy, blackish, spotted and completely barred white (barring incomplete in Eurasian Cuckoo). *Immature:* Above more tawny than adult, boldly barred and speckled with white; throat and breast buff, barred blackish. *Chick:* Naked, dark purplish with bright orange mouth lining.
Voice: Loud melancholy 2-syllabled *hoop-hoop,* very similar to call of African Hoopoe, second note barely perceptibly higher in tone than first, repeated up to 50 times; ♀ calls ringing high-pitched *wit-it-it-it-it.* Calls only September to December or January, then silent.

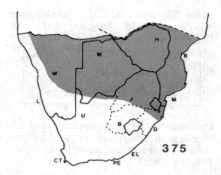

375

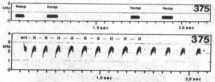

Distribution: Breeds from Zululand, n Kalahari Gemsbok National Park and n Namibia northward; migrates to tropical Africa.
Status: Uncommon to fairly common breeding intra-African migrant, August to April; rarely overwinters in s Africa.
Habitat: Woodland and *Acacia* thornveld.
Habits: Solitary; shy and elusive, so easily

overlooked unless calling. Poorly known.
Food: Almost entirely caterpillars.
Breeding: *Season:* September to December in Zimbabwe, November to January (mainly October) in S Africa. *Host:* Only authenticated host is Forktailed Drongo; host may reject up to 70% of poorly matching eggs. *Clutch:* Up to 6 eggs/♀ in a season; 1 egg/ host nest, laid when host clutch incomplete. *Eggs:* Pink, pinky buff, pale blue-green or cream, speckled with dark red-brown and mauve, forming ring around thick end; measure (6) 23,7–17,6 (23,2–24,8 × 17–18). *Incubation:* Between 11 and 17 days. *Nestling:* 22 days.

Ref. Tarboton, W. 1975. *Ostrich* 46:186–188.

---

376 (342)   **Lesser Cuckoo**   **Plate 35**
Kleinkoekoek
Cuculus poliocephalus

[Gackelkuckuck]

Measurements: Length 26–28 cm; wing (♂) 149–164, (♀) 149–153; tail 126–137; tarsus 17–19; culmen 24–25. Weight (4) 48–56–62 g.
Bare Parts: Iris brown; eyering yellow; bill blackish horn, base and gape yellow; legs and feet wax yellow.
Identification: Size small to medium; very similar to Eurasian Cuckoo, but somewhat smaller and more boldly barred on buffy belly; bill bright yellow at base (green in Eurasian Cuckoo); tail broadly and evenly barred brown.

376

323

Voice: Silent in s Africa; usual call when breeding is husky chattering *that's your CHOKY pepper* or *whip whip whip too*.

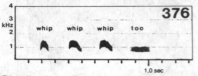

Distribution: Breeds e and se Asia and Madagascar; migrates to s Asia and Africa; recorded Zimbabwe (3 times) and Durban (once).

Status: Very rare nonbreeding Palaearctic migrant, January to April; very rare migrant from Madagascar, April to September. Palaearctic Lesser Cuckoo *C. poliocephalus* and Madagascar Lesser Cuckoo *C. rochii* now usually considered to be separate species. May be more regular than present records show.

Habitat: Forest edges and dense thickets.

Habits: Solitary; shy and elusive. Similar to European Cuckoo.

Food: Caterpillars.

Breeding: Extralimital.

---

377 (343)   **Redchested Cuckoo**   **Plate 35**
Piet-my-vrou
Cuculus solitarius

Mukuku (K), Tsheketani, Xiholowanye (Ts), Uphezukomkhono (X), uPhezukomkhono (Z), [Einsiedlerkuckuck]

Measurements: Length 28–30 cm; wing (17) 172–175–184; tail 145–160; tarsus 18–20; culmen 20,5–23. Weight (4 ♂) 71–75,3–81,2 g, (4 ♀) 66,5–68,4–74 g, (3 unsexed) 66,5–70,5–75 g.

Bare Parts: Iris brown; eyering yellow; bill blackish horn, base yellow; legs and feet yellow.

Identification: Size medium; above slate grey (darker than Eurasian and African Cuckoos); throat buffy grey, merging with deep rufous chest (diagnostic); rest of underparts barred black and white. *Immature*: Very dark blackish grey above and on throat; rest of underparts heavily barred black and buffy white. *Chick*: Naked blackish; back flat; inside of mouth orange; nostril round.

Voice: Highly distinctive ringing 3-note call, descending in pitch, *WIP, wip, weeu*, repeated many times; well expressed by Afrikaans *Piet-my-vrou*; heard September to February; also low gurgling sound by ♀; repeated *wik-wik-wik-wik* often heard in response to call of ♂, probably by ♀; fledgling calls incessant *zeep, zeep*.

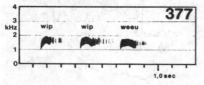

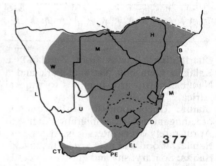

Distribution: Africa S of Sahara; populations breeding higher latitudes migrate to tropics, but movements not mapped; in s Africa absent from dry W and Kalahari sandveld, except as vagrant.

Status: Common breeding migrant, October to April.

Habitat: Forest, woodland, farmland with trees, parks, gardens, exotic plantations.

Habits: Usually solitary. Highly vocal in summer, especially after rain, and even at night; usually calls from hidden perch among leaves high in tree, seldom from exposed perch. Easily overlooked when not calling; sits still for long periods; often tame.

Food: Insects (especially caterpillars); also some seeds.

Breeding: *Season*: October to January. *Hosts*: Robins (Chorister, Heuglin's, Natal, Cape, Whitethroated, Starred, Swynnerton's, Bearded), chats (Boulder, Mocking, Stone), thrushes (Olive, Kurrichane, Cape Rock), Dusky Flycatcher, Cape Wagtail; accidentally also Cape Siskin; other possible hosts unconfirmed. *Eggs*: Usually plain olive green or chocolate brown; females parasitizing Boulder Chat lay greenish white eggs, speckled with red-brown; 1 egg per host nest (rarely 2); measure (21) 24,4 × 18,3 (22,9–25,5 × 17–19,7). *Incubation*: 13–15 days. *Nestling*: 17,5–22 days; chick hollows back while evicting host eggs and/or young within 4 days of hatching.

Ref. Liversidge, R. 1955. *Ostrich* 26:18–27.

378 (344) Black Cuckoo Swartkoekoek

Plate 35

Cuculus clamosus

Unomntanofayo (X), iNdodosibona (Z), [Schwarzkuckuck]

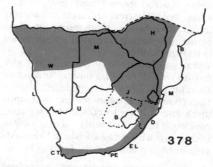

378

Measurements: Length 29–30 cm; wing (25) 167–176–184; tail 141–155; culmen 22–27. Weight (1 ♂) 90,2 g, (1 ♀) 89 g, (2 unsexed) 78–91,5 g.

Bare Parts: Iris dark brown; bill blackish horn; legs and feet dark pinkish brown.

Identification: Size medium; looks all black at distance; undertail barred with buff; underwing mottled and barred with white; edge of wing white; rare colour form barred with rufous on underparts. *Immature*: Sooty black to brownish; no white on tail. *Chick*: Naked dark purplish; nostril round, prominent; back flat (not hollowed).

Voice: Highly characteristic mournful monotonous mellow whistle of 2–3 syllables, rising in pitch on drawn-out last note, *hoop-hoo whooo*; sometimes *hoop whooo* or *hoop-hoo whooo whooo*; also wild whirling rolling notes rising and falling in pitch, *whirly-whirly-whirly-whirly* ....; fledgling begs with insistent *sweet* call.

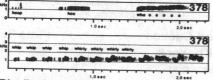

Distribution: Africa S of Sahara; in s Africa absent from most of dry W; regular in sw Cape.

Status: Fairly common breeding migrant from tropical Africa, September to April.

Habitat: Forest edges, woodland, riverine bush, exotic plantations, farmland, suburban areas.

Habits: Solitary and secretive. Seldom perches in open; usually calls from concealed perch high in leafy tree; posture somewhat hunched, most of body below perch. Flight fast and swerving.

Food: Insects (mainly caterpillars).

Breeding: *Season*: October to January. *Hosts*: Only *Laniarius* bush shrikes (Crimsonbreasted Shrike, Southern and Tropical Boubous). *Eggs*: 1 per host nest, matching closely those of host; white, pale green, greyish white, speckled with brown, red-brown and grey, forming zone at thick end; measure (9) 25,1 × 18,1 (23,6–27,3 × 17,5–19,1). *Incubation*: About 13–14 days. *Nestling*: 20–21 days; evicts host eggs and/or young within about 48 hours of hatching.

Ref. Jensen, R.A.C. & Clinning, C.F. 1974. *Living Bird* 13:5–50.

379 (344X)
Barred Cuckoo
Langstertkoekoek
Cercococcyx montanus

Plate 35

[Bergkuckuck]

Measurements: Length 33 cm; wing (11 ♂) 141–147,6–153, (2 ♀) 146–148; tail (10 ♂) 144–157,9–177, (2 ♀) 163–174; culmen (11 ♂) 22,5–24–25, (2 ♀) 23,5–24. Weight (1 ♂) 62,7 g.

Bare Parts: Iris brown; eyering yellow; bill blackish above, yellowish brown below; legs and feet yellow.

Identification: Size medium; tail long, boldly barred brown and white below; above barred brown and buff; below white, boldly barred with dark brown and throat and breast. *Immature*: Streaked below, not barred like adult; some scaly markings on breast.

Voice: In Zimbabwe ringing call, *wik wik hey ho* or *wik hey ho* (similar to song of Redchested Cuckoo); repeated downslurred *reeoo, reeoo* increasing in tempo, pitch and volume to crescendo, *ree-roo, ree-roo*, then suddenly dying away (similar to whirly call of Black Cuckoo); also bubbling call (probably by ♀).

Distribution: From e Zimbabwe and Zambezi Valley (Mana Pools National Park) to Tanzania.

Status: Common at Haroni-Lusitu junction, Zimbabwe; possibly migratory, but recorded Mozambique in June.

Habitat: Canopy of lowland evergreen and riverine forests.

Habits: Solitary; highly elusive; easily overlooked unless calling, usually from dense leafy canopy. Vocal only in summer, usually in evening and at night, or briefly at sunrise. Flight straight and fast. May forage near ground.

Food: Unrecorded.

Breeding: *Season*: Probably during rains. *Hosts*: Unrecorded, but African Broadbill suspected. *Eggs*: Only 1 known, laid in captivity; white, faintly spotted with redbrown around thick end; measures 21 × 15; another possibly authentic egg from African Broadbill nest measures 22 × 16,5. *Incubation*: Unrecorded. *Nestling*: Unrecorded.

Ref. Dean, W.R.J., Macdonald, I.A. & Vernon, C.J. 1974. *Ostrich* 45:188.

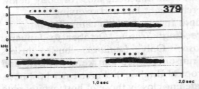

380 (346)
Great Spotted Cuckoo
Gevlekte Koekoek
Clamator glandarius

Plate 35

Haya (Sh), [Häherkuckuck]

Measurements: Length 37–40 cm. *C. g. choragium*: wing (10 ♂) 185–194–200, (10 ♀) 187–193–198,5; tail (10 ♂) 173–182–201,5, (10 ♀) 176–183–198; tarsus (29) 28–31; culmen (29) 26–33. *C. g. glandarius*: wing (10 ♂) 202–208–213, (10 ♀) 195–202–211; tail (10 ♂) 205–214–222, (10 ♀) 200–205–210.

Bare Parts: Iris brown; eyering reddish orange; bill dark horn, base of lower jaw pinkish grey; legs and feet brownish grey.

Identification: Size large; 2 subspecies indistinguishable in field; head markedly crested, pale grey; back dark greyish brown, spotted with white (no white spots in Thickbilled Cuckoo); throat and upper breast buff, extending around back of neck as collar (underparts white in Thickbilled Cuckoo); rest of underparts plain white (undertail coverts barred in Thickbilled Cuckoo); tail plain dark grey (banded black and grey in Thickbilled Cuckoo). *Immature:* Browner on back than adult, with smaller white spots; top of head black, crest small; throat and breast bright rufous buff; primaries chestnut.

Voice: Loud rasping *keow*, *kree-kree-krikrikrikri* quickly repeated; short *kawk* alarm note; ♀ calls bubbling *burroo-burroo*.

Distribution: Africa, s Europe, Middle East; *C. g. glandarius* breeds Palaearctic, migrates to s Africa; *C. g. choragium* breeds s Africa, migrates to tropical Africa (routes not mapped); in s Africa both subspecies occur from upper Natal, ne Orange Free State, Transvaal, Mozambique, Botswana, Zimbabwe and ne Namibia; mainly absent from dry W; vagrant to s and sw Cape.

Status: Nonbreeding Palaearctic migrant (*glandarius*) or breeding intra-African migrant (*choragium*), September to April; rarely overwinters; locally common.

Habitat: Woodland and savanna.

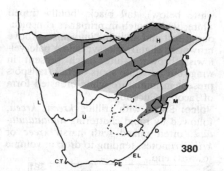

Habits: Solitary, in pairs or in scattered small groups. Noisy and conspicuous; spends much time in tops of trees, but descends to forage lower down, even to ground. Flight heavy.

Food: Mainly hairy caterpillars; also other insects.

Breeding: *Season:* August to January (mainly October-November) in Zimbabwe, October to December in Transvaal; also recorded September to February. *Hosts:* Mainly Pied Crow; also Black Crow, starlings (Longtailed, Blue-eared, Glossy, Burchell's, Pied, Redwinged, Palewinged, Indian Myna). *Eggs:* Up to 9 (rarely 13) cuckoo eggs in crow's nest, together with 5–7 crow's eggs; host's eggs often accidentally broken by hard-shelled cuckoo eggs; pale greenish, evenly speckled and spotted with brown and grey; measure (72) 31,4 × 22,9 (29–36 × 22,6–28). *Incubation:* About 14 days. *Nestling:* At least 18 days; does not evict young or eggs of host; all may be reared together, but late-hatched young of either host or parasite sometimes trampled to death.

Ref. Mundy, P.J. & Cook, A.W. 1977. *Ostrich* 48:72–84.

381 (347) Striped Cuckoo — Plate 35
Gestreepte Nuwejaarsvoël
Clamator levaillantii

Tihonyi, Tatamagoba (Ts), Khowela (Venda), [Kapkuckuck]

Measurements: Length 38–40 cm; wing (13) 176–181–187; tail 215–237; tarsus 27–30,5; culmen 27–31. Weight (2 ♀) 133–141 g, (1 unsexed) 71 g.

Bare Parts: Iris dark brown; bill black; legs and feet blue-grey.

Identification: Size medium; above glossy black; head distinctly crested; below white, boldly streaked black (white-breasted form of Jacobin Cuckoo plain white below); tail black, boldly tipped white; white patch in primaries conspicuous at rest and in flight. *Immature*: Above brownish, slightly glossy; below pale yellowish brown; white patch present in wing, but no white spots on tail (tailspots present in immature white-breasted form of Jacobin Cuckoo).

Voice: Starts with trilling *kreeu, kreeu*, followed by rapid chattering *tutututututu-tutu*, often mixed with harsh *kreee* or *krikrikri* notes, tending to drop in volume towards end.

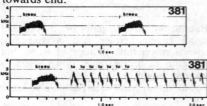

Distribution: Africa S of Sahara; in s Africa confined mainly to subtropics and tropics from Zululand, n Transvaal, n Botswana and n Namibia northward; vagrant to Ugab River, Namibia.

Status: Uncommon breeding intra-African migrant, September to May; some birds possibly resident in Zimbabwe.

Habitat: Woodland, riverine bush and forest edge; not open savanna.

Habits: Solitary; easily overlooked except when calling. Usually perches in dense leafy bush or tree.

Food: Caterpillars and other insects.

Breeding: *Season*: October to May. *Hosts:* Arrowmarked, Hartlaub's and Barecheeked Babblers; Lesser Masked Weaver also reported (needs authentication). *Eggs*: One (sometimes 2) per host nest; thick-shelled, finely pitted; glossy blue to greenish blue; measure (9) 26,1 × 21,1 (24,8–28,1 × 20,2–22,3). *Incubation*: 11–12 days. *Nestling*: At least 11 days; does not eject host's eggs or young, but tramples them to death; host and cuckoo young sometimes reared together; fed for at least 36 days after leaving nest.

Ref. Steyn, P. 1973. *Ostrich* 44:163–169.
Steyn, P. & Howells, W.W. 1975. *Ostrich* 46:258–260.
Vernon, C.J. 1982. *Honeyguide* 111/112: 10–11.

382 (348)   **Jacobin Cuckoo**   **Plate 35**
Bontnuwejaarsvoël
Clamator jacobinus

Hunyi, Mahleveni, Tatamagova (Ts), Ilunga Legwaba (X), iNkanku (Z), [Jakobinerkuckuck, Elsterkuckuck]

Measurements: Length 33–34 cm. *C. j. serratus* pale form: wing (27) 152–156,5–162; tail 173–182–195; tarsus 24–26; culmen 23,5–25,4–27. Weight (1 ♀) 77 g. *C. j. serratus* dark form: wing (16) 145–154–160; tail 165–175–192; tarsus 24–27; culmen 20–22,5–25. *C. j. jacobinus*: wing 135–150; tail 146–172. *C. j. pica*: wing 149–164; tail 173–197. Weight (3 ♂) 71,2–77,6–81 g, (3 ♀) 73,3–83,2–94 g.

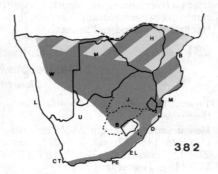

Bare Parts: Iris brown; bill black; legs and feet dark grey.

Identification: Size medium to large; above black, slightly glossy; head crested; short white wingbar at base of primaries visible in folded wing, conspicuous in flight; tail black, tipped white in all but dark form *serratus*; below white (*jacobinus* and *pica*), greyish white (pale form *serratus*) or black (dark form *serratus*). *Immature:* Brownish where adult black; pale form buffy below, with white tailspots (no white tailspots in immature Striped Cuckoo). *Chick:* Naked, dark purplish; mouth red.

Voice: Loud ringing *kleeu-wi-wip*, accented on first syllable, sometimes *kleeu-wip* or with several *wips*; *kruu-kru-kru-kleeuu* in courtship; *chuka-chuka-chuka* alarm call.

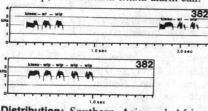

Distribution: Southern Asia and Africa; *C. j. jacobinus* breeds India, *C. j. pica* breeds N Africa, both migrating to s Africa; *C. j. serratus* breeds s Africa, migrating to African tropics. In s Africa absent only from dry W.

Status: Fairly common nonbreeding Palaearctic and Indian migrant (*pica* and *jacobinus*), September to April; common

breeding intra-African migrant (*serratus*), October to April (rarely to May).

Habitat: Thornveld, savanna, woodland, bushveld.

Habits: Usually solitary; sometimes 2–3 together. Noisy at start of breeding season; flies restlessly from tree to tree; less secretive than most other large cuckoos; flight fast and straight, usually low, ending in upward swoop into tree. When breeding, ♂ distracts host species so that ♀ can lay in host's nest, usually 1–3 hours after sunrise.

Food: Mainly hairy caterpillars; also termite alates and other insects.

Breeding: *Season:* October to November in Cape, September to February in Natal, October to March in highveld, October to May N of Limpopo and in Transvaal lowveld. *Hosts:* Mainly Cape, Blackeyed, Redeyed and Sombre Bulbuls, and Fiscal Shrike; also Forktailed Drongo; accidentally Cape White-eye; several other unconfirmed (probably accidental) hosts, including Speckled Mousebird, Terrestrial Bulbul, Arrowmarked Babbler, Fiscal and Paradise Flycatchers, Southern Boubou, Bokmakierie, Titbabbler, Cape Wagtail. *Eggs:* Usually 1 per host nest, but sometimes 2–4 (rarely up to 7); host's egg not removed; plain glossy white; measure (156) 26,2 × 21,7 (23–29 × 19–24); weigh 5,7–8 g. *Incubation:* 11 days. *Nestling:* 14 days; host's eggs and/or young not evicted, but trampled to death in nest.

Ref. Liversidge, R. 1971. *Ostrich Suppl.* 8:117–137.

383 (345)   **Thickbilled Cuckoo**   **Plate 35**
Dikbekkoekoek
Pachycoccyx audeberti

[Dickschnabelkuckuck]

Measurements: Length about 36 cm; wing (43 ♂) 214–224,6–240, (25 ♀) 213–223,1–236; tail (43 ♂) 161–181,6–210, (23 ♀) 168–178,8–198; tarsus 24–25; culmen (37 ♂) 16,5–17,7–19,5, (20 ♀) 16–17,2–19,5.

Bare Parts: Iris dark brown; eyering yellow; bill black above, yellow below, tip dusky; legs and feet yellow.

Identification: Size medium to large; above dark grey without white spots; no crest on head; below white, barred

under tail (undertail of Great Spotted Cuckoo plain white); tail dark grey broadly banded black, tipped white (no black bands on tail of Great Spotted Cuckoo). *Immature:* Above dark brown, spotted creamy white; large white spots on wing and tail; below white, washed buff on throat and flanks; undertail coverts barred brown; bill black; similar to Great Spotted Cuckoo adult, but spots bigger, no crest, undertail coverts barred and legs yellow (not blackish). *Chick:* Reddish brown to dark mauve;

THICKBILLED CUCKOO

bill black; mouth yellow; feet pale yellow; back broad and flat.

Voice: Raucous loud metallic *were-wik* display call; querulous *wheep-wheep-wheep*; drawn-out sharp rippling and vibrating *ti-ti-ti-ti-ti-ti*.

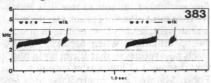

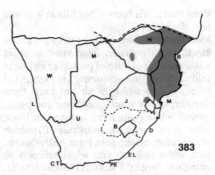

Distribution: Africa from Transvaal to w Zaire and Sudan; also Madagascar; in s Africa confined to Transvaal and Swaziland lowveld, e Zimbabwe, Mozambique and n Botswana; vagrant to Tuli, Botswana, and Ndumu Game Reserve, Zululand (1968 and 1977).

Status: Uncommon to rare resident or local migrant, September to February in Zimbabwe; migrations probably only altitudinal. Rare (RDB).

Habitat: Woodland, bushveld, savanna.

Habits: Solitary or in groups of 3–4 birds. Flight hawklike, wingbeats slow; display flight buoyant and floppy, accompanied by *were-wik* calls, sometimes in groups; makes exaggerated wingfolding movements on landing. Restless, often flying from tree to tree; posture hawklike; movements slow and deliberate.

Food: Mostly grasshoppers; also caterpillars and mantises.

Breeding: *Season*: September to January. *Host*: Redbilled Helmetshrike. *Eggs*: Usually 1 per host nest, rarely 2; pale cream, green or blue-green, spotted and blotched with pale brown, grey and lilac, mainly in zone at thick end; indistinguishable from host eggs; measure (5) 23,8 × 17,4 (22,5–25,4 × 17,2–17,8). *Incubation*: Maximum 13 days. *Nestling*: (3) 28–30 days; evicts host eggs and/or young within 5 days after hatching; dependent on foster parents for about 60 days after leaving nest.

Ref. Benson, C.W. & Irwin, M.P.S. 1972. *Arnoldia* 5(33):1–24.
Vernon, C.J. 1984. *Proc. 5th Pan-Afr. Orn. Congr.*:825–840.

384 (350)   Emerald Cuckoo   Plate 36
Mooimeisie
Chrysococcyx cupreus

Intananja (X), uBantwanyana (Z), [Smaragdkuckuck]

Measurements: Length 18–22 cm; wing (17 ♂) 108–113,2–115, (7 ♀) 103–107,3–111; tail (17 ♂) 85–97, (7 ♀) 75–83; tarsus (24) 14–20; culmen (16) 17–19. Weight (1 ♂) 33,7 g, (4 ♀) 32,5–38,2–40,3 g, (3 unsexed) 31–32,4–33,7 g.

Bare Parts: Iris dark brown; eyering blue-green; bill bright blue-green, tip dusky; legs and feet blue-grey (♂) or dark grey (♀).

Identification: Size small. *Male*: Bright metallic green, except for chrome yellow belly; undertail white, barred metallic green (Klaas's and Diederik Cuckoos males white below, barred on flanks; eye-

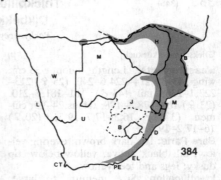

brow white). *Female*: Crown brown, barred with buff; rest of upperparts and wings metallic green, barred with brown (no white spots in wings and no whitish eyebrow as in ♀ Diederik Cuckoo); below white, finely barred with metallic green (♀ Klaas's Cuckoo barred with brown; barring much finer than in Diederik Cuckoo); outer tail feathers mainly white. *Immature*: Similar to adult ♀, but ♂ mottled with white on crown; otherwise very like immature Klaas's Cuckoo, but without white earpatch.

Voice: Highly characteristic sweet whistled 4-syllabled phrase *pretty georgie*, or *hullo Aunt Bet*, slurred downwards from 1st to 2nd notes, lower-pitched on 2nd and 3rd notes, slightly drawn-out on 3rd note, with slight pause between *pretty* and *georgie*; rarely explosive series of melodious notes.

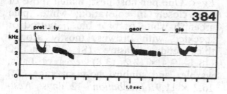

Distribution: Africa S of Sahara; in s Africa confined to SE, E and NE.

Status: Fairly common breeding intra-African migrant, September to January; possibly resident, but easily overlooked in forest when not vocal; some may overwinter even as far S as Natal.

Habitat: Canopy of evergreen and riverine forest, dense thickets, well developed woodland.

Habits: Solitary. ♂ calls from top of tall tree day after day; drives off conspecific males. Flight quick and undulating. ♀ seldom seen, highly secretive.

Food: Mainly caterpillars; also other insects, seeds, fruit (*Kiggelaria*).

Breeding: *Season*: October to about January. *Hosts*: Only authentic hosts in s Africa are Starred Robin, Bleating Warbler and Bluegrey Flycatcher, but other species possible. *Eggs*: One per host nest; white, plain or freckled and blotched with greyish brown, with ring of mauve-brown marks at large end; measure (5) 18,9 × 13,3 (18,3–19,6 × 12,8–14); weigh (1) 2,1 g. *Incubation*: About 14 days. *Nestling*: Unrecorded.

385 (351)   Klaas's Cuckoo   Plate 36
Meitjie
Chrysococcyx klaas

[Klaaskuckuck]

Measurements: Length 17–18 cm; wingspan 25 cm; wing (27 ♂) 96–101,7–106, (11 ♀) 98–103–106; tail (28) 69–80; tarsus (28) 14–17; culmen (38) 15–18. Weight (2 ♀) 26,4–27,4 g, (1 unsexed) 38,6 g.

Bare Parts: Iris brown to olive grey; bill slate grey, base tinged green, tip black; legs and feet greyish green.

Identification: Size small; white outer rectrices conspicuous in all plumages (looks like honeyguide in flight). *Male*: Above and on sides of chest bright metallic green; small white patch behind eye (Diederik Cuckoo has broad white eyebrow); outer tail feathers mainly white (mainly green with white spots in Emerald and Diederik Cuckoos); below white, barred metallic green on flanks (belly of Emerald Cuckoo plain bright yellow); iris brownish (bright

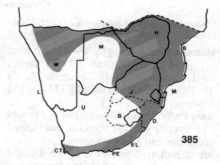

red in Diederik Cuckoo). *Female*: Similar to ♀ Emerald Cuckoo; above mainly brown, barred with metallic green on wings; outer tail feathers mainly white; below white finely barred with brown (barring green in ♀ Emerald Cuckoo, bolder in ♀ Diederik Cuckoo). *Immature*:

Similar to ♀ but darker; above barred green and brown; below whitish, densely barred blackish; earpatch pale.

Voice: Rather mournful high-pitched sweet whistle of 2–3 syllables, *wit-wheet-ki, wheet-ki* or *whee-eet-ki*, drawn-out on first note, staccato on second, repeated 2–3 times with pauses of 5–10 seconds between series; Afrikaans *meitjie* is onomatopoeic.

Distribution: Africa S of Sahara, s Arabia; in s Africa absent from dry W, except as vagrant.

Status: Uncommon to fairly common breeding intra-African migrant, September to April; S African breeding birds migrate at least to Zimbabwe, May to August; Zimbabwean breeding birds migrate northward; some resident, especially in lowland areas throughout range.

Habitat: Edges of riverine forest, thickets, dense woodland and savanna, wooded rocky hills.

Habits: Solitary. Easily overlooked when not calling; ♀ seldom seen; ♂ calls for long periods day after day, often from exposed perch, but usually hidden among leaves; much shyer than Diederik Cuckoo. Flight undulating.

Food: Mainly caterpillars; also other insects.

Breeding: *Season*: September to April in Zimbabwe, January to April in Namibia, October to March in S Africa. *Hosts*: 23 passerine species authenticated in s Africa; Stonechat, Barthroated Apalis, Longbilled Crombec, Yellowbellied Eremomela, Neddicky, Tawnyflanked Prinia, flycatchers (Dusky, Bluegrey, Fantailed), batises (Chinspot, Cape, Pririt), Puffback, and sunbirds (Malachite, Marico, Greater Doublecollared, Whitebellied, Dusky, Grey, Scarletchested, Black, Collared). *Eggs*: One per host nest; match those of host closely in coloration; white, pale greenish white or pale blue, spotted or speckled with browns, mostly around thick end; measure (8) 18,7 × 13,2 (18,1–19,4 × 12,2–13,8); eggs of batis, warbler and sunbird hosts average (74) 16,2 × 11,9. *Incubation*: 12 days. *Nestling*: 20–21 days; evicts young and/or eggs of host.

386 (352)   Diederik Cuckoo   Plate 36
Diederikkie
Chrysococcyx caprius

Umgcibilitshane (X), uNononekhanda (Z), [Diderikkuckuck, Goldkuckuck]

Measurements: Length 18–20 cm; wing (51) 114–118–125; tail 77–90; tarsus 16–17; culmen 16–19. Weight (32 ♂) 23–30,3–39 g, (21 ♀) 28–34,7–42,6 g, (31 unsexed) 29–34,6–48 g.

Bare Parts: Iris crimson (♂) or red-brown (♀); eyering red; bill blackish, base tinged grey; legs and feet dark grey.

Identification: Size small; above metallic green with bronze reflections (sometimes looks brownish); stripe on midcrown and eyebrow white (small white earpatch only in Klaas's Cuckoo); tail green, spotted with white (outer tail feathers mostly white in Klaas's Cuckoo); below white, heavily barred on flanks with metallic green; eye red (brown in other metallic

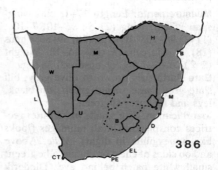

cuckoos); ♀ similar to ♂, but browner above; breast, eyebrow and crown stripe tinged buff. *Immature*: Very heavily streaked and barred below with metallic green; bill bright coral red (other metallic cuckoos have dark bills).

Voice: Persistent plaintive musical *dee-dee-deederik*, rising then falling in pitch; introductory *dees* vary in number; also rapid *di-di-di-di-di*; ♀ calls *deea-deea-deea*; fledgling calls *chee, chee* all day long.

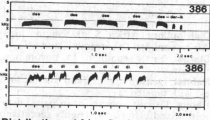

Distribution: Africa S of Sahara; also s Arabia; widespread in s Africa.
Status: Very common breeding intra-African migrant, October to April (rarely May), from tropical Africa; adults appear to leave breeding areas by end of February.
Habitat: Woodland, savanna, riverine bush, gardens, parks, farmland, exotic plantations, semi-arid scrub.
Habits: Solitary or in pairs. Neither shy nor secretive like most other cuckoos; ♂ calls for hours from conspicuous perch on top of tree; ♀ less bold, but often seen; in display ♂ swoops in wide arc over territory with raised head and tail; adjacent territorial males chase each other for up to

400 m. Flight direct with quick wingbeats; often calls and chases conspecifics in flight. ♂ feeds caterpillars to ♀ in courtship (sometimes erroneously reported as feeding own young).
Food: Mainly caterpillars; also other insects.
Breeding: *Season*: October to March. *Hosts*: 24 species authenticated; most heavily exploited are Cape Sparrow (21%), Masked Weaver (20%), Cape and Spottedbacked Weavers, Red Bishop (37%) and Cape Wagtail; others include Mountain Chat, Karoo, Kalahari and Whitebrowed Robins, Rattling Cisticola, Spotted Prinia, Titbabbler, Marico and Paradise Flycatchers, Great and Greyheaded Sparrows, Spectacled, Yellow, Golden, Lesser Masked and Redheaded Weavers, Whitewinged Widow and Goldenbreasted Bunting. *Eggs*: One per host nest (♀ removes and eats one host egg); usually match host eggs; blue, blue-green, pale green, white or cream, plain or variously spotted and blotched with browns and greys; measure (68) 21,3 × 15 (18,6–25 × 13,3–16). *Incubation*: 10–12 days. *Nestling*: 20–21 days; evicts eggs and/or young of host within 4 days of hatching; postnestling dependence up to 32 days.

Ref. Reed, R.A. 1953. *Ostrich* 24:138–140; 1968. *Ibis* 110:321–331.

---

387 (358)   **Green Coucal**   **Plate 35**
Groenvleiloerie
Ceuthmochares aereus

[Erzkuckuck]

Measurements: Length 30–35 cm; wingspan about 35 cm; wing (3 ♂) 124–127–131, (2 ♀) 123–126; tail (5) 190–199,2–210; tarsus (5) 28–30,2–34; culmen (5) 29–29,6–30. Weight (4 ♂) 63,1–69,5–79,2 g, (3 ♀) 60,4–65,6–72,4 g.
Bare Parts: Iris crimson; eyering greyish green; skin around eye blackish; bill bright yellow, base of culmen and gape darker; legs and feet blackish.
Identification: Size medium; above dull greenish grey; below light olive buff, shading to greenish grey on belly; tail long,

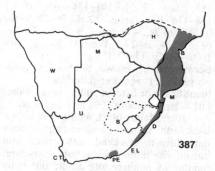

graduated, slightly iridescent dull green; bill large, bright yellow (diagnostic). *Immature*: Below brownish buff; wing coverts edged buff; bill dark horn; iris brown.

Voice: Sharp metallic *tsik-tsik, tsik, tsik-tsik*, becoming rapid *tsik-tsik-tsik-tsik*, merging into loud plaintive decrescendo *teew, teew, teew*, speeding up at end *wip-wipwipwipwip*; also repetitive mournful high-pitched *kweee-eep, kweee-eep* in breeding season; flight call *tsik-tsik*.

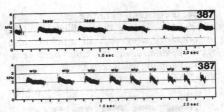

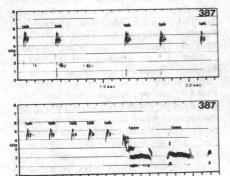

Distribution: Africa S of Sahara; in s Africa confined to extreme E and SE.

Status: Fairly common to uncommon resident.

Habitat: Dense evergreen and riverine forest with tangled creepers.

Habits: Usually solitary or in pairs; may join mixed bird party. Highly secretive; creeps about like large rat in tangled vegetation. Flight heavy. Easily overlooked, even when perched motionless in open; best located by voice.

Food: Insects, treefrogs, slugs.

Breeding: *Season*: October to December. *Nest*: Loose saucer of sticks, often with leaves attached; about 15 cm diameter; 2–5 m above ground in fork of tree or in tangled cover. *Clutch*: 2–4 eggs. *Eggs*: White; measure (9) 30,3 × 23 (27,8–31,9 × 21–25,9). *Incubation*: Unrecorded. *Nestling*: Unrecorded.

388 (353)　　**Black Coucal**　　**Plate 35**
Swartvleiloerie
Centropus bengalensis

[Tulukuckuck, Grillkuckuck]

Measurements: Length 32–37 cm; wing (9 ♂) 140–150–158, (14 ♀) 171–176,1–183; tail (7 ♂) 143–151–163, (9 ♀) 168–176–192; tarsus (12 ♂) 36–38,5–40, (9 ♀) 36–38,5–40; culmen (7 ♂) 22–23, (9 ♀) 24–25–27. Weight (6 ♂) 94–100,3–108 g, (1 ♀) 151 g.

Bare Parts: Iris brown; bill black to greyish pink; legs and feet slate black.

Identification: Size medium; sexes alike, but ♀ larger (about 50% heavier) than ♂. *Breeding*: Mainly black with tawny brown back and wings. *Nonbreeding*: Above dark brown, streaked with cream and barred with rufous; below buff. *Immature*: Similar to nonbreeding adult, but belly

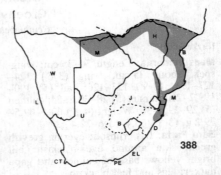

barred with brown. *Chick*: Skin black with long white wiry down, hanging like fringe over head.

Voice: *Dudu, dudu, dudu* advertising call; hooting *whoop, whoop*, about 1 note/second; bubbling *kokokokokok*; mellow *too loo loo; tuk tuk* alarm call.

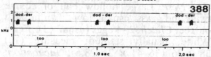

Distribution: Most of Africa S of Sahara; also tropical Asia; in s Africa from s Mozambique to e and n Zimbabwe to n Botswana.

Status: Locally common, but mostly uncommon breeding intra-African migrant, November to April; possibly moves N or to coastal Mozambique after breeding; rarely overwinters. Indeterminate (RDB).

Habitat: Tall rank grass in vleis.

Habits: Usually solitary or in pairs. Shy and elusive; usually stays low down in grass; sometimes perches on top of bush. Flight clumsy with fast wingbeats. Usually silent. ♀ may be polyandrous.

Food: Insects, spiders; possibly small reptiles, seeds.

Breeding: *Season*: December to March in Zimbabwe. *Nest*: Oval of dry grass and sedge, 18–26 cm diameter, lined with leaves; built into oval framework of living grass or sedge 15–45 cm off ground. *Clutch*: (16) 3–3,9–6 eggs (usually 4). *Eggs*: White; measure (18) 30,3 × 24,2 (27,2–35,5 × 23–25,6). *Incubation*: Unrecorded; by ♂ only; begins with first egg. *Nestling*: 18–20 days, but can leave nest at 11 days; flies at 28 days; cared for by ♂ only.

Ref. Vernon, C.J. 1971. *Ostrich* 42:242–258.

---

389 (354)   Copperytailed Coucal   Plate 35
Grootvleiloerie
Centropus cupreicaudus

Mukuku (K), [Angola-Mönchskuckuck]

Measurements: Length 44–50 cm; wing (25 ♂) 200–211–219, (23 ♀) 217–222–233; tail (19 ♂) 223–233–244, (23 ♀) 227–235–246; tarsus (25 ♂) 46–49–52, (24 ♀) 46–50–54; culmen (25 ♂) 33–36–39, (24 ♀) 35–38–42. Weight (6 ♂) 250–272–293 g, (5 ♀) 245–299–342 g.

Bare Parts: Iris red; bill, legs and feet black.

Identification: Size large; similar to Burchell's Coucal, but larger and with very heavy bill; top of head, mantle and tail black with coppery violet gloss; rump and wings bright rusty (mantle rusty, rump black in Senegal Coucal; mantle black, rump barred black-and-buff in Burchell's Coucal); underparts white (no fine barring on flanks and thighs as in Burchell's and Senegal Coucals). *Immature*: Rusty feathers of rump and wings barred with black; outer rectrices barred whitish; iris grey; bill horn.

Voice: Deep booming bubbling call (similar to that of Senegal Coucal, but slower); harsh crowing; low resonant *ku-ku-ku* contact call, answered by mate.

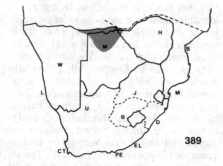

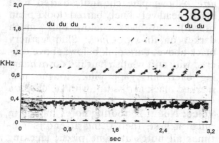

Distribution: Caprivi, n Botswana and Victoria Falls to Angola, Zambia, s Zaire and Tanzania.

Status: Fairly common resident.

Habitat: Swamps with reeds, Papyrus and other tall growth; also floodplains and riverine vegetation; sometimes moves to adjacent dry ground to feed.

Habits: Usually solitary. Shy and secretive; rarely seen except when sunning on top of reed or other high perch; flies seldom.

Food: Large insects, snails, small birds (up to size of Blue Quail), nestlings.

Breeding: *Season*: Not yet recorded in s Africa; September to February in Zambia. *Nest*: Large hollow ball of coarse twigs and grass; usually low down in bush or tree. *Clutch*: 2–4 eggs (usually 3). *Eggs*: White, usually stained; measure (12) 38 × 36 (36–41 × 24–28,6). *Incubation*: Unrecorded. *Nestling*: Unrecorded.

390 (355) Senegal Coucal   Plate 35
Senegalvleiloerie
Centropus senegalensis

Mukuku (K), Murenda (Sh), [Senegal-Spornkuckuck]

Measurements: Length 35–42 cm; wing (32 ♂) 163–169–176, (32 ♀) 170–176–186; tail (32 ♂) 190–200–220, (32 ♀) 191–211–232; tarsus (32 ♂) 36–38–40, (32 ♀) 36–38–40; culmen (32 ♂) 27–27,5–29, (32 ♀) 27–29–30. Weight (4 ♂) 160–169–178 g, (5 ♀) 141–169,8–180 g, (3 unsexed) 166–195 g.

Bare Parts: Iris scarlet (♂) or orange-red (♀); bill black; legs and feet lead grey.

Identification: Size medium to large; similar to Copperytailed Coucal (but much smaller) and to Burchell's Coucal. Top of head, rump and tail black (not with coppery gloss as in Copperytailed Coucal); mantle and wings bright rusty (mantle black, rump rusty in Copperytailed Coucal; rump and base of rectrices barred black and buff in Burchell's Coucal); below white, finely barred blackish on flanks and thighs (no barring on underparts of Copperytailed Coucal). *Immature*: Above pale chestnut, barred with black; head very finely barred (looks plain brown); tail black; below buff, much darker on throat. *Chick*: Skin leathery black above, dark pink below; above covered with stiff whitish hairlike down hanging over bill; gape pink; tongue red, marked black across tip, with small white spines.

Voice: About 20 tooting notes, falling in pitch at first, then rising at end; sometimes all notes at same pitch; clucking *tok-tok-tok-tok*; sometimes calls in duet, one bird answering the other; *guk guk* alarm call.

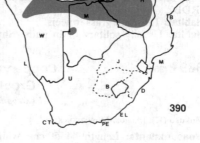

390

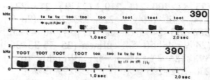

Distribution: Africa S of Sahara to Zimbabwe, n Botswana and ne Namibia.

Status: Uncommon to fairly common resident.

Habitat: Rank grass and thickets in woodland; also reedbeds and dense riverine bush.

Habits: Usually solitary. Similar to Burchell's Coucal, and often found in same habitat, but generally prefers drier country.

Food: Insects, small rodents, reptiles, birds, birds' eggs.

Breeding: *Season*: October to February in Zimbabwe. *Nest*: Ball of coarse dry grass, lined with leaves; up to about 4 m above ground in leafy bush or thorntree. *Clutch*: 2–5 eggs (usually 4). *Eggs*:

White; measure (37) 33,2 × 25,6 (30–38 × 24–27); weigh (5) 67,5–75,1–78 g. *Incubation*: 18–19 days; starts with first egg. *Nestling*: 18–20 days; ejects nause-ating brown liquid faeces when handled, but normally deposits faecal sac which parents carry away.

Ref. Steyn, P. 1972. *Ostrich* 43:56–59.

391 (356) Burchell's Coucal (Whitebrowed Coucal)   Plate 35
Gewone Vleiloerie
Centropus burchellii

Mukuku (K), Fukwani, Nfuku (Ts), Ubikhwe (X), uFukwe, umGugwane (Z), [Tiputip]

Measurements: Length 38–44 cm. *C. s. burchelli*: wing (38 ♂) 154–164–170, (21 ♀) 167–174–187; tail (59) 190–240; tarsus (59) 39–43; culmen (59) 30–35. *C. s. loandae*: wing (6 ♂) 160–164–172, (7 ♀) 170–176–180; tail (13) 195–230; tarsus (13) 37–43; culmen (13) 28–30. Weight (all races) (14 ♂) 133,5–160–213 g, (11 ♀) 153,3–178,9–212 g.

Bare Parts: Iris crimson; bill, legs and feet black or bluish grey.

Identification: Size medium. Southern and e birds (*burchellii* and *fasciipygialis*) very similar to Senegal Coucal, but do not overlap much with it; top of head and mantle glossy blue-black (mantle bright rusty in Senegal Coucal); back, rump, uppertail coverts and base of rectrices dark olive to blackish, barred with buffy white (no pale barring in either Senegal or Copperytailed Coucal); tail mostly black, narrowly tipped white (hard to see in field; no white tipping in other coucals); below creamy white, finely barred with dusky on flanks and thighs (no barring in Copperytailed Coucal). Northern birds (*loandae*) similar, but top of head brown, boldy streaked cream; bold creamy white eyebrow (hence Whitebrowed Coucal). Whitebrowed birds occur mainly where range overlaps with that of Senegal Coucal, so little chance of confusion. *Immature*: Above barred rusty and black; base of tail finely barred whitish; buffy rufous below, finely barred black on flanks; iris greyish brown. *Chick*: Black with long white down; tongue light red with subterminal black band and pink tip.

Voice: Series of rapid mellow hooting notes, first falling in pitch, then rising at end, about 17 notes, *du-du-du-du-du-du.....du du du*, sometimes slowing down

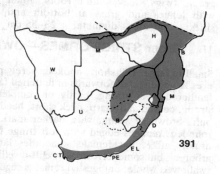

391

towards end of phrase; likened to water bubbling out of narrow-necked bottle; often calls before, during and after rain, hence popular name of Rainbird; also harsh tearing *kh-kh-kh-kh-kh*, rapidly repeated.

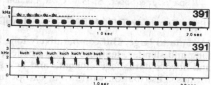

Distribution: Africa S of Sahara, s Arabia, Socotra; in s Africa confined mainly to extreme S, E and N, including Orange Free State, Transvaal, n Botswana, Kavango and Caprivi.

Status: Common resident. Whitebrowed race may be separate species *Centropus superciliosus*.

Habitat: Riverine and coastal bush, rank growth around streams and marshes, reedbeds, gardens, parks.

Habits: Usually solitary or in pairs. Skulks in dense vegetation; seldom seen unless flying across open space, or perched on top of bush or post, drying or sunning plumage; flight heavy, ending in glide into cover. Vocal when breeding, even on moonlit nights. Forages in vegetation or on ground; runs well. Partly crepuscular. **Food:** Insects, small frogs, reptiles, nestling birds (up to size of fully grown Laughing Dove), mammals, snails (broken open on "anvil" stone). **Breeding:** *Season:* September to February. *Nest:* Large untidy hollow ball of grass, twigs, leaves and roots, lined with leaves and grass at bottom and sides; outside diameter 23–55 cm (usually less than 30 cm), depth 15–22 cm; 0,5–1,5–10 m above ground (52 nests) in matted thornbush, creeper, tree, pile of brushwood. *Clutch:* (56) 2–3,6–5 eggs (usually 4). *Eggs:* White; measure (75) 33,6 × 26,4 (27,2–37,6 × 24,3–30,3). *Incubation:* 14–18 days, probably by both parents; starts with first egg. *Nestling:* 18–20 days, but does not fly until few days later; fed by both parents.

18. Order STRIGIFORMES—OWLS (Two families)

Small to large. Bill short, hooked, barely protruding beyond face; cere at base of bill; eyes large, directed forwards in flattened facial disc; legs medium to fairly long, usually feathered; toes strong, partly or completely feathered; outer toe reversible; claws strong, curved and sharp; neck short; head large; plumage cryptically coloured in grey, buff, brown or white, with darker markings; feathers soft; wings long, broad and rounded; remiges edged with soft fringe for silent flight; tail medium to short; sexes usually alike, but female sometimes larger than male; largely nocturnal; mostly arboreal, but some terrestrial or cliff-dwelling; food animals caught by active predation, swallowed whole; undigested remains regurgitated as firm pellets; usually solitary; nest in holes, burrows, old stick nests of other birds, ledges, or on ground—no nest built; eggs 1–7, white, rounded; chick downy (white), altricial; parental care by both sexes, but incubation usually by female only. Distribution almost worldwide.

Ref. Burton, J.A. (Ed.) 1984. *Owls of the world.* London: Peter Lowe.
Kemp, A. & Calburn, S. 1987. *The owls of southern Africa.* Cape Town: Struik Winchester.
Mendelsohn, J.M., Kemp, A.C., Biggs, H.C., Biggs, R. & Brown, C.J. 1989. *Ostrich* 60:35–42.
Sparks, J. & Soper, A. 1970. *Owls.* London: David & Charles.

18:1. Family 47 TYTONIDAE—BARN AND GRASS OWLS

Medium to large. Bill comparatively long and slender, mostly covered by bristles; legs long and slender, feathered; toes bristled; middle claw pectinate; eyes relatively small and always dark; face elongate and heart-shaped; other features as for Order Strigiformes. Distribution worldwide, except most of N America, Asia, New Zealand and some oceanic islands; about 10 species; two species in s Africa.

Ref. Vernon, C.J. 1972. *Ostrich* 43:109–124.

392 (359)   Barn Owl   Plate 37
Nonnetjie-uil
Tyto alba

Suunsu (K), Leribisi (NS), Sephooko (SS), Zizi (Sh), Madzukuya, Nsoo, Xoona (Ts), Lerubise, Morubitshe (Tw), Isikhova (X), isiKhova, umZwelele (Z), [Schleiereule]

Measurements: Length 30–33 cm; wingspan (11) 90,9 cm; wing (3 ♂) 290–298, (4 ♀) 235–287; tail (7) 115–130; tarsus (7) 58–67; culmen (7) 18–20. Weight (2 ♀) 218,8–221 g, (24 unsexed) 266–334,4–470 g.

Bare Parts: Iris dark brown; bill white to pale pink; toes pinkish.

Identification: Size medium; very pale generally; above tawny and grey (dark brown in Grass Owl) with small white spots; face and underparts white, with fine brown spots from breast to belly and wash of tawny buff across breast; brown eyes contrast with pale heart-shaped face; longish legs closely feathered white. Grass Owl similar, but darker upperparts contrast with pale underparts more than in Barn Owl; habitats different. *Immature*: Above darker than adult; below washed buffy. *Chick*: Pink, sparsely covered with white down.

Voice: Prolonged thin screeching *schreeee* by ♂ and ♀, sometimes with tremolo quality; hissing defence call; also snoring and wheezing notes by ♀, answered by staccato squeaks from ♂; chirruping contact call.

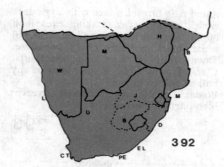

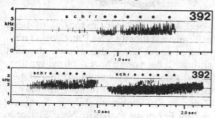

Distribution: Almost worldwide; widespread in s Africa.

Status: Locally common resident.

Habitat: Varied, but always near suitable roosting cavity in cliff, building, deep well, mineshaft, Sociable Weaver or Hamerkop nest, hole in tree, base of palm frond; from woodland to desert, but not forest.

Habits: Usually in pairs. Roosts by day in suitable cavity (see **Habitat**); when disturbed elongates body and almost completely closes eyes. Emerges at dusk to hunt by quartering ground in alternate flap-and-glide flight; may hover to scan ground, or beat bushes to disturb roosting birds; also hunts from perch. Weaves lowered head from side to side in threat display.

Food: Mainly rodents (75–97% of diet); in urban areas mainly small birds (up to 95%); also shrews, elephant shrews, lizards, frogs (rarely) and insects.

Breeding: *Season*: August to December in sw Cape, mainly February to March elsewhere in s Africa, but breeding possible in all months; mainly March-April and September in Zimbabwe. *Nest*: Unlined scrape or flat floor of cavity similar to roosting cavity (see **Habitat**); in nest of Hamerkop (50%), building (31%), hollow tree (8%); site used repeatedly if undisturbed. *Clutch*: (226) 2–5,6–13 eggs (usually 5); larger clutches in years of rodent plagues. *Eggs*: White; measure (116) 39,1 × 31,3 (36–43,1 × 28,9–34,5). *Incubation*: 30–32 days by ♀ only; starts with 1st egg, so chicks hatch over several days. *Nestling*: 50–55 days; as little as 45 days if food abundant; brooded and fed by ♀ only at first, on food brought by ♂; later ♀ hunts too. In years of rodent plagues, first egg of next clutch may be laid before young of current brood have left nest.

Ref. Coetzee, C.G. 1963. *Koedoe* 6:115–125.

---

393 (360)   **Grass Owl**   **Plate 37**
Grasuil
Tyto capensis

Suunsu (K), Makgohlo (NS), Sephooko (SS), Zizi (Sh), Musoho (Ts), Lerubise (Tw), Isikhova (X), isiKhova, umShwelele (Z), [Graseule]

Measurements: Length 34–37 cm; wing 325–342; tail 120–130; tarsus 70–78; culmen 19–23. Weight (8) 355–419,3–520 g.

Bare Parts: Iris brown; bill white to pale pink; feet yellowish pink.

Identification: Size medium; similar to Barn Owl, but dark brown above (Barn Owl light grey and tawny); below whitish with buffy breast (sometimes pale brownish; Marsh Owl always brownish below); upperparts and underparts contrast strongly (more so than in Barn Owl; hardly any contrast in Marsh Owl); white to pale brownish heart-shaped face contrasts with dark eyes (Marsh Owl has

round pale brownish face with large dark circles around eyes, making eyes look huge); face narrowly rimmed blackish; bill white (black in Marsh Owl). *Immature*: Tawny buff on face and underparts. *Chick*: Downy white at first; later downy buff or golden brown.
Voice: Usually silent; muted screech; high-pitched churring hiss.

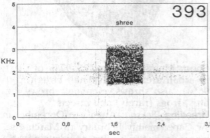

Distribution: Sw Cape to Ethiopia, s Asia, Australia; in s Africa confined to moister s and e parts.
Status: Uncommon to rare; local and irregular; numbers declining because of habitat destruction. Probably Vulnerable (RDB).
Habitat: Long grass, usually near water, vleis, marshes.
Habits: Usually in pairs or small loose groups of 4–5 birds. Roosts on ground in rank grass, making well-defined form where regurgitated pellets accumulate. Flushes reluctantly; flies up with legs dangling, soon dropping back into grass. Hunts by quartering low over grassland, dropping suddenly onto prey; rarely hunts from perch; mainly nocturnal, but occasionally hunts by day; prey usually eviscerated before being swallowed.

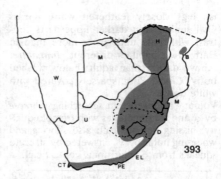

Food: Mostly rodents (up to 97% of diet); in Transvaal mostly Vlei Rat *Otomys irroratus* of about 120 g; also shrews, elephant shrews, bats, young hares, birds, reptiles, frogs, insects; prey weighs up to 100 g.
Breeding: *Season*: November to May in Zimbabwe, October to July in S Africa; mostly February to April. *Nest*: Flattened pad of grass at end of grassy tunnel in dense tuft; usually connected by other tunnels through grass to separate forms (Marsh Owl has only one form for nest). *Clutch*: (21) 3–3,9–5 eggs (rarely 6). *Eggs*: White; measure (44) 41,8 × 33,6 (39–45,3 × 31,3–35,8). *Incubation*: About 32 days, probably by ♀ only; all eggs may hatch within about 24 hours, or on consecutive days. *Nestling*: About 35 days; fly at about 42 days; brooded and fed by ♀ only at first, on food brought by ♂; later both parents hunt; postnestling dependence at least 30 days.

Ref. Davidson, I.H. & Biggs, H.C. 1974. *Ostrich* 45:31.
Earlé, R.A. 1978. *Ostrich* 49:90–91.

18:2. Family 48 STRIGIDAE—TYPICAL OWLS

Small to large. Bill short and strong; legs short to longish, naked in some species; middle claw not pectinate; eyes very large, often yellow or orange; ear openings asymmetrical; other features as for Order Strigiformes. Distribution worldwide except for some oceanic islands; about 125 species; 10 species in s Africa.

394 (362)   **Wood Owl**   **Plate 37**
Bosuil
Strix woodfordii

Kakuru (K), Zizi (Sh), Mankhudu (Ts), Lerubisana (Tw), Ibengwana (X), uMabhengwane (♀), uNobathekeli (♂) (Z), [Woodfordkauz]
Measurements: Length 30–36 cm; wing-span (6) 78,8 cm; wing (29) 233–248–264; tail 145–160; tarsus 38–47; culmen 17–20. Weight (3 ♂) 250–286,9–340 g, (1 ♀) 297 g.

Bare Parts: Iris brown; eyelids reddish; bill yellow; feet yellowish pink.

Identification: Size medium; deep red-brown above, spotted white on wings; tail barred, longish, extending well beyond wingtips at rest; below barred russet and white; face white, especially broad eyebrows, contrasting with dark crown and eyes. *Immature*: Similar to adult, but paler on head, with less well defined white facial markings. *Chick*: Downy white; bill pale cream; feet pink.

Voice: Syncopated hooting phrase *WHOO-hu, WHOO-hu-hu, hu-hu*, higher-pitched and accented on the *WHOO*, lower and staccato on the *hu*, with slight pause between each section of phrase; ♂ and ♀ may answer each other in duet; ♀ also calls *eeeyow*, answered by low gruff *hoo* from ♂; other soft hooting notes and bill-clacking alarm sounds.

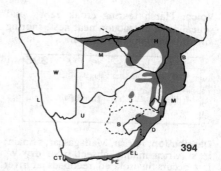

Distribution: Africa S of Sahara; in s Africa confined to extreme S, E, NE and N.

Status: Locally fairly common resident.

Habitat: Evergreen and riverine forest, dense woodland, coastal bush, pine plantations; seldom in savanna.

Habits: Usually in pairs. Strictly nocturnal; well camouflaged and easily overlooked when perched in tree by day; fairly tame; flushes reluctantly. Hunts by dropping onto prey from perch; may hawk insects in flight.

Food: Mainly insects; also rodents, frogs, birds, centipedes; rarely snakes.

Breeding: *Season*: August to November in Zimbabwe (one April record), July to October in S Africa. *Nest*: Floor of natural hole in tree; entrance may be from side or top; from 60 cm to 30 m above ground; rarely on ground at base of tree or under log. *Clutch*: (12) 2 eggs (less often 1 or 3). *Eggs*: White; measure (17) 43,4 × 37,6 (40–46 × 35,5–40,5). *Incubation*: (3) 31 days, probably by ♀ only; starts with first egg. *Nestling*: (3) 30–35–37 days; unable to fly for several days; postnestling dependence up to 120 days.

Ref. Scott, J. 1980. *Honeyguide* 103/4:4–8.
Steyn, P. & Scott, J. 1973. *Ostrich* 44:118–125.

395 (361)   Marsh Owl   Plate 37
Vlei-uil
Asio capensis

Kakuru (K), Sephooko (SS), Zizi (Sh), Xikhotlwani (Ts), Lerubise (Tw), iNkovane, umShwelele (Z), [Kapohreule]

Measurements: Length 36–37 cm; wingspan (2) 86,1–97 cm; wing (23) 270–285–300; tail 140–155; tarsus 47–52; culmen 16–19. Weight (14) 243–315,4–355 g.

Bare Parts: Iris brown; bill black; feet blackish.

Identification: Size medium; looks uniform brown at distance (Grass Owl markedly two-toned with dark upperparts contrasting with whitish underparts); face round, pale brown with black rim (face white or pale brown, heart-shaped in Grass Owl); eyes dark, surrounded by blackish feathering, giving them huge appearance; in flight looks long-winged; pale patches near wingtips conspicuous; short "eartufts" near centre of forecrown (between eyes) seldom visible in field. *Immature*: Like adult. *Chick*: Downy buff; bill black; feet pink.

Voice: Harsh tearing croak *zzrk*; loud squealing in distraction near nest; snoring *kor*; bill-snapping alarm sounds.

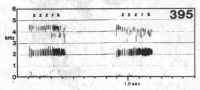

Distribution: Africa, Madagascar, s Spain; in s Africa mainly absent from dry W, but occurs in isolated reedbeds at river mouths on Namib coast.

Status: Common resident; somewhat nomadic, especially during grass burning in dry season.

Habitat: Grassland, vleis, edges of marshes.

Habits: Solitary or in pairs when breeding; sometimes in groups of up to about 40 birds. Roosts by day in hollow form under dense grasstuft, sometimes several birds close together; when flushed flies low, soon dropping into vegetation. Hunts by quartering in flight with steady wingbeats, twisting and dropping suddenly onto prey; rarely hovers; may hunt by day, especially when cloudy. Often perches on fenceposts along roads.

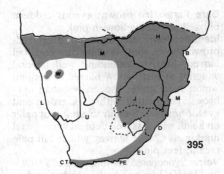

Food: Mainly small rodents, insects and birds; also shrews, elephant shrews, young hares, bats, frogs.

Breeding: *Season*: Mainly March to May, but breeding recorded all months except June. *Nest*: Hollow on ground, sparsely lined with dry grass; in dense grass which may be bent over to form canopy. *Clutch* : (32) 2–2,7–4 eggs (usually 3; rarely 5). *Eggs*: White; measure (55) 40 × 34,1 (37,9–43 × 32,4–36). *Incubation*: 27–28 days. *Nestling*: 14–18 days; makes temporary forms away from nest; flies weakly at 35–40 days; dependent on parents for further unknown period.

396 (363) **African Scops Owl** **Plate 37**
Skopsuil
Otus senegalensis

Kakuru (K), Chipotonho (Sh), Xokotlwa, Xikotlani (Ts), Lerubisana (Tw), [Afrikanische Zwergohreule]

Measurements: Length 13,5–18 cm; wingspan (14) 415–451–493; wing (27) 125–135–148; tail (16) 49–62,4–75; tarsus (15) 21–23,2–27; culmen (14) 9,2–11,9–16. Weight (2 ♀) 60,1–61,6 g, (17 unsexed) 45–64,5–97,4 g.

Bare Parts: Iris yellow; bill blackish, merging to greenish at base; feet brownish green.

Identification: Small (about size of Laughing Dove; smaller than Whitefaced Owl); face grey (white in Whitefaced Owl); outlined boldly in black; tail short, not projecting beyond wing at rest; long "eartufts" on head (can be folded down

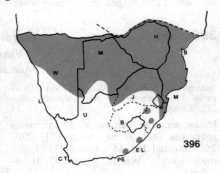

out of sight). *Grey form*: Above grey with two rows of white spots on back; below grey, streaked with black (Whitefaced

Owl white below). *Brown form*: Similar to grey form, but brown above. *Immature*: Like adult. *Chick*: Unrecorded.

Voice: High-pitched ventriloquial purring *prrrrup*, somewhat insectlike, given up to 40 times at about 14 notes/min.

Distribution: Africa S of Sahara, Socotra, Arabia, some w Indian Ocean islands; in s Africa absent from dry W and sw Cape.

Status: Sparse to locally common resident; some northward movement of S African birds into Zimbabwe possible; possibly conspecific with European Scops Owl *Otus scops*.

Habitat: Almost any woodland, but mainly drier savanna; absent from forest.

Habits: Solitary or in pairs. Nocturnal; roosts by day against trunk of tree; well camouflaged and easily overlooked; when disturbed elongates body, closes eyes almost completely. Vocal at dusk, ♂ and ♀ answering each other. Hunts by dropping onto prey from perch.

Food: Insects, scorpions.

Breeding: *Season*: September to November (also June) in Zimbabwe. *Nest*: Floor of natural hole in tree, about 30 cm from top; 1–9 m above ground; entrance vertically from above in 2 cases; also among sticks of old vulture nest, in old woodpecker hole or in nestbox. *Clutch*: (8) 2–2,8–3 eggs (usually 3). *Eggs*: White; measure (23) 29,5 × 25,4 (28–32,2 × 23,7–27). *Incubation*: 22–28 days, mainly by ♀; ♂ feeds ♀ at nest. *Nestling*: (2) 25–28 days; fed by ♀ on food brought by ♂ at first; later ♀ also hunts.

Ref. Brown, C.J., Riekert, B.R. & Morsbach, R.J. 1987. *Ostrich* 58:58–64.

397 (364) Whitefaced Owl — Plate 37
Witwanguil
Otus leucotis

Kakuru (K), Zizi (Sh), Xikhova (Ts), Lerubisana (Tw), uMandubulu (Z), [Weißgesicht-Ohreule]

Measurements: Length 25–28 cm; wingspan (5) 67,7 cm; wing (8 ♂) 190–194–198, (15 ♀) 195–199–206; tail (4) 86–94,3–100; tarsus (5) 25–30,6–37; culmen (23) 16–19. Weight (1 ♂) 192 g, (1 ♀) 206 g, (4 unsexed) 150–199,3–250 g.

Bare Parts: Iris orange to orange-yellow; bill greenish or bluish grey; feet greyish.

Identification: Size small to medium; bigger than Scops Owl; face white (grey in Scops Owl) with black border; above dove grey with row of white spots down each side of back; eyes orange (yellow in Scops Owl); tail short, not extending beyond wings at rest. *Immature*: Similar to adult, but face greyish; eyes yellow. *Chick*: Downy greyish white.

Voice: Rapid hooting *ku-ku-ku-ku-ku-WHOO-OO*, first few notes staccato, last one or two notes accented, slightly longer, drawn out and higher-pitched; snarling catlike alarm call; soft chirruping by ♀ to ♂ at nest.

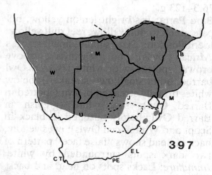

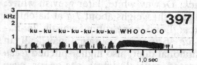

Distribution: Africa S of Sahara; in s Africa widespread except in S.

Status: Fairly common resident.

Habitat: Woodland, savanna, arid thornveld, riverine bush.

Habits: Solitary or in pairs. Nocturnal; perches by day in tree, but less well concealed than Scops Owl; when disturbed, elongates body and "eartufts" and closes eyes to slits. Hunts from perch, dropping onto prey.

Food: Up to 85% rodents (up to size of Bush Squirrel *Paraxerus cepapi*); also arthropods and birds (up to size of Laughing Dove).

Breeding: *Season*: May to November (mainly August-October) in Zimbabwe; also February in Namibia (where probably more opportunistic). *Nest*: Old nest of bird of prey, heron, lourie, or crow; also on top of nests of Scalyfeathered Finch, Cape Sparrow, Wattled Starling; also in multiple fork of tree with natural hollow. *Clutch*: (17) 2–2,4–4 eggs (usually 2–3). *Eggs*: White, rounded; measure (53) 38,8 × 32,3 (37–41,4 × 30,4–33,3). *Incubation*: (2) 30 days by both sexes; mostly by ♀. *Nestling*: At least 23 days; flies at about 33 days; fed by ♀ on food brought by ♂; postnestling dependence at least 2 weeks.

Ref. Worden, C.J. & Hall, J. 1978. *Honeyguide* 93:31–37.

398 (365) Pearlspotted Owl Plate 37
Witkoluil
Glaucidium perlatum

Kakuru (K), Zizi (Sh), Mankhudu (Ts), Lerubisana (Tw), iNkovana (Z), [Perlkauz]

Measurements: Length 17–21 cm; wingspan (28) 311–371–414; wing (48) 99–106–115; tail (30) 71–75,9–84; tarsus (30) 18,1–21,7–26; culmen (31) 9,6–11,3–13,4. Weight (7 ♂) mean 61,5 g, (4 ♀) 87,5–95,1–116 g, (45 unsexed) 61,5–76,3–123 g.

Bare Parts: Iris bright lemon yellow; bill pale green to dull yellow; feet dull yellow.

Identification: Size small (smallest of s African owls); no "eartufts"; above brown, spotted with white (Barred Owl barred, other small owls streaked); below white, broadly streaked brown (spotted in Barred Owl); face white (greyish in Barred Owl; boldly outlined in black in Scops and Whitefaced Owls); eyes yellow; back of head shows "false face" pattern of two dark spots surrounded by white. *Immature*: Lacks spots on head and back. *Chick*: Downy white, later greyish white; bill greyish; weighs about 7 g at hatching.

Voice: Loud penetrating whistle *tiu-tiu-tiu-tiu*, rising in volume; may call in antiphonal duet; also higher-pitched *teeeu* repeated several times; *pee-oo* or *peep peep* alarm notes; at start of breeding, ventriloquial *peep* by both sexes about every 30 seconds.

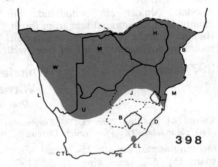

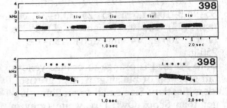

Distribution: Africa S of Sahara; widespread in s Africa, except S of Zululand, n Cape and s Namibia.

Status: Common resident.

Habitat: Bushveld, woodland, *Acacia* savanna.

Habits: Solitary or in pairs. Partly diurnal, but mainly nocturnal; tamer and more conspicuous than other small owls. Flicks or wags tail in alarm; stares at disturbance (unlike Scops and Whitefaced Owls which close eyes to slits). Flight fast, dipping, woodpeckerlike, with audible wingbeats

(most owls' wings silent). Hunts by dropping onto prey from perch, but can catch bats in flight.

Food: Mainly arthropods; also small rodents, bats, lizards, snakes, frogs, birds (up to size of dove), molluscs (*Namibiella* and *Xerocerastus*) after rain.

Breeding: *Season*: August to November (mainly September-October). *Nest*: Usually barbet or woodpecker hole in tree; sometimes natural tree-hole or nestbox; may line nest with green leaves; 1–10 m above ground. *Clutch*: 2–4 eggs (usually 3). *Eggs*: White; measure (25) 31 × 25,8 (28–33,8 × 24–27,2). *Incubation*: 28–29 days, possibly by both sexes. *Nestling*: About 27–31 days; fed by ♀ on food brought by ♂.

Ref. Steyn, P. 1979. *Bokmakierie* 31:50–60.

---

399 (366)

Barred Owl
Gebande Uil
Glaucidium capense

Plate 37

Kakuru (K), Zizi (Sh), Lerubisana (Tw), [Kapkauz]

Measurements: Length 20–21 cm; wingspan (4) 40,4 cm; wing (15) 134–139–143; tail 80–89; tarsus 21–24; culmen 12–14. Weight (1 ♂) 103 g.

Bare Parts: Iris lemon yellow; bill pale green or greenish yellow; feet greenish grey to dull yellow.

Identification: Size small; no "eartufts"; head large and puffy; above brown, narrowly barred with white; two rows of bold white spots down back, forming V pattern; below white, spotted with brown (streaked in Pearlspotted Owl); eyes yellow. *Immature*: Indistinctly spotted below; otherwise like adult. *Chick*: Undescribed; older nestlings have white down.

Voice: Repeated fairly high-pitched series of notes *purr purr piu piu piu piu*, rising slightly in volume, somewhat like notes of Cape Turtle Dove; also 2-syllabled slightly trilled *prr-purr, prr-purr*, second note slightly higher than first; soft mellow *twoo, twoo, twoo.*

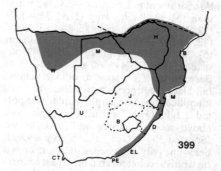

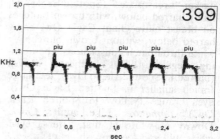

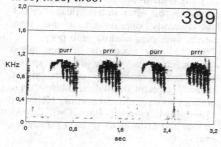

Distribution: From Zululand, Zimbabwe, n Botswana and Namibia (from Windhoek) to Zaire and Kenya; isolated population in e Cape (Kenton-on-Sea, Bathurst) and Transkei (Hluleka Nature Reserve); vagrant to Natal.

Status: Fairly common resident in N (subspecies *ngamiense* and *robertsi*); rare in s Cape and Transkei (subspecies *capense*). Rare (RDB).

Habitat: Riverine forest and coastal bush.

Habits: Similar to Pearlspotted Owl.

Partly diurnal. Hunts by dropping onto prey from perch.
Food: Poorly known; mainly arthropods; also small birds, lizards, frogs.
Breeding: *Season*: September to October. *Nest*: Natural hole in tree, with floor 15–30 cm below entrance; 5–6 m above ground. *Clutch*: (6) 3 eggs (possibly only 2 at times). *Eggs*: White; measure (11) 32,6 × 27,3 (30–34 × 26–28). *Incubation*: About 1 month. *Nestling*: About 33 days.

Ref. Carlyon, J. 1985. *Afr. Wildl.* 39:22–23.
Clancey, P.A. 1980. *Durban Mus. Novit.* 12:143–149.
Steyn, P. 1979. *Bokmakierie* 31:50–60.

400 (367)   Cape Eagle Owl   Plate 37
Kaapse Ooruil
Bubo capensis

Khuhunu, Phikuphiku, Xikhova (Ts), isiKhova-mpondo (Z), [Kapuhu]

Measurements: Length 48–53 cm; wing-span (5) 124,9 cm; wing (5 ♂) 330–357, (12 ♀) 363–392; tail (5 ♂) 155–215, (12 ♀) 169–240; tarsus (5) 62–65; culmen (5) 28–29. Weight (1 ♀) 1195 g, (7 un-sexed) 905–1115,4–1360 g.
Bare Parts: Iris orange to orange-yellow; bill black; feet greyish or yellowish.
Identification: Size large; similar to Spotted Eagle Owl; "eartufts" conspicuous; above mottled tawny and dark brown (Spotted Eagle Owl lightish grey above); below heavily blotched with dark brown on whitish, concentrated on breast to form darker "breastplates" (Spotted Eagle Owl finely barred below, with brown blotches on breast only; Giant Eagle Owl finely barred below, without brown blotching); white throatpatch conspicuous when calling; legs and feet feathered whitish (barred in Spotted Eagle Owl); feet large (much smaller in Spotted Eagle Owl); eyes orange (yellow in Spotted Eagle Owl). *Immature*: Like adult. *Chick*: Downy off-white at first, later greyish white; bill and feet greyish.
Voice: Mellow hooting, *hoo-boo, hoo-woo-woooh*, lower-pitched on the *boo*, drawn out on last note; also *hoooo-hu* or *hu-hoooo-hu*; resonant pigeonlike *koo-kook* in display; sharp *wak-wak* and bill-clacking alarm sounds; far-carrying wheezy *shreer* soliciting call by ♀ and large young.

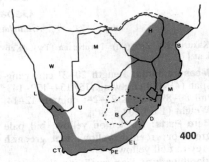

400

Distribution: S Africa to E Africa; in s Africa mainly confined to s and w Cape Province, through to Orange Free State, Natal, Lesotho and e Transvaal (*B. c. capensis*); much larger *B. c. mackinderi* occurs Zimbabwe and adjacent Mozambique.
Status: Uncommon to rare resident.
Habitat: Rocky and mountainous country, usually with dense woodland or bush nearby; in sw Cape inhabits mountain fynbos to sea level.
Habits: Usually solitary. Nocturnal; by day sits tight in secluded roost in cave or on ledge, less often in tree; flushes reluctantly; easily overlooked. Hunts from perch, swooping silently onto prey.
Food: Mostly mammals in most areas (hares, canerats, young dassies, spring-hares, genets, mongooses, smaller rodents, shrews, elephant shrews); also birds (up to 80% in some areas; francolins, Helmeted Guineafowl, pigeons, Barn Owl, doves), lizards and arthropods (insects, arachnids, crabs).

400

Breeding: *Season*: May to July in Zimbabwe, May to August in sw Cape. *Nest*: Unlined scrape on ground or ledge of cave, or under rock on hillside, well screened by vegetation. *Clutch*: 2 eggs (sometimes 1 or 3). *Eggs*: White, rounded; measure (21 *capensis*) 53 × 44 (50,6–54,8 × 42–46,8); (19 *mackinderi*) 57,8 × 46,5 (55–60,7 × 44–48,4). *Incu-*

bation: 38 days by ♀ only. *Nestling*: Leaves nest at about 45 days; flies at 70–77 days; fed at first by ♀ on food brought by ♂; later fed by both parents.

Ref. Brooke, R.K. 1973. *Ostrich* 44:137–139. Grobler, J.H. 1982. *Afr. Wildl.* 36:218–221. Steyn, P. & Tredgold, D. 1977. *Bokmakierie* 29:31–42.

401 (368)   Spotted Eagle Owl   Plate 37
Gevlekte Ooruil
Bubo africanus

Editika (K), Morubisi, Sephooko, Makhohlo, Sehihi (SS), Khukunu, Phikuphiku (Ts), Morubise, Mophoê, Makgotlwê (Tw), Ifubesi (X), isiKhovampondo (Z), [Fleckenuhu, Berguhu]

Measurements: Length 43–47 cm; wingspan (26) 113,3 cm; wing (36) 315–340–370; tail 176–220; tarsus 60–70; culmen 20–26. Weight (2 ♂) 540–751 g, (10 ♀) 446–593,7–729 g, (63 unsexed) 487–696,4–995 g.

Bare Parts: Iris yellow (orange in rufous form); bill blackish; soles of feet yellowish.

Identification: Size large; "eartufts" conspicuous. *Normal form*: Above grey, sparingly spotted white; below white, finely barred dark grey, including legs and feet, spotted with brown on breast only (Cape Eagle Owl heavily blotched with brown on breast, broadly barred on belly); eyes yellow (orange in Cape Eagle Owl). *Rufous form*: Rare; rufous instead of grey above; eyes orange. *Immature*: Similar to adult, but "eartufts" shorter; ventral barring blacker. *Chick*: Downy white at first, later downy grey.

Voice: ♂ has deep 2-syllabled hooting *vooo-hoo*, lower on second note; in ♀ first note just noticeably 2 syllables, *voowu-hoo*, the *wu* very short; may call in duet, one bird replying to other in lower tone; ♀ may use 3-syllabled *hoo-hoohoo*, middle note higher-pitched; wailing *keeyow* alarm call; also bill-clacking; hissing threat note.

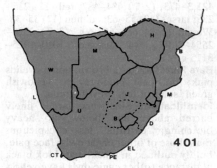

Distribution: Africa S of Sahara, s Arabia; throughout s Africa.

Status: Common resident.

Habitat: Rocky areas, woodland, forest edge, savanna, semidesert, towns.

Habits: Usually solitary or in pairs. Nocturnal; roosts by day on ground, on rocky ledge, or in tree; sits close; when disturbed may partly close eyes and raise "eartufts", relying on camouflage. Hunts from perch, dropping onto prey; commonly perches on fenceposts or telephone poles; often killed by cars at night; rarely catches bats in flight; also catches flying termites with feet, passing prey to bill in flight.

Food: Mostly arthropods; also birds (up to size of nearly full-grown guineafowl), reptiles, mammals, frogs, rarely fish.

Breeding: *Season*: July to January (mainly August-October); also May and June. *Nest*: Shallow scrape on ground under rock, on ledge of donga, cliff or building; also in hole in tree, old nest of raptor, or on top of nest of Hamerkop or Sociable

Weaver. *Clutch*: (297) 2–2,4–4 eggs (usually 2). *Eggs*: White, rounded; measure (80)   49,1 × 41,1   (47,1–54,2 × 39,1–44,4). *Incubation*: 30–32 days by ♀ only. *Nestling*: 40 days; postnestling dependence at least 5 weeks.

402 (369)   Giant Eagle Owl   Plate 37
Reuse Ooruil
Bubo lacteus

Editika (K), Zizi (Sh), Khuhunu, Phikuphiku, Xihina (Ts), Morubise, Mophoê, Makgotlwê (Tw), Ifubesi (X), isiKhova, iFubesi (Z), [Milchuhu, Blaßuhu]

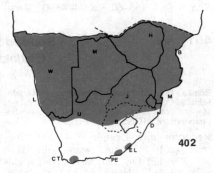

402

Measurements: Length 58–65 cm; wingspan (5) 143,2 cm; wing (4 ♂) 300–421,3–473, (2 ♀) 484–487; tail (12) 235–275; tarsus (12) 55–63; culmen (12) 35–38. Weight (2 ♂) 681–681,6 g, (3 ♀) 2525–2554–2610 g, (4 unsexed) 1010–1925–3115 g.

Bare Parts: Iris dark brown; upper eyelids pink; bill pale blue-grey to yellowish green; soles of feet greyish green.

Identification: Size very large; finely barred above and below; no heavy blotching; "eartufts" less conspicuous than those of other eagle owls; face pale, boldly outlined in black; eyes look black at distance (other eagle owls have yellow or orange eyes); pink eyelids conspicuous. *Immature*: Paler than adult. *Chick*: Downy white at first, later greyish.

Voice: Irregular gruff hooting *hru hru, hru-hru-hru, hru hru*, deep and somewhat booming; may call in duet; plaintive far-carrying ventriloquial *pseeeeeew* by ♀ and fledglings; weird resonant *ooo-aau-au* in distraction near nest; low *whock* and bill-clacking alarm sounds; hissing threat call.

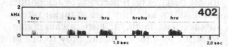

402

Distribution: Africa S of Sahara; in s Africa mainly from Orange River and Zululand northwards; small isolated populations in e Cape and De Hoop Nature Reserve, sw Cape.

Status: Rare and isolated in e Cape and Natal; fairly common to common from n Cape and n Transvaal northward; resident; vagrant to Bredasdorp.

Habitat: Woodland, savanna, tree-lined watercourses.

Habits: Solitary, in pairs, or family groups of 3 birds. Mostly nocturnal, rarely hunts in daylight; by day roosts in larger trees, preferably in shade; often tame. Flight buoyant; hunts by swooping onto prey from perch; may catch roosting birds in trees, or insects in flight.

Food: Very varied; mammals (up to size of Vervet Monkey; especially hedgehogs where available), birds (from white-eye to Secretarybird, including ducks, raptors, owls, korhaans and many others), reptiles, frogs, fish, arthropods.

Breeding: *Season*: March to September (mainly June-August). *Nest*: Top of nest of other bird species (raptors, Hamerkop, Sociable Weaver, Redbilled Buffalo Weaver, Pied Crow), hollow in tree. *Clutch*: 2 eggs (sometimes only 1). *Eggs*: White, rounded, sometimes with surface nodules; measure (38)   62,9 × 51,2 (58–67,3 × 48–54). *Incubation*: About 38–39 days by both sexes; mostly by ♀. *Nestling*: About 2 months; flies at about 3 months; remains with parents until following breeding season.

Ref. Avery, G., Robertson, A.S., Palmer, N.G. & Prins, A.J. 1985. *Ostrich* 56:117–122.
Pitman, C.R.S. & Adamson, J. 1978. *Honeyguide* 95:3–23; 26–43.

403 (370)

Pel's Fishing Owl
Visuil
Scotopelia peli

Plate 37

Dinidza (Sh), [Bindenfischeule, Fischeule]

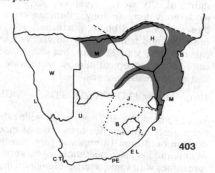

403

Measurements: Length about 63 cm; wingspan (1) 153 cm; wing 400–440; tail 230–260; tarsus 65–70; culmen 36–38. Weight (3) 2055–2141,7–2270 g.

Bare Parts: Iris brown; bill horn to black, base paler; legs and feet pinkish white.

Identification: Size very large; no "ear-tufts" on head, but crown feathers raised in alarm; above tawny rufous, barred black; below tawny buff, streaked and spotted with blackish brown; facial disc poorly defined; eyes look black at distance; legs unfeathered, white, hidden by belly feathers at rest. *Immature*: Paler than adult. *Chick*: Downy white at first, later buff.

Voice: Deep sonorous hooting preceded or followed by low grunt *hooommmmm-hut*; repeated horn-like *hoom, hoom*; resonance from inflated air sacs; sometimes ♂ and ♀ call in duet, ♂ starting with grunting *uh-uh-uhu* building up to high *hoommm*, answered by deeper hoot of ♀; high-pitched penetrating trill, followed by scream in distraction display; eerie wailing *eeeyooow* begging call by fledgling.

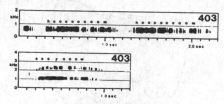

Distribution: Africa S of Sahara; in s Africa mainly from Zululand to Mozambique, Limpopo River valley, e and n Zimbabwe, n Botswana and Caprivi; rarely to Natal and e Cape.

Status: Rare in S; locally common in suitable habitat elsewhere (e.g. Okavango), especially in subtropical regions; resident. Rare (RDB).

Habitat: Forest bordering larger rivers and swamps, mainly in lowlands.

Habits: Usually in pairs or family groups of 3 birds. Largely nocturnal; roosts by day in shady (usually dark-leaved) tree up to 18 m above ground; unobtrusive and easily overlooked, but flushes readily, flying with noisy wingbeats; may perch on top of tree in full view; often mobbed by Fish Eagles. Hunts from perch on tree or bank about 1–2 m up, overlooking water, swooping down on surface fishes; long claws and spiny soles hold slippery prey.

Food: Mostly fish (up to 2 kg; mostly 100–250 g); also frogs, crabs, mussels, young crocodiles; fruits of Mobola Plum *Parinari curatellifolia* in Zimbabwe.

Breeding: *Season*: April, May and October in Zimbabwe, January to June (mainly February-April) in Okavango Delta, mainly March-April in Zululand and n Kruger National Park. *Nest*: Hollow about 30–40 cm diameter in broad fork, hole or cavity in large tree; 3–6–12 m above ground (12 nests); overlooking water or up to 200 m from water. *Clutch*: 2 eggs (sometimes only 1). *Eggs*: White, rounded; measure (13) 61,7 × 51,7 (58,8–65,1 × 49,2–53,5); weigh (4) mean 85 g. *Incubation*: Between 33 and 38 days, all or most by ♀. *Nestling*: 68–70 days; only 1 chick reared; dependent on parents for at least 4 months after leaving nest.

Ref. Liversedge, T.N. 1980. *Proc. 4th Pan-Afr. Orn. Congr.*:291–299.

19. Order CAPRIMULGIFORMES (Five families; one in s Africa)

Small to large. Bill short, deep or very small; gape wide; legs very short and weak; toes short, usually weak; eyes very large; neck short; wings long, usually pointed; tail moderately long to long; plumage cryptic and elaborately patterned in grey, buff, brown, white and black; nocturnal; arboreal or terrestrial; food mostly flying insects, some gleaned from bark or on ground (Oilbird, family Steatornithidae, of S America eats only fruit); flight silent, but some species clap wings in display. Distribution mainly tropical to subtropical, almost worldwide, except New Zealand, n N America, n Asia and most oceanic islands.

19:1. Family 49 CAPRIMULGIDAE—NIGHTJARS

Small to medium. Bill very small with tubular nostrils; gape very wide, sometimes with rictal bristles (in species texts, size of mouth given by mouth:wing index, calculated as mean mouth area (tomium × gape)/mean wing length); legs and feet very small and weak; middle claw pectinate; eyes very large; head large; wings long and pointed, sometimes with some remiges elongated in males for display; tail medium to long, variable in shape, usually square or rounded; plumage highly cryptic, elaborately patterned, sometimes with white spots or patches in wings and/or tail; hawk insects in flight; usually roost on ground; no nest; eggs 1–2, white or pale pink, usually spotted with reddish, laid on bare ground or leaf litter; chick downy, altricial; parental care by both sexes. Distribution as for Order Caprimulgiformes; about 70 species; seven species in s Africa.

Ref. Colebrook-Robjent, J.F.R. 1984. *Ostrich* 55:5–11.
  Jackson, H.D. 1984a. *Arnoldia (Zimbabwe)* 9(14):223–230; 1984b. *Smithersia* 4:1–55; 1985. *Bull. Brit. Orn. Club* 105:51–54.

404 (371)   **Eurasian Nightjar**   **Plate 38**
Europese Naguil
Caprimulgus europaeus

Rumbamba (K), Semanama (SS), Datiwa (Sh), Mahulwana, Ribyatsane (Ts), Tshogwi, Leubauba, Mmapheke (Tw), Udebeza (X), uZavolo, uMawewe (Z), [Ziegenmelker, Nachtschwalbe]

Measurements: Length 25–28 cm; wing (16) 184–194,5–200; tail 121–136,4–147; tarsus 15–17,1–19; culmen 8–9,9–11; mouth:wing index = 420. Weight (5 ♂) 56,7–62,4–71 g, (4 ♀) 50–69,7–87 g.

Bare Parts: Iris brown; bill dark horn; legs and feet pinkish brown.

Identification: See Plate 38 and nightjar key; ♀ lacks wingbar and tail patches.

Voice: Usually silent in s Africa; sharp *koo-ik* take-off and flight call; *wik-wik-wik* (♂) and *chuk* (♀) alarm calls; sustained vibrant churring in 2 tones (42 and 24 notes/second respectively), rising and falling in cadence.

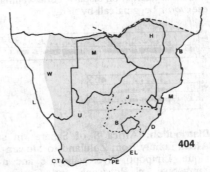

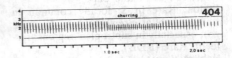

Distribution: Breeds Europe and Asia; migrates to Africa and s Asia; widespread in s Africa, except in dry W.

Status: Nonbreeding Palaearctic migrant, common in E, scarce in W; September to early April (mostly November-March); returns to same sites year after year.
Habitat: Woodland, savanna, tree-lined watercourses, plantations, gardens.

Habits: Usually solitary. Roosts by day parallel to horizontal branch, rarely on ground. Feeds over open ground at twilight and on moonlit nights.
Food: Flying insects.
Breeding: Extralimital.

405 (373) Fierynecked Nightjar   Plate 38
Afrikaanse Naguil
Caprimulgus pectoralis

Rumbamba (K), Leuwauwe (NS), Datiwa (Sh), Mahulwana, Ribyatsane, Riwuvawuva (Ts), Tshogwi, Leubauba, Mmapheke (Tw), Udebeza (X), uZavolo, uMawewe (Z), [Rotnacken-Nachtschwalbe]

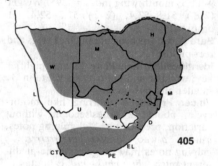

405

Measurements: Length 23–25 cm; wing (209) 142–161,2–176; tail (178) 104–120,4–136; white on outermost rectrix (128 ♂) 33–44,3–52, (84 ♀) 17–27,8–37; tarsus (230) 11–15,7–21; culmen (205) 8–11,6–15; mouth:wing index = 480. Weight (89 ♂) 37,4–54,2–66 g, (74 ♀) 41,2–53,5–66 g, (9 unsexed) 33–45,3–51 g.
Bare Parts: Iris brown; bill, legs and feet pinkish brown.
Identification: See Plate 38 and nightjar key; wingbar and tail patches white in ♂, smaller and buff in ♀.
Voice: Mellow whistled phrase introduced by 2 slurred notes with rising tone, ending with rapid, almost trilled, series of notes with falling tone, *koo-WEEU, koo-WIririri*; also set to words *good lord deliver us* (hence name of Litanybird), or *jag weg die wewenaar*; also clucking notes.

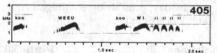

405

Distribution: Most of Africa S of Sahara; in s Africa absent from most of dry W.
Status: Common partial migrant; largely resident in lowlands; breeding summer migrant to higher elevations, mostly November to April.
Habitat: Dense woodland, plantations, gardens, thornveld, bushveld.
Habits: Usually solitary or in pairs. Cre-

puscular; by day lies up on ground in shade. Hawks prey from arboreal perch. Vocal mainly dusk and dawn, but throughout moonlit night.
Food: Insects (especially beetles) and spiders.
Breeding: *Season*: August to December (mainly September-November); may rear 2 broods/season. *Nest*: None; eggs laid on leaf litter and debris under trees. *Clutch*: (49) 1–1,9–2 eggs (usually 2). *Eggs*: Pale ivory, pinkish cream or pale salmon, plain or with tiny speckles or blotches of dark pink and lilac; measure (73) 27,4 × 20 (24,5–30 × 18,3–21,4); weigh (20) 4,9–5,9–6,8 g. *Incubation*: About 17–19 days by ♀ (day) and by ♂ (night). *Nestling*: Leaves nest at about 10 days; flies at about 24 days; brooded by ♀ until 37 days; fed by both parents until at least 40 days.

Ref. Jackson, H.D. 1985. *Ostrich* 56:263–276.
Steyn, P. & Myburgh, N.J. 1975. *Ostrich* 46:265–266.
Langley, C.H. 1984. *Ostrich* 55:1–4.

406 (372)   Rufoucheeked Nightjar   Plate 38
Rooiwangnaguil
Caprimulgus rufigena

Rumbamba (K), Semanama (SS), Datiwa (Sh), Mahulwana, Ribyatsane, Riwuvawuva (Ts), Tshogwi, Leubauba, Mmapheke (Tw), [Rostwangen-Nachtschwalbe]

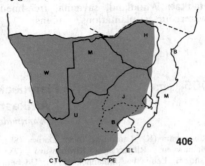

406

Measurements: Length 23–24 cm; wing (19 ♂) 157–164–176, (23 ♀) 149–160–167; tail (42) 114–130; white on outermost rectrix (10 ♂) 24–27,9–35, (10 ♀) 12–16,1–20; tarsus (42) 17–18; culmen (42) 9–11,5; mouth:wing index = 395. Weight (2 ♂) 51,8–52,4, (2 ♀) 51,3–52,4, (1 unsexed) 64,1 g.

Bare Parts: Iris brown; bill black; legs and feet pinkish.

Identification: See Plate 38 and nightjar key; wingbar and tail patches white in ♂, smaller and buff in ♀.

Voice: Prolonged churring like motorcycle, about 31 notes/second, without variation, preceded by 2–4 gulping notes, *q-woo, q-woo, q-woo, prrrrrrrrrr.....*; gulping notes may be given alone at different pitch; *chuk-chuk-chuk* callnotes.

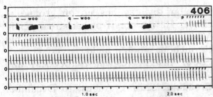

406

Distribution: S Africa to Ethiopia; in s Africa mainly in higher and drier parts, including sw Cape.

Status: Fairly common breeding intra-African migrant from N of equator, August to April (rarely to May).

Habitat: Open woodland, savanna, exotic plantations, semi-arid scrub, shrubby semidesert.

Habits: Usually solitary or in pairs. Crepuscular; by day lies up on ground in shade of tree or low shrub; when flushed, flies with irregular wingbeats and swooping flight, usually not far, landing suddenly on ground at base of bush or tree like other nightjars. Vocal at twilight, especially at start of breeding season.

Food: Flying insects.

Breeding: *Season*: September to January (mainly October-November). *Nest*: None; eggs laid on bare ground or leaf litter; nest site sometimes ringed with small stones. *Clutch*: (38) 1–1,97–2 eggs (usually 2). *Eggs*: Glossy, pale pinkish cream, indistinctly marbled with pale brick over lilac; very rarely pure white or scrawled with brick; measure (64) 27,2 × 20,1 (23,9–30 × 18,4–21,6); weigh (22) 4,1–5,7–7,2 g. *Incubation*: 16 days by ♀ only by day; possibly by ♂ at night. *Nestling*: Unrecorded.

407 (375)   Natal Nightjar   Plate 38
Natalse Naguil
Caprimulgus natalensis

Rumbamba (K), Tshogwi, Leubauba, Mmapheke (Tw), umHlohlongwane (Z), [Natalnachtschwalbe]

Measurements: Length about 23 cm; wing (8) 148–159,9–168; tail 96–101,3–107; tarsus 20–21,4–24; culmen 10–10,8–12; mouth:wing index = 480. Weight (1 ♂) 86,7 g.

Bare Parts: Iris brown; bill dark brown; legs and feet pinkish brown.

Identification: See Plate 38 and nightjar key.

Voice: Unmusical slow churring *chop-chop-chop-chop* at 4 notes/second; tremulous winnowing *wuwuwuwuwuwu*.

Distribution: Africa S of Sahara; in s Africa from e Cape to s Mozambique and e Transvaal lowveld; also Caprivi and n Botswana, marginally to Zimbabwe on S bank of Zambezi River above Katombora Rapids.
Status: Uncommon to locally fairly common resident. Vulnerable (RDB).
Habitat: Moist edges of lowland and coastal lagoons, vleis and swamps, often around palms.
Habits: Usually solitary or in pairs. Crepuscular; lies up by day in grass or among ferns; when disturbed may fly to patch of trees. Hawks prey in flight, sometimes low over ground; also perches on posts and roads.

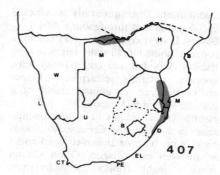

Food: Flying insects, especially beetles.
Breeding: *Season*: August to November. *Nest*: None; eggs laid on bare ground, usually in shelter of grasstuft or small bush. *Clutch*: (11) 2 eggs. *Eggs*: Pale pinkish white or off-white, faintly marked with slate grey; measure (10) 29,7 × 21,4 (28–31,2 × 20,8–22,2). *Incubation*: Unrecorded. *Nestling*: Unrecorded.

408 (374) Freckled Nightjar Plate 38
Donkernaguil
Caprimulgus tristigma

Datiwa (Sh), Mahulwana, Ribyatsane, Riwuvawuva (Ts), Tshogwi, Leubauba, Mmapheke (Tw), [Fleckennachtschwalbe]

Measurements: Length 27–28 cm; wing (20) 184–189,9–204; tail 124–132,3–143; tarsus 18–19,2–21; culmen 11–13,2–15; mouth:wing index = 550. Weight (3 ♂) 79–80,7–83 g, (6 ♀) 71–80–91 g, (1 unsexed) 65,7 g.
Bare Parts: Iris dark brown; bill, legs and feet dark horn.
Identification: See Plate 38 and nightjar key; overall dark grey coloration distinctive; ♂ has white wingbar and tail patches; ♀ has wingbar only. *Chick*: Mottled dark grey and off-white; bill and eyes black; eyes open on first day.
Voice: Series of somewhat ringing or yelping 2-syllabled *whip-wheeu*, occasionally 3-syllabled *whip-wheeu-wheeu*, higher in tone and slightly accented on second syllable, slurred down on first note (timbre reminiscent of that of Red-

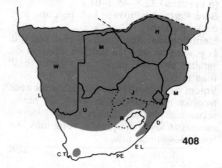

chested Cuckoo); also triple *kluk-kluk-kluk* when disturbed; long series of *woot-woot-woot* notes, probably as contact call.

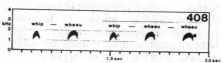

353

Distribution: Discontinuously in Africa S of Sahara; almost throughout s Africa.
Status: Locally common to very common resident; some birds locally migratory.
Habitat: Wooded and bushy rocky hills, koppies, outcrops, escarpments; especially abundant on granite shield of e Zimbabwe and in Matobo.
Habits: Usually singly or in pairs, sometimes in small groups. Crepuscular; roosts by day on bare or lichen-covered rocks where well camouflaged. Often sits on roads at night. Hawks insects by short flights out from perch on scarp or boulder, returning by glide to same perch.

Food: Flying insects (especially moths).
Breeding: *Season*: August to December (mainly September-November). *Nest*: None; eggs laid on bare rock or in gravel-filled hollow on rock; sometimes on flat rooftops (e.g. in Durban). *Clutch*: (10) 2 eggs (rarely 1). *Eggs*: White or greyish white, blotched with pale sepia and underlying pale lilac, forming zone at thick end; measure (20) 29,4 × 21,2 (27,5–31,1 × 20–22,6). *Incubation*: 18,5 days by ♀ by day, ♂ at night. *Nestling*: Flies at about 20 days; fed and brooded by both parents.

Ref. Steyn, P. 1971. *Ostrich Suppl.* 9:179–188.

409 (376) Mozambique Nightjar Plate 38
Laeveldnaguil
Caprimulgus fossii

Datiwa (Sh), Mahulwana, Ribyatsane, Riwuva-wuva (Ts), [Gabunnachtschwalbe]

Measurements: Length 23–24 cm; wing (24 ♂) 157–164,9–173, (26 ♀) 156–160,7–166; tail (34 ♂) 119–128,5–137, (36 ♀) 99–119,3–129; tarsus (20) 17–18,7–22; culmen (20) 9–10–11; mouth: wing index = 420. Weight (13 ♂) 39–59,4–74 g, (16 ♀) 38,5–60,8–77,4 g, (6 unsexed) 32,8–46,2–64 g.
Bare Parts: Iris brown; bill, legs and feet dusky pinkish.
Identification: See Plate 38 and nightjar key; wingbar and tail patches white in ♂, smaller and buff in ♀; tail shorter in ♀ than in ♂.
Voice: Sustained high-pitched somewhat froglike trill, varying in pitch, 24 notes/second at higher frequency, 18 notes/second at lower frequency; song may last for 100–400 seconds.

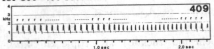

Distribution: From Natal to Ethiopia and Ghana; in s Africa confined to E, NE and N.
Status: Common resident in lowveld; less common breeding migrant to highveld from lowveld, September to May.
Habitat: Scrub with open sandy ground in savanna, riverine bush, coastal dunes.

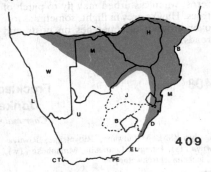

Habits: Usually solitary or in pairs. Crepuscular; hawks prey in short sallies from ground or perch, or in flight over ground or water. Often sits on roads and in clearings; seldom perches in trees.
Food: Insects (especially beetles; also termites, moths, bugs and ants).
Breeding: *Season*: August to November (mainly October-November). *Nest*: None; eggs laid on bare ground among plant debris, often under thornbush. *Clutch*: (47) 1–1,9–2 eggs (usually 2). *Eggs*: Deep cream to pink, heavily blotched and smeared with rich browns or warm deep brick; appear brown overall; rough-textured, matt to glossy; measure (80) 27 × 20 (24,5–31,1 × 18,5–21,5); weigh (17) 4,5–5,7–7 g. *Incubation*: 14–17 days by ♀ during day, by ♂ at night. *Nestling*: Unrecorded.

410 (377)   Pennantwinged Nightjar   Plate 38
Wimpelvlerknaguil
Macrodipteryx vexillaria

[Ruderflügel]

Measurements: Length 25–28 cm; wing ♂ 234–240, ♀ 190–196; wing with pennant 675–730; tail (5) 127–145; tarsus (5) 19–23; culmen (5) 8–12; mouth:wing index = 280. Weight (111 ♂) 59–68,6–86 g, (44 ♀) 40,2–74–91 g.

Bare Parts: Iris brown; bill dark brown; legs and feet pinkish to greyish brown.

Identification: See Plate 38 and nightjar key; only ♂ has long pennants in wing; ♀ lacks white wingbar; no pale tail patches in either sex. *Immature*: Like adult ♀.

Voice: High-pitched batlike twittering, rather like stridulating cricket; ♀ usually silent.

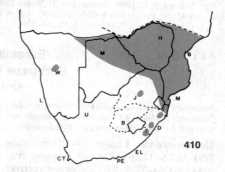

Distribution: Breeds Africa S of equator; migrates to N of equator; in s Africa mainly in subtropical NE, vagrant to Windhoek and Natal.

Status: Rare in S to locally common in N; breeding intra-African migrant, September to March (rarely August to May). Indeterminate (RDB).

Habitat: Stony hillsides, sandy ground in well developed woodland, mainly in lowveld.

Habits: Usually solitary; gregarious on migration. Partly diurnal; tends to forage earlier in evening than most nightjars, when smaller prey still visible. ♂ may fly fairly high in display with fluttering pennants, sometimes followed by ♀. Roosts on ground for most of day; at night often sits on roads; when flushed may perch lengthwise on branch. Males arrive before females, losing pennants immediately after breeding.

Food: Mainly small flying insects (especially termites).

Breeding: *Season*: September to November (sometimes to December). *Nest*: None; eggs laid on bare ground, in ploughed field, or among leaf and twig litter. *Clutch*: (111) 1–1,9–2 eggs (usually 2). *Eggs*: Pinkish cream, rose pink to salmon, blotched and streaked with darker pink, red-brown, grey and mauve, sometimes forming zones or cap; measure (176) 30,8 × 22 (26,4–34,4 × 20,4–23,6); weigh (58) 6–7,8–9,2 g. *Incubation*: 15–18 days by ♀ only. *Nestling*: Unrecorded.

20. Order APODIFORMES (Two families; one in s Africa)

20:1. Family 50 APODIDAE—SWIFTS

Small to medium. Bill very small, slightly decurved; gape wide; legs extremely short, tarsometatarsus sometimes feathered; toes very short, strong, with sharp, curved claws; two outer toes and two inner toes oppose each other in pairs for grasping; neck short; head and eyes large; wings extremely long, narrow and pointed; secondaries short; tail long or short, square or forked; plumage usually black, brown or grey, often with white on rump or underside; sexes alike; most gregarious; flight strong and fast; feed on aerial plankton (insects and spiders); colonial or solitary breeders; nest in holes, crevices, caves, under overhangs, or under palm leaves; nest a pad or ball of grass and feathers, or a half cup of twigs glued with saliva, sometimes made wholly of saliva (edible nests of cave swifts of SE Asia); eggs 1–6, white, elongate; chick naked when hatched, altricial; parental care by both sexes. Distribution worldwide, mostly tropical, avoiding high latitudes; about 75 species; 13 species in s Africa.

Ref. Brooke, R.K. 1969. *Bokmakierie* 21:39–40; 1970. *Durban Mus. Novit.* 9:13–24; 1971. *Ostrich Suppl.* 8:47–54; 1971. *Ostrich* 42:5–36; 1974. *Ostrich* 45:139–140.
Donnelly, B.G. 1974. *Ostrich* 45:256–258.

411 (378)   Eurasian Swift   Plate 39
Europese Windswael
Apus apus

Sisampamema (K), Lehaqasi (SS), Nkonjana (Ts), Pêolwane, Phêtla (Tw), Ihlabankomo, Ihlankomo (X), uHlolamvula, iJankomo (Z), [Mauersegler]

Measurements: Length 17–18 cm; wing (79) 162,5–171,9–182; tail (longest rectrix) (71) 65–73,6–83,5, (shortest rectrix) 43–48. Weight (2 ♂) 33,2–40,3 g, (3 ♀) 35,4–40–43,2 g, (mean of 2 000 unsexed) 43 g.
Bare Parts: Iris dark brown; bill black; feet dark pinkish.
Identification: Size medium; similar to Black Swift; throat whitish; from above wings and body uniform dark brown (in Black Swift dark body contrasts with paler inner wings); wingtips look slightly kinked inward. *Immature*: Finely scalloped with whitish below.
Voice: Normally silent in s Africa; high-pitched screaming when breeding.

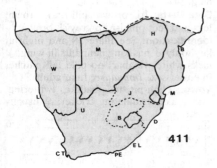

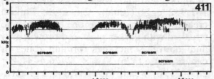

Distribution: Breeds Palaearctic region; migrates to Africa; throughout s Africa, but uncommon S of Orange River drainage.
Status: Common nonbreeding Palaearctic migrant, November to March; many s African birds from England and Netherlands; Asian birds also present, especially in Namibia.
Habitat: Mostly open country, but occurs almost anywhere.
Habits: Highly gregarious, usually in flocks of hundreds of birds, often in company with other species of swift. Usually flies high, except before or after storms; seldom lands, even sleeping in flight at great heights.
Food: Aerial arthropods; mainly insects.
Breeding: Extralimital.

Ref. Brooke, R.K. 1975. *Durban Mus. Novit.* 10:239–249.
Lack, D. 1956. *Swifts in a tower.* London: Methuen.

412 (380)   Black Swift   Plate 39
Swartwindswael
Apus barbatus

Sisampamema (K), Lehaqasi (SS), Nkonjana (Ts), Pêolwane, Phêtla (Tw), Ihlabankomo, Ihlankomo (X), iHlabankomo, iHlolamvula, iJankomo (Z), [Kapsegler]
Measurements: Length 18–19 cm; wing (40) 169–178,6–196; tail (longest rectrix) 71–77, (shortest rectrix) 47–52. Weight (19) 35–42,1–50 g.
Bare Parts: Iris dark brown; bill black; feet dark pinkish.

Identification: Size medium, similar to Eurasian Swift; throat whitish; below uniformly dark; from above dark body contrasts with paler inner wings. *Immature*: Has whitish edges to outer remiges.
Voice: Shrill twittering scream in displaying flocks.

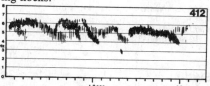

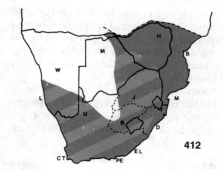

Distribution: Much of Africa S of Sahara, Comoros, Madagascar; throughout s Africa, especially moister parts.
Status: Very common; resident in Zimbabwe; mostly breeding intra-African migrant in S Africa, September to April, but some birds overwinter along e littoral.
Habitat: Mostly open country near mountains, cliffs and gorges, but ranges over any habitat.
Habits: Highly gregarious, flocks numbering hundreds of birds; often in company with other species of swift. Silent when feeding, but vocal in gregarious displays of spiralling clouds of birds, usually very

high. Similar to most other medium to large swifts.
Food: Aerial arthropods; mostly insects.
Breeding: *Season*: September to January in S Africa, September in Zimbabwe. *Nest*: Shallow pad of feathers and grass, stuck together with saliva; in horizontal or vertical crevice in overhanging cliff; usually colonial. *Clutch*: 2 eggs (sometimes only 1). *Eggs*: White; measure (4) 25,9 × 16,8 (23,3–27,5 × 15,3–17,4). *Incubation*: Unrecorded. *Nestling*: Unrecorded.

Ref. Brooke, R.K. 1970. *Durban Mus. Novit.* 8(19):363–374.

413 (381) Bradfield's Swift
Muiskleurwindswael
Apus bradfieldi
Plate 39

[Damarasegler]

Measurements: Length 18 cm; wing (30) 167–182; tail (longest rectrix) 70–77. Weight (2) 44–53 g.
Bare Parts: Iris dark brown; bill and feet black.
Identification: Size medium; mostly uniformly mousecoloured with contrasting blackish primaries and rectrices; pale edges to belly feathers visible only at close quarters; very little white under chin (much less than other all-dark swifts of similar size); wingtips less curved than in other swifts; looks pale, slender and narrow-winged; dark streak at base of upperwing.
Voice: Shrill scream.
Distribution: From Kimberley (Big Hole) through Namibia to w Angola; possibly also e Karoo (Cradock).

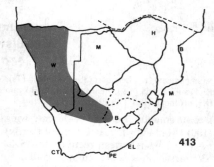

Status: Common resident. Possibly Rare (RDB).
Habitat: Mountains, cliffs, gorges; ranges into open country to forage.
Habits: Gregarious. Roosts in cracks in cliffs and in palm fronds; departs early in

357

morning and returns to roost shortly after sunset; performs aerial manoeuvres around roosting trees, possibly when about to breed. Rests on ground during foraging, taking off without difficulty. Rather poorly known.

Food: Aerial arthropods, including bees.

Breeding: *Season:* August to May in Namibia. *Nest:* Flat cup of dry grass, twigs, feathers and down, cemented with saliva; overall diameter 10 cm; central hollow 8,7 cm diameter, 2,4 cm deep; against back wall of crevice, about 1 m deep; colonially in horizontal rock fissures of caves and overhanging cliffs. *Clutch:* Usually 2 eggs. *Eggs:* White; measure (2) 26,5–27,4 × 16,8–17. *Incubation:* Unrecorded. *Nestling:* Unrecorded.

Ref. Brooke, R.K. 1970. *Durban Mus. Novit.* 8(19):363–374.

---

414 (379) **Pallid Swift** **Plate 39**
Bruinwindswael
Apus pallidus

[Fahlsegler]

Measurements: Length 16–18 cm; wing (20) 168–173,5–180; tail (longest rectrix) 65–73, (shortest rectrix) 40–45.

Bare Parts: Iris brown; bill black; feet purplish brown.

Identification: Size medium; very similar to Eurasian Swift, but wings proportionately shorter, head and body stockier, and tail less deeply forked; sooty grey with primaries paler from above; extensive white on throat; head relatively large; wingbeats relatively slow.

Voice: Similar to that of Eurasian Swift.

Distribution: Breeds Mediterranean region to Baluchistan; recorded once, Kuruman, February 1904; also s Zambia, December 1957.

Status: Probably very rare vagrant.

Habitat: Cliffs and adjacent open areas.

Habits: Gregarious, often in company with Eurasian Swift. Poorly known.

Food: Aerial arthropods.

Breeding: Extralimital.

---

415 (383) **Whiterumped Swift** **Plate 39**
Witkruiswindswael
Apus caffer

Sisampamema (K), Lehaqasi (SS), Nkonjana (Ts), Pêolwane, Phêtla (Tw), Ihlabankomo, Ihlankomo (X), uNonqane (Z), [Weißbürzelsegler]

Measurements: Length 14–17 cm; wing (100) 141–148,5–157; tail (longest rectrix) 67–77,1–86, (shortest rectrix) 40–45,4–53; tarsus 8–9,7–11; culmen 5–6,2–8. Weight (2 ♂) 22,4–25,8 g, (194 unsexed) 18–24,1–30 g.

Bare Parts: Iris brown; bill black; feet dark pinkish.

Identification: Size smallish to medium; build slender (less stocky than Horus and Little Swifts); black above and below;

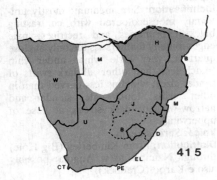

throat white; white on rump narrow and slightly V-shaped (broad and straight across in Little and Horus Swifts); tail longish, slender, deeply forked, looks pointed when held closed (tail with shallow fork in Horus Swift, square in Little Swift).

Voice: Shrill scream, sometimes in short bursts, *psrrit, psrrit*.

Distribution: Africa S of Sahara, w Mediterranean region; throughout most of s Africa, except Kalahari basin.

Status: Very common breeding intra-African migrant, August to April; rarely overwinters.

Habitat: Built-up areas, cliffs and bridges; forages over adjacent open ground.

Habits: Gregarious or in pairs; seldom in large flocks; often in company with other species of swifts and swallows. Forages high or low, depending on food supply;

silent when feeding, but vocal in and near nest sites.

Food: Aerial arthropods (beetles, bugs, wasps, flies, termites, spiders).

Breeding: *Season*: August to April (peak October-January); may rear 2–3 broods/season. *Nest*: Pad of feathers, cemented with saliva; usually in tunnel-and-bowl nest of swallow (swallows may be evicted); also in crevice or hole in rock face, or under eaves of building; not usually colonial. *Clutch*: (649) 1–2–5 eggs (usually 2; clutches larger than 3 eggs probably laid by more than 1 ♀). *Eggs*: White, elongate; measure (70) 23,1 × 14,9 (21,6–26,1 × 13,4–16,2). *Incubation*: 21–26 days by both sexes. *Nestling*: (8) 41–46–53 days (rarely to 69 days); fed by both parents.

Ref. Brooke, R.K. 1971. *Durban Mus. Novit.* 9(4):29–38.
Schmidt, R.K. 1965. *J. Orn.* 106:295–306.

416 (384)   Horus Swift   Plate 39
Horuswindswael
Apus horus

Sisampamema (K), Lehaqasi (SS), Nkonjana (Ts), Pêolwane, Phêtla (Tw), [Horussegler, Erdsegler]

Measurements: Length 14–17 cm; wing (102) 137–161; tail (longest rectrix) 56–60, (shortest rectrix) 43–49; tarsus 11, culmen 8. Weight (1 ♂) 34 g, (1 ♀) 34,2 g, (214 unsexed) 17–26,2–31,3 g.

Bare Parts: Iris dark brown; bill black; feet dark pinkish grey.

Identification: Size medium; stockier than Whiterumped Swift; body black; throat white; rump broadly white and straight across, wrapping around flanks (narrow, V-shaped and not onto flanks in Whiterumped Swift); tail slightly forked (looks square when spread, notched when folded; long and deeply forked in Whiterumped Swift, short and square in Little Swift); dark form in C Zimbabwe (and possibly nw Namibia) lacks white rump (and sometimes white throat), but distinguishable by notched tail.

Voice: Pleasant warbling trill, *preeeooo, preeeooo*, and variations.

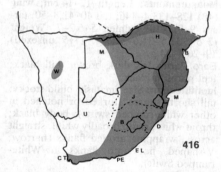

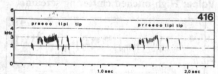

Distribution: S Africa to Ethiopia and Sudan; in s Africa mainly confined to e parts; breeds as far W as Ysterfontein, sw Cape; vagrant to Windhoek, Namibia.

HORUS SWIFT

Status: Locally common breeding intra-African migrant, October to April, in highveld; resident in tropical lowveld.
Habitat: Vertical sandbanks along rivers, dongas, minedumps; forages over adjacent open country.
Habits: Gregarious, but not usually in very large flocks (except at large breeding colonies). Seldom seen far from roosting and nesting burrows; roosts in abandoned burrows of bee-eaters, kingfishers, martins, chats and starlings for up to 2 months before breeding; both members of pair roost in nest burrow, even with young. Fly around nesting colony in evening until almost too dark to see.
Food: Aerial arthropods (termites, other insects, and spiders).
Breeding: *Season:* January to April (rarely May) in Transvaal, all months (mainly November to February) in Zimbabwe (summer on plateau, winter in lowveld). *Nest:* Flat pad of feathers, grass, dry mealie leaves, animal hair, moss and rags, outer rim of about 2 cm glued with saliva to form hard mat; in chamber at end of disused burrow of other species (see **Habits**); does not usurp occupied burrow; usually colonial; possibly 2 broods/season. *Clutch:* (38) 2–2,4–4 eggs (rarely 1). *Eggs:* White, elongate; measure (35) 22,8 × 15,1 (21,1–24,3 × 13,8–16,3). *Incubation:* About 28 days. *Nestling:* Unrecorded; fed by both parents.

Ref. Brooke, R.K. 1971. *Durban Mus. Novit.* 9(4):29–38.
Harwin, R.M. 1960. *Ostrich* 31:20–24.

---

417 (385)   Little Swift   Plate 39
Kleinwindswael
Apus affinis

Sisampamema (K), Lehaqasi (SS), Nkonjana (Ts), Pêolwane, Phêtla (Tw), [Haussegler]

Measurements: Length 12–14 cm; wing (48) 128–133,4–146; tail 40–41,8–50; tarsus 9–9,7–10; culmen 5–6,2–7. Weight (3 ♂) 31,5–31,6–31,7 g, (115 unsexed) 19–26,4–34 g.
Bare Parts: Iris dark brown; bill black; feet purplish black.
Identification: Size smallish; build stocky; tail short, square (forked or notched in other white-rumped swifts); body black; throat white; rump broadly white, straight across, wrapping around flanks (narrow, V-shaped, not onto flanks in White-rumped Swift).
Voice: High-pitched chittering scream.

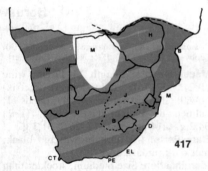

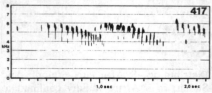

Distribution: Africa to s China and se Asia to Java; throughout s Africa, except most of Kalahari basin.

Status: Very common partial migrant; mostly resident; some highveld birds breeding migrants August to May.
Habitat: Built-up areas, cliffs, gorges, rocky hills; forages in adjacent open country.
Habits: Highly gregarious, often in flocks of hundreds of birds; frequently in company with other species of swift. Silent when feeding, but vocal in large flocks wheeling in display around roosting and nesting sites morning and evening, mostly 17:00–18:30. Roosts in nests or under eaves of buildings.

Food: Aerial arthropods.
Breeding: *Season*: September to May (mainly November-December) in Zimbabwe, September to April in S Africa. *Nest*: Closed bowl of grass and feathers glued with saliva, with small side-top entrance hole (one entrance may serve more than one nest chamber); under eaves or overhang of building, bridge or natural rock face; highly colonial, adjacent nests touching or overlapping. *Clutch*: (63) 1–2,3–3 eggs. *Eggs*: White, elongate; measure (14) 23 × 14,7 (21–25,4 × 14,2–15,3). *Incubation*: 21–24 days. *Nestling*: 36–40 days.

Ref. Brooke, R.K. 1971. *Durban Mus. Novit.* 9(7):93–103.

418 (386)   Alpine Swift   Plate 39
Witpenswindswael
Tachymarptis melba

Sisampamema (K), Lehaqasi, Lehaqasi-le-lephatsoa (SS), Nkonjana (Ts), Péolwane, Phêtla (Tw), Ubhantom, Ihlabankomo (X), [Alpensegler]

Measurements: Length 21–22 cm; wing (18 ♂) 200–210,8–223, (11 ♀) 203–209–215; tail (17) (longest rectrix) 78,7–92, (shortest rectrix) 54–66; tarsus (17) 17,2–19,2; culmen (19) 10–11,2–12. Weight (13) 67–77–91 g.
Bare Parts: Iris dark brown; bill black; feet horn.
Identification: Size large; above brown; below white with brown breastband (diagnostic); back and wings brown.
Voice: Loud high-pitched chittering around nesting cliffs.
Distribution: Africa, Madagascar, s Europe, s Asia to India and Sri Lanka; throughout s Africa.
Status: Common breeding intra-African migrant to S Africa, August to March (sometimes as late as June); mainly passage migrant through Zimbabwe, March-June and August-September.
Habitat: Mountains, gorges; forages over any type of country.
Habits: Gregarious, but seldom in very large flocks; often mixes with other species of swifts. Usually forages higher than

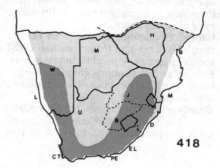

418

other swifts, but flies low before or after storms; attracted to grassfires. Extremely fast and powerful flier; wings make loud whooshing sound.
Food: Aerial arthropods.
Breeding: *Season*: October to April. *Nest*: Half-cup of feathers glued with saliva to inside of vertical crack in rock face; colonial, sometimes in same cliffs as Black Swift. *Clutch*: 1–2 eggs. *Eggs*: White; measure (3) 26,2 × 17 (25,7–26,5 × 16,8–17,4). *Incubation*: 17–23 days (Europe). *Nestling*: 53–66 days (Europe).

Ref. Brooke, R.K. 1971. *Durban Mus. Novit.* 9(10):131–143.

419 (382)   Mottled Swift   Plate 39
Bontwindswael
Tachymarptis aequatorialis

[Schuppensegler]

Measurements: Length about 20 cm; wing (9 ♂) 194–200,9–206, (7 ♀) 190–198–205, (87 unsexed) 188–203,1–213; tail (longest rectrix) 85–90, (shortest rectrix) about 55. Weight (1 ♂) 59,7 g, (1 ♀) 73 g, (5 unsexed) 83,8–87,9–92,6 g.
Bare Parts: Iris brown; bill and feet black.
Identification: Size large (barely smaller than Alpine Swift); generally dark dull

brown; mottled underparts visible at close quarters (Alpine Swift has white belly).
Voice: Rather quiet scream like that of Little Swift; high-pitched squeak; low-pitched harsh trill. Quite loud *prrpt-prrpt-prrpt* drumming produced by fanning tail sideways, always to the right, at start of dive towards water for drinking.
Distribution: Africa S of Sahara to Zimbabwe.
Status: Locally common resident; some postbreeding dispersal.
Habitat: Rocky overhangs in granite-shield country of Zimbabwe; forages further afield, especially when not breeding, even over urban areas.
Habits: Gregarious. Seldom seen further than about 50 km from roosting cliffs; roosts in crevices in cliffs after sunset. Flies up to 300 m above ground.
Food: Aerial arthropods (bees, termites, ants, beetles, flies).
Breeding: *Season:* June to November. *Nest:* Hard strong half-cup of feathers, seeds and leaves, 82–87 × 60–65 mm

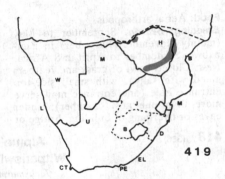

419

across, 25–48 mm deep; glued with saliva to rock face in vertical crevice with at least 6-m drop below, or in cave 1,8–2,4 m above floor; colonial, nests built close together, just beyond pecking range of neighbours. *Clutch:* 1–2 eggs. *Eggs:* White; measure (3) 29,6 × 19,2 (29,2–30 × 18,8–19,5). *Incubation:* Unrecorded; by both sexes. *Nestling:* Unrecorded.

Ref. Brooke, R.K. 1967. *Arnoldia (Rhod.)* 7(3):1–8; 1973. *Ostrich* 44:106–110.

---

420 (385X) **Scarce Swift** **Plate 39**
Skaarswindswael
Schoutedenapus myoptilus

[Maussegler]

Measurements: Length about 17 cm; wing 129–141; tail (longest rectrix) 58–72, (shortest rectrix) 37–41.
Bare Parts: Iris dark brown; bill and feet dusky.
Identification: Size small; uniform brownish grey; no white on throat or rump (otherwise similar to Whiterumped Swift); tail longish, deeply forked, but looks pointed when folded.
Voice: Metallic *tik* followed by few short trills (similar to call of Cardinal Woodpecker); also trill followed by nasal chittering, ending in high-pitched *tik*.
Distribution: Africa from Zimbabwe to Angola, Ethiopia and Nigeria; also Fernando Póo; in s Africa confined to e highlands of Zimbabwe.
Status: Locally common resident.
Habitat: Crags and precipices in high mountains (Inyanga and Chimanimani).

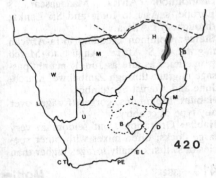

420

Habits: Gregarious, sometimes in large flocks. Poorly known.
Food: Aerial arthropods.
Breeding: Not recorded; probably breeds in fissures of cliff faces.

Ref. Dowsett, R.J. & Dowsett-Lemaire, F. 1978. *Scopus* 2:51–52.

421 (387)

Palm Swift
Palmwindswael
Cypsiurus parvus

Plate 39

Sisampamema (K), Nkonjana (Ts), [Palmensegler]

Measurements: Length 14–17 cm; wing (157 ♂) 120–131,6–148, (149 ♀) 115–128,4–142; tail (longest rectrix) (6) 76–96,7–105, (shortest rectrix) (6) 34–38,7–44; tarsus (6) 8–9,3–11; culmen (6) 5–6,3–8. Weight (12 ♂) 10–13,7–18,1 g, (16 ♀) 11–13,9–16,5 g, (80 unsexed) 10–13,4–18,1 g.

Bare Parts: Iris dark brown; bill black; feet brownish pink.

Identification: Size small; build very slender; uniform brownish grey; tail very long, pointed, deeply forked; wings long, slender, pointed. *Immature*: Scaled with rufous buff above and below; tail shorter than that of adult.

Voice: High-pitched thin querulous scream; faint *tseep*.

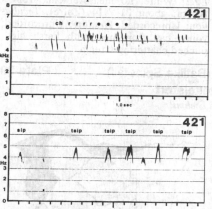

Distribution: Africa S of Sahara, Madagascar; in s Africa mainly in N and E; spreading westwards to sw Transvaal, n Cape (Kuruman) and s Namibia (Mariental, Auob River).

Status: Locally common resident; numbers increasing because of artificial planting of palm trees and increasing use of manmade structures for nesting.

Habitat: Palm trees, both indigenous and exotic, mostly at lower elevations; gardens, parks.

Habits: Gregarious, sometimes in company with other species of swifts and swallows. Roosts under or on palm leaves. Flight swift and graceful on stiff wings.

Food: Aerial arthropods, including termite alates.

Breeding: *Season*: All months, mainly August to February in Zimbabwe. *Nest*: Pad of feathers glued with saliva to midrib of underside or upperside of palm leaf, vertical wall of building or bridge member; as low as 2 m above ground, usually much higher; eggs glued with saliva to lower lip of pad. *Clutch*: 2 eggs (rarely 3). *Eggs*: White; measure (7) 19,2 × 12,6 (17,5–21 × 12–13,8). *Incubation*: 18–22 days; incubating parent clings vertically to nest, using sharp claws. *Nestling*: 28–33 days.

Ref. Brooke, R.K. 1972. *Durban Mus. Novit.* 9(15):217–231.

422 (388)

Mottled Spinetail
Gevlekte Stekelstert
Telacanthura ussheri

Plate 39

[Baobabsegler]

Measurements: Length about 14 cm; wing 141–151; tail 30. Weight 31–34,1–37,5 g.

Bare Parts: Iris dark brown; bill black; feet brownish black.

Identification: Size medium (much larger

than Böhm's Spinetail); sooty black; throat and breast mottled with white (Little Swift has plain white throat only); rump broadly white; narrow white band across vent (absent in Little Swift); tail square.

Voice: Quiet rippling *tt-rrit, tt-rrit, tt-rrit.*

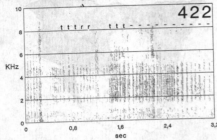

Distribution: Africa S of Sahara to Zimbabwe; lowlands of n and se Zimbabwe, Mozambique S to Limpopo basin; ne Transvaal lowveld.

Status: Sparse localized resident. Rare (RDB).

Habitat: Dry deciduous woodland, usually with baobabs; also forest edges; mainly in major river valleys.

Habits: Usually in pairs or small groups;

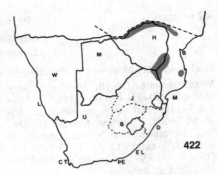

sometimes in company with Little Swift. Flight looks slow and laboured. Roosts in hollow baobab trees.

Food: Aerial arthropods.

Breeding: *Season:* April to May in Transvaal. *Nest:* Bracket-shaped cup, about 8 × 6 cm, of leaves and twigs stuck with saliva to vertical wall of hollow baobab; may nest on building. *Clutch:* 2–4 eggs *Eggs:* White; no measurements from s Africa; about 21 × 14 (Zaire). *Incubation:* Unrecorded. *Nestling:* Unrecorded; young call from nest with harsh high-pitched chattering scream.

423 (389) Böhm's Spinetail (Batlike Spinetail) Plate 39
Witpensstekelstert
Neafrapus boehmi

Sisampamema (K), [Fledermaussegler]

Measurements: Length about 10 cm; wing (22 ♂) 108–115,6–126, (16 ♀) 112–117,9–124; tail about 20; culmen 5,4. Weight (5 ♂) 12–13,5–15,5 g, (2 ♀) 13–15 g.

Bare Parts: Iris brown; bill black; feet purple.

Identification: Size small; looks tailless; broad wings look batlike in flight; throat and breast grey; belly and rump white.

Voice: High-pitched, relatively slow *tri-tri-tri-peep.*

Distribution: From ne Transvaal and s Mozambique to Zimbabwe, Caprivi, Angola, Zaire and s Somalia.

Status: Sparse resident; commoner than Mottled Spinetail. Rare (RDB).

Habitat: Lowland dry deciduous woodland, riverine forest, clearings and edges of lowland evergreen forest.

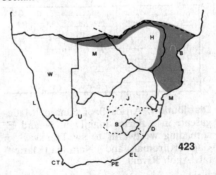

Habits: Solitary, in pairs or small groups. Flies lower than most swifts; forages in and around woodland and forest, often in company with Eastern Sawwing Swallow; flight fairly slow, highly manoeuvrable and jerky; wings flexible. Very large gape evident when feeding. Uses tail spines as prop against vertical walls of roosting and nesting sites.

Food: Aerial arthropods.

Breeding: *Season*: October to March or April (rarely as early as August). *Nest*: Almost circular cup of short thin unbranched twigs, glued together with blobs of saliva; externally 6,3–8 cm diameter, 2,5–6 cm deep; internally 5–5,6 cm diameter, 2,5 cm deep; stuck

to wall of well shaft, old mine tunnel, hollow baobab; may be 6 m or more below ground level; eggs not glued to nest. *Clutch*: 2–3 eggs. *Eggs*: White; measure (6) 17,1 × 11,9 (16,1–19 × 11,3–13). *Incubation*: About 17–18 days (possibly as little as 14). *Nestling*: About 40 days.

Ref. Brooke, R.K. 1966. *Arnoldia (Rhod.)* 29:1–18.

21. COLIIFORMES (One family)

21:1. Family 51 COLIIDAE—MOUSEBIRDS (COLIES)

Small, excluding long tail. Bill short, stout and conical, curved on culmen; cere around nostrils; legs short; toes long and strong, hind toe reversible; claws long and sharp; wings short and rounded; tail very long (more than twice length of body), stiff and sharply graduated; plumage soft and lax, mostly dull brown or grey; sexes alike; gregarious; arboreal; flight fast and direct; climb well with bill and feet; usually perch hanging below branch; roost communally, bunched together; food fruit, buds, leaves, etc.; breed solitarily; nest bowl-shaped of plant material in bush or tree; eggs 2–4, white or cream, plain or spotted (2–4 females may lay in one nest); chick sparsely downy at hatching, altricial, fed by regurgitation; parents eat faeces of young; parental care by both sexes. Distribution Africa S of Sahara; six species; three species in s Africa.

Ref. Rowan, M.K. 1967. *Ostrich* 38:63–115.

---

424 (390)   **Speckled Mousebird**   **Plate 42**
Gevlekte Muisvoël
Colius striatus

Ndlazi (Ts), Indlazi (X), iNdlazi (Z), [Braunflügel-Mausvogel]

Measurements: Length (39) 27–33–36 cm; wing (22 ♂) 87–93,1–99, (22 ♀) 85,5–92,5–97,5; tail (39) 182–204–228; tarsus (39) 19–21,9–25; culmen (39) 11–13,3–14,7. Weight (7 ♂) 42,4–50,3–57,5 g, (8 ♀) 38,4–50,9–65 g, (279 unsexed) 32–55–71 g.

Bare Parts: Iris brown; bill black above, bluish white below; legs and feet purplish brown to dull red.

Identification: Size small; tail long, pointed; almost uniform brown (fine barring visible only at very close range); face black (amount of black variable; red in Redfaced Mousebird); bill dark above, pale

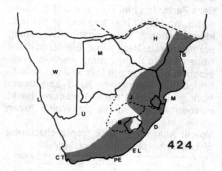

below (all dark in Redfaced Mousebird, pale with black tip in Whitebacked Mousebird). *Immature*: Like adult, but lacks black on face; bill pale greenish grey.

SPECKLED MOUSEBIRD

Voice: Harsh *zik, zik* alarm notes; sharp *chee chee chik chik*, probably contact call.

Distribution: Africa S of Sahara; in s Africa mainly in S and E.

Status: Common resident.

Habitat: Bushveld, tangled thickets, edges of dense vegetation, gardens, orchards.

Habits: Usually gregarious in flocks of 5–20 birds; mean flock size (10) is 9,2 birds, but 2–3 separate flocks may join temporarily to make combined flock of up to 30 birds. Flies fast and straight with rapid wingbeats alternating with stiff-winged glides; on landing, crashes into bush or tree. Hangs below perch; forages by clambering mouselike about branches. Roosts from just before sunset in bunches in bush or tree; departs just after sunrise; even by day up to 15 birds may cluster on branch for several minutes. Dust-bathes frequently.

Food: Fruit, leaves, seeds, nectar; occasionally insects (mainly termites).

Breeding: *Season*: July to February in sw Cape, all months in e Cape, July to April in Natal, July to March in Zimbabwe; mostly September-January throughout s Africa. *Nest*: Large untidy bowl of plant material, lined with soft material and leaves; internal diameter 6–8,5 cm, depth 2,5–5 cm; 1–7 m (usually 1–3 m) above ground in bush or tree. *Clutch*: (215) 1–3–7 eggs (mostly 2–4; larger clutches probably laid by more than 1 ♀). *Eggs*: White or cream; measure (201) 20,8 × 16,6 (19,5–24,2 × 14,6–18,4); weigh (5) mean 2,7 g. *Incubation*: 12–15 days by both sexes. *Nestling*: 17–18 days; may leave nest at 10–11 days to climb about branches; fed by regurgitation; parents eat faeces of young.

425 (391) Whitebacked Mousebird Plate 42
Witkruismuisvoël

Colius colius

Rramatsiababa, Mmamarungwane, Letsôrô (Tw), [Weißrücken-Mausvogel]

Measurements: Length (13) 29–31–32 cm; wing (13) 85–90–94; tail 196–211–220; tarsus 16–18,9–20; culmen 11–12,7–13,5. Weight (7 ♂) 37,2–43,7–54 g, (84 unsexed) 31–41,1–59 g.

Bare Parts: Iris blackish brown; bill bluish white, tip black; legs and feet bright red.

Identification: Size small; tail long, pointed; lower back white, bordered black (diagnostic in flight); rump maroon; combination of bright red legs and pale black-tipped bill distinctive; head and upper back grey; below buffy. *Immature*: Lacks maroon rump; bill bright bluish green above, blackish below.

Voice: Sharp *krik krik*; rapid chattering *chichichichi*; pleasant *zwee, weewit.*

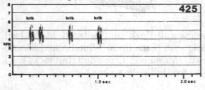

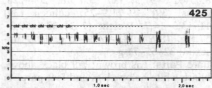

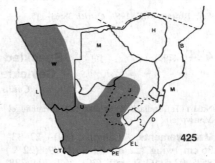

Distribution: Drier w parts of s Africa from Cape to Orange Free State, Transvaal, s Botswana and Namibia.

Status: Common resident.

Habitat: Arid to semi-arid scrub, riverine bush, farmyards, gardens, orchards.

Habits: Similar to Speckled Mousebird. Sometimes forages on ground.

Food: Fruit, flowers, leaves, nectar, seedlings.

Breeding: *Season*: Nearly all months (mainly September-December). *Nest*: Bowl of dry plant material, lined with wool and plant down; internal diameter

6 cm, depth 4,5 cm; 1–7 m (mostly 1–3 m) above ground in bush, tree or hedge. *Clutch*: (66) 1–3–6 eggs (usually 2–4); larger clutches, sometimes up to 8 eggs, laid by more than 1 ♀. *Eggs*: Chalky white; measure (52) 21,2 × 16,3 (19–23,3 × 15–17,6). *Incubation*: Unrecorded. *Nestling*: Unrecorded; fed by regurgitation by both parents.

426 (392) Redfaced Mousebird   Plate 42
Rooiwangmuisvoël
Urocolius indicus

Ediratoto (K), Letswiyobaba (NS), Shirapopo (Sh), Ncivovo, Xiavava (Ts), Letsibaba, Mmamarungwane, Letsôrô (Tw), Intshili (X), umTshivovo, umJombo (Z), [Rotzügel-Mausvogel]

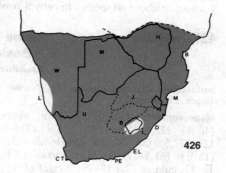

426

Measurements: Length (14) 30–32–37 cm; wing (14) 93–95,6–102; tail 185–210–240; tarsus 16–18,4–20,5; culmen 12,5–13,9–15. Weight (5 ♂) 58,4–61,8–64,9 g, (5 ♀) 48,4–51–55,5 g, (270 unsexed) 32,5–55,7–78,9 g.

Bare Parts: Iris greyish; facial skin purplish red to carmine; bill deep pinkish crimson, tip black; legs and feet rose red.

Identification: Size small; tail long, pointed; bare face red (other mousebirds have dark feathered faces); above bluegrey; below yellowish sandy. *Immature*: Bare face and bill greenish.

Voice: Musical *ti-wi-wi*, or *ti-wi-wi-wi*, falling in pitch, slightly accented on first syllable; high-pitched slurred *cheuwip*.

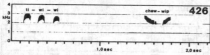

Distribution: S Africa to Angola, Zaire and Tanzania; in s Africa mostly absent from extreme dry W.

Status: Common resident; somewhat nomadic.

Habitat: Savanna with thickets, riverine bush, gardens, orchards.

Habits: Gregarious in small groups, seldom more than 8 birds, but sometimes up to 20; more wary than other mousebirds;

usually flies high from one feeding area to another; flight fast strong and direct. Otherwise similar to other mousebirds.

Food: Mainly fruit; also flowers, leaves, nectar.

Breeding: *Season*: June to February in sw Cape, July to February in Natal and Transvaal, August to February in w Transvaal, all months (mainly September-November) in Zimbabwe. *Nest*: Untidy bowl of plant material, and sheep's wool on base of twigs (often thorny); internal diameter 4,5–9 cm, depth 2–5,5 cm; 1–7 m (mostly 2–4 m) above ground in bush or tree. *Clutch*: (200) 1–2,6–7 eggs (usually 2–4; larger clutches probably laid by more than 1 ♀). *Eggs*: White or cream, usually scrolled or spotted with reddish brown; measure (133) 21,3 × 15,8 (18,7–24 × 14,4–17); weigh (1) 2,9 g. *Incubation*: 11–13–15 days. *Nestling*: About 14–17 days.

22. Order TROGONIFORMES (One family)

22.1. Family 52 TROGONIDAE—TROGONS, QUETZAL

Medium. Bill short, broad, curved on culmen; legs short; toes rather weak with unique arrangement of 1st and 2nd toes directed forwards, 3rd and 4th toes directed backwards; wings short, rounded; tail longish (very long in Quetzal *Pharomachrus mocino* of C America), graduated, square when folded, patterned ventrally with black-and-white; plumage soft, loosely attached to skin; above and on breast bright green, blue or violet with metallic sheen (African and S American species) or non-metallic red or pink (Asian species); below red, pink, orange or yellow; females duller than males, but colour pattern similar; flight light and buoyant, seldom sustained; perch for long periods in one place; arboreal in forest or dense woodland; pluck invertebrates, small vertebrates or fruits from leaves or branches, or hawk insects in flight; voice usually deep hooting; nest solitarily in unlined natural or self-excavated hole in tree, termite mound or wasp nest; eggs 2–3, rarely 4, usually plain white, sometimes buff, pale blue or pale green; chick naked at hatching, altricial; parental care by both sexes. Distribution Africa, Asia, S America; about 40 species (mostly S American); one species in s Africa.

---

427 (393)   **Narina Trogon**   **Plate 34**
                            Bosloerie
                         Apaloderma narina

Intshatshongo (X), umJenenengu (Z), [Narina-Trogon, Zügeltrogon]

Measurements: Length 29–34 cm; wing (46 ♂) 118,5–129,8–139, (21 ♀) 124–129–137,5; tail (42 ♂) 154–168,8–183, (13 ♀) 161,5–171,5–178,5; tarsus (25) 16–17; culmen (25) 18–20. Weight (1 ♂) 67 g, (2 ♀) 59,5–70 g.

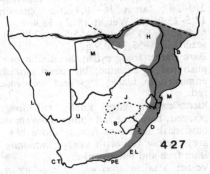

Bare Parts: Iris reddish brown to hazel; skin above and below eye and on throat light blue (breeding ♂) or slate (♀ and nonbreeding ♂); bill yellow, green or pale grey, base orange or yellow; legs and feet greyish pink.

Identification: Size medium. *Male*: Head, back and breast bright metallic green, washed gold on head and mantle; below bright red; outer rectrices white; bill yellow. *Female*: Similar to ♂, but face and throat pinkish rufous, shading to grey on breast; lower breast pinkish white, finely vermiculated with blackish; belly dull pink. *Immature*: Like ♀, but whiter below; wing coverts tipped white; bill dark.

Voice: Series of 10–15 paired hooting notes with slightly growling quality, *hroo-hoo, hroo-hoo, hroo-hoo*, second note of each pair slightly higher-pitched and more accented than first; various other hooting calls; ♂ also has low chattering display call; loud hiss from nestlings when alarmed.

Distribution: Africa S of Sahara; in s Africa confined to SE, E and NE.

Status: Uncommon to fairly common; mostly resident; some birds possibly breeding migrants from further N, but easily overlooked when not vocal.

Habitat: Evergreen and riverine forest, dense woodland, moist thornveld, coastal bush, valley bushveld (especially *Euphorbia*), wattle plantations.

Habits: Usually solitary or in pairs, occasionally 3 birds together; in breeding season groups of up to 12 males sing and display for up to 2 hours, then individuals disperse to their territories. Perches motionless for long periods, usually on high branch; posture somewhat hunched, ventral plumage fluffed so that red visible at sides even from behind; tail sometimes slowly raised and lowered; hard to see when green back towards observer. Forages by sallying out from perch, catching prey off leaves and branches or in air with highly manoeuvrable twists and turns; flight buoyant, strong, slightly dipping.

Responds to taped playback in breeding season, but not in winter, though sometimes calls in winter.

Food: Mainly insects; also fruit, chameleons.

Breeding: Monogamous. *Season*: October to January in S Africa, December to January in Zimbabwe. *Nest*: Natural hole in tree or dead stump; no material added. *Clutch*: (12) 1–2,6–4 eggs. *Eggs*: White, glossy; measure (10) 28,6 × 22,7 (26,8–31 × 21,2–23,8). *Incubation*: 16–17 days by ♀. *Nestling*: About 25 days in other trogon species.

Ref. Brosset, A. 1983. *Alauda* 51:1–10.
Harcus, J.L. 1976. *Ostrich* 47:129–130.

23. Order ALCEDINIFORMES (= HALCYONIFORMES)
(Four families; two in s Africa)

Mostly small to medium, a few large. Formerly combined with Order Coraciiformes. Bill rather long, straight or slightly decurved; usually pointed and laterally compressed; legs short, rather weak; feet small; front toes syndactyl (partly joined from base), adapted for perching; plumage usually brightly coloured in blue, green, red and yellow; sexes alike or different; wings short and rounded (but long and pointed in bee-eaters); tail variable; all eat small animals hunted in the air, in water, on ground or hawked from perch; solitary or gregarious; mostly arboreal; nest in self-excavated burrow in bank, some colonially, or more rarely in hole in tree; nest chamber unlined; eggs 2–7, white, rounded; chick naked at hatching, altricial; parental care by both sexes. Distribution worldwide, mainly tropical.

Ref. Fry, C.H., Fry, K. & Harris, A. 1992. *Kingfishers, bee-eaters & rollers*. Halfway House, South Africa: Russel Friedman Books.

23:1. Family 53 ALCEDINIDAE (=HALCYONIDAE)—KINGFISHERS

Small to large. Bill large, long, straight and pointed (occasionally hooked); legs very short; plumage often includes bright blue above and rufous below; solitary; food fish caught by diving, or land animals caught on ground; other features as for Order Alcediniformes. Distribution as for Order Alcediniformes; about 90 species; 10 species in s Africa.

Ref. Fry, C.H. 1979. *Living Bird* 18:113–160; 1980. *Ibis* 122:57–72.
Hanmer, D.B. 1980. *Ostrich* 51:129–150.
Harwin, R.M. 1984. *Proc. 5th Pan-Afr. Orn. Congr.*:387–394.

428 (394)   Pied Kingfisher   Plate 40
Bontvisvanger
Ceryle rudis

Muningi (K), Seinoli (SS), Chinyurirahove (Sh), Mavungana, N'waripetani, Xicelele (Ts), Seinôdi, Mmatlhapi (Tw), Isaxwila (X), isiQuba, isiXula, iHlabahlabane (Z), [Graufischer]

Measurements: Length 25–29 cm; wing (34) 132–140–146; tail 70–78; tarsus 9–11;

culmen 53–63. Weight (4 ♂) 69,9–72,7–77 g, (2 ♀) 70–71 g, (5 unsexed) 73,5–81,6–90 g.

Bare Parts: Iris dark brown; bill, legs and feet black.

Identification: Size medium; black-and-

PIED KINGFISHER

white coloration distinctive; breastband double in ♂, single in ♀. *Immature*: Like ♀; throat and breast scaled with black.
Voice: High-pitched twitters and squeaks; sharp *kwik-kwik-kwik*.

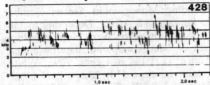

Distribution: Africa S of Sahara, Nile Valley, Middle East, s Asia to China; in s Africa absent from most of Kalahari sandveld and much of dry W.
Status: Common to very common resident.
Habitat: Rivers, lakes, dams, estuaries, canals, coastal waters.
Habits: Usually in pairs, but sometimes in loose groups. Hunts from perch or by hovering over water with body almost vertical and bill pointed downwards; dives with audible splash; beats prey on perch before swallowing; may forage up to 3 km from shore over Lake Kariba. Raises and lowers tail when perched. Tame and conspicuous. May associate with Clawless Otter for disturbed food.

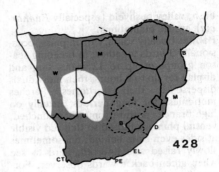

Food: Mostly fish of 1–2 g weight (up to 15 g); also crustaceans and insects.
Breeding: *Season*: August to November in S Africa; all months except May and June in Zimbabwe (mainly August-November). *Nest*: Burrow, 1–2 m long, excavated in earth or sandbank, with chamber at end; becomes lined with regurgitated fish bones and scales. *Clutch*: (20) 2–3,9–6 eggs. *Eggs*: White, rounded; measure (56) 29 × 23,1 (24,7–32,8 × 21–24,4). *Incubation*: Unrecorded. *Nestling*: Unrecorded; fed by both parents and sometimes 1–4 helpers.

Ref. Reyer, H.-U. 1986. *Behaviour* 82:277–303.

---

429 (395)   **Giant Kingfisher**   **Plate 40**
Reuse Visvanger
Megaceryle maxima

Esompwaningi (K), Seinoli (SS), Mavungana, N'waripetani, Xitserere (Ts), Seinôdi, Mmatlhapi (Tw), Uxomoyi (X), isiVuba (Z), [Riesenfischer, Rieseneisvogel]

Measurements: Length 43–46 cm; wing (24) 192–202–209; tail 110–123; tarsus 13–15; culmen 86–101. Weight (2 ♂) 338–355 g, (4 ♀) 363–380–405 g, (4 unsexed) 340–355,7–375 g.
Bare Parts: Iris brown; bill black, base horn; legs and feet blackish slate.
Identification: Size large (largest s African kingfisher); above finely spotted white on black; breast chestnut in ♂, spotted black on white in ♀; belly spotted black on white in ♂, chestnut in ♀. *Immature*: ♀

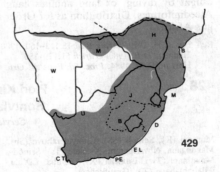

has white breast; ♂ has black speckling on chestnut breastband.

370

Voice: Loud ringing laughing yelps, *wak-wak-wak*, singly or in series of up to 4 notes, often varied with rapid notes falling in pitch, *wak-wak rirriri, wakririri*; somewhat like voice of Hamerkop, but sharper; hard mechanical rattle (yelps and rattles may be interspersed).

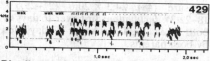

Distribution: Africa S of Sahara; in s Africa absent from most of dry W.

Status: Uncommon to locally common resident.

Habitat: Rivers, estuaries, lakes, wooded streams, sewage ponds, seashore.

Habits: Usually solitary; rarely in pairs. Shy and unobtrusive, unless calling; often calls in flight; flies high when travelling long distance between feeding areas (say more than 1 km). Perches motionless on rock, snag or low branch of tree over water; sometimes hovers, especially over sea. Often raises crest and bobs tail.

Food: Fish, crabs, frogs.

Breeding: *Season*: August to January in S Africa, May to October (also March) in Zimbabwe. *Nest*: Tunnel (19) 0,90–1,83–8,45 m long in earth bank along river or dam spillway; from 46 cm to 5 m above foot of bank (mean of 26 tunnels, 2,28 m); entrance usually about 1 m from top of bank; chamber at end 25–30 cm deep, lined with fish bones and crab carapaces; excavation by both sexes. *Clutch*: (35) 3–3,5–5 eggs. *Eggs*: White, glossy; measure (63) 45 × 35,1 (40,7–51 × 33,2–36,7). *Incubation*: Unrecorded. *Nestling*: 37 days; both parents feed young.

Ref. Arkell, G.B.F. 1979. *Ostrich* 50:176–181.
   Moynihan, M. 1987. *Malimbus* 9:97–104.

---

430 (396)   **Halfcollared Kingfisher**   **Plate 40**
Blouvisvanger

Alcedo semitorquata

Muningi (K), Mavungana, N'waripetani, Xitserere, Ntungununu (Ts), Seinôdi, Mmatlhapi (Tw), Isaxwila (X), isiXula (Z), [Kobalteisvogel]

Measurements: Length 19–20 cm; wing (67) 80–84,7–90; tail (27) 39–45; tarsus (27) 8–10; culmen (27) 42–50. Weight (2) 39 g.

Bare Parts: Iris brown; bill black; legs and feet orange to coral red.

Identification: Size smallish; above bright blue; throat, side of hindneck and line in front of eye white (no white eyeline in other small blue kingfishers); rest of underparts rich ochre-buff (brighter orange-chestnut in other small blue kingfishers); blue half collar on sides of chest diagnostic; bill black (similar to immature Malachite Kingfisher, but no chestnut on sides of head); line through eye black (diagnostic); feet red. *Immature*: Scaled blue-black on breast.

Voice: Shrill *teep* or *tseep-tseep; spip-ip-ip-ip-peep* alarm call.

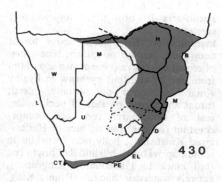

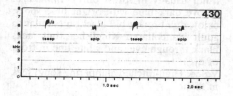

Distribution: S Africa to Angola and Ethiopia; in s Africa absent from dry W and Limpopo catchment.
Status: Uncommon resident.
Habitat: Fast-flowing perennial streams, rivers and estuaries, usually with dense marginal vegetation.
Habits: Usually solitary. Perches low down on branch or rock over water; rarely hovers. Flight fast, low and direct; after landing raises and lowers head and flicks tail.
Food: Fish, crabs, insects.

Breeding: *Season*: September to March in S Africa, July to March in Zimbabwe. *Nest*: Burrow about 7 cm diameter, 60 cm long, in river bank; usually 1–3 m above foot of bank, about 40 cm from top; chamber lined with fish bones. *Clutch*: (11) 2–3,5–5 eggs. *Eggs*: White, glossy; measure (48) 24,3 × 20,6 (21–25,5 × 18–22,3). *Incubation*: Just over 16 days by both sexes. *Nestling*: About 27 days; fed by both parents.

Ref. Moreau, R.E. 1944. *Ostrich* 15:161–177.

---

431 (397) **Malachite Kingfisher** **Plate 40**
Kuifkopvisvanger
Alcedo cristata

Seinoli (SS), Chinderera, Kanyururahove (Sh), Mavungana, N'waripetani, Xicelele, Ntungununu (Ts), Seinôdi, Mmatlhapi (Tw), Isaxwila (X), iNhlunuyamanzi, uZangozolo, isiKhilothi (Z), [Malachiteisvogel, Haubenzwergfischer]

Measurements: Length about 14 cm; wing (33) 54–57–60; tail 24–31; tarsus 7; culmen 31–37,5. Weight (2 ♂) 19,6–21 g, (6 ♀) 14,4–17,5–21,1 g, (36 unsexed) 12,7–17,9–21 g.
Bare Parts: Iris brown; bill, legs and feet scarlet.
Identification: Size small; above bright deep blue, greener on crown; blue-green of crown meets eye (blue crown separated from eye by chestnut eyebrow in Pygmy Kingfisher); crest not usually raised; throat and streak on side of neck white; rest of underparts and face orange-chestnut (no chestnut on face of Halfcollared Kingfisher); belly may be white in some Caprivi birds; bill and feet bright red (bill black in Halfcollared Kingfisher); entirely waterside habitat (Pygmy Kingfisher usually in forest only). *Immature*: Above dark blue with bright blue spots; below dull brown; bill blackish (similar to adult Halfcollared Kingfisher, but lacks black through eye, and white line in front of eye).
Voice: High-pitched chippering song; *seek* in flight.

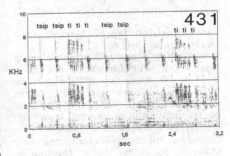

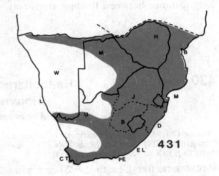

Distribution: Africa S of Sahara, Madagascar and adjacent islands; in s Africa absent from much of dry W; otherwise widespread.
Status: Common resident.

Habitat: Lakes, dams, streams, rivers, estuaries, irrigations canals, sewage ponds, with marginal vegetation.
Habits: Usually solitary. Perches low over water on branch or stem; dives for prey. Often bobs head and body when still-hunting from perch. When disturbed, flies straight and low, disappearing around bend in watercourse or shoreline.

Food: Fish, insects, tadpoles, frogs, crustaceans.
Breeding: *Season*: August to February. *Nest*: Tunnel, 30–90 cm long, in bank; chamber lined with regurgitated fish bones and arthropod exoskeletons. *Clutch*: (21) 3–3,7–6 eggs. *Eggs*: White, glossy; measure (87) 18,8 × 15,6 (17–20,5 × 14,6–16,7). *Incubation*: About 14–16 days. *Nestling*: About 25 days.

432 (398)   Pygmy Kingfisher   Plate 40
Dwergvisvanger
Ispidina picta

isiPhikeleli, iNhlunuyamanzi, uZangozolo, isiKhilothi (Z), [Natalzwergfischer]

Measurements: Length 12–13 cm; wing (55) 52–56,1–59; tail (62) 24–26,2–29; tarsus 7; culmen 24–28. Weight (20 ♂) 11,8–13,8–17,2 g, (14 ♀) 11,1–13,7–15,8 g, (69 unsexed) 11,3–14,6–18,9 g.
Bare Parts: Iris brown; bill, legs and feet scarlet.
Identification: Size small (smallest s African kingfisher); above bright deep blue (no greenish tinge on crown as in Malachite Kingfisher); blue crown separated from eye by chestnut eyebrow (blue of crown meets eye in Malachite Kingfisher); throat and faint stripe on side of neck white; patch behind ear coverts mauve (absent in Malachite Kingfisher). *Immature*: Above blackish, speckled with blue; bill blackish; otherwise like adult.
Voice: Thin squeaky *seek*.

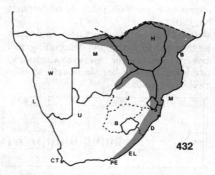

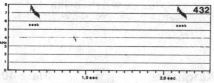

Distribution: Africa S of Sahara; in s Africa confined to extreme E and NE; also recorded Pretoria and n Transvaal.
Status: Locally fairly common breeding intra-African migrant, October to April (rarely to May); probably migrates to Zaire and coastal Mozambique.

Habitat: Edges and clearings in dense woodland, coastal bush and forest; also riverine forest, edges of cultivated lands in forest; dry savanna in Transvaal.
Habits: Usually solitary, occasionally in twos or threes. Unobtrusive, but not shy. Perches fairly low in bush or tree, flying to ground to pick up prey; sometimes catches insects in flight; rarely dives into water. Flight fast and straight; migrates at night; often found dead or stunned after flying into buildings.
Food: Insects, frogs, lizards, crustaceans, spiders.
Breeding: *Season*: Mainly October to December; also March. *Nest*: Tunnel, 30–60 cm long; in earth bank or wall of Antbear burrow. *Clutch*: (38) 3–3,8–6 eggs. *Eggs*: White, glossy; measure (87) 18 × 15,7 (16–19,3 × 14,3–16,5). *Incubation*: Unrecorded. *Nestling*: Unrecorded; fed by both parents.

433 (399) Woodland Kingfisher Plate 40
Bosveldvisvanger
Halcyon senegalensis

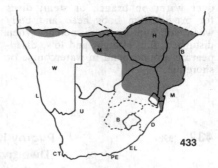

Muningi (K), uNongozolo (Z), [Senegalliest]

Measurements: Length 22–24 cm; wing (9) 110–112,4–116; tail 62–69; tarsus 13; culmen (9) 46–47,8–51. Weight (1 ♂) 61,8 g, (12 unsexed) 54,7–67,4–81 g.

Bare Parts: Iris dark grey; bill red above, black below, tip black; legs and feet black.

Identification: Size medium; above bright light blue; below white; large black patch on bend of wing; primaries blackish; upper half of bill red, lower half black (diagnostic; Mangrove Kingfisher has all-red bill). *Immature*: Similar to adult, but narrowly barred on sides of underparts; bill dusky.

Voice: Loud phrase, starting with staccato high note, followed by descending trill, *krit-trrrrrrr*, fading away towards end; harsh *kee-kee-kee-kee* alarm call; scolding *zwik-zwik-zwik*.

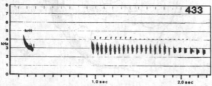

Distribution: Africa S of Sahara; in s Africa from Zululand and n Transvaal (Pretoria) to Zimbabwe and n Namibia; vagrant to Potchefstroom.

Status: Common breeding intra-African migrant, October to April.

Habitat: Woodland, denser savanna, riverine forest.

Habits: Solitary or in pairs. Perches low in tree, scanning ground for prey; rarely dives for fish in water. Highly vocal when breeding; displays by pivoting on perch with outspread wings flashing alternately blue and white. Migrates at night; often recovered dead or injured.

Food: Mainly insects; also millipedes, lizards, snakes, frogs; rarely fish, crabs, birds.

Breeding: *Season*: November to March in Transvaal, November to January in Mozambique and Zimbabwe. *Nest*: Usually in disused hole of barbet or woodpecker in tree; also under eaves of house; rarely in old nest of Little Swift; height of 10 nests 1,5–4,8–9 m. *Clutch*: 2–4 eggs (usually 3). *Eggs*: Glossy white; measure (27) 27,9 × 24,5 (25–30,5 × 22,1–25,6). *Incubation*: 13–14 days. *Nestling*: 15–22 days; fed by both parents.

Ref. Greig-Smith, P.W. 1978. *Ostrich* 49:67–75.
Milstein, P. le S. 1962. *Ostrich* 33(3):2–12.

434 (400) Mangrove Kingfisher Plate 40
Mangliedvisvanger
Halcyon senegaloides

uNongozolo (Z), [Mangroveliest]

Measurements: Length 23–24 cm; wing (12 ♂) 103,5–106,6–112, (3 ♀) 107–108,3–110; tail 57–68; tarsus 11–13; culmen 48–50. Weight 57–66 g.

Bare Parts: Iris brown; bill red; legs and feet black.

Identification: Size medium; very similar to Woodland Kingfisher, but bill all red (lower half of bill black in Woodland Kingfisher); above bright light blue, except for grey crown (crown blue in Woodland Kingfisher); below white; black patch on bend of wing. *Immature*: Similar to adult, but vermiculated with blackish on breast and flanks; bill brownish.

Voice: When breeding, loud chattering *kling-kling-kling-kling...*, speeding up towards end; when not breeding, raucous *chichoo-cha-cha-ch-ch-ch-ch-ch*, ending in trill; calls with wings raised.

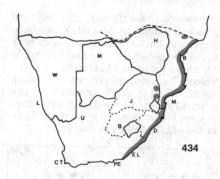

434

Distribution: E coast of Africa from Transkei to Kenya, Zanzibar and Pemba; further inland when breeding, as far as Kruger National Park.

Status: Uncommon local migrant, breeding inland from coast, about October to January; migrates to coastal habitats after breeding. Probably Vulnerable (RDB).

Habitat: Wooded streams when breeding; otherwise mangrove swamps in lagoons and estuaries; city parks with fishponds.

Habits: Solitary or in pairs; silent and secretive in winter; vocal September to April. Perches on branch to scan water or ground below.

Food: Insects, crabs, lizards; rarely fish.

Breeding: *Season*: December to January in Transkei (Kobonqaba River). *Nest*: Hole in tree up to 5 m above ground; also in burrow in bank. *Clutch*: 3 eggs. *Eggs*: White; measure about 25 × 23. *Incubation*: Unrecorded. *Nestling*: Unrecorded; fed by both parents.

---

435 (402) Brownhooded Kingfisher
Bruinkopvisvanger
Halcyon albiventris

Plate 40

Muningi (K), Undozela (X), iNdwazela, uNongozolo, uNongobotsha (Z), [Braunkopfliest]

Measurements: Length 22–24 cm; wing (53) 103–106–112; tail 63–70; tarsus 11,5–13; culmen 45–52. Weight (18 ♂) 49,6–60,2–69,4 g, (19 ♀) 45,6–63,1–80,5 g, (24 unsexed) 40–60,1–70 g.

Bare Parts: Iris brown; bill deep red, tip blackish; legs and feet dark pinkish red.

Identification: Size medium; crown brown (grey in Greyhooded Kingfisher, streaked in Striped Kingfisher); upper back black (♂) or brown (♀); lower back, rump, tail and wings blue (back all brown in Striped Kingfisher); below buffy white, washed ochre on breast and flanks (mainly bright

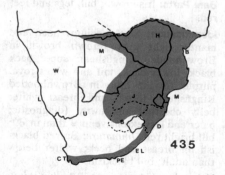

435

chestnut in Greyhooded Kingfisher); flanks streaked blackish (no streaks in

Greyhooded Kingfisher); bill all red (blackish above in Striped Kingfisher). *Immature*: Duller than adult; upper back brown; below whitish; marked with blackish across breast and hindneck.

Voice: Repeated phrase of 3–5 sharp notes, falling in pitch, accented on first note, *KI-ti-ti-ti, KI-ti-ti-ti*; also long series of even louder notes at same pitch, *ki-ki-ki-ki-ki-ki....*; trilling in display.

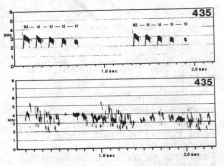

Distribution: S Africa to Gabon, Zaire, Kenya and Somalia; in s Africa absent from most of highveld and all of dry W and Kalahari sandveld.

Status: Common resident.

Habitat: Thickets in woodland and denser savanna, forest edge, riverine and coastal bush, gardens and parks.

Habits: Solitary or in pairs; pairs display to each other with open wings, bobbing, pivoting and calling. Perches on branch, post or telephone wire, scanning ground below for prey; sometimes dives for fish but less expertly than aquatic kingfishers.

Food: Mainly insects; also lizards (including chameleons), crabs, small rodents, birds (warblers, waxbills, sunbirds), small snakes (up to about 25 cm long), scorpions.

Breeding: *Season*: Mainly September to December, but as late as April in Natal. *Nest*: Tunnel, about 1 m long, in bank; about 1–3 m above ground level; chamber lined with regurgitated arthropod fragments. *Clutch*: (73) 2–3,7–5 eggs (rarely 6). *Eggs*: White; measure (141) 27,7 × 24,5 (24,2–30,1 × 22,6–26,6). *Incubation*: About 14 days. *Nestling*: Unrecorded; fed by both parents.

436 (401) Greyhooded Kingfisher Plate 40
Gryskopvisvanger
Halcyon leucocephala

Muningi (K), [Graukopfliest]

Measurements: Length about 20 cm; wing (14) 95–100–106; tail 49–65; tarsus 11–11,5; culmen 38–41. Weight (1 ♂) 37,5 g, (17 unsexed) 41–45,1–50 g.

Bare Parts: Iris brown; bill, legs and feet red.

Identification: Size medium; head and mantle light grey (crown brown in Brownhooded Kingfisher); upper back black; lower back, tail and wings royal purple (bright blue in Brownhooded Kingfisher); throat and breast white; belly chestnut or tawny (diagnostic; paler and less extensive in ♀ than in ♂); bill bright red. *Immature*: Barred blackish on breast and neck; whiter below than adult; bill blackish.

Voice: Loud chattering trill *trrrit-it-it-it-it*; loud *weep-weep woop* interspersed with weak twittering *trrr*.

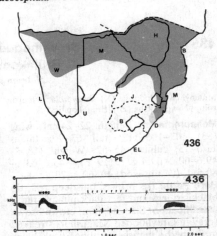

Distribution: Africa S of Sahara, s Arabia; in s Africa from Transvaal lowveld to nw Transvaal, Zimbabwe, n Botswana and n Namibia; vagrant to Durban.

Status: Uncommon to locally fairly common breeding intra-African migrant, September to April (rarely to May). Probably Rare (RDB).

Habitat: Well developed woodland, usually near water.

Habits: Solitary or in pairs. Perches for long periods on branch, scanning ground below; bobs head before diving to ground for prey; large prey beaten on perch before swallowing. Migrates at night; often killed by flying into buildings.

Food: Insects, lizards.

Breeding: *Season:* September to December in Zimbabwe and Mozambique. *Nest:* Burrow, 0,5–1 m long, in bank; about 30 cm from top; also in roof of Antbear burrow. *Clutch:* (10) 3–3,7–4 eggs (sometimes 5). *Eggs:* White; measure (68) 24,6 × 21,6 (22,7–28,2 × 19,1–24,1). *Incubation:* Unrecorded. *Nestling:* Just over 3 weeks; fed by both parents.

437 (403) Striped Kingfisher Plate 40
Gestreepte Visvanger
Halcyon chelicuti

Muningi (K), [Streifenliest, Gestreifter Baumliest]

Measurements: Length 17–19 cm; wing (16) 80–83–86; tail 42–48; tarsus 11–12; culmen 29–35. Weight (1 ♂) 42,7 g, (22 unsexed) 34–38,7–48 g.

Bare Parts: Iris brown; bill dark brown above, red below; legs and feet pinkish brown, pink behind.

Identification: Size smallish (smaller than Brownhooded Kingfisher); crown streaked black and whitish; mantle whitish; back brown; uppertail coverts, tail and edges of remiges bright blue; whitish patch on folded wing (diagnostic); below white, streaked black on flanks and across breast; bill blackish above, red below (diagnostic). *Immature:* Has pale patch on wing buffy; breast and flanks freckled and scaled blackish; bill dusky.

Voice: High-pitched *keep-kirrrr*, the final trill descending in pitch; trill may be frequently repeated on its own, *kirrrr, kirrrr, kirrrr*.

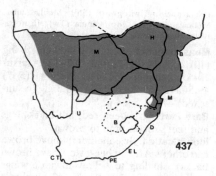

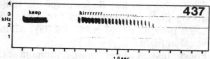

Distribution: Africa S of Sahara; in s Africa from Umfolozi Game Reserve and Windhoek northwards; absent from most of S and W.

Status: Common resident; some local movements.

Habitat: Almost any woodland and savanna; not forest or very dry *Acacia* thornveld.

Habits: Solitary or in pairs. Perches on branch, scanning ground below. Often bobs head and opens and closes wings while calling, showing black band on underwing of ♂; this display also performed by pair or groups of up to 6 birds together, making lots of noise; neighbouring birds answer calls until many calling together.

Food: Insects, small lizards.

Breeding: *Season:* Mainly September to October, but also to February. *Nest:* In hole in tree, 1,5–5 m above ground; rarely in nest of Lesser Striped Swallow. *Clutch:* (16) 2–3,4–6 eggs. *Eggs:* White; measure (49) 24,4 × 21 (22,8–27 × 19,5–22). *Incubation:* Unrecorded. *Nestling:* Unrecorded; fed by both parents.

Ref. Steyn, P. 1970. *Bokmakierie* 22:64–65.

23:2. Family 54 MEROPIDAE—BEE-EATERS

Small to medium. Bill long, rather slender, laterally compressed, decurved and sharply pointed; tail longish, variable in shape; plumage usually bright green with dark stripe through eye and patches of other colours on throat, belly crown or rump; sexes similar; hawk insects in air from perch or in flight pursuit; most gregarious; breed colonially or solitarily; nest a burrow excavated in bank or level ground, with unlined chamber at end; eggs 2–6, white; other features as for Order Alcediniformes. Distribution s Europe, Africa, Madagascar, s Asia to Australia; about 24 species; nine species in s Africa.

Ref. Fry, C.H. 1972. *Living Bird* 11:75–112; 1984. *The bee-eaters*. Calton: T. & A.D. Poyser.
Hanmer, D.B. 1980. *Ostrich* 51:25–38.

438 (404)   Eurasian Bee-eater   Plate 40
Europese Byvreter
Merops apiaster

Gamanyuchi, Hwirogwiro (Sh), Muhladzanhu, Muhlagambu (Ts), Morôkapula (Tw), [Europäischer Bienenfresser]

Measurements: Length 25–29 cm; wing (19) 137–148–157; tail 107–127; tarsus 10–12; culmen 36–41. Weight (5 ♂) 49,5–54,2–59,2 g, (1 ♀) 58,5 g, (6 unsexed) 47–54,5–64 g.

Bare Parts: Iris deep red; bill black; legs and feet greyish pink to brown.

Identification: Size medium; above brown (no other s African bee-eaters have brown backs), shading to yellow towards wings and rump; forehead whitish; eyebrow green; throat bright yellow, bordered by black collar; rest of underparts blue to blue-green; central rectrices elongate. *Immature*: Scaled with green above; no black collar or long central rectrices.

Voice: Trilled liquid *kwirri* or *kwirriri*; also sharp *kwip, kwip*.

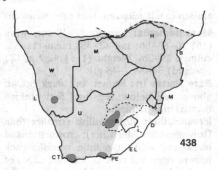

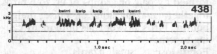

Distribution: Two populations (indistinguishable in appearance): one breeds s Europe, N Africa and s Russia, migrating mainly to Africa, including all of s Africa; other breeds s, sw and n Cape, s Orange Free State and s Namibia, migrating northward to C Africa.

Status: Palaearctic population sporadically common nonbreeding migrants, September to April (rarely to May); bird ringed Russia recovered in Zimbabwe; s African breeders locally common, wintering from n Transvaal to Rwanda; present September to February; birds seen in s Africa April-September likely to be s African breeders.

Habitat: Woodland, savanna, scrubby grassland.

Habits: Gregarious at all times. Roosts in flocks of up to 150 birds in tall trees. Circles high in air; flocks perch on telephone lines or dead trees, flying out to catch prey in air. Migrates by day; often vocal in flight.

Food: Insects (bees, wasps, dragonflies, grasshoppers, mantids, termites, butterflies).

Breeding: *Season*: September to December in sw Cape; October to January near Port Elizabeth. *Nest*: Narrow tunnel, up to 2 m long, in low earth or sandbank; chamber usually lined with insect remains;

colonial. *Clutch*: (6) 2–4,3–6 eggs. *Eggs*: White; measure (60) 25,8 × 21,8 (23,7–28 × 20–23). *Incubation*: About 20 days (Europe). *Nestling*: 30–31 days (Europe); dependent on parents for about 3 weeks after leaving nest.

439 (406)   Olive Bee-eater   Plate 40
Olyfbyvreter
Merops superciliosus

[Madagaskar-Bienenfresser, Madagaskarspint]

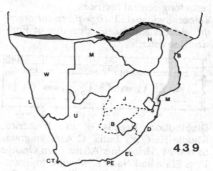

Measurements: Length 27–30 cm; wing (21 ♂) 133–139,6–145, (25 ♀) 129–134–141; tail (5) 131–162; tarsus (5) 9–11; culmen (18) 44,5–49,8–56,5. Weight (16 ♂) 43–45,4–49 g, (4 ♀) 37–41,3–46 g.

Bare Parts: Iris bright red; bill black; legs and feet brownish pink.

Identification: Size medium to large; body mostly green; crown brown (green in Bluecheeked Bee-eater); throat and cheeks brown (upper throat yellowish, cheeks blue in Bluecheeked Bee-eater); eyebrow whitish (bright blue in Bluecheeked Bee-eater); central rectrices elongate. *Immature*: Lacks long central rectrices; crown greenish.

Voice: Sharp syncopated twittering phrase *twip, twee-tittle-tirr, twee-tittle-tirr, teetirr*, uttered rapidly; similar to notes of Eurasian Bee-eater, but faster and sharper.

Distribution: Three populations: one breeds Madagascar, migrates to African mainland from ne Zululand to Angola and Ethiopia; another breeds Zambezi Valley, migrates northward within Africa; third breeds n Namibia and Angola, migrates northward within Africa; nonbreeding distributions of intra-African migrants not precisely known.

Status: Common breeding intra-African migrant, or nonbreeding migrant from Madagascar, September to April.

Habitat: Riverine woodland, *Acacia* around pans, mangroves.

Habits: Gregarious at all times. Roosts in reedbeds and mangrove swamps in huge flocks which wheel about in air when assembling at roost. Hawks insects from perch on dead tree, returning to swallow prey; large prey beaten on perch before being eaten; cruises about in air less than some bee-eaters; may rest on sandbanks between sallies.

Food: Insects (mainly bees; also butterflies, dragonflies, termites, etc.)

Breeding: *Season*: September to December in Namibia, Zimbabwe and Mozambique. *Nest*: Burrow in earth bank or dry ditch; colonial. *Clutch*: 2–3–4 eggs. *Eggs*: White; measure (5) 24 × 21,1 (23,3–24,7 × 20,5–21,8). *Incubation*: Unrecorded. *Nestling*: Unrecorded.

440 (405)   Bluecheeked Bee-eater   Plate 40
Blouwangbyvreter
Merops persicus

Muhladzanhu, Muhlagambu (Ts), isiThwelathwela (Z), [Blauwangenspint]

Measurements: Length 30–33 cm; wing (6) 143–159; tail 125–155; tarsus 10–11,5; culmen 41–45. Weight (3) 48–49–50 g.

Bare Parts: Iris bright red; bill black; legs and feet brownish pink.

Identification: Size medium to large; very similar to Olive Bee-eater; mainly green, including crown (crown brown in Olive

Bee-eater); eyebrow light blue (whitish in Olive Bee-eater); cheeks blue (brownish in Olive Bee-eater); throat brown, shading to yellow under chin (no yellow on brown throat of Olive Bee-eater); central rectrices elongate; underwing rufous-cinnamon. *Immature*: Duller than adult; lacks long central rectrices.

Voice: Syncopated *trree-preep-titi-preep-titi;* sharper and quieter than that of Eurasian Bee-eater.

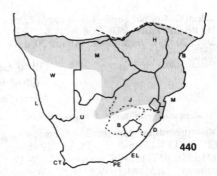

Distribution: Breeds W and N Africa, Middle East, nw India, C Asia; migrates to rest of Africa; in s Africa from Orange Free State and Natal northward to Transvaal, Zimbabwe, Mozambique n Botswana and n Namibia.

Status: Locally fairly common nonbreeding Palaearctic migrant, November to April.

Habitat: Mainly larger rivers; also woodland around pans and vleis.

Habits: Gregarious in small flocks. Hunts actively over open areas (such as mown lucerne fields). Perches regularly spaced on power lines; swoops out after prey; about 85% of sallies successful.

Food: Insects, including butterflies and dragonflies.

Breeding: Extralimital.

441 (407)   **Carmine Bee-eater**   **Plate 40**
Rooiborsbyvreter
Merops nubicoides

Muhembo (K), Muhladzanhu, Muhlagambu, Tinkonyane (Ts), iNkotha-enkulu (Z), [Scharlachspint]

Measurements: Length 33–38 cm; wing (14 ♂) 145–153–160, (3 ♀) 143–149, (170 unsexed) 145–151–160; tail (170, longest rectrix) 167–198–232, (170, shortest rectrix) 91–103–121; tarsus (170) 11–13–15; culmen (170) 36–41–46. Weight (1 ♀) 51 g, (864 unsexed) 51–61,2–75 g.

Bare Parts: Iris reddish brown; bill black; legs and feet pinkish brown.

Identification: Size large; mostly rose red; crown and undertail coverts blue; rump light green; central rectrices elongate. *Immature*: Duller than adult; no long central rectrices.

Voice: Rolling *rik-RAK* or *rik-rik-rik-RAK*, higher-pitched on last note; deeper *tirriktirriktirrik*.

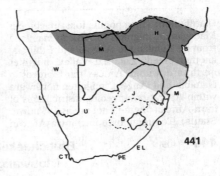

Distribution: Zululand and ne Namibia to Gabon, e Zaire and Kenya.
Status: Locally common breeding intra-African migrant to Zimbabwe, August to November; after breeding, birds disperse from Zimbabwe to S Africa, then move N in March to equatorial Africa; nomadic when not breeding.
Habitat: Major lowveld river valleys and floodplains; usually with vertical banks when breeding.
Habits: Highly gregarious at all times, in flocks of hundreds of birds. Roosts communally; by day scatters widely; hawks flying insects from perch over river, at grassfires, and around large mammals; may perch on back of Kori Bustard when foraging; also circles high in air. Bathes by splash-diving into water. Active mainly morning and evening; lethargic around midday.
Food: Large flying insects.
Breeding: *Season:* August to November in Zimbabwe, September to October in Mozambique. *Nest:* Straight, slightly declined burrow, 1,5–2 m long, in vertical river bank, less often in flat ground; chamber lined with insect remains; highly colonial. *Clutch:* (13) 2–3–5 eggs. *Eggs:* White; measure (48) 26,4 × 22,1 (23,9–28,4 × 20,8–23,4). *Incubation:* Unrecorded. *Nestling:* About 30 days.

442 (408) Böhm's Bee-eater Plate 40
Roeskopbyvreter

Merops boehmi

[Böhmspint]

Measurements: Length 21–22 cm; wing (39) 78–80,6–83; tail (39) 122–132,6–156; tarsus (1) 9; culmen (38) 28–29,9–31. Weight (43) 14,4–16,7–18,2 g.
Bare Parts: Iris red; bill, legs and feet black.
Identification: Size smallish; similar to Olive Bee-eater, but lacks white eyebrow; brown of throat more extensive; mostly green with throat and crown brown; stripe below eye bright blue; central tail feathers elongate. *Immature:* Paler than adult; crown pale orange-buff; below pale greenish grey and fawn; central rectrices and bill short; eye brown; adult coloration acquired at 5–6 months.
Voice: Shrill chirping *swee*; liquid trill.
Distribution: From Tete and Manica e Sofala in Mozambique, to Malawi, Tanzania, Zambia and Zaire.
Status: Uncommon local resident.
Habitat: Thickets, riverine forest.
Habits: Usually in pairs; not gregarious.

442

Fairly tame; sallies out from perch to catch flying insects; wags tail slowly while perched.
Food: Flying insects.
Breeding: *Season:* September to October in Mozambique. *Nest:* Tunnel, about 75–103 cm long, in bank, flat ground or roof of Antbear burrow. *Clutch:* 2–5 eggs. *Eggs:* White; measure (4) 18,9 × 15,7 (18–19,5 × 15–16,5). *Incubation:* Unrecorded. *Nestling:* Unrecorded.

443 (409) Whitefronted Bee-eater Plate 40
Rooikeelbyvreter

Merops bullockoides

Sitembandayi (K), Muhladzanhu, Muhlagambu (Ts), Morôkapula (Tw), iNkotha (Z), [Weißstirnspint, Weißstirn-Bienenfresser]

Measurements: Length 22–24 cm; wing (16) 111–114–119; tail 93–105; tarsus 7,5–9,5; culmen 32–39. Weight (2 ♂)

31,4–34,1 g, (3 ♀) 29,1–30,6–31,7 g, (43 unsexed) 27–34,4–38 g.

Bare Parts: Iris brown; bill black; legs and feet greyish pink to greenish black.

Identification: Size medium; crown and breast cinnamon; forehead and upper throat white; lower throat red (red-and-white throat diagnostic); rest of upper-parts and wings green; undertail coverts bright blue; no elongate central rectrices, tail square (diagnostic, but should not be confused with immatures of other species). *Immature*: Crown green; throat light red; rest of underparts green.

Voice: Squeaky nasal *weeep, zeeep, kriki-riki* and other creaking noises.

Distribution: From central and w Orange Free State, n Cape, Zululand, Transvaal, Mozambique, Zimbabwe and n Botswana to Gabon, Zaire and Kenya.

Status: Very common resident with some local movements.

Habitat: Woodland, especially along large rivers and lakes.

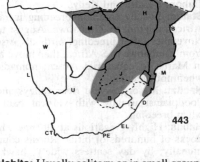

443

Habits: Usually solitary or in small groups by day; roosts communally at night in large flocks in trees. Sallies out from perch to catch flying insects in air or on surface of water; when perched swings tail slowly to and fro. Fairly tame.

Food: Flying insects, especially butter-flies.

Breeding: *Season*: September to October in S Africa, August to November in Zimbabwe (mainly September). *Nest*: Inclined burrow up to about 1 m long; in bank; colonial. *Clutch*: (138) 2–3,2–5 eggs. *Eggs*: White; measure (61) 22,1 × 18,6 (19,1–25 × 17–21,5). *Incubation*: About 20 days. *Nestling*: About 28 days; fed by both parents and 1 or more helpers.

Ref. Emlen, S.T. & Wrege, P.H. 1991. *J. anim. Ecol.* 60:309–326.
Hegner, R.E., Emlen, S.T. & Demong, N.J. 1982. *Nature* 298:264–266.

444 (410)   **Little Bee-eater**   **Plate 40**
Kleinbyvreter
Merops pusillus

Sitembandayi (K), Muhladzanhu, Muhlagambu (Ts), Morôkapula (Tw), iNkotha (Z), [Zwergspint, Zwergbienenfresser]

Measurements: Length 17–18 cm; wing (35) 77–81–84; tail 61–69; tarsus 7–9; culmen 23–29. Weight (3 ♂) 11–12,7–14,7 g, (4 ♀) 12,5–15–17,2 g, (270 un-sexed) 10,5–14,6–18,1 g.

Bare Parts: Iris red; bill black; legs and feet dark pinkish.

Identification: Size small; above green; eyebrow turquoise; throat yellow, bordered below by black collar; rest of under-parts bright yellow ochre (diagnostic); tail

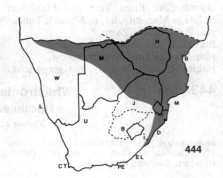

444

square or slightly notched (diagnostic). *Immature*: Above bluer than adult; more buff below; black collar faint or absent; bill shorter and straighter; eye brown; adult coloration acquired at 5 months.

Voice: High-pitched *kreee-kree*; sharp *kip*; seldom vocal.

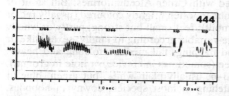

Distribution: Africa S of Sahara; in s Africa confined to NE from Natal to ne Botswana, Transvaal, Zimbabwe and Mozambique.

Status: Common resident.
Habitat: Bushveld, open woodland, savanna, streams, reedbeds.
Habits: Solitary or in pairs by day; at night sometimes roosts on branch in tightly bunched row of up to 15 birds. Hawks flying insects from perch on twig, reed or grass stem, returning to eat prey; uses same perches day after day.
Food: Flying insects.
Breeding: *Season*: September to November in S Africa, September to February (mainly October-November) in Zimbabwe. *Nest*: Small burrow, 50 cm to 1,3 m long in low bank or Antbear hole; solitary. *Clutch*: (60) 2–4–6 eggs. *Eggs*: White; measure (142) 18,7 × 15,7 (17–20,7 × 14,4–17). *Incubation:* 19–20 days, starting with first egg. *Nestling*: 29 days; fed by both parents.

445 (411) Swallowtailed Bee-eater
Swaelstertbyvreter
Merops hirundineus

Plate 40

Sitembandayi (K), Morôkapula (Tw), [Schwalbenschwanzspint, Gabelschwanzspint]

Measurements: Length 20–22 cm; wing (76) 89–95,1–102; tail (10) 90–106; tarsus (10) 8–9,5; culmen (76) 27–33,2–38. Weight (1 ♂) 22,5 g, (22 unsexed) 19–22,5–29 g.
Bare Parts: Iris deep red; bill black; legs and feet brown to blackish.
Identification: Size small; blue forked tail diagnostic; body mainly bright yellowish green; throat bright yellow, bordered below by blue band; white stripe below black face mask. *Immature*: Lacks yellow and blue throat; forked tail distinctive at all ages.
Voice: High-pitched piping and buzzing calls, *kweep kweepy bzzz, kweep*; sharp *kwit, kweet-kwit*.

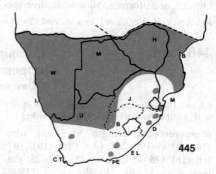

Distribution: Africa S of Sahara; in s Africa mostly absent S of Orange River, e Orange Free State, Lesotho, s Natal and south-central Transvaal.

Status: Locally common, usually resident; some seasonal movements; winter visitor to Natal and Zululand; rare S of Orange River as far E as Cradock.
Habitat: Arid *Acacia* savanna, riverine trees and scrub, clearings and edges of woodland.
Habits: Solitary or in pairs; nonbreeding birds sometimes in small groups. Usually perches low down in bush or tree; darts out to catch flying insects, sometimes with much swooping; often returns to same perch after each sally. May roost in small close-packed groups on branch. Silent and inconspicuous as a rule.

Food: Flying insects (bees, wasps, grass-hoppers, cicadas, etc.).
Breeding: *Season*: October to December in Zimbabwe, Namibia and Kalahari; September to November in Mozambique.

Nest: Tunnel, up to 1 m long, in low earth or sandbank; solitary. *Clutch*: 3–4 eggs. *Eggs*: White; measure (21) 20,8 × 18,2 (20–21,8 × 16,7–19,5). *Incubation*: Unrecorded. *Nestling*: Unrecorded.

24. Order CORACIIFORMES (Six families; four in s Africa)

Medium to very large. Formerly combined with Order Alcediniformes. Bill stout or slender, short or very large, decurved on culmen, often brightly coloured (usually red or yellow); legs short (except in Ground Hornbill); feet small but strong, partly or wholly syndactyl (toes joined from base); plumage variable according to family; sexes alike or different; wings rounded, flight heavy and flapping; tail medium to long and heavy; mostly arboreal; nest in unlined hole in tree (sometimes in crevice, or hole in ground), not excavated by birds themselves; eggs 3–6, usually plain white, but green, blue or brownish in hoopoes; chick naked at hatching in most species, downy in hoopoes, altricial; incubation usually by female only; young fed by both sexes. Distribution Africa, s Europe, s Asia to n Australia.

24:1. Family 55 CORACIIDAE—ROLLERS

Medium. Bill stout, broad, relatively short, decurved on culmen, slightly hooked at tip; legs very short; 2nd and 3rd toes united at base; wings long, rounded, bright blue in patches; tail medium or long, variously shaped; plumage usually with blue coloration associated with purple, green or brown; sexes alike; hawk from perch, flying to ground to catch small animals; other features as for Order Coraciiformes. Distribution as for Order Coraciiformes; 16 species; five species in s Africa.

Ref. Fry, C.H., Fry, K. & Harris, A. 1992. *Kingfishers, bee-eaters & rollers.* Halfway House, South Africa: Russel Friedman Books.

446 (412) **Eurasian Roller** **Plate 41**
Europese Troupant
Coracias garrulus

Gatawa (Sh), Bvebve, Tlekedwani (Ts), Letlêrê-tlêrê, Letlhakêla (Tw), iFefe (Z), [Blauracke]

Measurements: Length 30–31 cm; wing (10 ♂) 194–198–204, (8 ♀) 186–191–197; tail (18) 115–135; tarsus (18) 22–25; culmen (18) 33–40. Weight (2 ♀) 119,6–136 g, (1 unsexed) 147 g.

Bare Parts: Iris brown; bill black; legs and feet yellowish.

Identification: Size large; mainly sky blue; upper back light brown; tail square (Purple Roller also has square tail, but streaked white on purplish below; crown and back olive brown; tail shape variable in other species); outermost rectrices somewhat shorter and pointed at tips. *Immature*: Washed with olive above and below.

Voice: Usually silent; harsh raucous *ak-er-ak, rak-kak, kacker.*

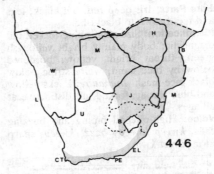

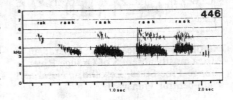

Distribution: Breeds Europe, Middle East and w Asia; migrates to Africa and India; in s Africa absent from most of dry W.
Status: Fairly common nonbreeding Palaearctic migrant, October to April or May; December to February in sw Cape.
Habitat: Woodland, savanna, grassveld with scattered trees.
Habits: Usually solitary; sometimes roosts communally. Perches on tele-phone wire, or other conspicuous perch; flies down to catch prey on ground, eating it there or carrying it back to perch; occasionally catches prey in flight. Flight sluggish but buoyant; wings longer than those of s African breeding rollers; wingbeats slow.
Food: Insects (beetles, locusts, crickets, bees), scorpions, frogs, lizards.
Breeding: Extralimital.

447 (413)   Lilacbreasted Roller   Plate 41
Gewone Troupant
Coracias caudata

Sikambu (K), Matlakela (NS), Gatawa (Sh), Bvebve, Muhlagambu (Ts), Letlêrêtlêrê, Letlha-kêla (Tw), iFefe (Z), [Gabelracke]

Measurements: Length 35–36 cm; wing (27) 157–166–174; tail (longest rectrices) 156–218, (shortest rectrices) 108–128; tarsus 20–24; culmen 29–37. Weight (1 ♂) 112 g, (3 ♀) 97–100,6–106,8 g, (2 unsexed) 99–107 g.
Bare Parts: Iris brown; bill black; legs and feet olive or greenish yellow.
Identification: Size large; crown light green; back light brown; rump blue; tail blue, forked, with long narrow outermost rectrices (not always easy to see in field, but good flight character); breast lilac; belly blue; in flight wings bright blue. *Immature*: Duller than adult; outer rectrices shorter.
Voice: Harsh *rak-zak-zaak, zak-zak-zak, rak-zaak*, etc. in display; otherwise largely silent.

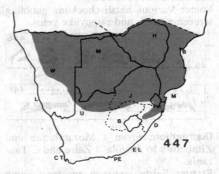

Distribution: S Africa to Angola and Ethiopia; in s Africa absent from extreme S and W, and from most of treeless high-veld.
Status: Common resident or local migrant; in some areas occurs only summer or winter; rare vagrant to e Cape.
Habitat: Savanna or open woodland.
Habits: Usually solitary or in pairs. Perches conspicuously on top of bush, tree or telephone wire; flies to ground to catch prey; flight fast and high; in display dives with wings almost closed, loops up and over, or flies upward, loops over and drops with open wings and legs extended. Rocks from side to side when diving to perch. Attracted to grassfires.
Food: Insects (locusts, beetles, caterpillars, ants, mealie borers), scorpions, centipedes, snails, frogs, small snakes, lizards, small birds and rodents.
Breeding: *Season*: August to December. *Nest*: Natural hole in tree, 2–6 m above ground. *Clutch*: (22) 2–2,8–4 eggs. *Eggs*: White; measure (78) 31,4 × 25,4 (28,4–34 × 21,4–28,5). *Incubation*: 17–18 days (or up to 25 days reported) by both sexes. *Nestling*: Over 20 days.

448 (414) Rackettailed Roller
Knopsterttroupant
Coracias spatulata

Plate 41

Sikambu (K), Gatawa (Sh), [Spatelracke]

Measurements: Length 36–38 cm; wing 159–176; tail (longest rectrices) 193–225, (shortest rectrices) 135–157; tarsus 20,5–21,5; culmen 30,5–35. Weight (1 ♀) 88 g.
Bare Parts: Iris light to yellowish brown; bill black; legs and feet yellowish to greenish yellow.
Identification: Size large; racket-shaped outermost rectrices diagnostic; above brown, except for blue rump; below bright light blue; wings darker blue. *Immature*: Browner and duller than adult; lacks spatulate outermost rectrices.
Voice: Various harsh chuckling gabbling screeching calls and puppylike yelps.

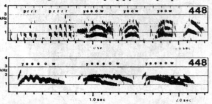

Distribution: From s Mozambique and Zimbabwe to Angola, s Zaire and C Tanzania.
Status: Fairly common resident; some local movement. Probably Rare (RDB).
Habitat: Well-developed woodland (denser

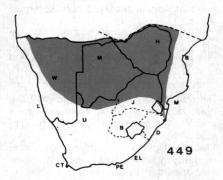

than that favoured by Lilacbreasted Roller), both mopane and *Brachystegia*.
Habits: Solitary or in groups of 2–4 birds; 2–3 birds may roost together on branch. Flight undulating; display flight rapid zig-zag, followed by vertical ascent of 5–7 m with closed wings, gentle loop, then dive with closed wings; accompanied by loud calls. Usually perches on low conspicuous branch or stump.
Food: Insects.
Breeding: *Season*: September to December (mainly October) in Zimbabwe. *Nest*: Natural hole in tree. *Clutch*: (7) 2–3–4 eggs. *Eggs*: White; measure (20) 32 × 26 (29,6–34,7 × 24,8–27,9). *Incubation*: Unrecorded. *Nestling*: Unrecorded.

449 (415) Purple Roller
Groottroupant
Coracias naevia

Plate 41

Sikambu (K), Gatawa (Sh), Bvebve, Tlekedwani (Ts), Letlêrêtlêrê, Letlhakêla (Tw), [Strichelracke]

Measurements: Length 35–40 cm; wing (23) 175–189–198; tail 135–152; tarsus 22–26; culmen 37–46. Weight (2 ♂) 157–167 g, (1 unsexed) 156 g.
Bare Parts: Iris brown; bill black; legs and feet olive brown.
Identification: Size large; general coloration dull compared with other rollers; tail square; above light brown (Eurasian Roller brown on back only; head and wings bright blue); rump and tail blue;

below light purple, streaked white; wing coverts light purple (bright blue in Eurasian Roller); rest of wing dark blue, *Immature*: Browner than adult, with broader white ventral streaks.

Voice: Loud, somewhat nasal, rasping, *chik-kaaa chik-kaaa, ka-ka-kaka* (similar to chattering of Redbilled Woodhoopoe); repeated snarling *keeow*.

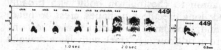

Distribution: Africa S of Sahara to Zululand, Transvaal, Cape Province N of Orange River and n Namibia.

Status: Uncommon to fairly common resident with local movements.

Habitat: Savanna and open woodland.

Habits: Usually solitary or in pairs. Rather quiet and sluggish; perches on conspicuous dead tree or telephone wire for long periods; catches prey on ground. Displays with rocking and rolling flight as if wings beating unevenly, first rising, then falling like paper kite out of control; display accompanied by calls.

Food: Insects, scorpions, small reptiles.

Breeding: *Season*: September to December in Zimbabwe, July in Namibia; possibly opportunistic after rain in drier savanna. *Nest*: Natural hole in tree, or old nest of woodpecker. *Clutch*: (15) 2–3,3–4 eggs. *Eggs*: White; measure (23) 34,5 × 28,2 (31–36,7 × 25,8–29,3). *Incubation*: Unrecorded. *Nestling*: Unrecorded; fed by both parents.

450 (416)   Broadbilled Roller   Plate 41
Geelbektroupant
Eurystomus glaucurus

[Zimtroller]

Measurements: Length 25–27 cm; wing (22) 170–176–183; tail 92–104; tarsus 15–19; culmen 22–22,5. Weight (♂) 94–114 g, (♀) 84–130 g.

Bare Parts: Iris brown; bill bright yellow; legs and feet olive brownish.

Identification: Size medium; yellow bill diagnostic; above rich hazel brown; rump and tail blue; below violet-purple; wings blue. *Immature*: Almost blackish above and on throat and breast; scaled rusty below.

Voice: Snarling nasal *keow, keow, keowrrrrr, keowrrrrr*; sharp chattering *kik-k-k-k-r-r-r-r*.

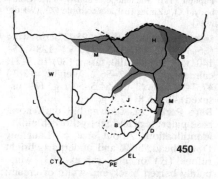

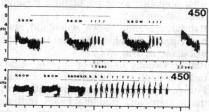

Distribution: Africa S of Sahara, Madagascar; in s Africa from Zululand to Mozambique, Transvaal lowveld, Zimbabwe n Botswana and Caprivi.

Status: Uncommon in more open woodland, fairly common elsewhere; breeding intra-African migrant, September to April.

Habitat: Mainly fringing forest in major river valleys and denser bushveld; locally in more open woodland.

Habits: Solitary or in pairs when breeding; sometimes in flocks of up to about 30 birds on migration. Perches on tops of trees, flying out to catch insects on the wing; often hunts moths at dusk. Looks like large bat in flight; chases other birds readily. See-sawing display flight accompanied by calls.

Food: Flying insects; also small rodents and young birds.
Breeding: *Season*: September to December. *Nest*: Natural hole in tree, up to 12 m above ground; also holes in tobacco barns. *Clutch*: (26) 2–2,7–4 eggs (usually 3). *Eggs*: White; measure (35) 32,3 × 26,5 (24,6–37,2 × 24,2–28,7). *Incubation*: Unrecorded. *Nestling*: Unrecorded.

24:2. Family 56 UPUPIDAE—HOOPOE

Medium. Bill long and very slender, somewhat decurved; legs short and slender; toes longish (3rd and 4th joined at base); wings broad and rounded, flight appears laboured; tail square, medium length; plumage cinnamon to chestnut on body with broadly banded black, white and buff wings and tail; long erectile fan-shaped crest on head, tipped with black; sexes similar; feed on ground; food small animals; nest in almost any kind of unlined hole; eggs 4–7, plain blue, green or brownish; chick with white down at hatching, altricial; other features as for Order Coraciiformes. Distribution Africa, Madagascar, s Europe, s Asia to Japan; one species (most closely related to wood-hoopoes, family Phoeniculidae).

451 (418) **African Hoopoe** **Plate 34**
Hoephoep
Upupa africana

Nduranganga, Kangungu (K), Kukuku (NS), Popopo (SS), Mhupupu (Sh), Marimamalanga, Pupupu (Ts), Mmadilêpê, Pupupu (Tw), Ubhobhoyi (X), uZiningweni, umZolozolo (Z), [Wiedehopf]

Measurements: Length 25–27 cm; wing (26 ♂) 132–140–145, (13 ♀) 128–135–140; tail (39) 84–100; tarsus (39) 16,5–21; culmen (39) 42–56. Weight (2 ♂) 47,7–63,6 g, (2 ♀) 54,5–56,1 g, (19 unsexed) 46–56,8–67,7 g.
Bare Parts: Iris brown; bill dark horn, base paler; legs and feet yellowish pink.
Identification: About size of Laughing Dove; head, back and underparts bright rufous (♂) or dull rufous (♀); wings boldly barred black and white or cream; tail mainly black, white at base; bill long, thin, slightly decurved; conspicuous pointed crest can be erected into fan shape when alarmed; legs short. *Immature*: Duller than adult ♀.
Voice: Mellow *hoop-hoop* or *hoop-hoop-hoop*, repeated several times in phrases of 2–3 syllables; quiet *zweee* on take-off and when alarmed; fledgling calls *sweet, sweet*.

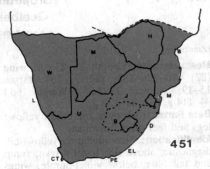

Distribution: Africa, Madagascar, Europe, tropical Asia; throughout s Africa, except extreme desert.
Status: Sparse to common resident; somewhat nomadic; some populations possibly seasonal migrants.
Habitat: Savanna, open woodland, gardens, parks, Kalahari thornveld; riverine woodland in arid areas.
Habits: Usually solitary or in pairs; sometimes in small groups when not breeding. Forages by walking on ground with short quick steps and nodding head, probing often with bill, especially in lawns. Flight heavy on broad floppy wings, somewhat butterflylike. Usually perches in tree when calling. Often raises crest after alighting.
Food: Insects (especially larvae, like cut-

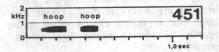

worms), earthworms, small snakes, frogs; sometimes hawks termites in flight.

Breeding: *Season*: July to December (mainly August-October); may rear 2–3 broods per season. *Nest*: Natural hole in ground, termite mound, stone wall, hollow tree, under eaves, burrow in bank; does not excavate own hole; nest un-lined, becoming foul-smelling after young hatch. *Clutch*: (26) 2–3,4–6 eggs (rarely 7). *Eggs*: Pale blue or olive green, fading to greyish or brownish with white pores; measure (73) 25,3 × 17,2 (22,2–27,6 × 15,8–18,5). *Incubation*: 17 days by ♀ only. *Nestling*: 26–32 days; fed by both parents.

24:3. Family 57 PHOENICULIDAE—WOODHOOPOES

Medium. Bill long, slender, decurved, red in some species; legs very short; toes longish with sharp, curved claws for hanging onto bark; wings rounded; tail long, graduated; plumage black with blue, purple or green gloss, with white patches in wings and tail; sexes similar, but female usually has shorter bill than male; usually gregarious, noisy; arboreal; food mostly arthropods probed out of crevices in bark and wood; nest in unlined hole in tree; eggs 3–4, green, blue or grey; chick downy, altricial; other features as for Order Coraciiformes. Distribution Africa S of Sahara (not Madagascar); eight species; three species in s Africa.

452 (419)   Redbilled Woodhoopoe   Plate 34
Gewone Kakelaar (Rooibekkakelaar)
Phoeniculus purpureus

Musokoto (K), Haya (Sh), Kolokolwana, Munyane (Ts), Foofoo (Tw), Intlekibafazi (X), iNhlekaba-fazi, uNukani (Z), [Steppenbaumhopf]

Measurements: Length 30–36 cm; wing (9 ♂) 131–137–142, (12 ♀) 125–133–137; tail (9 ♂) 162–187, (12 ♀) 160–170; tarsus (21) 20–24; culmen (9 ♂) 52–62, (12 ♀) 41–48. Weight (4) 61–70,8–75 g.

Bare Parts: Iris brown; bill, legs and feet scarlet.

Identification: Size medium; black with green iridescence, bluer on throat and wings, purplish on wrist and tail (Violet Woodhoopoe iridescent purple on mantle and underparts); bill and legs bright red; white spots on primaries, and white barring on rectrices visible in flight (less easily when perched); tail about 100 mm shorter than that of Violet Woodhoopoe. *Immature*: Duller than adult; bill black; throat buff.

Voice: Loud cackling, starting off slowly, then crescendo, several birds calling together; likened to laughter of women (hence Xhosa and Zulu names); call accompanies group display, birds rocking back and forth with lowered head.

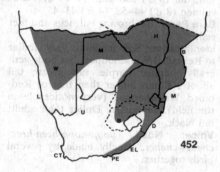

452

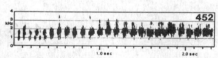

452

Distribution: Africa S of Sahara; in s Africa mainly absent from highveld and dry W.

Status: Common resident.

Habitat: *Acacia* thornveld, mixed woodland, edges of evergreen forest, exotic plantations, gardens, parks.

Habits: Gregarious in groups of 2–16 birds

(usually 3–9); each group includes only 1 breeding pair. Forages mostly by clambering about branches of trees, probing into loose bark and fissures; uses tail as prop, often dropping in stages, checking with tail; also feeds on ground in dry season; hawks termite alates in flight; probes nests of other birds (probably for insect larvae). Restless and noisy; flies in loose formation from tree to tree; may bow and fan tail while calling.

Food: Insects, millipedes, lizards; nectar of *Erythrina* flowers.

Breeding: *Season*: All months (mainly September-October) in Zimbabwe, July to March (mainly September-November)

in S Africa; may rear 2 broods a season. *Nest*: Usually old nest hole of barbet or woodpecker; also natural hole in tree; 1–22 m above ground. *Clutch*: (58) 2–3–5 eggs. *Eggs*: Pale olive green to turquoise blue, with fine white pores; measure (129) 24,9 × 17,3 (22,2–29,2 × 16–18,9). *Incubation*: About 18 days by ♀ only; starts with complete clutch; incubating ♀ fed by 1 or 2 males only. *Nestling*: About 30 days; fed by parents and up to 3 adult helpers, as well as possibly by young from previous brood.

Ref. Ligon, J.D. & Ligon, S.H. 1978. *Living Bird* 17:159–197.

---

453 (420)   **Violet Woodhoopoe**   **Plate 34**
Perskakelaar
Phoeniculus damarensis

[Damarabaumhopf]

Measurements: Length about 35 cm; wing (8 ♂) 148–157–164, (4 ♀) 149–152–158; tail (8 ♂) 230–262, (4 ♀) 210–242; culmen (8 ♂) 44–58, (4 ♀) 43–45.

Bare Parts: Iris brown; bill, legs and feet red.

Identification: Size medium; very similar to Redbilled Woodhoopoe, but body generally metallic purple, not green; tail about 100 mm longer than that of Redbilled Woodhoopoe (very noticeable in the field). *Immature*: Duller than adult; bill black.

Voice: Noisy *hoop-hoop-heea-heea-chatter-chatter*; usually made by several birds together.

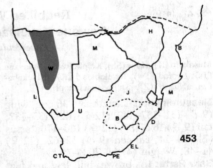

Distribution: North-central Namibia to extreme s Angola; also E Africa.

Status: Common resident; formerly considered subspecies of Redbilled Woodhoopoe, but occurs sympatrically with it S and W of Etosha Pan.

Habitat: Tall trees along dry watercourses.

Habits: Gregarious in groups of up to 10 birds. Noisy flocks fly from tree to tree, foraging on bark of branches and trunks. Similar to Redbilled Woodhoopoe.

Food: Insects.

Breeding: *Season*: December to January. *Nest*: Hole in tree or stump. *Clutch*: 3 eggs. *Eggs*: Olive green to bluish; measure about 26 × 18. *Incubation*: Unrecorded. *Nestling*: Unrecorded.

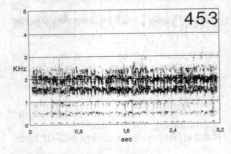

454 (421) Scimitarbilled Woodhoopoe Plate 34
Swartbekkakelaar
Rhinopomastus cyanomelas

Musokoto (K), Ndokotwana, Munyani (Ts), [Sichelhopf]

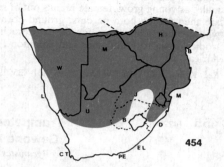

454

Measurements: Length 24–28 cm; wing (8 ♂) 110–113–122, (8 ♀) 100–103–106; tail (8 ♂) 125–133–147, (8 ♀) 113–118–132; culmen (8 ♂) 42–49, (8 ♀) 35–42,5. Weight (2 ♀) 33–36 g, (3 unsexed) 25,3–31,6–41,5 g.

Bare Parts: Iris dark brown; bill, legs and feet black.

Identification: Size smallish (smaller than other woodhoopoes). *Male:* All black with metallic blue sheen; tinged violet on back, green on underparts; bold white bar on each primary forms white stripe in flight; outer 3 rectrices with bold white spot near tip; bill black, sharply decurved (much more curved than in immature Redbilled and Violet Woodhoopoes). *Female:* Like ♂, but with face and underparts dark brown, without metallic sheen; bill more slender. *Immature:* Like adult ♀.

Voice: Somewhat mournful *wheep-wheep-wheep-wheep*, repeated in phrases of 3–5 syllables; sharp rapid *kwi-kwi-kwi-kwi*; squeaky *sweee-sweee*; rolling *krrr-krrr-krrr* alarm call.

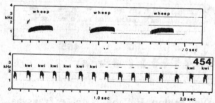

454

Distribution: S Africa to E Africa; in s Africa absent from extreme S and most of highveld.

Status: Common resident.

Habitat: *Acacia* thornveld, dry savanna, riverine bush.

Habits: Usually solitary or in pairs; sometimes in small family group. Forages mainly in outer branches of trees, less often also on bark of trunks like Redbilled Woodhoopoe; sometimes forages on ground; restless and agile, often hanging upside down while probing with bill in bark; often probes with lower jaw only and bill open. After feeding in treetop, descends in glide to lower parts of next tree; flight graceful and buoyant. Usually silent when feeding. Roosts at night vertically on bark of treetrunk or in groups of up to 4 birds in hole in tree.

Food: Insects (especially larvae), spiders; also seeds, buds, nectar.

Breeding: *Season:* August to December (mainly September-October). *Nest:* Natural hole in tree; also old nest hole of barbet or woodpecker. *Clutch:* (9) 2–2,7–4 eggs. *Eggs:* Greenish blue, with white pores, becoming nest-stained during incubation; measure (23) 22,3 × 15,8 (20,9–25,6 × 14,7–17,6). *Incubation:* 15–17 days by ♀ only; fed on nest by ♂. *Nestling:* 23–24 days; fed by both parents; nestling retains feather sheaths, especially on head, until nearly ready to leave nest; hisses and sways when threatened; defaecates foul-smelling fluid if handled.

Ref. Hoesch, W. 1933. *Orn. Monatsber.* 41:33–37.

24:4. Family 58 BUCEROTIDAE—HORNBILLS

Medium to very large. Bill huge, decurved, usually topped by a horny casque, often brightly coloured (yellow or red); neck fairly long; legs very short (except in Ground Hornbill) and rather stout; toes short, syndactyl; plumage usually black and white with grey and brown; face and throat usually bare and brightly coloured; sexes similar or different; most arboreal; food a great variety of animal and plant material; nest in unlined natural tree-hole, usually with entrance sealed from within by female, using material provided by male, leaving narrow vertical slit through which she is fed by male; as young grow, female breaks out of sealed entrance; young re-seal entrance and are then fed by both parents; ground hornbills do not seal nest entrance; eggs 1–6, white; other features as for Order Coraciiformes. Distribution Africa S of Sahara, tropical Asia to Philippines and Solomon Islands; about 45 species; nine species in s Africa.

Ref. Kemp, A.C. 1976. *Tvl Mus. Mem.* 20:1–125; 1978. *Living Bird* 17:105–136.

455 (422) Trumpeter Hornbill — Plate 41
Gewone Boskraai
Bycanistes bucinator

Gangambudzi (Sh), Nkorhondlopfu, Hakamila, N'an'ana (Ts), Kôrwê (Tw), Ilithwa (X), iKhunatha (Z), [Trompeter-Hornvogel]

Measurements: Length 58–65 cm; wing (33 ♂) 273–288–302, (37 ♀) 252–263–280; tail (19 ♂) 200–216–230, (25 ♀) 188–198–209; tarsus (19 ♂) 41–44–47, (23 ♀) 37–40–44; culmen from behind casque (25 ♂) 121–136–154, (35 ♀) 94–112–125; casque (11 ♂) 125–150, (14 ♀) 65–93. Weight (6 ♂) 607–737–941 g, (5 ♀) 565–616–670 g.

Bare Parts: Iris brown or red; skin around eye pink; bill and casque blackish; casque whitish behind; legs and feet black, soles whitish.

Identification: About size of crow, but tail long and heavy; mainly black; belly, tips of secondaries and of outer rectrices white (Silverycheeked Hornbill lacks white on secondaries; black extends to upper belly); casque blackish, pointed in front (whitish, truncated in Silverycheeked Hornbill); bare skin around eye pink; casque smaller in ♀ than in ♂; white rump conspicuous in flight. *Immature*: Like ♀, but feathers of face tipped brown.

Voice: Very loud braying, laughing, trumpeting, squealing and wailing calls, some drawn out, others rapidly staccato; often calls in groups.

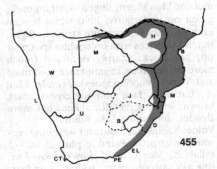

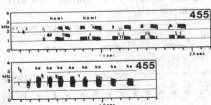

Distribution: E Cape, Natal, e Transvaal, Mozambique, Zimbabwe, n Botswana and n Namibia to Angola, Zaire and Kenya.

Status: Locally common resident; some local seasonal movements.

Habitat: Forest, dense woodland with tall trees, riverine bushveld.

Habits: Usually gregarious in flocks of up to 50 birds (groups of 2–5 birds more usual). Roosts in groups of 3–12, rarely up to 50 birds. Forages by bounding and hopping lightly among branches. Flight heavy, but can take off almost vertically in

dense forest. Vocal mostly morning and evening.
Food: Fruit (especially figs), large insects.
Breeding: *Season*: October to December. *Nest*: Natural hole in tree, less often in rock crevice; entrance sealed to form nar-row slit; up to 12 m above ground. *Clutch*: (11) 2–2,4–4 eggs. *Eggs*: White; measure (15) 49 × 35,2 (47–53,7 × 33,5–38,2). *Incubation*: Unrecorded. *Nestling*: Unrecorded; nestlings in same brood differ in size.

456 (423) Silverycheeked Hornbill Plate 41
Kuifkopboskraai
Bycanistes brevis

[Schopfhornvogel, Silberwangen-Hornvogel]

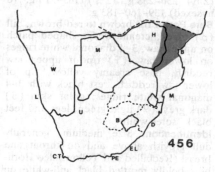

456

Measurements: Length 75–80 cm; wing (72 ♂) 345–369–395, (37 ♀) 321–340–360; tail (50 ♂) 256–276–295, (21 ♀) 245–260–280; tarsus (35 ♂) 50–55–60, (17 ♀) 47–50–52; culmen (43 ♂) 153–171–195, (21 ♀) 138–149–155; casque ♂ 162–205, ♀ 92–115. Weight (1 ♂) 1265 g, (2 ♀) 1058–1193 g.

Bare Parts: Iris brown to red; skin around eye black, blue, grey or pinkish; bill dull grey to blackish, line at base white to yellow; casque yellowish cream; legs and feet black.

Identification: Size large; mainly black; no white in upper wing (secondaries tipped white in Trumpeter Hornbill); underwing coverts white; rump, lower belly, under-tail, thighs and tips of outer rectrices white (whole belly white in Trumpeter Horn-bill); casque large, pale, contrasting with dark bill, truncated in front, especially in ♀ (less contrasting in colour and more pointed in front in Trumpeter Hornbill); head distinctly crested behind (not crested in Trumpeter Hornbill). *Immature*: Casque smaller than in adult; feathers around bill and sides of face edged brown.

Voice: Repeated *waak-waak-waak* like blast on toy trumpet, often in chorus; various braying, howling, screeching, bleating and barking calls; clattering call like that of Egyptian Goose.

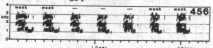

Distribution: Extreme n Transvaal low-veld, lower Limpopo River, e Zimbabwe, through E Africa to Ethiopia.

Status: Fairly common resident; vulnerable to habitat destruction; threatened in se Zimbabwe.

Habitat: Tall evergreen forest and *Brachystegia* woodland, mainly in canopy.

Habits: Usually in pairs; also gregarious in small groups or flocks of up to 50 or more birds; sometimes in company with Trumpeter Hornbill. May roost communally in flocks of hundreds of birds. Flight undulating, alternating flapping and gliding; wingbeats make loud whooshing sound.

Food: Fruit (mainly figs), insects, birds' eggs and nestlings, centipedes.

Breeding: *Season*: September, October and April in Zimbabwe. *Nest*: Natural hole in tall tree; up to 20 m or more above ground; entrance sealed to form narrow vertical slit. *Clutch*: 1–3 eggs. *Eggs*: White; measure (7) 46,8 × 33,7 (45,2–48,9 × 32,5–35); weigh (1) 50 g. *Incubation*: About 40 days by ♀ only. *Nestling*: 77–80 days; ♀ remains with young until they leave nest.

Ref. Moreau, R.E. & Moreau, W.M. 1941. *Auk* 58:13–27.

457 (424)

Grey Hornbill
Grysneushoringvoël
Tockus nasutus

Plate 41

Munkono (K), Goto, Hoto (Sh), Nkorhoxangu (Ts), Kôrwê (Tw), [Grautoko]

Measurements: Length 43–48 cm; wing (137 ♂) 210–225–250, (47 ♀) 187–206–225; tail (61 ♂) 184–201–218, (36 ♀) 167–183–200; tarsus (67 ♂) 34–38–42, (35 ♀) 32–35–39; culmen (68 ♂) 89–99–120, (40 ♀) 69–78–97. Weight (2 ♂) 230–258 g, (2 ♀) 163–215 g, (6 unsexed) 139–160–183 g.

Bare Parts: Iris brown to red-brown; bill (♂) black, cream wedge-shaped patch on upper jaw, 3–4 diagonal white ridges on lower jaw, (♀) tip of upper jaw reddish, base creamy yellow, tip of lower jaw reddish, rest black with 3–4 diagonal white ridges; gular skin (♂) dark grey, (♀) light green; legs and feet black, soles white.

Identification: Size medium; generally dull greyish above and on throat and breast (Redbilled and Yellowbilled Hornbills boldly mottled black-and-white on wings); rest of underparts whitish; tail brownish, tipped white (tail blackish in Yellowbilled and Redbilled Hornbills, outer rectrices all white); dark bill of ♂ diagnostic (other smaller hornbills have bright yellow or red bills); ♀ has dark lower jaw (Yellowbilled Hornbill has all-yellow bill); eyes dark (Yellowbilled Hornbill has yellow eyes, Redbilled Hornbill may have either yellow or brown); whitish streak down back in flight. *Immature*: Browner than adult; bill with white patch at base of upper jaw as in ♂; lacks casque.

Voice: High-pitched whistled call, starting off with few lower notes, *woop-woop-woop*, *weep-weep-weep-weep*, *weep-weep*, *weep-weep*, etc.; whistles sometimes interspersed with clicking sounds; often calls in chorus.

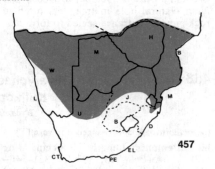

457

Distribution: Africa S of Sahara, s Arabia; in s Africa absent from most of highveld, Natal, Cape, s Namibia and treeless Kalahari sandveld.

Status: Common resident; some local seasonal movements in Zimbabwe.

Habitat: Bushveld, savanna, woodland.

Habits: In pairs when breeding; otherwise gregarious in small groups or large dry-season concentrations of 100 or more birds. Forages in trees, rarely on ground; hawks insects in flight. Flight undulating, buoyant and dextrous; tail raised on alighting. Frequents grassfires. When calling flaps wings and points bill upwards.

Food: Insects, solifugids, rodents, frogs, chameleons, seeds, fruit, peanuts.

Breeding: *Season*: September to December (mainly October-November) in Zimbabwe, February-March in Namibia (after rains), October to November in Transvaal. *Nest*: Natural hole in tree, lined mainly with bark flakes; 3–4 m above ground; usually with chimney or funkhole above entrance; floor of hole about 10 cm below entrance; minimum size of entrance hole 2,5 cm wide, 3,5 cm high; diameter of nest chamber (20) 15–23,2–32 cm. *Clutch*: (25) 3–4–5 eggs. *Eggs*: White; measure (34) 37,4 × 26,9 (33,9–40 × 25–28,3). *Incubation*: (5) 24–25–26 days by ♀ only. *Nestling*: (10) 43–45,5–49 days; ♀ breaks out of nest 19–24 days after first egg hatches; nestlings re-seal entrance unaided.

Ref. Kemp, A.C. 1976. *Tvl Mus. Mem.* 20:1–125.

458 (425)
Redbilled Hornbill
Rooibekneushoringvoël
Tockus erythrorhynchus

Plate 41

Rukoko (K), iKolo (Ndebele), Goto, Hoto (Sh), Nkorho, Manteveni (Ts), Kôrwê (Tw), umKho-lwane (Z), [Rotschnabeltoko]

Measurements: Length 42–50 cm; wing (5 ♂) 183–187–195, (9 ♀) 162–171–182; tail (14) 174–200; tarsus (14) 33–41; culmen (76 ♂) 51–63,5–71, (73 ♀) 44–51,2–59. Weight (2) 125–134 g.

Bare Parts: Iris yellow or brown; skin around eye pink; bill dull red, base of lower jaw black in ♂; gular skin pink; legs and feet black, soles whitish.

Identification: Size medium; no casque on red bill (bill yellow in Yellowbilled Hornbill); much white on head and neck (head and neck dark without white eyebrow in Crowned, Bradfield's and Monteiro's Hornbills); wings boldly mottled black-and-white (more uniform greyish in Grey Hornbill). *Immature*: Bill shorter than in adult; wings spotted buffy.

Voice: Sharp staccato trumpeting, starting off with some single notes, then speeding up into syncopated double notes, *wak, wak, wak, kawak-kawak-kawak*, etc.; clicking *xok*; growling *krrr*.

Distribution: W, E and s Africa; in s Africa confined to Zululand, Mozambique, Transvaal, Zimbabwe, n and e Botswana and n Namibia.
Status: Common resident; some local movements.

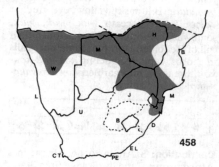

458

Habitat: Savanna, especially mopane woodland.
Habits: Usually gregarious in small flocks (rarely large flocks at waterhole) when not breeding; otherwise in pairs. Forages mainly on ground; digs for food in soil and dung. Tame. Flight buoyant, undulating. Displays by bobbing up and down with bowed head.
Food: Insects, seeds, scorpions, amphisbaenans, weaver eggs.
Breeding: *Season*: September to February (mainly January-February) in Zimbabwe, October-November in Transvaal. *Nest*: As for Grey Hornbill, but nest often lined with green leaves. *Clutch*: (82) 2–4,1–5 eggs (usually 4–5). *Eggs*: White, pitted; measure (35) 37,1 × 26,2 (31,8–40,9 × 23–29). *Incubation*: (6) 23–24–25 days by ♀ only. *Nestling*: (10) 39–45–50 days; ♀ leaves nest 20–23 days after first egg hatches; nestlings re-seal entrance unaided.

Ref. Kemp, A.C. 1976. *Tvl Mus. Mem.* 20:1–125.

459 (426)
Southern Yellowbilled Hornbill
Suidelike Geelbekneushoringvoël
Tockus leucomelas

Plate 41

Rukoko (K), Goto, Hoto (Sh), Nkorho, Manteveni (Ts), Kôrwê (Tw), [Gelbschnabeltoko]

Measurements: Length 48–60 cm; wing (58 ♂) 186–203,8–218, (41 ♀) 173–188,1–203; tail (33 ♂) 203–213,2–231, (25 ♀) 178–195,4–208; tarsus (26) 34–43; culmen (104 ♂) 58–74,8–97, (102 ♀) 50–62,4–83. Weight (75 ♂) mean 211 g, (75 ♀) mean 168 g.

Bare Parts: Iris yellow; skin around eye dark pink; bill yellow-orange to chrome yellow, black along cutting edges and gonys; gular skin dark pink; legs and feet black.

Identification: Size medium; similar to Redbilled Hornbill, but bill more massive and deep yellow (not red); eyes always yellow (eyes brown in Grey Hornbill). *Immature*: Bill dusky yellow; eye grey.
Voice: Loud staccato *wuk, wuk, wuk,* somewhat mellower and lower-toned than call of Redbilled Hornbill; sometimes calls in chorus; rapid trumpeting *kok-kok-kok-kok*, breaking into garbled *kowakowako-wakowak* in display.

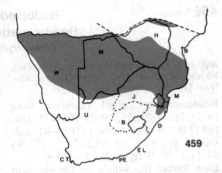

459

459

Distribution: S Africa to ne Africa; in s Africa from n Cape, w Orange Free State, Zululand, C Transvaal and ne Namibia northwards.
Status: Common resident.
Habitat: Bushveld, woodland, savanna, arid thornveld.
Habits: Solitary, in pairs, or in small groups. Forages mostly on ground, but also in trees; runs on ground. Calls with wings up and bill pointed downwards between feet. Similar to Redbilled Hornbill.

Food: Rodents, insects, scorpions, solifugids, centipedes, seeds, fruit.
Breeding: *Season*: September to March (mostly October-November) in Zimbabwe, February to March in Namibia. *Nest*: As in Grey Hornbill, but usually lined with dry grass and leaves. *Clutch*: (68) 2–3,7–5 eggs (usually 3–4). *Eggs*: White with conspicuous pores; measure (71) 36,8 × 26,2 (31,5–41 × 21,3–28,5). *Incubation*: (1) 24 days by ♀ only. *Nestling*: (7) 42–44–47 days; ♀ leaves nest 20–22 days after first egg hatches; nestlings re-seal entrance unaided.

Ref. Kemp, A.C. 1976. *Tvl Mus. Mem.* 20:1–125.

460 (427) Crowned Hornbill Plate 41
Gekroonde Neushoringvoël
Tockus alboterminatus

Rukoko (K), Kgoropo (NS), Goto, Hoto (Sh), Nkorhonyarhi (Ts), Umkholwane (X), umKholwane (Z), [Kronentoko]

Measurements: Length 50–54 cm; wing (30 ♂) 237–252–273, (14 ♀) 226–237–247; tail (9) 203–235; tarsus (9) 27–32; culmen (4 ♂) 91–99, (5 ♀) 77–90. Weight (1 ♂) 234 g.
Bare Parts: Iris yellow; skin around eye dark brown to black; bill red to redbrown, basal band creamy yellow; gular skin (♂) black, (♀) yellow, greenish to blue-green; legs and feet blackish, soles whitish.
Identification: Size medium to large; bill casqued (no other red-billed hornbills have casque); mainly sooty black; belly and tips of outer rectrices white; head

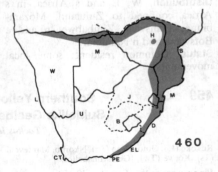

460

greyish, streaked white on nape. *Immature*: Lacks casque, bill yellow; no white on outer rectrices; eye grey.

Voice: High-pitched rapid ploverlike *pi-pi-pi-pi-pi*; short sharp whistled *pi-eee* with head thrown back.

Distribution: S Africa to ne Africa; in s Africa confined to extreme E, NE and N.
Status: Common resident; some local movements.
Habitat: Dense dry thorn thicket in lowland savanna, dense woodland, forest edge.
Habits: Usually in groups of 2–5 birds; rarely in flocks of up to 50. Flight slow but agile with pronounced dip after every few wingbeats; twists or tumbles just before alighting. Forages mainly in trees; hawks

insects in flight; nibbles food with billtip before swallowing. Hops on ground. Roosts communally on slender branches exposed from above. Pairs probably mate for life.
Food: Mainly fruit; also insects, diplopods, chameleons, small birds, seeds.
Breeding: *Season*: October to January in Zimbabwe; October-November in S Africa. *Nest*: Hole in tree or rock face; 2–14 m above ground; entrance sealed to form vertical slit. *Clutch*: (13) 2–3,5–5 eggs. *Eggs*: White; measure (18) 40,2 × 27,2 (37,1–42,4 × 26–28,4). *Incubation*: 25–30 days by ♀ only. *Nestling*: 50–53 days; nestlings remain 23–34 days after ♀ leaves nest, plastering entrance again unaided; young remain in parental territory for 6–8 months.

Ref. Ranger, G. 1949. *Ostrich* 20:54–65; 152–167; 1950. *Ostrich* 21:2–14; 1951. *Ostrich* 22:77–93; 1952. *Ostrich* 23:26–36.

461 (428) Bradfield's Hornbill Plate 41
Bradfieldse Neushoringvoël
Tockus bradfieldi

Rukoko (K), Goto, Hoto (Sh), Kôrwê (Tw), [Bradfieldtoko, Felsentoko]

Measurements: Length 50–57 cm; wing (17 ♂) 247–259–271, (12 ♀) 231–237–250; tail (17 ♂) 210–219–235, (12 ♀) 194–200–213; tarsus (11 ♂) 37–39–43, (8 ♀) 35–37–39; culmen (17 ♂) 85–99–111, (12 ♀) 80–86–91.
Bare Parts: Iris yellow; skin around eye black; bill orange to orange-red; gular skin (♂) grey, (♀) pale blue-green to yellow-green; legs and feet blackish brown to greenish slate.
Identification: Size medium to large; mainly greyish brown, feathers edged paler; no white in wings (much white in wings of Monteiro's Hornbill); belly white; bill large, orange without casque (bill smaller, dark or yellowish in Grey Hornbill); tail greyish brown, tipped white on all but central and outermost rectrices (Monteiro's Hornbill has blackish tail with outer rectrices all white); eye yellow (brown in Monteiro's Hornbill).
Voice: Plaintive whistling, almost identical to voice of Crowned Hornbill, *pi-pi-pi pi-pi-pi pi-pi-pi-peeeu*.

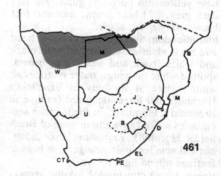

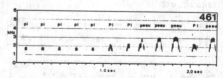

Distribution: From w Zimbabwe across n Botswana to n Namibia; also sw Zambia and s Angola.
Status: Uncommon resident; locally common in Hwange National Park at end of dry season.

Habitat: *Baikiaea* woodland on Kalahari sand, well developed mopane woodland, savanna, rocky plateau of Waterberg in Namibia (where known as *Felsentoko*).

Habits: In pairs or large nonbreeding flocks. Poorly known. Forages on ground in dry season; digs among elephant dung; hops on ground; forages arboreally in summer. Both sexes vocal at any time of day; calls with bill pointed upwards, rocking back and forth.

Food: Large insects, fruit, nuts, small reptiles.

Breeding: *Season*: September to November in Zimbabwe, November in Namibia. *Nest*: Hole in tree or rock face; rock hole may be 1 m deep; entrance plastered to form narrow vertical slit; usually about 3 m above ground. *Clutch*: (1) 3 eggs. *Eggs*: White; measure (4) 40,9 × 26,8 (39,1–43 × 26,5–27); weigh (1) 14,5 g. *Incubation*: Unrecorded; by ♀ alone. *Nestling*: Unrecorded.

462 (429)   Monteiro's Hornbill   Plate 41
Monteirose Neushoringvoël
Tockus monteiri

[Monteirotoko]

Measurements: Length 54–58 cm; wing (28 ♂) 204–215–224, (10 ♀) 181–194–203; tail (19 ♂) 219–231–245, (8 ♀) 192–207–215; tarsus (17 ♂) 44–47–50, (6 ♀) 43–44–46; culmen (23 ♂) 103–115–127, (11 ♀) 86–95–105.

Bare Parts: Iris dark brown to red-brown; skin around eye blackish; bill dark red, base yellow, tip purplish; gular skin (♂) dark grey, (♀) blue-green; legs and feet brown to purplish black.

Identification: Size medium to large; head and neck silver-grey, streaked with black and white; back and wings grey-brown, spotted white on wings; outer rectrices all white (white at tip only in Bradfield's Hornbill); bill large, deep red (orange in Bradfield's Hornbill); in flight inner secondaries white (no white in wing of Bradfield's Hornbill). *Immature*: Like adult, but bill smaller, pale orange; eye brown; feathers tipped light brown.

Voice: Harsh crowing *tok tok tok takaak, takaak*, etc.

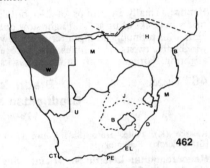

Distribution: From about Windhoek (Namibia) to Benguela (Angola), mainly in arid nw Namibia.

Status: Locally common resident.

Habitat: Arid rocky and hilly country with savanna woodland.

Habits: In pairs or nonbreeding flocks of up to 50 or more birds. Shy and wary; perches on tops of taller trees. Forages on ground, digging holes up to 30 cm across, 10 cm deep. When calling nods head with bill pointing downwards, tail slightly fanned and wrists slightly away from body, like Redbilled Hornbill. Flight direct, alternating flapping and gliding; bounds on ground (Redbilled and Yellowbilled Hornbills run on ground).

Food: Insects, rodents, fruit, shoots, pollen.

Breeding: *Season*: February to March (after good rains). *Nest*: Hole in rock face or in tree; up to 39 m above ground; entrance sealed, even when large, to form

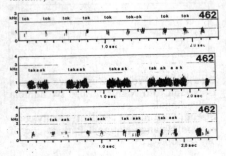

narrow vertical slit; sealing may take 14 days, using mud, faeces and nest debris; floor of nest hole lined with dry leaves, *Acacia* pods, grass, bark and snail shells brought by ♂. *Clutch*: (8) 3–4,4–5 eggs (rarely 2–6). *Eggs*: White, tinged greyish, with white pores; measure (18) 41 × 27,8 (37,2–43,7 × 26,3–29,2). *Incubation*: 24–25–27 days by ♀ only. *Nestling*: (5) 43–45–46 days.

Ref. Kemp, A.C. & Kemp, M.I. 1972. *Ann. Tvl Mus.* 27:255–268.

463 (430) Southern Ground Hornbill Plate 1
Bromvoël
Bucorvus leadbeateri

Dendera (Sh), Rhandzala (Ts), Lehututu (Tw), Intsikizi, Intsingizi (X), iNsingizi, iNgududu (Z), [Hornrabe]

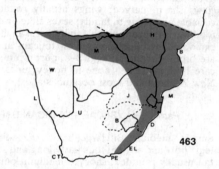

463

Measurements: Length 90–129 cm; wing (33 ♂) 469–560–618, (10 ♀) 495–528–550; tail (22 ♂) 300–345–360, (9 ♀) 290–324–340; tarsus (21 ♂) 130–143–155, (7 ♀) 130–135–140; culmen (30 ♂) 190–207–221, (10 ♀) 168–192–215. Weight (3 ♂) 3500–3671–3937 g, (2 ♀) 2230–2296 g.

Bare Parts: Iris yellow; skin of face, throat and wattles bright red, bluish on centre of throat in ♀; legs and feet black, soles whitish.

Identification: Size very large; turkeylike; mostly black; in flight primaries white; red wattles distinctive; ♀ usually has purplish blue also on face, orbital skin and wattles. *Immature*: Browner than adult; facial and gular skin light khaki; bill dark grey.

Voice: Deep booming territorial call of 4–5 syllables, falling in pitch, started by one bird, replied to by second bird in lower tone, bird A: *du, du, dududu*, bird B: *hu, hu huhu*, bird A: *du, du, dududu*, bird B: *hu, hu, huhu*, etc., repeated several times, bill pointing downwards, neck arched and inflated; soft *uhu* contact call; grating *squawk* high-intensity alarm or fear call.

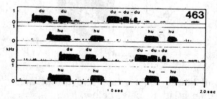

463

Distribution: Africa S of equator; in s Africa confined to E, NE and N.

Status: Locally common resident, but scarce in settled areas; some local movements. Vulnerable (RDB).

Habitat: Any woodland, savanna, open grassveld, agricultural lands.

Habits: In pairs or groups of usually not more than 8 birds (2–4 adults and 1–3 immatures); mean group size (290) 3,6 birds. Neighbouring groups chase each other in aerial pursuits. Forages on ground, walking with stiff rolling gait on terminal phalanges of toes; digs with bill for food. Vocal mostly early morning; also late afternoon. Flight powerful with deep wingbeats, little gliding. Roosts in groups at ends of branches, head tucked into shoulders, bill pointing upwards.

Food: Entirely carnivorous; reptiles (including tortoises), frogs, snails, insects; also mammals up to size of hare.

Breeding: *Season*: October to November. *Nest*: Usually hole in tree; also hole in rock face or wall of donga; height above ground (12) 4–5,7–7 m; one cliff nest 120 m above ground; lined with grass and leaves; cavity about 40 cm wide; entrance about 30 cm wide, not sealed as in other hornbills. *Clutch*: (37) 1–1,8–2 eggs.

Eggs: White, rough textured; measure (27) 73,9 × 51,3 (67,3–79 × 46,9–55,7). *Incubation*: (1) about 40 days by dominant ♀ only; ♀ fed by adult males and sometimes by immatures. *Nestling*: (1) 85–87 days; dependent on adults for food for 6–12 months.

Ref. Kemp, A.C. & Kemp, M.I. 1980. *Ann. Tvl Mus*. 32:65–100.

25. Order PICIFORMES (Seven families; four in s Africa)

Small to large. Bill variable according to family, usually strong, but slender in jacamars (Galbulidae) of S America; legs short; toes zygodactyl (1st toe absent in a few species); claws sharp, curved; wings usually rounded (rather pointed in honeyguides); tail variable according to family; sexes alike or different; mostly arboreal (a few terrestrial); food varies according to family; nest in hole in tree, bank or level ground, usually excavated by birds themselves (toucans and wrynecks use natural holes; honeyguides are brood-parasites); eggs 2–8, pure white; chick naked at hatching, altricial; parental care by both sexes (none in honeyguides). Distribution worldwide except Australia, New Zealand and most oceanic islands.

25:1. Family 59 LYBIIDAE—AFRICAN BARBETS

Small to medium. Bill large, heavy, of medium length, toothed or serrate, pointed at tip; legs short and strong; toes fairly long and strong, zygodactyl; wings short and rounded; tail usually rounded, short to medium; plumage usually with bright patches of colour; sexes mostly alike; mostly solitary; arboreal (some terrestrial); food mostly fruit; nest in self-excavated holes in trees, banks or ground, no lining; eggs 2–4, white; see also under Order Piciformes. Distribution Africa S of Sahara; about 38 species; 10 species in s Africa.

464 (431) Blackcollared Barbet Plate 42
Rooikophoutkapper
Lybius torquatus

Chikweguru (Sh), Nwagogosane (Ts), Kôpaôpê, Mmanku (Tw), Isinagogo (X), isiKhulukhulu, isiQonqotho (Z), [Halsband-Bartvogel]

Measurements: Length 19–20 cm; wing (126) 84–91–97; tail (42) 53–58,1–67,5; tarsus (22) 20–22,3–25,5; culmen (22) 21–22,7–24. Weight (17 ♂) 47,9–51,8–59,3 g, (16 ♀) 47,1–51,7–58,7 g, (96 unsexed) 44–55,2–71 g.

Bare Parts: Iris deep red or red-brown; bill black; legs and feet greenish grey to brown.

Identification: Size medium; face, throat and breast bright red (rarely yellow); hindcrown, mantle and broad band across lower breast black; back greyish olive; belly dull pale yellowish grey; wings and tail edged with yellow. *Immature*: Crown

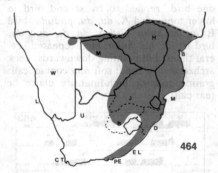

all black; red on face and throat duller than in adult; paler below.

Voice: Duet starting off with buzzing *skiz-skiz-skiz*, becoming loud ringing antipho-

nal *whoop-dudu, whoop-dudu*, first bird
(♂) giving *whoop*, second (♀) answering
dudu (or *dududu*) immediately; also written *two-puddly, two-puddly*, or *clean-
collar, clean-collar*; phrase repeated up to
about 8 times in quick succession; snarling
snaar threat note.

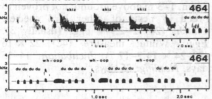

Distribution: Africa S of equator; in s
Africa mainly confined to E and NE;
apparently extending range westward to
Bloemfontein (Orange Free State) and
Rundu (Namibia).
Status: Common resident.
Habitat: Coastal bush, woodland, forest
edge, riverine forest, parks, gardens.

Habits: Solitary, in pairs or small groups.
Highly vocal, especially in summer; birds
bob up and down, opening and closing
wings as they call. Up to 11 birds may
roost together in nest hole. Flight fast,
direct, with whirring wings.
Food: Fruit (especially figs), insects.
Breeding: *Season*: August to April
(mainly September-November); may rear
4 broods a season. *Nest*: Hole excavated in
upright or sloping trunk or branch; up to
25 cm deep from entrance to floor.
Clutch: (38) 2-3,3-5 eggs. *Eggs*: White;
measure (63) 24,4 × 17,6 (21,2-27,1 ×
16,1-18,5). *Incubation*: (2) 18,5 days by
both sexes, starting with first egg. *Nestling*: 33-35 days; fed by both parents and
often also by 1-2 adult helpers; 2 pairs
may share nest hole.

Ref. Payne, R.B. & Skinner, N.J. 1970. *Ibis*
112:173-183.
Skead, C.J. 1950. *Ostrich* 21:84-96.

465 (432) Pied Barbet Plate 42
Bonthoutkapper
Tricholaema leucomelas

Sikuta (K), Serokolo (SS), Mogôrôsi (Tw),
[Rotstirn-Bartvogel]

Measurements: Length 17-18 cm; wing
(34 ♂) 78-82,8-86, (18 ♀) 75-79,7-85;
tail (8) 46-53; tarsus (8) 19-20; culmen
(8) 19-21,5. Weight (8 ♂) 33-35,6-
38,6 g, (12 ♀) 31,6-35,4-41,5 g, (196
unsexed) 23-32,4-45 g.
Bare Parts: Iris brown; bill blackish horn;
legs and feet blackish, soles white.
Identification: Size medium to smallish;
forehead bright red; hindcrown, broad
stripe through eye, broad bib from throat
to belly black; rest of underparts white;
back black streaked narrowly with yellow;
eyebrow yellow. *Immature*: Forehead
black.
Voice: Distinctive tin-trumpetlike *pehp,
pehp, pehp*, repeated up to about 12
times; Hoopoelike *toop-toop-toop-toop*,
with bill pointed downwards, throat
inflated, repeated up to 20 times in quick
succession (not in short phrases like Hoopoe), sometimes speeding up towards
end.

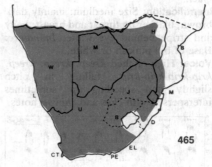

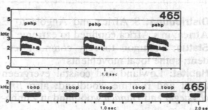

Distribution: Southern Africa and
Angola; expansion of range in s Africa
dependent on provision of nest sites and

fruits in alien plants, artificial waterholes and bush encroachment.
Status: Common resident.
Habitat: *Acacia* savanna, woodland on Kalahari sand (in Zimbabwe), riverine scrub, arid scrubland, gardens, orchards, farmyards.
Habits: Usually solitary or in pairs. Flight fast and direct, somewhat dipping. Vocal most daylight hours. Roosts in own nest holes, or in nests of Greater Striped Swallow, South African Cliff Swallow, Sociable Weaver, Cape Weaver and Masked

Weaver or in burrows of Brownthroated Martin.
Food: Fruit, nectar, seedpods of *Sophora japonica*, suet (takes fat off bones).
Breeding: *Season*: August to April. *Nest*: Hole excavated in soft or dead wood, often of willows *Salix* spp.; usually low down, 1–3 m above ground; not proven to breed in nests of other bird species. *Clutch*: (24) 2–2,9–4 eggs (usually 3). *Eggs*: White; measure (42) 22 × 16 (20–24 × 14,5–17,7). *Incubation*: 14–15 days. *Nestling*: 35 days.

466 (433) White-eared Barbet / Witoorhoutkapper
Stactolaema leucotis

Plate 42

iNtunjana (Z), [Weißohr-Bartvogel]

Measurements: Length 17,5–19 cm; wing (7) 88–92–95; tail 48–53; tarsus 20–22; culmen 19–20. Weight (2) 50 g.
Bare Parts: Iris brown; bill, legs and feet black.
Identification: Size medium; mainly dark brown, blacker on throat and breast; belly and stripe behind eye white. *Immature*: Base of bill pinkish or white.
Voice: High-pitched *kreep, kreep, kreep, krip-krip-krip-krip*, falling in pitch slightly, and speeding up; sometimes interspersed with *chip* and *chiwoo* notes.

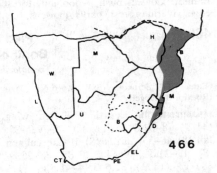

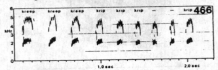

Distribution: S Africa and Angola to E Africa; in s Africa confined to extreme E.
Status: Common to very common resident; some local movements.
Habitat: Lowland and coastal evergreen forest and riverine woodland; also *Brachystegia* and *Uapaca* woodland in Zimbabwe.
Habits: In pairs or small groups. Flight straight and fast. Often frequents dead trees. Roosts communally in nest holes at

night; up to 11 birds in one hole. Members of pair bow to each other in display, giving twittering calls.
Food: Fruit (mainly figs) and insects; may hawk moths in flight.
Breeding: *Season*: October to January. *Nest*: Excavated in dead trunks and branches; entrance (1) 11,2 cm diameter; chamber 21–22 cm diameter, 70 cm deep from roof to floor. *Clutch*: (6) 3–4,3–6 eggs. *Eggs*: White; measure (16) 23 × 17,9 (22,1–24 × 17–18,4). *Incubation*: Unrecorded. *Nestling*: 39 days; fed by both parents and up to 2 adult helpers.

Ref. Oatley, T.B. 1968. *Lammergeyer* 8:7–14.
Short, L.L. & Horne, J.F.M. 1984. *Bull. Brit. Orn. Club* 104:47–53.

467 (434) Whyte's Barbet (Yellowfronted Barbet) Plate 42
Geelbleshoutkapper
Stactolaema whytii

[Spiegelbartvogel]

Measurements: Length about 19 cm; wing (60) 85,5–92,9–98, tail (47) 53,5–55,4–59; tarsus (20) 17–20,4–22,5; culmen (20) 18–19,8–21. Weight (3 ♂) 51,3–53–54,8 g, (7 ♀) 34,1–49–59,5 g, (39 unsexed) 45,3–53,5–63,6 g.

Bare Parts: Iris brown; bill, legs and feet black.

Identification: Size medium; mostly dull umber brown speckled with off-white; yellow forehead with blackish centre diagnostic; chin, stripe under eye, wingpatch and lower belly white; in flight shows white underwing and patch on wrist. *Immature*: Forehead black, speckled white; lower jaw paler than upper.

Voice: Quieter than most barbets; soft *koo* repeated at 1-second intervals for about 1 minute; also louder single *few*.

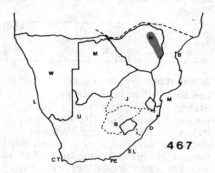

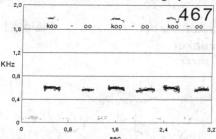

Distribution: South-central Africa; in s Africa confined to plateau and highlands of e Zimbabwe and adjacent Mozambique.

Status: Common resident in restricted range.

Habitat: *Brachystegia* woodland with fig trees; gardens in Harare; edges of dry forest and woodland in Zimbabwe highlands.

Habits: In pairs or small groups of up to 5 birds, often in tops of dead trees. Roosts communally in nest hole at night.

Food: Fruit (especially figs); young fed on insects.

Breeding: *Season*: September to January (mainly September-October). *Nest*: Hole excavated in dead trunk or branch; 3–6 m above ground. *Clutch*: 3–6 eggs (usually 4). *Eggs*: White; measure (10) 23,9 × 18,3 (22,9–25 × 17,5–19). *Incubation*: Unrecorded. *Nestling*: About 49 days recorded (probably only about 40 days).

468 (435) Green Barbet (Woodwards' Barbet) Plate 42
Groenhoutkapper
Stactolaema olivacea

[Olivbartvogel]

Measurements: Length 16–18 cm; wing (4) 86–89–91; tail (4) 49–50,5–53; tarsus (4) 23–23,5–24; culmen (3) 18–19,7–21.

Bare Parts: Iris dark hazel brown; bill, legs and feet black.

Identification: Size smallish to medium; mainly dull olive green, blackish brown on crown, paler below; eyebrow and ear coverts tinged yellow; underwing greenish or creamy white.

Voice: Monotonous piping *chop, chop,*

403

chop, repeated 1–3 seconds up to 22 times, sometimes in antiphonal duet; double *quop-quop*, second note shorter; high-pitched twittering between members of pair.

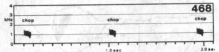

Distribution: Ngoye Forest, Zululand, and Rondo Plateau, Tanzania.

Status: Fairly common resident in restricted range. Rare (RDB).

Habitat: Canopy of evergreen forest.

Habits: Usually singly or in pairs; sometimes in groups at fruiting trees. Hard to see, but easily located by call; usually perches high in forest canopy. Flight swift and direct. Adults call to each other frequently. May roost communally in groups of up to 6 birds.

Food: Fruit (e.g. *Flagellaria guineenensis*, *Ficus*, *Cryptocarya*, *Macaranga*, *Syzigium*, *Schefflera*, *Canthium*, *Tarenna*), insects (moths, cockroaches), slugs.

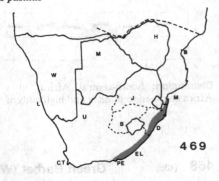

Breeding: *Season*: November to January. *Nest*: Hole excavated by both sexes in dead trunk or branch, 7–10 m above ground; entrance about 5 cm diameter, depth about 23 cm from roof to floor. *Clutch*: 4–5 eggs. *Eggs*: White; no authentic measurements available. *Incubation*: Unrecorded. *Nestling*: Unrecorded; makes continuous whirring noise in nest, audible from 25 m.

Ref. Holliday, C.S. & Tait, I.C. 1953. *Ostrich* 24:115–117.

469 (436) Redfronted Tinker Barbet Plate 42
Rooiblestinker
Pogoniulus pusillus

Unoqandilanga (X), isiKhuhlukhuhlu, uNogandi-langa, iPhengempe (Z), [Feuerstirn-Bartvogel]

Measurements: Length about 12 cm; wing (18) 58–59–62; tail 33–36; tarsus 14–16,5; culmen 12–13,5. Weight (1) 10 g.

Bare Parts: Iris dark brown; bill black; legs and feet greenish grey.

Identification: Size small; forehead red (orange or yellow in Yellowfronted Tinker Barbet); above black, boldly streaked pale yellow; face boldly striped black and white; golden patch on wing diagnostic (Yellowfronted Tinker Barbet has pale narrow wingbars only); below pale greenish yellow. *Immature*: Forehead black.

Voice: Monotonous clinking like hammer on small anvil, about 120–130 notes/minute (Yellowfronted Tinker Barbet has lower-pitched, somewhat slower series of notes); up to 355 notes consecutively.

Distribution: E Cape to Zululand, Swaziland and se Transvaal; separate population in ne Africa.

Status: Common resident.

Habitat: Coastal forest, riverine woodland, evergreen mistbelt forest, wooded kloofs and gorges; occasionally dense thornveld.

Habits: Usually solitary. Perches high in tree while calling most of day, including hot midday hours; more often heard than seen. Jerks head while searching vegetation thoroughly for food; often darts after insects and gleans foliage rather like white-eye.

Food: Fruit (including mistletoes), insects.

Breeding: *Season*: October to December. *Nest*: Hole excavated in dead trunk or underside of branch; sometimes low down; entrance about 2 cm diameter. *Clutch*: (9) 2–2,8–4 eggs (usually 3). *Eggs*: White; measure (7) 19 × 14 (18,5–19,7 × 13,7–14,4). *Incubation*: Unrecorded. *Nestling*: Unrecorded.

470 (437) Yellowfronted Tinker Barbet Plate 42
Geelblestinker
Pogoniulus chrysoconus

Sikuta (K), [Gelbstirn-Bartvogel]

Measurements: Length about 12 cm; wing (28 ♂) 55,5–61,3–65,5, (24 ♀) 56,5–61,2–64,5; tail (28 ♂) 28–32,5–35, (24 ♀) 29–32,2–35; tarsus (26) 12–15; culmen (28 ♂) 12,5–13,6–14,5, (24 ♀) 13–13,5–14,5. Weight (4 ♂) 11,3–12,7–14,2 g, (2 ♀) 11,4–12,3 g, (21 unsexed) 10,6–13,8–16,8 g.

Bare Parts: Iris dark brown; bill black; legs and feet brown.

Identification: Very similar to Redfronted Tinker Barbet, but forehead yellow to deep orange (not red); no golden patch on wing; paler below than Redfronted Tinker Barbet; inhabits more open woodland types than Redfronted Tinker Barbet. *Immature*: Forecrown black.

Voice: Monotonous *tink, tink, tink*, about 100–110 notes/minute (somewhat deeper-toned and slower than call of Redfronted Tinker Barbet); also high-pitched musical trill *trroo, trroo, trroo*; aggressive *kss kss*.

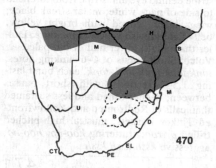

470

Distribution: Africa S of Sahara; in s Africa from Transvaal to Mozambique, Zimbabwe, n Botswana and n Namibia.

Status: Common resident.

Habitat: Woodland, especially *Brachy-*stegia and other broad-leaved savannas.

Habits: Usually solitary. Perches high in tree while calling, even during midday. Forages like warbler in vegetation, actively darting at insects and gleaning from foliage; also creeps up branches and trunks of trees like woodpecker; often joins bird parties.

Food: Fruit (especially of mistletoes), insects.

Breeding: *Season*: July to May (mainly September to December) in Zimbabwe; mainly October to December elsewhere. *Nest*: Hole excavated in dead trunk or underside of sloping branch of tree; entrance about 2 cm diameter. *Clutch*: 2–3 eggs. *Eggs*: White; measure (9) 18,5 × 14,8 (17,5–19,8 × 13,8–16,1). *Incubation*: Unrecorded. *Nestling*: Unrecorded; fed on fruit and insects by both parents.

405

471 (438)   **Goldenrumped Tinker Barbet**   **Plate 42**
Swartblestinker
Pogoniulus bilineatus

[Goldbürzel-Bartvogel]

Measurements: Length about 12 cm; wing (78) 55–57,5–60,5; tail (23) 29–31–33; tarsus (20) 14,5–16,5–19; culmen (21) 11–12,9–15. Weight (7 ♂) 11,8–13,3–15 g, (3 ♀) 13,8–15,2–16,6 g, (95 unsexed) 11–14,7–18,6 g.

Bare Parts: Iris brown; bill black; legs and feet greyish.

Identification: Size small; crown and upper back solid black (crown and back streaked with yellow in Redfronted and Yellowfronted Tinker Barbets); throat, stripe behind eye and stripe from forehead to side of neck white; malar streak black; wings black, edged with bright yellow; belly light greyish yellow. *Immature*: Duller than adult; lower half of bill pale.

Voice: Short bursts of 4–6 clinking notes, *tonk-tonk-tonk-tonk-tonk*, each burst lasting 1,5–2 seconds, with short pauses between; deeper-toned and less sustained than calls of Redfronted and Yellowfronted Tinker Barbets; musical high-pitched trilled *prrroo*; stuttering *hoo-ho, hoo-ho*; aggressive *kssh kssh kssh*.

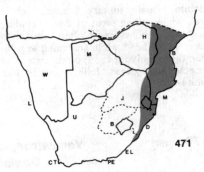

Distribution: Africa S of Sahara; in s Africa confined to extreme E from Natal northwards; uncommonly to Nelspruit and extreme s Kruger National Park.

Status: Common resident.

Habitat: Coastal forest, lowland evergreen forest; in Zimbabwe sometimes also montane evergreen forest.

Habits: Usually solitary or in pairs. Tends to perch in middle or upper strata of forest; often fairly tame. Forages actively, often darting after insects. Flight straight with whirring wings. Calls from treetops throughout daylight hours, mainly October to April.

Food: Fruit (including those of mistletoes; seeds regurgitated), insects.

Breeding: *Season*: September to March. *Nest*: Hole excavated in dead trunk or underside of sloping branch; entrance hole about 2,3 cm diameter, chamber 4–5 cm diameter; depth from roof to floor about 20–35 cm; excavated in as little as 10 days; usually low down. *Clutch*: (6) 2–3,3–5 eggs. *Eggs*: White; measure (6) 19,2 × 14,1 (17,8–19,8 × 13,7–14,7). *Incubation*: 12 days by both sexes. *Nestling*: 20 days; fed on insects and fruit by both parents.

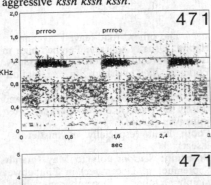

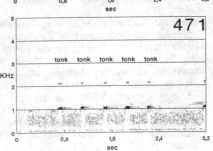

472 (438X)　　Green Tinker Barbet　　Plate 42
Groentinker
Pogoniulus simplex

[Schlichtbartvogel]

Measurements: Length about 12 cm; wing (6 ♂) 52–53,5–54,5, (5 ♀) 51,5–52,1–53.

Bare Parts: Iris brown; bill, legs and feet black.

Identification: Size small; above dull olive green; rump bright yellow; wing feathers edged yellow; below olive grey. *Immature*: More olive above and greyer below than adult.

Voice: About 6 staccato notes, *pop-op-op-op-op-op*, sometimes becoming trill; trill may be given alone.

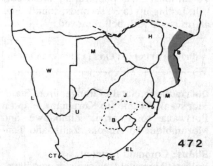

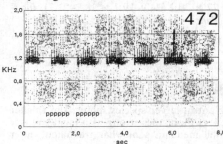

Distribution: E Africa to Mozambique, possibly to Limpopo River; in s Africa recorded only from Funhalouro, Sul do Save, Mozambique.

Status: Uncertain; possibly rare resident.

Habitat: Evergreen coastal forest.

Habits: Usually solitary. Keeps to treetops; highly vocal. Poorly known.

Food: Probably mainly fruit.

Breeding: Undescribed.

473 (439)　　Crested Barbet　　Plate 42
Kuifkophoutkapper
Trachyphonus vaillantii

Mbangura (K), Chizuvaguru (Sh), Xitsemahangoni (Ts), Kôpaôpê (Tw), iMvunduna (Z), [Haubenbartvogel]

Measurements: Length 23–24 cm; wing (40 ♂) 97–101,5–108, (10 ♀) 95–101,4–107; tail (38 ♂) 79–85,7–93, (10 ♀) 80,5–85,5–94; tarsus (43) 24–28; culmen (43) 21–26. Weight (1 ♂) 74,5 g, (1 ♀) 62,8 g, (76 unsexed) 58–71–83 g.

Bare Parts: Iris red-brown; bill yellow-green to greenish grey, tip dusky; legs and feet greenish grey.

Identification: Size medium to largish; head crested; back, tail and broad breast-band black, spotted and scalloped with white; head and face yellow, scaled with red; crest and nape black; rump red; belly yellow, broadly streaked red; bill pale; ♀

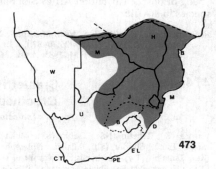

has less red in plumage than ♂, especially on head and belly where more black intrudes into yellow parts. *Immature*: Duller than adult; lacks white spots in collar;

bill yellow with dusky central band; iris grey-brown; forehead and cheeks redder than in adult.

Voice: Sustained penetrating unmusical trill, lasting up to 30 seconds; sounds like alarm clock with bell removed.

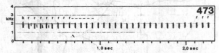

Distribution: Natal, Orange Free State, Transvaal, n Cape (to Kuruman), e and n Botswana to Caprivi, Zimbabwe and Mozambique to Angola, Zaire and Tanzania.

Status: Common resident.

Habitat: Thornveld, thickets in woodland, riverine bushveld, exotic plantations, parks, gardens.

Habits: Usually solitary or in pairs. Vocal throughout year, but especially in early summer. May roost in disused nests of Greater Striped Swallow and White-browed Sparrowweaver, but usually in own nest hole. Tame; comes to feeding trays and nestboxes in gardens. Forages in bushes and trees, and on ground; hops on ground.

Food: Insects (especially termites), worms, fruit, snails, birds' eggs.

Breeding: *Season*: All months except May and June in Zimbabwe, August to February elsewhere; may rear up to 4 broods per season. *Nest*: Hole excavated in dead trunk, stout branch, or length of *Agave* stem tied to tree or post; also uses nestboxes; rarely also natural hole in tree. *Clutch*: (17) 2-2,9-4 eggs (usually 3, rarely 5). *Eggs*: White; measure (44) 27 × 20,2 (24,9-29,1 × 18,1-21,7). *Incubation*: 17 days. *Nestling*: 27-30 days.

Ref. Prozesky, O.P.M. 1966. *Ostrich Suppl.* 6:171-182.

25:2. Family 60 INDICATORIDAE—HONEYGUIDES

Small. Bill short, stout or slender, rather blunt in larger species, pointed in smaller species; nostrils open as short tubes on bill; legs short; toes strong with long, strongly hooked claws; wings longish and pointed; tail medium, somewhat graduated, outer rectrices white with dark tips (all white in young birds); plumage dull brown, grey or olive, paler ventrally; sexes alike, except in Greater Honeyguide, females usually smaller than males; solitary; arboreal; Greater Honeyguide leads man to bees' nests, hence family name; food insects, beeswax; special gut bacteria may aid in wax digestion; brood-parasitic on hole-nesting birds or small passerines; eggs usually white; chick naked when hatched, equipped with hooks at tips of both jaws in all species for killing young of host. Distribution Africa S of Sahara, tropical Asia to Borneo; 14 species; six species in s Africa.

Ref. Friedmann, H. 1955. *U.S. Natn. Mus. Bull.* 208: 1-292.
Ranger, G.A. 1955. *Ostrich* 26:70-87.
Short, L.L. & Horne, J.F.M. 1985. *Amer. Mus. Novit.* 2825:1-46.

---

474 (440) **Greater Honeyguide** **Plate 36**
Grootheuningwyser
Indicator indicator

Kasoro (K), Tshetlo (NS), Tsehlo (SS), Mukaranga, Tsoro, Shezhu (Sh), Hlalala, Nhlampfu (Ts), Tshetlho (Tw), Intakobusi, Intaka Yenyosi (X), uNomtsheketshe, iNhlavebizelayo, iNgede (Z), [Großer Honiganzeiger, Schwarzkehl-Honiganzeiger]

Measurements: Length 19-20 cm; wing (25 ♂) 108-112-119, (18 ♀) 103-107-111; tail (43) 62-79; tarsus (43) 14-17; culmen (43) 12-16. Weight (1 ♀) 49 g, (17 unsexed) 28-46,7-62 g.

Bare Parts: Iris brown; bill (♂) light pink, (♀) black to horn; legs and feet grey to bluish green.

Identification: About size of Blackeyed or Redeyed Bulbul. *Male*: Above dark grey; below light grey; large white ear patch and black throat diagnostic; wrist patch golden yellow; upperwing coverts streaked whitish; outer rectrices white (conspicuous in flight). *Female*: Similar to ♂, but lacks white earpatch and black throat; larger than Lesser Honeyguide and greyer above (Lesser Honeyguide strongly tinged olive yellow on back and wings; lacks yellow wrist patch and white upperwing streaks). *Immature*: Browner than adults; otherwise similar to ♀, but with yellow ochre wash from chin to breast; yellow underparts retained for about 6 months.

Voice: ♂ has far-carrying repeated 2-note song phrase, *WHIT-purr, WHIT-purr, WHIT-purr*, higher-pitched and accented on first note; also written *VIC-torr*; guiding call is rattling *chitik-chitik-chitik* like matchbox shaken lengthwise; in display flight wings make resonant *voova-voova-voova* 3–4 times in quick succession as bird flies in circle of about 100-m diameter, each double note accompanying flight undulation; also swoops upward with spread tail making vibrating *bvooomm*.

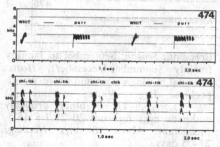

Distribution: Africa S of Sahara; in s Africa absent from dry W.
Status: Widespread but sparse resident.
Habitat: Woodland, savanna, forest edge, exotic plantations, orchards, farmyards.
Habits: Usually solitary. ♂ has fixed call-sites, usually high in tall tree, used year after year; such sites known to be used for over 20 years; when calling, ♂ stretches head upwards at angle, holds wrists slightly out, and jerks tail at each *WHIT* note. Males, females and immatures guide man to bees' nests, bobbing

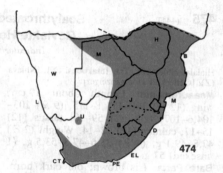

body, flirting tail, then flying in undulating flight to next perch where calling repeated, until hive reached; guiding attempts may last an hour or more; no satisfactory evidence for guiding of any other mammals. Silent and unobtrusive, except when singing, displaying or guiding. May hawk insects in flight from perch; sometimes forages in mixed bird parties.
Food: Insects (including adult and larval bees), beeswax; rarely eggs of other birds.
Breeding: *Season*: September to January (mainly September-October). *Hosts*: Only hole-nesting species; *Halcyon* kingfishers, Pygmy Kingfisher, Little, Whitefronted, Carmine, Olive, Böhm's and Swallowtailed Bee-eaters, Hoopoe, Redbilled and Scimitarbilled Wood-hoopoes, Blackcollared, Pied and Crested Barbets, Redthroated Wryneck, Goldentailed and Knysna Woodpeckers, Whitethroated, Redbreasted and Greater Striped Swallows, Banded Martin, Southern Black Tit, Anteating Chat, Glossy and Pied Starlings, Scarletchested Sunbird, Greyheaded and Yellowthroated Sparrows; possibly also Brownthroated Martin. *Clutch*: 4–8 eggs. *Eggs*: White; usually only 1 egg per host nest, rarely 2; ♀ often pecks 1 or more host eggs when laying; measure (12) 24,4 × 18,9 (21,7–26 × 17,4–20). *Incubation*: Unrecorded. *Nestling*: About 30 days; nestling kills host young with bill hooks which are lost at about 14 days; fed by host for up to 10 days after leaving nest.

475 (441)   Scalythroated Honeyguide   Plate 36
Gevlekte Heuningwyser
Indicator variegatus

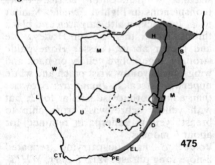

Hlalala, Nhlampfu (Ts), Intakobusi (X), iNhlava (Z), [Gefleckter Honiganzeiger]

Measurements: Length about 19 cm; wing (12 ♂) 108–111,1–115, (9 ♀) 103–104,6–107; tail (12) 59–70; tarsus (12) 15–17; culmen (12) 12–14. Weight (2 ♂) 47,8–49,1 g, (4 ♀) 35,6–47,3–53,5 g, (1 unsexed) 57 g.

Bare Parts: Iris brown; bill dark horn, shading to pink at base; legs and feet greenish grey.

Identification: Slightly smaller than Greater Honeyguide (between size of sparrow and bulbul); forecrown and breast grey, scaled with greenish or buffy white (diagnostic); back and wings olive greyish brown; belly buffy white; tail blackish, outer rectrices white (conspicuous in flight). *Immature:* Freckled black on breast.

Voice: Rolling froglike *prrrrrrrr*, lasting 3–4 seconds, rising in pitch towards end; call repeated about every 1–1,5 minutes; also high-pitched whistled *foyt-foyt-foyt*.

less for long periods on shady branch; easily overlooked unless calling; call sites used year after year. Guides man to bees' nests, but less often than does Greater Honeyguide. Forages for food on bark of trees; also hawks insects in flight. Flight dipping, like that of small woodpecker.

Food: Insects (including adult and larval bees), beeswax, honey, figs, seeds.

Distribution: S Africa to Ethiopia and Sudan; in s Africa confined to SE and E.

Status: Fairly common to uncommon local resident.

Habitat: Canopy of evergreen and taller riverine forest, bushveld, thickly wooded valleys, exotic plantations.

Habits: Usually solitary. Perches motion-

Breeding: *Season*: September to January (mainly September-December). *Hosts*: Cardinal, Goldentailed and Olive Woodpeckers. *Eggs*: White; measure (2) 20,7–21 × 16,5–17; 2 other probably authentic eggs measure 20–21,7 × 16,5. *Incubation*: About 18 days. *Nestling*: 27–35 days.

476 (442)   Lesser Honeyguide   Plate 36
Kleinheuningwyser
Indicator minor

Kasoro (K), Hlalala, Nhlampfu (Ts), Intakobusi (X), iNhlava (Z), [Kleiner Honiganzeiger]

Measurements: Length 15–16 cm; wing (82 ♂) 86–93–100, (72 ♀) 84–87,2–90,2; tail (10 ♂) 58,5–61,4–66, (12 ♀) 52,5–54,7–58,5; tarsus (34) 12–15–18; culmen (10 ♂) 12–12,7–14, (12 ♀) 11–11,7–12,5. Weight (9 ♂) 24,9–27,8–30,5 g, (6 ♀)

23,1–26,1–28,2 g, (153 unsexed) 21–28,2–39 g.

Bare Parts: Iris dark brown; bill blackish horn, base pinkish; legs and feet olive grey.

Identification: Size smallish (smaller than Greater and Scalythroated Honeyguides); head and breast grey, shading to white on belly; back olive grey with gold wash; tail dark, outer rectrices white (conspicuous in flight); malar stripe blackish. *Immature*: Darker below than adult; tail feathers pointed, outermost more extensively white.

Voice: Series of 10–30 far-carrying piping unmusical *ki-link ki-link ki-link* notes; pauses about half minute between series; each series starts with sharp *tweet* or *kew* note; display flight in undulating circles accompanied by single *whurrr*, probably made by tail feathers.

Distribution: Africa S of Sahara; in s Africa absent from most of dry W.
Status: Locally common resident.
Habitat: Most woodland, including parks and gardens; reedbeds in dry season during moult; absent from dry savanna and forest.
Habits: Usually solitary. Easily overlooked unless calling; perches motionless for long periods in hunched posture; call site used repeatedly. Forages by investigating holes and crevices in trees; hawks insects in flight. May forage or sing from isolated tree. Does not guide to bees' nests. Flight dipping or direct without dips.

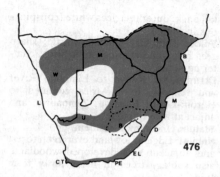

Food: Insects (including bees and their larvae), spiders, honey, *Acacia* gum, beeswax.

Breeding: *Season*: September to January (mainly October-November). *Hosts*: Blackcollared, Pied, White-eared and Crested Barbets; also reported to parasitize Goldentailed Woodpecker, Little Beeeater, Redbilled Woodhoopoe, Striped Kingfisher, Redthroated Wryneck, Whitethroated Swallow, Glossy and Plumcoloured Starlings, Cape Rock Thrush, Yellowthroated Sparrow, but these records require confirmation; ♀ may remove one host egg when laying her own. *Eggs*: White, glossy; measure (25) 21,7 × 17,1 (20,1–24 × 16,1–19,6). *Incubation*: Between 12 and 17 days. *Nestling*: About 38 days; nestling kills young of host with bill hooks.

477 (442X)

Eastern Honeyguide
Oostelike Heuningwyser
Indicator meliphilus

Plate 36

[Olivmantel-Honiganzeiger]

Measurements: Length about 13 cm; wing (4 ♂) 73–79–86, (3 ♀) 76–78–81; tail (4 ♂) 48–51,5–56, (3 ♀) 46–46,7–48; tarsus (4 ♂) 12–12,3–12,5, (3 ♀) 12–12,5–13; culmen (4 ♂) 7,5–8–9, (3 ♀) 8,5–8,8–9.
Bare Parts: Iris brown; bill blackish; legs and feet grey.
Identification: Size small; very similar to Lesser Honeyguide, but smaller and lacks malar stripe; grey head conspicuous; bill short and stubby; breast pale buffy white, faintly streaked olive grey;

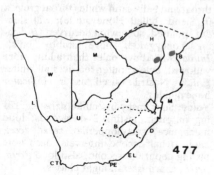

tail dark, outer rectrices white (conspicuous in flight).

Voice: Thin high-pitched whistle; sharp *zeet zeet* while chasing other birds; chattering notes.

Distribution: Kenya to Limpopo River and Angola; in s Africa confined to Haroni-Lusitu Junction, Zimbabwe, and adjacent Mozambique.

Status: Uncommon resident.

Habitat: Edge of lowland evergreen forest and adjacent well developed woodland; also solitary trees in fields away from forest.

Habits: Usually solitary. Easily over-

looked. Chases other small birds, following closely bill-to-tail while calling *zeet zeet*; spreads tail and swerves about in flight with great dexterity. Hawks insects in flight up to about 7 m from tree, often returning to same perch; moves head from side to side before hawking; gleans from bark, flowers and leaves. Poorly known. Does not guide to bees' nests.

Food: Insects, beeswax.

Breeding: *Season:* One record for January in Zimbabwe. *Hosts:* Only White-eared Barbet recorded so far. *Eggs:* White; measure (1) 21,4 × 17,4. *Incubation:* Unrecorded. *Nestling:* Unrecorded.

478 (443)   Sharpbilled Honeyguide   Plate 36
Skerpbekheuningvoël
Prodotiscus regulus

Kasoro (K), [Schmalschnabel-Honiganzeiger]

Measurements: Length 13–14 cm; wing (5 ♂) 79–81–84, (4 ♀) 71–76–82, (63 unsexed) 74–79–84; tail (56) 44–49,1–54; tarsus (9) 10–12; culmen (56) 11–12,4–14. Weight (1 ♂) 17,6 g, (1 ♀) 13,2 g, (20 unsexed) 12–14,1–16 g.

Bare Parts: Iris dark brown; bill black; legs and feet greyish.

Identification: Size small; warblerlike in general appearance, but white outer rectrices diagnostic (tipped brown in adult, all white in immature), conspicuous in flight only; tail looks white from below; above dull brownish; tuft of white feathers on either side of rump; below pale grey; throat and belly satin white (throat greyish in Slenderbilled Honeyguide); bill slender, pointed, somewhat decurved (*Indicator* honeyguides have stubby bills). *Immature:* Above paler than adult; more yellowish below; outer rectrices all white. *Chick:* Nostril raised as in *Indicator* honeyguides.

Voice: Song raspy insectlike *dzreeeee*, rising in pitch, lasting 3–4 seconds; loud mechanical grasshopperlike *zeeet, zeeet, zeeet* at half-second intervals, each note lasting about 0,5 second; also loud *prrrp, prrrp*; sharp *tseet* in flight chases.

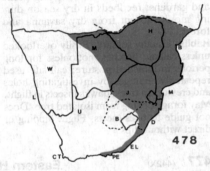

Distribution: S Africa to Ethiopia, Sudan and Nigeria; in s Africa absent from most of highveld and dry W.

Status: Uncommon local resident or possibly short-distance migrant.

Habitat: Woodland, exotic plantations, thornveld, coastal forest.

Habits: Solitary or in groups of 2–3 birds in one bush or tree. Forages by hawking insects in flight from perch, like flycatcher,

but seldom sits for long in one place; also gleans from branches, trunks and leaves down to about 30 cm above ground, sometimes in company with white-eyes and tits. Raises wings with bent wrist; bobs head sideways. Flight dipping, like tiny woodpecker, usually with spread tail; in display 2 birds chase each other in flight for up to 500 m with explosive *tseet* calls.
Food: Insects; possibly wax from scale-insects.
Breeding: *Season*: September to January.

Hosts: Bleating Warbler, Lazy Cisticola, Neddicky and Spotted Prinia; possibly also Cape White-eye and Yellowthroated Sparrow but these records require confirmation. *Eggs*: 2 white eggs from nest of Cape White-eye (Transvaal Museum) possibly of this species measure 15,3 × 12,5 and 15,7 × 12,5; host's eggs measure 17,5 × 12,4 and 17,6 × 12,6. *Incubation*: Unrecorded. *Nestling*: About 17–21 days.

Ref. Maclean, G.L. 1971. *Ostrich* 42:75–77.

479 (444) Slenderbilled Honeyguide Plate 36
Dunbekheuningvoël
Prodotiscus zambesiae

Kasoro (K), [Zwerghoniganzeiger]
Measurements: Length about 12 cm; wing 71–75; tail 47–50; tarsus 11,5; culmen 8,2–9. Weight (1 ♀) 10,5 g.
Bare Parts: Iris dark brown; bill blackish; gape greenish yellow; legs dark greenish grey.
Identification: Size small; warblerlike, but white outer rectrices diagnostic; above brownish olive green; below sooty grey, washed olive green; throat greyish (white in Sharpbilled Honeyguide); earpatch and belly whitish. *Immature*: Less greenish than adult; throat finely streaked. *Chick*: Naked at hatching, orange; heelpads and bill hooks present; nostrils raised as in *Indicator* honeyguides.
Voice: Harsh *skeee-aa* repeated during flight display; also sibilant metallic *tsit*; song *pee-ee-it*.
Distribution: Limpopo River to E Africa and Angola; in s Africa confined to Mozambique, Zimbabwe to Caprivi and Okavango.
Status: Sparse to fairly common resident; local movements in winter.
Habitat: Canopy of *Brachystegia* and *Baikiaea* woodland on broken rocky slopes with little ground cover; also gardens, cultivated lands; rarely in riverine forest; mostly above 1000 m in Zimbabwe.
Habits: Usually solitary or in pairs; in winter joins bird parties with white-eyes, warblers, ploceids and cuckooshrikes. Forages by settling on branch, peering about, pecking at prey, then hopping to new perch; gleans from bark, leaves,

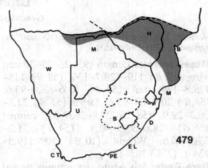

479

mosses and lichens; hawks insects in flight, fluttering and zigzagging; may forage as low as 2 m above ground. Bobs head up, down or sideways. Flight display direct, undulating, high above canopy; each dip sometimes accompanied by tail fanning; calls *skeee-aa* while flying. 2–4 birds sometimes chase each other in swerving flight, calling *tsit*; chasing bird raises wings vertically and fans tail in short glide.
Food: Insects (mainly scale-insects), spiders.
Breeding: *Season*: August to October in Zimbabwe. *Host*: Only Yellow White-eye in Zimbabwe. *Eggs*: White or turquoise blue, almost always matching those of host; honeyguide removes host egg when laying; measure about 15 × 12. *Incubation*: 13 days or less. *Nestling*: About 22 days; kills host young with bill hooks within 3 days of hatching; hooks lost by 7 days; sometimes 2 honeyguide chicks in host nest.

Ref. Vernon, C.J. 1987. *Honeyguide* 33:6–12.

25:3. Family 61 PICIDAE—WOODPECKERS

Small to large. Bill strong, straight, chisel-like; neck longish; legs short; toes zygodactyl, 1st toe sometimes absent; claws strong, hooked and pointed; wings rounded, flight strong and characteristically dipping; tail medium and stiff to act as support while perched vertically on trunk of tree; plumage variable, often barred, spotted or pied with red on head (especially in males); sexes usually different; usually solitary; mostly arboreal (a few terrestrial); food insects, fruit, nuts, sap of trees; nest in unlined self-excavated hole in tree or bank; eggs 2–8, pure white; other features as for Order Piciformes. Distribution worldwide except Madagascar, Australasia and most oceanic islands; about 210 species; nine species in s Africa.

Ref. Short, L.L. 1971. *Ostrich* 42:89–98; 1982. *Woodpeckers of the world*. Greenville, Del.: Delaware Museum of Natural History, Monograph Series No. 4.

480 (445) Ground Woodpecker Plate 43
Grondspeg
Geocolaptes olivaceus

Mohetle, Khatajoe (SS), Ungximde (X), umNqa-ngqandolo (Z), [Erdspecht]

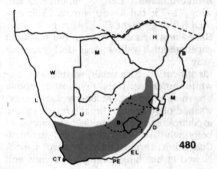

Measurements: Length (93) 23–25–30 cm; wing (57 ♂) 119–128,7–136, (58 ♀) 118–128,8–139; tail (56 ♂) 63,6–83,4–93,6, (58 ♀) 70,9–83–93,6; tarsus (57 ♂) 22,1–26,3–29,9, (58 ♀) 20,8–26,6–37; culmen (56 ♂) 28,6–35,9–40,8, (54 ♀) 31,3–35,5–40,6. Weight (10 ♂) 109–119,5–134 g, (2 ♀) 105–125 g.

Bare Parts: Iris white, sometimes tinged red or yellow around rim; bill blackish slate; legs and feet greenish grey to black.

Identification: Fairly large (about size of starling); head grey; back olive, spotted pale yellow on wings; rump bright red (conspicuous in flight); throat white; breast and belly pinkish red, darker in centre; tail olive, barred yellow; malar stripe flecked red in ♂. *Immature*: Paler than adult; below speckled, not as intensely pink as in adult.

Voice: Loud harsh rolling scream, *peeaaarrgh*, *peer*, or *peeo* alarm call; 2-note "saw-sharpening" *chik-ree, chik-ree* contact call; *chew-kee* call with head-swinging.

Distribution: Namaqualand, s and e Cape to Transvaal.

Status: Locally common resident.

Habitat: Mountains, rocky hillsides, dongas.

Habits: Usually in pairs or small groups of up to 6 birds. Perches on rocks where well camouflaged, often sidling around to far side and peering over top at intruder; may perch on fence post or sturdy bush. Flight undulating. Forages for about 30% of daytime, mainly on ground, pecking, digging and flicking with bill; probes with long sticky tongue into cracks, between stones or into dead wood; hops on ground and rocks; often jumps onto rock to look around while feeding.

Food: About 95% ants, including their larvae, pupae and eggs.

Breeding: *Season*: August to November (mainly October). *Nest*: Burrow in vertical wall of donga, river bank or cutting; also in compact earth on top of large rock or in rock face; tunnel 50–100 cm long,

7,5–8,4 cm diameter; terminal chamber about 15 cm diameter. *Clutch*: (18) 2–2,8–4 eggs (usually 3). *Eggs*: Glossy white; measure (60) 27,9 × 21,8 (24,4–30,2 × 20,2–22,9). *Incubation*: Unrecorded. *Nestling*: Unrecorded.

481 (446) Bennett's Woodpecker · Bennettse Speg
Plate 43
Campethera bennettii

Mbangura (K), Hohodza (Sh), Gogosana, Ngongondzwani (Ts), Kôkômere, Phaphadikôta (Tw), [Bennettspecht]

Measurements: Length 22–24 cm; wing (55 ♂) 116–123,6–131, (48 ♀) 116–122,9–134; tail (55 ♂) 60–67,3–75, (48 ♀) 61–69,9–74; tarsus (17) 18–21; culmen (55 ♂) 24–28,7–32, (48 ♀) 24–28,1–31. Weight (13) 67,4–72,3–83,5 g.

Bare Parts: Iris dark red; bill slate grey to black; legs and feet greenish grey.

Identification: Size medium; see woodpecker key; birds in n Namibia (*C. b. buysi*) have plain pale yellow rump. *Male*: Whole crown and malar stripe red; back barred; breast spotted black on buffy white; throat plain white. *Female*: Throat and stripe below eye brown (diagnostic); forecrown black, spotted white; hindcrown red; back barred; breast spotted. *Immature*: Similar to adult ♀, but ♂ may have some red in crown and malar stripe; mantle spotted with white.

Voice: Single long chattering series of kingfisherlike notes, *wi-wi-wi-wi-wi*, or double repeated *wirrit-wirrit-wirrit*, often in duet, sometimes starting with *churrr*.

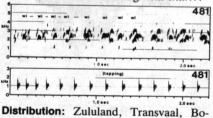

Distribution: Zululand, Transvaal, Botswana and n Namibia to Angola, s Zaire and Tanzania.

Status: Uncommon to common resident.

Habitat: Well developed woodland, bushveld.

Habits: Solitary or in pairs when breeding; otherwise sometimes in small groups. Forages about 70% of time on ground; also on branches and trunks of larger trees. Flight undulating. Often displays with wing flapping while calling.

Food: Insects (mostly ants and their eggs).

Breeding: *Season*: September to February (mainly October-November) in Transvaal and Zimbabwe. *Nest*: Hole excavated in trunk or branch; sometimes natural tree hole. *Clutch*: (14) 2–2,9–4 eggs (usually 3, sometimes 5). *Eggs*: White; measure (18) 24,4 × 18,9 (22,3–28,1 × 18–20,2). *Incubation*: Unrecorded; by both sexes. *Nestling*: Unrecorded; fed by both parents.

Ref. Irwin, M.P.S. 1978. *Honeyguide* 93:21–28.
Short, L.L. 1971. *Ostrich* 42:71–72.

482 (446X) Specklethroated Woodpecker · Tanzaniese Speg
Plate 43
Campethera scriptoricauda

[Schriftschwanzspecht]

Measurements: Length about 23 cm; wing 109–115, (7 ♂) mean 113, (11 ♀) mean 113; tail (7 ♂) mean 63, (11 ♀) mean 64; culmen (7 ♂) mean 27, (11 ♀) mean 25.

Bare Parts: Iris red; bill black, base yellowish; legs and feet olive green.

Identification: Size medium; very similar to Bennett's Woodpecker but throat speckled, not plain white; see woodpecker key. *Male*: Whole crown and malar stripe red; back barred; breast and throat spotted with black. *Female*: Forecrown spotted white on black; hindcrown red; back barred; throat and breast spotted with black; malar stripe spotted white on black.

Voice: Loud squeaky chatter, similar to call of Bennett's Woodpecker.

Distribution: Lower Zambezi River to e Tanzania.

Status: Common in restricted range; probably race of Bennett's Woodpecker.

Habitat: Open *Brachystegia* woodland with tall grass.

Habits: Poorly known. Rather quiet; unobtrusive.

Food: Insects (mainly ants and their larvae).

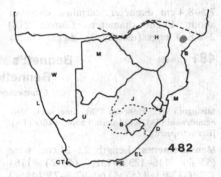

Breeding: Not recorded in s Africa. *Season*: October to November in Malawi. *Nest*: Hole excavated in dead tree, often in palm stem; cavity fairly deep, widening into slight chamber at bottom. *Clutch*: 3 eggs. *Eggs*: Glossy white; measure about 22,5 × 18,5.*Incubation*:Unrecorded.*Nestling*: Unrecorded.

483 (447) Goldentailed Woodpecker Plate 43
Goudstertspeg
Campethera abingoni

Mbangura (K), Hohodza (Sh), Gogosana, Ngongondzwani (Ts), Kôkômere, Phaphadikôta (Tw), isiQophamuthi, uSibagwebe (Z), [Goldschwanzspecht]

Measurements: Length 19–23 cm; wing (25 ♂) 110–117,5–123, (25 ♀) 110–118–124; tail (25 ♂) 59–64,2–69, (25 ♀) 61–65,9–72; tarsus (10) 17; culmen (25 ♂) 25–27–30, (25 ♀) 24–27,6–29. Weight (3 ♂) 63,2–67,4–74,5 g, (23 unsexed) 61,5–68,3–83 g.

Bare Parts: Iris red; bill slate grey, tip black; legs and feet greenish grey.

Identification: Size medium; see woodpecker key. *Male*: Forecrown mottled black and red; hindcrown and malar stripe red; back spotted and barred; breast heavily streaked (throat black and breast spotted in more westerly populations). *Female*: Forecrown spotted white on black; hindcrown red; malar stripe speckled white on black; back spotted and barred, breast streaked or spotted. *Immature*: Similar to adult ♀, but duller.

Voice: Loud wailing single *waaa*.

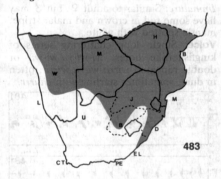

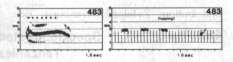

Distribution: Africa S of Sahara; in s Africa absent from most of highveld, Karoo, sw Cape and extreme arid W.

Status: Sparse, but widespread resident.

Habitat: Coastal forest, evergreen thickets, well developed woodland, riverine forest, bushveld, *Acacia* savanna.

Habits: Usually solitary or in pairs. Fairly silent, but call loud and distinctive. Forages on branches of trees, tapping for insect larvae in dead wood. Flight dipping.
Food: Insects (mainly ants and their larvae).
Breeding: *Season*: August to December

(mainly September-October). *Nest*: Hole excavated in living or dead branch. *Clutch*: (16) 2–2,9–4 eggs. *Eggs*: White; measure (20) 24,6 × 18,6 (23,2–26,4 × 17,6–19,5). *Incubation*: Unrecorded; by both sexes. *Nestling*: Unrecorded; fed by both parents.

Ref. Irwin, M.P.S. 1978. *Honeyguide* 93:21–28.

484 (448)   Knysna Woodpecker   Plate 43
Knysnaspeg
Campethera notata

Isinqolamthi (X), [Natalspecht]

Measurements: Length 20–21 cm; wing (10) 105–107–110; tail 67–75; tarsus 19–21; culmen 19–24.
Bare Parts: Iris reddish to brown; bill slate grey, tip black; legs and feet greenish grey.
Identification: Size medium; see woodpecker key. *Male*: Forecrown mottled black and red (looks pinkish); hindcrown and malar stripe red; back spotted; breast marked with heavy streaky blotches. *Female*: Forecrown spotted white on black; hindcrown red; malar stripe speckled white on black; back spotted; breast heavily marked with streaky blotches. *Immature*: Similar to adult female.
Voice: Somewhere between croak and whistle, *kra kra, kree kree kree kree, kra kra*; first 2 and last 2 notes lower-pitched than middle notes; repeated 3-syllabled lilting *wee-wi-wi*; shrill *shriek* like that of Goldentailed Woodpecker but higher-pitched.

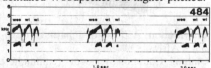

Distribution: From about Breede River

mouth in sw Cape to Oribi Gorge, Natal.
Status: Uncommon resident in restricted range.
Habitat: Coastal and riverine bush, evergreen forest, denser thornveld, *Euphorbia* scrub.
Habits: Usually solitary, in pairs or in small family groups; may join mixed bird parties. Forages mainly in middle layers of trees, on larger branches. Similar to Goldentailed Woodpecker, but poorly known.
Food: Ants, larvae of woodboring beetles.
Breeding: *Season*: August to October. *Nest*: Hole excavated in tree. *Clutch*: 2–4 eggs. *Eggs*: White; measure (7) 23,5 × 18,1 (22,7–24,5 × 17,5–18,7). *Incubation*: Unrecorded. *Nestling*: Unrecorded.

485 (449)   Little Spotted Woodpecker   Plate 43
Gevlekte Speg
Campethera cailliautii

[Tüpfelspecht]

Measurements: Length about 18 cm; wing 91–97; tail 58–66; tarsus 15–17; culmen 14–15. Weight (19) 34–41–55 g.

Bare Parts: Iris dark red to brown; bill blackish; legs and feet olive green.

Identification: Size smallish; see woodpecker key; no malar stripe in either sex.

LITTLE SPOTTED WOODPECKER

Male: Forecrown mottled black and red; hindcrown red; back and breast spotted. *Female*: Forecrown spotted white on black; hindcrown red; back and breast spotted. *Immature*: Similar to adult ♀; forehead more finely spotted; breast spots larger; somewhat barred on flanks.

Voice: High-pitched plaintive *heee* repeated 4–5 times at regular intervals.

Distribution: Limpopo River to Angola, Zaire and Uganda; in s Africa confined to e Zimbabwe and s Mozambique.

Status: Locally common resident.

Habitat: Dense *Brachystegia* and *Uapaca* woodland, edge of evergreen forest.

Habits: Solitary or in pairs. Shy; moves to off-side of tree when disturbed; easily overlooked unless calling or tapping. Forages in trees; opens seedpods for insects.

Food: Arboreal ants and termites.

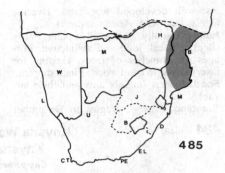

485

Breeding: *Season*: October to November. *Nest*: Hole excavated in tree. *Clutch*: 2–3 eggs. *Eggs*: White; measure (5) 23,9 × 18,2 (22,6–24,7 × 18–18,4). *Incubation*: Unrecorded; by both sexes. *Nestling*: Unrecorded; fed by both parents.

486 (450)   Cardinal Woodpecker   Plate 43
Kardinaalspeg
Dendropicos fuscescens

Mbangura (K), Hohodza (Sh), Gogosana, Ngo-ngondzwani (Ts), Kôkômere, Phaphadikôta (Tw), Isinqolamthi (X), iNqondaqonda (Z), [Kardinal-specht]

Measurements: Length 14–16 cm; wing (31 ♂) 89–92,5–97, (6 ♀) 89–92,4–97; tail (15) 44–51; tarsus (15) 15–17; culmen (15) 17,5–21. Weight (4 ♂) 26–33,4–37 g, (7 ♀) 19,5–28,9–37 g, (9 unsexed) 25–30,3–38 g.

Bare Parts: Iris brown to red-brown; bill greyish, tip black; legs and feet greyish green to olive.

Identification: Size small; see woodpecker key. *Male*: Forecrown brown (diagnostic); hindcrown red, malar stripe black; back barred; breast streaked. *Female*: Like male but with hindcrown black. *Immature*: Similar to adult, but hindcrown red to brick red in both sexes.

Voice: High-pitched rapid *kri-kri-kri-kri*; drums fast, rather quiet, mechanical rolled *trrrr*, often followed by call.

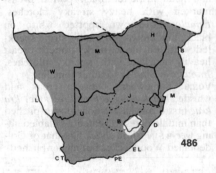

486

Distribution: Africa S of Sahara; throughout s Africa.

Status: Common resident (commonest arboreal woodpecker in s Africa).

Habitat: Any woodland, forest edge, exotic plantations, orchards, parks, gardens, riverine bush.

Habits: Usually in pairs; sometimes solitary. Forages on trunks and branches of trees, bushes and euphorbias; also on reed and maize stalks (for borers ?); usually lands low in tree and works up towards top, sometimes spiralling around branch; may join bird parties. Moves to off-side of

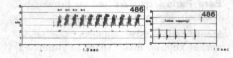

418

trunk or branch when disturbed. Flight fast, direct, undulating.
Food: Insects (especially beetle larvae).
Breeding: *Season*: All months except February and March; mainly August-October. *Nest*: Hole excavated in dead tree or branch. *Clutch*: (16) 1–2,4–5 eggs (usually 2). *Eggs*: White; measure (16) 20,9 × 16 (18,2–23 × 15–17,2). *Incubation*: 12–13 days by both sexes; starts with completed clutch. *Nestling*: About 27 days; fed by both parents.

Ref. Attwell, G.D. 1952. *Ostrich* 23:88–91.

---

487 (451)   Bearded Woodpecker   Plate 43
Baardspeg (Namakwaspeg)
Thripias namaquus

Mbangura (K), Hohodza (Sh), Gogosana, Ngo-ngondzwani (Ts), Kôkômere, Phaphadikôta (Tw), [Namaspecht]

Measurements: Length 23–25 cm; wing (19 ♂) 130–134–138, (16 ♀) 127–131–137; tail (35) 60–75; tarsus (35) 17–21; culmen (35) 27–36. Weight (1 ♀) 61,7 g, (10 unsexed) 67–81–89 g.

Bare Parts: Iris brown to deep red; bill slate grey, tip black; legs and feet olive grey.

Identification: Size large; see woodpecker key; forecrown spotted white on black; hindcrown red (♂) or black (♀); malar stripe broad, black, conspicuous (hence "bearded"); back and belly barred (diagnostic; no other s African woodpeckers have barred underparts). *Immature*: Similar to adult ♂, but duller.

Voice: Loud rapid chattering *wik-wik-wik-wik-wik* of 6–8 notes increasing in tempo towards end; drums loudly, somewhat deliberately, slowing down towards end, audible for up to 1 km; high-pitched *chip, chip, chip*.

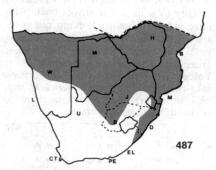

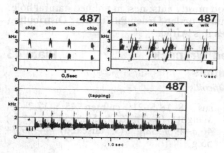

Distribution: S Africa to Sudan and Ethiopia; in s Africa absent from most of dry W, sw and s Cape, highveld and inland Natal, occurring as far S as lower Kei River.

Status: Fairly common to uncommon resident.

Habitat: Drier savanna and woodland.

Habits: Usually in pairs. Noisy, often calling or drumming on resonant wood; raps loudly also while feeding, usually high up on dead branches and trunks of larger trees.

Food: Insects (especially larvae); also spiders and geckoes.

Breeding: *Season*: June to November in Zimbabwe, May to July in S Africa. *Nest*: Hole excavated in dead tree; entrance hole characteristically oval, about 7,5 cm high, 5,5 cm wide. *Clutch*: 2–4 eggs (usually 3). *Eggs*: White; measure (6) 25,7 × 18,5 (25–26,4 × 17,5–19,4). *Incubation*: Unrecorded; by both sexes. *Nestling*: About 27 days; fed by both parents.

488 (452) Olive Woodpecker   Plate 43
Gryskopspeg
Mesopicos griseocephalus

Mbangura (K), [Goldrückenspecht]

Measurements: Length about 20 cm; wing (53 ♂) 104–109,1–114, (34 ♀) 102,5–105,7–110; tail (48) 60–69; tarsus (48) 17–20; culmen (48) 22–31. Weight (3 ♂) 47,5–48,8–49,5 g, (2 ♀) 49,6 g, (23 unsexed) 33–42–51 g.

Bare Parts: Iris brown; bill grey, tip black; legs and feet greenish grey.

Identification: Size medium; see woodpecker key; forehead grey; crown red (♂) or grey (♀); no malar stripe; back plain olive green (diagnostic); rump red (conspicuous in flight); breast golden (diagnostic); belly grey. *Immature*: Duller olive green than adult above and below.

Voice: Whistled *whee-whee-whee; tweet* take-off call; high-pitched *wer-chik, wer-chik* or *wicker, wicker* call in flight or perched, repeated 3–4 times.

Distribution: S Africa to E Africa; in s Africa from sw Cape, E to Transvaal escarpment; also e Caprivi (Katima Mulilo).

Status: Fairly common resident inland; scarce on coast.

Habitat: Evergreen forest, dense coastal and riverine bush; also into fynbos when foraging.

Habits: Usually in pairs. Looks like small stump when perched upright; hops up branches; prefers thinner branches high in large trees. Forages in fynbos on trunks of trees and bushes to near ground level; also on old *Protea* inflorescences. Shakes head from side to side while calling.

Food: Insects.

Breeding: *Season*: Mostly September to November; as late as April in e Cape and June in e Transvaal. *Nest*: Hole excavated in dead branch or trunk. *Clutch*: (3) 2–3 eggs. *Eggs*: White; measure (5) 24,3 × 18,4 (23,3–26,2 × 18–18,8). *Incubation*: Unrecorded; by both sexes. *Nestling*: Unrecorded.

Ref. Richardson, D. 1989. *Bokmakierie* 41:17–18.

25:4 Family 62 JYNGIDAE—WRYNECKS

Small. Bill short, slender, pointed; legs short; toes zygodactyl; wings rounded; tail medium (not stiff as in woodpeckers); plumage cryptically coloured in elaborate patterns of brown, grey, black or rufous to look like dry bark; sexes alike; solitary; arboreal, but sometimes feed on ground; food mostly ants; nest in unlined natural hole, usually in tree; eggs 2–6, white; other features under Order Piciformes. Distribution Africa and Eurasia; two species; one species in s Africa.

489 (453) Redthroated Wryneck   Plate 43
Draaihals
Jynx ruficollis

[Braunkehl-Wendehals, Rotkehl-Wendehals]

Measurements: Length 18–20 cm; wing (20) 90–92,7–96; tail 66–69,1–74; tarsus 18–18,5–21; culmen 15,5–17,2–18. Weight (5 ♂) 52,8–55,5–59 g, (4 ♀) 46,3–49,9–52 g, (9 unsexed) 44–49,8–55 g.

Bare Parts: Iris light umber brown to red-brown; bill bluish or greenish grey, culmen and tip dusky; legs and feet greenish grey.

Identification: About size of smallish woodpecker; deep rufous throat and breast diagnostic; above mottled greyish brown with conspicuous irregular dark stripe down midline; belly white, streaked with black. *Immature*: Duller rufous on throat and breast than adult.

Voice: ♂ calls loud harsh *week-week-week-week-week*; ♀ calls lower *ooit-ooit-ooit-ooit-ooit*; also low guttural *peegh-peegh-peegh*; in display up to 15 notes, *krok-krok-krok.....*; quiet *klik* alarm call.

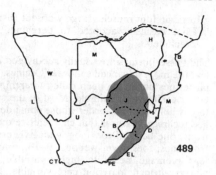

489

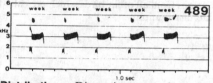

489

Distribution: Discontinuously from e Cape to Cameroon and Sudan; in s Africa from about Port Elizabeth through Natal to w Swaziland, e Orange Free State and Transvaal.

Status: Locally fairly common; generally uncommon; migratory in S, resident in N; passage migration northward through Natal in February-March, southward in spring (probably birds from e Cape).

Habitat: Thornveld, open bushveld, exotic plantations, gardens, farmyards.

Habits: Solitary or in pairs. Often perches high on exposed branch. Forages mostly on ground, walking with short steps; hops when moving fast; also gleans from trunks and branches of trees. Roosts at night in hole or sheltered crevice behind bark, or in dense foliage.

Food: Mostly ants (including their larvae, pupae and eggs); also termites and caterpillars.

Breeding: *Season*: August to February (peak October). *Nest*: Old nest hole of woodpecker or barbet, natural hole in tree, cavity under eaves, nestbox, hollow fencepost. *Clutch*: (37) 1–3,3–6 eggs (usually 3–4). *Eggs*: White; measure (24) 21,5 × 16,6 (19,8–23,5 × 15,1–17,5). *Incubation*: (4) 12–13–15 days by both sexes. *Nestling*: 25–26 days; fed by both parents; nestlings have snake-like display towards intruder.

Ref. Tarboton, W.R. 1976. *Ostrich* 47:99–112.

26. Order PASSERIFORMES—PASSERINES (about 65 families; 29 families in s Africa)

Small to large (mostly small to medium). The passerines comprise a complex of over 5 000 species of birds; the order is hard to define; for the expert the following diagnosis is provided:

a. Palate aegithognathous, vomer truncated anterior to posterior edge of maxillopalatines;

b. Tensor propatagialis brevis tendon from shoulder to extensor metacarpi radialis muscle of forearm, thence to insertion on humerus;

c. Spermatozoa in bundles; each cell coiled in head region with large acrosome;

d. Hallux and claw large in relation to other toes; no connection between major flexors (flexor digitorum longus (FDL) and flexor hallucis longus (FHL));

e. Type VII deep plantar tendons without connection (vinculum) between FDL and FHL;

f. Pubo-ischio-femoralis muscle arranged as pars lateralis and pars medialis (in non-passerines arranged as pars cranialis and pars caudalis respectively);

g. Intrinsic foot muscles largely absent (usually present in non-passerines);

h. Foot basically adapted to perching, but development of terrestrial habits not precluded.

The Passeriformes are usually subdivided into the more primitive suborder Suboscines, and the more advanced suborder Oscines, which together form a natural grouping. The passerines have also been called "perching birds" or "songbirds", neither term being either exclusive or suitable. Most of the commoner small birds that one sees from day to day belong to this order whose name derives from the Latin *passer*, a sparrow. Other less technical features that characterize the order are as follows: foot with three toes in front, one behind; toes not syndactyl, except in broadbills; hind toe at same level as front toes; toes never webbed; 9–10 primaries in wing; usually 12 rectrices in tail; bill, legs, plumage, nest, etc. highly variable; chick naked or sparsely downy at hatching, always altricial; parental care variable. In s Africa only two suboscine families are represented, the Eurylaimidae (broadbills) and the Pittidae (pittas), with a single species each. The remaining 27 families of birds in s Africa (and therefore in this book) are oscine passerines. A technical diagnosis is unhelpful for use in the field, but familiarity will enable one to sort out the passerines from all other birds which are called "non-passerines". Passerines are of worldwide distribution.

Ref. Ames, P.L. 1971. *Bull. Peabody Mus. Nat. Hist.* 37:1–194.
Maclean, G.L. 1990. *Tvl Mus. Bull. (Suppl.)* 22:1–11.
Maclean, G.L. & Vernon, C.J. 1976. *Ostrich* 47:95–98.
Markus, M.B. 1972. *Ostrich* 43:17–22.
Raikow, R.J. 1982. *Auk* 99: 431–445.
Sibley, C.G. 1970. *Bull. Peabody Mus. Nat. Hist.*, Yale 32:1–131.

26:1. Family 63 EURYLAIMIDAE—BROADBILLS

Small to medium. Bill rather large, broad and dorsoventrally flattened, with wide gape, hooked at tip; head relatively large; body stout; legs short; toes strong, syndactyl, fairly long; wings rounded; tail variable; plumage variable, Asian species often brightly coloured, African species mostly dull, streaked below, usually with exposable white patch on back (concealed when at rest); sexes usually different; solitary; arboreal in forest or open woodland; food highly varied, both plant and animal; nest a pendent structure of plant material with side entrance; eggs 2–5, white or pinkish, plain or spotted; chick naked at hatching; parental care by both sexes. Distribution subsaharan Africa, tropical Asia to Philippines and Borneo; 14 species; one species in s Africa.

490 (454)   African Broadbill   Plate 36
Breëbek
Smithornis capensis

[Kap-Breitrachen]

Measurements: Length about 14 cm; wing (18 ♂) 68–71,7–76, (10 ♀) 66,5–70,4–73; tail (18 ♂) 47–52,7–58,5, (10 ♀) 45–49–52,5; tarsus (10) 14,5–16; culmen (18 ♂) 16,5–18–19, (10 ♀) 16,5–17,7–19. Weight (10 ♂) 21–24,5–26,9 g, (8 ♀) 17,4–23,5–27,5 g.

Bare Parts: Iris brown; bill blackish horn above, pale pink below; legs and feet greenish grey.

Identification: About size of sparrow; forehead white; crown black (grey, streaked black in ♀); above greyish brown, streaked black and white on mantle; below creamy white, washed yellow on flanks, heavily streaked with black on breast and flanks (diagnostic); tail dark sooty; bill broad, flat, dark above, pale below. *Immature*: Yellower above than adult; no dark markings on back.

Voice: Froglike *prrrrrup*, rising in pitch; plaintive mewing *twee-oo* distress and alarm call.

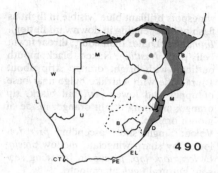

490

Distribution: Africa S of Sahara; in s Africa from s Natal to Mozambique, e and ne Zimbabwe, and Caprivi.
Status: Locally common, but increasingly scarce in Natal; resident. Vulnerable (RDB).
Habitat: Dense woodland, evergreen forest, deciduous thickets.
Habits: Usually solitary. Perches low down in dense vegetation; usually silent, inactive and easily overlooked. Performs display flight with froglike call in circle of about 60–100 cm diameter on vibrating wings, like large moth, puffing out white feather bases on back; in courtship display 2 birds hang upside down near each other for about 30 seconds, flicking wings and giving froglike call; up to 4 birds may display together, possibly as lek. Flicks wings when agitated. Catches insects in

flight from perch like flycatcher; also picks up prey from ground.
Food: Insects and spiders.
Breeding: *Season*: October to February (mainly November-December). *Nest*: Hanging tangle of leaves, bark, grass, moss and roots, bound with spider web, attached to low horizontal branch by broad band; slightly porched entrance at side leads to central chamber, below which hangs untidy tail of plant material; built by both sexes. *Clutch*: (20) 1–2,4–3 eggs. *Eggs*: White, glossy; measure (11) 21,2 × 15,1 (19–23,6 × 14,5–16); weigh (3) 2,6–2,7–2,8 g. *Incubation*: Unrecorded; by ♀ only, while ♂ keeps watch. *Nestling*: Unrecorded.

26:2. Family 64 PITTIDAE—PITTAS

Small to medium. Bill medium, strong, slightly curved on culmen; legs long and strong; feet large; wings short, rounded, usually with white patches showing in flight; tail very short; plumage usually with patches of bright colours; sexes similar or different; terrestrial in forest habitats; often migrate at night; food small vertebrates and invertebrates; nest a domed structure of twigs and rootlets from ground level up to about 3 m in tree or bush; eggs 2–4, whitish, spotted, glossy; chick naked at hatching; parental care by both sexes. Distribution Africa S of Sahara, tropical Asia, Australia, to Solomon Islands; about 25 species; one species in s Africa.

491 (455)

Angola Pitta
Angolapitta
Pitta angolensis

Plate 36

[Angolapitta]

Measurements: Length about 20 cm; wing 130–136; tail 50; tarsus 40; culmen 35–38. Weight (2 ♂) 93–100 g, (1 ♀) 89 g.

Bare Parts: Iris dark brown; bill blackish brown; legs and feet pinkish.
Identification: About size of quail; tail very short; legs long; head broadly striped buff and black; back green; throat pink; breast fawn; belly crimson; rump and

ANGOLA PITTA

wingspots brilliant blue (visible in flight as flash of blue, ending in downward flutter). *Immature*: Duller than adult; throat fawn; belly pink. *Nestling*: Naked, black; mouth outlined with bright orange strip about 1 mm wide with wartlike bulge near base of upper and lower jaw; bill black, tip orange; anal ring bright orange; inside of mouth orange.

Voice: Single short ascending *prrr* followed by sharp wingclap; mellow *pleeup* or *lop, lop, lop, pleeup* in breeding season; guttural *hggh* alarm note.

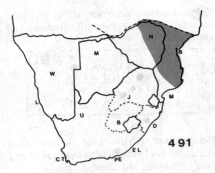

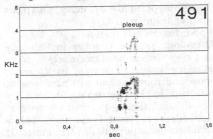

Distribution: Tropical Africa; rarely further S than Limpopo River; in s Africa confined to Zimbabwe and adjacent Mozambique; migrates to ne Zaire after breeding.

Status: Uncommon breeding intra-African migrant, October to April in Zimbabwe; spring movement SE across n Zimbabwe; autumn movement probably NE through Mozambique. Vagrant S of Limpopo River; recorded Port Elizabeth, Pietersburg, Pretoria, Potchefstroom, Pietermaritzburg.

Habitat: Lowland evergreen forest, deciduous thickets.

Habits: Usually solitary. Easily over-looked unless calling. Forages on ground in leaf litter and around termite mounds, flirting tail continually; runs well; sometimes bounds along; when disturbed sometimes flies into tree and crouches on branch. Flight fast and direct. In breeding display jumps vertically about 5 cm from horizontal branch, making *prrrup* sound with wings; crouches in threat display, with feathers fluffed, wings spread, bill pointing upwards. Migrates at night; often killed by flying into lighted buildings.

Food: Insects, molluscs.

Breeding: *Season*: November to December in Zimbabwe. *Nest*: Untidy dome of twigs and dry leaves with side entrance, like small coucal's nest; roof rather flat, rimmed with short twigs like upturned hatbrim; lined inside with finer material; in smaller branches of thorntree, 2–4 m above ground. *Clutch*: 2–4 eggs. *Eggs*: White or cream, spotted with dark and pale grey, more concentrated at thick end; measure (14) 28 × 23 (27,5–29 × 21,7–25); weigh (4) 7,2–7,7–8,2 g. *Incubation*: Unrecorded. *Nestling*: Unrecorded.

Ref. Masterson, A. 1987. *Bokmakierie* 39:23–25.

26:3. Family 65 ALAUDIDAE—LARKS

Small to medium. Bill short or long, curved on culmen, sometimes stout and conical; legs medium to longish, back of tarsometatarsus scaled (not usually a single smooth plate as in other passerines, but may become so in old birds); toes longish, hind claw long and often straight; wings longish, usually pointed, sometimes rounded; tail short to medium, rounded or square; no pessulus in syrinx (see Glossary), but most species sing well; plumage cryptically coloured brown, rufous, buff or grey dorsally (tending to be plain in desert species, patterned in grassland and savanna species), below white, black or rufous, usually marked on chest; sexes alike or different; terrestrial in desert, grassland and savanna; food mostly insects and seeds; nest cup-shaped of rootlets and grass on ground, domed in some genera, usually under shelter of plant or stone; eggs 2–6, whitish, spotted; chick downy, altricial, able to leave nest at 7–10 days after hatching, well before it can fly; mouth and tongue of nestling bright yellow with black spots on tongue and tips of jaws; parental care by both sexes. Distribution N, C and n S America, Africa, Madagascar, Eurasia to Philippines, Australasia (not New Zealand); about 76 species; 25 species in s Africa.

Ref. Dean, W.R.J. & Hockey, P.A.R. 1989. *Ostrich* 60:27–34.
Maclean, G.L. 1970a. *Ann. Natal Mus.* 20:381–401; 1970b. *Zool. afr.* 5:7–39.
Willoughby, E.J. 1971. *Zool. afr.* 6:133–176.

492 (456) Melodious Lark Plate 44
Spotlewerik
Mirafra cheniana

Maliberwani (NS), Sebotha (Tw), [Spottlerche]

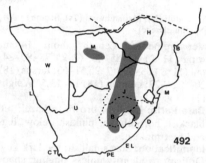

Measurements: Length about 12 cm; wing (10 ♂) 71–75,5–79, (7 ♀) 72–73,9–76; tail (17) 43–46,5–50, tarsus (17) 18–19,8–21,5; culmen (17) 12–12,9–14.

Bare Parts: Iris brown; bill horn, base yellowish; legs and feet pinkish.

Identification: Size smallish to medium; see lark key. Difficult to identify unless singing; looks somewhat like cross between lark and ♀ bishop; bill rather heavy, conical; primaries edged rufous, conspicuous in flight; belly and flanks buff (white in Monotonous Lark); breast heavily streaked and spotted; tail relatively short, black with conspicuous white outer rectrices showing up well in flight (somewhat similar to Shorttailed Pipit, but rufous wings distinctive).

Voice: Repetitive *chuk-chuk-chucker-chuk* alarm call; song mainly imitations of other bird species (at least 57 species recorded; francolins, guineafowl, plovers, coursers, louries, cuckoos, bee-eaters, swifts, larks, swallows, chats, warblers, pipits, longclaws, shrikes, starlings, sunbirds, ploceids, waxbills, canaries); sings in flight or from perch.

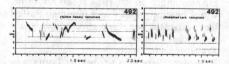

Distribution: Discontinuous; e Cape (Bedford, Queenstown, Jamestown, Aliwal North), Natal (Matatiele, Ladysmith, Winterton), Transvaal (N of Johannesburg, Pretoria), Botswana (Patlana Flats, Lake Ngami), Zimbabwe (Bulawayo).

Status: Uncommon resident; greatly reduced in numbers and range by habitat destruction.

Habitat: Open climax grassland, especially Rooigras *Themeda triandra*, sometimes with rocky outcrops; also cultivated fields of Teff *Eragrostis tef*; in Natal at 550–1750 m elevation, rainfall 400–800 mm/year.

Habits: Solitary or in pairs. In flight display rises to 20 m or more on rapidly beating wings, puffed up like carpenter bee, flying in circle about 50 m diameter for 25 minutes or more, alternately fluttering and singing with dip and rise, returning to original perch; may end display with sudden drop into grass, after chasing conspecific low over grass; fluffs plumage also when singing from perch. Easily overlooked when males not singing; sometimes hard to flush after landing;

on landing crouches for a while before creeping away through grasstufts.
Food: Insects, seeds.
Breeding: *Season*: October to November in e Cape, November in Natal, September to January in Zimbabwe. *Nest*: Domed cup of grass and rootlets set into scrape on ground among tall grass. *Clutch*: 3–4 eggs

(usually 3). *Eggs*: White to dull yellowish, heavily spotted with brown and grey-brown, sometimes in zone around thick end; measure (17) 19,2 × 14,3 (17,8–20,9 × 13,9–14,7). *Incubation*: Unrecorded. *Nestling*: Unrecorded.

Ref. Vernon, C. 1982. *Bee-eater* 33:45–47.

---

493 (457)   **Monotonous Lark**   **Plate 44**
Bosveldlewerik
Mirafra passerina

Yisimatuli (K), Mapuluhweni (Ts), Sebotha (Tw), [Sperlingslerche]

Measurements: Length about 14 cm; wing (11 ♂) 83–85–88, (7 ♀) 78–80–84; tail (11 ♂) 53–59, (7 ♀) 51–53; tarsus (18) 20–21,4–23; culmen (18) 12–13,5. Weight (1) 23 g.
Bare Parts: Iris light brown to hazel; bill blackish horn above, pinkish below; legs and feet pinkish.
Identification: Size smallish; see lark key. Difficult to identify unless singing; shape dumpy; bill short, conical; eyebrow white, not extending to base of bill; primaries edged rufous (conspicuous in flight); outer rectrices white; belly white (buff in Melodious Lark); white throat conspicuous when singing.
Voice: Invariable quick 5-syllabled phrase, *for syrup is sweet*, with rising intonation, repeated over and over; several males usual sing within earshot of each other; *chip chip* alarm note (similar to call of Croaking Cisticola).

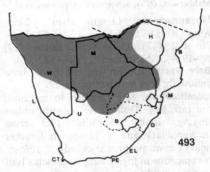

Distribution: Northern Cape, n Orange Free State, Transvaal, s and w Zimbabwe, Botswana, n Namibia (rarely to Angola).
Status: Common; highly nomadic, numbers fluctuating greatly from season to season and year to year; summer visitor to Transvaal lowveld; resident in some areas.
Habitat: Savanna with bare or stony ground and sparse grass cover, semi-arid savanna with stunted trees, stony ground in open woodland, eroded areas in mopane scrub.
Habits: Solitary or in pairs. Easily overlooked except when breeding. When disturbed rises suddenly; flies off jinking, then drops suddenly to ground and disappears. Males sing from tops of trees and bushes, even at night, but not during hot midday; perches with body at 45°, head forward, throat puffed out while singing. Display flight short; rises to about 15 m, wings beating rapidly and plumage fluffed like carpenter bee, then glides down again to perch.
Food: Insects, seeds.
Breeding: *Season*: October to January in Zimbabwe, January to April in Transvaal, December to March in Namibia; usually after good rains. *Nest*: Domed cup of dry

grass, set into side of grasstuft or between 2 tufts; growing grass in walls bent over to form roofed bower. *Clutch*: 2–4 eggs (usually 3). *Eggs*: Dull whitish, heavily mottled with brown and grey, usually zoned at thick end; measure (22) 19,2 × 14,2 (17,7–21 × 13,5–15,2). *Incubation*: Unrecorded. *Nestling*: Unrecorded.

494 (458) Rufousnaped Lark Plate 44
Rooineklewerik
Mirafra africana

Yisimatuli (K), Mapuluhweni (Ts), Sebotha (Tw), Igwangqa, Iqabathule (X), uNongqwashi, uNgqangendlela (Z), [Rotnackenlerche]

Measurements: Length ♂ 17,5 cm, ♀ 16 cm; wing (10 ♂) 95–100–105, (4 ♀) 89–92; tail (14) 58–71; tarsus (14) 27–32; hindclaw (14) 11–14; culmen (14) 18–23. Weight (1 ♂) 42,1 g, (3 unsexed) 39–45–51 g.

Bare Parts: Iris light hazel brown; bill blackish horn, base pinkish; legs and feet pinkish brown.

Identification: Size large; see lark key. Shape chunky; bill heavy; primaries edged bright rufous (conspicuous in flight); belly pale buffy rufous; rufous nape seldom visible in field. Birds in S and E darker, more rufous; in W and N paler, more pinkish. *Immature*: Less clearly spotted on breast than adult; upperparts more scaled.

Voice: Song from perch clear whistled phrase of 4 notes, run together in pairs (sometimes sounds like 2 notes), rising then falling in pitch, *tiree-tiroo*; given about every 4 seconds; between every 3–5 phrases, birds raises body on straight legs (or even lifts slightly off perch) as wings rattled, *phrrrp*; flight song sustained series of rambling whistles, tweets and trills, sometimes with imitations; also clear whistled *pew-it* or *peeet* (contact call ?); loud ringing *pree, pree* alarm call.

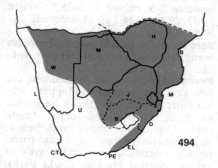

Distribution: S Africa to Somalia, Sudan and Nigeria; in s Africa absent from most of dry W and from extreme NE.

Status: Common resident.

Habitat: Open grassland with scattered perches (bushes, trees, fenceposts), *Acacia* savanna, cultivated lands.

Habits: Usually solitary; sometimes in pairs. Flushes reluctantly; flight bouncy with short bursts of wingbeats; drops suddenly into grass, then runs mouselike in crouched posture between grasstufts. Near nest flies about with thudding wingsnaps as distraction display. Easily overlooked when not breeding.

Food: Mainly insects; also millipedes, arachnids, seeds.

Breeding: *Season*: July to April (mainly November-January) throughout s Africa. *Nest*: Shallow domed cup of grass and rootlets set into ground at base of grasstuft, with wide side entrance. *Clutch*: (74) 2–2,4–4 eggs (usually 2–3). *Eggs*: Dull white to pale cream, spotted and blotched with shades of brown and grey, concentrated at thick end; measure (137) 22,2 × 15,8 (20,2–24,7 × 14,9–18,2). *Incubation*: Unrecorded. *Nestling*: Unrecorded.

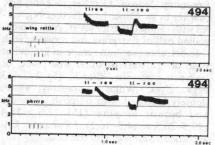

495 (466)

Clapper Lark
Hoëveldklappertjie
Mirafra apiata

Plate 44

Semote, 'Mote (SS), Sebotha (Tw), [Grasklapper-lerche]

Measurements: Length about 15 cm; wing (6) 84–92; tail 54–63; tarsus 18–23; hindclaw 7–9; culmen 13,5–15,5. Weight (3 ♂) 29,1–31–34,2 g, (4 unsexed) 26–30,5–33,8 g.

Bare Parts: Iris light brown; bill brownish horn, base paler; legs and feet pale pinkish.

Identification: Smallish to medium; see lark key. Very similar to Flappet Lark, but more rufous, less greyish (separable on flight displays and songs); bright rufous or tawny above and below, including underwing; w birds paler; heavily mottled above; crown grey or rufous, mottled blackish (looks dark); primaries edged bright rufous (conspicuous in flight); outer rectrices white (buff in Flappet Lark). *Immature*: Less clearly marked than adult.

Voice: Flight display every 15–30 seconds starts with steep climb producing loud wing-rattle at top, *prrrrr*, followed imme-

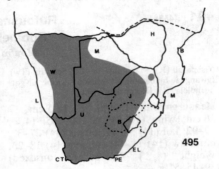

495

Status: Common resident.

Habitat: Highveld grassland, Kalahari sandveld with scattered bushes and tall grass, semi-arid karoo.

Habits: Usually solitary. Easily overlooked unless displaying (see **Voice**). Flushes reluctantly, sometimes perching on bush, but usually landing and running away through grass. Flight distraction near nest accompanied by loud wing-snaps.

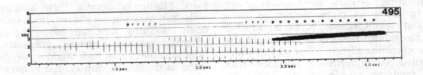

495

diately by dive accompanied by clear drawn-out whistled *poooeee*, rising in pitch (no whistle after rattle in Flappet Lark); climb-rattle-dive-whistle sequence may start from high cruising flight or from ground, sometimes ending in descent to ground or perch, or cruising may continue for many minutes; *peeek*, grating *chrk, chrk* and mewing alarm calls; imitates other bird species (francolins, plovers, warblers, waxbills, etc.).

Distribution: Southern Africa; absent only from E, NE and extreme N.

Food: Insects and seeds.

Breeding: *Season*: October to February, (earlier in sw Cape, later further N); varies with rainfall in drier areas. *Nest*: Thick-walled ball of fine grass and rootlets, with side entrance; set into scrape in ground at base of grasstuft or other low plant, or between grasstufts. *Clutch*: (5) 2–2,6–3 eggs. *Eggs*: White to creamy white, densely blotched with purplish, lavender and brown; measure (15) 22,6 × 15,4 (20,3–26,5 × 14,3–16,2). *Incubation*: Unrecorded. *Nestling*: Unrecorded.

496 (468)
Flappet Lark
Laeveldklappertjie
Mirafra rufocinnamomea

Plate 44

Yisimatuli (K), Chitambirmbuya (Sh), Mamhe-ngele, Matharhatharha, Phapharharha (Ts), Sebo-tha (Tw), uQaqashe (Z), [Baumklapperlerche, Zimtbaumlerche]

Measurements: Length 14–15 cm; wing (13) 75–80,7–82; tail 52–59; tarsus 21–24; culmen 13,5–15. Weight (1 ♂) 26 g.
Bare Parts: Iris brown; bill dark horn, base pinkish; legs and feet pinkish brown.
Identification: Size medium; see lark key. Very similar to Clapper Lark, but less rufous, more greyish (separable on flight displays and songs); above olive brown, mottled dark brown and scaled buff; throat white; rest of underparts buff, washed rufous on flanks and breast; breast spotted dark brown; primaries edged rufous (conspicuous in flight); outer rectrices buff (white in Clapper Lark). *Immature:* Duller than adult, somewhat barred above.
Voice: ♂ cruises high in air or rises from ground with 2–5 bursts of far-carrying muffled castanetlike wing-rattles at top of climb, *phrrrr-phrrr*, followed by thin wispy *chik-chik-a-wee*, very hard to hear between wingclaps and seems to come from some other source; whistled *tuee-tui* from ground.

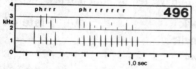

Distribution: Africa S of Sahara; in s Africa confined to NE from Zululand to n Botswana.

Status: Locally fairly common, but generally sparse resident.
Habitat: Savanna and grassy woodland with clearings or drainage lines; also coastal grassland.
Habits: Usually solitary. Shy and easily overlooked unless displaying, but may do so at any time of year; runs fast; flushes reluctantly. Rarely perches on low tree or bush. Starts display-flying (see **Voice**) in early morning, sometimes before sunrise; at end of display flight, dives to about 10 m above ground, levels off and then alights.
Food: Insects, seeds.
Breeding: *Season:* October to November in Zululand, October to April in Zimbabwe. *Nest:* Roofed cup of dry grass and rootlets set into scrape on ground at base of grasstuft. *Clutch:* (23) 2–2,2–3 eggs. *Eggs:* Dull white, streaked and spotted with brown and underlying grey; measure (41) 20,8 × 14,8 (18,5–22,4 × 13,7–16,1). *Incubation:* Unrecorded. *Nestling:* Unrecorded.

497 (459)
Fawncoloured Lark
Vaalbruinlewerik
Mirafra africanoides

Plate 44

Yisimatuli (K), Mapuluhweni (Ts), Sebotha (Tw), [Steppenlerche]

Measurements: Length about 14 cm; wing (9) 87,5–94; tail 57–65; tarsus 21–23; culmen 13–15. Weight 19–21,5 g.

Bare Parts: Iris light brown; bill light yellowish horn, base paler; legs and feet pinkish.
Identification: Size medium; see lark key. Above light to dark rufous (individually and regionally variable), lightly streaked

429

darker; broad white eyebrow; white streak below eye (no white below eye in Monotonous Lark); no dark line from gape to ear coverts (as in Karoo, Dune and Red Larks); below white, streaked brown on breast; primaries edged rufous (conspicuous in flight; no rufous in wing of Sabota Lark); outer edge of tail white. *Immature*: More spotted than streaked above; outer edge of tail more broadly white.

Voice: Song 4–5 staccato notes, followed by rapid jumbled phrase of musical twittering notes, ending with slightly drawn-out slurred note, *chip chip chip chiree, chiree, chiree, chweeer*, lasting 2–3 seconds; song phrases about 7–10 seconds apart; loud *peeek* alarm note.

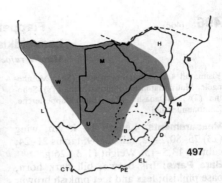

497

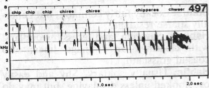

Distribution: S Africa to E Africa; in s Africa mainly on Kalahari sand, from n Namibia across Botswana, n Cape, w Orange Free State, w and C Transvaal, w and C Zimbabwe, to s Mozambique.
Status: Common resident.
Habitat: Scrub and savanna, usually with sandy soils.
Habits: Solitary or in pairs; sometimes in loose groups of 3–4 birds. Tame and con-

spicuous, especially when singing; often walks about on open ground, well away from cover, but flies or runs to shelter of vegetation when disturbed. Sings in cruising flight up to about 30 m above ground, or from perch on tree or bush; perches with body almost horizontal, head somewhat drawn into shoulders, legs flexed.
Food: Insects, seeds, millipedes.
Breeding: *Season*: September to February in Zimbabwe, January-April and August-November in n Cape and Botswana; breeds opportunistically after rain. *Nest*: Cup of dry grass and rootlets, roofed with dome of grass; set into soil at base of grasstuft. *Clutch*: (14) 2–2,5–3 eggs (rarely 4). *Eggs*: White, spotted and blotched with brown, yellow-brown and grey, somewhat concentrated at thick end; measure (35) 20,8 × 14,7 (17,2–23,4 × 11,9–15,6). *Incubation*: 12 days. *Nestling*: 10–14 days; fed by both parents.

498 (460)   **Sabota Lark**   **Plate 44**
Sabotalewerik
Mirafra sabota

Yisimatuli (K), Vhumakutata, Urimakutata (Ts), Sebotha (Tw), [Sabotalerche]

Measurements: Length 14–15 cm; wing (43) 76–90; tail 46–57; tarsus 19–22,5; culmen 12,2–15,8. Weight (2 ♂) 21,3–25 g, (13 unsexed) 22,6–25,1–26,7 g.
Bare Parts: Iris brown; bill dark horn, base pinkish; legs and feet pinkish brown.
Identification: Size medium; see lark key. Above reddish brown, greyish brown, buffy grey or whitish grey, depending on region (paler-coloured in drier regions; not bright rufous as in Fawncoloured Lark), boldly mottled with dark brown

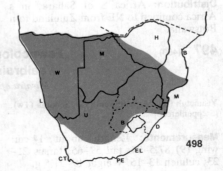

498

(not lightly streaked as in Fawncoloured Lark); throat white; rest of underparts buffy white, breast speckled dark brown; primaries edged buffy (not rufous); outer rectrices buffy white; bill heavy (heavier than that of Fawncoloured Lark), longer and heavier in S, shorter and more slender in N of range.

Voice: Jumble of rich fluty and trilled notes, somewhat canarylike, but highly variable and incorporating imitations of calls of over 60 other species of birds; loud *pip-pip-peeu* repeated every few seconds; thin *si si si* alarm call; also alarm calls of other bird species (larks, bulbuls, warblers, flycatchers, shrikes, buntings, etc.).

Distribution: S Africa to Angola and Cabinda; throughout s Africa except extreme S and NE.

Status: Common resident.

Habitat: Semi-arid savanna, especially on rocky slopes with bushes and trees, fringes of dry watercourses, thorny bushveld with tall grass.

Habits: Usually solitary. May forage on open ground, often away from cover; walks with flexed legs and somewhat crouched posture. Often perches and sings on top of bush or tree, with body nearly horizontal, head drawn into shoulders and legs flexed; sometimes sings in flight several metres above ground.

Food: Seeds (60%), insects (40%); does not drink water.

Breeding: *Season*: October to February (mainly November-December) in Zimbabwe, February-March in Kalahari, November in Natal, December in Transvaal lowveld, January to May in Namibia; opportunistically after rains in arid regions. *Nest*: Cup of grass and rootlets, roofed over with dome of grass; set in foundation of small stones on ground against grasstuft or shrub, often among larger stones on slope. *Clutch*: (36) 2–2,6–4 eggs. *Eggs*: White, spotted with brown, yellow-brown and grey, concentrated at thick end; measure (49) 20,6 × 14,8 (18,6–23 × 13,9–15,5). *Incubation*: Unrecorded. *Nestling*: Unrecorded.

---

499 (473)

Rudd's Lark
Drakensberglewerik
Mirafra ruddi

Plate 45

[Spornlerche]

Measurements: Length about 14 cm; wing (10 ♂) 73,5–74,9–77,5, (7 ♀) 69–71–74; tail (17) 38–45; tarsus (17) 24–26; hindclaw (17) 12–20; culmen (17) 13–15.

Bare Parts: Iris hazel; bill dark brownish horn, base pinkish; legs and feet pinkish.

Identification: Size smallish (somewhat larger than Pinkbilled Lark); looks like small Spikeheeled Lark or large cisticola; see lark key. Tail narrow and short (diagnostic); outer rectrices strikingly white in flight; white median stripe from forehead to crown (diagnostic); long crown feathers extend to nape; looks big-headed, thin-necked; above dark brown, boldly scaled

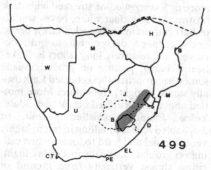

with whitish; wings broad, dull reddish brown (good flight character); posture upright (looks like small Spikeheeled Lark).

431

RUDD'S LARK

Voice: In flight display bird takes off at about 60°, rises to about 15–30 m, flutters in air for many minutes while singing clear phrase of 3–4 notes, *is-it-wee, is-it-wee-prr* or *for-see-is-it-wee*, in each case accented and rising in pitch on the *ee*; each phrase uttered on rising flutter about 5 seconds apart; then descends again at same angle to take-off point; may also fly up, whistle plaintively at about 4 m, then drop into grass; faint *chik-chik* alarm call in flight.

Distribution: 2 separate populations in s Africa and Somalia; in s Africa confined to Lesotho, e Orange Free State, se Transvaal highveld, Natal to Ncora Dam, Transkei.

Status: Generally uncommon resident; locally common (e.g. Wakkerstroom region). Vulnerable (RDB).
Habitat: High-altitude and montane grassveld above about 1700 m, usually on crowns and ridges without rocks and with dense grass cover up to 50 cm tall.
Habits: Usually solitary, but several adjacent males may display simultaneously (see **Voice**). In flight fans tail; flight fast; on landing crouches or stands upright; may run several metres. On ground stands bolt upright; does not appear to perch on fences or stones. Poorly known.
Food: Unrecorded.
Breeding: *Season:* November in Orange Free State, January in Transvaal. *Nest:* Domed cup of grass in tussock. *Clutch:* 3 eggs. *Eggs:* Pinkish, heavily spotted with light brown and grey, concentrated at thick end; measure (1) 21,1 × 15,2. *Incubation:* Unrecorded. *Nestling:* Unrecorded.

---

500 (475)   **Longbilled Lark**   **Plate 45**
Langbeklewerik
Mirafra curvirostris

[Langschnabellerche]
Measurements: Length ♂ 19–20 cm, ♀ 16–17 cm; wing (5 ♂) 104–107,4–113, ♀ 90–97; tail (5 ♂) 73–82; tarsus (5 ♂) 27,5–30; hindclaw (5 ♂) 11–15,2; culmen (5 ♂) 29,5–33.
Bare Parts: Iris brown; bill blackish horn, base pinkish; legs and feet pinkish brown.
Identification: Size large; see lark key. Above brown, rufous or greyish brown, more or less mottled or streaked with dark brown; eyebrow clear white; below whitish or buff (rufous in Spikeheeled lark); breast finely streaked darker; bill longish, decurved; tail relatively long (short in Spikeheeled Lark); posture on ground usually somewhat crouched (Spikeheeled Lark usually stands upright). *Immature:* More mottled above and speckled below than adult.
Voice: Plaintive whistled *peeeuu*, or 2-syllabled *mee-too*, falling in pitch; highly ventriloquial and hard to locate when calling on ground; also calls in display flight, rising almost vertically from ground or perch, whistles at top of trajectory, closes wings, drops vertically, then opens wings just before landing; also chattering call-notes, *churr-wee-wurr* or *pee-hee-hee*.

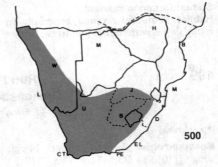

Distribution: Mountainous and arid parts of s Africa to Angola (Benguela).
Status: Common resident.
Habitat: Open short grassveld or desert from coastal Namib dunes and karoo shrub to high mountains and stony hills and ridges.
Habits: Usually solitary or in pairs. For-

432

ages mostly on open areas or at base of plants, digging with long bill; posture on ground typically crouched with flexed legs. Often perches on top of stone or mound when disturbed or to look around; less often perches on bushes. Display flight characteristic (see **Voice**).

Food: Insects, seeds, *Lycium* fruits.

Breeding: *Season*: August to April (mostly September-December; earlier in sw Cape, later in E); variable in arid regions according to rainfall. *Nest*: Domed cup of grass on ground under stone or grasstuft; lined with finer material. *Clutch*: (6) 2–2,7–3 eggs (usually 3). *Eggs*: Dull white to pinkish white, evenly speckled and spotted with yellowish brown and grey; measure (16) 23,3 × 16,7 (21,8–24,9 × 15,8–17,5). *Incubation*: Unrecorded. *Nestling*: Unrecorded.

501 (465) Shortclawed Lark Plate 44
Kortkloulewerik
Mirafra chuana

[Betschuanalerche]

Measurements: Length about 19 cm; wing ♂ 105, ♀ 91; tail (3) 75–79; tarsus (3) 26–27,5; hindclaw (3) 7–8,5; culmen (3) 16,5–20,5.

Bare Parts: Iris brown; bill brownish horn, base paler; legs and feet pinkish brown.

Identification: Size large (larger than Rufousnaped Lark), rather pipitlike but shape chunkier and markings very bold; see lark key. Similar to Rufousnaped Lark, but bill longer, looks rather straight in field; primaries edged rufous (not easily visible in flight; no rufous in wing of Longbilled Lark), above tawny brown, boldly streaked black; slight rufous crest; eyebrow white, conspicuous; throat off-white; breast buff, clearly streaked brown; tail all dark (no white tip as in Spikeheeled Lark); belly buffy white.

Voice: Callnote loud clear rising whistle *pooeeeep*, usually uttered repeatedly in flight; song shrill clear *pip-peeu-peeu, peeuweeu, wip peee prrr pip peeet pree* and variations of other clear whistles; *kwert-kwert* alarm call from top of low bush; harsh warning *krerr-krerr-krerr*.

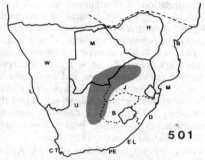

Distribution: Northern Cape (Kuruman), se Botswana, adjacent Transvaal; possibly also nw Orange Free State.

Status: Mostly uncommon resident, but locally common around Pietersburg, n Transvaal and in se Botswana. Probably Rare (RDB).

Habitat: Open ground in semi-arid scrub of Karee (*Lycium* and *Rhus* species) and Vaalbos *Tarchonanthus camphoratus*; grassland 30–40 cm tall with scattered *Acacia* thorntrees, or taller open grassland in n Transvaal, usually with open patches of shorter grass; fallow lands. Shares grassy habitat with Rufousnaped Lark.

Habits: Usually solitary or in pairs. Displays in fluttering flight, low over grass, clapping wings; when disturbed may fly to top of bush and gives alarm or warning call, but more often lands in grass; not usually shy. Flight floppy, 2–4 m above grass, often accompanied by whistled call-notes. Walks with typical crouched *Mirafra* posture and short steps. Poorly known.

Food: Insects and grass seeds.

Breeding: *Season*: March (1 possible record, n Transvaal), October–January in se Botswana. *Nest*: Cup of grass stems, leaves and roots in hollow in ground at base of herb or shrub in overgrazed grassveld; measures (12) 7,5–8,4–11,5 cm diameter, 3–4–6 cm deep. *Clutch*: (13) 2–2,7–3 eggs. *Eggs*: Dull white to buffy brown, spotted and blotched evenly with shades of brown and grey; measure (9)

433

21,2 × 15,6 (18,7–22,4 × 15,1–16). *Incubation*: Unrecorded; by ♀ only. *Nestling*: Unrecorded; fed by both parents.

Ref. Herremans, M. & Herremans, D. 1992. *Babbler* 23:6–17.

Hustler, K. 1985. *Honeyguide* 31:109–110.

502 (461)   Karoo Lark   Plate 44
Karoolewerik
Mirafra albescens

[Karrulerche]

Measurements: Length about 17 cm; wing (5) 83–85,4–89; tail 52–54,2–56; tarsus 24–24,6–26; culmen 13–13,9–15.

Bare Parts: Iris brown; bill blackish horn, base paler; legs and feet grey-brown.

Identification: Size medium; see lark key. Bill fairly light (not conical or decurved; lighter than that of Red Lark); above grey to rufous, heavily streaked (Dune Lark paler, very lightly streaked or almost plain; Red Lark deep plain rufous); dark line from gape to ear coverts (none in Fawncoloured Lark); eyebrow and line below eye white; below white, breast heavily streaked (lightly streaked in Dune Lark); tail dark, square, shortish; flight rather heavy. *Immature*: More spotted than streaked above.

Voice: Stereotyped phrase of 2–3 staccato notes, one high-pitched buzzy note and one lower-pitched final bubbling trill, *tip-tip-tip-zree-trrr*; also *cheepy-cheepy-rrr*.

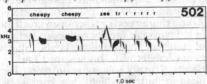

Distribution: Sw Cape and Karoo to Namaqualand; n limits uncertain, but probably overlaps with Dune Lark in n Namaqualand and s Namib Desert.

Status: Common resident.

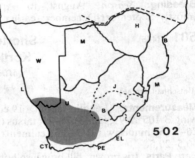

502

Habitat: Shrubby semi-desert on stony or sandy ground, coastal dunes.

Habits: Usually solitary or in pairs. Forages on ground in hunched posture, legs well flexed; digs for food in sand by shaking vigorously with bill, especially at base of plants. When disturbed may run mouse-like among shrubs, or flies up to perch on bush. Sings from perch or in flight on rapidly vibrating wings, often almost hovering in one place.

Food: Seeds, arthropods, berries.

Breeding: *Season*: August to March (mainly August-November in winter-rainfall area); in more arid parts probably opportunistically after rain. *Nest*: Cup of grass with domed roof, set into ground at base of plant; built by both sexes. *Clutch*: 2–3 eggs. *Eggs*: White, spotted with brown, red-brown and grey; measure (8) 21,3 × 16 (19,8–22,8 × 14,7–19,6). *Incubation*: Unrecorded. *Nestling*: Unrecorded.

503 (–)   Dune Lark   Plate 44
Duinlewerik
Mirafra erythrochlamys

[Dünenlerche]

Measurements: Length about 17 cm; wing (4 ♂) 87–88,3–89, (4 ♀) 81–81,8–82, (5 unsexed) 83–85,6–88; tail (5) 61–62,6–64; tarsus (5) 25–26,2–28; culmen (5) 14–15–16. Weight (8 ♂) 26,3–29,4–33,1 g, (10 ♀) 24,8–26,8–28,9 g.

Bare Parts: Iris brown; bill brownish horn, base paler; legs and feet pinkish brown.

Identification: Size medium; see lark key. Similar in build to Karoo Lark; above rufous, faintly streaked or almost plain

(Karoo Lark heavily streaked; Red Lark deeper rufous, unstreaked); dark line from gape to ear coverts (none in Fawncoloured Lark); below white, lightly streaked on breast (streaks heavy in Karoo Lark).
Voice: Similar to that of Karoo Lark, but with longer series of about 5 introductory staccato notes, *tip-tip-tip-tip-tip-zree-trrr*, lasting 2–3 seconds; during nestbuilding ♂ sings *tip tip tip* introductory notes of phrase ending with 3 *tew tew tew* notes, with wings drooped and sometimes fluttered, but not rattled; mellow bubbling notes in display flight (see **Habits**); buzzing threat note in territorial dispute; alarm call loud *prrr-t-t-t-t-t*.

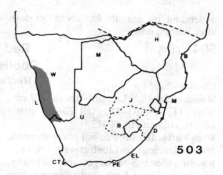

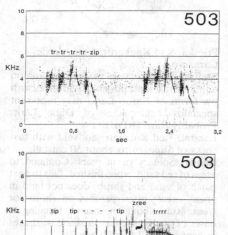

rapidly from side to side with bill to expose seed-rich lower layers, especially at bases of plants; runs quickly from one grasstuft to another. Shelters for about 3 hours in heat of day inside clumps of grass, then active again in late afternoon. Sings from perch on mound or grass stem, or in flight; displays by flying slowly around with slow deep wingbeats, 3–20 m above ground; also hovers with dangling legs and flicking tail at about 3 m giving rapid series of mellow bubbling notes.
Food: Insects (68%; mostly ants), seeds (32%; mostly grass seed); also succulent leaves and buds of *Trianthema hereroensis*.
Breeding: *Season*: August to May (peak January-February); breeding territory 2–4 ha. *Nest*: Cup of grass (mainly dead leaves of *Stipagrostis sabulicola*) and rootlets, with domed roof attached to adjacent plant; overall height (10) 11,5–12,9–16 cm, overall width (10) 11–12,1–14,5 cm, internal height (9) 5,5–7,5–10 cm, internal diameter (9) 6,5–7,4–10 cm; entrance height (9) 5,5–7,5–10 cm, width (9) 6–6,9–10 cm, usually facing SE; lined with fine plant material, feathers, hair and shed reptile skin, often plastered and felted with spider web; set into sand at base of grasstuft at top of small hummock or on side of hummock or steep dune; built by ♀ only in 7–9 days. *Clutch*: (11) 1–1,9–2 eggs. *Eggs*: White, densely spotted with dark red-brown and some pale purplish grey, concentrated at thick end into ring or cap; measure (16) 22 × 15,9 (20,1–23,7 × 14,3–17,5); weigh (10) 2,5–2,9–3,4 g. *Incubation*: (3) 13–14 days by ♀ only. *Nestling*: 12–14 days; fed by both parents; young

Distribution: From n Namaqualand and lower Orange River inland from coastal dunes to about Walvis Bay, Namibia (n limits uncertain).
Status: Common resident.
Habitat: Sand dunes or sandy flats with low shrubs or sparse tufts of coarse grass (*Stipagrostis sabulicola* and *S. lutescens*).
Habits: Solitary, in pairs or in groups of 4–8 birds. Active from about 20 minutes after sunrise, foraging singly for insects from surface of sand or plants; moves down dune to form groups of up to 6 birds, foraging for seeds by flicking sand

dependent on parents for about 30 days after leaving nest.

Ref. Boyer, H.J. 1988. *Ostrich* 59:30–37.
Cox, G.W. 1983. *Ostrich* 54:113–120.

504 (479)   Red Lark   Plate 45
Rooilewerik
Mirafra burra

[Oranjelerche]

Measurements: Length about 19 cm; wing (11) 95–103–112; tail 72–83; tarsus 26–30; culmen (2) 11–13.

Bare Parts: Iris brown; bill blackish horn, base paler; legs and feet greyish brown.

Identification: Size large; see lark key. Similar to Dune Lark, but deeper rufous above, not streaked (browner and streaked from Brandvlei eastwards); face boldly patterned; dark line from gape to ear coverts; eyebrow and stripe below eye white; below white, heavily streaked dark brown on breast; bill heavy (heavier than in either Dune or Karoo Lark); ♂ larger and more richly red than ♀, markings on face and breast more distinct (♀ looks more like Karoo Lark). *Immature*: Streaked dusky on back (similar to Karoo Lark).

Voice: Slightly husky pleasing whistled *trrridly-woo-tu-wee*, accented on first and last syllables; musical trill; rattling alarm call with hovering alarm flight near nest.

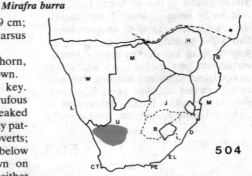

504

Prieska, S to Kenhardt, Vanwyksvlei and Carnarvon.

Status: Locally rare to fairly common nomadic resident; possibly hybridizes with nw forms of Karoo Lark; may represent specialized subspecies of Dune Lark. Probably Rare (RDB).

Habitat: Red Kalahari sandveld with tussocks of *Stipagrostis* about 50 cm tall.

Habits: Solitary or in pairs. Confined to areas of red sand; when flushed, flies to next patch of sand and shrub; does not land in grassy areas; often perches on shrubs or trees. Runs about on ground, foraging at bases of plants; shelters in shade of shrubs in heat of day. Little known.

Food: Mostly grass seeds; also seeds of forbs, *Lycium* fruits and insects.

Breeding: *Season*: October to January. *Nest*: Cup of grass stems lined with fine grass leaves and flowers; 2,5 cm deep; 7,5–8,5 cm diameter; with domed or half-domed roof of dry grass; entrance about 9 cm high; on red sand between grasstufts. *Clutch*: (1) 3 eggs. *Eggs*: White, speckled with sepia, brown and greyish brown, slightly concentrated at thick end; measure (1) 23,3 × 16,8. *Incubation*: Unrecorded. *Nestling*: Unrecorded; fed by both parents.

Ref. Dean, W.R.J. 1989. *Ostrich* 60:158.
Dean, W.R.J., Milton, S.J., Watkeys, M.K. & Hockey, P.A.R. 1991. *Biol. Conserv.* 58:257–274.
Myburgh, N. & Steyn, P. 1989. *Birding S. Afr.* 41:114–115.

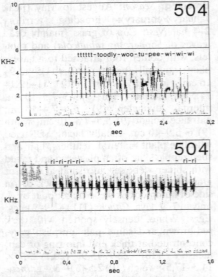

Distribution: From S bank of Orange River in Bushmanland (Bushman Flats) to

505 (464)   Dusky Lark   Plate 44
Donkerlewerik
Pinarocorys nigricans

Yisimatuli (K), Xihelagadzi (Ts), [Drossellerche]

Measurements: Length 18–19 cm; wing (2) 115–118; tail 76; tarsus 26–27,5; hindclaw 7–8; culmen 15–15,5.
Bare Parts: Iris brown; bill dark horn, base yellowish; legs and feet whitish.
Identification: Size large; see lark key. Above brownish grey to dark brown, lightly scaled with buff; bold brown and white head pattern; below white, heavily spotted on breast (looks thrushlike). *Immature*: More distinctly scaled above with tawny.
Voice: Soft *wek-wek-wek* repeated 3–6 times, or *chuk* or *churruk* in flight; *zhree zhree zhree* repeated in song-flight display.

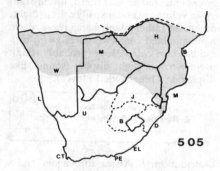

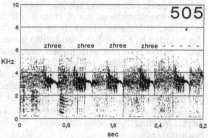

Distribution: Africa S of equator; breeds tropical Africa to n Angola; migrates to s Mozambique, Transvaal, n Natal, Zululand, Zimbabwe, e Botswana.

Status: Uncommon nonbreeding intra-African migrant, October to May (or June).
Habitat: Short grass in savanna and open woodland; also parks, lawns.
Habits: Usually in small flocks on passage migration; sometimes in flocks of hundreds. Forages on ground; walks about quickly, stops, flicks wings and continues walking; movements vigorous. Flight undulating; in flight display rises in slow spiral to about 30 m, circles for about 2 minutes, flapping and gliding; then descends in series of stalling glides to tree; throughout display sings *zhree*. Often perches in trees.
Food: Insects.
Breeding: Extralimital.

Ref. Dean, W.R.J. 1974. *Durban Mus. Novit.* 10:109–125; 1979. *Ostrich* 50:60–62.

506 (474)   Spikeheeled Lark   Plate 45
Vlaktelewerik (Vlakvoëltjie)
Chersomanes albofasciata

Ungqwembe, Ungqembe (X), [Zirplerche]

Measurements: Length ♂ 15 cm, ♀ 13 cm; wing (9 ♂) 89–91,3–95, (4 ♀) 80–83; tail (9 ♂) 50–59, (4 ♀) 43–49; tarsus (9 ♂) 27–31, (4 ♀) 25–28; culmen (13) 19,5–21. Weight (21 ♂) 22,5–27,4–32 g, (14 ♀) 19,5–22–27,6 g, (2 unsexed) 27–31 g.
Bare Parts: Iris brown; bill blackish horn, base paler; legs and feet pinkish brown.

Identification: Size medium; see lark key. Long decurved bill, rufous belly and relatively short white-tipped tail diagnostic; above brown, rufous, pinkish or light greyish (variable with range; deeper rufous or brown and more heavily marked in S and E, paler and more lightly marked in dry W), mottled dark brown, scaled buffy; eyebrow rufous (never white); throat white; rest of underparts rufous; tail blackish, tipped white (conspicuous

437

SPIKEHEELED LARK

when fanned in flight). *Immature*: Mottled with whitish above and below.

Voice: Mellow chatter or trill, *piree-piree-piree*, repeated several times, usually falling in volume at end; usually calls in flight, otherwise rather silent; harsh *cheee* alarm note; jumbled *chip-kwip-kwip-kwip, ti-ti-ti-ti-ti, chirri-chirri-chirri* (probably song); *trrr-trrr-trrr* in flight display (sounds like displaying Threebanded Plover).

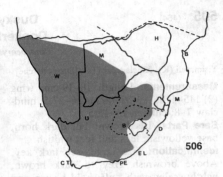

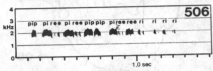

Distribution: S Africa to Angola and s Tanzania (rarely to Kenya); in s Africa mainly confined to highveld and dry W.

Status: Common resident; somewhat nomadic.

Habitat: Sparse grassland, overgrazed areas, shrubby semidesert to desert edge.

Habits: In pairs or groups of up to 10 birds. Runs or walks quickly while foraging, digging in soft soil at base of plants; posture usually rather upright. Flight bouncy, accompanied by trilling calls and characteristically fanned tail. When disturbed creeps away among shrubs, or flies away for short distance and lands on ground; seldom perches on shrubs. In display flight rises to about 2 m, then glides down with wings stretched upwards, giving display call (see **Voice**).

Food: Insects, solifugids and other arthropods (84%), seeds (16%), some green plant material; does not drink water.

Breeding: *Season*: Mainly August to December; any month in arid regions according to rainfall. *Nest*: Cup of dry grass and rootlets, about 6,4 cm diameter, 3,2 cm deep (27 nests), set into scrape in soil; in foundation of small stones, clods or sticks; at base of grasstuft or shrub on shady side (E, SE or S); foundation sometimes partly covered with mixed sand and spider web. *Clutch*: (67) 2–2,3–3 eggs. *Eggs*: White or greyish white, speckled or spotted with brown, usually concentrated at thick end; measure (136) 20,9 × 14,8 (19,2–22,5 × 13,7–16,3). *Incubation*: 12 days. *Nestling*: At least 10 days; fed by both parents.

---

507 (488)   **Redcapped Lark**   **Plate 45**
                   Rooikoplewerik
                   Calandrella cinerea

Tsiroane, Thetsa-balisana (SS), Intibane, Intutyane (X), umNtoli (Z), [Rotscheitellerche]

Measurements: Length 15–16 cm; wing (83 ♂) 90–95,8–105,5, (67 ♀) 85,5–90,1–98; tail (8) 58–67; tarsus (8) 19–21,5; culmen (8) 12–14. Weight (6 ♂) 22,4–25,7–28,9 g, (5 ♀) 24–26,4–28,9 g, (28 unsexed) 21,9–25,9–30,4 g.

Bare Parts: Iris brown; bill and inside of mouth black; legs and feet black to brown.

Identification: Size medium; see lark key. Crown and pectoral patches plain bright rufous (diagnostic); back light brown, streaked darker; below white, breast

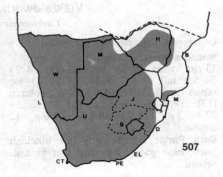

438

faintly brownish, flanks buff to tawny; no spots or streaks on breast as in most other lark species; tail dark, square, outer rectrices white; bill rather slender and pipit-like, but all black (pipits' bills pale at base); flight pipitlike. *Immature*: Above dark brown, spotted whitish; below whitish, breast heavily spotted dark brown.

Voice: Flight song jumbled varied high-pitched and somewhat trilled *treee, treee, tip-tip, tippy, tippy, tippy*, etc.; may imitate other birdcalls; callnote sharp high-pitched *tsreee* or sparrowlike *chreep*.

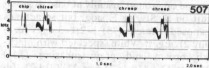

Distribution: S, E and N Africa, s Europe, C Asia to Manchuria; in s Africa widespread, but absent from lowveld regions except as vagrant.

Status: Common, but numbers fluctuate; highly nomadic; resident in some areas.

Habitat: Open grassland, bare ground, burnt and overgrazed veld, cultivated lands, semidesert.

Habits: Usually gregarious, in flocks of hundreds (rarely thousands) when not breeding; otherwise in pairs or small flocks of 20–30 birds. In display flight dips and twists while singing (see **Voice**). Forages on ground in short runs or quick walking steps, calling often. When disturbed flies low, showing white outer rectrices, then drops to ground and runs; flies high on nomadic treks.

Food: Mainly seeds; also many insects, up to 12 mm long.

Breeding: *Season*: March to December (mainly August-September) in Zimbabwe, February to October in w Transvaal, August to November in Natal; several broods/season. *Nest*: Neat cup of dry grass in scrape on ground; sometimes near plant or clod of earth, but often fully exposed; sometimes with foundation of small clods; built in about 5 days. *Clutch*: (161) 1–2,1–4 eggs (usually 2). *Eggs*: Creamy white, spotted with grey and some brown; measure (86) 21,2 × 15,1 (17–23,3 × 13,2–16,8). *Incubation*: 13–15 days. *Nestling*: (6) 10–12 days; fed by both parents.

Ref. Borrett, R.P. & Wilson, K.J. 1971. *Ostrich* 42:37–40.
Winterbottom, J.M. & Wilson, A.H. 1959. *Ostrich Suppl.* 3:289–299.

508 (490) Pinkbilled Lark
Pienkbeklewerik
Spizocorys conirostris

Plate 45

Ruruworo, Tjowe (K), [Rotschnabellerche]

Measurements: Length 12–13 cm; wing (24) 73–76,7–81; tail 39–48; tarsus 15–19; culmen 10–12,5.

Bare Parts: Iris pinkish brown to yellowish brown; bill pink; legs and feet pinkish.

Identification: Size small; see lark key. Similar to Botha's Lark, but bill stouter, and belly uniformly plain light rufous (in Botha's Lark, rufous of belly fades to whitish in centre and under tail); above rufous brown mottled and streaked dark brown; throat white; breast streaked blackish; flanks not streaked (streaked blackish in Botha's Lark); bill conical, pink. *Immature*: Darker than adult;

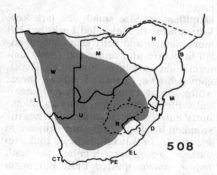

more speckled above and below; bill blackish.

439

Voice: Flight call characteristic quick musical chirp of 2–3 syllables, *si-si-si* repeated often; alarm call similar, but accented on first syllable, *SI-si-si*.

Distribution: Southern Africa from e Cape and upland Natal through highveld to Botswana and n Namibia.

Status: Common nomad; numbers fluctuate greatly.

Habitat: Open short grassland in highveld, tall grass in Kalahari sandveld, cultivated lands.

Habits: In pairs when breeding; otherwise gregarious in flocks of 5–20 or more birds. Unobtrusive and easily overlooked unless calling in flight or drinking at water. Forages by walking or running in short bursts on open ground, often in upright posture. When disturbed at nest, often flutters over site, giving alarm call.

Food: Seeds and insects.

Breeding: *Season*: All months (opportunistic after rain); mainly October to May in E. *Nest*: Cup of dry grass and rootlets with apron of coarser grass and sticks around rim; diameter of cup 5,3 cm, depth 3,5 cm (means of 54 nests); set into scrape on ground; usually at base of grass-tuft on S, SE, or E side, but sometimes exposed. *Clutch*: (75) 1–2,1–3 eggs (usually 2). *Eggs*: White, speckled with blackish brown and grey; measure (144) 18,5 × 13,6 (16,1–24,6 × 11,8–14,7). *Incubation*: 11–12–13 days. *Nestling*: 10 days.

509 (472)   Botha's Lark   Plate 45
Vaalrivierlewerik
Spizocorys fringillaris

[Finkenlerche]

Measurements: Length about 12 cm; wing (6 ♂) 78,3–80,8–82,9, (4 ♀) 78,4–80,5–82,3; tail (6 ♂) 39,2–41,8–43,8, (4 ♀) 38,2–40,3–43; tarsus (6 ♂) 19,5–20,9–22,2, (4 ♀) 19,5–20,9–21,9; hindclaw (6 ♂) 9,5–10,2–11,8, (4 ♀) 10,1–11–12; culmen (6 ♂) 9,9–10,5–11, (4 ♀) 10,5–11,2–13. Weight (6 ♂) 15,7–17,9–19,2 g, (3 ♀) 20,2–20,5–21 g.

Bare Parts: Iris brown; bill, legs and feet pink.

Identification: Size small; see lark key. Very similar to Pinkbilled Lark, but bill more slender and belly shading to whitish in centre and under tail (belly uniform light rufous in Pinkbilled Lark); above brown, streaked black; throat white; throat, centre of belly and undertail white; breast, upper belly and flanks buffy rufous; breast and flanks heavily streaked blackish (flanks not streaked in Pinkbilled Lark); bill conical, pink, tip darker. *Immature*: Similar to adult below; above spotted buff; bill horn; legs and feet pink.

Voice: Melodious *chiree* repeated several times; flight call irregular *chuk*.

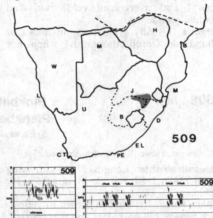

Distribution: Mainly Vaal River catchment from ne orange Free State to se Transvaal around Amersfoort and Wakkerstroom; distribution patchy.

Status: Uncommon resident (possibly common locally). Probably Rare (RDB).

Habitat: Heavily grazed grassy uplands in sour grassveld (avoids valley bottoms, vleis, pastures, cultivated lands and rocky areas).

Habits: Solitary, in pairs or in groups of up to 10 birds. Usually undemonstrative and inconspicuous; no aerial display recorded; flushes readily; fans tail on take-off, showing buff outer rectrices, then flies in wide circle calling; flight undulating, followed by vertical dive to land in grass. Forages by walking about briskly with upright stance, looking at ground, sometimes darting after prey or jumping into air after flying insect; does not dig for food.

Food: Insects (including beetles and moths); possibly also seeds when not breeding.

Breeding: *Season*: November to December. *Nest*: Cup of shredded dry grass, lined with finer material, sometimes with sheep's wool; overall diameter (6) 7,8–8,6–10 cm, inside diameter (11) 5,1–5,8–6,1 cm, inside depth (8) 3,1–3,4–4,5 cm; set into scrape on ground between grasstufts or among sheep droppings, exposed above. *Clutch*: (9) 2–2,1–3 eggs (usually 2). *Eggs*: Cream, heavily speckled with brown and grey, concentrated at thick end; measure (11) 18,7 × 12,6 (17,7–19,6 × 12,1–14,5). *Incubation*: Unrecorded. *Nestling*: Unrecorded; fed by both parents.

Ref. Allan, D.G., Batchelor, G.R. & Tarboton, W.R. 1983. *Ostrich* 54:55–57.
Herholdt, J.J. & Grobler, N.J. 1987. *Mirafra* 4:61–62.

510 (491) Sclater's Lark / Namakwalewerik

Plate 45

Spizocorys sclateri

[Sclaters Kurzhaubenlerche]

Measurements: Length about 14 cm; wing (6 ♂) 83–86, (6 ♀) 80–84; tail (12) 42–49; tarsus (12) 16–17,5; culmen (12) 13–14,2.

Bare Parts: Iris brown; bill brownish horn, tip darker; legs and feet light brown.

Identification: Size smallish to medium; see lark key. Build stocky; looks big-headed and short-tailed; dark tear-drop mark below eye diagnostic; above buff, broadly streaked dusky; throat white; breast and belly fawn, breast streaked dusky; head not crested (as in Stark's Lark). *Immature*: Paler and greyer than adult; more spotted than streaked above.

Voice: Flight call *trit-trit-trit* like calls of Spikeheeled Lark; song phrase *trip-trip-trip-trip cheeeu*; twittering notes while feeding.

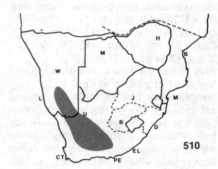

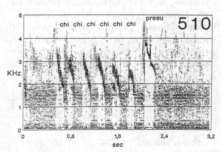

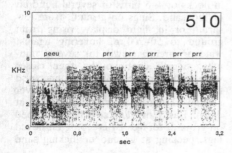

Distribution: Southern Namibia, nw Cape (Brandvlei, Vanwyksvlei, Prieska) to karoo (Carnarvon, Beaufort West, De Aar, Philipstown, Prince Albert); borders of distribution inadequately known.

Status: Uncommon resident; nomadic

within restricted range. Possibly Rare (RDB).

Habitat: Arid stony plains with low sparse shrubs.

Habits: In pairs when breeding; otherwise gregarious in flocks of up to 25 birds. Drinks often, flying to water in small groups; often keeps eyes partly closed. Turns over small flat stones while foraging. Poorly known.

Food: Harvester ants (*Messor* sp.), harvester termites (*Hodotermes*), seeds.

Breeding: *Season*: July to November (probably opportunistically after rain). *Nest*: Neat cup of thickly padded dry grass with fringe of material around rim flush with hollow on ground, surrounded by small stones; fully exposed among shale far from cover; cup diameter 5–5,9 cm, depth (4) 2,5–2,9–3 cm. *Clutch*: (19) 1 egg. *Eggs*: Off-white, finely spotted with greyish brown concentrated at thick end; measure (7) 21,1 × 14,9 (20–23,4 × 13,9–15,5). *Incubation*: Unrecorded; by both sexes. *Nestling*: 10–11 days; stones placed in nest after chick hatches; chick leaves nest unable to fly; fed by both parents.

Ref. Steyn, P. & Myburgh, N. 1989. *Birding S. Afr*. 41:67–69; 1991. *Birding S. Afr*. 43:73–76.

511 (492) Stark's Lark · Woestynlewerik · Plate 45
Spizocorys starki

[Starks Kurzhaubenlerche]

Measurements: Length about 14 cm; wing (14 ♂) 76–80,9–85, (8 ♀) 76–77,6–79,5; tail (22) 39–51; tarsus (22) 14,5–18; culmen (22) 11,5–14. Weight (40 ♂) 16–18,5–21,2 g, (30 ♀) 15,5–18,6–22,5 g.

Bare Parts: Iris brown; bill whitish horn; legs and feet pinkish white.

Identification: Size smallish to medium; see lark key. Crown feathers long, often raised as crest (diagnostic); above sandy buff, broadly streaked dusky; below white, breast streaked dusky; bill rather heavy, pale whitish (diagnostic); no pale eyebrow, but eye surrounded by whitish ring. *Immature*: Spotted whitish above.

Voice: Simple mellow trilled song of mixed notes, *prrr, prrr, preee, preee, prrr, prrr, preee, preee*, or *chur-chirr-cheer-chor-cheer-reelo*; flight call *trree* repeated irregularly.

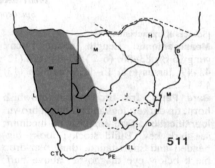

Distribution: Arid w parts of s Africa to sw Angola.

Status: Common nomad; numbers fluctuate greatly.

Habitat: Sparsely shrubby stony semi-desert, thinly grassed stony or gravelly plains.

Habits: In pairs when breeding; otherwise in flocks of 4–5 birds or several hundred or thousand. Sings on ground, from low shrub, or in flight display, rising from ground to 50–200 m, hovering against wind or circling slowly for several minutes, singing continuously; then closes wings and drops vertically to ground; also flutters slowly with dangling legs low over ground while singing; starts displaying at dawn. Easily overlooked when crouched on ground; forages by creeping on flexed legs, pecking at ground or flicking sand

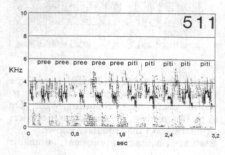

sideways with bill to uncover food, often squatting while nibbling food; seeks shade in heat of day, rarely perching on top of shrub or rock.
Food: Seeds (75%), arthropods (20%), green plant material (5%); drinks in hot weather.
Breeding: *Season*: August to November in Kalahari, April to May in Namib; breeds opportunistically after rain. *Nest*: Cup of fine silky grass in slight depression in soil;

internal diameter 5,5 cm, depth 3,4 cm (means of 15 nests); set in foundation of small clods or stones; usually at base of plant or stone, on S or SE side, sometimes exposed; often in loose colonies. *Clutch*: (19) 2–2,3–3 eggs. *Eggs*: White, spotted with pale pinky brown and some grey; measure (13) 19,7 × 14,3 (19–20,4 × 13,4–14,8). *Incubation*: 11–12–13 days by both sexes. *Nestling*: 10 days; fed by both parents.

512 (463)   Thickbilled Lark   Plate 44
Dikbeklewerik
Galerida magnirostris

[Dickschnabellerche]

Measurements: Length about 18 cm; wing (67 ♂) 95,5–104,9–111,5, (39 ♀) 92,5–98,8–104; tail (44 ♂) 60,1–65,8–70,5, (19 ♀) 56,7–61–66,1; tarsus (7) 25–27; hindclaw (7) 13–17; culmen (71 ♂) 18,7–21,2–23,5, (34 ♀) 17,1–20,5–23,1.
Bare Parts: Iris brown; bill dark brown, base yellow; legs and feet pinkish brown.
Identification: Size large; see lark key. Heavy bill with yellow base diagnostic, usually held up at slight angle; above light brown, heavily mottled with black; below whitish (sometimes buffy white), heavily streaked black on breast; may raise prominent crest at back of crown, especially when singing; tail dark, square. *Immature*: Above brown, lightly scaled whitish, forming 2 pale wingbars; crown spotted with tawny (crest often raised); below washed bright tawny, streaked blackish on breast; base of lower jaw whitish.
Voice: Fluty rolling phrase of 4–8 syllables run quickly together, *tee-triddly-pee* or *whit-titwiddliddle-widdly*, repeated many times; also imitates calls of other grassland birds (at least 13 species recorded) in fine sustained song.

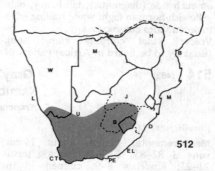

Distribution: Interior and SW of S Africa, including Lesotho.
Status: Common resident.
Habitat: High montane grassland, semi-arid karoo, fynbos, cultivated lands.
Habits: Usually solitary or in pairs. Often perches on fence, termite mound, rock or bush; sings from perch or in fluttering display flight. Forages by walking about with flexed legs. Conspicuous when calling.
Food: Insects, seeds, bulbs.
Breeding: *Season*: August to December. *Nest*: Cup of grass and rootlets set in foundation of small sticks; at base of grasstuft or shrub. *Clutch*: (18) 2–2,2–3 eggs. *Eggs*: White or pale cream, heavily spotted with brown and grey; measure (62) 23,2 × 16,6 (20,9–25,7 × 15,4–17,4). *Incubation*: Unrecorded. *Nestling*: Unrecorded; fed by both parents.

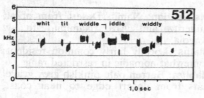

443

513 (487)   Bimaculated Lark   Plate 77
Swartborslewerik
Melanocorypha bimaculata

[Bergkalanderlerche]

Measurements: Length 17–19 cm; wing ♂ 117–127, ♀ 107–117; tail 50–61; tarsus 25–27; hindclaw 14; culmen 17–19.
Bare Parts: Iris brown; bill pale yellowish horn; legs and feet pinkish brown.
Identification: Size large (not included in lark key); build stocky; above buff, streaked blackish brown on head and back; rump plain buff; eyebrow white, broad; tail blackish, edged buff, tipped white; throat and belly white; flanks buff; breast buff, streaked dark brown, with large black patch on each side (diagnostic); bill heavy, pale yellowish horn; in flight white trailing edge to secondaries conspicuous.
Voice: Nasal chirping *klitra*; song (unlikely to be heard in Africa) variety of musical notes interspersed with imitations of other birdcalls.
Distribution: Breeds N Africa, s Europe, Middle East and C Asia; migrates to Egypt, Sudan and Ethiopia; vagrant to Namibia.
Status: Very rare vagrant, collected once, Swakopmund, Namibia, September 1930; probably an escaped aviary bird.
Habitat: Semidesert steppe, short grassland.
Habits: Likely to be solitary in s Africa, but usually in flocks when not breeding. Flight buoyant. Sings in circling display flight, then drops silently to ground.
Food: Seeds, insects.
Breeding: Extralimital.

Ref. Brooke, R.K. 1988. *Ostrich* 59:76–77.

514 (483)   Gray's Lark   Plate 45
Namiblewerik
Ammomanes grayi

[Namiblerche]

Measurements: Length about 14 cm; wing ♂ 82–85, ♀ 76,5; tail 49; tarsus 22–23; hindclaw 8–9; culmen 13–16. Weight (37 ♂) 19,3–22,7–26,5 g, (35 ♀) 17,5–20,2–23 g.
Bare Parts: Iris olive brown; bill grey, tip black; legs and feet grey.
Identification: Size small; see lark key. Very pale overall; above plain pinkish grey; eyebrow whitish; below white (no markings on breast); bill fairly slender and short. *Immature*: Above obscurely mottled.
Voice: Callnotes high-pitched *tseet* and mellow *tew* between members of flock; sings mainly at night, high-pitched tinkling notes and loud up-slurred whistles; sings also in aerial display, alternating song phrases with bursts of reedy wing-whirring in undulating flight.

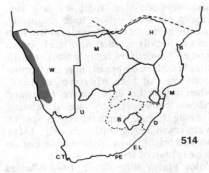

Distribution: Namib Desert from about Lüderitz and Aus (Namibia) to sw Angola.
Status: Locally fairly common resident; somewhat nomadic in restricted range.
Habitat: Barren pale pinkish grey gravel flats from desert edge to near coast,

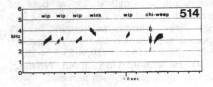

with or without sparse grass or low succulent shrubs; favours areas of grass
15–50 cm tall with much bare ground
between.

Habits: Usually in loose groups of 3–30
birds, foraging on ground, especially
around rodent burrows; picks food from
surface, or uncovers it by flicking sand
sideways with bill. Extremely difficult to
see; crouches when alarmed; flushes reluctantly, seldom flying far. May shelter in
rodent burrows in heat of day; also stands
on stones or low twigs to escape heat of
desert floor.

Food: Seeds (60%), arthropods (mainly
insects, 36%), green plant food (such as

bases of grass stems, 3%); does not drink
water; nestlings fed insects only.

Breeding: *Season:* Usually March to May,
sometimes to September; opportunistically after rain. *Nest:* Deep cup of fine
dry grass, sometimes thickly felted; inside
diameter 5,7 cm, depth 3,5–5 cm; in
scrape on gravel flat, usually next to stone
or sparse grasstuft, or under shrub; scrape
may be unlined. *Clutch:* (5) 2–2,6–3 eggs.
Eggs: White, finely speckled with pinky to
greyish brown and grey, concentrated at
thick end; measure (6) 21,3 × 14,8 (20,3–
21,9 × 14,5–15,7). *Incubation:* Unrecorded. *Nestling:* Unrecorded; leaves nest well
before flying age.

515 (484) Chestnutbacked Finchlark Plate 45
Rooiruglewerik
Eremopterix leucotis

Ruruworo, Tjowe (K), 'Mamphemphe, 'Maliberoane (SS), [Weißwangenlerche]

Measurements: Length 12–13 cm; wing
(20) 78–82,8–86; tail 43–49; tarsus 14–18;
culmen 10–13. Weight (2 ♂) 20–21 g,
(1 ♀) 23,8 g, (1 unsexed) 13,5 g.

Bare Parts: Iris brown; bill bluish to whitish horn; legs and feet pale grey.

Identification: Size small; see lark key.
Male: Head and underparts black; back
chestnut; large earpatch, narrow collar on
hindneck, thighs and heavy bill white (no
white patch in centre of crown as in ♂
Greybacked Finchlark); rump pale in flight.
Female: Head, back and breast mottled buff
and sooty brown; upperwing coverts chestnut; centre of belly black (no black on belly
of ♀ Blackeared Finchlark); faint whitish
collar on hindneck; flanks, thighs and
undertail white; bill heavy, whitish; plumage altogether darker than that of ♀ Greybacked Finchlark; rump pale in flight.
Immature: Similar to ♀ but paler; above
mottled with buffy white.

Voice: Rattling *chirp, chip-cheew*; song
varied and musical, usually in fluttering
flight.

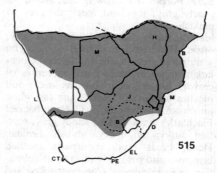

Distribution: Africa S of Sahara; in s
Africa absent from dry W, extreme SE
and extreme NE.

Status: Common nomad; numbers fluctuate greatly.

Habitat: Bare areas with scattered trees or
bushes in savanna and bushveld, burnt
grassland, airstrips, fallow lands, roadside
verges.

Habits: In pairs when breeding; otherwise
gregarious in flocks of up to 50 birds
(rarely in hundreds). Runs on ground
while foraging; posture often erect. Flight
low and jinking; lands suddenly. Rarely
perches in trees. Performs bouncing flight
over nest when disturbed.

Food: Seeds and insects.

Breeding: *Season:* February to September
in Zimbabwe (peak in May), February to

July in ♀ Transvaal; season irregular; probably opportunistic after rain. *Nest*: Scrape in soil, lined with cup of dry grass and rootlets; ♀ continues to add material after eggs laid; usually on S, SE or E of clod, stone or grasstuft. *Clutch*: (47) 1–1,9–2 eggs. *Eggs*: Greyish white, freckled with brown, concentrated at thick end; measure (16) 18,9 × 13,5 (17,6–19,9 × 12,9–14,2). *Incubation*: 11 days by both sexes; nest relief every 0,5–3 hours by day; only ♀ incubates at night. *Nestling*: Unrecorded.

Ref. Chittenden, H.N. & Batchelor, G.R. 1977. *Ostrich* 48:112.

516 (485) Greybacked Finchlark   Plate 45
Grysruglewerik
Eremopterix verticalis

Ruruworo, Tjowe (K), 'Maliberoane (SS), [Nonnenlerche]

Measurements: Length 13 cm; wing (33 ♂) 79–83,4–87, (26 ♀) 76,5–79,8–84; tail (37) 40–48; tarsus (37) 15–17,5; culmen (37) 9,5–12. Weight (7 ♂) 17,3–18,8–21,2 g, (7 ♀) 16,4–18–20,5 g, (57 unsexed) 12,5–17–21,1 g.

Bare Parts: Iris brown; bill bluish to pearly grey; legs and feet pale grey to pinkish grey.

Identification: Size small; see lark key. *Male*: Head and underparts black (no white on thigh as in Chestnutbacked Finchlark); large earpatch, patch in centre of crown, broad collar on hindneck and patches on sides of chest white (no white on crown or chest of ♂ Chestnutbacked Finchlark); back dark or sandy grey, mottled dusky; bill heavy, whitish. *Female*: Head, breast and upperparts mottled brownish and pale grey (no rufous coloration as in females of Chestnutbacked and Blackeared Finchlarks); centre of belly black (diagnostic in combination with greyish back); bill heavy, whitish. *Immature*: Similar to ♀, but mottled with buff above.

Voice: Sharp tinkling song *twip twip chik* in flight; sharp *pruk* alarm note; chirping flight calls, *chip chreep chip chip chreep*.

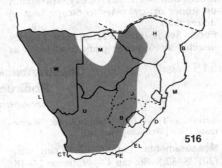

516

Distribution: Highveld and dry W of s Africa to arid coastal Angola.

Status: Very common nomad; numbers fluctuate greatly.

Habitat: Arid gravelly or stony ground with sparse shrubs and grass, open shortgrass plains, bare pans, burnt areas, fallow lands.

Habits: Gregarious, even when breeding; flocks number tens or hundreds of birds. In aerial display flies in circles 15–30 m diameter, a few metres above ground, often with dangling legs; flight display may or may not end in vertical dive to ground. Posture often upright when walking or running on ground; forages in loose flocks in open. Flight jerky and erratic; performs bouncing flight over nest when disturbed.

Food: Seeds (91%), insects (8%), green plant material (1%); drinks water frequently, especially in hot weather.

Breeding: *Season*: All months; opportunistically after rain. *Nest*: Cup of dry grass and rootlets, internal diameter 5,4 cm, depth 3 cm (means of 139 nests); set in scrape in soil, or substantial foundation of stones, clods and a few twigs; usually at

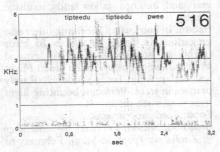

base of plant, stone or clod, on S, SE, or E side; built by ♀ only in 4–5 days; not colonial, but nests may be several metres apart. *Clutch*: (204) 2–2,1–3 eggs (86% of 2 eggs). *Eggs*: Dull white, speckled with brownish yellow, brown and grey, concentrated at thick end; measure (314) 19,3 × 13,9 (16,9–21 × 12,3–15,7). *Incubation*: 11–12–13 days by both sexes. *Nestling*: 7–10 days; fed by both parents.

517 (486) Blackeared Finchlark Plate 45
Swartoorlewerik
Eremopterix australis

[Schwarzwangenlerche]

Measurements: Length about 13 cm; wing (3 ♂) 79–80, (3 ♀) 73–78; tail (6) 43–48; tarsus (6) 15,5–17; culmen (6) 9,5–10.
Bare Parts: Iris orange-red to red-brown; bill bluish white; legs and feet brownish to greyish white.
Identification: Size small; see lark key. *Male*: Head and underparts solid black; back dull chestnut; bill heavy, whitish; broad black wings conspicuous in flight. *Female*: Above dull rufous, streaked with dark brown; faint whitish ring around eye; below white, spotted and streaked blackish; no black patch in centre of belly (as in other ♀ finchlarks); bill heavy, whitish. *Immature*: Similar to ♀, but barred above with buff and blackish; below mottled dusky and off-white on breast and flanks.
Voice: Buzzing notes in display flight; short canarylike song from ground; sharp *dzee* or *preep* alarm notes; *chee-chee-chee* distress call.

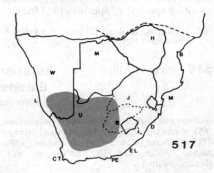

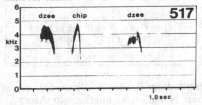

Distribution: Arid interior of S Africa, se Namibia and s Botswana.
Status: Locally common nomad; numbers fluctuate greatly.
Habitat: Shrubby karoo and Kalahari sandveld, especially associated with *Rhigozum* and *Galenia* shrub species; mostly confined to plains of red sandstone and red Kalahari sand.

Habits: Gregarious even when breeding; flocks may number 50–100 birds. Forages in open places among shrubs and stones; flies readily when disturbed, in typically bouncing erratic flight. Display flight butterflylike with exaggerated wingbeats in circles over territory, sometimes with legs dangling. ♂ performs elaborate injury-feigning distraction displays at nest.
Food: Insects and seeds; does not drink water.
Breeding: *Season*: July to November, also February in Kalahari; opportunistically after rain, so can breed at any time. *Nest*: Cup of fine grass and rootlets, inside diameter 5,2 cm, depth 3,3 cm (means of 50 nests); set in foundation of small sticks around scrape at base of shrub or grass-tuft; built by ♀ only; rim of cup and stick foundation covered with felted mixture of sand and spider web brought by ♂, applied by ♀. *Clutch*: (56) 2–2,1–3 eggs (usually 2). *Eggs*: White, finely speckled with pinky brown, forming wreath around thick end; measure (103) 18,3 × 13,4 (16,7–20,6 × 12,3–14,9). *Incubation*: 11–12–13 days by both sexes. *Nestling*: 7–10 days; fed by both parents.

26:4. Family 66 HIRUNDINIDAE—SWALLOWS AND MARTINS

Small to medium (including longish tail). Bill small, flattened; gape wide; legs very short and weak, feathered in some species; toes small and slender, partly joined at base, feathered in some species; body slender, streamlined; wings very long and pointed; tail medium to long, square or forked, outer rectrices sometimes very long; plumage black or brown dorsally, often with blue or green gloss, ventrally black, white, brown or rufous; sexes similar; aerial feeders on insects (some rarely eat fruit); most gregarious, at least when not breeding; nest solitarily or colonially; nest a pad of feathers and grass in chamber at end of self-made burrow in bank or in level ground, hole in tree, or in mud nest (half-cup or bowl-and-tunnel) under overhang; eggs 1–6, white, plain or spotted; chick sparsely downy at hatching; parental care by both sexes. Distribution worldwide; about 75 species; 22 species in s Africa.

Ref. Turner, A. & Rose, C. 1989. *A handbook to the swallows and martins of the world.* London: Christopher Helm.

518 (493)   **Eurasian Swallow**   **Plate 46**
                                   Europese Swael
                                   Hirundo rustica

Sisampamema (K), Lefokotsane, 'Malinakana (SS), Nyenganyenga (Sh), Mbawulwana, Nyenga (Ts), Pêolwane, Phêtla (Tw), Inkonjane, Udlihashe, Ucelizapholo (X), iNkonjane (Z), [Rauchschwalbe]

Measurements: Length about 20 cm; wing (17 ♂) 118,5–123,9–127, (16 ♀) 112–121,1–126,5, (143 unsexed) 112–122,2–130; tail, longest rectrix (41) 61–72–105, shortest rectrix (10) 42–46; tarsus (101) 10–11,6–12,7; culmen (102) 5,2–6,5–11. Weight (344) 13,9–17,9–22,2 g.

Bare Parts: Iris brown; bill, legs and feet black.

Identification: Size medium (see swallow key); above metallic blueblack; forehead and throat rufous; throat bordered below by blueblack band (in *H. r. gutturalis* rufous of throat extends into black collar, even replacing it in centre); belly creamy white or buff; tail deeply forked, black with white windows (outer rectrices particularly long in newly moulted adults). *Immature:* Brownish with faint blueblack wash where adult blueblack; forehead and throat buff or whitish (but collar much broader than in Whitethroated Swallow); belly whiter than in adult; outer rectrices not very long.

Voice: Various high-pitched twittering and creaking notes; large flocks make considerable noise.

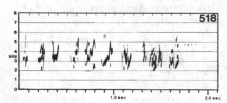

Distribution: Breeds N Africa, Europe, n Asia, N America; migrates to Africa, s Asia, Australasia and S America; throughout s Africa (mostly *H. r. rustica; H. r. gutturalis* occurs only as far S as Transvaal and Natal).

Status: Abundant nonbreeding Palaearctic migrant, September to April (sometimes to May); most s African birds come from w Russia and Britain, others from Europe and e Russia.

Habitat: Almost anywhere outside of forest; especially common over water, open grassland, cultivated lands, pastures and vleis.

Habits: Highly gregarious; flocks scatter by day. Roosts at night in reedbeds in flocks of hundreds of thousands or even millions of birds; also roosts in maize fields. Flight quick and agile, often low over ground; forages at all heights, often in company with other swallows and swifts. Before northward departure in March and April gathers in hundreds or thousands on utility lines, twittering excitedly; may fly 12 000 km in 34 days (Johannesburg to n hemisphere).

Food: Arthropods (mostly flying insects, but also spiders and amphipods); plucks bollworms from cotton heads and army worms from grass heads in flight, and ants from ground in flight (up to 120 per stomach); arils of *Acacia cyclops* seeds.

Breeding: Extralimital.

Ref. Mendelsohn, J.M. 1973. *Ann. Tvl Mus.* 28:79–89.

519 (494) Angola Swallow — Angolaswael — Plate 77

Hirundo angolensis

Sisampamema (K), [Angolaschwalbe]

Measurements: Length about 14–15 cm; wing 114–128; tail, longest rectrix 65, shortest rectrix 45; culmen 9.

Bare Parts: Iris brown; bill, legs and feet purplish black.

Identification: Size smallish (smaller than Eurasian Swallow; see swallow key); similar to coloration to Eurasian Swallow, but rufous on throat extends onto upper breast, collar narrower and broken, belly greyish brown (not creamy white or buff), outer rectrices relatively much shorter; above metallic blueblack; forehead and throat rufous; tail forked, black, with white windows. *Immature*: Duller than adult.

Voice: Warbling song, often uttered in flight.

Distribution: Gabon, Zaire, Tanzania, Malawi, n Zambia and w Angola, S to Kunene and Okavango Rivers and Caprivi.

Status: Uncommon to rare resident; some

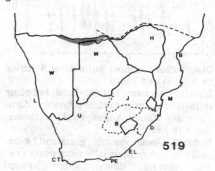

local altitudinal migration possible; vagrant to s Africa.

Habitat: Montane grassland, perennial rivers, forest, human habitations.

Habits: Usually solitary or in pairs. Similar to Eurasian Swallow, but less active flier. Often sings in display flight with downcurved quivering wings. Poorly known.

Food: Aerial insects.

Breeding: Extralimital.

520 (495) Whitethroated Swallow — Witkeelswael — Plate 46

Hirundo albigularis

Sisampamema (K), Lefokotsane, 'Malinakana (SS), Nyenganyenga (Sh), Mbawulwana, Nyenga (Ts), Pêolwane, Phêtla (Tw), Inkonjane (X), iNkonjane (Z), [Weißkehlschwalbe]

Measurements: Length 14–17 cm; wing 118–128,5–136; tail, shortest rectrix 40–44,3–54, longest rectrix 55–70–84; tarsus 10–12–15; culmen 8–9,7–10,5. Weight (10 ♂) 20,1–22,8–28,6 g, (54 unsexed) 16–21,3–28 g.

Bare Parts: Iris brown; bill, legs and feet black.

Identification: Size medium (see swallow

449

key); above metallic blueblack; forehead chestnut (forehead blueblack in Pearlbreasted Swallow); below white; complete blueblack collar on lower throat, 10–12 mm wide (narrower in centre than at sides; even width in Eurasian Swallow; Pearlbreasted Swallow has incomplete or no collar); tail deeply forked, black, with white windows (no windows in Pearlbreasted Swallow); wing broader than that of European Swallow. *Immature*: Less metallic than adult; no chestnut on forehead; collar brownish.

Voice: Sharp twittering alarm notes; warbling song.

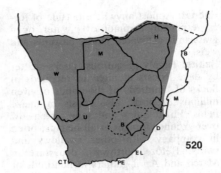

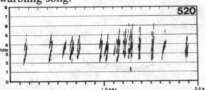

Distribution: Almost throughout S Africa to Angola and Zaire.

Status: Common, but localized, breeding intra-African migrant from Angola, Zambia and s Zaire, August to April (sometimes to May).

Habitat: Open country, grassland, especially in highveld; usually near water (rivers, streams, dams); often around manmade structures (bridges, dam walls, buildings).

Habits: Usually solitary or in pairs; some-times in family groups. Flight quick and agile, similar to that of Eurasian Swallow; often hawks prey over water, but also over open grassland. Perches on posts or stumps in water.

Food: Aerial arthropods.

Breeding: *Season*: August to March (mainly September-January); double-brooded. *Nest*: Half-cup of mud pellets mixed with grass, lined with feathers and rootlets; stuck to wall of bridge, culvert, building, dam wall, rock face, silo; usually close to overhang or roof; same site used year after year. *Clutch*: (79) 2–2,8–4 eggs (usually 3). *Eggs*: White, speckled with red-brown and some grey; measure (176) 20,1 × 14,2 (18,1–23 × 12,9–15,8). *Incubation*: 15–16 days. *Nestling*: 20–21 days; fed by both parents; fledglings return to nest for about 12 days after initial departure.

521 (497)   **Blue Swallow**   **Plate 46**

Blouswael

Hirundo atrocaerulea

[Stahlschwalbe]

Measurements: Length 20–25 cm; wing (47 ♂) 103,5–113,4–119,5, (19 ♀) 101–107,4–111; tail, longest rectrix (46 ♂) 92,6–132,6–160, (18 ♀) 60–71,4–81, shortest rectrix (48 ♂) 35,4–39,8–46,7, (19 ♀) 35–40,4–49; tarsus (48 ♂) 9,2–10,3–12,5; (19 ♀) 9,1–10–10,6; culmen (45 ♂) 5,5–6,7–7,5, (19 ♀) 5,8–6,4–7.

Bare Parts: Iris brown; bill, legs and feet black.

Identification: Size medium (see swallow key); wholly metallic blueblack, brighter in ♂ (white streaks on rump and flanks not

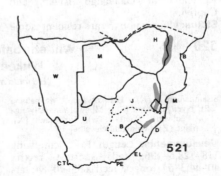

450

easily seen in field); outermost rectrices very long, especially in ♂; no white windows in tail. *Immature*: Sooty black (not glossy); throat brownish.

Voice: Wheezy somewhat nasal call of 1–2 syllables; warbling trill; song 6–8 clear notes at same pitch (sounds like distant alarm notes of Wattled Plover).

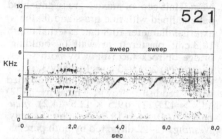

Distribution: Breeds inland Natal, e Transvaal, e Zimbabwe highlands and adjacent Mozambique, to Malawi, ne Zambia, sw Tanzania and se Zaïre; migrates to tropical Africa as far N as Uganda.

Status: Uncommon to rare breeding intra-African migrant, September to April; at most 5–6 pairs/km². Endangered (RDB).

Habitat: Moist montane grassland (mostly above 1500 m in Zimbabwe, lower further S), usually with sinkholes, dongas and potholes, often close to evergreen mistbelt forest, usually with nearby stream; habitat rapidly being destroyed by planting of exotic timber trees.

Habits: Solitary or in small groups of up to 9 birds. Flight graceful, usually low over grass, seldom sustained; perches more than most swallow species, on leafless treetops, wires or posts; hawks prey over open grassland, vleis and forest edges.

Food: Aerial arthropods.

Breeding: *Season*: September to February (mainly December-January); up to 3 broods/season. *Nest*: Half-cup of mud mixed with fine grass; lined with grass, rootlets, feathers and plant down; stuck to wall of pothole, donga or antbear burrow, from 30–100 cm below ground level, with clear flight path unobstructed by vegetation; less often on manmade site like culvert or building. *Clutch*: (23) 2–2,9–3 eggs (usually 3). *Eggs*: White, lightly spotted with rufous, yellowish brown, brown and grey; measure (15) 18,5 × 13,1 (17,3–19,6 × 12,5–13,8). *Incubation*: 15 days by ♀ only. *Nestling*: 20–26 days; fed by both parents.

Réf. Allan, D.G. (Ed.) 1987. *Report on the Blue Swallow in South Africa and Swaziland*. Cape Town: Blue Swallow Working Group. Earlé, R.A. 1987. *Ostrich* 58:182–185. Snell, M.L. 1963. *Bokmakierie* 15:4–7; 1969. *Ostrich* 40:65–74; 1979. *Bokmakierie* 31:74–78.

522 (496) Wiretailed Swallow · Draadstertswael · Plate 46

Hirundo smithii

Sisampamema (K), Nyenganyenga (Sh), Mbawu-lwana, Nyenga (Ts), iNkonjane (Z), [Rotkappenschwalbe]

Measurements: Length about 17 cm; wing (7) 103–107–110; tail, longest rectrix (4 ♂) 71–75–81,5, (5 ♀) 51–68, shortest rectrix (6) 30–35; culmen (6) 7,5–9,5. Weight (1 ♂) 13,1 g, (1 ♀) 12,6 g, (9 unsexed) 11–12,5–14 g.

Bare Parts: Iris brown; bill, legs and feet black.

Identification: Size smallish (see swallow key); crown reddish chestnut; rest of upperparts, including broad stripe from bill to nape metallic blueblack; below white, sometimes tinged pinkish on throat and breast; incomplete blueblack band

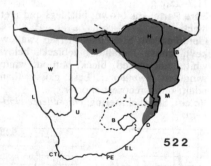

under base of tail; tail black with white windows, forked, outer rectrices very long. *Immature*: Duller than adult; crown brown; throat and neck light rufous.

Voice: Usually silent; double chirp, *che-che*; twittering song, *chirrik-weet, chirrik-weet*, repeated about every 2 seconds from perch near nest.

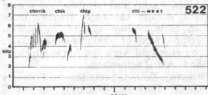

Distribution: Most of Africa S of Sahara, C and s Asia, Burma, Thailand, Laos, Vietnam; in s Africa confined to e Natal, Mozambique, e and n Transvaal, Zimbabwe and n Botswana to Caprivi.

Status: Common resident; may have seasonal movements at higher elevations; rare above 1000 m.

Habitat: Rivers, streams and dams, usually in woodland and around buildings.

Habits: Solitary or in pairs; sometimes in loose groups while feeding; forages over water, grassland and cultivated fields. Flight quick and agile, alternating rapid wingbeats with swoops and glides. May roost in buildings or in reedbeds. Perches on bridge railings and parapets.

Food: Small aerial arthropods.

Breeding: *Season*: All months, mainly August-October and February-April. *Nest*: Half-cup of mixed grass and mud pellets, lined with fine grass and feathers; external diameter 10,8 cm, external depth 10,3 cm; plastered to wall of building, bridge or rock face; built by both sexes. *Clutch*: (9) 2–2,9–3 eggs (usually 3, rarely 4). *Eggs*: White, spotted and speckled with reddish brown; measure (32) 18,4 × 12,9 (17–19,5 × 12,5–14,2). *Incubation*: (5) 14,5–18,5 days by ♀ only. *Nestling*: 15–22 days; fed by both parents; fledglings return to nest for several days after initial departure.

Ref. Moreau, R.E. 1939. *Proc. Zool. Soc. Lond.* 109:109–125.

523 (498)   Pearlbreasted Swallow   Plate 46
Pêrelborsswael
Hirundo dimidiata

Sisampamema (K), Nyenganyenga (Sh), Mbawulwana, Nyenga (Ts), Pêolwane, Phêtla (Tw), Lefokotsane (SS), iNkonjane (Z), [Perlbrustschwalbe]

Measurements: Length 13–14 cm; wing (27) 97,5–102,7–110; tail, longest rectrix (8) 57–70, shortest rectrix (8) 40–44; culmen (8) 7–7,5. Weight (23) 10–11,7–15,2 g.

Bare Parts: Iris brown; bill, legs and feet black.

Identification: Size smallish (see swallow key); above metallic blueblack; below white; tail forked, black, without white windows. *Immature*: Less glossy than adult; outer rectrices shorter.

Voice: Song chittering *chip-cheree-chip-chip*.

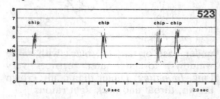

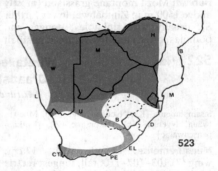

Distribution: S Africa to Angola, Zaire, Zambia, Malawi and Tanzania; in s Africa absent from most of Natal, e Orange Free State, Lesotho and s Mozambique.

Status: Sparse to fairly common; resident in Zimbabwe, Namibia and Transvaal lowveld; breeding intra-African migrant to sw Cape, August to April; nonbreeding winter visitor to Johannesburg (possibly from Cape); some S African birds may migrate in winter to Zimbabwe where

great increase in numbers from May to August; movements inadequately mapped.
Habitat: Edges and clearings of *Brachystegia* and other woodland, semi-arid scrub, farmland; often around human settlement.
Habits: In pairs or small loose groups. Often perches on dead twigs on treetops. Flight quick and agile, somewhat like that of Eurasian Swallow; forages over grassland, in clearings, or over cultivated fields. Usually rather quiet and unobtrusive.

Food: Aerial arthropods.
Breeding: *Season*: August to February; double-brooded. *Nest*: Half-cup of mud pellets, often built up to ceiling at sides, lined with fine grass, hair and feathers; stuck to wall of building, culvert, well, rock face or burrow of Antbear or Brown Hyaena. *Clutch*: (9) 2–2,4–3 eggs (rarely 4). *Eggs*: Plain white; measure (38) 17,3 × 12,6 (14,8–19,5 × 11,3–14). *Incubation*: (4) 16–17 days. *Nestling*: 20–23 days.

Ref. Schmidt, R.K. 1959. *Ostrich* 30:155–158.

524 (501) Redbreasted Swallow Plate 46
Rooiborsswael
Hirundo semirufa

Sisampamema (K), Nyenganyenga (Sh), Mbawu-lwana, Nyenga (Ts), Pêolwane, Phêtla (Tw), [Rotbauchschwalbe]

Measurements: Length about 24 cm; wing (55 ♂) 127–133–142, (55 ♀) 124–130–136; tail, longest rectrix (51 ♂) 99,5–131,9–157, (50 ♀) 80,3–116,8–136,8; tail, shortest rectrix (52 ♂) 46,5–53,1–60,5, (54 ♀) 46,9–54,1–60; tarsus (55 ♂) 13,6–16–17,9, (55 ♀) 14–15,9–18; culmen (49 ♂) 7,4–8,2–9,8, (54 ♀) 6,9–8,1–9,2. Weight (22 ♂) 25,7–30,9–36 g, (28 ♀) 24,5–29,5–40 g, (4 unsexed) 28–30–34 g.
Bare Parts: Iris brown; bill, legs and feet black.
Identification: Size large (see swallow key); above metallic blueblack, extending to below eye (dark crown of Mosque Swallow extends to level of eye only); rump and underparts bright rufous (no white on throat as in Mosque Swallow); tail deeply forked, black with white windows. *Immature*: Above brownish, with little lustre; below paler than adult; innermost secondaries tipped buff; outer rectrices shorter than those of adult.
Voice: Callnote plaintive *seeurrr-seeurrr* or *chik-chitrrrperree*; *weet-weet* alarm notes; song soft and gurgling.

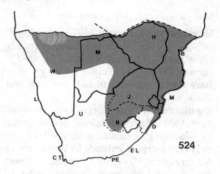

Distribution: Africa S of Sahara; in s Africa from n Cape (Barkly West) and parts of Orange Free State, Natal (from Durban), Transvaal, ne Botswana, Zimbabwe and n Namibia; rarely to Mozambique.
Status: Scarce in S to fairly common in subtropics; breeding intra-African migrant from tropical Africa, July to May (most birds arrive August, depart March-April).
Habitat: Sweet grassveld, vleis, open bushveld, thornveld; absent from areas without suitable nest sites.
Habits: Solitary or in pairs. Flight comparatively slow and leisurely, with much gliding. Forages over open grassland and clearings, sometimes also on ground. Perches on wires and leafless twigs.
Food: Aerial arthropods.
Breeding: *Season*: August to April (mainly September-February) in Zim-

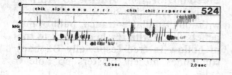

babwe, September to March in S Africa (mainly October to February in highveld); begins to breed after rains when temperature reaches mean maximum of 20 °C. Two broods/season. *Nest*: Bowl of outside diameter (18) 16–20–22 cm, with tubular entrance 10–37 cm long, built of mud pellets; lined with grass, feathers and wool throughout incubation; stuck to roof of culvert, Antbear burrow, hollow termite mound, hole in bank; usually only 1 m or

less above ground; not usually over water; built in 13–16 days. *Clutch*: (161) 3–3,5–6 eggs. *Eggs*: White, slightly glossy; measure (192) 22,1 × 15,4 (19,6–25,2 × 13,7–16,6); weigh (75 fresh eggs) 2,4–2,8–3,4 g. *Incubation*: (15) 16–16,5 days by ♀ only. *Nestling*: (11) 23–24–25 days.

Ref. Earlé, R.A. 1989. *Ostrich* 60:13–21.
Earlé, R.A. & Brooke, R.K. 1989. *Ostrich* 60:151–158.

---

525 (500)   Mosque Swallow   Plate 46
Moskeeswael
Hirundo senegalensis

Sisampamema (K), [Senegalschwalbe]

Measurements: Length 24–25 cm; wing ♂ 142–145, ♀ 137–142; tail, longest rectrix (7) 83–117, shortest rectrix (7) 45–50; culmen (7) 10–11. Weight (1) 43 g.

Bare Parts: Iris brown; bill, legs and feet black.

Identification: Size large (see swallow key); looks like small falcon; above metallic blueblack, extending to level of eye only (dark crown extends to below eye in Redbreasted Swallow); rump, lower breast and belly bright rufous; sides of face, throat and upper breast white (no white on underparts of Redbreasted Swallow); tail deeply forked, black with white windows. *Immature*: Duller than adult; inner secondaries tipped buff.

Voice: Guttural nasal trill, *harrrp*, sometimes drawn out; also guttural chuckling.

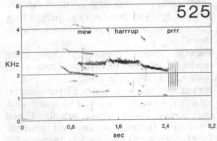

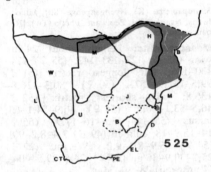

Distribution: Africa S of Sahara; in s Africa from Zululand (Cape Vidal) to e Transvaal lowveld, Mozambique, e and n

Zimbabwe, Zambezi Valley, Caprivi and Ovamboland.

Status: Uncommon resident; vagrant in Zululand.

Habitat: Dense woodland, especially in major river valleys; less often open woodland.

Habits: Usually solitary or in pairs, but sometimes in small groups of around 6 birds; roosts in flocks of up to 50 birds in trees. Flight slow and leisurely, with quick flutter of wings followed by glide; forages usually fairly high above treetops. Less attracted to human settlements than most other swallows.

Food: Aerial arthropods.

Breeding: *Season*: August to April in Zimbabwe; double-brooded. *Nest*: Bowl with long tubular entrance, built of mud pellets; lined with feathers; stuck to roof of hollow in tree (especially Baobab); sometimes merely plasters up hole in tree or roof of building to suitable size, lining inside hollow with feathers. *Clutch*: 3–4 eggs. *Eggs*: Plain white; measure (11) 21,7 × 14,7 (21–22,1 × 14–15). *Incubation*: Unrecorded. *Nestling*: Unrecorded.

526 (502)   Greater Striped Swallow   Plate 46
Grootstreepswael
Hirundo cucullata

Sisampamema (K), Lefokotsane, 'Malinakana (SS), Nyenganyenga (Sh), Mbawulwana, Nyenga (Ts), Pêolwane, Phêtla (Tw), Inkonjane (X), iNkonjane (Z), [Große Streifenschwalbe]

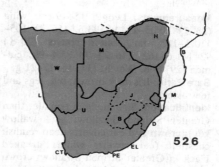

526

Measurements: Length 18–20 cm; wing (10) 117–125–131; tail, longest rectrix ♂ 101–108, ♀ 90–99, shortest rectrix (8) 46–54; culmen (8) 8–9. Weight (34) 19–27–35 g.

Bare Parts: Iris brown; bill black; legs and feet brown.

Identification: Size medium (larger than Lesser Striped Swallow; see swallow key); crown chestnut (narrow blueblack streaks not visible in field), not including ear coverts; back metallic blueblack; rump pale tawny orange (paler than that of Lesser Striped Swallow); below (including ear coverts) white, narrowly streaked black (streaks bold in Lesser Striped Swallow; ear coverts chestnut); tail deeply forked, black with white windows. *Immature*: Similar to adult, but less metallic on back; outer rectrices much shorter.

Voice: Chuckling phrase of 2–3 introductory short notes followed by gargled trill, *trip trip trirrr*, uttered perched or flying, with head thrown back and throat puffed out; mellow *chissik* callnote.

526

Distribution: Breeds s Africa; migrates to Angola, sw Zaire, Zambia and sw Tanzania; throughout s Africa, except n Botswana, Zambezi Valley and Mozambique.

Status: Common breeding intra-African migrant, August to April (rarely as late as June; some birds rarely overwinter).

Habitat: Open country, especially grassy highveld; also grasslands to sea level; avoids dense woodland and forest.

Habits: Solitary or in pairs when breeding; in family groups towards end of breeding season; in flocks of 30 or more birds after breeding, often in company with other swallows and swifts. Flight relatively slow and leisurely with much gliding between wingbeats; forages over open grassveld and water, rarely on ground.

Food: Aerial arthropods; arils of *Acacia cyclops* seeds.

Breeding: *Season*: August to March (rarely to April) in most areas, September to December in sw Cape; at least 2 broods/season. *Nest*: Bowl with long tubular entrance, built of mud pellets; lined with grass, feathers and bits of cloth; plastered to roof of building, rock overhang, culvert, bridge, underside of fallen tree; same site used year after year; built by both sexes in 2–3 weeks. *Clutch*: (48) 2–3–4 eggs (usually 3). *Eggs*: White, usually plain, rarely with few brownish spots; measure (104) 21,7 × 15,1 (19,1–24,5 × 13,5–16,5). *Incubation*: (17) 16–17,6–20 days by ♀ only; both sexes sleep in nest at night. *Nestling*: 23–30 days; fed by both parents; fledglings return to nest for about 9 days after initial departure.

Ref. Schmidt, R.K. 1962. *Ostrich* 33:3–8.

527 (503)   Lesser Striped Swallow   Plate 46
Kleinstreepswael
Hirundo abyssinica

Sisampamema (K), Nyenganyenga (Sh), Mbawu-lwana, Nyenga (Ts), Pêolwane, Phêtla (Tw), Inkonjane (X), iNkonjane (Z), [Kleine Streifen-schwalbe]

Measurements: Length 15–19 cm; wing (23 ♂) 105,5–114,9–123,5, (16 ♀) 105–110,3–117; tail, outer rectrix (20 ♂) 92–111,6–162, (16 ♀) 73–85,4–99; culmen (29) 6–8. Weight (11) 16–17–21 g.

Bare Parts: Iris dark brown; bill, legs and feet black.

Identification: Size medium (smaller than Greater Striped Swallow; see swallow key); crown and ear coverts deep reddish chestnut (ear coverts white, streaked black in Greater Striped Swallow; crown finely streaked black); back metallic blue-black; rump deep orange-rust (darker than that of Greater Striped Swallow), extending to ventral surface at base of tail; below white, heavily streaked black (streaks light in Greater Striped Swallow); tail deeply forked, black with white windows. *Immature*: Similar to adult, but duller; outer rectrices much shorter than those of adult.

Voice: Loud squeaky grinding song of 9–10 notes, *chip-chip-chwip, kreek, kree-kree, kreep, chwip, kreeee.*

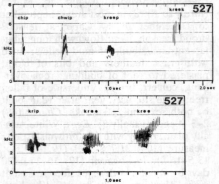

Distribution: Africa S of Sahara; in s Africa from Jansenville, Steytlerville and Tarkastad (Cape Province), E to Natal, Swaziland, Mozambique, Transvaal, Zim-

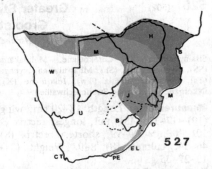

babwe, Botswana and Caprivi; recorded Waterberg Plateau, Namibia.

Status: In S Africa common breeding intra-African migrant, July to March (sometimes to April); some populations breeding Zimbabwe depart northwards in about March, to be replaced by birds from S Africa which overwinter, but many birds resident.

Habitat: Varied; woodland, savanna, forest edge, urban and suburban areas, open grassland; usually at lower elevations.

Habits: In pairs when breeding; otherwise in flocks, often in company with other swallows and swifts. Forages over woodland or grassland; flight more agile and darting than that of Greater Striped Swallow, but not as quick as that of Eurasian Swallow, and with more gliding. Highly vocal both flying and perched; often perches on wires or leafless twigs on treetops.

Food: Aerial arthropods; arils of *Acacia cyclops* seeds.

Breeding: *Season*: July to April in S Africa, all months in Zimbabwe (mainly September-January); at least 2 broods/season. *Nest*: Bowl with long tubular entrance, built of mud pellets; lined with grass and feathers; stuck under roof of building, bridge, rocky overhang, or under stout branch of tree; at least 2 m above ground or water; built by both sexes; building may take up to 7 weeks, but usually less. *Clutch*: (63) 2–3–4 eggs (usually 3). *Eggs*: White, usually plain, but sometimes sparsely speckled with reddish brown in ring around thick end; measure (72) 19,7 × 13,9 (17,3–21,8 × 12,5–15,4). *Incubation*: About 14 days. *Nestling*: 17–28 days; fed by both parents.

528 (504)   South African Cliff Swallow   Plate 46
Familieswael
Hirundo spilodera

Sisampamema (K), Lefokotsane (SS), Pêolwane, Phêtla (Tw), [Klippenschwalbe]

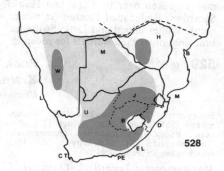

Measurements: Length 14–15 cm; wing (226 ♂) 105–111,3–118, (136 ♀) 105–111,7–119; tail (172 ♂) 45–50,5–56, (99 ♀) 45,4–51,5–57,2; tarsus (127 ♂) 11,7–13,9–16,8, (77 ♀) 12,3–13,8–17,8; culmen (47 ♂) 7,4–8,1–9,2, (29 ♀) 7–8,1–9,1. Weight (500 ♂) 16–20,4–24,2 g, (500 ♀) 16,5–20,7–26 g, (1 867 unsexed) 13–20,6–26 g.

Bare Parts: Iris dark brown; bill, legs and feet black.

Identification: Size medium (see swallow key); tail square or notched (not forked as in most metallic swallows), black without white windows; crown sooty; narrow band on forehead and lores light rufous (sometimes absent on forehead); back metallic blueblack, lightly streaked and mottled whitish; rump light rufous (buff in worn plumage); below pale rufous or whitish, darker on breast, spotted black on throat and breast (gives dark-throated look in field); undertail cinnamon. *Immature*: Less glossy than adult on back; paler on rump and underparts.

Voice: Chattering series of warbles by members of flock, each bird uttering 3–4 twittering syllables, *chor-chor-chor-chur*; also various threat and alarm calls, sharp and high-pitched.

Distribution: Breeds s Africa from e Cape and e Karoo to highveld of Natal, Orange Free State and Transvaal, across Botswana to n Namibia; intermittently small breeding colonies near Bulawayo, Zimbabwe; migrates to tropical Africa as far N as Zaire.

Status: Locally common breeding intra-African migrant, August to April; bird ringed Transvaal recovered Zaire, 2 273 km N; few birds rarely overwinter.

Habitat: Open grassland, sparse savanna, usually close to breeding sites under bridges and buildings.

Habits: Highly gregarious in flocks of tens or hundreds at all times. Usually seen foraging over open veld near breeding colonies, mostly less than 2 m above ground, often disturbing prey from bushes; flight fluttering and agile, about 33 km/h; spends up to 7 hours/day foraging; may settle on ground to feed on Harvester Termites and locust hoppers; highly vocal, especially near nests; when disturbed, birds fly from nests and whole colony circles above site in close group, higher and higher until almost out of sight. Roosts in nests, usually in pairs; before breeding, birds occupy nests from 11:00–15:00, leaving colony for rest of daylight hours to forage.

Food: Aerial and terrestrial arthropods (see **Habits**).

Breeding: *Season*: August to February (rarely to March), depending on rainfall. *Nest*: Hollow ball of mud pellets with side entrance near top, usually with short downward-facing entrance tube; length (6) 14–18–21 cm, height (8) 7,7–9,1–12,6 cm, inside diameter of chamber (14) 10,9–13,2–15,5 cm, entrance height (11) 2,5–3–3,7 cm, entrance width (11) 3,4–4,3–5,7 cm; lined with plant down, sheep's wool and feathers; usually under angled top of culvert, bridge (often over water), roof of building, water tower, etc.; also under rock overhang; densely colonial, nests clustered together, touching each other and overlapping; built by both sexes in up to 7 days, starting with floor and ending with entrance tunnel; nests may be taken over by Cape and House Sparrows, Redheaded Finches (in winter only), Whiterumped and Little Swifts for breeding, or by Pied Barbets for roosting.

Clutch: (1045) 1–2,4–4 eggs (usually 2–3). *Eggs*: White, spotted and blotched with red-brown, purple and grey, concentrated at thick end; rarely pure white; measure (280) 20,4 × 14,1 (18,3–24,7 × 12,9–15,2); weigh (26) 1,5–2,2–2,6 g. *Incubation*: (16) 14–14,6–16 days by both sexes. *Nestling*: (21) 23–24,1–26 days; fed by both parents.

Ref. Earlé, R.A. 1985. *Navors. nas. Mus., Bloemfontein* 5:1–8; 21–36; 37–50; 53–66; 1986. *Ostrich* 57:56–59; 138–156.

529 (506)   Rock Martin   Plate 46
Kransswael
Hirundo fuligula

Sisampamema (K), Lekabelane (SS), Nyenganyenga (Sh), Mbawulwana, Nyenga (Ts), Pêolwane, Phêtla (Tw), Inkonjane, Unongubende, Unongubendala (X), iNhlolamvula (Z), [Felsenschwalbe, Steinschwalbe]

Measurements: Length 12–13 cm. *H. f. pretoriae*: wing (49 ♂) 123–131,6–139, (40 ♀) 123–131–139; tail (47 ♂) 50–53,5–57, (39 ♀) 51–53,8–58; tarsus (5) 11–11,5–12; culmen (5) 8–8,8–10. *H. f. fusciventris*: wing (18) 108–112,9–117; tail (19) 43–45,2–47. Weight (7) 16–22,4–30 g.

Bare Parts: Iris brown; bill black; legs and feet pinkish brown.

Identification: Size medium (smallish in Zambezi Valley subspecies *fusciventris*); see swallow key; above greyish brown; below pinkish cinnamon or ochre; tail square, dark brown with white windows. *Immature*: Above scaled with buff; rectrices edged buff.

Voice: High-pitched *twee*; various twittering calls and clicking notes.

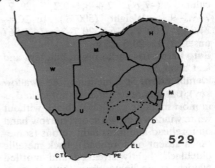

Distribution: Africa S of Sahara; in s Africa absent only from most of C and n Botswana and Caprivi.

Status: Common resident; some altitudinal movement to lower elevations in winter.

Habitat: Rocky cliffs, gorges, quarries, buildings; mostly in highveld, but also to sea level.

Habits: Usually solitary or in pairs; sometimes in loose flocks when not breeding, often in company with other swallows and swifts. Seldom seen far from cliffs, gorges and tall buildings (or almost any building in flatter, more open country). Flight looks slow and leisurely with much gliding, but cruises easily at 80 km/h; white windows in tail conspicuous when turning in flight. Often perches on rock and window ledges.

Food: Aerial arthropods.

Breeding: *Season*: August to April over most of s Africa; almost any month after rain in Kalahari; 2–3 broods/season. *Nest*: Neat half-cup of mud pellets, lined with grass and feathers; against vertical wall of building, culvert, bridge or rock face, close under overhang or roof; usually 2 m or more above ground, but sometimes less; built by both sexes in up to 40 days; used for successive broods in same season and in successive seasons. *Clutch*: (60) 2–2,8–6 eggs (usually 2–3). *Eggs*: White, speckled and spotted with reddish brown and grey; measure (83) 21,4 × 14,1 (17,3–23,5 × 13,3–15,3). *Incubation*: 16–17 days by both sexes. *Nestling*: 25–30 days; fed by both parents.

Ref. Brooke, R.K. & Vernon, C.J. 1961. *Ostrich* 32:51–52.

Irwin, M.P.S. 1977. *Honeyguide* 91:10–19.

530 (507) House Martin
Huisswael
Delichon urbica

Plate 46

Sisampamema (K), [Mehlschwalbe]

Measurements: Length 14–15 cm; wing (11) 107–113–123; tail, longest rectrix (7) 55–62, shortest rectrix (7) 42–46; culmen (7) 7–8. Weight (1 ♂) 19,8 g, (3 unsexed) 18–18,4–19 g.

Bare Parts: Iris brown; bill black; legs and feet pinkish, covered with fine white feathers.

Identification: Size smallish (see swallow key); above metallic blue-black; rump white; below white; tail deeply forked, black without white windows. *Immature*: Above brown, slightly metallic on mantle; throat and undertail densely freckled greyish brown; somewhat similar to Grey-rumped Swallow, but rump whiter, tail less deeply forked, size larger.

Voice: Harsh twittering *chirrup*; shrill *tseep* alarm note.

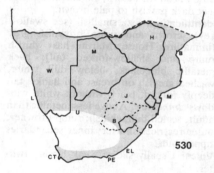

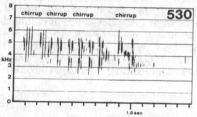

Distribution: Breeds mostly in Europe, N Africa and Asia; migrates to Africa S of Sahara and s Asia.

Status: Locally common; mostly non-breeding Palaearctic migrant, October to April; some irregular breeding in s Africa; one Russian-ringed bird recovered Ceres, sw Cape. Indeterminate (RDB).

Habitat: Usually around steep hillsides, rocky places, high manmade structures (grain silos, dam walls); also open grasslands and cultivated fields.

Habits: Usually gregarious in flocks of several to several thousand birds, often in company with other swallows and swifts. Forages over open grasslands fields and water; flight quick, fluttery and agile. Before migration in April thousands gather on telephone lines at roadsides. May roost in reedbeds in small flocks.

Food: Aerial arthropods.

Breeding: *Localities*: Cape Town (1892), Otjiwarongo (1928), Keiskammahoek (for several years up to 1946), Kokstad (1967), Somerset West (1969). *Season*: September, October, December, January and May. *Nest*: Rounded or oval hollow of mud pellets built into angle of wall and roof of building, with rounded entrance at top against roof; built by both sexes; lined with grass and feathers; solitary or in small colonies of up to 10 nests. *Clutch*: 1–3,5–5 eggs (England). *Eggs*: White, measure (100, Europe) 19,4 × 13,4; weigh (207, Europe) 1–1,7–2,3 g. *Incubation*: 13–14,5–16 days (England) by both sexes. *Nestling*: 30–31 days (England); fed by both parents.

Ref. Bryant, D.M. 1975. *Ibis* 117:180–216.

531 (499)   **Greyrumped Swallow**   **Plate 46**
Gryskruisswael
Pseudhirundo griseopyga

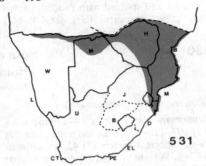

531

Sisampamema (K), Nyenganyenga (Sh) [Graubür-zelschwalbe]

Measurements: Length about 14 cm; wing (9) 91–95,4–101; tail, longest rectrix 63–90, shortest rectrix 35–42; culmen 6. Weight (3) 9–9,5–9,8 g.

Bare Parts: Iris brown; bill black; legs and feet dark pinkish to pale brown.

Identification: Size smallish (see swallow key); crown and rump brownish grey (immature House Martin has whitish rump and shallow-forked tail); back metallic blueblack; below dull white, washed greyish on breast and flanks; tail deeply forked, black without white windows. *Immature*: Above less metallic than adult, scaled dull whitish; rump browner; outer rectrices shorter; inner secondaries tipped buff.

Voice: Usually silent; weak hissing twitter.

Distribution: Africa S of Sahara; in s Africa from Zululand to Swaziland, Transvaal lowveld, Mozambique, Zimbabwe, n Botswana and Caprivi.

Status: Common resident or local migrant; usually present April to October on breeding grounds in Zimbabwe (commonest breeding swallow on Mashonaland Plateau), moving to lower elevations in rainy season.

Habitat: Dry or burnt grassland, bare ground at edges of vleis, clearings in woodland, fallow lands, polo fields, golf courses.

Habits: Gregarious at all times; usually in small loose flocks when breeding; non-breeding flocks may number up to 3 000 birds before migration. Roosts communally in reedbeds. Forages over open ground and in woodland clearings; flight fluttering and darting. Often perches on leafless twigs or grass stems.

Food: Aerial arthropods.

Breeding: *Season*: July to November (mainly August) in Zimbabwe; March to July in S Africa (80% in June and July, during dry season when flooding unlikely). *Nest*: Pad of soft dry grass in rodent burrow; also in old nest hole of kingfisher or Little Bee-eater, or in funnel of termite mound. *Clutch*: (6) 3–3,3–4 eggs. *Eggs*: White, glossy; measure (17) 16 × 11,9 (14,3–17,6 × 11–12,9). *Incubation*: Unrecorded. *Nestling*: Unrecorded.

532 (508)   **Sand Martin**   **Plate 46**
Europese Oewerswael
Riparia riparia

Sisampamema (K), Nyenganyenga (Sh), [Europäische Uferschwalbe]

Measurements: Length 13–14 cm; wing (126) 99–105,8–115; tail, longest rectrix (41) 46–52,2–60, shortest rectrix (1) 41; tarsus (43) 9,8–11–11,8; culmen (44) 4,2–4,6–5,5. Weight (589) 9,2–13,8–19,8 g.

Bare Parts: Iris dark brown; bill black; legs and feet brownish pink.

Identification: Size small (see swallow key); above greyish brown; below white; narrow breastband and underwing greyish brown (Brownthroated Martin has throat and upper breast brown; Banded Martin much bigger, with broader better-defined breast-

460

band and white underwing coverts); tail brown, slightly forked or notched (square in Banded Martin); small tuft of feathers at back of tarsus above hind toes can be seen in hand (absent in Brownthroated Martin). *Immature*: Above scaled with buff.

Voice: Weak twittering similar to that of Brownthroated Martin; shrill *chirrp* callnote; short *brrit* alarm note.

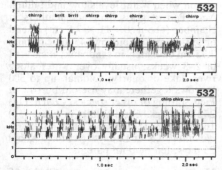

Distribution: Breeds Europe, Asia, Japan, N America; migrates to Africa, s Asia and S America; in s Africa from Cape Recife, Bushman's River and Grahamstown (e Cape) to Natal, Transvaal, Mozambique, Botswana, Zimbabwe and n Namibia; vagrant to Kleinmond (w Cape).

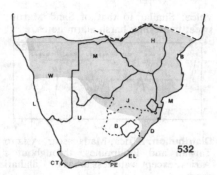

Status: Fairly common nonbreeding Palaearctic migrant, October to March (rarely as early as August); numbers increasing since 1950s.

Habitat: Moist open grassveld, inland waters, reedbeds, irrigated pastures and crops.

Habits: Highly gregarious in flocks of 50–100 birds by day; roosts at night in reedbeds in flocks of up to 2 000 birds. Forages over open grassland and water with flitting flight (less darting than larger swallows), sometimes quite high, often in company with other swallows; attracted to grassfires.

Food: Aerial insects.

Breeding: Extralimital.

533 (509)   Brownthroated Martin   Plate 46
Afrikaanse Oewerswael
Riparia paludicola

Sisampamema (K), Lekabelane, Sekatelane (SS), Nyenganyenga (Sh), Mbawulwana, Nyenga (Ts), Pêolwane, Phêtla (Tw), [Braunkehl-Uferschwalbe, Afrikanische Uferschwalbe]

Measurements: Length 12–13 cm; wing (62) 97–104,2–114; tail, longest rectrix (15) 49–59, shortest rectrix (15) 41–50; culmen (15) 6–7. Weight (121) 11–13,3–15 g.

Bare Parts: Iris brown; bill black; legs and feet brownish pink.

Identification: Size small (see swallow key); smoky brown except for white belly to undertail (Sand and Banded Martins have white throats, brown breastbands); belly brown in about 10% of birds (distinguished from Rock Martin by notched tail); underwing brown (coverts white in Banded Martin); tail slightly forked or

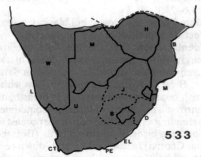

notched (square in Banded Martin); no tuft of feathers on back of tarsus as in Sand Martin. *Immature*: Above scaled buffy; tinged buff on belly.

461

Voice: Similar to that of Sand Martin; sweet twittering; harsh alarm notes.

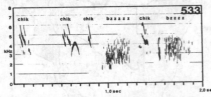

Distribution: Africa, Madagascar, Asia to Taiwan and Philippines; throughout s Africa, except waterless areas of Kalahari sandveld.
Status: Common resident; disperses after breeding.
Habitat: Rivers, streams, lakes, estuaries, reedbeds.
Habits: Usually gregarious in flocks of a few to 1 000 birds or more. Forages over water and open grasslands, usually near water; flight fluttering (less dashing than

that of larger swallows). Often perches on shoreline vegetation (reeds, grass, bushes).
Food: Aerial insects, including dragonflies up to 2,5 cm long.
Breeding: *Season*: June to September in Zimbabwe, March to November in Natal, August to February in sw Cape, February to October in Transvaal; breeds in dry season when water levels low and falling. *Nest*: Pad of grass, hair and feathers in chamber (about 9 × 11 × 7,5 cm) at end of self-excavated burrow, 45–60 cm long, 3,75 cm diameter, in sandbank; excavated in 2–3 weeks; usually over water along river, lake or quarry; colonial, up to 500 burrows together; may use old burrow of Pied Starling or other species. *Clutch*: (14) 2–2,9–4 eggs. *Eggs*: White; measure (50) 16,9 × 12,2 (15,3–18,7 × 10,5–13,8). *Incubation*: About 12 days. *Nestling*: About 25 days; fed by both parents.

534 (510)   Banded Martin   Plate 46
Gebande Oewerswael
Riparia cincta

Sisampamema (K), Lekabelane (SS), Nyenganyenga (Sh), Mbawulwana, Nyenga (Ts), Pêolwane, Phêtla (Tw), [Bindenschwalbe, Weißbrauenschwalbe, Gebänderte Uferschwalbe]

Measurements: Length 17–18 cm; wing (30 ♂) 126–131,3–139, (22 ♀) 123–129,1–133,5; tail (30 ♂) 56–59,6–63, (22 ♀) 57–59,3–62; culmen (11) 9–10. Weight (1 ♀) 21,4 g, (17 unsexed) 20,6–24,8–29,7 g.
Bare Parts: Iris brown; bill black; legs and feet dark pinkish brown to blackish.
Identification: Size medium (see swallow key); above mouse brown; lores black; eyebrow white (no white eyebrow in Sand or Brownthroated Martins); below white with broad brown breastband (breastband narrow in Sand Martin), sometimes extending as small line onto upper breast in southern birds; in northern birds (Botswana, Caprivi) breastband extends down centre of belly as broad brown stripe; flanks washed brown; underwing coverts white (brown in Sand and Brownthroated Martins); tail brown, square (notched in Sand and Brownthroated Martins). *Immature*: Above scaled with rufous buff.

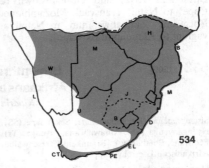

Voice: Song subdued squeaky warble sometimes ending in trill; various *chirps* at different pitch; chippering in flight.

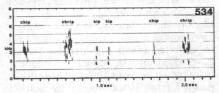

Distribution: S Africa to Ethiopia and Sudan; in s Africa absent from dry W.

Status: Uncommon and local breeding intra-African migrant, September to April; migrates to Angola, Zaire, n Mozambique, Zambia, Malawi, Tanzania and Kenya; rarely overwinters in Zimbabwe and Botswana.
Habitat: Grassland and vleis near streams and dongas with vertical banks.
Habits: Usually solitary or in pairs; sometimes in small family groups; non-breeding birds gregarious, especially on migration, up to 1 000 birds together at times. Forages low over grassveld and vleis; may pick insects off grass inflorescences; flight less fluttering, more leisurely than that of other martins; perches on telephone wires, fences and grass stems.
Food: Insects.
Breeding: *Season*: August to October in s Cape, November to February in Natal, September to February in Zimbabwe. *Nest*: Pad of grass, rootlets and feathers in chamber at end of self-excavated burrow, 60–90 cm long, in vertical bank of stream, donga or river; may use old burrow of kingfisher; usually solitary, sometimes in colony of Pied Starlings. *Clutch*: (15) 2–3,2–4 eggs (usually 3–4; rarely 5). *Eggs*: White; measure (26) 21,1 × 15 (19–23,9 × 14,1–16). *Incubation*: Unrecorded. *Nestling*: 21–24 days; fed by both parents.

535 (504X)   Mascarene Martin   Plate 46
Gestreepte Kransswael
Phedina borbonica

[Maskarenenschwalbe]

Measurements: Length about 12 cm; wing (4 ♂) 106–110,4–113,5, (5 ♀) 102–106,6–112; tail (4 ♂) 52–53,5–55, (5 ♀) 50–52,5–54,5; tarsus (9) 13–14; culmen (9) 6–7. Weight (4 ♂) 21,3–22,1–22,9 g, (5 ♀) 17,9–20,3–22,7 g.
Bare Parts: Iris brown; bill, legs and feet black.
Identification: Size smallish to medium (not included in swallow key); above smoky brown; throat to belly streaked blackish and white (Brownthroated Martin not streaked with white on breast; tail notched); lower belly and undertail white; underwing smoky brown; tail blackish, notched (looks square in flight); in flight wings blackish; flight slow and fluttering. Somewhat similar to Lesser Striped Swallow, but tail not deeply forked and without white windows; size slightly larger. *Immature*: Secondaries broadly tipped white.
Voice: Wheezy *phree-zz*.
Distribution: Breeds Madagascar, Mauritius, Reunion; Madagascan population migrates to African mainland (Mozambique, Malawi), Aldabra and Pemba; in s Africa recorded only from Inhaminga, Manica e Sofala Province, Mozambique,

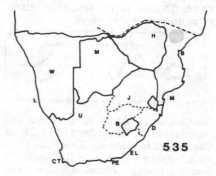

535

June-July 1968; unconfirmed sight records from Lundi River, e Zimbabwe.
Status: Locally common non-breeding migrant from Madagascar; possibly occurs annually.
Habitat: Clearings and cultivated fields in woodland.
Habits: Gregarious, often in company with other swallows and swifts. Flight rather slow, alternating fluttering with gliding; forages low in cloudy weather, otherwise high in air. Perches on dead twigs on treetops. Poorly known.
Food: Aerial insects.
Breeding: Extralimital.

Ref. Clancey, P.A., Lawson, W.J. & Irwin, M.P.S. 1969. *Ostrich* 40:5–8.

536 (511)   **Black Sawwing Swallow**   **Plate 46**
Swartsaagvlerkswael
Psalidoprocne holomelas

Sisampamema (K), Inkonjane, Unomalahlana (X),
[Sundevalls Sägeflügelschwalbe]

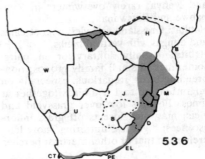

Measurements: Length 17–18 cm; wing
(9 ♂) 105–110,3–118, (2 ♀) 98–104; tail,
longest rectrix (9 ♂) 82–85,6–92, (3 ♀)
63–71,3–82, shortest rectrix (5 ♂) 40–44,
(1 ♀) 39; culmen (6) 5,5–6,3. Weight
(1 ♂) 11,3 g.
Bare Parts: Iris dark brown; bill black;
legs and feet purplish.
Identification: Size small (see swallow
key); solid sooty black all over, with slight
greenish sheen; tail deeply forked, outer
rectrices sharply pointed; in hand, outer
web of first primary of ♂ serrated ("sawwing"). *Immature*: Like adult, but lacks
sheen.
Voice: Usually silent; soft *chirp* alarm
note; nasal *chirr chirr cheeu*.

Distribution: S Africa to E Africa and
Nigeria; in s Africa confined to S, E from
Cape Town to s and nw Zimbabwe (Victoria Falls), and extreme n Botswana.
Status: Locally fairly common, but
uncommon in Zimbabwe; resident in
some areas, breeding intra-African
migrant in most of S Africa and Zimbabwe, September to April, probably wintering in Mozambique.

Habitat: Streams, vleis and clearings in
forest, dense woodland and exotic plantations.
Habits: Usually solitary or in pairs; sometimes in loose groups of 6–10 birds. Flight
swift, graceful and agile, skimming
between trees, across clearings and along
forest tracks; perches often, mainly on
dead twigs on treetops.
Food: Aerial arthropods.
Breeding: *Season*: October to March.
Nest: Pad of grass, pine needles, lichens or
moss in chamber, about 7,5 cm ×
13 cm × 7 cm, at end of self-excavated
burrow, about 2,5 cm diameter, 45 cm
long, sloping upwards; in earth bank of
stream, road cutting, quarry, low sandy
cliff on shore; bank may be as little as
45 cm high; burrow takes up to 3 weeks to
excavate. *Clutch*: (16) 1–1,9–3 eggs.
Eggs: White; measure (16) 18,7 × 12,8
(17,9–20,7 × 11,9–14,3). *Incubation*:
About 14–15 days. *Nestling*: At least 25
days; fed by both parents.

537 (512)   **Eastern Sawwing Swallow**   **Plate 46**
Tropiese Saagvlerkswael
Psalidoprocne orientalis

[Reichenows Sägeflügelschwalbe]

Measurements: Length about 15 cm;
wing (9 ♂) 104–108,9–113, (5 ♀) 95–
97,6–99; tail, longest rectrix (9 ♂) 77–
82,1–89, (5 ♀) 65–67,2–69, shortest rectrix (3) 40–42; culmen (3) 6. Weight (1 ♂)
11,9 g, (14 unsexed) 9,5–11,2–12 g.

Bare Parts: Iris brown; bill black; legs
dusky.
Identification: Size small (see swallow
key); very similar to Black Sawwing Swallow, but underwing coverts white or light
grey (conspicuous in flight); rest of plumage sooty black with greenish sheen.

Immature: Duller black than adult; under-wing coverts washed dusky.

Voice: Low twitter; whistling *mew*; nasal *tseeu tseeu tsee-ip*.

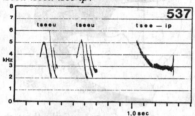

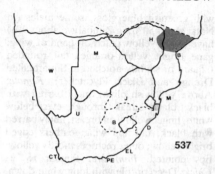

Distribution: Angola, Mozambique and Zimbabwe to E Africa; in s Africa restricted to e highlands of Zimbabwe as far W as Rusape and Marondera, and adjacent Mozambique; also Gorongoza; normally does not overlap with Black Sawwing Swallow in s Africa; vagrants reported from Harare, Chinhoyi, Caprivi and Natal (Zinkwazi Beach).

Status: Locally common resident with altitudinal movement downwards in winter.

Habitat: Edges of evergreen forest, vleis, open hillsides, *Brachystegia* woodland.

Habits: In pairs or small groups. Similar to Black Sawwing Swallow, flitting about among trees and over grassland, usually low down; perches often on dead twigs on treetops.

Food: Aerial arthropods.

Breeding: *Season*: July to April in Zimbabwe. *Nest*: Pad of lichen in chamber at end of narrow tunnel in low earth bank (streamside, roadside cutting, etc.). *Clutch*: Usually 2 eggs. *Eggs*: White; measure (2) 18,3–18,4 × 12–12,2. *Incubation*: Unrecorded. *Nestling*: Unrecorded.

26:5. Family 67 CAMPEPHAGIDAE—CUCKOOSHRIKES AND MINIVETS

Small to medium. Bill medium, rather heavy, slightly to strongly hooked at tip; legs short; feet small; wings longish, rather pointed; flight undulating, wings often shuffled on alighting; tail moderately long, sometimes forked; dorsal feathers dense, partially erectile, with rigid pointed shafts, easily shed (for defence?); plumage coloration broadly divisible into four groups: (a) grey, black and white, often with barring (*Coracina* and *Pteropodocys*), (b) black and white, sometimes washed rufous (trillers—*Lalage, Chlamydochaera* and *Hemipus*), (c) males black, females brown and yellow with barring (*Campephaga*) and (d) males bright red, orange or yellow, females grey (a few species without bright colours) (minivets—*Pericrocotus*); only *Campephaga* and *Coracina* represented in s Africa; sexes usually different; arboreal in forest or savanna (one Australian species largely terrestrial); food insects and fruit; nest a saucer-shaped pad of plant material bound with spider web on branch of tree; eggs 2–4, white, green or blue with markings; chick very sparsely downy at hatching; parental care by both sexes. Distribution Africa S of Sahara, tropical Asia, Australia, Papuan region to Samoa; 72 species; three species in s Africa.

538 (513)   Black Cuckooshrike   Plate 47
Swartkatakoeroe
Campephaga flava

Rankwitsidi (NS), Umthethi, Usinga Olumnyama (X), iNhlangu (Z), [Kuckuckswürger]

Measurements: Length 19–22 cm; wing (25 ♂) 100–105–113, (21 ♀) 97–103–109; tail (46) 95–105; tarsus (46) 18–21; culmen (46) 14–16. Weight (6 ♂) 28,9–32,3–36,1 g, (5 ♀) 30,4–32,2–33,3 g.

Bare Parts: Iris brown; bill black, base pinkish; swollen gape yellow-orange; legs and feet blackish.

Identification: Size medium. *Male*: Black

with greenish blue gloss; some males (in Natal about 50%, in Zimbabwe about 9%) have bright yellow patch on bend of wing; gape bright yellow-orange; tail rounded (square or slightly notched in Squaretailed Drongo and Black Flycatcher). *Female*: Above yellowish olive, finely barred with black; black streak through eye; below white, tinged yellow on breast, finely barred with black; tail and wing feathers edged bright yellow; outer rectrices mostly yellow, tips pointed. *Immature*: Similar to ♀. *Chick*: Deep purple with long white down. **Voice:** Very high-pitched prolonged insectlike trill, *krrreee*; lower-pitched rolling *kreeu, kreeu*; hissing *ssseeu, ssseeu*; unmusical *chup* or *tsip, tsip*.

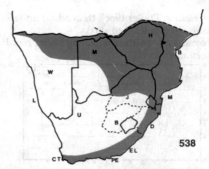

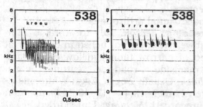

Distribution: S Africa to E Africa; in s Africa confined to wooded areas of S, E and N; absent from highveld and dry W, but recorded Waterberg Plateau, Namibia.
Status: Uncommon to fairly common resident or local migrant; disperses into drier areas after rain and to lower altitudes in winter.
Habitat: Any woodland, edge of evergreen forest, exotic plantations; sparse in open savanna.
Habits: Usually solitary or in pairs. Quiet and unobtrusive; perches for long periods in dense vegetation. Creeps quietly through thick foliage, gleaning insects from leaves and twigs of canopy and in bark of trunks; sometimes hovers to pick prey off leaf; rarely feeds on ground; may join bird parties. Flight floppy, undulating. Often flicks wings up and down when perched.
Food: Insects (mainly caterpillars), fruit.
Breeding: *Season*: September to February (mainly October-December) in Zimbabwe, October to January in e Cape, September to December in Natal. *Nest*: Small shallow saucer of felted moss and lichen, bound with spider web, lined with finer fibres, hair or leaf midribs; outside diameter 7–10 cm, inside diameter 4–4,5 cm, inside depth 1,3–2 cm; moulded into fork or saddle of branch, often high in tree, easily overlooked; built by ♀ only; ♂ accompanies ♀ during building. *Clutch*: (37) 1–1,9–3 eggs. *Eggs*: Blue-green or yellow-green, spotted with dark brown and purplish grey, somewhat concentrated at thick end; measure (42) 23,8 × 17,3 (21,5–25,9 × 16,2–18,4). *Incubation*: (3) 20 days by ♀ only; ♂ feeds ♀ on nest. *Nestling*: (7) 20–23 days; fed by both parents; brooded by ♀ only.

Ref. Skead, C.J. 1966. *Ostrich* 37:71–75.

539 (515)   **Whitebreasted Cuckooshrike**   **Plate 47**
Witborskatakoeroe
Coracina pectoralis

[Weißbrust-Raupenfänger]

Measurements: Length about 27 cm; wing (13 ♂) 136–141–149, (5 ♀) 138–141–146; tail (18) 107–117; tarsus (18) 22–24; culmen (18) 18–21.
Bare Parts: Iris dark brown; bill black; legs and feet dark grey.
Identification: About size of Laughing Dove; upperparts and throat light grey, paler on head; rest of underparts white, sharply divided from grey of throat, giving hooded appearance; wings and outer rectrices blackish; throat of ♀ paler than that of ♂. *Immature*: Above barred black and white on grey; below spotted blackish; wings edged white in flight; outer rectrices pointed. *Chick*: Steel grey with coarse white down above.

Voice: Soft whistled *duid-duid* (♂); long trilled *chreeeee* (♀); also weak squeak.

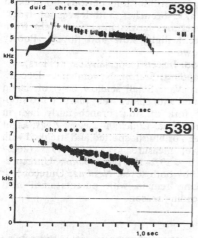

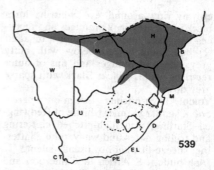

Distribution: Africa S of Sahara; in s Africa confined to NE and N.

Status: Uncommon resident, territorial throughout year; some dispersal after breeding. Rare (RDB).

Habitat: Canopy of well developed woodland (Grey Cuckooshrike inhabits forest, not woodland).

Habits: Usually solitary or in pairs; sometimes in mixed bird parties. Forages by gleaning from trunks or branches, by hawking prey in air, or less often on ground; bounds through treetops, stopping at times to examine twigs and leaves for prey. Flight flapping and gliding.

Food: Insects (especially caterpillars).

Breeding: *Season*: August to December (mainly September-November) in Zimbabwe. *Nest*: Shallow bowl of leaf petioles, covered outside with *Usnea* and other lichens and spider web; one nest measured outside diameter 113 mm, inside diameter 81 mm, depth of cup 38 mm; 6–20 m above ground on branch of tall tree; hard to see from below; built by both sexes in about 5 days. *Clutch*: 1–2 eggs. *Eggs*: Pale bluish green or dull green, heavily spotted with dark brown and underlying grey; measure (13) 27,3 × 19,5 (26,1–30 × 18,9–20,1). *Incubation*: 23 days by both sexes. *Nestling*: 30 days; fed by both parents; postnestling dependence about 2–3 months; young remain with parents until next breeding season.

Ref. Whittingham, A.P. 1964. *Ostrich* 35:63–64.

540 (516) **Grey Cuckooshrike** **Plate 47**
Bloukatakoeroe
Coracina caesia

Usinga, Umsimpofu (X), iKlebedwane (Z), [Grauer Raupenfänger, Waldraupenfänger]

Measurements: Length 25–27 cm; wing (9 ♂) 129–131–133, (11 ♀) 126–128–131; tail (20) 107–118; tarsus (20) 22–25; culmen (20) 18–21.

Bare Parts: Iris brown; bill, legs and feet black.

Identification: About size of Laughing Dove (somewhat smaller than Whitebreasted Cuckooshrike); blue-grey all over (♀ distinctly paler than ♂), sometimes whitish over forehead and sides of

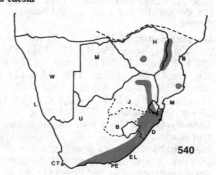

crown; ring around eye whitish; lores black in ♂, grey in ♀; remiges and rectrices blackish. *Immature*: Similar to adult ♀, but finely barred below with buffy grey; edges of remiges and tips of outer rectrices white. *Chick*: Black with sparse grey down.

Voice: High-pitched drawn-out *peeee-oooo*, similar to quiet whistle of Redwinged Starling; also high-pitched chittering and trilling notes and weaverlike chattering; sneeze-like *chi-oo*; usually silent.

Distribution: S Africa to Cameroon and Ethiopia; in s Africa confined to extreme S and E.

Status: Uncommon resident; some fairly extensive local movements after breeding.

Habitat: Canopy of evergreen forest and coastal bush.

Habits: Usually solitary or in pairs; accompanies mixed bird parties. Perches still for long periods. Forages on trunks, branches and leaves of trees, sometimes hawks insects in flight from perch; flight slow and floppy. Poorly known.

Food: Insects (especially caterpillars).

Breeding: *Season*: November to December. *Nest*: Small shallow bowl of lichen bound with spider web; plastered to sloping fork or stout branch fairly high in forest tree. *Clutch*: 1–2 eggs. *Eggs*: Light green or bluish, spotted and streaked with olive; measure (3) 27,6 × 19,3 (26,2–29,9 × 19,2–19,5). *Incubation*: Unrecorded; by both sexes. *Nestling*: Unrecorded; young remain with parents until next breeding season.

26:6. Family 68 DICRURIDAE—DRONGOS

Small to medium (not including very long tail feathers of some species). Bill robust, broad, somewhat hooked at tip, notched behind hook, culmen arched; legs short; toes strong; wings longish, rounded or somewhat pointed; flight undulating; tail fairly long, square or forked, sometimes with elongate and decorative outer rectrices; head large; eyes usually red; plumage usually glossy black, sometimes grey, or occasionally with white patches; some species crested; sexes alike; arboreal in forest or savanna; solitary or in small loose flocks; food insects, small vertebrates, rarely nectar; nest a thin hammock-like saucer of plant fibres bound with spider web in horizontal fork of branch; eggs 2–4, white or pink, plain or marked; chick naked at hatching; parental care by both sexes. Distribution Africa, tropical Asia to Australia and Solomon Islands; 20 species; two species in s Africa.

---

541 (517)   **Forktailed Drongo**   **Plate 47**
Mikstertbyvanger
Dicrurus adsimilis

Ntene (K), Theko (NS), Nhengu, Nhengure (Sh), Matengu, Ntengu (Ts), Kuamosi (Tw), Intengu (X), iNtengu (Z), [Trauerdrongo, Gabelschwanzdrongo]

Measurements: Length ♂ 25 cm, ♀ 22,5–24 cm; wing (58 ♂) 123–134–143, (32 ♀) 120–130,7–139; tail (34 ♂) 104–116,4–126, (18 ♀) 102–114,1–124; tarsus (38) 21–24; culmen (38) 19–23. Weight (4 ♂) 38,1–40–42,4 g, (1 ♀) 23,7 g, (14 unsexed) 37,7–50,1–58 g.

Bare Parts: Iris deep red; bill, legs and feet black.

Identification: Size medium; black with purplish sheen all over; tail longish, deeply notched or forked (less so in ♀); in

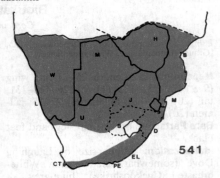

moult, tail often has double fork until fully grown out; in flight wings pale, translucent, almost whitish; albinos and partial albinos rarely occur. Similar to Black Flycatcher but somewhat larger; bill heavier, deeper at base, hooked at tip; forehead tends to slope back from bill (forehead higher and more rounded in Black Flycatcher); tail more deeply forked (but sometimes fairly deeply notched in Black Flycatcher); perches with legs flexed, belly on branch (Black Flycatcher often perches high on legs); eye red (visible in good light only; brown in Black Flycatcher). Larger than Squaretailed Drongo, with more deeply forked tail; inhabits open woodland (Squaretailed Drongo inhabits forest). *Immature*: Below grey, densely speckled pale grey.

Voice: Song loud jumble of strident twanging, creaking and rasping sounds like unoiled wooden wagonwheels; imitates other birdcalls; callnote single trumpetlike *twank* or *twillang*; vocal on moonlit nights gentle *tweep* flight call.

Distribution: Africa S of Sahara; almost throughout s Africa, except w Karoo and Namaqualand.

Status: Common resident; may have some short-distance local movements.

Habitat: Woodland, savanna, riverine *Acacia*, exotic plantations, farmyards, gardens, parks, open grassveld with perches (e.g. fences, isolated trees), forest edge; avoids forest interior.

Habits: Usually solitary or in pairs; sometimes in groups of up to 20 birds; may join bird parties. Perches on conspicuous branch, post or large herbivorous mammal; sallies out to catch prey in flight or on ground, often returning to same perch; attracted to grassfires. Flight buoyant, undulating and agile. Mobs larger raptors, owls, hornbills, crows, small mammals; aggressive at nest, even attacking man; may rob food from other birds; kills and carries small birds in feet or bill; may feed by holding prey with foot and tearing with hooked bill. Bathes by plunge-diving from air or perch; drinks by sucking and raising head to swallow.

Food: Insects (especially bees, when available), small birds (white-eyes, mannikins, canaries), fish (caught by plunging like kingfisher), nectar.

Breeding: *Season*: October to January in Natal, August to January (mainly September-November) in Zimbabwe; 2–3 broods/season; only known host of African Cuckoo. *Nest*: Strongly woven, thin-walled, often transparent, shallow saucer of rootlets, tendrils and twigs, neatly bound with spider web; usually suspended hammocklike in horizontal fork of tree, well away from main trunk; less often more substantial bowl of plant material or sheep's wool placed on top of horizontal branch; 2–12 m above ground. *Clutch*: (172) 2–2,8–4 eggs (usually 3). *Eggs*: Highly variable; white, cream or pink, plain or spotted with dark pink, reddish brown or blackish; measure (336) 24,3 × 18,2 (21,2–28,3 × 16,7–20,1). *Incubation*: 16–17 days. *Nestling*: 17–18 days.

542 (518)   **Squaretailed Drongo**   **Plate 47**
Kleinbyvanger
Dicrurus ludwigii

Intengwana (X), iNtengwana (Z), [Geradschwanzdrongo, Kleiner Drongo]

Measurements: Length about 19 cm; wing (26 ♂) 100–103,4–107,5, (26 ♀) 95–98,8–103,5; tail (11) 88–93; tarsus (12) 14–18; culmen (12) 17–21,5.

Bare Parts: Iris deep red; bill, legs and feet black, soles whitish.

Identification: Size smallish (smaller than Forktailed Drongo); overall black with greenish blue sheen (♀ duller than ♂); tail slightly notched (deeply forked in Forktailed Drongo, rounded in Black Cuckooshrike); forest habitat (Black Cuckooshrike, Forktailed Drongo and Black Flycatcher inhabit more open woodland); eye red (brown in Black Flycatcher); underwing lightly marked with white feather tips (not good field character). *Immature*: Like adult ♀, but speckled pale greyish below.

Voice: Highly vocal; various tweets and whistles interspersed with loud strident twanging 3-syllabled *tswing-tswing-tswing* phrases.

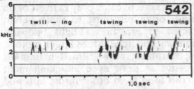

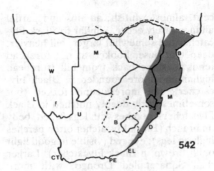

Distribution: Africa S of Sahara; in s Africa confined to SE (e Cape) and E.
Status: Locally common resident.
Habitat: Mid-stratum of evergreen forest.
Habits: Usually solitary or in pairs; often in mixed bird parties, especially with Forest Weaver. Perches on branch and darts out at flying insects; twitches tail sideways when perched. Seldom ventures out of forest interior. Aggressive and noisy, especially near nest; mobs larger birds; may steal food from other birds.
Food: Insects, nectar.
Breeding: *Season*: October to April

in Natal, September to January in Zimbabwe. *Nest*: Small neat cup of twigs, plant fibres and lichens bound with spider web; slung hammocklike in horizontal fork of slender branch in forest interior. *Clutch*: (33) 2–2,6–3 eggs (usually 3). *Eggs*: White, plain or spotted with purplish brown and grey; measure (34) 21,4 × 15,8 (20,1–22,8 × 15–16,5); weigh (2) 2,3–2,4 g. *Incubation*: Unrecorded. *Nestling*: Unrecorded.

26:7. Family 69 ORIOLIDAE—OLD-WORLD ORIOLES

Small to medium. Bill medium, strong, slightly hooked at tip, often reddish; legs medium to short; toes medium, strong; wings moderately long, pointed; flight swift and undulating; tail medium, rounded or square; plumage largely yellow, green, red or chestnut with black in wings, tail and head region; sexes alike or different; arboreal in forest canopy or open woodland; solitary; food insects, fruit, nectar; nest a deep cup suspended in horizontal fork, usually high in tree; eggs 2–5, white, pink or green, marked; chick sparsely downy at hatching; parental care by both sexes. Distribution Africa, s Europe, s Asia, Australasia (not New Zealand) and Philippines; about 27 species; four species in s Africa.

543 (519) **Eurasian Golden Oriole** **Plate 47**
Europese Wielewaal
Oriolus oriolus

Nkulivere (K), Ndukuzani (Ts), [Europäischer Pirol]
Measurements: Length 22,5–24 cm; wing ♂ 146–155, ♀ 144–150; tail (6) 80–87; tarsus (6) 20–23; culmen (6) 25–27,5. Weight (2) 64–65 g.
Bare Parts: Iris crimson; bill dark pink; legs and feet grey.
Identification: Size medium (about size of smaller starlings). *Male*: Mainly yellow; wings and tail mostly black (mainly yellow in African Golden Oriole); lores black

(African Golden Oriole has black line from base of bill through eye to ear coverts). *Female*: Above yellowish green; below mainly white, washed yellow on flanks, streaked dusky; undertail yellow. *Immature*: Like adult ♀, but more heavily streaked below; bill dusky.
Voice: Usually silent in s Africa; distinctive pleasant flutelike *weelawoo* or *who-are-you*, sometimes with harsher nasal quality; harsh rattling *chrrr* alarm note.

470

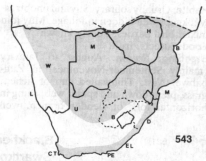

543

Distribution: Breeds Europe and w Asia to India; migrates to Africa and India; widespread in s Africa, but largely absent from drier W.

Status: Fairly common, but elusive, non-breeding Palaearctic migrant, October to April; females and immatures far outnumber adult males.

Habitat: Coastal scrub, savanna, riverine *Acacia*, bushveld, drier woodland, exotic plantations, orchards.

Habits: Usually solitary; sometimes in small groups. Shy and secretive, keeping to tops of trees; usually seen flying from one tree to another; flight buoyant and undulating, up to 40 km/h. Bathes by plunge-diving from perch.

Food: Insects, fruit.

Breeding: Extralimital.

544 (520)   African Golden Oriole   Plate 47
Afrikaanse Wielewaal
Oriolus auratus

Nkulivere (K), Ndukuzani (Ts), [Schwarzohrpirol]

Measurements: Length about 24 cm; wing 132–143; tail 78–84; tarsus 21–23; culmen 26,5–28. Weight (6) 70–73,7–79,4 g.

Bare Parts: Iris ♂ deep red, ♀ brown; bill ♂ dark brownish pink, ♀ black; legs and feet grey.

Identification: Size medium. *Male:* Bright yellow except for black central rectrices, eyestripe and wingtips (Eurasian Golden Oriole has black lores, not eyestripe, black wings and black tail with yellow tip only). *Female:* More greenish yellow above than ♂; below dull yellow, streaked olive. *Immature:* Similar to adult ♀; wing coverts edged greenish yellow; eyestripe olive (no yellow feather edging or olive eyestripe in immature Eurasian Golden Oriole).

Voice: Indistinguishable from that of Blackheaded Oriole; far-carrying liquid piping and bubbling notes, *wee-er-er-wul*; drawn-out *aa-aa-aa-er*; harsh *mwaa* alarm note.

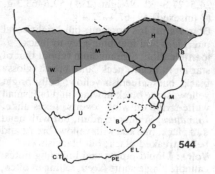

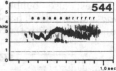

544

Distribution: Africa S of Sahara; in s Africa confined to N.

Status: Uncommon breeding intra-African migrant, August to April (rarely to May); winters tropical Africa, but some birds over-winter in s Africa, especially in lowveld.

Habitat: Mainly canopy of *Brachystegia* woodland; also dense bush around hills, riverine forest of major river systems; less often also in savanna.

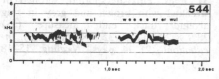

544

471

Habits: Usually solitary. Shy and unobtrusive; keeps well hidden in foliage. May join mixed bird parties. Poorly known.

Food: Insects, fruit.

Breeding: *Season*: August to January (mainly September-November) in Zimbabwe. *Nest*: Thinwalled cup of lichen, grass, plant down and spider web; slung in horizontal fork of slender branch, well away from trunk of tree; 5–13 m above ground. *Clutch*: (14) 2–2,3–3 eggs (usually 2). *Eggs*: Buffy pink, boldly spotted with chestnut, brown and grey, suffused with deeper pink around each brown spot; measure (45) 28,5 × 20,5 (26–32,9 × 19,2–21,8). *Incubation*: Unrecorded. *Nestling*: Unrecorded; fed by both parents; brooded by ♀ only.

---

545 (521) **Blackheaded Oriole** **Plate 47**
Swartkopwielewaal
Oriolus larvatus

Nkulivere (K), Gotowa (Sh), Nkodyo, Ndukuzama (Ts), Umkro, Umqokolo (X), umQoqongo, umBhicongo (Z), [Maskenpirol]

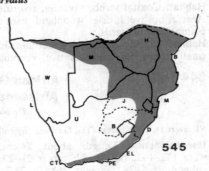

Measurements: Length 24–25 cm; wing (25 ♂) 130–138,8–143,5, (24 ♀) 127–134,7–142; tail (25 ♂) 79–89,1–100, (24 ♀) 77,5–87,3–93,5; tarsus (18) 21–24; culmen (25 ♂) 25,5–28,5–33, (24 ♀) 24,5–27,8–32. Weight (2 ♂) 59,6–63,3 g, (7 unsexed) 59–67,4–72,4 g.

Bare Parts: Iris crimson; bill bright coral pink; legs and feet blue-grey to black.

Identification: Size medium (about that of starling); head, neck and breast glossy black; back greenish yellow; belly bright yellow; some black in wings and tail; small white stripe on wing coverts; sexes alike. *Immature*: Similar to adult, but with head dull black, marked with yellow; breast and belly streaked black; bill blackish.

Voice: Liquid piping and bubbling notes; callnote single short *kleeu*, falling in pitch, repeated several times; also bubbling *klupklop, kiddlywop* and variations; harsh *kwaar* alarm note; song jumble of rich melodious notes.

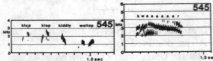

Distribution: S Africa to E Africa; in s Africa confined to e third from s Cape eastwards.

Status: Common resident; some local seasonal movement to concentrated food supplies, e.g. flowering aloes.

Habitat: Almost any woodland, forest edge, riverine and coastal bush, exotic plantations, parks, gardens, farmyards with big trees.

Habits: Usually solitary or in pairs; forms loose groups at good food source (fruit, nectar). Keeps mostly to tops of tall trees; highly vocal, especially in early morning. Flight fast, undulating.

Food: Insects, fruit, nectar.

Breeding: *Season*: September to February (mainly September-November) in Zimbabwe, September to December in Natal. *Nest*: Deep cup of *Usnea* lichen, moss, tendrils, grass and spider web; bound hammocklike to horizontal fork of slender branch, well away from trunk of tree; built by ♀ only; 5–13 m above ground; often built among growing *Usnea* and hard to see. *Clutch*: (61) 2–2,4–3 eggs (rarely 4 or 5). *Eggs*: Pinkish, spotted, scrolled or streaked with brown and grey in ring around thick end; measure (88) 28,9 × 20,2 (26,1–32,7 × 16,7–22,3). *Incubation*: (2) 14 days. *Nestling*: 15–18 days.

546 (521X)

Greenheaded Oriole
Groenkopwielewaal
Oriolus chlorocephalus

Plate 47

[Grünkopfpirol]

Measurements: Length about 24 cm; wing (8 ♂) 125–138,4–144, (4 ♀) 126–132–134,5; tail (8 ♂) 90–103,8–108, (4 ♀) 93–99,1–103; tarsus (4 ♂) 22–23,5–25, (2 ♀) 22–23; culmen (4 ♂) 25–26,8–29, (2 ♀) 22–27.

Bare Parts: Iris red-brown; bill reddish brown; legs and feet light bluish grey.

Identification: Size medium; head, back and tail mossy olive green; underparts and collar on hindneck deep yellow; wings light blue-grey with white wingpatch (no white speculum in populations further N); sexes alike. *Immature*: More greenish yellow than adult; streaked below with green.

Voice: Similar to voice of Blackheaded Oriole, possibly clearer and more liquid; also distinctive nasal whining *heee-eee-aaa*.

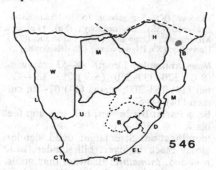

5 4 6

Distribution: Discontinuously from se Kenya to Gorongosa, Mozambique; isolated subspecies, *O. c. speculifer* characterized by white wingpatch, found on Mt Gorongosa only.

Status: Fairly common resident in restricted range.

Habitat: Canopy of montane evergreen forest, 750–2000 m above sea level.

Habits: Similar to those of Blackheaded Oriole; solitary except at concentrated food source. Poorly known.

Food: Insects, fruit, flowers.

Breeding: *Season*: Unrecorded in s Africa. *Nest*: Deep baglike cup of *Usnea*; slung in slender lateral fork, about 10 m above ground in forest tree. *Clutch, Eggs, Incubation, Nestling*: Unrecorded.

Ref. Clancey, P.A. 1970. *Bokmakierie* 22:53–54.

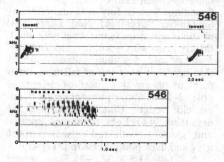

26:8. Family 70 CORVIDAE—CROWS, JAYS, MAGPIES, ETC.

Small to large (include the largest of the passerines). Bill strong, slender or very heavy; nostrils covered by bristles; legs strong, short to moderately long; feet large and strong; wings pointed or rounded, usually broad; tail variable, usually medium, square, rounded or graduated; plumage black, white and grey in crows, more brightly coloured in most jays which may also be barred and spotted; sexes usually alike; some gregarious; omnivorous; breed solitarily or colonially; nest an open bowl in tree, on ledge or in hole (roofed with sticks in magpies and *Zavattariornis*); eggs 2–9, white or coloured with markings; chick naked or sparsely downy at hatching; parental care by both sexes. Distribution worldwide; about 100 species; four species in s Africa (one introduced).

Ref. Goodwin, D. 1976. *Crows of the world*. London: British Museum (Natural History).
Winterbottom, J.M. 1975. *Ostrich* 46:236–250.

547 (523)

Black Crow
Swartkraai
Corvus capensis

Plate 47

Ekorova (K), Segogobane (NS), Mokhoabane, Lekhoaba (SS), Chikungubaya (Sh), Gunguva, Xikhunguba, Qugwana (Ts), Lehukubu (Tw), Unomyayi (X), iNgwababane (Z), [Kapkrähe]

Measurements: Length 48–53 cm; wing (8 ♂) 320–330–350, (6 ♀) 293–321–338; tail (14) 163–200; tarsus (14) 62–70; culmen (14) 54–63.

Bare Parts: Iris brown; bill, legs and feet black.

Identification: Size large; build slender; glossy black all over; bill slender; head rounded. *Immature*: Browner than adult.

Voice: Highly vocal; loud harsh *kraa, kraa*; liquid bubbling *kwollop, kwollop*; deep *grrrr*; often mixes repertoire in "conversational" calling.

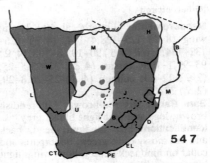

547

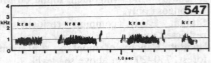

beats; displays in flight with rapid little wingbeats well below body, while uttering gargling call. Non-territorial birds may roost in flocks of up to 600 in trees or on telephone poles.

Food: Omnivorous; insects, frogs, fallen grain, fruit; also carrion (but less of a scavenger than Pied Crow).

Distribution: S Africa to Ethiopia and Sudan; widespread in s Africa, but absent from n Botswana, nw Zimbabwe, s Mozambique.

Status: Common to fairly common resident.

Habitat: Open grassland, afroalpine meadows, cultivated fields, exotic plantations, *Acacia* savanna, riverine trees in desert.

Habits: Usually in pairs with permanent territory; sometimes solitary or in flocks of up to 50 birds. Forages on ground, walking with long strides, often in ploughed fields. Calls from perch in tall tree, on telephone pole or earth mound, bowing puffed-up head, raising tail and flicking wings. Flies with deep wing-

Breeding: *Season*: July to January (mainly September-November). *Nest*: Large bowl of sticks and twigs (sometimes wire also), thickly lined with wool, fur, cloth, string, feathers and dry dung; usually among thin branches near top of tall tree, outer fork of thorn tree, top of telephone pole; 2–24 m above ground; rarely builds on cliff ledge. *Clutch*: (162) 1–3,5–6 eggs (usually 4). *Eggs*: Light pink, spotted and speckled with red-brown, purplish grey and dark pink; measure (217) 45,4 × 31,1 (40–53,5 × 27,6–34,3); weight 17–18,6–20 g. *Incubation*: 18–19 days by both sexes. *Nestling*: 36–39 days; fed by both parents; dependent on parents for food for up to 3 months after leaving nest; may remain with parents for up to 6 months.

548 (522)

Pied Crow
Witborskraai
Corvus albus

Plate 47

Ekorova (K), Legokobu (NS), Mohakajane (SS), Gunguwo (Sh), Ukuuku, Xikhunguba (Ts), Legakabê (Tw), Igwangwa, Igwarhube (X), iGwababa, uGwabayi (Z), [Schildrabe]

Measurements: Length 46–52 cm; wing

(17) 328–356–388; tail 175–200; tarsus 55–61; culmen 51–58. Weight (5 ♀) 421–519,2–581 g, (? unsexed) 545,6–567,9–612 g.

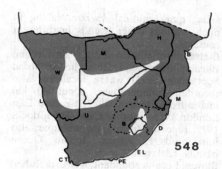

548

Bare Parts: Iris brown; bill, legs and feet black.

Identification: Size large; build stockier than that of Black Crow; shiny black with white breast and broad white collar on hindneck (Whitenecked Raven has white on hindneck only); bill fairly heavy (heavier than that of Black Crow, but not as deep as that of Whitenecked Raven). *Immature:* Less glossy than adult; white feathering tipped dusky.

Voice: Harsh deep *kraah* or *kroh*; snoring *khrrrr*.

Distribution: Africa S of Sahara, and Aldabra; in s Africa largely absent from C Kalahari basin and se Namibia; otherwise widespread.

Status: Common to abundant resident.

Habitat: Farmland, savanna, urban areas, rubbish dumps, verges of roads and railways.

Habits: Usually in pairs or small flocks; sometimes highly gregarious in flocks of up to 300 birds (rarely 500). Forages mainly on ground or in litter bins; walks on ground, but hops when moving fast; largely scavenger; can catch small birds in flight. May damage maize crops by perching on stalks, but not major pest; sometimes digs up sown grain; may injure weakened small stock or newborn calves. Flies with deep regular wingbeats. Flocks roost in trees. Gathers in groups of up to 150 birds to perform aerial spiralling flights to 100 m or more. Wary but often bold.

Food: Primarily plant material (seeds, fruit, roots); also arthropods, molluscs, frogs, reptiles, fish, birds (including eggs and nestlings), small mammals, ectoparasites from game mammals, carrion (such as road kills).

Breeding: *Season:* July to January (mainly September-October) throughout s Africa. *Nest:* Large bowl of sticks, twigs and wire (some nests mainly of wire, weighing up to 20 kg), thickly lined with fur, wool, rags, dry dung; 3–30 m above ground in stout fork of isolated tall tree, telephone pole or windmill platform; rarely on cliff ledge; built by both sexes. *Clutch:* (140) 1–4,1–7 eggs (usually 4–5). *Eggs:* Light green, blotched and spotted with dark brown, olive and grey; measure (187) 44,7 × 30,5 (39–51 × 26,2–33). *Incubation:* 18–19 days, about 80% by ♀, 20% by ♂. *Nestling:* 35–45 days; fed by both parents.

Ref. Brooke, R.K. & Grobler, J.H. 1973. *Arnoldia* 6(10):1–13.

---

549 (523X)

House Crow
Huiskraai

Corvus splendens

Plate 47

[Glanzkrähe, Hauskrähe]

Measurements: Length about 43 cm; wing ♂ 266–284, ♀ 252–282; tail ♂ 162–175, ♀ 154–175; tarsus ♂ 45–51, ♀ 44–48; culmen ♂ 51–56, ♀ 45–50. Weight (2 ♂) 310–362 g, (5 ♀) 252–304 g, (2 unsexed) 266–280 g.

Bare Parts: Iris brown; bill, legs and feet black.

Identification: Size medium to large; smaller than Black Crow; build fairly slender; mainly shiny black, with sooty grey breast, nape and mantle; bill medium (somewhat heavier than that of Black Crow). *Immature:* Lighter grey than adult on breast and mantle; dull brownish black elsewhere.

Voice: Shrill *kwaa, kwaa* or nasal *kaan,*

475

kaan; quiet musical *kurrrrr*, falling in pitch; various other sounds in different contexts.

Distribution: Iran to India, Pakistan and Burma; introduced Durban (first recorded September 1972) where localized; also recorded Camperdown, about 40 km inland from Durban, 1973; 1 record East London 1975, another Cape Town docks 1979; reported from s Mozambique; also introduced E Africa, Indian Ocean islands, Malaysia.

Status: Locally abundant, well established resident; control measures implemented 1990 in Durban in attempt to eradicate local populations.

Habitat: Urban, especially industrial and southern suburbs of Durban (Mobeni, Chatsworth).

Habits: Usually gregarious in flocks of up to 50 birds; in pairs when breeding. Forages on ground; walks with perky gait; sometimes hops and flicks wings. Flight straight, wingbeats rather slow and shallow; performs aerial manoeuvres. Roosts communally in trees.

Food: Omnivorous: grain, fruit, nectar, birds (including eggs and nestlings), small mammals, lizards, fish, insects, crabs, carrion, scraps, offal.

Breeding: Poorly documented in S Africa; first recorded Durban about 1972. *Season*: October. *Nest*: Large bowl of sticks and wire, lined with soft plant and animal fibres; outside diameter 25–30 cm, inside diameter 12–15 cm, inside depth 7–10 cm; about 3–4 m above ground in thin vertical fork or outer branches of tree; less often on building or telephone pole; material collected by both sexes, built by ♀ only. *Clutch*: 3–6 eggs (usually 4–5). *Eggs*: Pale blue-green, speckled and streaked with brown, red-brown and grey; measure (200, India) 37,2 × 27 (33–40 × 24–29). *Incubation*: (17) 16–16,1–17 days by both sexes, mostly by ♀; only ♀ incubates at night; young hatch at intervals of 24–48 hours. *Nestling*: 3–4 weeks; fed by both parents; dependent on parents for several weeks after initial departure.

Ref. Clancey, P.A. 1974. *Ostrich* 45:31–32.
Lamba, B.S. 1963. *J. Bombay Nat. Hist. Soc.* 60:122–133.

550 (524)   **Whitenecked Raven**   **Plate 47**
                             Withalskraai
                             Corvus albicollis

Lekhoaba, Moqukubi (SS), Gwavava, Ukuuku (Ts), Ihlungulu, Umfundisi, Irhwababa (X), iHubulu, iWabayi (Z), [Geierrabe]

Measurements: Length 50–54 cm; wing (4) 376–430; tail 180–184; tarsus 72–79; culmen 61–66. Weight (1 ♀) 865 g, (1 unsexed) 762 g.

Bare Parts: Iris dark brown; bill black, tip white; legs and feet black.

Identification: Size large; glossy black with white collar on hindneck (sometimes hard to see in flight); bill massive, arched, tip white; in flight wings broad, tail broad and short; voice distinctive (see **Voice**). *Immature*: Browner than adult; narrow whitish breastband; white hindneck sometimes flecked black.

Voice: Characteristically high-pitched, almost falsetto *kraak-kraak-kraak*, usually given in quick series; also some deeper notes seldom heard.

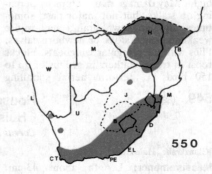

Distribution: S Africa to Kenya; in s Africa confined mainly to SW, S and E,

but absent from most of s Mozambique.
Status: Locally common resident, though generally uncommon.
Habitat: Mainly mountains, gorges, cliffs; forages in more open country at times.
Habits: Usually singly or in pairs; sometimes in flocks of up to 150 birds at good food source, often in company with other scavengers (crows, kites, vultures); usually arrives first at carcass. Soars well; wingbeats shallower than those of other corvids; performs aerobatics; patrols roads seeking animals killed by vehicles. Often vocal in flight.
Food: Carrion, insects, birds' eggs, fruit,

grain, birds, mammals, reptiles; drops tortoises from air to break shells.
Breeding: *Season*: July to November (mainly September-October) throughout s Africa. *Nest*: Large bowl of sticks, lined with grass, hair, wool and other soft material; on inaccessible cliff ledge or pothole (rarely in tree). *Clutch*: (12) 2–3,4–5 eggs (usually 4; rarely 1 or 6). *Eggs*: Light green, streaked and spotted with brown, olive and grey; measure (24) 51 × 33,3 (45–56,9 × 31,6–35). *Incubation*: 19–21 days. *Nestling*: Unrecorded.

Ref. Uys, C.J. 1966. *Bokmakierie* 18:38–41.

26:9. Family 71 PARIDAE—TITS

Small. Bill short, slender or fairly stout, blunt at tip; nostrils covered by bristles; legs short to medium, strong; feet strong; wings somewhat rounded, fairly short; tail medium; plumage variable, but usually with black and white (especially about head and face) associated with grey, blue or yellow; sexes alike or nearly so; often gregarious when not breeding; arboreal; food invertebrates, nuts and seeds; breed in natural holes in trees, rocks or earth; nest a bulky pad of plant material and feathers; eggs 2–4 in s hemisphere, up to 15 in n hemisphere, whitish with reddish speckles; chick naked at hatching; parental care by both sexes, incubation usually by female only. Distribution N and C America, Eurasia, African mainland; 46 species; six species in s Africa.

TABLE 2

IDENTIFICATION OF GREY TITS

Feature	Species		
	Southern Grey	Ashy	Northern Grey
Head and bib	Blueblack	Blueblack	Sooty black, bib narrower
Hindneck	Pinkish buff*	White	White
Back	Dull brown*	Bluish grey	Bluish grey
Malar stripe	Clear white	Clear white	Dull buffy white*
Flanks	Dull pinkish buff	Grey*	Chalky pinkish white
Outer rectrix and tail tip	White	White	Buff*

*Diagnostic feature.

551 (525)   **Southern Grey Tit**   **Plate 48**
Piet-tjou-tjou-grysmees
Parus afer

[Kapmeise]
Measurements: Length 14–15 cm; wing (13) 69–73–77; tail 53–60; tarsus 17–21; culmen 13–15. Weight (14) 17,3–20,2–22,4 g.

Bare Parts: Iris dark brown; bill black; legs grey.
Identification: Size small (about sparrow-sized); very similar to Ashy and Northern Grey Tits (see identification Table 3 for

grey tits); crown, nape, bib and belly-stripe blueblack; broad white malar stripe; flanks pinkish buff (grey in Ashy Tit, whitish in Northern Grey Tit); hindneck pinkish buff (white in other grey tits); back dull brown (bluish grey in other grey tits). *Immature*: Remiges buff-edged; back browner than that of adult; crown slightly brownish black.

Voice: Penetrating ringing *wit-wit-wit-wit tseeu tseeu* or *wittee-wittee-wittee* ; harsh rapid vibrating *tsitsi-kr-kr-kr-kr* (faster than corresponding callnote of Southern Black Tit).

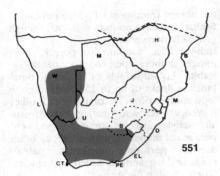

551

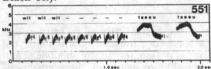

Distribution: Southern Namibia, Namaqualand, sw Cape, Karoo, to Port Elizabeth, ne Cape, Lesotho highlands and sw Orange Free State.
Status: Uncommon to fairly common resident.
Habitat: Karoid scrub.
Habits: In pairs or small family groups.

Forages restlessly on branches and among foliage of trees and bushes, hopping about and hanging upside down; calls often while feeding. Flight bouncing with quick bursts of wingbeats.
Food: Insects.
Breeding: *Season*: August to March. *Nest*: Thick pad of hair and grass in bottom of hole in tree, bank, rock, wall or fence pole. *Clutch*: (6) 2–3,3–5 eggs. *Eggs*: White, spotted with reddish, purple and grey; measure (3) 19,2 × 14,6 (18,9–19,5 × 14,5–14,6). *Incubation*: Unrecorded. *Nestling*: Unrecorded; fed by 2–4 adults, on caterpillars only.

552 (–)   **Ashy Tit**   **Plate 48**
                         Acaciagrysmees
                         Parus cinerascens

[Aschenmeise]

Measurements: Length about 15 cm; wing 72–79–84; tail 55–64; tarsus 17–20; culmen 12–14. Weight (3) 18,5–19,4–20,1 g
Bare Parts: Iris brown; bill black; legs and feet grey.
Identification: Size small (about sparrow-sized); very similar to Southern and Northern Grey Tits (see identification Table 3 for grey tits); crown, nape, bib and belly-stripe blueblack; hindneck white (pinkish buff in Southern Grey Tit); back bluish grey (brown in Southern Grey Tit); malar stripe white (buff in Northern Grey Tit); flanks grey (pinkish buff in Southern Grey Tit, whitish in Northern Grey Tit);

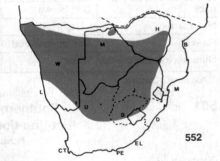

552

outer rectrix and tail tip white (buff in Northern Grey Tit).
Voice: Probably indistinguishable from voice of Southern Grey Tit.

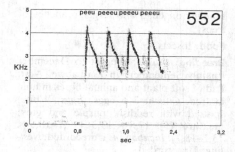

peeu peeeu peeeu peeeu

552

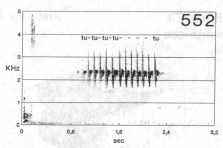

552

tu-tu-tu-tu- - - - tu

Distribution: Sw Angola, Namibia, n and nw Cape to just S of Orange River, Botswana, w Transvaal and s Zimbabwe; overlaps with Northern Grey Tit in s Zimbabwe and s Namibia.

Status: Fairly common to uncommon resident.

Habitat: Acacia savanna, dry thornbush, Kalahari scrub, bushy watercourses.

Habits: Similar to those of Southern Grey Tit. May join mixed bird parties, rarely in company with Northern Grey Tit. May roost at night in nest of Sociable Weaver or in burrow of Brownthroated Martin.

Food: Insects, especially caterpillars.

Breeding: *Season*: September to November in Zimbabwe; probably opportunistically in arid regions. *Nest*: Pad of soft plant and animal fibres in hole in tree. *Clutch*: 3–4 eggs. *Eggs*: White, spotted with reddish, purple and grey; measure (11) 18,8 × 13,9 (17,8–19,7 × 13,6–14,2). *Incubation*: Unrecorded. *Nestling*: Unrecorded.

553 (526) Northern Grey Tit (Miombo Grey Tit) Plate 48
Miombogrysmees
Parus griseiventris

[Miombomeise]

Measurements: Length about 15 cm; wing 74–82; tail 56–63; tarsus 18–20; culmen 11–12,5.

Bare Parts: Iris brown; bill black; legs and feet grey.

Identification: Size small (about sparrow-sized); very similar to Southern Grey and Ashy Tits (see identification Table 3 for grey tits); crown, nape, bib and belly-stripe sooty black (not shiny as in other grey tits); bib narrower than in Ashy Tit; small patch on hindneck whitish or grey (larger white patch in Ashy Tit); back bluish grey; wing paler than in Ashy Tit; malar stripe dull buffy white (clear white in Ashy Tit); flanks chalky pinkish white (grey in Ashy Tit); outer rectrix and tail tip buff (white in other grey tits); bill much smaller than in other grey tits.

Voice: Rolling *swip-ji-ji-ji-ji*; similar variety of ringing and harsh vibrating calls to those of Ashy Tit.

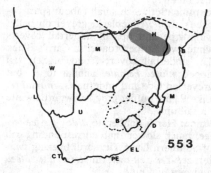

553

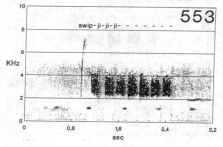

swip-ji-ji-ji- - - - - -

553

Distribution: Most of Zimbabwe, except extreme S, Mozambique N of Save River, to Angola and Tanzania.
Status: Uncommon to fairly common resident.
Habitat: Endemic to *Brachystegia* (miombo) woodland; canopy of large woodland trees.
Habits: Similar to habits of Ashy Tit, mostly ecologically separate, though sometimes found in mixed bird parties with Ashy Tits where habitats adjoin.

Forages on dead and larger branches of trees.
Food: Insects.
Breeding: *Season*: August to December (mainly September) in Zimbabwe. *Nest*: Pad of soft plant and animal fibres in hole in tree. *Clutch*: 3–5 eggs. *Eggs*: White, spotted with reddish, purple and grey; measure (5) 17,8 × 13,3 (17,1–18,5 × 13,2–13,7). *Incubation*: Unrecorded. *Nestling*: Unrecorded.

554 (527)   **Southern Black Tit**   **Plate 48**
Gewone Swartmees
Parus niger

Vayivayi (Ts), Isicukujeje, Isicubujeje (X), [Mohrenmeise]

Measurements: Length 15–16 cm; wing (87 ♂) 80–85,2–91,5, (61 ♀) 76,5–80,3–85,5; tail (55 ♂) 66,5–72,8–78, (40 ♀) 64–69,4–75; tarsus (53) 17–21; culmen (53) 10–12. Weight (11 ♂) 19,7–21,9–26 g, (11 ♀) 17,2–21,1–24,8 g, (2 unsexed) 19,4–20,3 g.
Bare Parts: Iris brown; bill black; legs and feet blue-grey.
Identification: Size small (about sparrow-sized). *Male*: Blueblack, greyer on belly; wingstripe and tips of undertail coverts white (wingstripe broader in Carp's Black Tit, undertail coverts solid black); tail tipped white. *Female*: Similar to ♂, but greyer on face and underparts. *Immature*: Like ♀, but buffier grey below; little white on tail tip.
Voice: Harsh deliberate *diddy-jee-jee-jee-jee*, much slower than corresponding call of Southern Grey Tit; shrill buzzing twitter, *zeu-zeu-zeu-twit*; ringing *teeu teeu teeu* and *pitu pitu pitu*.

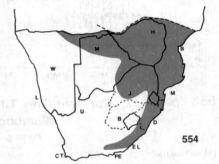

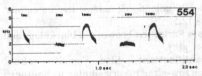

Distribution: Eastern Cape to Natal, Transvaal, ne Botswana, Caprivi and ne Namibia, Zimbabwe and Mozambique (to Zambia and Malawi).
Status: Common resident.
Habitat: Almost any woodland, gardens, parks, dense thornveld, edges of evergreen forest, exotic plantations.
Habits: Usually in pairs or small groups of about 6 birds. Forages restlessly on branches, under bark and in foliage in middle and upper levels of trees and bushes; holds seed pods in foot while tapping with bill to extract insect larvae; calls intermittently while feeding; may join mixed bird parties. Flight bouncing and quick.

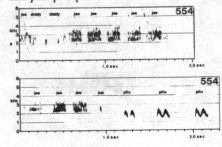

Food: Insects, especially larvae.
Breeding: *Season*: August to December (mainly September-October) in Zimbabwe, October to January in Transvaal; usually 1 brood/season. *Nest*: Soft pad of grass, lichen and hair, 6–9 cm thick; in natural hole in main trunk of tree, about 2–5 m above ground; cavity usually 15–40 cm deep from entrance; built by ♀ alone. *Clutch*: (39) 2–3,6–5 eggs. *Eggs*: White, speckled with reddish, brown and grey, concentrated at thick end; measure (82) 18 × 13,9 (16,6–20,7 × 13–14,6). *Incubation*: 15 days by ♀ only; fed by ♂ and up to 4 male helpers; incubating ♀ hisses like snake and lunges when disturbed. *Nestling*: 24 days; brooded by ♀ only; fed by both parents and up to 4 ♂ helpers.

Ref. Tarboton, W.R. 1981. *Ostrich* 52:216–225.

555 (528) Carp's Black Tit
Ovamboswartmees
Parus carpi
Plate 48

[Rüppellmeise]

Measurements: Length about 15 cm; wing (12 ♂) 80–94, (7 ♀) 74,5–92; tail (♂) 62–70 (♀) 61–68,5; culmen (♂) 11–12,5, (♀) 11,5–12.
Bare Parts: Iris brown; bill black; legs and feet grey.
Identification: Size small (about sparrow-sized); very similar to Southern Black Tit, mainly glossy black, but white areas on wing more extensive; below glossier black than Southern Black Tit; undertail coverts solid black (edged white in Southern Black Tit); ♂ and ♀ less differently coloured below than in Southern Black Tit.
Voice: Similar to voice of Southern Black Tit; various trilling and rasping notes.

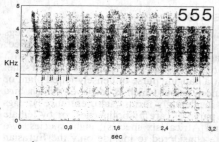

Distribution: Highlands and Namib edge of n Namibia to Kavango and sw Angola (Novo Redondo).

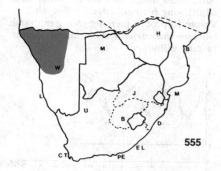

Status: Common resident.
Habitat: Bush and tree savanna, especially along dry watercourses and on hills and escarpments.
Habits: In pairs or small groups. Forages restlessly among lower branches of trees and bushes; flies quickly from tree to tree with dipping flight. Similar to Southern Black Tit.
Food: Insects; at times feeds mainly on seeds.
Breeding: *Season*: November to January. *Nest*: Pad of soft material in natural hole in tree. *Clutch*: 4–5 eggs. *Eggs*: White, tinged pink, densely spotted with reddish brown; measure 20,5 × 14,5. *Incubation*: Unrecorded. *Nestling*: Unrecorded.

481

556 (529)   **Rufousbellied Tit**   **Plate 48**
Swartkopmees
Parus rufiventris

[Rotbauchmeise]

Measurements: Length 14–15 cm; wing
(46 ♂) 83–85,5–89, (27 ♀) 77,5–81,6–86;
tail (46 ♂) 61–64,8–73, (25 ♀) 58–
62,3–66,5; tarsus 18–20; culmen 10–11.
Bare Parts: Iris brown to pale brown
(cream-coloured from Zambezi northwards); bill black; legs and feet blue-
grey.
Identification: Size small (about sparrow-
sized); head and breast glossy black; back
grey; wing black, edged with white, forming white wingbars; tail black, edged and
tipped white; belly pale rufous to pinkish
buff; sexes alike. *Immature*: Duller than
adult; wing feathers edged yellowish.
Voice: Repeated piercing *chik-wee*; harsh
chweerr-chweerr-chweerr alarm note;
rasping callnotes.

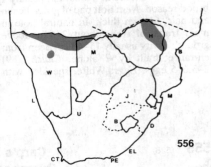

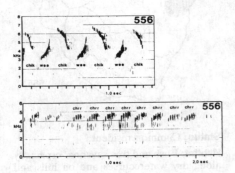

Distribution: Zimbabwe, extreme n Namibia, to Angola, Zaire and Tanzania.
Status: Fairly common to uncommon
resident.
Habitat: Canopy of well developed *Brachystegia* and *Uapaca* woodland.
Habits: In pairs or small groups; sometimes in mixed bird parties with Northern
Grey Tits and flycatchers. Forages among
high branches of trees. Poorly known.
Food: Insects (mainly caterpillars).
Breeding: *Season*: September to December in Zimbabwe. *Nest*: Soft pad of plant
fibres in natural hole in tree; usually
1–2 m above ground. *Clutch*: 2–4 eggs
(usually 3). *Eggs*: White or cream, heavily
speckled and spotted with chestnut and
grey; measure (12) 17,2 × 13,4
(15,8–19,5 × 12,8–14,1). *Incubation*:
Unrecorded. *Nestling*: Unrecorded.

26:10. Family 72 REMIZIDAE—PENDULINE TITS

Small. Bill short, slender, finely pointed at tip; nostrils covered with bristles; legs
medium; feet slender, but strong; one foot used a grasping organ; wings short, rounded;
flight bouncing; tail medium to short; plumage mostly dull brown, grey and white with
yellow or rufous patches; sexes similar; arboreal in arid savanna or bushveld; food small
arthropods, fruit; somewhat gregarious; nest a hanging purse of densely felted plant or
animal fibres with closeable tubular entrance, below which is ledge on which bird
perches to open entrance tube (and which incidentally forms "false entrance"); eggs
3–6, plain white; chick naked at hatching; parental care by both sexes, or by female
only. Distribution Eurasia (two species) and Africa (six species); eight species; two
species in s Africa. The Remizidae are here considered to include only the Eurasian
genus *Remiz* and the African genus *Anthoscopus*, though the American Verdin
Auriparus and Asian Firecapped Tit *Cephalopyrus* also use one foot as a grasping organ
and so may be related.

557 (531)

Cape Penduline Tit
Kaapse Kapokvoël
Anthoscopus minutus

Plate 54

Unothoyi, Unogushana (X), [Kapbeutelmeise]

Measurements: Length 9–10 cm; wing (17 ♂) 47–51–53, (9 ♀) 47–50–52; tail (26) 33–37; tarsus (26) 13–15; culmen (26) 7–9. Weight (4) 6,9–7,5–8,6 g.

Bare Parts: Iris yellowish brown; bill black, horn, grey to blue-grey, edges paler; legs and feet black, slate or dark cobalt blue.

Identification: Size very small; warblerlike appearance; above light brownish grey; forehead marked black-and-white (diagnostic; forehead plain buff in Grey Penduline Tit, plain grey in Yellowbellied Eremomela); stripe through eye black; eyering, face and throat white; breast and belly pale yellow. *Immature:* Below paler yellow than adult.

Voice: Bell-like *tillink* or *tillilink* contact call; sharp *tsik-tsik*; loud raspy *zizzit*; plaintive *tswee, tswee*; thin *tsee-tsee-tsee-tsee*.

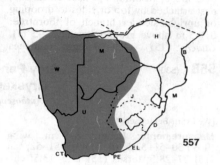

557

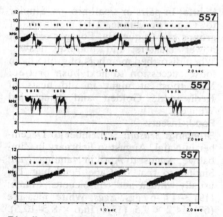

557

557

557

Distribution: Most of s Africa, except extreme E, to sw Angola.

Status: Fairly common resident.

Habitat: *Acacia* savanna, secondary thornbush, semi-arid scrub.

Habits: In pairs or small groups of 10–20 birds. Usually tame. Forages by flitting and hopping restlessly among branches of bushes and trees; contact maintained by calls between members of flock. Flight bouncy. Up to 18 birds may roost in nest after breeding; during breeding up to 6 adults may roost in nest with eggs; may also roost in old Masked Weaver nests at night.

Food: Small insects, insect eggs, berries.

Breeding: *Season:* June to December in Cape, October to February in Zimbabwe, August to March in Kalahari; probably largely opportunistic after rain in arid areas. *Nest:* Oval bag of soft, tightly-felted woolly plant and animal fibres, with tubular entrance spout near top; usually

whitish, but blackish where Karakul sheep occur; 14–15 cm overall height, 7–8 cm widest outside diameter; inside diameter of main chamber 5–6 cm, about 11 cm from roof to floor; walls vary from 0,5 cm thick at top to 2 cm thick at bottom; entrance tube 2–6 cm long, 2 cm diameter, thin-walled, soft and collapsible, facing slightly downwards; small curved ledge, about 3 cm wide, below entrance tube, used as perch by incoming bird as it opens entrance with one foot; entrance tube closes automatically forming roof over ledge, resulting in "false entrance"; nest attached by top or sides to drooping or upright slender branch of thorntree, 0,3–5 m above ground (usually 2–3 m). *Clutch*: (15) 4–4,9–10 eggs (clutches larger than 5 eggs possibly laid by 2 females). *Eggs*: White; measure (38) 14,1 × 9,8 (13,2–14,9 × 9,3–11,1). *Incubation*: 13–14 days. *Nestling*: 22–24 days; young probably fed cooperatively by helpers.

Ref. Skead C.J. 1959. *Ostrich Suppl.* 3:274–288.

558 (530)   Grey Penduline Tit   Plate 54
Gryskapokvoël
Anthoscopus caroli

[Weißstirn-Beutelmeise]

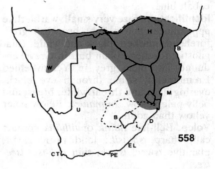

Measurements: Length 8–9 cm; wing (9 ♂) 50–51–52,5, (6 ♀) 49,5–51–52; tail (15) 27–28,5; tarsus (15) 12,5–13,5: culmen (15) 7,5–9. Weight (3 ♂) 6–6,4–6,6 g, (5 ♀) 6–6,4–6,9 g.

Bare Parts: Iris brown; bill black above, grey below; legs and feet slate grey.

Identification: Size very small; warblerlike appearance; above ashy to slaty grey, paler on forehead (no black-and-white pattern on forehead as in Cape Penduline Tit); below buff, whitish on throat, yellowish on breast; underwing white. *Immature*: Like adult.

Voice: Raspy *chiZEE-chiZEE-chiZEE* or *chikiZEE-chikiZEE-chikiZEE*.

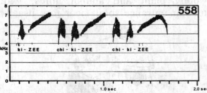

Distribution: S Africa to E Africa; in s Africa confined to NE (from Ladysmith, Natal) and N (Caprivi and n Namibia; recorded Waterberg Plateau, Namibia).

Status: Common to fairly common resident.

Habitat: *Acacia* savanna, riverine *Acacia*, *Brachystegia* woodland.

Habits: In pairs or small groups. Similar to Cape Penduline Tit; members of groups call frequently. Forages often at flower clusters and budding leaves. When disturbed members of group fly in loose succession to next bush or tree. May roost at night in old nests of Redheaded, Golden and Spectacled Weavers.

Food: Insects.

Breeding: *Season*: September to December in Natal, August to February in Zimbabwe, August to April in Namibia. *Nest*: Similar to that of Cape Penduline Tit; usually whitish and conspicuous. *Clutch*: (19) 3–4,4–6 eggs. *Eggs*: White; measure (67) 14,2 × 9,5 (13,3–16,6 × 8,5–10,5). *Incubation*: Unrecorded. *Nestling*: Unrecorded; fed by both parents.

26:11. Family 73 SALPORNITHIDAE—SPOTTED CREEPER

Small. Bill long, slender, decurved; legs short but strong; toes long, strong, with sharply curved claws; wings long, pointed; flight undulating; tail medium, soft, not used for support when perched; plumage brown above, spotted with white, off-white below, barred with brown; sexes alike; solitary; arboreal in woodland; food insects; nest a cup of plant material and spider web on branch; eggs 2–3, bluish green, spotted; chick sparsely downy at hatching; incubation by female; care of young by both sexes. Distribution Africa and India; one species.

559 (532)   Spotted Creeper   Plate 48
Boomkruiper
Salpornis spilonotus

[Fleckenbaumläufer, Stammsteiger]

Measurements: Length about 15 cm; wing (40 ♂) 89–94,1–100, (28 ♀) 87–92,1–98,5; tail 50–60; tarsus 16; culmen 17–20. Weight (1) 16 g.

Bare Parts: Iris brown; bill dusky, base whitish; legs and feet greyish to purplish brown.

Identification: Size small (smaller than sparrow); above blackish, boldly spotted white; eyebrow broadly white; below buffy white, barred black; bill longish, slender, decurved; feet large. *Immature*: Below whiter than adult; less sharply barred with black.

Voice: High-pitched wispy *sweepy-swee-seepy* or *sweepy-swip-swip-swip*, rather sunbirdlike; 5–6 high croaking *kek-kek-kek-kek-kek* notes.

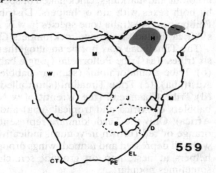

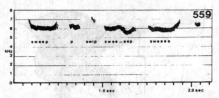

Distribution: Africa S of Sahara, and India; in s Africa confined to Mashonaland Plateau of Zimbabwe and Manica Platform (Mozambique); 1 specimen collected Bangu Gorge, central Kruger National Park, may represent relict population.

Status: Sparse localized resident in Zimbabwe.

Habitat: *Brachystegia* woodland in Zimbabwe; deciduous forest in Kruger National Park.

Habits: Usually singly or in pairs. May join mixed bird parties; forages on trunks and larger branches of trees, starting near bottom, fluttering and clambering quickly up towards top, stopping now and then to investigate crevice, then flying off to next tree. Flight undulating, woodpeckerlike; lands heavily, pitching onto trunk with wings open. When disturbed moves to far side of trunk; easily overlooked, well camouflaged on bark.

Food: Insects (moths, caterpillars, beetles, woodborers, bugs), spiders.

Breeding: *Season*: August to October in Zimbabwe. *Nest*: Small cup of grass, leaf petioles, bark chips, lichens, bound with spider web and covered with bark and lichens; lined with soft cobwebs, cocoons and plant down; inside diameter about 4,5 cm, depth about 4,5 cm; bound with spider web to horizontal branch, often against vertical branch; 3–12 m above ground. *Clutch*: 1–3 eggs (usually 3). *Eggs*: Pale bluish green, speckled and blotched with brown and grey, concentrated at thick end; measure (5) 17,9 × 13,4 (16,2–19,5 ×12,9–13,8). *Incubation*: Unrecorded; by ♀ only; ♀ fed by ♂. *Nestling*: Unrecorded.

Ref. Masterson, A. 1970. *Honeyguide* 61:35–36.
Steyn, P. 1974. *Bokmakierie* 26:80–82.

26:12.   Family 74 TIMALIIDAE—BABBLERS

Small to medium. Bill variable, usually medium, sometimes long and decurved, stout or slender; legs and toes moderately long and strong; wings short, rounded; tail variable; plumage highly variable, soft, lax, long and dense on lower back, with brown, black and white predominating in most species; sexes alike or different; most gregarious; highly vocal; arboreal or terrestrial, usually in undergrowth, in forest or open woodland; food arthropods and other small animals, some fruit; breed solitarily or with helpers at communally built nest; nest an open cup or domed with side entrance; eggs 2–5, variable in colour and markings; chick naked or sparsely downy at hatching; parental care usually by both sexes with aid of helpers. Distribution Africa, Madagascar, tropical Asia to Philippines, Australia (one species in w N America); about 250 species; eight species in s Africa, including the two rockjumpers *Chaetops*, presently included in the Turdidae.

The Timaliidae may not be an altogether natural family as it stands; it is divided into six tribes: (a) Tribe Pellorneini (jungle babblers of tropical Asia; one African species), (b) Tribe Pomatorhinini (scimitar babblers and wren-babblers of tropical Asia and Australia), (c) Tribe Timaliini (shortbilled babblers of tropical Asia and Madagascar), (d) Tribe Chamaeini (the Wrentit of w N America), (e) Tribe Turdoidini ("typical" babblers of Africa and tropical Asia) and (f) Tribe Picathartini (rockfowl of tropical Africa). Only the Turdoidini are represented in s Africa; eyes in adults usually yellow, orange or red (brown in young), indicative of status; call raucously in chorus; display with tail depressed and fanned, wings drooped and quivered, rump exposed; usually 3–5 helpers at nest; hop on ground; scratch directly (not over wing); eggs turquoise, sometimes nodular.

560   (533)   **Arrowmarked Babbler**   **Plate 49**
                                    Pylvlekkatlagter
                                    Turdoides jardineii

Siwerewere (K), Hochahocha, Dywedywe (Sh), Mayokoyokwani, Ngayakaya (Ts), Letshêganôga (Tw), iHlekehle (Z), [Braundroßling]

Measurements: Length 23–25 cm; wing (42) 103–110–116; tail 105–111; tarsus 31–33; culmen 23–25. Weight (1 ♂) 70,6 g, (1 ♀) 56,3 g, (10 unsexed) 61,3–72,2–81,5 g.

Bare Parts: Iris orange with red outer ring, or yellow with orange outer ring; bill, legs and feet black.

Identification: Size medium; above ashy brown, streaked blackish, indistinctly spotted whitish; rump plain greyish brown; below brownish grey, streaked with white arrowhead markings; wings and tail dark brown; eye looks light orange in field. *Immature*: Buffy; lacks white streaks; spotted dusky below; eye brown.

Voice: Nasal whirring *ra-ra-ra-ra-ra*, usually in chorus; harsh *chak-chak-chak*; 1 or 2 birds start calling, others join in crescendo, then calling dies away.

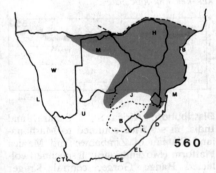

560

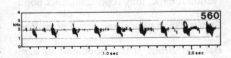

Distribution: S Africa to Kenya and Cabinda; in s Africa from Natal to Transvaal, n Orange Free State, e Botswana, ne Namibia, Mozambique and Zimbabwe.

Status: Very common resident.
Habitat: Thickets with long grass and bushes in woodland, savanna and bushveld, riverine reedbeds, secondary bushy growth at edges of cultivation, denser Kalahari woodland, exotic plantations.
Habits: Gregarious in noisy groups of up to 10 birds. Forages on ground and by clambering and jumping through lower bushes and undergrowth, every now and then calling in chorus; forms mixed parties with Whiterumped Babbler where ranges overlap. Flight straight with alternating fluttering and gliding; members of flock follow each other in loose succession from bush to bush. Roosts communally.
Food: Insects (up to 35 mm long—grasshoppers, termites, moths, caterpillars, flies, ants, beetles), spiders, solifugids,

snails, lizards, seeds, fruit (larger fruits like loquats held in foot while being eaten), nectar.
Breeding: *Season*: October to March in Natal, all months in Transvaal lowveld and in Zimbabwe (mainly September to April). *Nest*: Mass of grass and twigs with bowlshaped hollow on top, lined with fibres and rootlets; 0,5–3,5 m above ground in dense bush or tree, pile of driftwood, dense reeds or cavity in dead tree; built by up to 7 helpers (at least 3 adults and perhaps 2 immatures). *Clutch*: (34) 2–2,8–4 eggs (usually 3). *Eggs*: Plain turquoise or greenish blue; measure (75) 24,9 × 18,6 (22–28,1 × 17,3–19,7). *Incubation*: Unrecorded; helpers also incubate. *Nestling*: Unrecorded; fed by parents and up to 5 helpers.

---

561 (534)   **Blackfaced Babbler**   **Plate 49**
Swartwangkatlagter
Turdoides melanops

Siwerewere (K), Letshêganôga (Tw), [Dunkler Droßling, Schwarzzügeldroßling]

Measurements: Length about 28 cm; wing (4 ♂) 118,5–121,4–123, (4 ♀) 109–115,6–119; tail 118–125; tarsus 32; culmen (11) 26–31.
Bare Parts: Iris light yellow to greenish yellow; bill black; legs and feet slaty black.
Identification: Size medium (somewhat larger than Arrowmarked Babbler; paler overall than Whiterumped babbler); crown dusky, scaled white; back brown; lores black; below light brown, faintly scaled paler, throat whitish (no white streaks below as in Arrowmarked Babbler); underwing blackish (visible in flight; underwing tawny to buff in Arrowmarked and Whiterumped Babblers); wings and tail dark brown; eye yellow. *Immature*: Less clearly marked than adult; eye brown.
Voice: Chattering nasal *pa-pa-pa-pa* and *jeu-jeu-jeu*, crescendo, often in chorus; catlike yells, *wha-u*, and bleating squeaks.

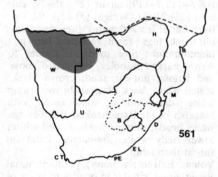

561

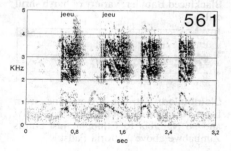

Distribution: Northern Namibia, n Botswana (Okavango), to Angola, Zaire and Kenya (absent from Zambia).
Status: Locally common, but generally uncommon; resident.
Habitat: Underlying grass and thickets in dense *Acacia* and *Commiphora* savanna.
Habits: Gregarious in small groups of 5–7 birds. Forages low down in grass and on ground, often tossing leaf litter aside with bill. Inquisitive but shy, keeping to dense cover. Roosts communally. Poorly known.

Food: Insects, reptiles, fruit.

Breeding: *Season:* December in Etosha. *Nest:* Bowl of grass, lined with finer fibres; looks like roughly made thrush nest; about 5 m above ground in upper outer branches of *Commiphora*. *Clutch:* 4 eggs. *Eggs:* Deep turquoise with finely nodular surface; measure (2) 26,5–28,5 × 19–19,5. *Incubation:* Unrecorded. *Nestling:* Unrecorded; may be up to 4 helpers at nest.

---

562 (535) **Hartlaub's Babbler** (Whiterumped Babbler) **Plate 49**
Witkruiskatlagter

Turdoides hartlaubii

Siwerewere (K), Letshêganôga (Tw), [Weißbürzeldroßling]

Measurements: Length about 26 cm; wing (10 ♂) 115,5–119–122,5, (10 ♀) 113–118,3–124, (23 unsexed) 105–117–121; tail (10 ♂) 106–113,4–119, (10 ♀) 108,5–113,7–119; tarsus (23) 35–39; culmen (23) 21–24. Weight (3) 83,1–92,3 g.
Bare Parts: Iris red with yellow inner rim; bill black; legs brown; feet dark brown.
Identification: Size medium; similar to Arrowmarked Babbler, but scaled above and below, not streaked; crown black, scaled white; back blackish brown; rump white (diagnostic in combination with blackish head; Barecheeked Babbler has white head); below brown, scaled white; lower belly white. *Immature:* Paler on throat than adult.
Voice: Extremely noisy; petulant nasal *pa-pa-pa-pa*, similar in quality to voice of Blackfaced Babbler; variety of harsh shrill calls.

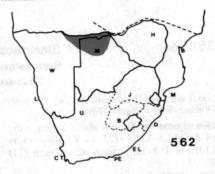

Status: Common resident.
Habitat: Edges of riverine forest, reedbeds and papyrus swamps, thickets on termitaria; usually between woodland and drainage lines.
Habits: Gregarious in flocks of up to 20 birds. Forages on ground or in trees along larger rivers, often in mixed parties with Arrowmarked Babblers, which it resembles in habits. Flight direct, alternating flutter and glide. Fairly tame, but keeps to dense vegetation. Roosts in reedbeds.
Food: Unrecorded.
Breeding: *Season:* December in Botswana. *Nest:* Untidy bowl of coarse plant material, lined with finer fibres; in bush or reedbed. *Clutch:* 2–3 eggs. *Eggs:* Deep greenish blue; measure (2) 25,5 × 18,4–18,5. *Incubation:* Unrecorded. *Nestling:* Unrecorded.

Distribution: Extreme n Botswana, from Lake Ngami and Botletle River, Caprivi and ne Namibia to Ethiopia; just enters Zimbabwe above Victoria Falls.

563 (536)

Pied Babbler
Witkatlagter
Turdoides bicolor

Plate 49

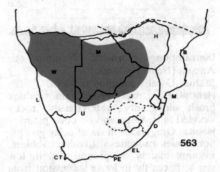

Letshêganôga (Tw), [Elsterdroßling]

Measurements: Length about 26 cm; wing (10) 108–113–118; tail 106–117; tarsus 33–36; culmen 24–25,5. Weight (2) 69,2–82,4 g.

Bare Parts: Iris reddish orange to orange-yellow; bill black; legs and feet black to brown.

Identification: Size medium; white with black wings, tail and bill. *Immature*: Mostly brown, paler on lower belly, darker on wings and tail; resembles immature Arrowmarked Babbler; adult plumage acquired at about 4 months.

Voice: Various harsh chattering notes, often in chorus, *cha-cha-cha, keeyi-keeyi-keeyi, kawa-kawa-kawa*, etc.; also crowing notes.

Distribution: Semi-arid interior of s Africa from N of Orange and Vaal Rivers to w Transvaal, Botswana (to Moremi), sw Zimbabwe and n Namibia.

Status: Locally common resident.

Habitat: Semi-arid savanna and woodland, riverine *Acacia* and associated bushy undergrowth.

Habits: Gregarious in noisy groups of up to about 12 birds, usually of 3–7 adults and up to 3 immatures. Forages mainly on ground, lifting leaves like thrush; creeps through tangled undergrowth; flies in loose formation from bush to bush. Forms bird parties with Redbilled Buffalo Weavers and Crimsonbreasted Shrikes. Roosts communally in huddled row on branch.

Food: Insects.

Breeding: *Season*: August to January in Zimbabwe, October to April in Namibia; probably opportunistic after rain in more arid areas. *Nest*: Bowl of sticks and grass, with cupshaped cavity neatly lined with hair, soft fibres and rootlets; in fork of bush or thorntree. *Clutch*: (8) 2–2,8–3 eggs (usually 3; rarely 4–5). *Eggs*: Pale blue, smooth at ends, nodular over middle area; measure (23) 26 × 19 (23,5–27,5 × 18–20,1). *Incubation*: Unrecorded. *Nestling*: Unrecorded; attended by up to 12 birds, including parents and 1 or more helpers; usually 2 or more helpers at nest.

564 (537)

Barecheeked Babbler
Kaalwangkatlagter
Turdoides gymnogenys

Plate 49

Siwerewere (K), [Nacktohrdroßling]

Measurements: Length about 24 cm; wing (6) 110–117; tail 100–110; tarsus 33–36; culmen 24–25.

Bare Parts: Iris lemon yellow; bill and skin under eye black; legs and feet dusky grey.

Identification: Size medium; crown, rump and underparts white; back brown faintly scaled paler; sides of neck, flanks and underwing tawny; wings and tail dark brown; bare skin from bill under eye to earcoverts, and small bare patch on ear coverts, black. Similar to Wattled Starling at distance, but keeps low down near ground. *Immature*: Mottled brown and tawny on crown.

Voice: Continuous low grating *chuk-chuk*, taken up by all members of flock; very similar to voice of Arrowmarked Babbler.

Distribution: Northern Namibia to Angola (Novo Redondo).
Status: Locally common resident.
Habitat: Bare rocky ground among thick brush along dry watercourses, rocky wooded hills, woodland on open plains.
Habits: Gregarious in small noisy groups. Sometimes associates with other babblers. Forages mainly on ground and in low scrub; flocks fly in loose succession from bush to bush. Similar to other *Turdoides* babblers.
Food: Unrecorded.
Breeding: Only 2 nests known. *Season*: November and December in Namibia.

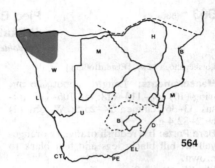

Nest: Bulky loosely-built bowl of dry grass and herb stems, lined with finer grass; outside diameter 12,5 cm, inside diameter 8 cm, inside depth 5 cm; about 2 m above ground in upright multiple fork of *Spirostachys* or *Terminalia* tree. *Clutch*: 2 eggs. *Eggs*: Turquoise; glossy and smooth; measure (2) 26,4–26,6 × 20,2. *Incubation*: Unrecorded. *Nestling*: Unrecorded.

565 (542)   Bush Blackcap   Plate 48
Rooibektiptol
Lioptilus nigricapillus

[Buschschwarzkäppchen]

Measurements: Length 16–18 cm; wing (17) 76–81–88; tail 68–83; tarsus 22–25; culmen 12–15.
Bare Parts: Iris reddish brown; bill pale orange or coral pink; legs and feet dull pink.
Identification: Size small (little bigger than sparrow); top of head to mantle jet black; back brown; chin black; rest of underparts light grey, shading to pale brown on flanks; bill pink (contrasts strikingly with black cap).
Voice: Usually silent; variety of bulbul-like notes in lively song in summer, *peeu peeu peeu whit-whit-whit-whit*, etc.; fairly loud guttural *burgg* alarm note.

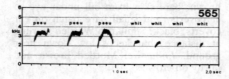

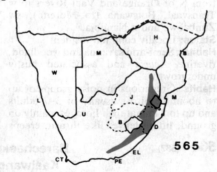

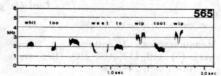

Distribution: Eastern Cape, Natal interior, w Zululand, w Swaziland, e Orange Free State (Ficksburg area), e and n Transvaal.

Status: Generally uncommon; locally fairly common in isolated forest patches; resident, but locally nomadic; some seasonal altitudinal movement.
Habitat: Evergreen mistbelt and montane forest and adjacent scrubby hillsides, especially with *Leucosidea*.
Habits: Solitary, in pairs or small groups. Quiet and unobtrusive, but tame and inquisitive; responds well to spishing. Creeps about middle layers of forest edge or low down in scrub with slow deliberate

movements. Flight direct, somewhat undulating. Poorly known.
Food: Fruit.
Breeding: *Season*: November to January. *Nest*: Cup of twigs and moss, lined with rootlets; 1–2 m above ground in fork of tree at edge of clearing, often in boggy ground. *Clutch*: 2 eggs. *Eggs*: Dull white, streaked light brown, concentrated at thick end; measure (3) 23,4 × 16,8 (23–24,3 × 16,5–17). *Incubation*: Unrecorded. *Nestling*: Unrecorded.

26:13. Family 75 PYCNONOTIDAE—BULBULS

Small to medium. Bill short to medium, notched just behind tip of upper jaw, sometimes hooked at tip, arched on culmen; legs short; toes medium, strong in terrestrial species; wings rounded, short to medium, flight appears weak; tail medium, square or rounded in most species; plumage soft with long lower-back feathers and hairlike feathers on nape; mostly dull coloured in green and brown, but *Pycnonotus* species have patches of red or yellow under tail, and sometimes on face; sexes similar; some gregarious; arboreal (a few terrestrial) in forest or open woodland; food fruit, insects and nectar; nest a flimsy cup in tree or bush; eggs 2–4, white, pink or cream, spotted; chick naked at hatching; parental care by both sexes. Distribution Africa, Madagascar, tropical Asia to Philippines; about 118 species; 10 species in s Africa.

566 (543)   **Cape Bulbul**   **Plate 48**
                              Kaapse Tiptol
                              Pycnonotus capensis

[Kapbülbül]

Measurements: Length 19–21 cm; wing (7 ♂) 94–96–98,5, (6 ♀) 90–91–92; tail (7 ♂) 84–86,9–89, (6 ♀) 80,5–82,1–83; tarsus (13) 20–23; culmen (7 ♂) 20,5–21–22, (6 ♀) 21–21,4–22,5. Weight (355) 26–38,8–48 g.
Bare Parts: Iris reddish brown; wattle around eye white; bill, legs and feet black.
Identification: Size smallish; upperparts and breast sooty brown, darker on head; head slightly crested; conspicuous white eye wattle (diagnostic, even at distance); belly shades from brown to white; undertail lemon yellow. *Immature*: Has smaller eye wattle than adult.
Voice: Cheerful sounding liquid call of 2 or more varied notes, *pit-peet-pitmajol, piet-piet-patata*, etc.; often rather higher-pitched and slightly less rich than calls of other *Pycnonotus* bulbuls.

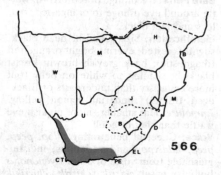

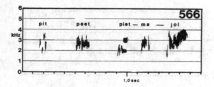

Distribution: Sw Cape, N to orange River mouth, E to about Sundays River, e Cape.
Status: Common resident.
Habitat: Taller fynbos, coastal and riverine scrub, thickets of exotic wattles (Rooikrans *Acacia cyclops* and Port Jackson Willow *A. saligna*), gardens.
Habits: Usually in pairs; forms loose groups at good food source (feeding tray, fruiting plants). Noisy and conspicuous, often perching on top of bush. Flight somewhat jerky and bouncing. Becomes tame in gardens. Forehead sometimes covered with pollen when feeding on nectar from flowers.

Food: Fruit and nectar.
Breeding: *Season*: Mainly August to December; breeds opportunistically after late rains in February and March. *Nest*: Strongly built shallow cup of roots, twigs and other plant fibres; 1–4 m above ground in fork of bush or tree, usually well concealed. *Clutch*: (57) 2–2,5–3 eggs. *Eggs*: White, tinged pink, spotted with dark red and purplish grey; measure (44) 23,7 × 16,9 (21,7–26 × 15,9–18). *Incubation*: 12–14 days by ♀ only. *Nestling*: Unrecorded.

Ref. Liversidge, R. 1966. *Ostrich Suppl.* 6:419–424.

567 (544)   Redeyed Bulbul   Plate 48
Rooioogtiptol
Pycnonotus nigricans

Mburukutji (K), Hlakahlotoana, Kaka-hlotoana (SS), Rramorutiakolê (Tw), [Maskenbülbül]

Measurements: Length 19–21 cm; wing (58 ♂) 90–97,8–109, (47 ♀) 84–92,8–99,5; tail (36 ♂) 77–83,3–91, (30 ♀) 74–79,3–91; tarsus (39) 19–23; culmen (36 ♂) 18,5–20,1–22, (30 ♀) 18–19,3–22. Weight (316) 21,6–30,8–37,4 g.
Bare Parts: Iris orange or red-brown; wattle around eye orange to orange-red; bill, legs and feet black.
Identification: Size smallish; head black, slightly crested; eyering bright orange-red (diagnostic); back greyish brown; breast blackish, shading to white on belly (but more contrasty than underparts of Blackeyed Bulbul); undertail lemon yellow. *Immature*: Has smaller, more pinkish eye wattle than that of adult.
Voice: Cheerful penetrating *tillop, peep, peep, tiddlypop* and variations; indistinguishable from voice of other *Pycnonotus* bulbuls; nasal *chirrik, chirrik, chirrikik* alarm notes.

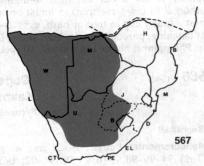

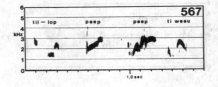

Distribution: Drier parts of s Africa from Karoo, through highveld to Botswana (as far N as Chobe National Park) and Namibia, N to extreme w Zimbabwe, sw Zambia and sw Angola.
Status: Very common resident.
Habitat: Savanna, drier woodland, semi-arid scrub, riverine bush, farmyards, gardens, orchards; always near water.
Habits: In pairs or small loose groups. Tame, vocal and conspicuous; often calls from top of bush or tree; flicks wings and flirts tail while singing and when alarmed. Forages mostly arboreally, often hanging sideways and upside down, seldom on ground; visits feeding trays; drinks frequently; hawks insects in flight.

Food: Fruit, nectar, insects.
Breeding: *Season*: September to March; timing may vary with rainfall. *Nest*: Neat cup of dry grass, fine twigs and rootlets; 1–4 m above ground in fork of tree or bush, often well hidden. *Clutch*: (9) 2–2,3–3 eggs

(usually 3; rarely 4). *Eggs*: Pale pink, spotted and speckled with dark red, brown and purplish grey; measure (42) 22,5 × 16,3 (19,7–25,4 × 14,7–17,5). *Incubation*: (2) 11–12 days by ♀ only. *Nestling*: 13 days; fed by both parents.

---

568 (545)   **Blackeyed Bulbul**   **Plate 48**
Swartoogtiptol
Pycnonotus barbatus

Mburukutji (K), Rankgwetšhe (NS), Hlakahlotoana (SS), Chigwenhure, Mugweture, Bwoto (Sh), Bokota, Byitana, Phyandlane (Ts), Rramorutiakolê (Tw), Ikhwebula (X), iPhothwe, iPogota (Z), [Graubülbül, Gelbsteißbülbül]

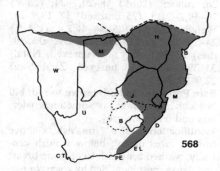

568

Measurements: Length 20–22 cm; wing (86 ♂) 89,5–98,7–107, (80 ♀) 86–94,2–103,5; tail (60 ♂) 78–88,4–99, (51 ♀) 74,5–84,3–97,5; tarsus (55) 20–23; culmen (60 ♂) 17,5–20,4–23, (51 ♀) 18,5–19,8–22. Weight (109 ♂) 26–40,4–49,5 g, (91 ♀) 29–35,8–44,8 g, (989 unsexed) 21,1–38,6–52,9 g.
Bare Parts: Iris dark brown; eyering, bill, legs and feet black.
Identification: Size smallish; head black, slightly crested; no coloured eye wattle (diagnostic; wattle white in Cape Bulbul, orange to red in Redeyed Bulbul); back greyish brown; breast dark brown, shading to whitish belly; undertail lemon yellow. *Immature*: Duller and paler than adult; back tinged buff or rusty.
Voice: Lively liquid notes, indistinguishable from those of other *Pycnonotus* bulbuls; *klip*, *klop*, *kollop* and variations; repeated *klip*, *klip*, *klip*; nasal *chirrik chirrik* alarm notes.

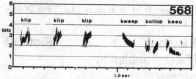

Distribution: Africa and Arabia; in s Africa confined to moister E, NE and N.
Status: Very common resident.
Habitat: Woodland, forest edge, riverine bush, dense montane scrub (e.g. *Leucosidea*), exotic plantations, gardens, parks.

Habits: Usually in pairs; sometimes in loose groups at good food source. Highly vocal, restless and conspicuous; often calls from top of bush or tree. Forages arboreally, picking fruit and gleaning insects from leaves; also feeds on ground and hawks insects in flight. Calls loud alarm in presence of cat, snake or mongoose, usually attracting other bird species.
Food: Fruit, nectar, insects, small lizards.
Breeding: *Season*: September to April throughout s Africa (mainly September-December). *Nest*: Neat strong, often thinwalled cup of dry grass, plant fibres, rootlets and small twigs; lined with finer materials and hair; 2–12 m above ground in fork of tree, often far from trunk. *Clutch*: (178) 2–2,6–3 eggs (usually 3; one clutch of 6 probably laid by 2 females). *Eggs*: White to pale pink, spotted, speckled and blotched with dark red, purplish, brown and grey; measure (221) 22,4 × 16,3 (19,8–25,6 × 15,2–18,1). *Incubation*: 12–14 days by ♀ only (♂ rarely incubates, but feeds ♀ on nest). *Nestling*: 10–12 days in S Africa, 15–17 days in Zimbabwe; fed by both parents.

569 (546) Terrestrial Bulbul   Plate 48
Boskrapper
Phyllastrephus terrestris

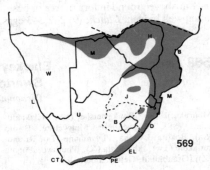

569

Ikhalakandla, Umnqu, Ugwegwegwe (X), [Laub-bülbül]

Measurements: Length 20–22 cm; wing (67 ♂) 86–91–100, (71 ♀) 76–82,7–87; tail (45 ♂) 85–93,9–101, (54 ♀) 71–87,4–95; tarsus (26 ♂) 21–23,5–28, (28 ♀) 20–22,8–25, (25 unsexed) 22–24,2–26; culmen (26 ♂) 18–20,7–24, (28 ♀) 16–19,2–21,5, (25 unsexed) 17–18,9–23. Weight (154 ♂) 29,5–34–44,2 g, (154 ♀) 24–29–38,2 g, (111 unsexed, several localities) 23–30,6–41 g, (16 unsexed, Natal) 33–39,6–47 g, (14 unsexed, Zimbabwe) 22,9–27,8–33 g.

Bare Parts: Iris reddish brown to red; bill blackish horn, lower jaw sometimes paler; legs and feet slate grey.

Identification: Size smallish; above brown; lores dusky; below whitish centrally, washed brownish to olive on breast and flanks; best identified by voice. *Immature*: Paler overall; wing feathers fringed rufous; iris washed greyish; bill pale horn.

Voice: Harsh churring chattering *wak, wak, wakkity wakkity wakkity, kra-kra-kra*, etc.; often calls in groups; song warbled *wicherwer-wicherwer*.

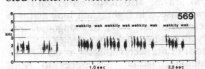

569

Distribution: S Africa to E Africa (Kenya); in s Africa confined to extreme S, E, NE and N.

Status: Sparse to fairly common resident.

Habitat: Evergreen forest, mainly in low-lands, riverine bush and forest, dense thickets.

Habits: Usually in small groups of 3–6 birds. Forages on forest floor among leaf litter, often in gloomy interior; rustles leaves while scratching for food; often vocal, but seldom seen; easily called up by spishing (see Glossary). Perches low down in undergrowth.

Food: Insects, snails, fruit.

Breeding: *Season*: October to January in Natal, October to March in Mozambique, September to April in Zimbabwe. *Nest*: Shallow, frail-looking cup of dark plant fibres, lined with rootlets; slung between twigs of low bush at edge of thicket; about 1 m above ground. *Clutch*: (47) 1–2,1–4 eggs (mostly 2). *Eggs*: Glossy white, streaked and blotched with dark olive brown and grey, concentrated at thick end; measure (41) 24 × 16,9 (20,9–26,9 × 15,5–18). *Incubation*: Unrecorded. *Nestling*: Unrecorded.

Ref. Harwin, R.M. & Manson, A.J. 1989. *Honeyguide* 35:6–11.

570 (547) Yellowstreaked Bulbul   Plate 48
Geelstreepboskruiper (Geelstreeptiptol)
Phyllastrephus flavostriatus

[Gelbstreifen-Laubbülbül]

Measurements: Length 18–21 cm; wing (149 ♂) 88–98–104, (129 ♀) 80,5–85,4–94; tail (122 ♂) 83–92,2–99,5, (86 ♀) 75–80,5–89; tarsus (209) 20–23,5–27; culmen (14 ♂) 23–25–27, (18 ♀) 20–21,9–24, (212 unsexed) 13,5–19,2–23. Weight (156 ♂) 30,1–34,7–39,8 g, (112 ♀) 21,4–26,5–39,1 g, (4 unsexed) 25,6–29–35 g.

Bare Parts: Iris brown; bill black; legs and feet bluish slate.

Identification: Size smallish; crown and face grey; back olive; below white, faintly streaked pale yellow, washed ochre on belly, olive on flanks; ♀ noticeably smaller than ♂. *Immature*: Tinged olive on breast; centre of belly light yellow.

Voice: Noisy; penetrating nasal notes, *winky-wink winky-wink chink CHANK chow, chink CHANK chow*, final note often repeated *chow, chow, chow*, up to about 10 times; sharp *wititi-ti-ti*, like call-note of Blackeyed Bulbul; yapping *yow-yow-yow*.

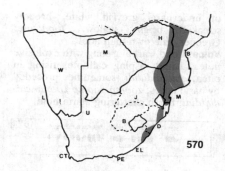

570

Distribution: S Africa to Zaire and Tanzania; in s Africa confined to extreme E from Ngoye Forest (Natal) northward.

Status: Fairly common, but localized resident.

Habitat: Evergreen forest.

Habits: Solitary or in pairs, sometimes in mixed bird parties. Forages in middle and top layers of forest trees, running along branches, clambering among creepers, probing into accumulated debris, often hanging upside down or clinging to tree trunks; sometimes forages also on rotting logs of forest floor. Flicks wings open, one at a time.

Food: Insects (including eggs and larvae), spiders, berries.

Breeding: *Season*: October to January (mainly November-December) in Zimbabwe, December to February in Transvaal, October to January in Natal. *Nest*: Cup of twigs, rootlets and other plant fibres, bound with spider web and covered with moss, often with flakes of *Milletia* bark in walls; lined with roots of *Microsorum* fern; slung in fork, or placed in tangled creepers or dense foliage; usually low down. *Clutch*: (6) 2–2,3–3 eggs. *Eggs*: Pinkish, grey or mauve, spotted and streaked with brown, purple, red-brown and slate grey; measure (11) 22,7 × 16,5 (21–23,9 × 15,4–17); weigh (3) 3,3–3,4–3,4 g. *Incubation*: Unrecorded. *Nestling*: Unrecorded.

571 (548)

Slender Bulbul
Kleinboskruiper (Kleintiptol)

Phyllastrephus debilis

Plate 48

[Kleiner Gelbstreifen-Laubbülbül]

Measurements: Length about 14 cm; wing (2 ♂) 66–67,5, (3 ♀) 62–63; tail (5) 60–64; tarsus (5) 16,5–18; culmen (5) 13,5–15. Weight (7 ♂) 13,3–14,9–16,5 g, (11 ♀) 12,5–13,2–15 g.

Bare Parts: Iris red-brown to yellow; bill dusky above, paler below and on edges; legs and feet grey.

Identification: Size small (smallest bulbul in s Africa); build and habits rather warblerlike; top of head grey (paler than in Yellowstreaked Bulbul); back bright olive green; tail brownish; throat white; rest

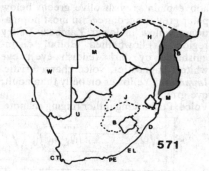

571

of underparts greyish white, broadly streaked bright yellow. *Immature*: Greener on crown than adult.

Voice: Loud warbling song with explosive notes; harsh rasping callnote, rising in pitch, *chididididi*, sometimes preceded by nasal notes, *zoomp zoomp zoomp chididididi*; harsh chattering alarm note.

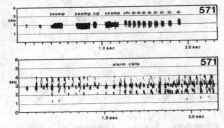

Distribution: From Limpopo River to Kenya; in s Africa confined to e lowlands of Zimbabwe and coastal Mozambique N of Limpopo River.

Status: Very common resident.

Habitat: Lowland evergreen forest.

Habits: Solitary or in pairs. Gleans insects from surface of vegetation, creeping about in tangled undergrowth like warbler.

Food: Mainly insects.

Breeding: *Season*: October to January in Zimbabwe. *Nest*: Small neat cup of lichens, grass inflorescences, ferns and dry leaves, bound with spider web; outside depth 6,5 cm, inside depth 3,5 cm, inside diameter 5 cm; slung in fork of small tree or in outer branches of bush, about 2 m above ground. *Clutch*: (2) 2 eggs. *Eggs*: Light blue, ringed at thick end with dark and light brown and grey spots and blotches; measure (7) 18,6 × 13,5 (18,4–18,9 × 13,4–13,7). *Incubation*: Unrecorded. *Nestling*: Unrecorded.

---

572 (551)   Sombre Bulbul   Plate 48
Gewone Willie
Andropadus importunus

Inkwili (X), iWili (Z), [Kap-Grünbülbül]

Measurements: Length 19–23 cm; wing (74 ♂) 87–90,9–97, (75 ♀) 80–86,1–95; tail (18) 86–95; tarsus (18) 22–25; culmen (49) 17–21. Weight (26 ♂) 26–31,4–40 g, (22 ♀) 24–26,6–30 g, (113 unsexed) 26–32,6–44,5 g.

Bare Parts: Iris white to pale cream; bill black; legs and feet greyish black.

Identification: Size smallish to medium; above plain greyish olive green; below paler grey, tinged green in most populations, yellow in lower Zambezi Valley region (Yellowbellied Bulbul distinguishable by dark reddish eye); eye white (diagnostic); voice characteristic. *Immature*: Yellower on belly than adult; eye grey.

Voice: Penetrating rather ringing callnote, *willie*; song starts with callnote, runs into jumbled phrase, and usually ends with plaintive drawn-out whistle, *willie, come and have a fight, (or are you) sca-a-a-ared?*

Distribution: S Africa to E Africa; in s Africa confined to S and E from Cape Town to Mozambique, e Zimbabwe and Zambezi Valley.
Status: Common resident.
Habitat: Forest, coastal and riverine bush, dense thickets.
Habits: Usually solitary or in pairs. Keeps to dense foliage; elusive and easily overlooked unless calling, but usually highly vocal; hard to see, even when calling, but sometimes perches on top of tree; easily called up by spishing (see Glossary). Forages mostly in upper branches of trees, sometimes also in undergrowth or on ground among leaf litter.
Food: Insects, fruit, small snails.

Breeding: *Season*: October to April in Natal, October to January in Transvaal, September to March in Mozambique, October to February in Zimbabwe. *Nest*: Thin shallow cup of twigs, rootlets and tendrils, lined with fine grass inflorescences and hairlike plant fibres; 1–4 m above ground in fork of sapling or bush, usually at edge of clearing or thicket; nest sometimes poorly concealed. *Clutch*: (96) 1–1,9–3 eggs (usually 2). *Eggs*: Dull whitish or cream, with cloudy spots and scrolls of greenish brown and grey; measure (59) 23,1 × 16,7 (20,7–26,8 × 15,3–18,2). *Incubation*: 15–17 days by ♀ only; sitting ♀ sometimes sits very closely, but deserts easily if disturbed. *Nestling*: 14–16 days.

573 (549) Stripecheeked Bulbul   Plate 48
Streepwangwillie (Streepwangtiptol)
Andropadus milanjensis

[Strichel-Grünbülbül]

Measurements: Length 19–21 cm; wing (132 ♂) 86,5–95,8–101,5, (98 ♀) 84–91,9–96; tail (115 ♂) 81,5–88,9–95, (93 ♀) 78–85,4–91; tarsus (127) 20,5–23,8–27; culmen (131) 15,5–18,1–22. Weight (157 ♂) 32,4–38,4–45,9 g, (129 ♀) 30,7–36,8–43,9 g, (20 unsexed) 32,8–48,9 g.
Bare Parts: Iris umber brown; bill black; legs and feet greyish brown.
Identification: Size smallish (about size of Sombre Bulbul); crown blackish grey, shading to lighter grey on face (crown and back of Yellowbellied Bulbul uniform brownish olive); ear coverts blackish, streaked white (diagnostic at close range; no streaking in Yellowbellied Bulbul); narrow eyering white; back olive green (browner in Yellowbellied Bulbul); below bright greenish yellow, shading to greyer on throat; eye dark (Sombre Bulbul has white eye). *Immature*: Greener on crown than adult.
Voice: Slightly guttural phrase, *chowp chowp chop-chop, chipchipchip, chrrrr*, speeding up and ending in churring trill.

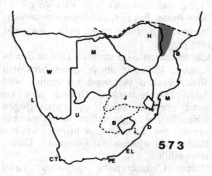

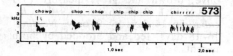

Distribution: Eastern Zimbabwe and adjacent Mozambique to Kenya.
Status: Common to very common resident; some seasonal altitudinal migration from highlands.
Habitat: Evergreen forest, mostly above 1 400 m in Zimbabwe.
Habits: Usually solitary; rather silent skulker in dense foliage, but voice diagnostic. Forages at all levels in forest, even to bushes of undergrowth and into neighbouring *Brachystegia* woodland, especially after rain. When calling, sidles along branch with little hops. When disturbed disappears into dense undergrowth.
Food: Insects, worms, fruit, seeds.

Breeding: *Season*: October to March in Zimbabwe (mainly November-December). *Nest*: Thin, neatly rounded cup of coarse twigs, roots and grass, lined with tree-fern fibres; 4–7 m above ground in bush, creeper, fork of sapling or thin branch. *Clutch*: (3) 2 eggs (sometimes only 1). *Eggs*: White, densely spotted, streaked and marbled with chocolate, brown and grey; measure (6) 25,1 × 17,8 (24,3–26 × 17,5–18,1). *Incubation*: Unrecorded. *Nestling*: Unrecorded.

---

574 (550)   **Yellowbellied Bulbul**   **Plate 48**
Geelborswillie (Geelborstiptol)
Chlorocichla flaviventris

iBhada (Z), [Gelbbrustbülbül]

Measurements: Length 20–23 cm; wing (20 ♂) 99–104,6–109, (23 ♀) 91,5–97–100; tail (18) 87–105; tarsus (18) 21–25; culmen (19) 18–24. Weight (26 ♂) 34,5–41,9–51,2 g, (18 ♀) 31,9–37,3–51,2 g, (42 unsexed) 32,9–40,8–46 g.

Bare Parts: Iris red, red-brown or brown; bill purplish slate, edges paler; legs and feet grey.

Identification: Size smallish (about size of Sombre Bulbul); above plain brownish olive, washed yellowish on mantle and rump (Stripecheeked Bulbul grey on head, green on back); eye partly ringed white; below bright yellow; wings and tail brown; eye dark (red or brown; Sombre Bulbul has white eye). *Immature*: Duller than adult.

Voice: Characteristic querulous nasal *pão-pão-pão-pão*, rather like small yapping dog, increasing in pitch and tempo when alarmed; several birds often call together.

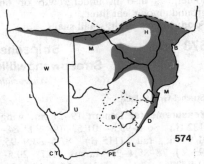

Distribution: S Africa to Angola and Kenya; in s Africa confined to E, NE and N.

Status: Common resident.

Habitat: Coastal and riverine forest and bush, inland evergreen forest, deciduous thickets.

Habits: In pairs or in groups of 5–6 birds. Vocal but shy, keeping to dense tangles, usually low down in forest; seldom emerges at edge of forest, except to sun itself on winter mornings. Forages at all levels of forest, but usually lower ones; hawks insects in flight; may associate with other bulbul species at good fruit supply.

Food: Fruit, insects, flowers, seeds.

Breeding: *Season*: October to December (also June) in Natal, September to March (mainly October-December) in Zimbabwe, November to January in Mozambique. *Nest*: Loosely built cup of twigs, tendrils, grass and plant fibres, lined with grass blades; usually low down (up to 4 m) in densely foliaged tree; built by both sexes in about 7 days. *Clutch*: (26) 2–2,1–3 eggs (usually 2). *Eggs*: White, cream or pale olive, heavily blotched and spotted with olive, brown and grey; measure (33) 24,8 × 17,1 (21,6–26,9 × 15,9–18). *Incubation*: 14 days by ♀ only. *Nestling*: 16–18 days; fed and brooded by both parents.

575 (725)   **Yellowspotted Nicator**   **Plate 48**
Geelvleknikator
Nicator gularis

[Bülbülwürger]

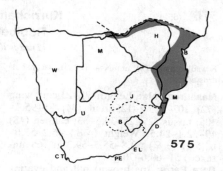

575

Measurements: Length ♂ about 23 cm, ♀ about 20 cm; wing (32 ♂) 104–108,9–116, (22 ♀) 88–91,1–95; tail (26 ♂) 101–106–114, (20 ♀) 83,5–89,3–95; tarsus (8 ♂) 27–31, (4 ♀) 25–28; culmen (8 ♂) 20–22, (4 ♀) 18,5–20. Weight (10 ♂) 50–55,7–63 g, (11 ♀) 33,6–37,3–41,3 g.

Bare Parts: Iris brown to yellow-brown; bill dark horn, edges paler; legs and feet blue-grey.

Identification: Smallish (about size of Sombre Bulbul, but looks larger because of longish tail); above yellowish olive, crown greyer; lores and ear coverts whitish; wing coverts boldly spotted white or yellow (diagnostic); below buffy white, washed olive grey on breast; undertail and underwing yellow; tail longish, tipped pale yellow; bill relatively heavy. *Immature:* Duller than adult; primaries tipped yellow; outer rectrices pointed. *Fledgling:* Has naked face.

Voice: Loud jumble of rich penetrating notes, *wip chip chop rrup chopchopchop krrip krrrr*, etc.; *churrr* or ringing *zokh* alarm note; *chuk* callnote.

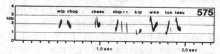

Distribution: Zululand to Somalia; in s Africa from Lower Umfolozi River to lowveld of Swaziland, Transvaal, Mozambique and e Zimbabwe; vagrant to Durban.

Status: Fairly common resident.

Habitat: Riverine forest, thickets in bushveld.

Habits: Usually solitary; females may join mixed bird parties, but not males. Skulks in tangled and dense vegetation; easily overlooked unless calling. Forages in low vegetation and on ground among leaf litter. Dives into cover and flicks wings when alarmed. Sings from concealed perch in upper branches of tree.

Food: Insects; probably also other invertebrates.

Breeding: *Season:* November to January. *Nest:* Shallow saucer of twigs, roots and moss; well concealed, low down in fork of dense bush. *Clutch:* 1–4 eggs (usually 2). *Eggs:* Dull pinkish cream, buffy or bluish, heavily blotched and spotted with brown and lilac; measure (10) 25,5 × 17,5 (24,7–27 × 16,6–19,5). *Incubation:* Unrecorded. *Nestling:* Unrecorded.

26:14. Family 76 TURDIDAE—THRUSHES, CHATS, ROBINS, ETC.

Small to medium. Bill medium to longish, slender, arched on culmen; legs moderately long and strong; toes usually fairly long and strong; wings usually short, rounded (rarely long and pointed); tail medium, square or rounded in most species (sometimes very short or long, graduated or forked); adult plumage highly variable; juvenile plumage always spotted; sexes alike or different; usually solitary; arboreal or terrestrial in wide variety of habitats from forest to desert (mostly forest or woodland); food varied, both plant and animal; nest an open cup (seldom domed) in bush or tree, hole in bank, rock or tree, or on ground; eggs 2–6, variable in colour (usually greenish), usually spotted;

chick naked or sparsely downy at hatching; nestling lacks black tongue-spots; incubation by both sexes or by female only; chicks cared for by both sexes. Distribution worldwide, except New Zealand and some oceanic islands; 305 species; 44 species in s Africa.

576 (552)   Kurrichane Thrush   Plate 49
Rooibeklyster
Turdus libonyana

N'wadlodloma (Ts), umuNswi (Z), [Rotschnabel-drossel]

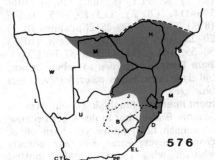

576

Measurements: Length 21–23 cm; wing (72) 107–115,2–125; tail (34) 85–95,3–105; tarsus (25) 25–30,5–33; culmen (48) 19–22,1–24,5. Weight (4 ♂) 46,2–55,6–64,5 g, (3 ♀) 50,8–55,3–59,3 g, (65 unsexed) 51–60,6–70 g.

Bare Parts: Iris brown; bill and eyering bright orange; billtip dusky; legs and feet pinkish to pale yellow.

Identification: Size smallish to medium; above greyish olive brown, rump greyer (Orange Thrush has 2 white wingbars); throat white with 2 bold black malar stripes (diagnostic; Orange Thrush has orange throat, breast and flanks; Olive Thrush has white throat, streaked blackish); breast greyish; centre of belly white, sides bright orange (whole belly dull yellow in Olive Thrush); undertail white; bill orange (yellow in Olive Thrush). *Immature:* Above spotted rusty buff; below spotted black.

Voice: Piercing 2-syllabled callnote *witteet, witteet,* often uttered on take-off; song rather deliberate, well-spaced short phrases of 4–10 varied sweet whistled notes, *sweety-weet-weet* or *wip-weedle, weedle, weety-wip-weet* with variations.

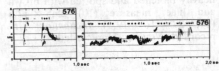

Distribution: S Africa to Angola, Zaire and Tanzania; in s Africa from Natal to Mozambique, Transvaal, Zimbabwe, e and n Botswana and Caprivi.

Status: Common resident.

Habitat: Woodland, exotic plantations, valley bushveld, riverine bush, gardens, parks; avoids forest and arid savanna.

Habits: Usually solitary or in pairs. Forages on ground, running in short bursts, stopping and pecking vigorously; tosses leaves aside to expose prey. When disturbed flies off with 2-note call, usually landing in tree. Sings well after rain, mostly in spring and early summer, often before dawn in moonlight.

Food: Insects, spiders, worms, molluscs, lizards, fruit (e.g. of *Rhus* species).

Breeding: *Season:* August to December (mainly October-November) in Natal, September to February (mainly October-November) in Transvaal, August to March (mainly September-December) in Zimbabwe; 2–3 broods/season. *Nest:* Bowl of coarse plant material, paper strips, cotton, roots; lined with mud and rootlets; inside diameter 6,5–7 cm, depth 3,5–4 cm; built by ♀ only in 1–2 days, often with wet material which dries hard; 1–3,7–7 m above ground (33 nests) in stout fork of large tree, usually against trunk. *Clutch:* (363) 1–2,9–4 eggs (usually 3). *Eggs:* Pale green, rather sparingly spotted or speckled with light red-brown and grey; measure (146) 26,5 × 19,3 (22,3–30 × 17–21,3); weigh (9) 4,8–5,2–5,6 g. *Incubation:* 13–14 days by ♀ only. *Nestling:* 13–14 days; fed by both parents; ♂ may feed fledglings while ♀ incubates next clutch.

Ref. Chittenden, H. 1982. *Bokmakierie* 34:67–68.

577 (553)

Olive Thrush
Olyflyster

Turdus olivaceus

Plate 49

Umswi (X), umuNswi (Z), [Kapdrossel, Kapamsel]

Measurements: Length about 24 cm; wing (77 ♂, Zimbabwe) 108–115,9–120,5, (73 ♀, Zimbabwe) 101–111,5–115,5, (108 unsexed, S Africa) 110,5–125,6–140; tail (73 ♂, Zimbabwe) 80–85,9–90,5, (73 ♀, Zimbabwe) 62–81,2–86, (101 unsexed, S Africa) 80–89,8–104,5; tarsus (166, Zimbabwe) 26–30,4–37; culmen (165, Zimbabwe) 19–22,2–24,5. Weight (19 ♂, S Africa) 59,5–72–81,5 g, (74 ♂, Zimbabwe) 59,4–66,4–76,4 g, (4 ♀, S Africa) 65,5–70,5–79,5 g, (78 ♀, Zimbabwe) 57,4–66,1–78,9 g, (179 unsexed, S Africa) 60–78,1–98 g.

Bare Parts: Iris brown; bill deep yellow, culmen and base dusky; legs and feet ochre yellow.

Identification: Size smallish to medium; above dark olive grey-brown (darker than Kurrichane Thrush); throat white, streaked blackish brown; breast olive grey; belly dull yellow, washed olive at sides (no white in centre of belly as in Kurrichane Thrush). *Immature*: Below spotted blackish; streaked rufous above.

Voice: Thin *tseep* alarm and take-off call; song phrases of varied fluty and slightly trilled notes, rather longer, faster and less deliberate than those of Kurrichane Thrush, e.g. *weety-weety-weety*, *prrr*, *tweet-weet*, *weety*; sings mainly spring and autumn, mostly silent midsummer.

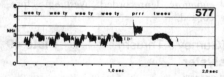

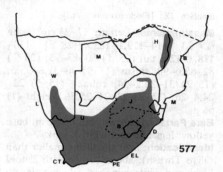

Status: Common resident; some altitudinal movement in montane regions.

Habitat: Evergreen forest in E; elsewhere in riverine bush, exotic plantations, gardens, parks, orchards.

Habits: Usually singly or in pairs. Forages on ground, running, stopping and pecking at ground or leaf litter. Shy in forest habitats, otherwise becomes tame, feeding on open lawns and in shrubberies. When disturbed, flies up with *tseep* call, usually landing in tree. Starts singing before dawn.

Food: Insects, molluscs, spiders, small lizards (including chameleons), fish, nestling birds, fruit, seeds.

Breeding: *Season*: All months in w Cape (mainly August-November), September to January (mainly November) in Natal, August to March (mainly September-December) in Transvaal, September to January in Zimbabwe. *Nest*: Large bowl of coarse leaves, twigs, grass and moss; lined with mud and dry grass; 1,5–20 m above ground (usually 2–5 m) in fork of bush or tree, usually against trunk. *Clutch*: (95) 1–2,1–4 eggs (usually 2). *Eggs*: Rich greenish blue, blotched and spotted with brown, red-brown and grey (richer in colour and more heavily marked than eggs of Kurrichane Thrush); measure (114) 29,3 × 21,6 (25–34,1 × 18,9–23,5). *Incubation*: (2) 14 days by ♀ only. *Nestling*: 16 days; fed by both parents.

Distribution: Africa S of Sahara; in s Africa over most of Cape Province to s Namibia (N to Hardap Dam), Natal, highveld of Orange Free State and Transvaal, along Drakensberg escarpment to Zoutpansberg, montane forests of Mozambique and Zimbabwe.

Ref. Winterbottom, M.G. 1966. *Ostrich* 37:17–22.

578 (558) Spotted Thrush Plate 49
Natallyster
Zoothera guttata

umuNswi (Z), [Fleckengrunddrossel]

Measurements: Length 22–23 cm; wing
(27 ♂)   114–119,1–125,   (28 ♀)   110–
118,1–120; tail (23 ♂) 80–87–93, (20 ♀)
82–85,6–90; tarsus (15 ♂) 30–31,8–33,5,
(15 ♀) 31–32,2–34; culmen (15 ♂) 23–
24,4–26, (15 ♀) 23–24–25,5. Weight (1)
56 g.

Bare Parts: Iris brown; bill blackish, base
yellow; legs and feet whitish pink.

Identification: Size smallish (smaller than
Olive Thrush); above brown with 2 bold
black-and-white wingbars (diagnostic; no
wingbars in Groundscraper Thrush); face
white with bold black border around ear
coverts; underparts white, heavily spotted
black; forest habitat (Groundscraper
Thrush inhabits open woodland). *Immature*: Above spotted buff; more finely
spotted below than adult.

Voice: Clear fluty song of shortish phrases
with brief pauses between, *swee-toot-
toodle*, *pree-pree-swee*, *swee-toot-toodle*,
etc.; sibilant *tsee-tsee* callnote.

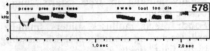

Distribution: Discontinuously from S
Africa to E Africa; in s Africa confined to
littoral from e Cape (East London) to
Zululand.

Status: Locally fairly common to uncommon; resident in Natal; e Cape populations appear to migrate to Natal in winter.
Vulnerable (RDB).

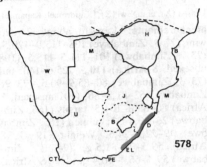

Habitat: Coastal and lowland evergreen
forest.

Habits: Usually solitary, but sometimes in
loose groups. Elusive and seldom seen.
Forages on forest floor among leaf litter.
When disturbed flies away with great agility, twisting and turning through forest
before alighting in tree. Migrates at night;
many killed by flying into buildings.

Food: Insects, molluscs.

Breeding: *Localities*: Ngoye Forest, Oribi
Gorge, Isipingo, Ndumu Game Reserve,
Nquleni Forest (Transkei). *Season*:
November to December. *Nest*: Bowl of
leaves, roots, grass, twigs, moss and mud,
lined with finer plant fibres; 7–10 m above
ground in fork of tree, usually where
slender branch emerges from bole;
favours *Garcinia gerrardii* in Ngoye Forest. *Clutch*: 2–3 eggs. *Eggs*: Greenish
blue, heavily blotched with dark red-
brown and greenish brown; measure (7)
25,5 × 19,2 (23,3–28 × 17,6–20,3). *Incubation*: Unrecorded. *Nestling*: Unrecorded.

579 (556) Orange Thrush (Gurney's Thrush) Plate 49
Oranjelyster
Zoothera gurneyi

[Gurneys Grunddrossel]

Measurements: Length 21–23 cm; wing
(58 ♂) 97–105,8–114, (61 ♀) 66–102,2–
112, (32 unsexed) 105–109,8–116; tail
(53 ♂) 75–80,2–90, (56 ♀) 70–76,5–88,
(14 unsexed) 77–86,6–93; tarsus (3 ♂) 34,

(4 ♀) 33–34,3–36, (22 unsexed) 31–
33,9–35; culmen (3 ♂) 21,5–23,2–25,
(4 ♀) 22,5–23–23,5, (12 unsexed) 20–
23,4–25. Weight (54 ♂) 44,5–54,4–
64,5 g, (56 ♀) 48,5–54,9–70,2 g, (25
unsexed) 58,7–64–70 g.

Bare Parts: Iris dark brown; patch behind eye cream; bill black; legs whitish pink.
Identification: Size smallish to medium; above dark brown; 2 bold white wingbars (no wingbars in Kurrichane or Olive Thrushes); lores and underparts orange; centre of belly and undertail white (whole belly dull yellow in Olive Thrush); bill black (orange in Kurrichane Thrush, deep yellow in Olive Thrush). *Immature*: Speckled buff above; wingbars present; mottled with black below.
Voice: Sustained song of varied mellow whistling notes, less broken up into phrases than songs of other thrush species, easily confused with song of Brown Robin; sibilant trilling callnote.

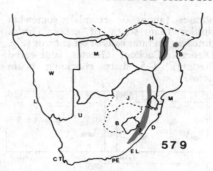

579

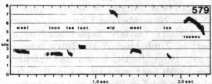

579

Distribution: S Africa to E Africa; in s Africa confined to montane evergreen forest from e Cape (Buffalo River) to Natal, Swaziland, e Transvaal escarpment, e highlands of Zimbabwe and adjacent Mozambique, and Gorongosa.
Status: Locally scarce to fairly common resident; some seasonal altitudinal movement.
Habitat: Moist evergreen montane forest, especially along streams.
Habits: Solitary or in pairs. Shy and elusive. Forages mainly on forest floor in gloomy interior. Partly crepuscular; vocal mainly in early morning and at dusk. Poorly known.
Food: Insects, molluscs, worms, fruit.
Breeding: *Season*: October to January in Natal and Transvaal, October to November in Transvaal, November to January in Zimbabwe. *Nest*: Deep bowl of roots, twigs, moss and ferns, lined with finer fibres; outside diameter 18–20 cm, inside diameter 3–8,5 cm, inside depth 4,5–5 cm (5 nests); on horizontal branch or in fork of slender forest tree, or among vines against treetrunk, often near footpath or over stream; 30 cm to 3 m above ground. *Clutch*: (23) 1–2–3 eggs (usually 2). *Eggs*: Turquoise blue, spotted with red-brown and grey, usually concentrated at thick end; measure (18) 28,4 × 20,5 (24–31,2 × 19,2–21,8). *Incubation*: 15 days; parent sits very tight. *Nestling*: 14–19 days; young brooded until almost fully fledged.

Ref. Earlé, R.A. & Oatley, T.B. 1983. *Ostrich* 54:205–212.

580 (557) Groundscraper Thrush Plate 49
Gevlekte Lyster
Turdus litsitsirupa

Mugendasikarapi (K), Nwadlodloma (Ts), Letsetserôpa, Letsotsonôpo (Tw), [Akaziendrossel]

Measurements: Length 20–22 cm; wing ♂ 130–133, ♀ 122–128; tail (39) 63–76; tarsus (39) 31–35; culmen (39) 22,5–27–30,5. Weight (7) 67–74,4–82,2 g.
Bare Parts: Iris brown; bill black, base yellow; legs and feet yellowish pink to yellowish brown.
Identification: Size smallish to medium; above light olive grey (no wingbars as in Spotted Thrush); face white; ear coverts boldly ringed black; below white, heavily spotted black; in flight wing shows large panel of orange-buff. *Immature*: Above spotted whitish; below more finely spotted than adult.
Voice: Varied phrases of a few quickly whistled and harsh notes, *sweet sweet wip-wip, wooeet-tzz-tzz-wooeet, wheee-toot-kzkzkzkz, putreeu treep treee putreeu,* etc., with fairly long pauses between

phrases (about 3 seconds); somewhat shriller than songs of other *Turdus* thrushes; imitates calls of other birds (e.g. Diederik Cuckoo, Greater Blue-eared Starling); 4–5 sharp chuckling alarm notes.

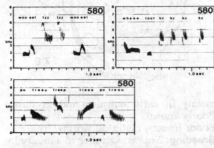

Distribution: S Africa to NE Africa; in s Africa absent from S, most of dry W and s Mozambique.
Status: Fairly common resident, usually of local and sporadic occurrence.
Habitat: Savanna woodland, thornveld, exotic plantations, cultivated clearings, farmyards.
Habits: Solitary or in pairs. Usually quite bold, especially around human settlements, foraging on lawns, short grassland, clearings and plantation floors; runs well on ground; flicks one wing at a time every now and then. When disturbed flies to tree or post with chuckling callnote.

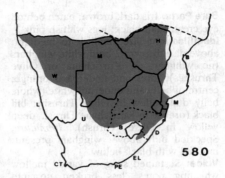

580

Food: Insects, molluscs and other invertebrates.
Breeding: *Season*: September to November in Natal, August to January (mainly October-November) in Transvaal, August to January (mainly September-November) in Zimbabwe. *Nest*: Bulky bowl of grass, twigs, herbs, leaves and feathers, lined with finer material; no mud; 2–6 m above ground in fork of tree; often near active nest of Forktailed Drongo. *Clutch*: (55) 2–2,7–4 eggs (usually 2–3). *Eggs*: Pale green, spotted with red-brown and blotched with lilac; measure (142) 27,5 × 20,3 (24,7–31,9 × 18–22,4). *Incubation*: Unrecorded. *Nestling*: Unrecorded; may be fed by parents and up to 2 adult helpers.

---

581 (559)   **Cape Rockthrush**   **Plate 49**
Kaapse Kliplyster
Monticola rupestris

Thume (SS), Igwagwa, Unomaweni (X), isiHlalamatsheni, iKhwelematsheni (Z), [Klippenrötel]

Measurements: Length 21–22 cm; wing (21 ♂) 110–113–119, (12 ♀) 106–109–115; tail (33) 72–88; tarsus (33) 28–31; culmen (33) 21–25. Weight (1 ♂) 60,5 g, (2 ♀) 60–63,7 g.
Bare Parts: Iris brown; bill black; legs and feet pinkish brown to black.
Identification: Size smallish to medium. *Male*: Head, throat and upper breast bright blue-grey (whole breast blue-grey in Sentinel Rockthrush; crown almost white in Shorttoed Rockthrush); back

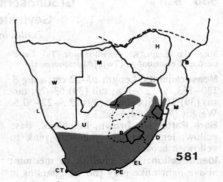

581

mottled dark brown and rufous (plain blue-grey in Sentinel and Shorttoed Rockthrushes); breast and belly rich orange-rufous (breast blue-grey in Sentinel Rockthrush); tail orange with black centre. *Female*: Above brown, streaked black; face and throat mottled white and brownish (♀ Shorttoed Rockthrush has more extensive area of white on throat); rest of underparts rich orange-rufous (mottled brown and white in ♀ Sentinel Rockthrush); tail as in ♂. *Immature*: Above brown, mottled buff; below rufous, mottled black.

Voice: Both sexes sing variable mellow whistling notes in phrases, *weetleoo pee pee chitrrr, whittoo chu whee chu chrruuchrruu*, etc., each phrase ending in buzzing trill, with pauses of 2–3 seconds between phrases; guttural *burrr* alarm note.

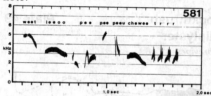

Distribution: Cape Province S of Orange River, e Orange Free State, Lesotho, Natal, Swaziland, e Transvaal escarpment to Zoutpansberg, Lebombo Range into sw Mozambique; also w Transvaal and se Botswana.

Status: Locally common resident.

Habitat: Rocky gorges, cliffs, boulder-strewn hillsides, scree slopes, usually with scattered low trees, bushes and aloes.

Habits: Solitary or in pairs. Perches on top of rock, bush or tree when alarmed, or to sing; sometimes flicks wings after landing. Forages mostly on ground, by hopping; attracted to burnt areas; also feeds on flowering aloes. Tame around human settlements.

Food: Insects, spiders, millipedes, centipedes, molluscs, small frogs, nectar, fruit, seeds.

Breeding: *Season*: September to February. *Nest*: Untidy mass of grass, twigs, roots and soil, with cup-shaped cavity on top, lined with rootlets; in crevice or on ledge of rock. *Clutch*: (23) 2–3,1–4 eggs (usually 3). *Eggs*: Light blue, plain or sparingly spotted with pale rust; measure (41) 27,3 × 19,7 (25,5–29,8 × 19,1–20,7). *Incubation*: Unrecorded. *Nestling*: Unrecorded; fed by both parents.

582 (560) Sentinel Rockthrush Langtoonkliplyster   Plate 49

Monticola explorator

Thume (SS), Umganto (X), [Langzehenrötel]

Measurements: Length 16,5–18 cm; wing (16) 97–102–108; tail 56–65; tarsus 32–35; culmen 19–22,5.

Bare Parts: Iris brown; bill black; legs and feet brown to black.

Identification: Size small (smaller than Cape Rockthrush). *Male*: Upperparts, throat and breast bright blue-grey (breast rufous in Cape Rockthrush; crown whitish in Shorttoed Rockthrush); rest of underparts rich orange-rufous; tail orange with black centre. *Female*: Above brown, faintly mottled buff; below mottled brown and white (♀ Cape and Shorttoed Rockthrushes

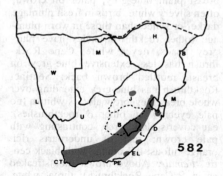

plain bright rufous on belly); tail as in ♂. *Immature*: Above spotted whitish; below scaled dark brown.

Voice: Lively whistled song in short phrases, similar to that of Cape Rockthrush, but less penetrating.

Distribution: Sw Cape and s Karoo, to highlands of ne Cape, Lesotho, Natal and se Transvaal; vagrant to e Cape, Zululand, n and C Transvaal.

Status: Common resident in lowlands; in highlands subject to seasonal altitudinal movement, breeding mostly above 1 200 m, some birds moving downward in winter to about 600 m.

Habitat: High rolling grasslands, rocky slopes, burnt areas, felled plantations.

Habits: Solitary, in pairs or small loose groups. Active and conspicuous, hopping rapidly over open ground; perches on stones, rocks or termite mounds in upright posture. May frequent human habitations at higher elevations.

Food: Insects (especially ants), fruit, seeds.

Breeding: *Season*: September to December. *Nest*: Untidy foundation of grass, twigs, and roots, with cup-shaped cavity on top, lined with fine grass and rootlets; in rock crevice, on rock ledge, on ground under rock (sometimes sheltered by vegetation), or under dense grasstuft on open grassy slope. *Clutch*: (8) 3 eggs (rarely 4). *Eggs*: Plain greenish blue; measure (18) 26,5 × 19,1 (24,2–28,5 × 18,3–20,4). *Incubation*: 13–14 days. *Nestling*: 16 days; fed by both parents.

---

583 (561)   **Shorttoed Rockthrush**   **Plate 49**
                              Korttoonkliplyster
Monticola brevipes

[Kurzzehenrötel]

Measurements: Length about 18 cm; wing 96–108; tail 60–67; tarsus 25–27; culmen 20–22.

Bare Parts: Iris brown; bill, legs and feet black.

Identification: Size smallish to medium. *Male*: Upperparts, throat and upper breast plain blue-grey, paler on crown, often silvery white, birds in fresh plumage darker-crowned than those in worn plumage (other rockthrush males have blue-grey heads, never white; Cape Rockthrush has less extensive blue-grey on breast, mottled brown back: Sentinel Rockthrush has blue-grey extending over whole breast); eyebrow always whitish (no pale eyebrow in other ♂ rockthrushes); ear coverts dark grey, contrasting with pale crown; rest of underparts rich orange-rufous; tail orange with black centre. *Female:* Above brown (not streaked as in ♀ Cape Rockthrush); throat white, mottled with brown (more extensively white than that of ♀ rockthrushes); rest of underparts rich rufous (♀ Sentinel

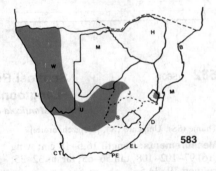

Rockthrush mottled brown and whitish below); tail as in ♂. *Immature*: Spotted with buff and black above and below.

Voice: Clear jumbled sweet whistled song phrases, similar to those of other rockthrushes; imitates other bird species.

Distribution: Northern Karoo, n Cape, w and C Transvaal, se Botswana, w half of Orange Free State, most of Namibia to sw Angola (Mossamedes); isolated population Siteki, Swaziland.

Status: Fairly common to common localized resident.

Habitat: Rocky outcrops, koppies, escarpments, inselbergs, river valleys, usually with scattered bushes and low trees; also towns and villages.
Habits: Usually solitary or in pairs. Keeps mostly to rocky places, hopping about on rocks and perching in trees; in towns perches on buildings. Usually rather shy in open country, becoming tame around human settlement.

Food: Insects, scorpions, seeds.
Breeding: *Season*: September to January in Transvaal. *Nest*: Cup of dry grass and rootlets; under rock or among dense roots of climbing fig on rock face. *Clutch*: 2–3 eggs (usually 3). *Eggs*: Plain sky blue to greenish blue; mea:ure (7) 22,7 × 17,3 (21,1–24,2 × 17,1–18,3). *Incubation*: Unrecorded. *Nestling*: Unrecorded.

584 (562) Miombo Rockthrush (Angola Rockthrush) Plate 49
Angolakliplyster
Monticola angolensis

Mugendasikarapi (K), [Großes Waldrötel, Miomborötel]

Measurements: Length about 18 cm; wing (10 ♂) 98–101,2–102, (10 ♀) 92–97,7–101, (32 unsexed) 94–100–108; tail (32) 59–69; tarsus (32) 23–28,5; culmen (32) 19,5–22,5. Weight (2) 44–44,7 g.
Bare Parts: Iris dark brown; bill, legs and feet black.
Identification: Size smallish; not a bird of rocky habitat like other rockthrushes. *Male*: Above blue-grey, mottled black (diagnostic; no other ♂ rockthrushes have mottled upperparts); throat and upper breast plain blue-grey; lower breast and flanks bright rufous, shading to white in centre of belly and undertail (other ♂ rockthrushes all rufous on belly); tail orange with black centre. *Female*: Above mottled buff and black; throat white with dark-mottled malar stripes; breast and flanks light rufous, shading to white in centre of belly and undertail; tail as in ♂. *Immature*: Similar to ♀, but mottled black-and-white below.
Voice: Sweet and varied whistled song of relatively high-pitched notes; fluty 2-note whistled callnote, second syllable higher-pitched; chattering alarm call; mimics other bird species.

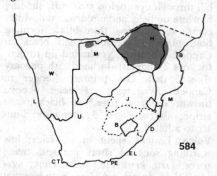

584

Distribution: Zimbabwe, adjacent Mozambique, Botswana, Zambia, Angola, Malawi, Zaire and Tanzania.
Status: Locally common resident.
Habitat: Endemic to *Brachystegia* woodland; also in *Baikiaea* woodland; usually in hilly country.
Habits: Solitary, in pairs or small loose groups. Forages mainly on ground. When disturbed flies into tree, perches motionless for a while, then flies away.
Food: Insects (mainly ants and termites).
Breeding: *Season*: August to December (mainly September-October). *Nest*: More or less substantial foundation of coarse grass and twigs with cup-shaped cavity on top, lined with finer grass; foundation sometimes absent; in shallow cavity in tree trunk, on stump or on branch. *Clutch*: 3–4 eggs. *Eggs*: Turquoise blue, plain or sparingly spotted with red-brown; measure (18) 23,8 × 17,8 (20,4–26 × 16,8–19). *Incubation*: Unrecorded. *Nestling*: Unrecorded; fed by both parents.

584

585 (563)
Eurasian Wheatear
Europese Skaapwagter
Oenanthe oenanthe
Plate 50

[Steinschmätzer]

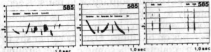

Measurements: Length about 15 cm; wing (5) 93–96,6–100; tail 56–57,2–58; tarsus 27–28,3–31,5; culmen 17,5–19,1–20. Weight (3) 25–25,7–27 g.

Bare Parts: Iris brown; bill, legs and feet black.

Identification: Size small; ♀ very similar to immature Capped Wheatear, but more lightly built. *Male*: Above grey; eyebrow and rump white; broad black stripe from bill through eye; below rich buff, shading to white on belly and undertail; tail white, centre and terminal third black, forming bold black T (terminal half black in Capped Wheatear, graduated up to centre, not T-shaped); in hand, 5th primary shorter than 2nd primary (longer in Capped Wheatear). *Female*: Above brown; eyebrow pale; no black facial stripe; otherwise as in ♂. *Immature*: Similar to adult ♀.

Voice: Usually silent in s Africa; low warbling song of short phrases, *tseeu, tswee, krrit, krrit*, etc.; harsh *chak, weet chak-chak*, or *stsk, tsk* alarm note like that of Stonechat or Familiar Chat.

Distribution: Breeds n Palaearctic and Nearctic; migrates to Africa S of Sahara; in s Africa recorded only scattered localities in Zimbabwe and once in Transvaal.

Status: Rare vagrant, seldom S of 18 °S, October to December.

Habitat: Bare ground, cattle kraals, cleared woodland, fallow fields, always with low perches.

Habits: Solitary. Perches upright on prominent post, wall or termite mound; flies from perch to perch when disturbed, bowing and bobbing after landing; fans and flicks tail up and down; shy and wary, hard to approach. Forages on ground; moves in long hops; also hawks insects in air by jumping from ground.

Food: Insects, millipedes; rarely seeds, berries.

Breeding: Extralimital.

Ref. Borrett, R.P. & Jackson, H.D. 1970. *Bull. Brit. Orn. Club* 90:124–129.

586 (564)
Mountain Chat
Bergwagter
Oenanthe monticola
Plate 50

Letsoanafike, Letsoana-tsoana, Khaloli (SS), [Bergschmätzer]

Measurements: Length 17–20 cm; wing (6 ♂) 106–110–116, (4 ♀) 102–104,5–110; tail (18 ♂) 70–80, (8 ♀) 65–73; tarsus (8) 28–31; culmen (26) 17,5–23. Weight (2 ♀) 35,5–38,5 g, (3 unsexed) 30,8–32,6–35 g.

Bare Parts: Iris brown; bill, legs and feet black.

Identification: Size smallish. *Male*: Black or grey; wrist patch, rump and outer rectrices white (all conspicuous in flight), but white wrist patch may be very small in grey males; black males may have grey or white crown and nape, and white belly

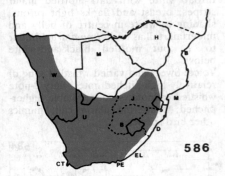

5 8 6

(about 1 out of 4,5 black males have white belly). *Female*: Sooty black or blackish

brown (looks black at distance); rump and outer rectrices white, tipped black. *Immature*: Similar to adult ♀.

Voice: Usually rather silent; ♂ has loud song of jumbled fluty notes, somewhat trilled, in phrases with pauses between, *tsi-tsuru-wi-tsi-wi*, etc.; mimics other birdcalls, including Eurasian Bee-eater, Greater Striped Swallow, Olive Thrush, Cape Wagtail, Pied Starling, bulbuls, sparrows and canaries; ♀ calls whistled *tyeeoop*; rasping *chit-chit* alarm notes.

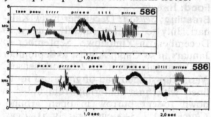

Distribution: Highveld and dry w parts of S Africa, Lesotho, sw Botswana and Namibia to sw Angola (Benguela).
Status: Locally common to fairly common resident.
Habitat: Rocky outcrops, hills, koppies, valley slopes, escarpments; usually with grass and/or shrubs and bushes; also riverine bush, farmyards and gardens.

Habits: Usually solitary or in pairs; sometimes in small groups of 3–4 birds. Flies restlessly from rock to rock, usually low down, showing conspicuous white patches; moves with long hops over rocks; also perches on termite mounds or in trees. Forages on ground or by darting into air to catch flying prey. Becomes tame around human settlements, even visiting feeding trays. Often sings on moonlit nights.
Food: Insects, spiders, table scraps.
Breeding: *Season*: June to March (mainly September-November); opportunistically after rain in arid areas; 2–3 broods/season. *Nest*: Rather untidy foundation of spider web, grass, wool, earth, twigs and small stones, with cup-shaped cavity on top, neatly lined with hair or soft plant material; under rock on ground, in hole in rock, wall or building, or in nestbox; built by ♀ only, in 4–14 days. *Clutch*: (50) 2–2,8–4 eggs. *Eggs*: Pale bluish green, finely speckled with pinkish rust, concentrated at thick end; measure (204) 23,5 × 16,8 (20,9–26,4 × 15,8–19). *Incubation*: 13–14 days by ♀ only. *Nestling*: 16–17 days; fed by both parents.

Ref. Plowes, D.C.H. 1948. *Ostrich* 19:80–88.
Taylor, J.S. 1946. *Ostrich* 17:248–253.

587 (568) **Capped Wheatear** **Plate 50**
Hoëveldskaapwagter
Oenanthe pileata

Kasinganzwi (K), Thoromeli (SS), Ntidi (Tw), Isixaxabesha, Inkotyeni (X), iSangwili (Z), [Erdschmätzer]

Measurements: Length 16–18 cm; wing (27 ♂) 91–98–104, (9 ♀) 88–90–92; tail (27 ♂) 57–68, (9 ♀) 50–59; tarsus (27 ♂) 29–34, (9 ♀) 26–32; culmen (36) 15–16. Weight (1 ♀) 23,9 g, (1 unsexed) 32,5 g.
Bare Parts: Iris brown; bill, legs and feet black.
Identification: Size smallish (about size of Cape Robin); crown and face black; forehead and broad eyebrow white; back brown; rump white; below white with broad black breastband, passing around sides of neck to join black face and nape; flanks deep buff; tail white on basal half, black on terminal half, graduated to all-

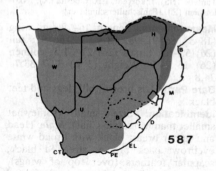

black central rectrices (Eurasian Wheatear has only terminal third of tail black, forming bold T-shaped pattern, not graduated to form V). *Immature*: Above brown, spotted buff; below off-white, mottled brown on breast and flanks; somewhat similar to ♀ Eurasian Wheatear, but tail pattern diagnostic (see above).

Voice: Song of mixed harsh and melodious whistling notes, including imitations of other birdcalls; clicking alarm notes.

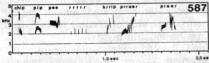

Distribution: S Africa to E Africa; throughout s Africa except e Cape, Natal, Lesotho, Mozambique littoral and most of Kaokoveld.

Status: Common breeding intra-African migrant in sw Kalahari, November to June; in Zimbabwe mainly nonbreeding migrant from sw s Africa, May to December (but many birds breed there); possibly resident in some areas, but overall status uncertain.

Habitat: Open semidesert, burnt grassland, cultivated fields, eroded or overgrazed veld, stockyards and kraals.

Habits: Usually solitary; sometimes in pairs or family groups. Perches in upright posture on stone, bush or termite mound; flies to ground to catch prey, moving in long hops, then flying back to perch; on landing bows exaggeratedly and flicks or swings tail up and down. Displays by flying up and hovering on fluttering wings, body nearly horizontal, head drawn back and tail cocked, accompanied by song; also has bobbing display with clicking calls when perched (alarm?).

Food: Insects.

Breeding: *Season*: December in sw Kalahari, July to January (mainly August to December) in Zimbabwe, September to January in sw Cape, August to September in Transvaal; may rear 2 broods/season. *Nest*: Cup-shaped pad of grass and roots, lined with finer material; from 0,3–1 m down rodent burrow in open ground. *Clutch*: (6) 2–3–4 eggs (rarely 5). *Eggs*: Pale greenish or bluish white, plain or faintly speckled with pink; measure (44) 23,4 × 17,4 (20,9–27 × 15,5–20,4). *Incubation*: Unrecorded. *Nestling*: Unrecorded.

---

588 (569) **Buffstreaked Chat** **Plate 50**
Bergklipwagter
Oenanthe bifasciata

Tantabe (NS), Inkotyeni, Isixaxabesha (X), iNkolotsheni (Z), [Fahlschulterschmätzer]

Measurements: Length 16–17 cm; wing (18 ♂) 86–91–98, (8 ♀) 82–86–91; tail (26) 53–65; tarsus (26) 27–31,5; culmen (26) 16,5–19. Weight (3 ♀) 32,7–33,7–34,8 g.

Bare Parts: Iris brown; bill, legs and feet black.

Identification: Size small (somewhat smaller than Mountain Chat). *Male*: Head and upper breast black with broad white eyebrow; back brown, streaked black; scapular feathers (over top of wings), rump and belly bright orange-buff; tail and wings black. *Female*: Above brown, lightly streaked darker; eyebrow pale buff, narrow; rump orange-buff; below cinnamon-buff, streaked brownish; tail

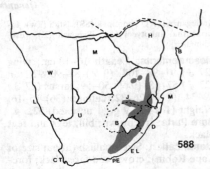

black. *Immature*: Similar to adult ♀, but spotted with buff above; below scaled with blackish.

Voice: Song by both sexes of short quick phrases, starting with sharp clicking notes like stones knocked together, followed by penetrating whistling notes, *klitik tweeoo, trrrpeetoo* (pause), *klitik tritri tweeoo, tritritri*, etc.; sometimes mimics other bird-calls.

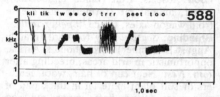

Distribution: Eastern Cape (around Grahamstown), se and ne Orange Free State (along Vaal River to Parys), Transkei, inland Natal, e and n Transvaal.
Status: Locally fairly common resident; generally uncommon.
Habitat: Rocky slopes of hills, ridges, escarpments and mountain foothills, with rolling grassland and low scattered bushes.
Habits: Usually solitary or in pairs; in small groups when not breeding. Lively and conspicuous, perching on rocks

1,5–3 m high, and flying restlessly from one to another, often flirting wings and tail on alighting or when alarmed; may perch in treetop if disturbed. Forages for about 70% of day when not breeding, on ground among rocks and bushes or by making aerial sallies from rock to catch flying insects; often also in fallow lands, along roadsides and around kraals and farmyards. Gait on ground is bounding hop. Becomes tame around human settlement; otherwise wary.
Food: Insects (mostly ants, grasshoppers, beetles and termite alates), nectar.
Breeding: *Season*: September to February (mainly October-November). *Nest*: Cup of fine grass and hair in bulky foundation of grass and roots; under rock or in hole in rock or wall. *Clutch*: (18) 2–2,8–3 eggs (rarely 4). *Eggs*: White or pale bluish white, speckled with rufous and grey, forming cap at thick end; measure (20) 23,1 × 16,5 (21–25,2 × 15,1–17,3). *Incubation*: Unrecorded. *Nestling*: Unrecorded.

Ref. Tye, A. 1988. *Ostrich* 59:105–115.

---

589 (570)   **Familiar Chat**   **Plate 50**
                    Gewone Spekvreter
                    Cercomela familiaris

Letlerenyane, Letleretsane (SS), Isikretyane, Unongungu (X), umBexe (Z), [Rostschwanzschmätzer, Rostschwanz]

Measurements: Length about 15 cm; wing (22 ♂) 85–88–92, (24 ♀) 79–82–85; tail (46) 55–68; tarsus (42) 22,5–26; culmen (54) 13–19. Weight (7 ♂) 21–22,2–23 g, (3 ♀) 19,5–22,3–28 g, (45 unsexed) 17–21,5–28,8 g.
Bare Parts: Iris brown; bill, legs and feet black.
Identification: Size small; smoky brownish grey, paler below; ear coverts tinged rufous (not always good field character); rump and tail dull orange-rufous; centre and tip of tail blackish brown, forming dark T on orange background (diagnostic with orange rump in flight, but orange not visible when perched; other small chats have paler orange, white or grey on rump

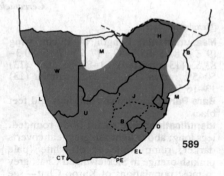

and tail with black area graduated to form solid V-shape); flicks wings 1–4 times on landing, stopping, or merely turning around on perch (other chats do not flick wings so constantly or deliberately).

FAMILIAR CHAT

Immature: Above spotted with buff; below scaled with blackish.

Voice: Harsh *chak-chak* or *peep-chak-chak* when alarmed; song usually rather quiet garbled series of peeps, chuckles and churrs, *peep-churr-churr, peep-chak-churr, peep-peep*, etc.

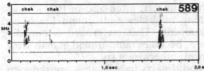

Distribution: Africa S of Sahara; throughout s Africa except n Botswana and Caprivi.

Status: Common resident, especially in drier areas; uncommon in moist e littoral.

Habitat: Variable; rocky outcrops, mountains, koppies, valley slopes, escarpments; woodland in Zimbabwe; tree-lined watercourses in arid regions; farmyards, gardens, dongas.

Habits: Solitary or in pairs. Tame, especially around human settlement. Perches on almost any raised object (tree, bush, rock, windmill, termite mound, building); flies to ground to catch prey, flicking wings on landing; hops on ground, flicking wings at every stop; returns to perch, flicks wings and usually slowly raises tail once or twice.

Food: Insects, fruit (fallen mulberries), bread, animal fat (formerly ate grease from wagon axles, hence "*Spekvreter*").

Breeding: *Season*: July to April (mainly August-December) throughout s Africa; opportunistic in arid areas, breeding after rain. *Nest*: Neat cup of hair, wool, feathers or soft plant material in thick pad of soft grass, string, fluff, paper, etc.; on bulky foundation of clods of earth, small stones (most weighing 5–6 g), bits of bark; in hole in ground, wall of donga, rock face, building, old burrow of bee-eater, disused Sociable Weaver nest chamber, crevice or hole in tree; also in nestbox, or other manmade object. *Clutch*: (95) 2–3,1–4 eggs (usually 3). *Eggs*: Bright greenish blue, sparingly speckled with rusty red, concentrated at thick end; measure (186) 20,4 × 15,1 (18–23,6 × 14,1–16,6). *Incubation*: (6) 13–15 days. *Nestling*: (4) 15–18 days; fed by both parents.

Ref. Steyn, P. 1966. *Ostrich* 37–176–183.

---

590 (571)   **Tractrac Chat**   **Plate 50**
         Woestynspekvreter
         Cercomela tractrac

[Namibschmätzer]

Measurements: Length 14–15 cm; wing (9 ♂) 81,5–85,5–89, (7 ♀) 79,5–80,3–83,5, (13 unsexed) 81–83–85; tail (13) 50–55; tarsus (13) 26–29,5; culmen (13) 13–16,5.

Bare Parts: Iris brown; bill, legs and feet black.

Identification: Size small; body rounded, legs long; above light ash grey; ear coverts darker; rump white or off-white (pale pinkish orange in Sicklewinged Chat, grey in most populations of Karoo Chat—see below); tail white with solid triangle of black from tip towards centre (tail of Sicklewinged Chat similar, but rusty white; black of tail in Karoo Chat meets grey rump in centre); below white (all other *Cercomela* chats are greyish below,

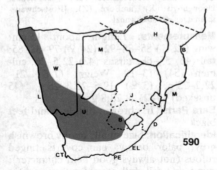

590

except Namib race of Karoo Chat which is buff). Karoo races of Tractrac and Karoo Chats easily separable, but Namib races difficult; black in central rectrices of Karoo Chat meets pale rump; bases of central rectrices in Tractrac Chat white; tail of Tractrac Chat always about 10–20 mm shorter than that of Karoo Chat. *Immature*: Speckled with buff and black above and below.

Voice: Usually silent; jumbled song of slurred and chirping notes; sharp *trak-trak* when alarmed.

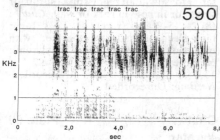

Distribution: Ne Cape, s Orange Free State, Karoo, Namaqualand, s and w Namibia to Kaokoveld; also to sw Angola (Mossamedes).

Status: Fairly common resident.

Habitat: Open shrubby plains in desert, semidesert, karoo and stubbly grassveld; also straggly bushes along dunes or dry watercourses.

Habits: Usually solitary or in pairs; loosely territorial, 6–10 birds sometimes visible at once over wide area. Perches on top of low shrub or stone; flies to ground to catch prey; runs fast on ground. Flicks wings and jerks tail almost as regularly as, but less deliberately than Familiar Chat. Tame and inquisitive; when alarmed, hovers briefly then drops to ground or perch.

Food: Insects (including tenebrionid beetles killed by motor vehicles on roads).

Breeding: *Season*: August to April (season varies with rainfall, but mostly September-October). *Nest*: Neat cup of soft grass and hair in foundation of sticks and twigs; on ground under stone or shrub, or inside gnarled *Welwitschia* plant. *Clutch*: 2–3 eggs. *Eggs*: Greenish blue, plain or finely speckled with red-brown; measure (14) 22,1 × 16,1 (19,5–24,2 × 15–16,9). *Incubation*: Unrecorded. *Nestling*: Unrecorded.

591 (572)   Sicklewinged Chat   Plate 50
Vlaktespekvreter
Cercomela sinuata

[Oranjeschmätzer]

Measurements: Length about 15 cm; wing (8 ♂) 78,5–80,6–85, (7 ♀) 72–76,1–78,5; tail (15) 48–57; tarsus (15) 26–30; culmen (15) 13–16. Weight (2 ♀) 17,4–19,7 g.

Bare Parts: Iris brown; bill, legs and feet black.

Identification: Size small; similar to Familiar Chat, but altogether paler; rump and tail pale rusty with solid triangle of blackish, graduated up towards central feathers (not orange-rufous with dark T-shape as in Familiar Chat or white with black triangle as in Tractrac Chat); above smoky greyish brown; below greyish buff, flanks tawny buff; flicks wings, but less than does Familiar Chat; in hand, 2nd primary remex notched back narrowly from tip, sickle-shaped. *Immature*: Spotted above with buff; below scaled with dusky on buff; remiges broadly tipped buff.

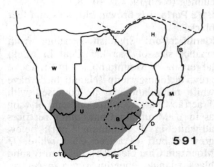

Voice: Usually silent; quiet *chak-chak*.

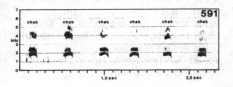

Distribution: Sw and n Cape, Karoo, e Cape and Transkei to Matatiele, Namaqualand, s Namibia, Orange Free State, Lesotho and Natal border, sw Transvaal.

Status: Common resident; some altitudinal movement from higher elevations in winter.

Habitat: Karoo, drier fynbos, shrubby semidesert, montane grasslands, alpine slopes (in Lesotho); also cultivated lands, well-grazed pastures.

Habits: Solitary or in pairs. Perches on top of low shrub or fence; drops to ground to catch prey; sometimes flicks wings on landing, but less regularly and deliberately than does Familiar Chat (more twinkling than flicking movement). Flies low from perch to perch; hops rapidly on ground.

Food: Insects.

Breeding: *Season:* August to March (mostly October to January). *Nest:* Cup of soft dry grass and plant down in foundation of coarser grass and twigs; set into soil under grasstuft, shrub or stone, or in hole in rock or wall. *Clutch:* (8) 2–2,5–3 eggs (rarely 4). *Eggs:* Light blue-green, indistinctly speckled with pale rust, concentrated at thick end; measure (47) 20,1 × 14,7 (18,5–22,5 × 13,6–15,6). *Incubation:* Unrecorded. *Nestling:* Unrecorded.

592 (566)   Karoo Chat   Plate 50
Karoospekvreter
Cercomela schlegelii

[Bleichschmätzer, Wüstenschmätzer]

Measurements: Length 15–18 cm. *C. s. schlegelii* (Namib region): wing (6 ♂) 94,5–95,6–97, (5 ♀) 83,5–86,7–90; tail (6 ♂) 65–68, (5 ♀) 59–62; tarsus (11) 26–30; culmen (11) 13–16,5. *C. s. pollux* (Namaqualand): means only, wing (5 ♂) 108, (12 ♀) 101; tail (4 ♂) 78, (11 ♀) 72; culmen (6 ♂) 19, (12 ♀) 18.

Bare Parts: Iris brown; bill, legs and feet black.

Identification: Smallish (grading from smaller size of Familiar Chat in N, to larger size of Mountain Chat in S); above grey, including rump (Namib birds have white rump and can be confused with Tractrac Chat; no white on bend of wing as in ♂ Mountain Chat; outer rectrices all-white in ♂ Mountain Chat); below grey to buff (Tractrac Chat white, ♀ Mountain Chat blackish); tail mainly solid black triangle, meeting rump in centre, with white panels at base on either side, conspicuous in flight (more extensive white on tail of Tractrac Chat; black in centre does not meet rump); tail 10–20 mm longer than that of Tractrac Chat. *Immature:* Above spotted with buff; below scaled blackish.

Voice: Rattling *tirr-tit-tat* or *tirr-tit-tat-tut* or *zip-zip-zik-zik-chirp*.

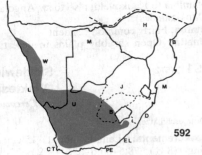

592

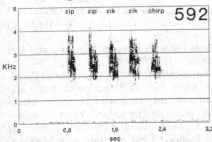

592

Distribution: From Matatiele through n Transkei to ne Cape, Karoo, n Cape, sw Transvaal, Namaqualand, s and w Namibia.

Status: Common resident in Karoo; less common in Namib region.

Habitat: Karoo, scrubby and bushy plateaus and stony hillsides.

Habits: Solitary or in pairs. Perches on top of bush, shrub, rock or telephone wire; on landing flutters wings until balanced; sometimes flicks wings, but not as regularly as does Familiar Chat. Forages on ground or by dropping to ground from perch. When disturbed flies low from bush to bush; flight wavy.

Food: Insects, seeds.

Breeding: *Season*: August to March (season may vary with rainfall). *Nest*: Cup of dry grass and plant down on foundation of sticks and twigs; on ground under rock, bush or grasstuft. *Clutch*: (10) 2–2,6–4 eggs. *Eggs*: Pale greenish blue, heavily freckled with rusty red; measure (40) 20,7 × 15,4 (19,1–24 × 14,3–16,5). *Incubation*: Unrecorded. *Nestling*: Unrecorded.

593 (573)   Mocking Chat   Plate 50
Dassievoël
Thamnolaea cinnamomeiventris

iQumutsha-lamawa (Z), [Rotbauchschmätzer]

Measurements: Length 20–23 cm; (15 ♂) 109–115,3–122,5, (13 ♀) 103–109–115; tail (29) 90–100; tarsus (30) 27,5–31,5; culmen (30) 18–22. Weight (3 ♀) 46,7–48,4–51,1 g, (5 unsexed) 40,7–47,7–51 g.

Bare Parts: Iris dark brown; bill, legs and feet black.

Identification: Size medium (about size of smallish starling). *Male*: Mainly glossy black, except for bright rufous rump and belly, and white wrist patch. *Female*: Slaty black where ♂ glossy black; wings and tail black; deep chestnut where ♂ bright rufous; no white patch on wing. *Immature*: Similar to adults, but duller.

Voice: Fine rich song of 2 types, (a) clear powerful fluty warble with little or no imitation of other birdsong, (b) quieter rapid jumble of imitated calls and songs of other bird species (at least 30 different species recorded); both sexes sing equally well, sometimes in duet; variable sibilant callnote, *istsisisi*; harsh *kraat* alarm note.

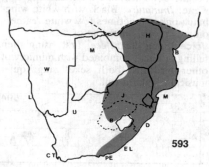

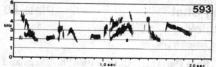

Distribution: Africa S of Sahara; in s Africa from e Cape to Natal, most of n Orange Free State, Swaziland, Transvaal, Zimbabwe and Gorongosa.

Status: Locally common resident.

Habitat: Well wooded rocky gorges, dongas, cliffs, boulder-strewn hillsides.

Habits: Usually in small groups of 4–5 birds. Runs quickly on ground, rock or thick branch, sometimes with tail raised; bounds about in trees. Forages by dropping to ground from perch, or searching branches for fruit. Flight low with gliding and flapping; wings make soft swishing; on landing raises and lowers tail slowly and exaggeratedly. Becomes tame around human settlements.

Food: Insects, fruit.

Breeding: *Season*: August to December (mainly September-November) throughout s Africa. *Nest*: Felted bowl of dassie (hyrax) or antelope hair, on foundation of leaves, feathers, twigs and roots; usually in nest of Lesser Striped Swallow (swallows may be ousted, and original lining, with or without eggs or young, pulled out); built by both sexes in 1–3 weeks; hair may be obtained from living antelopes. *Clutch*: (36) 2–2,8–4 eggs (usually 3). *Eggs*: White, cream, pale green or bluish, spotted with pale red-brown and mauve; measure (28) 25,6 × 18,2 (24–27,6 × 17–19,1). *Incubation*: 14–16 days by ♀ only. *Nestling*: 19–21 days; fed by both parents.

Ref. Farkas, T. 1961. *Ostrich* 32:122–127; 1966. *Ostrich Suppl*. 6:95–107.

594 (574)   Arnot's Chat   Plate 50
Bontpiek
Thamnolaea arnoti

Mandlakeni (Ts), [Arnotschmätzer]

Measurements: Length about 18 cm; wing (14) 97–102–107; tail 63–76; tarsus 26–30; culmen 14–17.

Bare Parts: Iris brown to red-brown; bill, legs and feet black.

Identification: Size smallish. *Male*: Jet black; crown and bend of wing white. *Female*: Jet black; throat and bend of wing white. *Immature*: Black with white wing-patch only; sometimes few white feathers on crown of ♂ or throat of ♀.

Voice: Song clear *feee*, first rising then falling in pitch, combined with mimicry of other birdcalls; both sexes sing; quiet musical *fik* alarm call.

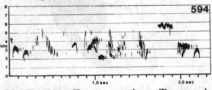

Distribution: Eastern and ne Transvaal, Zimbabwe and ne Botswana to s Zaire and Tanzania.

Status: Locally common resident; numbers reduced by destruction of habitat, especially *Brachystegia*. Rare (RDB).

Habitat: Well developed *Brachystegia, Baikiaea* and mopane woodland.

Habits: In pairs or small groups. Somewhat thrushlike; lively and conspicuous.

Forages low down among gnarled trunks of trees, sometimes hanging sideways on bark; pounces on prey on ground from perch about 3 m up. Flies with audible wingbeats.

Food: Insects and spiders.

Breeding: *Season*: August to December (mainly October-November) in Zimbabwe. *Nest*: Bowl-shaped hollow on foundation of coarse plant material; lined with grass, leaf petioles and feathers; inside diameter 8 cm, depth 4 cm; in natural hole in tree, 2–4 m above ground. *Clutch*: 2–4 eggs. *Eggs*: Pale bluish or greenish, heavily speckled with rufous and mauve; measure (12) 22,6 × 16,6 (20,9–24 × 15,2–17,5). *Incubation*: Unrecorded. *Nestling*: Unrecorded.

Ref. Barbour, D. 1972. *Bokmakierie* 24:16.

595 (575)   Anteating Chat   Plate 50
Swartpiek
Myrmecocichla formicivora

Thume, Thoromeli (SS), Leping (Tw), Isanzwili (X), [Termitenschmätzer, Ameisenschmätzer]

Measurements: Length about 18 cm; wing (103 ♂) 93–98,9–107, (70 ♀) 87,2–94,8–102,7; tail (89 ♂) 48,1–59,3–65, (59 ♀) 48–56,6–62,9; tarsus (90 ♂) 29,8–33,4–36,6, (59 ♀) 29,2–32,5–35,5; culmen (90 ♂) 15,1–17,9–20,5, (59 ♀) 12–17–20,5. Weight (31 ♂) 41,5–49,4–60,8 g, (24 ♀) 40,5–45,8–59 g, (63 unsexed) 35–42,2–51,1 g.

Bare Parts: Iris dark brown; bill, legs and feet black.

Identification: Size smallish; round-bodied and long-legged; sooty blackish brown all over (looks black at distance); in flight primaries show as white window, fluttering rapidly below level of body; ♂ has small white patch on bend of wing, usually concealed when perched. *Immature*: Dark brown, washed rusty; little white in wings.

Voice: Clear plaintive whistled *peeeek* call or alarm note, sometimes rising slightly in pitch; song cheerful jumble of whistling and rasping notes, fairly sustained; sometimes imitates other birdcalls.

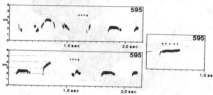

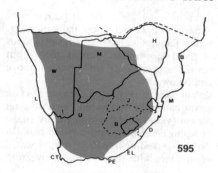

Distribution: Highveld and semi-arid w parts of S Africa, Lesotho, Botswana, sw Zimbabwe and Namibia.
Status: Common resident.
Habitat: Open grassveld, rolling grassy hills, Kalahari sandveld, shrubby semi-desert; usually with termite mounds, dongas and Antbear burrows.
Habits: Solitary, in pairs or in small groups of 6 or more birds. Perches on termite mound, bush, fence or telephone wire, especially along country roads; flies with blur of white wings, hovering, swerving and dropping to ground or perch; often raises tail after landing; rarely flicks wings. Forages by hopping or running on ground (mainly winter) or by dropping onto prey from perch (mainly summer). Calls in flight or when perched.
Food: Insects (including ants, termites, beetles, bugs and caterpillars), solifugids, millipedes, fruit; ants taken mostly in winter.
Breeding: *Season*: August to February (mainly October-November). *Nest*: Bowl of dry grass and fine rootlets; in chamber at end of self-excavated burrow (17) 0,35–0,92–1,5 m long, in wall of donga, stream bank, road-cutting or quarry, or in roof of Antbear or hyaena burrow in open veld; entrance (17) 5,5–7,9–12 cm diameter; excavation and building by both sexes; soil dug with bill and removed with feet; completed in 8–10 days; rarely builds in nest of Greater Striped Swallow under road culvert, sometimes evicting swallows. *Clutch*: (65) 2–3,7–5 eggs (usually 3). *Eggs*: White, rarely with few brown spots; measure (47) 23,9 × 17,9 (21,7–28,5 × 16,5–19,4); weigh 3,8–4,1–4,2 g. *Incubation*: (5) 14–14,5–15 days, by ♀ only. *Nestling*: (5) 15–16,6–18 days; fed by both parents and sometimes by helpers from earlier broods; chicks return to nest after initial departure; fed for up to 7 days after leaving nest.

Ref. Earlé, R.A. & Herholdt, J.J. 1988. *Ostrich* 59:155–161.

---

596 (576)   **Stonechat**   **Plate 50**
                    Gewone Bontrokkie
                    Saxicola torquata

Tlhatsinyane, Hlatsinyane (SS), Isangcaphe, Ingcaphe (X), isAnqawane, isAncaphela, isiChegu (Z), [Schwarzkehlchen]

Measurements: Length about 14 cm; wing (63 ♂) 66–70,4–76, (50 ♀) 64–67,8–72,5; tail (53 ♂) 46–51,6–56, (41 ♀) 47–50–54; tarsus (28) 20–21,6–24; culmen (29) 10–12,5–15,5. Weight (35 ♂) 12,8–14,9–17,1 g, (29 ♀) 12,2–14,7–18 g.

Bare Parts: Iris dark brown; bill, legs and feet black.
Identification: Size small. *Male*: Head, back and tail black, faintly scaled rufous on back; patches at sides of neck, on wing and on rump white; breast and flanks bright chestnut, shading to white in centre of belly and undertail. *Female*: Above mottled light and dark brown; rump and

517

patch on wing white; throat buff; rest of underparts light cinnamon, paler on belly. White patches in both sexes conspicuous in flight. *Immature*: Similar to ♀, but heavily spotted buff and blackish above and below.

Voice: Sharp repeated *seep-chak-chak* alarm call; song somewhat canarylike set phrase (varies slightly among individuals) of piping and trilling notes, *sweep-twiddle-dee sweep-twiddle-tree-deeee trrr*, repeated many times with short pauses between.

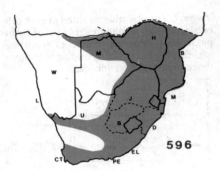

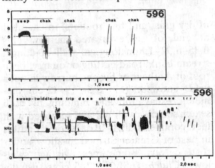

Distribution: Africa, Madagascar, Europe, Asia; in s Africa absent only from dry W, but extends down Orange River to Atlantic coast.

Status: Very common in highveld and montane areas; fairly common elsewhere; resident in some areas; otherwise seasonal altitudinal migrant from higher country to lower; possibly some migration between Zimbabwe and S Africa.

Habitat: Alpine grassland, lush grassy slopes and hills, edges of vleis, canefields, fallow lands, road verges, karoo scrub,

irrigated fields and pastures, riverine scrub.

Habits: Usually in pairs; sometimes solitary. Perches on top of bush, weed, stump, fence or telephone line; drops to ground to catch prey; hops on ground, but soon returns to perch; flicks wings and tail on landing. Flight jerky, showing conspicuous rump and wing patches. Usually quite tame, but exceedingly wary when nesting.

Food: Insects.

Breeding: *Season*: August to December (mainly August-October) in Transvaal and Natal, July to December (mainly August-November) in Zimbabwe. *Nest*: Cup of coarse grass, neatly lined with finer material and hair; on ground or in low earth bank, well hidden under or inside dense clump of grass, rushes or reeds. *Clutch*: (50) 2–3,2–5 eggs (usually 3–4). *Eggs*: Bluish green, lightly speckled with rusty red, concentrated at thick end; measure (87) 18,9 × 14,2 (17,4–20,4 × 13,2–15,6). *Incubation*: 14–15 days by ♀ only. *Nestling*: 13–16 days; fed by both parents; young dependent on parents for at least 2–3 weeks after initial departure.

597 (577)   Whinchat   Plate 50
Europese Bontrokkie
Saxicola rubetra

[Braunkehlchen]

Measurements: Length 13–14 cm; wing 70–84; tail 43–50; tarsus 20–24; culmen 11–12.

Bare Parts: Iris brown; bill, legs and feet black.

Identification: Size small; above streaked buff and black; face black (brown in ♀); eyebrow and malar stripe white (diagnos-

tic; no white stripes on head of ♀ Stonechat); wingpatch and base of tail white (rump white in Stonechat; no white in tail); below rich rufous buff, shading to white on throat and belly.

Voice: Callnote *tik-tik* or *fwee-tik-tik*, similar to that of Stonechat; song short jumbled phrase, *prrr swippy tseeu*, etc.

518

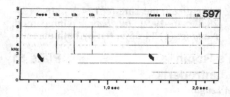

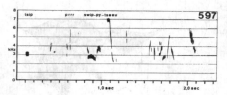

Distribution: Breeds w Palaearctic; migrates to Africa; in s Africa collected Swakopmund 1925; sight records Natal and Zululand 1961, and Zimbabwe 1949 and 1950.

Status: Rare nonbreeding Palaearctic migrant; vagrant, seldom migrating S of Zambia and Malawi.

Habitat: Moist grassland, ploughed fields, with scattered bushes and small trees.

Habits: Solitary or in small groups. Similar to Stonechat.

Food: Insects.

Breeding: Extralimital.

598 (578)   Chorister Robin   Plate 51
Lawaaimakerjanfrederik
Cossypha dichroa

Ugagasisi (X), uMananda (Z), [Lärmrötel]

Measurements: Length 19–20 cm; wing (75 ♂) 95–101,9–107, (36 ♀) 91–97,7–102,5; tail (56 ♂) 75–84,4–93, (24 ♀) 74–81,6–85,5; tarsus (29) 27,5–32; culmen (29) 16,5–19. Weight (17) 38,2–40,3–43,8 g.

Bare Parts: Iris dark brown; bill black; legs and feet pinkish brown.

Identification: Size smallish; above blackish slate; rump and underparts orange; tail orange with black centre. Heuglin's Robin similar, but has white eyebrow. *Immature:* Above spotted buff; below scaled dusky on buff.

Voice: Ratchetlike *chr-r-r-r*, *chr-r-r-r* alarm note; rich whistled *tleetoo* callnote; song rich melodious piping trills and whistles, incorporating much imitation of other forest bird species; easily confused with song of Natal Robin.

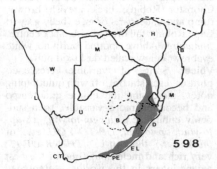

Distribution: S and e Cape, Natal, w Swaziland and e Transvaal to Zoutpansberg.

Status: Locally common resident; some seasonal altitudinal movement at higher elevations.

Habitat: Evergreen forest, especially in mist belt.

Habits: Usually solitary. More often heard than seen; keeps to dense foliage in forest canopy; may forage on ground in winter, sometimes catching insects flushed by foraging molerats. Highly vocal in summer; can be called up by spishing (see Glossary).

Food: Mainly insects; also millipedes, spiders, ticks; fruit in winter.

Breeding: *Season:* October to January (mainly November). *Nest:* Shallow cup of rootlets and other plant fibres; in hole or

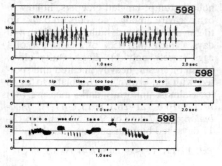

519

cavity in treetrunk, up to 12 m above ground. *Clutch*: (28) 2–2,9–3 eggs (usually 3). *Eggs*: Plain glossy chocolate brown or olive green; measure (66) 24,5 × 18,7 (23–28,8 × 16–19,9). *Incubation*: Unrecorded. *Nestling*: (1) 14 days; fed by both parents.

599 (580)   Heuglin's Robin   Plate 51
Heuglinse Janfrederik
Cossypha heuglini

Tepa (K), [Weißbrauenrötel]

Measurements: Length 19–20 cm; wing (42 ♂) 94–98,1–105, (58 ♀) 85–90–95; tail (21 ♂) 83–91,5–100, (36 ♀) 76–82,4–88,3; tarsus (35) 27–30,6–35; culmen (36) 14–16,5–19. Weight (51 ♂) 30,5–39–46,5 g, (64 ♀) 27,3–32,8–41,9 g, (182 unsexed) 27,3–35,9–46,5 g.

Bare Parts: Iris brown; bill black; legs and feet dark pinkish brown.

Identification: Size smallish; top of head black; bold white eyebrow (no eyebrow in Chorister Robin); back greyish brown; rump and underparts orange (belly grey in Cape Robin); tail orange with black centre. *Immature*: Above spotted buff; no white eyebrow; below scaled dusky on buff.

Voice: Song of variable crescendo phrases, each starting off with quiet piping notes, increasing in volume and tempo and becoming more variable, then suddenly ending, e.g. *it's-up-to-you, it's-up-to-you , up-to you, UP-TO-YOU*, etc., or *think-of-it, think-of-it, THINK-OF-IT*; very rich and melodious (one of the best avian singers in the world); stereotyped call, *don't-you-DO-it*; also sings in duet; imitates other birds' alarm calls near nest; harsh *tserrk-tsrek* alarm call.

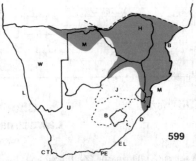

Distribution: S Africa to Sudan and Chad; in s Africa confined to NE and N, as far S as Zululand.

Status: Locally common resident.

Habitat: Dense riverine bush, evergreen thickets, gardens.

Habits: Usually solitary. Keeps to thick cover, seldom seen. Forages mainly on ground; at least partly crepuscular, coming into clearings and more open places to feed. Sings from low perch in tree or bush; vocal mainly dawn and late evening.

Food: Insects, spiders, centipedes, worms, fruit, small frogs and lizards.

Breeding: *Season*: September to January (mainly November) in Natal and Zimbabwe; may raise 2 broods/season. *Nest*: Cup of leaves, twigs and moss, lined with rootlets and finer plant fibres; among dense shoots of coppicing bush or tree, or in hollow stump, tangled creepers, hollow in bank, cavity among tree roots on bank; up to 2 m above ground; built by ♀ only in 4–5 days. *Clutch*: (48) 95% of 2 eggs, 5% of 3 eggs (rarely only 1). *Eggs*: Buffy olive, bluish or cream, heavily smeared and spotted with red-brown or chocolate so as to look almost uniformly dark; measure (84) 22,9 × 16,6 (21–26,1 × 15,1–17,7). *Incubation*: 14–17 days by ♀ only. *Nestling*: 13–17 days; fed by both parents, mostly by ♀.

Ref. Farkas, T. 1973. *Ostrich* 44:95–105.

600 (579)

Natal Robin
Nataljanfrederik
Cossypha natalensis

Plate 51

Nyarhututu (Ts), [Natalrötel]

Measurements: Length 17,5–20 cm; wing (42 ♂) 88–94,3–98, (40 ♀) 83–88,4–94,5; tail (33 ♂) 72,5–77,7–81, (35 ♀) 60–70,2–76; tarsus (69) 25–27,4–31; culmen (66) 14–16,3–19. Weight (34 ♂) 27,3–32,2–34,8 g, (36 ♀) 24,9–29–33 g, (78 unsexed) 24,4–30,8–40 g.

Bare Parts: Iris dark brown; bill black; legs and feet pinkish brown.

Identification: Size small; above brownish to bluish grey (Zimbabwean birds rufous on crown, hence called "Redcapped Robin"; Chorister Robin much darker slaty black above); below dull orange, including face (Chorister Robin has blackish face and crown); tail orange with black centre. *Immature*: Spotted dark brown and buff above and below.

Voice: Monotonous froglike 2-syllabled (rarely 3-syllabled) *preep-prrup* or *preep-preep-prrup* callnote, second syllable lower-pitched, call rising and falling in volume and pitch for minutes on end like squeaky seesaw; rich melodious whistled song involving much imitation of over 30 other species of birds, similar in quality to song of Chorister Robin and easily confused with it; guttural *gurr* alarm note (softer than alarm note of Chorister Robin).

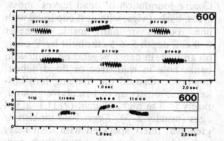

Distribution: S Africa to Kenya, Sudan and Cameroon; in s Africa confined to E and N in lowlands, including Limpopo and Zambezi Valleys and e Caprivi.

Status: Scarce to common; mostly resident; in highlands of Zimbabwe migrates

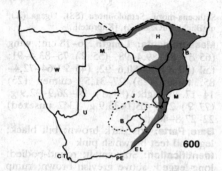

to Mozambique, May to August, but some stragglers remain.

Habitat: Usually evergreen forest; also deciduous thickets, riverine forest, parks and large gardens.

Habits: Usually solitary. Elusive, more often heard than seen; keeps mostly to undergrowth of forest; forages on ground, especially at dusk, sometimes taking insects disturbed by foraging molerats; moves seasonally to higher forest strata when fruits ripen. Sings from low perch, sometimes with slightly raised quivering wings.

Food: Insects, spiders, centipedes; fruit mainly in winter.

Breeding: *Season*: September to January (mainly November) in Natal and Zimbabwe, November-December in Transvaal. *Nest*: Cup of dead leaves, twigs and moss, lined with fine rootlets and other plant fibres; in hollow stump, rock crevice, niche in wall, hanging creeper or on ground. *Clutch*: (120) 1–2,8–4 eggs (usually 3). *Eggs*: Variable; plain chocolate brown or olive green, or turquoise blue, heavily mottled with brown or olive; measure (278) 22,4 × 16,6 (20–24,9 × 15–18); weigh (2) 2,7 g. *Incubation*: 13,5–15 days by ♀ only; incubating ♀ fed by ♂. *Nestling*: (2) 12 days; sometimes 17 days; fed by both parents.

Ref. Farkas, T. 1969. *Ibis* 111:281–292.

601 (581)

Cape Robin
Gewone Janfrederik
Cossypha caffra

Plate 51

Sethoena-moru, Setholo-moru (SS), Ugaga (X),
umBhekle, uGaga (Z), [Kaprötel]

Measurements: Length 16–18 cm; wing
(65 ♂) 82–89,4–98, (55 ♀) 75–83,4–91;
tail (50 ♂) 70–80,6–92, (45 ♀) 64–72,4–
85; tarsus (25) 27–31,5; culmen (25)
14–17. Weight (84 ♂) 24–26,9–32,9 g,
(77 ♀) 21,9–25,1–33,9 g, (342 unsexed)
22–27,8–40 g.

Bare Parts: Iris dark brown; bill black;
legs and feet brownish pink.

Identification: Size small; round-bodied,
long-legged; above greyish brown; rump
orange; conspicuous white eyebrow; face
black; throat and breast light orange; belly
grey (Chorister Robin wholly orange
below); undertail yellowish buff; tail
orange with black centre. *Immature*: Spotted buff and dark brown above and below.

Voice: Harsh low 3-syllabled alarm note,
WA-deda, slightly accented on first syllable; song of somewhat variable short
passages, each starting with same down-
slurred whistle, continuing with musical
phrase of 2–10 sweet clear notes, likened
to someone reading shopping list, *teeu
teetoo, teeu tiddly-too, teeu teetoo teetoo*,
etc., with brief pause between each
phrase; imitates over 20 other bird species.

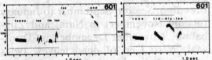

Distribution: S Africa to Uganda and
Sudan; throughout most of S Africa
(except much of n Cape) and s Namibia
(N to Hardap Dam); isolated population
in e Zimbabwe, adjacent Mozambique
and Gorongosa.

Status: Common resident inland, scarce
coastally in E; some altitudinal migration
from highlands in winter.

Habitat: Forest edge, wooded kloofs,
riverine bush (especially in semi-arid
areas), montane scrub, gardens, parks,
farmyards, regenerating wattle and *Eucalyptus* plantations.

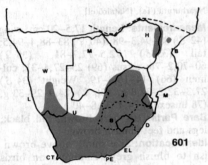

Habits: Usually solitary or in pairs. Keeps
mostly to dense undergrowth, but often
forages in open at edge of thicket to which
it retreats when disturbed; hops on
ground; rarely wades in shallow water.
Flight jerky; on alighting flicks wings and
fans tail briefly, showing orange-and-black
pattern. Sings from perch, sometimes
exposed on top of bush or tree.

Food: Insects, spiders, worms, small
frogs, lizards, fruit.

Breeding: *Season*: June to December
(mainly August-October) in sw and e
Cape, August to January (mainly
September-December) in summer-rainfall
areas, September to December (mainly
October-November) in Zimbabwe. *Nest*:
Coarse foundation of dead leaves, moss,
grass, bark, twigs, with nest cup lined with
fine rootlets or hair; inside diameter
6–8 cm, depth 5–6,5 cm; built by ♀ only;
on ground, in dense vegetation, hollow in
bank, hole in wall, tree or flood debris,
flowerpot, disused tin, hanging fern basket, etc.; mostly up to 1 m above ground,
rarely to 3 m high. *Clutch*: (711) 1–2,3–4
eggs (usually 2–3). *Eggs*: Pale pinkish or
greenish, finely speckled with light rusty
red and grey, forming cap at thick end;
measure (290) 23,1 × 16,6 (20,3–
25,8 × 13,7–18,3). *Incubation*: 14–18
days by ♀ only. *Nestling*: 14,5–16–18
days; fed by both parents.

Ref. Rowan, M.K. 1969. *Living Bird* 8:5–32.

602 (582)

Whitethroated Robin
Witkeeljanfrederik
Cossypha humeralis

Plate 51

[Weißkehlrötel]

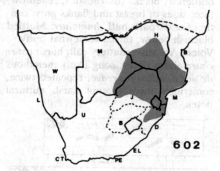

602

Measurements: Length 16–18 cm; wing (14 ♂) 77–81–85, (4 ♀) 73–74,5–76; tail (14 ♂) 70–79, (4 ♀) 63–70; tarsus (18) 26–29; culmen (18) 15–17. Weight (14 ♂) 20,2–22,4–24,7 g, (9 ♀) 19–20,7–23,1 g, (14 unsexed) 18,5–23–28,5 g.

Bare Parts: Iris dark brown; bill, legs and feet black.

Identification: Size small; above slate grey; rump dull orange; face, sides of neck and wing black; eyebrow and wingstripe white (diagnostic; no other robin has white wingstripe); below white, shading to orange-buff on flanks and undertail (Bearded Robin has orange across breast, bold black malar stripes, tail black with white tip); tail orange with black centre and tip (other *Cossypha* robins lack dark tip). *Immature:* Spotted buff and dark brown above and below.

Voice: Song sustained jumble of piping, twittering and other musical notes, including imitation of other birdcalls, each bout lasting up to 10 seconds without pause; grating *grrr* and high-pitched *peep* alarm notes (somewhat like calls of Familiar Chat).

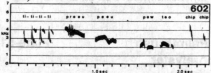

Distribution: Zululand, Swaziland, Mozambique S of Save River, s and C Zimbabwe, Transvaal and e Botswana.

Status: Locally common, especially in drier parts of range.

Habitat: Thorn thickets, riverine bush and forest, low dense woodland with understory of grass and herbs, gardens.

Habits: Solitary or in pairs. Retiring; keeps to dense cover; forages on ground, moving with quick hops; most active in late evening. Flirts wings and tail. Vocal mainly during winter months.

Food: Insects, other invertebrates (including spiders and centipedes), berries.

Breeding: *Season:* September to October in Natal, September to December in Transvaal and Zimbabwe (mainly October-November). *Nest:* Neat cup lined with petioles and grass in foundation of sticks and dead leaves set level with soil; on ground, well hidden between roots of tree, under bank or low branch. *Clutch:* (69) 2–2,7–3 eggs. *Eggs:* Cream, pinkish cream, greenish white or reddish brown; spotted and blotched with darker red-brown and pale grey, sometimes forming ring at thick end; measure (134) 20,9 × 15,1 (19–23,3 × 14–16,1). *Incubation:* 14–15 days. *Nestling:* 14 days.

603 (593)

Collared Palmthrush
Palmmôrelyster
Cichladusa arquata

Plate 51

[Morgenrötel]

Measurements: Length about 20 cm; wing (5) 86–88,6–91; tail 85–92; tarsus 25–27; culmen 16–17,5. Weight (8) 31–34–37 g.

Bare Parts: Iris grey, greyish white or yellowish grey; bill black; legs and feet olive grey to brown.

Identification: Smallish (slightly smaller than thrush); robinlike on ground, other-

523

wise somewhat like bulbul in build; above brown; rump, wings and tail bright chestnut; throat and centre of breast buff, bordered black (diagnostic); eyebrow, face, sides of breast and flanks grey; centre of underparts buff. *Immature*: Mottled blackish below, throat somewhat buffy.

Voice: Abrasive chattery call; harsh *churr churr* alarm notes; song lively melodious *de dee doodle-oo deedee*, repeated twice, sometimes incorporating harsh guttural notes.

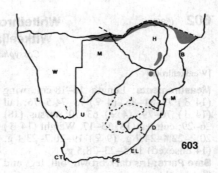

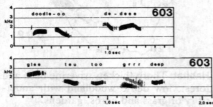

Distribution: Limpopo River to E Africa; in s Africa confined to Limpopo, Sabi and Zambezi valleys; sight record from Letaba Camp, Kruger National Park.

Status: Locally common resident.

Habitat: Thickets with *Phoenix, Hyphaene* and *Borassus* palms; less often around human settlements in *Combretum* and mopane woodland.

Habits: In pairs or small groups. Forages mouselike among palms, or by hopping on ground like robin; often flicks and fans tail, or waves it up and down with chatlike wing-flicking. Wings make loud *prrrup, prrrup* noise in flight. Tame around human settlement; may nest and roost under eaves.

Food: Insects.

Breeding: *Season*: October to March. *Nest*: Cup-shaped shell of mud, lined with woven palm-leaf fibres (somewhat like nest of swallow); inside depth of cup 2,5 cm; at base of palm frond, *Dracaena* leaf, or under eaves of building. *Clutch*: Usually 2 eggs, sometimes 3. *Eggs*: Faint greenish or bluish white, plain or faintly spotted with red-brown; measure 27 × 15. *Incubation*: Unrecorded. *Nestling*: Unrecorded.

Ref. Donnelly,B.G. 1967. *Ostrich* 38:230–232.

604 (593X)   **Rufoustailed Palmthrush**   **Plate 51**
Rooistertmôrelyster
Cichladusa ruficauda

[Graubruströtel]

Measurements: Length about 17 cm; wing (47) 85–93; tail 72–85; tarsus 24–27; culmen 13–16.

Bare Parts: Iris red to red-brown; bill black; legs and feet light brown to purplish blue.

Identification: Size small; similar to Collared Palmthrush, but lacks collar; above red-brown to chocolate; rump and tail bright rufous; underparts buff in centre, grey at sides. *Immature*: Mottled buff and blackish below.

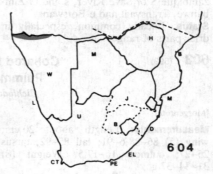

Voice: Song loud melodious whistled phrases, often in duet; imitates other bird-calls; harsh *churr* alarm note.

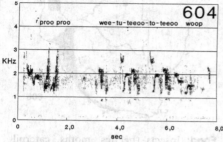

Distribution: Kunene River to Gabon; in s Africa confined to lower Kunene River, n Namibia.

Status: Locally common resident.
Habitat: Lowland plains with thick brush, especially with *Borassus* palms; also riverine bush.
Habits: Usually in pairs. Highly vocal, but rather retiring. Roosts in palms at night. Poorly known.
Food: Insects.
Breeding: Not recorded in s Africa. *Season*: January and May in Angola. *Nest*: Deep rounded cup of mud; in crown of palm, crevice in trunk of baobab, under eave or on ledge of building. *Clutch*: 2 eggs. *Eggs*: Pale greenish white, speckled dull rufous at thick end; measure (2) 23,7–24,1 × 16,4–16,2. *Incubation*: Unrecorded. *Nestling*: Unrecorded.

605 (591X) Whitebreasted Alethe Plate 51
Witborsboslyster
Alethe fuelleborni

[Weißbrust-Alethe]

Measurements: Length about 22 cm; wing 102–112; tail (1) 79; tarsus (1) 32; culmen (1) 23. Weight (14) mean 49,4 g.
Bare Parts: Iris brown; bill black; legs pinkish.
Identification: Size smallish; above brown, shading to russet on rump and tail; below white; sides of neck and flanks olive grey. *Immature*: Above spotted black and rufous; below scaled blackish.
Voice: Melodious piping *fweet-her-hee-her-hee-her*.

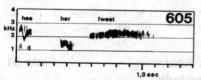

Distribution: Gorongosa and Beira to ne Tanzania.

Status: Rare, probably resident.
Habitat: Evergreen forest.
Habits: Solitary. Hops on ground; skulks in tangled undergrowth; highly elusive. Poorly known.
Food: Insects, fruit.
Breeding: *Season*: November in Zambia. *Nest, Clutch, Eggs, Incubation, Nestling*: Unrecorded.

606 (589) Starred Robin Plate 51
Witkoljanfrederik
Pogonocichla stellata

[Sternrötel]
Measurements: Length ♂ 15–16–17 cm; ♀ 13,5–14–14,5 cm; wing (118 ♂) 84–

90,2–95, (92 ♀) 79–83–88, (15 unsexed) 75–78,5–85; tail (110 ♂) 58–67–72, (99 ♀) 55–59,7–66; tarsus (222) 23–

STARRED ROBIN

24,7–31; culmen (226) 12,5–14,4–17. Weight (127 ♂) 16,9–21–24,2 g, (105 ♀) 16,4–19,9–24 g.

Bare Parts: Iris brown; bill black; legs and feet pinkish.

Identification: Size small; whole head and throat slaty black (white frontal and throat spots or "stars" seldom visible); back green; wings bluish slate; rest of underparts bright yellow; tail golden yellow with black centre and tip. *Immature:* First plumage spotted buff and black above, mottled black on pale yellow below; second plumage olive green above, light yellow below; tail as in adult, but duller.

Voice: Piping callnote, *too-twee* in Natal, or *terwheh dada weeyoo* in Transvaal and Zimbabwe; song quiet stereotyped piping phrase of about 6 notes, ending in slightly drawn-out whistle; soft guttural rattling anxiety call.

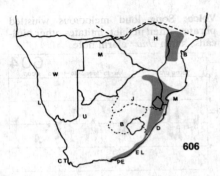

606

606

Distribution: Discontinuously from S Africa to E Africa; in s Africa restricted to SE, E and NE.

Status: Locally common; mostly altitudinal migrant; few birds resident.

Habitat: Montane evergreen forest, September to February; lowland evergreen forest February to August.

Habits: Usually solitary. Quiet and retiring; can be called up by spishing (see Glossary). Forages on ground, or gleans from leaves, twigs and bark; hawks flying prey in air, especially after sunset.

Food: Insects (beetles, moths, caterpillars, ants, flies, bugs, wasps, crickets, grasshoppers), centipedes, spiders, amphipods; fruit mainly in winter.

Breeding: *Season:* October to December in Natal, September to December in Transvaal, October to January in Zimbabwe (mainly October-November throughout). *Nest:* Domed cup of skeletonized leaves, lined with finer material; inside diameter of cup 5–6,5–8,5 cm, depth 2,5–4–5 cm; entrance about 5,5 cm wide, 4,5 cm high; usually on gently sloping ground, rarely in steep bank, often against boulder or base of tree, well hidden by forest litter. *Clutch:* (114) 2–2,9–3 eggs. *Eggs:* White, spotted with pinkish brown and some lilac, forming cap at thick end; measure (152) 22 × 16 (19,6–24 × 14,8–17,2); weigh (18, fresh) 2,7–3–3,2 g. *Incubation:* 16–18 days by ♀ only. *Nestling:* (9) 13,5–14,5–15,5 days; fed by both parents.

Ref. Oatley, T.B. 1982. *Ostrich* 53: 135–146; 193–205; 206–221.

---

607 (590)   Swynnerton's Robin   Plate 51
Bandkeeljanfrederik
Swynnertonia swynnertoni

[Swynnertonrötel]

Measurements: Length 13–14 cm; wing (106 ♂) 66–70,4–73, (41 ♀) 65–67,3–70; tail (98 ♂) 43–49,8–52, (37 ♀) 41–44,2–47; tarsus (164) 23–26,1–28; culmen (164) 12–14–16. Weight (105 ♂) 13,8–15,8–20,4 g, (44 ♀) 14,4–16,3–19,5 g, (1 unsexed) 16,8 g.

Bare Parts: Iris brown; bill black; legs and feet pinkish grey.

Identification: Small (warbler-sized); whole head and throat blue-grey, crown washed dark olive green in ♀; back green; throat bordered below by white crescent and black collar (diagnostic, but not easily seen unless in display; no collar in Starred

526

Robin); rest of underparts ochre yellow (not bright yellow as in Starred Robin); tail plain dusky (Starred Robin has golden tail with black T-pattern). *Immature*: Above spotted with buff; below white; collar dull light grey-white and brown.

Voice: Song clear high-pitched piping 4-syllabled phrase, *pee-pee, sweetsweee*, frequently repeated; drawn-out quavering alarm call like high-pitched monotonous purring; low sibilant *si-si-si* callnote; quiet chirruping greeting call.

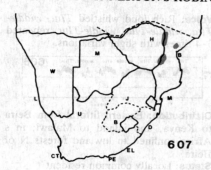

6 07

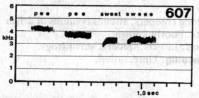

Distribution: Scattered localities, totalling about 1 000 ha, in e highlands of Zimbabwe and adjacent Mozambique; also Gorongosa Mountain and Tanzania.
Status: Locally very common resident, up to 6 pairs/ha; vulnerable to destruction of limited habitat.
Habitat: Evergreen forest, usually montane above 900 m; associated with *Dracaena fragrans* when breeding.
Habits: Usually solitary; males territorial all year, females only out of breeding season. Keeps to deepest shade. Alert, inquisitive and tame; seldom perches higher than about 1 m above ground; forages by hopping about on forest floor and fallen logs, turning over dead leaves;

attends columns of driver ants; movements quick, accompanied by flicking of wings and tail. Wingbeats audible in flight.
Food: Mainly insects (beetles, ants, termites, bugs, flies, caterpillars); also spiders, centipedes, small berries.
Breeding: *Season*: October to January (82% of nests November-December); at least 2 broods/season. *Nest*: Neat cup of well woven fine roots, dead leaves, moss and fine stems; lined with coarse brown fibres from treeferns; outside diameter 12 cm, inside diameter 5 cm, inside depth 2,5 cm; at base of *Dracaena* frond, in densely foliaged tree or bush, hollow stump, cavity in bank; 1–2 m above ground. *Clutch*: (4) 2 eggs (rarely 3). *Eggs*: Pale blue-green or buff, spotted with red-brown, concentrated at thick end; measure (3) 21,2 × 14,4 (20–23 × 14–15). *Incubation*: 16 days by ♀ only. *Nestling*: Unrecorded.

Ref. Manson, A.J. 1990. *Honeyguide* 36:5–13.

608 (591) **Gunning's Robin** **Plate 51**
Gunningse Janfrederik
Sheppardia gunningi

[Blauflügel-Akalat]

Measurements: Length about 13 cm; wing (6 ♂) 69,5–72,9–75; tail (6 ♂) 51–53–54; tarsus (2 ♂) 20–23; culmen (2 ♂) 12,5–13. Weight (4) 15–17,6–20 g.
Bare Parts: Iris greyish brown; bill blackish, base paler; legs and feet pale pinkish mauve.

Identification: Small (warbler-sized); above olive brown, shading to russet on rump; short white eyebrow, not projecting behind eye (sometimes indistinct); below orange, shading to white in centre of belly; tail dusky, edged dull rufous. *Immature*: Mottled with black and buff above and below.

Voice: Rich loud whistled *TItu, widdle-TItu, widdle-TItu, widdle-TItu*, repeated 3–4 times with slight variations.

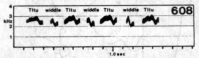

Distribution: Eastern littoral from Beira to Kenya, and inland to Malawi; in s Africa confined to lowland forests N of Beira.
Status: Locally common resident.
Habitat: Lowland evergreen forest.
Habits: Apparently usually solitary. Forages mainly on or near forest floor among debris, especially around moss-covered logs, but also into middle layers of forest

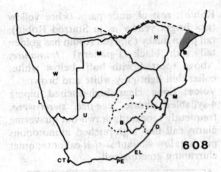

among creepers; attends columns of driver ants. Poorly known.
Food: Insects, spiders, small frogs.
Breeding: Unrecorded.

609 (592)   Thrush Nightingale   Plate 51
Lysternagtegaal
Luscinia luscinia

[Sprosser]

Measurements: Length 16–18 cm; wing ♂ 84–95, ♀ 83–90; tail (12) 63–71; tarsus (12) 25–28; culmen (12) 16–17. Weight (2) 20,5–28 g.
Bare Parts: Iris brown; bill pale brown, culmen and tip darker; legs and feet pinkish brown.
Identification: Size smallish; no obvious distinguishing marks; above brown, shading to rufous on rump and tail (distinguishes it from *Acrocephalus* warblers; River Warbler greener above); below off-white with cloudy brown mottling on chest (visible at close range only); best identified by song.
Voice: Rich melodious song, usually starting with sharp *chuk-chuk-chuk* and interspersed with *chuk* notes.

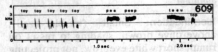

Distribution: Breeds n Palaearctic; migrates to Africa and s Arabia; in s Africa recorded scattered localities in Transvaal, Zimbabwe, Botswana, Namibia and Mozambique.

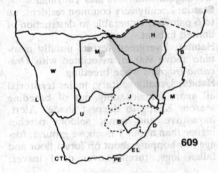

Status: Locally common, but generally uncommon; nonbreeding Palaearctic migrant, December to April.
Habitat: Thickets of bushy plants like *Grewia flava* and *Lantana camara*; also riverine bush.
Habits: Usually solitary. Sings from concealed low perch in bush; stops singing when disturbed. Darts quickly from one thicket to another; generally shy and hard to see.
Food: Insects, spiders, worms, snails.
Breeding: Extralimital.

Ref. Van Nierop, F. 1976. *Bokmakierie* 28:39.

610 (538)

Boulder Chat
Swartberglyster
Pinarornis plumosus

Plate 50

[Steindroßling]

Measurements: Length 23–27 cm; wing (3) 110–118; tail 114–132; tarsus 27–31; culmen 18,5–20,5. Weight (1 ♂) 65,8 g.

Bare Parts: Iris brown; bill, legs and feet black.

Identification: Medium (about size of starling); overall sooty blackish brown with white-tipped tail; throat barred whitish (barely visible in field); in flight broad white bar across wing (not visible at rest). *Immature*: Like adult.

Voice: Sustained series of 3-note phrases like squeaky wheel, falling in pitch by almost 3 tones; 1 phrase/second for up to 17 minutes; also pleasant warbling or piping note with bill pointed upwards.

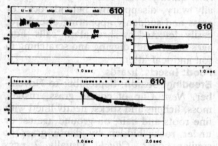

Distribution: Granite shield of Zimbabwe and adjacent Botswana.

Status: Locally fairly common resident.

Habitat: Hills and rocky outcrops with boulders on lower slopes, even isolated clumps of rocks 0,5 ha in area; usually in granite regions with some woodland canopy.

Habits: In pairs or small family groups.

Very like rockjumper in build and habits; perches on top of rock; now and then squats on tarsi, stands up, fluffs rump, then squats again. Runs over rocks, gliding from one to another; raises and lowers tail on landing.

Food: Insects and small lizards.

Breeding: *Season*: September to December (mainly October-November). *Nest*: Neatly lined cup of leaf petioles, 9 cm diameter, 4 cm deep, set in foundation of bark, small clods, dry leaves and twigs; on ground, half hidden under stone, boulder or log near base of koppie. *Clutch*: (13) 2–2,8–3 eggs (usually 3). *Eggs*: Greenish white, speckled with red-brown, concentrated at thick end, sometimes forming cap; measure (40) 27 × 18,9 (25–32,7 × 17,6–19,9). *Incubation*: Unrecorded. *Nestling*: 16–20 days; fed by both parents; when disturbed feathered young leave nest and squat under boulders.

Ref. Grobler, J.H. & Steyn, P. 1980. *Ostrich* 51:253–254.

611 (540)

Cape Rockjumper
Kaapse Berglyster
Chaetops frenatus

Plate 49

[Kap-Felsenspringer]

Measurements: Length 23–25 cm; wing 90–96; tail 100–115; tarsus 38–40; culmen 20–21.

Bare Parts: Iris red to orange-red, bill, legs and feet black.

Identification: Size medium; legs and tail longish; feet large. *Male*: crown and back grey, streaked black; wing black, spotted and barred white; rump chestnut; tail longish, black, tipped white; face, throat and upper breast black; broad white eye-

529

brow and malar stripe (conspicuous in field); rest of underparts chestnut (light orange-rufous in Orangebreasted Rockjumper). *Female*: Similar to ♂, but dull rufous where ♂ chestnut; eyebrow and malar stripe streaked with black; throat and upper breast greyish (paler in ♀ Orangebreasted Rockjumper). *Immature*: Similar to adult ♀, but shorter-tailed. *Chick*: Densely covered with slate grey down.

Voice: Shrill piping *pee-pee-pee-pee…* falling in pitch, like alarm clock running down; variety of loud piping alarm, anxiety or contact calls, *peeurip tri-tri-trip chitreeeprip*, etc.

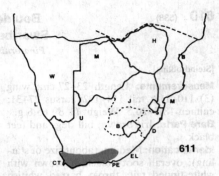

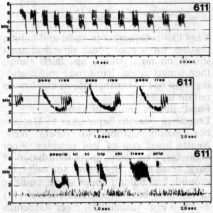

Distribution: Mountains of sw and s Cape from Cedarberg to E of Port Elizabeth (e limits not clear).

Status: Fairly common resident. Genus *Chaetops* should be in family Timaliidae (babblers), not Turdidae.

Habitat: Steeper rocky slopes from sea level to mountain tops.

Habits: Usually in pairs; sometimes in small family group. Perches on top of rock, often with tail slightly cocked; bounds or flies from one rock to another; flight alternating fluttering and gliding; runs quickly over rocks or ground. Usually wary, disappearing behind rocks or grass and suddenly appearing elsewhere; easily detected by shrill alarm calls. Forages on ground, digging and scratching in soil and leaf litter.

Food: Insects, lizards.

Breeding: *Season*: September to November. *Nest*: Cup of coarse grass, rushes, moss, lichens and sticks, neatly lined with fine roots and hair; on ground against or under rock, hidden by dense grass or similar cover. *Clutch*: Usually 2 eggs (sometimes 3, rarely 4). *Eggs*: Plain white; measure (4) 26,1 × 19,7 (25,4–26,4 × 19,6–19,8). *Incubation*: Unrecorded. *Nestling*: Unrecorded; fed by both parents; 1 extra ♂ may help to feed young.

612 (541) Orangebreasted Rockjumper Plate 49
Oranjeborsberglyster
Chaetops aurantius

Molisa-lipela, 'Mamolisa-lipela (SS), [Natal-Felsenspringer]

Measurements: Length 21–22 cm; wing (5 ♂) 89–95, (3 ♀) 84–88; tail (8) 80–100; tarsus (8) 36–41; culmen (8) 18–23,5.
Bare Parts: Iris red to brown; bill, legs and feet black.

Identification: Size medium; similar to Cape Rockjumper, but rump and breast of ♂ lighter orange-rufous (not chestnut); throat of ♀ pale buffy white (not greyish); belly of ♀ light orange-buff (paler than in ♀ of Cape Rockjumper). *Immature*: Similar to adult ♀, but with shorter tail.

Voice: Very similar to voice of Cape Rockjumper; loud *teep-teep-teep* rapidly repeated; variable strident piping calls, *pee-TEE-teep*, *prreee-pree-pree*, etc.

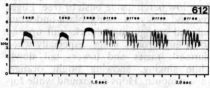

Distribution: Eastern Cape from around Graaff-Reinet to Lesotho and Natal Drakensberg, mostly above 1000 m.

Status: Fairly common resident; some seasonal altitudinal movement at highest elevations in Lesotho. Genus *Chaetops* should be in family Timaliidae, not Turdidae.

Habitat: Steeper rocky slopes, low escarpments, tumbled scree, with grass and low shrubs or bushes.

Habits: Usually in pairs or family groups. Similar to Cape Rockjumper. Leaps from rock to rock, often with little wing action, but flies and glides well. Runs fast, sometimes with tail cocked.

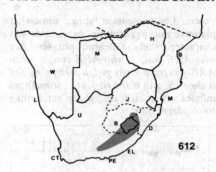

Wary and vocal when disturbed, especially near nest or young, running to and fro, disappearing and reappearing at different places.

Food: Insects.

Breeding: *Season*: October to December. *Nest*: Bowl of coarse grass and sticks, neatly lined with finer grass, rootlets and hair; on ground under or against rock, well hidden by grass or shrub. *Clutch*: 1–3 eggs. *Eggs*: Plain white; measure (10) 26,4 × 19,4   (24,2–27,9 × 18,6–20,2). *Incubation*: Unrecorded. *Nestling*: Unrecorded; fed by both parents.

---

613 (588)   **Whitebrowed Robin**   **Plate 51**
                     Gestreepte Wipstert

Erythropygia leucophrys

Eherekete (K), [Weißbrauen-Heckensänger]

Measurements: Length about 15 cm; wing ♂ 67–73, ♀ 64–68, (29 unsexed) 62–67,2–73; tail (16) 57–62,6–73; tarsus (16) 22–25,2–27,5; culmen (16) 14–15,4–18,5. Weight (14 ♂, Zimbabwe) 12,9–17–20,3 g, (5 ♀, Zimbabwe) 15–16–17,9 g, (63 unsexed) 16,2–18,8–22,9 g.

Bare Parts: Iris brown to red-brown; bill blackish brown, base yellowish pink; legs and feet pinkish brown to greyish.

Identification: Size small; above light brown, faintly streaked darker; rump bright orange-rufous; tail blackish, tipped white (Kalahari Robin has orange tail, tipped white, with black subterminal band); below white, streaked black on

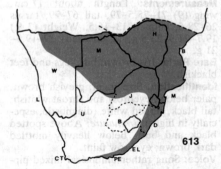

breast and flanks, with dark malar streaks (Kalahari Robin plain buffy white below). *Immature*: Spotted buff and dark brown above and below.

531

WHITEBROWED ROBIN

Voice: Loud pleasant song, somewhat plaintive and penetrating, of variable but characteristically repeated phrases, *hey who-ARE-you, who-ARE-you, who-ARE-you*, or *a pretty girl, a pretty girl, and is she rich, and is she rich,* etc.; sometimes mimics other birdcalls; sharp ratchetlike *tskirr* alarm note.

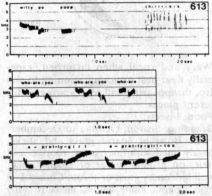

Distribution: S Africa to Uganda and Ethiopia; in s Africa absent from dry W and most of highveld.

Status: Common resident.

Habitat: Woodland and savanna with thickets and tall grass.

Habits: Usually solitary. Retiring and usually hard to see, even when singing; sings from low perch inside bush or tree. Flight low and jerky, showing black-and-white tail and orange rump; flicks tail up and down and droops wings, especially when alarmed; raises and lowers tail slowly while singing, showing bright orange-yellow mouth. Hops on ground while foraging; also catches insects in flight.

Food: Mainly insects and spiders; in winter also berries and aloe nectar.

Breeding: *Season:* September to January (mainly October-November) in Natal and Zimbabwe, October to January (also March and May) in Transvaal. *Nest:* Bulky cup of coarse grass stems, neatly lined with finer grass and rootlets; usually near ground in dense grasstuft, shrub, or other low matted vegetation, but sometimes up to 1,5 m above ground; well concealed. *Clutch:* (146) 2–2,7–4 eggs (usually 3). *Eggs:* White, spotted with light brown and grey, mainly at thick end; measure (124) 19,9 × 14,4 (17,1–22,9 × 13,2–15,5). *Incubation:* Unrecorded. *Nestling:* (3) 11–12 days.

---

614 (583) Karoo Robin Plate 51
Slangverklikker
Erythropygia coryphaeus

[Karruheckensänger]

Measurements: Length about 17 cm; wing (9) 71–75,5–79; tail 67–79; tarsus 26–28,5; culmen 13–15,5. Weight (3 ♀) 19,7–21,9–23,5 g, (4 unsexed) 19–19,9–21 g.

Bare Parts: Iris brown; bill, legs and feet blackish.

Identification: Size small; greyish brown, paler below; eyebrow and throat whitish; tail black, tipped white (diagnostic, especially in flight). *Immature:* Above spotted black and buff; below heavily mottled dark brown; eyebrow faint.

Voice: Song rather unmusical mixed piping and harsh notes, *sweep-sweep-chip, switip-switip-tweety, sweep-sweep-chrr,* etc.; prolonged harsh churring, almost hissing, alarm call, especially when mobbing.

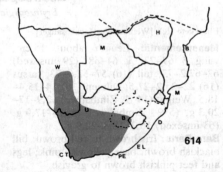

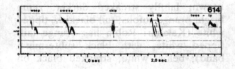

Distribution: Confined to sw parts of s Africa, from sw Cape to Karoo, s Namibia, s and e Orange Free State.
Status: Fairly common to common resident.
Habitat: Dry fynbos, karoo, thorny riverine scrub, bushy hillsides.
Habits: Usually solitary or in pairs. Bold, inquisitive and excitable; when disturbed perches on top of bush or rock, flicking tail and calling loudly; flies with fanned tail (showing black and white pattern) to cover of bush if alarmed. Forages on ground or among low branches of bushes; runs well, rarely hops. Readily mobs predators, calling harshly (see **Voice**).
Food: Insects, worms, *Lycium* fruits.

Breeding: *Season*: July to January (mainly October); probably opportunistic after rain in drier parts. *Nest*: Cup of coarse sticks, dry succulent stems and grass, neatly lined with hair, rootlets and sometimes plant down; internal diameter 3,8 cm, depth 3,8 cm; on ground under bush or other dense plant; well hidden. *Clutch*: (24) 2–2,4–4 eggs (usually 2–3). *Eggs*: Pale greenish blue, spotted and blotched with light red-brown and purplish grey, concentrated at thick end; measure (101) 20 × 14,8 (16,5–22 × 13,7–16,1). *Incubation*: (2) 14–15 days; ♂ feeds ♀ on nest, so probably only ♀ incubates. *Nestling*: (2) 13–14,5 days.

615 (586) Kalahari Robin   Plate 51
Kalahariwipstert
Erythropygia paena

Phênê (Tw), [Kalahariheckensänger]

Measurements: Length 16–17 cm; wing (15 ♂) 67–70,7–74, (7 ♀) 67–69,3–72; tail (22) 60–69; tarsus (22) 22–27; culmen (22) 14–16,5. Weight (2 ♂) 18,9–20 g, (2 ♀) 19,5–20,8 g, (29 unsexed) 16,5–19,5–22,5 g.
Bare Parts: Iris brown; bill black; legs and feet greyish black.
Identification: Size small; light sandy brown, paler below and over eye, shading to orange-rufous on rump; tail orange with broad black subterminal band and white tip (diagnostic; Whitebrowed Robin has orange on rump only; tail all dark with white tip). *Immature*: Spotted black and buff above and below.
Voice: Lively sustained song of mixed musical and harsh notes, each repeated 2–8 times, e.g. *preep, chitik, chitikik, peeo, peeo, tepeeu, tepeeu, tepeeu, preep, wip-wip-wip-wip*, etc.; grating alarm call.

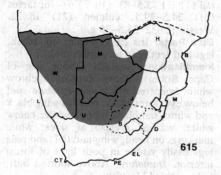

615

615

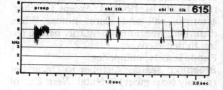

Distribution: Dry W from n Cape, w Orange Free State (from Bloemfontein), w Transvaal and sw Zimbabwe to Botswana (Chobe National Park), most of Namibia and sw Angola (Mossamedes).
Status: Fairly common to common resident.
Habitat: Open scrub and *Acacia* savanna

533

on Kalahari sands, usually with bare ground.
Habits: Solitary or in pairs. Runs fast on ground, stops now and then, flicks tail up, and runs on; may flick and droop wings. Flies low to bottom of bush, showing bright tail pattern. Sings from low concealed perch, mostly morning and evening.
Food: Insects (mainly termites, beetles, ants), spiders, centipedes, small fruits.
Breeding: *Season*: September to December or January in Zimbabwe, July to Jan-

uary (mainly October-December) in Transvaal; elsewhere opportunistically after rain (e.g. July, August, December, March-May in sw Kalahari). *Nest*: Untidy cup of coarse grass stems, neatly lined with finer grass, rootlets and sometimes hair; in low bush, tree, bunch of mistletoe or even grasstuft, from ground level to 2,5 m above ground. *Clutch*: (26) 2–2,4–3 eggs. *Eggs*: White, spotted with red-brown and grey; measure (45) 20,4 × 14,7 (18,3–23,4 × 13,8–15,6). *Incubation*: Unrecorded. *Nestling*: Unrecorded.

616 (584) Brown Robin Plate 51
Bruinwipstert
Erythropygia signata

[Natalheckensänger]

Measurements: Length 18–19 cm; wing (11 ♂) 81–86,5–92, (10 ♀) 79–81,6–88; tail (11 ♂) 73,5–83, (10 ♀) 67–76; tarsus (21) 24,5–29,5; culmen (21) 18–22. Weight (5) 32–33,5–35 g.
Bare Parts: Iris dark brown; bill black; legs and feet grey to whitish pink.
Identification: Smallish (about size of Cape Robin); above brown; eyebrow white, bordered black above; white spot below eye; lores black; bend of wing black and white; tail black, tipped white; below white, washed greyish at sides; white markings on head, wing and tail, and pale legs easily visible in poor light of forest interior. *Immature*: Above spotted buff; below scaled blackish.
Voice: Rapid *tritritritritri* call and alarm notes (diagnostic); song fairly high-pitched sweet notes in variable phrases of 6–20 notes with short pauses between, *sweet-twee-too twit-twit tree-ip*, etc., sometimes interspersed with warbling trills (higher-pitched than song of Natal Robin, but easily confused with song of Orange Thrush).

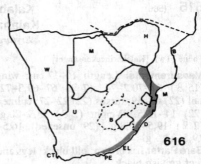

616

Distribution: Narrow forest belt from s Cape (about Humansdorp) to Zululand, Swaziland, s Mozambique (to Limpopo River) and e Transvaal.
Status: Locally fairly common resident; some local movements possible.
Habitat: Coastal, lowland and some mist-belt evergreen forest.
Habits: Usually solitary. Forages on ground in areas clear of undergrowth in dimmest forest interior, hopping along and tossing leaves aside like thrush; catches insects flushed by foraging mole-rats. Easily overlooked, except for characteristic call and alarm notes. When disturbed, freezes momentarily before flying to dense cover.
Food: Insects, millipedes.
Breeding: *Season*: October to December (mainly November) in Natal. *Nest*: Cup of

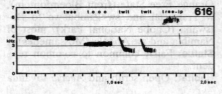

grass and roots; in hole or niche of old stump, or in dense bush, up to 3 m above ground. *Clutch*: (19) 2–2,4–3 eggs. *Eggs*: White or pale greenish blue, spotted and blotched with brown and purplish grey; measure (10) 22,6 × 16,5 (21,6–24 × 16,1–17). *Incubation*: Unrecorded. *Nestling*: Unrecorded.

617 (585) Bearded Robin Plate 51
Baardwipstert
Erythropygia quadrivirgata

[Brauner Bartheckensänger]

Measurements: Length 16–18 cm; wing ♂ 81–84, ♀ 79–81; tail 66–79; tarsus 26–29; culmen 16–18. Weight (20 ♂) 23,4–26,6–30,7 g, (12 ♀) 21,2–25,6–31,2 g, (14 unsexed) 21–24,4–29,5 g.

Bare Parts: Iris dark brown; bill black to horn; legs and feet pinkish to purplish pink.

Identification: Size small; above brown, shading to rufous on rump; eyebrow white, bordered above and below with black; black-and-white pattern on bend of wing; below white with bold black malar stripes (diagnostic, combined with bold eyebrow pattern); breast and flanks tawny; tail black, tipped white. *Immature*: Spotted and scaled with buff and dark brown above and below.

Voice: Rich sustained song of variable piping and fluting notes, involving much mimicry of songs of other bird species; harsh *chek-chek-cherrr* alarm call; low *chuk* callnote.

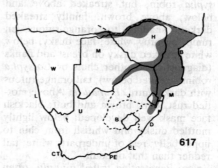

Distribution: Eastern Africa from Zululand to Somalia; in s Africa confined to lowlands on e littoral plain and Limpopo, Sabi, Lundi and Zambezi basins.

Status: Fairly common resident.

Habitat: Lowland and riverine mixed woodland, forest and thickets, especially with thorny and grassy tangles along streams and dongas.

Habits: Solitary or in pairs. Secretive and seldom seen, but sings loudly, mostly September-December; neighbouring birds often sing in reply. Forages in low bushes or by hopping on ground, tail somewhat cocked, scratching among leaf litter; active mostly dawn and dusk, and on overcast days; inactive in heat of day, keeping to dense cover.

Food: Insects (beetles, ants, termites, etc.), spiders, centipedes.

Breeding: *Season*: September to December in Zimbabwe, September to November in Natal; mainly October. *Nest*: Cup of roots, twigs and stems, lined with shredded bark and hair; in crevice or cavity of tree, or behind loose bark; usually 1–3 m above ground. *Clutch*: (33) 2–2,8–3 eggs. *Eggs*: Light blue-green, heavily spotted and blotched with dark brown, red-brown and mauve; measure (67) 20,3 × 14,8 (18,2–21,9 × 13,8–15,7). *Incubation*: (2) 13–14 days. *Nestling*: (1) 15 days.

618 (660)

Herero Chat
Hererospekvreter
Namibornis herero

Plate 50

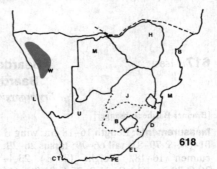

618

[Namibschnäpper]

Measurements: Length about 17 cm; wing (4 ♂) 90–95, (6 ♀) 89–91; tail (2) 69–72; tarsus (2) 21–22; culmen (2) 14–15.

Bare Parts: Iris brown; bill, legs and feet black.

Identification: Size small; similar to *Cossypha* robin, but streaked above and below; above brown, faintly streaked darker, shading to orange-rufous on rump; eyebrow white; face dusky; below white streaked dusky on breast and flanks (diagnostic; no other chats or *Cossypha* robins streaked below); tail orange-rufous with dark centre. *Immature*: Above mottled rust, dark brown and buff; blackish face mask well developed; below lightly mottled dusky and whitish from chin to upper belly; rest of underparts white; tail redder than that of adult.

Voice: Penetrating trilled *ji-ju-jiiu*, often repeated; song mellow trilled warble of short jumbled phrases; harsh *churrr* alarm note.

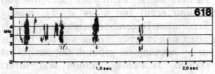

618

Distribution: Nw Namibia in Naukluft Mountains.

Status: Locally fairly common resident.

Habitat: Mountain slopes and hillsides along Namibian escarpment, with mixed *Acacia* and *Commiphora* trees 3–4 m tall, ground almost bare, rainfall 75–250 mm/year; some local movement westward into Namib after good rains.

Habits: Solitary, in pairs or small groups of up to 5 birds. Hunts from low perch in bush or tree, picking food off ground; hops on ground. Flight wavy; flicks wings 1–3 times on landing. Not usually shy, perching on outer branches of bushes.

Food: Small insects (including ants), berries of *Commiphora saxicola*, scraps at picnic sites.

Breeding: *Season*: February to April. *Nest*: Bulky cup of dry grass, fibres and rootlets, bound with silky seeds and spider web, sometimes lined with cottony material; inside diameter 5,5 cm, depth 3,5 cm; overall diameter about 8 cm, depth about 6 cm; in outer twigs of bush or tree, 1,3–4 m above ground. *Clutch*: 1–2 eggs. *Eggs*: Pale greenish white, speckled with dark red-brown, sometimes concentrated at thick end; measure (4) 22,5 × 16,1 (21–23,2 × 15,1–16,6). *Incubation*: Unrecorded. *Nestling*: Unrecorded.

Ref. Jensen, R.A.C. & Jensen, M.K. 1971. *Ostrich Suppl.* 8:105–116.

26:15. Family 77 SYLVIIDAE—WARBLERS, CISTICOLAS, PRINIAS, ETC.

Small to medium (mostly small). Bill usually small and slender, sometimes stout, sometimes moderately long, arched on culmen, or nearly straight; legs slender, short to long; toes slender, moderately long; wings usually medium and rounded (sometimes pointed); flight usually jerky or bouncing; tail variable, usually medium, square or rounded; plumage typically dull coloured; sexes usually similar; arboreal to grassland or semi-terrestrial in wide variety of habitats; solitary or gregarious; nest cup-shaped or domed in tree, bush, grass or on ground; eggs 2–10 (usually 3–5), variable in colour and markings, sometimes plain; chick usually naked at hatching; mouth and tongue of nestling yellow with two or three black spots on tongue in most species; incubation by both sexes or by female only; young cared for by both sexes. Distribution Africa, Eurasia, Australasia, most of N America, tropical S America; about 340 species; 71 (possibly 73) species in s Africa. The Sylviidae are here considered to exclude the Australian wren-warblers (Maluridae) and thornbills (Acanthizidae). Because of their small size, dull colours, closed habitat and often skulking habits, warblers present identification difficulties, even to experts. A combination of habitat, plumage, behaviour and voice is usually necessary for certain identification, especially among the reed warblers (*Acrocephalus*), cisticolas (*Cisticola*, sometimes considered to form their own family, the Cisticolidae) and the small Palaearctic migrant warblers of the genera *Sylvia*, *Hippolais*, and *Phylloscopus*.

619 (595)   Garden Warbler   Plate 54
Tuinsanger
Sylvia borin

Niini (K), Timba (Sh), [Gartengrasmücke]

Measurements: Length 14–15 cm; wing (30 ♂) 78–80,7–84, (16 ♀) 77–80,7–85, 135 unsexed) 72–79,2–84; tail (30 ♂) 52,5–55,7–58,5, (17 ♀) 53–55,5–60, (108 unsexed) 48–56,1–62,5; tarsus (119) 16–20,6–25; culmen (119) 9–12,4–15,5. Weight (31 ♂) 17,1–19,5–29,2 g, (19 ♀) 15,1–18,5–21,2 g, (616 unsexed) 15–19,2–29 g.

Bare Parts: Iris brown to greyish brown; bill blackish to brown, base pinkish to yellowish; legs and feet blue-grey to grey-brown.

Identification: Size small; build fairly robust; no distinctive markings; above brown, including wings; below greyish white (not yellowish as in Willow Warbler); head rounded; bill relatively short; tail square or slightly rounded (not notched as in Willow Warbler); no white eyebrow or outer rectrices as in Olive-tree Warbler. See also under **Status**.

Voice: Rapid babbling jumble of mellow chirping, bubbling, chirruping and zipping notes, with pauses (less sustained than song of Whitethroat); sharp *chak-chak* callnote; harsh *charrr* alarm note.

Distribution: Breeds n Europe and n Asia; migrates to Africa; in s Africa absent from Cape Province S of Orange River and from extreme dry W; vagrant to Grahamstown.

Status: Common nonbreeding Palaearctic migrant, September to April; returns to

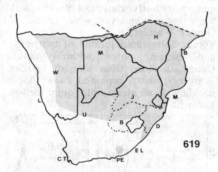

619

same areas in successive seasons. *S. b. borin* from w Palaearctic (browner above; throat and breast pale creamy white; wing more than 79 mm) commoner in Zimbabwe (about 60%), less common in drier W; *S. b. woodwardi* (more olive above, crown darker; throat white) less common in Zimbabwe (about 40%), but much commoner in dry W.

Habitat: Woodland, thickets (including *Lantana*), riverine bush and forest, montane forest edges, gardens.

Habits: Usually solitary; sometimes 2–3 birds together. Not shy, but easily overlooked unless singing; sings from concealed position deep within bush or brushwood. Forages among foliage of trees and bushes.

Food: Insects, soft fruits (mulberries, blackberries, *Asparagus*, *Lantana*, figs).

Breeding: Extralimital.

537

620 (594)   Whitethroat   Plate 54
Witkeelsanger
Sylvia communis

Niini (K), Timba (Sh), [Dorngrasmücke]

Measurements: Length about 15 cm; wing (7) 70,5–72,3–74; tail 57–64; tarsus 20–22; culmen 11–11,5. Weight (9) 13–16,4–22 g.

Bare Parts: Iris brown to yellowish brown; bill greyish brown, base paler; legs and feet pinkish brown.

Identification: Size small; above brown, head brownish grey in ♂, brown in ♀; wings edged rusty brown (diagnostic in most populations); throat white; breast washed pinkish in ♂, buff in ♀ (contrasting with white throat; diagnostic); rest of underparts buffy white; tail blackish with white outer edges (no white in tail of Garden Warbler).

Voice: Song rapid jumble of twittering and chirping notes, without pauses (more sustained than song of Garden Warbler); sharp repeated *chuk*; harsh scolding *sharrr* alarm note; quiet mellow *voit-voit wit-wit*.

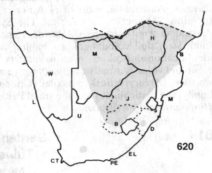

620

Distribution: Breeds N Africa, Europe and Asia; migrates to Africa and s Asia; in s Africa from Orange Free State, Transvaal and N Cape northwards; vagrant elsewhere.

Status: Generally sparse nonbreeding Palaearctic migrant, November to April. Three subspecies occur: *S. c. communis* (wing ♂ 66–72,5, ♀ 65,7–72; wing coverts and secondaries edged brown) widespread Botswana and Zimbabwe; *S. c. volgensis* (wing 66,3–77; wing coverts and secondaries edged pale rufous) in Transvaal, Botswana and Zimbabwe; *S. c. icterops* (wing ♂ 73–77,5; wing coverts and secondaries edged rusty) in Transvaal, Zimbabwe, Botswana, n Cape, Namibia.

Habitat: Savanna woodland (usually drier than habitat of Garden Warbler).

Habits: Usually solitary. Active and restless; often raises crown feathers and fans tail. Forages among foliage of trees, or catches insects in flight.

Food: Insects, fruit (including *Rhus pyroides*).

Breeding: Extralimital.

621 (658)   Titbabbler   Plate 55
Bosveldtjeriktik
Parisoma subcaeruleum

[Meisensänger]

Measurements: Length 14–16 cm; wing (29 ♂) 62–66,9–71, (17 ♀) 62–64,9–69; tail (46) 62–74; tarsus (46) 19–23; culmen (46) 10–13,5. Weight (6 ♂) 13,2–15,5–16,8 g, (5 ♀) 14,7–15,5–16,2 g, (175 unsexed) 11–14,4–18,6 g.

Bare Parts: Iris white, greyish white or cream; bill black; legs and feet slaty black.

Identification: Size small; above dull bluegrey; tail black, tipped white, conspicuous in flight; throat white, boldly streaked black (not always easy to see in field); breast and belly grey; undertail bright chestnut (diagnostic); eye white (conspicuous at close range). *Immature*: Below uniform grey (no black-and-white streaking on throat).

Voice: Commonest callnote sharp *cheriktik* or *cheriktiktik* (hence Afrikaans name), often answered by conspecific; song loud melodious piping and bubbling notes, interspersed with *chrrr* or *cheriktik* phrases; imitates other bird species, including Diederik Cuckoo, Greater Honeyguide, Southern Grey Tit, Longbilled Crombec, Spotted Prinia, Cape and Pririt Batises, Fiscal Shrike, Bokmakierie, Cape White-eye, Whitethroated Canary and Cape Bunting.

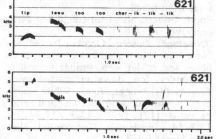

Distribution: Southern Africa (except wetter e and ne parts) to Angola.
Status: Common resident.
Habitat: Thornveld, riverine bush and scrub, semi-arid scrub, bushy hillsides, thickets in savanna.
Habits: Usually solitary or in pairs. Forages by hopping restlessly through foliage and branches of bushes and smaller trees, calling often; gleans preferentially off bare branches; rather titlike in habits; flies low from bush to bush. Inquisitive; can be called up by spishing (see Glossary). Display flight with head raised, somewhat larklike.
Food: Insects, spiders, fruit.
Breeding: *Season:* August to December in sw Cape, August to March (mainly October-December) in Transvaal, October to January in Natal, September to March (mainly September-November) in Zimbabwe, December to April in sw Kalahari (where probably partly opportunistic after rain). *Nest:* Thin-walled cup of dry grass, rootlets and spider web, lined with fine plant fibres and down; 1,5–3 m above ground in smaller branches of bush or outer twigs of tree; often in bunch of mistletoe. *Clutch:* (45) 2–2,5–4 eggs (usually 2–3). *Eggs:* White, spotted with greenish brown, brown and blue-grey concentrated at thick end; measure (155) 18,2 × 13,8 (16,3–20,3 × 12,6–14,8). *Incubation:* (2) 13–15 days. *Nestling:* (2) 14–15 days.

622 (659)   **Layard's Titbabbler**   **Plate 55**
Grystjeriktik
Parisoma layardi

[Layards Meisensänger]

Measurements: Length 14–16 cm; wing (7 ♂) 64–65,7–67, (3 ♀) 64–66,5; tail (10) 61–64; tarsus (10) 18–21; culmen (10) 10,5–12. Weight (3 ♂) 14–14,8–15,5 g.
Bare Parts: Iris white to yellowish white; bill, legs and feet black.
Identification: Size small; similar to Titbabbler, but undertail white; above dull grey; below white, streaked black on throat, washed greyish on flanks; tail black, tipped white (obvious in flight); eye white (conspicuous at close range). *Immature:* Lacks streaks on throat.

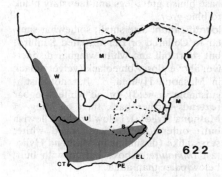

539

Voice: Song similar to that of Titbabbler, but mellower, less sustained and variable—*chrr peetu-peetu-peetu, chitititi peetu peetu peetu peetu chichichichip*, in crescendo bursts, sweet and melodious. Less vocal than Titbabbler.

Distribution: Highveld and dry w parts of s Africa from Lesotho and Natal border, through Karoo to sw Cape, s and w Namibia.

Status: Locally fairly common, but generally scarce.

Habitat: High montane or arid to semi- arid scrub and bushes in ravines, on steep mountainsides and rocky slopes.

Habits: Usually solitary or in pairs. Somewhat skulking, so easily overlooked, but inquisitive and can be called up by spishing (see Glossary); forages low down in thick bushes and shrubs, mainly from leaves and twigs. May snap wings in flight from bush to bush, usually in high arc, seldom in straight line; in display flight bounds into air, singing at each bound, then descends steeply on stiff wings. Also sings from perch.

Food: Insects; also fruit (including *Ficus cordata*).

Breeding: *Season*: October-November. *Nest*: Neat thin-walled cup of grass, plant fibres and spider web, similar to nest of Titbabbler; low down in matted bush. *Clutch*: (4) 3 eggs. *Eggs*: White, fairly evenly spotted with brown and grey; measure (12) 17,8 × 13,3 (17,2–19 × 12,7–14). *Incubation*: Unrecorded. *Nestling*: Unrecorded.

623 (670)   Yellowbreasted Hyliota   Plate 58
Geelborshyliota
Hyliota flavigaster

[Gelbbauch-Hyliota]

Measurements: Length about 13 cm; wing (22 ♂) 65,5–71,2–78, (10 ♀) 68– 71,6–74,5; tail (22 ♂) 42–46,5–52,5, (10 ♀) 42–46,7–49; tarsus (5) 17–19; culmen (22 ♂) 15–15,9–17, (10 ♀) 15– 15,8–16,5. Weight (1) 11,7 g.

Bare Parts: Iris dark brown; bill black, base bluish grey; legs and feet slaty black to blue-grey.

Identification: Size small; somewhat similar to Collared or Bluethroated Sunbird, but short bill and white wingbar distinctive; above glossy blueblack (velvety black in Mashona Hyliota ♂, but not distinguishable in field); broad white wingbar (extends further back than on wing of Mashona Hyliota); below bright yellowish buff; outermost rectrices edged white; sexes alike (dissimilar in Mashona Hyliota). *Immature*: Above barred with buff; below paler than adult.

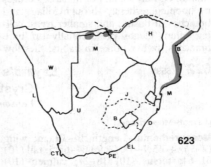

Voice: Quiet 2-syllabled whistle, frequently uttered; excited chattering.

Distribution: Africa S of Sahara to Limpopo and Okavango Rivers; in s Africa confined to Mozambique littoral and e Caprivi.

Status: Fairly common resident.

Habitat: Open woodland, mainly *Brachystegia*.

Habits: Usually solitary or in pairs; often

in mixed bird parties. Forages in canopy of trees by gleaning from leaves, flowers and branches; movements quick and restless; may hawk insects in flight. Inconspicuous and easily overlooked. Poorly known.

Food: Insects.

Breeding: *Season*: October to December in Mozambique and Zambia. *Nest*: Small open cup of moss, stems, and lichens (somewhat like nest of *Batis*); in tree at almost any height above ground. *Clutch*: 2 eggs. *Eggs*: Dull white, with zone of brown and lilac spots and squiggles around thick end; measure about 17 × 13. *Incubation*: Unrecorded. *Nestling*: Unrecorded.

624 (668)

Mashona Hyliota
Mashonahyliota
Hyliota australis

Plate 58

[Maschona-Hyliota]

Measurements: Length about 12 cm; wing (39 ♂) 66,5–70,5–76,5, (25 ♀) 64–68,3–74; tail (25 ♂) 43–47–50,5, (12 ♀) 41–45,1–49; tarsus (9) 16–19,5; culmen (25 ♂) 14–14,7–15,5, (12 ♀) 14–14,9–16. Weight (1 ♂) 12,4 g, (1 ♀) 12,3 g.

Bare Parts: Iris dark brown; bill black, base bluish grey; legs and feet black.

Identification: Size small to very small; similar to Yellowbreasted Hyliota. *Male*: Above dull velvety black (glossy blue-black in Yellowbreasted Hyliota); broad white wingbar conspicuous in flight (but straight across, not extending backwards as in Yellowbreasted Hyliota); below bright yellowish buff; outermost rectrices edged white. *Female*: Similar to ♂, but brownish grey above; more white in outer rectrices than in ♂. *Immature*: Similar to adult ♀, but paler below.

Voice: Repeated squeaking whistles, followed by warbling trill; twittering contact call; sharp high-pitched *zik* or *tsik*.

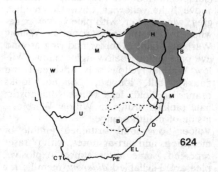

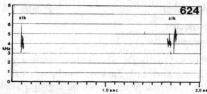

Distribution: Eastern and C Africa; in s Africa confined to Zimbabwe as far S as Matobo Hills, W to Mabali crossroads on Bulawayo-Victoria Falls road, and Mozambique as far S as Limpopo River.

Status: Uncommon resident; some seasonal altitudinal movement possible at higher elevations.

Habitat: Canopy of *Brachystegia* woodland; also riverine *Acacia albida*.

Habits: Usually solitary or in pairs or family groups with year-round territories; joins mixed bird parties. Forages in crowns of trees, gleaning from leaves and branches; may hawk insects in flight. Flight rapid, zigzag; usually lands out of sight behind branch. Quiet and easily overlooked, but aggressive near nest, chasing away other bird species.

Food: Insects.

Breeding: *Season*: August to January (mainly September) in Zimbabwe. *Nest*: Neat deep cup of lichens, somewhat like nest of *Batis*; in lichen-covered fork of topmost branches of tree, 6–7,5 m above ground. *Clutch*: 2–4 eggs. *Eggs*: Pinkish white, minutely spotted with brown and slate concentrated in ring around thick end; measure (10) 17,2 × 13,2 (15–18,9 × 11,5–14,6). *Incubation*: Unrecorded. *Nestling*: Unrecorded.

625 (596)   Icterine Warbler   Plate 54
Spotvoël
Hippolais icterina

Niini (K), Timba (Sh), [Gelbspötter]

Measurements: Length 14–15 cm; wing (7) 69,5–75,7–81; tail 51–56; tarsus 19–22; culmen 13–14,5. Weight (7) 7,6–12,1–14 g.

Bare Parts: Iris brown; bill brown above, yellow below; legs and feet blue-grey.

Identification: Size small; build robust (somewhat like *Acrocephalus* warbler); above light yellowish olive to greenish grey; wing darker, with pale yellow panel when folded (no pale panel in Willow Warbler); faint eyebrow and ring around eye pale yellow; below light yellow (Willow Warbler yellow only on breast and flanks); bill, longish, pointed, looks orange in field; legs bluish (diagnostic; pale pinkish brown in Willow Warbler); inside of mouth orange.

Voice: Song loud sustained jumble of melodious and jarring notes, with phrases repeated, some notes almost explosive; pleasant 3-syllabled *dideroit*; metallic *tek* callnote; short harsh *chirr* alarm note.

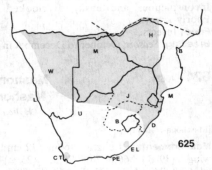

625

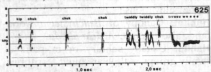

largely absent from S, much of highveld and dry W; sometimes recorded as far S as East London; vagrant to Cape of Good Hope Nature Reserve, w Cape.

Status: Sparse to common nonbreeding Palaearctic migrant, October to April; possibly commoner than records show.

Habitat: Usually *Acacia* savanna and thorn thickets; also mixed woodland and exotic plantations.

Habits: Usually solitary. Conspicuous because of frequent loud song; sings from exposed perch, with bill wide open and pointed upwards; also sings while foraging, creeping and hopping quickly along branches. Easily overlooked when not singing.

Food: Insects, spiders, berries.

Breeding: Extralimital.

Distribution: Breeds Europe and w Asia; migrates to Africa and Arabia; in s Africa

626 (597)   Olivetree Warbler   Plate 54
Olyfboomsanger
Hippolais olivetorum

[Olivenspötter]

Measurements: Length 16–18 cm; wing (13) 80–90; tail 65–71; tarsus 22–24,5; culmen (10) 15,5–17,5. Weight (3) 20,2–23,4 g.

Bare Parts: Iris greyish brown; bill horn brown, paler below; legs and feet yellowish to pinkish brown or pinkish grey.

Identification: Large (about size of Cape Reed Warbler); above brownish grey, wings and tail darker; eyebrow indistinct; closed wing shows pale grey panel on secondaries; outer rectrices edged white (conspicuous in flight in fresh plumage only); below whitish; bill longish, pointed.

Voice: Song loud slow jumble of harsh and grating churring and gurgling notes, krek-krek, krak, krak, krok-krek krek, etc.; subsong like that of Great Reed Warbler; harsh *chuk-chuk* alarm notes; soft *tuk* callnote.

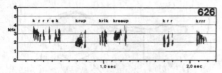

Distribution: Breeds se Europe and Middle East; migrates to Africa; in s Africa recorded mainly from scattered localities in Zimbabwe, Transvaal and Natal; also Botswana.
Status: Uncommon and local nonbreeding Palaearctic migrant, December to March.
Habitat: *Acacia* savanna and thorn thickets.

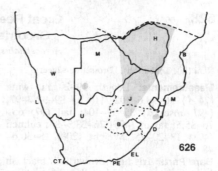

Habits: Usually solitary. Forages about 2–3 m above ground in thick cover. Skulking and easily overlooked.
Food: Insects, fruit.
Breeding: Extralimital.

Ref. Sinclair, J.C. 1976. *Bokmakierie* 28:19.

627 (598)   River Warbler   Plate 52
Sprinkaansanger
Locustella fluviatilis

[Schlagschwirl]

Measurements: Length 13–15 cm; wing 67–80; tail 57–58; tarsus 21–22; culmen 12–14.
Bare Parts: Iris greyish brown; bill brown, base yellow; legs and feet pale pink to pale horn.
Identification: Very difficult to identify in field. Size small; above plain olive brown; eyebrow pale; below whitish, faintly streaked dark brown on breast and flanks; tail broad, rounded or somewhat wedge-shaped.
Voice: Harsh widely-spaced *klak klak*, or *ziki-ziki-ziki-ziki*, sometimes faster, sometimes slower (likened to sound of distant steam locomotive), ending with 4–5 *swee* notes; strident callnote.

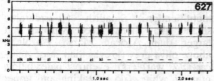

Distribution: Breeds e Europe and w Russia; migrates to Africa; in s Africa

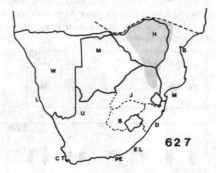

recorded from scattered localities in Transvaal, Botswana, Zimbabwe and Mozambique.
Status: Rare nonbreeding Palaearctic migrant, about December to February.
Habitat: Dense riverine vegetation; also short grass in *Brachystegia* woodland.
Habits: Usually solitary. Skulking and easily overlooked; forages low down near ground. Flies reluctantly. Sings from exposed perch, often in shade of large tree.
Food: Insects.
Breeding: Extralimital.

628 (603)   Great Reed Warbler   Plate 52
Grootrietsanger
Acrocephalus arundinaceus

Niini (K), Timba (Sh), [Drosselrohrsänger]

Measurements: Length 19–20 cm; wing (24 ♂) 96–98,6–102, (16 ♀) 89–92,7–97, (497 unsexed) 85–97–104; tail (97) 65–76–85,5; tarsus (495) 26–28,3–33; culmen (495) 18–20–25. Weight (200) 18–30,6–48 g.

Bare Parts: Iris light brown; bill blackish brown above, pinkish yellow below; legs and feet greenish grey, brown or pinkish, soles yellow.

Identification: Large (about size of Cape Robin); bill heavy; above plain brown; eyebrow pale, thin, well-defined; below white; spreads tail in flight. *A. a. arundinaceus*: above darker, below creamy white; lower throat faintly streaked grey; flanks deeper buff (commoner in S Africa); *A. a. zarudnyi*: above paler, more olive brown; below whiter (commoner in Zimbabwe).

Voice: Song rather harsh creaking and scraping sounds, *gruk-gruk kree kree chitip chitip, kip krip kreek krip gruk gruk,* etc.; rather ventriloquial.

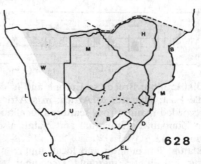

628

Distribution: Breeds Europe and Asia; migrates to Africa, s Asia, Australasia; in s Africa absent from most of Cape Province S of Orange River, Lesotho and driest w parts.

Status: Locally common nonbreeding Palaearctic migrant, November to March (sometimes to April).

Habitat: Reedbeds, rank vegetation along watercourses, gardens, canefields; not necessarily near water.

Habits: Solitary. Flies low with fanned tail; plunges somewhat heavily into cover. Forages low down in dense vegetation, often rustling reeds as it moves; rarely perches in open, even on tree or telephone line.

Food: Insects, spiders, tiny frogs.

Breeding: Extralimital.

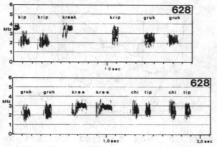

629 (–)   Basra Reed Warbler   Plate 52
Basrarietsanger
Acrocephalus griseldis

[Basra-Rohrsänger]

Measurements: Length about 16–17 cm; wing (157) 73–81,7–88; tarsus (154) 22–24,6–28; culmen (154) 17–18,7–24. Weight (143) 15,5–23,5 g.

Bare Parts: Iris brown; bill brown above, pinkish horn below; legs and feet brownish grey.

Identification: Smallish (considerably smaller than Great Reed Warbler, but larger than African Marsh Warbler); above olive grey (greyer than most *Acrocephalus* warblers); eyebrow pale; below creamy white (no streaking on upper breast as in Great Reed Warbler); flanks washed buff; bill relatively long (finer and narrower than bill of Great Reed Warbler).

Voice: Very similar to that of Great Reed Warbler (small greyish *Acrocephalus* singing like Great Reed Warbler is probably Basra Reed Warbler).

Distribution: Breeds Iraq; migrates mainly to E Africa; in s Africa collected only lower Zambezi Valley, Mozambique, and Empangeni, Zululand; sight records from 80–90 km N of Beira.

Status: Very rare nonbreeding Palaearctic migrant, at very edge of range; formerly considered subspecies of Great Reed Warbler.

Habitat: Tall weedy growth in woodland, secondary forest.

Habits: Solitary. Similar to other *Acrocephalus* warblers. Poorly known in nonbreeding area.

Food: Insects.

Breeding: Extralimital.

---

630 (604X)   Eurasian Reed Warbler   Plate 52
Hermanse Rietsanger
Acrocephalus scirpaceus

[Teichrohrsänger]

Measurements: Length about 13 cm; wing (13) 60–63,8–68; tail (27) 49–55; tarsus (27) 23–24; culmen (13) 17–18,1–19,4; width of bill at nostrils (13) 3,6–4,1–4,4. Weight (Africa, 13) 8,5–10–12 g, (Europe, 347) 9–11,3–17 g.

Bare Parts: Iris light brown; bill dark horn above, pale pinkish or yellowish horn below; legs and feet brown to greyish horn.

Identification: Small (about size of African Marsh Warbler); very similar to Eurasian Marsh Warbler, but bill longer, more slender, forehead more sloping; wing longer and more pointed than in African Marsh Warbler, otherwise almost identical in the field; above plain brown, tinged rufous; eyebrow indistinct; below buff, paler in centre of belly; legs usually dark brown (pink in Eurasian Marsh Warbler).

Voice: Song rather squeaky unmusical series of notes, each repeated 2–3 times, *churr-churr-churr*, *cherek-cherek-cherek*, etc. (song of Eurasian Marsh Warbler) more melodious); deep *chak* or shrill *skarr* alarm notes.

Distribution: Breeds Europe and w Asia; migrates to Africa; in s Africa recorded from Klip River, Transvaal (December 1975), Windhoek, Namibia (January 1965), Bushmanland (January 1986), Kavango (February 1986, December 1986, February 1987); normally not further S than Zambia, but possibly regular in s Africa.

Status: Very rare nonbreeding Palaearctic migrant, February; possibly visitor to s Africa only in some years; may be conspecific with African Marsh Warbler.

Habitat: *Phragmites* reedbeds, riverine trees, dense bush, tall dry grass.

Habits: Solitary. Spreads tail in low flight over water or ground. Fairly shy, keeping to dense cover.

Food: Insects, spiders; rarely also berries.

Breeding: Extralimital.

Ref. Komen, J. & Myer, E. 1988. *Ostrich* 59:142–143.

631 (606) **African Marsh Warbler** **Plate 52**
Kleinrietsanger
Acrocephalus baeticatus

Niini (K), Timba (Sh), [Gartenrohrsänger]

Measurements: Length 12–13 cm; wing (427) 51,5–57,6–63; tail (93) 43–48–54; tarsus (82) 19,5–21,6–24; culmen (82) 12–13,7–16,5. Weight (8 ♂) 9,3–10,3–11,2 g, (3 ♀) 8,8–10,4–11,8 g, (523 unsexed) 7,3–10,3–15 g.

Bare Parts: Iris light brown; bill blackish horn to brown above, yellowish below; legs and feet greenish horn to yellowish grey, soles yellow.

Identification: Size small (one of the smallest *Acrocephalus* species; smaller than Eurasian Marsh Warbler; wing shorter and more rounded than in Eurasian Reed Warbler, but almost indistinguishable in the field); above light medium brown (faintly more rufous than Eurasian Marsh Warbler); eyebrow indistinct; below buffy white, faintly washed cinnamon-buff across breast and flanks; legs pale; tail smoky brown, lightly tipped buff. *Immature*: Like adult.

Voice: Song sustained grating and squeaky notes varying in pitch, *chuk-chuk-chuk, chrr-chrr-chrr, chirruk-chirruk-chirruk, cheeek cheeek*, etc.; similar to song of Eurasian Reed Warbler; lacks fluty bubbling notes of Cape Reed and Eurasian Marsh Warblers; harsh scolding alarm note.

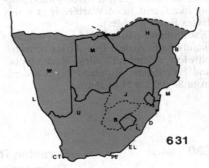

631

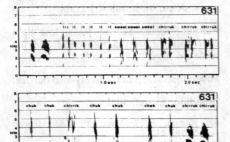

Distribution: Whole of s Africa, to E Africa.

Status: Common breeding intra-African migrant; winters in C Africa; may be conspecific with Eurasian Reed Warbler.

Habitat: Mostly reedbeds, tall grass, rank weeds, swampy areas, margins of sewage ponds, willow groves on rivers and dams; also rank vegetation away from water, gardens, exotic wattles in sw Cape.

Habits: Usually solitary or in pairs. Skulks low down in dense vegetation, but can be called up by spishing (see Glossary); emerges briefly to investigate intruder, then dives back into vegetation; when alarmed flirts tail and repeatedly jerks head and body first up then down, peering over and under foliage. Forages low down in undergrowth or higher in trees, rustling reeds and sedges as it moves.

Food: Insects.

Breeding: *Season*: September to November in Cape, October to February (mainly December-January) in Transvaal, November to January in Natal, November to March in Zimbabwe. *Nest*: Neat cup of grass and reed blades, lined with finer grass; firmly bound to upright stems of weeds sedges, reeds or arum lilies, or to leaves and inflorescences of large sedges or drooping branches of willow; usually but not always well hidden; 0,3–3 m above ground. *Clutch*: (23) 2–2,7–3 eggs (usually 3). *Eggs*: White, greyish white or pale bluish, spotted with greyish brown and grey; measure (82) 17,6 × 13,2 (16–18,7 × 12,4–14,5). *Incubation*: 12,5–14 days. *Nestling*: 14 days.

632 (–)

Cinnamon Reed Warbler
Kaneelrietsanger
Acrocephalus cinnamomeus

Plate 52

[Zimtrohrsänger]

Measurements: Length 12–13 cm; wing (8) 53–53,8–55,5; tail 42–43,5–44,5; tarsus (1) 22; culmen (8) 15–16–17.
Bare Parts: Iris light brown; bill dark horn above, yellowish below; legs and feet brownish to yellowish pink.
Identification: Size small; very similar to African Marsh Warbler, possibly not safely separable in field; above brown, faintly more reddish over mantle (darker, less rufous overall than African Marsh Warbler); below white, faintly washed buffy over breast and flanks; wings and tail darker brown than back (in hand, markedly shorter than wings and tail of African Marsh Warbler).
Voice: Unrecorded; probably very similar to that of African Marsh Warbler.
Distribution: From Maputo (Mozambique) to s Malawi, e Zambia, se Zaire, and most of Africa to Eritrea and Senegal; vagrant to Natal (Umvoti Vlei).
Status: Uncommon resident or local migrant; formerly considered subspecies

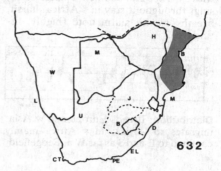

of African Marsh Warbler, but ranges overlap in Mozambique.
Habitat: Reedbeds.
Habits: Similar to those of African Marsh Warbler. Poorly known.
Food: Unrecorded; probably insects.
Breeding: Unrecorded in s Africa. *Season*: February in Zambia. Other information unrecorded.

Ref. Clancey, P.A. 1975. *Arnoldia* 7(20):1–14.

633 (607)

Eurasian Marsh Warbler
Europese Rietsanger
Acrocephalus palustris

Plate 52

[Sumpfrohrsänger]

Measurements: Length 13–14 cm; wing (2 ♂) 68–70, (114 unsexed) 58–66,2–72; tail (95) 44,5–51,4–61,5; tarsus (93) 19–22,1–24; culmen (93) 11,5–13,8–17. Weight (3 ♂) 11,2–11,9–12,9 g, (3 ♀) 10,4–11,6–12,8 g, (118 unsexed) 8,7–11,5–16 g.
Bare Parts: Iris olive brown; bill dark horn above, pinkish horn below; legs and feet brownish or yellowish pink.
Identification: Size smallish; very similar to Eurasian Reed Warbler, but legs pale pinkish (not dark brown), bill shorter and stouter, forehead more steeply sloping; above plain olive brown (less rusty brown than in Eurasian Reed Warbler); pale

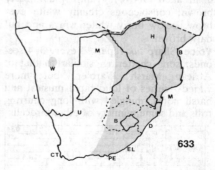

eyebrow distinct; below buffy white, washed yellowish (diagnostic at close range), darker on flanks.

547

Voice: Song musical and varied with canarylike trills, including wide range of mimicry of other birdcalls, interspersed with *chirrups* and distinctive nasal notes; sings throughout stay in s Africa; harsh, breathy *tcchhh* alarm note (highly distinctive).

Distribution: Breeds Europe and w Asia; migrates to Africa; in s Africa mainly confined to E and S as far W as Sedgefield,

Cape; specimens collected Windhoek, 1975.

Status: Uncommon to fairly common nonbreeding Palaearctic migrant, November to April.

Habitat: Thickets in various types of woodland and forest, reedbeds, rank vegetation, gardens with dense cover.

Habits: Solitary. Skulking and easily overlooked, but distinctive alarm note gives away presence; sings fairly often from concealed perch; can be called out briefly by spishing (see Glossary).

Food: Insects, berries (including *Rhus pyroides*).

Breeding: Extralimital.

---

634 (608)　　　**Eurasian Sedge Warbler**　　　**Plate 52**
Europese Vleisanger
Acrocephalus schoenobaenus

Niini (K), [Schilfrohrsänger]

Measurements: Length 12,5–14 cm; wing (257) 61–65,9–72; tail (126) 42–48,4–53,5; tarsus (110) 18,5–21–23; culmen (111) 10,5–12,7–15. Weight (493) 8,7–12,2–18,8 g.

Bare Parts: Iris brown; bill blackish horn above, yellowish pink below; legs and feet greenish grey to light brown.

Identification: Size small; crown and back greyish to olive brown, streaked black (diagnostic; all other *Acrocephalus* species unstreaked above); rump plain rusty brown; conspicuous creamy white eyebrow; below buffy white; wings and tail dark brown.

Voice: Sharp *tuk* repeated every 3–4 seconds; song chattering, similar to that of African Marsh Warbler, but more varied—series of loud rapid musical and harsh notes, mingled with long churring trills and some mimicry of other birdcalls.

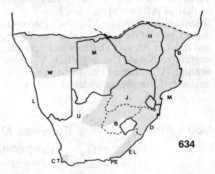

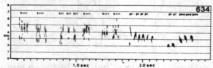

Distribution: Breeds Europe and Asia; migrates to Africa and s Asia; in s Africa

largely absent from dry W and Kalahari basin, but extends to Atlantic coast at Walvis Bay; vagrant to w Cape.

Status: Fairly common nonbreeding Palaearctic migrant, November to early May; very common in s Transvaal.

Habitat: Low emergent aquatic vegetation, swamps and sewage ponds with rank growth and sedges, weedy areas in abandoned fields.

Habits: Solitary. Forages low down in dense vegetation; easily overlooked except for song and callnote; often calls in response to disturbance.

Food: Insects, spiders; occasionally berries.

Breeding: Extralimital.

635 (604)

Cape Reed Warbler
Kaapse Rietsanger
Acrocephalus gracilirostris

Plate 52

Niini (K), Timba (Sh), [Kaprohrsänger]

Measurements: Length 17–18 cm; wing (72 ♂) 64–69,4–78, (51 ♀) 61–65,1–69; tail (54 ♂) 57–63–69, (42 ♀) 54–58,8–65,5; tarsus (99) 22–25,6–29; culmen (99) 12,5–16,3–19. Weight (74 ♂) 12,9–16,1–20,2 g, (50 ♀) 11,3–14,2–17 g, (100 unsexed) 11,3–18,6–22 g.

Bare Parts: Iris brown; bill blackish horn, base yellowish; legs and feet dark greenish or bluish horn, soles yellow.

Identification: Size fairly large (larger than African Marsh Warbler); build robust; above brown (darker than African Marsh Warbler); eyebrow fairly distinct; below buffy white, flanks dull rufous (diagnostic); legs dark brown (paler in most *Acrocephalus* warblers). *Immature*: Like adult.

Voice: Song distinctive richly melodious phrases of bubbling and trilling notes with pauses between (somewhat thrushlike; not sustained as in most other *Acrocephalus* warblers), *tewip prr-tititititi pr trrr troorreee* and variations; harsh alarm note.

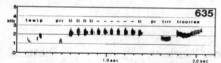

Distribution: Africa S of Sahara; most of s Africa, except Kalahari basin and most of Namibia (but present extreme n Ovamboland and Caprivi, and in S as far N as Naute Dam near Keetmanshoop).
Status: Locally common resident.
Habitat: Beds of reeds and bulrushes in standing water of lagoons, estuaries, rivers, dams, pans, marshes, vleis, lakes.
Habits: Solitary or in pairs. Forages low down in reeds, often just above water; sidles nimbly up and down vertical stems. Inquisitive, responds well to spishing (see Glossary). Highly vocal in summer.
Food: Insects, small frogs.
Breeding: *Season*: September to December in Cape, September to January (mainly December) in Natal, August to February (mainly October to January) in Transvaal, August to May (mainly November-March) in Zimbabwe. *Nest*: Neat cup of grass and reed blades, tapered below to form cone-shaped shell, lined with fine grass; firmly plaited around vertical reed stems; usually 20–120 cm above water; sometimes under nest of larger bird species. *Clutch*: (30) 2–2,3–3 eggs. *Eggs*: White to greenish or bluish white, heavily spotted with black, brown and grey; measure (31) 18,7 × 14,2 (16–21,2 × 12,6–15,3). *Incubation*: Unrecorded; by both sexes. *Nestling*: Unrecorded.

636 (604Y)

Greater Swamp Warbler
Rooibruinrietsanger
Acrocephalus rufescens

Plate 52

[Papyrusrohrsänger]

Measurements: Length about 18 cm; wing 71–85; tail 62–74; tarsus 26–30; culmen 18–20.
Bare Parts: Iris hazel to light red-brown; bill dark brown above, grey below, base yellow; legs and feet grey to blue-grey, soles yellow.

Identification: Size fairly large (larger than Cape Reed Warbler); above dark olive brown; no pale eyebrow; lores pale; throat and centre of belly white; rest of underparts light greyish brown (diagnostic; not rufous on flanks as in Cape Reed Warbler).

Voice: Song loud gurgling *churr-churr, chirrup, chuckle*, etc.; harsh *chirr* or *chirr-up* callnote.

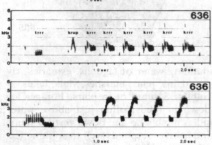

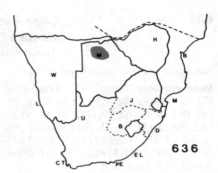

Distribution: Africa S of Sahara; in s Africa confined to Okavango region of n Botswana.

Status: Locally common resident.

Habitat: Extensive papyrus swamps.

Habits: Solitary. Skulks in papyrus, so easily overlooked. Forages by climbing up and down stems. Poorly known.

Food: Insects.

Breeding: Not recorded in s Africa. *Season*: October to February in Zambia. *Nest*: Deep cup of papyrus and grass strips, usually unlined; bound inside papyrus inflorescence or between upright stems of *Typha* over water. *Clutch*: (6) 1–1,6–2 eggs (Senegal). *Eggs*: White to pale bluish green, or pale bluish grey, sparsely or heavily spotted with grey and blackish concentrated at thick end (similar to eggs of Cape Reed Warbler); measure 20,3–21,2 × 15,1–15,5. *Incubation*: Unrecorded. *Nestling*: Unrecorded.

Ref. De Naurois, R. 1985. *Alauda* 53:181–185.

---

637 (666)   **African Yellow Warbler**   **Plate 52**
Geelsanger
Chloropeta natalensis

[Schnäpperrohrsänger]

Measurements: Length 14–15 cm; wing (17 ♂) 59–61,6–64, (7 ♀) 59–60–61, (68 unsexed) 55–61–65; tail (53) 55–60,3–66; tarsus (46) 19–21,2–23; culmen (47) 11,5–13,2–16. Weight (3 ♂) 12,1–12,3–12,5 g, (68 unsexed) 9–11,7–13,6 g.

Bare Parts: Iris brown to greyish brown; bill dark brownish horn, base yellowish; legs and feet slate grey.

Identification: Size medium; build similar to that of *Acrocephalus* warblers; above yellowish olive brown, rump yellower; ear coverts dark; below bright yellow, con-

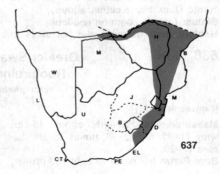

trasting with brown back; ♀ duller, less contrasting than ♂. *Immature*: Like adult ♀, but buffier.

Voice: Song shortish phrases of rich throaty and fairly shrill notes, with pauses between, very like song of Cape Reed Warbler, but less melodious—*chip chip titit reet-reet-reet-reet, rip krupkrupkrup krrrr*, etc.; sharp *chip* or *chirr* alarm note.

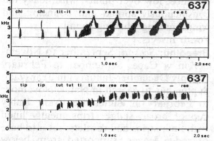

Distribution: S Africa to Cameroon and Ethiopia; in s Africa confined to extreme E as far S as Transkei; also up Zambezi Valley to e Caprivi.

Status: Locally common to scarce resident; some seasonal altitudinal movements possible at higher elevations.

Habitat: Rank vegetation and bracken along streams and gulleys, in vleis and other moist situations in woodland or at forest edges.

Habits: Usually solitary or in pairs. Keeps low down in vegetation, so easily overlooked unless singing; sings from exposed perch on top of tall plant, or from just beneath canopy; when disturbed drops into vegetation and creeps away. Forages fairly low down, snapping at insects while hopping from stem to stem; sidles up and down stems like reed warbler. Very like *Acrocephalus* warblers in habits.

Food: Insects (especially caterpillars).

Breeding: *Season*: October to February in Natal, November to February in Transvaal, January in Mozambique, September to February (mainly December) in Zimbabwe. *Nest*: Neat cup of broad grass blades, lined with finer grass; inside diameter 6 cm, depth 5 cm; firmly bound to upright stems or upright fork of herbaceous plant such as *Leonotis leonurus*; usually 30–90 cm above ground; very like nest of *Acrocephalus* warbler. *Clutch*: (11) 1–1,4–2 eggs. *Eggs*: White, sparingly spotted with pinkish brown around thick end; measure (15) 18,4 × 13,5 (17–19 × 12,7–14,1). *Incubation*: 12 days, mostly by ♀; ♂ incubates seldom. *Nestling*: 14–16 days; fed by both parents (mostly by ♀); postnestling dependence up to about 30 days.

---

638 (609)   **African Sedge Warbler**   **Plate 52**
Kaapse Vleisanger
Bradypterus baboecala

Unomakhwane (X), [Sumpfbuschsänger]

Measurements: Length 15–19 cm; wing (174) 53–58,6–66,5; tail (126) 56,5–65,5–79; tarsus (45) 19–21,5–24; culmen (126) 11–15,6–19. Weight (83) 11,2–14–17 g.

Bare Parts: Iris umber brown; bill blackish horn, base pinkish or yellowish; legs and feet pinkish, brownish or greyish.

Identification: Size medium; above dark smoky brown (much darker than any *Acrocephalus* warbler), tinged rusty towards rump; eyebrow buff; below greyish white, faintly streaked dusky on breast (diagnostic at close range only); flanks and undertail dull rufous; tail broad, rounded

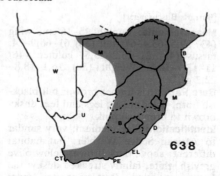

(good field character). *Immature*: Tinged yellowish below.

551

Voice: Song striking series of sharp notes in same pitch, speeding up towards end, *krrak krrak krrak krak krak-krak-krak-krak*, ending as bubbling trill and stopping abruptly; somewhat like stick held in spokes of wheel turning faster and faster, then stopped; song sometimes followed by brief *prrrr-prrrr-prrrr* wing-rattling flight display above sedges, lasting 2–3 seconds; nasal catlike *meew* alarm note.

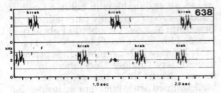

Distribution: S Africa to Chad and Ethiopia; in s Africa absent from dry W and most of Kalahari basin.

Status: Locally common resident; some local seasonal movements dictated by available water.

Habitat: Reeds and other swamp vegetation, especially sedges (*Cyperus*) and

bulrushes (*Typha*), around lagoons, marshes, sewage ponds, dams and vleis.

Habits: Usually solitary or in pairs. Very shy and hard to see; can be called up briefly by spishing (see Glossary), but quickly drops back into vegetation; may perch on exposed reed top in early morning. Forages low down over ground or water. Flies reluctantly and for only short distance, low over plants, with heavy tail conspicuously spread and bouncing and wings making whirring sound.

Food: Insects.

Breeding: *Season:* September to November in w Cape, September to February (mainly December-January) in Transvaal, September to March in Natal, November to February in Zimbabwe. *Nest:* Bulky cup of broad sedge strips, neatly lined with finer strips and rootlets; set into base of sedge leaves, supported from below (not bound around leaves as in *Acrocephalus* warblers); usually less than 70 cm above ground. *Clutch:* (9) 2–2,4–3 eggs. *Eggs:* Dull white to creamy white, spotted with yellowish to pinkish brown and light grey concentrated at thick end; measure (7) 19,2 × 13,7 (18,5–20,4 × 13,5–13,9). *Incubation:* 12–14 days. *Nestling:* 12–13 days.

---

639 (610)   **Barratt's Warbler**   **Plate 52**
                              Ruigtesanger
                              Bradypterus barratti

[Barratts Buschsänger]

Measurements: Length 15–16 cm; wing (43) 59,5–63,4–67; tail (36) 61–66,9–74; tarsus (45) 21–23,2–25,5; culmen (46) 11–13,9–16,5. Weight (36) 16,1–18,8–22,2 g.

Bare Parts: Iris umber brown; bill blackish horn, paler below; legs and feet dusky brown to brownish pink.

Identification: Size medium; very similar to African Sedge Warbler, but habitat different; above dark brown; below olive greyish white, faintly streaked dusky; tail heavy, rounded. Best separated from Knysna Warbler by song; both species occur together coastally from autumn to

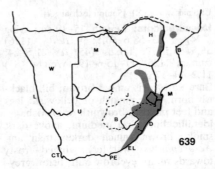

spring. *Immature:* Above more olive than adult; below yellowish.

552

Voice: Loud warbling trilling song, starting with deliberate high-pitched notes, followed by lower notes speeding up into blurred trill, *tsip-tsip-tsip-trip-tsiptsiptsiptrrrrrrrll*; quiet growling *chrr-chrr* alarm notes.

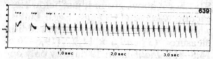

Distribution: Discontinuously from se Cape through Natal, ne Orange Free State (to Golden Gate), s Mozambique and Swaziland to e Transvaal and Zoutpansberg; also e Zimbabwe, adjacent Mozambique and Mount Gorongosa.
Status: Locally fairly common to very common resident; moves to lower altitudes in winter (e.g. to East London from Amatola Mountains).

Habitat: Dense tangled vegetation along streams, in kloofs, on forest edges; clumps of bush on coast; also montane scrub and heathlands in Zimbabwe.
Habits: Usually solitary. Forages low down in dense vegetation, or on ground; runs, does not hop. Hard to see, keeping to dense undergrowth as quiet shadowy mouselike form; presence revealed by song and callnotes.
Food: Insects and other small invertebrates.
Breeding: *Season:* October to December throughout s Africa. *Nest:* Bulky cup of leaves, stems and grass; low down in tangled scrub, well hidden. *Clutch:* (3) 2 eggs. *Eggs:* Pinkish white, thinly speckled with yellowish brown and blue-grey; measure (8) 20,5 × 15,5 (19,6–21,4 × 14,5–16,5). *Incubation:* Unrecorded. *Nestling:* Unrecorded.

---

640 (611) **Knysna Warbler** **Plate 52**
Knysnaruigtesanger
Bradypterus sylvaticus

[Sundevalls Buschsänger]

Measurements: Length 14–15 cm; wing (4) 56–58,8–62; tail (2) 57–61; tarsus (2) 19–19,5; culmen (2) 13.
Bare Parts: Iris brown; bill brown, paler below; legs and feet olive brown.
Identification: Size smallish (larger than white-eye); olive brown, paler below (looks uniform chocolate brown in shade); bill longish, pointed; tail broad, slightly fan-shaped, graduated. Best separated from Barratt's Warbler by song; both occur together along Transkei coast from autumn to spring.
Voice: Song loud ringing deliberate *wit, wit, wit, wit*, sometimes ending in bubbling trill, *wit-wit-wit-tr-r-r-r-r-r*; song very similar to that of Barratt's Warbler, but louder, less blurred, with notes more stuttered; low *churr* alarm note; soft *trr...up* call note.

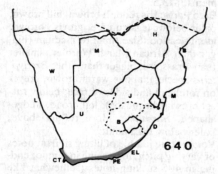

Distribution: Extreme s Cape from Cape Town through Transkei to Natal as far N as Umhlanga Rocks; in s Cape also at Oubos, Grootvadersbosch and Garcia.
Status: Rare and local; mostly resident; moves northwards in coastal Natal in winter.

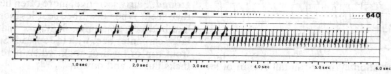

Habitat: Lowland and coastal evergreen forest with dense tangled undergrowth; also thickets in gullies and in riverine forest.

Habits: Usually solitary. Keeps to darkest parts of undergrowth, so seldom seen; presence revealed by song. Forages on ground by walking slowly and uncovering prey by fluttering in leaf litter to scatter it with wings and tail spread; may also use fluttering as distraction display without vocalization. Scurries mouselike on ground.

Food: Insects.

Breeding: *Season*: September to October. *Nest*: Bowl of dry plant material, lined with finer fibres; inside diameter 5 cm, depth 4,2 cm, outside diameter 13 cm, overall depth 10 cm (means of 3 nests); well concealed in matted branches, 50–120 cm above ground, just below leafy canopy. *Clutch*: (1) 3 eggs. *Eggs*: Pinkish white, speckled and spotted with reddish; measure (3) 19,8 × 14,9 (19,6–20 × 14,8–15). *Incubation*: 19 days by only one parent (probably ♀). *Nestling*: 12–14 days; fed by both parents.

Ref. Pringle, J.S. 1977. *Ostrich* 48:112–114.

---

641 (612)   **Victorin's Warbler**   **Plate 52**
Rooiborsruigtesanger
Bradypterus victorini

[Rostbrust-Buschsänger]

Measurements: Length 15–17 cm; wing (4) 53–55; tail 74–77; tarsus 21–22; culmen 13–13,5.

Bare Parts: Iris reddish brown; bill brown, paler below; legs and feet greyish brown.

Identification: Size small to medium (bigger than African Marsh Warbler, smaller than Grassbird; bigger than other *Bradypterus* species); above warm brown, greyer on forehead and sides of face; below russet brown (diagnostic); tail broad, wedge-shaped. *Immature*: More rufous above, paler below than adult.

Voice: Song jumble of lilting sibilant notes of varying pitch, increasing in tempo, ending in 4–5 sucking notes (somewhat like song of Grassbird), *twiddy twee twit, twiddy twee...seep seep seep seep*; sharp *chip chip* alarm notes; piercing *teep* and rasping *chorrr* (like alarm note of Cape Sparrow) callnotes.

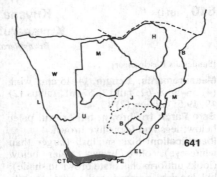

641

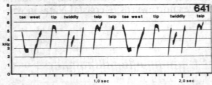

Distribution: Winter-rainfall region of sw

and s Cape from n Cedarberg, E to Witteklip Mountain, 20 km W of Port Elizabeth.

Status: Locally common resident.

Habitat: Forest edge, coastal scrub, scrubby mountain slopes with rocky kloofs and streamside vegetation; usually on moist south-facing slopes.

Habits: Usually solitary. Forages low down in dense vegetation and on ground among grass and shrubs; walks or hops on ground. Fairly secretive, more often heard than seen. When disturbed scuttles mouselike between grasstufts; flight like that of large carpenter bee, with tail spread. Sings from top of bush or rock; when perched flicks tail up and down.

Food: Unrecorded; probably insects.
Breeding: *Season*: September to October.
Nest: Cup of bark and dead leaves in foundation of coarse grass, lined with fine grass and some plant down; on ground or up to 30 cm above ground, well hidden in dense grasstuft. *Clutch*: 2 eggs. *Eggs*:

Pinkish white, spotted with red concentrated at thick end; measure (2) 20,8–21 × 15–15,3. *Incubation*: 21 days. *Nestling*: Unrecorded; fed by both parents.

Ref. McLeod, N., Stanford, W.R. & Broekhuysen, G.J. 1958. *Ostrich* 29:71–73.

---

642 (616)

Broadtailed Warbler
Breëstertsanger
Schoenicola brevirostris

Plate 53

Qovo (Ts), Umvokontshi (X), [Breitschwanzsänger]

Measurements: Length 15–16 cm; wing (7 ♂) 60–61,6–63, (3 ♀) 56–62; tail (10) 69–81; tarsus (10) 16,5–19,5; culmen (10) 10–12,5. Weight (1) 17 g.
Bare Parts: Iris light brown; bill blackish horn above, greyish below, base yellowish; legs and feet pinkish.
Identification: Size smallish; tail broad, blackish, tipped white (diagnostic; looks very heavy in flight); above buffy brown to rusty brown; eyebrow indistinct, buff; below white, washed buff on breast and flanks; undertail coverts greatly elongated, boldly scaled black and white. *Immature*: Below yellowish.
Voice: Song slow deliberate, fairly high-pitched metallic piping *twink, twink, twink* or *zink, zink, zink* or soft ringing *tseenk, tseenk*, like small frog; 3-syllabled *jur-jur-jur* callnote; alarm notes sharp *tik, tik, tik.*

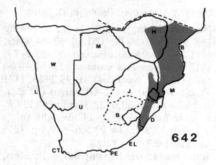

642

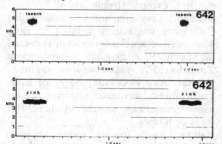

Distribution: S Africa to Ethiopia and Cameroon; in s Africa confined to moister e parts as far S as Dwesa, Transkei.

Status: Sparse and local; resident below about 1 000 m; at higher elevations breeding migrant, November to April. Indeterminate (RDB).
Habitat: Vleis, marshy grassland, moist grassy hillsides, boggy drainage lines, coarse high grassland.
Habits: Usually solitary or in pairs. Skulks low down in dense grass and shrubby vegetation, but sometimes also perches exposed on grass stalk, bush or even telephone wire, especially early morning; flicks wings when perched. Sings in flight up to about 15 m above ground in wide circles, with body at angle, tail jerking up and down, and wings snapping; on landing dives into grass. More visible and vocal in wet or misty weather. Seldom flies far when disturbed; looks tail-heavy in flight.
Food: Insects.
Breeding: *Season*: November to March. *Nest*: Bulky cup, loosely woven of coarse dry grass, sometimes lined with finer grass; outside diameter 7,5–9 cm; overall

555

depth 6,5–6,9 cm; inside diameter 4,5–6 cm, inside depth 2,5–5 cm; very well hidden in dense rank grasstuft or reeds 0,7–1 m tall, 10–30 cm above ground, often over moist ground or even water. *Clutch*: (4) 2–2,8–3 eggs. *Eggs*: White to creamy white, speckled with red-brown and grey concentrated at thick end; measure (4) 18,4 × 13,7 (17,9–18,9 × 13,5–13,9). *Incubation*: Unrecorded. *Nestling*: Unrecorded; fed by both parents.

Ref. Took, J.M.E. 1959. *Ostrich* 30:138–139.

---

643 (599)   **Willow Warbler**   **Plate 54**
Hofsanger
Phylloscopus trochilus

Niini (K), Timba (Sh), Unothoyi (X), [Fitis]

Measurements: Length 11–12 cm; wing (13 ♂) 70–70,8–72, (20 ♀) 63–64,9–69, (111 *P. t. trochilus* unsexed) 57–65,2–74, (117 *P. t. acredula* unsexed) 59–67,4–76; tail (112 *P. t. trochilus*) 41–49,2–58, (121 *P. t. acredula*) 42–51–60; tarsus (32 *P. t. trochilus*) 18,5–20,6–22,5; culmen (137 *P. t. trochilus*) 9,5–11,7–14. Weight (6 ♂) 7,1–9,1–13,2 g, (14 ♀) 6,6–8–9,3 g, (215 unsexed) 6,7–8,6–12 g.

Bare Parts: Iris brown; bill dark horn, base yellow; legs and feet pinkish brown.

Identification: Size very small; above greenish to brownish grey; eyebrow pale yellow (distinctive; no pale eyebrow in Garden Warbler); throat and breast light yellow shading to whitish belly (Icterine Warbler all yellow below); tail notched (squarish or rounded in Garden Warbler). Three subspecies, somewhat different in coloration: *P. t. trochilus* (about 30%) dull greenish olive above, more uniform yellow below, eyebrow yellow; *P. t. acredula* (about 55%) darker and browner above, eyebrow, throat and breast yellow, belly white, undertail yellow; *P. t. yakutensis* (about 15%) less greenish above (browner), eyebrow dull white, little or no yellow below, undertail white.

Voice: High sweet quick *sweet-sweetu* or *sweetu* callnote; song simple musical little warbling, becoming purer in tone and slower in tempo, then falling away — *si-si-si-si-swee-swee-su-su-sweet-sweet-sweetu*.

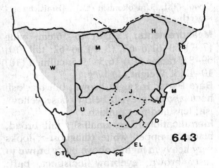

643

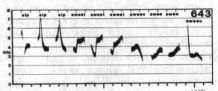

Distribution: Breeds Europe, Asia, Alaska; migrates to Africa; widespread in s Africa, except extreme arid W.

Status: Very common nonbreeding Palaearctic migrant, September to early May. All 3 subspecies common in Transvaal in March; *P. t. acredula* commonest in Zimbabwe, *P. t. yakutensis* least common.

Habitat: Any woodland, edges of evergreen forest, savanna, gardens, parks, exotic plantations; almost anywhere with trees or bushes.

Habits: Usually solitary; sometimes joins mixed bird parties. Forages by restlessly gleaning off leaves and branches in middle and upper strata of trees and bushes; not as quick and jerky as white-eye. Sings mostly from about February, but subsong heard at any time.

Food: Insects (including aphids).
Breeding: Extralimital.

644 (671) Yellowthroated Warbler Plate 58
Geelkeelsanger
Seicercus ruficapillus

Umbese (X), [Rotkopf-Laubsänger]

Measurements: Length 10–12 cm; wing (14 ♂) 52–55,5–57, (16 ♀) 49–51–53,5, (87 unsexed) 47–54,9–61; tail (87) 35–42,1–48; tarsus (97) 18–20,1–22; culmen (98) 8,5–10,8–15. Weight (94) 6,2–7,7–9,5 g.

Bare Parts: Iris brown; bill dusky brown above, yellowish below; legs and feet horn to greyish brown.

Identification: Size very small (smaller than white-eye); crown rufous brown; back olive grey, shading to olive green on rump; black line through eye; wings greenish; eyebrow, throat, breast and undertail bright lemon yellow; belly white. *Immature:* Greener on breast than adult.

Voice: Gentle high-pitched *wittee* and tremulous *zit-zit*; louder *tweety-tweety-tweety-twit*; metallic *tsip-tsop-tsop*; sings in duet, *tsee* answered by *tsik, tsee-tsik-tsee-tsik*, etc.

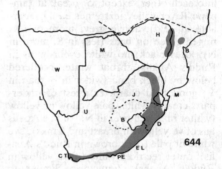
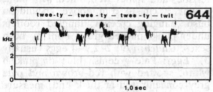

Distribution: Discontinuously from S Africa to E Africa; in s Africa confined to extreme S and SE, along Drakensberg escarpment to Zoutpansberg; also in e Zimbabwe, adjacent Mozambique and Gorongosa Mountain.

Status: Common resident.

Habitat: Middle layers of evergreen forest (mostly montane forest).

Habits: Usually singly or in pairs; sometimes in small groups; may join mixed bird parties of other warblers and flycatchers. Forages mostly in middle to upper strata of forest, but sometimes also in shrubby undergrowth; moves restlessly, gleaning off leaves and twigs like Willow Warbler or white-eye; sometimes hovers to take prey off leaf.

Food: Insects.

Breeding: *Season:* October to December. *Nest:* Domed cup of moss, leaf skeletons and other plant fibres, lined with grass and some feathers; on ground, well hidden in niche of mossy bank; less often in low shrub or (once) in solitary nest of weaver. *Clutch:* 2–3 eggs. *Eggs:* White or pale pink; spotted with light red; measure (8) 16,2 × 12 (15,1–16,5 × 11–12,6). *Incubation:* (1) 17 days. *Nestling:* (1) 16 days.

645 (622) Barthroated Apalis Plate 55
Bandkeelkleinjantjie
Apalis thoracica

Xinyamukhwarani, N'walanga (Ts), Ugxakhweni (X), uMabhelwane (Z), [Halsband-Feinsänger]

Measurements: Length 12–13 cm; wing (205) 45–52,8–58; tail (204) 41–50,7– 60,5; tarsus (91) 18–21,2–24; culmen (97) 11–13,1–15,5. Weight (25 ♂) 9,1–10,3– 11,6 g, (15 ♀) 8,3–10,2–11,9 g, (263 unsexed) 7,9–10,3–12,8 g.

Bare Parts: Iris creamy white to pale yellow; bill black; legs and feet brownish pink.

Identification: Size very small; variable in amount of green on back and yellow on belly (13 subspecies recognized, grading into each other, except for break at Limpopo River valley; extremes easily separable in field); above grey, more or less tinged green on back (less in S, more in N); lores black; no white eyebrow as in Rudd's Apalis; throat white, bordered below by black band (wider in ♂ than in ♀; good field character); rest of underparts creamy white, pale yellow or yellow (whiter in S, yellower in N; Rudd's Apalis has olive yellowish breast and flanks); eye white or pale (dark brown in Rudd's Apalis); outer rectrices white (olive yellow in Rudd's Apalis). *Immature*: Similar to adult, but throat band indistinct.

Voice: Penetrating, quickly repeated *tlip-tlip-tlip-tlip-tlip*; drawn out *chwee chwee* or 2-syllabled *gully gully gully*; calls in duet; also snaps bill.

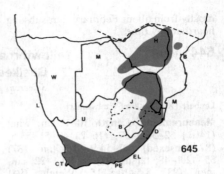

645

645

bird parties. Forages at all heights in denser vegetation, from shrubby undergrowth to canopy, gleaning insects from flowers, buds, leaves and treetrunks; also sometimes on ground or on lichen-covered rocks. Not usually shy; responds well to spishing (see Glossary); inquisitive and fairly tame, even near nest.

Food: Insects (especially caterpillars).

Breeding: *Season*: August to December in Cape, August to January (mainly November-December) in Natal, September to January in Transvaal, August to March (mainly September-January) in Zimbabwe. *Nest*: Long oval with side-top entrance; built of rootlets, silky plant material, fine grass, moss (highly characteristic) and spider web, lined with plant down; 30 cm to 3 m above ground in bush, hanging creeper, tangled rootlets under bank, matted grass; built by both sexes. *Clutch*: (79) 2–2,7–4 eggs (usually 3). *Eggs*: Pale greenish blue or pinkish white, spotted with red-brown and pale grey concentrated at thick end; measure (106) 17,2 × 12,2 (15,5–19,1 × 11,2–13,5). *Incubation*: (1) 17–18 days. *Nestling*: (2) 17–18 days.

Distribution: S Africa to E Africa; in s Africa mainly confined to S and E, excluding subtropical lowveld.

Status: Common resident; some seasonal altitudinal movement at higher elevations.

Habitat: Edges of evergreen forest and bush, well wooded kloofs, bushy hillsides, moist woodland, gardens.

Habits: Usually in pairs; often joins mixed

---

646 (623X)　　　　**Chirinda Apalis**　　　　**Plate 55**
　　　　　　　　　　　Gryskleinjantjie

Apalis chirindensis

[Selinds Feinsänger]

Measurements: Length about 13 cm; wing (36 ♂) 46–50,3–52, (19 ♀) 47–52,5–58; tail (31 ♂) 51–58,3–66, (15 ♀) 50–52,6–57; tarsus (14) 18–20,3–22; culmen (34 ♂) 13–13,9–15, (15 ♀) 13–13,8–15. Weight (4 ♂) 7,6–8,1–8,9,

(1 ♀) 7,5 g, (10 unsexed) 7,1–8,3–10,1 g.

Bare Parts: Iris orange-brown; bill black (in n birds; base sometimes pinkish in ♀) or pale horn above, pinkish below (in s birds); legs and feet pink.

Identification: Size very small (same as Barthroated Apalis); above grey; below whitish, washed grey on breast; tail blackish, narrowly tipped white; eye orange; legs pink; no black collar.

Voice: Long series of *wik-wik-wik-wik* contact notes; chattering chipping song (similar to that of Roberts's Prinia); rapid bill snapping.

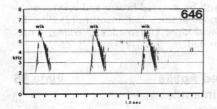

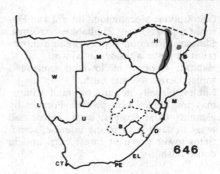

Distribution: Eastern Zimbabwe, adjacent Mozambique and Gorongosa Mountain.
Status: Uncommon resident; some local altitudinal movements from higher elevations in winter.

Habitat: Canopy of middle to highland evergreen forest.
Habits: In pairs or small groups. Movements lively with much darting about. Poorly known.
Food: Unrecorded.
Breeding: Unrecorded; birds in breeding condition October to February; fledglings under parental care in December (Mutare).

---

647 (623) **Blackheaded Apalis** **Plate 55**
Swartkopkleinjantjie
Apalis melanocephala

[Schwarzkopf-Feinsänger]

Measurements: Length 13–14 cm; wing (19 ♂) 45–49–52, (11 ♀) 46–47,5–49; tail (12 ♂) 58–60,8–66, (11 ♀) 47–49,6–51; culmen (18 ♂) 13,5–14,1–15, (11 ♀) 13,5–14,14,5. Weight (1) 9,5 g.

Bare Parts: Iris yellowish brown to greyish brown; bill and inside of mouth black; legs and feet pinkish.

Identification: Size very small; looks clearly 2-toned; above blackish (crown black); below creamy white, washed buffy on breast; tail longish, black, tipped white; eye yellowish; black mouth conspicuous when singing. *Immature*: Paler than adult.

Voice: Song *ping ping ping*, repeated 30–40 times, ending with single short *pik*; sharp burring *territ-territ* or *durr-irr-irr-irr*; quiet *seet* callnote; calls in duet.

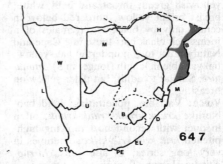

Distribution: Mozambique littoral and Haroni-Lusitu region of Zimbabwe, to Kenya.
Status: Common resident; some movement to lower altitudes in winter.
Habitat: Canopy of lowland evergreen forest, dense riverine bush.
Habits: Usually in pairs or small groups; may join mixed bird parties. Forages by gleaning from flowers, buds, leaves and twigs in canopy of forest interior, sometimes lower down at forest edge and in dense bush.

Food: Insects.
Breeding: *Season*: November to February. *Nest*: Thick-walled oval with side-top entrance; built of moss and lichen bound with spider web, lined with plant down; well hidden in foliage of tree, fairly high above ground. *Clutch*: 2–3 eggs. *Eggs*: Bluish green, boldly spotted and speckled with brown, red-brown and grey concentrated at thick end; measure (2) 19 × 13. *Incubation*: Unrecorded. *Nestling*: Unrecorded.

---

648 (625)　　　　　**Yellowbreasted Apalis**　　　　　**Plate 55**
Geelborskleinjantjie
Apalis flavida

Xinyamukhwarani, N'walanga (Ts), [Gelbbrust-Feinsänger]

Measurements: Length 12–13 cm; wing (217 ♂) 45–50,8–55, (34 ♀) 45–48,5–52; tail (217 ♂) 42,5–50,8–58,5, (34 ♀) 41–46,4–53; tarsus (15) 18–21; culmen (79 ♂) 13–14,6–16, (34 ♀) 13,5–14,1–15. Weight (2 ♀) 7,3–7,4 g, (5 unsexed) 7–7,7–8,8 g.
Bare Parts: Iris brown; bill blackish; legs and feet pinkish brown.
Identification: Size very small (smaller than Barthroated Apalis); head grey variably washed greenish (greener in N); back yellowish green; throat and belly white; breast bright yellow, bordered below in centre only by black bar (females of n forms lack black bar; those in e Cape and Natal similar to ♂); undertail pale yellow; tail variable in length (longer in S). *Immature*: Similar to adult, but paler yellow on breast.
Voice: Variable, penetrating; loud babblerlike *krunk-krunk-krunk-krunk*, often in duet with second bird replying high-pitched *krik-krik-krik-krik*, sometimes in very long series; ♂ also calls *chirrup-chirrup-chirrup*, ♀ replies *twee-twee-twee* in duet; buzzy *churr* or sharp *krit-krit* alarm notes; also bill snapping.

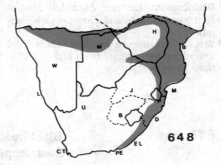

Distribution: Africa S of Sahara; in s Africa confined to E and N.
Status: Locally fairly common resident.
Habitat: Riverine forest, moist bushveld, mixed woodland, mature thornveld, thickets, middle to lowland evergreen forest, regenerating scrub; less often *Brachystegia* woodland.
Habits: Usually in pairs; sometimes in small groups; may join mixed bird parties. Forages restlessly like Willow Warbler, gleaning insects from leaves and twigs of bushes and trees at all levels. Highly vocal; voice surprisingly loud for tiny bird. When alarmed cocks and flicks tail and droops wings; may also snap wings and bill.
Food: Small insects, fruit, nectar.
Breeding: *Season*: October to January in Natal and Zimbabwe, possibly to February. *Nest*: Oval with side-top entrance; built of lichen and moss, bound with

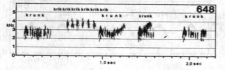

spider web, lined with plant down and soft seedpods; inside diameter about 4 cm, height 5–7 cm; overall length 8–10 cm; in leafy bush or tree up to 5,6 m above ground, between twiggy upright branches. *Clutch*: (27) 2–2,9–3 eggs (usually 3).

Eggs: White or pale greenish, spotted with red-brown and grey concentrated at thick end; measure (35) 15,8 × 11,3 (14,2–17,7 × 10–12). *Incubation*: 12–14 days by both sexes, mostly by ♀. *Nestling*: 15–17 days; fed by both parents.

649 (624)   Rudd's Apalis   Plate 55
Ruddse Kleinjantjie
Apalis ruddi

[Rudds Feinsänger]

Measurements: Length 12,5–13 cm; wing (4 ♂) 47,5–50, (1 ♀) 48; tail (4 ♂) 54–56, (1 ♀) 49; tarsus (5) 18,5–22; culmen (5) 11–13.

Bare Parts: Iris brown; bill black; legs and feet pinkish brown.

Identification: Size very small; similar to Barthroated Apalis, but darker overall; head dark grey; back yellowish olive; short buffy eyebrow (none in Barthroated Apalis); lores and below eye black (forming small facemask); below white with black collar below throat and greenish yellow wash across breast and flanks; tail olive, tipped yellowish.

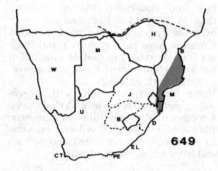

Voice: Rattling *chooky-chooky-chooky* like knocking on wood; also anvillike *klink-klink* tapping notes, like those of tinker barbets; low-toned *churg-churg* contact call; also bill snapping.

Distribution: Zululand from Umfolozi River to e Swaziland and Mozambique to Save River.

Status: Uncommon resident.

Habitat: Flat coastal bushveld, small forest patches, thickets around vleis and in woodland.

Habits: Usually solitary or in pairs. For-
ages by creeping and hopping restlessly about in thickets, gleaning from leaves; sometimes hawks insects in flight; moves quickly through canopy. May snap bill and wings in alarm. Similar to Yellowbreasted Apalis.

Food: Insects, flower buds.

Breeding: *Season*: September to January. *Nest*: Oval with side-top entrance; of lichen and moss, bound with spider web and silk from caterpillar cocoons; lined with thistle-down; concealed among leaves of tree or low bush, suspended from thin twigs 0,25–2,5 m above ground; built in about 10 days. *Clutch*: 2–3 eggs. *Eggs*: Bright turquoise to pale greenish blue, boldly marked with blotches of rust concentrated at thick end; measure (5) 17 × 12,2 (16,5–17,8 × 11,9–12,7). *Incubation*: Unrecorded. *Nestling*: Unrecorded.

Ref. Beven, G. 1944. *Ostrich* 15:178–187.

650 (621X)   Redfaced Crombec   Plate 53
Rooiwangstompstert
Sylvietta whytii

[Whytes Sylvietta]

Measurements: Length about 10 cm; wing (24 ♂) 55–58,8–62, (17 ♀) 53,5–
57–65; tail (12 ♂) 22–25,4–27, (11 ♀) 21–24,4–28; tarsus (12 ♂) 16–17,7–19, (11 ♀) 16–17,1–18; culmen (12 ♂)

11,5–12,6–14, (11 ♀) 11,5–12,4–14.
Weight (5 ♂) 9,1–10–10,4 g, (3 ♀)
9,2–9,7–10,1 g, (17 unsexed) 8–9–10,5 g.
Bare Parts: Iris yellow to hazel; bill dark
brown, paler below, darker on culmen;
legs and feet reddish to ochre brown.
Identification: Size very small; tail very
short (looks tailless); body rounded;
very similar to Longbilled Crombec and
easily confused with it; above pale grey;
face and underparts rufous (brighter
than in Longbilled Crombec); no pale
eyebrow (tropical races of Longbilled
Crombec have pale eyebrow); bill longish (but shorter than that of Longbilled
Crombec). *Immature*: Fawn grey above,
dappled fawn on wings.
Voice: Far-carrying tripping trill, *wit-wit-
wit-wit-wit* (similar to voice of Redcapped
Crombec); also insectlike trill *prrrrrrr*;
phrase of 3–7 whistled syllables on same
key, *see-si-si-seee*, not trilled; *chik* contact
call between members of pair.

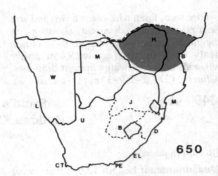

650

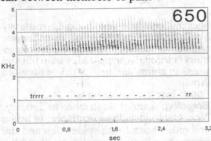

Distribution: Mozambique (N of Save
River) and Zimbabwe, to Malawi and E
Africa.
Status: Sparse to common resident.
Habitat: Canopy of woodland, edges of
lowland evergreen and riverine forest.

Habits: Usually in pairs; often joins
mixed bird parties. Forages by creeping
about with quick little steps on twigs
and small branches, examining lichens,
crevices and curled leaves; posture
hunched, head drawn into shoulders.
Movements quicker than those of Longbilled Crombec.
Food: Insects, spiders.
Breeding: *Season*: August to December
(mainly September-November). *Nest*:
Hanging purse of bark, grass, tendrils,
dead leaves, lichen, flowers and seedpods
bound with spider web, lined with plant
down and spider web; suspended by rim
from drooping branch in centre of tree,
0,6–3 m above ground. *Clutch*: (6)
1–1,7–2 eggs (usually 2, very rarely 3).
Eggs: White, spotted, freckled and
blotched with browns and greys; measure
(10) 17,8 × 12,3 (16,6–19,6 × 11,5–13).
Incubation: 13–14 days by both sexes.
Nestling: 14–17 days; fed by both parents.

Ref. Donnelly, B.G. & Irwin, M.P.S. 1969. *Arnol-
dia (Rhod.)*. 16(4):1–15.
Irwin, M.P.S. 1959. *Occ. Pap. Natn. Mus. S.
Rhod.* 3(23B):286–294; 1968. *Bonner zool.
Beitr.* 19:249–256.

651 (621) **Longbilled Crombec** **Plate 53**
Bosveldstompstert
Sylvietta rufescens

Simpanda (K), Ngunhu (Ts), iNdibilitshe (Z),
[Langschnabel-Sylvietta, Kurzschwanz-Sylvietta]
Measurements: Length 10–12 cm; wing
(82 ♂) 58–62,5–67,5, (72 ♀) 55–64,3–63;
tail (11 ♂) 27–29,3–33, (8 ♀) 24–26,8–
30; tarsus (9 ♂) 18,5–19,3–20, (6 ♀)
18,5–18,8–19; culmen (82 ♂) 14,5–16,5–

19, (68 ♀) 13–15,8–18. Weight (6 ♂)
10,1–11,3–12,7 g, (3 ♀) 9,2–10,8–12,4 g,
(76 unsexed) 8–11,6–23 g.
Bare Parts: Iris light brown; bill blackish
horn, base pinkish; legs and feet pinkish
to yellowish brown.
Identification: Size very small; tail very

short (looks tailless); above light grey; pale eyebrow in tropical races (none in Redfaced Crombec); ear coverts and underparts pale tawny (lighter than in Redfaced Crombec); bill long (much longer than that of Redfaced Crombec). *Immature*: Similar to adult.

Voice: Trilled, fairly high-pitched syncopated *chi-rrr-it, chi-rrr-it* or *prru tree-ree, prru tree-ree* repeated several times; rolling *trrrt trrrt*; song tripping *chirrit chirrit chirrit titrr trrt chip chip tria-tria-tria-tria-tria chiploi chiploi chiploi.*

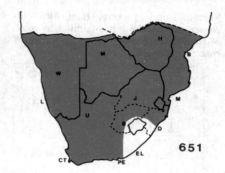

651

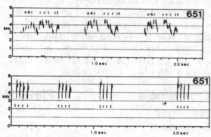

Distribution: S Africa to Angola and Zaire; widespread in s Africa, except Lesotho, parts of e Cape, Transkei and s Natal.

Status: Common to fairly common resident.

Habitat: Drier savanna with scattered trees and bushes, light mixed woodland and thornveld, usually with well-developed understory of vegetation and secondary growth; avoids forests.

Habits: Usually solitary or in pairs; joins mixed bird parties. Forages with rest-less agile hops on trunks, leaves, twigs and branches, usually starting low down and working up to canopy. Flight bouncy.

Food: Insects.

Breeding: *Season*: August to December in Cape, October to January in Natal, September to March (mainly October-January) in Transvaal, August to March (mainly September-December) in Zimbabwe. *Nest*: Hanging bag of grass, fibres, plant down and spider web; suspended from drooping branch or bunch of leaves inside bush or in lower branches of tree, about 1 m above ground. *Clutch*: (72) 1–1,8–3 eggs (usually 2, rarely 3). *Eggs*: White, spotted with greenish slate, olive and brown or red-brown; measure (106) 18,6 × 12,4 (17,1–20,9 × 11–13,7). *Incubation*: 14 days. *Nestling*: 14 days.

Ref. Donnelly, B.G. & Irwin, M.P.S. 1969. *Arnoldia (Rhod.)* 16(4):1–15.
Irwin, M.P.S. 1959. *Occ. Pap. Natn. Mus. S. Rhod.* 3(23B):286–294.

652 (621Y)   **Redcapped Crombec**   **Plate 53**
Rooikroonstompstert
Sylvietta ruficapilla

[Rotohr-Sylvietta]

Measurements: Length about 12 cm; wing (33 ♂) 62–66,5–72, (39 ♀) 60–63,5–70; tail (15 ♂) 24–26,1–28, (15 ♀) 21–22,5–25; tarsus (15 ♂) 19–19,7–21, (15 ♀) 17–18,1–19; culmen (15 ♂) 12–12,9–14, (15 ♀) 11–12,4–13.

Bare Parts: Iris yellow; bill horn above pinkish below; legs and feet red-brown.

Identification: Size very small; tail very short (looks tailless); above ashy grey; ear coverts chestnut (diagnostic); throat white, lightly streaked grey; breast washed chestnut; rest of underparts buffy grey, paler in centre.

Voice: Loud ringing *richi-chichi-chicheeer*, repeated 6 times (similar to voice of Redfaced Crombec in quality); *chip* or *chik* contact call.

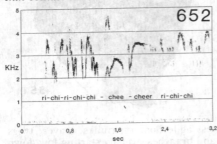

Distribution: Angola, Zambia, s Zaire, n Mozambique; recorded only once in s Africa from Nampini Ranch, W of Victoria Falls, Zimbabwe.

Status: Uncommon; may be more common than records show; probably resident.
Habitat: Canopy of *Brachystegia* woodland on Kalahari sand; less often also canopy of adjacent forest.
Habits: Poorly known, but probably similar to other species of *Sylvietta*.
Food: Unrecorded.
Breeding: Not recorded in s Africa. *Season*: September to October in Zambia. *Nest*: Hanging purse of grass, leaves and flowers, bound with spider web; suspended by rim from drooping branch high in canopy of tree; may nest in association with tree ant, *Oecophylla*. *Clutch*: 2 eggs. *Eggs*: White, spotted with dark brown and grey concentrated at thick end; measure about 18 × 11,5. *Incubation*: Unrecorded. *Nestling*: Unrecorded.

653 (600) Yellowbellied Eremomela   Plate 54
Geelpensbossanger
Eremomela icteropygialis

Niini (K), Timba (Sh), [Gelbbauch-Eremomela]

Measurements: Length 10–11 cm; wing (13) 54–55,8–59; tail (21) 32–42; tarsus (13) 16,5–18; culmen (21) 9–12. Weight (4 ♂) 7,6–8,5–9,4 g, (3 ♀) 6,7–7,4–8,5 g, (5 unsexed) 7,5–8,4–9,3 g.
Bare Parts: Iris red-brown to brown; bill dark horn, base pinkish; legs and feet slate grey.
Identification: Size very small; somewhat similar to Cape Penduline Tit, but yellow confined to lower belly only; above light olive grey, eyebrow paler (no black-and-white forehead pattern as in Cape Penduline Tit; no white eyering as in white-eyes); dark line through eye (absent in Cape Penduline Tit); throat, breast and upper belly greyish white; rest of underparts light yellow (paler than in Cape Penduline Tit). *Immature*: Duller yellow than adult.
Voice: Quick phrase of 2–5 syllables repeated 2–3 times, *chichichrr, chichichrr, chichichrr*, slightly accented on first syllable, dropping in pitch on third; song similar, but incorporates other notes also; rapid twittery *wee tri-tri-tri-tri-tri*, rising in pitch with each note; plaintive whistled

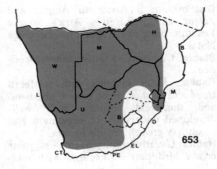

alarm note, *peee* or *pee-reee*, rising in pitch; rapid warbling *toodle-oodle-oodle-oo tee-ree-ree* near nest; harsh *dzzz* before take-off.

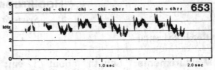

Distribution: Africa S of Sahara; widespread in s Africa, especially in drier parts; absent from extreme S, e Cape, most of Natal, most of highveld and extreme NE.

Status: Fairly common resident; nomadic in driest areas.

Habitat: Almost any woodland, bushveld, arid shrub and open scrub; riverine scrub in arid regions.

Habits: Usually solitary or in pairs; sometimes joins mixed bird parties. Forages very like Cape Penduline Tit by hopping restlessly among twigs and leaves of bushes and trees, searching diligently from bottom to top; sometimes forages by hopping on ground. Tame and confiding. Rather poorly known.

Food: Small insects.

Breeding: *Season:* October to March in Kalahari (after rain), October to January in Transvaal, August to April in Zimbabwe. *Nest:* Neat thin-walled cup of dry grass and other plant fibres, bound with spider web and plant down, inside diameter 4,1 cm, depth 4,1 cm; suspended between horizontal twigs of small tree or shrub, 60 cm to 2,7 m above ground; very like nest of white-eye. *Clutch:* (35) 2–2,3–3 eggs. *Eggs:* White, spotted with greenish brown, red-brown and chocolate concentrated at thick end; measure (69) 15,8 × 11,4 (14,3–18 × 10,4–12,2). *Incubation:* 13–14 days. *Nestling:* 15–16 days; fed by both parents.

654 (626) Karoo Eremomela (Green Eremomela) Plate 54
Groenbossanger
Eremomela gregalis

[Langschwanz-Eremomela]

Measurements: Length about 12 cm; wing (4 ♂) 52–56, (6 ♀) 50–56; tail (4 ♂) 47–53, (6 ♀) 45–54; tarsus (9) 16,5–18,5; culmen (19) 8–12.

Bare Parts: Iris bright lemon yellow; bill black; inside of mouth black in ♂, pink in ♀; legs and feet blackish brown.

Identification: Size very small; above green, yellower on rump; below white, duller in ♀ (dull greyish white in Bleating Warbler); undertail yellow (white in Bleating Warbler); eye bright yellow (diagnostic). *Immature:* Above browner than adult.

Voice: Song high-pitched *seewip seewip* repeated continuously at about 2 notes/ second for up to 2 minutes (audible for at least 400 m); sharp *twink* contact call; *chwit* alarm note; group-contact call *zii-zii-zii.*

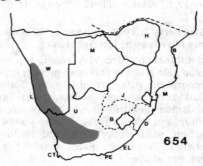

654

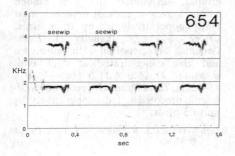

654

Distribution: Western Karoo, Namaqualand and s Namibia.

Status: Locally fairly common resident.

Habitat: Karoo scrub, shrubby desert to semidesert, low bushes along watercourses and on rocky hillsides in very arid regions.

Habits: Usually solitary or in pairs; sometimes in groups of up to 7 birds. Forages among branches of low bushes and shrubs or on ground. Secretive and hard to locate, slipping quickly from bush to bush. Sings before sunrise.

Food: Small insects.

Breeding: *Season:* August to December (mainly October-November). *Nest:* Thick-walled cup of thin twigs, grass and felted plant down, thickly lined with soft downy seeds; outside diameter 7,8–12 cm, inside diameter 4 cm; wall of cup

565

up to 4 cm thick; in fork of small bush, below canopy, about 30–40 cm above ground; nest supported from below (not slung from rim as in Yellowbellied Eremomela). *Clutch*: 3–4 eggs. *Eggs*: Pale blue, spotted with red-brown and pale lilac mainly at thick end; measure (4) 16 × 11,3 (15,5–16,3 × 11–11,5). *Incubation*: Unrecorded. *Nestling*: Unrecorded.

Ref. Frost, P.G.H. & Vernon, C.J. 1978. *Ostrich* 49:87–89.

655 (602) Greencapped Eremomela (Duskyfaced Eremomela) Plate 54
Donkerwangbossanger
Eremomela scotops

Niini (K), Timba (Sh), [Grünkappen-Eremomela]

Measurements: Length 11–12 cm; wing (23) 54–57,3–61,5; tail 43–51; tarsus 16–19,5; culmen 11–12. Weight (1 ♂) 9,2 g.

Bare Parts: Iris yellowish white; bill black; legs olive brown; feet light russet.

Identification: Size very small; top of head pale green to yellowish grey; rest of upperparts pale greenish grey; lores dusky; below light yellow, paler on abdomen (whitish in w birds); chin white; eye whitish (diagnostic in combination with dusky face and yellow breast). *Immature*: Paler than adult, greener above.

Voice: Song loud monotonous rapidly repeated *twip-twip-twip-twip*; loud churring alarm note; also rapid chattering.

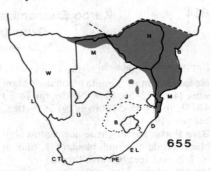

Distribution: S Africa to Zaire and Kenya; in s Africa confined mainly to NE from Zululand to Caprivi; also n Transvaal.

Status: Fairly common resident.

Habitat: Canopy of woodland and bushveld.

Habits: Usually in small groups of 2–8 birds (breeding groups average 3,3 birds, nonbreeding flocks average 4,7 birds). Forages in groups among leaves of woodland canopy; also catches insects in flight with bill-snap. Roosts communally, huddled in row on twig. Highly vocal; sings dawn to sunrise; also snaps bill and wings in chasing displays between groups.

Food: Small insects.

Breeding: *Season*: July to February (mainly September-November). *Nest*: Small cup of white plant down and rusty sepals of *Brachystegia* buds, bound with spider web; 6–7 m above ground, suspended and well hidden among leaves at ends of branches; nest built cooperatively by up to 5 birds. *Clutch*: 2–3 eggs (usually 2). *Eggs*: Greenish blue, spotted with red-brown and lilac concentrated at thick end; measure (4) 16,6 × 11,6 (16,4–16,8 × 11–12,1). *Incubation*: Unrecorded. *Nestling*: Unrecorded; fed cooperatively by up to 5 birds.

Ref. Vernon, F.J. & Vernon, C.J. 1978. *Ostrich* 49:92–93.

656 (601)

Burntnecked Eremomela
Bruinkeelbossanger
Eremomela usticollis

Plate 54

Niini (K), Timba (Sh), [Rostkehl-Eremomela, Rostband-Eremomela]

Measurements: Length 10–11 cm; wing (37) 52,5–54,3–59; tail 38–45; tarsus 18,5–21; culmen 10–11,5. Weight (5) 7,3–8,3–9,3 g.

Bare Parts: Iris cream to light yellow; bill horn, base yellowish pink; legs and feet pinkish.

Identification: Size very small (smallest eremomela species); above dark bluish grey; below buffy white; cheeks, ear coverts and collar on throat rusty. *Immature*: Lacks rusty face and collar.

Voice: Very high-pitched rapidly repeated *twee-twip-ti-ti-ti-ti-ti* varying in tempo and dropping in pitch like callnotes of Spectacled Weaver, but higher-pitched, sometimes becoming trilled *tirrrrr*.

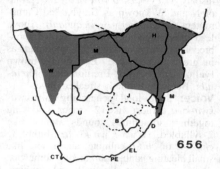
656

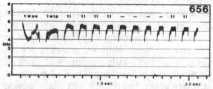
656

Distribution: S Africa to Angola and Malawi; in s Africa from s Namibia, n Botswana and Zululand northwards.

Status: Common in N, uncommon in S; resident.

Habitat: *Acacia* savanna, mixed woodland, riverine thornbush.

Habits: Usually in pairs or small groups of up to 5 birds; joins mixed bird parties with other warblers, penduline tits and white-eyes. Forages off leaves and twigs in canopy of thorntrees; highly active. Poorly known.

Food: Small insects.

Breeding: *Season*: October to April in Transvaal, September to April in Zimbabwe. *Nest*: Cup of felted plant down bound with spider web and covered with dry leaves or insect egg capsules; 36 mm diameter, 25 mm deep; slung in fork in topmost branches of tree 3–6 m above ground. *Clutch*: (6) 2–2,6–4 eggs. *Eggs*: Pale greenish white, sparingly spotted with light brown; measure (12) 16 × 11,8 (14–17,3 × 10,5–12,6). *Incubation*: Unrecorded. *Nestling*: Unrecorded.

Ref. Tarboton, W.R. 1970. *Ostrich* 41:212–213.

657 (627)

Bleating Warbler
Kwê-kwêvoël
Camaroptera brachyura

Plate 53

Niini (K), Unomanyuku, Unome (X), umBuzana, iMbuzi-yehlathi, uVinyothi (Z), [Meckergrasmücke (Grünrücken-Camaroptera, Graurücken-Camaroptera)]

Measurements: Length 12–13 cm; wing (65) 47–53,5–58; tail (21) 36–41,1–45; tarsus (19) 21–22,3–25,5; culmen (21) 11,2–13,5–15. Weight (20 ♂) 9,2–10,8–12,1 g, (15 ♀) 9–10,1–11,5 g, (66 unsexed) 5,1–10,8–13,9 g.

Bare Parts: Iris brown to orange-brown; bill blackish horn, base pinkish; legs and feet pinkish brown.

Identification: Size very small; body rounded; tail often cocked upwards. Two distinct, but intergrading colour types: (a) *Green-backed* (*brachyura* group of S and E): Above mossy green to yellowish olive; below dull greyish

567

white (white in Karoo Eremomela); undertail white (yellow in Karoo Eremomela), often conspicuously puffed out in display. *Grey-backed (brevicaudata* group of N and W known as Greybacked Camaroptera *Camaroptera brevicaudata).* Above lead grey (breeding) or ashy brown (nonbreeding); wings mossy green; underparts as in green-backed type. Eye orange-brown (yellow in Karoo Eremomela). *Immature:* Below indistinctly streaked olive.

Voice: Song loud penetrating *kwit-kwit-kwit-kwit* almost like 2 stones knocking together; sometimes sounds almost like 2-syllabled, *k'wit-k'wit-k'wit;* bubbling *chit-it-it* or *chit-it* callnote; alarm note like small bleating lamb, *maaa* or *kwê,* somewhat drawn out; various other calls and combinations of above vocalizations.

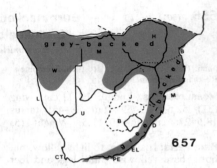

6 57

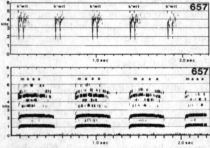

Distribution: Africa S of Sahara; in s Africa absent from highveld and dry W.

Status: Common resident. Green-backed and grey-backed forms may be separate species.

Habitat: Thickets in woodland, forest edges, gardens, parks, tangled riverine bush; green-backed forms favour moist woodland, grey-backed forms drier woodland.

Habits: Usually solitary or in pairs. Forages low down in undergrowth, or even on ground, hopping restlessly about. Rather secretive, but located easily by bleating alarm call; responds well to spishing (see Glossary). Male displays by flying in loop over perch, making whirring sound; sings from concealed perch among leaves at very top of tall tree.

Food: Small insects.

Breeding: *Season:* September to March throughout s Africa (mainly November-December); sometimes as late as April in Transvaal. *Nest:* Ball of growing leaves sewn together with spider web poked through tiny holes; inner shell of pieces of stiff dry grass, lined with soft plant down; in low herbs, bush or leafy tree; from ground level to 1,3 m above ground (rarely as high as 6 m). *Clutch:* (60) 2–2,8–4 eggs (mostly 3). *Eggs:* White, usually plain, rarely dotted with red-brown; measure (52) 17,1 × 12,4 (14–19 × 10,8–13,8). *Incubation:* 14–15 days by both sexes, mostly by ♀. *Nestling:* 14–15 days; fed by both parents.

Ref. Earlé, R.A. 1980. *Ostrich* 51:128.

---

658 (614)   **Desert Barred Warbler**   **Plate 53**
                Gebande Sanger
                Calamonastes fasciolatus

[Bindensänger]

Measurements: Length 13–15 cm; wing (39 ♂) 57–61,1–64, (23 ♀) 54–58,1–62; tail (11 ♂) 52–57,5, (9 ♀) 47–52; tarsus (20) 20–23; culmen (20) 12–14,5. Weight (1 ♀) 13,8 g, (23 unsexed) 10,6–13–14,3 g.

Bare Parts: Iris grey; bill black to blackish brown; legs and feet pinkish brown.

Identification: Size small to medium; similar to Stierling's Barred Warbler;

tail longish, usually held cocked and fanned over back. *Breeding* ♂: Above rich brown; throat and breast plain brown (white, barred with dusky in Stierling's Barred Warbler); rest of underparts buffy white, barred dusky; undertail plain buff (underparts barred from chin to undertail in Stierling's Barred Warbler). *Female and nonbreeding* ♂: Above rich brown; below brownish white, barred with dusky from chin to belly; undertail plain buff (Stierling's Barred Warbler whiter below, undertail barred); eye pale (dark in Stierling's Barred Warbler). *Immature*: Above more rufous brown than adult; breast washed yellowish.

Voice: 2–5 high-pitched froglike trilling bleats, *preep-preep-preep* (rather like squeak of bicycle pump); rapid piping *weee-ti-ti-ti-ti-ti*, repeated several times.

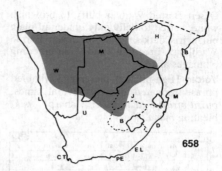

Distribution: Kalahari basin from n Cape and nw Orange Free State (Hoopstad) to w Transvaal, Botswana, n Namibia and sw Zimbabwe; beyond to sw Angola.

Status: Common to fairly common resident.

Habitat: Dense bush and tree savanna, especially with small-leaved thorny bushes and patchy ground cover, semi-arid savanna with *Acacia, Combretum* and *Commiphora* trees.

Habits: Usually in pairs or small groups. Forages inside cover of bush from bottom to top, flying to bottom of next bush and repeating upward pattern; birds maintain contact with each other by calling. Ascends vertically in display flight, swooping downward with purring wings.

Food: Unrecorded; probably small insects.

Breeding: *Season:* November to March in Transvaal, December to January in Namibia. *Nest:* Oval of plant down, grass and rootlets, with side-top entrance; sewn into growing leaves of herb, shrub or tree by plugging spider web through small holes pierced in leaves which almost hide entrance; 1–3 m above ground. *Clutch:* (6) 2–2,8–4 eggs. *Eggs:* Bluish white or cream, evenly speckled with lilac and purplish brown; measure (16) 16,8 × 12,4 (15,2–18,5 × 11,4–13,5). *Incubation:* Unrecorded. *Nestling:* Unrecorded.

659 (615)   Stierling's Barred Warbler   Plate 53
Stierlingse Sanger
Calamonastes stierlingi

Xingede (Ts), [Stierling-Bindensänger]

Measurements: Length about 14 cm; wing (61 ♂) 56–63–67, (55 ♀) 51–58,1–65; tail 40–49; tarsus 19,5–22; culmen 12–13. Weight (3 ♂) 12,3–13,2–14 g, (1 ♀) 13,1 g.

Bare Parts: Iris orange to red-brown; bill black; legs and feet brownish pink.

Identification: Size medium; very similar to Desert Barred Warbler; above rufous brown; below white, barred with dusky from chin to undertail (underparts of

Desert Barred Warbler buffy to brownish white, barred to belly only; undertail plain buff); iris darkish (pale in Desert Barred Warbler); breeding and non-breeding plumages alike.

Voice: High-pitched piercing 3-syllabled phrase repeated quickly several times, *biririt-biririt-biririt-biririt*; sharp *tsik*; bleating *maaa*.

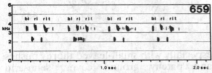

Distribution: S Africa to Tanzania; in s Africa confined to NE, from Zululand to e Transvaal and Swaziland, Mozambique, most of Zimbabwe and extreme n Botswana.

Status: Common resident.

Habitat: Mainly *Brachystegia* and *Baikiaea* woodland, thickets on termite mounds.

Habits: Very similar to Desert Barred Warbler. Forages most on or near ground; when disturbed ascends to canopy. In

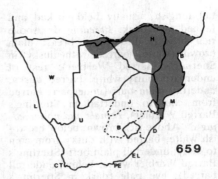

display flies fast, dodging between trees, first high then low near ground, but always below canopy, singing as it goes.

Food: Unrecorded; probably insects.

Breeding: Season: September to March. *Nest:* Similar to that of Desert Barred Warbler; oval of plant down and spider web plugged into holes in drooping leaves. *Clutch*: (4) 2–2,5–3 eggs. *Eggs*: Undescribed; measure (10) 17,2 × 12,3 (15,5–18,3 × 11,5–13,1). *Incubation*: Unrecorded. *Nestling*: Unrecorded.

660 (613)   **Cinnamonbreasted Warbler**   **Plate 53**
Kaneelborssanger
Euryptila subcinnamomea

[Zimtbrustsänger]

Measurements: Length 13–14 cm; wing (3) 53–54; tail 57,5–58; tarsus 19–20,5; culmen 12,5–13.

Bare Parts: Iris brownish grey or dull olive; bill, legs and feet blackish horn.

Identification: Size smallish; forecrown, rump, undertail and broad band on upper belly bright chestnut or cinnamon; rest of upperparts warm russet-brown; eyebrow and face speckled black-and-white; throat and breast grey; lower belly blackish grey; tail black, often held cocked up (diagnostic in combination with cinnamon breast and distinctive habitat). *Immature*: Above more rufous than adult; cinnamon belly band paler, grading into rufous flanks.

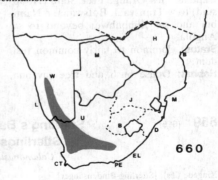

Voice: Drawn-out *dweee-dweee* (similar to whistle of Diederik Cuckoo); quick piping *twi-twi-twi-twi;* string of rapidly stuttered notes (like those of prinia).

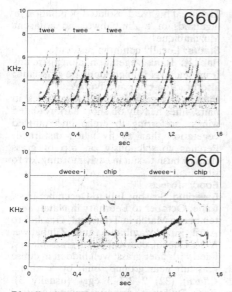

Distribution: Karoo from De Aar to w Cape, Namaqualand and s Namibia to Naukluft Mountains; distribution discontinuous.

Status: Locally fairly common to uncommon resident.

Habitat: Boulder-strewn hillsides and mountainsides with low shrubs and grasstufts.

Habits: Usually solitary or in pairs. Forages over rocks, in bushes and in clefts with quick thoroughness, darting about like white-eye; movements jerky like clockwork toy, flicking tail up, down and sideways, sometimes partly or wholly fanned; clings to rock face at any angle. Tame and confiding, but lands inconspicuously behind rock and runs or creeps about on rock face; may bound from boulder to boulder. Flies quickly from bush to bush, sometimes perching on top.

Food: Small insects, including grasshoppers.

Breeding: *Season*: July to August. *Nest*: Thick-walled oval with side-top entrance; built of grass stems, thickly padded and interwoven with plant down and sheepswool, bound with spider web and thickly lined with plant down; entrance 3–3,5 cm diameter; overall diameter 10–11,5 cm; near ground in tuft of grass or *Restio* at foot of rock, usually concealed by bush. *Clutch*: 2–4 eggs (usually 2–3). *Eggs*: Pale bluish white, dotted with lilac concentrated at thick end; measure (2) 18,4–19 × 13,1–13,8. *Incubation*: Unrecorded. *Nestling*: Unrecorded.

Ref. Martin, J. & Martin, R. 1965. *Ostrich* 36:136–137.

661 (618) Grassbird Plate 53
Grasvoël
Sphenoeacus afer

Itshitshi, Udwetya (X), uVuze (Z), [Kap-Grassänger]

Measurements: Length 19–23 cm; wing (8) 64–67,8–70; tail 98–106; tarsus 21–23,5; culmen 15–17,5. Weight (1 ♂) 32,3 g, (3 ♀) 27,7–29,9–33,7 g.

Bare Parts: Iris brown; bill blackish horn, base paler; legs and feet brownish to greyish.

Identification: Fairly large (almost robinsized); crown bright rusty red, streaked with black on hindcrown and nape; back streaked buff and black (no streaks on upperparts of Moustached Warbler); rump plain rufous; below buff, paler on throat, streaked black on flanks; 2 con-

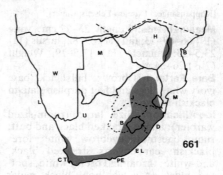

spicuous black malar stripes on each side (diagnostic with red crown; only 1 malar stripe in Moustached Warbler); rectrices rufous, longish, sharply pointed (diagnostic, especially in flight). *Immature*: Duller than adult; whole crown streaked with black.

Voice: Song rapid jumbled phrase of twittering, fairly musical notes ending in single down-slurred trill or whistle (similar to song phrases of Fawncoloured Lark and Stonechat), *chu-tee-ree chwiddly-chwiddly-chwiddly-chreeeu*; song phrase repeated at intervals of about 5 seconds; catlike *meeew* alarm note, rising in pitch.

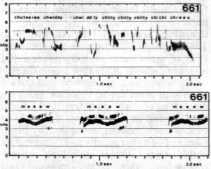

Distribution: Sw Cape to Lesotho, Natal, e Orange Free State, w Swaziland and Transvaal highveld; isolated population in highlands of e Zimbabwe and adjacent Mozambique.

Status: Locally common resident.

Habitat: Rank vegetation along streams from sea level to high montane grassland; also bracken-brier and fynbos.

Habits: Usually solitary, sometimes in pairs. Flies heavily on short dark rounded wings, preferring to creep into tangled vegetation than to fly when disturbed. Perches conspicuously on top of grass stem or bush to sun in early morning, or to sing.

Food: Insects.

Breeding: Season: July to December in sw Cape, October to February in Natal, September to March in Transvaal, October to April in Mozambique and Zimbabwe. *Nest*: Cup of coarse curled grass blades, lined with finer grass; well hidden in dense grasstuft near ground; built by ♀ alone. *Clutch*: (32) 2–2,7–3 eggs (usually 3). *Eggs*: Dull white or greyish white, spotted with brown and grey concentrated at thick end; measure (52) 22 × 15,8 (20–24 × 14,8–17). *Incubation*: 14–17 days. *Nestling*: 14–16 days; fed by both parents.

---

662 (539)   **Rockrunner**   **Plate 53**
Rotsvoël

Achaetops pycnopygius

[Klippensänger, Damara-Felsenspringer]

Measurements: Length 23–27 cm; wing (19) 66–69–73; tail (11) 69–82; tarsus (11) 23,5–25; culmen (11) 17,5–19. Weight (7 ♂) 26–34 g.

Bare Parts: Iris brown; bill black, base ivory white; legs and feet purplish slate to blackish brown.

Identification: Size large (robin-sized warbler); above streaked black and buff; rump chestnut; eyebrow white; lores blackish; ear coverts streaked black-and-white; throat and breast white, spotted black at sides; bold black malar stripe (diagnostic); belly and undertail bright rufous (diagnostic); tail black.

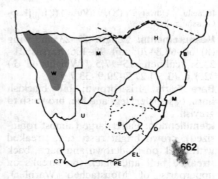

Immature: Less distinctly marked than adult.

Voice: Song rapid rich warbling *tip tip tootle titootle tootle too* (number of *tootles* varies), somewhat like throaty *Acrocephalus* song; also mimics calls of other bird species; *tootle-tootle* or *hoo-boy, hoo-boy* anxiety call; sharp *ti-tip ti-ti-ti-ti-ti....*; harsh drawn-out *cheerrrrr* alarm note.

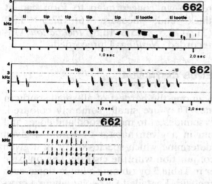

Distribution: Central Namibia E of Namib Desert to Waterberg Plateau and sw Angola.
Status: Uncommon to rare resident.

Habitat: Lower rocky slopes of hills and mountains, especially along dry water-courses.
Habits: Usually solitary or in pairs. Both sexes sing from top of boulder or bush in early morning and evening. Fairly easily located by watching skyline for bird to show up in silhouette; not shy when singing; otherwise flies from rock to rock, or skulks in crevices and between rocks.
Food: Insects (beetles and grasshoppers).
Breeding: Season: December to March. *Nest:* Thick-walled cup of grass, lined with soft fine grass; inside diameter 6,3–7,6 cm, depth 5,7 cm; well hidden in centre of large grasstuft. *Clutch:* 2–3 eggs. *Eggs:* Pale buffy pink, with small red-brown spots and underlying slaty blotches forming ring around thick end; measure (14) 21,4 × 15,4 (20,9–22,7 × 15–16,5). *Incubation:* Unrecorded. *Nestling:* Unrecorded; young leave nest early and run about like mice.

Ref. Clinning, C.M. & Tarboton, W.R. 1972. *Madoqua Ser. 1*, 5:57–61.

663 (617)   **Moustached Warbler**   **Plate 53**
Breëstertgrasvoël
Melocichla mentalis

[Bartgrassänger]

Measurements: Length 18–20 cm; wing (6 ♂) 76–78,5–82, (2 ♀) 80–83; tail (6 ♂) 83–87,2–90, (2 ♀) 84–87; tarsus (6 ♂) 27,5–28,7–30, (2 ♀) 28–29; culmen (6 ♂) 17,5–18,8–20, (2 ♀) 17,5–18,5.
Bare Parts: Iris brown to yellowish; bill black above, dark grey below; legs and feet blue-grey.
Identification: Size medium (smaller than Grassbird); forehead and ear coverts chestnut; crown and back plain rufous brown (streaked in Grassbird); rump rufous; wings and tail blackish brown, remiges edged rufous (showing as rusty patch when wing folded); eyebrow white; throat white with single black malar stripe (2 black stripes in Grassbird); breast to undertail light russet (streaked in Grassbird). *Immature:* Lacks chestnut forehead; innermost secondaries tipped buff.

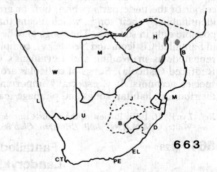

Voice: Song rich melodious jumbled phrase, *tip-tip-tip-tip-twiddle-iddle-eeee* (rather thrushlike).

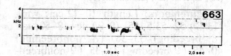

573

Distribution: Eastern highlands of Zimbabwe to Ethiopia and Guinea Bissau.
Status: Rare local resident.
Habitat: Marshy ground along streams and among scattered trees at edges of montane evergreen forest, with rank grass, bracken or bushes.
Habits: Usually solitary. Skulks behind vegetation; sometimes perches on top of grass to sun or to sing (very like Grassbird). Poorly known.

Food: Insects (mantids, grasshoppers, beetles).
Breeding: Season: January in Zimbabwe. *Nest:* Thin shallow bowl, loosely built of grass and rootlets; well hidden in grasstuft, up to 30 cm above ground. *Clutch:* 2 eggs. *Eggs:* Pinkish white, marbled with red-brown concentrated to form cap at thick end; measure (6) 22,5 × 15,9 (21,5–22,5 × 15,3–16,5). *Incubation:* Unrecorded. *Nestling:* Unrecorded.

THE CISTICOLAS, GENUS *CISTICOLA*

The cisticolas (pronounced sis-TIK-o-las) are among the hardest of all small southern African passerines to identify by sight alone. They are small, sombrely coloured, quick-moving warblers of grassy habitats from semidesert to moist woodland edges and vleis. The number of species to choose from in a given habitat or within a given distribution is limited: Table 3 will help to determine which species occur in a given region in a given habitat (use this Table in conjunction with the cisticola key on page lxxiii). Check distribution and habitat together in Table 3 by running a finger down each of these two columns at the same time, starting with Fantailed Cisticola; where a cross occurs in both the distribution and the habitat columns, that species of cisticola is likely to occur in that combination of region and habitat, but check also the map in the text to see if that species is supposed to occur in the area you are dealing with. A maximum of eight species is theoretically possible in a marshy lowveld habitat, but seldom will three or four species (at most) be apparent at any one time in most habitats in a given distribution. Plumage features to look for include the colour of the crown (plain rufous, faintly streaked black-on-rufous, plain buff, or boldly streaked blackish on buff), the colour of the back (grey or buff, streaked or plain), the length of the tail (long, medium or short; tails of all species are noticeably longer in winter than in summer) and the colour of the underparts (white, buff or grey). Cisticolas are most easily and certainly identifiable by their songs, which means that positive identification of many of them is possible only in summer. The songs may be simple (one note repeated several times, as in Fantailed Cisticola and Neddicky), complex and stereotyped (a set phrase, sometimes repeated, as in Wailing and Levaillant's Cisticolas) or complex and variable (as in Redfaced Cisticola). Songs of cisticolas are clearly reproduced in the sonagrams in the species accounts. It is especially important in this group of birds, therefore, to use distribution, habitat, songs and plumage features in combination for sure identification.

Ref. Lynes, H. 1930. Review of the genus *Cisticola*. *Ibis* 6 (12th Series), *Cisticola Supplement*.
White, C.M.N. 1960. *Bull. Brit. Orn. Club* 80:124–132.

664 (629)   Fantailed Cisticola   Plate 56
Landeryklopkloppie
Cisticola juncidis

Tangtang (NS), Motintinyane (SS), Kadhi-idhi-i, Timba (Sh), Matinti (Ts), Unoqandilana, Unozwi (X), uNcede (Z), [Zistensänger]

Measurements: Length 10–12 cm; wing (13 ♂) 52–53,5–55, (8 ♀) 46–48–50; tail (♂ breeding) 33–36, (♂ nonbreeding) 40–45, (♀ breeding) 31–35, (♀ nonbreeding) 35–38; tarsus (21) 17–19; culmen (21) 9,5–10,5. Weight (10) 7–9,4–13 g.
Bare Parts: Iris light brown; bill dark horn, base yellowish; legs and feet pinkish brown.
Identification: Size small; above tawny buff, streaked blackish brown (paler in

TABLE 3

CISTICOLA DISTRIBUTION AND HABITATS

Species	Distribution			Habitats											
	'Lowveld' (under 500 m a.s.l.)	'Middleveld' (500–1 200 m a.s.l.)	'Highveld' (over 1 200 m a.s.l.)	Bushveld	Savanna	Shrub or scrub	Rank vegetation (weeds, *etc.*)	Tall grassveld	Marshy or streamside vegetation	Open rank grassveld	Open short grassveld	Cultivated fields	Gardens	Mountains and rocks	Desert and semidesert
Fantailed	+	+	+					+	+	+	+	+			+
Desert			+							+	+				+
Cloud		+	+								+				
Ayres'		+	+					+			+			+	
Palecrowned	+	+							+	+					
Shortwinged	+			+	+										
Neddicky	+	+	+	+	+	+							+	+	
Greybacked	+	+				+								+	
Wailing	+	+	+				+	+	+					+	
Tinkling	+	+	+		+										+
Rattling	+	+		+	+	+		+							
Singing	+			+	+	+	+		+						
Redfaced	+			+			+		+						
Blackbacked	+						+		+						
Chirping	+	+							+						
Levaillant's	+	+	+				+	+	+						
Croaking	+	+		+				+	+	+					
Lazy	+	+	+	+			+	+	+					+	

winter, streaks more distinctly continuous; Desert Cisticola paler overall); rump plain bright tawny; below white, washed yellowish buff on breast and flanks (breast white when breeding); tail medium, fanned in flight, blackish brown, tipped black and white, the only cisticola with spotted fan pattern on tail at all seasons (tail much shorter in Cloud, Ayres' and Palecrowned Cisticolas; black subterminal band not visible from above in Desert Cisticola). *Immature*: Below pale yellow. **Voice:** Song monotonous *klink, klink, klink* or *zit, zit, zit, zit* repeated about every second in dipping display flight, one note at each dip; alarm rapidly repeated *chik-chik-chik* or *tik-tik-tik*.

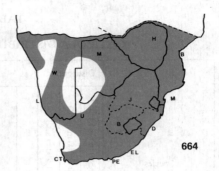

664

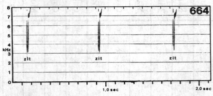

Distribution: Africa, s Europe, s Asia, Australia; widespread in s Africa, except most of dry W.
Status: Very common resident; some local movements.
Habitat: Open grassveld, vleis, cultivated fields (lucerne, *Eragrostis* , wheat), fallow lands, edges of cultivation, airfields, golf courses.
Habits: Usually solitary or in pairs. Conspicuous in display flight, about 10–15 m above ground over nesting territory in summer (see **Voice**). Forages low down in grass and weeds, or on ground; when disturbed perches on thin stem, flicking tail sideways; flight bouncing, with fanned tail jerking at each bounce. Snaps wings loudly when alarmed near nest, even while carrying building material or food.

Food: Small insects (mainly grasshoppers).
Breeding: *Season*: September to March (mainly November-January) in Natal, October to March (mainly December-February) in Transvaal, November to April (mainly December-March) in Zimbabwe. *Nest*: Unique vertical bottle of plant down and spider web, narrow at top entrance (2,5–3,6–4,5 cm diameter), wider at base; chamber diameter 5–5,9–7 cm, internal depth from rim of entrance to floor of chamber 13 cm, maximum overall height 8–10,9–14,5 cm (dimensions of 7 nests); bound to green grassblades, 2–20 cm above ground; lining material added after egglaying, so walls thicken with time. *Clutch*: (120) 2–3,3–5 eggs (usually 3–4). *Eggs*: White, pale cream, pale blue, greenish blue, turquoise or pinkish cream, rarely plain, usually spotted light brown or chocolate and lilac; sometimes finely speckled; measure (181) 15,1 × 11,4 (13,3–16,5 × 10,4–12,4); weigh (mean) 1,1 g. *Incubation*: 12–15 days. *Nestling*: About 11–14 days; nestlings make sharp hiss when nest touched.

Ref. Penry, E.H. 1985. Ostrich 56:229–235.

---

665 (630)   **Desert Cisticola**   **Plate 56**
Woestynklopkloppie
Cisticola aridula

Motintinyane (SS), Kadhi-idhi-i, Timba (Sh), Matinti (Ts), [Kalahari-Zistensänger]
Measurements: Length 10–12 cm; wing (12 ♂) 50–51–52, (5 ♀) 47–52; tail (♂ breeding) 35–40, (♂ nonbreeding) 39–45, (♀ breeding) 33–35, (♀ nonbreeding) 41–43; tarsus 17,5–19,5; culmen 10–11,5. Weight 7,8–10,1 g.

Bare Parts: Iris light brown; bill dark horn, base greyish pink; legs and feet pinkish.

Identification: Size small; very similar to Fantailed Cisticola; above streaked blackish on buff; below white, washed buff on breast and flanks; tail medium, dusky above, spotted below, tipped white (Fantailed Cisticola has subterminal black band visible from above; tail looks longer). *Immature*: Paler than adult; not yellow below.

Voice: Song monotonous high-pitched tinkling *ting-ting-ting* about every half-second, changing in pitch after every few notes; staccato clicking *chik-chik-chik* or bell-like *jing-jing-jing* alarm notes, often in aerial display while bouncing like yo-yo, with marked wing-snap at each bounce.

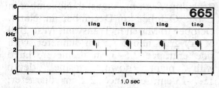

Distribution: Africa S of Sahara; in s Africa widespread in drier grasslands of interior.

Status: Locally common to fairly common resident; some local nomadic movements.

Habitat: Arid short grassland, dry edges of vleis.

Habits: Usually solitary or in pairs. Forages low in grass or on ground. Male conspicuous in erratic display flight low over grass; sings in flight or when perched. Female snaps wings in alarm near nest or fledglings. Somewhat similar to Fantailed Cisticola but prefers drier grassland with narrow-leaved species.

Food: Small insects (especially grasshoppers).

Breeding: *Season*: October to March (mainly November-December) in Natal, October to April (mainly December-March) in Transvaal, November to April (mainly December-January) in Zimbabwe. *Nest*: Ball of dry grass and plant down, with large side-top entrance; roof somewhat loosely built; in tuft of dry grass up to 30 cm above ground (rarely to 60 cm). *Clutch*: (35) 2–3,4–5 eggs (usually 3–4). *Eggs*: White or pale blue, plain or finely speckled with purplish brown, red-brown and lilac sometimes concentrated into ring around thick end; measure (47) 15 × 11,3 (13,9–15,9 × 10,8–12). *Incubation*: (2) 14 days. *Nestling*: 18 days; nestlings make sharp hiss when nest touched.

---

666 (631)   **Cloud Cisticola**   **Plate 56**
Gevlekte Klopkloppie
Cisticola textrix

Motintinyane (SS), Igqaza (X), iBhoyibhoyi (Z), [Pinkpink]

Measurements: Length 9–10 cm; wing (31 ♂) 50–52,7–57, (23 ♀) 45–47,9–50; tail (♂ breeding) 25–28, (♂ nonbreeding) 35–37, (♀ breeding) 26–28, (♀ nonbreeding) 31–34; tarsus (10 ♂) 21–22,5, (10 ♀) 18,5–20; culmen (54) 9–11,5.

Bare Parts: Iris light brown; bill dark horn, base yellowish pink; legs and feet pinkish brown.

Identification: Size very small; tail very short, especially when breeding, black above, spotted below (spotted above and below in Fantailed Cisticola); similar to Ayres' Cisticola, but body more robust and legs much longer; voice diagnostic; above tawny, broadly streaked blackish (more blobbed than Fantailed Cisticola, especially when breeding); crown almost plain light brown in breeding ♂; below white, washed buff on flanks, slightly streaked dark brown on sides of breast (whole breast and flanks streaked in birds from s Cape and e Orange Free State; diagnostic). In hand: 1st primary remex very short and pointed, as in Ayres' Cisticola. *Immature*: Below bright lemon yellow.

Voice: Song, always in high cruising flight, rapid high-pitched set phrase, *tik-tik-tik-tik see-see chik-chik-chik-chik* or *pi-pi-pi-pi chikchikchikchikchik*, repeated about every 2–3 seconds for several minutes on end (regional variations occur, but always much faster than song phrase of Ayres' Cisticola); cruising flight ends in vertical dive accompanied by rapid *chik-chikchikchik* (without wingsnaps as in Ayres' Cisticola).

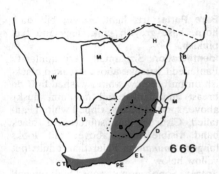

666

666

Distribution: S Africa to Angola and Zaire; in s Africa confined to extreme SW, S and highveld to n Transvaal.

Status: Common resident.

Habitat: Very short grassland, usually with bare patches between tufts; also flat estuarine marshland in s Cape.

Habits: Usually solitary. Forages on ground; inconspicuous unless singing in flight display; ♂ rises with whirring wings at about 45°, often to beyond range of normal human vision, cruising about for many minutes, giving song phrases (see **Voice**), sometimes swooping about with *chickichik* call; at end of dive (see **Voice**), checks just above ground and lands.

Food: Small insects (especially grasshoppers).

Breeding: *Season*: August to November in Cape, October to December in Natal, October to March in Transvaal. *Nest*: Ball of dry grass about 7,5 cm diameter, with side entrance 2,5–3 cm diameter, lined with plant down; inside depth 11,7–13 cm; entrance 2,2 cm diameter; internal diameter about 5,5 cm; on or near ground, inside or under grasstuft, with living grass woven into roof. *Clutch*: (23) 2–3,1–4 eggs (rarely 5). *Eggs*: Pale pink, turquoise or greenish, speckled and spotted with red-brown concentrated at thick end; measure (58) 15,7 × 11,6 (14–17,8 × 10,8–12,5). *Incubation*: Unrecorded. *Nestling*: 15–16 days.

---

667 (634)   **Ayres' Cisticola**   **Plate 56**

Kleinste Klopkloppie

Cisticola ayresii

Motintinyane (SS), Igqaza, Unogqaza, Uqandiliso (X), iBhoyibhoyi (Z), [Zwergpinkpink]

Measurements: Length 9–10 cm; wing (10 ♂) 49–50,5–52, (11 ♀) 42–46–48; tail (♂ breeding) 24–27, (♂ nonbreeding) 34–35, (♀ breeding) 24–28, (♀ nonbreeding) 33; tarsus (10 ♂) 18,5–19,5, (11 ♀) 17,5–18,5; culmen (21) 9–10,5. Weight (3) 9–10,1–12 g.

Bare Parts: Iris light brown; bill dark horn, base yellowish pink; legs and feet pinkish brown.

Identification: Size very small; very similar to Cloud Cisticola (probably not safely separable in field by sight alone), but less robustly built, and streaked only on sides of breast; tail very short, especially when breeding, black above; legs much shorter than those of Cloud Cisticola; voice diagnostic. In hand: 1st primary remex very short and pointed, as in Cloud Cisticola. *Immature*: Duller than adult; below pale yellow.

Voice: Song, given only in high cruising flight lasting many minutes, rather slow and deliberate set phrase of 3–7 notes (very much slower than song of Cloud Cisticola), *chitik chitik tsi tsi tsi*, or *chiki pee pee pee*, or simply *tee tee tee* or *ser SIT sue*, repeated many times, now and then interspersed by diving flight accompanied by loud rapid *tiktiktiktik*, sometimes with wing-snaps (but not always); some regional variation; in ne Cape song sometimes shorter *pi pi teep teep* interspersed with wing-snapping; in Natal song may be repeated *willy weety weety*, interspersed with sharp *tsiktsiktsik* notes in dive; flight display ends in vertical dive with rapid *tiktiktik* notes and wing-snaps, sometimes ending in swerving flight just above grass before landing; rapid squeaky *chiki chiki chiki* accompanied by loud wing-snaps in alarm near nest or fledglings.

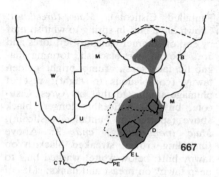

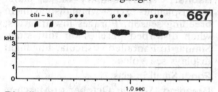

667

Distribution: S Africa to Gabon and Sudan; in s Africa confined to SE, e Transvaal and parts of Zimbabwe.

Status: Common resident; some local movement, especially away from burnt grassland in winter.

Habitat: Short grassland, usually at lower elevations than that of Cloud Cisticola in Natal, but not in Lesotho; prefers slightly denser grass than does Cloud Cisticola, but also requires bare ground between tufts.

Habits: Usually solitary or in pairs. Very similar to Cloud Cisticola. For displays see **Voice**. Female highly secretive, especially when nesting, but may give distraction display by flying from nest low over grass, dropping 5–6 times into grass; display silent without wingsnaps. Generally inconspicuous unless ♂ in flight display, usually at great height above ground, close to limits of human vision, cruising back and forth with rapidly beating wings.

Food: Small insects.

Breeding: *Season*: October to March in Natal and Zimbabwe, September to March in Transvaal. *Nest*: Ball of dry grass, plant down and spider web, 7–7,5 cm diameter, with side entrance 2–3,5 cm diameter; on ground under small grasstuft or broad leaf of low composite herb (rarely up to 5 cm above ground in grasstuft), usually with growing grass curled into structure of roof; often faces onto small bare patch of soil. *Clutch*: (30) 2–3,3–4 eggs (usually 3–4). *Eggs*: White or very pale greenish, sparsely speckled with brown or pinkish brown, mostly at thick end; measure (27) 15,2 × 11,6 (13,2–16,5 × 10,5–12). *Incubation*: At least 11 days by ♀ only. *Nestling*: Unrecorded.

668 (635)   **Palecrowned Cisticola**   **Plate 56**
Bleekkopklopkloppie
Cisticola brunnescens

Kadhi-idhi-i, Timba (Sh), [Blaßkopfpinkpink]
Measurements: Length 10–11 cm; wing ♂ 52–56, ♀ 48–50; tail (breeding) 29–35, (nonbreeding) 33–37; tarsus 20,5–22; culmen 10–12.

Bare Parts: Iris light brown; bill dark horn, base yellowish pink; mouth of breeding ♂ black; legs and feet pinkish brown.

Identification: Size small (larger than Cloud and Ayres' Cisticolas; about size of

579

Fantailed Cisticola). *Male (breeding)*: Crown olive buff in spring to whitish buff by end of summer (diagnostic); lores and area around eye blackish, forming diagnostic face mask; rump bright golden tawny (conspicuous in flight); rest of plumage similar to that of Ayres' Cisticola, but tail noticeably longer, black above (spotted in Fantailed Cisticola). *Male (nonbreeding) and ♀*: Above (including crown) streaked blackish on tawny buff; below white, washed buff to deep tawny on breast and flanks; sides of breast streaked blackish (probably not safely separable from Fantailed Cisticola on appearance alone, except for streaks on sides of breast). *Immature*: Below bright lemon yellow.

Voice: Song of ♂ (usually in flight display, sometimes also from perch) high-pitched slow *teee teee teee* (3–7 times in level flight), then somewhat faster *chree-chree-chree-chree* (up to 13 times in steep dive), then *chree chree* (twice after pulling suddenly out of dive by upward swoop into level flight again); may sing *teee teee* several times while rising to displaying height, but sometimes rises silently; display sometimes accompanied by barely audible wingsnaps; after several display bouts, nose-dives silently (no calls or wingsnaps) to grass; alarm call of ♂ high-pitched single *tee* or *twee* 1–2 seconds apart, sometimes accompanied by loud wingsnaps near young; alarm call of ♀ quiet *chitty chitty chitty*.

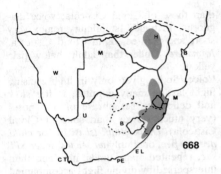

668

Distribution: S Africa to Cameroon and Ethiopia; in s Africa discontinuously from Transkei, ne Orange Free State, se Transvaal to e Zimbabwe.

Status: Locally fairly common to uncommon; resident in some areas; in Natal midlands summer breeding visitor only.

Habitat: Moist, but fairly short grassland, edges of grassy drainage lines and vleis.

Habits: Usually solitary or in pairs. Inconspicuous except when displaying in breeding season. Forages low in grass; when disturbed perches on thin stem. Similar to Fantailed Cisticola. For flight displays see **Voice**.

Food: Small insects.

Breeding: *Season*: October to March in Natal, November to May in Zimbabwe. *Nest*: Oval (not ball) of spider web and living grass (very little dead grass) about 20 cm high and 6 cm wide, with side-top entrance about 4 cm diameter; inside height about 7 cm; tops of living grass blades mostly left pointing upwards, but some woven into fabric of roof; thickly lined with plant down; 5–15 cm above ground in lush green grass; quite different from nests of Cloud and Ayres' Cisticolas. *Clutch*: (16) 2–3,1–5 eggs (mostly 3). *Eggs*: White, pale blue or turquoise, spotted with red-brown, chocolate, purplish and grey; measure (20) 15,6 × 11,5 (14,7–16,7 × 10,9–12). *Incubation*: 11–13 days. *Nestling*: 12–14 days.

Ref. Penry, E.H. 1985. *Ostrich* 56:229–235.

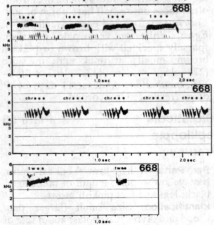

669 (638)

Greybacked Cisticola
Grysrugtinktinkie
Cisticola subruficapilla

Plate 57

[Bergzistensänger]

Measurements: Length 11–13 cm; wing (32 ♂) 53–55–59, (25 ♀) 47–49,5–52; tail (32 ♂) 51–59, (25 ♀) 46–55; tarsus (32 ♂) 17–19, (25 ♀) 16–18; culmen (32 ♂) 11–12, (25 ♀) 10–11. Weight (3 ♀) 9,6–10,5–12 g.

Bare Parts: Iris brown; bill grey, culmen blackish brown; legs and feet pinkish.

Identification: Size medium (larger than Fantailed Cisticola); very similar to Wailing Cisticola, but breast greyish white (not buff); crown dark rufous merging with grey of back, faintly streaked blackish (streaking not usually visible in field); eyebrow indistinct; back grey, finely streaked black; rest of underparts dull whitish (clearly spotted darker in sw Cape birds; spots vestigial in other populations); tail longish, dusky, tipped pale brown, subterminal band black. Birds in drier areas paler and less distinctly streaked than those further E. *Immature*: Similar to adult; only faintly washed yellowish below (much brighter yellow in immature Wailing Cisticola).

Voice: Song similar to that of Wailing Cisticola, but more musical loud *prrreee tee tee tee tee* (somewhat like song of Levaillant's Cisticola with components reversed); tinkling *trrrrink* callnote (similar to introductory trill of song); buzzy *zt-bzeet* or *bzeet* alarm call; piping *tee tee tee* anxiety (?) call.

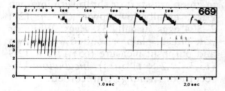

Distribution: Mainly dry W of s Africa from e Karoo and ne Cape to Angola.

Status: Common resident; may be conspecific with Wailing Cisticola.

Habitat: Semi-arid shrubby plains and scrubby slopes, fynbos, Karoo, montane grassland with tussocky drainage lines.

Habits: Usually in pairs, sometimes solitary. Forages low down in shrubs and grasstufts, but often perches conspicuously on top of vegetation. Highly vocal at all seasons, but sings only in breeding season; sings only from perch. Very similar to Wailing Cisticola, but habitat somewhat different.

Food: Small insects.

Breeding: *Season*: August to December. *Nest*: Ball of dry grass and plant down with side entrance; on or near ground in grasstuft or low shrub, with growing grass incorporated into roof and walls. *Clutch*: (12) 2–2,8–4 eggs. *Eggs*: Whitish to pale blue, spotted with red-brown, brown and purplish; measure (78) 15,9 × 11,9 (14,2–17,1 × 10,6–13). *Incubation*: Unrecorded. *Nestling*: Unrecorded.

Ref. Vernon, C.J. 1982. *Bee-eater* 33:29–30.

670 (639)

Wailing Cisticola
Huiltinktinkie
Cisticola lais

Plate 57

Kadhi-idhi-i, Timba (Sh), Ngonhavarimi (Ts), Iqobo (X), uQoyi (Z), [Trauerzistensänger]

Measurements: Length ♂ 13–14 cm, ♀ 12–13 cm; wing (17 ♂) 60–66, (13 ♀) 51–55; tail (17 ♂) 55–66, (13 ♀) 44–54; tarsus (17 ♂) 20–22,5, (13 ♀) 17,5–20,5; culmen (17 ♂) 11,5–13, (13 ♀) 10,5–12. Weight (21 ♂) 13,1–14,7–17,3 g, (14 ♀)

10,7–10,9–12,3 g, (8 unsexed) 10–12,2–15,5 g.

Bare Parts: Iris light brown; bill blackish horn, base whitish pink; legs and feet pinkish.

Identification: Size medium (larger than Fantailed Cisticola); very similar to Greybacked Cisticola, but breast buff (not grey), sometimes streaked in birds from s Cape; crown rufous, contrasting with grey of back (lightly streaked blackish when not breeding; n Transvaal birds have crown streaked at all times); back grey, streaked black (streaks broader than in Greybacked Cisticola); clear rufous bar on folded wing (formed by rusty edges of remiges; less clear in Greybacked Cisticola); tail reddish brown, tipped light brown, subterminal band black; rest of underparts dull whitish. *Immature*: Yellowish on face, throat and breast (only faintly yellow in Greybacked Cisticola); crown brown (not rufous).

Voice: Song similar to that of Greybacked Cisticola (less musical, more wailing), long raspy note followed by 4–6 high-pitched piping notes, *sreee teep teep teep teep*, loud and penetrating; some regional variation; also rich bubbling *wititi peep peep peep peep*; loud wailing *pweee* or *prrrweee* or *peeweet* with rising intonation, or harsh *jree jree jree* alarm calls; loud bubbling *wititi wititi* callnote.

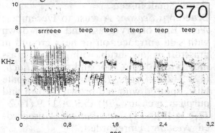

Distribution: S Africa to Angola and Kenya; in s Africa mainly in montane

country, discontinuously from sw Cape to e Zimbabwe, adjacent Mozambique and Gorongosa Mountain.

Status: Common resident; may be conspecific with Greybacked Cisticola.

Habitat: Montane grassland with bracken and some scattered shrubs, usually on steep rocky slopes; also long grassland on steep rocky coastal slopes with bracken and fynbos.

Habits: Usually in pairs; sometimes solitary; in small groups when not breeding. Very similar to Greybacked Cisticola. Forages low down in dense grass and rank shrubby vegetation; often perches conspicuously on top of bracken or low shrub. Highly vocal, but sings only when breeding; sings from perch.

Food: Small insects.

Breeding: *Season*: September to January in Natal, October to March in Transvaal, October to February (mainly December-January) in Zimbabwe. *Nest*: Ball of dry grass and plant down with side entrance; in green grasstuft or shrub with ingrown grass, usually low down. *Clutch*: (27) 2–3–4 eggs (usually 3). *Eggs*: White or pale bluish, plain or spotted with brown and purplish; measure (65) 17,2 × 12,9 (15,3–19,2 × 11,5–14). *Incubation*: Unrecorded. *Nestling*: Unrecorded.

Ref. Vernon, C.J. 1982. *Bee-eater* 33:29–30.

671 (641)   **Tinkling Cisticola**   **Plate 57**
Rooitinktinkie

Cisticola rufilata

Harudeve (K), [Rotschwanz-Zistensänger]

Measurements: Length 13–14,5 cm; wing (15 ♂) 54–57–60, (11 ♀) 51–52–53; tail (15 ♂) 51–60, (11 ♀) 48,5–57; tarsus (26) 18–22; culmen (26) 11–13,5. Weight

(1 ♂) 14,7 g, (1 ♀) 11,8 g, (23 unsexed) 8–11,3–14,7 g.

Bare Parts: Iris brown to yellowish brown; bill blackish, shading to grey below; mouth black; legs and feet pinkish.

Identification: Medium (about size of Rattling Cisticola); similar to Rattling Cisticola but altogether more rufous, including tail; crown, eyering and ear coverts bright russet; conspicuous buff lores and eyebrow; back streaked buff or brown and blackish; below buff, shading to white in centre of throat and belly; tail bright rufous (diagnostic; dusky brown in Rattling Cisticola), with white tip and subterminal black band. *Immature*: Duller than adult; no yellow below.

Voice: Song of ♂ series of distinctive high tinkling bell-like notes, *tweee, tweee, tweee, tweee*; high twittering alarm call, *chirrrrrr*; also snaps bill and wings.

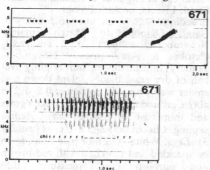

Distribution: Northern Cape to Angola and Zaire; in s Africa from Kuruman District to C and n Transvaal, Botswana, n Namibia and w and C Zimbabwe.

Status: Local and uncommon resident; usually commonest where Kalahari sand predominates.

Habitat: Transitional (ecotonal) zones;

scrub in semi-arid savanna, mainly on Kalahari sand, open grassland with scattered bushes and trees; also edges of *Baikiaea, Burkea, Terminalia, Brachystegia* and other woodland and secondary growth around cultivation.

Habits: Usually solitary; in family groups after breeding. Secretive and relatively silent, especially nesting ♀; dives into cover when alarmed; may drop to ground and run mouselike for several metres before flying; hard to see.

Food: Small insects.

Breeding: *Season*: November-December in Transvaal, October to March (mainly December-January) in Zimbabwe; may rear 2 broods/season. *Nest*: Ball of dry greyish grass blades and thickly felted plant down, with side entrance; well hidden in dense herbs, grass or low shrub, up to about 30 cm above ground. *Clutch*: 3–4 eggs. *Eggs*: White or pale blue, usually boldly spotted with pinkish brown and purplish grey forming cap at thick end; measure (70) 17 × 12,6 (16–18,8 × 11,4–13,2). *Incubation*: Unrecorded; by ♀ only. *Nestling*: Unrecorded; fed by both parents; postnestling dependence at least 35 days, when cared for by ♂ if ♀ starts second clutch.

672 (642)   **Rattling Cisticola**   **Plate 57**
Bosveldtinktinkie
Cisticola chiniana

Harudeve (K), Timba (Sh), Lekgere (Tw), iNqoba (Z), [Rotscheitel-Zistensänger]

Measurements: Length ♂ 14–16 cm, ♀ 12–13 cm; wing (37 ♂) 58–65,1–71, (13 ♀) 51–55,3–60; tail (18 ♂) 54–59,8–69, (8 ♀) 48,5–54–60; tarsus (14 ♂) 21–24, (5 ♀) 19,5–20, (19 unsexed) 22–24,1–26,5; culmen (21) 12–13,8–16. Weight (26 ♂) 13,2–17,9–21,4 g, (12 ♀) 11,1–13,7–18,5 g, (19 unsexed) 13–17,9–21,2 g.

Bare Parts: Iris light brown; bill blackish horn, base pinkish; mouth black in breeding ♂; legs and feet pinkish brown.

Identification: Size medium; somewhat similar to Greybacked and Wailing Cisticolas, but larger and in completely different habitat; crown deep russet; back greyish brown (more rufous in winter), streaked dusky; below creamy white; tail dusky brown (rufous in Tinkling Cisticola), tipped white, subterminal band black. *Immature:* Duller than adult; no yellow below.

Voice: Song loud repeated phrase of 2–4 high-pitched notes followed by bubbling trill, *tsee tsee tsee tr-r-r-r-r* and variations; trill may be discrete notes, *di-di-di-di*; harsh *cheee, cheee, cheee* alarm call.

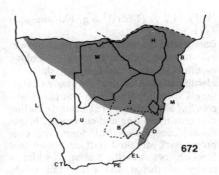

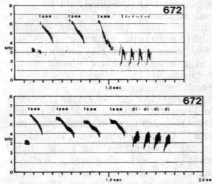

Distribution: S Africa and E Africa to Eritrea; in s Africa from Natal, Transvaal, Botswana and n Namibia northwards.

Status: Common resident.

Habitat: *Acacia* savanna, drier woodland, coastal scrub.

Habits: In pairs or small groups. Highly vocal, especially when breeding; black palate of ♂ conspicuous when singing from top of tree; ♀ secretive, except when alarm-calling near nest; ♂ readily gives alarm call at any time to human intruder.

Food: Insects, nectar of aloes.

Breeding: *Season:* October to January in Natal, October to March (mainly November-December) in Transvaal, October to April (mainly November-January) in Zimbabwe. *Nest:* Slightly oval ball of dry grass blades, plant down and spider web with side entrance; 0,2–1,2 m above ground in dry grasstuft, mixed grass and thornbush or fork of small *Acacia* sapling. *Clutch:* (89) 2–3,1–5 eggs (usually 3). *Eggs:* White, green or pale blue, plain or speckled and blotched with red-brown and purplish grey; measure (105) 16,9 × 12,4 (14,7–18,8 × 10,9–13,3). *Incubation:* Unrecorded; by ♀ only. *Nestling:* 14 days.

673 (643)   Singing Cisticola   Plate 57
Singende Tinktinkie

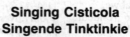

Cisticola cantans

[Grauer Zistensänger]

Measurements: Length 11,5–14 cm; wing (45) 44–52,5–56,5; tail (41) 38–49,9–64; tarsus (56) 19–22,7–25,5; culmen (55) 11–12,8–14,5. Weight (4 ♂) 11,1–12,6–14,6 g, (1 ♀) 10,2 g, (43 unsexed) 8,9–11,8–13,9 g.

Bare Parts: Iris light brown; bill blackish, base greyish; legs and feet brownish pink.

Identification: Size small to medium; very similar to Redfaced Cisticola; crown dull rufous, contrasting with brown back (browner, less contrasting, in Redfaced Cisticola); spot below lores black; eyebrow and face white (face light rufous in Redfaced Cisticola); back plain earth brown, rustier in winter (streaked in Tinkling Cisticola); below creamy white; tail greyish brown (more russet in Redfaced Cisticola), tipped white, subterminal band black. *Immature:* Duller than adult; no yellow below.

Voice: Song loud musical 2-syllabled *ju-hee* or *whee-choo*, somewhat variable; may be 3 syllables, *o-ki-wee* or *chewit-prrr-chewit*; other varied stuttering metallic and musical callnotes; also loud ringing metallic *plin plin* at intervals of 2–3 seconds; sibilant cicadalike *srrt srrt srrt*; thin *tsit tsit* or mournful drawn-out *cheerr cheerr* alarm calls (less harsh, more drawn-out than alarm calls of Redfaced Cisticola).

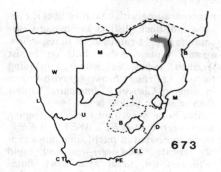

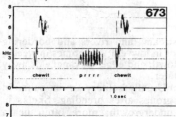

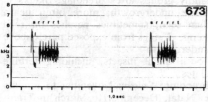

Distribution: Zimbabwe to E and W Africa; in s Africa confined to e Zimbabwe, adjacent Mozambique and Mount Gorongosa.

Status: Locally fairly common to very common resident.

Habitat: Bracken-brier and similar moist vegetation with trees and bushes along streams about 1000–1750 m above sea level; also forest edges in gullies.

Habits: Usually solitary or in pairs; in family groups after breeding. Inconspicuous and secretive, except when ♂ sings from prominent perch in breeding season; ♂ calls readily in response to human intrusion. Forages in low undergrowth; ♀ creeps silently away when disturbed, often into nearby thicket or forest; more often heard than seen.

Food: Small insects.

Breeding: *Season:* November to April (mainly December-January) in Zimbabwe and Mozambique. *Nest:* Oval of dry grass with side-top entrance, lined with plant down (further lining added after egg-laying); overall height about 14 cm; overall width 7,5 cm; depth of cup from threshold about 5 cm; sewn into broad leaves of herb or bush up to 90 cm (usually below 60 cm) above ground. *Clutch:* (43) 2–2,7–4 eggs (usually 2–3). *Eggs:* White to pale turquoise, boldly blotched with pale red-brown and grey; measure (61) 17 × 12,3 (15,9–19,5 × 11,9–13,1). *Incubation:* 12–14 days by ♀ only. *Nestling:* About 16 days; fed by both parents.

674 (644)   **Redfaced Cisticola**   **Plate 57**
                        Rooiwangtinktinkie

Cisticola erythrops

Harudeve (K), Timba (Sh), [Rotgesicht-Zisten-sänger]

Measurements: Length ♂ about 14 cm, ♀ about 12–13 cm; wing (81 ♂) 51–56,3–62, (84 ♀) 48–51,9–56; tail (22 ♂ breeding) 44,5–49,6–57, (24 ♂ nonbreeding) 48,5–54,5–62,5, (17 ♀ breeding) 38,5–45,5–52, (18 ♀ nonbreeding) 43–49,9–55; tarsus (60) 19–22,6–25; culmen (59) 11–14–17,5. Weight (28 ♂) 13,7–15,8–17,8 g, (43 ♀) 11,2–14–15,9 g, (141 unsexed) 11,2–14,3–19 g.

Bare Parts: Iris pale brown; bill blackish horn, base pinkish white; mouth black in breeding ♂; legs and feet pinkish.

Identification: Size smallish to medium; very similar to Singing Cisticola; forecrown rusty buff, grading into light olive grey on rest of upperparts (no streaking; crown less russet than in Singing Cisticola, not contrasting with colour of back); eyebrow indistinct (distinct in Singing Cisticola); face light rufous at all times; below creamy white, washed buff on breast (washed tawny in winter, including throat); tail russet brown (greyish brown in Singing Cisticola). *Immature*: Duller than adult; no yellow below.

Voice: Song very loud crescendo piping *weet-weet-weet-WEET-WEET-WEET*, rising somewhat in pitch; sometimes simply repeated loud *weet-weet-weet*; rapid *wit-wit-wit-wit*; nasal *nyaa nyaa*; notes mostly rich and full-toned or somewhat metallic; loud drawn-out *tearr* alarm call, louder in ♂ (harsher, higher-pitched and shorter than alarm call of Singing Cisticola).

Distribution: Africa S of Sahara; in s Africa confined to E and NE.
Status: Locally common to fairly common resident.
Habitat: Tall rank vegetation in marshes,

674

along streams and rivers and bordering reedbeds in lowveld; sometimes in weeds, rank growth and edges of canefields away from water.

Habits: Usually solitary or in pairs; in family groups after breeding. Skulks in dense undergrowth; more often heard than seen; sometimes perches on reed stems. ♂ sings from exposed perch above undergrowth.

Food: Small insects, including termite alates.

Breeding: *Season*: November to January in Natal, December to March in Transvaal, October to March (mainly December-February) in Zimbabwe. *Nest*: Oval ball of leaves with cup of dry grass, plant down and spider web, with side-top entrance; built by both sexes; sewn into broad leaves of herb or shrub; up to 50 cm above ground. *Clutch*: (20) 2–2,9–4 eggs (usually 3). *Eggs*: Turquoise, blotched with red-brown and grey concentrated at thick end; highly glossed and distinctively coloured; measure (45) 17,5 × 12,6 (16–18,8 × 11,6–13,5). *Incubation*: 12–16 days mostly by ♀. *Nestling*: 14–16 days; fed by both parents.

675 (645)   **Blackbacked Cisticola**   **Plate 57**
Swartrugtinktinkie
Cisticola galactotes

Harudeve (K), [Schwarzrücken-Zistensänger]

Measurements: Length 11–15 cm; wing (10 ♂) 55–59–62, (7 ♀) 52–53,5–55; tail (♂ breeding) 47–54, (♂ nonbreeding) 57–69, (♀ breeding) 46–52, (♀ nonbreeding) 53–61; tarsus (17) 20–23; culmen (17) 12–14. Weight (3) 10–13–15 g.

Bare Parts: Iris hazel; bill blackish, base pinkish grey; mouth black in breeding ♂; legs and feet pinkish.

Identification: Size medium; similar to Levaillant's and Chirping Cisticolas, but voice diagnostic; crown and nape dull rufous; eyebrow buff (rusty in Chirping

Cisticola); lores dusky; back black, scaled grey when breeding (scaled buff in Levaillant's Cisticola); back tawny, streaked black when not breeding; rump plain grey; below buff, paler on throat and centre of belly; tail grey (bright rufous brown in Levaillant's Cisticola) with clear pale tips (indistinct in Chirping Cisticola) and white outer rectrices. *Immature*: Similar to adult, but streaked blackish on crown; below light lemon yellow.

Voice: Variable, but highly vocal; loud piping *tskooee, tskooee* with rising tone; sharp *skit-skit-skit* or *tsrit-tsrit-tsrit*; monotonous rasping *zzreee*; penetrating *tee tee*, loud *PRRIT PRRIT* or rattling chatter (like machinegun) when alarmed.

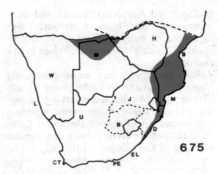

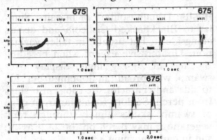

Distribution: Africa S of Sahara; in s Africa confined to extreme E and extreme N.

Status: Fairly common resident, sometimes with seasonal movements.

Habitat: Reedbeds and rank grass along lakes and rivers and in permanent or semipermanent pans; also maize fields and canefields next to reedbeds.

Habits: Usually solitary or in pairs. Inconspicuous when not breeding, skulking low in dense vegetation or shorter grass at edges of swamp. Breeding ♂ sings from exposed perch on reed stem, or in slow floppy flight display back and forth or in wide circle about 15 m above reeds; black mouth conspicuous while singing.

Food: Insects.

Breeding: *Season*: October to February (also June) in Natal, January in Zimbabwe. *Nest*: Ball of grass with side entrance, lined with grass inflorescences and decorated outside with plant down and cocoons; 0,6–1,2 m above water or ground suspended in grass or other plants; growing grass woven into fabric of nest. *Clutch*: (24) 2–2,9–4 eggs (usually 3). *Eggs*: Plain deep glossy terra-cotta or brick red; rarely pinkish white, densely freckled with pale brick red; measure (24) 17 × 12,5 (15,9–18,3 × 11,5–13,3). *Incubation*: 12–13 days by ♀ only. *Nestling*: 15–17 days; fed by both parents.

---

676 (645X)   **Chirping Cisticola**   **Plate 57**
Piepende Tinktinkie
Cisticola pipiens

Harudeve (K), [Sumpfzistensänger]

Measurements: Length 13–15 cm; wing (7 ♂) 60–61,6–66, (4 ♀) 53–56–60; tail, breeding 56–60, nonbreeding 62–70; tarsus 23–25; culmen 13–14. Weight 16–17,1 g.

Bare Parts: Iris brown; bill blackish brown, paler greyish below; legs and feet pinkish.

Identification: Size medium (looks slightly larger than Blackbacked Cisticola; otherwise similar, but voice diagnostic); crown and nape dark rusty brown; eyebrow faint, rusty (buff in Blackbacked Cisticola); blackish spot on lores; back greyish buff (greyer when breeding, more rufous otherwise), broadly streaked black; rump plain grey; tail dusky brown (greyer in

587

Blackbacked Cisticola), broad and conspicuous in flight; below rusty buff, paler in centre of belly (paler buff in Blackbacked Cisticola). *Immature*: White below and on face.

Voice: Song variable; most commonly *chip chip-chip chrrrrr* or bubbling *tik tik-tik-turr*; also 4-syllabled croaking twanging phrase *trrit-trrit-tree-treeei*; opening notes similar to those of Redfaced Cisticola; ratchetlike *krrrrr*; alarm calls similar to those of Levaillant's Cisticola.

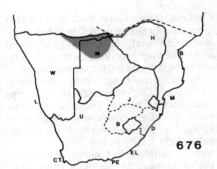

676

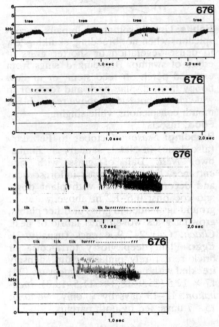

Distribution: Northern Botswana (Okavango region) to Angola, Zambia and s Zaire.

Status: Fairly common resident.

Habitat: *Papyrus* beds in swamps and along rivers, flooded grassland, floodplains.

Habits: Usually solitary or in pairs. Similar to Blackbacked Cisticola and occurs alongside it, but usually in taller vegetation. Unobtrusive except when breeding ♂ sings in zig-zag flight display over swamp, with broad tail flopping from side to side and characteristic song; also sings from perch. Seldom found far from edge of swamp; skulks nimbly through rank vegetation; may perch on top of grass to sun in early morning.

Food: Small insects (especially green grasshoppers).

Breeding: *Season*: About February to April in Botswana (October to April in Zambia, November to March in Angola). *Nest*: Ball of dry grass with side entrance, decorated with cocoons and lined with cocoons and plant down; well hidden in dense undergrowth. *Clutch*: 3–4 eggs. *Eggs*: Glossy salmon pink, marbled and clouded with terra-cotta; measure (10) 17,8 × 12,7 (15,7–19,1 × 12–13). *Incubation*: Unrecorded. *Nestling*: Unrecorded.

677 (646)   **Levaillant's Cisticola**   **Plate 57**

Vleitinktinkie

Cisticola tinniens

Motintinyane (SS), Timba (Sh), Matinti (Ts), Umvila, Imvila (X), [Uferzistensänger]

Measurements: Length 12–15 cm; wing (37 ♂) 50–53,5–58, (20 ♀) 46–49–51; tail (37 ♂) 51–66, (20 ♀) 46–60; tarsus (57) 17,5–20; culmen (57) 10–12. Weight (20) 8–11,4–18,5 g.

Bare Parts: Iris light brown; bill blackish horn, base pinkish; mouth black when breeding; legs and feet pinkish.

Identification: Size medium; similar to Blackbacked Cisticola, but voice diagnostic; crown bright russet, lightly streaked blackish on hindcrown (streaks bolder and

588

over whole crown when not breeding); back black, scaled light greyish buff (scaled greyer in Blackbacked Cisticola); rump dull olive buff, streaked black (plain grey in Blackbacked Cisticola); eyebrow, face and underparts buffy white; tail rusty brown and blackish (grey and blackish in Blackbacked Cisticola). *Immature*: Duller than adult; throat and breast washed pale lemon yellow.

Voice: Song bubbling *tseep* (or *tseeoo*) *tsirrirrooree*, rising slightly in pitch at end; sometimes up to 3 *tseep* notes before trill; loud *tee tee tee* callnotes, more plaintive as alarm call.

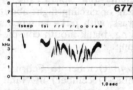

Distribution: S Africa to Angola and Kenya; in s Africa from sw Cape through highveld to n Transvaal; also in higher parts of Zimbabwe.

Status: Locally common resident.

Habitat: Vleis, marshy areas along smaller rivers and streams, edges of reedbeds, moist grassland.

Habits: Usually in pairs; sometimes solitary or in family groups. Highly vocal and conspicuous at all times, but sings only in summer months. Forages low down in vegetation; when disturbed perches high

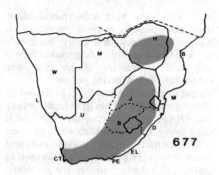

677

on tall stem or weed to view intruder, often giving alarm notes; may fly back and forth, jerking tail and calling; also flicks tail sideways when perched.

Food: Small insects.

Breeding: *Season*: August to October in sw Cape, October to March in Natal, September to April (mainly November-January) in Transvaal, September to May (mainly November-March) in Zimbabwe. *Nest*: Oval ball with side-top entrance, of broad dry grass blades, roots and spider web, lined with plant down; in standing or drooping grasstuft or weeds, in water or hanging over edge of stream or pond, up to 60 cm above water or ground. *Clutch*: (70) 2-3,5-5 eggs (usually 3-4). *Eggs*: White, pale green or blue, plain or spotted with pinkish brown, red-brown and grey; measure (134) 16 × 12 (13,8-17,6 × 10,9-13,3). *Incubation*: Unrecorded. *Nestling*: 14 days.

678 (647)   **Croaking Cisticola**   **Plate 57**
Groottinktinkie
Cisticola natalensis

Harudeve (K), Timba (Sh), Matinti (Ts), Ubhoyibhoyi, Igabhoyi (X), iBhoyi (Z), [Strichelzistensänger]

Measurements: Length ♂ 14-16 cm, ♀ 12,5-15 cm; wing (21 ♂) 69-72-76, (19 ♀) 58-60,5-63; tail (♂ breeding) 48-57, (♂ nonbreeding) 59-72, (♀ breeding) 46-60, (♀ nonbreeding) 56-66; tarsus (21 ♂) 27-30, (19 ♀) 23,5-27; culmen (40) 12-15,5. Weight (2 ♂) 21-24,8 g, (6 ♀) 14-16,4-18,2 g, (18 unsexed) 15-22 g.

Bare Parts: Iris light brown; bill (breeding) blackish, paler below, (nonbreeding) pinkish, culmen darker; mouth of breeding ♂ black; legs and feet pinkish.

Identification: Size large (♂) to medium (♀); build robust; general coloration greyish without any rufous tones; above grey (breeding) or olive buff (nonbreeding), streaked blackish; below creamy white, breast washed pale yellow (breeding) or buff (nonbreeding); tail grey, broadly tipped white (breeding) or buff (nonbreeding), with very bold subterminal black band (conspicuous in field, especially in flight); bill heavy, markedly decurved, black when breeding (diagnostic, especially in ♂). *Immature*: Duller and paler than adult; below bright yellow.

Voice: Loud rolling croaking, preceded by clicking sound like Zulu *q*; in flight display *q-q-RRRP, q-q-RRRP, q-q-RRRP* about once every 1,5–2 seconds; when perched *q-RRRRRRRP*, much drawn out and given only every 2–3 seconds (also used as alarm call); faster *qrr-qrr-qrr-qrr* when perched or flying.

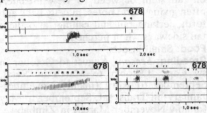

Distribution: S Africa to Sudan and Guinea Bissau; in s Africa confined to E and NE, from Kei Mouth northwards.

Status: Common resident or local migrant.

Habitat: Rank open moist grassland, edges of vleis, usually with scattered bushes or trees; also in clearings and edges of forest and regenerating secondary growth.

Habits: Usually solitary; sometimes in pairs. Unobtrusive unless breeding; highly

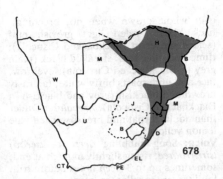

vocal; when disturbed perches on top of bush or tree, giving loud alarm calls. ♂ displays in zig-zag or circling flight about 2–3 m above grass, with jerky wingbeats and croaking song; black mouth conspicuous when singing.

Food: Insects.

Breeding: *Season*: October to February (mainly November-December) in Natal, November to February in Transvaal, November to March (mainly December-February) in Zimbabwe. *Nest*: Oval ball of dry grass and plant down with side entrance; in bower of dense green grass, 10–25 cm above ground (sometimes less); growing grass woven into roof and walls. *Clutch*: (65) 2–3,3–5 eggs (usually 3–4). *Eggs*: White or pale blue, spotted with tan, pale brown or red-brown and grey; measure (105) 18,7 × 13,7 (16–20,6 × 12,4–14,7). *Incubation*: Unrecorded; by ♀ only. *Nestling*: About 14 days.

679 (648) **Lazy Cisticola** **Plate 57**
Luitinktinkie
Cisticola aberrans

Timba (Sh), Matinti (Ts), Ungxengezi, Uqume (X), uNgcede (Z), [Smiths Zistensänger]

Measurements: Length 13–15 cm; wing (14 ♂) 53–56–59, (12 ♀) 48–51,5–54; tail (14 ♂) 61–72, (12 ♀) 56–64; tarsus (26) 19–23; culmen (26) 11–13. Weight (12 ♂) 13,1–15,2–16,9 g, (9 ♀) 12–13,7–15,9 g, (17 unsexed) 10,5–12,2–14,1 g.

Bare Parts: Iris brown; bill dark horn, base pinkish; legs and feet pinkish.

Identification: Size smallish to medium; tail relatively long (Neddicky has shortish tail); crown and nape plain dull russet; back dull olive grey (rustier when breed-

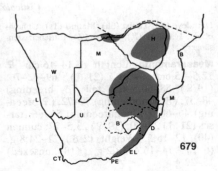

ing; streaks very faint, so looks plain-backed); eyebrow, face and underparts buff, darker on flanks and breast (Neddicky lacks pale eyebrow; light grey below); tail buffy olive (looks greyish), tipped buff (tip not clear in field). *Immature*: Similar to adult or slightly duller.

Voice: Most commonly heard note is loud petulant rising *weeee-ee* alarm call, sometimes followed by penetrating *peet-peet-peet*; song loud clear *twink twink twink*, thinner *tsee tsee tsee*, metallic crescendo *tu-whee-tu-whee-tu-whee*; rapid clicking *q-q-q-q-q* (as in Zulu *q*); somewhat variable; also sharp clinking *kweee* and *kwee-et* callnotes; in Zimbabwe clear *sping* callnote and sharp zipping *krrt* and *krrrrr* alarm notes.

Distribution: Africa S of Sahara; in s Africa from Great Fish River (e Cape) through Natal to Transvaal and extreme se Botswana; also most of Zimbabwe.

Status: Locally common to fairly common resident.

Habitat: Rocky outcrops in woodland, open hill and mountain slopes with rocky substratum and patchy grass and herb cover, usually with some scattered bushes and trees (also called Rock Cisticola), rank grass and weeds bordering bush and forest, usually on moist ground near streams; thick scrub and grass, especially near the feet of hills.

Habits: Usually solitary or in pairs. Forages low down in vegetation or on ground and rocks, running about like mouse; flirts tail like prinia. Generally keeps to cover, but inquisitive and responds well to spishing (see Glossary). ♂ sings from conspicuous perch; no flight displays (hence "Lazy").

Food: Small insects (especially grasshoppers and caterpillars).

Breeding: *Season*: October to February in Natal, to March in Transvaal, September to April (mainly October-November) in Zimbabwe. *Nest*: Ball of grass and plant down with side entrance; near ground in grasstuft, living grass built into roof. *Clutch*: (16) 2–3,1–4 eggs. *Eggs*: Pale greenish blue, finely spotted with brown and reddish; measure (14) 16,6 × 12 (15,2–17,9 × 11,1–12,9). *Incubation*: 14 days. *Nestling*: 14 days; postnestling dependence at least 21 days.

---

680 (636) **Shortwinged Cisticola** **Plate 56**
Kortvlerktinktinkie
Cisticola brachyptera

[Kurzflügel-Zistensänger]

Measurements: Length 11–12 cm; wing ♂ 48–52, ♀ 43–45; tail, breeding 29–36, nonbreeding 35–41; tarsus 17–17,5; culmen 10,5–12,5. Weight 9 g.

Bare Parts: Iris brown; bill whitish to pinkish grey, darker on culmen; mouth black in breeding ♂; legs and feet dusky pink.

Identification: Size small; Somewhat similar to Neddicky, but posture hunched, whitish (not grey) below and lacks rufous crown; above dull rusty brown, somewhat streaked in nonbreeding plumage; eyebrow, face and underparts buff; tail dusky, rather short (looks

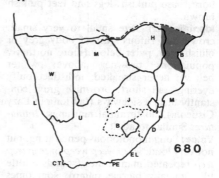

broader-tailed than Neddicky). *Immature*: Below yellow.

Voice: Song series of up to 9 feeble siffling *see see see* or *skwip, skwip, skwip* notes, falling in pitch; weak *chik chik chik* (♂) or repeated rapid wispy (♀) alarm notes; call 5 or more repeated notes *chip chip chip-ey chip*, sometimes in display flight.

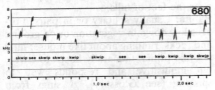

Distribution: Africa S of Sahara; in s Africa confined to Mozambique N of Save River, and adjacent e Zimbabwe.
Status: Common resident.
Habitat: Clearings in *Brachystegia* and other woodland or savanna, especially with dead trees; also thickets on termita-ria, edges of cultivation, open ground between river and woodland.
Habits: Usually solitary. ♂ sings from top of dead tree up to 15 m above ground, or in aerial cruise with fanned tail, up to 50 m above ground, ending in vertical dive and final upward and sideways swoop before landing. Otherwise quiet and unobtrusive; forages low down in grass. When disturbed hops to top of bush to observe intruder.
Food: Small insects.
Breeding: *Season*: November to March in Zimbabwe. *Nest*: Ball of dry grass covered with dry leaves; with side entrance, thickly lined with plant down; in grasstuft or low herbs, 8–20 cm above ground. *Clutch*: 2–4 eggs. *Eggs*: White, greenish or blue, plain or spotted with rust; measure (6) 16,6 × 12 (15,5–17 × 11,8–12,2). *Incubation*: 14 days. *Nestling*: About 17 days; fed by both parents.

681 (637) Neddicky Plate 56
Neddikkie
Cisticola fulvicapilla

Harudeve (K), Motintinyane (SS), Kadhi-idhi-i, Timba (Sh), Matinti (Ts), Incede (X), iNcede, uQoyi (Z), [Brauner Zistensänger]

Measurements: Length 10–11 cm; wing (64 ♂) 46,5–50,6–54, (53 ♀) 43–46,7–50; tail (37) 37–47; tarsus (37) 16–18,5; culmen (37) 10–11,5. Weight (4 ♂) 8,4–8,8–9,3 g, (1 ♀) 8,1 g, (108 unsexed) 7–9,3–15 g.
Bare Parts: Iris light brown; bill dark horn, base pinkish; legs and feet pinkish brown.
Identification: Size small to very small; crown dull rufous; rest of body grey or bluish grey, paler below (more northerly populations browner above, whiter below); never streaked; indistinct buffy eyering; tail short, brownish grey, constantly flicked sideways (tail long in Lazy Cisticola), no terminal markings. *Immature*: Similar to adult.
Voice: Song monotonous penetrating, but not very loud, *weep weep weep* or *teep teep teep* repeated many times (sounds a little like squeaky bicycle pump); sometimes combines piping tone of song and unmusical tone of alarm call into harsher

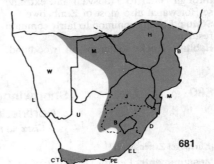

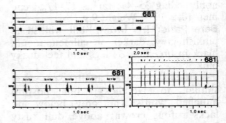

krrip krrip krrip; ratchetlike prolonged *krrrrrr-r-r-r-r* alarm call, like running fingernail across teeth of comb.

Distribution: S Africa to Kenya; in s Africa largely absent from dry W.

Status: Common resident.

Habitat: Understory of woodland and thornveld; scrub, brushwood and secondary growth at edges of forest, plantations or roadsides; scrub and rank grass on rocky slopes; gardens with low shrubs and trees; regenerating plantations of exotic trees with grassy understory.

Habits: Usually solitary or in pairs when breeding; otherwise sometimes in small family groups; may join mixed bird parties. Forages low down in undergrowth or brushwood, or on ground, hopping jerkily about like clockwork toy. When alarmed flies up to perch, flicking tail and giving alarm call. Male sings from high perch on treetop, telephone wire or tall bush, often on leafless branch; sings mostly from Sep-tember to March, but also intermittently in winter.

Food: Small insects.

Breeding: *Season*: September to December in Cape, October to February (mainly October-December) in Natal, October to March (mainly November-January; also May) in Transvaal, October to March (mainly November to February) in Zimbabwe. *Nest*: Ball of dry grass, spider web and plant down, with side entrance; usually in mixed grass and low thorny shrub or green weeds, or in dense grasstuft at base of tree or bush; 6–35 cm above ground. *Clutch*: (142) 2–3–4 eggs (usually 3, rarely 5); one clutch of 7 eggs from 2 females in same nest. *Eggs*: White, pale blue or pale pink, sparingly spotted with pinkish brown and red-brown; measure (177) 15,2 × 11,5 (13,3–16,9 × 10,5–12,6). *Incubation*: 12–14,5 days. *Nestling*: (4) 12–14 days.

---

682 (620)   Redwinged Warbler   Plate 53
Rooivlerksanger
Heliolais erythroptera

[Sonnensänger, Sonnenprinie]

Measurements: Length about 14 cm; wing (4 ♂) 49,5–52, (2 ♀) 48–49; tail (6) 50–64; tarsus (6) 20–21,5; culmen (6) 13–15. Weight (2 ♂) 12,4–13 g, (3 ♀) 10,6–11,6–12,3 g, (1 unsexed) 12,9 g.

Bare Parts: Iris brown to yellowish brown; bill blackish (breeding) to light brown or horn (nonbreeding); legs and feet yellowish ochre.

Identification: Size medium to smallish; very like prinia, but more robustly built, with heavier bill; above greyish brown (tinged rusty in nonbreeding season); face grey; wing feathers edged bright rufous (diagnostic); below creamy white, flanks and thighs deep buff; tail longish, greyish brown with subterminal blackish spots. *Immature*: Paler than adult.

Voice: Musical tinkling callnotes; thin twittering *tseek-tseek-tseek* or downslurred *tseeu-tseeu-tseeu*; shrill chirping whistles.

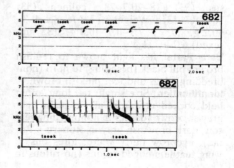

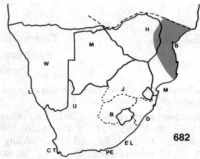

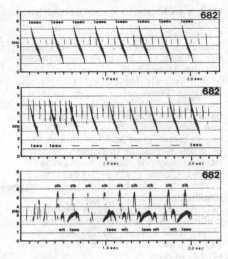

Habitat: *Brachystegia* woodland with understory of tall grass; rank vegetation at edges of lowland evergreen forest; bamboo thickets.

Habits: Usually in pairs or small family groups of up to 6 birds. Members of group keep in touch with constant tinkling calls. Restless and lively; forages low down in understory; when disturbed flies to treetop.

Food: Unrecorded; probably insects.

Breeding: *Season*: November to January in Zimbabwe, December in Mozambique. *Nest*: Upright thin-walled oval of dead grey grass, lined with feathery grass tops, with side-top entrance; bound together with spider web; about 45 cm above ground in shrub among rank grass and weeds. *Clutch*: (4) 2–2,5–3 eggs. *Eggs*: Very pale green with many fine streaks of pale rusty red concentrated at thick end; measure (9) 17,5 × 12,5 (16,5–19 × 12–13). *Incubation*: Unrecorded. *Nestling*: Unrecorded.

Distribution: Africa S of Sahara; in s Africa confined to Mozambique N of Limpopo River, and adjacent e Zimbabwe.

Status: Generally uncommon resident.

Ref. Plowes, D.C.H. 1972. *Honeyguide* 69:34–35.

683 (649)   **Tawnyflanked Prinia**   **Plate 55**
Bruinsylangstertjie
Prinia subflava

Harudeve (K), Timba (Sh), Matsinyani (Ts), Ungcuze (X), [Rahmbrustprinie]

Measurements: Length 10–15 cm; wing (26 ♂) 48–51–53, (22 ♀) 45–48–50, (54 unsexed) 42–50,7–56; tail (♂ breeding) 54–57, (♂ nonbreeding) 65–81, (♀ breeding) 47–53, (♀ nonbreeding) 64–70; tarsus (33) 18–20,7–23; culmen (33) 10–11,7–13. Weight (7 ♂) 8,1–9,3–10,2 g, (7 ♀) 7,1–8,7–10,4 g, (82 unsexed) 6,7–9–11,4 g.

Bare Parts: Iris light brown to reddish brown; bill black (breeding) to horn (nonbreeding); legs and feet pinkish brown.

Identification: Size small; tail long, often held cocked upwards; above plain light greyish brown (darker in nonbreeding season; dark brownish grey in Roberts's Prinia); eyebrow buffy white; lores dusky; wing feathers edged rufous (no rufous in

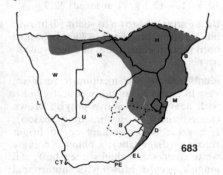

wing of Blackchested or Roberts's Prinias); below buffy white, washed creamy buff to tawny on breast, flanks and undertail (breast buffy white in nonbreeding season; grey in Roberts's Prinia; belly light lemon yellow in nonbreeding Blackchested Prinia); tail brown with dark sub-terminal spots and pale tip (tail plain greyish brown in Roberts's Prinia). *Immature*: Below tinged lemon yellow; bill yellowish.

Voice: Monotonous *przzt przzt przzt*; loud piping *teep teep teep*, or sharper *tsip tsip tsip*; harsh mewing *zbeee* alarm note much repeated.

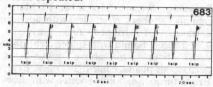

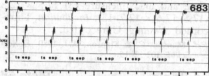

Distribution: Africa S of Sahara, s Asia to Java; in s Africa confined to moister E, NE and N; recorded Waterberg Plateau, Namibia.

Status: Common resident.

Habitat: Rank grass, weeds or bushes among scattered trees, usually along streams and sewage ponds; gardens, edges

of old cultivated lands; more arboreal in winter than in summer.

Habits: Usually in pairs; sometimes in small groups or mixed bird parties, keeping contact with cheerful calls. Forages low down in bushes, shrubs and grass, but also in trees (especially in dry season). Lively and active, swinging and wagging cocked tail sideways, especially when alarmed. Usually tame.

Food: Insects, nectar.

Breeding: *Season*: September to March (mainly November-January) in Natal and Transvaal, August to April (mainly November-March) in Zimbabwe; rarely as late as July. *Nest*: Thin-walled oval with side-top entrance, woven of narrow green grass blades which dry firm and brown; sometimes unlined, usually lined with soft grass flowers; 60–180 cm above ground in weeds, bush or small tree, sometimes sewn into broad leaves; may also use old nest of Red Bishop. *Clutch*: (192) 2–3,1–5 eggs (usually 3–4). *Eggs*: Highly variable; cream, blue, green or pink, boldly blotched, scrawled and marbled with black, red-brown and brown sometimes concentrated at thick end; measure (222) 16 × 11,4 (14,1–17,9 × 10,5–12,8). *Incubation*: 13–14 days. *Nestling*: 13–17 days (usually 14–15 days).

684 (649X) Brier Warbler (Roberts's Prinia) Plate 55
Woudlangstertjie
Oreophilais robertsi

[Roberts-Prinie]

Measurements: Length 14–15 cm; wing (246) 46,5–50,2–54; tail, breeding (10) 59–61,7–65, nonbreeding (13) 61–63,8–67, (235) 40–62,2–71; tarsus (246) 19–22,3–25; culmen (253) 10–12,8–15,5. Weight (3 ♂) 8,7–9,1–9,5 g, (2 ♀) 8,3–9,7 g, (252 unsexed) 7–8,9–11,4 g.

Bare Parts: Iris light yellow ochre; bill dark horn to black above, paler horn to black below; mouth blackish; legs and feet light brown to pinkish.

Identification: Size small; similar to Tawny-flanked Prinia, but crown slate brown, no pale eyebrow, no dark spots near end of tail, no rufous in wing; above dark brown-

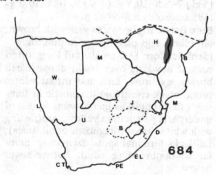

ish grey; dark line through eye; below pale grey, shading to white on belly, rufous on flanks; eye light yellow (diagnostic).

Immature: Similar to adult, but eye brown to grey.

Voice: Harsh shrill chattering and chirruping *cha-cha-cha-cha*; scolding *zizz-zizz*.

Distribution: Highlands of e Zimbabwe and adjacent Mozambique, mostly above 1400 m, but down to 1200 m in S of range. **Status:** Locally common resident. Has only 8 rectrices; genus *Prinia* has 10 rectrices.
Habitat: Edges and clearings of montane forest, dense vegetation (heath, brackenbrier, streamside growth) away from forest, thickets among exotic pine trees;

prefers denser cover than does Tawny-flanked Prinia.
Habits: Usually solitary or in pairs when breeding; otherwise in fairly large groups. Forages low down in dense undergrowth; less often also in trees at forest edge, but not in forest interior; highly vocal, keeping contact with noisy chattering.
Food: Small insects.
Breeding: *Season*: September to March (mainly October). *Nest*: Oval with side-top entrance, of stripped fine grass inflorescences, bound with spider web; unlined; about 1 m above ground in herbaceous plants. *Clutch*: 2–3 eggs. *Eggs*: Bright turquoise, boldly spotted with chocolate and lilac; measure (3) 17,5 × 12,8 (17,5–17,6 × 12,7–13). *Incubation*: Unrecorded. *Nestling*: Unrecorded.

Ref. Manson, C. & Manson, A.J. 1980. *Honeyguide* 102:12–15.

685 (650) **Blackchested Prinia** **Plate 55**
Swartbandlangstertjie
Prinia flavicans

Harudeve (K), Motintinyane (SS), Tôntôbane (Tw), [Brustbandprinie]

Measurements: Length 13–15 cm; wing (83 ♂) 50–53,8–58, (73 ♀) 47,5–51,2–55,5; tail (53 ♂) 54–76,6–93, (48 ♀) 57–74,5–86,5, (♂ breeding) 62–68, (♂ nonbreeding) 72–94, (♀ breeding) 50–58, (♀ nonbreeding) 76–81; tarsus (39) 19,5–22, culmen (39) 9–11,5. Weight (5 ♂) 7–8,8–10,5 g, (4 ♀) 9–10,1–10,6 g, (195 unsexed) 6,8–9–12 g.
Bare Parts: Iris brown to yellowish brown; bill black; legs pale brown to pinkish.
Identification: Size small; tail long, often cocked upwards over back; above earth brown; eyebrow, face and throat white; broad black chestband diagnostic in summer (absent or indistinct in winter); rest of underparts pale lemon yellow, contrasting with white throat (diagnostic at all times); tail lacks terminal spots. *Immature*: Similar to nonbreeding adult, but yellower below.
Voice: Loud sharp, almost explosive, *chip-chip-chip-chip* or *kzee-kzee-kzee-kzee*, repeated 10–30 times; longer ratchetlike *zrrrrrt*; weeping alarm call.

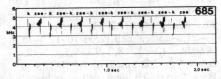

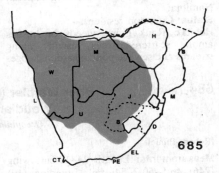

Distribution: Drier parts of s Africa from Orange River and highveld northwards and westwards to sw Zambia and s Angola.
Status: Common resident.
Habitat: Kalahari and other semi-arid scrub, *Acacia* savanna with low bushes, old cultivated fields with tall weeds in

open grassland, bushes and shrubs in dry watercourses, gardens.
Habits: Usually in pairs. Forages by hopping about in bushes, also often on ground, often wagging long tail from side to side, or flicking tail up and down. Inquisitive and tame; perches on top of bush or weed when disturbed, cocking tail and calling.
Food: Small insects.
Breeding: *Season*: August to May (mainly October-March) in Transvaal, September to March in Zimbabwe, almost any month in Kalahari and arid W (breeds opportunistically in winter

after late rains, even without black chestband). *Nest*: Oval with side-top entrance, woven of thin green grass blades which dry firm and brown; lined with plant down, mostly after egglaying; 90–150 cm above ground in upright stems of weed, bush, shrub or grass; built in up to 11 days. *Clutch*: (36) 2–3,3–6 eggs (usually 3–4). *Eggs*: Pale fawn, pale blue, pale greenish or turquoise, blotched, scrolled, clouded and marbled with black, browns, greys and mauve; measure (115) $16 \times 11,6$ $(13,7–17,8 \times 10,5–12,4)$. *Incubation*: 12–13 days. *Nestling*: 14 days.

686 (651) Spotted Prinia Plate 55
Geelpenslangstertjie
Prinia hypoxantha

Motintinyane (SS), Ujiza (X), [Gelbbauchprinie, Fleckenprinie]

Measurements: Length 13–15 cm; wing (16 ♂) 47–53–58, (12 ♀) 48–50,5–53; tail (28) 60–80; tarsus (28) 19–22; culmen (28) 10,5–12. Weight (2 ♂) 8,2–10 g, (1 ♀) 11,1 g, (47 unsexed) 6–9,4–20 g.
Bare Parts: Iris light brown; bill blackish; legs and feet pinkish brown.
Identification: Size small; tail long, often cocked over back; above warm brown; eyebrow, face and throat whitish; rest of underparts yellowish white to lemon yellow (nonbreeding birds deeper yellow), throat, breast and flanks clearly streaked black (diagnostic); tail tipped pale brown, with subterminal blackish spot. *Immature*: Above tinged rufous; below primrose yellow with dusky streaks.
Voice: Loud explosive *kli-kli-kli-kli*, similar to calls of Blackchested Prinia, but somewhat more ringing; rasping *krrrt krrrt*; various chipping and reedy piping notes.

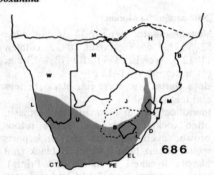

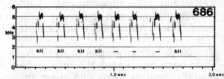

Distribution: Most of Cape Province, s Namibia, e Orange Free State, Lesotho

and higher parts of Natal, Swaziland and Transvaal.
Status: Common resident; eastern birds from East London to Zoutpansberg more yellowish buff below and inhabit moister habitats (Spotted Prinia *Prinia hypoxantha*); western birds whiter below, inhabit fynbos and karoo, so may be separate species (Karoo Prinia *Prinia maculosa*).
Habitat: Karoo, fynbos, coastal and montane scrub, rank grass and thickets along streams and edges of forest, woodland and exotic plantations, tall weeds in fallow lands and on roadsides, gardens.
Habits: Usually in pairs when breeding; otherwise in small groups. Forages low down in grass, weeds and bushes; sometimes hawks insects in flight. When disturbed perches on top of tall plant, flicking

tail and calling; responds well to spishing (see Glossary); when closely approached, dives into vegetation and disappears. Becomes tame in gardens.
Food: Small insects.
Breeding: *Season*: July to December in sw Cape, October to March in e Cape, October to February (mainly December-January) in Natal and Transvaal; rarely to April. *Nest*: Oval with side-top entrance, woven of thin green grass blades which dry firm and brown; lined with plant down; 30–55–100 cm above ground (370 nests) in bush or dense grasstuft; rarely uses old nests of Red Bishop or Yellowrumped Widow. *Clutch*: (296) 2–3,7–5 eggs (usually 4). *Eggs*: Pale blue, spotted and blotched with greyish brown, chestnut and lilac mainly at thick end; measure (328) 16,4 × 11,7   (14,5–20 × 10,8–12,8). *Incubation*: (17) 13–14–17 days by both sexes. *Nestling*: (14) 13–14–16 days; fed by both parents.

Ref. James, H.W. & Brooke, R.K. 1972. *Ostrich* 43:137–138.
Rowan, M.K. & Broekhuysen, G.J. 1962. *Ostrich* 33(2):6–30.

687 (653)   Namaqua Warbler   Plate 55
Namakwalangstertjie
Phragmacia substriata

[Namasänger, Namaprinie]

Measurements: Length 13–14 cm; wing 52–56; tail 65–78; tarsus 20–22; culmen 11–12,5. Weight (3 ♂) 11,5–12,4–13,2 g, (11 unsexed) 9–11–13 g.
Bare Parts: Iris grey; bill blackish; legs and feet pinkish.
Identification: Size small; tail longish, often cocked over back; above rufous brown; eyebrow, face and underparts white, breast lightly streaked black (not heavily streaked as in Spotted Prinia), washed brownish on flanks and undertail (Spotted Prinia pale yellow below); tail plain brown (no terminal spots).
Voice: Song sharp *chit chit-churrr*, or *chit-churrr; chewi chewi chewi* alarm call lasting for 2 minutes or more; *chit* contact call.

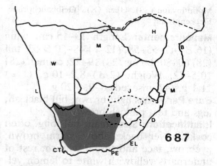

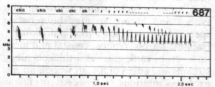

Distribution: Karoo, Namaqualand, lower Orange River to C Orange Free State.
Status: Locally fairly common resident; nest architecture and other features indicate that it is not a *Prinia* species as formerly thought.

Habitat: Thornbush (essentially *Acacia*) along rivers and streams in karoo; overgrown gardens and orchards along watercourses.
Habits: Usually solitary or in pairs; in small family groups after breeding. Keeps largely to dense bushy growth, but ♂ sings from high in tree. Forages by gleaning from branches, twigs and leaves in tangled vegetation, less often on ground, in flood wrack and into adjacent open karoo. Movements quick and restless.
Food: Insects; fruit of *Lycium* and *Atriplex*.
Breeding: *Season*: August to April. *Nest*: Deep open cup of grass and strips of bark bound to upright stems with green grass; lined with rootlets, feathers, fluffy seeds and hair; camouflaged with bits of bark,

dead leaves, lichen and twigs; outside diameter 6–10 cm, outside depth 7–9 cm, inside diameter 4 cm, inside depth 4 cm; 30–150 cm above ground in tall grass, thistles, bulrushes, or in flood debris against small bush on river bank. *Clutch*: 2–4 eggs (usually 3). *Eggs*: Pale to deep

blue, blotched and spotted with dark red-brown and grey; measure (18) 16,5 × 11,4 (14,2–17,1 × 10,5–12,7). *Incubation*: About 16 days. *Nestling*: At least 15 days.

Ref. Brooke, R.K. & Dean, W.R.J. 1990, *Ostrich* 61:50–55.

688 (619)   Rufouseared Warbler   Plate 53
Rooioorlangstertjie
Malcorus pectoralis

[Rotbackensänger]

Measurements: Length 14–16 cm; wing (4) 48,5–51; tail 75–80; tarsus 19,5–20; culmen 10–12,5. Weight (10) 8–10–11,5 g.

Bare Parts: Iris reddish hazel; bill black; legs and feet pinkish.

Identification: Size small; tail long, often cocked over back like that of prinia; above buffy grey, streaked black (prinias unstreaked); eyebrow whitish; lores, face and ear coverts brick red (brighter in ♂; diagnostic); below white or off-white, washed buff on flanks; narrow black collar on throat (bolder in ♂; diagnostic). *Immature*: Similar to adult; black collar may be absent.

Voice: Song monotonous penetrating piping *tee-tee-tee-tee-tee*, about 4 notes/ second; plaintive *peeeee* alarm note.

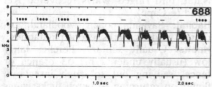

Distribution: Dry W of s Africa from ne Cape (Barkly East) and e Orange Free State, through Karoo to Namaqualand, sw Transvaal, n Cape, sw Botswana and most of Namibia.

Status: Common resident.

Habitat: Low shrubby vegetation on dry mountain slopes, karoo and Kalahari plains and in dry watercourses along Namib edge.

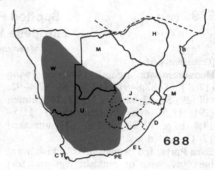

Habits: Usually solitary or in pairs. Forages mainly on ground; also low down in shrubs, gleaning from twigs like whiteeye; hops and bounds quickly over ground with tail cocked, especially when disturbed, disappearing between bushes. ♂ sings from top of low bush or tall shrub; ♂ displays to ♀ with jerking body and tail, fluttering wings and song.

Food: Insects, including ants.

Breeding: *Season*: Breeds opportunistically after rain in any month. *Nest*: Untidy oval with side-top entrance, of dry grass leaves and stems; lined with plant down; entrance about 3,4 cm diameter, usually facing E, SE or S; 20–120 cm above ground in shrub or bush. *Clutch*: (41) 2–3,6–7 eggs (usually 3–4; clutches larger than 5 eggs possibly laid by 2 females). *Eggs*: Plain white or very pale bluish white; measure (53) 15,5 × 11,4 (14,2–17,1 × 10,5–12,3). *Incubation*: 12–13 days. *Nestling*: 11–13 days.

Ref. Maclean, G.L. 1974. *Ostrich* 45:9–14.

599

26:16. Family 78 MUSCICAPIDAE—OLD-WORLD FLYCATCHERS

Mostly small, a few medium. Bill typically shortish, broad, dorsoventrally flattened; legs short; feet small and relatively weak; wings short and rounded, or long and pointed; flight usually agile; tail variable; plumage variable, juvenile typically spotted; sexes alike or different; arboreal in forest or open woodland; feed on insects caught in air or on ground, usually by hawking from perch; usually solitary; nest cup-shaped on branch, in hole or on ledge; eggs 2–6, pale ground colour, spotted; chick naked or sparsely downy at hatching; incubation by both sexes or by female only; young cared for by both sexes. Distribution Africa, Eurasia, Australasia; 134 species; 22 species in s Africa. The family Muscicapidae is here taken to exclude the Australasian wren-warblers (Maluridae), fantails (Rhipiduridae), monarchs (Monarchidae) and whistlers (Pachycephalidae), though the genera *Batis, Platysteira, Stenostira, Erythrocercus, Trochocercus* and *Terpsiphone* may belong to the Monarchidae (or even to the Malaconotidae).

Ref. Fraser, W. 1983. *Ostrich* 54:150–155.

689 (654) Spotted Flycatcher Plate 58
Europese Vlieëvanger
Muscicapa striata

[Grauschnäpper]

Measurements: Length 14–15 cm; wing (17 ♂) 85–87,8–91, (12 ♀) 86–87,4–92; tail (29) 58–63; tarsus (29) 13–16; culmen (29) 11,5–14,5. Weight (5 ♂) 11,5–14,4–16 g, (2 ♀) 14,1 g, (47 unsexed) 12–15,2–18,6 g.

Bare Parts: Iris brown; bill blackish horn, base yellowish or pinkish; legs and feet dark pinkish grey.

Identification: Size small (rather larger than Dusky Flycatcher); above brownish grey (more lead grey in Dusky Flycatcher), streaked darker on crown (streaks barely visible in Dusky Flycatcher); no whitish eyering as in Dusky Flycatcher; below white, streaked dark grey on chest and sides of throat (streaks less distinct in Dusky Flycatcher).

Voice: Thin sibilant *seep*; harsh *chirrt* and *tek-tek* alarm notes; song thin quick *sip-sip-see-sitti-see-see*.

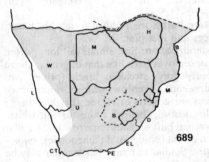

Distribution: Breeds Palaearctic (N Africa, Europe and w and C Asia); migrates to Africa.

Status: Common nonbreeding Palaearctic migrant, October to March (sometimes April); birds ringed Helsinki (Finland) recovered Johannesburg, Swaziland and Natal; bird ringed Wales recovered Kei Road (e Cape).

Habitat: Savanna, open woodland, orchards, gardens, parks, exotic plantations.

Habits: Usually solitary. Perches fairly low (usually under 2 m) on branch or fence, sallying out to catch insects in flight; on returning to perch flicks wings more often than other flycatchers. Usually quiet and unobtrusive; returns to same set of perches day after day and to same locality in successive seasons. Sings March-April in Transvaal and Zimbabwe.

Food: Small insects; also kernels of sunflower seeds (stolen from Whitethroated Canary), fruit of *Ochna pretoriensis, Trema orientalis*.

Breeding: Extralimital.

690 (655)

Dusky Flycatcher
Donkervlieëvanger
Muscicapa adusta

Plate 58

Unomaphelana (X), [Dunkelschnäpper]

Measurements: Length 12–13 cm; wing ♂ 65,5–70, ♀ 64–66; tail (26) 48–55; tarsus (26) 14,5–16,5; culmen (26) 10–12. Weight (1 ♀) 9,6 g, (4 unsexed) 9,6–11,6–12,9 g.

Bare Parts: Iris dark brown; bill dark brownish horn to blackish, base dull yellow; legs and feet brownish pink, greyish to black.

Identification: Size small; similar to Spotted Flycatcher but size smaller, back greyer (less brownish), spotting on head and breast indistinct; above olive grey, crown faintly streaked (looks uniform grey); eyering buffy white (diagnostic at close range; Spotted Flycatcher lacks pale eyering); below dull white, lightly streaked greyish on breast and flanks. *Immature*: Above speckled buff on greyish; below off-white, spotted brown.

Voice: Thin very high-pitched drawn out *tseeee*, repeated several times; sharp repeated *tsip-tsip-tsirrrrt*.

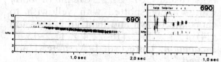

Distribution: S Africa to Cameroon and Ethiopia; in s Africa confined to S and E.

Status: Locally common; some populations resident, most locally migratory; breeding visitor to sw Cape, September to April (always absent mid-May to mid-August).

Habitat: Evergreen and riverine forest, patches of forest in dense woodland; exotic plantations, well wooded gardens.

Habits: Usually solitary or in pairs. Forages by hawking in air from low shady perch at forest edge, catching prey on ground, gleaning from leaves, hovering at branches, and catching off branches in flight. When perched flicks wings, but less often than does Spotted Flycatcher. Rather quiet and unobtrusive; usually noticed when hawking prey.

Food: Insects (including moths), small fruits (e.g. of *Vepris undulata*).

Breeding: *Season*: September to January (mainly October-December) throughout s Africa. *Nest*: Small neat thick-walled cup of grass, plant fibres, rootlets, lichen, moss and bark; lined with hair, rootlets and small feathers; up to 9 m above ground in hole in bank or tree, among creepers or in niche in wall, on rocky ledge, in hanging fern basket. *Clutch*: (40) 2–2,7–3 eggs. *Eggs*: Pale greenish white, densely speckled and spotted with pinkish to reddish brown concentrated at thick end; measure (35) 18,2 × 13,4 (16,4–19,3 × 12,8–14,6). *Incubation*: 14–15 days. *Nestling*: Unrecorded.

Ref. Skead, C.J. 1966. *Ostrich* 37:143–145.

691 (656)

Bluegrey Flycatcher
Blougrysvlieëvanger
Muscicapa caerulescens

Plate 58

[Schieferschnäpper]

Measurements: Length 14–15 cm; wing (14 ♂) 72–76,7–82,5, (4 ♀) 70–72,8–76; tail (18) 56,5–62; tarsus (18) 15,5–17; culmen (18) 11–12. Weight (9 ♂) 11,7–16,5–18,4 g, (3 ♀) 16,3–16,4–16,4 g, (7 unsexed) 15–17 g.

BLUEGREY FLYCATCHER

Bare Parts: Iris brown; bill blackish, base pinkish to grey; legs and feet dark grey to blackish.

Identification: Size small; above blue-grey (less brownish or smoky grey than Spotted and Dusky Flycatchers); lores black (diagnostic at close range); eyering white; below pale grey, shading to whitish grey on throat and lower belly (no streaking as in Spotted and Dusky Flycatchers); tail plain dark grey (no white as in Fantailed Flycatcher). *Immature*: Speckled all over with dark brown and buff.

Voice: Song quick sibilant stuttering *tsip tsip tsip tsip tseep tslipsipsipsip*; somewhat variable; husky *zayt*; 3–4-syllable callnote, *pit pit pit pit*, starting high and dying away down scale.

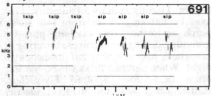

Distribution: Africa S of Sahara; in s Africa confined to E and NE.

Status: Locally common resident.

Habitat: Edges of lowland evergreen forest, upper strata of riverine woodland, thickets in drier woodland, moister savanna, wooded gorges.

Habits: Solitary or in pairs; may join mixed bird parties. Hawks insects in flight, darting out from perch; flicks wings on return to perch; catches insects on ground and gleans from bark; often perches sideways on vertical treetrunk. Usually quiet and easily overlooked, but not shy; perches motionless for long periods.

Food: Insects, small fruits.

Breeding: *Season*: October to December in Natal, November-December in Transvaal, September to January in Zimbabwe. *Nest*: Cup of matted plant fibres and green moss strands, lined with rootlets and finer fibres; in niche of tree trunk, crevice of bark, shallow hole in stump, narrow fork of thick branches. *Clutch*: (17) 2–2,8–3 eggs (usually 3). *Eggs*: Cream or buffy white, finely spotted with yellowish to chocolate brown and light grey; measure (24) 19,2 × 14,2 (18–21,4 × 13,2–15,4). *Incubation*: Unrecorded. *Nestling*: Unrecorded.

692 (655X) Collared Flycatcher Plate 58
Withalsvlieëvanger
Ficedula albicollis

[Halsbandschnäpper]

Measurements: Length 12,5–13 cm; wing 77–84; tail 52–55; tarsus 16–17; culmen 10–12.

Bare Parts: Iris brown; bill, legs and feet black.

Identification: Size small; forehead, collar on hindneck (may be absent in nonbreeding plumage), broad wingstripe and wingbar, rump and underparts white; rest of plumage, including tail, black to dark brown (♂) or greyish brown (♀); ♀ also greyish brown on chest. *Immature*: Lacks white collar; otherwise like adult ♀.

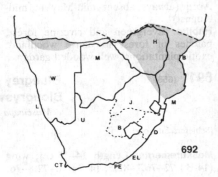

602

Voice: Zip callnote; *tik-tik-tik-tik* alarm notes; song simple brief *tsit-tsit-tsit-shu-si*.

Habitat: Savanna and woodland.
Habits: Usually solitary. Forages like

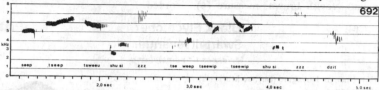

Distribution: Breeds Europe and w Asia; migrates to Africa; in s Africa recorded isolated localities in Transvaal, Namibia and Zimbabwe.
Status: Rare nonbreeding Palaearctic vagrant, October to March; seldom occurs S of Zambia and Malawi.

typical flycatcher, darting out from perch to catch prey in flight, then returning to same or different perch. Tends to perch higher than does Spotted Flycatcher.
Food: Insects.
Breeding: Extralimital.

693 (657) Fantailed Flycatcher Plate 58
Waaierstertvlieëvanger
Myioparus plumbeus

[Meisenschnäpper]

Measurements: Length about 14 cm; wing (11 ♂) 65–66,8–69, (12 ♀) 61–63,4–66; tail (23) 56–67; tarsus (23) 16–18; culmen (23) 11–12. Weight (1) 21 g.
Bare Parts: Iris brown; bill blackish, base pinkish; legs and feet slate.
Identification: Size small; similar to Bluegrey Flycatcher, but with white in tail; also resembles Sharpbilled Honeyguide, but eyering white, tail longer, upperparts more blue-grey (not so brown); above blue-grey; tail black, outermost rectrices white, often fanned like cards being shuffled (Bluegrey Flycatcher has no white in tail, does not fan tail); below whitish grey. *Immature*: Spotted brown and buff above and below; distinguished from immature Bluegrey Flycatcher by white in tail.
Voice: Penetrating quavering whistle *peely-peeerr*, or drawn-out *peeerrrp*, rather plaintive, very similar to song phrase of Rufousnaped Lark.

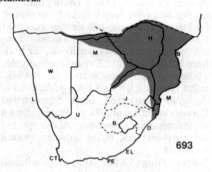

Distribution: Africa S of Sahara; in s Africa confined to NE from Zululand to n

Ovamboland; vagrant to Johannesburg and Pretoria.
Status: Local and uncommon resident.
Habitat: Bushveld, savanna, *Brachystegia* woodland, riverine forest, edges of lowland evergreen forest.
Habits: Usually solitary, but may join mixed bird parties. Gleans from leaves and twigs like warbler. Constantly raises and lowers and fans tail.
Food: Insects (including caterpillars and beetles).
Breeding: *Season*: October to December in Natal and Zimbabwe. *Nest*: Scant cup of fine straws, roots, shredded bark, lichens and feathers; in old nest hole of barbet or woodpecker, or in natural hole in branch, up to 6 m above ground.

Clutch: 2–3 eggs. *Eggs*: Dull white or greenish white, thickly spotted with olive brown and greyish brown; measure (4) 17,2 × 13 (17–17,5 × 12,5–13,3). *Incubation*: Unrecorded. *Nestling*: Unrecorded.

694 (664) Black Flycatcher   Plate 58
Swartvlieëvanger
Melaenornis pammelaina

Ndiru (K), Nhengu, Nhengure (Sh), umMbesi (Z), [Drongoschnäpper]

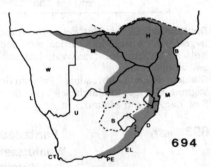

694

Measurements: Length 19–22 cm; wing (42 ♂) 100–108–117,5, (34 ♀) 97–105,1–114; tail (27 ♂) 82,5–91,4–100, (24 ♀) 81–90,8–101; tarsus (24) 20,5–25; culmen (27 ♂) 16,5–18,3–20, (25 ♀) 17–18,3–19,5. Weight (8) 24,2–29,8–32,4 g.

Bare Parts: Iris dark brown; bill, legs and feet black.

Identification: Size large (slightly smaller than Forktailed Drongo); glossy blue-black all over (♀ duller, greyer below, than ♂); tail notched (not deeply forked like that of Forktailed Drongo); bill slender (deep at base in Forktailed Drongo); forehead usually high and rounded (usually sloping back from bill in Forktailed Drongo); wings pale, whitish, in flight (similar to those of Forktailed Drongo); iris dark brown (dark red in drongos). Separated from Squaretailed Drongo by different habitat. Partial albinos sometimes occur. *Immature*: Above spotted pale rusty on black; below browner, spotted with buff.

Voice: Song rather thin high-pitched *tseep-tseep-tsoo, tseep-cheeu, tseep-twee-twee, tseep-tititititi*, etc., somewhat variable, occasionally lightly trilled; imitates other birdcalls; persistent *chair* in evening before roosting.

Distribution: S Africa to Kenya; in s Africa mainly confined to SE, E and NE from e Cape to Caprivi and n Ovamboland.

Status: Common resident.

Habitat: Any woodland, forest edge, exotic plantations, gardens.

Habits: Usually in pairs; sometimes small groups of up to 5 birds, often in association with Forktailed Drongo which it closely resembles in appearance and habits (mimicry of more aggressive drongo undoubtedly adaptive). Catches insects in flight, or (mostly) on ground, returning to perch; perches at almost any height above ground, usually on leafless branch, fencepost or wire; hops on ground. Usually sits higher on legs than does drongo when perched.

Food: Insects, nectar of aloes, small fruits (e.g. *Solanum nigrum*).

Breeding: *Season*: September to January (mainly October-November) in Natal, September to February (mainly October-November) in Transvaal, August to January (mainly September-October) in Zimbabwe. *Nest*: Shallow cup of twigs and stems, neatly lined with rootlets; in top of broken stump or fire-blackened tree hollow, in niche behind bark or in wall, at base of large aloe leaf, in top of drainpipe, in old nest of thrush, bulbul or Redheaded Weaver, or in bunch of bananas; usually 1,5–5 m above ground (rarely up to 9 m; mean of 71 nests = 2,6 m). *Clutch*: (66) 2–2,6–4 eggs (usually 3). *Eggs*: Pale greenish white, heavily spotted with red-brown and grey-brown; measure (160) 21,6 × 15,9 (19,5–24,3 × 14,7–17,2). *Incubation*: 13–14 days. *Nestling*: 15 days.

695 (661) Marico Flycatcher · Plate 58
Maricovlieëvanger
Melaenornis mariquensis

Kapantsi (Tw), [Maricoschnäpper]

Measurements: Length about 18 cm; wing (32) 80–85,4–92; tail 71–81; tarsus 19–24; culmen 12–14. Weight (2 ♀) 26,2–28,5 g, (14 unsexed) 22,3–23,8–27,2 g.

Bare Parts: Iris dark brown; bill, legs and feet black.

Identification: Size medium (smaller than Black and Chat Flycatchers); above fawn-brown (Pallid Flycatcher mousy grey-brown); black spot in front of eye (present also in Pallid Flycatcher); below pure silky white (diagnostic; Pallid Flycatcher off-white, washed greyish buff across breast and flanks). *Immature:* Spotted buff and brown above and below.

Voice: Song harsh unmusical *chreep chi-chu chreep*, etc.; sharp *chiu, CHIKichiu* anxiety calls near nest; thin *tsee tsee* alarm calls to fledglings.

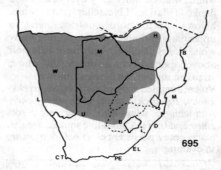

695

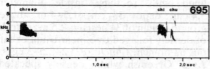

Distribution: Orange Free State, Transvaal and n Cape to Botswana, Namibia, sw Zimbabwe, sw Zambia and s Angola.

Status: Common resident; uncommon in Transvaal lowveld.

Habitat: *Acacia* savanna.

Habits: Usually in pairs or small groups of 4–5 birds. Perches fairly low on outer leafless branch of tree, or on fence; flies to ground to catch prey; may hop about on ground to feed on emerging insects; rarely hawks insects in flight. On ground holds tail and body perkily up; may flick tail after landing on perch or ground.

Food: Insects (including termites and large black ants); rarely small fruits (e.g. *Rhus pyroides*).

Breeding: *Season*: August to February (mainly October-December) in Transvaal, August to November (also June) in Kalahari, July to March (mainly September-December) in Zimbabwe; breeds opportunistically after rain in drier areas. *Nest*: Shallow bowl of twigs, grass stems and coarse roots, lined with finer plant fibres, feathers and wool; inside diameter 5,9 cm, depth 3,8 cm; about 1,5–5 m above ground (mean of 71 nests = 2,6 m) in horizontal fork of *Acacia* tree, or in cluster of parasitic plants. *Clutch*: (16) 2–2,9–3 eggs (usually 3). *Eggs*: Pale greenish to light olive, faintly speckled with greyish forming indistinct ring at thick end; rough-textured; measure (80) 20,2 × 14,5 (18–22 × 13,2–15,7). *Incubation*: Unrecorded. *Nestling*: Unrecorded; sometimes fed by 3 adults or by 2 adults and young from previous brood; dependent on adults for up to 2 months after leaving nest.

696 (662) Pallid Flycatcher · Plate 58
Muiskleurvlieëvanger
Melaenornis pallidus

[Fahlschnäpper]

Measurements: Length 15–17 cm; wing (20 ♂) 89–92,8–96, (20 ♀) 83–87,2–94; tail (20 ♂) 68–73, (20 ♀) 60–74; tarsus (40) 17,5–21; culmen (40) 13–15. Weight (2 ♂) 22,3–23,2 g, (1 ♀) 21,1 g.

Bare Parts: Iris chestnut brown; bill, legs and feet blackish.

Identification: Size medium; somewhat similar to Marico Flycatcher, but mousy grey-brown above (not fawn); below off-white, washed buffy grey over breast and flanks (Marico Flycatcher pure white below—much more contrast between upperparts and underparts); eyering buffy white; lores blackish. *Immature*: Pale buff above, spotted brown; below dull white, streaked and scaled blackish brown.

Voice: Jumbled song of raspy notes, *treeky-treeky, trip-tricky, treeky chip chippy-chee, witti-wttittee, witty witty witty*, etc.; soft *churr* and thin mammal-like squeak, *see see*, alarm notes; persistent *chrrr* before roosting in evening.

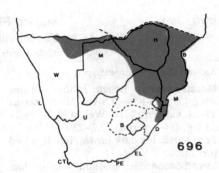

696

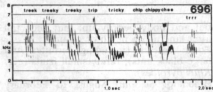

Distribution: S Africa to Sudan and Ethiopia; in s Africa confined to NE and N from Zululand to Ovamboland.

Status: Common resident.

Habitat: Mainly broadleaved woodland, and savanna with well developed understory; less often *Acacia* savanna if Marico Flycatcher absent.

Habits: Usually in pairs when breeding; otherwise in small groups (exceptionally of up to 12 birds). Perches on low outer branch at edge of clearing, dropping to ground to catch prey; sometimes hawks insects in flight. Somewhat chatlike; flicks wings. Tame, unobtrusive and rather silent.

Food: Insects (especially beetles, caterpillars, termites), small fruits (e.g. *Rhus pyroides*).

Breeding: *Season*: September to January (mainly October-November) in Natal, August to February (mainly October) in Transvaal, August to January (mainly September-November) in Zimbabwe; may rear 2 broods/season. *Nest*: Thin-walled bowl of roots, grass and twigs, lined with rootlets; inside diameter 3,4 cm, depth 3,4 cm; 1,5–4 m above ground (mean of 34 nests = 2,5 m) in fork of densely foliaged tree, near trunk or far out on branch. *Clutch*: (82) 2–2,5–3 eggs. *Eggs*: Greenish white, densely speckled with red-brown, yellow-brown and grey concentrated to form ring at thick end; measure (169) 19,8 × 14,8 (17,8–23,4 × 12,9–16,5). *Incubation*: 14 days. *Nestling*: 17 days; fed by both parents; young remain with parents for several months after leaving nest.

697 (663)   **Chat Flycatcher**   **Plate 58**
Grootvlieëvanger
Melaenornis infuscatus

[Drosselschnäpper]

Measurements: Length about 20 cm; wing (42 ♂) 101–116,4–124,5, (26 ♀) 98–108–121,5; tail (42 ♂) 73–83–93, (26 ♀) 74–80,8–90; tarsus (5) 27–32; culmen (42 ♂) 19,5–21,7–28, (26 ♀) 20–22,7–26,5. Weight (1) 37 g.

Bare Parts: Iris dark brown; bill, legs and feet black.

Identification: Size large (biggest flycatcher; slightly bigger than Cape Robin; considerably bigger than Marico Flycatcher); build robust, chatlike; whole plumage ash brown, slightly paler below; eyering buffy white. *Immature*: Heavily streaked brown and white above and below (not spotted as in most other young flycatchers of similar size).

Voice: Song slightly musical chirruping

notes, *chirr chirr cheep chirr chirr chirr cheep cheep*, etc.; thin *tsee tsee* anxiety call; harsh buzzing *krzzzt* or *kzzt kzzt kzzt peep* alarm calls; loud *chek chek* alarm near nest.

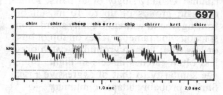

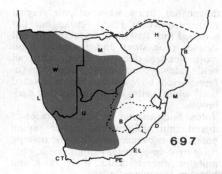

Distribution: Dry w parts of s Africa to sw Angola.

Status: Common resident.

Habitat: Arid scrub and shrub on open plains.

Habits: Usually solitary or in pairs; seldom in small groups of about 4 birds. Perches on top of shrub, bush, fence or telephone wire (not on low branch as Marico and Pallid Flycatchers usually do), dropping with heavy flight onto prey on ground; hops on ground with wings partly spread; prey eaten on ground or taken back to perch. Flight somewhat wavy, but not dipping. Conspicuous when hunting; highly secretive when nesting.

Food: Insects (including grasshoppers and ants), small reptiles (including *Typhlops* species).

Breeding: *Season*: October to November in Transvaal, all months according to rainfall in more arid W. *Nest*: Untidy bowl of plant stems, coarse grass and twigs, lined with rootlets and soft furry leaves of *Helichrysum* and other herbs; inside diameter 6,6 cm, depth 4,5 cm; 0,6–2,5 m above ground in fork of shrub or bushy tree (especially *Rhigozum, Boscia* and *Acacia*; mean of 30 nests = 1,2 m); built in about 8 days. *Clutch*: (44) 2–2,6–3 eggs. *Eggs*: Bright blue-green, boldly spotted with red-brown and grey concentrated at thick end; measure (83) 23,6 × 17,2 (20–25,9 × 16,2–18,2). *Incubation*: (2) 14 days. *Nestling*: (3) 11–12 days.

---

698 (665)   **Fiscal Flycatcher**   **Plate 58**
Fiskaalvlieëvanger
Sigelus silens

Icola (X), [Würgerschnäpper]

Measurements: Length 17–20 cm; wing (24 ♂) 91–95,6–98, (8 ♀) 87–89,8–93; tail (32) 73–89; tarsus (32) 21–24,5; culmen (32) 13,5–17,5. Weight (12 ♂) 22,9–25,6–31 g, (10 ♀) 23,6–26,9–37 g, (163 unsexed) 21–26,2–34,7 g.

Bare Parts: Iris reddish brown; bill, legs and feet black.

Identification: Large (about robin-sized); above jet black (♂) or sooty blackish brown (♀) to below eye; bold white wingstripe; tail black with large rectangular white windows (conspicuous in flight;

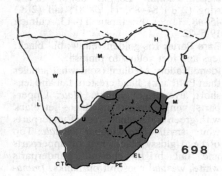

diagnostic); below white or pale greyish white; similar to Fiscal Shrike but tail rounded (not longish and graduated), bill slender (not stout and hooked), head more slender; does not perch with tail held sideways as does Fiscal Shrike. *Immature*: Above reddish brown, spotted buffy white; below off-white, spotted dark brown.

Voice: Song shorter or longer phrases of mixed thin sibilant and richer piping notes, *tsip tsip chuk tweeu-kik-rrr, tswippy tswip trree-up-up, tsippy tsip twee-up*, etc.; imitates other birdcalls; sharp *skisk* and *kirr-kirr-kirr* alarm calls.

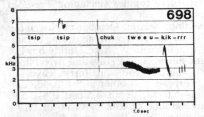

Distribution: Most of S Africa, Lesotho, Swaziland, extreme se Botswana and extreme s Mozambique.

Status: Common resident subject to much local movement in winter; winter visitor to lowland Natal and Mozambique, May to September.

Habitat: Thornveld, bushveld, semi-arid scrub, karoo, riverine bush, small dense patches of trees or bushes (including exotic species) in scrub and grassland, gardens in smaller towns and suburbs.

Habits: Usually singly or in pairs; sometimes in groups of up to 10 in suitable fruiting tree in winter. Usually silent; conspicuous and tame; perches on top of bush or low tree; flies to ground to catch prey; less often catches insects in flight. Plumage similarity to that of aggressive Fiscal Shrike probably adaptive mimicry.

Food: Insects, fruit (of *Cotoneaster, Euonymus, Chrysanthemoides monilifera* and *Halleria lucida*), nectar of aloes, porridge from dogbowl.

Breeding: *Season*: September to January in Cape, October to December in Natal, August to January (mainly September-November) in Transvaal. *Nest*: Bulky shallow bowl of twigs, grass, weeds and lichen, lined with plant down and rootlets; up to 6 m above ground in fork of small tree or bush, or base of aloe leaf. *Clutch*: (31) 2–2,8–4 eggs (usually 3). *Eggs*: Pale greenish blue, finely speckled with reddish brown or olive brown concentrated at thick end; measure (92) 21,4 × 15,9 (18,5–24,2 × 14,4–17). *Incubation*: (3) 13–15 days. *Nestling*: Unrecorded.

---

699 (667) **Vanga Flycatcher** **Plate 58**
Witpensvlieëvanger
Bias musicus

[Vangaschnäpper]

Measurements: Length about 16 cm; wing (2 ♂) 84–85, (1 ♀) 81; tail (2 ♂) 45–48, (1 ♀) 49; tarsus 11–13; culmen 19,5–22.

Bare Parts: Iris golden yellow; bill black; legs and feet yellow to pinkish.

Identification: Medium (somewhat smaller than Puffback); head crested; tail and legs short; eye bright yellow. *Male*: Upperparts, wings, breast and thighs jet black with green iridescence; rest of underparts white; small white wingbar. *Female*: Top of head glossy black; rest of upperparts and tail bright chestnut; underparts white, washed chestnut on flanks. *Imma-*

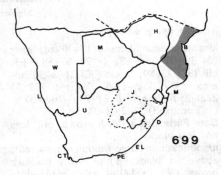

ture: Like adult ♀, but streaked brown on head.

Voice: Song variety of loud sharp notes, *chi-KIK-yoo*, *we-chip*, *we-chip*, often repeated; also *wit-tu-wit-tu-tu-tu-tu*, first rising then falling in pitch; harsh *churr* in flight.

Distribution: Africa S of Sahara; in s Africa confined to lowlands of Mozambique to Inhambane, and adjacent Zimbabwe.

Status: Uncommon resident; possibly makes seasonal movements in Mozambique; occasional in Zimbabwe.

Habitat: Evergreen and riverine forest.

Habits: Usually in pairs or small groups.

Keeps to canopy of forest; highly vocal and conspicuous. Flight slow and flapping, rather like that of Yellowrumped Widow; courtship flight fluttering. ♂ flies in slow circles around nesting tree; aggressive towards other birds.

Food: Unrecorded; probably insects.

Breeding: *Season*: October in Zimbabwe. *Nest*: Small shallow cup of plant fibres, strips of bark and rotten wood, bound with spider web; lined with leaf petioles and flowers; on stout horizontal branch or in fork of tree about 30 m above ground, sometimes overhanging river; built by ♀ only. *Clutch*: 2 eggs. *Eggs*: Greyish white to pale bluish green, spotted with brown and grey concentrated at thick end; measure about 19–21 × 15–16. *Incubation*: Unrecorded. *Nestling*: Unrecorded.

THE GENUS *BATIS*

Flycatchers of the genus *Batis* are all small, large-headed and relatively short-tailed birds of forest, woodland, savanna or bush. In all but Woodwards' Batis, the ♂ has a black breastband, the ♀ a chestnut or ochre breastband; the females usually have chestnut or ochre on the throat also. The upperparts are grey (sometimes mottled with white), the wings blackish with a white or rusty wingbar. The face is black, bordered above by a white eyebrow (not in ♂ Cape Batis) and below by the white, chestnut or yellow throat. The tail is always black with white outer edges and tips. The flight is quick and bouncing. Batises forage by catching insects in flight or by gleaning from leaves and twigs, catching prey with a loud bill snap. The song of the ♂ is a distinctive short piping phrase, usually rising or falling in pitch; alarm calls are quiet stuttering *ch-ch-ch-ch* sounds. There are 5 species in southern Africa. The genus *Batis* may be related to the bush shrikes or helmetshrikes.

700 (672)   **Cape Batis**   **Plate 59**
                        Kaapse Bosbontrokkie
                           Batis capensis

Ingedle, Unongedle (X), umNqube, uDokotela (Z), [Kapschnäpper]

Measurements: Length 12–13 cm; wing (19 ♂) 57–60,3–63, (19 ♀) 56,5–60,3–63, (85 unsexed) 56–61,5–65; tail (83) 35–43,5–46; tarsus (174) 15,5–20,6–24; culmen (176) 10–13,7–16. Weight (101 ♂) 9,3–11,8–14,5 g, (200 ♀) 8,9–11,5–13,9 g, (11 unsexed) 9,3–12–14,2 g.

Bare Parts: Iris yellow, orange or scarlet; bill, legs and feet black.

Identification: See *Batis* account. *Male*: Black breastband very broad; flanks chestnut to tawny (diagnostic); rest of under-

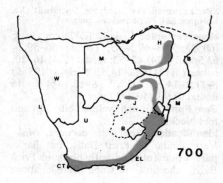

700

parts white; no white eyebrow (diagnostic); wingbar tawny (white in all other ♂ batises with black breastbands). *Female*: Similar to ♂ but throat and breast tawny, deeper chestnut on breastband; short white eyebrow (eyebrow extends from bill to sides of neck in ♀ Woodwards' Batis). *Immature*: Like adult ♀, but without black facemask; above more olive. *Fledgling*: Spotted brown and buff above; white below with buff throat.

Voice: Song variable piping phrases; monotonous *tu-tu-tu-tu* or *tu-tu-tu-tee-tee* or *tu-tu-tu-tee-tee-tee*, last 2–3 notes higher pitched than first series; rapid *ch-ch-ch-chwee-oo* of 2–3 hoarse notes, followed by 2 bell-like notes, rising a tone on *chwee*, falling about 6 tones on *oo*; ringing musical *tu-wit*, repeated about 12 times every 5 seconds; harsh rolling ratchetlike *chi-chi-chi-chi-chu-chiriri*; single repeated *reep-reep-reep* callnote; grinding *prrit prrit* alarm note like 2 stones rubbed together.

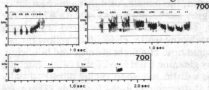

Distribution: Discontinuously in s Africa from sw Cape to Natal, thence inland to escarpments of Swaziland and Transvaal; also s and e Zimbabwe.

Status: Common resident; some seasonal altitudinal movement.
Habitat: Lower levels of evergreen forest, densely wooded gorges and exotic plantations in summer; in winter may spread to more open woodland and savanna.
Habits: Usually in pairs; sometimes in groups of up to 9 birds (sometimes all females); may join mixed bird parties. When alarmed flies with bursts of whirring wingbeats. Usually tame especially at nest.
Food: Insects.
Breeding: *Season*: September to December in w Cape, November to March in e Cape, September to December in Natal, September to February (mainly October-December) in Zimbabwe. *Nest*: Small strong neat cup of dry plant material, bound with spider web and covered outside with lichen moulded to site; in fork of twig or sapling, on horizontal branch, or against trunk of tree; 1–9,5 m above ground (mean of 27 nests about 4,1 m); built by both sexes. *Clutch*: (65) 1–2,1–3 eggs (usually 2). *Eggs*: Salmon pink to pinkish or greenish white, spotted and blotched with browns and grey concentrated at thick end; measure (40) 18 × 13,9 (16,3–21 × 12,6–15,2). *Incubation*: 17–21 days by ♀ only. *Nestling*: About 16 days; fed by both parents; young may remain with parents for at least a year.

Ref. Broekhuysen, G.J. 1958. *Ostrich* 29:143–152.

701 (673) **Chinspot Batis** **Plate 59**
Witliesbosbontrokkie
Batis molitor

Xibirhimangwani (Ts), Undyola, Unondyola (X), umNqube (Z), [Weißflankenschnäpper]

Measurements: Length 12–13 cm; wing (60 ♂) 57,5–60,5–65, (64 ♀) 56–59,2–62,5; tail (124) 42–52; tarsus (124) 16–20; culmen (124) 11–14,5. Weight (95 ♂) 8–11,2–14 g, (95 ♀) 8–12,1–14 g, (6 unsexed) 9,9–10,6–12 g.
Bare Parts: Iris light yellow; bill, legs and feet black.
Identification: See *Batis* account. *Male*: Very similar to Pririt Batis, but flanks pure white (marked with black in Pririt Batis, chestnut in Cape Batis); above

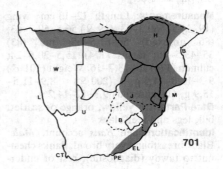

grey; below white with neat black breast-band; wingbar white; short white eye-brow. *Female*: Similar to ♂, but breastband and central spot on throat chestnut (throat and breast of ♀ Pririt Batis rich yellow ochre). *Immature*: Similar to adult ♀, but washed rusty above; ♂ has buff chinspot and breastband, sometimes mixed with black. *Fledgling*: Spotted buff and blackish above.

Voice: Song of ♂ somewhat plaintive piping of 2–3 syllables, dropping by about quarter-tone, *weep-woop* or *weep-woop-wurp*; sometimes with rolling quality, *kreep-kroop*, or with variations, *kreep-kroop-chowp* or *weep-woop-chuk*; rapid *ch-ch-ch-ch* alarm notes, rather like fine sandpaper on wood; churring and bill-snapping in display.

Distribution: S Africa to Kenya; widespread in SE, NE and N; avoids highveld and dry W.

Status: Common; mostly resident, but undergoes some local seasonal movement.

Habitat: Woodland, savanna, bushveld and riverine thickets; rarely forest edge.

Habits: Usually solitary or in pairs; may join mixed bird parties in winter. Forages mostly in canopy of trees. Fairly tame; confiding near nest. Displays above tree-tops and over open spaces with noisy wingsnaps, bouncing at each snap.

Food: Insects and spiders.

Breeding: *Season*: September to October in e Cape, October to December in Natal, August to February (mainly October-December) in Transvaal, August to February (mainly September-November) in Zimbabwe. *Nest*: Small strong cup of plant fibres bound with spider web, decorated outside with flakes of lichen moulded onto site; usually on horizontal branch of tree, or in vertical fork of sapling; 1–4 m above ground (mean of 14 nests = 2,3 m), usually in *Acacia* species or *Ziziphus mucronata*; built by both sexes in up to 14 days. *Clutch*: (88) 1–1,7–4 eggs (almost invariably 2). *Eggs*: Pale greenish or blue-green, spotted and blotched with blackish, brown and grey sometimes concentrated into ring around thick end; measure (92) 17,3 × 13 (15,4–19 × 11,9–14,2). *Incubation*: (6) 16–18 days by ♀ only. *Nestling*: 16–18 days; fed by both parents; postnestling dependence 6–14 weeks.

---

702 (675)   **Mozambique Batis**   **Plate 59**
Mosambiekbosbontrokkie
Batis soror

[Sansibarschnäpper]

Measurements: Length 10,5–11,5 cm; wing 50–62; tail 32–42; tarsus 17,5–19; culmen 12–14. Weight (36 ♂) 8,8–9,6–11 g, (38 ♀) 8–9,5–13,1 g.

Bare Parts: Iris yellow; bill, legs and feet black.

Identification: See *Batis* account; smaller than Chinspot Batis. *Male*: Similar to Chinspot Batis ♂, but back more mottled with white and grey, white eyebrow more extensive and black breastband narrower. *Female*: Similar to Chinspot Batis ♀, but chestnut on throat diffuse (not neat spot), and breastband paler, less well defined.

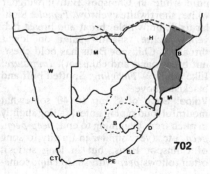

702

Voice: Song long series of deliberate piping notes, *tlop-tlop-tlop-tlop*, sometimes interspersed with higher-pitched *wit* or *wit-wit*; also jarring alarm notes.

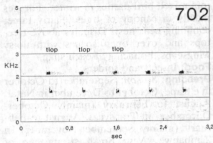

Distribution: Littoral of e Africa from s Mozambique (Limpopo River) and adjacent e Zimbabwe, to Kenya.
Status: Fairly common resident; formerly considered subspecies of Chinspot Batis, because of similar appearance, but overlaps with it marginally in Zimbabwe.
Habitat: Lowland savanna and denser woodland (replaces Chinspot Batis on moister e slopes of Zimbabwe highlands).
Habits: Very similar to those of Chinspot Batis. Poorly known in s Africa. Forages mostly in mid-canopy, flicking tail at each movement; often joins mixed bird parties, especially in winter.
Food: Insects.
Breeding: *Season*: October to November in Zimbabwe. *Nest*: Similar to that of Chinspot Batis; up to 8 m above ground. *Clutch*: (3) 2–3 eggs (usually 2). *Eggs*: Undescribed. *Incubation*: Unrecorded. *Nestling*: Unrecorded; fed by both parents.

703 (674)   **Pririt Batis**   **Plate 59**
Priritbosbontrokkie
Batis pririt

[Priritschnäpper]

Measurements: Length about 12 cm; wing (23 ♂) 55–56,4–58, (22 ♀) 52–55–57,5; tail (10 ♂) 44–48, (8 ♀) 42–45; tarsus (45) 16–19; culmen (10 ♂) 14–15, (8 ♀) 13–14. Weight (12 ♂) 8–9–10 g, (21 ♀) 8–9,7–14 g, (7 unsexed) 7,5–8,3–9 g.
Bare Parts: Iris light yellow to ivory white; bill, legs and feet black.
Identification: See *Batis* account; slightly smaller than Chinspot Batis. *Male*: Above grey; below white with neat black breastband and black markings on flanks (flanks pure white in Chinspot Batis); wingbar white; short white eyebrow. *Female*: Similar to ♂, but whole throat and breast rich yellow ochre, slightly paler on lower throat (♀ Chinspot Batis has bold chestnut breastband and chinspot). *Immature*: Like adult ♀. *Fledgling*: Spotted buff and blackish above.
Voice: Song of ♂ up to 40 somewhat mournful loud piping notes, falling slightly in pitch from beginning to end, *peep-peep-peep*, etc. (very similar in quality to song of Chinspot Batis, but in long series); often follows *peep* with sharp *chip*; some-

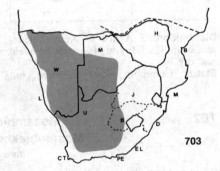

times reminiscent of initial singing attempts of immature Bokmakierie; sharp *chuk* alarm note.

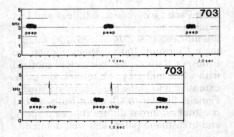

Distribution: Dry w parts of s Africa from Karoo to sw Angola.
Status: Common resident.
Habitat: *Acacia* savanna, riverine bush (especially with dense stands of *Tamarix usneoides*); thickets around waterholes.
Habits: Usually in pairs or family groups. Forages in middle to lower layers of bushes or trees, seldom higher than about 5 m, usually in scrubbier growth than do other batises, but sometimes also in canopy of larger *Acacia* trees. Performs wing-snapping display flight across open spaces between thickets, bouncing at each snap. Usually tame. In breeding season ♂ sings for long periods.
Food: Insects.
Breeding: *Season*: July to March (pos-

sibly any month, according to rainfall). *Nest*: Small strong cup of plant fibres, bound with spider web and cocoons; decorated outside with small bits of bark; usually on rather slender horizontal branch of *Acacia* tree or *Tamarix* bush, often against small vertical twig; looks like knot or gall on branch; usually in shade, from about 1–3 m above ground. *Clutch*: (35) 1–4 eggs (usually 2). *Eggs*: White, cream or greenish white, spotted and blotched with shades of brown and grey; measure (24) 16,5 × 12,7 (15,7–18,1 × 12–13,3). *Incubation*: 17 days by ♀ only. *Nestling*: 17 days; fed by both parents; fledgling dependent on parents for about 6 weeks after leaving nest.

---

704 (676) **Woodwards' Batis** **Plate 59**
Woodwardse Bosbontrokkie
Batis fratrum

[Woodwardschnäpper]

Measurements: Length 10,5–11,5 cm; wing (13 ♂) 58,5–60,9–64, (14 ♀) 59–60,5–62; tail (13 ♂) 31,5–33,8–38, (14 ♀) 33–34,1–36; tarsus (8) 17,5–19; culmen (13 ♂) 15–16,5–17,5, (14 ♀) 15–15,6–16,5. Weight (43 ♂) 10,4–12,2–13,8 g, (23 ♀) 10,3–11,7–13,6 g.
Bare Parts: Iris yellow; bill, legs and feet black.
Identification: See *Batis* account; smaller than Chinspot Batis. *Male*: Above grey; below white with tawny breastband and flanks (throat all white; other ♂ batises have black breastbands); short eyebrow and wingbar white. *Female*: Similar to ♀ Pririt Batis, but wingbar tawny (not white); white eyebrow extends from bill to sides of neck (short, to eye only, in ♀ Cape Batis); throat, breast and flanks tawny (not chestnut as in ♀ Cape Batis). *Immature*: Like adult ♀, but eyebrow buff; no black facemask. *Fledgling*: Spotted brown and buff above.
Voice: Song rather slow and deliberate ringing *poo-poo-poo* of up to 6 notes; rapid rasping jerky *prer-rer-rer-rer-rer-rert*.

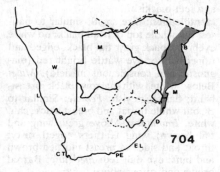

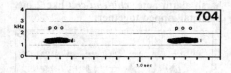

Distribution: Zululand from about Richards Bay to Mozambique N of Zambezi River, and extreme e lowlands of Zimbabwe.
Status: Locally fairly common resident. Possibly Rare (RDB).

Habitat: Middle to lower levels of lowland and coastal evergreen forest; less often riverine forest on littoral plain.
Habits: In pairs or small groups; joins mixed bird parties. Similar to other batises, but less tame and vocal than most.
Food: Insects.
Breeding: *Season*: October to November in Zululand, November in Zimbabwe.

Nest: Small rather loosely constructed cup of fine grass and moss, bound with spider web; not as tidy as nests of other batises; well hidden in fork of tree or bush. *Clutch*: (7) 1–2,4–3 eggs. *Eggs*: Cream or white, spotted and blotched with shades of brown and grey; measure (8) 18,1 × 13,1 (16,3–19,3 × 12,4–14,1); weigh (2) 1,8 g. *Incubation*: Unrecorded. *Nestling*: Unrecorded.

705 (677)   Wattle-eyed Flycatcher   Plate 59
Beloogbosbontrokkie
Platysteira peltata

[Schwarzkehl-Lappenschnäpper]

Measurements: Length about 13 cm; wing (38 ♂) 63–65,1–70, (32 ♀) 62–64,6–67; tail (5) 51–54; tarsus (5) 17–19; culmen (5) 14–16. Weight (60 ♂) 11,4–13,6–17 g, (56 ♀) 10–13,8–18,8 g.
Bare Parts: Iris brown, purplish or grey peripherally, white around pupil; wattle above and before eye bright red; bill, legs and feet blackish.
Identification: Size small; similar to batises, but whole top of head black; no white eyebrow; back grey; tail black, edged and tipped white; eye wattle bright red (diagnostic and conspicuous in field). *Male*: Below white with narrow black breastband; flanks greyish. *Female*: Similar to ♂, but whole throat and breast black; chin white. *Immature*: Above grey; wing and tail brown; wing feathers edged rusty; throat and sides of breast mottled brown and buff; eye dull red. *Fledgling*: Barred brown and rufous above.
Voice: Harsh *jip-jip zik-keek, zik-keek, zik-keek*; tinkling *er-er-fee, er-er-fee-fu*; harsh alarm note, *chit-chit-chit* like 2 bits of metal tapped together.

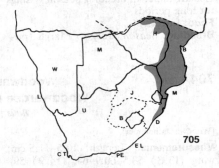

705

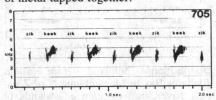

705

Distribution: S Africa to Kenya; in s Africa confined to extreme e littoral belt from Natal to Transvaal lowveld, Mozam-

bique and adjacent Zimbabwe; also up Limpopo Valley, probably as far as Tuli in Botswana.
Status: Locally common resident. Probably Rare (RDB).
Habitat: Riverine woodland, lowland evergreen forest, evergreen thickets in Sabi and Limpopo Valleys, mangrove swamps; usually low in understory near water.
Habits: Usually in pairs. Similar to batises in foraging methods (see *Batis* account). Less vocal than batises. Aggressive towards other birds when nesting; displaying ♂ makes *frip frip* sounds with wings.
Food: Insects, especially moths.
Breeding: *Season*: October to December in Natal, July to March (mainly September-November) in Zimbabwe and ne Transvaal. *Nest*: Small neat cup of fine twigs and grass fibres, bound with spider web; sometimes lined with plant down or *Usnea* lichen; not always decorated with lichen; not as deep as nest of Paradise Flycatcher; 0,7–9 m above ground in small fork of tree, or on drooping branch;

built by both sexes, mostly by ♀. *Clutch*: (6) 2–3 eggs (usually 2). *Eggs*: Grey-green, green or blue with spots and blotches of red-brown, purple and grey; measure (8) 18 × 13,7 (16,5–18,5 × 13–14,3). *Incubation*: Usually 18 days (rarely only 16 days) by both sexes. *Nestling*:

13–16 days; fed by both parents; dependent on parents for at least 1 week after leaving nest; may remain with parents for further 6 months.

Ref. Brooke, R.K. & Manson, A.J. 1979. *Honeyguide* 97:15–17.
Scott, J.A. 1984. *Honeyguide* 30:72–74.

706 (678)   Fairy Flycatcher   Plate 59
Feevlieëvanger
Stenostira scita

[Elfenschnäpper]

Measurements: Length 11–12 cm; wing (27 ♂) 49–51,8–56, (21 ♀) 48,5–51,6–55; tail (27 ♂) 50–53,3–55,5, (21 ♀) 48–52,7–56; tarsus (23) 16–19; culmen (27 ♂) 12,5–13,7–15, (21 ♀) 12–13,1–14. Weight (48) 4–5,9–8 g.

Bare Parts: Iris dark brown; bill, legs and feet black.

Identification: Size very small; build slender; looks like slim batis; above blue-grey; facemask black; eyebrow white; wing black with conspicuous white stripe; tail longish (proportionately much longer than tail of batis), black, edged and tipped white; breast soft blue-grey; rest of underparts white, tinged salmon pink on throat and upper belly. *Immature*: Above rusty brown; below buff, darker on breast.

Voice: Thin squeaky *tsee-tsi-zee tseepy-tsweeu, tseepy-zzzzz*, and variations (somewhat sunbirdlike); sibilant *kisskiss-skiss* callnote of 2–3 syllables; harsh *zrrt zrrt* (alarm?).

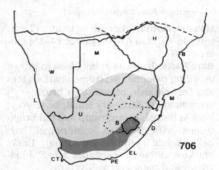

706

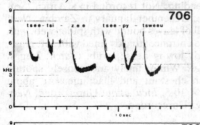

706

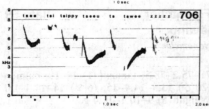

706

Distribution: Breeds mostly w Cape, Karoo, Lesotho highlands, upper Drakensberg; migrates in winter to lower regions and further N to s Namibia, n Cape, Orange Free State, n and w Transvaal, upland Natal, Swaziland and extreme sw Mozambique; vagrant to s Zimbabwe and e Transvaal mainly in dry years.

Status: Common seasonal migrant over most of range, moving from S to N and from high elevations to lower from April to October.

Habitat: *Breeding*: Fynbos, karoo scrub, bushy hillsides. *Nonbreeding*: *Acacia* savanna, riverine thornbush, scrubby hillsides, exotic plantations, gardens.

Habits: In pairs when breeding; otherwise usually solitary. Forages inside leafy canopy of bushes and trees, darting restlessly about like white-eye or warbler, gleaning insects from twigs and leaves. Often droops wings and slightly raises and spreads tail.

Food: Small insects.

Breeding: *Season*: October to December. *Nest*: Small cup with thick compact walls of bark shreds, grass and dead leaves, bound with spider web; thickly lined with wool, hair, feathers or plant down; inside diameter 3 cm, depth 3–3,8 cm; sometimes covered outside with lichen; as low as 20 cm above ground in bush, among fallen branches, or in drifted debris; well camouflaged; built by ♀ only in about 4 days. *Clutch*: (10) 2–2,3–3 eggs. *Eggs*: Dull white to cream or greenish buff, zoned with darker shade, sometimes speckled with greenish brown; measure (21) 15,2 × 11,5 (14,5–16,9 × 10,8–12,7). *Incubation*: 17–18 days. *Nestling*: Unrecorded.

Ref. James, H.W. 1922. *Ibis* 4 (11th Series):254–256.

707 (679) Livingstone's Flycatcher Plate 58
Rooistertvlieëvanger
Erythrocercus livingstonei

[Livingstones Rotschwanzschnäpper]

Measurements: Length about 12 cm; wing 45–50; tail 47–48; tarsus 14–15; culmen 8–9.

Bare Parts: Iris brown; bill black to brown or white, paler below, culmen darker; legs and feet pinkish, brownish or black.

Identification: Size very small; head grey; back yellowish green; rump and tail bright rufous with blackish subterminal bar; belly bright yellow. *Immature*: Lacks blackish tailbar; back duller green; hindcrown and nape greenish yellow.

Voice: Song high-pitched *wit* and *tweet* notes in warbling burst, *wit-ti-ti-ti-ti-wee-tu-tu-wee*; also sharp *zert* and *chip* (alarm?) notes.

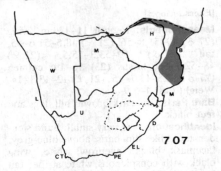

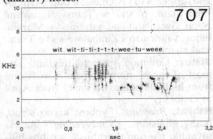

Distribution: From Limpopo River to E Africa; in s Africa confined to extreme NE in Mozambique and adjacent Zimbabwe up Zambezi Valley.

Status: Fairly common resident.
Habitat: Riverine forest and nearby woodland and thickets.
Habits: Usually in pairs or small groups; sometimes in mixed bird parties. Forages like eremomela, creeping, hopping and darting about in upper layers of trees or bushes; sometimes hawks insects in flight; fans and flirts rufous tail continuously.
Food: Insects.
Breeding: Not recorded in s Africa. *Season*: December-January in Zambia. *Nest*: Ball of leaves bound with spider web, with side entrance; thickly lined with soft grass; fairly low in dense scrub. *Clutch*: 2 eggs. *Eggs*: White, finely and densely spotted with chestnut and lilac; measure about 13 × 10,5. *Incubation*: Unrecorded. *Nestling*: Unrecorded.

708 (680) Bluemantled Flycatcher Plate 59
Bloukuifvlieëvanger
Trochocercus cyanomelas

Igotyi (X), [Blaumantel-Schopfschnäpper]

Measurements: Length about 15 cm; wing (28 ♂) 64–66,9–70,5, (3 ♀) 63–64,4–65; tail (20 ♂) 72,5–77,6–83, (10 ♀) 71–75,2–78,5; tarsus (11) 16–19; culmen (20 ♂) 13,5–14,4–15, (6 ♀) 14–14,4–15. Weight (5) 9–10,1–11,4 g.

Bare Parts: Iris brown; bill, legs and feet slate blue.

Identification: Size medium (slightly smaller than Paradise Flycatcher). *Male*: Whole head, crest and throat glossy blue-black; back grey; wingbar and rest of underparts white; tail black. *Female*: Similar to ♂, but crest shorter; head less glossy; face, throat and breast vaguely mottled grey and white, shading to white on belly; wingbar white (diagnostic; no wingbar in Whitetailed Flycatcher); tail black (no white as in Whitetailed Flycatcher). *Immature*: Similar to adult ♀, but more washed with olive buff; wingbar buff.

Voice: Zipping *zweet-zwa* or *zweet-zweet-zwa* alarm call (almost indistinguishable from that of Paradise Flycatcher), sometimes interspersed with thin twittering *tititititi* notes; song loud ringing *tsee-yoyoyoyoyoyo*, or mellower slower *kew-ew-ew-ew-ew*, often preceded or interspersed with harsher *zweet* notes.

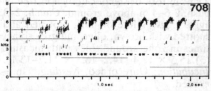

Distribution: S Africa to C and E Africa (Somalia); in s Africa confined to narrow strip between coast and lower or more northerly escarpments (Winterberg, Natal Midlands, n Drakensberg, Zoutpansberg, Zimbabwe highlands) from sw Cape to Mozambique, e Transvaal, Limpopo Valley and e Zimbabwe, Victoria Falls and in Caprivi at confluence of Cuito and Kavango Rivers.

Status: Uncommon and local resident; may have seasonal movements.

Habitat: Middle to lower layers of coastal, lowland and mid-altitude evergreen forest (even very small forest patches); also thickets in riverine forest.

Habits: Usually solitary or in pairs; occasionally joins mixed bird parties. Forages with restless flitting and hopping among branches, constantly fanning tail open and closed and swinging body from side to side; catches prey in flight or off twigs and leaves. Quite vocal, usually detected first by raspy callnotes.

Food: Small insects.

Breeding: *Season*: October to December in Natal, October to January in Zimbabwe. *Nest*: Thick-walled neat cup of bark fibres, fine grass, moss and lichens, bound with spider web; 1–8 m above ground in leafy fork of tree or bush. *Clutch*: (9) 2–2,2–3 eggs. *Eggs*: White, cream or pinkish, blotched and spotted with red-brown, greenish brown and purplish grey often in ring around thick end; measure (10) 18,8 × 13,8 (15,8–22,9 × 12,2–15,1). *Incubation*: Unrecorded. *Nestling*: Unrecorded.

709 (681)   **Whitetailed Flycatcher**   **Plate 59**
                         Witstertvlieëvanger
                         Trochocercus albonotatus

[Weißschwanz-Schopfschnäpper]

Measurements: Length 14–15 cm; wing (12 ♂) 61–63,7–66, (11 ♀) 60–62,3–65, (125 unsexed) 54–62,8–69; tail (10 ♂) 70–72,8–79, (9 ♀) 67,5–70,8–76, (118 unsexed) 64–72,3–84; tarsus (127) 15–18,1–21; culmen (10 ♂) 12,5–13,8–14, (9 ♀) 12–13,5–14, (128 unsexed) 7,5–10,3–13. Weight (7 ♂) 7,3–8,6–9,5 g, (4 ♀) 7–7,9–8,7 g, (128 unsexed) 6,2–8,2–10,8 g.

Bare Parts: Iris dark brown; bill, legs and feet black.

Identification: Size smallish to medium; similar to ♀ Bluemantled Flycatcher, but

617

lacks white wingbar, and has white edges and tip to tail (conspicuous when fanned); head, crest and throat slightly glossy black; back, breast and flanks dark grey, shading to white on belly (♂ Bluemantled Flycatcher has black and white of underparts sharply demarcated). *Immature*: Dark grey on throat and sides of head. *Chick*: Covered with scanty short grey down; inside of mouth plain yellow.

Voice: Song stuttering series of thin sharp twittering whistled notes, *chrit-it-it-it-it*; thin 2-syllabled callnote.

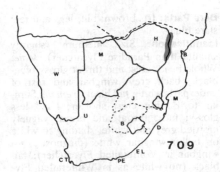

7 0 9

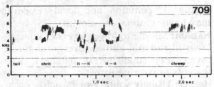

Distribution: Zimbabwe to Kenya and Uganda; in s Africa confined to e highlands of Zimbabwe, adjacent Mozambique and Mount Gorongosa.
Status: Common resident; some altitudinal movement.
Habitat: Middle layers of montane and mid-altitude evergreen forest, even quite small isolated patches and adjacent scrub.
Habits: Usually in pairs. Similar to Bluemantled Flycatcher, foraging restlessly

among branches, often pursuing insects in flight; constantly fans tail. Flight jerky. ♂ droops wings and raises tail in courtship. Highly vocal, often detected first by callnotes; tame.
Food: Insects.
Breeding: *Season*: October to January (mainly November-December) in Zimbabwe. *Nest*: Goblet-shaped cup of felted moss and spider web, sometimes with lichen on outside; internal diameter about 4 cm; in fork of slender branch in tree or bush, 0,6–4 m above ground. *Clutch*: 2–3 eggs. *Eggs*: White or buff, blotched and spotted with brown, olive and grey sometimes in zone around thick end; measure (3) 15,5 × 12,4 (14,2–16,3 × 11,7–13,1). *Incubation*: Unrecorded. *Nestling*: Unrecorded.

---

710 (682)   **Paradise Flycatcher**   **Plate 59**
Paradysvlieëvanger
Terpsiphone viridis

Mmakgwadi (NS), Dzwedzwe, Ridantswe, Dzindzo (Ts), Ujejane, Unomaphelana (X), uVe, iNzwece (Z), [Paradiesschnäpper]

Measurements: Length ♂ (including long tail) 23–41 cm, ♀ 16–18 cm; wing (29 ♂) 76,5–82,1–88, (25 ♀) 73–78,6–85,5; tail, outermost rectrix (11 ♂) 67–80, (5 ♀) 68–70, longest (central) rectrix (17 ♂) 101–237,4–352, (8 ♀) 83–98,4–112; tarsus (15) 13,5–16–17,5; culmen (14) 12–14,8–17,5. Weight (35 ♂) 11,1–14,4–17,9 g, (24 ♀) 11,6–14–16,5 g, (16 unsexed) 12–14,8–17 g.
Bare Parts: Iris brown; bill, gape and

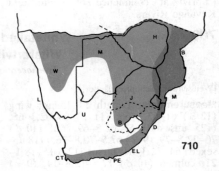

710

wattle around eye bright blue to greenish blue, billtip blackish; mouth greenish yellow (♂); legs and feet bluish slate.

Identification: Size medium (smaller than Black Flycatcher); whole head, crest, mantle, throat and breast metallic greenish black (black restricted to top of head only in ♀; nape and throat grey); rest of upperparts and tail bright orange-rust; tail very long in ♂, more than twice length of body; rest of underparts grey, shading to white on belly. *Immature*: Similar to adult ♀, but duller on head.

Voice: Song quick rippling phrase of piping notes *tzzeee switty-sweety-tsweep-sweepy-taweep*, and variations; raspy *zweet-zwayt* or *zweet-zweet-zwayt* alarm call.

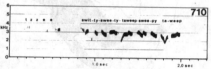

Distribution: Africa S of Sahara and sw Arabia; widespread in s Africa except in highest and drier parts.

Status: Common breeding intra-African migrant, September to March or May (rarely to June); one bird ringed Pietermaritzburg recovered Vila Junqueiro, Mozambique; present in all months in Zululand, Mozambique and e and n Zimbabwe.

Habitat: Riverine and coastal forest, forest edge, thickets in savanna and other types of woodland, gardens, exotic plantations.

Habits: Solitary or in pairs. Hawks insects in quick sallies from perch; flight undulating and graceful; ♂ looks like swooping orange rocket. Quite vocal, often detected first by voice, despite bright coloration; tame but unobtrusive. Bathes by plunge-diving into water.

Food: Insects.

Breeding: *Season*: October to January in Cape, September to March (mainly October-December) in Natal, October to March (mainly October-January) in Transvaal, September to February (mainly October-December) in Zimbabwe. *Nest*: Neat shallow cup of bark, roots and grass, bound with spider web, lined with rootlets; often decorated outside with bits of lichen; 1,5–4,5 m above ground on fork of slender drooping or sloping branch, often over water or dry streambed; usually in shade. *Clutch*: (197) 1–2,4–4 eggs (usually 2–3). *Eggs*: Creamy or pinkish white, sparingly spotted with reddish brown in zone around thick end; measure (111) 18,8 × 14,1 (17,3–21,5 × 13–15,1). *Incubation*: (10) 12–13,7–15 days; rarely up to 17 days. *Nestling*: 10–12 days, rarely to 16 days; fed by both parents; dependent on parents for at least 1 week after leaving nest.

Ref. Little, J. de V. 1964. *Ostrich* 35:32–41.
Skead, C.J. 1967. *Ostrich* 38:123–132.

26:17.   Family 79 MOTACILLIDAE—WAGTAILS, PIPITS, LONGCLAWS

Small to medium. Bill medium, slender, pointed, somewhat arched on culmen; legs medium to moderately long, slender or stout; toes medium to very long, with extremely long claws in longclaws (genus *Macronyx*); hind claw typically long, but not straight as in many larks; wings medium, pointed or somewhat rounded; tail medium to longish, outer rectrices white or tipped with white; tail wagged up and down in wagtails and pipits; plumage usually grey, black and white in wagtails (*Motacilla*), brown and white with streaks in pipits (*Anthus*) and brown above, yellow, orange or pink below with black collar in longclaws (*Macronyx*), but with some overlap between groups (wagtails comprise subfamily Motacillinae, pipits and longclaws subfamily Anthinae); sexes mostly similar, but female often duller; primarily terrestrial on shorelines, streams, grassland or semidesert; song-flight displays common; food mostly small invertebrates; gregarious when not breeding;

nest an open cup on ground or in bank, hole, crevice or creeper; eggs 2–7, white or yellowish, mottled or spotted; chick downy at hatching; incubation by both sexes or by female only; young cared for by both sexes. Distribution worldwide, but predominantly Old World; about 55 species; 23 species in s Africa.

Ref. Clancey, P.A. 1990. *Durban Mus. Novit.* 15: 42–72.
Winterbottom, J.M. 1964. *Ostrich* 35:129–141.

711 (685) African Pied Wagtail Plate 60
Bontkwikkie
Motacilla aguimp

Kamukombo (K), Motjoli (SS), Umcelu, Umventshane, Umvemve (X), umVemve, umCishu (Z), [Witwenstelze]

Measurements: Length about 20 cm; wing (7) 91–95,3–98; tail 96–103; tarsus 23–26; culmen 13,5–15,5. Weight (55) 23–27–30,5 g.

Bare Parts: Iris brown; bill, legs and feet black.

Identification: Size large (largest wagtail in s Africa); upperparts, tail and broad breastband black (sooty in ♀; upperparts grey in Cape and Longtailed Wagtails); eyebrow, patch on side of neck, bold wingstripe, outer rectrices and rest of underparts white; outer rectrices conspicuous in flight. *Immature*: Brownish where adult black; flanks washed brownish.

Voice: Song sustained jumble of high-pitched and mellow piping notes *tsip weet-weet, twip-twip-twip, weep-weep, tip-tip-tip, weet-woo-woo*, etc.; short whistled *tuwhee* callnote.

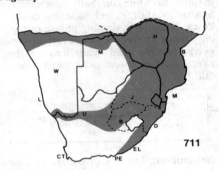

711

Habitat: Rocks and sandbanks of larger rivers, sewage ponds, playing fields, golf courses, parks, gardens.

Habits: Solitary or in pairs when breeding; otherwise in groups of a few to several dozen birds. Walks briskly about, running now and then after prey, and jumping or flying into air to catch flying insects; on alighting, stopping, or when agitated, wags tail up and down.

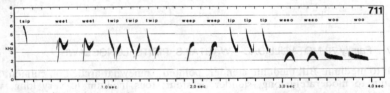

711

Distribution: Africa S of Sahara; in s Africa mainly confined to E, and along Vaal/Orange and Kunene/Okavango river systems to Atlantic coast; vagrant to sw Cape.

Status: Common to scarce; mostly resident; breeding migrant to e Cape in summer months; nonbreeding migrant to much of Transvaal in winter (April-August).

Tame, especially around human settlements.

Food: Insects, breadcrumbs, meal.

Breeding: *Season*: June to April (mainly September-October) in S Africa, all months except May (mainly August to October) in Zimbabwe. *Nest*: Bulky foundation of rags, string, leaves, roots, grass and other dry plant material, with neat cup lined with finer grass, hair and small feathers; in niche of river bank, pile of flood debris, thatch of roof, on ledge of building or moored boat, rock shelf in cave, in hole in tree, or among creepers. *Clutch*: (70) 2–3,2–5 eggs (usually 3–4). *Eggs*: Dull white or greyish white, vaguely marked with brown and grey; measure (45) 21,8 × 15,9 (19,4–24,9 × 14,6–16,6). *Incubation*: 13 days by both sexes (mainly by ♀). *Nestling*: 15–16 days; fed by both parents.

Ref. Nhlane, M.E.D. 1990. *Ostrich* 61:1–4.

712 (688) Longtailed Wagtail Plate 60
Bergkwikkie
Motacilla clara

Umcelu, Umventshane, Umvemve (X), umVemve, umCishu (Z), [Langschwanzstelze]

Measurements: Length 19–20 cm; wing (11) 76–79–81,5; tail 90–103; tarsus 20–22; culmen 14–15,5.
Bare Parts: Iris brown; bill and mouth black, lower jaw sometimes tinged greyish; legs and feet pinkish to greyish brown.
Identification: Size smallish; build slender (looks smaller than Cape Wagtail, but longer-tailed); above light blue-grey (dull olive grey in Cape Wagtail); face, narrow breastband, wings and tail black; eyebrow, underparts, outer rectrices and edges of wing feathers white (underparts off-white in Cape Wagtail). *Immature*: Similar to adult, but browner; mouth yellow.
Voice: Song musical piping *tsweu-tsweee, trrrip, tee-tu-wee-twi-twi*; loud chissik call-note on take-off; single high-pitched *teep* contact call.

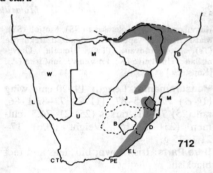

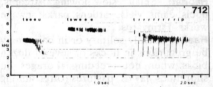

Distribution: Africa S of Sahara; in s Africa discontinuously from e Cape to e Transvaal, n Transvaal, e and n Zimbabwe, adjacent Mozambique and Mount Gorongosa.
Status: Sparse; resident on permanent streams and rivers; nomadic on seasonal tributaries.
Habitat: Fast-flowing well-wooded rocky streams and rivers, larger forested rivers; sometimes also smaller quiet tributaries, or streams in forest with pools and waterfalls.
Habits: Usually in pairs; unmated birds solitary; in family groups after breeding. Lively and quick, running about on rocks in midstream or wading up to belly-deep in water; catches insects in flight. Wags tail incessantly. When disturbed flies low and fast over water with undulating flight and fanned tail. Usually about 1 pair/0,5 km of pristine river; about 1 pair/km of unclean river. Threatens conspecifics with puffed body plumage and raised tail.
Food: Insects (mostly larvae of dragonflies and mosquitoes).
Breeding: *Season*: August to January (mainly September-October) in S Africa, August to November (mainly December) in Zimbabwe; up to 4 broods/season. *Nest*: Bulky foundation of leaves, moss and grass, started with material wet; with neat deep cup lined with dry fine rootlets and thin plant stems (no hair or down); inside diameter 5,5–6 cm, depth of cup 6 cm; on rock ledge or in niche of stream bank, usually

concealed by hanging vegetation; rarely under bridge or in tree; from ground level to 5 m up, usually 1–2 m above water; up to 9 m from river; built by both sexes in as little as 4 days; same sites used year after year. *Clutch*: (28) 1–2,1–3 eggs (usually 2, rarely 4 eggs). *Eggs*: Dull greyish, spotted with brown concentrated at thick end; measure

(43) 20,2 × 15,1 (17,4–21,9 × 14,2–16); weigh (8) 2,1–2,5–2,8 g. *Incubation*: 13–14 days by both sexes. *Nestling*: 14–18 days; fed by both parents; post-nestling dependence 28–32 days in 1st brood, up to 60 days in last brood.

Ref. Piper, S.E. 1989. *Ostrich Suppl.* 14:7–15; 123–131.

713 (686) Cape Wagtail — Plate 60
Gewone Kwikkie
Motacilla capensis

Kamukombo (K), Moletašaka (NS), Motjoli (SS), Matsherhani, N'wapesupesu, Mandzedzerekundze (Ts), Mokgôrônyane (Tw), Umcelu, Umventshane, Umvemve (X), umVemve, umCishu (Z), [Kapstelze]

Measurements: Length 19–20 cm; wing (14 ♂) 77–82,5–87, (11 ♀) 77–82,1–86; tail (25) 77–91; tarsus (25) 21–24,5; culmen (25) 13–15. Weight (206) 17–21,1–25 g.

Bare Parts: Iris brown; bill, legs and feet blackish.

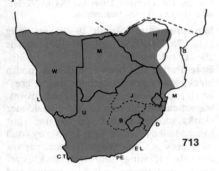

713

Identification: Size medium (looks less robust than African Pied Wagtail, but chunkier than Longtailed Wagtail); above dull olive grey (light blue-grey in Longtailed Wagtail); no black face-mask (as in Longtailed Wagtail); underparts dull off-white, washed grey on flanks, with slate grey breastband (collar may be partly or completely absent in northern birds, sometimes showing as central breast spot only); eyebrow, outer rectrices and edges of wing feathers creamy white (no white wing-stripe as in African Pied Wagtail). *Immature*: Above browner than adult; tail shorter.

Voice: Sharp piping *tweep* callnote; song jumble of sweet piping and twittering notes, *tweep, tweep-tweep, wi-ti-ti-ti-ti, cheep, tweep-tweep*, etc.

Distribution: S Africa to Angola and Kenya; throughout s Africa.

Status: Common to very common resident in s Namibia and S Africa; uncommon elsewhere; some local seasonal movements; numbers declining in many areas.

Habitat: Small slow-flowing streams, pools, dams, vleis, gardens, parks, sewage works, farmyards.

Habits: Usually solitary or in pairs; may be gregarious in flocks of several dozen birds when not breeding. Forages on shorelines, lawns, pastures (often among cattle), paved yards, in gutters, cowsheds and shallow streams, walking purposefully about; runs or flies to catch moving prey; may take prey in flight from surface of water; calls frequently while foraging. Wags tail on alighting, or when standing, especially if anxious. Sings from perch on rock, tree or building; calls on take-off, showing white outer rectrices, unless flying off nest when leaves silently with folded tail.

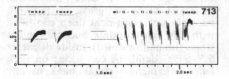

May roost communally when not breeding.

Food: Insects, small crustaceans, fish up to 2 cm long, tadpoles, food scraps.

Breeding: *Season*: All months in S Africa (mainly August-December), August to February in Zimbabwe; up to 4 broods/season. *Nest*: Bulky foundation of grass, stems, weeds, rags and roots with neat cup lined with hair, fine rootlets and feathers; in niche of stream bank, jetty or wall, in dense grasstuft or flood debris on bank, on ground under rock, under eaves of building, in trucks or trailers; in natural sites usually well hidden behind hanging vegetation; usually less than 1,5 m above ground level, but sometimes up to 6 m; built by both sexes in 2–10 days. *Clutch*: (590) 1–2,8–7 eggs (usually 3). *Eggs*: Dull yellowish or putty coloured, clouded with brownish at thick end, or obscurely mottled with brownish; measure (240) 21 × 15,4 (18,6–25,5 × 14–16,8). *Incubation*: (25) 14 days by both sexes. *Nestling*: 14–21 days (usually 14 days); fed by both parents.

Ref. Skead, C.J. 1954. *Ibis* 96:91–103.
Winterbottom, J.M. 1964. *Ostrich* 35:129–141.

714 (689) Yellow Wagtail Plate 60
Geelkwikkie
Motacilla flava

[Schafstelze]

Measurements: Length 16–18 cm; wing ♂ 80–87, ♀ 75,5–81; tail (11) 67–73; tarsus (11) 21,5–23,5; culmen (11) 12–13,5. Weight (224 ♂) 13–17,1–21,5 g, (230 ♀) 12,8–16,5–21,6 g.

Bare Parts: Iris brown; bill, legs and feet black.

Identification: Medium (about size of Cape Wagtail); head coloration variable according to race (4 subspecies, *M. f. flava*, *M. f. thunbergi*, *M. f. feldegg* and *M. f. lutea*). *Male (breeding)*: Similar to breeding ♂ Grey Wagtail, but back greenish (not grey) and throat yellow (not black); crown grey (*flava* and *thunbergi*), black (*feldegg*) or yellow (*lutea*); back yellowish olive green; eyebrow white (*flava*), yellow (*lutea*) or absent; malar stripe white (*flava* and *thunbergi*) or yellow (*feldegg* and *lutea*); face dark grey (*flava*), black (*thunbergi* and *feldegg*) or yellow (*lutea*); below bright chrome yellow; tail black, outer rectrices white. *Male (nonbreeding)*: Uniformly yellow below, throat paler (Grey Wagtail bright yellow only on undertail coverts); wing coverts edged pale whitish or yellow, forming pattern on folded wing (uniformly dark in Grey Wagtail); tail about 30% shorter than in Grey Wagtail; posture horizontal; legs black (pale brownish pink in Grey Wagtail); white eyebrow broad (narrow in Grey Wagtail). *Female*: Similar to non-breeding ♂, but throat yellowish; breast usually spotted brownish. *Immature*: Above similar to adult ♀; below dull whitish with black malar stripe joining black collar below throat.

Voice: Song simple piping *tsip-tsip-tsipsi*; pleasant *psee-ip* or *tseer* callnote.

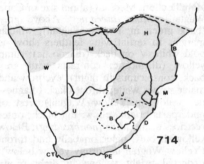

Distribution: Breeds N Africa, Europe, n Asia and Alaska; migrates to rest of Africa, s Asia and Australasia; widespread in s Africa, except in highveld and dry W.

Status: Locally common, but generally scarce nonbreeding Palaearctic migrant, October to April; most birds belong to race *M. f. flava*, but several subspecies may occur together in one flock.

Habitat: Moist short grasslands and pastures, edges of vleis and pans with exposed mud and short-cropped grass, newly planted canefields near water.

Habits: Usually in small groups, less often solitary. Forages like other wagtails by walking about on ground; attends herds of grazing cattle and antelopes, catching disturbed insects.

Food: Insects.

Breeding: Extralimital.

Ref. Smith, S. 1950. *The Yellow Wagtail.* London: Collins.

715 (–)   Grey Wagtail   Plate 60
Gryskwikkie
Motacilla cinerea

[Gebirgstelze]

Measurements: Length 18 cm; wing 80–88; tail 95–105; tarsus 20–22; culmen 11,5–12,5.

Bare Parts: Iris brown; bill black; legs and feet dark red-brown to brownish pink.

Identification: Medium (about size of Cape Wagtail). *Male (breeding)*: Above grey (back green in Yellow Wagtail); whitish margins to tertial wing feathers show as bold white V on back (diagnostic); rump yellow (diagnostic; contrasts with grey back, conspicuous in flight); eyebrow and malar stripes white; throat black (diagnostic; yellow in Yellow Wagtail); rest of underparts bright yellow; tail black, outer rectrices white. *Male (nonbreeding)*: Below yellowish buff, paler on belly and throat (Yellow Wagtail uniformly yellow below); undertail bright yellow; in flight shows white line through middle of wing; folded wing almost uniformly dark (pale pattern in Yellow Wagtail); tail about 40% longer than Yellow Wagtail; posture upright; legs pale pinkish brown (black in Yellow Wagtail); white eyebrow narrow (broad in Yellow Wagtail). *Female*: Similar to nonbreeding ♂, but crown tinged greenish; throat and flanks white. *Immature*: Similar to adult ♀, but duller; below yellower; undertail bright yellow.

Voice: Metallic *tsillip* callnote; shrill *si-heet* alarm call; song variable jumble of piping and trilling notes.

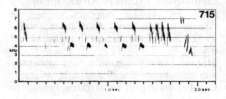

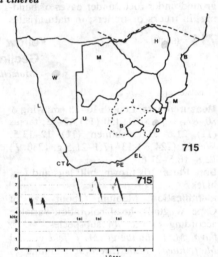

Distribution: Breeds N Africa, s Europe, C and e Asia; migrates to Africa (usually as far S as Malawi), s Asia and Indonesia; in s Africa only in isolated localities in Zimbabwe, Natal (4 records) and Namibia (1 record at Avis Dam, Windhoek).

Status: Very rare nonbreeding Palaearctic vagrant in summer months.

Habitat: Wooded rocky streams, both coastal and montane.

Habits: Always solitary or in pairs, but may roost communally in small flocks in trees. Forages by running about on stones and edges of streams, sometimes darting up to catch flying prey; wags tail vigorously at each pause or after landing. Flight typically undulating.

Food: Insects.

Breeding: Extralimital.

Ref. Frost, P.G.H. & Cyrus, D.P. 1981. *Ostrich* 52:107.
Herremans, M. 1992. *Babbler* 23:36–38

PIPITS

Pipits are smallish to medium ground birds of grassy habitats. They are nearly all brown above and whitish or buff below, streaked on the breast and usually also on the upperparts with dark brown. Apart from the Yellowbreasted and Golden Pipits they are among the hardest of all birds to identify with certainty in the field; some are hard to identify even in the hand. Useful visual field characters are the colour of the outer rectrices (white or buff), the colour of the underparts (white or buff), the markings on the breast (heavy or light; clear, obscure or absent) and the markings on the upperparts (present or absent). Even more useful, though, are the song and flight display in some species, but these are apparent only when the birds are breeding. In the absence of any unmistakable features, it is better not to try to make a decision about pipit identification. Habitat is sometimes another useful criterion, but not foolproof. In the hand the pattern of emargination of the primary flight feathers (Plate 60) is diagnostic for several species, especially when used in conjunction with measurements and plumage features; in the following accounts the primaries are numbered P1-P7 from outside inwards (which is the opposite of the usually accepted practice today, but more convenient for quick reference).

Ref. Borrett, R. 1969. *Honeyguide* 57:15–22.
Clancey, P.A. 1985. *Ostrich* 56:157–169.

---

716 (692)   **Grassveld Pipit** (Richard's Pipit)   **Plate 60**
Gewone Koester
Anthus cinnamomeus

Tšase (SS), Icelu, Icetshu (X), umNgcelu, umNgce-lekeshu (Z), [Weidelandpieper, (Spornpieper)]

Measurements: Length 16–17 cm; wing (60 ♂) 83–89,2–94,5, (19 ♀) 80,5–84,7–88,5; tail (52) 58–70; tarsus (52) 23–28,5; hindclaw (51) 10–13; culmen (12,5–15,5). Weight (1 ♀) 24,6 g, (20 unsexed) 21–24,5–28,5 g.

Bare Parts: Iris brown; bill blackish brown, base pale yellow; legs and feet pinkish to yellowish.

Identification: Size medium; very similar to Mountain, Longbilled, Plainbacked and Buffy Pipits; paler and yellower than Mountain Pipit; above brown, distinctly streaked; throat and flanks plain buffy greyish, shading to white on belly, tawny on breast; breast and malar stripe spotted dark brown (malar stripe often darker and heavier in Longbilled Pipit); outer rectrices white (buff in other similar pipits); posture erect, long-legged. *In hand*: Outermost 3 primaries about equal; P5 much shorter than P4; P2–4 emarginate. *Immature*: Above darker than adult, scalloped with

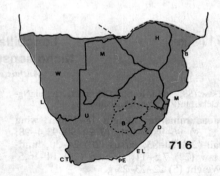

off-white; below whiter with rounder spots.

Voice: Song phrase of 3–7 identical notes, *tree-tree-tree-tree*, repeated at intervals of 2–3 seconds with each upward loop of flight display, starting from take-off to height of about 30 m, followed by steep dive accompanied by repeated *tree-tree-tree-tree-tree* until bird lands on ground or perch; sharp *chissik* callnote, usually on take off; buzzing *zzz-zzz-zzz* during distraction display at nest.

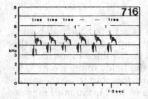

Distribution: Throughout s Africa to Angola.

Status: Common resident, especially in highveld; some local movements (moves down from montane grasslands in Zimbabwe from February to October); nomadic in dry W. Formerly regarded as Richard's Pipit *Anthus novaeseelandiae*.

Habitat: Open grassland and savanna, cultivated lands, airfields, playing fields, parks with big lawns, grassy sidewalks and road verges.

Habits: Solitary or in pairs when breeding; otherwise sometimes in small loose flocks, often in company with other small ground birds on burnt grassland. Runs in short bursts; dips tail 1–3 times at each pause.

Perches on fence or bush when disturbed. Flight display (see **Voice**) mainly August to September at start of breeding season.

Food: Insects, other arthropods; some seeds.

Breeding: *Season*: October to December in Cape, August to January (mainly September-November) in Natal, August to April (mainly October-December) in Transvaal, May to February (mainly September-December) in Zimbabwe. *Nest*: Cup of dry grass, lined with fine rootlets and hair; set into soil at base of grasstuft or low shrub, usually well hidden. *Clutch*: (66) 2–2,7–4 eggs (usually 3). *Eggs*: White or pale cream, closely speckled with grey and shades of brown; measure (182) 20,7 × 15,3 (18,8–23,4 × 13,9–16,9). *Incubation*: 12–13 days by both sexes, mostly by ♀. *Nestling*: 12–17 days, unless disturbed; fed by both parents.

Ref. Borrett, R.P. & Wilson, K.J. 1971. *Ostrich Suppl.* 8:333–341.
Clancey, P.A. 1984. *Durban Mus. Novit.* 13:189–194.

717 (693)   Longbilled Pipit   Plate 60
Nicholsonse Koester
Anthus similis

Tšase (SS), Icelu, Icetshu (X), umNgcelu, umNgcelekeshu (Z), [Langschnabelpieper]

Measurements: Length 18–19 cm; wing (11 ♂) 96–98,7–104, (9 ♀) 90–93,4–98; tail (20) 70–83; tarsus (20) 24–30; hindclaw (20) 7,5–11; culmen (20) 14–16,5. Weight (5) 22–23–25 g.

Bare Parts: Iris dark brown; bill dark horn, base yellowish pink; legs and feet light pinkish brown.

Identification: Size medium (slightly bigger than Grassveld Pipit); bill distinctly longer than that of Grassveld Pipit; above brown, streaked dark brown (upperparts darker than in Grassveld Pipit, but less distinctly streaked); eyebrow buff; below pale buff, darker on flanks and breast; malar stripe, lower throat and breast spotted dark brown (malar stripe often darker and bolder than that of Grassveld Pipit);

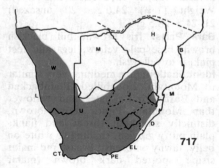

outer rectrices pale buff or greyish (white in Grassveld Pipit). *In hand*: P1 slightly shorter than P2–4, but longer than P5 = 5 mm shorter than P2 and P3; P6 much shorter than P1–5; P2–5 emarginate; tail usually more than 71 mm long.

Immature: Similar to adult, but paler and more heavily spotted above and below.

Voice: Clear metallic 2-syllabled *killink* callnote, especially on take-off; song similar to that of Plainbacked Pipit, sparrowlike *chip, chreep, chroop, chreep, chip,* etc., repeated several times from perch on rock or from ground, more rarely in flight.

Distribution: Natal (except for e littoral), Transvaal highveld, Orange Free State, Lesotho, Cape Province (except for extreme N) and most of Namibia.

Status: Fairly common resident; some seasonal altitudinal movement.

Habitat: Lightly grassed or shrubby hilly or mountainous terrain with outcrops of rocks and boulders.

Habits: Usually solitary or in pairs; in small groups in winter, often in company with other ground passerines. Perches readily on rocks, mounds, bushes and trees. Attracted to grass fires. Performs injury-feigning distraction display near nest, like most pipits. Does not wag tail like Grassveld Pipit.

Food: Insects and spiders.

Breeding: *Season*: October in Natal, October to December in Transvaal. *Nest*: Bowl of dry grass, lined with rootlets; on ground, well hidden under grasstuft or rock. *Clutch*: (6) 2–2,8–4 eggs (usually 2–3). *Eggs*: White, densely spotted with shades of brown and grey; measure (13) 21,1 × 15,9 (20,1–22,5 × 14,8–16,6). *Incubation*: Unrecorded. *Nestling*: Unrecorded.

718 (694)   Plainbacked Pipit   Plate 60
Donkerkoester
Anthus leucophrys

Tšase (SS), Xihitagadzi (Ts), Icelu, Icetshu (X), umNgcelu, umNgcelekeshu (Z), [Braunrückenpieper]

Measurements: Length 16–18 cm; wing (14 ♂) 92–98,6–105, (7 ♀) 92–94,4–98; tail (20) 64–80; tarsus (21) 25,5–29; hindclaw (21) 8,5–14; culmen (21) 14–17. Weight (8) 21–23,9–26 g.

Bare Parts: Iris brown; bill blackish, base pale yellow; legs and feet pinkish brown.

Identification: Size medium (looks larger than Grassveld Pipit; very similar to Buffy Pipit, but darker above, more cinnamon below); above plain brown (sometimes faintly streaked on crown); eyebrow and malar stripe buffy white (no bold dark malar stripe as in Grassveld and Longbilled Pipits); below cinnamon-buff, shading to whitish in centre of belly, darkest on breast; breast faintly streaked darker brown, or plain; wing coverts edged pale, centres showing as rows of darker spots; outer rectrices buff; base of lower jaw yellowish (pinkish in Buffy Pipit). *In hand*: P1-P4 more or less equal, but much longer than P5; P2–5 emarginate. *Immature*: Above heavily mottled with dark and light brown.

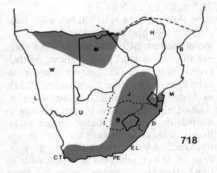

718

Voice: Song rather sparrowlike *chrrip-chreep, chrrip-chreep* from ground or low perch (not in display flight); thin, quiet *tsip-tsip* flight call (also used in alarm); thin *t-t-t-tit* on take-off.

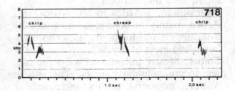

Distribution: Africa S of Sahara; in s Africa discontinuously from sw Cape to n and e Transvaal and s Mozambique; also extreme nw Zimbabwe to n Botswana to n Namibia.

Status: Locally scarce to fairly common resident; some populations subject to local nomadic or migratory movements, not yet mapped.

Habitat: Flat or hilly short grassland, especially where overgrazed or burnt, usually with termite mounds or scattered rocks; also pastures, cultivated fields.

Habits: Solitary or in pairs when breeding; otherwise gregarious in loose flocks of up to about 20 birds. Similar to Grassveld Pipit.

Food: Insects, seeds.

Breeding: *Season*: October to December in Cape and Natal, September to December in Transvaal. *Nest*: Cup of grass, lined with rootlets; set into soil at base of overhanging grasstuft; also between clods in ploughed field. *Clutch*: (19) 2–2,7–3 eggs (usually 3, sometimes 4). *Eggs*: White, thickly smeared with brown or yellowish brown, or closely spotted with shades of brown and grey; measure (54) 21,5 × 15,6 (19,3–24,8 × 14,3–16,6). *Incubation*: Unrecorded. *Nestling*: Unrecorded.

719 (695)   Buffy Pipit   Plate 60
Vaalkoester
Anthus vaalensis

Tšase (SS), [Vaalpieper]

Measurements: Length 18–19 cm; wing ♂ 102–109, ♀ 98–102,5; tail (10) 73–77; tarsus (10) 25,5–29; hindclaw (10) 8–11; culmen (10) 13,5–15,5. Weight (1 ♂) 28,5 g, (2 ♀) 25,7–29,7 g.

Bare Parts: Iris brown; bill blackish, base pinkish; legs and feet pinkish brown.

Identification: Size medium to large (bigger than Grassveld Pipit); above lightish brown without streaks (greyer than Grassveld Pipit; paler than Plainbacked Pipit); eyebrow buffy white; below whitish, washed buff, darker on breast, shading to whitish on centre of belly; breast indistinctly streaked, sometimes almost unstreaked; outer rectrices buff or greyish; base of lower jaw pinkish (yellowish in most other similar pipits); wags tail more than other pipits. *In hand*: P1–4 about equally long; P5 much shorter than P4; P2–5 emarginate. *Immature*: Above spotted dark and light brown; more boldy spotted below than adult.

Voice: Usually silent; quiet *chissik* in flight; song undescribed.

Distribution: S Africa to NE Africa; in s Africa mainly in central area, generally avoiding coastal lowlands, Lesotho highlands and most of dry W.

Status: Mostly uncommon resident; subject to nomadic movements, especially in winter; numbers greatly increased in

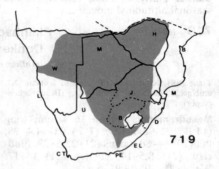

stock-farming areas where grass well grazed.

Habitat: Bare ground and sparse grassland, such as overgrazed areas, edges of vleis, arid grasslands, burnt canefields; usually with low perches like termite mounds, rocks, contour ridges or ploughed furrows.

Habits: Usually solitary or in pairs; when not breeding also in small loose groups, but less gregarious than most other similar grassland pipits. Forages by running about on ground; stands bolt upright and wags tail between runs. Perches in trees or on mounds, rocks, fences and telephone wires, especially when disturbed, but usually only briefly.

Food: Insects and other arthropods; also some seeds.

Breeding: *Season*: August to December in

most of S Africa, July to February (mainly September-December) in Zimbabwe. *Nest*: Bulky cup of dry grass, lined with rootlets and finer grasses; set into soil under grasstuft; well concealed. *Clutch*: 2–3 eggs. *Eggs*: Dull white, closely spot-ted with browns and greys; measure (21) 22 × 15,3 (20,4–24,4 × 14,9–17,2). *Incubation*: Unrecorded. *Nestling*: Unrecorded; fed by both parents.

Ref. Borrett, R.P. & Wilson, K.J. 1971. *Ostrich Suppl.* 8:333–341.

720 (696) Striped Pipit Plate 60
Gestreepte Koester
Anthus lineiventris

Intsasana (X), [Streifenpieper]

Measurements: Length 17–18 cm; wing (20 ♂) 85–87,7–91, (20 ♀) 81–83,3–85; tail (20 ♂) 60–65,3–70, (20 ♀) 58–63–68; tarsus (15) 26–29; hindclaw (15) 7–9,5; culmen (15) 14,5–17. Weight (2 ♂) 30,3–34,8 g, (2 ♀) 31,8–34,8 g.

Bare Parts: Iris brown; bill blackish, base pinkish; legs and feet pinkish brown.

Identification: Medium (about size of Grassveld Pipit); easy to identify; above buffy olive (less brown than most pipits), boldly streaked with very dark brown; eyebrow yellowish white; below buffy white, darker on breast, boldly streaked on breast and flanks with blackish brown (diagnostic; much more boldly streaked than other pipits); wing and tail feathers edged yellow (diagnostic); outermost rectrix mostly white, next 2 pairs broadly tipped white. *In hand*: Underwing buff, streaked with lemon yellow; P1–4 about equally long; P5 slightly shorter than P4; P6 much shorter than P5; P2–5 emarginate. *Immature*: Paler than adult; more spotted above.

Voice: Song melodious piping of variable phrases, *whip tew-tew, whitty pee tee-tee, whip-tee*, etc., similar in tone to song of Whitebrowed Robin but more sustained.

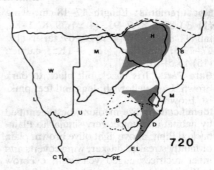

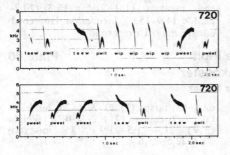

Distribution: S Africa to Angola and Tanzania; in s Africa from Komgha and East London to Natal, Swaziland, s Mozambique and Transvaal; also e Botswana and most of Zimbabwe and adjacent Mozambique.

Status: Uncommon to locally fairly common resident with some local seasonal movements.

Habitat: Rocky woodland, usually on steep slopes of gorges, hills and mountains.

Habits: Usually solitary or in pairs; sometimes in small loose groups when not breeding. Fairly tame. Forages on ground among stones and grasstufts, and commonly along roadsides. When disturbed runs quickly away or perches in tree; also walks about in trees as does Wood Pipit. Sings from branch in tree, usually in spring and early summer.

Food: Insects.

Breeding: *Season*: September to November in Natal, December to January in Transvaal, September to January in Zimbabwe. *Nest*: Cup of grass, lined

629

with fine rootlets; on ground under rock or dense grasstuft. *Clutch*: (9) 2–2,8–3 eggs (usually 3). *Eggs*: Creamy white, spotted with red-brown and shades of grey; measure (29) 22,5 × 16,4 (19,7–24,5 × 14,8–17,5). *Incubation*: Unrecorded. *Nestling*: Unrecorded.

721 (697) Rock Pipit Plate 60
Klipkoester
Anthus crenatus

Tšase-ea-thaba, Tšase-tatalana (SS), [Klippen-pieper]

Measurements: Length 17–18 cm; wing (11 ♂) 82,5–87,7–93, (4 ♀) 79–82,1–85; tail (11 ♂) 65–71, (4 ♀) 62–69; tarsus (15) 27–29,5; hindclaw (15) 9–11,5; culmen (15) 15,5–18.

Bare Parts: Iris hazel; bill black to dark brown, base yellowish; legs and feet pinkish brown.

Identification: Size medium; best identified by habitat and voice; very similar to Plainbacked Pipit; above light olive brown, plain or faintly streaked darker; wing coverts and inner rectrices edged yellowish; eyebrow buffy white; below pale buff, shading to whitish on throat and centre of belly, breast darker, more or less streaked greyish brown; outer rectrices dull white (not buff as in Plainbacked Pipit). *In hand*: P1–4 subequal; P5 slightly shorter than P4; P6 much shorter than P5; P2–5 emarginate. *Immature*: Undescribed.

Voice: Song sweet 2-syllabled phrase, second note somewhat trilled, *whee-tsrreeu, whee-tsrreeu*, repeated several times, falling in pitch on second note; also slower, rather quavering *wheeu-prrreeu*, falling in pitch.

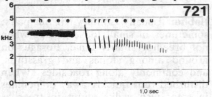

Distribution: Inland S Africa from w Karoo to Swaziland; also recorded Suikerbosrand, Transvaal.

Status: Locally fairly common resident.

Habitat: Rocky hills and mountains, and lower rocky slopes of escarpments such as Winterberg and Drakensberg; also koppies and rocky outcrops in karoo (where called "Koppie Lark").

Habits: Usually solitary or in pairs. Forages on ground but often perches on rock; sings from top of rock, standing erect with bill pointing upwards; also sings in flight. Poorly known.

Food: Insects, spiders, seeds.

Breeding: *Season*: November to January. *Nest*: Cup of grass and roots, lined with finer material; on ground under grasstuft or stone. *Clutch*: 3–4 eggs. *Eggs*: White or greyish white, densely speckled with browns and greys concentrated at thick end; measure (15) 21,5 × 15,3 (20,7–22,2 × 14,9–15,9). *Incubation*: Unrecorded. *Nestling*: Unrecorded.

722 (698) Tree Pipit Plate 60
Boomkoester
Anthus trivialis

[Baumpieper]

Measurements: Length about 14 cm; wing (15) 83–87,1–91,5; tail (7) 57–62,9–65; tarsus (7) 20–22,1–23; hindclaw (10) 7–9; culmen (7) 8,2–9,9–14. Weight (3 ♀) 21,4–21,5–21,7 g, (5 unsexed) 20,2–22,5–25,6 g.

Bare Parts: Iris brown; bill dark horn, base pinkish; legs and feet brownish pink.
Identification: Size medium; overall appearance crisp and neat; above light brown to olive brown, clearly but finely streaked blackish; eyebrow white; throat white; bold black malar stripe; rest of underparts buffy, breast darker, heavily streaked blackish down to sides of belly (diagnostic in combination with pure white throat; throat buffy in Striped and Bushveld Pipits); outer rectrices white; bill looks short in field. *In hand*: Rectrices somewhat pointed; P1–3 about equally long; P4 3–4 mm shorter than P3; P5 much shorter than P4; P2–4 emarginate; hindclaw short, curved.
Voice: Rather silent; single *tseep* in flight; sharp *tik-tik-tik* alarm call; song seldom heard in s Africa, pleasant canarylike phrase of jumbled notes.

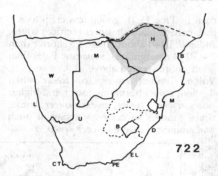

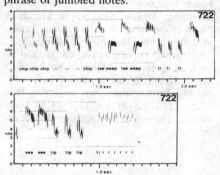

Distribution: Breeds Europe and C Asia; migrates to Africa and India; in s Africa confined to Zimbabwe, adjacent Mozambique, e Botswana and n Transvaal.
Status: Fairly common (in Zimbabwe) to rare nonbreeding Palaearctic migrant, October to March or April.
Habitat: Savanna and edges of woodland, grassy hillsides with scattered bushes, edges of exotic plantations, gardens.
Habits: Solitary, in pairs or in small flocks. Easily overlooked. Walks on ground and in trees, with bent legs in low-bellied stance; wags tail up and down when pausing. When disturbed flies into tree; flight undulating, like that of wagtail.
Food: Insects, seeds, nectar of *Erythrina*.
Breeding: Extralimital.

---

723 (699)   **Bushveld Pipit**   **Plate 60**
Bosveldkoester
Anthus caffer

[Buschpieper]

Measurements: Length 13–14 cm; wing ♂ 72–78, ♀ 68–72; tail (25) 49–56,5; tarsus (25) 16–19; hindclaw (25) 5–7; culmen (25) 10–13. Weight (1) 16 g.
Bare Parts: Iris brown; bill blackish, base pinkish; legs and feet pinkish brown.
Identification: Size small; looks somewhat like ♀ bishop (*Euplectes*); above brown, boldly streaked blackish; below buffy white, looking white in field (only throat white in Tree Pipit), washed darker on breast and flanks; breast and flanks boldly streaked blackish (streaks more confluent

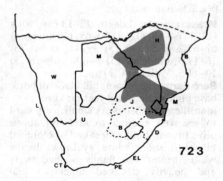

than in Tree Pipit, giving less crisp look); malar stripe blackish; outer rectrices white. *In hand*: P1–4 about equal; P5 shorter than P4; P2–4 emarginate. *Immature*: Paler than adult; more spotted above.

Voice: Sibilant *see-eep* or *tseeer* when flushed; song alternating lower and higher notes, *zweeep tseeer, zweeep tseeer*; sometimes 3 notes successively rising in pitch and sibilance, *zweeep tseeer seeep*.

ing; otherwise in small loose flocks. Somewhat wary and easily overlooked; when disturbed flies into tree or disappears with erratic zigzag flight. Forages on ground among leaf litter and grasstufts, walking with deliberate steps in somewhat crouched posture, body horizontal; does not run with quick steps, nor stand so upright as do most other pipits.

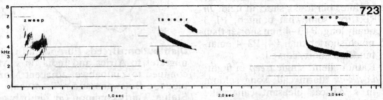

Distribution: S Africa to NE Africa; in s Africa from Zululand to s Mozambique, Transvaal (common in Pilanesberg), e Botswana and Zimbabwe.
Status: Locally fairly common to common resident.
Habitat: Parklike savanna and bushveld with broadleaved trees and patchy ground cover; also *Acacia* savanna with short grass.
Habits: Solitary or in pairs when breed-

Food: Insects.
Breeding: *Season*: October to March in Natal, November to February in Transvaal, November to January in Zimbabwe. *Nest*: Small cup of grass; on ground at base of grasstuft. *Clutch*: (28) 2–2,5–3 eggs. *Eggs*: White, spotted with red-brown, brown and grey; measure (65) 18,5 × 14 (16,5–21,4 × 13,1–14,5). *Incubation*: Unrecorded. *Nestling*: Unrecorded.

---

724 (700)   **Shorttailed Pipit**   **Plate 60**
Kortstertkoester
Anthus brachyurus

[Kurzschwanzpieper]

Measurements: Length 12–13 cm; wing (12 ♂) 64–68, (12 ♀) 60–65, (10 unsexed) 62–65,2–67,5; tail (5) 39–41; tarsus (5) 16–17,5; hindclaw (5) 5–6,8; culmen (5) 10–11,5. Weight (1 ♀) 13,5 g.

Bare Parts: Iris brown; bill blackish horn, base pinkish; legs and feet pinkish.

Identification: Size very small; very hard to see well enough to identify; above olive brown, boldly streaked or blotched blackish; short white eyebrow; below white, breast and flanks washed buffy and heavily streaked blackish (dia-

gnostic, especially in flight from below); outer rectrices white (diagnostic in flight; looks like dark Sharpbilled Honeyguide when flying away, but grassland habitat diagnostic). *Immature*: More rufous than adult.

Voice: Nasal buzzy *bzeent* repeated in flight display in wide circles (anxiety?); soft nasal *tseep* or *stee-ip*; song rolling *tip-pi-reep-prip-rip*.

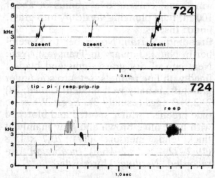

Distribution: Discontinuously in se and C Africa; in s Africa patchily distributed from Natal and Zululand to Transvaal highveld; also s Mozambique around Beira.

Status: Uncommon to rare; subject to considerable local movements, appearing in an area for some months, then not again for several years; movements not understood. Rare (RDB).

Habitat: Grassy hillsides or flats.

Habits: Solitary or in pairs. Flushes reluctantly, flying up at one's feet, then in jerky dipping flight in wide circles; or flies right away in zigzag flight for 20–30 m, about 3–5 m above ground, landing in grass; flushes again 2–5 m from landing place if pursued. Never lands on perch; rarely lands in open.

Food: Insects and grass seeds.

Breeding: *Season*: October to January in Natal and Transvaal. *Nest*: Cup of coarse dry grass, lined with fine rootlets; inside diameter 6–7 cm, depth 3,5 cm; overall diameter 9–12 cm; on ground between grasstufts, not necessarily well hidden, but grass pulled down over nest to form bower. *Clutch*: (3) 2–2,7–3 eggs. *Eggs*: White, creamy or pinkish white, finely speckled with light olive brown and slate grey; measure (7) 17,3 × 13,3(16,1–18,4 × 12,6–14,3). *Incubation*: Unrecorded. *Nestling*: Unrecorded.

725 (701) Yellowbreasted Pipit   Plate 60
Geelborskoester
Hemimacronyx chloris

Iguru, Iguru-guru (X), [Gelbbrustpieper]

Measurements: Length 16–18 cm; wing (7 ♂) 84,5–87,4–89, (9 ♀) 80–84,2–87,5; tail (7 ♂) 65–72, (9 ♀) 61–72; tarsus (16) 22,5–26; hindclaw (16) 10–13,5; culmen (16) 13–14,5.

Bare Parts: Iris hazel; bill dark horn, base paler; legs and feet yellowish pink.

Identification: Size medium; similar to Grassveld Pipit, but pale face and yellow underparts diagnostic; above buffy brown, streaked and spotted dark brown; eyebrow white; below lemon yellow, shading to buff on flanks and undertail; breast lightly streaked blackish; outer rectrices white. *Immature*: Below buff; paler buffy brown above than adult.

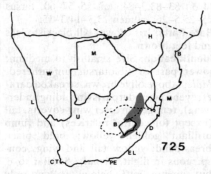

Voice: Song of ♂ repeated double *swee-ip, swee-ip, swee-ip* or single down-slurred whistled *tseeu*; rapid rather quiet *chik-chik-chik* alarm call (similar to that of Longtailed Widow).

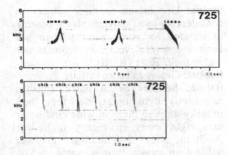

Distribution: Breeds above 1800 m in ne Cape, upland Natal, Lesotho, e Orange Free State and extreme se Transvaal; migrates downwards in winter as far as Natal and Zululand coast (sight records Enseleni Nature Reserve, Umfolozi Game Reserve) and Swaziland.

Status: Rare in Transkei and e Cape; otherwise locally common to fairly common altitudinal migrant. Vulnerable (RDB).

Habitat: Flat to gently rolling lush montane grassland when breeding; lowland grassland to bushveld in winter.

Habits: Usually solitary or in pairs when breeding; in winter in small flocks of up to 14 birds. Rather shy; keeps to shelter of grasstufts, running from one to next when approached; flushes reluctantly. ♂ sings from perch or in display flight, rising to 20–25 m above ground with rapid floppy wingbeats, cruising over radius of about 100 m, then plunging vertically into grass.

Food: Insects.

Breeding: *Season*: November to December in Natal, January in Transvaal. *Nest*: Neat cup of dry grass stems and blades, lined with fine rootlets; set into soil under grasstuft, usually well hidden. *Clutch*: (8) 2–2,9–3 eggs (usually 3). *Eggs*: White to pale greenish white, spotted and blotched with light olive brown and grey mainly at thick end; measure (17) 20,7 × 15,8 (19,2–22,4 × 15,2–16,6). *Incubation*: Unrecorded. *Nestling*: Unrecorded.

726 (702)   **Golden Pipit**   **Plate 60**
Goudkoester
Tmetothylacus tenellus

[Goldpieper]

Measurements: Length 14–16 cm; wing (4 ♂) 83–83,3–84; tail 55–57–60; tarsus 25–25,5–26; culmen 13,5–14,3–15.

Bare Parts: Iris brown; bill blackish; legs and feet brown.

Identification: Size smallish to medium; lower part of tibiotarsus unfeathered. *Male*: Above olive brown, streaked darker; eyebrow, underparts (including underwing), remiges, greater wing coverts, tail (except for central rectrices) and rump brilliant golden yellow; bold black breastband; yellow tail and wings conspicuous in flight. *Female*: Similar to ♂ but mostly buff below; yellow only on centre of belly, wing and outer rectrices. *Immature*: Feathers of upperparts edged whitish; breast sometimes spotted brown.

Voice: Probably mainly silent in s Africa;

song of ♂ set phrase in fluttering display flight or from ground, *dzip-dzip-dzippy-zippy-peet* rising on last note.

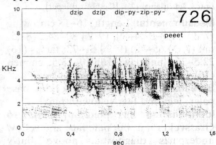

Distribution: NE Africa, straggling southwards; recorded Transvaal lowveld (1906, 1986, 1988, 1989) and once in Hwange National Park, Zimbabwe (1972).

Status: Very rare nonbreeding vagrant, November, January and March.

Habitat: Arid thornbush.

Habits: Usually in pairs when breeding; otherwise in small family groups or loose flocks. Often perches on trees and bushes; wags tail like wagtail when perched. Rather shy and hard to approach. Displays by gliding from treetop to ground, holding wings in V over back.

Food: Insects.
Breeding: Extralimital (unlikely in s Africa).

Ref. Brooke, R.K. 1972. *Bokmakierie* 24:53.
Brooke, R.K. & Irwin, M.P.S. 1972. *Bull. Brit. Orn. Club* 92:91.

727 (703)   Orangethroated Longclaw   Plate 60
Oranjekeelkalkoentjie
Macronyx capensis

Lethoele, 'Mantlhake, Mahlakali (SS), Holiyo, Hwiyo (Ts), Inqilo (X), iNqomfi (Z), [Kapgroßsporn]

Measurements: Length 19–20 cm; wing (24 ♂) 97–100–105, (12 ♀) 91–95,5–100; tail (36) 61–73; tarsus (36) 31–37; hindclaw (36) 14–22; culmen (36) 17–20. Weight (4 ♂) 41,3–47,5–50,8 g, (2 ♀) 45,2–47 g, (8 unsexed) 40–44–49.
Bare Parts: Iris brown; bill blackish to dark brown, base greyish; legs and feet pinkish brown.
Identification: Size large (robin-sized; bigger than pipits); build chunky; legs and toes long; above buffy brown, boldy spotted and streaked dark brown; throat bright orange (paler in ♀); eyebrow and underparts bright mango yellow, shading to buff on flanks; bold black collar separates throat from breast (narrower in ♀); tail brown, tipped white (conspicuous when spread in flight). *Immature*: Above scalloped whitish on dark brown; below buffy yellow; breastband indistinct, spotted.
Voice: Loud catlike *meew* alarm call, given in flight or from ground or perch; piping 2-syllabled *deewit, deewit* (sometimes calls in duet, *deewit, meew; deewit, meew*; often preceded by staccato *choi-choichoik*), usually in flight; mellow high-pitched far-carrying whistled *tweeee* song and/or contact call.

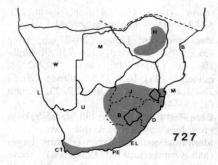

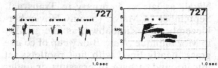

Distribution: Discontinuously from sw Cape to e Karoo, highveld of Orange Free State, Lesotho, Natal, s Transvaal, Zimbabwe and s Mozambique.
Status: Common resident.
Habitat: Moist short grassland, vleis, seasonally flooded grassland; usually without trees, above 600 m.
Habits: Usually in pairs; when not breeding also in small loose groups of up to 5 birds. Forages by walking with big steps across ground or tufty grass; scratches open termite tunnels with feet, chases insects on ground or hawks them in air; beats larger prey on ground before swallowing; at times stands on top of tuft or low mound to look around. When alarmed crouches low; if pressed flies off with bouncing quail-like flight, short bursts of stiff wingbeats alternating with glides; tail usually spread in flight. In display rises to about 10 m above ground, fluttering and singing; then drops to grass again; also sings from perch on low mound or fence. Droops wings and fans tail in threat posture.
Food: Insects; some grass seed.
Breeding: *Season*: August to December, also April, in w Cape, September to March (mainly November-December) in Natal, August to April (mainly November-

January) in Transvaal, September to March (mainly November-January) in Zimbabwe. *Nest*: Bulky bowl of coarse grass, neatly lined with rootlets; inside diameter 8,3–8,5 cm, depth 5,7 cm; set into soil at base of grasstuft or broad-leaved plant; well hidden. *Clutch*: (71)

2–2,9–4 eggs (usually 3). *Eggs*: White to creamy white, with large spots of browns and greys concentrated at thick end (very different from eggs of Yellowthroated Longclaw); measure (113) 24,4 × 17,8 (22,4–26,7 × 16,5–18,9). *Incubation*: 13–14 days. *Nestling*: 16–17 days.

728 (704) Yellowthroated Longclaw Plate 60
Geelkeelkalkoentjie
Macronyx croceus

Holiyo, Hwiyo (Ts), iNqomfi, iGwili (Z), [Gelbkehlgroßsporn, Safrangroßsporn]

Measurements: Length 20–21 cm; wing (26 ♂) 93–98,9–103, (20 ♀) 91–95,2–100; tail (28) 67–86; tarsus (28) 32–38; hindclaw (28) 16,5–23,5; culmen (20 ♂) 20–21,4–23,5, (20 ♀) 20–21,2–23. Weight (3) 53–54,7–58 g.

Bare Parts: Iris brown; bill blackish, base grey; legs and feet pinkish brown.

Identification: Size large (slightly larger than Orangethroated Longclaw); above greyish buff, mottled and streaked with dark brown; malar streak white; eyebrow and underparts brilliant yellow (duller in ♀); bold black breastband; breast streaked black (plain yellow in Fülleborn's Longclaw); outer rectrices and tail tip white (conspicuous when spread in flight). *Immature*: Above scalloped whitish on dark brown; below buffy yellowish; breastband indistinct.

Voice: Song far-carrying whistled *tir-rEEoo, trip-tritri, trip-tritri* and variations; alarm call loud piping *whip pipipipi, tuwhip pipipipi* (3–7 *pi* notes, depending on intensity of alarm), usually from top of tree; loud whistled *tirreeo* in flight.

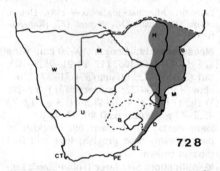

728

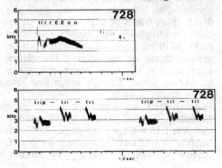

Distribution: Africa S of Sahara; in s Africa confined to E.

Status: Locally common resident; some irregular local movement away from breeding areas in winter; as far W as Kobonqaba, Transkei, June to January.

Habitat: Rank grass, edges of vleis, swampy drainage lines, with scattered trees and bushes or in savanna or light woodland.

Habits: Usually in pairs or small groups of up to 5 or 6 birds. Forages on ground among tufty grass, walking with long strides. When disturbed may crouch on ground, but usually flies to top of tree, bush or telephone wire; sings from perch. Calls frequently in flight. Extremely wary when nesting.

Food: Insects.

Breeding: *Season*: October to February in Natal, as late as February in Transvaal, September to March (mainly November-December) in Zimbabwe, as late as May in Mozambique. *Nest*: Bulky cup of coarse grass, neatly lined with fine rootlets; set into ground at base of grasstuft or under broadleaved herb; well concealed. *Clutch*: (25) 2–3–4 eggs (usually 3). *Eggs*: Dull white, finely streaked and speckled with pale grey (very different from eggs of Orangethroated Longclaw); measure (31) 24,1 × 18,2 (22,4–26,3 × 17,1–19,3). *Incubation*: 13–14 days, all or mostly by ♀. *Nestling*: 16–17 days; fed by both parents; young hardly able to fly on leaving nest, but run well.

729 (–)   Fülleborn's Longclaw   Plate 60
Angolakalkoentjie
Macronyx fuelleborni

[Füllebornpieper, Fülleborns Großsporn]

Measurements: Length 19–20 cm; wing (50) 95–110; tail 75–85; tarsus 36–40; culmen 17–19.

Bare Parts: Iris brown; bill blackish, base grey; legs and feet pinkish brown.

Identification: /Size large; very similar to Yellowthroated Longclaw, but lacks black streaking on breast; above greyish brown, mottled and streaked dark brown; below yellow (breast and belly not as bright as in Yellowthroated Longclaw), washed dull buffy brown on flanks, lower belly and undertail; tail tipped white (conspicuous in flight). *Immature*: Below buffy brown; breastband indistinct.

Voice: Song 2-syllabled *tiwoo-preet, tiwoo-preet*; monotonous whistled *jee-o-wee* or *zeeee* (alarm?) from top of bush; sparrowlike chirping *chwee*.

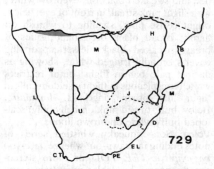

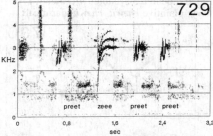

Distribution: Angola, s Zaire to Tanzania; in s Africa confined to extreme n Namibia along Angola border.
Status: Common resident in Angola; probably vagrant to Namibia.
Habitat: Short moist grassland with scattered bushes, marshy meadows and hollows, usually in highlands.
Habits: Very similar to Yellowthroated Longclaw. Not well documented.
Food: Insects.
Breeding: Not recorded in s Africa; probably extralimital.

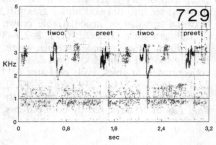

730 (705)   Pinkthroated Longclaw   Plate 60
Rooskeelkalkoentjie
Macronyx ameliae

[Rotkehlgroßsporn, Karmesinpieper]
Measurements: Length 19–20 cm; wing (41 ♂) 86–91–95, (20 ♀) 82–86,6–91; tail (41 ♂) 65–70,6–82, (20 ♀) 65–67,9–77;

tarsus (41 ♂) 28–30,6–33, (20 ♀) 29–30,3–33; culmen (39 ♂) 15,5–17,1–19, (20 ♀) 15–16,6–19.

Bare Parts: Iris brown; bill blackish, base yellowish pink; legs and feet pinkish to yellowish brown.

Identification: Large (about size of Yellowthroated Longclaw); above buff, mottled and streaked blackish; eyebrow white, with slight pink streak in front of eye; below bright cerise pink, shading to whitish on flanks; broad black breastband; sides of breast streaked black; lesser upperwing coverts broadly fringed white, showing as distinct pale bar in flight; outer rectrices white (conspicuous in flight); seldom calls in flight like other longclaws. *Immature:* Below buff, tinged pink on belly only; scalloped buffy white on brown above.

Voice: Song squeaky whistled series of notes ending in drawn-out wheeze, *teee-yoo tyip-tyip-tyip-TEE YOO* or more stereotyped repeated 3-syllabled *preet-tewy, preet-tewy*; plaintive *chewit, chewit* alarm call.

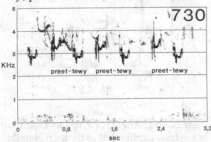

Distribution: Discontinuously from S Africa to Kenya; in s Africa patchily distributed from n Natal and Zululand to Mozambique littoral; e highlands of Zimbabwe and adjacent Mozambique; n Botswana and Caprivi.

Status: Locally rare to fairly common resident; numbers fluctuate greatly, but mostly sedentary. Vulnerable (RDB).

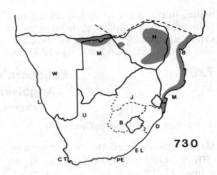

730

Habitat: Waterlogged grassland, permanent vleis, seasonally flooded tussocky grassland, edges of vleis or lakes with fine grass (*Sporobolus subtilis, S. virginicus* and *Paspalum vaginatum*), often where grazed short by hippos and antelopes.

Habits: Usually solitary or in pairs. Crouches when disturbed; flushes reluctantly; does not fly far, lands in grass, then mounts tussock to look around; may also perch in low tree or on termite mound. Flight stiff-winged like that of other longclaws; sings in hovering flight display, sometimes high above ground, often with dangling legs; may display before dawn. Shy and local. Runs fast on ground.

Food: Insects.

Breeding: *Season*: October to December in Natal, November to April (mainly December-February) in Zimbabwe. *Nest*: Deep cup of dry grass, neatly lined with rootlets; set into dry soil under grasstuft, between tussocks or inside friable crown of old grasstuft. *Clutch*: (17) 2–2,7–3 eggs. *Eggs*: White to pale greenish white, heavily spotted with dark brown and grey concentrated at thick end; measure (21) 22,4 × 16,3 (21,1–23,8 × 15,5–17,3). *Incubation*: 13–14 days by ♀ only. *Nestling*: About 16 days; fed by both parents.

26:18. Family 80 LANIIDAE—SHRIKES

Small to medium. Bill shortish, stout, hooked and toothed; legs short, strong; feet strong, capable of grasping and carrying prey; claws sharp, curved; head large; wings medium, rounded; tail moderately to very long and narrow; plumage mainly combinations of black, white, grey and rufous; juvenile typically finely barred above and below; sexes similar or different; arboreal in open woodland; solitary; hunt prey by dropping onto it from perch; bold and aggressive; food small vertebrates and invertebrates; prey often impaled on thorns; nest a bulky cup of plant material in bush or tree; eggs 2–8, variable in colour, usually spotted; chick naked or sparsely downy at hatching; parental care by both sexes. Distribution N America, Africa, Eurasia; 26 species; five species in s Africa. The family Laniidae here includes only the genera *Lanius* and *Corvinella*.

Ref. Harris, T. & Arnott, G. 1988. *Shrikes of southern Africa*. Cape Town: Struik Winchester.

731 (706)   Lesser Grey Shrike   Plate 61
Gryslaksman
Lanius minor

Nankuwo (K), Juka, Rhiyani (Ts), [Schwarzstirn-würger]

Measurements: Length 20–22 cm; wing (20) 110–116–122; tail 85–94; tarsus 23–26; culmen 16–18. Weight (33) 28,6–47,5–62,9 g.

Bare Parts: Iris brown; bill black, base paler; legs and feet black.

Identification: Size medium (looks slightly chunkier than Fiscal Shrike); above grey (Fiscal Shrike black above with broad white V on back); forehead, face, wings and tail black (forehead grey, eyebrow white in Sousa's Shrike); small wingpatch and outer rectrices white (conspicuous in flight); below white, flanks grey. *Immature*: Above light brownish grey; whiter below than adult, breast tinged buff; no black on forehead (black confined to ear coverts only).

Voice: Variable sustained twittering song with some harsh notes, somewhat drongolike in quality, *cheep-roop zweep chip tswe-ip tswe-ip zank zank*, etc.; harsh *chek* callnote.

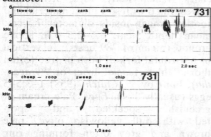

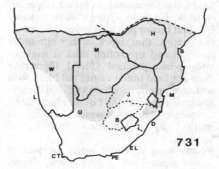

Distribution: Breeds Europe and w Asia; migrates to Africa; in s Africa absent from most of highveld, Cape Province, s Natal and s Namibia.

Status: Fairly common nonbreeding Palaearctic migrant, October to April; some birds overwinter in se lowveld of Zimbabwe; vagrant to e Cape.

Habitat: *Acacia* savanna, open grasslands.

Habits: Usually solitary; rarely several birds in loose association. Perches on top of bush or telephone wire; drops to ground to catch prey; impales prey on thorns. Similar to Fiscal Shrike, but flies faster.

Food: Insects.

Breeding: Extralimital.

Ref. Dowsett, R.J. 1971. *Ostrich* 42:259–270.

732 (707)   Fiscal Shrike   Plate 61
Fiskaallaksman
Lanius collaris

Nankuwo (K), Tšemeli (SS), Korera (Sh), Juka, Rhiyani (Ts), Tlhômêdi (Tw), Inxanxadi, Umxhomi (X), iQola, iLunga (Z), [Fiskalwürger]

Measurements: Length 21–23 cm; wing (14) 93–98,9–103; tail (10) 100–113; tarsus (10) 25–30; culmen (14) 16–25. Weight (34 ♂) 34,7–41,8–50 g, (5 ♀) 34,9–37,6–43 g, (107 unsexed) 31–41,6–58 g.

Bare Parts: Iris brown; bill, legs and feet black.

FISCAL SHRIKE

Identification: Size medium; build some-what more slender than that of Lesser Grey Shrike; above black to below eye, bold white V on back; no white eyebrow in e and s birds, broadly white in *L. c. subcoronatus* and *L. c. aridicolus* from about C Orange Free State and n Cape westwards to Atlantic coast; rump grey or white; below white, washed grey on flanks and sometimes on breast (especial-ly in w Cape to Orange River); small chestnut brown patch on lower flank of ♀; tail longish, slim, black, with white outer rectrices and tips, often held at angle to body when perched (Fiscal Flycatcher does not hold tail at angle; tail black with rectangular white windows); bill heavy, hooked (slender in Fiscal Flycatcher). *Immature*: Above brownish grey, barred buffy; buffy greyish below, finely barred blackish.

Voice: Song repeated varied phrases of mixed piping and grating notes, *chippy chippy ghree-jur chitik, ghree-jur, chippy*, etc.; often imitates other birdcalls as part of sustained song interspersed with own harsh notes; loud harsh grating *ghree, ghree, ghree* alarm and threat notes; fledglings have insistent rasping *cheee, cheee* while being fed.

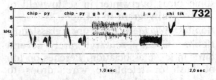

Distribution: Africa S of Sahara; through-out most of s Africa, except C Botswana, nw Zimbabwe and most of Mozambique.

Status: Common to very common resi-dent; sporadic appearance of white-browed birds around Pretoria and Johannesburg may indicate some local movements.

Habitat: Open grassland with scattered bushes, fences or other perches, bushy hillsides, savanna, farmyards, gardens, edges of plantations.

Habits: Usually solitary; sometimes in pairs. Perches conspicuously on bush, fence, telephone wire or tree, dropping to ground to catch prey; on returning to perch often wags tail from side to side;

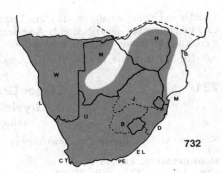

carries prey in bill or feet; may impale prey on thorn, sharp twig or barbed wire fence, returning to feed on it later if necessary. Often aggressive towards other birds. Hops on ground; flight direct with rapid wingbeats.

Food: Insects, spiders, small rodents, small birds (sparrows, wagtails, Laughing Doves, guineafowl chicks up to 30 g, nest-lings), small frogs, lizards, snakes; also seeds, food scraps (bread, porridge from dogbowls). Regurgitates pellets of undi-gested material.

Breeding: *Season*: All months except February throughout s Africa (mainly August to December); several broods/season. *Nest*: Thick-walled, often bulky, bowl of grass, twigs, leafy herbs (espe-cially *Helichrysum*), rags, string and leaves, lined with soft plant material and rootlets; mean inside diameter 7,5 cm, mean depth 5 cm; 0,6–2,5–6 m above ground (mean of 789 nests), in vertical or horizontal fork of bush or tree (often thorny, like *Acacia*, brier or *Pyracan-tha*); built by ♀. *Clutch*: (958) 1–3,5–5 eggs (usually 3–4). *Eggs*: Pale cream or greenish, speckled and spot-ted with dull yellowish olive, pale brown and grey often forming ring around thick end; measure (630) 23,5 × 17,7 (19,6–28,5 × 15,6–19,9). *Incu-bation*: 15–16,5 days by ♀ only. *Nest-ling*: 17–21 days; fed by both parents (mostly by ♀); dependent on parents for up to 30 days after leaving nest; young remain in parental territory for up to 5 months.

Ref. Cooper, J. 1970. *Ostrich* 42:166–178.

733 (708)

Redbacked Shrike
Rooiruglaksman
Lanius collurio

Plate 61

Nankuwo (K), Juka, Rhiyani (Ts), Ihlolo (X), [Neuntöter]

Measurements: Length 17–18 cm; wing ♂ 90–93, ♀ 87–91; tail (12) 71–81; tarsus (12) 22–25; culmen (12) 13–17. Weight (46 ♂) 23,8–29–46 g, (31 ♀) 20,7–28,4–36,4 g, (32 unsexed) 22–27,5–35 g.

Bare Parts: Iris brown; bill blackish, base pinkish; legs and feet black.

Identification: Medium (about size of Fiscal Shrike, but shorter-tailed). *Male*: Crown, mantle and rump blue-grey, eyebrow paler; forehead and facemask black; back bright russet (no white V on back as in Sousa's Shrike); below white, breast and flanks washed pinkish; tail black with white side panels. *Female*: Above reddish grey-brown, finely barred buffy; no black facemask; below white, finely barred blackish; tail dark rufous, outer rectrices edged white. *Immature*: Similar to adult ♀.

Voice: Song jumbled phrase of chirping and harsher notes, *chu-wee-chur, chittip chittip, weechurp, chittip-wee-chur*, etc., sometimes incorporating imitations of European bird species; harsh *chak* call and alarm note, often repeated.

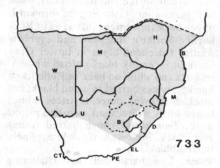

733

Status: Uncommon (in S) to common (in N) nonbreeding Palaearctic migrant, October to April (rarely to May in Zimbabwe); bird ringed Zambia recovered Czechoslovakia; bird ringed Germany recovered Malawi.

Habitat: Savanna, scrubby woodland.

Habits: Usually solitary; sometimes several in loose association. Similar to Fiscal Shrike, but usually perches lower down on outer branches of bush or tree, seldom right on top; also perches on fences.

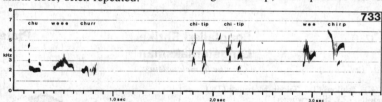

733

Distribution: Breeds Europe and w Asia; migrates to Africa and Arabia; throughout most of s Africa except much of Karoo, s and w Cape and high Drakensberg.

Drops to ground to catch prey; impales prey on thorns.

Food: Insects, small reptiles, nestling birds.

Breeding: Extralimital.

734 (708X)

Sousa's Shrike
Sousase Laksman
Lanius souzae

Plate 61

Nankuwo (K), [Souzawürger]

Measurements: Length 16,5–17 cm; wing (22 ♂) 78–81,3–87, (24 ♀) 78–81,6–85; tail 72–87; tarsus 19–23; culmen 12,5–14. Weight (12 ♂) 21–27–30 g, (11 ♀) 22–25,7–30 g, (1 unsexed) 33 g.

Bare Parts: Iris brown; bill, legs and feet black.

Identification: Size smallish (smaller than Fiscal Shrike, shorter-tailed); head and mantle grey shading to brownish upper back (not bright rufous as in Redbacked Shrike); forehead and eyebrow whitish (forehead black in Lesser Grey Shrike); facemask black; broad white V on back (no white on back of Redbacked Shrike); wings barred rust and black; tail blackish brown, outer rectrices white; below buffy white, flanks washed rufous in ♀. *Immature*: Above barred rufous and black; below buffy white, finely barred black.

Voice: Low harsh calls and chattering alarm notes.

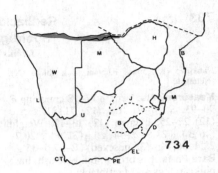

Distribution: Angola, Zaire, Zambia, Malawi, n Mozambique, Tanzania; in s Africa only along Kunene, Okavango and Chobe Rivers; possibly also extreme nw Zimbabwe.

Status: Sparse and local resident; some local movements in some populations.

Habitat: Almost endemic to *Brachystegia* woodland; also *Burkea* and *Baikiaea* woodland.

Habits: Usually solitary. Similar to other *Lanius* species, but perches inconspicuously below canopy, dropping to ground to catch prey. Poorly known.

Food: Insects.

Breeding: Not recorded in s Africa. *Season*: September to November in Zambia, September in Angola. *Nest*: Bulky cup of twigs, grass and lichens, sometimes bound with spider web; in fork of small tree or bush. *Clutch*: 3–4 eggs. *Eggs*: Cream or pale greenish white, spotted with brown, purple and grey concentrated in ring around thick end; measure (10) 21 × 16,4 (19,5–23,2 × 15,6–17,1). *Incubation*: Unrecorded. *Nestling*: Unrecorded.

---

735 (724)   Longtailed Shrike   Plate 61
Langstertlaksman
Corvinella melanoleuca

Muruli (K), Tshiloni (Ts), Tilodi, Motsilodi (Tw), umQonqotho (Z), [Elsterwürger]

Measurements: Length 40–50 cm; wing (42) 122–134–143; tail (25 ♂) 225–350, (17 ♀) 215–340; tarsus (42) 31–35,5; culmen (42) 16,5–20,5. Weight (22 ♂) 54,8–82,3–97,1 g, (12 ♀) 70,9–82,4–96 g, (4 unsexed) 86–92,6–97 g.

Bare Parts: Iris brown; bill, legs and feet black.

Identification: Size large; tail very long (about two-thirds length of body); whole plumage black except for bold white V on lower back, grey rump, white patch on primaries (conspicuous in flight) and white tips to innermost remiges; ♀ also has

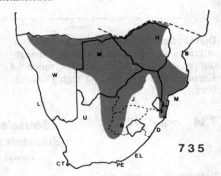

white patches on flanks. Albinos occur. *Immature*: Browner than adult.

Voice: Sonorous piping *tlee-teeooo*, often by several birds in chorus; harsh scolding alarm notes.

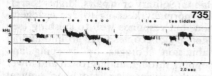

Distribution: S Africa to Kenya; in s Africa mainly in wooded areas from Zululand to Zimbabwe and s Mozambique, and from n Karoo to w Transvaal, Botswana and n Namibia.

Status: Locally common to very common resident.

Habitat: *Acacia* savanna, bushveld.

Habits: Usually in small groups of 3–12 birds; rarely solitary. Perches on top of bush or tree, or on outer branch, dropping to ground for prey. Flight fast, somewhat dipping, ending in upward swoop to perch. Long tail jerked while calling.

Food: Insects, small reptiles.

Breeding: *Season*: October to March in Zululand, August to February (mainly October-November) in Transvaal and Zimbabwe. *Nest*: Bulky cup of twigs, grass stems and roots, lined with finer rootlets and stems of creepers. *Clutch*: (55) 2–3,3–6 eggs (usually 3–5). *Eggs* : Buff or yellowish stone, speckled and spotted with reddish brown, dark brown and grey mainly at thick end; measure (166) 26,8 × 19,7 (23,1–29,9 × 18,3–20,7). *Incubation*: Unrecorded. *Nestling*: Unrecorded; fed by up to 4 adults (2 parents and 2 helpers).

26:19. Family 81 MALACONOTIDAE—BUSH-SHRIKES

Small to medium. Bill medium, heavy or slender, hooked and notched; legs medium to long, strong; feet relatively large and strong; wings medium, rounded or pointed; tail medium, rounded or square; plumage variable—black, white and grey, sometimes with rufous, red or yellow (*Laniarius, Nilaus, Dryoscopus, Lanioturdus*), green with yellow, red, black and grey (*Malaconotus, Telophorus*), rusty on wings with bold head and tail pattern (*Tchagra*); sexes alike or different; arboreal, but some feed on ground, in forest or open woodland; food small vertebrates and invertebrates; nest cup-shaped in tree or bush; eggs 2–4, green, blue or cream, spotted; chick naked at hatching; mouth of nestling deep yellow, sometimes with two dark tongue spots; parental care by both sexes. Distribution Africa S of Sahara; 44 species; 17 species in s Africa.

Ref. Harris, T. & Arnott, G. 1988. *Shrikes of southern Africa*. Cape Town: Struik Winchester.

736 (709)   **Southern Boubou**   **Plate 61**
Suidelike Waterfiskaal
Laniarius ferrugineus

Hwilo, Samjukwa, Xighigwa (Ts), Igqubusha (X), iBhoboni, iGqumusha (Z), [Flötenwürger]

Measurements: Length 21–23 cm; wing (9 ♂) 95–99,9–101, (10 ♀) 92–94,5–97; tail (19) 91–104; culmen (19) 22,5–26; bill depth (19) 8,8–10. Weight (S Africa and Zimbabwe, *L. f. ferrugineus* and *L. f. natalensis*) (11 ♂) 53–60,2–68,8 g, (7 ♀) 54,1–57,5–61,9 g, (s Mozambique, *L. f. savensis*) (3 ♂) 44,2–50–53,2 g, (5 ♀) 42,1–44,7–51 g.

Bare Parts: Iris brown; bill black; legs and feet blue-grey.

Identification: Size large (but rather

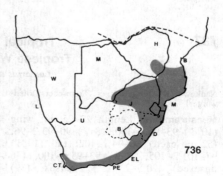

smaller than Tropical Boubou in zone of overlap); above black to below eye, back duller, somewhat slaty (♀ all slaty greyish above; Tropical Boubou glossy black above with whitish rump); bold white wingstripe; below pinkish or creamy white, with rufous wash on flanks (♂ and ♀) and belly (♀ only; Tropical Boubou plain cream or pinkish white below, without rufous wash; Swamp Boubou pure white below); tail black. *Immature*: Above spotted black and rust; below whitish, barred brown.

Voice: Highly variable; loud ringing bell-like notes, sometimes harsh buzzing notes, usually in antiphonal duet, one bird alternating with another several times; (A) *wheep-wheeo*, (B) *kokoko*; (A) *swooop*, (B) *twheee*; (A) *kooee*, (B) *hollyonk*; (A) *bizzykizzkizz*, (B) *hoowee*; (A) *hoop hoowhee*, (B) *bobobo*; duet started by either sex, answered by different call from opposite sex; harsh scolding *bizzykizzkizz* or *skhaaa* alarm calls.

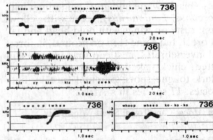

Distribution: Sw and s Cape to Natal, s and e Transvaal, se Botswana, Swaziland and Sul do Save (Mozambique).
Status: Common resident.

Habitat: Dense bush and tangles in coastal and riverine bush, scrub thickets, forest edge, gardens; also exotic plantations.
Habits: Solitary or in pairs. Highly secretive, normally keeping to dense vegetation, but responds well to spishing (see Glossary); becomes tame around human habitation. Forages by creeping and hopping through undergrowth and lower branches, venturing into open only at very edge of thicket; hops on ground. Highly vocal; members of pair keep in constant touch by duetting.
Food: Insects (including bees; sting rubbed off before swallowing), birds' eggs, nestling and fledgling birds, grain, fruit, porridge.
Breeding: *Season*: August to January (rarely to March) in sw Cape, September to December (mainly October-November) in Natal, August to February (rarely in winter) in Transvaal. *Nest*: Shallow bowl of roots, twigs and grass, bound with spider web; sometimes lined with finer material; usually well hidden about 1–4 m above ground (rarely to 8 m) in dense bush, tree or creeper; rarely in exposed leafless fork; built by ♀ only in about 6 days. *Clutch*: (77) 2–2,5–3 eggs. *Eggs*: Pale greenish white, finely speckled with shades of brown and grey forming ring around thick end; measure (90) 24,6 × 18,1 (22–27,4 × 16–19,2). *Incubation*: 16–17 days by both sexes. *Nestling*: 16–17 days; fed by both parents; post-nestling dependence at least 54 days; young accompany parents for at least 80 days after initial departure from nest.

Ref. Langley, C.H. 1983. *Ostrich* 54:172–173.

737 (–)   Tropical Boubou   Plate 61
Tropiese Waterfiskaal
Laniarius aethiopicus

Nankuwo (K), [Orgelwürger, Tropischer Flötenwürger]

Measurements: Length 23–25 cm; wing (10 ♂) 93–96,6–100, (8 ♀) 90–93,2–96, (52 unsexed) 86–94,7–102; tail (10 ♂) 97–101,2–105, (8 ♀) 93–95,6–100, (36 unsexed) 90,5–23–25,5; tarsus (19) 30,5–33,7–37,5; culmen (19) 19–23–25,5. Weight (26 ♂) 42,4–52,5–69 g, (24 ♀) 40,1–47,5–57 g, (51 unsexed) 42,9–49,9–61 g.
Bare Parts: Iris reddish brown; bill black; legs and feet bluish slate.
Identification: Size large (rather bigger

than sympatric forms of Southern Boubou in Mozambique); sexes alike (somewhat different in Southern Boubou); above glossy blueblack (Southern Boubou greyish black on back); rump whitish (diagnostic in flight); bold white wingstripe; below plain cream or pinkish (not washed rufous on flanks as in Southern Boubou; Swamp Boubou pure white below). *Immature*: Duller than adult; above spotted tawny.

Voice: Similar duetting to that of Southern Boubou, combining ringing and harsh calls; *ko-tzz ko-tzz*, mellow *hoo-hee-hoo*, quavering *hooooo*, harsh *zweo zweo krrrr*, scraping *shrang-shrang*, etc.; possibly incorporates more harsh notes than does Southern Boubou; differences between calls of boubou species not well documented; *chuk* contact call at nest.

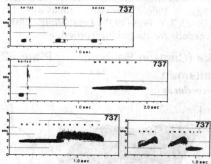

Distribution: Africa S of Sahara; in s Africa confined to extreme n Transvaal and Botswana to upper Limpopo River (Mmabolela), Caprivi, Zimbabwe and Mozambique.

737

Status: Common resident. Rare (RDB).
Habitat: Riverine forest, thickets on termite mounds, forest edge, gardens; usually near water.
Habits: Usually in pairs. Similar to Southern Boubou; skulks in dense cover, but can be approached fairly closely. Flight heavy, with fairly rapid wingbeats. Hops on ground when foraging.
Food: Insects, small reptiles, nestlings and eggs of birds, young rodents.
Breeding: *Season*: All months (mainly September–January) in Zimbabwe. *Nest*: Shallow thin-walled bowl of twigs, tendrils and roots, lined with fine fibres; 0,5–15 m (usually about 3 m) above ground in fork of bush or tree, not always well hidden; built by both sexes, mostly by ♀. *Clutch*: (7) 2–2,6–3 eggs. *Eggs*: Blue-green to greenish buff, spotted with brown and lilac; measure (19) 25 × 18,3 (22,3–26,8 × 16,7–19,1). *Incubation*: 15 days by both sexes. *Nestling*: 14–16 days; fed by both parents; young remain with parents 4–6 months after leaving nest.

738 (710)   **Swamp Boubou**   **Plate 61**
Moeraswaterfiskaal
Laniarius bicolor

Nankuwo (K), [Zweifarbenwürger]

Measurements: Length 23–25 cm; wing (4 ♂) 108–108,8–109, (2 ♀) 100–106, (6 unsexed) 90–100–110; tail (4) 95–110; tarsus (4) 32–34; culmen (4) 24–25. Weight (5 ♂) 47,8–53,3–56,7 g, (4 ♀) 43–52,1–58,2 g.
Bare Parts: Iris brown; bill black; legs and feet slate-blue.

Identification: Size large (somewhat larger than Tropical Boubou); sexes alike; above deep glossy blue-black (greyish black in Southern Boubou); underparts and wingstripe pure white (cream, pinkish or rufous in other boubous). *Immature*: Above spotted buffy; below barred dusky.
Voice: Duetting of mellow hooting and

harsh notes, usually synchronous, *hoooo-kh-kh-kh-kh-kh*, less variable than in other boubous; harsh notes may follow immediately after hoot or may overlap.

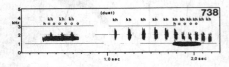

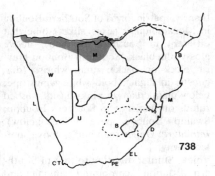

738

Distribution: Western tropical Africa from Gabon to Angola, Caprivi and Oka-vango system, Botswana.
Status: Fairly common resident.
Habitat: Reedbeds, riverine thickets and bush.
Habits: Usually solitary or in pairs. Similar to other boubous; skulks low down in vegetation, but may sometimes perch conspicuously on top of papyrus or reed. Highly vocal, members of pair calling and answering frequently. Forages by hopping on ground and flicking debris aside with bill, or by gleaning from trunks, branches, leaves and reeds.
Food: Insects, small fruits.
Breeding: *Season*: October to December. *Nest*: Bowl of plant material; in fork of tree or bush, or at base of palm frond; 1,5–4 m above ground. *Clutch*: (1) 2 eggs. *Eggs*: Pale greenish; measure (2) 23–23,7 × 19,8–19,9. *Incubation*: Unrecorded. *Nestling*: Unrecorded.

739 (711) Crimsonbreasted Shrike (Crimson Boubou) Plate 62
Rooiborslaksman

Laniarius atrococcineus

Etwakura (K), Kgorogoro, Kgaragoba (Tw), [Rot-bauchwürger, Reichsvogel, Kaiservogel]

Measurements: Length about 23 cm; wing (23 ♂) 98–100–105, (13 ♀) 93–97–101; tail (36) 90–109; tarsus (36) 30–34; culmen (36) 20,5–26. Weight (41) 40–48,3–55 g.
Bare Parts: Iris brown; bill, legs and feet black.
Identification: Size large; above jet black; wingstripe white; below crimson, rarely yellow. *Immature*: Above dull black, barred buff; below barred dusky and whitish; undertail crimson.
Voice: Loud penetrating bell-like, fluty, zipping or tearing sounds, singly or in duet, *kirik-dzui-kirik, chopchop-kizzee-chopchop, keo-kizzee-keo-kizzee*, etc.; various other snarling and clicking notes.

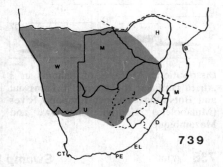

739

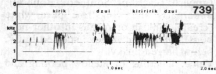

739

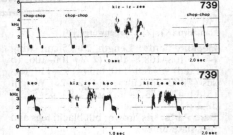

739

Distribution: Dry interior and W of s Africa; also sw Angola.

Status: Common resident.

Habitat: *Acacia* savanna, riverine thornbush, semi-arid scrub.

Habits: Solitary or in pairs. Forages mostly by running about on ground like thrush, but also searches rough-barked trunks and branches of trees. Not shy, but fairly secretive; responds to spishing (see Glossary). Fairly vocal, more often heard than seen. Flies fairly high between patches of bush or trees, showing bright red underparts.

Food: Insects.

Breeding: *Season*: September to April in Transvaal, September to January (mainly October-November) in Zimbabwe, October to January in arid W; 2 or more broods/season. *Nest*: Bowl of bark stripped from branches, secured to site with spider web; lined with finer fibres and roots; usually 1,5–3 m above ground (often to 8 m), in fork of bush or tree, or on stout horizontal branch; built by both sexes. *Clutch*: (30) 2–2,7–3 eggs. *Eggs*: White, buff, pale green or pale blue, rarely plain, usually spotted with shades of brown and grey concentrated at thick end; measure (69) 23,7 × 17,5 (22–25,5 × 16,3–19,7). *Incubation*: 16–19 days by both sexes; may start with first egg. *Nestling*: 18–20 days; fed by both parents.

Ref. Tarboton, W.R. 1971. *Ostrich* 42:271–290.

---

740 (712)   **Puffback**   **Plate 61**

Sneeubal

Dryoscopus cubla

Nankuwo (K), Unomaswana, Intakembila (X), iBhoboni (Z), [Schneeballwürger]

Measurements: Length 17–18 cm; wing (62 ♂) 76,5–81,8–88, (41 ♀) 75–78,8–85; tail (36 ♂) 60–66,7–73, (36 ♀) 61–66,7–74,5; tarsus (31) 21–24; culmen (31) 17,5–21. Weight (125 ♂) 19,3–27,1–36 g, (98 ♀) 21–25,4–30,4 g, (2 unsexed) 27–32 g.

Bare Parts: Iris yellow, orange or red; bill black; legs and feet grey.

Identification: Size smallish to medium (smaller than Fiscal Shrike); tail relatively short; mainly black-and-white. *Male*: Above black; rump greyish white; no white eyebrow; wings black-and-white; below white; tail black. *Female*: Similar to ♂, but less intensely black; white areas more buff or greyish white. *Immature*: Deep buffy olive where adults white.

Voice: Usual call loud 2-syllabled click-whistle phrase (click like sharp Zulu *q*), *q-weeu*, *q-weeu*, *q-weeu*, repeated 10 times or more; various sharp tearing, rasping, clicking and piping sounds, *tzzzzzrrr*, *dzweep*, *q-k-wooo*, etc.; loud bill-clicking in threat.

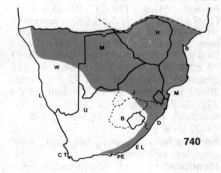

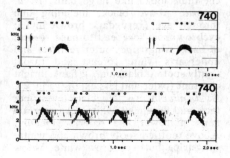

Distribution: S Africa to E Africa; in s Africa absent from highveld and dry W, occurring as far S as George.

Status: Fairly common to common resident.

Habitat: Canopy of woodland, riverine forest, edges of lowland evergreen forest, exotic groves and plantations.

Habits: Usually in pairs, sometimes in small family groups; joins mixed bird parties. Forages high in trees, seldom lower down in bushes, hopping about gleaning from foliage, branches and twigs. Usually silent when feeding, otherwise fairly vocal; easily overlooked unless calling. Male raises and fluffs spectacular white rump plumes during courtship (hence English and Afrikaans names). Flight bouncy with loud wingbeats.

Food: Insects.

Breeding: *Season*: October to December in Natal, September to January (rarely June) in Transvaal, all months except May (mainly September-December) in Zimbabwe. *Nest*: Small neat cup of grass, roots and bark, firmly felted with spider web; lined with fine grass; in slender upright fork of tree, 2–12 m above ground; built in 6–11 days by ♀ only, but ♂ may collect material also. *Clutch*: (34) 2–2,7–3 eggs. *Eggs*: White, cream or pink, spotted and streaked with dark brown and grey concentrated at thick end; measure (52) 22,2 × 15,9 (19,2–24,4 × 14,9–17,7). *Incubation*: 13 days by both sexes. *Nestling*: 17 days; fed by both parents; young remain with parents until start of next breeding season.

741 (731) Brubru Plate 61
Bontroklaksman
Nilaus afer

[Brubru]

Measurements: Length 14–15 cm. *N. a. brubru*: Wing (10 ♂) 87–88,4–90,5, (10 ♀) 83–86–91,5, (60 unsexed) 80–84–91; tail 52–63; tarsus 20–24; culmen 14–17,5. Weight (4) 23,6–24,6 g. *N. a. miombensis*: Wing (10 ♂) 79–82,4–84,5, (10 ♀) 77,5–80,5–84, (14 unsexed) 77–81,3–86; tail 47–57; tarsus 20–22,5; culmen 15–17. Weight (3 ♂) 22,6–24,7–27,1 g, (1 ♀) 24,9 g; (race not specified) (32 ♂) 17–23,2–32 g, (26 ♀) 18–22,8–30 g.

Bare Parts: Iris brown; bill black, base grey; legs and feet grey.

Identification: Size smallish; tail relatively short; mainly black, white and chestnut; looks like large batis. *N. a. brubru*: Above black, including line through eye (very dark brown in ♀); eyebrow from forehead to nape, centre of back, wingstripe, outer rectrices and underparts white (breast and throat lightly spotted black in ♀); flanks bright chestnut (paler and less extensive in ♀). *N. a. miombensis*: No black eyestripe; face and forehead white; chestnut on flank narrower and paler. *Immature*: Above mottled sooty brown and white; wingstripe buff; eyebrow white; below

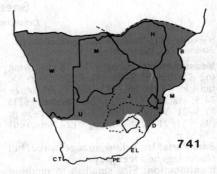

741

white, barred dull brown; adult plumage acquired at about 60 days after leaving nest.

Voice: Male has far-carrying high-pitched trill, usually preceded by 1–5 quick clicks or chucks, *chuk-prrrreeee*, or *chukchuk-prrrreeee*; often in antiphonal duet, ♀ answering with squeaky *skweeu; prrrreeee* and *skweeu* may be synchronous.

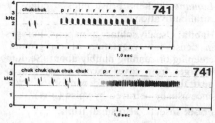

Distribution: Africa S of Sahara; in s Africa absent only from extreme S, Karoo and high country. Subspecies *brubru* and similar *solivagus* occur over most of s Africa; *miombensis* occurs from Zululand to Mozambique and e lowlands of Zimbabwe.

Status: Uncommon to fairly common resident.

Habitat: Canopy of woodland, savanna and riverine *Acacia*.

Habits: Usually solitary; in pairs when breeding; territory about 30–40 ha; may join mixed bird parties. Forages high in trees, gleaning from foliage and branches; easily overlooked unless calling; more often heard than seen.

Food: Insects.

Breeding: *Season*: September to December in Natal, August to January in Transvaal, September to January (mainly September-November) in Zimbabwe, October to November in Namibia. *Nest*: Shallow saucer of small twigs, leaf petioles, bits of bark, soft plant material and lichens, moulded and bound with spider web to sloping saddle of stout fork; outside diameter 6,5–7 cm, inside diameter 4,5 cm, inside depth 2 cm; very well camouflaged, blending with colour and contour of site; 2,5–4,9–9 m above ground (21 nests) in large tree, often *Acacia, Terminalia* or *Burkea*; built by both sexes; early nests often destroyed before being laid in. *Clutch*: (59) 2 eggs (very rarely 1 or 3). *Eggs*: Dull white, greenish or greyish, densely smeared and streaked with dull greyish brown and grey; measure (44) 20,2 × 15,4 (18,6–22,3 × 14,3–16,8). *Incubation*: (1) 19 days by both sexes; ♀ incubates at night. *Nestling*: (2) 21–22 days; fed by both parents; young accompany parents up to 55 days after initial departure from nest.

Ref. Tarboton, W. 1984. *Ostrich* 55:97–101.

742 (713)   Southern Tchagra   Plate 62
Grysborstjagra
Tchagra tchagra

Umguphane (X), [Kaptschagra]

Measurements: Length 20–22 cm; wing (9) 79–81,2–83; tail 83–96; tarsus 26–30; culmen 24–26,5. Weight (22) 38–47,2–54,3 g.

Bare Parts: Iris brown; bill black; legs and feet bluish grey.

Identification: Size large (larger than Threestreaked Tchagra); above greyish brown (darker than other tchagras), tinged rusty on crown (crown black in Blackcrowned Tchagra, dull brown in Threestreaked Tchagra); eyebrow and face white (eyebrow bordered above by narrow black line in Threestreaked Tchagra, and by black crown in Blackcrowned Tchagra); line through eye black; wings bright chestnut; below greyish white, flanks darker; tail black, broadly tipped

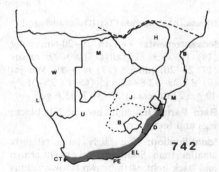

white (conspicuous in flight), central rectrices brown. *Immature*: Below tinged olive; tail tipped buff.

Voice: In flight display low over bushes, wing-rattling *prrr-prrr-prrr-prrr* followed by harsh *churr churr churr*, then loud whistled   *trrr-t-t-t-t-tew-tew-tew-tew-tew*, slowing in tempo towards end (corresponding call of Threestreaked Tchagra very similar, but distinctly 2-syllabled and falling somewhat in pitch towards end); harsh scolding *jeee jeee* alarm notes, possibly those rendered *tcha-tcha-tcha-gra* by Levaillant in 1799, from which these bush shrikes get their name.

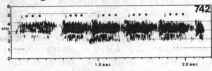

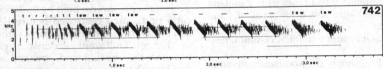

Distribution: Sw, s and e Cape, s Karoo to Colesberg, Cradock and Graaff-Reinet, Natal, Swaziland, and extreme s Mozambique.
Status: Fairly common in S, local and sparse in N; resident.
Habitat: Thorny riverine scrub, dense coastal bush, edges of coastal dune forest, *Lantana* thickets, brush piles at edges of rural cultivation.

Habits: Usually solitary or in pairs. Forages in dense low vegetation or on ground, creeping or running nimbly about. Seldom emerges from cover except to fly low to next thicket, with rapid wingbeats. Presence usually betrayed by voice (*q.v.*).

Food: Insects; also small fruits.

Breeding: *Season*: August to December in Cape, October to December in Natal. *Nest*: Shallow cup of stems, twigs and roots, lined with finer rootlets; about 1 m above ground in fork of matted bush or shrub; well hidden. *Clutch*: (17) 2–2,2–3 eggs (usually 2). *Eggs*: White, spotted and scrolled with dark red-brown and purplish grey; measure (19) 24,3 × 18,4 (22,9–26,7 × 17–19,7). *Incubation*: 15,5–16 days. *Nestling*: 13–15 days; fed by both parents.

---

743 (714) **Threestreaked Tchagra** **Plate 62**
Driestreeptjagra (Rooivlerktjagra)
Tchagra australis

Eyimba (K), Mugubani (Ts), [Damaratschagra]

Measurements: Length 19–20 cm; wing (19) 71–76,3–81; tail (17) 90–99; tarsus (17) 23–26; culmen (17) 16,5–19. Weight (91 ♂) 27–32,8–45,8 g, (68 ♀) 25–31,7–40 g, (22 unsexed) 27–31,7–33,6 g.

Bare Parts: Iris light brown; bill black; legs and feet grey.

Identification: Size fairly large (slightly smaller than Southern Tchagra); crown and back light earth brown (crown rufous brown in Southern Tchagra, black in Blackcrowned Tchagra); eyebrow white, bordered above and below by black line (diagnostic at close range; no black line above eyebrow of Southern Tchagra); wings bright chestnut; below buffy to

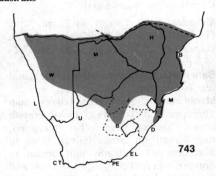

greyish white, throat paler; tail black, tipped white (conspicuous in flight), central rectrices brown. *Immature*: Rectrices more pointed than those of adult, tipped buff.

650

Voice: In flight display rises with loud bursts of quivering wings, just above vegetation, *prrr prrr prrr prrr*, followed by gliding descent with spread tail and about 15 melodious double whistles dropping in tone but rising in volume, *pa-reeu pa-reeu pa-reeu*, etc.; sharp *chirrp, chirrp* alarm and anxiety calls.

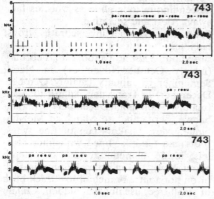

Distribution: Africa S of Sahara; in s Africa absent from S, highveld and most of dry W; widespread elsewhere.
Status: Fairly common resident.
Habitat: Woodland (not *Brachystegia*), thornveld, bushveld, especially with thorny thickets.
Habits: Usually solitary or in pairs. Forages mainly on ground or low down in thickets and tangles; hops or runs on ground; somewhat larklike; flies reluctantly, usually running into cover and creeping away through branches. Has characteristic song-flight (see **Voice**).
Food: Insects; other invertebrates, young rodents.
Breeding: *Season:* October to November in Natal, September to March (mainly October-November) in Transvaal, September to April (mainly October-December) in Zimbabwe. *Nest:* Neat shallow thin-walled cup of stems, roots and fibres, bound with spider web; lined with fine rootlets; usually low down in mixed bush and tall grass, or up to 3 m above ground in fork of bush or tree; built by both sexes in 5–10 days. *Clutch:* (72) 2–2,4–4 eggs (usually 2–3). *Eggs:* White or pinkish white, spotted and blotched with brown and grey concentrated at thick end; measure (133) 21,7 × 16,3 (19,4–25,3 × 14,9–18,3). *Incubation:* About 14–16 days by both sexes, mostly by ♀. *Nestling:* 14,5–16 days; fed by both parents; young remain with parents for at least 5 months after leaving nest.

744 (715) Blackcrowned Tchagra Plate 62
Swartkroontjagra
Tchagra senegala

Eyimba (K), Nyamaburo, Chisamaura (Sh), Mugubani (Ts), Umnguphane (X), umNguphane (Z), [Senegaltschagra]

Measurements: Length 21–23 cm; wing (36 ♂) 82–86,6–93, (33 ♀) 82–86,4–90; tail (69) 91–112; tarsus (69) 26–31; culmen (69) 20,5–25. Weight (46 ♂) 33–53,5–59 g, (35 ♀) 35–53,6–61,8 g, (4 unsexed) 32–51,8–67 g.
Bare Parts: Iris brown; bill black; legs and feet greenish grey.
Identification: Large (same size as Southern Tchagra); crown black (brown in Threestreaked Tchagra, reddish brown in Southern Tchagra); eyebrow white, bordered below by black line through eye; back brown, rump greyer; wings rusty; below white, creamy white or greyish white, paler on throat and undertail; tail

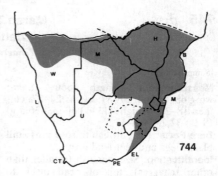

black, tipped white (conspicuous in flight), central rectrices brown; voice diagnostic (*q.v.*). *Immature:* Crown mottled brown and black; rectrices more pointed than those of adult, tipped buff; bill horn.

Voice: Usual song loud cheerful mellow whistled phrase in 2 or 3 parts, each of 2–3 somewhat variable lilting syllables, each succeeding part pitched lower, *wee-tee, wee-too*, or *sa-wee-tee, sa-wee-too, sa-woo-too*; also growling or rolling notes followed by whooping whistles, *kwirrrr-sweeeoo, krrup-kweeo, turrrrrrr-kweeo*, etc. often in duet; trill sometimes prolonged like that of nightjar; harsh *churr* alarm call; *chuk* anxiety note.

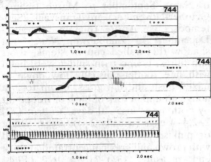

Distribution: Africa S of Sahara, NW Africa, s Arabia; in s Africa from about East London through Natal to Transvaal, e and n Botswana, n Namibia (from Otjiwarongo), Zimbabwe and Mozambique.
Status: Common resident.
Habitat: Bush and scrub, especially in thornveld; also woodland in Zimbabwe.

Habits: Usually solitary or in pairs. More arboreal than Threestreaked Tchagra, but forages largely on or near ground; runs well. Flies low between clumps of bush with bursts of fluttery wingbeats. Vocal mostly in early mornings in spring and early summer; may sing in display flight with purring wingbeats and whistling (see **Voice**), rising high above bush and descending in long glide as whistles fade away. Alert and secretive.
Food: Insects; other invertebrates, frogs, tadpoles.
Breeding: *Season*: October to February (mainly October-November) in Natal, September to January (mainly October-December) in Transvaal, August to April (mainly September-December) in Zimbabwe, September to March in Mozambique. *Nest*: Shallow cup of fine twigs, roots and tendrils, lined with finer rootlets; inside diameter about 8 cm, depth about 4 cm; 1–4 m above ground in fork or on horizontal branch of low thick bush or small tree, usually well hidden. *Clutch*: (100) 2–2,5–4 eggs (usually 2–3). *Eggs*: White to pinkish white, spotted and blotched with dark red-brown, grey and lavender concentrated at thick end; measure (184) 24,6 × 18 (21,9–27,5 × 17–19,4). *Incubation* : 12–15 days, mostly by ♀. *Nestling*: 14–16 days; fed by both parents.

---

745 (716) **Marsh Tchagra** **Plate 62**
Vleitjagra
Tchagra minuta

[Sumpftschagra]

Measurements: Length about 18 cm; wing 68–81; tail 67–87; tarsus 24–27; culmen 18–22. Weight (13 ♂) 30–33–36,5 g, (5 ♀) 32,2–34,7–36,5 g.
Bare Parts: Iris purplish to rose pink; bill black; legs and feet lead grey.
Identification: Size smallish (smaller than other tchagras); top of head black to below eye (narrow white eyebrow in ♀); rest of upperparts light rusty to yellowish brown; wings chestnut; tail black, edged and tipped white; below yellowish buff, shading to whitish in centre of throat and

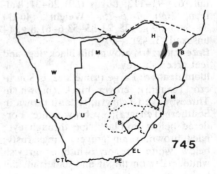

belly. *Immature*: Mottled blackish and buff; mantle spotted black.

Voice: Song of 4–6 whistling notes sounding like *today or tomorrow* or *pirree ti-weep peeeu*, preceded by wing-rattling, sometimes in duet; sharp *chrrr* of ♂ answered by harsh bleat from ♀; cheerful *chillep chee chin*, similar in tone to call of Blackeyed Bulbul.

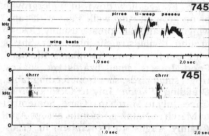

Distribution: Africa S of Sahara; in s Africa confined to extreme e Zimbabwe, adjacent Mozambique, Mount Gorongosa, Beira and Dondo.

Status: Uncommon resident.

Habitat: Rank vegetation in marshy places, streams with reeds.

Habits: Solitary or in pairs. Skulks low down in dense cover, but quite often perches on top of bush or tall grass stem. Flies reluctantly when disturbed. In display flies level, then shoots suddenly up to about 3 m on fluttering wings with shrill whistled song (see **Voice**).

Food: Insects.

Breeding: *Season*: November to March. *Nest*: Neat cup of tendrils, stems and roots, usually with sloughed snakeskin built into wall; 60–90 cm above ground in fork of bush or woven into upright grass stalks. *Clutch*: (5) 1–3 eggs (usually 2). *Eggs*: White, spotted and streaked with reddish, purple and grey mainly at thick end; measure (12) 22,5 × 17 (19,4–26,6 × 15,7–18,9). *Incubation*: Unrecorded; by both sexes. *Nestling*: Unrecorded.

---

746 (722)   Bokmakierie   Plate 62
Bokmakierie
Telophorus zeylonus

Psempsetle (NS), Pjempjete (SS), Ingqwangi (X), iNkovu (Z), [Bokmakiri]

Measurements: Length 22–24 cm; wing (35 ♂) 92,5–98,8–104, (32 ♀) 89–97–105; tail (25) 92–105; tarsus (13 ♂) 32–36, (12 ♀) 29–34; culmen (25) 21–26,5. Weight: *T. z. zeylonus*, S Africa (12 ♂) 57–65,1–71,3 g, (11 ♀) 48–61,2–76,1 g, (19 unsexed) 52–66,6–76 g.; *T. z. restrictus*, Zimbabwe (5 ♂) 67,8–69,4–71,3 g, (4 ♀) 63,8–68,4–76,1 g.

Bare Parts: Iris brown, purplish or greyish; bill black; legs and feet blue-grey.

Identification: Size large; top of head grey; back bright olive green; eyebrow and underparts bright chrome yellow; broad collar on upper breast, black; tail black, tipped chrome yellow (diagnostic in flight), central rectrices dull olive. *Immature*: Above dark olive; below dull greyish

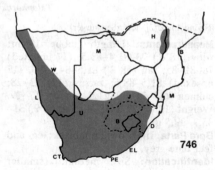

yellow, finely barred with grey; no black collar.

Voice: Very variable loud ringing song, almost invariably in duet, *kwit-kwit-kwit-kwit, wikiri, wikiri, ka-weet, ka-weet, ka-weet, bokmakiri, bokmakiri, koki-*

koki-koki, etc., in any combination; either bird may change song phrase in mid-song; notes sometimes trilled or clicked, *prrr-too, prrr-too* or *tok-weet, tok-weet*; immatures often sing flat or off-key; harsh *krrrr* alarm note; knocking *tok-tok-tok* warning call.

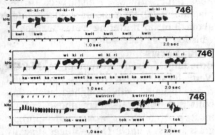

Distribution: Mainly confined to extreme S and SE, Karoo, highveld and dry W; isolated population of only about 400 birds (*T. z. restrictus*) in Chimanimani Mountains of Zimbabwe, and adjacent Mozambique.

Status: Common resident over most of range; uncommon in Zimbabwe and Namib Desert.

Habitat: Very variable; bushy hillsides with rocks, aloes and *Euphorbia*, riverine scrub, thickets in open grassveld, exotic groves and plantations, gardens, farmyards, dense shrubs along dry watercourses; in Zimbabwe and Mozambique well-wooded boulder-strewn ravines, mosaic of grassland and rocky areas with heaths and proteas.

Habits: Solitary or in pairs. Sings all year round from top of bush, tree, post, fence or roof, head thrown back and bill wide open. Forages low down in undergrowth or on ground; runs well. Flies with rapid wingbeats and tail spread, usually close to ground, diving straight into cover. Shy in wild, but tame around human settlement.

Food: Insects, small lizards and snakes, frogs, small birds, suet from feeding table.

Breeding: *Season*: July to October in sw Cape, July to March in e Cape, September to March in Natal, all months except April (mainly August to November) in Transvaal, November to January in Zimbabwe. *Nest*: Bulky bowl of twigs, stems, roots and herbs; in dense hedge, bush or fork of leafy tree; from ground level to about 2 m above ground. *Clutch*: (54) 2–3–6 eggs (usually 3). *Eggs*: Bright greenish blue, spotted with reddish brown; measure (194) 25,6 × 19,3 (22,9–29,3 × 16,5–20,8). *Incubation*: (4) 14–17 days. *Nestling*: (3) 17–19 days; fed by both parents.

747 (721)   Gorgeous Bush Shrike   Plate 62
Konkoit
Telophorus quadricolor

iNgongoni (Z), [Vierfarbenwürger]

Measurements: Length about 19 cm; wing (18 ♂) 78–81,4–83,5, (17 unsexed) 78–81–85; tail (18 ♂) 81,5–84,9–90, (17 unsexed) 81,5–88,5; tarsus (17) 23–28; culmen (13 ♂) 19–21,5, (4 ♀) 17–19. Weight (19 ♂) 29,6–38–40,5 g, (7 ♀) 31–35,7–39,5 g.

Bare Parts: Iris brown; bill black; legs and feet blue-grey.

Identification: Size medium (smaller than Bokmakierie; about size of Orange-breasted Bush Shrike); above bright olive green; short yellow streak in front of eye; lores black; throat bright red, bordered below by broad black collar (diagnostic; collar narrower in ♀); rest of underparts bright yellow, tinged red

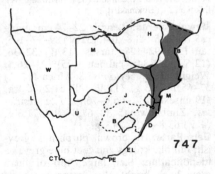

on upper belly and undertail in ♂; tail olive green (♀) or black (♂). *Immature*: Above duller green than adult; below light yellowish, breast finely barred dusky.

Voice: Loud bell-like *kong-kowit-kowit*, or *kong-kong-kowit*, higher-pitched on the *wit* notes, often preceded by faint *klink* and followed by brief rattling clicking sound; similar in tone to calls of Southern Boubou, but less variable; harsh guttural *graak-graak* alarm call.

Distribution: S Africa to E Africa; in s Africa confined to extreme E, from about Sezela (Natal) to Zoutpansberg (n Transvaal), s Mozambique and extreme e Zimbabwe.

Status: Locally common to fairly common resident.

Habitat: Dense thickets at edges of lowland to mid-altitude evergreen forest and fairly dry woodland, dune forest, riverine bush, tangles of secondary growth.

Habits: Usually solitary or in pairs. Wary and hard to see, despite bright coloration. Forages low down in undergrowth and on ground, turning over leaves like thrush. Creeps into densest vegetation when disturbed. Responds to spishing (see Glossary).

Food: Insects.

Breeding: *Season:* October to November in Natal, October in Transvaal, October to February in Zimbabwe, November to December in Mozambique. *Nest:* Shallow, loosely built bowl of twigs, stalks, grass and roots, lined with petioles; 0,6–1,5 m (usually about 1 m) above ground in tangled creeper or dense bush; well hidden. *Clutch:* (13) 2 eggs. *Eggs:* Light greenish blue or whitish blue, streaked and spotted with grey-brown and purplish grey; measure (10) 23,3 × 16,9 (22,4–24,6 × 15,9–18,3). *Incubation:* Unrecorded. *Nestling:* Unrecorded; young remain with parents for at least 4 months after leaving nest.

748 (719)   Orangebreasted Bush Shrike   Plate 62
Oranjeborsboslaksman
Telophorus sulfureopectus

uHlaza (Z), [Orangewürger, Orangebrustwürger]

Measurements: Length 18–19 cm; wing (37) 84–88,3–94; tail 81–96; tarsus 24–29; culmen 14,5–17,5. Weight (34 ♂) 24–27,5–30,5 g, (21 ♀) 19,5–26,4–30,2 g, (13 unsexed) 26–29,1–32 g.

Bare Parts: Iris brown; bill black; legs and feet blue-grey.

Identification: Size medium (smaller than Bokmakierie); crown, nape, mantle and ear coverts grey (olive form of Olive Bush Shrike wholly green above); forehead and eyebrow bright yellow (diagnostic; no yellow eyebrow in Olive or Blackfronted Bush Shrikes); lores black (whitish or yellow in Olive Bush Shrike); rest of upperparts yellow-green; below bright yellow, breast orange; tail yellow-green, tipped yellow (tail black, tipped yellow in Olive Bush Shrike). *Immature:* Lacks yellow and black on face; no orange on breast; throat sometimes paler yellow than rest of underparts; barred blackish above and below.

Voice: Usual call 5–8 ringing notes in quick phrase, first note slightly lower-pitched than rest, *poo-ti-ti-ti-ti-ti-ti*; individually variable in pitch and tempo; clicking and rasping alarm calls.

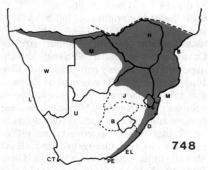

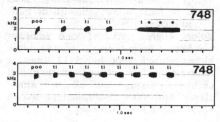

Distribution: Africa S of Sahara; in s Africa absent from extreme S, highveld and drier w parts.
Status: Fairly common resident.
Habitat: Riverine *Acacia* bush, dense thornveld, thickets, edges of riverine and lower-altitude evergreen forest.
Habits: Usually solitary or in pairs; may join mixed bird parties. Highly vocal, but hard to see; tends to keep to tops of leafy trees, gleaning food from branches and leaves. Responds well to spishing (see Glossary), coming very close with clicking calls.
Food: Insects, including hairy caterpillars.
Breeding: *Season*: October to December in e Cape, September to January (mainly October-November) in Natal, August to January in Transvaal, all months except May and August (mainly October-December) in Zimbabwe. *Nest*: Flimsy saucer of twigs and roots, lined with finer roots and petioles, almost like dove's nest; in multiple fork of thorntree or bush, usually lower than 4 m above ground, sometimes as high as 10 m. *Clutch*: (33) 1–1,8–3 eggs (usually 2). *Eggs*: Dull light green or greenish white, thickly streaked and spotted with shades of brown and grey mainly at thick end; measure (51) 22 × 16,1 (19,5–24 × 14–18). *Incubation*: Unrecorded; by both sexes. *Nestling*: 12 days; fed by both parents.

749 (720)   Blackfronted Bush Shrike   Plate 62
Swartoogboslaksman
Telophorus nigrifrons

[Schwarzstirn-Buschwürger]

Measurements: Length about 19 cm; wing 83–95; tail 83–95; tarsus 25–26; culmen 17,5–19. Weight (12 ♂) 31,4–35,2–37,6 g, (4 ♀) 31,6–33,6–36,4 g.
Bare Parts: Iris bright red; bill black; legs and feet blue-grey.
Identification: Medium (about size of Orangebreasted Bush Shrike); crown, nape and mantle grey (olive form of Olive Bush Shrike wholly green above); back and tail yellow-green (tail black, tipped yellow in ♂ Olive Bush Shrike); lores, ear coverts and sides of neck black (diagnostic; ♀ lacks black ear coverts; no yellow eyebrow as in Orangebreasted Bush Shrike; lores yellow or white in Olive Bush Shrike); below orange, grading to yellow on belly (♀ less extensively orange than ♂; Orangebreasted Bush Shrike orange on breast only). *Immature*: Lacks black on face; below yellowish or buff, barred dusky.
Voice: Highly variable; loud resonant bell-like *whoop-tweeup*, second note higher-pitched, repeated 8–12 times at intervals of 3–5 seconds; snarling and clicking phrase, *klitik-skreeu, klitik-skreeu*; drawn out nasal *twaang*; resonant *krooooo* and *kwo-kwo-kwo*.

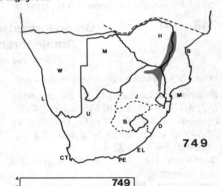

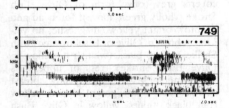

Distribution: S Africa to E Africa; in s Africa restricted to e and n Transvaal, e Zimbabwe and adjacent Mozambique; also Mount Gorongosa.
Status: Locally common to uncommon resident. Indeterminate (RDB).

Habitat: Canopy of well developed evergreen forest, thickets and tangles at forest edge.

Habits: Usually solitary; sometimes joins mixed bird parties. Vocal but seldom seen. Forages in middle to higher strata of forest, gleaning from trunks, branches and leaves; works its way up one tree, then glides down to next.

Food: Unrecorded.

Breeding: *Season*: February in Zimbabwe, January in Mozambique. *Nest*: Shallow saucer of twigs and tendrils; well hidden in creepers or other dense vegetation; about 20 m above ground. *Clutch*: (3) 2 eggs. *Eggs*: Pale whitish green, heavily streaked with dark brown and blue-grey forming cap at thick end; measure (2) 22,3–22,4 × 17–17,3. *Incubation*: Unrecorded. *Nestling*: Unrecorded.

750 (717) Olive Bush Shrike Plate 62
Olyfboslaksman
Telophorus olivaceus

Umthethi (X), [Olivwürger]

Measurements: Length 17,5–19 cm; wing (55 ♂) 83–85,9–89, (34 ♀) 72–82,6–86,5, (42 unsexed) 76–84,7–87; tail (55 ♂) 78,5–83–86,5, (34 ♀) 74–79,9–85; tarsus (120) 23–26,4–29,5; culmen (119) 16–18,5–22,5. Weight (103 ♂) 31,1–34,5–38,8 g, (56 ♀) 24,6–32,7–43,6 g, (3 unsexed) 26–32–38 g.

Bare Parts: Iris brown; bill black; legs and feet blue-grey.

Identification: Size medium (slightly smaller than Orangebreasted Bush Shrike); 2 colour forms. *Olive form*: Above olive green (no grey on head as in Orangebreasted and Blackfronted Bush Shrikes); face and ear coverts black (♂) or grey (♀); lores, stripe behind ear, underparts and tail tip bright yellow, suffused orange on breast in ♂; tail mainly black (♂) or green (♀), tipped yellow. *Ruddy form*: Crown to mantle grey; rest of upperparts olive green; face and ear coverts black (♂) or grey (♀); lores, stripe behind ear coverts, throat and lower belly buffy white, faintly barred olive green on flanks; breast and upper belly light buffy rufous; tail as in olive form. *Immature*: Similar to adults, but barred olive brown below.

Voice: Loud piping phrase starting with high note followed by up to 7 quick notes, *peep-whit-whit-whit-whit-whit-whit-whit*, varying somewhat in pitch and tempo, sometimes starting with 2 high notes, *peep-peep-hoop-hoop-hoop-hoop*, etc; penetrating high-pitched *tew-tew-tew-tew*; grating alarm notes.

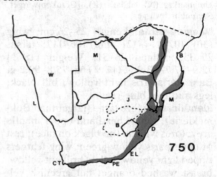

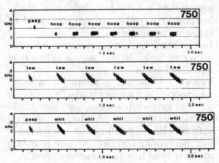

Distribution: S Africa to Malawi; in s Africa confined to forest belt from sw Cape to Natal, Swaziland, e and n Transvaal, Mozambique and extreme e Zimbabwe.

Status: Locally fairly common to common resident.

Habitat: Canopy of evergreen forest, tall dense bush, riverine forest.

Habits: Usually solitary or in pairs. Forages high in treetops, gleaning from branches and leaves; rarely comes to lower tangles at forest edge. More often heard than seen.

Food: Insects, fruit (figs).

Breeding: *Season*: December to January in e Cape, September to December in Natal, November to February in Transvaal, October to January in Zimbabwe, November to December in Mozambique.

Nest: Flimsy saucer of stems, roots and tendrils; in fork of bush or tree, up to 3 m above ground. *Clutch*: (11) 1–1,6–2 eggs. *Eggs*: Pale greenish white, heavily smeared with streaks of brown and grey; measure (18) 21,6 × 15,9 (19,4–23 × 14,3–17). *Incubation*: Unrecorded. *Nestling*: Unrecorded.

751 (723) Greyheaded Bush Shrike Plate 62
Spookvoël
Malaconotus blanchoti

Umbhankro (X), uHlaza (Z), [Graukopfwürger, Riesenbuschwürger]

Measurements: Length 25–26 cm; wing (30) 107–114–121; tail 106–117; tarsus 29–35; culmen 26–31. Weight (18 ♂) 72,9–77,7–83,9 g, (17 ♀) 65–75,8–99,2 g.

Bare Parts: Iris light yellow; bill black; legs and feet blue-grey.

Identification: Size large (larger than Bokmakierie); top of head and upper mantle grey; lores whitish (no black on face); rest of upperparts yellow-green; wing feathers tipped light yellow; below brilliant yellow, breast washed orange; tail greenish yellow, tipped pale yellow; bill huge, black, hooked; eye yellow (diagnostic at close range in combination with huge bill and lack of black on face). *Immature*: Mottled brown on head; lighter yellow below than adult; bill horn.

Voice: Mournful hooting whistle, *whooooooo*; sometimes varied by rise in pitch at very end, *whoooo-up*; also clacking notes (sounding like hedge clippers) with or without hooting, *tuk-tuk whooooooop*; screaming *skreeep, skreeep*; may sing in duet; loud hoarse *skwaark* at nest.

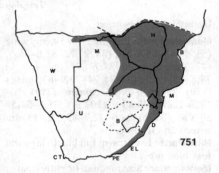

751

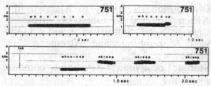

Distribution: Africa S of Sahara; in s Africa confined to SE, E and NE from e Cape to Natal, Transvaal, e Botswana, Caprivi, Zimbabwe and Mozambique.

Status: Mostly uncommon; common in some localities; mostly resident; some local seasonal migrations in Natal.

Habitat: Woodland and savanna with scrub and thickets, riverine forest, gardens.

Habits: Usually solitary or in pairs. Easily overlooked, except for loud calling. Forages at all levels in vegetation from near ground to canopy, hopping and bounding through branches. May be mobbed by smaller birds. Enters suburban gardens especially on migration.

Food: Insects (including wasps), frogs, lizards, small mammals and birds, birds' eggs and nestlings.

Breeding: *Season*: September to January in Natal, August to January in Transvaal, July to April (mainly September-November) in Zimbabwe. *Nest*: Shallow loosely built bowl of stout twigs, roots, grass and leaves, lined with tendrils, rootlets and bark fibres; inside diameter 7 cm; in fork of bush or smallish tree, often fairly conspicuous; several metres above ground. *Clutch*: (32) 2–2,9–4 eggs. *Eggs*: Pinkish, cream or buff, finely spotted and clouded with brown and grey; measure (69) 29,4 × 20,6 (26,5–32,1 × 19,3–21,8). *Incubation*: 15–18 days. *Nestling*: About 20–21 days; usually only 2 young reared; may remain with parents for up to a year after leaving nest.

752 (726) Whitetailed Shrike Plate 61
Kortstertlaksman
Lanioturdus torquatus

[Drosselwürger]

Measurements: Length about 15 cm; wing (8) 82–84,8–92; tail (1 ♂) 41, (3 ♀) 33–36; tarsus (5) 28,5–30; culmen (8) 18–21. Weight (26) 22,5–29–45 g.

Bare Parts: Iris bright yellow, greenish yellow or orange-yellow; bill, legs and feet black.

Identification: Size smallish; looks big-headed, round-bodied, long-legged and short-tailed; boldly pied black, white and grey; crown, face, nape, breastband, base of tail and wingtips black; forehead, throat, narrow nape band, tail, wingpatches and lower belly white; back and lower breast grey; tail tipped black in centre; white wingpatches conspicuous in flight; at rest wingtips reach almost to tip of tail. *Immature*: Black breastband narrower than in adult; nape mottled; eye brown.

Voice: Loud piping and churring notes, often in duet, *chiu-chiu-(kirr)-chiu*; ringing boubou-like *poo-eee* and *cheeeu* calls, mixed with harsh nasal *krank-krank* and rattling *chuk-k-k-k-k notes*; harsh *skwee, skwee* alarm notes.

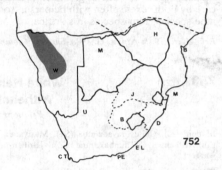

752

trees, gleaning from branches and foliage up to 25 m above ground, in bushes and on ground; hops on ground with large bounds. Restless and active; keeps to dense vegetation, but perches on top of bush or tree when alarmed.

Food: Insects.

Breeding: *Season*: January to April in Namibia; November to December in Angola. *Nest*: Neat deep cup of grass and bark strips bound with spider web, lined with fine grass stems; several metres above ground in fork of tree, usually in

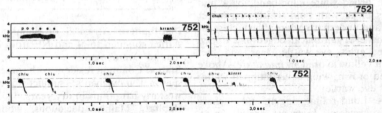

752

Distribution: From S of Windhoek (Tsondab and Sossus Rivers at Namib edge), Namibia, to sw Angola.

Status: Common resident; some local seasonal movements.

Habitat: Scrubby savanna and thornbush.

Habits: Usually in pairs or small groups of 12 or more birds. Flight somewhat laboured, but direct, usually not far. Forages in canopy. *Clutch*: (16) 1–3 eggs (usually 2–3). *Eggs*: White, greyish green or bluish white, sparingly spotted with red-brown and blue-grey mainly in zone around thick end; measure (9) 20,4 × 15,8 (20,2–20,9 × 15,4–16,8). *Incubation*: 15 days by ♀ only. *Nestling*: (4) 19–21 days; fed by both parents; dependent on parents for about 2 weeks after leaving nest.

26:20. Family 82 PRIONOPIDAE—HELMETSHRIKES

Small to medium. Bill medium, fairly stout, hooked at tip; legs fairly short and strong; wings medium to longish, rounded; tail medium, rounded; plumage boldly patterned in black, white, grey and brown; coloured, comb-like eye-wattles in some species (genus *Prionops*); sexes similar; gregarious in open woodland; food insects, some fruit; breed solitarily or with helpers; nest a small neat cup of plant material and spider web on a branch; eggs 3–5, white or greenish, spotted; chick sparsely downy at hatching; parental care by both sexes, often with helpers in some species. Distribution Africa S of Sahara; nine species; four species in s Africa.

Ref. Harris, T. & Arnott, G. 1988. *Shrikes of southern Africa*. Cape Town: Struik Winchester.

753 (727) **White Helmetshrike** **Plate 61**
Withelmlaksman
Prionops plumatus

Muduni (K), Chiteveravadzimba (Sh), Muriyane (Ts), iPhemvu, uThimbakazane (Z), [Brillen-würger]

Measurements: Length 19–20 cm; wing (82 ♂) 98–106,3–116, (73 ♂) 103–108,9–115; tail (81 ♂) 78–84,7–90, (73 ♀) 79–86–91; tarsus (40) 19–23; culmen (78 ♂) 18,5–19,9–22, (70 ♀) 18,5–19,9–22. Weight (44 ♂) 27,3–32,7–35,8 g, (41 ♀) 29,7–34,9–39,8 g, (25 unsexed) 24,5–29,5–37 g.

Bare Parts: Iris yellow; serrated eye-wattle deep yellow to orange-yellow; bill black; legs and feet orange-yellow.

Identification: Size medium to smallish; boldly pied black, white and grey; crown grey, forming slightly bushy crest on forehead; broad white nape-band; back and wings black with bold white wingstripe; face and underparts white; black crescent behind eye; tail black, edged and tipped white; eyes, eye-wattle, legs and feet bright yellow to orange. *Immature*: Above tinged brown; wing coverts tipped white; lacks eye wattle.

Voice: Loud rolling ringing and ratchety calls, *krawow, krawow, kreee, kreee, kreepkrow, kreepkrow*, etc., usually in chorus; also bill-snapping and growling sounds.

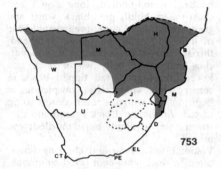

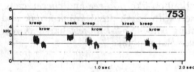

Distribution: Africa S of Sahara; in s Africa confined to N and NE from Zululand to Ovamboland.

Status: Common resident with some local seasonal movements; subject to major westerly irruptions in dry years.

Habitat: Mainly deciduous woodland when breeding; disperses into other kinds of woodland and *Acacia* savanna after breeding.

Habits: Gregarious at all times in groups of 2–22 birds (mean of 1 096 groups = 7 birds), usually including siblings from previous broods; sometimes joins mixed bird parties. Forages in canopy, on branches and trunks, and on ground; rest-

less, hopping about and calling while foraging. Flight fairly fast low and undulating, usually silent. Roosts communally in huddled row on branch.
Food: Insects, spiders; rarely lizards.
Breeding: Cooperative in groups. *Season*: October to November in Natal, September to December in Transvaal, August to April (mainly September-December) in Zimbabwe. *Nest*: Neat compact cup of bark shreds, felted and bound outside with spider web; (11 nests) outside diameter 8,1–8,4–9 cm, outside depth 3,5–5–6,5 cm, inside diameter 6,3–6,8–7,1 cm, inside depth 2,4–2,6–2,8 cm;

2–10 m m above ground (mostly 3–6 m) on horizontal branch or fork of tree; nests always solitary, never in neighbouring trees, usually more than 50 m apart. *Clutch*: (299) 2–3,8–9 eggs in groups with more than 1 ♀; (29) 2–5 eggs in groups with only 1 ♀. *Eggs*: Pale greenish, pinkish or buff, spotted and blotched with purplish red, brown and grey mainly at thick end; measure (271) 20,6 × 16 (18,5–23,5 × 14,5–18). *Incubation*: (8) 17 days (rarely 21 days) by all members of group. *Nestling*: (8) 17–20–22 days; fed by all members of group; post-nestling dependence at least 70 days.

---

754 (728) Redbilled Helmetshrike Plate 61
Swarthelmlaksman
Prionops retzii

[Dreifarbenwürger, Dreifarb-Brillenwürger]

Measurements: Length 20–23 cm; wing (54 ♂) 121–130–137, (55 ♀) 121–130,5–142; tail (56 ♂) 85–92,6–99, (55 ♀) 87–93,3–102; tarsus (5) 22–23; culmen (34 ♂) 22–23,5–26, (34 ♀) 22,5–24–26. Weight (19 ♂) 37,9–43,1–48 g, (19 ♀) 38,4–44,6–49,2 g, (41 unsexed) 38–47,8–53,5 g.
Bare Parts: Iris orange; serrated eye-wattle orange, red or rose pink; bill red to orange-red, tip yellow; legs and feet pink, orange-red or scarlet.
Identification: Size medium (somewhat smaller than Bokmakierie); all black except for brown back, white-tipped tail and white undertail; white wingpatch visible only in flight; bill, eyering and legs red. *Immature (1st year)*: Brown where adult black; bill dull horn; no eye-wattles; otherwise similar to adult. *Immature (2nd year)*: Bill and eye-wattle orange; black of adult plumage acquired only in 3rd year.
Voice: Many weird grating and churring calls; short *cheer, cheer, cheer*, rolling *krreeer*, lilting *whip-reer, whip-reer, whip-reer*, etc., often in chorus; also bill-snapping sounds.

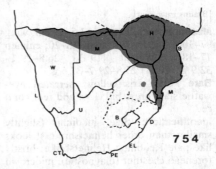

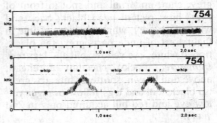

Distribution: S Africa to E Africa; in s Africa mainly in NE from Zululand to Ovamboland.
Status: Fairly common to common resident or nomad.
Habitat: Mainly deciduous woodlands when breeding; otherwise disperses into

Acacia savanna and other dry woodland types.

Habits: Gregarious at all times in small groups; nonbreeding flocks (220) 2–4,9–15 birds, breeding flocks (52) 2–4,7–11 birds; in Zululand flocks may number up to 17 or even 30 birds. Forages mainly on larger branches and on trunks of trees; also hawks insects in flight or on ground. Mobs predators (snakes, owls, raptors, monkeys and small carnivores), snapping bill and alarm-calling. Flight fast, low, somewhat undulating. Roosts communally in huddled row on branch.

Food: Insects, lizards.

Breeding: Cooperative in small groups. *Season:* September to December in Transvaal, August to June (mainly September-November) in Zimbabwe. *Nest:* Neat shallow cup of grass, bark, tendrils and lichens, firmly and smoothly bound with spider web; outside diameter 10–11 cm, outside depth 3,5–5 cm, inside diameter 7–7,7 cm, inside depth 1,5–3 cm; 3–20 m above ground on stout horizontal branch of large tree (especially *Pterocarpus rotundifolia*). *Clutch:* (33) 2–3,2–5 eggs (usually 3). *Eggs:* Pale bluish or buffy green, spotted and lined with black, brown, reddish and grey mainly at thick end; measure (36) 24,4 × 17,1 (22,7–25,8 × 15,6–18,2). *Incubation:* At least 17 days (but less than 21 days) by all members of breeding group. *Nestling:* About 20 days; fed by all members of group.

Ref. Tarboton, W. 1963. *Bokmakierie* 15:1–3.

755 (729) **Chestnutfronted Helmetshrike** **Plate 61**
Stekelkophelmlaksman
Prionops scopifrons

[Braunstirnwürger]

Measurements: Length 17,5–19 cm; wing 97–104; tail 75–79; tarsus 18–20; culmen 17–18,5. Weight (19 ♂) 26,8–29,1–32,9 g, (20 ♀) 25,8–29,7–37,5 g.

Bare Parts: Iris yellow; serrated eye-wattle slate grey; bill, legs and feet coral red.

Identification: Size medium (slightly smaller than other helmetshrikes); looks like pale Redbilled Helmetshrike; bristly forehead chestnut (diagnostic); midcrown grey; chin, undertail and spot in front of eye white; rest of head black; back and wings dark grey, white wingspot visible in flight; rest of underparts grey; tail black, tipped white; eye yellow; bill and legs red. *Immature:* Lacks chestnut forehead; above dull brown, spotted white; iris greyish black; bill and legs yellow-orange (yellow eye and red bill acquired only in 2nd year).

Voice: Various whirring, gobbling and chucking calls, *chair-rer wit wit chirro, tree, tree, tree*, etc.; sharp *shuk*; also bill-snapping.

Distribution: S Africa to E Africa; in s Africa from Zululand to Mozambique and extreme e lowlands of Zimbabwe.

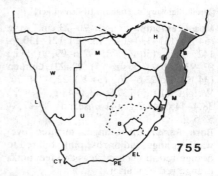

755

Status: Sparse resident or nomad S of Save River; commoner northwards.

Habitat: Canopy of lowland evergreen and riverine forest, adjacent woodlands, dense bushveld.

Habits: Gregarious in small groups of 3–10 birds when breeding, up to 30 birds when not breeding; often in company with Redbilled Helmetshrike and other species in mixed bird parties in winter. Forages like tit, gleaning from foliage in canopy; also gleans from branches and trunks of trees. Readily mobs birds of prey.

Food: Insects; *Ochna* fruits fed to young.

Breeding: Cooperatively in small groups. *Season:* October to December in Zimbabwe, October in Mozambique. *Nest*: Neat shallow cup of plant fibres (grasses and thin bark), felted outside with spider web; outside diameter 6,3 cm; inside depth 2,4 cm; 4,5–20 m above ground on stout horizontal branch or saddled in fork of tree (mainly *Brachystegia spiciformis*). *Clutch*: (2) 3 eggs. *Eggs*: Very pale grey, tinged turquoise, liberally spotted and flecked lavender, brick and grey, forming ring around middle; measure (3) 19,5 × 15,3 (19–20 × 15,2–15,3); weigh (3) 2,3–2,4–2,4 g.. *Incubation*: Unrecorded; by all members of breeding group. *Nestling*: Unrecorded; young fed by all members of group.

Ref. Britton, P.L. & Britton, H.A. 1977. *Scopus* 1:86.

---

756 (730)   **Whitecrowned Shrike**   **Plate 61**
Kremetartlaksman
Eurocephalus anguitimens

[Weißscheitelwürger]

Measurements: Length 23–25 cm; wing (22) 130–136–143; tail 100–116; tarsus 22–26; culmen 15–20. Weight (13 ♂) 55,7–68–76,5 g, (9 ♀) 59–70,1–84 g, (3 unsexed) 51–63,5–70 g.

Bare Parts: Iris brown; bill blackish horn; legs and feet blackish brown to light brown.

Identification: Size medium to large; crown, nape, throat and breast white; face and sides of neck black (contrasting with white head; diagnostic); wings and tail black; back and belly ashy brown; rump white (conspicuous in flight). *Immature*: Mottled brownish on crown, whitish on ear coverts; wing coverts tipped buff; breast brown like belly.

Voice: Loud somewhat nasal *skwee-skwee, skwee-kwee-kwee*, often in chorus; brief *chut*.

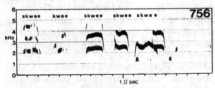

Distribution: Northern Transvaal, C and w Zimbabwe,Botswana (except dry W), n Cape, n Namibia (rare in S, but recorded Mariental and Windhoek) and s Angola.

Status: Fairly common to common resident; some local or nomadic movements.

Habitat: Woodland and savanna, often with Baobab trees.

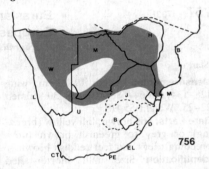

756

Habits: Solitary, in pairs or small groups of up to 12 birds. Perches conspicuously on top or outer branch of tree. Flight strong, direct, with shallow quick wingbeats; calls on take-off. Forages by watching from perch and dropping to ground for prey; walks on ground.

Food: Insects; also berries.

Breeding: *Season*: October to December in Transvaal, September to January (mainly October-November) in Zimbabwe. *Nest*: Neat small compact thick-walled cup of plant fibres, firmly bound and felted with spider web; on horizontal branch or fork several metres above ground. *Clutch*: (21) 2–3,3–5 eggs (usually 2–4; rarely up to 8). *Eggs*: White or cream, spotted with grey and brown; measure (94) 27,2 × 21,3 (23–30 × 17–22,8). *Incubation*: Unrecorded. *Nestling*: Unrecorded; fed by parents and up to 3 adult helpers.

26:21. Family 83 STURNIDAE—STARLINGS

Mostly small to medium, some large. Bill medium to moderately long, arched on culmen, strong; legs moderately long, strong; feet large and strong; wings variable, short and rounded to long and pointed; tail medium to long, rounded, square or graduated; body robust; plumage variable, but usually more or less black with iridescence (highly glossy in some species) and silky texture; sexes alike or different; gregarious, at least when not breeding; arboreal or terrestrial; most feed on ground; omnivorous; breed solitarily or colonially; nest not highly variable—pad of soft material in hole in tree, rock, bank or building, or in self-made burrow, or bowl-shaped nest on rock ledge, or mass of sticks with side entrance, or hanging woven nest in tree; eggs 2–5, green or blue, plain or spotted; chick sparsely downy at hatching; incubation by both sexes or by female only; young fed by both sexes. Distribution Africa, Eurasia, n Australia, Pacific islands to Tuamotu Archipelago; several species introduced to N America, Australia and New Zealand; 106 species; 14 species in s Africa (two introduced).

757 (733)   Eurasian Starling   Plate 63
Europese Spreeu
Sturnus vulgaris

[Star]

Measurements: Length 19–22 cm; wing 128–134; tail 64–68; tarsus 28–30; culmen 22–25. Weight 55–96 g.

Bare Parts: Iris brown; bill yellow (breeding) or grey to greenish brown (non-breeding); legs and feet reddish brown.

Identification: Size small; shorter-tailed than any other starling; whole head and body iridescent black with green and violet reflections, faintly spotted buff on back, whitish on belly (less iridescent and more heavily spotted when not breeding); wings and tail edged with brown; bill sharply pointed, yellow (grey when not breeding). *Immature*: Brownish grey; throat whitish.

Voice: Jumble of high-pitched squeaks, creakings and pipings, sometimes incorporating imitations of other birdcalls; harsh alarm scream; sharp *klik klik* anxiety calls near nest; insistent *churr churr* from begging fledglings.

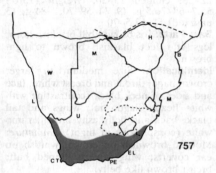

757

Distribution: Originally Europe and Asia; introduced to s Africa, N America, Australia and New Zealand; w, sw, s, e and ne Cape, Karoo and s Natal (to Durban); northward expansion apparently slowing down towards Natal; also introduced N America, Australia, New Zealand and some oceanic islands.

Status: Very common resident in Cape, straggler Natal; introduced from Britain to Cape Town by C.J. Rhodes in 1899; spread to Clanwilliam by 1950, Port Elizabeth by 1955, King William's Town by 1961, East London by 1966, ne Cape and Kleinzee (Namaqualand) by 1970, Durban by 1973.

Habitat: Urban areas, farmyards.

Habits: Usually gregarious, often in flocks of hundreds of birds when not breeding;

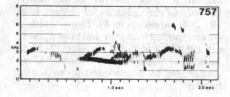

757

otherwise in smaller flocks. Forages on lawns, playing fields and mown grasslands, walking with perky gait, probing frequently with bill in grass, opening bill to expand hole; also raids orchards and vineyards for fruit; may attend grazing cattle in pasture. Flight fast and direct with rapid wingbeats; flocks highly synchronized in flight movements; foraging flock may take off, settle in nearby trees, then return to ground in unison. Roosts in vast flocks on buildings or in tall trees. Sings with bill pointed up, wings shivering.

Food: Fruit, seeds, fallen grain, insects, spiders, worms, molluscs, lizards.

Breeding: *Season*: September to December; first layings of season highly synchro-

nized in sw Cape. *Nest*: Loose bowl of grass, pine needles and straw, lined with grass, feathers, wool and moss; in hole in wall or tree, under eaves of building, in pipes and gutters; sometimes in hollow among accumulated debris in tree; built by ♀ only (♂ may help with foundation). *Clutch*: 3–6 eggs. *Eggs*: Pale blue; measure (68) 29,6 × 21,3 (27,5–32,9 × 19,7–22,4); weigh about 7 g. *Incubation*: 12–13 days by both sexes, mostly by ♀; ♀ incubates at night. *Nestling*: About 20 days; fed by both parents.

Ref. Quickelberge, C.D. 1972. *Ostrich* 43:179–180.
Winterbottom, J.M. & Liversidge, R. 1954. *Ostrich* 25:89–96.

758 (734) Indian Myna   Plate 63
Indiese Spreeu
Acridotheres tristis

[Hirtenmaina]

Measurements: Length 21–25 cm; wing ♂ 138–153, ♀ 138–147; tail ♂ 81–95, ♀ 79–86; tarsus ♂ 34–42, ♀ 35–41; culmen ♂ 25–30, ♀ 25–28. Weight (22) 82–110,2–138 g.

Bare Parts: Iris brown or red-brown, mottled with white; bill, facial skin, legs and feet yellow.

Identification: Size medium; head and breast glossy black; remiges black with large white patch (conspicuous in flight); tail black, broadly tipped white; rest of plumage rich brown, shading to white under tail; bill, bare face and legs yellow (diagnostic and conspicuous). *Immature*: Paler than adult, otherwise similar.

Voice: Song sustained jumble of squawks, whistles, croaks, creaks and whines, most notes repeated 2–4 times each, *krr-krr-krr, chi-ri-ri-ri, krrup-chip-krrup, chirri-chirri-chirri, grr-grr, cheee*, etc.; loud *radio-radio-radio* callnotes; harsh swearing *kharr* alarm note.

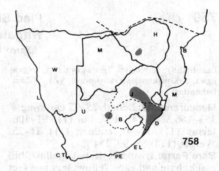

758

Distribution: Originally India, Turkestan, Afghanistan, Baluchistan, Burma, Thailand and SE Asia; introduced to s Africa; Natal, Transkei, Johannesburg, Pretoria; also introduced to Madagascar, parts of Australia, New Zealand, many oceanic islands.

Status: Abundant resident; introduced from India to Durban between 1888 and 1900; reached (or introduced to) Wit-

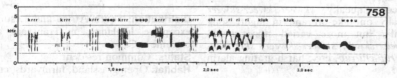

watersrand about 1938, Kimberley 1964.
Habitat: Cities, towns, villages; always near human settlement.
Habits: In pairs when breeding; otherwise in small groups or flocks of up to about 30 birds. Roosts communally in large trees in flocks of hundreds or thousands of birds, making tremendous noise even long after nightfall. Forages on lawns, playing fields, mown grasslands, streets, sidewalks, railway yards, stockpens, etc., walking with determined tread, or bounding in long strides; often probes with bill in grass. Sings throughout year from perch or ground, often bowing and nodding head; pairs display to one another with bowing and feathers raised. Neighbouring pairs fight furiously, often locking claws. Flight fast, slightly undulating. Exceedingly wary, but may become tame in gardens.

Food: Insects, fruit, seeds, worms, nectar, millipedes, snails, birds' eggs, table scraps, young mice, small frogs and lizards.
Breeding: *Season*: September to January in Natal, October to December in Transvaal. *Nest*: Bowl-shaped hollow on top of large foundation of grass, roots, leaves, paper, string, twigs, snakeskin, bits of plastic, etc.; usually lined with finer straws, petioles or paper strips; nest may weigh several kilograms; in hole under eaves, in wall, pipe or tree, in damaged street light. *Clutch*: (26) 2–3,9–5 eggs (sometimes 6). *Eggs*: Greenish blue or turquoise; measure (35) 29,2 × 21,5 (26,3–32,9 × 20,2–22,5). *Incubation*: 17–18 days by both sexes. *Nestling*: 22–24 days; fed by both parents; young accompany parents for several weeks after leaving nest.

759 (746)   Pied Starling   Plate 63
Witgatspreeu
Spreo bicolor

Leholi (SS), Igiyo-giyo, Igiwu-giwu (X), iNgwa-ngwa, iKhwikhwi, iGwayigwayi (Z), [Zweifarbenstar]

Measurements: Length 25–27 cm; wing ♂ 153–166,5, ♀ 147–157; tail (11) 91–106; tarsus (11) 37–40; culmen (11) 21–25. Weight (114) 88–99–154 g.
Bare Parts: Iris white to pale yellow; bill black, base and gape yellow; legs and feet black.
Identification: Size large; mainly blackish brown with oily sheen, glossed green on tail; undertail and lower belly white; eye white; gape yellow (conspicuous in field). *Immature*: Like adult, but dull charcoal without sheen until first moult at few months of age; eye dark brown; gape white; in 2nd year eye mixed brown and white; gape yellow; birds may breed at this age.
Voice: Squeaky *skweer-skweer-skweer* usually on take-off and in flight; song similar but more varied *skwee-skwee-skwee, skwik, skweer-skweer, skik-skik, chirrup-chirrup*, etc.; harsh grating alarm note.

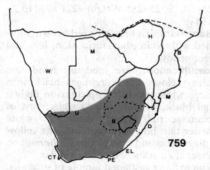

Distribution: South Africa and Lesotho, except e lowlands, n Transvaal and extreme n Cape.
Status: Common resident.
Habitat: Open grassland, farmyards, culti-

vated fields, rolling foothills, especially with dongas and eroded banks.

Habits: Highly gregarious at all times, usually in flocks of 10–20 birds. Roosts communally in trees and reedbeds, often in flocks of hundreds of birds. Forages on ground, walking or running after prey; follows plough for exposed insect larvae; often accompanies grazing cattle and will remove ectoparasites; rarely raids orchards for fruit. When disturbed flies off calling; flight wavy, somewhat dipping; may perch on fence, telephone line or bush.

Food: Insects, ticks, centipedes, small lizards, seeds, fruit, aloe nectar.

Breeding: *Season*: Mainly August to January; also April to June in Transvaal; usually 2 broods/season. *Nest*: Flattish pad of grass, feathers, paper, snakeskins, leaves and other materials, in chamber at end of burrow 0,3–1,5 m long, 1,5 m or more above ground level in vertical bank of river, donga, quarry or cutting; also under eaves of buildings; built by both sexes; usually colonial. *Clutch*: (55) 2–4,2–6 eggs (usually 4–5). *Eggs*: Bright blue-green, plain or sparingly spotted with brownish red; measure (131) 30,3 × 21,3 (26,9–35,3 × 19,6–22,5). *Incubation*: 14–16 days by ♀ only; starts before clutch complete. *Nestling*: 21–26 days; fed by both sexes and up to 7 helpers (mainly immatures and subadults).

Ref. Craig, A. 1983. *Ibis* 125:114–115; 346–352; 1985. *Ostrich* 56:123–131; 1987. *Ostrich* 58:176–180.

---

760 (735) **Wattled Starling** **Plate 63**
Lelspreeu
Creatophora cinerea

Uwambu, Unowambu (X), iMpofazana (Z), [Lappenstar]

Measurements: Length 21–22 cm; wing (15 ♂) 118–122–127, (17 ♀) 114–117–120; tail (32) 61–71; tarsus (32) 27–30; culmen (32) 21–24. Weight (134) 56–67,5–92 g.

Bare Parts: Iris brown; bill pale pink; (breeding ♂) head and wattles blackish except for yellow area on hindcrown, over ears to cheeks; legs and feet brown.

Identification: Small (about size of Laughing Dove); mainly pale whitish grey; rump white (diagnostic; conspicuous in flight); remiges and tail black; wing coverts white (♂) or black (♀), but variable; breeding ♂ has head bare, mainly black with large black wattle on forehead and throat; hindcrown bright yellow. *Immature*: Like adult ♀, but browner; throat bare, yellow or greenish.

Voice: Song high-pitched jumble of thin squeaky notes, *tsip-tsip, tseep, tseeee, tseep-tseep*, etc. (something like song of Eurasian Starling); usually silent when not breeding; 3-syllabled flight call; nasal *graaah* alarm call.

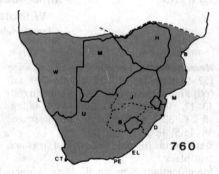

Distribution: S Africa, E Africa and s Arabia; throughout s Africa.

Status: Locally abundant nomad, seldom staying long in any one place; regular seasonal movements in some areas.

Habitat: Open woodland, savanna, farmland.

Habits: Highly gregarious at all times; rarely solitary or in small groups of 3–10 birds. Roosts and nests communally in trees in flocks of hundreds or thousands of birds. May form combined flocks with metallic starlings (*Lamprotornis*) or Pied Starlings. Forages by walking about on ground, catching live prey or picking up offal from rubbish tips and abattoirs; perches on sheep's or rhinos' backs to catch disturbed insects. Appears and disappears erratically, usually in response to food supply, such as locust swarms. Flies with rapidly beating wings, often in tight flocks.

Food: Insects (locusts less important than previously believed), offal, snails, fruit (*Royena, Ziziphus*, mulberries), nectar of flowering trees and aloes, worms.

Breeding: *Season*: Any month depending on food supply and rainfall, but mainly August to February. *Nest*: Large untidy ball of sticks with side or top entrance; chamber floor lined with pad of grass and feathers; at almost any height in thorntree or bush, or on telephone pole; highly colonial, adjacent nests usually touching and piled up on top of each other; built by both sexes. *Clutch*: (13) 2–3,6–5 eggs. *Eggs*: Pale blue, usually plain, sometimes sparingly spotted with brown; measure (48) 28,3 × 20,5 (26,4–31,9 × 18,3–21,9). *Incubation*: About 11 days by both sexes. *Nestling*: 13–16 days, but flies only at about 19–22 days; fed by both parents.

Ref. Liversidge, R. 1961. *Ann. Cape Prov. Mus.* 1:71–80.
Uys, C.J. 1977. *Bokmakierie* 29:87–89.

---

761 (736)   **Plumcoloured Starling**   **Plate 63**
Witborsspreeu
Cinnyricinclus leucogaster

[Amethystglanzstar]

Measurements: Length 17,5–19 cm; wing (57 ♂) 104–108–113, (3 ♀) 104–109; tail (60) 57–64; tarsus (60) 19–22; culmen (60) 13–17. Weight (4 ♂) 39,5–44,4–48,2 g, (5 ♀) 32,7–44,7–55,6 g, (6 unsexed) 38–45,5–48 g.

Bare Parts: Iris pale yellow; bill, legs and feet black.

Identification: Size small. *Male*: Upperparts, throat, breast and tail iridescent purple, varying with angle of light from black to rose pink; rest of underparts, and outer edge of tail white. *Female*: Above light brown, streaked black; below white, heavily streaked dusky; eye yellow. *Immature*: Similar to ♀, but eye brown, narrowly ringed yellow.

Voice: Song repeated phrases of 9–15 somewhat drongolike twanging notes and thrushlike pipings, tweng *tweng-tweng trippy-treea-skwee-trang, treng tring-tring trippy skeea pree-pree*, etc.; twittering flight calls; usually silent.

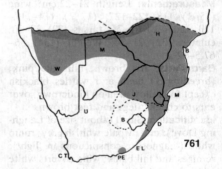

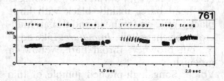

Distribution: Africa S of Sahara, sw Arabia; in s Africa confined to E, NE and N.

Status: Fairly common to scarce breeding intra-African migrant, October to April in S Africa, September to March in Zim-

babwe. Nonbreeding birds disperse then migrate northwards, probably mainly to Zambia and Angola (possibly to Sudan and Ethiopia); some overwinter in n Transvaal and Zimbabwe, May to July.
Habitat: Woodland, savanna, bushveld, riverine forest.
Habits: In pairs when breeding; gregarious in small flocks when not breeding, often of females and young only, or of males only. May accompany flocks of Wattled and Glossy Starlings. Forages arboreally, less often on ground; also hawks insects in flight. Often perches conspicuously on top of tree or bush; flicks wings like chat after alighting. Flight swift and direct.
Food: Mainly fruit; also insects.

Breeding: *Season:* October to February in Natal, September to February in Transvaal, October to January in Zimbabwe. *Nest:* Pad of fresh green leaves on foundation of grass, hair and dry dung; in natural hole in tree or in pipe; 1–10 m above ground; built by ♀; both sexes add green leaves throughout incubation. *Clutch:* (35) 2–2,6–4 eggs (usually 2–3). *Eggs:* Pale greenish blue, spotted with red-brown and purple somewhat concentrated at thick end; measure (72) 24,5 × 17,4 (22–26,7 × 15,5–18,7). *Incubation:* About 12 days by ♀ only. *Nestling:* About 21 days; fed by both parents.

Ref. Traylor, M.A. 1971. *J. Orn.* 112:1–20.

METALLIC STARLINGS, GENUS *LAMPROTORNIS*

The metallic (or "glossy") starlings are all characterized by black plumage with intense green, blue and purple lustre. They range in size from medium to large. Of the 7 s African species, 5 have bright yellow, orange or red eyes and relatively short tails; the other 2 species (Burchell's and Longtailed Starlings) have dark brown eyes and relatively long tails. Identification of the orange-eyed group is often difficult. Distinctions lie in the degree of sheen (highly satin-glossed to fairly dull metallic), amount of contrast between ear coverts and rest of head, amount of iridescence on belly, and voice. Distribution and habitat must also be carefully compared.

762 (743)　　　　　**Burchell's Starling**　　　　　**Plate 63**
　　　　　　　　　　　Grootglansspreeu
　　　　　　　　　　　Lamprotornis australis

Ndjundju (K), Khololwane, Khwezu (Ts), Legô-dilê (Tw), [Riesenglanzstar, Glanzelster]

Measurements: Length 30–34 cm; wing (12 ♂) 162–183–191, (4 ♀) 150–166–173; tail (10 ♂) 150–175, (4 ♀) 142–157; tarsus (14) 40–49; culmen (14) 20–23,5. Weight (1 ♂) 130,6 g.
Bare Parts: Iris dark brown; bill, legs and feet black.
Identification: Size large; build heavy; iridescent blue-green, blacker on face and ear coverts; tail long, rounded (longer, floppier and strongly graduated in Longtailed Starling), heavy, purplish, barred black in good light; legs and feet long and strong; wings very broad and rounded, flight laboured. *Immature:* Duller than adult; belly blackish.
Voice: Loud harsh high-pitched croaking, *kriki-krik, krak-krik, kruk, chirree-krrr, chirri-kwirri-krrr,* etc., with pauses be-

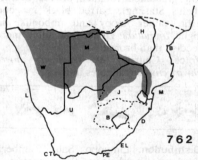

tween each group of notes; noise almost deafening in chorus at roost.

Distribution: Interior and w parts of s Africa, to Angola.
Status: Fairly common to abundant resident.
Habitat: Parklike woodland and savanna.
Habits: Usually solitary or in pairs or small groups, sometimes in company with other metallic starlings; roosts communally in large flocks in trees or reedbeds, performing synchronized aerobatics before settling. Flight looks slow and heavy on big floppy wings. Forages on bare ground, walking with long strides. Becomes tame in game reserves; otherwise rather shy.

Food: Insects, other invertebrates, fruit.

Breeding: *Season*: September to March (mainly October to January) in Transvaal, November to March in Namibia. *Nest*: Pad of grass in natural hole in tree, usually fairly high above ground; sometimes as low as 2 m. *Clutch*: 2–4 eggs. *Eggs*: Bright sky blue to pale greenish blue, plain or sparsely spotted with reddish purple mainly at thick end; measure (14) 29,2 × 20,5 (27,5–31,7 × 19,8–22,1). *Incubation*: Unrecorded. *Nestling*: Unrecorded.

763 (742)   Longtailed Starling   Plate 63
Langstertglansspreeu
Lamprotornis mevesii

Ndjundju (K), Mwazea (Sh), [Meves-Glanzstar]

Measurements: Length 30–34 cm; wing (32 ♂) 142–149,7–159, (23 ♀) 131,5–138,2–145; tail (14 ♂) 185–210, (7 ♀) 182–190; tarsus (21) 31–40; culmen (21) 17,5–20,5. Weight (29) 55,7–64,2–77 g.
Bare Parts: Iris brown; bill, legs and feet black.
Identification: Size large; less heavily built than Burchell's Starling; iridescent bluish bronze, washed purple on upper back and belly, gold on lower back; tail long, narrow, graduated (rounded, broader in Burchell's Starling), barred black in good light, rather floppy and ribbonlike in flight. *Immature*: Duller than adult, more reddish than bronze.
Voice: Churring *chwirri-chwirr chwee chwirr chweer* callnotes in flock.

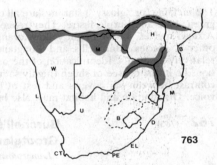

763

Distribution: Limpopo, Sabi, Zambezi, Okavango and Kunene River systems, n Namibia; also Angola, Zambia and Malawi.
Status: Locally common resident. Indeterminate (RDB).
Habitat: Semi-arid savanna, mopane woodland, usually with sparse and/or overgrazed ground cover.
Habits: Usually in small groups; some-

times in flocks of up to 150 birds. Flies fairly high between treetops. Forages on ground, walking or running about on bare areas. Roosts communally in large flocks, performing aerobatics before settling in reedbeds.
Food: Insects, fruit.
Breeding: *Season*: November to April in Zimbabwe. *Nest*: Pad of dry plant fibres and twigs in natural hole in tree, or in hollow fence post or ventilation pipe; up to 4 m above ground; ♀ may excavate own nest hole in soft wood; nest built by ♀ alone; solitary (never colonial). *Clutch*: 3–4 eggs. *Eggs*: Pale greenish blue; measure about 28,5 × 20. *Incubation*: Unrecorded. *Nestling*: 22 days; fed by both parents and by helpers from previous year's brood; post-nestling dependence several weeks.

Ref. Dowsett, R.J. 1967. *Bull. Brit. Orn. Club* 87:157–164.

764 (737)   Glossy Starling   Plate 63
Kleinglansspreeu
Lamprotornis nitens

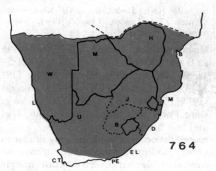

Ndjundju (K), Legodi (NS), Leholi-piloane (SS), Hwirikwiri (Sh), Khololwane, Khwezu (Ts), Legôdi, Leswêdi (Tw), Inyakrini, Inyakrili (X), iKhwinsi, iKhwezi (Z), [Rotschulter-Glanzstar]

Measurements: Length 22–23 cm; wing (50 ♂) 127–135,9–148, (38 ♀) 120–128,3–140; tail (18) 84–96; tarsus (18) 32–36; culmen (18) 21–26. Weight (1 ♂) 91 g, (2 ♀) 78,3–80 g, (25 unsexed) 67–83,8–104,8 g.

Bare Parts: Iris orange-yellow; bill, legs and feet black.

Identification: Size medium; similar to Greater and Lesser Blue-eared Starlings, but less brilliantly lustrous; best identified by voice (*q.v.*); entirely metallic blue-green, washed faintly purplish on ear coverts (ear coverts not contrasting with head as much as in blue-eared starlings); small purplish copper area on wrist (not diagnostic); 2 rows of dark spots on wing coverts (similar to Greater Blue-eared Starling; Lesser Blue-eared Starling has only 1 row of dark spots); eye bright orange-yellow. *Immature*: Similar to adult, but duller; iris greyish or greenish.

Voice: Distinctive 2-syllabled deep, but somewhat muffled, slurred rolling *turr-rreeu* callnote, always uttered on take-off; sometimes preceded by staccato note, *tup-turr-rreeu*; song fairly pleasant sustained jumbled throaty warbling, incorporating *turr-rreeu* callnotes, often in chorus.

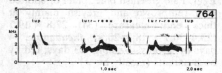

Distribution: S Africa to Zambia, Angola, Zaire and Gabon; throughout s Africa except extreme sw Cape and Mozambique N of Save River.

Status: Common to fairly common resident; nomadic in arid areas; only species of *Lamprotornis* over most of highveld and arid W.

Habitat: *Acacia* savanna, riverine bush, semi-arid scrub, forest edges, farmyards, exotic plantations, towns, parks, gardens; usually prefers sparse ground cover.

Habits: In pairs when breeding; otherwise more or less gregarious in small flocks of about 6–10 birds (other metallic starlings more gregarious). Forages arboreally or on ground; runs well on longish legs. Flight fast and fairly direct, though somewhat laboured with loud whooshing wing noises produced by notched primaries. Sings from perch inside or on top of tree. Usually shy.

Food: Insects, fruit, nectar of aloes, bonemeal from feeding tray.

Breeding: *Season*: October to February in Natal, September to March (mainly October to January) in Transvaal (rarely also April, June and July in lowveld), September to December (mainly October-November) in Zimbabwe, November to February in dry W. *Nest*: Pad of grass, snakeskin, paper, dung and other soft materials; in natural hole in tree, under eaves of building, in chimney, in vertical pipe used as gatepost; from 1,5–5 m above ground. *Clutch*: (53) 2–2,8–6 eggs (usually 3). *Eggs*: Light greenish blue, sparingly speckled with light rusty red; measure (128) 28,1 × 20 (25,4–32,5 × 19–22,5). *Incubation*: Unrecorded. *Nestling*: (2) 19–20 days; fed by both parents and by young of past 1–3 seasons.

Ref. Craig, A. 1983. *Ibis* 125:114–115; 346–352.

765 (738)   Greater Blue-eared Starling   Plate 63
Groot-blouoorglansspreeu
Lamprotornis chalybaeus

Ndjundju (K), Hwirikwiri (Sh), Khololwane, Khwezu (Ts), Legôdi, Leswêdi (Tw), [Grünschwanz-Glanzstar]

Measurements: Length 21–23 cm; wing (206 ♂) 130–148,1–152, (117 ♀) 121,5–135,3–146; tail (19) 82–98; tarsus (19) 30–33,5; culmen (19) 18–21. Weight (191 ♂) 79–94–106 g, (109 ♀) 66–79–96 g.
Bare Parts: Iris bright orange; bill, legs and feet black.
Identification: Size medium; very similar to Glossy Starling, but more satiny lustrous all over; dark blue ear coverts contrast strongly with green head colouring (much less contrast in Glossy Starling); best identified by voice (*q.v.*); entirely shiny blue-green, belly glossed royal blue (glossed magenta in Lesser Blue-eared Starling, blue-green in Glossy Starling); ear coverts deep purple; wrist purplish copper; 2 rows of black spots on wing coverts (as in Glossy Starling; only 1 row in Lesser Blue-eared Starling); eye bright orange. *Immature*: Dull brownish black with only slight gloss; eye grey.
Voice: Somewhat querulous drawn-out nasal *skweer* or *skwee-weer*; song jumble of squeaks and squawks with same whining tone as callnote, *chuk, skwik, skwee-weer, chiweep, chuk, krrrk, skwee-weer*, etc.; harsh *shwarr* alarm note.

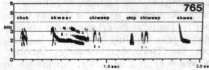

Distribution: Africa S of Sahara; in s Africa confined to NE from Zululand, Transvaal lowveld and Mozambique to Limpopo Valley, Zimbabwe, n Botswana and n Namibia.

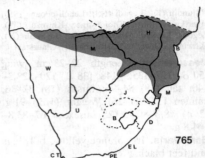

765

Status: Common resident; commonest of yellow-eyed metallic starlings in Zimbabwe; nomadic at edges of range.
Habitat: Open woodland, savanna, riverine forest, bushveld; usually with fairly tall dense ground cover.
Habits: In pairs when breeding; otherwise gregarious in large flocks. Forages mostly by running about on ground; tame in game reserve camps, taking scraps from tables. Flocks sing in chorus from perches in trees. Flight fast and direct with loud swishing wingbeats. Roosts communally in trees or reedbeds.
Food: Fruit, insects, seeds.
Breeding: *Season*: August to November in Transvaal, August to January (mainly September-November) in Zimbabwe. *Nest*: Pad of grass, feathers and snakeskin; in natural hole in tree or in hollow fence pole. *Clutch*: 2–5 eggs (usually 3–4). *Eggs*: Pale greenish blue, plain or spotted with red-brown and greyish mainly at thick end; measure (34) 27,8 × 19,7 (23,4–30,7 × 18,3–20,9). *Incubation*: 14 days by ♀ only. *Nestling*: 23 days; fed by both parents (mostly by ♀).

766 (739)   Lesser Blue-eared Starling   Plate 63
Klein-blouoorglansspreeu
Lamprotornis chloropterus

Ndjundju (K), Hwirigwiri (Sh), [Messingglanzstar]

Measurements: Length 18–20 cm; wing (3 ♂) 120–126, (2 ♀) 112–115; tail (5)

68–72; tarsus (5) 24–27; culmen (5) 17–19.
Bare Parts: Iris chrome yellow to golden yellow; bill, legs and feet black.

Identification: Size medium to smallish (slightly smaller than Greater Blue-eared Starling); much more lustrous than Glossy Starling; best identified by voice (*q.v.*); entirely shiny blue-green, belly glossed magenta (royal blue in Greater Blue-eared Starling, blue-green in Glossy Starling); 1 row of black spots on wing coverts (2 rows in Glossy and Greater Blue-eared Starlings); wrist violet-copper; eye bright orange-yellow. *Immature*: Above blackish grey, sometimes with slight iridescence; below brownish rufous (diagnostic); eye grey.

Voice: Clear *wirri-gwirri* on take-off; song lively phrases of 6–12 notes, *chip chirrew kwip krrreeup kwip krip cheeu*, without querulous quality of Greater Blue-eared Starling, or rolling quality of Glossy Starling; harsh *chair* alarm note.

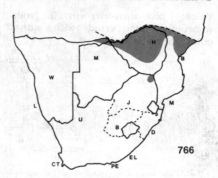

766

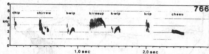

766

Distribution: Africa S of Sahara; in s Africa confined to extreme NE; also recorded n Kruger National Park.

Status: Common resident; somewhat nomadic in places; commonest yellow-eyed metallic starling on Mashonaland Plateau.

Habitat: Mainly *Brachystegia* woodland

when breeding; otherwise also other types of woodland or savanna.

Habits: In pairs when breeding; otherwise forms large flocks of up to 800 birds (more gregarious than Greater Blue-eared Starling). Forages in canopy of trees and on ground. Very similar to Greater Blue-eared Starling.

Food: Insects, seeds, fruit, flowers.

Breeding: *Season*: September to November in Zimbabwe, October in Mozambique. *Nest*: Mass of straw and leaves with bowl-shaped hollow on top; in natural hole or woodpecker's hole in tree or behind loose bark. *Clutch*: 3–5 eggs. *Eggs*: Light blue-green, sparingly spotted with rusty red and greyish; no authentic measurements available. *Incubation*: Unrecorded. *Nestling*: Unrecorded.

767 (741)

Sharptailed Starling
Spitsstertglansspreeu

Lamprotornis acuticaudus

Plate 63

[Keilschwanz-Glanzstar]

Measurements: Length 21–25 cm; wing (3 ♂) 123–127,3–130; tail, central rectrices (3 ♂) 89–93,7–101, (45 unsexed) 85–91–110, outermost rectrices (3 ♂) 67–70,7–75; tarsus (45) 25–28; culmen (45) 20–22.

Bare Parts: Iris bright red or orange (dark brown in immature), inner rim brown; bill, legs and feet black.

Identification: Size medium; similar to other "yellow-eyed" metallic starlings, but tail graduated or wedge-shaped (diagnostic; rounded in other species); entire plumage metallic blue-green; ear coverts glossy blue; wrist purplish copper; eye red (diagnostic; eye yellow to orange in other small

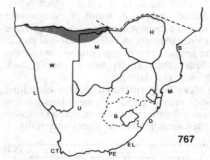

767

metallic starlings). *Immature*: Above dull blackish, sometimes with slight gloss; below dusky, scaled light greyish; eye dark brown, becoming yellow.

673

Voice: Noisy *wirri-wirr-wirri* in group, sometimes interspersed with slurred notes, *wirri-wee-wee*.

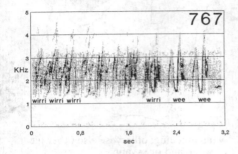

Distribution: Northern Ovamboland and Caprivi to Angola, Zambia and Zaire.
Status: Locally common resident.
Habitat: Open woodland (habitat usually drier than that of Lesser Blue-eared Starling).
Habits: In pairs when breeding; otherwise gregarious. Roosts communally; flocks perform aerobatics before settling. Poorly known.
Food: Insects, fruit.
Breeding: Not recorded in s Africa. *Season*: August to October in Angola, October in Zambia. *Nest, Clutch, Eggs, Incubation, Nestling*: Unrecorded.

---

768 (740)   **Blackbellied Starling**   **Plate 63**
Swartpensglansspreeu
Lamprotornis corruscus

Intenenengu, Isithenenengu (X), iKhwinsi, iKhwezi (Z), [Schwarzbauch-Glanzstar]

Measurements: Length 20–21 cm; wing (6 ♂) 106–110,5–112, (8 ♀) 99–105,5–110; tail (14) 72–82; tarsus (14) 21,5–24; culmen (14) 16,5–19.
Bare Parts: Iris bright orange-yellow; bill, legs and feet black.
Identification: Size smallish to medium; darker than other yellow-eyed metallic starlings; above metallic blue-green, shading to purplish over rump; no violet-purple patch on wrist as in other small metallic starlings; throat and breast metallic blue-green; belly dark violet-purple in ♂, matt black in ♀ (looks black when shaded, purple in sunlit ♂; diagnostic; other yellow-eyed metallic starlings have mainly blue-green bellies); tail dull metallic purple; eye orange-yellow. *Immature*: Duller than adult; below mainly dark brown; eye dark grey.
Voice: Song sustained jumble of trilling and rather harsh piping notes, interspersed with imitations of other birdcalls; often sings in chorus; flocks very noisy.

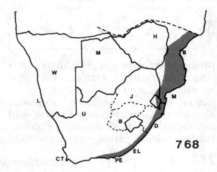

Distribution: Extreme e parts of Africa from Knysna (s Cape) through Natal, Swaziland, se Transvaal lowveld, Mozambique, extreme e lowlands of Zimbabwe, to E Africa.
Status: Very common resident; some local migration; present Zimbabwe only October to January.
Habitat: Canopy of lowland evergreen forest and adjacent dense woodland.
Habits: In pairs when breeding; otherwise gregarious in compact flocks of 20–30 birds. Forages mainly in canopy of trees; seldom comes to ground. Flight fast and direct with loud swishing wingbeats. Highly vocal at all times. Usually shy and hard to approach.
Food: Mainly fruit; also insects, flowers.

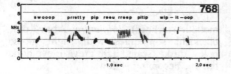

Breeding: *Season*: December in e Cape, August to December in Natal, December in Zimbabwe, October to January in Mozambique. *Nest*: Pad of hair, grass and feathers; in natural hole or old nest hole of barbet or woodpecker in tree, usually fairly high above ground. *Clutch*: (15) 2–2,9–4 eggs. *Eggs*: Pale greenish blue, plain or faintly spotted with brownish; measure (36) 25,7 × 19 (24,2–27,2 × 17,9–19,8). *Incubation*: Unrecorded. *Nestling*: Unrecorded.

769 (745)   Redwinged Starling   Plate 63
Rooivlerkspreeu
Onychognathus morio

Letomila, Letoemila (SS), Gwitso (Sh), Isomi (X), iNsomi, iSomi (Z), [Rotschwingenstar]

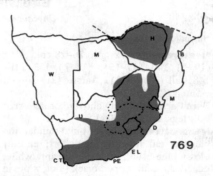

Measurements: Length 27–29 cm; wing (24 ♂) 144–151,5–160, (26 ♀) 138–146–154; tail (50) 115–138; tarsus (50) 31–35; culmen (50) 27–30. Weight (34 ♂) 115–137,9–155 g, (23 ♀) 110–129,2–151 g, (27 unsexed) 91–134,5–148 g.

Bare Parts: Iris dark red; bill, legs and feet black.

Identification: Size large; build slender and elegant; legs short; tail longish. *Male*: Entirely glossy blueblack; primaries rich chestnut, edged black (diagnostic and conspicuous in flight; primaries of Palewinged Starling creamy white, edged pale rusty, tipped black, looking white in flight); eye dark (bright yellow to orange in Palewinged Starling). *Female*: Similar to ♂, but head, upper breast and upper mantle dark grey, streaked blueblack (sexes alike in Palewinged Starling). *Immature*: Similar to adult ♂, but duller (no grey head in immature ♀).

Voice: Various mellow sweet whistled *peeeo, wheo teetoo, piroo titoo taroo* callnotes; song variable mellow whistles, *wheeo peetu, whirripeetu teeooo*, etc.; harsh jarring *skharrr* alarm note.

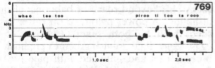

Distribution: S Africa to Malawi; in s Africa confined mainly to moister e parts of S Africa, Orange River to below Upington, w Swaziland and e Transvaal escarpment; also most of Zimbabwe and w Mozambique; overlaps with Palewinged Starling at edge of Karoo.

Status: Common to abundant resident; disperses widely after breeding.

Habitat: Mountains, cliffs, gorges, rocky hills, buildings (rural and urban); after breeding also inhabits coastal bush.

Habits: In pairs when breeding; otherwise more or less gregarious in flocks of a few birds to many hundreds or even up to 3 000; sometimes associates with Palewinged Starlings. Forages arboreally or on ground; moves with bounding hops on relatively short legs (does not walk); also perches on backs of Klipspringers *Oreotragus oreotragus* and cows, probing ears and under tail to search for ectoparasites; perches on sheep as lookout only, not for ectoparasites. Flight fast and direct; clings agilely to cliff faces or vertical walls. Members of flock maintain contact with whistled callnotes. Highly aggressive near nest, often divebombing carnivores and man.

Food: Fruit, insects, ticks, millipedes, lizards, aloe nectar.

Breeding: *Season*: October to March in Cape, October to February in Natal, September to February in Transvaal, September to March (mainly October-November) in Zimbabwe; usually 2 broods/season. *Nest*: Bowl of mud bound with plant fibres, plugged in centre with coarser material and neatly lined with hair, pine needles, roots or *Casuarina* stems; on ledge or in hole or crevice of cliff, cave, building or mineshaft, usually under overhang; sometimes also at base of palm frond; built by both sexes in about 9 days. *Clutch*: (75) 2–3,1–4 eggs (usually 3, rarely 5). *Eggs*: Bright light blue-green, sparingly spotted with rusty red; measure (138) 33,8 × 23,2 (21,8–38,6 × 20,3–28,5). *Incubation*: (14) 12,5–16–23 days by ♀ only. *Nestling*: (14) 22–26–28 days; fed by both parents.

Ref. Broekhuysen, G.J. 1951. *Ostrich* 22:6–16.
　Craig, A. 1983. *Ibis* 346–352.
　Rowan, M.K. 1955. *Ibis* 97:663–705.

770 (744)　Palewinged Starling　Plate 63
Bleekvlerkspreeu
Onychognathus nabouroup

Ndjundju (K), [Bergstar]

Measurements: Length 26–28 cm; wing (17 ♂) 140–145–154, (14 ♀) 133–141–148; tail (21) 98–112; tarsus (21) 30–33; culmen (21) 21–26.

Bare Parts: Iris light yellow to orange-red; bill, legs and feet black.

Identification: Size large; build slender and elegant; tail longish; legs short; entirely glossy blue-black; primaries creamy white, edged chestnut, tipped black (look white in flight, rusty when folded; diagnostic and conspicuous in flight; primaries rich chestnut in Redwinged Starling); eye yellow (diagnostic; dark brown in Redwinged Starling); sexes alike (♀ Redwinged Starling has grey head). *Immature*: Duller than adult.

Voice: Song sustained churring, chirruping and twittering notes (not mellow and musical as in Redwinged Starling; more like song of Glossy Starling); harsh alarm note.

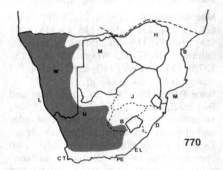

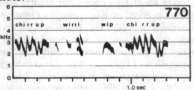

Distribution: Dry western S Africa to Namibia and arid sw Angola.

Status: Locally common resident.

Habitat: Cliffs, gorges, rocky hills and mountains in arid to semi-arid country, mostly between 100-mm and 300-mm isohyets.

Habits: Gregarious even when breeding; nonbreeding flocks bigger; sometimes associates with Redwinged Starlings. Forages arboreally or on ground, hopping with big strides (does not walk); perches on Klipspringers *Oreotragus oreotragus* (and occasionally other mammals) to search for ectoparasites. Flies high to water, usually morning and evening; flight fast and direct with alternating wingbeats and short glides with closed wings. Usually shy, but becomes tame at picnic sites.

Food: Insects, ticks, fruit, table scraps (such as cheese).

Breeding: *Season*: September to April (variable according to rains). *Nest*: Bowl of grass, lined with fine rootlets and horsehair; usually in deep vertical crevice of rocky cliff beyond reach of baboons; also in hollow in power pylon, or on rafter of shed; built by both sexes. *Clutch*: 2–5 eggs. *Eggs*: Pale greyish green to greenish blue, dotted and smudged with pale redbrown; measure (18) 31,4 × 21,7 (29,2–35,2 × 20,7–23). *Incubation*: Unrecorded; probably by ♀ only. *Nestling*: Unrecorded.

Ref. Brooke, R.K. 1968. *Bull. Brit. Orn. Club* 88:113–116.
　Craig, A. 1983. *Ibis* 125:346–352.

26:22. Family 84 BUPHAGIDAE—OXPECKERS

Small to medium. Bill stout and deep, yellow or red, medium length, slightly hooked at tip, arched on culmen, laterally flattened; legs short and stout; feet strong, toes longish, claws sharply curved and pointed; wings long, pointed; tail moderately long, stiff, used as support when perched on side of large mammal; plumage olive brown, paler below and on rump; sexes alike; inhabit savanna and bushveld where they spend most of their time on large game mammals (hence sharp curved claws); food ectoparasitic arthropods (ticks, insects), loose skin and wound tissue of host mammal; gregarious; breed solitarily, sometimes with helpers; nest a pad of mammalian hair, grass and feathers in hole in tree, bank or building; eggs 2–3, white, pale pink or blue, spotted; chick sparsely downy at hatching; parental care by both sexes. Distribution Africa S of Sahara; two species, both in s Africa.

Ref. Stutterheim, I.M. & Panagis, K. 1985. *S. Afr. J. Zool.* 20:10–14; 237–240.

---

771 (747)   **Yellowbilled Oxpecker**   **Plate 63**
                         Geelbekrenostervoël
                            Buphagus africanus

Kamugcara (K), Tsande (Sh), iHlalankomo, iHla-lanyathi (Z), [Gelbschnabel-Madenhacker]

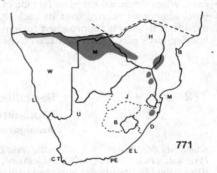

771

Measurements: Length 22–23 cm; wing (22) 128,5–131,1–136; tail (66) 88–105; tarsus (66) 20–23; culmen (66) 14–18.

Bare Parts: Iris orange or scarlet; bill yellow basally, red apically; mouth blood red; eyering yellow; legs and feet brown.

Identification: About size of Plumcoloured Starling; build slender; tail rather pointed; upperparts, head and throat brown, shading to paler yellowish buff on rump and rest of underparts (pale rump diagnostic; Redbilled Oxpecker almost uniform brown above); wings and tail dark brown; bill heavy, basal half yellow, expanded into broad flanges on either side of lower jaw (diagnostic; no such expansion in red bill of Redbilled Oxpecker), tip red. *Immature:* Darker brown on throat than adult; finely barred with black above and on throat and breast; eye brown; bill dusky or yellowish; legs and feet light blue-grey; tail short.

Voice: Hissing cackling *kriss, kriss*.

Distribution: Savannas of Africa S of Sahara; in s Africa confined to patches in e Transvaal (Kruger National Park), s and w Zimbabwe, n Botswana and n Namibia; formerly also as far S as Zululand; reintroduced to Hluhluwe Game Reserve, Zululand. Restricted mainly to larger game reserves.

Status: Common in Caprivi (about 61% of oxpecker population, Redbilled Oxpecker about 39%); in Zimbabwe common only in Hwange and Chizarira National Parks and w Matetsi in NW, and in Gonarezhou National Park in SE; successfully reintroduced into Matobo National Park; elsewhere uncommon to rare. Numbers declining over entire s African range because of game eradication and reduction of ticks by cattle dipping. Reintroduced into Umfolozi-Hluhluwe Game Reserve Complex, Natal, 1986. Listed as "Extinct" in

South Africa (RDB), but naturally re-established in Kruger National Park.

Habitat: Savanna and woodland, mainly along watercourses and on floodplains in Caprivi.

Habits: Usually in small groups of 4–6 birds, even when breeding, but as many as 20 birds in winter. Most important hosts are Giraffe and Cape Buffalo; in Matobo National Park, Zimbabwe, forages in descending order of preference on Cape Buffalo, White Rhinoceros, Eland, Burchell's Zebra, Giraffe, Sable, Wildebeest, Impala and Warthog; also forages on Kudu, Roan Antelope and Hippopotamus; domestic stock in descending order of preference include donkeys, horses and cattle; goats seldom used; clambers about host using tail as prop, gleaning ectoparasites. When disturbed keeps on far side of host, sometimes peering over its back at intruder; if closely approached neighbouring birds may gather on back of one

mammal, bills raised, before flying off in flock with cackling notes. Roosts on host mammals, mainly Giraffes, up to 9 birds/mammal; less often on Kudu and Roan Antelope.

Food: Ticks and other ectoparasitic invertebrates; also wound tissue and fluids of host mammal. Prey plucked with bill (Redbilled Oxpecker uses scissorlike bill action).

Breeding: *Season:* October to March in Zimbabwe. *Nest:* Pad of grass, feathers and mammal hair (taken from backs of live hosts) in natural hole in tree. *Clutch:* 2–3 eggs. *Eggs:* White or pale bluish, plain or spotted with shades of brown and grey; measure (5) 24,8 × 17 (23,4–26,6 × 16,6–18); weigh (3) about 45 g. *Incubation:* At least 13 days. *Nestling:* About 25 days; fed by both parents and 1–2 adult helpers.

Ref. Mundy, P.J. & Cook, A.W. 1975. *Ibis* 117:504–506.

---

772 (748) **Redbilled Oxpecker** **Plate 63**
Rooibekrenostervoël
Buphagus erythrorhynchus

Kamugcara (K), Tsande (Sh), Ndzandza, Yanda (Ts), Kala (Tw), Ihlalanyathi (X), iHlalankomo, iHlalanyathi (Z), [Rotschnabel-Madenhacker]

Measurements: Length 20–22 cm; wing (61 ♂) 110–119–128, (55 ♀) 107–115,8–121; tail (59 ♂) 87–96,8–107, (53 ♀) 84–94,6–103; tarsus (60 ♂) 20,2–22,2–26,8, (55 ♀) 20,5–22,1–26,6; culmen (61 ♂) 16–17,4–18,8, (55 ♀) 15,8–17,2–18,6. Weight (61 ♂) 45–51–56 g, (55 ♀) 42–50,5–59 g.

Bare Parts: Iris yellow to red; eyering bright yellow; bill and inside of mouth scarlet; legs and feet dark brown.

Identification: About size of Plumcoloured Starling; build slender; tail somewhat pointed; upperparts, throat and breast brown, rump slightly paler (rump much paler in Yellowbilled Oxpecker), shading to creamy buff on rest of underparts; bill red (diagnostic; base yellow in Yellowbilled Oxpecker). *Immature:* More sooty

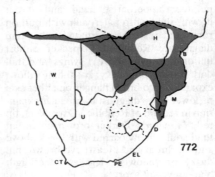

brown than adult; bill dark olive, yellowish in centre, later turning all dark; bill reddens at 4 months, fully red at 7 months; eye brown; adult plumage acquired at 6 months.

Voice: Sharp hissing *kssss, kssss* (similar to voice of Yellowbilled Oxpecker); staccato *tsik tsik* sounding like twittering chorus in flight.

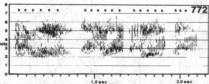

Distribution: S Africa to NE Africa; in s Africa confined mainly to NE from Zululand to n Transvaal, n Botswana, Zimbabwe and Mozambique; formerly also e Orange Free State, Lesotho lowlands and e Cape to Grahamstown.
Status: Common resident in and around larger game reserves; rare to absent elsewhere.
Habitat: Savanna and bushveld.
Habits: Usually in small groups of 2–6 birds. Forages mainly on Giraffe when available; also on Kudu, Sable, Hippopotamus, Nyala, Impala, Cape Buffalo, Eland, Burchell's Zebra, rhinoceroses and large domestic stock (cattle, horses, donkeys, pigs); clambers about host mammal, using tail as prop, gleaning ectoparasites. Moves to far side of host when disturbed, peering over its back and finally flying off with chittering calls. Flight fast, direct, slightly undulating. Roosts by preference in palm trees; less often on larger game mammals (not Cape Buffalo) at night; also roosts communally in reedbeds.
Food: Ticks, horseflies and other ectoparasitic invertebrates; also wound tissue and dry skin flakes of host. Uses scissorlike bill action (Yellowbilled Oxpecker tends to pluck at prey).
Breeding: *Season*: September to February in Natal, October to March in Transvaal, November to December in Zimbabwe; may raise 3 broods/season. *Nest*: Cupshaped pad of hair (over 90% of material) on foundation of dung, grass and rootlets; in natural hole in tree, 1,2–8,1–15 m above ground (mean of 43 nests). *Clutch*: (85) 1–2,7–5 eggs (usually 2–3). *Eggs*: Pinkish white, finely and heavily speckled with red-brown, purple and lilac; measure (47) 24 × 17,2 (22,5–26,5 × 15,8–18,6). *Incubation*: (6) 12–12,6–13 days by both sexes; ♀ incubates alone at night. *Nestling*: (4) 26–30 days; fed by both parents and up to 3 helpers.

Ref. Grobler, J.H. 1980. *Koedoe* 23:89–97.
Stutterheim, C.J. 1977. *Ostrich* 48:119–120; 1980a. *Ostrich* 51:107–112; 1980b. *Lammergeyer* 30:21–25; 1981. *Koedoe* 24:99–107; 1982. *Ostrich* 53:79–90.

26:23. Family 85 PROMEROPIDAE—SUGARBIRDS

Small to medium (not including long tail). Bill long, slender, decurved; legs medium, strong, toes medium, strong; wings short, rounded; tail long to very long, flexible, graduated; plumage brown above, dull white below with brown or rufous on chest, undertail coverts yellow; sexes similar, but female's tail shorter; arboreal in fynbos (macchia or Cape flora) with proteas; food arthropods, nectar; solitary; nest built by female, a bowl of plant material, usually in protea bush; eggs 2, cream or rufous, spotted; chick sparsely downy at hatching; incubation by female only; young fed by both sexes. Distribution s Africa; two species. Formerly placed with the Australasian honeyeaters in the family Meliphagidae, then considered a separate family with possible affinities with the starlings (Sturnidae), but now more likely to be related to the thrushes (Turdidae) or to the sunbirds (Nectariniidae).

Ref. Olson, S.L. & Ames, P.L. 1984. *Ostrich* 55:213–218.
Sibley, C.G. & Ahlquist, J.E. 1974. *Ostrich* 45:22–30.
Skead, C.J. 1967. *The sunbirds of southern Africa; also the sugarbirds, the white-eyes and the Spotted Creeper*. Cape Town: Balkema.

773 (749)   **Cape Sugarbird**   **Plate 63**
Kaapse Suikervoël
Promerops cafer

[Kap-Hongifresser]
Measurements: Length ♂ 37–44 cm, ♀ 24–29 cm; wing (67 ♂) 86–93,5–101, (46 ♀) 77–82,7–84; tail (59 ♂) 121–258,9–360, (40 ♀) 85–124,8–188; tarsus (11) 21–24; culmen (52 ♂) 28,3–31,4–

34,7, (40 ♀) 28–30,1–32,2. Weight (57 ♂) 30,5–37,5–43,5, (46 ♀) 26–32,2–39 g.

Bare Parts: Iris dark brown; bill, legs and feet black.

Identification: About size of Blackeyed Bulbul, but with long bill and tail; upperparts, face and breast brown, streaked darker above, more rufous on breast (but not as strongly russet as breast of Gurney's Sugarbird which also has russet crown); malar stripe brown, bordered above by white stripe and below by white throat; belly white, flanks streaked dusky; undertail bright yellow; tail long (♀) or very long (♂), strongly graduated, brown, pliable (much longer than in Gurney's Sugarbird); tail of moulting male may be as short as tail of female in October and November. *Immature*: Lacks dark flank streaks; undertail pale brown; colour of breast and belly not sharply defined; bill pinkish at base; gape bright yellow for first year; tail relatively short.

Voice: Song of ♂ somewhat drongolike grating chirping, chipping and twanging notes in fairly sustained series; sustained *klak-klak-klak*, and various hissing and more musical callnotes; rasping alarm call, like rusty metal hinge; also tearing alarm note at higher intensity.

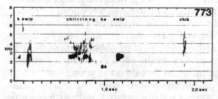

Distribution: Extreme sw and s Cape from Cedarberg to Buffalo River near East London.

Status: Common resident.

Habitat: Fynbos from sea level to mountains, especially where dominated by *Protea* species.

Habits: Solitary or in pairs when breeding; otherwise sometimes in groups of up to about 12 birds at good food supply; may fly up to 50 km for food. Male often perches on top of conspicuous protea bush to advertise territory by song, wing-flicking displays and chasing; long

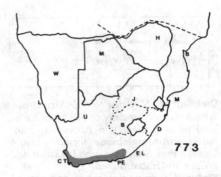

tail blows about in wind; in display ♂ flies up from perch, beats wings rapidly and jerks body to flick tail repeatedly over back; quivers wings in threat display. Forages arboreally; probes protea inflorescences and flowers of other plants for nectar and insects; hovers or perches while probing; also hawks insects in flight. Flight fast and direct, tail streaming out behind.

Food: Insects, spiders, nectar (mainly of proteas; also of heaths, *Tecomaria, Watsonia, Kniphofia, Agave* and *Eucalyptus*).

Breeding: *Season*: February to August (mainly April-May in sw Cape, June-July in e Cape). *Nest*: Untidy cup of twigs, grass, bracken, rootlets and pine needles, neatly lined with brown protea down held in place with fine plant fibres; internal diameter (77) 5,5–7–8 cm; depth (77) 4–6–7 cm; height above ground (91) 0,3–1,2–2,4 m; in fork or tangled branches in interior of protea or other bush or tree with large leaves and dense foliage; built by ♀ only in 5–10 days. *Clutch*: (80) 2 eggs (rarely only 1). *Eggs*: Cream, buff or pinkish white, blotched, spotted and scrawled with grey, brown, purplish black and chocolate often concentrated at thick end; measure (100) 23,4 × 17,5 (21,4–25 × 16,5–18,7). *Incubation*: (11) 17 days by ♀ only. *Nestling*: (6) 17–19–21 days; fed by both parents.

Ref. Broekhuysen, G.J. 1959. *Ostrich Suppl.* 3:180–221.

Burger, A.E., Siegfried, W.R. & Frost, P.G.H. 1976. *Zool. afr.* 11:127–158.

Mostert, D.P., Siegfried, W.R. & Louw, G.N. 1980. *S. Afr. J. Sci.* 76:409–412.

774 (750)

Gurney's Sugarbird
Rooiborssuikervoël
Promerops gurneyi

Plate 63

[Gurneys Honigfresser]

Measurements: Length ♂ 25–29 cm, ♀ about 23 cm; wing (62 ♂) 86–94,5–101, (80 ♀) 79–87,4–96; tail (62 ♂) 94–149,7–186, (80 ♀) 88–111,6–136; tarsus (62 ♂) 19,4–21,7–23,8, (80 ♀) 17–20,8–25,3; culmen (62 ♂) 25,8–28,9–31,9, (80 ♀) 25,2–27,7–30,6. Weight (62 ♂) 30–37–42,8 g, (81 ♀) 26,5–32,8–43 g.

Bare Parts: Iris dark brown; bill, legs and feet black.

Identification: About size of Blackeyed Bulbul, but bill and tail long; crown and breast deep russet (diagnostic); back and malar stripe brown; cheek stripe, throat and belly white; belly and back streaked dusky; undertail bright yellow; tail long, graduated, pliable, dark brown; secondary remiges edged white; in hand adult ♂ shows bulge on 6th primary remex measuring 13,1–15,9 mm maximum width; bulge in adult ♀ measures 9,9–12 mm. *Immature*: Secondary remiges edged brownish; breast greenish russet; undertail greenish yellow; gape yellow for few months after leaving nest.

Voice: Rapid high-pitched jumble of twittery and twanging notes, less grating than those of Cape Sugarbird; tearing threat call; harsh *sskirrit* alarm note.

774

Habits: Usually solitary or in pairs; sometimes in small loose groups at good food source. Probes all kinds of tubular flowers for nectar and insects; also hawks insects in flight. Often perches on top of bush or tree. Flight fast with tail streaming out behind; does flip-jump on alighting or leaving perch; ♂ displays by flying steeply up from perch and suddenly diving down almost vertically; also raises wings to show white underside of remiges. Bulge on 6th primary remex makes loud *frrrt* noise in flight. Flicks wings jerkily in alarm.

Food: Insects, nectar (of proteas, aloes, *Watsonia, Eucalyptus* and other flowers).

Distribution: Eastern Cape, s and inland Natal, Drakensberg escarpment to n Transvaal, Zoutpansberg and Waterberg; also e highlands of Zimbabwe and adjacent Mozambique.

Status: Locally common resident; uncommon in Zoutpansberg and Waterberg; local movements determined by flowering plants; some altitudinal movement in winter.

Habitat: Montane scrub with *Protea* and *Aloe*; also gardens and *Protea* nurseries.

Breeding: *Season*: June to February in Natal, November to February in Transvaal, July, October and April in Zimbabwe. *Nest*: Neat shallow cup of stems, twigs, grass and bark fibres, compactly lined with brown protea fluff and fine grass; inside diameter 5,8 cm, depth 4,4 cm; in multiple fork or old inflorescence of protea, usually well hidden among leaves; 1–6 m above ground. *Clutch*: (17) 1–1,6–2 eggs (usually 2). *Eggs*: Cream, buff or pale brownish, spotted, scrawled, blotched and clouded with browns and purple; measure (16) 22,5 × 16,7 (20,9–23,4 × 16–17,5). *Incubation*:

Unrecorded; by ♀ only. *Nestling*: Unrecorded; fed by both parents. *Ref.* Skead, D.M. 1963. *Ostrich* 34:160–164.

26:24. Family 86 NECTARINIIDAE—SUNBIRDS AND SPIDERHUNTERS

Small (not including long tail of some species). Bill long, slender, decurved; legs medium, slender; toes medium to moderately long, strong; wings short, rounded; tail usually medium, square, sometimes long or with central rectrices very long; tail short in Malaysian spiderhunters (*Arachnothera*); plumage often brightly coloured with metallic green or bronzy reflections especially in male, most females dull without iridescence; sexes usually different; males of most species have yellow, red or orange pectoral tufts used in display, but otherwise concealed; arboreal in forest, woodland, savanna or fynbos (macchia or Cape flora); food arthropods, nectar, some fruit; usually solitary; nest a purse of plant material bound with spider web, with side entrance, suspended from end of branch or creeper; eggs 1–3, white, grey or greenish, speckled; chick naked at hatching; incubation by female alone; young fed by both sexes or by female only. Distribution Africa S of Sahara, Madagascar, Middle East, tropical Asia to Philippines, n Australia; 118 species; 21 species in s Africa.

Ref. Hanmer, D.B. 1981. *Ostrich* 52:156–178.
   Skead, C.J. 1967. *The sunbirds of southern Africa*. Cape Town: Balkema.

775 (751)   **Malachite Sunbird**   **Plate 64**
Jangroentjie
Nectarinia famosa

Tale-tale, Tala-pinyane (SS), Ingcungcu Eluhlaza (X), iNcwincwi, iNcuncu, uHlazazana (Z), [Malachitnektarvogel]

Measurements: Length ♂ 24–26 cm (including long tail), ♀ about 15 cm; wing (19 ♂, S Africa) 76–77,7–86, (20 ♂, Zimbabwe) 73–76,3–80,5, (4 ♀, S Africa) 66–69,5–72, (10 ♀, Zimbabwe) 61,5–70,2–76; tail (longest rectrices, 17 ♂, S Africa) 118–142, (5 ♂, Zimbabwe) 124–142,3–158, (basic rectrices, 17 ♂, Zimbabwe) 49–54,2–60, (11 ♀) 38,5–47,7–55; tarsus (37) 15,5–17,4–19; culmen (39) 29,5–32,2–34,5. Weight (24 ♂, S Africa) 15,5–17–21 g, (27 ♀, S Africa) 12–14,7–16,2 g, (24 ♂, Zimbabwe) 13–15,5–18,7 g, (14 ♀, Zimbabwe) 11,5–13,9–17,5 g.

Bare Parts: Iris brown; bill, legs and feet black.

Identification: Size large. *Breeding ♂*: Entirely bright metallic green, with coppery sheen on back (Bronze Sunbird bronze and amethyst, much darker); pectoral tufts bright yellow; central rectrices greatly elongated. *Nonbreeding ♂*: Mostly

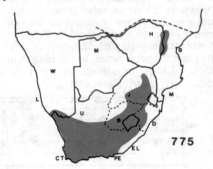

similar to ♀, sometimes with few metallic green feathers; long central rectrices present or absent; large size and voice diagnostic. *Female*: Above yellowish grey; malar stripe and cheek yellow (diagnostic in combination with large size); below yellowish grey, shading to whitish on belly; tail dusky, edged white (conspicuous in flight); no long central rectrices. *Immature*: Similar to adult ♀.

Voice: Loud piping *tsip-tsip* callnote, sometimes of 3 or more syllables; song usually introduced by piping callnotes, followed by rapid high-pitched *tseepy-tseepy-tseepy* and other twittering notes; when not breeding may sing quietly for long periods.

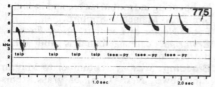

Distribution: S Africa to Ethiopia; in s Africa throughout most of Cape Province, extreme s Namibia, Lesotho, inland Natal, s and e Orange Free State, w Swaziland, Transvaal; also e highlands of Zimbabwe and adjacent Mozambique.

Status: Common; resident in lower-lying areas; seasonal migrant from higher regions in winter, especially from Lesotho highlands to e Orange Free State and Natal midlands.

Habitat: Variable; scrubby hillsides in mountainous country, alpine grasslands, succulent arid steppe of Namaqualand, riverine thornbush, gardens, parks, exotic plantations (especially when *Eucalyptus* in flower).

Habits: Usually solitary; in pairs when breeding. Probes flowers for nectar; hawks insects in flight with snap of bill. Active, conspicuous and aggressive, often chasing conspecifics and other sunbirds;

flight dashing, long rectrices of ♂ streaming or whipping up and down. ♂ displays to ♀ with raised tail and shivering wings. ♂ sings from inside bush, or calls loudly from top of conspicuous perch.

Food: Nectar (especially of *Leonotis*, aloes, proteas, *Kniphofia*, *Watsonia*), insects, spiders.

Breeding: *Season*: May to November in sw Cape, August to January in e Cape, October to April (mainly December-January) in Natal, November to January in Lesotho, August to January in Orange Free State, August to December in Transvaal, August to March in Zimbabwe. *Nest*: Oval of grass, leaves, twigs, fronds and roots, bound with spider web, with side-top entrance; lined with fine grass, hair, plant down and feathers; entrance usually with porch; overall height about 14 cm; suspended from grasstuft, hanging branch, upright fork or between upright weeds; sometimes in mass of driftwood or dead branches; often overhanging stream, gully or cliff face; 15 cm to over 20 m above ground (usually 1–2 m); built by ♀ only in 7–21 days. *Clutch*: (62) 1–1,9–3 eggs (usually 2). *Eggs*: Pale brownish, cream, greenish buff or whitish, mottled, clouded and spotted with shades of brown and grey; measure (120) 19,6 × 13,6 (17,9–22,2 × 12,8–15). *Incubation*: 13 days by ♀ only. *Nestling*: 18–21 days; fed by both parents; young return to roost in nest for 1–2 nights after initial departure.

776 (752)   **Bronze Sunbird**   **Plate 64**
Bronssuikerbekkie
Nectarinia kilimensis

[Bronzenektarvogel]
Measurements: Length ♂ about 23 cm (including long rectrices), ♀ about 15 cm; wing (17 ♂) 70–71,9–75, (23 ♀) 63–65,8–69; tail (longest rectrices, 14 ♂) 102–115,9–122, (basic rectrices, 11 ♂) 54,5–60,5–67, (longest rectrices, 12 ♀) 55–58,7–63, (basic rectrices, 15 ♀) 48–53,9–63; tarsus (44) 16–18,4–20,5; culmen (10 ♂) 27,5–29, (4 ♀) 24,5–26, (47 unsexed) 25,5–29,1–31,5. Weight (20 ♂) 13,5–15,4–18 g, (21 ♀) 11,7–13,9–16,1 g.
Bare Parts: Iris dark brown; bill, legs and feet black.

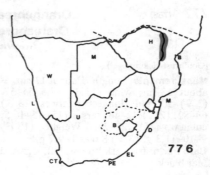

776

BRONZE SUNBIRD

Identification: Size large; similar to Malachite Sunbird. *Male*: Entirely metallic bronze and amethyst (not green like Malachite Sunbird), looks blackish in some lights; central rectrices elongate; no eclipse plumage. *Female*: Above olive grey; eyebrow whitish; below greyish yellow (brighter than ♀ Malachite Sunbird), streaked dusky on throat and flanks (diagnostic; ♀ Malachite Sunbird not streaked). *Immature*: Similar to adult ♀ but more olive above and on breast; throat mottled grey and white; not streaked below.

Voice: Loud pleasant piping *tseeptseweep, cheep, cheep*; both sexes sing, but ♂ is louder; loud *chee-wit-chee chee wit wit* threat call to conspecific.

Male highly aggressive towards conspecifics and other sunbirds, chasing them from territory; active throughout daylight, even in midday heat. Probes flowers for nectar; forages for arthropods on leaves, by hovering in front of webs, and in flight. Similar to Malachite Sunbird.

Food: Nectar of *Leonotis, Aloe, Fuchsia, Erythrina*, cannas, bananas and other flowers; insects, spiders.

Breeding: *Season*: September to May in Zimbabwe. *Nest*: Oval of grass stems and inflorescences, lichen and bark shreds bound with spider web, with porch over side-top entrance; overall length 11,5 cm; internal diameter 4,5–5 cm; entrance 3–3,5 cm diameter; depth from entrance lip to floor 5 cm;

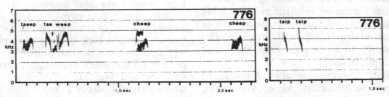

Distribution: Zimbabwe to Kenya; in s Africa confined to e highlands of Zimbabwe and adjacent Mozambique.

Status: Common; largely resident; some seasonal movement dictated by flowering plants.

Habitat: Edges of montane evergreen forest, dense shrubby and herbaceous mountainsides.

Habits: Usually solitary; sometimes in pairs when breeding; ♂ displays to ♀ with wings drooped and tail raised at angle.

lined with plant down up to 2,5 cm thick in floor; 3–12 m above ground at end of branch of bush or tree, or between reeds; often over gully; built by ♀ only in 4,5 days, sometimes up to 14 days or more. *Clutch*: Usually 1 egg, rarely 2. *Eggs*: Whitish or pale bluish cream, spotted and blotched with grey and shades of brown; measure (1) 20 × 13,5. *Incubation*: 14–15 days by ♀ only. *Nestling*: 16 days; fed by ♀ only.

Ref. Löhrl, H. 1979. *J. Orn.* 120:441–450.

777 (753) **Orangebreasted Sunbird** **Plate 64**
Oranjeborssuikerbekkie
Nectarinia violacea

[Goldbrust-Nektarvogel]

Measurements: Length ♂ about 17 cm, ♀ about 13 cm; wing (13 ♂) 52,5–54–57, (2 ♀) 50; tail (longest rectrices, 13 ♂) 68–82, (2 ♀) 42–46; tarsus (15) 15–16,5; culmen (15) 20–23. Weight (15 ♂) 9–10–11,3 g, (3 ♀) 8,6–9,1–9,7 g.

Bare Parts: Iris dark brown; bill, legs and feet black.

Identification: Size small. *Male*: Head, throat and mantle bright metallic green; rest of upperparts olive green; upper breast metallic violet; lower breast bright deep orange, shading to lighter orange and yellow on belly; tail blackish, central rectrices elongated. *Female*: Above olive greenish grey; below olive yellowish, paler on belly (yellower than ♀ Lesser Doublecollared Sunbird; best separated by voice); wings and tail blackish. *Immature*: Similar to adult ♀.

Voice: Tinny twangy sibilant *sshraynk* or *sskrang* callnote, often repeated 2 or more times; ♂ calls sharp *ke-ke-ke-ke* when chasing ♀; song subdued rapid warble lasting up to 60 seconds, interspersed with characteristic twangy callnotes.

Distribution: Western and sw Cape from near Vanrhynsdorp to e Cape around Port Elizabeth; vagrant to East London.

Status: Common resident.

Habitat: Fynbos with *Protea* and *Erica* in winter-rainfall region, from sea level to bleak mountain slopes.

Habits: Solitary or in pairs when breeding; otherwise gregarious in loose flocks of up to 100 birds at good food supply. At rest often perches with tail drooped, bill slightly raised and plumage fluffed. Aggressive towards conspecifics and other birds. ♂ has flitting and hovering display flight. Commonly bathes in dew on leaves. Hawks prey in flight.

Food: Nectar (especially of *Erica* spp.), insects, spiders.

Breeding: *Season*: February to November (mainly May to August); rarely January. *Nest*: Rounded oval of rootlets, fine leafy twigs and grass, bound with spider web; lined with brown protea fluff and other

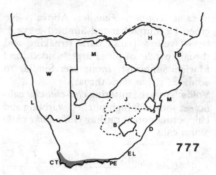

777

plant down; side-top entrance lacks porch; external height 9–12 cm, internal height 5–8 cm; entrance diameter (97) 2,5–3,6–5 cm; usually less than 1 m above ground in low shrub or bush (mainly proteaceous); sometimes as high as 10 m in tree; built by ♀ alone in 5–18 days. *Clutch*: (250) 1–1,7–2 eggs (usually 2). *Eggs*: White, cream or greyish green, clouded, spotted, lined and blotched with shades of brown and grey; measure (122) 16,5 × 12,4   (14,9–18,2 × 10,8–13,5). *Incubation*: 14–15 days by ♀ only. *Nestling*: (13) 15–19–22 days; fed by both parents, mostly by ♀; young return to nest for 5–15 days after initial departure.

Ref. Broekhuysen, G.J. 1963. *Ostrich* 34:187–234.

778 (754) Coppery Sunbird — Plate 64
Kopersuikerbekkie
Nectarinia cuprea

Kalyambya (K), Tsodzo, Dzonya (Sh), [Kupfer-nektarvogel]

Measurements: Length 11–12 cm; wing (66 ♂) 61–64,3–67, (45 ♀) 56–58,8–61; tail (7 ♂) 42,5–47,3–51, (7 ♀) 36–40,8–45; tarsus (7 ♂) 15,5–16,3–18,5, (7 ♀) 15–16,5–18,5; culmen (7 ♂) 19–19,5–20, (7 ♀) 18–19,4–21. Weight (70 ♂) 8,4–9,8–11,4 g, (48 ♀) 7,3–8,8–10,2 g.

Bare Parts: Iris dark brown; bill, legs and feet black.

Identification: Size small. *Breeding* ♂: Upperparts, throat and breast metallic golden copper with purple and red reflections, more purplish on lower back (♂ Purplebanded and Marico Sunbirds metallic green with metallic purple breastband);

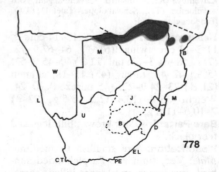

778

rest of underparts, wings and tail black. *Nonbreeding* ♂: Similar to ♀, but wings and tail black; wing coverts and rump m₌tallic copper. *Female*: Above olive green (♀ Purplebanded Sunbird greyer); below yellow (lacks dark streaking and throat patch of ♀ Purplebanded and Marico Sunbirds). *Immature*: Similar to adult ♀; ♂ has dark throat.

Voice: Hoarse stuttering *chit-chit-chit* call-notes; song soft high-pitched warbling and chippering notes; rattling *chiki-chiki-chiki* alarm calls.

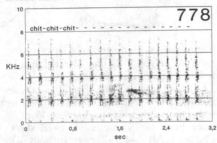

Distribution: Africa S of Sahara; in s Africa confined to n and ne Zimbabwe and Zambezi Valley into Mozambique and Caprivi.

Status: Uncommon; mainly breeding migrant, September to March; few winter records in Zambezi Valley.

Habitat: Edge of riverine forest; sometimes also woodland and montane regions with bush and woodland in marshy ground; also parks, gardens.

Habits: Solitary or in pairs when breeding; otherwise in small groups. Roosts communally in trees; may join mixed bird parties. Flits jerkily from bush to bush while foraging; punctures flowers at base of tube; hawks prey in flight.

Food: Nectar (including that of *Eucalyptus, Jacaranda* and *Bougainvillea*), insects, spiders.

Breeding: *Season*: November to March in Zimbabwe. *Nest*: Oval of fibres, grass, stems, lichen, leaf litter, cocoons and bark, bound with spider web, lined with plant down; side-top entrance has projecting porch; tail of nest material often hangs below nest; external height 13–14 cm; entrance diameter 3–5 cm; 0,6–3 m above ground, suspended from drooping branch of small tree or shrub; built by ♀ only. *Clutch*: 2 eggs. *Eggs*: Cream, buff or pale greyish, streaked, spotted and clouded with blackish and shades of brown; measure (15) 16,6 × 11,7 (15,6–17,6 × 11–12,2). *Incubation*: 13,5–14 days by ♀ only. *Nestling*: 15–16 days; fed by both parents.

Ref. Howells, W.W. 1971. *Ostrich* 42:99–109.
Manson, C. & Manson, A. 1981. *Honeyguide* 105:9–12.

779 (755) Marico Sunbird   Plate 64
Maricosuikerbekkie
Nectarinia mariquensis

Kalyambya (K), Ntsotsotso, Xidyamhangani, Xinwavulombe (Ts), Senwabolope, Talêtalê (Tw), [Bindennektarvogel]

Measurements: Length ♂ 13–14 cm, ♀ 11,5–13 cm; wing (61 ♂) 64–67,9–72, (7 ♀) 58–61,3–63; tail (23 ♂) 40–45,9–52, (5 ♀) 42–43; tarsus (45) 15–18; culmen (21 ♂) 23–24,9–27, (45 unsexed) 20–24. Weight (36 ♂) 10,4–12,2–13,5 g, (22 ♀) 7–10,6–11,8 g.

Bare Parts: Iris dark brown; bill, legs and feet black.

Identification: Size smallish to medium. *Male*: Very similar to Purplebanded Sunbird, but larger and longer-billed; somewhat similar to Coppery Sunbird, but greener, with purple breastband; head, breast and upperparts brilliant metallic

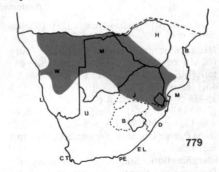

green, shading to peacock blue on rump; broad breastband metallic blue shading to metallic violet; rest of underparts, wings and tail black; no eclipse plumage.

Female: Above olive grey (somewhat paler than ♀ Purplebanded Sunbird); below pale yellow, streaked dusky (slightly darker yellow and more heavily streaked than ♀ Purplebanded Sunbird). *Immature*: Similar to adult ♀; throat blackish in ♂.

Voice: Song loud high-pitched staccato piping *tsip-tsip-tsip*, starting deliberately, then running together in stuttering series, often becoming pleasant rolling warble; song somewhat canarylike but faster and higher-pitched; may imitate other birdcalls; sharp *chip-chip* callnotes.

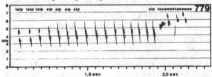

Distribution: S Africa to Ethiopia; in s Africa from Zululand and Swaziland to extreme s Mozambique, Transvaal, sw half of Zimbabwe, most of Botswana and n Namibia (as far S as Hardap Dam).

Status: Common resident; some local movements dictated by flowering plants.

Habitat: *Acacia* savanna, riverine forest, gardens.

Habits: Usually solitary or in pairs; larger numbers gather at good food source, but not in flocks. ♂ typically restless and aggressive towards other sunbirds, but less active than ♂ Purplebanded Sunbird. Probes flowers and gleans arthropods from plants and in flight.

Food: Nectar (of mistletoes, *Leonotis, Aloe, Erythrina, Thevetia, Acacia*, etc.), insects, spiders.

Breeding: *Season*: October to November in Zululand, August to February in Transvaal, September to December in Zimbabwe, July in Mozambique. *Nest*: Oval of plant down reinforced with grass, bark, seeds, resin, fibres and feathers, bound with spider web; side-top entrance has well-built porch; lined with feathers; external height 13 cm; entrance diameter 4 cm; attached to thin branch of tree or shrub (especially thorny species), 2–8 m above ground; usually in centre of canopy; built by ♀ only in up to 12 days. *Clutch*: (5) 2 eggs (rarely 3). *Eggs*: Pale cream, greyish or greenish white, streaked, smeared, scrolled and spotted with black, browns, greys and olive; measure (20) 18,4 × 12,1 (16,8–20 × 11–13,6). *Incubation*: 13,5–14,5 days by ♀ only. *Nestling*: Unrecorded; fed by both parents, mostly by ♀.

---

780 (756)   **Purplebanded Sunbird**   Plate 64
Purperbandsuikerbekkie
Nectarinia bifasciata

Kalyambya (K), Tsodzo, Dzonya (Sh), [Kleiner Bindennektarvogel]

Measurements: Length ♂ 11–12 cm, ♀ 10–11 cm; wing (63 ♂) 52–57,2–62, (10 ♀) 48–51,3–53; tail (63 ♂) 35–39,6–46, (6 ♀) 30–33,3–35; tarsus (14) 12,5–14; culmen (26 ♂) 17–18,4–19,5, (7 ♀) 16,5–19. Weight (73 ♂) 6–7,6–8,9 g, (22 ♀) 6–6,8–8 g.

Bare Parts: Iris dark brown; bill, legs and feet black.

Identification: Size small; similar to Marico Sunbird, but smaller and shorter-billed. *Breeding* ♂: Head, breast and upperparts brilliant metallic green, washed bronzy on head, peacock blue on rump; breastband metallic blue, bordered

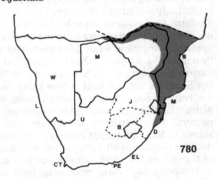

below by metallic violet; rest of underparts, wings and tail black. *Nonbreeding* ♂: Similar to ♀, but wings and tail black;

rump metallic blue-green. *Female*: Above greyish olive (darker than ♀ Marico Sunbird); below yellowish white, streaked dusky (paler yellow, less heavily streaked than ♀ Marico Sunbird); tail black, edged and tipped whitish.

Voice: Characteristic 4-syllabled callnote *tsikit-y-dik*, not repeated in succession; song high-pitched short phrase of deliberate introductory notes, followed by somewhat variable trill, *tsip tsip tsip tsip tsippity tsirrily tsirrily, tseep*, with pauses between each phrase, not sustained as in Marico Sunbird; also trilling buzz *brrrz*.

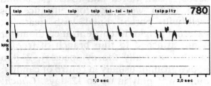

Distribution: S Africa to Gabon and Kenya; in s Africa confined to E and NE from Zululand to Zambezi Valley and Caprivi.

Status: Locally common resident; some nomadic movements; vagrant to s Kruger National Park and to Durban.

Habitat: Edges of riverine forest, thickets in savanna, coastal bush, edges of lowland evergreen forest.

Habits: Usually solitary or in pairs, but numbers gather at favourable food source. Very restless, flitting quickly from flower to flower; also catches prey in flight and by hovering at spider webs under eaves. Aggressive towards other sunbirds.

Food: Nectar (especially of mistletoes, *Syzigium cordatum* and *Mimusops caffra*), insects, spiders.

Breeding: *Season*: October to November in Natal; September to December in Mozambique, September to March in Zimbabwe. *Nest*: Small neat oval of grass, fronds, leaves, wood chips, lichen and plant down, bound with spider web, sometimes with "tail" beneath; lined with feathers and plant down; side-top entrance; external height 10 cm; suspended from projecting branch of tree, from creeper or bamboo; often over watercourse or roadway, 1,2–5 m above ground. *Clutch*: (31) 1–2–3 eggs (usually 2). *Eggs*: Grey, white or buff, spotted, streaked and smeared with grey, purplish brown and black mainly at thick end; measure (47) 15,5 × 10,7 (14,5–18,1 × 10,3–12). *Incubation*: Unrecorded. *Nestling*: Unrecorded; fed by both parents.

THE "DOUBLECOLLARED" SUNBIRDS

The five species of so-called doublecollared sunbirds include Shelley's, Neergaard's, Lesser Doublecollared, Miombo Doublecollared and Greater Doublecollared. They are confusingly similar in appearance but, except for the Greater and Lesser Doublecollared Sunbirds, and possibly Miombo Doublecollared and Shelley's Sunbirds, their ranges do not overlap. It is therefore essential to check the distribution maps before starting to try to identify any member of this group. The males are all brilliant metallic green on head, throat and back; they all have a bright red breast separated from the green throat by a narrow band of metallic blue, but the width of the red varies and can be diagnostic; all but Shelley's Sunbird have a blue rump (actually the upper tail coverts); the colour of the belly (black or grey) in combination with body size, length and curvature of bill, width of red breast, and rump coloration, is helpful in identification. All have yellow pectoral tufts, but these are seldom seen. The males of most species have not been shown to have an eclipse plumage, but some, such as the Lesser Doublecollared, may do. The females of all 5 species are very similar and can be separated only on the length of the bill, and in some cases by voice; it is safest (but not always possible) to see them in company with their more diagnostic males before making a decision about their identification. The species accounts give further details about field characteristics, but they should always be identified with caution.

Ref. Clancey, P.A. & Irwin, M.P.S. 1978. *Durban Mus. Novit.* 11:331–351.

781 (757)

Shelley's Sunbird
Swartpenssuikerbekkie
Nectarinia shelleyi

Plate 77

[Shelleys Nektarvogel]

Measurements: Length 12–13 cm; wing ♂ 61–68, ♀ 56–59; tail 31–43; tarsus 16–17; culmen 18–23.

Bare Parts: Iris dark brown; bill, legs and feet black.

Identification: Size smallish to medium. *Male*: Head, throat and upperparts brilliant metallic green with golden sheen (rump blue in Neergaard's Sunbird); breast brilliant red, bordered above by narrow metallic blue band (breast metallic purple in Marico and Purplebanded Sunbirds); belly, wings and tail black (grey in doublecollared sunbirds). *Female*: Similar to ♀ Marico Sunbird, probably not safely separable in field, but smaller, greyer above, less yellow below. *Immature*: Similar to adult ♀, but throat blackish.

Voice: Song nasal *chibee-cheeu-cheeu*; call-note distinctive rapid diminuendo chattering *di-di-di-di*; high-pitched *seep seep*.

Distribution: Zambezi River to Tanzania; although reported from Beira and Zambezi River, not certainly identified S of Zambezi, but could occur there and W of Victoria Falls.

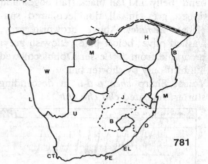

781

Status: Fairly common around Livingstone, Zambia; uncommon vagrant S of Zambezi; resident or with unmapped seasonal movements.

Habitat: *Brachystegia* woodland; less often also *Baikiaea* woodland.

Habits: Usually solitary or in pairs. Male sings from treetop. Forages in canopy. Poorly known.

Food: Nectar (especially of mistletoes; also of *Tecomaria, Holmskioldia* and *Lagerstroemia*), insects, spiders.

Breeding: Not recorded in s Africa. *Season*: September to October in Zambia. *Nest*: Oval of old leaves, leaf midribs, bark and grass, bound with spider web; lined with feathers; side-top entrance 3 cm diameter; internal height 10–12 cm; 2–3 m above ground in leafy bush or tree. *Clutch*: (1) 2 eggs. *Eggs*: Dull greyish, finely speckled with purplish; measure (2) 17–17,5 × 11,5–12.*Incubation*:Unrecorded. *Nestling*: Unrecorded.

782 (761)

Neergaard's Sunbird
Bloukruissuikerbekkie
Nectarinia neergaardi

Plate 64

[Neergaards Nektarvogel]

Measurements: Length 10–11 cm; wing (4 ♂) 54–55,4–57,5, (1 ♀) 52; tail (2 ♂) 35–40; tarsus (2 ♂) 15–16; culmen (2 ♂) 17–18. Weight (7 ♂) 6,2–6,5–7,1 g, (2 ♀) 5,6–5,9 g.

Bare Parts: Iris dark brown; bill, legs and feet black.

Identification: Size small; very similar to Lesser Doublecollared Sunbird, but slightly smaller, bill shorter, belly blackish (not grey). *Male*: Head, throat and back bright metallic green (less bronzy green than Lesser Doublecollared Sunbird); lower rump blue (rump metallic green in Shelley's Sunbird, grey band separates

689

green back and blue rump in Miombo Doublecollared Sunbird); breast crimson, bordered above by narrow metallic blue band; belly and tail black (tail edged and tipped grey in all doublecollared sunbirds). *Female*: Above brownish grey, washed olive; below pale yellowish grey; separable from ♀ Lesser Doublecollared Sunbird only by shorter bill.

Voice: Sharp *chee ti-ti-ti* in descending stutter; repeated *chit chit chit*.

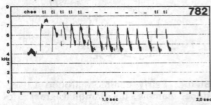

Distribution: Eastern littoral from Lake St Lucia, Zululand to Inhambane, Mozambique.

Status: Fairly common to uncommon resident. Rare (RDB).

Habitat: Dense coastal bush, dune forest, sand forest and adjacent *Acacia* woodland.

Habits: Forages in company with Black Sunbirds in flowering trees in abandoned

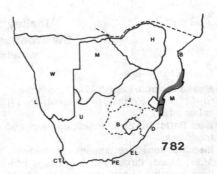

African kraals, and in undergrowth and scrub of riverine *Brachystegia* woodland. Poorly known; probably similar to habits of doublecollared sunbirds.

Food: Nectar (e.g. of *Schotia capitata* and *Syzigium cordatum*); probably also insects.

Breeding: *Season*: July, October, November in Zululand. *Nest*: Compact oval of feathers, plant down, lichen and exoskeletons of insect larvae, with porched sidetop entrance; suspended from outer branch of tree, 6 m above ground. *Clutch*: (8) 2 eggs. *Eggs*: Pale bluish grey, spotted with dark grey; measure (14) 16,2 × 11,1 (15,4–17,5 × 10,4–12,3). *Incubation*: Unrecorded. *Nestling*: Unrecorded.

---

783 (760)   **Lesser Doublecollared Sunbird**   **Plate 64**
Klein-rooibandsuikerbekkie
Nectarinia chalybea

Ingcungcu (X), iNcuncu (Z), [Halsband-Nektarvogel]

Measurements: Length 11–13 cm; wing (59 ♂) 52–56,1–59,5, (24 ♀) 47–51–53,5; tail (37 ♂) 40–43,5–47, (20 ♀) 33,5–36,1–40; tarsus (10 ♂) 16–17, (4 ♀) 16; culmen (37 ♂) 18–21,7–24, (20 ♀) 17–18,8–20. Weight (31 ♂) 6–8,7–10,2 g, (25 ♀) 6–7,4–9,5 g.

Bare Parts: Iris dark brown; bill, legs and feet black.

Identification: Size smallish; similar to Miombo Doublecollared Sunbird, but no grey on rump, wings greyer, belly darker; similar to Greater Doublecollared Sunbird, but smaller, shorter-billed, red breastband narrower; similar to Neer-

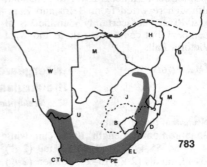

gaard's Sunbird, but belly grey. *Male*: Head, throat and back bright metallic golden green (more bluish green in Neer-

690

gaard's Sunbird); lower rump blue (not separated by grey from green back as in Miombo Doublecollared Sunbird); belly brownish grey; breast bright red, about 8 mm wide (18–23 mm wide in Greater Doublecollared Sunbird), bordered above by narrow metallic blue band; tail black, edged and tipped grey (no grey on tail of Neergaard's Sunbird); may have eclipse plumage. *Female*: Above brownish grey; below light yellowish grey; probably not safely separable in field from ♀ Neergaard's Sunbird, but bill rather longer. *Immature*: Similar to adult ♀.

Voice: Very high-pitched jumble of swirling sizzling tinkling notes, rising and falling in pitch and tempo for 3–5 seconds or more, *ssipity zweeta sweeta sweeta sweeta sweeta tsip tsip tsip*; quite variable, sometimes interspersed with harsher metallic notes; sharp *swik swik* and drawn-out *tseeet* callnotes; usually weaker and huskier than voice of Greater Doublecollared Sunbird.

Distribution: S Africa from Namaqualand (and possibly extreme s Namibia) through Karoo to e Cape, Natal and e Transvaal to Zoutpansberg.

Status: Locally common to fairly common resident.

Habitat: Evergreen forest and bush, *Eucalyptus* plantations, gardens.

Habits: Solitary, in pairs, or in small groups of 5–6 birds. Forages in forest canopy or lower down in bush, often hovering to take spiders out of webs, or to catch insects in air; flight quick and erratic.

Food: Nectar of indigenous and exotic flowers, juice of overripe figs, insects, spiders.

Breeding: *Season*: April to November (mainly July-September) in sw Cape, July to December in e Cape, October to December in Natal, June and October in Transvaal. *Nest*: Oval of grass, lichen, twigs (especially fruiting stalks of *Galium tomentosum* in sw Cape) and rootlets, bound with spider web, lined with wool, plant down and feathers; side-top entrance with or without porch; external height 11–13 cm; diameter entrance 3–3,5 cm; 15 cm to 10 m above ground (mostly under 1,2 m), suspended from branch or built into foliage of shrub, bush or tree; sometimes on electric wires near building; built by ♀ only in 7–30 days. *Clutch*: (55) 2–2,3–3 eggs (rarely only 1). *Eggs*: Cream, pale grey or pale green, spotted, streaked, mottled and clouded with black, browns and greys; measure (40) 16,3 × 11,6 (14,6–18,3 × 10,7–12,8). *Incubation*: (5, sw Cape) 14–15 days, 13 days in Natal, by ♀ only. *Nestling*: (7) 15–16,6–19 days; fed by both parents; post-nestling dependence up to 27 days.

Ref. Schmidt, R.K. 1964. *Ostrich* 35:86–94.
Martin, R. 1983. *Bokmakierie* 35:67.

784 (–) Miombo Doublecollared Sunbird Plate 64
Miombo-rooibandsuikerbekkie
Nectarinia manoensis

Tsodzo, Dzonya (Sh), [Miombonektarvogel]

Measurements: Length about 13 cm; wing (32 ♂) 60,5–63,1–66,5, (20 ♀) 54–57,7–64; tail (25 ♂) 39–44,3–48, (11 ♀) 34,5–39,4–42; tarsus (18) 15–16,7–19; culmen (15 ♂) 21–22,3–25,5, (9 ♀) 18–19–21,5, (20 unsexed) 17,5–22,3–27,5. Weight (67 ♂) 7–10–12 g, (61 ♀) 6–8,9–11,2 g.

Bare Parts: Iris dark brown; bill, legs and feet black.

Identification: Size smallish; very similar to Lesser Doublecollared Sunbird, but slightly larger, upper rump greyish in ♂. *Male*: Head, throat and back metallic golden green; upper rump dull olive grey (metallic green in Lesser Doublecollared Sunbird); lower rump blue (metallic green in Shelley's Sunbird); breast bright red, bordered above by narrow metallic blue band; belly grey (black in Shelley's Sunbird). *Female*: Like ♀ of other doublecollared sunbirds. *Immature*: Like adult ♀.

Voice: Song very high-pitched rapid twittering, probably indistinguishable from song of Lesser Doublecollared Sunbird; also sharper *chip* and *chak* notes.

Distribution: Zimbabwe to Tanzania; in s Africa confined to Zimbabwe, adjacent Botswana, Mount Gorongosa.

Status: Common resident; local movements governed by flowering plants. Formerly considered subspecies of Lesser Doublecollared Sunbird.

Habitat: Canopy of *Brachystegia* woodland, montane woodland, gardens; *Acacia* savanna in winter only.

Habits: Similar to those of Lesser Doublecollared Sunbird. Usually solitary or in pairs when breeding; larger numbers gather at good food source, especially in gardens and around *Tapinanthus* flowers in *Acacia* savanna in winter. Sings vigorously from perch in tree, bill opened wide and pointed somewhat down, sometimes with pectoral tufts displayed.

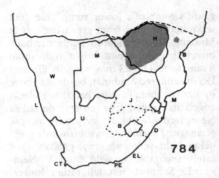

Food: Nectar (especially of mistletoes and *Bauhinia*), insects.

Breeding: *Season*: All months (mainly August-November) in Zimbabwe; may rear 2 broods/season. *Nest*: Similar to that of Lesser Doublecollared Sunbird. *Clutch*: (90) 1–1,9–3 eggs (usually 2). *Eggs*: Cream or greyish white, spotted, streaked, mottled and clouded with black, browns and greys; measure (78) 16,2 × 11,5 (14,6–18,1 × 10,6–12,5). *Incubation*: Unrecorded. *Nestling*: Unrecorded.

---

785 (758)   Greater Doublecollared Sunbird   Plate 64
Groot-rooibandsuikerbekkie
Nectarinia afra

Ntsotsotso, Rithweethwee, Xidyamhangani (Ts), Ingcungcu (X), iNcwincwi, iNcuncu (Z), [Großer Halsband-Nektarvogel]

Measurements: Length 14–15 cm; wing (70 ♂) 61–67–72, (22 ♀) 58–60,7–64,5; tail (24 ♂) 48–52,4–61, (8 ♀) 42–47; tarsus (46 ♂) 17,5–19, (8 ♀) 16–17; culmen (24 ♂) 25–27,1–29, (8 ♀) 24–26. Weight (10 ♂) 11–12,2–13,3 g, (6 ♀) 8,1–9,8–11,3 g.

Bare Parts: Iris dark brown; bill, legs and feet black.

Identification: Size medium; similar to Lesser Doublecollared Sunbird, but larger, longer-billed and with broader red breastband. *Male*: Head, throat and back brilliant metallic green; rump blue; breastband bright red, 18–23 mm wide (only about 8 mm wide in Lesser Doublecollared Sunbird), bordered above by narrow

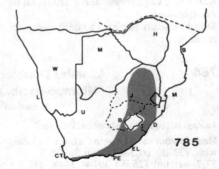

metallic blue band; belly smoky grey. *Female*: Above brownish grey; below light yellowish grey; separable from ♀ Lesser Doublecollared Sunbird only by much longer bill and larger size. *Immature*: Similar to adult ♀.

Voice: Song sustained jumble of tweeting, twittering and chipping notes, louder and richer than song of Lesser Doublecollared Sunbird, usually starting with husky *zhyeet* or *zheet-eet*; characteristic harsh *sskert* callnote; excited *ch ch ch cher-rreee* by ♂ when chasing ♀; stuttering hissing *ss ss ss* alarm notes.

Distribution: From sw Cape to n Transvaal; not Lesotho.
Status: Common resident; vagrant to Transvaal bushveld and lowveld.
Habitat: Coastal and riverine bush, forest edge, montane scrub, *Protea* savanna, parks, gardens.
Habits: Usually solitary or in pairs; gathers in loose groups of 6–7 birds at good food source, sometimes in company with other bird species, including other sunbirds. Male often sings from exposed perch, but also from inside bush; both sexes often chase conspecifics and other sunbirds. Hovers in front of webs to extract spiders.
Food: Nectar (e.g. *Erythrina, Schotia, Protea, Erica, Salvia, Plumbago* and many exotic garden flowers), insects, spiders.
Breeding: *Season*: All months (peak October-November) in e Cape, June to January in Natal, June, July and October in Transvaal; probably most months throughout S Africa; up to 3 broods/season. *Nest*: Oval of grass, *Usnea* lichen, rootlets, bark, wool, cotton, fur, plant down, twigs, rags, dried fruits, leaf mould, etc., bound with spider web; lined with hundreds of feathers; side-top entrance always with porch; external height 13–15 cm; entrance diameter 3–4 cm; built by ♀ only in 10–24 days. *Clutch*: (20) 1–1,8–2 eggs (usually 2). *Eggs*: White, greenish white to pale grey, spotted, mottled, clouded and scrawled with brown, olive and grey; measure (24) 18,6 × 12,4 (17–20,4 × 11,8–13,1). *Incubation*: 15–16 days by ♀ only. *Nestling*: Unrecorded; fed by both parents.

786 (762) Yellowbellied Sunbird · Plate 65
Geelpenssuikerbekkie
Nectarinia venusta

Tsodzo, Dzonya (Sh), [Gelbbauch-Nektarvogel]

Measurements: Length ♂ 11 cm, ♀ 10 cm; wing (71 ♂) 48–52,1–55, (86 ♀) 47–48,7–52; tail (71 ♂) 31–36,9–41, (86 ♀) 30–32,9–39; tarsus (66) 14,5–16,1–18,5; culmen (145) 16,5–19–22. Weight (312 ♂) 5,4–7,3–9,3 g, (296 ♀) 5,1–6,8–10 g.

Bare Parts: Iris dark brown, bill, legs and feet black.

Identification: Size small. *Male*: Head, throat and upperparts brilliant metallic green; breast metallic purple (Collared Sunbird ♂ has narrow purple collar below throat only); rest of underparts bright yellow; wings and tail blackish; pectoral tufts orange; bill long (much shorter in Collared Sunbird); no eclipse plumage.

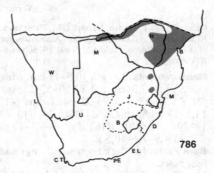

Female: Above greyish brown (♀ Collared Sunbird metallic green); below yellow (♀ Whitebellied Sunbird white). *Immature*: Similar to adult ♀; throat blackish in ♂.

Voice: Song short bursts of melodious rippling twitters and whistles, *chewip chewip ti-ti-ti-ti....*; clicking flight calls; 3-syllabled *tsiu-tse-tse* callnote; drawn-out *cheer cheer* alarm call.

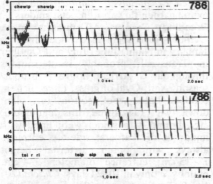

Distribution: Africa S of Sahara; in s Africa confined to e highlands of Zimbabwe and adjacent Mozambique; isolated population in Zambezi Valley to e Caprivi; sight records from Kruger National Park.

Status: Very common resident (commonest sunbird in e Zimbabwe); vagrant S of Limpopo River; seasonal movements in Zimbabwe.

Habitat: Rank herbaceous vegetation, bracken-brier, edges of evergreen forest, riverine bush, thickets around rocky outcrops; usually in areas of higher rainfall.

Habits: Usually in pairs or small groups; may join mixed bird parties at good food source. Highly active and restless; males chase each other in groups. Often hawks insects in flight.

Food: Nectar (of *Leonotis, Protea, Erythrina, Kniphofia,* mistletoes, etc.), insects, spiders.

Breeding: *Season:* All months (mainly August-November) in Zimbabwe, April to November in Mozambique. *Nest:* Untidy oval of grass, bark fibres and dead leaves, bound with spider web, lined with plant down; side-top entrance always porched; external height 12–13 cm; entrance diameter 2,5 cm; suspended from thin branch, creeper, weed or bracken; usually 1–2 m above ground, sometimes up to 3 m; often conspicuous; built by both sexes, mainly by ♀, in 14–21 days. *Clutch:* (11) 1–1,7–2 eggs (usually 2). *Eggs:* Buff, white or greyish white, finely freckled, streaked and marbled with fawn, brown and grey; measure (54) 15,8 × 11,3 (13,9–17,3 × 10,4–12,1). *Incubation:* About 14 days, most or all by ♀. *Nestling:* 14–15 days; fed by both parents.

787 (763) Whitebellied Sunbird Plate 64
Witpenssuikerbekkie
Nectarinia talatala

Kalyambya (K), Tsodzo, Dzonya (Sh), Ntsotsotso, Rithweethwee, Xidyamhangani, Xinwavulambe (Ts), Senwabolope, Talêtalê (Tw), [Weißbauch-Nektarvogel]

Measurements: Length 10,5–11 cm; wing (33 ♂) 54–57,3–60, (12 ♀) 50–52–55; tail (31 ♂) 38–43, (10 ♀) 32–38; tarsus (41) 14,5–17; culmen (31 ♂) 21,5–24, (10 ♀) 19–20. Weight (163 ♂) 6–8,2–10 g, (79 ♀) 4,8–7,1–10,5 g.

Bare Parts: Iris dark brown; bill, legs and feet black.

Identification: Size small. *Male:* Head, throat and upperparts bright metallic green (metallic purple in ♂ Violetbacked Sunbird; bill much shorter); breastband dark metallic purple (visible only in good light); belly white (yellow in Collared and

787

Yellowbellied Sunbirds); no eclipse plumage. *Female:* Above brownish grey; below greyish white, indistinctly streaked on breast (♀ Dusky Sunbird lacks streaking,

but probably not safely separable in field).
Immature: Similar to adult ♀.

Voice: 1–7 highly characteristic strident *chewy-chewy-chewy* callnotes; loud *chak-chak-chak* alarm notes; song husky canarylike warbling, starting with deliberate *chewy chwi shrip*, then breaking into rolling jumble of notes, often trilled, usually in fairly short phrases with pauses between; sometimes incorporates imitations of other birdcalls.

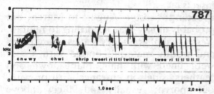

Distribution: S Africa from Bloemfontein and Transkei to Angola and n Mozambique; in s Africa absent mainly from Cape Province, highveld and dry W.

Status: Common resident; some altitudinal seasonal movements.

Habitat: Drier woodland, *Acacia* savanna, riverine bush, parks, gardens.

Habits: Usually solitary or in pairs; larger numbers gather at good food source. Active and restless, darting about foraging or chasing other sunbirds. Highly vocal at all times; may sing intermittently for 30 minutes or more from perch inside bush.

Food: Nectar of many indigenous and exotic flowers (especially of aloes and mistletoes); insects, spiders.

Breeding: *Season*: July to February (mainly August-December) in Natal, July to October in Mozambique, July to March (mainly September-November) in Transvaal, June to March (mainly September-November) in Zimbabwe. *Nest*: Oval of grass, leaves and plant down, bound with spider web, lined with plant down and some feathers; side-top entrance has well-built porch; external height 13 cm; entrance diameter 2,5 cm; 0,3–3 m above ground (usually 0,5–1,5 m), in thorny tree or shrub, or in low herbaceous plants; often on *Opuntia* (prickly pear) stem, suspended from thorns; built by ♀ only, in 5–8 days. *Clutch*: (81) 1–1,9–3 eggs (usually 2). *Eggs*: White, cream, greyish or dull greenish, spotted, smeared, scrolled and clouded with black and shades of brown and grey; measure (167) 16,2 × 11,3 (14,3–18 × 10,5–12,9); weigh (7) 1,9 g when fresh. *Incubation*: 13–14 days by ♀ only. *Nestling*: (11) 14–15 days; fed by both parents, mostly by ♀.

Ref. Earlé, R.A. 1982. *Ostrich* 53:65–73.

788 (764)   Dusky Sunbird   Plate 64
Namakwasuikerbekkie
Nectarinia fusca

[Rußnektarvogel]

Measurements: Length about 11 cm; wing (22 ♂) 54–57–59, (8 ♀) 48–50–52; tail (8) 38–41; tarsus (8) 15,5–17; culmen (8) 18–22. Weight (1 ♂) 10 g, (2 unsexed) 8 g.

Bare Parts: Iris dark brown; bill, legs and feet black.

Identification: Size small. *Breeding* ♂: Head, back, throat and breast dull black with faint metallic reflections, breast usually irregularly black in centre only, white at sides (head, throat and back bright green in Whitebellied Sunbird); belly white; pectoral tufts brilliant orange. *Nonbreeding* ♂: Above dark grey; below white with broad irregular black area from

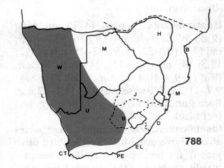

chin to breast. *Female*: Above light brownish grey; below dull white (no streaks on breast as in ♀ Whitebellied Sunbird, but probably not safely separable in field). *Immature*: Similar to adult ♀, but ♂ has blackish throat.

Voice: Harsh tearing *skrrrrrr-chek-chek* and stuttering *ts-ts-ts-ts-ts* callnotes; song weak husky jumble of rolling warbles, usually starting off slowly and speeding up towards end.

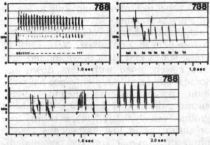

Distribution: Arid w parts of s Africa from Bloemfontein and Karoo to sw Angola (Benguela).

Status: Common resident; nomadic according to food supply; severe drought may cause irruptions into adjacent regions (e.g. into extreme sw Cape in July-August 1978).

Habitat: Desert to semidesert with shrubs, aloes or sparse bushes; trees and scrub along watercourses.

Habits: Usually solitary or in pairs; loose flocks of up to 20 birds (sometimes all males) may gather at good source of nectar, sometimes in company with other sunbird species. Highly restless; active even in midday heat; flight jerky and fluttering.

Food: Nectar (especially of *Aloe* species, *Nicotiana glauca*, mistletoes and *Lycium*), insects.

Breeding: *Season*: August to March, but probably at any time according to rainfall. *Nest*: Oval of grass, dry leaves, plant fibres and woolly material, bound with spider web; lined with hair, plant down and feathers; side-top entrance with or without porch; usually 40–90 cm above ground in low shrub, sometimes suspended from branch over watercourse; ♀ may build several preliminary nests before egglaying. *Clutch*: (23) 2–2,7–3 eggs. *Eggs*: White, spotted, clouded and mottled with greys and browns mostly at thick end; measure (25) 15,4 × 11 (14,1–16,1 × 10,6–11,6). *Incubation*: 13 days by ♀ only. *Nestling*: 13–14 days.

---

789 (765)   **Grey Sunbird**   **Plate 65**
Gryssuikerbekkie
Nectarinia veroxii

[Graunektarvogel]

Measurements: Length 14–15 cm; wing (9 ♂) 59–62,9–66,5, (7 ♀) 56–58,6–61,5; tail (7 ♂) 48–52, (5 ♀) 42–45; tarsus (12) 15,5–18; culmen (12) 24–26,5. Weight (8 ♂) 9,4–10,4–11,5 g, (10 ♀) 8,6–9,7–11,7 g, (20 unsexed) 9,5–11,1–12,6 g.

Bare Parts: Iris dark brown; bill, legs and feet black.

Identification: Size medium to large; sexes alike; above greyish (Olive Sunbird olive green), feathers edged metallic green (not usually visible in field); below paler grey, tinged olive, washed yellowish on flanks (Olive Sunbird much yellower below); wings and tail black; pectoral tuft scarlet (yellow in Olive Sunbird); lacks yellow

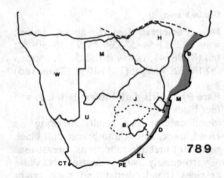

malar stripes of ♀ Malachite Sunbird (but habitats different anyway); voice usually diagnostic (*q.v.*). *Immature*: More olive below than adult.

696

Voice: Song loud monotonously repeated sparrowlike *chip chip chip jip-jip-jip-jip-jeep*, sharting off quietly and deliberately, ending loudly and fast; or penetrating rapid piping *ti-ti-ti-ti-ti-ti-tu-jip*; song always in short phrases, not usually sustained; quiet sustained subsong of twittering notes; various sharp *zit*, *tsip* and *tseep-chip-cha* callnotes; sharp *skiree-riree-riree* alarm calls.

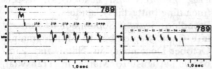

Distribution: S Africa to Somalia along E coast; in s Africa confined to e littoral from Port Elizabeth northwards.
Status: Fairly common resident; subject to some local movements.
Habitat: Coastal bush and evergreen forest; seasonally into adjacent dense thornveld for flowering plants.
Habits: Usually solitary. Shy and easily overlooked except when singing, usually from perch high in forest tree; jerks wings and body when singing, sometimes exposing pectoral tufts; highly vocal, often for long periods; may perch in one place for many minutes. Forages both in canopy and low down at forest edge, flying restlessly from flower to flower, probing quickly; hawks insects in flight; gleans spiders by hovering in front of webs; flight fast and jinking.

Food: Nectar (e.g. *Leonotis, Schotia*, mistletoes, *Strelitzia, Scadoxus, Erythrina*), insects, spiders, spider eggs.
Breeding: *Season*: December to January in e Cape, September to January (mainly November) in Natal, October in Mozambique. *Nest*: Fairly tidy oval of bark fibres, *Marasmius* strands, rootlets, twigs and dead leaves, sometimes bound with spider web; lined with dry grass inflorescences; side-top entrance hidden by overhanging porch; external height 12 cm; entrance diameter 3–4 cm; attached by long neck (about 11 cm) of material to branch or stem of shrub or tree, often over gully, usually under shelter of leafy canopy, overhanging bank or roof of derelict building; about 2–6 m above ground. *Clutch*: (45) 1–2,2–3 eggs (usually 2–3; rarely 4). *Eggs*: Plain buff, coffee or chocolate brown, usually darker at thick end; measure (24) $18,1 \times 12,5$ ($16,5$–$19,6 \times 11,9$–$13,2$). *Incubation*: Unrecorded. *Nestling*: Unrecorded.

---

790 (766)

Olive Sunbird
Olyfsuikerbekkie
Nectarinia olivacea

Plate 65

[Olivnektarvogel]

Measurements: Length ♂ 15–16 cm; ♀ 13–14 cm; wing (69 ♂) 61–64,9–69, (47 ♀) 53–58,9–63; tail (53 ♂) 48–54,5–62, (38 ♀) 38–45,5–54; tarsus (27) 16–18; culmen (51 ♂) 24–27,3–31, (36 ♀) 22–26,1–30,5. Weight (126 ♂) 9,2–12,6–14 g, (112 ♀) 7,8–9,8–11,8 g, (192 unsexed) 9–11,8–14,7 g.
Bare Parts: Iris dark brown; bill, legs and feet black.
Identification: Size medium to large; sexes alike; similar to ♀ Malachite Sunbird, but more olive green, less contrast between upper and underparts; habitat different; above olive green, faintly metallic in good light (Grey Sunbird greenish grey); below

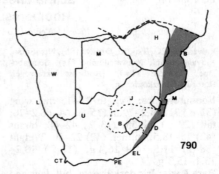

olive yellow, sometimes washed rusty on throat (Grey Sunbird grey below); pectoral tufts yellow (in most subspecies) or absent (in *N. o. sclateri* of e highlands of

697

Zimbabwe and adjacent Mozambique; scarlet in Grey Sunbird); voice usually diagnostic. *Immature*: Washed gold and rufous on throat.

Voice: Loud piping phrases of comparatively deliberate notes, starting slowly then speeding up slightly, falling in pitch towards end, *tip tip tip ti-tu-tu-tu-tiup tippy tuti*; advertising call by ♂ when breeding, monotonous froglike *peep peep peep* or cricketlike *slik-slik-slik*, often for many minutes on end; highly characteristic insistent *fit-zeet* repeated every 1–2 seconds; various sharp and twanging alarm notes; *tsip-tsip* flight calls.

Distribution: S, E and W Africa; in s Africa confined to extreme E from around East London northwards; vagrant to Grahamstown.

Status: Common resident.

Habitat: Evergreen and riverine forest, coastal bush, adjacent thornveld, parks, gardens, banana plantations.

Habits: Usually solitary; loosely gregarious in groups of up to 20 birds at good nectar course. Easily overlooked except for distinctive voice; groups of up to 10 males may sing in chorus in same tree.

Perches for long periods in one place, flicking wings at times. Forages in all layers of forest and gloomy forest interior (unlike other sunbirds), darting quickly from flower to flower; hawks insects in flight; gleans spiders by hovering in front of webs.

Food: Nectar (especially of *Strelitzia nicolai, Burchellia, Erythrina, Scadoxus, Halleria, Leonotis* and mistletoes), insects (including butterflies), spiders.

Breeding: *Season*: September to January in e Cape, September to March (mainly October-December) in Natal and Zimbabwe, August to March in Transvaal, October to March in Mozambique. *Nest*: Long untidy oval of grass, plant fibres, twigs, moss, lichen and leaves, bound with spider web; lined with plant down, feathers, fine grass or tendrils; side-top entrance with porch; external height 13 cm; entrance diameter 4 cm; mostly 1–1,5 m (up to 2 m) above ground on drooping branch or exposed roots against bank or rockface; also on wires or light fittings in buildings; built by ♀ only. *Clutch*: (50) 1–2–3 eggs (usually 2). *Eggs*: White, buff, pale brown or bluish, spotted, scrolled and marbled with shades of brown and grey; measure (31) 17,9 × 12,8 (16,8–20,1 × 11,7–13,6). *Incubation*: 16 days by ♀ only. *Nestling*: 14 days; fed by ♀ only.

791 (774) **Scarletchested Sunbird** **Plate 65**
Rooiborssuikerbekkie
Nectarinia senegalensis

Kalyambya (K), Tsodzo, Dzonya (Sh), Ntsotsotso, Xidyamhangani, Xinwavulombe (Ts), Senwabolôpe, Talêtalê (Tw), [Rotbrust-Nektarvogel, Rotbrust-Glanzköpfchen]

Measurements: Length 13–15 cm; wing (31 ♂) 71–74,2–79,5, (15 ♀) 64–68,2–70; tail (29 ♂) 48–55, (13 ♀) 42–48; tarsus (42) 15–18,5; culmen (42) 22–30. Weight (38 ♂) 11,5–14,9–16,4 g, (17 ♀) 10,2–13,1–15,3 g.

Bare Parts: Iris dark brown; bill, legs and feet black.

Identification: Size medium to large. *Male*: Mostly sooty black; crown and throat brilliant metallic green (throat ame-

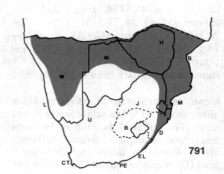

thyst in Black Sunbird); lower throat and breast scarlet; no eclipse plumage; no pectoral tufts. *Female*: Above greenish grey-brown; malar stripe buffy white; throat, breast and upper belly brown, mottled yellow (♀ Black Sunbird heavily streaked blackish on cream); rest of underparts dull yellow (much yellower than ♀ Black Sunbird). *Immature*: Similar to adult ♀, sometimes with some green and red on throat and breast in ♂.

Voice: Loud piercing piping phrases of 3–5 deliberate notes, *tip teeu tip tip*, or *syip tyip syip, syip chip-chip syip*, or *syip, chip-chip CHIP-chip*, repeated every few seconds for up to 1 hour; husky *sship* callnote; loud *chak chak* alarm call.

Distribution: Africa S of Sahara; in s Africa absent from most of Cape Province, highveld and dry W, except along major rivers (e.g. Fish River in Namibia).
Status: Common resident; some seasonal fluctuations in some areas.
Habitat: Woodland, savanna, riverine bush, gardens.

Habits: Solitary or in pairs, except at good food source. Aggressive and vocal, chasing conspecifics. Male sings from conspicuous perch on top of tree. Takes nectar by hovering, perching or hanging upside-down.
Food: Nectar (especially of *Erythrina* and *Aloe* species), spiders, insects.
Breeding: *Season*: August to January in Natal, August to March in Transvaal, July to April (mainly September-December) in Zimbabwe, September to March in Mozambique, November to March in Namibia. *Nest*: Untidy oval of grass, leaves, wool, string, paper, feathers, etc., bound with spider web; lined with plant down, hair or feathers; side-top entrance has porch; external height 13–16 cm; entrance diameter 3,5–4 cm; suspended from branch of bush or tree, often over water or dry gully; from 1,5–10 m above ground, usually high; also hung on wire or light fitting under porch of building. *Clutch*: (53) 1–2–3 eggs (almost always 2). *Eggs*: White, cream, grey, bluish or greenish, mottled, spotted, streaked and clouded with black and shades of grey and brown; measure (66) 19,2 × 13,2 (17,1–20,6 × 12–14,1). *Incubation*: 13,5–15 days by ♀ only. *Nestling*: 15,5–19 days; fed by both parents, mostly by ♀.

792 (772) Black Sunbird Plate 65
Swartsuikerbekkie
Nectarinia amethystina

Kalyambya (K), Tsodzo, Dzonya (Sh), Ntsotsotso, Xidyamhangani, Xinwavulombe (Ts), Senwabolôpe, Talêtalê (Tw), Ingcungcu (X), [Amethyst-Glanzköpfchen]

Measurements: Length 14–15 cm; wing (107 ♂) 61–71,7–77, (61 ♀) 59–65,6–69,5; tail (49 ♂) 42–46,6–54, (36 ♀) 36–42,3–46,5; tarsus (32) 14,5–16,2–18; culmen (36 ♂) 29–30,9–33, (20 ♀) 28–29–31, (30 unsexed) 20–23,9–27. Weight (157 ♂) 9,2–13–17 g, (112 ♀) 8,2–12–16,9 g.
Bare Parts: Iris dark brown; bill, legs and feet black.
Identification: Size medium to large. *Male*: Mostly sooty black; forecrown bright metallic green; throat, small patch on bend of wing, and rump metallic purple

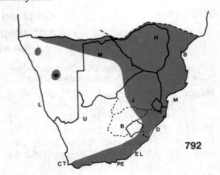

(looks pink, violet or black according to light; *N. a. kirkii* of Mozambique, n Zimbabwe and n Botswana lacks purple rump); usually no pectoral tufts (yellow tufts rarely present); no eclipse plumage. *Female*: Above grey, tinged olive; below creamy white, heavily streaked on throat and breast with blackish (♀ Scarletchested Sunbird yellower below, mottled brownish). *Immature*: Similar to adult ♀; ♂ may have black throat with some purple iridescence; adult plumage acquired at 15–17 months.

Voice: Song sustained series of very high-pitched twittering chattering notes, somewhat canarylike, but often very fast, *keep keep kyep koop*; sometimes sings for hours with only short pauses; highly characteristic penetrating monotonous stuttering *chak chak chak* or *chyek chyek* callnotes, varying in tempo and repeated for many minutes; rapidly stuttered *t-t-t-t-t-t* alarm notes.

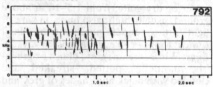

Distribution: S Africa to Kenya; in s Africa absent from sw Cape, Karoo, highveld and most of dry W; recorded Etosha National Park and Windhoek, Namibia.

Status: Common resident; numbers fluctuate seasonally.

Habitat: Forest edge, woodland, savanna, riverine bush, parks, gardens.

Habits: Usually solitary or in pairs; small loose groups gather at good food source, often in company with other nectar-feeding birds. Restless and aggressive unless singing; bobs head slightly when perched. Flight fast and jerky; often commutes long distances for food, even over open grassveld. Often hovers while feeding; flies backwards to withdraw bill from flower.

Food: Nectar of many indigenous and exotic flowers; insects, spiders.

Breeding: *Season*: July to April in e Cape, August to March and June in Natal, August to March (mainly September-December) in Transvaal and Zimbabwe. *Nest*: Oval of lichen, grass, down, stalks, hair, bark and leaves, bound with spider web; lined with plant down, rarely with feathers; side-top entrance porched with grass inflorescences; external height 13–17 cm; entrance diameter 3,5–5,5 cm; suspended from drooping branch of bush, tree or creeper, 2–6 m above ground (rarely up to 15 m in *Eucalyptus* trees); also builds on wires, fern baskets and light fittings around houses; built by ♀ only in 7–36 days. *Clutch*: (81) 1–1,8–3 eggs (usually 2). *Eggs*: White, cream, grey or greenish, spotted, streaked smudged and mottled with black and shades of brown and grey; measure (71) 19,3 × 12,9 (17,4–21 × 11,6–14). *Incubation*: 13–18 days by ♀ only. *Nestling*: 14–18 days; usually fed by ♀ only (rarely also by ♂).

Ref. Skead, C.J. 1953. *Ostrich* 24:159–166.

793 (771)   **Collared Sunbird**   **Plate 65**
Kortbeksuikerbekkie
Anthreptes collaris

Kalyambya (K), Inqathane (X), iNtonso, iNqwathane (Z), [Waldnektarvogel, Stahlnektarvogel]

Measurements: Length 10–11 cm; wing (54 ♂) 46–53,1–57, (37 ♀) 46–50,4–53; tail (38 ♂) 30,5–38,3–43, (26 ♀) 30–34,8–37; tarsus (12 ♂) 16–17, (9 ♀) 14–15,5, (78 unsexed) 14–16,2–18; culmen (79) 13–14,9–17. Weight (167 ♂) 6,3–7,8–9,4 g, (113 ♀) 5,8–7–9,7 g.

Bare Parts: Iris dark brown; bill, legs and feet black.

Identification: Size small; bill short, only slightly decurved. *Male*: Upperparts and throat brilliant metallic green; throat bor-

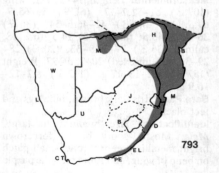

dered by narrow bluish purple band; rest of underparts yellow; pectoral tufts lemon yellow; no eclipse plumage. *Female*: Similar to ♂, but lacks green and blue throat, underparts wholly yellow. *Immature*: Similar to adult ♀.

Voice: Song reedy high-pitched chattering *chirri chirri chirri*, sometimes drawn out into trill; rolling duet, *chippery chippery*; thin *tsip, chirri* or *chipperi* callnotes; feeble *seep seep* alarm notes.

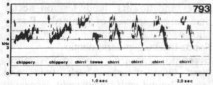

Distribution: S Africa to Kenya and Senegal; in s Africa confined to extreme S, E and N, from Humansdorp to Caprivi, including Limpopo Valley and e Zimbabwe.

Status: Locally common resident.

Habitat: Riverine and lowland evergreen forest, coastal bush, especially with tangled creepers.

Habits: Almost always in pairs; rarely in small groups of 3–4 birds. Often joins mixed bird parties. Inquisitive; responds well to spishing. Somewhat warblerlike; forages for invertebrates in creepers, dead leaves and spider webs; sometimes hovers to take food; hawks insects in flight; also probes shallow flowers, or slits tubular flow-

ers with short bill to get at nectar. Flight fast and direct, without typical jinking of larger sunbirds. Flicks wings in alarm.

Food: Nectar (e.g. of *Schotia, Erythrina, Xeromphis*), insects, spiders, snails, small berries (e.g. of *Trema orientalis, Chrysanthemoides monilifera*), seeds.

Breeding: *Season*: All months (mainly September-January) in e Cape, July to February (mainly October to December) in Natal, November and February in Transvaal, April-May and September-January in Mozambique, September to April (mainly September-December) in Zimbabwe. *Nest*: Oval of grass, leaves, twigs, rootlets and tendrils, bound with spider web; lined with wiry plant fibres, horsehair, rootlets and some feathers; side-top entrance porched; usually with untidy tail of material hanging below; external height 9–16,5 cm; entrance diameter 2,5–3 cm; suspended by neck of material to drooping branch of leafy tree or shrub at edge of forest, often over roadway or gully, at 1–4 m above ground; built by ♀ only in 2–6 days. *Clutch*: (112) 1–2,2–4 eggs (usually 2–3). *Eggs*: White pale pink, green, blue or cream, mottled, streaked, spotted and blotched with black, violet, greys and browns; measure (86) 15,9 × 11,2 (14,5–17,8 × 10,3–12). *Incubation*: 14 days by ♀ only. *Nestling*: About 17 days; fed by both parents; postnestling dependence up to 24 days.

Ref. Skead, C.J. 1962. *Ostrich* 33(2):38–40.

794 (769)   **Bluethroated Sunbird**   **Plate 65**
Bloukeelsuikerbekkie
Anthreptes reichenowi

[Blaukehl-Nektarvogel]

Measurements: Length about 10 cm; wing (3 ♂) 55–56, (3 ♀) 52–53; tail (3 ♂) 40–41, (3 ♀) 34–36; tarsus (6) 15–17; culmen (6) 15–16.

Bare Parts: Iris dark brown; bill, legs and feet black.

Identification: Size small; bill short (long in Yellowbellied Sunbird). *Male*: Above light green (not metallic as in Collared Sunbird); below yellow, including broad malar stripe (diagnostic; no yellow malar stripe in Collared Sunbird); forehead, throat and upper breast metallic blueblack

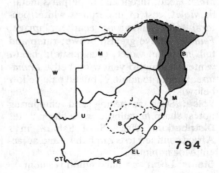

(green in Collared Sunbird); pectoral tufts yellow; no eclipse plumage. *Female*: Similar to ♂, but without blueblack forehead and throat; above greener than ♀ Yellowbellied Sunbird, not metallic like ♀ Collared Sunbird. *Immature*: Similar to adult ♀, but more olive above.

Voice: Song rambling twittering warble, *tsee tsee tsee chippee-chippee-chippee tweeu t-t-t-t-t*; sometimes resembles song of Willow Warbler; 2-syllabled *tik-tik* callnote.

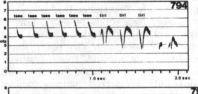

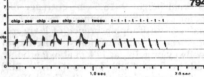

Distribution: Mozambique to Kenya; in s Africa confined to Mozambique and e Zimbabwe; isolated records from n Zululand and e Transvaal await confirmation.
Status: Uncommon to rare inland, common coastally; resident. Indeterminate (Rare) (RDB).
Habitat: Thickets at edge of lowland evergreen forest, riverine bush.
Habits: Usually in pairs; may join mixed bird parties. Forages like warbler among leaves and flowers; feeds less on nectar than larger species of sunbirds. Poorly known.
Food: Insects, spiders, nectar.
Breeding: *Season*: October to November. *Nest*: Oval of grass, bark, twigs and leaves, bound with spider web; decorated outside with cocoons; side-top entrance porched; suspended from branch. *Clutch*: (4) 1–2–3 eggs (usually 2). *Eggs*: White, spotted with red-brown and mauve; measure (6) 15,7 × 10,9 (15–16,2 × 10,4–11,4). *Incubation*: Unrecorded. *Nestling*: Unrecorded.

795 (770)   Violetbacked Sunbird   Plate 64
Blousuikerbekkie
Anthreptes longuemarei

Tsodzo, Dzonya (Sh), [Violettmantel-Nektarvogel]

Measurements: Length 12,5–13 cm; wing (130) 61–85; tail 40–60; tarsus 15,5–19; culmen 14–18. Weight (5 ♂) 12–12,3–13 g, (4 ♀) 12,1–12,7–13,4 g.
Bare Parts: Iris dark brown; bill dark horn brown to black; legs and feet black.
Identification: Size smallish; bill short. *Male*: Head, throat and upperparts metallic violet; rest of underparts white; pectoral tufts yellow; no eclipse plumage. *Female*: Above greyish brown; rump and tail metallic violet (diagnostic); below white, shading to yellow on belly. *Immature*: Similar to adult ♀, but all pale yellow below.
Voice: Song twittering and chippering notes; sharp *tit* callnote; *skee* alarm note.
Distribution: Africa S of Sahara; in s Africa confined to e Zimbabwe and adjacent Mozambique.
Status: Local and uncommon resident.

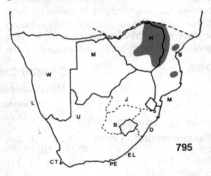

Habitat: Canopy of *Brachystegia* and *Uapaca* woodland.
Habits: Usually in pairs, sometimes solitary; congregates in loose groups of 12 or more birds at good food source, with much chasing of conspecifics and other birds; also joins mixed bird parties. Forages warblerlike in foliage and loose bark; agile and restless, often hanging upside

down. Flight direct and buoyant on fluttering wings.
Food: Insects, spiders, nectar (of *Erythrina, Bauhinia*, etc.).
Breeding: *Season*: August to December in Zimbabwe. *Nest*: Oval of plant fibres, silky down, grass and twigs, bound with spider web; outside decorated with leaves; lined with plant down; external height 15 cm; side-top entrance diameter 4 cm; 4–21 m above ground (usually 6–10 m) at end of branch or among dry leaves or cluster of spider web. *Clutch*: 1–2 eggs (usually 2). *Eggs*: White, pale blue, buff or pale grey, spotted, streaked and smudged with black, brown and grey; measure (14) 19,1 × 12,8 (18,1–20,2 × 12–13,3). *Incubation*: Unrecorded. *Nestling*: Unrecorded; fed by both parents.

26:25. Family 87 ZOSTEROPIDAE—WHITE-EYES

Small. Bill short to medium, slender, pointed, slightly arched on culmen; legs medium, slender, strong; toes medium; wings somewhat pointed, 10th primary remex vestigial; tail medium, square; plumage dull green or yellow, often with grey, white or rufous on belly, usually with conspicuous white eye-ring; sexes alike; arboreal in savanna and forest; gregarious; food insects, nectar, fruit, buds; breed solitarily; nest a tiny cup of plant and animal fibres bound with spider web, usually suspended in horizontal fork of branch; eggs 2–4, plain white or pale greenish blue; chick naked at hatching (downy plumes above eyes only); parental care by both sexes. Distribution Africa S of Sahara, Madagascar, tropical Asia, Japan, Philippines, Australasia to Fiji; about 80 species; two species in s Africa.

Ref. Clancey, P.A. 1967. *Ibis* 109:318–327.
Skead, C.J. 1967. *The sunbirds of southern Africa; also the sugarbirds, the white-eyes and the Spotted Creeper*. Cape Town: Balkema.

796 (775)   **Cape White-eye**   **Plate 65**
Kaapse Glasogie
Zosterops pallidus

Manqiti (Ts), Intukwane (X), uMehlwane, umBicini (Z), [Oranjebrillenvogel]

Measurements: Length 10–13 cm; wing (504) 52–60,6–68; tail (393) 40–47,6–56; tarsus (392) 15–17,2–20; culmen (393) 9–11–15. Weight (20 ♂) 7,7–10,3–14,6 g, (31 ♀) 8,4–11,8–14 g, (1 516 unsexed) 8–11,1–20 g.
Bare Parts: Iris brown; bill black, base blue-grey; legs and feet blue-grey.
Identification: Size small; bill short, warblerlike; above greyish green (Yellow White-eye greenish yellow above); eyering white; throat and undertail yellow; rest of underparts variable according to distribution—greenish yellow with green wash on breast, grey, or whitish with rufous flanks (underparts uniform bright yellow in Yellow White-eye). *Immature*:

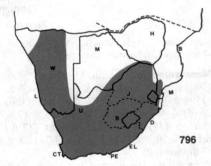

Duller than adult; white eyering develops at about 5 weeks.
Voice: Song longish jerky phrases of sweet reedy notes, varying in pitch, volume and tempo, usually starting off with *teee teee* or

pirrup pirrup notes, then becoming jumble of *tee tippee tweee yip yip twee,* etc., often incorporating brief imitations of other birdcalls; sweet piping or slightly trilled *pee, prree,* or *pirree* callnotes between members of flock; shrill *chip-chirrrrr* and *chrrree* alarm calls.

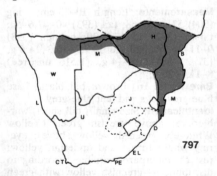

Distribution: S Africa, Lesotho, Swaziland, extreme s Mozambique, s Botswana and Namibia.

Status: Very common resident.

Habitat: Forest, woodland, savanna, parks, gardens, exotic plantations, riverine scrub and bush.

Habits: In pairs when breeding; otherwise gregarious in smaller or larger flocks (up to 100 birds in winter). Forages restlessly in foliage from canopy to undergrowth, on branches, at bases of flower and leaf buds, in brushwood and sometimes on ground, hopping and hanging agilely in all kinds of postures; also probes or slits tubular flowers for nectar. Drinks and bathes frequently in streams, birdbaths, puddles and dew on foliage. Highly vocal at all times; often sings from same place throughout breeding season, starting at dawn. Roosts together in pairs on branch. Flight straight, slightly undulating.

Food: Insects, spiders, spider eggs, nectar, fruit, fleshy flower petals and sepals, honeydew from aphids; also orange pulp, sugar and jam from table or feeding tray.

Breeding: *Season*: August to April in Cape Province, July to March in Natal, June to February in Transvaal; mainly October to December throughout. *Nest*: Small neat thin-walled cup of fine grass, stems, roots, hair and strands of lichen, bound with spider web; thinly lined with plant down or few feathers held down with fine rootlets and hair; internal diameter 3,7–4,5 cm, depth 4,1–5,1 cm; suspended by rim from thin horizontal fork (rarely supported within vertical fork) of shrub, bush, tree or creeper; 0,6–10 m above ground (usually 1–6 m); built by both sexes in 5–10 days. *Clutch*: (211) 2–2,5–4 eggs (usually 2–3). *Eggs*: Plain white, pale blue or pale green; measure (140) 16,8 × 12,3   (14,6–19,1 × 10,9–13,6). *Incubation*: 10,5–12 days by both sexes. *Nestling*: 12–13 days; fed by both parents.

Ref. Skead, C.J. & Ranger, G.A. 1958. *Ibis* 100:319–333.

797   (777)   Yellow White-eye   Plate 65
Geelglasogie
Zosterops senegalensis

Kahwarameso (Sh), Manqiti (Ts), umBicini, uMehlwane (Z), [Senegalbrillenvogel]

Measurements: Length 11–12 cm; wing (36 ♂) 54–59,2–63, (28 ♀) 54–59,3–63,5, (159 unsexed) 53–59,7–65; tail (136) 36–41,4–45; tarsus (24) 14–15,8–17,5; culmen (24) 9–10,5–12. Weight (17 ♂) 8,1–9,8–10,9 g, (24 ♀) 8,1–9,7–11,8 g, (346 unsexed) 7,4–9,9–14 g.

Bare Parts: Iris brown; bill black, base blue-grey; legs and feet blue-grey.

Identification: Size small; bill warblerlike; similar to Cape White-eye, but much yellower all over; above greenish yellow (Cape White-eye much greener, often tinged greyish); below bright yellow, faintly washed green across breast (Cape White-eye grey, whitish or greenish yellow, flanks darker, sometimes washed rufous); eyering white. *Immature*: Paler below than adult.

Voice: Song melodious whistled warble, similar to song of Cape White-eye or Willow Warbler, *tsee-tseer-tsi-tsi-tseer-tsi-tsi-tsi-tseer-tsee*, followed by pause before next phrase; soft piping and twittering contact calls, rather tinny.

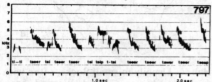

Distribution: Africa S of Sahara; in s Africa mainly confined to NE from Zululand to Ovamboland; recorded Waterberg Plateau, Namibia.

Status: Common resident. Probably Rare (RDB).

Habitat: Evergreen and riverine forest, woodland (especially *Brachystegia* and *Baikiaea*), *Eucalyptus* plantations, gardens.

Habits: Similar to Cape White-eye. In pairs or small flocks of up to 20 birds. Usually forages in canopy, gleaning prey from leaves and stems, keeping up constant twittering between members of flock; hawks insects in flight. Joins mixed bird parties. Roosts in pairs or threes on branch. Often bathes in water. Walks or hops on ground.

Food: Insects, nectar, fruit.

Breeding: *Season*: October to November in Zululand, August to February (mainly September-October) in Zimbabwe. *Nest*: Small neat cup of fine bark strips, grass blades, tendrils and lichen strands, bound with spider web; built by both sexes in about 7 days; slung by rim in horizontal fork of leafy shrub, bush or tree, 1–3,5 m above ground. *Clutch*: (17) 2–2,8–4 eggs (usually 3). *Eggs*: Plain white, pale blue or turquoise; measure (45) 15,3 × 11,7 (13,2–16,9 × 11,3–12). *Incubation*: 11 days by both sexes. *Nestling*: About 14 days; fed by both parents.

26:26.   Family 88 PLOCEIDAE—WEAVERS, SPARROWS, BISHOPS, WIDOWS, ETC.

Small to medium. Bill short to medium, conical, pointed, adapted for seed-eating; legs short to medium, strong; feet strong, toes longish; wings short and rounded to long and pointed; tail highly variable, mostly medium, square; plumage variable, males often brightly coloured; sexes usually different; eclipse plumage frequent in males; mostly gregarious, at least when not breeding; arboreal or terrestrial in wide variety of habitats; food seeds, fruit, insects, nectar, etc.; breed colonially or solitarily; many species polygynous; nest rather variable, but always roofed or in a hole: large communal structure of sticks and grass with chambers inside (buffalo weavers, sociable weavers), oval of dry grass with bottom entrance, sometimes colonial (sparrowweavers), oval of plant material with side entrance (sparrows), suspended ball of woven green plant strips with bottom entrance (true weavers), ball of dry grass with side entrance woven into living plants (bishops, widows, queleas); eggs 2–6, variable, usually spotted; chick naked or sparsely downy at hatching; incubation by female only; young fed by both sexes or by female only; one species (Cuckoo Finch) brood-parasitic. Distribution Africa, Eurasia (several species introduced to much of the rest of the world); 141 species; 35 species in s Africa (one introduced).

Ref. Summers-Smith, J.D. 1988. *The sparrows*. Calton: T. & A.D. Poyser.

798   (779)   **Redbilled Buffalo Weaver**   **Plate 66**
                                     Buffelwewer
                                     Bubalornis niger

Kamugcara (K), Mawilu (Ts), Mabônyana, Pônyane (Tw), [Büffelweber].

Measurements: Length 23–24 cm; wing (60 ♂) 116,5–123,1–127, (16 ♀) 109,5–114–118; tail (49 ♂) 95–102,9–109,5; tarsus (15) 27–32; culmen (15) 22–25. Weight (1 ♂) 80 g, (1 unsexed) 81,3 g.

Bare Parts: Iris dark brown; bill coral red to orange; legs and feet pinkish brown to pale orange.

Identification: Large (about size and shape of starling, but bill conical, bright orange). *Male*: Black, lightly mottled white on flanks; white wingpatch conspicuous in flight. *Female*: More brownish black than ♂, otherwise similar; throat, breast and undertail mottled with white. *Immature*: Below white, streaked dark brown. *Subadult*: Similar to adult ♀, but more mottled with white below; bill horn.

Voice: ♂ calls loud *lookatit-lookatit-lookatit* or *widdla-widdla-widdla-widdla* or *chika-chika-chika*; ♀ calls musical *chwee*; sounds something like fast Forktailed Drongo song.

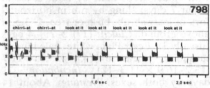

Distribution: S Africa to NE Africa; in s Africa discontinuously from s Mozambique and Kruger National Park to Limpopo Valley, se and w Zimbabwe, e and n Botswana and n Namibia; vagrant to Zululand.

Status: Locally common; mostly resident, but summer visitor to edges of range; in Transvaal lowveld present mainly October to April, males arriving shortly before females.

Habitat: Semi-arid savanna to dry bushveld, especially with large trees like Baobabs; in w Zimbabwe associated with Camelthorn *Acacia erioloba*.

Habits: Usually in small flocks, often with Greater Blue-eared and Wattled Starlings. Forages on ground by walking or hopping. Roosts communally in large stick nests in trees, dispersing by day and assembling again at night. Highly vocal.

Food: Insects, seeds, fruit.

Breeding: *Season*: October to April in Transvaal, September to April (mainly January-February) in Zimbabwe. *Nest*: Large untidy communally built mass of thorny twigs and sticks, each mass with 2 or more vertical entrance tunnels each leading to nest chamber lined with grass, roots and leaves; on branch of large tree, or on windmill; ♂ builds stick shell, ♀ lines chamber. *Clutch*: (16) 2–3,3–4 eggs (usually 3–4). *Eggs*: Dull greenish white, thickly and evenly spotted and mottled with grey and olive; measure (25) 28,3 × 19,9 (25,6–32,5 × 19–20,9). *Incubation*: 11 days by ♀ only, starting with first egg. *Nestling*: 20–23 days; fed by ♀ only.

Ref. Kemp, A. & Kemp, M. 1974. *Bokmakierie* 26:55–58.

799 (780) Whitebrowed Sparrowweaver Plate 66
Koringvoël
Plocepasser mahali

Mogale (Tw), [Mahaliweber]

Measurements: Length 16–18 cm; wing (33 ♂) 101–105,4–109, (42 ♀) 98–101,5–104; tail (33 ♂) 61–63,5–67, (42 ♀) 58–62,2–65; tarsus (33 ♂) 25–26,5–28,3, (42 ♀) 23,5–26,2–27,1; culmen (33 ♂) 15,6–16,9–18,2, (42 ♀) 14,6–16,3–17,5. Weight (72 ♂) 43–48,6–53,5 g, (90 ♀) 40,3–46,3–54,5 g.

Bare Parts: Iris reddish brown; bill black (♂) or horn (♀); legs and feet light brown.

Identification: Size medium; crown and face blackish brown; sides of head and back brown; broad eyebrow, rump and underparts white (diagnostic; rump conspicuous in flight); breast in n birds (n Zimbabwe and Tete District, Mozambique, *P. m. pectoralis*) marked with brown triangular spots; wings and tail blackish brown, edged white. *Immature*: Similar to adult; bill pinkish brown.

Voice: Song loud jumble of rich rolling

notes, *chewip cheepy cheew chup chee-prrr cheerrr cheew churr krrrup*, etc.; harsh *chik chik* callnotes.

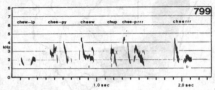

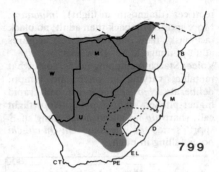

Distribution: S Africa to NE Africa; widespread in s Africa, except extreme arid w Namibia, w and s Cape, and moister e regions.

Status: Mostly very common resident; often somewhat local.

Habitat: *Acacia* savanna, Mopane woodland, bushy hillsides, farmyards with clumps of trees in open grassveld.

Habits: Usually in pairs or small groups of up to 9 birds (mean 4,2 birds/group in South Africa and 5,4 birds/group in Zimbabwe) consisting of one dominant ♂ and ♀ and 1–7 helpers; pair or group occupies one tree or several adjacent trees with several nests, each with 2 entrances, one more horizontal, one facing more downwards from rounded chamber; nests tend to be on W side of tree. Forages on ground, usually not far from nesting tree, often in overgrazed or bare disturbed areas along roads, around kraals or windmills; walks, runs or bounds. When disturbed flies into tree. Highly vocal. Roosts singly in nests at night.

Food: Insects, seeds.

Breeding: *Season*: May to February (mainly October-December) in Transvaal, November to May in Botswana (opportunistically after rain), August to April (mainly September-February) in Orange Free State and Zimbabwe; up to 4 broods/season. *Nest*: Bulky untidy oval of grass stems (looks like bunch of straw), about 23 cm long, 15 cm wide, 18 cm high, with entrance up to 30 cm long, 7 cm diameter; second entrance from chamber closed up in one nest/colony; chamber thickly lined with soft grass, feathers and woolly material; 2–8 m above ground in outer branches of tree, rarely also on telephone pole in treeless areas; nests built by all members of group. *Clutch*: (38) 1–2–3 eggs. *Eggs*: White or pale pink, speckled and clouded with pink, red-brown and grey often concentrated at thick end; markings sometimes indistinct; measure (116) 24,8 × 16,3 (22,6–27,6 × 14,6–17,5); weigh (9) 2,2–3–4,1 g. *Incubation*: (3) 14 days by dominant ♀ only. *Nestling*: (5) 21–22–23 days; fed by all members of group, more by females than by males.

Ref. Collias, N.E. & Collias, E.C. 1978. *Auk* 95:472–484.
Earlé, R.A. 1983. *Navors. nas. Mus., Bloemfontein* 4:177–191.
Lewis, D.M. 1982. *Ibis* 124:511–522.

800 (783)   **Sociable Weaver**   **Plate 66**
Versamelvoël (Familievoël)
Philetairus socius

Tlhantlagane (NS), Kgwêrêrê (Tw), [Siedelweber]

Measurements: Length about 14 cm; wing (73 ♂) 68,1–71,7–77,8, (43 ♀) 68,1–70,7–74,1; tail (73 ♂) 36,7–41–45,5, (43 ♀) 37,6–40,8–45,1; tarsus (73 ♂) 15,8–17,1–18,7, (43 ♀) 15,6–17–18,5; culmen (73 ♂) 13,5–14,9–16,3, (43 ♀) 13,7–14,9–16,1. Weight (89 ♂) 20,8–27,5–32 g, (62 ♀) 20,9–26,9–32 g.

Bare Parts: Iris dark brown; bill, legs and feet light blue-grey.

Identification: Medium (about size of Cape Sparrow); crown and rump buffy brown; back and wings blackish brown, neatly scaled buff; facemask black (diagnostic in combination with bluish bill); underparts deep buff; bold black chevrons on flanks; tail blackish with buff central rectrices (diagnostic in flight). *Immature*: More spotted on back than adult; no black facemask; flank chevrons faint; acquires adult plumage at 16–18 weeks.

Voice: Staccato chipping notes, somewhat metallic, varying in pitch and tempo; deliberate *chip chip* contact call; rapid higher-pitched *chip-chip-chip-chip* flight call; sharp *tip tip* alarm notes; song of ♂ short series of pleasing *chi-chi-chi-chi* notes falling in pitch.

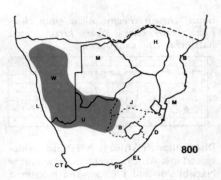

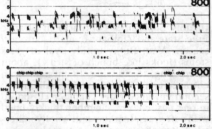

Distribution: Most of Namibia, sw Botswana, n Namaqualand, n Cape, w Orange Free State and sw Transvaal.

Status: Common resident.

Habitat: Arid *Acacia* savanna, riverine *Acacia*, semidesert with scattered Kokerboom *Aloe dichotoma*.

Habits: Highly gregarious at all times in colonies of about 6–300 birds; each colony associated with communally built nest mass, or set of masses on stout branch of *Acacia* tree, fork of *Aloe dichotoma*, windmill platform, crosspiece of telephone pole, or (rarely) cliff ledge; very little movement of birds between colonies. Forages on ground within about 1,5 km of nest tree, usually hopping quickly; uncovers food by flicking sand aside with bill. When disturbed flock flies to top of bush, tree or fence. Calls frequently in flight and at nest, less often while feeding. Roosts communally in nest chambers at night and in heat of day. Builds onto nest throughout year and most of day, carrying one stick or straw at a time; nest chambers used for roosting and/or nesting by Pygmy Falcon, Pied Barbet, Ashy Tit, Familiar Chat, Rosyfaced Lovebird and Redheaded Finch.

Food: Insects (16–80%), seeds (20–84%); seldom drinks water; young fed only insects.

Breeding: *Season*: Any month according to rainfall; one season may last up to 9 months; up to 4 broods/season. *Nest*: Large mass, up to 4 m deep and 7,2 m long, of dry grass straws enclosing 5–50 adjacent, but separate, rounded nest chambers 10–15 cm diameter, lined from floor to ceiling with soft plant material, fur, cotton and fluff, each with vertical entrance tunnel up to 25 cm long, 6–7 cm diameter; threshold of chamber reinforced with pliable stems; grass straws point diagonally downwards into entrance tunnel to form effective barrier against human hand or larger predator (but eggs and young heavily preyed on by Cape Cobra *Naja nivea* and Boomslang *Dispholidus typus*); whole mass roofed with coarse twigs and sticks 10–30 cm long, often thorny; from 1,6–16 m above ground. *Clutch*: (632) 2–3,6–6 eggs (usually 3–4; clutch varies with amount of rain). *Eggs*: Dull white, densely spotted with shades of grey; measure (76) 20,9 × 15,1   (18,1–22,8 × 13,2–15,9). *Incubation*: 13–14 days by both sexes, starting with 1st or 2nd egg. *Nestling*: 21–24 days; fed by both parents and at least one adult helper; in good season nestlings fed by parents and up to 9 young of previous broods of same season; fledgling dependent on parents for at least 16 days after initial departure.

Ref. Bartholomew, G.A., White, F.N. & Howell, T.R. 1976. *Ibis* 118:402–410.

Collias, E.C. & Collias, N.E. 1978. *Ibis* 120:1–15.

Ferguson, J.W.H. 1988. *S. Afr. J. Zool.* 23:266–271.

Maclean, G.L. 1973. *Ostrich* 44:176–261.

801 (784) **House Sparrow** **Plate 66**
Huismossie
Passer domesticus

Enzunge (K), Serobele (SS), Tswere (Tw), [Haussperling]

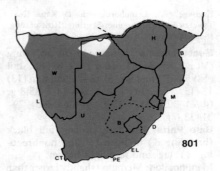

801

Measurements: Length 14–15,5 cm; wing ♂ 73–78,5, ♀ 71–78; tail 54–56; tarsus 19; culmen 12–14. Weight (110 ♂) 20,4–24,7–29,6 g, (94 ♀) 20,3–26,2–32,8 g, (143 unsexed, w Transvaal) 20,4–24,3–30,2 g.

Bare Parts: Iris brown; bill black (breeding ♂) or horn (♀ and nonbreeding ♂); legs and feet pinkish brown.

Identification: Medium (size of Cape Sparrow); rump grey (diagnostic in flight; indigenous species of *Passer* all have rufous rumps); similar to Great Sparrow, but less rufous above. *Male:* Crown and nape grey in centre, chestnut at sides; forehead, eyestripe, throat and upper breast black, scaled white on breast; mantle tawny, streaked black; wingbar white; rest of underparts dull white. *Female:* Above buffy brown, streaked black on back; eyebrow buffy white; face grey; dusky line through eye; below off-white. *Immature:* Similar to adult ♀ but paler and duller.

Voice: Sharp penetrating *chi-chip, chichiririp, cheep* callnotes; song repeated combinations of callnotes; loud rattling twitter, *ji-ji-ji-ji-ji*, alarm call.

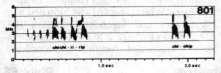

Distribution: Originally Europe and Asia; introduced and spread almost throughout s Africa to Malawi; also introduced N and S America, Australia, New Zealand and many oceanic islands.

Status: Very common resident; *P. d. indicus* introduced Durban between 1893 and 1897 and East London about 1930; spread from one human settlement to next, especially along roads and railways; reached Orange Free State and Transvaal by 1949–1952, n Cape by 1956, Botswana, Namibia and Zimbabwe by 1957–1960.

Habitat: Urban, suburban and rural human settlements in all habitats.

Habits: In pairs or family groups when breeding; otherwise more or less gregarious, sometimes in flocks of hundreds of birds. Forages by hopping on ground; may hawk flying termites and moths. Highly vocal except when feeding. Tame but wary; becomes confiding in city centres.

Food: Seeds, soft buds, fruit, insects (adults and larvae), spiders, scraps from feeding tray.

Breeding: *Season:* All months throughout s African range; mainly September-December. *Nest:* Untidy rounded mass of grass, wool, feathers and other soft materials, with side entrance; in hole in building or tree, under eaves or in thatched roof. *Clutch:* (31) 2–3,5–6 eggs (usually 3–4). *Eggs:* Pale blue, grey or white, heavily spotted and blotched with browns and greys; measure (68) 21,5 × 15,2 (19–24 × 13,6–19,7). *Incubation:* 12–14 days by both sexes, mostly by ♀. *Nestling:* About 15 days; fed by both parents.

Ref. Niethammer, G. 1971. *Ostrich Suppl.* 8:445–448.

802 (785)   Great Sparrow   Plate 66
Grootmossie
Passer motitensis

Enzunge (K), Lemphorokgohlo la Kapa (NS), Tswere (Tw), [Rotbrauner Sperling, Rostsperling, Riesensperling]

Measurements: Length 15–16 cm; wing (10 ♂) 83–84–85, (8 ♀) 79–81–85; tail (18) 56–67; tarsus (18) 18–21; culmen (18) 13–15. Weight (3 ♂) 34–34,7–35,8 g, (4 ♀) 30,6–31,5–32 g, (8 unsexed) 29–31–32,6 g.

Bare Parts: Iris dark brown; bill black (breeding ♂) or horn (♀ and nonbreeding ♂); legs and feet light brown.

Identification: Medium (slightly larger than Cape Sparrow); similar to House Sparrow, but rump rufous (conspicuous in flight; grey in House Sparrow). *Male*: Centre of crown, nape and mantle grey; stripe in front of eye and cheeks white; eyestripe black; broad curved stripe from above eye to side of neck tawny; back tawny, streaked black; wing-stripe white; broad bib from chin to upper breast black; rest of underparts white. *Female*: Similar to ♂, but paler, duller, and lacking tawny on sides of head; eyebrow cream; throat grey. *Immature*: Similar to adult ♀, but ♂ has black throat.

Voice: Harsh twittering *chreep, cheep* and *chirititit* callnotes; song repeated series of varied callnotes; almost indistinguishable from voice of House Sparrow.

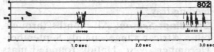

Distribution: Africa S of Sahara; in s Africa confined to Kalahari basin, Namibia and n Cape.

Status: Mostly uncommon to rare resident or nomad; locally commmon.

Habitat: Arid to semi-arid savanna and scrub.

Habits: Usually solitary or in pairs; small groups may gather to drink at waterholes. Quieter than most sparrows, easily overlooked. Shy; has not adapted to human settlement. Poorly known.

Food: Seeds, insects.

Breeding: *Season*: September to February in Zimbabwe and Botswana, December to February in Namibia. *Nest*: Large untidy thick-walled hollow ball of grass and *Asparagus* leaves, with side entrance; thickly lined with fine grass and feathers; 3–4 m above ground in thorntree or bush. *Clutch*: (9) 2–3,3–4 eggs (sometimes up to 6). *Eggs*: White, spotted and blotched with slate grey and lavender; measure (82) 20,5 × 15 (18,5–22,2 × 14–16,1). *Incubation*: Unrecorded. *Nestling*: Unrecorded.

803 (786)   Cape Sparrow   Plate 66
Gewone Mossie
Passer melanurus

Serobele (SS), Tswere (Tw), Undlunkulu, Unondlwane, Ingqabe (X), uNdlunkulu, uPhenyane (Z), [Kapsperling]

Measurements: Length 14–16 cm; wing (24 ♂) 72–78,4–86, (13 ♀) 73–76,6–82; tail (33) 53–64; tarsus (33) 17,5–21; culmen (33) 12–14. Weight (56 ♂) 25–29,6–34 g, (34 ♀) 22–29,4–38 g, (452 ♂)

mean 26 g, (466 ♀) mean 25,4 g, (466 unsexed) 20–24,5–37 g.

Bare Parts: Iris dark brown; bill black (breeding ♂) or horn (♀ and nonbreeding ♂); legs and feet brown.

Identification: Size medium. *Male*: Head and breast black with broad semicircles of white from behind eyes to sides of throat, not quite meeting in centre; mantle greyish; back, rump and upperwing coverts bright rufous; conspicuous white wingbar; rest of underparts white. *Female*: Somewhat like ♂, but duller; head and breast dark grey with paler semicircles from behind eyes to throat (Greyheaded Sparrow has plain grey head); wingbar dull white (Greyheaded Sparrow has short clear white wingbar). *Immature*: Like adult ♀; head darker in ♂.

Voice: Much more mellow and pleasing than voice of other sparrows; rolling musical *chreep, chirreep, chirrichreep* call-notes; song repeated jerky rolling chirps varying in pitch—*chip chirreep, chip chirreep*, or *chreep chroop, chreep chroop*, or *chip chollop tlip tlop*, etc.

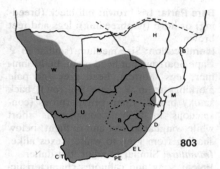

Distribution: Widespread in s Africa as far as sw Angola, except most of E, NE and N.
Status: Very common resident; nomadic in arid regions.
Habitat: Arid and semi-arid savanna, thornbush along watercourses, farmland in highveld, exotic plantations, gardens, parks, towns, cities; usually near water.
Habits: In pairs or family groups when breeding; otherwise more or less gregarious, sometimes in flocks of hundreds of birds. Forages by hopping on ground, often in company with other sparrows, weavers and doves; may hawk flying insects; drinks regularly. Roosts in pairs in specially built roosting nests, or communally in trees in flocks of up to 100 birds. Adapts well to human settlement, becoming fairly tame. Vocal all year; starts singing at dawn.

Food: Mainly seeds; also insects (adults and larvae—mainly small caterpillars), ovaries of deciduous fruit blossom, buds, scraps from feeding tray.
Breeding: *Season*: All months throughout range (mainly August-March). *Nest*: Large untidy hollow ball of grass, weeds, feathers, string, cotton, cloth and other soft material, with side entrance tunnel; thickly lined with feathers; from 2–20 m above ground in bush, tree, hollow fence pipe, chicken-wire fence, telephone pole crossbar, creeper, under eaves of building, in old swallow's nest; often colonial in arid regions, up to 30 nests in one tree (but not all occupied at once); built by both sexes. *Clutch*: (77) 2–3,5–5 eggs (usually 3–4; rarely 6). *Eggs*: White, greenish or bluish, usually densely spotted and blotched with dark brown and grey-brown often concentrated as cap at thick end; measure (267) 19,7 × 14,3 (16,5–22,4 × 13,2–15,8). *Incubation*: 12–14 days by both sexes, mainly by ♀; ♀ incubates at night. *Nestling*: 16–25 days; fed by both parents; postnestling dependence 1–2 weeks.

Ref. Immelmann, K. 1970. *Beitr. Vogelk.* 16:195–204.
Rowan, M.K. 1966. *Ostrich. Suppl.* 6:425–434.

804 (787)   **Greyheaded Sparrow**   **Plate 66**
Gryskopmossie
Passer diffusus

Enzunge (K), Serobele (SS), Tswere (Tw), [Graukopfsperling]
Measurements: Length 15–16 cm; wing (14 ♂) 79–82,5–88, (11 ♀) 77–80,1–83; tail (21) 58–65; tarsus (21) 16–19; culmen (21) 11–12,5. Weight (4 ♂) 21,5–24,2–25,5 g, (17 ♀) 22–24–25,8 g, (222 unsexed) 17,1–24,2–29,6 g.

GREYHEADED SPARROW

Bare Parts: Iris brown; bill black (breeding) or horn (nonbreeding); legs and feet brown.

Identification: Size medium (similar to ♀ Cape Sparrow, but head plain, build slimmer, legs shorter); head grey (no pale markings as in ♀ Cape Sparrow); back smoky brown; rump bright rufous (conspicuous in flight); conspicuous short white wingbar at rest and in flight; below shading from grey to white; sexes alike. *Immature*: Similar to adult, but duller.

Voice: Song and callnotes characteristically tinny, *chirrip cheeu chiriritit cheeu*, etc.; similar to notes of other sparrows, but thinner and higher-pitched.

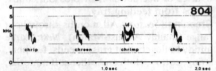

Distribution: Africa S of Sahara; throughout s Africa as far W as Montagu and Matjiesfontein; spreading westward in Karoo and s Cape at about 75 km/year; absent from extreme sw and w Cape and sw Namibia.

Status: Fairly common to uncommon in E, becoming common to locally abundant in W; resident, but nomadic in drier parts.

Habitat: *Acacia* savanna, dry woodland, exotic plantations, farmyards.

Habits: Solitary or in pairs when breeding; otherwise gregarious, especially in dry W

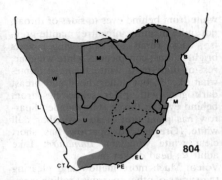

804

where flocks may number 50–60 birds (rarely over 500 birds), sometimes in company with other seed-eating species. Forages by walking on ground with small shuffling steps (other *Passer* species hop). Less adapted to human habitation than Cape Sparrow.

Food: Seeds, insects.

Breeding: *Season*: September to April (mainly November-March) throughout s Africa; rarely also June in Zimbabwe. *Nest*: Pad of grass, wool, hair and feathers in hole in tree (natural or made by barbet or woodpecker) or wall, hollow fence post, eave of building, thatched roof or old nest of Little Swift or striped swallow. *Clutch* : (33) 2–3,3–5 eggs (usually 3–4). *Eggs*: White, bluish or greenish, heavily blotched and spotted with brown and grey, often almost uniform chocolate or olive brown; measure (103) 19,2 × 14,3 (17–21,3 × 13,1–15,2). *Incubation*: Unrecorded. *Nestling*: Unrecorded.

805 (788)   Yellowthroated Sparrow   Plate 66
Geelvlekmossie
Petronia superciliaris

Enzunge (K), Inzwa-unzwe (Sh), Tswere (Tw), [Gelbkehlsperling]

Measurements: Length 15–16 cm; wing (73 ♂) 88–94,3–99, (47 ♀) 83,5–88,4–93; tail (52 ♂) 53–58,8–65, (23 ♀) 52–55,8–60; tarsus (41) 18–20; culmen (41) 13,5–14,5. Weight (3 ♂) 21–23,4–25,9 g, (2 ♀) 23,4–26 g, (12 unsexed) 25,3–27,5–29,8 g.

Bare Parts: Iris brown; bill dark horn, base pinkish; legs and feet brown.

Identification: Medium (about size of

Cape Sparrow); above greyish brown, streaked dusky on back (no rufous rump as in other indigenous s African sparrows); broad straight buff eyebrow, narrower in front, broader behind (diagnostic; Streakyheaded Canary has narrow curved white eyebrow); two pale bars on folded wing; below greyish, shading to off-white in centre of belly; yellow throat spot seldom shows in field; sexes alike. *Immature*: Similar to adult, but lacks yellow throat spot.

Voice: 3–4 loud evenly-pitched penetrating piping chirps, *chi-chi-chi* or *tri-tri-tri-tri* in quick phrase repeated several times with long pauses between.

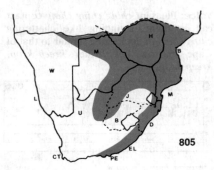

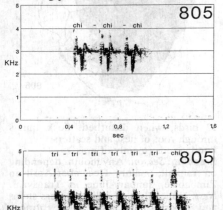

Distribution: S Africa to Zaire, Tanzania and Malawi; in s Africa absent from highveld and dry W.

Status: Generally uncommon resident; locally fairly common.

Habitat: Woodland, savanna, bushveld, riverine bush, exotic plantations (especially wattles); usually with sparse ground cover.

Habits: Solitary or in pairs. Quiet and unobtrusive; easily overlooked unless ♂ singing. Forages by walking on ground in small steps, or by gleaning from branches of canopy; flies into tree when disturbed. Often flicks wings and tail on alighting on branch, especially when alarmed.

Food: Insects, seeds, nectar of *Aloe* and *Tapinanthus*.

Breeding: *Season*: October to January in e Cape and Natal, August to December in Transvaal, August to March (mainly August-November) in Zimbabwe, January and February in Namibia. *Nest*: Pad of grass, wool, hair and feathers in hole in tree (natural, or old nest of barbet of woodpecker), or niche behind loose bark. *Clutch*: (26) 2–3,1–5 eggs (usually 3–4). *Eggs*: Greenish white, heavily streaked and blotched with dark brown, sometimes almost uniform chocolate brown; measure (70) 19,2 × 14,3 (16,3–21,3 × 13,4–15,9). *Incubation*: Unrecorded; by ♀ only. *Nestling*: 18–19 days; fed by both parents.

---

806 (789)   **Scalyfeathered Finch**   **Plate 69**
                       Baardmannetjie
                       Sporopipes squamifrons

Thaga (NS), Letsetsenkana, Raêuwanêng (Tw), [Schnurrbärtchen]

Measurements: Length 10–11 cm; wing (9 ♂) 57–57,5–58,5, (15 ♀) 52–56–58; tail (24) 34–40; tarsus (24) 14–16; culmen (24) 9–10. Weight (2 ♂, Orange Free State) 8,5–12,6 g, (2 ♀, Orange Free State) 10–11,5 g, (19 unsexed, Botswana) 8,9–10,3–12,2 g, (66 unsexed, w Transvaal) 10,4–12,4–13,7 g.

Bare Parts: Iris brown; bill rose pink; legs and feet pinkish to greyish brown.

Identification: Small (about size of waxbill; forecrown black, scaled white (hence "Scalyfeathered"); rest of upperparts light brownish grey; wings and tail black, edged white (conspicuous in flight); below whitish with bold black malar stripes (good field character, hence "*Baardmannetjie*"). *Immature*: Lacks scaling on forehead; bill dusky or horn-yellow.

713

Voice: Pleasant *ching ching ching* contact call in flight, sounding like chattering *chirri chirri* in flock; song similar to that of Cape Sparrow, but shriller, *kreep krop, kreep krop*.

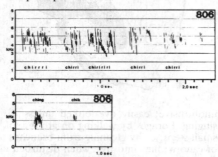

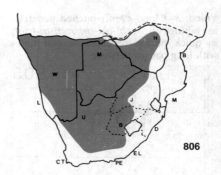

Distribution: Drier C and w parts of s Africa, to sw Angola.

Status: Common to very common nomadic resident.

Habitat: *Acacia* savanna, arid scrub, bushes along dry watercourses, farmyards.

Habits: Usually gregarious in flocks of 6–20 birds. Forages on ground, hopping quickly; seldom drinks water; when disturbed flies onto shrub or bush. Calls frequently. Tame and confiding; incubating birds sit very close. Roosts at night on branch in tight group of 3–4 birds, or in thin-roofed roosting nest in group of up to 12 birds; when disturbed, flock bursts through roof of nest and scatters.

Food: Seeds (mainly of grass).

Breeding: *Season*: Any month, depending on rainfall; mainly December-April in Zimbabwe, January-June in Transvaal. *Nest*: Hollow ball of pale dry grass stems and inflorescences, with side entrance tube; lined with fine grass flowers; 0,9–1,7–4,2 m above ground (50 nests) in thin branches of thornbush or tree (usually *Acacia* species); may roof over old nest of flycatcher or shrike. *Clutch*: (63) 2–4,1–7 eggs (usually 3–5). *Eggs*: Pale greenish, heavily clouded and spotted with greyish brown (like small eggs of Cape Sparrow); measure (106) 15,7 × 11,3 (13,9–17,7 × 10,3–12,7). *Incubation*: 10–12 days. *Nestling*: (8) 14–16–18 days.

---

807 (804)   **Thickbilled Weaver**   **Plate 66**
Dikbekwewer

Amblyospiza albifrons

[Weißstirnweber]

Measurements: Length ♂ 18–19 cm, ♀ 17–18 cm; wing (11 ♂) 94–96–101, (9 ♀) 83–85,8–90; tail (9 ♂) 65–71, (7 ♀) 58–65; tarsus ♂ 24–26, ♀ 21–23; culmen ♂ 24–26, ♀ 21–23. Weight (3 ♂) 43,3–50,4–60 g, (3 ♀) 31,4–37,1–45 g, (2 unsexed) 29,6–64,4 g.

Bare Parts: Iris brown; bill black (♂) or straw-yellow (♀); legs and feet grey to blackish.

Identification: Size large (somewhat smaller than Plumcoloured Starling); bill huge, very deep at base. *Male*: Mostly

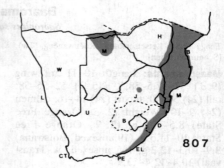

714

dark chocolate brown; frontal patches white (lost in eclipse); white wingpatch conspicuous in flight. *Female*: Above olive brown, scaled buff; below white, heavily streaked dark brown (distinguished from ♀ Plum-coloured Starling by heavy bill and un-streaked upperparts); no white wingpatch. *Immature*: Similar to adult ♀, but more rufous above, buffy below; bill dark horn.
Voice: Usually silent; chirping and twittering flight calls; quiet chatter from colony in reedbed; song jumble of simple pleasant chirps by ♂.

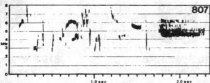

Distribution: Africa S of Sahara; in s Africa confined mainly to SE (from about Gamtoos River), e lowlands and midlands, and Okavango region of Botswana; isolated population on Witwatersrand.
Status: Common coastally and in tropics; locally common further inland in Natal; uncommon in e Cape; resident, but disperses widely after breeding.
Habitat: Reedbeds in breeding season; otherwise evergreen forest, groves of exotic Bugweed *Solanum mauritianum*.
Habits: Usually gregarious in flocks of 10–50 birds; rarely solitary or in smaller groups. Forages in canopy of forest, commuting up to 30 km from breeding grounds to feed; flight high, straight and slightly undulating; drops husks and shells of fruit to ground after opening with strong bill; holds husk in foot against perch while extracting seeds. Roosts at night in reed-beds in flocks of 400 birds or more, often in company with bishops and waxbills.
Food: Insects, fruit (e.g. *Celtis africana*, *Chaetacme aristata*), seeds (including *Sesbania*, *Melia* and *Lantana camara*), small molluscs.
Breeding: *Season*: September to March (mainly November-January) throughout s African range. *Nest*: Neatly woven oval of fine strips of grass, rush, sedge and palm leaves with small circular side-top entrance (unfinished nest has large entrance, Fig. 13); without lining; external height 17 cm, width 10 cm; walls about 1,5 cm thick, floor about 3 cm thick; woven around 2–6 upright stems of *Typha* and *Phragmites* (rarely in overhanging bush or tree); 1–1,5 m above water; built almost entirely by ♂ in 2–12 days; ♀ builds only inside nest; colonial, up to 50 nests/colony; rarely solitary; reeds or rushes around nest cut down by ♂ for radius of about 1 m; males usually monogamous. *Clutch*: (180) 2–3,1–4 eggs. *Eggs*: White to pink, spotted with red, purple and brown; measure (165) 23,6 × 16,2 (21,1–26,4 × 15,1–17,4); weigh (10) 2,3–2,7–3,1 g. *Incubation*: (5) 14–15–16 days by ♀ only. *Nestling*: About 20 days; fed by ♀ only on regurgitated seeds, snails and insects.

Ref. Laycock, H.T. 1979. *Ostrich* 50:70–82; 1984. *Proc. 5th Pan-Afr. Orn. Congr.*:413–424.

THE TRUE WEAVERS (GENUS *PLOCEUS*)

The genus *Ploceus* comprises a group of weavers from sparrow-sized to rather larger, breeding males of which are mostly yellow, with or without facemasks (the Chestnut Weaver is exceptional in being chestnut and black). The females are usually dull greenish above, yellowish or whitish below; eclipse males of most species resemble the females (the Forest, Oliveheaded and Spectacled Weavers are exceptional in that the females are very similar to the males which have no eclipse plumage). Breeding males present few identification problems (see the key on page lxxix)—look for colour and extent of facemask (black, brown, orange, green, none), iris colour (brown, red, yellow, white) and back colour and pattern (black, green or yellow; patterned or plain). Female weavers (apart from the exceptions already mentioned) are difficult to identify with certainty in the field, especially in winter when the males are not in breeding plumage. Features to look for are extent of yellow on belly, colour and pattern of back and relative size of body and bill. Several female weavers are probably not safely identifiable in the field, except on the basis of distribution and habitat. All but the Forest, Oliveheaded and Spectacled Weavers are gregarious colonial breeders.

WEAVER NESTS

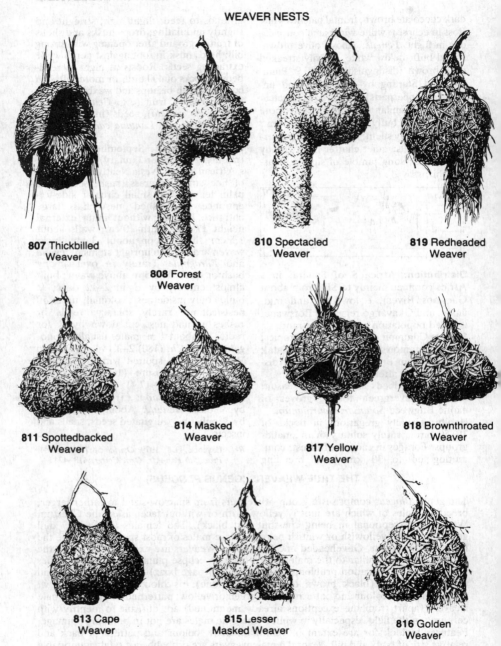

807 Thickbilled
Weaver

808 Forest
Weaver

810 Spectacled
Weaver

819 Redheaded
Weaver

811 Spottedbacked
Weaver

814 Masked
Weaver

817 Yellow
Weaver

818 Brownthroated
Weaver

813 Cape
Weaver

815 Lesser
Masked Weaver

816 Golden
Weaver

Figure 13. Types of nests of weavers of the genera *Ploceus* (the "true" weavers) and *Anaplectes* (the Redheaded Weaver). (Drawn by Jill Adams)

808 (790) Forest Weaver Plate 67
Bosmusikant
Ploceus bicolor

Ingilikingci (X), iTilongo (Z), [Waldweber]

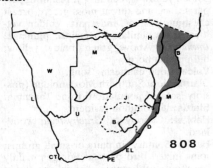

808

Measurements: Length 16–19 cm; wing (60 ♂) 82,5–87,7–94, (52 ♀) 78–83,4–87; tail (51 ♂) 52–56,6–61,5, (46 ♀) 50,5–54,4–57; tarsus (11) 21–33; culmen (11) 20–21.

Bare Parts: Iris brown; bill blue-grey or horn, cutting edges whitish; legs and feet pinkish brown.

Identification: Size medium to largish; sexes alike; above glossy black or brownish black; forehead speckled with white in subspecies *P. b. stictifrons*; below brilliant deep yellow, barred darker on throat. *Immature*: Above matt black with dark brown feather edges; throat not barred; flanks tinged olive.

Voice: Song fairly long phrases of mixed high-pitched musical and unmusical creaking notes, *tee-too-ti-kzzzrrree wee-too-tee-too-tee kzzzrrree*, etc., somewhat like rusty gate hinge; sings in duet, both sexes singing same song simultaneously; high-pitched bell-like *ting ting* and *zzrree* call-notes; rapid *tsi-tsi-tsi-tsi-tsi* alarm notes.

Distribution: Africa S of Sahara; in s Africa confined to extreme SE and E.

Status: Locally common resident.

Habitat: Upper and middle layers of evergreen forest, riverine forest and adjacent thickets.

Habits: Solitary, in pairs or small groups of up to 10 birds; pairs usually occupy fixed territories; young remain with parents to form family group, possibly until start of next breeding season; may join mixed bird parties. Forages high in trees, searching on mossy branches, in epiphytic plants and accumulated debris, creeping about and often hanging upside down. Easily overlooked unless calling. Tame and confiding.

Food: Insects, fruit, nectar (of *Aloe* and *Erythrina*).

Breeding: *Season*: October to January (mainly November) in Natal, September to February in Zimbabwe, August to December in Mozambique. *Nest*: Woven ball of vines and pliable twigs, with long vertical entrance spout (Fig. 13); lined with *Usnea* lichen; suspended from drooping branch of tree about 6–10 m above ground, often over clearing or roadway; built by ♂; solitary (not colonial). *Clutch*: (46) 2–3–4 eggs (usually 3). *Eggs*: Pinkish white, spotted with reddish, olive brown and slate; measure (54) 22,7 × 15,4 (20,9–25,4 × 14–16,6). *Incubation*: Unrecorded. *Nestling*: 22 days (captivity); independent of parents at 40 days.

Ref. Schmidl, D. 1988. *Gef. Welt* 112:44–47.
Wickler, W. & Seibt, V. 1980. *Z. Tierpsychol.* 52:217–226.

809 (791X) Oliveheaded Weaver Plate 67
Olyfkopwewer
Ploceus olivaceiceps

[Olivenkopfweber]

Measurements: Length about 16 cm; wing (11 ♂) 79–82,2–83,5, (9 ♀) 76,5–77,6–78,5; tail (11 ♂) 41,5–42,9–45, (9 ♀) 39,5–41,2–42; culmen (11 ♂) 14–14,8–16, (9 ♀) 14–14,6–15,5. Weight (11 ♂) 20,6–24 g, (8 ♀) 17,5–21,6 g.

Bare Parts: Iris ruby red; bill black; legs and feet greyish pink.

Identification: Size medium; forecrown golden yellow (green in ♀); rest of upperparts, face and throat moss green; breast chestnut; rest of underparts golden yellow; sexes similar; no eclipse plumage. *Immature*: Above green; below yellow; bill pinkish horn.

Voice: Loud chattering song.

Distribution: Southern Mozambique (possibly isolated population) to ne Tanzania.

Status: Uncommon resident.

Habitat: Canopy of *Brachystegia* woodland.

Habits: Solitary, in pairs or small groups; joins mixed bird parties. Forages mainly in canopy, off branches and foliage and in clumps of *Usnea* lichen, moving quickly and actively. Poorly known.

Food: Insects.

Breeding: Not recorded in s Africa. *Season*: September and October in Malawi.

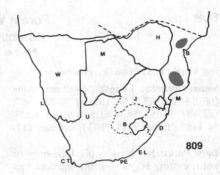

809

Nest: Oval of woven *Usnea* lichen with vertical entrance (no spout); suspended from stout branch fairly high above ground; usually inconspicuous. *Clutch*: 2–3 eggs. *Eggs*: Plain bright turquoise; measure about 20 × 15. *Incubation*: Unrecorded. *Nestling*: Unrecorded.

Ref. Clancey, P.A. & Lawson, W.J. 1966. *Durban Mus. Novit.* 8:35–37.

810 (791) Spectacled Weaver Plate 67
Brilwewer
Ploceus ocularis

Jesa (Sh), Sowa (Ts), Thaga (Tw), Ikreza (X), iGelegekle, iGeleja, umDweza (Z), [Brillenweber]

Measurements: Length 15–16 cm; wing (50 ♂) 71–75,4–82, (51 ♀) 69,5–73,3–77,5; tail (22 ♂) 58–61,3–66, (32 ♀) 56–60,5–64; tarsus (27) 23–26; culmen (10 ♂) 17–19,1–21, (13 ♀) 16–18–20. Weight (51 ♂) 21,2–26–33 g, (48 ♀) 20,3–24,8–29 g.

Bare Parts: Iris yellow; bill black; legs and feet blue-grey.

Identification: Size medium (see weaver key); crown and underparts golden yellow, shading to orange around black eyestripe (hence "Spectacled"; diagnostic) and black throat (in ♂; throat golden yellow in ♀); rest of upperparts yellow-green; rest of underparts bright yellow. *Immature*: Like adult ♀, but no orange on face; bill horn.

Voice: Characteristic sweet piping *tee-tee-tee-tee-tee* falling in pitch; harsh *chit* alarm note; twanging song by ♂ when approaching ♀.

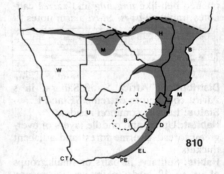

810

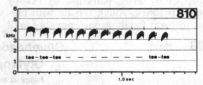

810

Distribution: S Africa to Guinea and Ethiopia; in s Africa confined to extreme SE and moister e parts.

Status: Fairly common resident.

Habitat: Riverine forest, adjacent thickets, edges of evergreen forest, dense scrub, gardens, parks.

Habits: Usually solitary or in pairs; sometimes in family groups. Forages in canopy, dense tangles, creepers, undergrowth, hedges and shrubberies, somewhat warblerlike; creeps up and down stems, often hanging upside-down. Members of pair call intermittently with descending piping phrase while feeding. Seldom emerges from cover.

Food: Insects, spiders, millipedes, nectar (mainly of *Aloe*), fruit, seeds.

Breeding: *Season*: September to February (mainly October-January) in Natal, October to January in Transvaal, September to March (mainly October-January) in Zimbabwe. *Nest*: Thin-walled ball of woven plant fibres (sometimes of horsehair, nylon thread or fishing line) with vertical entrance spout about 25–30 cm long (exceptionally up to 2 m long, Fig. 13); usually unlined or thinly lined with fine grass and plant down; tied to drooping branch of tree, bush or creeper, often overhanging dry gully or pool; about 3–6 m above ground or water; built by both sexes (mostly by ♂) in 2–3 weeks. *Clutch*: (90) 2–2,6–4 eggs (usually 3). *Eggs*: Greenish or pinkish white, speckled, spotted and streaked with grey and brown; measure (113) 21,9 × 14,8 (19,5–24,7 × 13,5–15,7). *Incubation*: 13,5 days by both sexes. *Nestling*: 18–19 days; fed by both parents.

Ref. Craig, A.J.F.K. 1984. *Proc. 5th Pan-Afr. Orn. Congr.*:477–483.
Skead, C.J. 1953. *Ostrich* 24:103–110.

---

811 (797)   Spottedbacked Weaver   Plate 67
Bontrugwewer
Ploceus cucullatus

Thaga (NS), Letholopje (SS), Jesa (Sh), Sowa (Ts), Thaga (Tw), Ihobo-hobo (X), iHlokohloko (Z), [Textor, Dorfweber]

Measurements: Length 15–17 cm; wing (209 ♂) 78–86,2–94, (174 ♀) 74–80–91; tail (142 ♂) 45–51,6–62, (135 ♀) 42–47,9–55; tarsus (17 ♂) 21–22,4–24, (2 ♀) 21,5–22; culmen (46 ♂) 16–19,8–22,5, (32 ♀) 17–19,1–22,5. Weight (227 ♂) 25,1–37,2–45,3 g, (166 ♀) 26–31,9–42,9 g.

Bare Parts: Iris red (♂) or brown (♀); bill black (breeding ♂) or pinkish horn (♀ and nonbreeding ♂); legs and feet brownish pink.

Identification: Size medium. *Breeding* ♂: Whole crown, sides of neck and underparts yellow (forehead black in Masked and Lesser Masked Weavers; whole head black, sometimes with yellow eyebrow, in n race of Spottedbacked Weaver *P. c. nigriceps* in Botswana and most of Zimbabwe and Mozambique); face and throat black, ending in point in centre of breast (as in Masked Weaver; Lesser Masked Weaver has rounded bib); rest of upperparts yellow, heavily spotted black (diagnostic for all races; other "masked" weavers have plain or faintly streaked green backs). *Female and nonbreeding* ♂: Crown olive; back and rump mottled grey; eyebrow dull yellow; throat yellow; rest of underparts white, washed grey on breast and flanks; ♂ recognizable by red eye. *Immature*: Similar to adult ♀.

Voice: Rolling swizzling song, very similar to that of Cape and Masked Weavers, but slightly less harsh, *cheee cheee shrrrrr, zzzzzrrr, cheee, ch-ch-ch-ch*, etc.; song characterized by wheezy "inhaling" sound

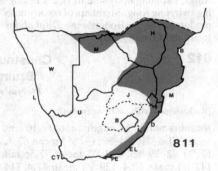

at end (songs of Cape and Masked Weavers just peter out); sharp *zit* alarm note; *chip chip* flight calls.

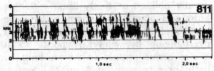

Distribution: Africa S of Sahara; in s Africa confined mainly to SE, NE and N.
Status: Common to very common resident; nomadic in winter.
Habitat: Edges of riverine forest, urban or suburban parks and gardens; usually near water.
Habits: Gregarious at all times; foraging flocks about 10–20 birds; breeding colonies up to 100 or more. Forages on ground or among leaves and flowers of trees; large food items held in foot while pecking with bill; flips fallen leaves with bill. Flight fast and direct with bursts of rapid wingbeats and intermittent flight calls. Male displays by hanging below nest, slowly fluttering wings, swinging body side to side and singing swizzling song. Members of colony mob predators (e.g. Boomslang *Dispholidus typus* and Gymnogene).

Food: Small insects (especially beetles), nectar (especially of *Aloe* and *Schotia*), stamens, green ovaries of flowers, seeds, food scraps from feeding tray.
Breeding: Males average 2 females each when breeding. *Season*: June to February (mainly September-December) in Natal, August to February in Transvaal, August to April (mainly September-February) in Zimbabwe. *Nest*: Horizontal oval woven by ♂ of strips of grass, reed, sedge and palm leaves, with vertical entrance (with or without very short spout, Fig. 13); roof thatched by ♂ with tree leaves; inside lined by ♀ with grass inflorescences; tied to drooping branch of tree (especially large exotics) or to upright reeds, from about 2 m or less above water (in reeds) to 20 m or more above ground (in trees); colonial, often aggregated around occupied nest of Hadeda Ibis or Pied Crow; ♂ strips nesting branches of leaves. *Clutch*: (139) 2–2,6–5 eggs (usually 2–3). *Eggs*: White, pale green or pale blue, plain or faintly speckled with red-brown; measure (180) 23,1 × 14,9 (20,5–25,1 × 13,4–16,9). *Incubation*: About 12 days by ♀ only. *Nestling*: 17–21 days; fed by both parents (mostly by ♀).

Ref. Collias, N.E. & Collias, E.C. 1971. *Koedoe* 14:1–27.

812 (796)   Chestnut Weaver   Plate 67
Bruinwewer
Ploceus rubiginosus

[Rotbrauner Weber, Maronenweber]

Measurements: Length about 16 cm; wing (10 ♂) 81–84–89, (42 ♂) mean 83,7, (7 ♀) 72–79–83, (29 ♀) mean 77,5; tail (42 ♂) mean 52,4, (29 ♀) mean 47,4, (14 unsexed) 48–65; tarsus (42 ♂) mean 22,9, (29 ♀) mean 21,4, (14 unsexed) 21–23; culmen (42 ♂) mean 20,9, (29 ♀) mean 19,6 (14 unsexed) 18–21.
Bare Parts: Iris orange to cinnamon-brown; bill black (breeding) or horn (non-breeding); legs and feet pale grey.
Identification: Size medium. *Breeding ♂*: Whole head and upper breast black; rest of body light chestnut; rump grey; wing and tail blackish, edged pale buff. *Female and nonbreeding ♂*: Crown light greenish grey, streaked blackish; eyebrow yellow-

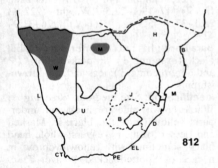

ish; rest of upperparts greyish brown, streaked dusky; below white, breast washed light brown (diagnostic). *Immature*: Similar to adult ♀, but breast streaked.

Voice: Loud chattering at breeding colonies; high-pitched *teep, cheep,* and *chip-chip* notes; chattery *tip-tip-tip*.

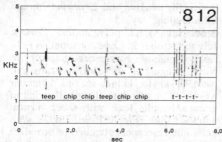

Distribution: Northern Namibia (from around Windhoek and Naukluft) and Angola, to E and NE Africa; occasional in Botswana around Maun and Gumare.
Status: Common breeding local migrant, present Namibia all year round.
Habitat: *Acacia* savanna.
Habits: Gregarious at all times; flocks compact, may be of one sex only. Flight fast and dashing. Shy, especially females. Poorly known.
Food: Unrecorded.

Breeding: *Season:* December to May (mainly January to March). *Nest:* Untidy but strongly woven ball of grass stems, with vertical entrance spout (26) 3–6–10 cm long; external length (26) 15–16–21 cm; external height (26) 12–15–18 cm; lined by ♀ with grass inflorescences (mainly *Stipagrostis uniplumis*) and some feathers; attached to outer branches of tall trees and bushes (mostly *Acacia, Albizia* and *Colophospermum;* also *Eucalyptus*); highly colonial, up to 200 or more nests/colony, sometimes in company with Masked Weaver. *Clutch:* (51) 2–3,3–6 eggs (61% of 3 eggs). *Eggs:* Plain white, turquoise or greenish blue; measure (181) 22,2 × 15,7 (20,3–24,5 × 14,1–17,2); weigh (27) 2–2,6–3,1 g. *Incubation:* (45) 11–14 days by ♀ only. *Nestling:* 13–16 days; weighs 2,1 g at hatching; fed by ♀ only; males may leave breeding colonies while young still in nests.

Ref. Berry, H.H., Archibald, T.J. & Berry, C.U. 1987. *Madoqua* 15:157–162.
Komen, J. 1990. *Cimbebasia* 12:69–74.
Komen, J. & Buys, P.J. 1990. *Cimbebasia* 12:63–67.

813 (799)   Cape Weaver   Plate 67
Kaapse Wewer
Ploceus capensis

Letholopje, Talane, Thaha (SS), Ihobo-hobo (X), [Kapweber]

Measurements: Length 17–18 cm; wing ♂ 89–95, ♀ 84–85; tail 53–61; tarsus 21–24; culmen 21–24. Weight (70 ♂) 42,2–47,5–52 g, (49 ♀) 36–40,3–45 g, (527 unsexed) 23–43,3–64 g.
Bare Parts: Iris yellow, cream, white (♂) or brown (♀; sometimes cream when breeding); bill black (breeding ♂) or pinkish horn (♀ and nonbreeding ♂); legs and feet pinkish brown.
Identification: Size medium to largish; bill relatively long; head slopes smoothly back from tip of bill to top of crown. *Breeding* ♂: Head brownish orange, shading to yellow underparts and yellowish green upperparts, faintly streaked darker olive on back; lores dusky; iris yellowish white (diagnostic; Lesser Masked Weaver has black facemask; Golden Weaver lacks

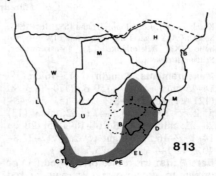

orange face). *Female and nonbreeding* ♂: Above greyish olive, lightly streaked dusky; throat and breast buff, shading to white over rest of underparts; flanks washed olive; breeding ♀ brighter yellow below; white eye of ♂ diagnostic at all times. *Immature:* Similar to nonbreeding ♀.

CAPE WEAVER

Voice: Harsh penetrating swizzling, less rolling than that of Spottedbacked Weaver and lacking wheezy final note; sings all year round; sharp *chip chip* alarm notes.

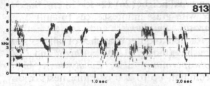

Distribution: Western, s and e Cape, Natal, Lesotho and most of Transvaal.
Status: Common resident; some altitudinal movement downwards in winter.
Habitat: Open woodland, wooded rivers, streams and kloofs, reedbeds near trees, farmland, parks, gardens.
Habits: Usually gregarious in small flocks; sometimes solitary. Forages on ground and in trees, gleaning from bark and foliage and probing flowers (forehead often coloured orange or yellow by pollen); visits bird tables. Large and aggressive; chases other birds at food source. Flicks wings vigorously when alarmed. Flight

fast and direct, 30–40 km/h. Similar to Spottedbacked Weaver.
Food: Insects, seeds, flower parts, nectar (especially of *Aloe* and *Erythrina*), bread from feeding tray.
Breeding: Males polygamous. *Season*: July to October in Cape, October to February (mainly November-January) in Natal, August to January in Transvaal. *Nest*: Oval to kidney-shaped chamber woven by ♂ of relatively broad strips of grass and palm leaf, with short vertical entrance tube (Fig. 13); lined by ♀ with grass inflorescences; attached to drooping branches of trees, upright reeds or telephone lines; usually about 2 m above water, 4–10 m above ground; colonial in groups of up to about 10 nests, sometimes aggregated around occupied nest of Hadeda Ibis; ♂ strips nesting branches of leaves. *Clutch*: (135) 2–2,6–4 eggs (usually 2–3). *Eggs*: Plain bright blue-green, often darker at thick end; measure (97) 24,7 × 16,1 (22,2–26,9 × 15,5–17,8). *Incubation*: 13,5 days by ♀ only. *Nestling*: 17 days; fed by both sexes, mostly by ♀.

Ref. Skead, C.J. 1947. *Ostrich* 18:1–42.

814 (803)   **Masked Weaver**   **Plate 67**
Swartkeelgeelvink
Ploceus velatus

Kambara (K), Letholopje, Thaha (SS), Jesa (Sh), Sowa (Ts), Thaga, Talê, Thaga-talê (Tw), Ihobohobo (X), iHlokohloko (Z), [Maskenweber, Schwarzstirnweber]

Measurements: Length ♂ 15–16 cm, ♀ 14–15 cm; wing (150 ♂) 70–78,3–90 (121 ♀) · 65–72,1–81; tail (51 ♂) 48–51,2–55, (56 ♀) 44,5–47,6–52; tarsus (13) 20–22; culmen (47 ♂) 14–16–18,5, (20 ♀) 14–15,2–16,5. Weight (596 ♂) 17–27,8–40 g, (2 144 ♀) 16,8–25,5–35,6 g.
Bare Parts: Iris red to orange-red (♂) or brown to grey-brown (♀; may be red when breeding); bill black (breeding ♂) or pinkish horn (♀ and nonbreeding ♂); legs and feet brownish pink.
Identification: Size medium. *Breeding* ♂: Forecrown, face and throat black, ending in point on centre of breast (whole crown yellow in Spottedbacked Weaver; bib rounded in Lesser Masked Weaver); hind-

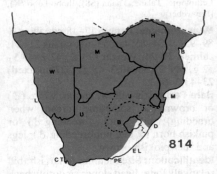

crown and nape yellow; rest of upperparts yellowish green, faintly streaked darker (heavily spotted black on yellow in Spottedbacked Weaver); rest of underparts bright yellow; eye red (pale yellow in Lesser Masked Weaver). *Female and nonbreeding* ♂: Above dull olive, streaked

722

darker on upper back; throat yellowish white, shading to buff on breast and white on belly (breeding ♀ deeper buff on throat and breast); ♂ distinguishable by red eye. *Immature*: Similar to nonbreeding ♀.

Voice: Harsh swizzling, possibly more rasping than that of Spottedbacked and Cape Weavers, but scarcely distinguishable, *zzzzrrrrr chik chik chik chik zzzrrr zweee*, etc., sometimes starting with introductory *chik* notes; song lacks wheezy final note heard in Spottedbacked Weaver; sharp *chuk* alarm note.

Roosts in unlined nests at night. Similar to Spottedbacked Weaver.

Food: Insects, seeds, flower parts, nectar, table scraps.

Breeding: *Season*: July to April (mainly September-February) throughout s Africa; often earlier in suburban areas than rural areas because of available building material; nestbuilding may continue into May; up to 8 successful broods/season for each polygamous ♂. *Nest*: Neat rounded oval woven by ♂ of strips of grass and reed leaves; vertical entrance with or without tube 8–12 mm long (Fig. 13); lined by ♀

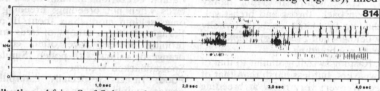

Distribution: Africa S of Sahara; throughout s Africa except most of coastal and s Natal, and parts of se Cape.

Status: Common resident; nomadic in winter.

Habitat: Almost all habitats except evergreen forest and coastal bush; mostly savanna, farmland with clumps of trees, exotic plantations, semi-arid scrub, riverine thickets, woodland edges; often near water, but also in waterless Kalahari and Namibia.

Habits: Gregarious; foraging flocks usually 5–20 birds; breeding colonies often much larger. Forages on ground or in trees, gleaning from bark and leaves; visits bird tables. Breeding and nonbreeding birds of both sexes display by hanging under nest, fanning wings and swizzling (see **Voice**). Males may acquire full breeding plumage in June, but many begin to build in eclipse plumage.

with grass inflorescences and leaves; attached to drooping branch of tree or between upright reed stems, over water when available; at almost any height above water or ground; nests not accepted by ♀ destroyed by ♂ only; colonial, sometimes aggregated around occupied nest of Pied Crow; ♂ may have up to 12 nests at one time, up to 36 nests/season, but up to 9 different males may display at one nest. *Clutch*: (196) 2–2,6–4 eggs (mostly 2–3). *Eggs:* Variable; white, pale blue, greenish blue or pale pink, plain or spotted with shades of brown and grey; measure (418) 21,2 × 14,5 (17,5–26,6 × 12,4–19,6). *Incubation*: Unrecorded; by ♀ only. *Nestling*: Unrecorded; fed by ♀ only.

Ref. Clancey, P.A. 1974. *Durban Mus. Novit.* 10:67–79.
Howman, H.R.G. & Begg, G.W. 1983. *S. Afr. J. Zool.* 18:37–44; 1987. *Honeyguide* 33:83–96.

815 (792)   Lesser Masked Weaver   Plate 67
Kleingeelvink
Ploceus intermedius

Kambara (K), Jesa (Sh), Sowa (Ts), Thaga (Tw), umZwingili (Z), [Cabanisweber]

Measurements: Length 14–15 cm; wing (16 ♂) 71–73,8–75, (17 ♀) 67–69–73; tail (29) 46–56; tarsus (29) 18–22; culmen (29) 14–17. Weight (4 ♂) 20,7–21,2–21,6 g, (4 ♀) 17,6–19,3–21,5 g, (22 unsexed) 14–21,9–28 g.

Bare Parts: Iris pale yellow to cream (♂) or brown (♀); bill black (♂) or pinkish horn (♀ and nonbreeding ♂); legs and feet blue-grey.

LESSER MASKED WEAVER

Identification: Size smallish; blue-grey legs and feet diagnostic in all plumages (pinkish brown in other similar weavers). *Breeding* ♂: Forecrown, face, throat and upper breast black, rounded below (pointed in centre of breast in Masked and Spottedbacked Weavers; whole crown yellow in Spottedbacked Weaver); nape and rest of underparts yellow; back green, streaked blackish (boldly spotted black on yellow in Spottedbacked Weaver); eye yellowish white (red in other black-masked weavers). *Female and nonbreeding* ♂: Above yellowish green, lightly streaked on back; throat and breast yellow, shading to whitish on belly (wholly yellow below when breeding). *Immature*: Similar to nonbreeding ♀.

Voice: Rasping swizzling similar to that of other weavers, but less harsh than that of Masked Weaver; very noisy at breeding colony.

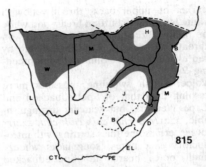
815

Distribution: S Africa to NE Africa; in s Africa from C Natal (around Pietermaritzburg) to Mozambique, e Transvaal, upper Limpopo River to Mmabolela, Zimbabwe, n Botswana and n Namibia.

Status: Locally common resident.

Habitat: *Acacia* savanna, bushveld, dry woodland, riverine trees; usually near water.

Habits: Gregarious in small flocks of 5–6 birds when not breeding; breeding colonies seldom more than about 10 pairs. Forages mostly in canopy of trees and by probing flowers; face often coloured orange or yellow with pollen. Similar to Spottedbacked Weaver.

Food: Insects (especially caterpillars), nectar (mainly of aloes), seeds.

Breeding: *Season*: October to February in Natal and Transvaal, August to March (mainly September-February) in Zimbabwe. *Nest*: Neat rounded oval woven by ♂ of fine strips of grass, reed or palm leaves (rarely of pine needles), with vertical entrance tube 2,5–7,5 cm long (Fig. 13); short lengths of building material (up to 2,5 cm long) sticking out all over give nest prickly appearance; suspended from branch on outside or inside of tree, often over water or up to 18 m above ground; sometimes also in reeds or low bushes; in small colonies of 10–20 nests, sometimes in association with Spottedbacked, Masked or Yellow Weavers. *Clutch*: (35) 2–2,5–4 eggs (usually 2–3). *Eggs*: Plain white or pale bluish white; measure (47) 21,3 × 14,6 (18,5–23,5 × 13,8–15,6). *Incubation*: Unrecorded. *Nestling*: Unrecorded; fed by both parents.

---

816 (801)   Golden Weaver   Plate 67
Goudwewer
Ploceus xanthops

Kambara (K), Jesa (Sh), Sowa (Ts), Thaga (Tw), iHlokohloko (Z), [Großer Goldweber, Safranweber]

Measurements: Length 17–18 cm; wing (139 ♂) 84–91,4–97, (108 ♀) 80–85,2–89; tail (78 ♂) 64–69,9–76, (71 ♀) 59–65,2–71,5; tarsus (34 ♂) 22–26–29, (30 ♀) 22–24,7–28; culmen (42 ♂) 18–20,8–22,5, (37 ♀) 17–19,8–22,5. Weight (124 ♂) 38–44–50,5 g, (101 ♀) 30,5–37,3–43 g.

Bare Parts: Iris yellow to pale orange; bill black (breeding) or pinkish horn (non-breeding); legs and feet pinkish brown.

Identification: Size medium to largish; yellow to light orange eye and heavy bill diagnostic in both sexes (eye red in Yellow Weaver). *Breeding* ♂: Forecrown and face golden yellow, shading to chrome yellow on underparts, centre of throat and upper breast washed orange (Yellow Weaver lemon yellow without orange wash); rest of upperparts golden green without streaking (faintly streaked in Yellow Weaver). *Female and nonbreeding* ♂: Above yellowish green, including forehead (back not streaked as in ♀ Yellow Weaver); below lemon yellow. *Immature:* Similar to adult ♀.

Voice: Sustained swizzling as in other weavers; sharp *chip* alarm note.

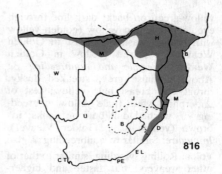

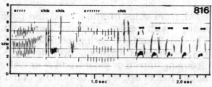

Distribution: S Africa to Zaire, Kenya and Uganda; in s Africa from s Natal to Swaziland, e Transvaal, Mozambique, Zimbabwe, n Botswana and n Ovamboland.

Status: Uncommon resident; possibly altitudinal migrant in Mozambique highlands (Mucrera Valley).

Habitat: Rank vegetation, reeds and bushes along streams and rivers, forest edge.

Habits: In pairs when breeding, otherwise gregarious in small groups, sometimes in company with other bird species. Forages in trees and dense bush along streams, sometimes in forest interior. Usually shy. Roosts in nest at night.

Food: Insects, fruit, seeds.

Breeding: *Season*: October to February in Natal, September to January in Transvaal, August to April (mainly September-February) in Zimbabwe. *Nest*: Large roughly woven ball of coarse strips of grass and palm leaves, with untidy grass inflorescences protruding through entrance (diagnostic) (Fig. 13); tied to drooping branch or upright reeds about 1–6 m above water; usually solitary, sometimes several nests in loose aggregation, but not truly colonial. *Clutch*: (30) 2–2,3–3 eggs. *Eggs*: White or light blue, plain or spotted with red-brown, violet and grey; measure (55) 24,1 × 16,2 (22,2–25,5 × 15,3–17,1). *Incubation*: Unrecorded. *Nestling*: 19–21 days; fed by both parents, mostly by ♀.

Ref. Mattocks, T. 1971. *Honeyguide* 67:32–34.

---

817 (800)   **Yellow Weaver**   **Plate 67**
                              Geelwewer
                           Ploceus subaureus

Intletlekwane (X), [Kleiner Goldweber]

Measurements: Length 16–17 cm; wing (11 ♂) 80–82,7–86, (4 ♀) 75–77,5–80; tail (13) 53–61; tarsus (13) 21–22,5; culmen (13) 17,5–19,5. Weight (4 ♂) 28,4–30,2–31,5 g, (5 ♀) 21–24,6–27,6 g.

Bare Parts: Iris red to pale orange (♂) or reddish brown to brown (♀); bill black (breeding ♂) or pinkish horn (♀ and nonbreeding ♂); legs and feet pinkish brown.

Identification: Size medium (smaller than Golden Weaver); head rounded. *Breeding* ♂: Crown golden yellow, shading to yellow-green on back; dark line through eye; below lemon yellow (golden yellow with orange wash on breast in Golden Weaver); eye red (yellow in Golden Weaver). *Female and nonbreeding* ♂: Above greenish grey, streaked dusky; throat and breast pale yellow; rest of underparts white (pale yellow in breeding ♀), washed dull buff on flanks; iris brown (yellow in ♀ Golden Weaver). *Immature*: Similar to nonbreeding ♀.

Voice: Rolling swizzling, similar to that of other weavers, but faster and higher-pitched; harsh *chik* alarm note.

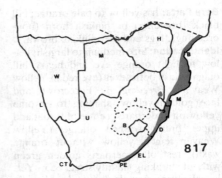

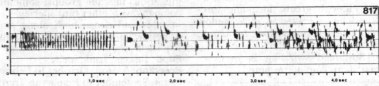

Distribution: S Africa to E Africa; in s Africa confined to littoral and adjacent inland from about Uitenhage northwards.
Status: Locally common resident.
Habitat: Reeds and reedbeds in dams, pans and estuaries when breeding; otherwise *Acacia* savanna and open woodland.
Habits: Gregarious at all times; flocks large when not breeding. Highly vocal at breeding colonies. Forages in trees. Similar to Masked Weaver.
Food: Insects, seeds, fruit.
Breeding: *Season*: September to February in Natal. *Nest*: Neat rounded oval woven by ♂ from strips of grass, reed and palm leaves, with vertical entrance (no spout; Fig. 13); lined by ♀ with grass inflorescences; suspended between upright reeds, drooping branch or palm frond over water about 1–2 m up; leaves of nesting branch stripped by ♂; colonial, sometimes in company with Lesser Masked Weavers. *Clutch*: (147) 2–2,4–4 eggs (usually 2–3). *Eggs*: White or pale blue; plain or spotted with black, brown, violet and grey; measure (53) 23 × 15,1 (21–26 × 14,1–16,3) *Incubation*: Unrecorded. *Nestling*: Unrecorded.

818 (802) Brownthroated Weaver Plate 67
Bruinkeelwewer
Ploceus xanthopterus

[Braunkehlweber]

Measurements: Length about 15 cm; wing (126 ♂) 68–72,3–80, (105 ♀) 61–64,4–70; tail (119 ♂) 44–47,6–54, (104 ♀) 38–42,8–46; tarsus (6) 18–22; culmen (119 ♂) 17–17,9–19, (103 ♀) 15–16,8–18. Weight (119 ♂) 23–24,9–28 g, (103 ♀) 16–19,1–24 g.
Bare Parts: Iris red-brown (♂) or brown (♀); bill black (breeding ♂) or pinkish horn (♀ and nonbreeding ♂); legs and feet pinkish (breeding) to brownish (nonbreeding).

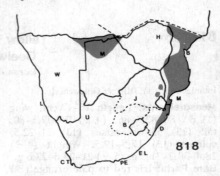

Identification: Size smallish; head rather square-shaped; tail short. *Breeding* ♂: Bright yellow, tinged green on back; face and throat chestnut brown (diagnostic). *Female and nonbreeding* ♂: Crown olive; back and rump olive washed cinnamon; throat, breast and flanks buffy yellow; rest of underparts white (underparts lemon yellow in breeding ♀). *Immature*: Similar to nonbreeding ♀.

Voice: Jumble of nasal twanging, buzzing, trilling and sibilant notes, *zeep seep zzzz swirrr zeep sweeu*, etc.

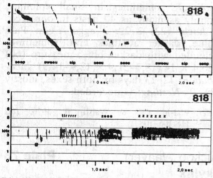

Distribution: S Africa to E Africa; in s Africa confined to extreme e lowlands

from S of Durban northwards, Okavango region and Zambezi River W of Victoria Falls.

Status: Uncommon resident.

Habitat: *Phragmites* reedbeds in rivers and estuaries when breeding; otherwise also riverine forest and thickets.

Habits: Gregarious at all times. Forages in trees and bushes, especially in winter. Similar to Yellow Weaver, but poorly known.

Food: Seeds, grain, berries, insects.

Breeding: Males may have up to 3 females. *Season*: October to December in Natal, October to January in Zimbabwe; sometimes 2 broods/season. *Nest*: Neat oval woven by ♂ from strips of reed leaves, lined with reed inflorescences; vertical entrance without tube (Fig. 13); tied to reed stems, up to 3 m above water; in colonies of 10–300 nests. *Clutch*: (29) 2–2,5–4 eggs (usually 2–3). *Eggs*: Deep chocolate or olive brown, or blue-green, plain or spotted with brown; measure (38) 21 × 14,6 (19,1–23 × 14–15). *Incubation*: (14) 14–16 days by ♀ only. *Nestling*: (11) 14–17 days; fed by ♀ only.

Ref. Hanmer, D.B. 1984. *Proc. 5th Pan-Afr. Orn. Congr.*:121–148.

---

819 (793)   **Redheaded Weaver**   **Plate 66**
Rooikopwewer
Anaplectes rubriceps

Sowa (Ts), [Scharlachweber]

Measurements: Length 14–15 cm; wing (25 ♂) 80–82–85, (11 ♀) 76–77,6–80; tail (42) 48–54; tarsus (42) 18–20; culmen (42) 16–18,5. Weight (1 ♂) 24,6 g, (1 ♀) 20,3 g, (9 unsexed) 14,4–19,1–20,8 g.

Bare Parts: Iris reddish (breeding) or brown (nonbreeding); bill red to orange (breeding ♂) or pinkish to orange (♀ and nonbreeding ♂); legs and feet pinkish brown.

Identification: Size smallish; bill rather slender. *Breeding* ♂: Head, breast and upper back brilliant scarlet; rest of upperparts grey (Cardinal and Redheaded Queleas red on head only); back heavily streaked; wings dusky, edged yellow; rest

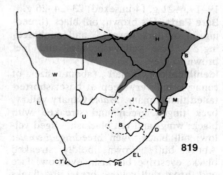

of underparts white. *Female and nonbreeding* ♂: Scarlet replaced by dull orange above, pale yellow to buff below. *Immature*: Similar to adult ♀.

Voice: Song rapid high-pitched squeaky swizzling *chi-chi-chi-chi swizz-swizz-swizz swee-swee ssss chhhrrrr sip-sip-sip*, etc.

Distribution: Africa S of Sahara; in s Africa confined to NE from Zululand to Caprivi; recorded Etosha and Waterberg Plateau, Namibia.
Status: Common to fairly common resident; summer breeding visitor to some areas.
Habitat: Woodland, bushveld, savanna; usually not far from water.
Habits: Usually solitary or in pairs; may join mixed bird parties. Forages off foliage, dry fruit capsules and branches of trees, somewhat woodpeckerlike. Usually quiet and easily overlooked, but presence indicated by nests which last many months.

Food: Mainly insects and spiders; also seeds and fruit.
Breeding: *Season*: October to January in Transvaal, July to February (mainly August-December) in Zimbabwe. *Nest*: Ball of woven sticks, twigs, tendrils and leaf midribs, thatched with broad leaves (built mainly by ♂, less by ♀), lined with grass (probably by ♀); vertical entrance with spout about 20 cm long (Fig. 13); attached by woven stalk to branch of tree, telephone wire or windmill vane, usually several metres above ground; usually solitary, sometimes in small colonies, rarely as many as 40 nests in one tree. *Clutch*: (23) 2-2,5-3 eggs. *Eggs*: Pale blue, darker at thick end, sometimes clouded with darker blue; measure (60) 20,4 × 14 (18,7-21,9 × 12,9-14,9). *Incubation*: 12-13 days by both sexes, mostly by ♀. *Nestling*: Unrecorded.

Ref. Walsh, J.F. & Walsh, B. 1976. *Ibis* 118:106-108.

820 (854) Cuckoofinch (Cuckoo Weaver) Plate 73
Koekoekvink
Anomalospiza imberbis

[Kuckucksweber]

Measurements: Length about 13 cm; wing (86 ♂) 68-71,3-76,5, (26 ♀) 68,5-69,8-73; tail 36-44; tarsus 17-18; culmen 12-14. Weight (8 ♂) 18-19,8-21 g, (6 ♀) 19-19,6-21 g, (4 unsexed) 23-24-26 g.
Bare Parts: Iris brown; bill black (breeding ♂) or dark horn (♀ and nonbreeding ♂), base yellowish; legs and feet brown to grey.
Identification: Small (about size of canary); bill very deep at base; shorter-tailed than canary. *Male*: Canary yellow, back tinged green and streaked with black; wings and tail blackish, edged yellow; bill black when breeding. *Female*: Above buffy brown, boldly streaked black; eyestripe blackish; eyebrow, face and throat dull yellow; breast and flanks pale brown shading to white on belly; heavy bill diagnostic. *Immature*: Similar to adult ♀. *Chick*: Dark purplish above, dark pinkish below (cisticola chicks mostly

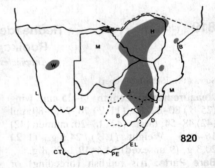

light pinkish); sparse tufts of white down on back and wings; mouth pinkish purple (yellow in cisticolas, with black tongue spots) with orange-yellow gape.
Voice: Song of ♂ slightly rasping *tseep krrik krrik krrik krrik* or *seedle-eedle-eedle-thrush-thrush* (somewhat like raspy song of Neddicky); ♂ also makes swizzling sounds in display; chattering and warbling contact calls in flock.

Distribution: Africa S of Sahara; in s Africa mainly inland Natal (from about Pietermaritzburg), Transvaal and Zimbabwe; also Caprivi; vagrant to Mozambique.

Status: Generally uncommon summer breeding visitor; locally common; probably resident but nomadic in Zimbabwe.

Habitat: Open or lightly wooded grassland, vleis, cultivated land.

Habits: Solitary, in pairs or in small flocks when breeding; in Zimbabwe roosts communally in reedbeds in flocks of 300–500 (even up to 1200) birds when not breeding. Except for heavy dark bill, easily confused with canaries, so often overlooked. Forages on inflorescences of grasses and weeds in open veld. Usually fairly shy; flight fast, direct and weaverlike.

Food: Seeds.

Breeding: *Season*: September to March in Transvaal, November to March in Zimbabwe. *Hosts*: Cisticolas (Fantailed, Desert, Ayres', Palecrowned, Croaking, Singing, Levaillant's and Redfaced) and prinias (Tawnyflanked and Blackchested). *Clutch*: (11) 1–2,9–4 eggs; 1–2 eggs in each host nest; one or more host eggs removed when laying. *Eggs*: Pale bluish white, plain or speckled with brick red; measure (6) 16,9 × 12,5 (15,4–18,1 × 11,6–13); mean weight 1,59 g (mean weight of Fantailed Cisticola eggs 1,07 g). *Incubation*: 14 days. *Nestling* : 18 days; 2 Cuckoofinch young may be reared together, but host young usually trampled to death; rarely host and parasite chicks reared together.

Ref. Vernon, C.J. 1964. *Ostrich* 35:260–263.

821 (805) Redbilled Quelea Plate 69
Rooibekkwelea
Quelea quelea

Enzunge (K), Lerwerwe (NS), Thaha (SS), Chimokoto (Sh), Xihlolavayeni, Vurhiyana, Nghatzi (Ts), [Blutschnabelweber]

Measurements: Length 11–13 cm; wing (279 ♂) 61–67,2–72, (129 ♀) 58–63,7–69; tail (245 ♂) 32–36,8–41, (111 ♀) 33–35,5–39; tarsus (39) 17–19; culmen (144 ♂) 13–14–15. Weight (2 003 ♂) 15–19,9–27,6 g, (950 ♀) 12,6–18,7–26,3 g.

Bare Parts: Iris brown; bill bright red (yellowish horn in breeding ♀); legs and feet pinkish.

Identification: Size small; red bill diagnostic in all adults, except breeding females which have yellow bill (other ♀ quelea species have dull horn-coloured bills at all seasons; *Euplectes* females never have red or yellow bills). *Breeding ♂:* Head and face variable; (a) forehead, face and throat black (about 90 % of population), surrounded by pink or light yellow from crown to breast, (b) face and throat white (about 10% of population) surrounded by pink or yellowish buff from top of head to breast; about equal numbers of pink and

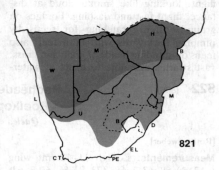

821

yellow birds, regardless of facial mask colour; rest of upperparts streaked black and buff; rest of underparts white, lightly mottled brownish on breast and flanks. *Female and nonbreeding ♂:* Above streaked greyish buff and brown; eyebrow off-white; below white, breast mottled greyish; bill red or yellow (female and eclipse ♂ whydahs also have red bill, but head boldly striped buff and blackish). *Immature*: Similar to adult ♀; bill pinkish horn.

Voice: Usually silent away from breeding colony; metallic chattering from members of colony; song mixed chattering and wheezy *tsssrreeee* and *chee-chee* notes; shrill *chak-chak* alarm call.

Distribution: Africa S of Sahara; widespread in s Africa, except in most of Cape S of Orange River, and extreme arid w Namibia.

Status: Locally abundant; highly nomadic, numbers varying greatly in time and place; southern populations migratory, sometimes breeding in southern part of range; seasonally reaches plague proportions in croplands.

Habitat: Savanna, agricultural land.

Habits: Highly gregarious, flocks sometimes numbering thousands or millions of birds, incurring serious crop losses. Flocks densely packed and highly synchronized in flight, looking like smoke cloud at distance; flight fast and dashing. Forages on ground, often scratching for seeds by jumping backwards with both feet; also feeds on standing heads of grain and grass; vast swarms assemble to drink at water-holes, sometimes breaking branches with sheer weight; drinking flock may fly over water, lowest birds dropping into water to drink and fly up again, so that flock "rolls" over water surface.

Food: Seeds, grain; insects fed to nestlings.

Breeding: *Season*: November to April in e Cape, December to May in Transvaal, November to April (mainly January-February) in Zimbabwe. *Nest*: Small rounded thin-walled ball with large side entrance, woven by ♂ from fine strips of grass; little or no lining added; usually in thorntrees, but also in reedbeds; colonial, usually in enormous numbers, sometimes up to 500 nests/tree; colony may cover several hectares. *Clutch*: (785) 1–2,8–5 eggs (usually 2–4). *Eggs*: Pale greenish blue or bluish white; measure (86) 18,8 × 13,2 (16,1–21 × 11,3–14,8). *Incubation*: 9,5–12 days by both sexes; ♀ incubates at night; no incubation on hot days. *Nestling*: 11–13 days; fed by both parents; mortality high, many young falling from nests and preyed on or scavenged by raptors, vultures, carnivorous mammals and monitor lizards.

Ref. Jones, P.J. & Ward, P. 1976. *Ibis* 118:547–574.
Naudé, T.J. 1959. *Ostrich Suppl.* 3:264–270.
Ward, P. 1965. *Ibis* 107:326–349; 1971. *Ibis* 113:275–297.

822 (806) Redheaded Quelea Plate 69
Rooikopkwelea
Quelea erythrops

[Rotkopfweber]

Measurements: Length 11–12 cm; wing (113 ♂) 58–63,7–68, (73 ♀) 55–60,8–63; tail (13) 31–36; tarsus (13) 16–18; culmen (13) 13,5–15. Weight (36 ♂) 17,5–21,1–25,5 g, (63 ♀) 15–17,7–22 g.

Bare Parts: Iris brown; bill black (breeding ♂) or horn (♀ and nonbreeding ♂); legs and feet pinkish.

Identification: Size small. *Breeding ♂*: Head, nape and throat bright red (red extends to upper breast in Cardinal Quelea); throat barred blackish, visible at close range only (no black on throat of Cardinal Quelea; nape streaked like

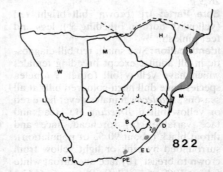

back); rest of upperparts streaked buff and dark brown; rest of underparts off-white, washed tawny across breast; bill black. *Female and nonbreeding ♂:* Similar to breeding ♂, but without red on head; eyebrow yellowish white; face orange-buff in breeding ♀; throat and breast light orange-buff (♀ Redbilled Quelea mottled greyish on breast); bill horn (red or yellow in ♀ Redbilled Quelea); probably not safely separable from ♀ Cardinal Quelea in field. *Immature:* Similar to nonbreeding ♀.

Voice: Song churring or buzzing; chattering calls at breeding colony.

Distribution: Africa S of Sahara; in s Africa mostly confined to littoral of Mozambique; vagrant S to Natal as far inland as Pietermaritzburg, and e Cape; has bred as far S as Durban; migrates to tropical Africa.

Status: Uncommon breeding migrant, about September to April.

Habitat: Rank weeds, grass and reedbeds near water in woodland and savanna.

Habits: Gregarious at all times; flocks much smaller than those of Redbilled Quelea, well coordinated in fast direct flight. Takes seeds from flowering tops of grass and tall herbs. Similar to Redbilled Quelea.

Food: Seeds, grain; insects fed to young.

Breeding: Has bred at St Lucia, Zululand 1985 and has built nests in Pietermaritzburg. *Season:* December to April. *Nest:* Ball of fine tightly woven grass or thin strips of *Typha* leaf, with large side entrance; 9–11 cm overall height, 7–10 cm wide; entrance 4–4,5 cm wide (10 nests); suspended between 2 reed stems, grass or herbs in swamp; 0,5–2 m above water, mostly 1,8 m; unlined; started by ♂, completed by ♀; colonial, up to 2 000 birds in colony. *Clutch:* (915) 1–2,1–4 eggs (84% of 2 eggs). *Eggs:* Plain pale greenish blue; measure (53) 18,9 × 13,4 (17,4–20,7 × 12,5–14,3). *Incubation:* Unrecorded; by ♀ only. *Nestling:* 12–14 days; fed by ♀ only.

Ref. Grimes, L.G. 1977. *Ibis* 119:216–220.
McLean, S. & Taylor, R.H. 1986. *Ostrich* 57:60–61.
Tree, A.J. 1965. *Bull. Brit. Orn. Club* 85:159–161.

823 (807) Cardinal Quelea Plate 69
Kardinaalkwelea
Quelea cardinalis

[Kardinalweber]

Measurements: Length 10–11 cm; wing 57–63; tail 30–37; tarsus 15–18; culmen 11–13.

Bare Parts: Iris brown; bill black (breeding ♂) or horn (♀ and nonbreeding ♂); legs and feet pinkish brown.

Identification: Size small. *Breeding ♂:* Head, throat and upper breast bright red (throat barred black in Redheaded Quelea; breast buff); nape and back streaked tawny and blackish (nape red in Redheaded Quelea); rest of underparts creamy white, streaked on flanks. *Female and nonbreeding ♂:* No red on head; crown streaked like back; eyebrow buff; throat and breast yellowish buff (breast mottled greyish in ♀ Redbilled Quelea); belly white; probably not safely separable from ♀ Redheaded Quelea in field. *Immature:* Below deeper buff than in adult ♀; breast lightly spotted with dusky.

Voice: Song of ♂ rapid swizzling *chit chit chit chichichichit*, like fingernail run fast over teeth of comb.

Distribution: Middle Zambezi Valley, Mozambique (and possibly Zimbabwe), Zambia and Malawi to Kenya.

Status: Uncertain, not definitely recorded within s African limits; possibly rare straggler at edge of range; nomadic after breeding.

Habitat: Rank grass in shallow valleys, vleis and swamps, often in drier areas than those favoured by Redheaded Quelea.

Habits: Gregarious, sometimes in large flocks. ♂ sings and displays from top of tall reed or bush, fluffing plumage, quivering wings and jerking fanned tail. Similar to other queleas.

Food: Seeds.

Breeding: Not recorded in s Africa; males polygamous. *Season:* February in Zambia. *Nest:* Upright oval, compactly woven of grass, with side-top entrance 4–5 cm in diameter; lined with fine grass inflorescences; tied to upright stems of grasses or herbs in marshy ground; about 60–90 cm above ground; colonial. *Clutch*: 2–3 eggs.

Eggs: White, blue or greenish, spotted with dark brown, red-brown and greyish mauve; measure (4) 18,2 × 12,4 (17–19,3 × 11,7–13). *Incubation*: 12–14 days by ♀ only. *Nestling*: 16–17 days.

THE BISHOPS AND WIDOWS, GENUS *EUPLECTES*

The technical difference between a bishop and a widow is that a male widow replaces its rectrices (tail feathers) in the pre-breeding moult, while a bishop does not. This is clearly of no use in the field. Most, but not all, male widows have long tails in the breeding season; bishops have short tails at all times. All *Euplectes* species are highly dimorphic sexually, breeding males being combinations of black, red, yellow and white; the females are streaked above with blackish on buff or brown, and are whitish below with darker-streaked breasts. The males have an eclipse plumage that resembles that of the female to a great extent, but males are often noticeably larger than females and may retain a flash of red, yellow or white on the rump or in the wing in some species. Breeding males are mostly highly distinctive and easily identifiable in the field; breeding females and many males in eclipse plumage are not so easy (see the key on page lxxiv); indeed some are probably not safely separable in the field except by an expert, even when they move about in large mixed-species flocks in winter. All species tend to be gregarious at all times, but in the breeding season females appear to outnumber males several fold because the males are polygamous. Most *Euplectes* species inhabit grassland, marshes, vleis, reedbeds and cultivated lands, at least when breeding. They have somewhat rasping swizzling songs, rather like those of the true weavers (*Ploceus*), but thinner and less carrying. The males have characteristic flight displays over their nesting territories with fluffed plumage and/or depressed long flexible rectrices. All are more or less colonial breeders, depending on the habitat.

Ref. Johnson, D.N. & Horner, R.F. 1986. *Bokmakierie* 38:13–17.

824 (808)   **Red Bishop**   **Plate 68**
Rooivink
Euplectes orix

Kambara Gomugeha (K), Thagalehlaka (NS), Thaha-khube, Khube, Thaha-khubelu (SS), Chikenya (Sh), Thaga, Mohubê (Tw), Umlilo, Intakomlilo, Ucumse (X), iBomvana, isiGwe, inTakansinsi (Z), [Oryxweber]

Measurements: Length ♂ 12–13 cm, ♀ 11–12 cm; wing (192 ♂) 65–71–79, (222 ♀) 59–63,1–68,5; tail (153 ♂) 35–39,8–45,5, (147 ♀) 30,5–34,9–42; tarsus (29) 20–23; culmen (20 ♂) 15–16, (9 ♀) 13,5–14. Weight (860 ♂) 15,3–24,6–26 g, (593 ♀) 13,5–19,8–25,2.

Bare Parts: Iris brown; bill black (breeding ♂) or pinkish horn, culmen dusky (♀ and nonbreeding ♂); legs and feet pinkish brown.

Identification: Size medium to smallish; very similar to Firecrowned Bishop. *Breeding* ♂: Forecrown, face and throat black (forecrown scarlet in Firecrowned

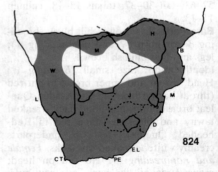

824

Bishop; only forehead narrowly black); rest of head, breast, lower belly and rump brilliant orange-scarlet; upper belly black; mantle orange-brown; wings and tail brown (black in Firecrowned Bishop). *Female and nonbreeding* ♂: Above boldly streaked buff and dark brown; eyebrow whitish; below white, washed buff and streaked brown on breast and flanks; wings and tail dark brown (black in Firecrowned Bishop). *Immature:* Similar to adult ♀, but yellower on throat and breast.

Voice: Sharp *chiz chiz* callnotes; song wheezy whining *chsssss zeeeee tsarippy-tsarippy-tsarippy ts-ts-ts-ts-ts zwipzwaay,* etc.

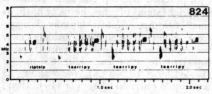

Distribution: Africa S of Sahara; throughout most of s Africa except central Kalahari basin and nw Namibia.

Status: Very common resident, less common in dry W; nomadic in winter.

Habitat: Rank grass, reedbeds, bullrushes and sedges in marshes, vleis, dams and rivers; also gardens, orchards, cultivated fields, open grassland.

Habits: Gregarious at all times, nonbreeding flocks sometimes numbering hundreds of birds, causing losses to grain crops. Forages on ground, walking in short steps; also visits feeding trays. Male displays from perch or in beelike cruising flight on rapidly beating wings, plumage puffed out, uttering swizzling song; sometimes several males display simultaneously in different parts of reedbed. Males often chase females and rival males.

Food: Seeds, grain; insects fed to young.

Breeding: Males polygamous, with up to 7 females each. *Season:* July to December in sw Cape, September to March in s Cape, October to April (mainly December-February) in Natal and Transvaal, November to April (mainly December-March) in Orange Free State, Lesotho and Zimbabwe. *Nest:* Thin-walled upright oval woven by ♂ of fine strips of grass and reed leaves, with porched side-top entrance; thinly lined by ♀ with soft grass flowers; attached to upright reed, grass or weed stems (also built in maize fields), or thin vertical branches of tree; usually 1–2 m above ground or water, less often up to 8 m up in tree; usually colonial, sometimes solitary. *Clutch:* (1060) 2–2,7–5 eggs (usually 3; 7 eggs in one nest probably laid by 2 females). *Eggs:* Plain greenish blue; measure (268) 19,2 × 14,1 (14,6–21,6 × 11,8–15,7); weigh (15) mean 1,73 g. *Incubation:* 12–13 days by ♀ only. *Nestling:* (17) 12–13,5–16 days; fed by ♀ only.

Ref. Brooke, R.K. 1966. *Ostrich Suppl.* 6:223–235.
Craig, A.J.F.K. 1974. *Ostrich* 45:149–160; 1982. *Ostrich* 53:182–188.
Skead, C.J. 1956. *Ostrich* 27:112–126.
Woodall, P.F. 1971. *Ostrich* 42:205–210.

825 (809)   **Firecrowned Bishop** (Blackwinged Bishop)   **Plate 68**
Vuurkopvink
Euplectes hordeaceus

[Feuerweber, Flammenweber]

Measurements: Length 13–15 cm; wing (14 ♂) 70–76,5–86, (6 ♀) 57–66,5–75; tail 34–50; tarsus 18–22; culmen 14–17. Weight (2 ♀) 18,8–19 g.

Bare Parts: Iris brown; bill black (breeding ♂) or horn (♀ and nonbreeding ♂); legs and feet brown.

Identification: Size smallish; very similar to Red Bishop. *Breeding ♂:* Crown, nape, breast, rump and lower belly brilliant orange-scarlet; narrow forehead band, face and throat black (forecrown black in Red Bishop); mantle orange-brown;

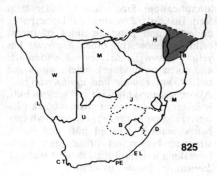

upper belly black; wings and tail black (diagnostic; brown in Red Bishop). *Female and nonbreeding ♂:* Above streaked black and buff; eyebrow yellowish white; below white, washed buff and streaked dark brown on breast and flanks; wings and tail brown as in Red Bishop. *Immature:* Similar to adult ♀, but buffier above.

Voice: Similar to that of Red Bishop.

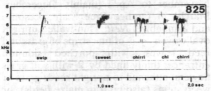

Distribution: Africa S of Sahara; in s Africa confined to extreme e and n Zimbabwe and Mozambique N of Save River.
Status: Local and uncommon resident.
Habitat: Rank vegetation with bushes and trees, usually along streams; also cultivated lands.

Habits: Usually in pairs or small groups. Very similar to Red Bishop, but less gregarious.

Food: Seeds, grain, insects.

Breeding: Males polygamous. *Season:* December to May in Mozambique, January to April in Zimbabwe. *Nest:* Upright oval woven by ♂ of green grass strips, with porched side-top entrance; attached to upright stems of grass, herbs or bush; in small colonies. *Clutch:* Usually 3 eggs. *Eggs:* Light greenish blue, usually plain but sometimes sparsely spotted with brown or violet; measure (20) 18,6 × 13,9 (17,4–19,9 × 12,9–14,4). *Incubation:* 13 days by ♀ only. *Nestling:* (2) 11–12 days; fed by ♀ only.

Ref. Fuggles-Couchman, N.R. 1943. *Ibis* 85:311–326.
Lack, D. 1935. *Ibis* 77:817–836.

826 (812) Golden Bishop Plate 68
Goudgeelvink
Euplectes afer

Kambara (K), Thaha-pinyane, Thaha-tsehle, Tsehle (SS), Mantunje, Xikhungumala (Ts), [Tahaweber, Napoleonweber]

Measurements: Length about 12 cm; wing (18 ♂) 62–64,2–67,5, (4 ♀) 61–61,8–63; tail (18) 33–40; tarsus (18) 16,5–18; culmen (18) 12–13. Weight (10 ♂) 12,8–16,3–19,8 g, (5 ♀) 13,5–14,8–16,6 g, (6 unsexed) 14–15,6–16,5 g.
Bare Parts: Iris brown; bill black (breeding ♂) or horn (♀ and nonbreeding ♂); legs and feet brown.
Identification: Size small (smaller than Red Bishop). *Breeding ♂:* Upperparts, undertail and patch at sides of breast brilliant yellow (no other *Euplectes* has yellow crown); face, rest of underparts and collar on hindneck black; wings and tail brown. *Female and nonbreeding ♂:* Above streaked blackish and greyish buff; line through eye to ear coverts black (distinctive at close range); eyebrow whitish; below whitish, washed buff and lightly streaked brown on breast and flanks (streaking less bold than in Red Bishop). *Immature:* Similar to adult ♀.

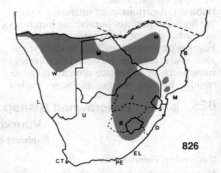

Voice: High-pitched rasping buzzing swizzling *zzzzzz zzit zzit zzzzz, etc.,* especially in flight display; sharp *tsip tsip* callnotes (and alarm?).

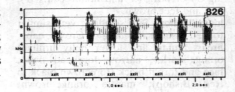

Distribution: Africa S of Sahara; in s Africa mainly confined to highveld above about 600 m, from ne Cape to Zimbabwe, n Botswana and Ovamboland to Caprivi as far east as Katima Mulilo.

Status: Locally common resident; nomadic in winter.

Habitat: Moist grassland, vleis, seasonally flooded pans, fields of standing wheat, maize or sorghum, rank weedy vegetation bordering dams and in valley bottoms.

Habits: Gregarious at all times, sometimes in flocks of hundreds of birds, often in company with other *Euplectes* species. Forages on inflorescences of standing grass and herbs, as well as on ground. Male displays back and forth over territory with slow beelike flight on rapidly beating wings, plumage fluffed like gold-and-black ball, giving buzzing song.

Food: Seeds, insects; nestlings fed mainly on small caterpillars at first.

Breeding: Males polygamous. *Season*: December to February in Natal and Orange Free State, December to May (mainly December-March) in Transvaal, December to March in Zimbabwe. *Nest*: Thin-walled upright oval woven by ♂ of fine grass strips, with porched side-top entrance; lined with fine grass flowers; attached to upright stems of grass, weeds, wheat or rushes in vlei, moist grassy slope or cultivated field; usually less than 60 cm above water or ground; tops of grass may be woven into roof of nest; usually in small loose colony. *Clutch*: (35) 2–3,2–5 eggs (usually 3; clutch of 7 in one nest probably laid by 2 females). *Eggs*: White, finely speckled with black (unique among *Euplectes* species); measure (88) 17,9 × 12,8 (16,2–21,7 × 11,9–13,6). *Incubation*: 12–14 days by ♀ only. *Nestling*: (1) 11 days in captivity; fed by both parents.

---

827 (810) Yellowrumped Widow Plate 68
Kaapse Flap
Euplectes capensis

Enzunge (K), Thaha (SS), Mantunje, Xikhungu-mala (Ts), Isahomba, Isakhomba (X), [Samtweber]

Measurements: Length ♂ 14 cm, ♀ 12,5 cm; wing (55 ♂) 66–72,6–91, (53 ♀) 59–64,1–83; tail (27 ♂) 48–52,9–60, (27 ♀) 41–45,6–51; tarsus (5 ♂) 22–24, (1 ♀) 21, (13 unsexed) 17–21–25; culmen (5 ♂) 17,5–19, (1 ♀) 16,5, (14 unsexed) 12–13,6–15. Weight (16 ♂, w Cape) 25–31,6–38 g, (9 ♀, w Cape) 28–30,2–34 g, (59 ♂, Zimbabwe) 17,3–20,4–25,1 g, (70 ♀, Zimbabwe) 12,1–16,9–21,3 g.

Bare Parts: Iris brown; bill black (breeding ♂) or horn, base pinkish (♀ and non-breeding ♂); legs and feet pinkish brown.

Identification: Size medium (larger than Red Bishop); yellowish rump and wing coverts diagnostic in all plumages; ♀ smaller than ♂. *Breeding ♂*: Mostly black; bend of wing, lower back and rump bright yellow; brown patch on each side of upper back (whole upper back and upperwing yellow in Yellowbacked Widow); tail shortish (long in Yellowbacked Widow).

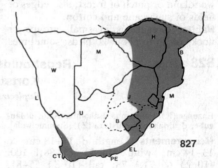

827

Nonbreeding ♂: Above streaked blackish brown on buff; rump and bend of wing bright yellow; wings and tail blackish; eyebrow buff; below white, washed buff and heavily streaked brown on breast and flanks (bishops more narrowly or more faintly streaked). *Female*: Similar to non-breeding ♂, but rump and bend of wing olive yellow, streaked blackish. *Immature*: Similar to adult ♀, but less yellowish on rump and bend of wing.

Voice: Thin *seep* and *tsip* notes; in display loud wing rattling alternated with rhythmic nasal *zimp zitit zeemp*, repeated several times.

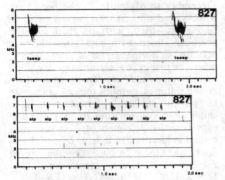

Distribution: S Africa to Ethiopia and Nigeria; in s Africa confined mainly to S and E; also sw and w Cape, and e Caprivi.
Status: Locally common resident; nomadic in winter.
Habitat: Rank grass or marshy places on steep slopes or in valley bottoms in mountainous or hilly country, usually with scattered trees and bushes, often at edge of woodland or patch of forest; also edges of fields of sugarcane and cotton.
Habits: Gregarious in small groups or flocks of up to about 20 birds; sometimes in company with other *Euplectes* species in winter; less gregarious than most *Euplectes* species. Male sings and displays with ruffed neck and rump plumage, either from perch or in buzzing flight accompanied by swizzling song and wing rattling. Forages from standing inflorescences of grass and other plants.
Food: Seeds, insects.
Breeding: Males polygamous with 2–3 females each. *Season*: August to November in sw Cape, December to February in Natal, November to February in Transvaal, December to April (mainly January-February) in Zimbabwe. *Nest*: Oval shell with slightly hooded side-top entrance, loosely woven by ♂ of grass strips, incorporating surrounding growing grass; lined with dry grass by ♀; usually about 60 cm above ground (sometimes up to 2 m) in dense grass and herbage; not usually in colony, nests of one ♂ several metres apart. *Clutch*: (60) 2–2,7–4 eggs (usually 3). *Eggs*: Pale greenish or bluish white, streaked, blotched and clouded with brown, greyish olive and grey; measure (136) 19,3 × 13,9 (16,8–22,4 × 12,7–15,6). *Incubation*: 13–16 days by ♀ only. *Nestling*: 15–16 days (up to 20 days); fed by both parents, mostly by ♀.

Ref. Mouritz, L.B. 1913. *J. S. Afr. Orn. Union* 9:79–83.

828 (816)   Redshouldered Widow   Plate 68
Kortstertflap
Euplectes axillaris

Enzunge (K), Isakhomba, Isahomba (X), ♂ uMangube, ♂ uMahube, ♀ iNtaka (Z), [Stummelwida]

Measurements: Length ♂ 17–18 cm, ♀ 13–14 cm; wing (14 ♂) 81–88,1–100, (10 ♀) 66–71,1–78; tail (10 ♂) 55–81, (6 ♀) 40–43; tarsus (10 ♂) 23–24, (6 ♀) 19–20; culmen (16) 15–18. Weight (268 ♂) 28,1–29,5–30,5 g, (406 ♀) 21,2–22–23 g.
Bare Parts: Iris brown; bill pale blue-grey (breeding ♂) or horn (♀ and nonbreeding ♂); legs and feet black (breeding) or brown (nonbreeding).
Identification: Size medium to large; ♂ much bigger than ♀. *Breeding ♂*: Black; bend of wing scarlet bordered below with buff (concealed unless displaying or flying

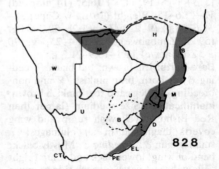

when conspicuous); tail medium, broad (very long in breeding ♂ Longtailed Widow). *Nonbreeding ♂*: Above streaked blackish on buff; eyebrow buffy white; bend of wing scarlet (diagnostic); below whitish, washed buff and streaked brown on breast and flanks; tail shorter than in breeding ♂, brown. *Female*: Similar to nonbreeding ♂, but smaller; bend of wing golden brown, streaked blackish (diagnostic at close range). *Immature*: Similar to adult ♀.

Voice: Husky rolling rhythmic *shreep skrik skrik wirra skreek skreek wirrily wirrily wirrily chink chink chink*, rather weak, without carrying power; more silent than other *Euplectes* species.

exaggeratedly flapping and rocking flight, tail spread and uttering weak song, checking suddenly and swerving to perch on top of bush, fence or tall grass stalk, displaying red epaulettes and spread tail, hindneck fluffed like ruff.

Food: Seeds, grain, insects.

Breeding: Males polygamous. *Season*: October to January in e Cape, October to March (mainly November-January) in Natal, October to November in Transvaal, October to end of summer in Mozambique. *Nest*: Shell of green grass with hooded side-top entrance, woven by

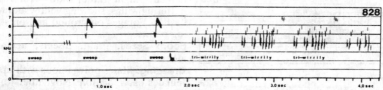

Distribution: Africa S of Sahara; in s Africa confined to lowlands and midlands of extreme SE and E, and Okavango region.

Status: Common resident; nomadic in winter.

Habitat: Open moist grassland, edges of vleis, rank grassy hillsides, marshes, edges of sugarcane fields.

Habits: Gregarious at all times, usually in smallish flocks when breeding, larger flocks in winter, often in company with other *Euplectes* species. Forages in grassland and fallow fields, mostly on ground. Breeding ♂ patrols territory with slow

♂ into living grass and weeds; lined by ♀ with ball of dry grass inflorescences; in green grasstuft, herb or small shrub mixed with grass, 2,5–19–60 cm above ground (mean of 22 nests); not colonial; neighbouring nests usually several metres apart. *Clutch*: (115) 2–2,8–4 eggs (usually 3). *Eggs*: Light greenish or blue-green, clouded and blotched with olive grey and brown; measure (69) 19,7 × 14,1 (17,7–22,4 × 13,3–15). *Incubation*: 12–13 days by ♀ only. *Nestling*: 15–16 days; fed by ♀ only.

Ref. Skead, C.J. 1959. *Ostrich* 30:13–21.

829 (814) Whitewinged Widow Plate 68
Witvlerkflap
Euplectes albonotatus

Enzunge (K), ♀ iNtakansinsi (Z), [Spiegelwida]

Measurements: Length (breeding ♂) 16 cm, (nonbreeding ♂) 14 cm, ♀ 12 cm; wing (143 ♂) 68–75,6–82, (68 ♀) 62–65,5–72; tail (61♂, breeding) 69–87,3–106, (63♂, nonbreeding) 43–52,2–60, ♀ 40–45; tarsus ♂ 19–22, ♀ 17–19; culmen 13–15. Weight (139 ♂) 16,9–20,8–27,5 g, (62 ♀) 13,9–17,6–22,2 g, (44 unsexed) 16,2–18,9–22,8 g.

Bare Parts: Iris brown; bill silver grey (breeding ♂) or pinkish horn (♀ and non-

breeding ♂); legs and feet black (breeding ♂) or pinkish brown (♀ and nonbreeding ♂).

Identification: Size medium to smallish; breeding ♂ looks larger because of fairly long broad tail. *Breeding ♂*: Black; bend of wing brilliant yellow; primary coverts white, showing as conspicuous flash in flight (diagnostic). *Nonbreeding ♂*: Above streaked blackish on buff; eyebrow yellow (buffy white in other *Euplectes* species); below whitish, washed buff and finely streaked brown on breast and flanks (much more lightly streaked than most *Euplectes* species); yellow and white flashes present on wing (diagnostic); tail medium, brown. *Female*: Similar to non-breeding ♂, but much smaller; bend of wing olive yellow (diagnostic at close range); primary coverts margined buffy white (show as pale flash in flight; diagnostic). *Immature*: Similar to adult ♀.

Voice: Song papery rustling *shrrr*, followed by 2–3 zinging chirps; twittering contact calls; usually rather silent.

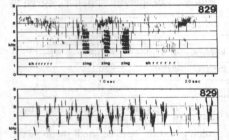

Distribution: S Africa to NE Africa; in s Africa from Natal throughout most of NE (except most of Mozambique and e Zimbabwe) to Caprivi.

Status: Uncommon to locally fairly common resident; nomadic in winter.

Habitat: Rank grass and weeds along road verges, edges of cultivated lands, moist valley bottoms; usually in thornveld.

Habits: Gregarious in small flocks, often in company with other *Euplectes* species, even when breeding. Male displays from perch by singing with tail conspicuously

fanned. Flight rather slow with rapidly fluttering wings, showing yellow and white flashes. Forages on ground and on standing plants.

Food: Seeds, grain, insects, nectar of aloes.

Breeding: Males polygamous with up to 4 females each. *Season*: November to May (mainly December-January) in Natal, October to March (mainly December-February) in Transvaal, December to April (mainly January-February) in Zimbabwe). *Nest*: Oval of rather dry grass blades and living plant material, lined with dry grass inflorescences protruding through side-top entrance; attached to rank weeds and grass, 1–1,5 m above ground. *Clutch*: (71) 2–2,6–5 eggs (usually 2–3). *Eggs*: Greenish white or greenish blue, spotted, smeared and blotched with olive and grey; measure (49) 18,5 × 13,6 (15,6–20 × 12,1–14,2). *Incubation*: 12–14 days by ♀ only. *Nestling*: 11–13,5 days.

Ref. Hornby, H.E. 1967. *Ostrich* 38:5–10; 1970. *Ostrich* 41:225–231; 1977. *Honeyguide* 89:13–18.

830 (815)   **Yellowbacked Widow**   **Plate 68**
Geelrugflap
Euplectes macrourus

[Gelbschulterwida]

Measurements: Length ♂ 18–22 cm, ♀ 13–14 cm; wing (4 ♂) 76–82,3–88, (4 ♀) 64–68,3–77; tail (breeding ♂) 108–117, (1 ♀) 51; tarsus ♂ 21,5–23,5, ♀ 19–20; culmen 15–16.

Bare Parts: Iris brown; bill blue-black (breeding ♂) or horn (♀ and nonbreed-

ing ♂); legs and feet black (breeding ♂) or brown (♀ and nonbreeding ♂).

Identification: Size medium. *Breeding ♂*: Black; upper back and wing coverts bright yellow, forming complete yellow band; tail fairly long and heavy. *Nonbreeding ♂*: Above streaked blackish and buff; bend of wing bright yellow (diagnostic; no yellow on rump as in Yellowrumped Widow); primaries black; below whitish, washed yellowish buff and faintly streaked dusky on breast and flanks; tail short. *Female*: Similar to nonbreeding ♂, but without yellow on bend of wing; rump not yellowish as in ♀ Yellowrumped Widow; tail short. *Immature*: Similar to adult ♀.

Voice: High-pitched *tswip* and *tsweep* calls; thin buzzing *zeeeee*.

Distribution: Africa S of Sahara; in s Africa confined to Mashonaland Plateau, Zimbabwe, above 1 200 m.
Status: Locally fairly common resident.
Habitat: Marshy grassland, vleis with short grass.
Habits: Gregarious, especially when not breeding, often in company with other *Euplectes* species in winter. In flight display ♂ jerks tail up and down; also

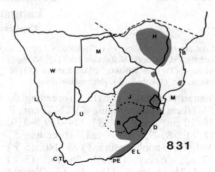

perches on tall grass stems. Shy and unapproachable.
Food: Seeds, insects.
Breeding: *Season*: December to March. *Nest*: Thin-walled upright rounded oval woven of fine grass, lined by ♀ with dry grass, even after egglaying; contents can be seen through walls at first; side-top entrance lacks porch; 15–60 cm above ground or water in short vlei grass. *Clutch*: 2–3 eggs. *Eggs*: Pale blue-green, very finely streaked and speckled with shades of grey and brown; measure (15) 19,4 × 14,2 (16,9–21 × 13,5–14,9). *Incubation*: Unrecorded. *Nestling*: Unrecorded.

831 (813) Redcollared Widow
Rooikeelflap
Euplectes ardens
Plate 68

♂ Molepe, ♂ Tjobolo, ♀ Thaha (SS), Muswewadepa (Sh), ♂ Ujobela, ♀ Intakazana (X), ♂ uJojo, ♀ iNtaka (Z), [Schildwida]

Measurements: Length (breeding ♂) 25–30 cm, (nonbreeding ♂) 12–13 cm, ♀ 12 cm; wing (158 ♂) 65–73,6–79, (189 ♀) 60,5–64,5–70; tail (breeding ♂) 180–251, (53 ♂, nonbreeding) 41–51,6–58,5, (160 ♀) 39–43,4–48; tarsus (22 ♂) 21–23, (7 ♀) 19–22; culmen (29) 14–15. Weight (400 ♂) 15,6–21,2–25 g, (512 ♀) 13,1–17,2–20,3 g.
Bare Parts: Iris brown; bill black (breeding ♂) or horn, base pinkish (♀ and nonbreeding ♂); legs and feet black (breeding ♂) or pinkish brown (♀ and nonbreeding ♂).
Identification: Size smallish. *Breeding ♂*: Black; tail very long, graduated, flexible, blows about in wind; collar on lower throat scarlet (visible only in good light; diagnostic). *Female and nonbreeding ♂*: Above buff, streaked blackish; eyebrow yellow (buff in bishops and most other widows); throat and breast yellowish, shading to buff on flanks, white in centre

of belly, unstreaked (diagnostic; all other eclipse and ♀ *Euplectes* streaked below); undertail light brown, mottled with black (♂) or white (♀); wings and tail black (♂) or brown (♀). *Immature*: Similar to adult ♀.

Voice: Song rapid high-pitched *chisisisi chisisisi chisisisi*, rather insectlike, usually in flight display with faintly rustling wings; also hissing *skheeee* (sounds like Puffadder *Bitis arietans*) from ♂ on alighting on treetop.

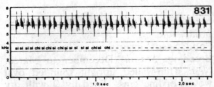

Distribution: Africa S of Sahara; in s Africa confined to moister SE and highveld of Natal, Lesotho, Orange Free State and Transvaal; also scattered localities in s Mozambique; also most of e and highveld Zimbabwe.

Status: Locally common resident; nomadic in winter.

Habitat: Rank grass in vleis, valleys, *Acacia* savanna, hillsides and streams; bracken-brier and streams in montane areas; edges of cultivated lands.

Habits: Gregarious at all times, especially after breeding; often in company with other *Euplectes* species. Forages on ground or on standing grass inflorescences. Male displays in slow flight from perch to perch over territory, with rapidly beating wings and tail depressed and keeled to form inverted sickle shape; ♂ also makes short flights low over nesting area, flopping intermittently into grass with tail feathers flying. Normal flight fast and direct with tail streaming straight out behind.

Food: Seeds and insects.

Breeding: Males polygamous with up to 3 females each. *Season*: October to March in Natal, November to March in Transvaal, December to April (mainly January) in Zimbabwe. *Nest*: Oval shell of woven living grass, lined by ♀ with oval of dry grass stems and inflorescences protruding through side-top entrance to form hooded porch; woven into tall dense grass, leafy bush or fine reeds, 30–56–200 cm above ground (mean of 8 nests); in small loose colonies of 3–4 nests. *Clutch*: (121) 2–2,4–6 eggs (usually 3). *Eggs*: Pale greenish blue, spotted, mottled and blotched with shades of olive brown concentrated at thick end; measure (149) 18,9 × 13,6 (17,1–21,5 × 12,8–14,6). *Incubation*: 12–15 days by ♀ only. *Nestling*: About 16 days; fed by ♀ only.

832 (818)   Longtailed Widow   Plate 68
Langstertflap
Euplectes progne

Lephaka (NS), ♂ Molepe, ♂ Tjobolo, ♀ Lepau, ♀ Lehelo (SS), Cilori, Ncilakulondza (Ts), Molopê, Molepê (Tw), ♂ Ibhaku, ♀ Intakazana (X), ♂ iBhaku, ♂ iSakabuli (Z), [Hahnschweifwida]

Measurements: Length (breeding ♂) 55–60 cm, (nonbreeding ♂) 22–23 cm, ♀ 18–20 cm; wing (54 ♂) 124–139,5–160, (7 ♀) 89–93–103; tail (breeding ♂) 310–490, (nonbreeding ♂) 88–140, (5 ♀) 57–62; tarsus (23 ♂) 25–29, (5 ♀) 22,5–24; culmen (28) 16–19. Weight (38 ♂) 33–41,6–46 g, (32 ♀) 25–32–39 g.

Bare Parts: Iris brown; bill pale blue-grey (breeding ♂) or horn, base pinkish (♀ and nonbreeding ♂); legs and feet dark brown to black (breeding ♂) or pinkish brown (♀ and nonbreeding ♂).

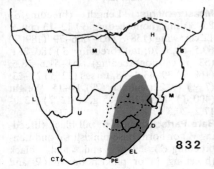

Identification: Size large; ♂ much larger than ♀; broad floppy wings diagnostic in all plumages; short floppy tail diagnostic in ♀ and eclipse ♂. *Breeding* ♂: Black; tail extremely long, floppy, graduated; bend of wing scarlet, bordered below by broad whitish band; bill whitish. *Nonbreeding* ♂: Above heavily streaked black on deep buff; bend of wing orange, bordered below by broad buff band; primaries black; eyebrow whitish; below buffy white, streaked dark brown on breast and flanks. *Female*: Similar to nonbreeding ♂; no orange and buff band on bend of wing, but broad buff margins of wing coverts form pale wingpatch; primaries brown. *Immature*: Similar to adult ♀.

Voice: Usually silent; ♂ calls sharp *zik zik zik zik* in flight display and in alarm; also sings repeated phrase of 4 lower and 4 higher notes *twi-twi-twi-twi-zizizizi*.

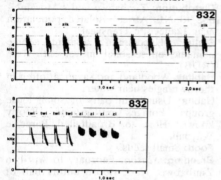

Distribution: Discontinuously from S Africa to Kenya; in s Africa from e Cape to highveld and n Transvaal.

Status: Common to very common resident; nomadic in winter.

Habitat: Open grassveld, especially in moister areas (vleis, mountain slopes); also pastures and scrub savanna.

Habits: Gregarious at all times, especially in winter. Forages mainly on ground, walking with short steps. Flight heavy and laboured on broad wings; breeding ♂ performs slow display flight low over territory, wings flapping slowly and erratically, long tail depressed and keeled like inverted bustle; perches on bush, grasstuft, termite mound or fence between flights. Breeding males roost communally in reedbeds at night, flying high to and from breeding grounds, long tails streaming out behind.

Food: Seeds, insects.

Breeding: Males polygamous with up to 6 females each. *Season*: November to March in e Cape, October to June (mainly January) in Natal, October to April (mainly December-February) in Transvaal. *Nest*: Ball of dry grass inflorescences, with wide side entrance; living grass pulled down over roof; 5–20 cm above ground in dense grasstuft, very well hidden; framework started by ♂, rest built by ♀. *Clutch*: (63) 2–3–4 eggs (usually 3). *Eggs*: Dull greenish white, spotted and blotched with olive brown and grey; measure (110) 21,6 × 15,7 (19–23,7 × 14,6–16,6). *Incubation*: 14 days by ♀ only. *Nestling*: 17 days; fed by ♀ only.

Ref. Andersson, M. 1982. *Nature* 299:818–820.

26:27. Family 89 ESTRILDIDAE—WAXBILLS, MANNIKINS, TWINSPOTS, FIREFINCHES, ETC.

Small. Bill very short, stout, conical, adapted for seed-eating, often red; legs and toes short and slender; wings short, rounded; tail short to moderately long, rounded or graduated; plumage variable but often brightly coloured in red, blue, yellow, orange or green; many species barred or spotted; usually gregarious, at least when not breeding; breed solitarily; nest an oval of dry grass with side entrance tube in bush, tree, hole or on ground (sometimes in old nest of another species); eggs 2–7, pure white; chick downy at hatching, with characteristic pattern of spots or patches on gape and in mouth; parental care by both sexes. Distribution Africa S of Sahara, Madagascar, Middle East, tropical Asia to Australia (many species introduced into other parts of the world); 124 species; 27 species in s Africa.

Ref. Goodwin, D. 1982. *Estrildid finches of the world*. London: British Museum (Natural History) and Oxford University Press.
Kunkel, P. & Kunkel, I. 1975. *Ostrich* 46:147–153.
Skead, D.M. 1975. *Ostrich Suppl*. 11:1–55.

833 (829)　　　　　**Goldenbacked Pytilia**　　　　**Plate 69**
Geelrugmelba (Geelrugsysie)
Pytilia afra

Matemate (K), [Wiener Astrild]

Measurements: Length about 11 cm; wing (8) 55–60–64; tail (6) 34–38; tarsus (6) 14–16; culmen (6) 10–11,5. Weight (1 ♂) 14,7, (1 ♀) 15,5 g, (4 unsexed) mean 14,5 g.

Bare Parts: Iris red to red-brown; bill red (♂) or orange (♀) below, brown above; legs and feet yellowish to pinkish brown.

Identification: Size small (smaller than Melba Finch). *Male*: Face, forecrown, throat, rump and tail bright red (face grey in Melba Finch); rest of upperparts light golden olive (nape grey in Melba Finch); wings orange (olive in Melba Finch); lower throat and sides of neck grey; breast golden olive; rest of underparts barred white and golden olive (barred blackish and white in Melba Finch); bill brown above (all red in Melba Finch). *Female*: Similar to ♂, but head grey; breast barred grey and white; bill brown. *Immature*: Similar to adult ♀, but rump orange-red. *Chick*: Palate reddish with or without dark central spot; lateral spots violet.

Voice: Callnotes like peeping of domestic chick; song starts with 2–3-syllabled rattling notes, then series of soft fluting notes, ending with short crackling *kay*.

Distribution: Zimbabwe and s Mozambique to NE Africa; isolated population near Tzaneen, e Transvaal.

Status: Uncommon resident; some nomadic or seasonal movement. Rare (RDB).

Habitat: Woodland and savanna, often in thorny tangles near water.

Habits: Usually in pairs or small loose groups. Forages on ground. Poorly known. Host to Broadtailed Paradise Whydah.

Food: Small seeds.

Breeding: *Season*: February to April in Zimbabwe. *Nest*: Loose untidy ball of fine dry yellowish grass and weed stems, with side entrance; lined with feathers; 1–3 m above ground in fork of bush, usually in dense shady cover. *Clutch*: 3–5 eggs (usually 3–4). *Eggs*: White; measure (4) 15,7 × 13,2 (15,5–16,1 × 13–13,4); weigh (mean) 1,42 g. *Incubation*: 12–13 days by both sexes. *Nestling*: About 21 days.

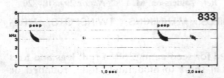

834 (830)　　　　　**Melba Finch**　　　　**Plate 69**
Gewone Melba (Melbasysie)
Pytilia melba

Matemate (K), [Buntastrild]

Measurements: Length 13–14 cm; wing (28 ♂) 57–59–62,5; (14 ♀) 57–58,5–62; tail (40) 46–53; tarsus (40) 14–17; culmen (40) 12–14. Weight (326 ♂) 10,7–15,3–17,9 g, (316 ♀) 10–14,9–18,4 g.

Bare Parts: Iris reddish orange, red-

brown to scarlet; bill orange-red, culmen dark horn in ♀ and nonbreeding ♂; legs and feet pinkish to greyish brown.

Identification: Size smallish (larger than Goldenbacked Pytilia). *Male*: Forecrown, throat and cheeks scarlet; hindcrown, face and nape grey (face red, hindcrown

golden olive in Goldenbacked Pytilia);
back and wings golden olive (wings orange
in Goldenbacked Pytilia); rump red; tail
dusky, edged red; breast greenish gold;
rest of underparts barred blackish and
white (olive and white in Goldenbacked
Pytilia), shading to buff in centre and
undertail. *Female*: Similar to ♂, but whole
head and face grey; throat and breast
barred blackish and white. *Immature*:
Washed olive on head and throat; below
plain greyish, paler in centre of belly and
undertail; bill black; eye red-brown.
Chick: Dark with sandy-white down;
mouth has central black palate spot, 2
lateral blue spots, whitish gape tubercles;
lower region blackish; tongue partly dark.
Voice: Song quiet string of notes lasting
up to 16 seconds, starting with 2–3 sounds
like drops falling into water accompanied
by ratchetlike *krik krik*, then trilled whistles, first on rising pitch, then on falling
pitch, mixed with insectlike *krik* and *krr-
ree* notes, *plink plink krip poorrrreeee krip
prrreeeeeoooo*, etc.; somewhat variable,
sometimes ending with 3 fluty notes; short
wik callnote.

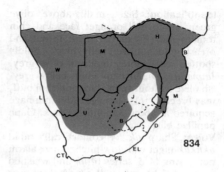

834

Habits: Usually in pairs or small family
groups; does not form large flocks. Forages in low brushy vegetation, but mostly
on ground, often in clearings or on roads;
otherwise rather secretive and seldom
seen; presence revealed by callnote.
Drinks regularly in winter. Host to Paradise Whydah.
Food: Seeds, insects (especially termites).
Breeding: *Season*: September to March
in Natal, September to July in Transvaal, all months (mainly January to
May) in Zimbabwe. *Nest*: Thin-walled

834

Distribution: Africa S of Sahara; widespread in s Africa, except most of Cape S
of Orange River, extreme arid w Namibia,
moister parts of of Natal, Lesotho and se
Transvaal.
Status: Common to fairly common resident.
Habitat: Thickets with rank grass in *Acacia* savanna, scrub savanna or grassland;
edges of riverine forest and bush in more
arid regions.

untidy ball of dry grass stems, with side
entrance about 5 cm diameter; lined
with feathers or plant down; on ground
or in bush up to 3 m above ground
(mean about 1,2 m). *Clutch*: (17)
2–3,8–5 eggs (usually 4–5, sometimes
6). *Eggs*: White; measure (52) 16,2 ×
12,5 (14,1–17,7 × 11,5–13,4); weight
(mean) 1,41 g. *Incubation*: 12–13 days
by both sexes. *Nestling*: 21 days; fed by
both parents.

835 (827)   Green Twinspot   Plate 70
Groenkolpensie (Groenrobbin)
Mandingoa nitidula

[Grüner Tropfenastrild]
Measurements: Length 10–11 cm; wing ♂
51,5–55,5, ♀ 49,5–53,5; tail 28–38; tarsus
13,5–14,5; culmen 9–12. Weight (12 ♂)

8,3–9–10 g, (13 ♀) 8,1–9,5–11,2 g, (26
unsexed) 8–9,4–11 g.
Bare Parts: Iris brown; bill black, tip
orange; legs and feet pinkish brown.

743

GREEN TWINSPOT

Identification: Size small; above olive green; rump dull orange; face and chin tomato red (♂) or buff (♀); throat and breast golden olive; belly black, boldly spotted with white; undertail olive grey. *Immature:* Duller than adult; below greyish olive without spots; face and chin buff; may breed in this plumage; adult plumage acquired at about 3 months. *Chick:* Gape papillae blue.

Voice: Sharp *tik tik* contact call; rapid *tiktiktik* flight call; low-pitched *tirrr* alarm note; song of ♂ series of *tik* and whistled notes, variable, *chrrr tik tik tik cheer weet weet weet teeu wooee tseeeu.*

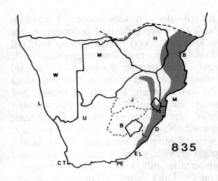

835

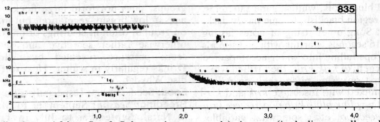

Distribution: Africa S of Sahara; in s Africa confined to extreme E, Drakensberg escarpment and Zoutpansberg.

Status: Locally fairly common resident.

Habitat: Mature evergreen forest, secondary growth around cultivation, gardens near dune forest, exotic plantations.

Habits: Solitary, in pairs or in small groups of up to 10 birds (probably family groups); pairs stay together for more than one season. Secretive, silent and easily overlooked; ascends into surrounding vegetation when disturbed. Forages low down in vegetation or with hopping walk on ground in clearings and at forest edges; gleans insects from leaves and stems rather like white-eye; also hawks flying insects by short sally in air.

Food: Seeds (especially green grass seeds), insects (including woolly aphids).

Breeding: *Season:* December to April in Natal, October to November in Zimbabwe and Mozambique. *Nest:* Oval, about 15 cm long, 12,5 cm deep, of grass stems, skeletonized leaves, rootlets, twigs and lichens, with wide side entrance 4–7 cm diameter, with or without tube; lined with feathers, fine grass, wool and string; covered externally with leaves, especially underneath; 3–8,5–15 m above ground (14 nests) in crown of tall tree, rarely in understory, well concealed in dense foliage or creeper; built by both sexes. *Clutch:* 4–6 eggs. *Eggs:* White; measure (4) 15,9 × 12 (15,2–16,6 × 11,3–12,3). *Incubation:* 12–14 days. *Nestling:* 17 days (21–23 days in captivity); fed by regurgitation by both parents; young return to nest for up to 7 days after initial departure.

836 (828)   Redfaced Crimsonwing   Plate 70
Rooirugsaadvretertjie (Rooirugrobbin)
Cryptospiza reichenovii

[Reichenows Bergastrild]

Measurements: Length about 12 cm; wing (138 ♂) 52–56,8–60, (119 ♀) 52–56,8–59,5; tail (133 ♂) 38–42,9–46,5, (113 ♀) 38,5–42,6–48,5; tarsus (192) 16–18,7–21,5; culmen (190) 10–12,6–14,5. Weight (152 ♂) 11,5–13,5–16,2 g, (125 ♀) 11,2–13,3–17,4 g, (6 unsexed) 13,5–14,6 g.

Bare Parts: Iris brown; bill black; legs and feet dark brown; soles of feet yellowish.
Identification: Size smallish. Patch around eye bright red in ♂ (head and throat red in Nyasa Seedcracker), olive in ♀; crown to mantle and underparts brownish olive; rest of upperparts and wings dark red (Nyasa Seedcracker has red on lower rump only); tail black (red in Nyasa Seedcracker); undertail spotted red in 65% of ♂ and 18% of ♀. *Immature*: Less red above than in adult. *Chick*: Palate yellow with 5 black spots; 2 black spots on tongue and 2 inside lower jaw; 4 iridescent gape tubercles outlined with black, 3 above, 1 below.
Voice: Song very soft, thin and high-pitched (not audible beyond about 10 m), 4 drawn-out notes falling in pitch, each followed by *chirp*; high-pitched *tsweep, tsweeer, sip sip sip* and *chik-chik-chik* call-notes.

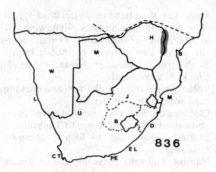

especially in wetter localities; rather scarce in Chimanimani Mountains.
Habitat: Interior, edges and clearings of montane forest with patches of undergrowth and/or scrub, tall *Philippia*, bracken-brier and other dense cover; also exotic pine plantations.
Habits: In pairs or small groups. Forages on ground, in croplands near forest, or in pine trees up to 15 m or more, feeding on seeds from cones. Does not fly far when disturbed; usually keeps well hidden in dense cover; silent and easily overlooked.
Food: Seeds (of grass, *Pinus patula*, etc.)
Breeding: *Season:* October to March in Mozambique, November to March in Zimbabwe. *Nest:* Oval of fine grass and skeletonized leaves with wide side entrance facing 'slightly upwards; lined with soft grass inflorescences; about 3–6 m above ground in treefern, thorny bush or sapling in forest; often in *Maytenus heterophylla* under overhanging branch. *Clutch:* 3–4 eggs. *Eggs:* White; measure (5) 16,9 × 12 (16,7–17,1 × 11,8–12.2). *Incubation:* Unrecorded; by both sexes. *Nestling:* About 21 days.

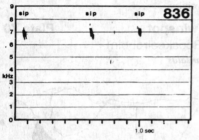

Distribution: Extreme e Zimbabwe, adjacent Mozambique and Mount Gorongosa, to Ethiopia and Cameroon.
Status: Common resident in Vumba,

Ref. Manson, A.J. & Harwin, R.M. 1990. *Honeyguide* 37: 9–13.

837 (819)   **Nyasa Seedcracker**   **Plate 70**
Rooistertsaadvretertjie (Rooistertrobbin)
Pyrenestes minor

[Kleiner Purpurastrild]

Measurements: Length about 14 cm; wing (2 ♂) 58–60, (5 ♀) 59–61; tail (7) 50–56; tarsus (7) 17,5–19,5; culmen (7) 8,5–9,5.

Bare Parts: Iris brown; bill black; legs and feet dark brown.
Identification: Large (about sparrow-sized). *Male:* Forecrown, face, throat, upper breast, rump and tail crimson (only eyepatch crimson in ♂ Redfaced Crimson-

wing; no red on head of ♀; tail black); rest of body earth brown (body olive, wing red in Redfaced Crimsonwing). *Female*: Similar to ♂, but less red on head; breast earth brown. *Immature*: No red on head. *Chick*: Undescribed.

Voice: Sharp sparrowlike *zeet* and clicking *qap*; song trilled chittering.

Distribution: Mozambique N of Save River, and extreme se Zimbabwe, to Tanzania.

Status: Uncommon to locally common resident.

Habitat: Tall rank grass and coarse weedy vegetation at edges of lowland evergreen forest and woodland; also reedbeds, and secondary growth around primitive cultivation.

Habits: Usually in pairs. Keeps low down in vegetation, not always in dense cover; quiet, skulking, easily overlooked. Poorly known.

Food: Grass seeds.

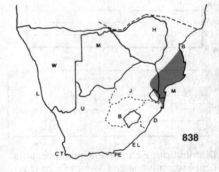

837

Breeding: *Season*: January in Zimbabwe, July in Mozambique. *Nest*: Loosely built untidy oval, up to 20 cm long, of grass, leaves and fronds; in fork of tree. *Clutch*: 3–6 eggs. *Eggs*: White; no measurements available (about 17 × 13). *Incubation*: 15 days by both sexes. *Nestling*: 20 days in captivity.

838 (831)   Pinkthroated Twinspot   Plate 70
Rooskeelkolpensie (Rooskeelrobbin)
Hypargos margaritatus

Katjikilili (K), [Perlastrild]

Measurements: Length 12,5–13 cm; wing ♂ 52–56, ♀ 52–54; tail (8) 50–54; tarsus (8) 15,5–17; culmen (8) 11–12.

Bare Parts: Iris dark brown; eyering cobalt blue; bill dark slate blue; legs and feet blackish.

Identification: Size smallish to medium; crown to back brown (crown grey in Redthroated Twinspot); lower rump dull red; face, throat and upper breast deep rose pink (♂) or light grey (♀) (red in Redthroated Twinspot); belly black, boldly spotted with pale pink (♂) or white (♀); tail dark red. *Immature*: Similar to adult ♀, but plain buff below; mouthspots still visible at 1 month old. *Chick*: Naked, flesh-pink, head downy; palate yellow with 3 black spots in triangular form; gape tubercles blue, 2 on each side; gape swellings white, becoming bluegreen internally after 3 days, blue at fledging; rest of mouth and tongue reddish; bill black.

Voice: Similar ringing trill to that of firefinch, *tsrrrrip*; song 2–6 soft fluty notes, similar to that of Redbilled Firefinch.

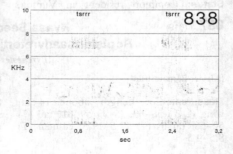

838

Distribution: From Lake St Lucia, Zululand, N to Swaziland, se Transvaal and Mozambique S of Save River.
Status: Fairly common resident.
Habitat: Thorny scrub and tangles at edge of evergreen forest, or bush and palm scrub.
Habits: Usually in pairs or small groups. Forages on ground, mostly in dense cover; darts into thickets when disturbed, sometimes pausing briefly at edge before disappearing. Shy and easily overlooked.
Food: Seeds.
Breeding: *Season*: January in Zululand (1 record). *Nest*: Oval of leaf ribs and skeletons, mixed with leaves, inflorescences and spider web, with side entrance 4–6 cm diameter; lined with palm fibre; near ground at base of palm frond. *Clutch*: (1) 3 eggs. *Eggs*: White; measure (3) 15,4 × 12 (15–15,6 × 12). *Incubation*: Unrecorded. *Nestling*: Unrecorded.

839 (832) **Redthroated Twinspot** **Plate 70**
Rooikeelkolpensie (Rooikeelrobbin)
Hypargos niveoguttatus

[Rotkehl-Tropfenastrild]

Measurements: Length about 13 cm; wing (28 ♂) 53–56,4–59, (26 ♀) 52–55,5–58; tail (28 ♂) 49,5–53,2–57, (26 ♀) 47–51,4–56; tarsus (9) 16–17,5; culmen (9) 12–13,5. Weight (23 ♂) 13,1–15–17,1 g, (23 ♀) 12,5–14,9–17,9 g.
Bare Parts: Iris dark brown; bill blue-black; legs and feet slate grey.
Identification: Size medium. *Male*: Crown and nape grey, washed red on nape (plain brown in Pinkthroated Twinspot); back and wings brown; lower rump dark red; tail black, edged crimson; face, throat and upper breast deep crimson; rest of underparts black, boldly spotted with white on flanks. *Female*: Above as in ♂; face grey; throat buff, shading to light red on breast; rest of underparts grey, boldly spotted white on flanks. *Immature*: Above similar to adult ♀; below russet without white spots; centre of belly black or dark grey. *Chick*: Pink with greyish down; skin turns blackish within 24 hours; 3 dark spots on palate; faint dark crescent on lower jaw; tongue plain; gape pale yellowish orange.
Voice: Tinkling trilled *trrreeee* callnote, somewhat cricketlike; song very high-pitched insectlike trill, preceded by 2–3 pure gurgled fluty whistles, *sip tooo tsssrrrrrr*; thin *tsisi*.

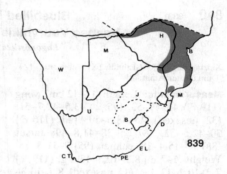

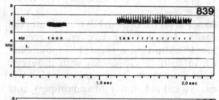

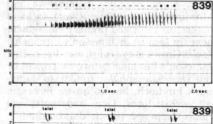

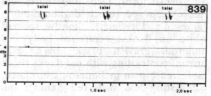

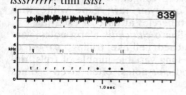

Distribution: Eastern Africa from Limpopo River to Kenya; in s Africa from extreme ne Transvaal (n Kruger National Park) to Mozambique, e and n Zimbabwe to Victoria Falls.
Status: Mostly common resident.
Habitat: Riverine forest and neighbouring thickets, edges of lowland evergreen forest.
Habits: Usually in pairs or small groups. Forages on ground, often at edge of clearing or on road. Quiet but often tame and inquisitive.
Food: Seeds.

Breeding: *Season*: January to April in Zimbabwe, June in Mozambique. *Nest*: Oval of grass, rootlets, fern stalks, skeletonized leaves and dry moss with side entrance, sometimes with incomplete "cock's nest" on top; lined with dry moss or feathers; chamber about 8 cm high; entrance 4 cm diameter; exterior covered with decomposing leaves; well camouflaged on ground or low down in bush or tree. *Clutch*: 3–6 eggs. *Eggs*: White; measure (3) 15,7–16 × 12,2–12,5. *Incubation*: 12–13 days by both sexes. *Nestling*: 21 days; fed by both parents.

840 (833)   **Bluebilled Firefinch**   **Plate 70**
Kaapse Vuurvinkie (Kaapse Robbin)
Lagonosticta rubricata

Xidzingirhi (Ts), Isicibilili (X), ubuCubu (Z), [Dunkelroter Amarant]

Measurements: Length 11–12 cm; wing (119 ♂) 46–49–53, (95 ♀) 43,5–47,7–51, (32 unsexed) 46–48,5–50; tail (116 ♂) 30–42,5–52, (87 ♀) 38–41,8–49; tarsus (88) 12–15,4–18; culmen (95) 9–11,3–14. Weight (147 ♂) 8,3–10,5–13,1 g, (119 ♀) 7,9–10,2–12,3 g, (12 unsexed) 8,7–10,3–11,6 g.
Bare Parts: Iris brown; bill bluish slate, tip darker; legs and feet dark pinkish grey.
Identification: Size small; bill looks bluish in field; 2 subspecies with different head coloration, *L. r. rubricata* (S Africa, Swaziland and s Mozambique) and *L. r. haematocephala* (Zimbabwe and Mozambique N of Save River); in hand outermost full-sized primary emarginate near tip (not so in Jameson's Firefinch). *Male*: Crown grey (*rubricata*; diagnostic; Jameson's Firefinch brown on crown) or red (*haematocephala*; similar to Jameson's Firefinch, but no brown in centre of crown); lores, face, underparts and rump deep red (much darker than in Jameson's Firefinch), lightly spotted white on flanks; centre of belly and undertail greyish black; back dark brown, contrasting with red flanks (back more red-brown in Jameson's Firefinch, contrasting less with red flanks); tail

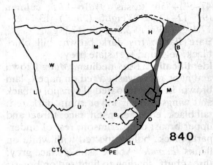

840

black, edged red. *Female*: Above similar to ♂; face grey (*rubricata*) or deep pink (*haematocephala*), lores bright red; throat and breast pale red; rest of underparts tawny, shading to black undertail, lightly spotted white on flanks; ♀ Jameson's Firefinch altogether paler above and below. *Immature*: Below more rufous than adult ♀; no red on lores. *Chick*: Dark with little whitish down; palate whitish with 5 black spots; black bar across tongue; black crescent on inside of lower jaw; gape white with bluish tubercles at base of each jaw.
Voice: Sharp *chit chitik* alarm notes; very high-pitched bell-like trilling, *trrrrr-t* or *trrritit*; song variable jumble of trills, tinkles and *chit* notes, often given 3 times each.

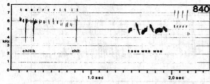

Distribution: Africa S of Sahara; in s Africa from s Cape (near Humansdorp) to Natal, Swaziland, Transvaal, Mozambique and extreme e Zimbabwe.
Status: Common resident.
Habitat: Rank grass and weedy vegetation, bracken-brier, edges of thickets, evergreen forest and riverine bush, brushwood around exotic plantations, secondary growth along roads and edges of cultivation.
Habits: Usually in pairs or small groups, sometimes in company with other firefinch

species. Forages on ground or low down in dense cover; flies low from one thicket to next, seldom staying in open; easily overlooked except for characteristic tinkling calls. Shy, taking to nearest cover when disturbed. Host to Black Widowfinch.
Food: Seeds, insects.
Breeding: *Season*: November to April throughout s Africa. *Nest*: Loosely built ball of dry yellow grass stems and coarse blades, with side entrance; thickly lined with feathers; 0,5–2,5 m above ground, well hidden in thorny tangle, pile of brushwood, or debris at base of tree. *Clutch*: (16) 2–3,7–5 eggs (usually 3–5). *Eggs*: White; measure (27) 15,1 × 11,5 (13,9–16 × 10,2–12); weigh (mean) 1,16 g. *Incubation*: About 11 days by both sexes by day, only ♀ at night. *Nestling*: 15–16 days; fed by both parents.

841 (835) Jameson's Firefinch Plate 70
Jamesonse Vuurvinkie (Jamesonse Robbin)
Lagonosticta rhodopareia

Xidzingirhi (Ts), [Rosenamarant, Jamesons Amarant]

Measurements: Length 11–12 cm; wing (89 ♂) 43,5–48,4–53,5, (103 ♀) 44–48–52; tail (32 ♂) 40,5–42,9–49, (28 ♀) 39–42,7–48,9; tarsus (10) 11–13,3–14,5; culmen (29) 9–10,4–13. Weight (91 ♂) 7,5–9,3–13 g, (101 ♀) 7,1–9,3–11,2 g.
Bare Parts: Iris brown; bill bluish slate, cutting edges black; legs and feet blackish grey.
Identification: Size small; similar to Bluebilled Firefinch and easily confused in field, but upperparts redder, less contrasting with pinker underparts; in hand outermost full-sized primary not emarginated near tip as in Bluebilled Firefinch. *Male*: Centre of crown and nape brown; rest of head, sides of neck and underparts dull dusty rose red (Bluebilled Firefinch deep red), lightly spotted white on flanks; centre of belly and undertail black; back light reddish brown; rump deep red. *Female*: Similar to ♂, but underparts pinkish buff; lores red; centre of belly and undertail buff, barred black under tail; flanks very sparingly spotted white. *Immature*: More rusty below than ♀; no red on lores.

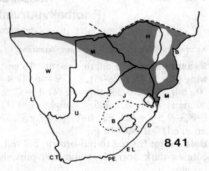

Chick: Dark with little down; gape violet and blue; angle of mouth red with violet tubercles.
Voice: Tinkling *trrr trr trt* alarm notes; musical *t'we-t'we-t'we* contact call; thin plaintive *fweeee* in display; sharp *zik-zik-zik-zik*.

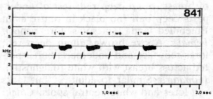

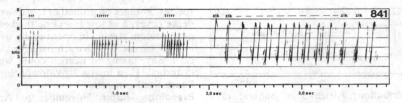

Distribution: S Africa to Ethiopia and Chad; in s Africa mostly confined to NE and N, from Zululand to Ovamboland.
Status: Common resident.
Habitat: Rank grass, edges of thickets, secondary growth, cultivated lands, edges of riverine forest, bushy gullies and rocky hillsides.
Habits: In pairs or small groups, sometimes in company with other small seed-eating birds. Forages on ground. Very similar to Bluebilled Firefinch. Host to Purple Widowfinch.

Food: Seeds.
Breeding: *Season*: March in Zululand, December to April in Transvaal, all months (mainly February-April) in Zimbabwe. *Nest*: Untidy loosely built oval of dry grass, with side entrance; lined with grass inflorescences and feathers; low down in bush or shrub mixed with growing grass. *Clutch*: (11) 2–3,6–5 eggs (usually 3–4). *Eggs*: White; measure (38) 14,6 × 11,2 (12,9–16,2 × 9,9–12,4); weigh (mean) 1,04 g. *Incubation*: 12 days (captivity), by both sexes. *Nestling*: 19 days (captivity).

842 (837) Redbilled Firefinch Plate 70
Rooibekvuurvinkie (Rooibekrobbin)
Lagonosticta senegala

Xidzingirhi (Ts), [Senegal-Amarant, Amarant]

Measurements: Length about 10 cm; wing (73 ♂) 46,5–49–51, (11 ♀) 46–47,4–50; tail (24) 32–38; tarsus (24) 11–12,5; culmen (24) 8,5–9,5. Weight (30 ♂) 6–8,3–9,5 g, (23 ♀) 6–7,7–10,2 g, (57 unsexed) 7,2–8,6–10 g.
Bare Parts: Iris red to red-brown; bill red, culmen dark horn; legs and feet pinkish brown.
Identification: Size very small; red bill diagnostic in both sexes (red only along sides in Brown Firefinch); most sexually dimorphic of all firefinches. *Male*: Centre of crown and nape, mantle and back brown; forehead, face, throat and breast dull rose red, faintly spotted white at sides of breast; rump deep red; rest of underparts deep buff (no black in centre as in Bluebilled and Jameson's Firefinches). *Female*: Above brown; rump deep red; lores red; face and underparts buff, spotted across breast with white (diagnostic). *Immature*: Similar to adult ♀, but lacks red lores and white ventral spots. *Chick*:

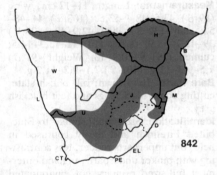

Yellowish orange with profuse whitish down; palate pale with 3 black spots; tongue yellow; black half-moon below tongue; white tubercle at base of each jaw; purplish blue tubercle on each side of gape.
Voice: Sharp *tzet, tzet, tzet* alarm notes; soft *fweet fweet* callnotes; song simple melodious phrase of 2–6 soft fluty notes, rising slightly in pitch towards end, preceded by sharp *tzet* note; some individual variation.

750

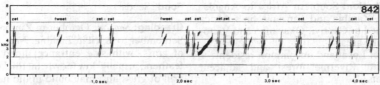

Distribution: Africa S of Sahara; widespread in s Africa from Orange River mouth through most of Karoo, Orange Free State, Transvaal, Zululand, Mozambique, Zimbabwe, n Botswana and n Namibia.
Status: Generally common; largely resident, but has seasonal movements in some areas (e.g. e Orange Free State where mainly winter visitor).
Habitat: Rank grass and thickets, especially in *Acacia* thornveld with patches of bare ground; also gardens and African villages.
Habits: Usually in pairs or small groups. Forages on ground in clearings and on roads; flies to nearest cover when disturbed, giving callnotes. Tame and confid-ing; drinks and bathes frequently. Host to Steelblue Widowfinch.
Food: Seeds, insects, crumbs.
Breeding: *Season*: January to March in Natal, December to April in Transvaal, all months (mainly December-April) in Zimbabwe. *Nest*: Ball of dry grass stems, with side entrance; lined with hair and feathers; in low bush, palm, thatched roof, hole in low wall, or on ground among rank herbage. *Clutch*: (10) 2–3,4–4 eggs (usually 3–4, sometimes 5–6). *Eggs*: White; measure (20) 13,3 × 10,6 (12–15,1 × 9,9–12); weigh (mean) 0,84 g. *Incubation*: 11–12 days by both sexes. *Nestling*: (6) 14–19 days; fed by both parents.

Ref. Payne, R.B. 1980. *Ibis* 122:43–56.

843 (836) Brown Firefinch Plate 70
Bruinvuurvinkie (Bruinrobbin)
Lagonosticta nitidula

[Großer Pünktchenamarant]

Measurements: Length about 10 cm; wing (41) 45–55; tail 33–42; tarsus 12–16; culmen 9–11.
Bare Parts: Iris brown to red-brown; bill steel blue above, red below, base purple; legs and feet slate grey.
Identification: Size very small; sexes similar, ♀ slightly paler than ♂; above brown, rump greyer (red in other firefinches); face, eyebrow, throat and upper breast light wine-red, spotted white across breast; rest of underparts pale brown; tail blackish. *Immature*: Lacks red on plumage and bill. *Chick*: 5 spots on palate; gape violet-blue with large pale yellow tubercle at base of each jaw, looking as if filled with opaque fluid.
Voice: High-pitched *weet-weet-weet* contact call; rolling *trrr* take-off call; song variable *tsee-kee-dee-tswee-dee-tswee*, sometimes with trills; not bell-like as in other firefinches.

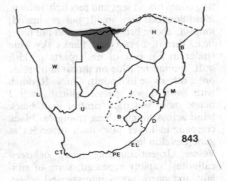

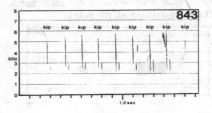

BROWN FIREFINCH

Distribution: Southern Africa to Angola, Zaire, Zambia and Tanzania; in s Africa confined to Caprivi, Okavango and Victoria Falls areas.
Status: Local and uncommon resident.
Habitat: Riverine forest and adjacent thickets.
Habits: In pairs or small groups. Forages on ground, often in clearings and cultivated fields. Normally shy, but becomes tame around human settlements. Poorly known. Host to Violet Widowfinch.

Food: Seeds.

Breeding: *Season*: October in Zimbabwe, September to April in Zambia. *Nest*: Oval of grass, with side entrance; lined with feathers; usually low down in thicket or wall of grass hut; may build in old nest of sunbird or weaver. *Clutch*: 3–7 eggs. *Eggs*: White; no measurements available (about 16 × 10,5). *Incubation*: 11–13 days by both sexes. *Nestling*: 18–19 days; fed by both parents.

---

844 (839)　　　**Blue Waxbill**　　　**Plate 71**
Gewone Blousysie
Uraeginthus angolensis

Katjikilili Gomuburau (K), Kasisi (Sh), Xidzingirhi (Ts), [Angola-Schmetterlingsfink]

Measurements: Length 12–13 cm; wing (78 ♂) 47–52,3–56, (54 ♀) 48–51,9–54, (97 unsexed) 48–52–58; tail (60 ♂) 46,5–53–59,5, (41 ♀) 44,5–50,7–56,5, (57 unsexed) 45–50,2–61; tarsus (31) 13–15; culmen (31) 9–11. Weight (197 ♂) 6,3–9,9–13 g, (177 ♀) 7,3–10–12,6 g.
Bare Parts: Iris red-brown to red; bill pink, mauve or bluish slate, tip and cutting edges black; legs and feet light brown.
Identification: Size small; tail graduated, longish; above brown; rump and tail blue; face, throat, breast and flanks sky blue (paler in ♀); rest of underparts pinkish buff. *Immature*: Blue on throat and breast only; otherwise like adult. *Chick*: Reddish with fawn down; palate whitish with 3 black spots and dark central line; black band across tongue; long triangular black crescent in lower jaw; dark tubercles at gape develop late.
Voice: Urgent-sounding *sweep* or *tseep* callnotes, rapidly repeated; song of sibilant and harsh notes interspersed, *chreu chreu chittywoo weeoo wee,* etc.; harsh stuttering rattling alarm notes.

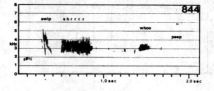

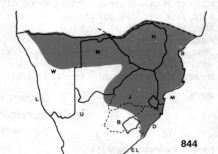

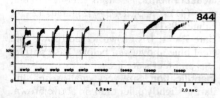

Distribution: S Africa to Angola and Tanzania; in s Africa from Natal to Transvaal, n and e Botswana, n Namibia, Zimbabwe and Mozambique.
Status: Locally common resident; somewhat nomadic.
Habitat: Open thornveld with grass and bushes, riverine bush, secondary growth around cultivation, gardens; sometimes edge of evergreen forest.
Habits: In pairs when breeding; otherwise gregarious in flocks of up to 40 or more birds. Forages on ground, but may hawk insects in flight. When disturbed flies to

nearest tree or bush, with rattling wing-beats; soon returns to ground when disturbance ceases. In courtship ♂ holds straw in bill while singing and bouncing up and down. Tame around human settlement.
Food: Seeds, insects.
Breeding: *Season*: October to March in Natal, October to June in Transvaal (peak in January), all months (mainly December-April) in Zimbabwe. *Nest*: Ball

of dry grass stems, with side entrance about 3 cm diameter; lined with fine grass and feathers; 0,5–1,7–4 m above ground in bush or tree, often near wasp nest. *Clutch*: (30) 2–3,5–7 eggs (usually 4–5). *Eggs*: White; measure (103) 14,4 × 10,8 (13,3–16,4 × 9,8–11,8). *Incubation* 11–12 days by both sexes. *Nestling*: 17–21 days; fed by both parents.
Ref. Goodwin, D. 1965. *Ibis* 107:285–315.

845 (840) Violeteared Waxbill   Plate 71
Koningblousysie
Uraeginthus granatinus

Katjikilili (K), Xidzingirhi (Ts), [Granatastrild, Blaubäckchen]
Measurements: Length 14–15 cm; wing (36 ♂) 55,5–58,1–61, (27 ♀) 55–56,8–59; tail (20 ♂) 66,5–78,6–82; tarsus (19) 15–17; culmen (19) 10–12. Weight (121 ♂) 8,6–11,7–15 g, (143 ♀) 9,5–11,7–13,9 g.
Bare Parts: Iris red-brown to red; eyering orange; bill red, base purple; legs and feet purplish brown to black.
Identification: Size medium; tail longish, graduated, black, conspicuous in flight. *Male*: Mostly rich chestnut brown; forehead and rump bright blue; face violet; throat, centre of belly and undertail black. *Female*: Light rusty buff where ♂ chestnut; forehead and rump blue; face pale violet; no black on throat or underparts. *Immature*: Similar to adult ♀, but without violet on face; rump only slightly blue; eye red (♂) or brown (♀). *Chick*: Blackish with long whitish down; palate orange with 5 black spots; tongue orange or yellow with black band; gape tubercles blue; black V on lower jaw.
Voice: Repeated *tiu-woo-wee* call; song tinkling canarylike twittering.

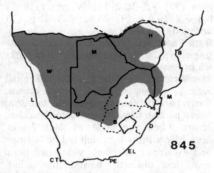

845

Distribution: Northern Cape, w Orange Free State, w and n Transvaal, extreme s Mozambique, Zimbabwe, Botswana, Namibia; also Angola and Zambia.
Status: Locally common resident.
Habitat: Dry savanna, especially *Acacia*, with thickets and denser riverine thornbush; also edges of cultivation.
Habits: Usually solitary or in pairs; sometimes in small groups of up to 10 birds; may associate with Blue Waxbill. Forages on ground, often in interior of low thickets; when disturbed flies into dense bush; often seen at waterholes. Wings make buzzing sound during courtship. Host to Shafttailed Whydah.
Food: Seeds, insects.
Breeding: *Season*: December to June in Transvaal, October to May (mainly January-February) in Zimbabwe. *Nest*: Loosely built ball of dry grass stems, with side entrance 4–5 cm diameter; lined with feathers; from near ground to 3 m above ground (mean 1 m) in thornbush. *Clutch*: (9) 3–6 eggs (usually 4–5). *Eggs*: White;

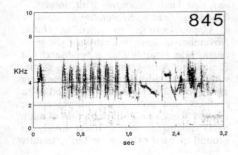

845

measure (36) 15,6 × 11,4 (14,2–17,2 × 9,2–13); weigh (mean) 1,25 g. *Incubation*: 12–13 days by both sexes. *Nestling*: 16–18 days; fed by both parents.

846 (843)   Common Waxbill   Plate 71
Rooibeksysie (Rooibekkie)
Estrilda astrild

Katjikilili (K), Borahane (SS), Xidzingirhi (Ts), Intshiyane (X), iNtiyane (Z), [Wellenastrild]

Measurements: Length 11–12 cm; wing (98 ♂) 45–48,1–54, (89 ♀) 44–47,6–51, (148 unsexed) 45–48,8–53,5; tail (97 ♂) 43–49,6–54, (83 ♀) 42–48,6–55, (97 unsexed) 47–52,3–60; tarsus (28) 14–16; culmen (97) 9,5–10,2–11. Weight (118 ♂) 6,4–8,2–10,6 g, (97 ♀) 6,3–8,1–11 g, (73 unsexed) 6–8,8–11 g.

Bare Parts: Iris brown; bill wax red, cutting edges darker; legs and feet dark pinkish brown.

Identification: Size small; sexes alike; tail longish, graduated; above greyish brown, finely barred blackish; eyestripe crimson; below pinkish white, finely barred blackish; centre of belly red; undertail black. *Immature*: Below buffy with dull red belly stripe and eyestripe; bill black with white basal spot; less distinctly barred than adult. *Chick*: Palate pinkish with 5 black spots; black crescent in lower jaw; 2 black marks on tongue nearly meet; 2 bluish white, black-centred swellings on each side of base of upper jaw; bluish white, black-ringed tubercle on each side of base of lower jaw.

Voice: Somewhat nasal *ching ching ching* callnotes; song repeated quick harsh phrase *di-di-di-JEE, di-di-di-JEE, di-di-di-JEE*; fledgling calls repeated *chiCHEE chiCHEE*.

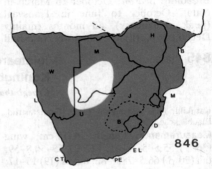

846

Distribution: Africa S of Sahara, Madagascar, some Indian Ocean islands; introduced to many parts of world; throughout s Africa, except C Kalahari basin.

Status: Common resident.

Habitat: Rank vegetation, usually in grass, reeds and rushes near water; also gardens, rank growth around cultivation, tangled vegetation along watercourses.

Habits: In pairs or family groups when breeding; otherwise gregarious in flocks of up to 30 or more birds. Roosts communally in reedbeds, sometimes in hundreds, perching in rows on stalks. Forages on ground, at feeding tray, in trees, or on standing grass inflorescences; flies into bush or tree when disturbed; flight fast and direct, but bounces with heavy tail when alighting. Flicks tail side to side when alarmed. Host to Pintailed Whydah.

Food: Seeds (including grass and *Casuarina*), ripe *Ficus sycomorus* fruit, insects.

Breeding: *Season*: September to January in Cape, October to April in Natal, November to June in Transvaal, November to May (mainly December-March) in Zimbabwe. *Nest*: Oval of dry grass stems, with tubular side entrance 7–10 cm long and about 2,5 cm diameter; lined with feathers and soft grass inflorescences; smaller "cock's nest" built on roof of main nest, sometimes also sparsely lined; on ground at base of grass or bush, usually

with bare patch of earth at entrance; sometimes low down in tangled vegetation. *Clutch*: (42) 3–4,9–9 eggs (usually 4–6). *Eggs*: White; measure (72) 13,9 × 10,6 (12,5–16,1 × 9,9–11,7); weigh (mean) 0,87 g. *Incubation*: 11–12 days by both sexes. *Nestling*: 17–21 days; fed by both parents.

847 (841) Blackcheeked Waxbill Plate 71
Swartwangsysie
Estrilda erythronotos

Siguye (K), Xidzingirhi (Ts), Sentsipitsipi (Tw), [Elfenastrild]

Measurements: Length about 13 cm; wing (27) 52–54–58; tail 53–60; tarsus 13–16; culmen 9–10,5. Weight (2 ♂) 7,7–8,4 g, (2 ♀) 7,9–8,6 g, (150 unsexed) 7,6–9,2–10,9 g.
Bare Parts: Iris red; bill blueblack; legs and feet black.
Identification: Size smallish; sexes alike, but ♀ paler on belly; tail black, graduated, longish; crown grey; back reddish grey, finely barred black; rump wine-red; chin and ear coverts black (diagnostic); throat and breast pinkish, finely barred black; belly wine-red; centre of belly and undertail black. *Immature*: Similar to adult ♀, but less red below; eye brown. *Chick*: Palate pale with 5 black spots; 2 black spots on tongue nearly meet in middle; lower jaw with or without black crescent; gape tubercles yellowish white with large black spot inside.
Voice: Repeated musical 2-note whistle *pee-tyee*, rising in pitch on second note, somewhat like high-pitched version of song of Rufousnaped Lark; contact call of ♀ sibilant *psyee* with no upward inflection; song jumble of warbled notes.

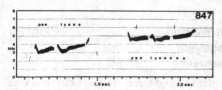

Distribution: S Africa to Angola, Ethiopia and Somalia; in s Africa from w Orange Free State and w Transvaal to Botswana, sw Zimbabwe and most of Namibia.
Status: Locally common resident.
Habitat: Mainly *Acacia* savanna, riverine thornbush, especially in drier areas.
Habits: Usually in small flocks of up to 12 birds; in pairs when breeding. Forages low down in tangled vegetation, or on ground; flies into bushes when disturbed. Roosts in nest (sometimes of weavers) at night.
Food: Seeds, insects, green plant material, nectar of aloes.
Breeding: *Season*: December to March in Transvaal, January in Botswana, September to April in Zimbabwe. *Nest*: Large ball of dry grass stems, with downward-pointing side entrance tube about 10 cm long; lined with fine grass; 3–9 m above ground in thorntree. *Clutch* : 3–6 eggs. *Eggs*: White; measure (23) 14,8 × 10,8 (13,9–15,9 × 10,1–11,4). *Incubation*: 12 days. *Nestling*: 22 days.

848 (842) Grey Waxbill Plate 71
Gryssysie
Estrilda perreini

[Schwarzschwanz-Schönbürzel]
Measurements: Length 10,5–11 cm; wing (9) 47–49–51; tail (7) 43–49; tarsus (7) 14,5–15,5; culmen (7) 8–9. Weight (2 ♂) 7,2–7,6 g, (1 ♀) 7,5 g, (3 unsexed) 6,1–7,4–9 g.

Bare Parts: Iris red; bill blue-grey, tip and cutting edges black; legs and feet greenish black.

Identification: Size small; sexes alike; tail longish, graduated, black; mostly grey, paler below; chin and eyestripe black (eyestripe red in Common Waxbill); rump crimson, conspicuous in flight (grey in Common Waxbill); undertail blackish. *Immature*: Lacks black eyestripe; rump duller red.

Voice: Thin, slightly explosive *pseeu pseeu* callnotes; ♂ has plaintive drawn-out whistle, *fweeeee*, sometimes followed by up to 5 shorter notes.

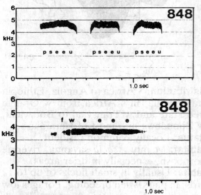

Distribution: S Africa to Angola, Zaire and Gabon; in s Africa confined to extreme E, from s Natal northwards; also inland in Transvaal to Haenertsburg and Magoebaskloof.

Status: Scarce in S of range; locally com-

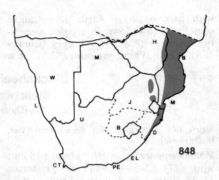

mon elsewhere; very common in e Zimbabwe.

Habitat: Edges of lowland and mid-altitude evergreen forest, coastal bush, riverine forest, thickets, dense secondary growth, and adjacent woodland.

Habits: Solitary or in pairs. Inconspicuous and easily overlooked. Forages off standing grass inflorescences or on ground, usually in or close to dense cover; may also forage in canopy. Poorly known.

Food: Seeds (probably mainly of grasses), insects, nectar.

Breeding: *Season*: October to February in Natal, October to April in Zimbabwe. *Nest*: Oval of dry grass tops and ferns, with side entrance tube about 7,5 cm long; lined with fine grass and feathers; 1,5–4 m above ground in bush or tree; sometimes in old nest of Forest Weaver. *Clutch*: (12) 2–4,3–5 eggs (usually 4–5). *Eggs*: White; measure (30) 14,6 × 11,4 (13,7–15,4 × 10,5–11,5). *Incubation*: 12 days (captivity), by both sexes. *Nestling*: 19–21 days.

---

849 (842X)   **Cinderella Waxbill**   **Plate 71**
Swartoogsysie
Estrilda thomensis

[Cinderella-Schönbürzel]

Measurements: Length about 11 cm; wing 50; tail 40; tarsus 14; culmen 8.

Bare Parts: Iris red; bill red, tip and lower surface black; legs and feet black.

Identification: Size small; similar to Grey Waxbill, but paler; mainly pale grey, washed rosy on mantle and breast (♀ duller); eyestripe black; rump and flanks bright red; lower belly black in ♂, grey in ♀ (Grey Waxbill all grey below); centre of belly and undertail black; tail black, graduated, longish; bill red (grey in Grey Waxbill). *Immature*: Similar to adult, but lacks red on flanks; belly of ♂ less intensely black; bill dull whitish, tip and cutting edges pink.

Voice: Soft trilling *tree* or *krr* callnotes; song of ♂ drawn-out whistled *see-eh see-eh sueee*; ♀ calls simple *seee*.

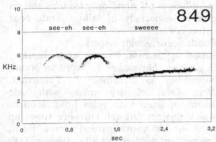

849

see-eh   see-eh   sweeee

KHz

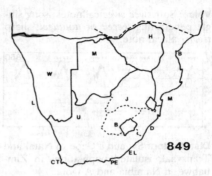

849

Distribution: Southern Angola to Kunene River, Namibia.
Status: Locally fairly common.
Habitat: Riverine bush, savanna, mopane woodland.
Habits: Usually in pairs; sometimes in small groups of up to 25 birds. Keeps to low bushes. Poorly known.
Food: Unrecorded.

Breeding: *Season*: Unrecorded. *Nest*: In captivity, large ball of grass, with side entrance tube about 12 cm long; sometimes builds "cock's nest" (in which ♂ may roost) on top of main chamber. *Clutch* : (2) 3–4 eggs (captivity). *Eggs*: White. *Incubation*: 12,5–14 days (captivity). *Nestling*: 17–21 days (captivity); fed by both parents; fledgling fed for up to 10 days after leaving nest.

---

850 (825)   **Swee Waxbill**   Plate 71
                      Suidelike Swie
                      Estrilda melanotis

Katjikilili (K), Xidzingirhi (Ts), ubuSukuswane (Z), [Gelbbauchastrild]

Measurements: Length 9–10 cm; wing (177) 40–44,2–50; tail (156) 27–35,3–39; tarsus (67) 12–13,4–15,5; culmen (68) 6,5–8,3–10. Weight (12 ♂) 5,7–7,5–8,4 g, (8 ♀) 7,2–8–8,4 g, (160 unsexed) 5–6,25–8,8 g.
Bare Parts: Iris red; bill black above, red below; legs and feet pinkish brown.
Identification: Size very small. *Male:* Crown, nape and breast grey; face and throat black (diagnostic; no black in ♂ East African Swee); back and wings light golden olive (diagnostic); rump bright red (diagnostic in flight); tail black; rest of underparts buff to light yellow. *Female:* Similar to ♂, but face and throat whitish, contrasting with grey ear coverts (face and throat grey in east African Swee); similar to both sexes of East African Swee, but

850

buff or yellow rather than orange on belly. *Immature*: Similar to adult ♀, but bill all black; less red on rump. *Chick*: Palate plain; black swelling bordered with white at base of each side of upper jaw; 2 white tubercles on black background at each side of base of lower jaw; dark band across tongue.

757

Voice: Soft *swee swee* callnotes; song single penetrating *teeeeit* or *tuuuueet*; sharp *teerrrr* alarm note.

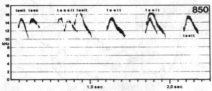

Distribution: Sw and s Cape to Natal and Transvaal; isolated populations in Zimbabwe, n Namibia and Angola.

Status: Common resident; some seasonal altitudinal movement in Natal Drakensberg and Thongaland.

Habitat: Edges of evergreen forest, exotic plantations, gardens, bushy hillsides, farmyards, thick streamside bush.

Habits: Usually in pairs or small groups. Fairly quiet and easily overlooked because of small size, but often tame and confiding. Forages off standing grass tops and on ground, especially in fallow lands near dense cover.

Food: Seeds, small insects.

Breeding: *Season*: November to January in e Cape, November to April in Natal, November to December in Transvaal. *Nest*: Oval of dry grass, with side entrance; lined with grass inflorescences which project through entrance tube; up to about 2 m above ground in tree, bush, creeper or garden pergola. *Clutch*: (18) 3–4,7–9 eggs (usually 4–5). *Eggs*: White; measure (34) 13,7 × 10,4 (12,2–16,3 × 9,9–11). *Incubation*: (6) 12–13 days by both sexes (captivity). *Nestling*: (6) 19–22 days; fed by both parents (captivity).

---

851 (826)　　　**East African Swee**　　　**Plate 71**
　　　　　　　　　Tropiese Swie
　　　　　　　　　Estrilda quartinia

[Grünastrild]

Measurements: Length 9–10 cm; wing 42–45,5; tail 35–38; tarsus 12,5–13; culmen 8–9. Weight (2 ♂) 5,7–6,2 g, (2 ♀) 7–7,2 g.

Bare Parts: Iris red; bill black above, red below; legs and feet blackish brown.

Identification: Size very small; sexes alike; similar to ♀ Swee Waxbill; head and breast grey (face and throat whitish in ♀ Swee Waxbill); back golden olive; rump red; tail black; rest of underparts light orange (buff or yellow in Swee Waxbill). *Immature*: Similar to adult, but bill all black; less red on rump.

Voice: Song variable jumble of notes, *tee-tee-tee-tuuueeh* or *teeku-teehleeeke-hleekee*, etc.; sharp *teeerrr* alarm note; weak *sree* callnote.

Distribution: Eastern Zimbabwe and adjacent Mozambique, to Ethiopia.

Status: Locally common resident; some seasonal movements possible.

Habitat: Bracken-brier and other dense montane vegetation, edges of highland

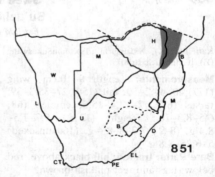

evergreen forest, regenerating exotic pine plantations.

Habits: In pairs or small groups of up to 12 birds. Forages on ground or from standing grass tops; when disturbed flies twittering into nearby bush, but soon returns to feed. Similar to Swee Waxbill.

Food: Seeds.

Breeding: *Season*: December-January in Zimbabwe, December to April in Mozambique. *Nest*: Ball of dry coarse grass, with side entrance; lined with fine grass inflorescences and some feathers; in leafy branch of tree, 2–5 m above ground; built in 7–10 days by both sexes. *Clutch*: 4–6 eggs. *Eggs*: White; measure (19) 13,6 × 10,5 (12,6–14,4 × 10–10,8). *Incubation*: 12–13 days by both sexes. *Nestling*: 14–16 days; fed by both parents.

852 (844) Quail Finch
Gewone Kwartelvinkie
Ortygospiza atricollis

Plate 71

Mukadi Gonon (K), Lekolukotoana, Lekolikotoana (SS), Unonkxwe (X), iNxenge, uNonklwe (Z), [Wachtelastrild]

Measurements: Length about 10 cm; wing (42 ♂) 52–55,3–58, (45 ♀) 52,5–55–58; tail (15) 25–31; tarsus (15) 13–15; culmen (15) 9–10. Weight (4 ♂) 10,5–11,4–12 g, (8 ♀) 10–10,6–11,5 g.

Bare Parts: Iris orange-brown; bill red (♂), dusky brown above, pink or red below (♀); legs and feet light brown.

Identification: Size very small; tail short; above grey; eyepatch and chin white; forehead, malar stripe and throat black in ♂, grey in ♀; breast and flanks barred black and white; belly light rufous, shading to white undertail. *Immature*: Below light brown, without barring. *Chick*: Palate yellowish with 6 black spots; 3 black marks on tongue; black crescent on inside of lower jaw; 3 iridescent opalescent tubercles on black skin at base of each side of upper jaw, and one at base of lower jaw.

Voice: Irregular *tink, tink-tink, tirrilink* or *tee tee tink-tink*, somewhat bell-like flight and take-off call; song rapid rattling rambling *klik klak kloik klik kluk klek*.

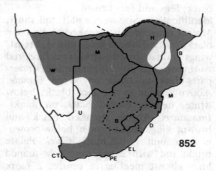

852

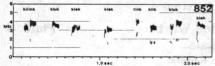

Distribution: Africa S of Sahara; widespread in s Africa, except arid W and highlands of Zimbabwe and adjacent Mozambique.

Status: Common resident; nomadic after breeding.

Habitat: Open short grassveld, vleis, edges of dams and pans, open grassy hillsides, dry Kalahari sandplains; usually with patches of bare ground.

Habits: In pairs when breeding; otherwise gregarious in small flocks of up to 20 or more birds. Entirely terrestrial and very hard to see; sits close, taking off at one's feet with clinking calls, usually flying with erratic jerky flight for some distance before landing; nesting bird takes off without calling. Forages on ground; catches termites in flight; drinks frequently. Flies high between feeding grounds; in display ♂ flies high, then plummets down with clicking song.

Food: Seeds, insects, spiders.

Breeding: *Season*: November to April (mainly January to March) in e Cape and Natal, October to February in Orange Free State, all months except October in Transvaal (80% of nests January-March), December to May (mainly January-April) in Zimbabwe. *Nest*: Ball of dry grey grass blades, with side entrance; thickly lined with soft grass and feathers; on ground at base of grasstuft or between 2 tufts, with small patch of bare ground at entrance. *Clutch*: (46) 3–4,2–6 eggs. *Eggs*: White; measure (115) 14,4 × 11,1 (12,7–16,5 × 10,4–12,9). *Incubation*: About 14 days by both sexes. *Nestling*: 19–21 days.

853 (845) Locust Finch Plate 71
Rooivlerkkwartelvinkie
Ortygospiza locustella

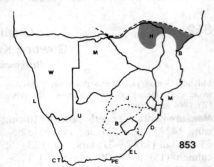

853

[Heuschreckenastrild]

Measurements: Length 9–10 cm; wing (25) 43–47; tail 27–31; tarsus 13–16; culmen 7–9.

Bare Parts: Iris yellow; bill red, culmen black; legs and feet brown.

Identification: Size very small; tail short. *Male*: Crown brown, streaked black; back black, spotted white; face, throat, breast, wings and rump red (darkest on face; red wings conspicuous in flight); rest of underparts black; tail black, edged red. *Female*: Above similar to ♂; face black; below white, heavily barred black on flanks. *Immature*: Above streaked black and brown; wings edged brown; below browner than adult ♀; bill black. *Chick*: Palate bright red with 2 opposing bow-shaped lines almost meeting in centre; 2 more lines at right angles to these on either side; tongue has 3 raised red lobes overlapping edges; 2 flat red protruding lobes on either side of gape.

Voice: Less vocal than Quail Finch; squeaky querulous *chip chip* flight call.

Distribution: Northeastern Zimbabwe and n Mozambique, to Zaire.

Status: Local and usually uncommon resident; makes seasonal movements in search of moist habitat.

Habitat: Vleis and moist grassland with tufts of short wiry grass and patches of bare ground, preferably on sandy soils; also old cultivated lands and burnt grassland in dry season.

Habits: In pairs when breeding; otherwise gregarious in small flocks of 3–16 birds. Completely terrestrial; forages on ground between grasstufts; never perches. Sits tight, flying off at last moment when disturbed, rising high and flying fast and erratically for up to 100 m before landing. Pair roosts in nest at night. Similar to Quail Finch.

Food: Seeds.

Breeding: *Season*: January to May in Zimbabwe (and Zambia). *Nest*: Ball, about 7–8 cm diameter, of fine dry grass, with high side entrance about 2,5 cm diameter; lined with grass inflorescences, green grass and feathers; on ground between grasstufts. *Clutch*: 2–8 eggs (usually 4–7). *Eggs*: White; measure (2) 12,2–12,9 × 9,9–10. *Incubation*: Unrecorded; mostly by ♀. *Nestling*: Unrecorded.

854 (838) Orangebreasted Waxbill Plate 71
Rooiassie
Sporaeginthus subflavus

Katjikilili (K), Borahane (SS), Xidzingirhi (Ts), [Goldbrüstchen]

Measurements: Length 9–10 cm; wing (277 ♂) 41–45,4–49, (187 ♀) 42–45,2–49; tail (233 ♂) 31–34,6–37,5, (161 ♀) 30,5–34,2–38; tarsus (13 ♂) 11,5–12,1–12,5, (5 ♀) 12,5–12,8–13; culmen (13 ♂) 7,5–8,5–9, (5 ♀) 8,5–8,9–9. Weight (287 ♂) 5,7–7,3–10,3 g, (192 ♀) 5,2–7,6–10,9 g.

Bare Parts: Iris red to orange-red; bill red, culmen and lower edge black; legs and feet pinkish brown.

Identification: Size very small; tail medium. *Male*: Above dull grey; eyebrow, rump and undertail scarlet; below orange-yellow, breast darker, barred brownish on flanks. *Female*: Similar to ♂, but lacks red eyebrow; underparts yellow. *Immature*: Similar to adult ♀, but buff below; rump tinged rufous; flanks not barred. *Chick*: Mouth mainly whitish with black markings; 3 spots on palate; horseshoe-shaped mark and 2 lateral spots in lower jaw; tongue broadly tipped black with 2 lateral spots; 2 confluent spots on each side of both upper and lower gape.

Voice: Rapid *trip-trip-trip* on take-off; soft *chit-chit* contact calls; soft *tink* flight call, 1–2 notes/second; loud metallic *chink* alarm note; song jumbled series of high-pitched notes, *chip chit cheet chink cheup chink*, etc., often sustained for several minutes.

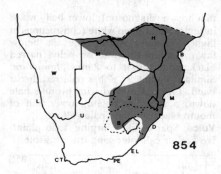

854

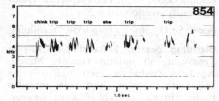

854

Distribution: Africa S of Sahara; in s Africa mainly in e half from e Cape and Orange River northwards to Zambezi and Okavango Rivers.

Status: Locally common resident.

Habitat: Tall rank grass in grassland or savanna, usually near water; reedbeds in vleis; also rank herbaceous vegetation bordering lowland forest.

Habits: Usually gregarious in flocks of up to about 20 birds; members of feeding or flying flock give short contact calls repeatedly. Forages on ground or on standing grass inflorescences, constantly flicking tail and wings and hopping about restlessly; when disturbed members of flock fly off short distance in small straggling groups. Flocks usually well synchronized in fast swerving flight when moving

between feeding grounds. Roosts in rushes and rank grass. Flies to water to drink and bathe, mainly mid-afternoon.

Food: Small dry or green grass seeds, insects, soft shoots.

Breeding: *Season*: January to May in Natal, January to July (mainly February-April) in Transvaal, December to July (mainly March-April) in Zimbabwe. *Nest*: Usually (about 95%) lines old nest of bishop (mostly Red Bishop), widow, weaver or cisticola with dry grass and feathers; in reedbed or rank grass near water; also builds own oval nest of grass, lined with soft grass inflorescences, feathers and plant down; outside height about 10 cm; inside chamber about 12 cm diameter; side entrance 3–5 cm diameter; 23–71–140 cm above ground (28 self-built nests); built by both sexes. *Clutch*: (110) 3–5–7 eggs (usually 4–6). *Eggs*: White; measure (273) 13,6 × 10,2 (11,8–15,3 × 9,3–11,2); weigh (25) 0,6–0,77–0,85 g. *Incubation*: 13 days by both sexes. *Nestling*: 17–19 days; fed by both parents; postnestling dependence about 2 weeks.

Ref. Colahan, B.D. 1982. *Ostrich* 53:1–30.

855 (821) **Cutthroat Finch** **Plate 69**
Bandkeelvink
Amadina fasciata

Enzunge (K), [Bandfink]

Measurements: Length about 12 cm; wing (11) 63–66–67,5; tail 39–42; tarsus 12,5–14; culmen 10,5–11. Weight (4) 17,4–17,6–17,9 g.

Bare Parts: Iris brown; bill blue-grey; legs and feet pale pinkish.

Identification: Medium to large (somewhat smaller than sparrow); bill heavy; tail rounded. *Male*: Above light brown, barred black (Redheaded Finch plain above); chin white; throat band red (diagnostic); breast and flanks fawn, barred black and white; patch in centre of belly rich brown (diagnostic); lower belly white in centre; tail tipped white (conspicuous in flight). *Female*: Above like ♂; below fawn, shading to white on belly, barred black from throat to flanks. *Immature*: Similar to adult ♀; ♂ has pale red throat band. *Chick*: Covered with profuse pale down; 5 spots on palate; lower half of mouth blackish; gape pale yellow.

Voice: Sparrowlike chirping; loud plaintive *kee-air* callnote; song fruity warble.

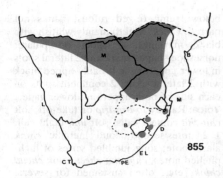

855

woodpeckers, or in natural holes. Quiet and easily overlooked.

Food: Seeds, insects (especially termites).

Distribution: Africa S of Sahara; in s Africa from Transvaal to Zimbabwe, n Mozambique, ne Botswana and n Namibia; straggler to Natal.

Status: Uncommon to fairly common resident; nomadic.

Habitat: Savanna and drier woodland (in areas of higher rainfall than for Redheaded Finch).

Habits: In pairs when breeding; otherwise gregarious, sometimes in large flocks. Forages mainly on ground. Roosts (and breeds) in disused nests of weavers or

Breeding: *Season*: December to May in Transvaal, all months (mainly March-April) in Zimbabwe. *Nest*: Ball of grass and feathers, with short side entrance tunnel, in old nest of *Ploceus* weaver, Redbilled Buffalo Weaver or Redheaded Weaver, hole in fencepost or tree. *Clutch*: (7) 2–4–7 eggs (usually 4–6). *Eggs*: White; measure (30) 16,8 × 13 (16–18 × 12,3–14,6). *Incubation*: 12–13 days by both sexes. *Nestling*: 21–23 days; fed by both parents.

856 (820)   Redheaded Finch   Plate 69
Rooikopvink
Amadina erythrocephala

Kafilita (K), Jeremane (SS), [Rotkopfamadine]

Measurements: Length about 14 cm; wing (32) 70–72,5–75; tail 46–55; tarsus 14–17; culmen 11–12,5. Weight (5 ♂) 19,7–21,6–23 g, (5 ♀) 22–23,6–25,5 g, (105 unsexed) 19–23,2–30 g.

Bare Parts: Iris brown; bill whitish horn; legs and feet pinkish brown.

Identification: Large (about size of Cape Sparrow); bill very heavy; tail rounded. *Male*: Whole head bright red; rest of upperparts greyish brown, faintly barred on rump (whole upperparts barred in Cutthroat Finch); breast and flanks fawn, spotted with white, each spot outlined in black; lower belly white; undertail barred black, white and brown. *Female*: Similar

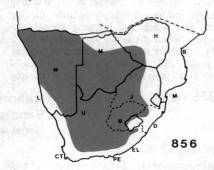

856

to ♂, but head brown above, barred black and white on throat; ♀ Cutthroat Finch barred black above. *Immature*: Similar to adults, but duller; ♂ has only trace of red on head. *Chick*: Palate pale with 5 black spots; throat and lower half of mouth black.

Voice: Nasal *chink chink* call and alarm note (also in flight); song whirring or buzzing notes with throat puffed out.

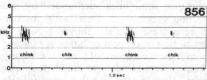

Distribution: Southern Africa from Karoo and inland Natal to Botswana, sw Zimbabwe and Namibia to Angola, excluding higher-rainfall areas.

Status: Common to very common resident; highly nomadic, numbers fluctuating greatly in time and space.

Habitat: Open grassland with clumps of trees or small plantations, dry savanna, farmyards, cultivated fields.

Habits: In pairs or small colonies when breeding; otherwise gregarious, sometimes in flocks of hundreds of birds; often in company with other seedeating species of birds. Forages on ground; drinks frequently, dipping and raising bill very fast; gathers in large flocks at waterholes. When disturbed flies to tree, fence or other perch; flight fast and undulating; flocks well coordinated. May roost at night in nests of Whitebrowed Sparrow-weaver.

Food: Seeds, insects.

Breeding: *Season*: Mainly winter months throughout s Africa, February to September; almost any month in Kalahari, according to rainfall. *Nest*: Pad or ball of grass and feathers; in old nest of sparrow, *Ploceus* weaver (especially of Chestnut Weaver in n Namibia), Redbilled Buffalo Weaver, Sociable Weaver, or in hole in tree or building; solitary or in small colony of 2–3 pairs in adjacent nest chambers. *Clutch*: (46) 2–4,2–11 eggs (usually 4–6). *Eggs*: White, rounded; measure (72) 18,3 × 14,7 (16,9–21,3 × 13,2–15,6). *Incubation*: 12–14 days by both sexes. *Nestling*: 15–21 days; fed by both parents.

857 (823)   Bronze Mannikin   Plate 69
Gewone Fret
Spermestes cucullatus

Zadzasaga (Sh), Rijajani (Ts), Ungxenge, Ingxenge (X), [Kleinelsterchen]

Measurements: Length 9–10 cm; wing (369) 45–49–53; tail (367) 25–30,5–35,5; tarsus (250) 12–14,1–16; culmen (250) 8–9,8–12. Weight (423) 7,2–9,8–12,2 g.

Bare Parts: Iris brown; bill black above, blue-grey below; legs and feet blackish brown.

Identification: Size very small; sexes alike; head, throat and upper breast blackish, washed dull metallic green (Redbacked Mannikin blacker on breast, contrasting more with white belly); back and wings greyish brown (deep chestnut in Redbacked Mannikin, barred black and grey in Pied Mannikin), upperwing with metallic green spots (seen only in good light); rump barred black and white; tail black; rest of underparts white, barred blackish on flanks and undertail. *Immature*: Plain buff, paler below; bill blackish.

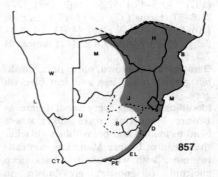

Voice: High-pitched rapid *tsree-tsree-tsree* contact call; sharp *chuk-chuk-chuk* alarm call; song rising and falling *chi-chi-chi-chu-chu-chu*, etc.

Distribution: Africa S of Sahara; in s Africa confined to e half from e Cape to Caprivi.

Status: Very common resident.

Habitat: Edges of thickets in savanna or

open woodland, secondary growth around cultivation, parks, gardens, farmyards; usually where water available.

Habits: In pairs or family groups when breeding; otherwise gregarious in compact, well coordinated flocks of up to about 30 birds. Forages on ground, off standing grass inflorescences or at feeding tray; drinks often. When disturbed flies into nearest bush or tree; wings make tiny whirring sound; flies in any direction and hovers well. Flicks wings and tail, especially when anxious or alarmed. Small groups rest in clusters on branch by day; roosts communally in nests at night, sometimes building special roosting nest in winter. Courting ♂ presents ♀ with grass stem.

Food: Seeds, insects, green plant material, nectar, algae.

Breeding: *Season*: September to April in Natal, August to April in Transvaal, August to May (mainly December-April) in Zimbabwe. *Nest*: Ball of dry grass, with tubular side entrance about 40 cm diameter; external height 16 cm, width 12,5 cm; entrance sometimes surrounded by projecting grass stems; lined with grass inflorescences; 1–3 m above ground in bush, tree or on post or beam of building; sometimes occupies old nest of bishop, weaver or waxbill; may build near wasp nest. *Clutch*: (50) 2–4,9–8 eggs (usually 3–6). *Eggs*: White; measure (86) 14,4 × 10,2 (12,9–16,1 × 9,6–12,2); weigh (28) 0,6–0,8–0,9 g. *Incubation*: 14–16 days by both sexes. *Nestling*: 17–23 days; fed by both parents.

Ref. Woodall, P.F. 1975. *Ostrich* 46:55–86.

---

858 (824)　　　　**Redbacked Mannikin**　　　　**Plate 69**
Rooirugfret
Spermestes bicolor

Rijajani (Ts), [Glanzelsterchen]

Measurements: Length 9–10 cm; wing (102) 40,5–48,1–52,5; tail (89) 27–31,8–37; tarsus (47) 12–14–17,5; culmen (50) 9–10,5–12. Weight (4 ♂) 8,4–8,9–9,3 g, (6 ♀) 8–8,6–9,8 g, (121 unsexed) 7,3–9,2–11,3 g.

Bare Parts: Iris brown, outer rim reddish; bill greyish horn; legs and feet blackish grey.

Identification: Size very small (same as Bronze Mannikin); sexes alike; whole head to mantle and breast black (blacker than head of Bronze Mannikin, contrasting more with white belly); back deep chestnut (diagnostic; grey-brown in Bronze Mannikin, barred in Pied Mannikin); rump barred black and white; rest of underparts white, barred black on flanks; bill uniform grey (half dark, half pale in Bronze Mannikin). *Immature*: Above dull red-brown; below white, washed buff on breast and flanks.

Voice: Twittering and whistling callnotes; also sharp *tsik tsik*.

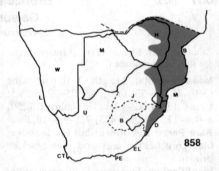

858

Distribution: Africa S of Sahara; in s Africa confined to extreme E from Transkei northwards, and to Zoutpansberg, Transvaal.

Status: Locally fairly common to common.

Habitat: Riverine forest, moist thickets, edges of coastal, lowland to midland evergreen forest, sometimes with tall grass.

Habits: In pairs when breeding; otherwise gregarious in small flocks of up to about 12 birds. Forages on ground and on standing grass inflorescences in clearings and edges of dense cover; hawks insects in flight; when disturbed flies to nearest bush or tree. Roosts communally in nest which may be used later by pair for breeding.

Food: Seeds, nectar of *Schotia* flowers, insects, algal filaments.

Breeding: *Season*: October to December in Natal, February in Transvaal, November to May in Zimbabwe, May in Mozambique. *Nest*: Ball of dry grass, with side entrance partly concealed by grass tops; in tree, usually fairly high above ground. *Clutch*: (8) 2–4,8–7 eggs (usually 4–6). *Eggs*: White; measure (27) 14,8 × 10,3 (13,4–16 × 9,7–11,1). *Incubation*: 12 days (captivity). *Nestling*: 17 days (captivity).

859 (822)   Pied Mannikin   Plate 69
Dikbekfret
Spermestes fringilloides

[Riesenelsterchen]

Measurements: Length 11–12 cm; wing (8) 57–60,8–66; tail (4) 33–36,2–40; tarsus (4) 13,5–15,3–17; culmen (4) 15–16–17. Weight (3 ♂) 16,1–17,5–18,9 g, (2 ♀) 16,2–17 g.

Bare Parts: Iris brown; bill blackish above, grey below; legs and feet black.

Identification: Size smallish to medium (larger than Bronze Mannikin); sexes alike; head, nape and throat black (black not extending to breast as in other mannikins); back barred buff and brown (plain in other mannikins); rump and tail black, tipped and edged white; below white; incomplete black collar on breast (diagnostic); flanks mottled black and buff (barred black and white in other mannikins). *Immature*: Above plain olive brown; below buffy white.

Voice: Cheerful *peu-peu-peu* flight call; song soft and bubbling; shrill alarm note.

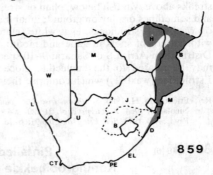

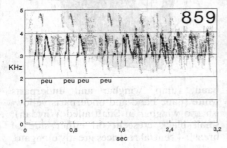

Distribution: Africa S of Sahara; in s Africa confined to extreme E from Natal northwards, including e Zimbabwe.

Status: Rare to uncommon and highly local resident; nomadic according to food supply. Indeterminate (RDB).

Habitat: Mainly Bindura Bamboo *Oxytenanthera abyssinica* thickets along rivers and on margins of lowland evergreen forest in Zimbabwe; elsewhere edges of evergreen bush, clearings in dense woodland and around African villages and gardens.

Habits: In pairs when breeding; otherwise gregarious in flocks of up to about 10 birds; rarely in flocks of up to 500 birds in Zimbabwe. Forages on standing grass and bamboo inflorescences. Similar to Bronze Mannikin.

Food: Seeds, grain (including rice); in

Zimbabwe mainly seeds of *Oxytenanthera abyssinica* measuring 12,5–16 × 2–2,5.
Breeding: *Season*: April in Natal (1 record), October to June in Zimbabwe (possibly dependent on flowering time of Bindura Bamboo), October to March in Mozambique. *Nest*: Ball of dry or green grass, sometimes with other leaves, with porched side entrance 1,5–3,5 cm long, 2–5 cm diameter; lined with fine grass and bamboo flowers; outside length 12,5–

20 cm, width 11–13 cm, height 12–13 cm; 2–5 m above ground in tree; built in 7–10 days. *Clutch*: 2–9 eggs (usually 4–6). *Eggs*: White; measure (25) 16,2 × 11,5 (14,6–17,8 × 10,9–12,3). *Incubation*: 14–16 days. *Nestling*: 19–22 days; independent at 49–55 days.

Ref. Brickell, N., Huntley, B. & Vorster, R. 1980. *Bokmakierie* 32:9–12.
Jackson, H.D. 1972. *Rhod. Sci. News* 6:342–348.

26:28. Family 90 VIDUIDAE—WHYDAHS AND WIDOWFINCHES (INDIGOBIRDS OR COMBASSOUS)

Small (excluding long tails). Bill very short, stout, conical, adapted for seedeating, often red or white; legs short and slender; feet small; wings short and rounded; tail medium, square, or with four central rectrices greatly elongated in breeding males of several species; plumage of breeding males black with some blue or green sheen, often with white, yellow or rufous on belly; plumage of females and eclipse males buffy with darker streaks above, whitish below, plain or streaked on chest; gregarious; arboreal, but feed and sometimes display on ground; inhabit mainly savanna; polygynous; brood-parasitic on waxbills (Estrildidae); eggs white (clutch size 1–4 eggs); chick downy at hatching, with pattern of spots in gape and mouth, resembling those of chicks of host species. Distribution Africa S of Sahara; 9–10 species; eight species in s Africa. The Viduidae may be related to the euplectine ploceids (bishops and widows), and not to the Estrildidae (waxbills) which comprise their hosts.

Ref. Friedmann, H. 1960. *Smithson. Inst. U.S. Natn. Mus. Bull.* 223:1–196.
Nicolai, J. 1964. *Z. Tierpsychol.* 21:129–204.
Payne, R.B. 1971. *Bull. Brit. Orn. Club* 91:66–76; 1977. *Ecology* 58:500–513.

860 (846)   **Pintailed Whydah**   **Plate 72**
Koningrooibekkie (Koningweduweetjie)
Vidua macroura

Harusira (K), ♂ 'Mamarungoana, Selahlamarungoana (SS), Tsikidzamutsetse, Mutsetse (Sh), N'waminungu (Ts), Ujobela, Uhlakhwe (X), uHlekwane (Z), [Dominikanerwitwe]

Measurements: Length ♂ 26–34 cm, ♀ 12–13 cm; wing (106 ♂) 65–73–79, (56 ♀) 64–67,2–71; tail (breeding ♂, longest rectrix) 163–264, (♂, shortest rectrix) 47–52, (13 ♂, nonbreeding) 42–48,5–52,5 (13 ♀) 39–45,7–50; tarsus (29 ♂) 16–18, (14 ♀) 15–16; culmen (29 ♂) 9,5–11, (14 ♀) 9–10,5. Weight (27 ♂) 12,5–15–18,7 g, (37 ♀) 10,6–14–15,9 g.

Bare Parts: Iris brown; bill red (♂) or brownish red (♀); legs and feet blackish grey.

Identification: Size small (smaller than sparrow). *Breeding* ♂: Above black; nape

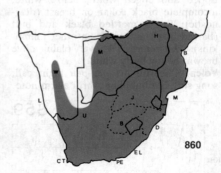

band, rump, wingbar and underparts white (nape band and underparts yellowish, no wingbar in Shafttailed Whydah); small black crescent on either side of breast; 4 central rectrices greatly elongate, black (diagnostic); ♂ breeds only in second year. *Female and nonbreeding* ♂: Top of head broadly striped black and tawny (not finely streaked as in *Euplectes* and Shafttailed Whydah); rest of upperparts tawny, streaked black; below white, washed buff on throat and breast, streaked black on flanks; red bill diagnostic (queleas finely streaked on head). *Immature*: Above plain light brown; below plain buff; bill dusky.

Voice: Song sustained high-pitched jerky *si swirt sweeu see sweep swip tsik tsweet*, etc.; *tsip-tsip* flight call.

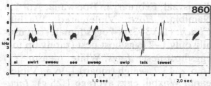

Distribution: Africa S of Sahara; in s Africa absent from most of Namibia, nw Cape and w Botswana.
Status: Common resident; nomadic in winter.
Habitat: Open savanna, grassland or hillsides with scattered trees and bushes, canefields, farmyards, gardens.
Habits: Gregarious in small flocks of about 20–30 birds; breeding groups usually of 1 adult ♂ and about 5–6 females and young males; average ratio is 1 ♂:2,2 ♀. Forages on ground or at feeding tray; scratches for food by jumping backwards with both feet to scatter sand; may hawk insects in flight. Breeding ♂ aggressive towards all birds at feeding station. In display ♂ bounces in air with tail flipping up and down, moving in circle around ♀, and singing; ♀ responds with wing-shivering; ♂ also sings from perch on bush, fence or tall grass stalk.
Food: Mainly seeds; also insects.
Breeding: Male polygamous with up to 6 females. *Season*: November to December in e Cape and Natal, November to April in Transvaal, November to March in Zimbabwe. *Hosts*: Mainly Common Waxbill; also Bronze Mannikin, Orangebreasted Waxbill, Redbilled Firefinch, Swee Waxbill, Neddicky and Tawnyflanked Prinia; egg of host removed for each egg of parasite. *Clutch*: (26) 2–3,1–4 eggs/female, but usually only 1–2 (rarely 3) eggs/host nest. *Eggs*: White; measure (15) 16,2 × 11,8 (14,4–16,8 × 11,3–12,5); weigh (mean) 1,34 g (eggs of Common Waxbill average 0,87 g). *Incubation*: 11 days. *Nestling*: 17–21 days; young of parasite reared together with young of host.

861 (847) Shafttailed Whydah Plate 72
Pylstertrooibekkie (Pylstertweduweetjie)
Vidua regia

Harusira (K), [Königswitwe]

Measurements: Length (breeding ♂) 30–34 cm, ♀ about 12 cm; wing (17 ♂) 70–72,5–75, (3 ♀) 68–70; tail (breeding ♂, longest rectrix) 210–243, (♂, shortest rectrix) 37–42, (3 ♀) 37–43; tarsus (17 ♂) 14,5–16,5, (3 ♀) 14–15; culmen (20) 9–10. Weight (6 ♂) 11,9–14–15,7 g, (3 ♀) 14,5–14,8–15,2 g, (10 ♀) mean 15,7 g.
Bare Parts: Iris brown; bill, legs and feet orange-red (♂) or dull brownish red (♀).
Identification: Size small (smaller than sparrow). *Breeding* ♂: Above black; nape band and underparts tawny yellow (white in Pintailed Whydah); 4 central rectrices

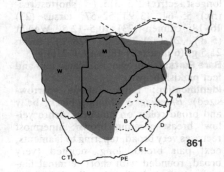

very long, thin, with broadened ends (diagnostic); bill and legs bright red. *Female and nonbreeding* ♂: Above buff, streaked black (Pintailed Whydah boldly striped on head); below white, washed buff on breast and flanks; bill and legs dull red. *Immature*: Dull rufous all over, streaked black on black. *Chick*: Palate has 3 black spots; black semicircle on floor of mouth.

Voice: Song short phrases of sharp quick canarylike notes, *tsip-tsreepy-tsri-trri-trripy-tsrreepy* repeated at short intervals; somewhat variable; incorporates imitations of song and callnotes of Violeteared Waxbill.

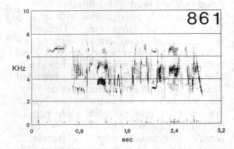

Distribution: Drier w parts of s Africa from n Karoo to Zambia and Angola.

Status: Common resident; nomadic in winter.

Habitat: Dry *Acacia* savanna.

Habits: Gregarious in small flocks; breeding group consists of 1 ♂ and several females and immature males. Forages on ground, scratching sand or leaf litter away by jumping forwards then backwards with both feet together. Similar to Pintailed Whydah.

Food: Seeds.

Breeding: *Season*: December to May in Transvaal, February in Botswana, April in Namibia. *Host*: Violeteared Waxbill. *Clutch*: (11) 3–3,1–4 eggs/female, but usually only 1–2 eggs/host nest (rarely up to 5 eggs/host nest). *Eggs*: White; measure (1) 16,5 × 13,2; weigh (mean) 1,36 g (Violeteared Waxbill eggs average 1,25 g). *Incubation* : 12–13 days. *Nestling*: 16 days; fledgling resembles host young very closely, but lacks blue on rump.

862 (852)   **Paradise Whydah**   **Plate 72**
Gewone Paradysvink
Vidua paradisaea

Harusira (K), Nyamubundu (Sh), Maningele, Nkapa (Ts), uJojokhaya (Z), [Spitzschwanz-Paradieswitwe]

Measurements: Length (breeding ♂) 33–38 cm, ♀ 15 cm; wing (20 ♂) 79–81–84, (35 ♀) 73–75,7–79; tail (breeding ♂, longest rectrix) 255–315, (♂, shortest rectrix) 55–64, (3 ♀) 52–57; tarsus (23) 16–18; culmen (23) 10,5–12,5. Weight (5 ♂) 20,2–21,2–22 g, (28 ♀) mean 21,5 g, (6 unsexed) 18,9–19,9–21,4 g.

Bare Parts: Iris brown; bill black; legs and feet pinkish brown.

Identification: Large (about sparrow-sized). *Breeding* ♂: Mainly black; belly and broad collar on hindneck ochre yellow; breast chestnut brown; innermost rectrices very broad, tapering to filaments; next pair broad, long, pointed (very broad, rounded with short terminal filaments in Broadtailed Paradise Whydah). *Female and nonbreeding* ♂: Very similar to Broadtailed Paradise Whydah, probably not separable in field, but darker and

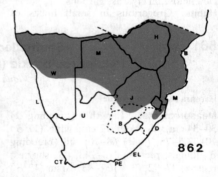

more broadly streaked; bill of breeding ♀ blackish to dark grey, paler below (pinkish grey, much paler below in ♀ Broadtailed Paradise Whydah); head boldly striped buff and dark brown (bolder in ♂ than in ♀); rest of upperparts buff, streaked dark brown; below buffy white, darker on breast and flanks; Pintailed Whydah has red bill and streaked flanks. *Immature*: Above plain buffy grey, faintly streaked on mantle, whiter in centre of belly.

Voice: Sharp *chip* callnote; song jumble of sparrowlike chirping notes interspersed with high-pitched drawn out *pseeee* and piping *tsee-tsee-tweet-tweet* notes; imitates song of Melba Finch.

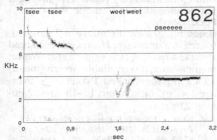

Distribution: Africa S of Sahara; in s Africa confined to n parts from Zululand, n Orange Free State, Botswana (except SW) and n Namibia northwards; vagrant to Kokstad and Kimberley.

Status: Fairly common resident.

Habitat: *Acacia* savanna, dry open woodland, cultivated lands, gardens.

Habits: Gregarious in flocks of up to 60 birds. Forages on ground, often on paths and tracks. ♂ displays with bouncing flight upwards at 45–60°, to 20–100 m above ground, levelling off and flying with rapid wingbeats, broad central rectrices raised, long streamers straight out behind, ending in swooping descent to perch; rectrices rustle in flight. Males display all day, feeding only in evening, in company with females and young males. ♀ attracted to song of Melba Finch. ♂ often perches conspicuously on telephone wire or dead twigs on treetop, neighbouring males gathering in flocks at twilight.

Food: Seeds, insects.

Breeding: Male polygamous. *Season*: January to June in Transvaal, January to April in Zimbabwe. *Host*: Melba Finch. *Clutch*: (21) 3–3,4–4 eggs/female, but only 1–3 parasite eggs/host nest; one female may lay up to 22 eggs/season. *Eggs*: White; measure (17) 18,2 × 14 (17,5–19,5 × 13–14,3); weigh (mean) 1,63 g (Melba Finch eggs average 1,41 g). *Incubation*: 12–13 days. *Nestling*: 16 days; independent at 27–30 days.

Ref. Nicolai, J. 1969. *J. Orn.* 110:421–447.
Payne, R.B. 1971. *Bull. Brit. Orn. Club* 91:66–76.

863 (853) Broadtailed Paradise Whydah Plate 72
Breëstertparadysvink
Vidua obtusa

Harusira (K), Nyamubundu (Sh), [Breitschwanz-Paradieswitwe]

Measurements: Length (breeding ♂) about 30 cm, ♀ about 15 cm; wing (38 ♀) 77–80–86; tail (breeding ♂, longest rectrix) length 176–225, breadth 33–37, (♂ and ♀, shortest rectrix) 54–58; tarsus 16–17; culmen 11,5–13. Weight (6 ♀) mean 19,5 g.

Bare Parts: Iris brown; bill black (♂) or greyish above, paler below (♀); legs blackish brown.

Identification: Large (about sparrow-sized). *Breeding ♂*: Similar to ♂ Paradise Whydah (*q.v.*), but longest rectrices equally broad throughout, except for short terminal filament (tapering and pointed in Paradise Whydah). *Female and nonbreeding ♂*: Similar to those of Paradise Whydah (*q.v.*), probably not separable in field, but paler

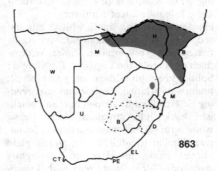

and more finely streaked; bill of breeding ♀ pinkish grey, grey or blackish above, much paler below (darker, usually blackish in ♀ Paradise Whydah). *Immature*: Paler than immature Paradise Whydah, but probably not separable in field.

Voice: Soft fluting *woooeeee* or *weetseeo*, similar to call of Goldenbacked Pytilia; song jumbled twittering *dwee chirrup weet-eet weetseeo*, etc.

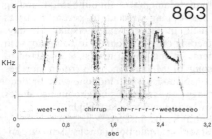

Distribution: Eastern Transvaal, n and e Zimbabwe, extreme n Botswana, e Caprivi, Mozambique (except extreme S), to Tanzania and Kenya.

Status: Uncommon resident. Rare (RDB).
Habitat: Savanna and woodland (usually in more wooded areas than Paradise Whydah).
Habits: Similar to those of Paradise Whydah, but poorly known. Gregarious in flocks of up to 60 birds, often in company with Goldenbacked Pytilias. Display flight not developed as in Paradise Whydah.
Food: Seeds.
Breeding: *Season*: February in Transvaal, March in Zimbabwe. *Host*: Goldenbacked Pytilia. *Clutch*: (2) 3 eggs. *Eggs*: White; no measurements available; weigh (mean) 1,64 g (Goldenbacked Pytilia eggs average 1,42 g). *Incubation*: 12–13 days. *Nestling*: 21 days.

Ref. Nicolai, J. 1969. *J. Orn.* 110:421–447.
Payne, R.B. 1967. *Bull. Brit. Orn. Club* 87:93–95; 1971. *Bull. Brit. Orn. Club* 91:66–76.

864 (849) Black Widowfinch — Plate 71
Gewone Blouvinkie
Vidua funerea

[Purpur-Atlaswitwe]

Measurements: Length 11–12 cm; wing (6 ♂) 65–68,6–71,5, (6 ♀) 64–66,2–69; tail 37–40; tarsus 12–14; culmen 9–10. Weight (7 ♂) 14–15,2–16,5 g, (17 ♀) 12–14,1–16,1 g, (17 ♀) mean 13,4 g.
Bare Parts: Iris brown; bill white (breeding ♂) or whitish horn (♀ and nonbreeding ♂); legs and feet coral red.
Identification: Size small; whitish bill and red legs and feet diagnostic in adults (except for very similar Violet Widowfinch of Angola and Caprivi). *Breeding ♂*: Solid glossy blue-black or green-black; underwing whitish. *Female and nonbreeding ♂*: Head boldly striped buff and blackish; back buff, streaked black; below white, greyish on breast and flanks. *Immature*: Similar to adult ♀, but almost plain above; crown all dark; mantle lightly streaked. *Chick*: Palate pink with 3 purplish black spots; gape pink with dark blue tubercles and lavender flange.
Voice: Harsh rapid *chichichichi* callnotes; song short variable phrases of chirping notes, *chip cheepy chirpy chippy chippy sweepy*, repeated several times, some-

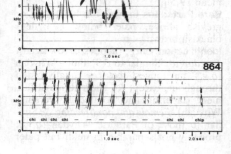

times interspersed with tinkling notes of Bluebilled Firefinch.

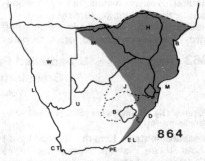

Distribution: S Africa to E Africa; in s Africa absent from most of highveld and dry W.
Status: Locally common to fairly common; nomadic in winter.
Habitat: Grassy hills, roadsides, edges of cultivation and gardens in savanna and bushveld.
Habits: Gregarious in winter; otherwise solitary or in small groups. Forages on ground or at feeding tray; males aggressive towards each other in breeding season, but several may gather at good food source; scratches in sand by jumping back-

wards with both feet. Breeding ♂ sings from perch for long periods, often on treetop or telephone wire; ♂ displays to ♀ with bobbing flight.
Food: Seeds; termites caught in flight.
Breeding: Male polygamous. *Season*: January to March in Transvaal, March to April in Zimbabwe. *Host*: Bluebilled Firefinch. *Clutch*: (23) 1–3–4 eggs/female, but usually only 1 parasite egg/host nest. *Eggs*: White; measure (1) 13,2 × 10,5; weigh (mean) 1,33 g (Bluebilled Firefinch eggs average 1,16 g). *Incubation*: Unrecorded. *Nestling*: Unrecorded.

865 (850)   **Purple Widowfinch**   **Plate 71**
Witpootblouvinkie
Vidua purpurascens

[Weißfuß-Atlaswitwe]

Measurements: Length about 12 cm; wing (39 ♂) 68–69,8–73, (7 ♀) 65–66,7–69; tail 37–40; tarsus 12–14; culmen 9–10. Weight (2 ♂) 12,6–13,2 g, (4 ♀) 11,7–12,9–13,7 g, (13 unsexed) 11,4–13,3–14,6 g.
Bare Parts: Iris brown; bill, legs and feet whitish to very pale pink.
Identification: Size small (smaller than sparrow); white bill, legs and feet diagnostic in adults. *Breeding ♂*: Glossy blue-black to matt black; bill, legs and feet may be white, pale mauve or pinkish. *Female and nonbreeding ♂*: Head boldly striped rufous-buff and black; back blackish brown, scaled deep rufous; below off-white, washed greyish on breast. *Immature*: Above scaled brighter rufous than ♀; below dark tawny; crown plain blackish. *Chick*: Palate pink with 3 purplish black spots; gape pink with dark blue tubercles and lavender flange.
Voice: Song mixed harsh notes and imitations of song of Jameson's Firefinch.

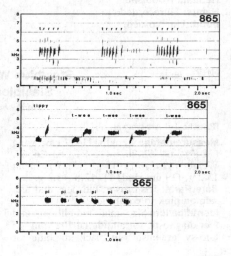

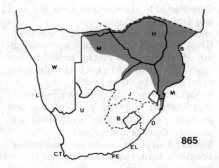

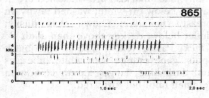

Distribution: S Africa to E Africa; in s Africa confined to NE from Zululand to Caprivi.
Status: Uncommon to rare resident.
Habitat: Savanna and bushveld, often around edges of cultivation.
Habits: Similar to those of Black Widowfinch. ♂ sings from dead twigs in treetop. Poorly known.
Food: Seeds.

Breeding: *Season*: December to March in Transvaal, January to April in Zimbabwe; males still in breeding plumage in Mozambique in June. *Host*: Jameson's Firefinch. *Clutch*: (13) 2–3,1–4 eggs. *Eggs*: White; measure (2) 14–15,2 × 12–12,2; weight (mean) 1,3 g (Jameson's Firefinch eggs average 1,04 g). *Incubation*: Unrecorded. *Nestling*: Unrecorded.

866 (–)   Violet Widowfinch   Plate 77
Persblouvinkie
Vidua wilsoni

[Nicolai-Atlaswitwe]

Measurements: Length about 12 cm; wing (1 ♂) 69.
Bare Parts: Iris brown; bill white (?); legs and feet light pinkish.
Identification: Size small; very similar to Black Widowfinch in all plumages; breeding ♂ dark violet-black; probably not separable from Black Widowfinch in field, except by voice (*q.v.*).
Voice: Imitates song of Brown Firefinch.
Distribution: Caprivi, ne Namibia and probably nw Zimbabwe to Angola and possibly Zambia and s Zaire.
Status: Unknown; probably uncommon. Formerly known as *Vidua incognita*.
Habitat: Woodland.
Habits: Unrecorded.
Food: Unrecorded.

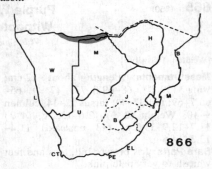

866

Breeding: *Season*: Unrecorded. *Host*: Brown Firefinch. *Clutch*, *Eggs*, *Incubation*, *Nestling*: Unrecorded.

Ref. Nicolai, J. 1972. *J. Orn.* 113:229–240.

867 (851)   Steelblue Widowfinch   Plate 71
Staalblouvinkie
Vidua chalybeata

[Rotschnabel-Atlaswitwe]

Measurements: Length 11–12 cm; wing (71 ♂) 64–67–70, (12 ♀) 63–66–68. Weight (2 ♂) 11–13 g, (51 ♀) mean 13,2 g, (19 unsexed) 11–12,8–15,2 g.
Bare Parts: Iris brown; bill, legs and feet salmon pink to coral red.
Identification: Size small; red bill, legs and feet diagnostic for all adults. *Breeding ♂*: Glossy greenish blueblack to blue or purplish black. *Female and nonbreeding ♂*: Head boldly streaked tawny and dusky; back blackish brown, scaled bright tawny; below off-white, washed tawny on breast. *Immature*: Crown plain dusky; duller below, darker above than adult ♀. *Chick*: Palate yellow with 3 or 5 black spots; gape orange with white tubercles and dark blue flange; mouth coloration retained until bill turns red.

Voice: Song incorporates imitations of song of Redbilled Firefinch, *chip chree chiririririri-chiri-sweeu-cheerr*; more sustained than song of Black Widowfinch; also loud clear *tswee* callnotes.

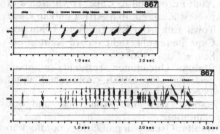

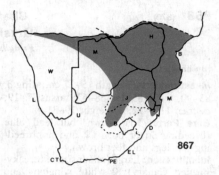

Distribution: Africa S of Sahara; in s Africa confined to NE from Zululand across Transvaal to Orange Free State (as far S as Bloemfontein) and n Botswana to Caprivi; extends as far S as Bloemfontein, Orange Free State.

Status: Common resident; highly nomadic when not breeding.

Habitat: Savanna, secondary growth around cultivation, dry thickets with rank grass, often with patches of bare ground.

Habits: Gregarious when not breeding, often in quite large flocks; otherwise solitary or in small groups; sometimes in company with host species, Redbilled Firefinch. Similar to other widowfinches.

Food: Seeds.

Breeding: *Season:* December to March in Transvaal, March to April in Zimbabwe. *Host:* Redbilled Firefinch. *Clutch:* 1–3–4 eggs/female, but only 1–3 eggs/host nest (rarely 5–6 in W Africa); each ♀ lays 1 egg in different host nest, but more than 1 ♀ may lay in same host nest; one ♀ may lay about 26 eggs/season. *Eggs:* White, larger and rounder than host eggs; measure (12) 15,2 × 12,6 (Redbilled Firefinch mean 13,5 × 10,2); weigh (mean) 1,27 g (Redbilled Firefinch eggs average 0,84 g). *Incubation:* 10–11 days. *Nestling:* Unrecorded; independent from foster parents at about 30 days.

Ref. Payne, R.B. 1985. *Z. Tierpsychol.* 70:1–44.

26:29. Family 91 FRINGILLIDAE—CANARIES, BUNTINGS, ETC.

Small (a few medium). Bill short, conical, usually stout, adapted for seed-eating; legs short to medium; toes short to medium; wings short and rounded to moderately long and pointed; tail mostly medium, square or slightly notched; plumage very variable, often brightly coloured, especially with green and yellow, but also with red and blue; sexes alike or different; arboreal or terrestrial; food mostly seeds; solitary or gregarious, especially when not breeding; breed solitarily; nest cup-shaped in bush or tree, or on rock ledge or on ground; eggs 2–6, variable, usually spotted; young sparsely downy at hatching; incubation and nest-building by female; young fed by both sexes usually. Distribution worldwide, except Madagascar, Australia and Oceania; 443 species, 20 species in s Africa (one introduced). The family Fringillidae is here considered to include the subfamilies Fringillinae (Old World finches), Carduelinae (canaries, etc.), Emberizinae (Old World buntings and New World cardinals, sparrows and finches) and Cardinalinae (New World grosbeaks and buntings).

Ref. Milewski, A.V. 1978. *Ostrich* 49:174–184.
Skead, C.J. 1960. *The canaries, seedeaters and buntings of southern Africa.* Cape Town: Trustees of the South African Bird Book Fund.

868 (870)

Chaffinch
Gryskoppie
Fringilla coelebs

Plate 72

[Buchfink]

Measurements: Length 15–17 cm; wing ♂ 83–90, ♀ 78–85; tail 58–67; tarsus 17–19; culmen 11,5–12,5. Weight 19–31 g.

Bare Parts: Iris brown; bill lead blue (breeding ♂) or horn (♀ and nonbreeding ♂); legs and feet brown.

Identification: Large (about size of Streakyheaded Canary); 2 white wingbars and blackish tail with white outer rectrices diagnostic in both sexes. *Male*: Crown, nape and sides of neck grey; back dark chestnut; rump green; face and underparts brownish rose, shading to white on belly and undertail. *Female*: Above brown; eyebrow pale; below paler brown, shading to whitish on throat and belly. *Immature*: Similar to adult ♀; bill horn.

Voice: Loud repeated *pink pink*, somewhat metallic; song repeated cascade of about 12 tumbling notes, *tee-tee-tee-tee-wi-wi-wi-woo treeeer*, increasing in tempo, falling in pitch but rising again at end; short *chip* flight call.

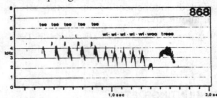

Distribution: Originally Europe and w Asia; introduced to Cape Town area and to New Zealand; in S Africa only in Cape Town area from Kloof Nek to Tokai and Cape Peninsula; sight record Kenton-on-Sea, e Cape, 1961.

Status: Uncommon resident; numbers declining since 1960s; introduced about 1898 by C.J. Rhodes.

Habitat: Gardens, parks, pine and oak plantations.

Habits: Usually in pairs; does not flock in winter as in Europe. Forages in trees and on ground.

Food: Seeds, grain, small fruits, leaf buds, green plant material, insects, spiders, worms, snails.

Breeding: *Season*: September to November. *Nest*: Compact cup of moss, rootlets, stems and hair, bound with spider web, decorated outside with lichen and bits of paper; lined with hair, wool and feathers; outside diameter 9–10 cm, depth 7–8 cm; inside diameter about 5 cm, depth 4–5 cm; 3–10 m above ground in stout fork of bush or tree. *Clutch*: 3–6 eggs. *Eggs*: Brownish, bluish white or greenish grey, spotted and lined with shades of brown, grey and violet; measure (27) 19,4 × 14,6 (17,8–21 × 14,3–15,2); weigh about 2 g. *Incubation* : 12–13 days by ♀ only. *Nestling*: 12–13 days.

869 (859)

Yelloweyed Canary
Geeloogkanarie
Serinus mozambicus

Plate 73

Nsense, Kandingo (K), Tšoere (SS), Risunyani, Ritswiri, Manswikidyane (Ts), Unyileyo (X), umBhalane (Z), [Mossambikgirlitz]

Measurements: Length about 12 cm; wing (135 ♂) 63–68,9–75, (78 ♀) 65–68,6–73; tail (116 ♂) 37–42,1–48, (69 ♀) 37–41,4–45,5; tarsus (31) 12–14; culmen (32) 8–11. Weight (97 ♂) 9,3–11,8–16,2 g, (45 ♀) 10–11,6–13,6 g, (110 unsexed) 8,5–13,3–16,2 g.

Bare Parts: Iris brown; bill horn, base pinkish; legs and feet pinkish brown.

Identification: Size small; see canary key; sexes alike. Eyebrow, cheeks, rump and underparts light yellow (underparts white in Lemonbreasted Canary); crown to back dull green, streaked dark brown; eyestripe and malar stripe black (better defined than in Yellow Canary); flanks greyish (diagnostic); yellow rump and white-tipped tail diagnostic in flight (Black-throated Canary streaked grey and dusky on back). *Immature*: Paler than adult; breast and flanks streaked brownish.

Voice: Whistled chirp, *tseeu* or *tswirri* callnote; typical canarylike song of twittering and whistled notes in fairly short phrases, not sustained as in most other canaries; notes somewhat shriller than those of other canaries.

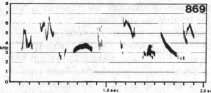

Distribution: Africa S of Sahara; in s Africa confined to SE, NE and N from about Uitenhage, e Cape, and Bloemfontein, Orange Free State, to ne Namibia.
Status: Common resident.
Habitat: Any woodland, thornveld, riverine bush, gardens, parks, exotic plantations.
Habits: In pairs or small family groups when breeding; gregarious in flocks of 20–30 birds (rarely up to 100) in winter, sometimes in company with other small seedeating birds. Forages on ground or in bushes and trees; may hawk insects in air; when disturbed takes off for nearest bush with bouncing flight and tweety callnotes. Male sings from conspicuous perch; several males may sing in concert and chase each other aggressively. Common cagebird in Mozambique.

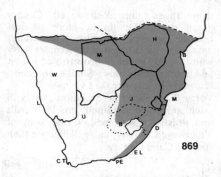

Food: Seeds (including *Casuarina*), insects, flowers, leaves of *Hibiscus*.
Breeding: *Season*: September to April in Natal, October to April in Transvaal, September to May (mainly December-March) in Zimbabwe, September to March in Mozambique. *Nest*: Small cup of grass, herbs and roots, bound with spider web; lined with plant down and fine rootlets; diameter of cup about 5 cm, depth about 5 cm; 1–6 m above ground in fork of bush, tree or creeper; built by both sexes. *Clutch* : (86) 2–3,2–5 eggs (usually 3–4). *Eggs*: White or very pale blue, plain or sparingly speckled with pink, brown or black mainly at thick end; measure (86) 16,3 × 12,1 (14,6–18,5 × 11,1–13,8). *Incubation*: 13–14,5 days by ♀ only. *Nestling*: 16–24 days; fed by both parents.

870 (860) Blackthroated Canary Plate 73
Bergkanarie
Serinus atrogularis

Nsense, Kandingo (K), Tšoere (SS), Ngodzi (Ts), [Angolagirlitz]

Measurements: Length 11–12 cm; wing (91) 65–71,2–77; tail (40 ♂) 40–43–48, (40 ♀) 40–42,9–46; tarsus (11) 11–14; culmen (11) 8–10,5. Weight (4 ♂) 8,7–10,8–11,8 g, (4 ♀) 10,7–11,9–12,8 g, (206 unsexed) 8–11,4–14 g.
Bare Parts: Iris brown; bill horn, base pinkish; legs and feet pinkish brown.
Identification: Size small; tail relatively short, tipped and edged white; sexes alike; above buffy grey streaked dusky; rump bright yellow (diagnostic in flight with

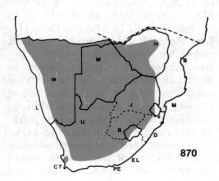

white-tipped tail; Yelloweyed Canary green on back); throat more or less heavily spotted blackish (sometimes hardly any black); rest of underparts buffy white, lightly streaked brownish on breast and flanks. *Immature*: Similar to adult, but more boldly streaked below.

Voice: Very sweet *twee* callnote, rising in pitch; song rich sustained jumble of trills and whistles, more mellow than' song of Yelloweyed Canary, more deliberate than song of Cape Canary.

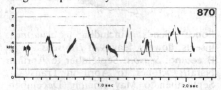

Distribution: S Africa to NE Africa and sw Arabia; widespread in inland s Africa, especially highveld and arid regions.

Status: Common to fairly common resident; some local seasonal movements.

Habitat: Savanna, open woodland, wooded farmyards in grassy highveld, riverine bush in semidesert, gardens, cultivated lands; always where drinking water available.

Habits: In pairs when breeding; otherwise in smaller or larger flocks of up to 60 birds, especially at waterholes in arid areas. Forages mainly on ground, but also in bushes or trees; may hawk insects in flight. Flight light and bouncing. Quiet and easily overlooked unless singing. Similar to Yelloweyed Canary.

Food: Seeds, insects, flowers.

Breeding: *Season*: October to April in Orange Free State, all months except May in Transvaal, September to June (mainly November-January) in Zimbabwe. *Nest*: Cup of dry grass, fine twigs and tendrils, bound with spider web; lined with cotton, plant down, wool, hair or feathers; cup diameter 4,5 cm, depth 3,2 cm; 1,2–15 m above ground in fork of tree, often in conifer, or at base of lopped palm frond, on rafter of shed, in notch of tree trunk, etc.; built by both sexes. *Clutch*: (9) 2–3–4 eggs (usually 3). *Eggs*: White or pale greenish blue, plain or sparingly spotted with black, brown and purple mainly at thick end; measure (22) 16,7 × 12,4 (15,5–18 × 11,4–13,2). *Incubation*: 12–13 days by ♀ only. *Nestling*: 15,5–17 days; fed by both parents.

---

871 (860X) **Lemonbreasted Canary** **Plate 73**
Geelborskanarie
Serinus citrinipectus

[Gelbbrustgirlitz]

Measurements: Length about 12 cm; wing (25 ♂) 62–65–68, (8 ♀) 61,5–64–67; tail (25 ♂) 36–38,1–41,5, (8 ♀) 35–37,4–40; tarsus (9 ♂) 13–13,6–14, (1 ♀) 14; culmen (9 ♂) 11–11,5–12, (1 ♀) 11.

Bare Parts: Iris dark brown; bill dark pinkish horn; legs and feet brown.

Identification: Size small; similar to Blackthroated Canary, but black malar patch diagnostic in both sexes. *Male*: Above pale grey, heavily streaked blackish; rump bright yellow; cheek patch, streak behind eye and throat to breast yellow; small white spot above and below base of bill; rest of face blackish; rest of underparts white, washed buff and

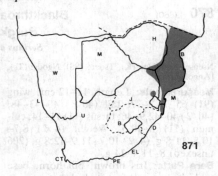

streaked brown on flanks (underparts yellow in Yelloweyed Canary). *Female*: Above similar to ♂; no yellow on face or underparts; eyebrow dull whitish; black malar patch distinctive; below buff, lightly streaked on breast and flanks.

Voice: Song typical high-pitched canary-like twittering.

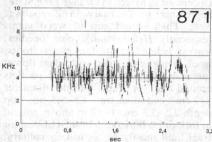

Distribution: Littoral plain from about Stanger (Natal) to Mozambique, se Zimbabwe, to s Malawi.

Status: Uncommon to locally fairly common resident. Rare (RDB).

Habitat: Dry savanna and woodland, Ilala

Palm *Hyphaene natalensis* savanna with short grass, often around cultivation and human settlement.

Habits: In pairs when breeding; otherwise in small flocks, often in company with commoner Yelloweyed Canary. Poorly known.

Food: Seeds.

Breeding: *Season*: December in Natal, January in Zimbabwe. *Nest*: Cup of dead creeper stems and shredded bark bound with caterpillar silk; lined with hair-like palm fibres; inside diameter 4,5–5,5 cm. *Clutch*: 3–4 eggs (in captivity). *Eggs*: White, lightly streaked or sparsely spotted with reddish brown, mainly at thick end; measure (1) 16 × 12. *Incubation*: 12–14 days by ♀ only (captivity). *Nestling*: 14–16 days (captivity).

Ref. Brickell, N. 1983. *Avicult. Mag.* 89:159–160.
Clancey, P.A. & Lawson, W.J. 1960. *Durban Mus. Novit.* 6(4):61–64.

872 (857) Cape Canary Plate 73
Kaapse Kanarie
Serinus canicollis

Tswere (NS), Tšoere (SS), Risunyani, Ritswiri. Vusunyani (Ts), Umlonji (X), umZwilili (Z), [Gelbscheitelgirlitz]

Measurements: Length 13–14 cm; wing (30) ♂ 75–79–82, ♀ 72–75–79, (35 unsexed) 72–76,7–81; tail (36) 49–53,8–60,5; tarsus (48) 13,5–15,2–17; culmen (48) 9–10,1–12,5. Weight (3 ♂) 12,4–14,7–17,5 g, (129 unsexed, S Africa) 10–15,1–19,5 g, (37 unsexed, Zimbabwe) 11,9–13,9–15,9 g.

Bare Parts: Iris brown; bill horn; legs and feet dark pinkish brown.

Identification: Size medium; build slender; tail longish, distinctly notched; sexes similar but ♀ duller than ♂, slightly streaked brown above; crown and face greenish gold; nape and mantle blue-grey (diagnostic; grey meets on breast of ♀); back light olive, finely streaked; rump dull yellow; below deep yellow, washed greenish on throat and breast (paler in ♀; breast blue-grey); tail olive, margined yellow. *Immature*: Buff, heavily streaked dark brown above and below.

Voice: Very sweet *peet, swee-eee* or *pee-eee* callnotes, rising in pitch, sometimes stut-

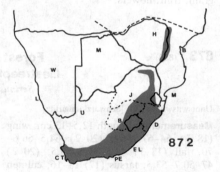

tered or trilled *pit-it-it-it*; song rich loud clear and fast jumble of rolling warbles, trills and twitters, often in chorus of several males in adjacent trees; much more sustained than songs of other canaries.

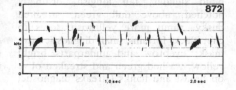

Distribution: S Africa to NE Africa; in s Africa confined mainly to S and E from w Cape to Zimbabwe; isolated population in sw Angola.

Status: Very common resident; some altitudinal and other seasonal migrations or nomadism.

Habitat: Montane grassland, brackenbrier, scrubby hillsides with *Philippia*, *Protea*, *Leucosidea* and other bushes, edges of open grassland with trees, gardens, parks, exotic plantations, cultivated fields.

Habits: In pairs or small family groups when breeding; otherwise in more or less large flocks, sometimes of hundreds of birds, especially at concentrated food source like ripe sunflower crop; often in company with other species of small seed-eating birds. Forages on ground or by perching on stems of seeding plants. Flight undulating, but less bouncy than that of smaller canaries; in courtship ♂ performs slow-winged "butterfly" flight.

Food: Seeds (grasses, *Senecio* species, *Cephalaria*, etc.), buds of *Buddleia*, fallen grain, fruit, flowers.

Breeding: *Season*: August to December in sw Cape (mainly September-October), July to December in e Cape, August to December in Natal and Transvaal, December to March in Orange Free State, September to February in Zimbabwe. *Nest*: Thick-walled cup of weed stems (especially *Helichrysum*), pine needles, leaves, lichen, moss, fine twigs, roots, wool, string, etc.; lined with plant down, fur and feathers, with rim of rootlets around top of cup; outside diameter 8–9 cm, cup diameter 4,5–5,5 cm, cup depth 2,5–3,3 cm; 1–18 m above ground in fork or on horizontal branch of bush or tree; built mostly by ♀; usually solitary, but sometimes in loose colony of up to 10 nests, some only 3–5 m apart. *Clutch*: (74) 2–3,2–5 eggs (usually 3–4). *Eggs*: White to pale greenish white, plain or spotted, blotched and scrolled with black, brown and grey; measure (60) 17,2 × 12,8 (15,8–18,9 × 11,6–13,6). *Incubation*: 12–16 days (usually 12–14) by ♀ only. *Nestling*: 15,5–18,5 days; fed by both parents.

Ref. Skead, C.J. 1948. *Ostrich* 19:17–44.

---

873 (858) **Forest Canary** **Plate 73**
Gestreepte Kanarie
Serinus scotops

Unotswitswitswi (X), [Schwarzkinngirlitz]

Measurements: Length 12,5–13 cm; wing (18 ♂) 64–67,5–69, (20 ♀) 64,5–66,6–70; tail (18 ♂) 48,5–51,5–53,5, (20 ♀) 47–50,7–53,5; tarsus (17) 14–16; culmen (17) 10–12. Weight (3 ♂) 14,8–15,3–15,6 g, (3 ♀) 14,6–15,1–16 g, (21 unsexed) 13,8–15,8–18 g.

Bare Parts: Iris brown; bill horn, base pinkish; legs and feet pinkish brown.

Identification: Size smallish to medium; build slender; tail longish, distinctly notched; above dull green, streaked dusky, rump more yellowish; lores to chin black, forming small diagnostic facemask; eyebrow and underparts bright yellow, washed green and streaked olive on breast and flanks (streaks diagnostic;

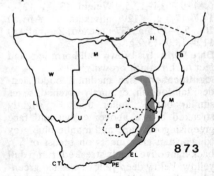

873

other "yellow" canaries unstreaked below except as immatures); ♀ duller than ♂, face greyish. *Immature*: Resembles adult ♀, but more heavily streaked.

Voice: Quiet *tsik, tsip-tsip* or stuttered *tsit-itit* callnotes; song sustained for 11–16 seconds, similar to that of Cape Canary, but higher-pitched and more sibilant, less richly rolling and warbling, with frequent down-slurred *sweeeu* notes.

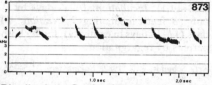

Distribution: Confined to forested areas from sw Cape (Kirstenbosch), to Natal, Drakensberg escarpment and Zoutpansberg.
Status: Locally fairly common resident.
Habitat: Evergreen forest and adjacent exotic plantations, fynbos, rank secondary growth and well-wooded gardens.
Habits: Usually in pairs; sometimes in small groups of up to about 12 birds. Forages in middle to upper layers of forest trees; members of pair or group maintain contact with quiet calls, but generally rather silent and easily overlooked. Poorly known.
Food: Seeds, small fruits, overripe figs (*Ficus* sp.), bases of leaf petioles.
Breeding: *Season:* October to March in e Cape, October to January in Natal. *Nest:* Cup of moss and fine stems, lined with fibrous lichen; 1–5 m above ground in fork of bush or tree, well hidden in foliage; built by ♀ only; ♂ may carry building material. *Clutch:* 2–4 eggs. *Eggs:* White to pale bluish white, spotted sparingly with browns and greys mainly at thick end; measure (6) 17,3 × 12,6 (16,9–18,3 × 12,2–13,3). *Incubation:* (2) 14 days by ♀ only (captivity). *Nestling:* (4) 15–17,5–19 days; fed by ♀ only, but ♂ brings food to nest (captivity).

874 (855)   Cape Siskin   Plate 73
Kaapse Pietjiekanarie
Pseudochloroptila totta

[Hottentottengirlitz]

Measurements: Length 12,5–13 cm; wing (5 ♂) 66,5–68,4–70, (6 unsexed) 68–72; tail (6) 49–53; tarsus (6) 14–15,5; culmen (6) 9–10,5.

Bare Parts: Iris brown; bill brownish horn, paler below; legs and feet pale brown.

Identification: Size smallish; white tips to wing and tail feathers diagnostic for both sexes especially in flight (white outer rectrices only in Drakensberg Siskin). *Male:* Crown and nape light brown streaked darker; back brown; rump greenish yellow; below greenish yellow, washed brownish on flanks. *Female:* Above similar to ♂; throat and breast yellowish green, throat streaked brown; rest of underparts lime green. *Immature:* Similar to adult ♀.

Voice: Twanging *chwing chwing chwing* contact call; song quiet, canarylike; *tswirri* flight call (similar to that of Yelloweyed Canary).

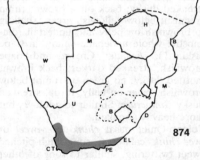

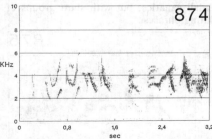

Distribution: Western and s Cape from n Cedarberg to Kei River.

Status: Fairly common resident.
Habitat: Rocky slopes and mountains with fynbos, from sea level to mountain tops; also pine plantations.
Habits: In pairs or small groups. Forages in bushes and trees or on ground and rocks. Shy and unobtrusive, flying off when disturbed; usually silent. Poorly known.
Food: Seeds, buds, insects.
Breeding: *Season*: September to December; 2 broods/season. *Nest*: Shallow cup of fine dry grass and rootlets, lined with finer grass, plant down, wool and some hair; cup diameter 5,1 cm, depth 2 cm; in niche of rocky ledge or pothole, often concealed by fern or other vegetation; built by ♀ only; ♂ accompanies her on collecting trips. *Clutch*: 3–5 eggs. *Eggs*: Plain white; measure (7) 17,9 × 13,3 (16,4–19,5 × 12,8–14,1). *Incubation*: 16–17 days by ♀ only; ♂ feeds incubating ♀. *Nestling*: 20 days (17–18 days in captivity); fed by both parents by regurgitation.

Ref. Schmidt, R.K. 1982. *Bokmakierie* 34:54–55; 86.

875 (856)   Drakensberg Siskin   Plate 73
Bergpietjiekanarie
Pseudochloroptila symonsi

Tšoere (SS), [Drakensberggirlitz]

Measurements: Length 13–14 cm; wing (6 ♂) 75–76,6–79; tail 54–59; tarsus 16–17; culmen 10,5–11.
Bare Parts: Iris brown; bill brownish horn, paler below; legs and feet brown.
Identification: Size small; no white in wings and on tip of tail (as in Cape Siskin); white outer rectrices diagnostic in flight. *Male*: Crown and nape dull olive green, streaked dusky; back olive brown; rump greenish; below yellowish green, shading to brownish on belly and undertail (diagnostic; whole underside yellow in Cape Siskin ♂). *Female*: Crown and nape brownish, streaked darker; back brown, mottled dusky; no green on rump; below brownish, paler on belly, throat streaked dusky. *Immature*: Similar to adult ♀, but more heavily streaked.
Voice: Quiet nasal *chink-tweet-tweet* or *twee-chink* callnotes; song high-pitched sweet twittering, similar to song of other small canaries, but with short groups of lilting phrases.

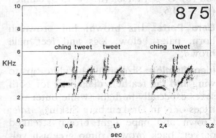

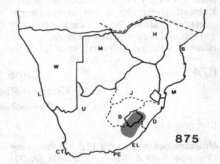

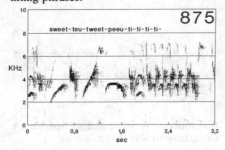

Distribution: Mountains of ne Cape, Transkei, Lesotho, e Orange Free State and upland Natal.
Status: Locally common resident; some altitudinal movement downwards in winter.
Habitat: Montane scrub, afroalpine grassland and mountainsides.
Habits: In pairs when breeding; otherwise in small flocks. Forages largely on ground among rocks and low vegetation and on

gravelly roadsides; well camouflaged and hard to see until it flies; also feeds in-bushes and trees. When disturbed does not fly far. Poorly known.
Food: Seeds, buds, insects, soft bases of *Erythrina* flowers.
Breeding: *Season*: November to January.
Nest: Shallow cup of dry grass, lined with

hair; on rock ledge or in pothole of low rocky cliff, sometimes concealed by grass-tuft or other plant. *Clutch*: 2–4 eggs. *Eggs*: White to pale greenish blue, spar-ingly spotted with brown and grey mainly at thick end; measure (9) 18 × 13,4 (16,4–19 × 12,8–13,9). *Incubation*: Un-recorded. *Nestling*: Unrecorded.

876 (861)   Blackheaded Canary   Plate 73
Swartkopkanarie
Serinus alario

[Alariogirlitz]

Measurements: Length 11,5–15 cm; wing (12 ♂) 62–67–71, (4 ♀) 63–64; tail (10) 42–49; tarsus (10) 13–15; culmen (10) 8–9. Weight (4) 11–11,8–13 g.
Bare Parts: Iris brown; bill grey, paler below; legs and feet slate.
Identification: Size medium; no yellow in plumage; 2 subspecies with variable amount of black and white on head of ♂, *S. a. alario* in Karoo and ne Cape, *S. a. leucolaema* in n Cape and s Namibia (subspecies overlap in w Cape when not breeding). *Male*: Head and centre of breast black, forming inverted V on breast (*alario*) or with white eyebrow, eyering, earpatch and throat and black bar on breast only (*leucolaema*); rest of upper-parts and tail chestnut; nape band and rest of underparts white, variably mottled black on flanks in *alario*. *Female*: head and back greyish brown, faintly streaked darker; rump and wing coverts dull chestnut; below light brownish, shading to buff on belly and undertail, faintly speckled on throat. *Imma-ture*: Similar to adult ♀, but more tawny, with bolder streaks above and below.
Voice: Musical *tweet* and *pee-chee* call-notes, rising in pitch; song pleasant but rather unmelodious jumble of gargling, twanging and skizzing notes.

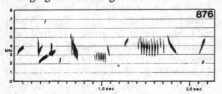

Distribution: Northeastern Cape, Karoo, s Orange Free State, n and w Cape and s Namibia.

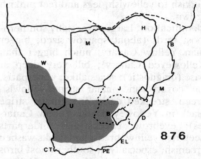

Status: Locally common to uncommon resident; nomadic after breeding.
Habitat: Arid shrubby hillsides and kop-pies, subalpine rocky slopes with bushes, w Cape strandveld, cultivated lands, gar-dens.
Habits: In pairs or small family groups when breeding; otherwise somewhat greg-arious in small flocks, especially at water. Forages on ground, in shrubs or on seed-ing herbs and grasses. Often tame. Male sings from perch on top of bush or shrub.
Food: Seeds.
Breeding: *Season*: July to April; season probably varies with rainfall. *Nest*: Deep cup of dry grass and fine twigs, lined with plant down and wool; sometimes rimmed with horsehair; 30–100 cm above ground in small shrub or bush, often overhanging ditch or rock face; built by ♀ only; ♂ accompanies ♀ on collecting trips. *Clutch*: (14) 2–2,7–4 eggs (usually 3, rarely 5). *Eggs*: White or pale bluish green, spotted and blotched with red-brown and brown mostly at thick end; measure (38) 16,5 × 12,4 (15–18,2 × 11,5–13,3). *Incu-bation*: About 13 days. *Nestling*: About 20–21 days (15 days in captivity).

877 (863)

Bully Canary
Dikbekkanarie
Serinus sulphuratus

Plate 73

Indweza Eluhlaza (X), [Schwefelgirlitz]

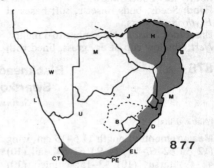

877

Measurements: Length 15–16 cm; wing (213) 72–77,6–85,5; tail (162) 54–59,1–64; tarsus (26) 15,5–17,3–19; culmen (27) 10,5–12,2–14. Weight (32, s Cape) 25–28,7–33 g, (10, Natal) 22–25,8–30,2 g, (236, Zimbabwe) 17,1–20,9–26,4 g.

Bare Parts: Iris brown; bill horn, base pinkish to yellowish; legs and feet pinkish brown.

Identification: Large, especially southernmost birds (about sparrow-sized; bigger than Yellow Canary; much bigger than Yelloweyed Canary); bill very deep at base (diagnostic); sexes alike; upperparts, ear coverts and malar stripe yellowish green, streaked dark olive (malar stripe black in Yelloweyed and Yellow Canaries); eyebrow, cheeks and underparts deep rich yellow, breast and flanks washed greenish, especially in southernmost birds (no greenish wash in Yellow or Yelloweyed Canaries; forehead yellow in Yellow Canary). *Immature:* Greyer than adult, paler yellow below; breast and flanks faintly streaked brown.

Voice: Song jumble of chirps, whistles, warbles and trills, rather deeper-pitched than songs of other canaries, and mixed with harsh *churr* and *chirrup* notes, in phrases lasting 5–8 seconds, with pauses of 8–10 seconds; trilled *swirriwirrit* and *chirrirrip* callnotes; deep *poy* or *see-it* alarm notes by ♀.

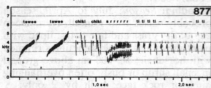

877

Distribution: S Africa to E Africa; in s Africa confined to narrow belt from w Cape to e Transvaal, Mozambique and most of Zimbabwe.

Status: Uncommon to fairly common resident; nomadic in winter.

Habitat: Bushy streamside vegetation, coastal bush, thickets, wooded kloofs, forest clearings, montane scrub, gardens, cultivated lands with rank secondary growth.

Habits: Usually solitary or in pairs; gregarious in groups of 4–12 birds when not breeding, sometimes flocks of 20–30 birds at good food source, often in company with other canaries. Forages on ground, hopping or running briskly, and in bushes and trees; cracks open large hard seeds with heavy bill. Flight fast and less undulating than that of other canaries. Usually quiet and unobtrusive.

Food: Seeds, fruit (e.g. of *Lycium, Ehretia, Scutia, Euphorbia ingens, Ficus burtt-davyi* and *Ligustrum*), leaves (e.g. of *Senecio*).

Breeding: *Season:* July to November in w Cape, May to December in e Cape, October to January in Natal, July to March (mainly August-October) in Zimbabwe. *Nest:* Cup of grass, weed stems and inflorescences, fine twigs and tendrils, lined with fine fibres, plant down, rags and wool; cup diameter 5 cm, depth 4 cm; 1,5–6 m above ground in bush or tree. *Clutch:* (30) 2–2,8–4 eggs. *Eggs:* White, pale blue or pale green, spotted and streaked with brown, purple and black; measure (52) 19,3 × 14 (17,4–21,5 × 13,1–15,3). *Incubation:* (6) 12,5–14,5–17 days by ♀ only; ♂ feeds ♀ on nest. *Nestling:* 15–21 days; fed for first 4 days by ♀ only, but ♂ brings food to nest; later fed by both parents.

878 (866)

Yellow Canary
Geelkanarie
Serinus flaviventris

Plate 73

Nsense, Kandingo (K), Tšoere (SS), [Gelbbauch-girlitz]

Measurements: Length 13–14 cm; wing (107 ♂) 68–74,6–77, (51 ♀) 66–73–80; tail (103 ♂) 46–51,8–59, (37 ♀) 49–52–58; tarsus (103 ♂) 15–18,4–23, (37 ♀) 14–18,2–21; culmen (103 ♂) 13–14–16, (37 ♀) 12–13,9–15. Weight (32 ♂) 14,7–17,4–19,9 g, (27 ♀) 14,7–16,5–18,7 g.

Bare Parts: Iris brown; bill horn, base pinkish; legs and feet dark pinkish brown.

Identification: Size medium (larger than Yelloweyed Canary, smaller than Bully Canary). *Male*: Above dull yellowish green, streaked dark olive, rump more yellowish; forehead, eyebrow, cheek and underparts bright yellow (not washed greenish on breast as in Bully Canary; flanks not greyish as in Yelloweyed Canary; forehead green in Bully Canary); malar stripe blackish; bill much smaller than that of Bully Canary; tail not tipped white as in Yelloweyed Canary. *Female*: Above greyish brown, streaked darker; rump yellow; eyebrow, cheek and underparts off-white, streaked dusky on breast and flanks (Whitethroated Canary greyer on belly, not streaked below). *Immature*: Similar to adult ♀, but more boldly streaked below.

Voice: Song sustained jumble of fast trilling and warbling notes, shriller than songs of other canaries; characteristic rolling *tirriyip* callnote, especially on take-off and when alarmed.

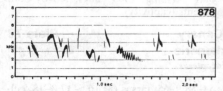

Distribution: Western half of s Africa, to sw Angola; vagrant to Swaziland.

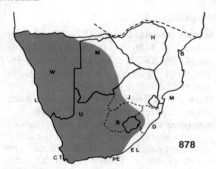

Status: Common resident; nomadic in winter.

Habitat: Montane shrub and grassland, karoo, arid savanna and scrub, fynbos; shrubby desert plains and hills, rocky hillsides with scattered bushes, farmyards, gardens.

Habits: In pairs when breeding; otherwise in small loose flocks; gathers in larger flocks at water. Forages on ground and in bushes or trees. ♂ sings from perch on top of bush or concealed inside tall tree. Flight fast and fairly direct, less undulating than that of smaller canaries.

Food: Seeds, flowers, nectar, insects, small crustaceans.

Breeding: *Season*: July to October in sw Cape, September to March in e Cape, November to February in Orange Free State, August to April in Transvaal, any month in arid W according to rainfall. *Nest*: Shallow cup of dry stalks, roots, tendril and grass stems, lined with plant down; cup diameter about 5 cm, depth about 4 cm; from ground level to about 3 m above ground (mostly 30–120 cm) in fork of shrub or tree; built by ♀ only in as little as 3 days. *Clutch*: (30) 2–3–4 eggs (usually 3, rarely 5). *Eggs*: Usually white, sometimes pale blue or green, plain or sparsely spotted and lined with shades of brown, purple and black; measure (99) 18 × 13,2 (16,1–20,6 × 12,2–14,6). *Incubation*: (2) 12–14 days (captivity) by ♀ only. *Nestling*: (2) 15–19 days (captivity); fed by both parents.

879 (865)

**Whitethroated Canary
Witkeelkanarie**
Serinus albogularis

Plate 73

[Weißkehlgirlitz]

Measurements: Length 13,5–15 cm; wing (17) 74–79,4–86; tail (6) 53–57,5–61; tarsus (4) 18–20–22; culmen (5) 12–14,2–16. Weight (1 ♂) 23,6 g, (2 ♀) 26–28,1 g, (59 unsexed) 21–27,1–32 g.

Bare Parts: Iris brown; bill horn, paler below; legs and feet blackish brown.

Identification: Medium to large (about sparrow-sized); build robust; sexes alike; above greyish brown, streaked dusky (no wingbars as in Protea Canary); rump bright greenish yellow to lemon yellow (diagnostic; conspicuous in flight; no yellow rump in Streakyheaded Canary; tinged olive yellow in Protea Canary); eyebrow and throat white (diagnostic, contrasting with grey of head and breast); breast light grey (much paler in Streakyheaded Canary), shading to pinkish buff belly and white undertail; tail notched; bill heavy (much lighter in Streakyheaded Canary). *Immature*: Similar to adult, but rump olive yellow.

Voice: Distinctive deep *skweeyik* callnote; song usually fairly short phrases of jumbled trilling and warbling notes with harsh nasal *frrra* interspersed, *weetle weetle frrra weetle frree tee chipchipchip*, highly variable; pauses between phrases usually very short.

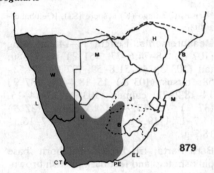

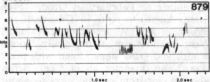

Distribution: Mainly dry W, from e Cape and Orange Free State to w Namibia and sw Angola.

Status: Common resident, especially in w parts of range; nomadic at all times.

Habitat: Riverine thornbush and scrub in semi-arid to arid grassveld and desert; also coastal bush; usually near water.

Habits: Usually solitary or in pairs; sometimes in small groups of up to 8 birds; flocks of up to 30 birds may gather at water; drinks often. Forages on ground, aloes and bushes. Usually rather quiet, except for callnote on take-off.

Food: Seeds (e.g. grass, *Senecio*, sunflowers, aloes), berries, buds, insects.

Breeding: *Season*: August to April; season probably varies with rainfall. *Nest*: Cup of fine twigs and grass stems; lined with plant down; 1,2–3 m above ground in fork of bush or low tree; built by ♀ only. *Clutch*: (25) 2–3,3–4 eggs (usually 3–4). *Eggs*: White, pale greenish, bluish or pinkish cream, plain or spotted and scrolled with browns, purple and black, often at thick end only; measure (144) 19,8 × 14,3 (17,2–22,1 × 12,8–16,6). *Incubation*: 13–14 days (captivity), by ♀ only. *Nestling*: 15–17 days; fed by both parents (captivity).

880 (869)

**Protea Canary
Witvlerkkanarie**
Serinus leucopterus

Plate 73

[Proteagirlitz]

Measurements: Length ♂ 16 cm, ♀ 15–16 cm; wing (18) 69–72,6–78; tail (12) 54–58,9–65; tarsus (3) 16,5–17,3–18; culmen (13) 12–12,7–14,5. Weight (15) 18,3–22,2–24 g.

Bare Parts: Iris brown; bill pinkish to whitish, darker above; legs and feet blackish brown to grey.

Identification: Large (about sparrow-sized); sexes alike; above greyish brown, dappled sooty brown (no white eyebrow as in Whitethroated and Streakyheaded Canaries); rump tinged olive yellow (bright yellow in Whitethroated Canary; grey in Streakyheaded Canary); wing dusky with 2 faint white bars (diagnostic when perched; no wingbars in Whitethroated Canary); chin blackish (diagnostic at close range); throat white, showing as white bar; rest of underparts dull greyish, breast faintly mottled darker, paler in centre of belly.

Voice: Song rich, rather slow and deliberate, short phrases of mellow notes interspersed with nasal wheezy *jeeer* notes, *weety weety chipip cheewee witty wipwipwip chiriri cheewip jeeer*; sometimes incorporates imitations of other birdsong; 3-syllabled *tree-lee-loo* callnote, sometimes only 2 syllables.

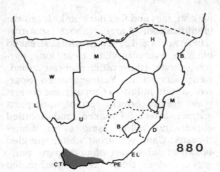

880

Distribution: Confined to mountains of s Cape from Cedarberg to Baviaanskloof W of Port Elizabeth.

Status: Uncommon resident.

Habitat: Mainly *Protea*-covered mountain slopes (mountain fynbos); also bushy kloofs, evergreen forest patches.

Habits: Solitary, in pairs or in small groups of up to 10 birds; rarely forms flocks of up to 40 birds. Forages mainly on standing bushes and other plants, some-times also on ground. Flight fast and direct, often over some distance, usually low over top of scrub. Not shy, but keeps to dense cover; unobtrusive and difficult to observe. Sings from exposed perch, allowing close approach.

Food: Seeds (of *Protea, Restio, Senecio, Erica, Rhus, Geranium*, grasses, sedges and many other plants); also nectar of *Protea, Halleria* and *Salvia*; fruit, flowers, buds, young pine needles.

Breeding: *Season*: August to October. *Nest*: Cup of dry plant stems, lined with plant down held in place with fine wiry grass; cup diameter 5,3–5,8 cm, depth 3,5–4,7 cm; 3–5 m above ground in *Protea*, pine or other low tree. *Clutch*: 2–4 eggs. *Eggs*: Ivory white to very pale blue, spotted and lined with browns and black mainly at thick end; measure (6) 20,6 × 14,6 (19–21,7 × 14,4–14,9). *Incubation*: 17 days. *Nestling*: At least 14 days; fed by both parents.

Ref. Fraser, M. & Richardson, D. 1989. *Birding S. Afr.* 41:86–87.
MacLeod, J.G.R. & Stanford, W.P. 1958. *Ostrich* 29:153–154.
Milewski, A.V. 1978. *Ostrich* 49:174–184.

881 (867)   **Streakyheaded Canary**   **Plate 73**
Streepkopkanarie
Serinus gularis

Indweza (X), umBhalane, umDendeliswe (Z), [Brauengirlitz]

Measurements: Length 14,5–16 cm; wing (20 ♂) 77–79–82, (20 ♀) 77–78,1–81, (120 unsexed) 72–77,4–83; tail (20 ♂) 56–59,5–62, (20 ♀) 56–58,4–61, (83 unsexed) 49,5–60,3–66; tarsus (16) 13–16–18; culmen (17) 10–11,7–13,5. Weight (3 ♂, Zimbabwe) 14,3–15,2–16,8 g, (5 ♀, Zimbabwe) 10,5–15,9–19,5 g, (67 unsexed, Cape) 20–21,9–26 g, (50 unsexed, Transvaal) 17–20,1–25 g, (172 unsexed, Zimbabwe) 11,4–16–21 g.

Bare Parts: Iris brown; bill horn, base

pinkish; legs and feet dark pinkish brown.
Identification: Large (about sparrow-sized); sexes alike; crown white, streaked blackish; eyebrow white, clear, long, narrow, curved (diagnostic; eyebrow broad, wedge-shaped in Yellowthroated Sparrow, absent in Protea Canary); ear coverts plain greyish brown; rest of upperparts greyish brown, streaked and mottled darker (no yellow rump as in Whitethroated Canary); throat white, speckled brown at sides; rest of underparts buffy grey (paler than in Whitethroated Canary). *Immature*: Similar to adult; boldly streaked brown below.
Voice: Song loud clear, fairly sustained, variable jumble of musical and harsh notes, often preceded by callnote repeated 2–3 times, usually ending in trill; sometimes sings set phrase *tseeu tseeu tirririt-tirik* repeatedly; 3-syllabled *chiririt* callnote.

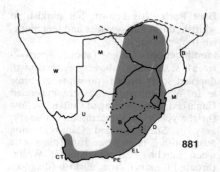

881

on ground. When disturbed flies into bush or tree; flight leisurely, undulating. Often raises crown feathers.
Food: Seeds (including those of *Opuntia*), fruit of *Euphorbia ingens*, berries (e.g. of *Lantana*), buds, flowers, nectar of *Aloe*, *Erythrina* and *Tecomaria*.

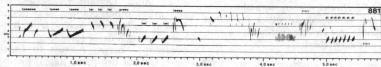

881

Distribution: Africa S of Sahara; in s Africa confined mainly to S and E, including Orange Free State, Transvaal and Zimbabwe, but absent from most of Mozambique.
Status: Fairly common resident; nomadic in winter.
Habitat: Savanna, open woodland, secondary growth around cultivation, riverine bush, open hillsides with scattered trees, gardens.
Habits: Usually solitary, in pairs or small groups of up to 8 birds; seldom gregarious in flocks of up to 20 or even 50 birds; may join mixed bird parties, or associate with other species of canary. Quiet and unobtrusive; easily overlooked. Forages on ground or in bushes, aloes and trees; hops

Breeding: *Season*: September to February in Natal, October to January in Transvaal, September to March in Zimbabwe. *Nest*: Cup of grass, dead leaves, twiglets, bark and paper, lined with outer layer of thin strips of bark and inner layer of plant down, wool and other soft material; cup diameter 5–7,5 cm, depth 2,6–3,9 cm; 1,5–12 m above ground (mostly 3–5 m) in fork of bush or tree, in cluster of pine cones, behind peeling bark, usually well hidden. *Clutch*: (52) 2–2,5–4 eggs (usually 3). *Eggs*: White or pale blue, plain or spotted sparingly with browns, purple and black; measure (54) 18,5 × 13,8 (17–21,2 × 12,6–15). *Incubation*: 12,5–15 days by ♀ only. *Nestling*: About 17 days; fed by both parents.

Ref. Irwin, M.P.S. 1977. *Honeyguide* 92:17–23.

882 (868) **Blackeared Canary** **Plate 73**
Swartoorkanarie
Serinus mennelli

[Schwarzwangengirlitz]
Measurements: Length 12,5–14 cm; wing (20 ♂) 79–82,1–82, (20 ♀) 78–80,5–82; tail (20 ♂) 49–51,9–54, (20 ♀) 49–51,8–54; tarsus (5) 12,5–14,5; culmen (5) 10–12,5. Weight (9) 13–15,3–17,7 g.
Bare Parts: Iris, bill and legs brown; feet slate grey.

Identification: Size medium; very similar to Streakyheaded Canary, especially females in worn plumage; crown white, heavily streaked blackish; ear coverts blackish brown (diagnostic in ♂; paler, more greyish brown in ♀); back grey, heavily blotched sooty brown; wings and tail blackish brown, edged paler; chin speckled white and blackish (no markings in Streakyheaded Canary); throat white; rest of underparts buff, heavily streaked sooty brown (Streakyheaded Canary hardly streaked below).

Voice: 3-syllabled sizzling *see-see-see* call-notes; song twittering whistled *de-ree-te-rue-se-ree-sue* or *fweee chip-chip-chip preeeu pilly twee pilly* rapidly repeated over and over, 2nd note higher than others.

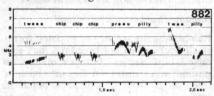

Distribution: Mozambique and Zimbabwe, to Angola, Zambia, Zaire and Malawi.

Status: Uncommon to fairly common resident; some seasonal movements, occurring around Masvingo (Fort Victoria) only September to March.

Habitat: *Brachystegia* and *Baikiaea* woodland (not in secondary growth or cultivation like Streakyheaded Canary).

Habits: Usually solitary, in pairs or small groups of 3–5 birds; forms large flocks when not breeding; may join mixed bird parties,

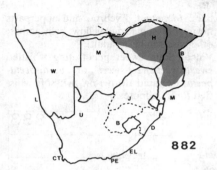

especially of other canaries. Male sings from perch or in flight; ♂ displays with swooping dives from air, interspersed with "butterfly" fluttering. Forages on ground by hopping or walking; strips seeds from standing grass inflorescences; also forages in trees and on aloes; hawks insects in flight.

Food: Seeds, nectar, insects, leaves and flowers of *Brachystegia*, small fruits.

Breeding: *Season:* November to February. *Nest:* Cup of *Usnea* lichen and other dry plant material, bound with spider web; lined with rootlets, fine grass, moss and lichen; decorated outside with bark and feathers; inside diameter 4,5 cm, depth 2 cm; 1–9 m above ground, usually in outer fork of tree. *Clutch:* 2–4 eggs (usually 3). *Eggs:* Pale bluish or greenish white, spotted with slate, brown, purple and black at thick end; measure 20,2 × 14,8 (17,2–22 × 13,2–16). *Incubation:* 13 days (captivity). *Nestling:* 18 days (captivity).

Ref. Irwin, M.P.S. 1977. *Honeyguide* 92:17–23.
Vernon, C.J. 1979. *Honeyguide* 99:12–15.

883 (875)   **Cabanis's Bunting**   **Plate 72**
Geelstreepkoppie
Emberiza cabanisi

[Cabanisammer]

Measurements: Length 16–17 cm; wing (6) 78–86; tail 68–75; tarsus 18,5–20,5; culmen 12–14. Weight (1 ♂) 22,3 g, (7 unsexed) 13,7–21,3–25,5 g.

Bare Parts: Iris brown; bill pale pinkish horn, culmen and tip black; legs and feet dull pinkish.

Identification: Large (about sparrow-sized); tail longish, rounded, black, tipped and edged white (conspicuous in flight); head black with central white stripe, white eyebrow and white line below black face (diagnostic; Golden-breasted Bunting has white line below eye, giving more striped effect, but lacks white line below face); back grey streaked brown and blackish (back rufous in Goldenbreasted Bunting); below bright yellow, shading to white undertail (no orange wash on breast as in Goldenbreasted Bunting); 2 conspicuous white wingbars. *Immature*: Eyebrow and upperparts tawny; breast pale dull yellow; belly amber; otherwise similar to adult.

Voice: Song sweet penetrating whistled *sweet-sweet-sweet-sweet* or *peetu-peetu-peetu*, or rapid *twi-twi-twi-twi*; soft whistled *turee* callnote.

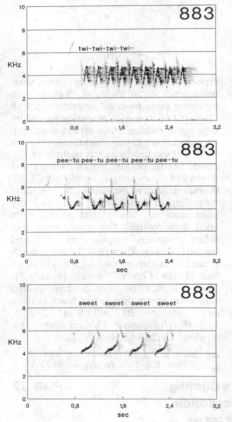

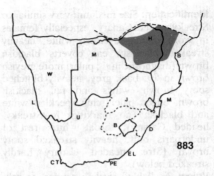

Distribution: Africa S of Sahara; in s Africa confined to Zimbabwe Plateau and adjacent Mozambique.

Status: Uncommon and local resident.

Habitat: *Brachystegia* woodland.

Habits: Usually solitary or in pairs; forms small flocks when not breeding; may join mixed bird parties. Forages mainly on ground; when disturbed flies into bush or tree. Sings from conspicuous perch in tree.

Food: Mainly insects (grasshoppers, beetles); also seeds, fallen grain.

Breeding: *Season*: September to March (mainly October-November) in Zimbabwe. *Nest*: Shallow cup of roots, twigs, grass stems and weed stalks, lined with fine grass and rootlets; 1–5 m above ground in bush or tree, usually hidden among foliage; built by ♀ only. *Clutch*: 2–3 eggs. *Eggs*: White or pale greenish, scrolled, lined and blotched with brown and grey often in ring around thick end; measure (17) 19,5 × 14,5 (18–21,9 × 13,5–15,1). *Incubation*: (1) 14 days (captivity). *Nestling*: (1) 16 days (captivity).

884 (874)   **Goldenbreasted Bunting**   **Plate 72**
Rooirugstreepkoppie
Emberiza flaviventris

Mavotiyo (Ts), Intsasa (X), umNdweza (Z), [Gelbbauchammer]

Measurements: Length 15–16 cm; wing (84 ♂) 79–83,8–93, (39 ♀) 76,5–80,1–85,5; tail (50 ♂) 61–70,5–80,5, (29 ♀) 58–68,5–77; tarsus (52) 16–19; culmen (52) 12–13,5. Weight (5 ♂) 15,1–18,5–20,5 g, (7 ♀) 16,1–18,2–21,2 g, (13 unsexed) 16,9–19,6–22 g.

Bare Parts: Iris dark brown; bill pale greyish pink, culmen and tip blackish; legs and feet dull greyish pink.

Identification: Size medium to large (slightly smaller than sparrow); build slender; tail longish, rounded, black, tipped and edged white (conspicuous in flight); head black; stripe on crown, eyebrow and stripe below eye white (Cabanis's Bunting lacks stripe below eye, but has white line below black face); back rufous, streaked black (back greyish in Cabanis's Bunting); rump plain grey; below bright yellow, washed deep orange on breast (diagnostic; no orange wash in Cabanis's Bunting); 2 conspicuous white wingbars. *Female*: Head stripes more buff than white. *Immature*: Duller and paler than ♀; breast streaked brown.

Voice: Plaintive whistled *pretty-cheeer*, often only *cheeer* audible, falling in pitch; song loud penetrating piping phrases *chippy chippy chippy chippy*, crescendo, or *chip-chip-chip-chip-tseeu-ti-ti-ti-ti*, or *prettyboy, prettyboy, prettyboy* repeated quickly; quiet *chip* flight call.

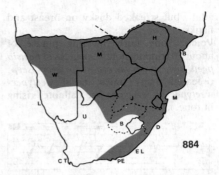
884

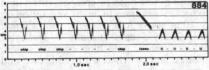

Distribution: Africa S of Sahara, except much of W Africa; widespread in s Africa except most of dry W.

Status: Uncommon to fairly common resident.

Habitat: Woodland, savanna, exotic plantations, riverine bush, farmyards, gardens.

Habits: Usually solitary or in pairs; sometimes gregarious in flocks of up to 20 birds when not breeding; forms mixed bird parties with other buntings and canaries. Forages mainly on ground, walking with small steps; sometimes hops. Sings from perch in tree, but not usually in open. Flight deeply undulating; flicks tail up on alighting.

Food: Insects (beetles, termites, ants), seeds, buds.

Breeding: *Season*: September to March (mainly November-December) in e Cape, October to February (mainly October-December) in Natal and Transvaal, September to April (mainly October-December) in Zimbabwe. *Nest*: Shallow, loosely-built cup of grass stems and roots, lined with fine rootlets and sometimes hair; cup diameter 5 cm, depth 3,8 cm; 45–150 cm above ground in horizontal fork of small tree or low bush, seldom concealed. *Clutch*: (133) 2–2,4–4 eggs (usually 2–3). *Eggs*: White, pale cream, greenish or bluish, spotted, scrolled and lined with black, brown and grey mainly around thick end; measure (206) 20,3 × 14,3 (15,5–22,5 × 13,1–15,3). *Incubation*: 12,5–13 days by ♀ only. *Nestling*: 16–17 days; fed by both parents.

885 (873) Cape Bunting Plate 72
Rooivlerkstreepkoppie
Emberiza capensis

'Maborokoane (SS), umNdweza (Z), [Kapammer]

Measurements: Length 15–16 cm; wing (22 ♂) 75–79,9–88, (11 ♀) 71–75,8–82; tail (10) 58–72; tarsus (10) 19–20; culmen (10) 10,5–12. Weight (3 ♂) 18,2–20,9–23,6 g, (1 ♀) 22,5 g, (31 unsexed) 17–20,7–24 g.

Bare Parts: Iris brown; bill slate black, base bluish or pinkish; legs and feet dark horn.

Identification: Size medium; build slender; crown and back grey streaked blackish; sides of head boldly striped black and white; wings bright rusty (diagnostic); throat white; rest of underparts grey, paler on belly (diagnostic; cinnamon in Rock Bunting). *Immature*: Similar to

CAPE BUNTING

adult, but streaked dusky on breast and flanks.

Voice: Song fairly piercing phrase of about 10 tripping notes, *tswip tswip peetsip peets swip tseep tsweep swip tseep tseep*, repeated many times; nasal *weetypee-weetypee* or *weetypee-pee* callnote, rising in tone.

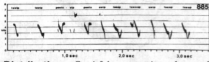

Distribution: S Africa to Angola and Malawi; widespread in s Africa except Kalahari basin and s and e littoral.

Status: Common to fairly common resident; uncommon in Zimbabwe.

Habitat: Rocky places from high mountains to coast, including riverine gorges, even in arid country; usually near water.

Habits: Usually solitary or in pairs; sometimes in small family groups; does not flock. Forages on ground, walking with short steps, or hopping. Sings from top of rock or low bush, sometimes opening and closing wings. Flight low and somewhat jerky, not sustained; on alighting often does quick about-turn. Becomes tame around human settlement. Easily overlooked except when calling; well camouflaged on rocks.

Food: Seeds, insects, spiders.

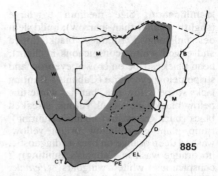

Breeding: *Season*: July to January (mainly September-October) in w Cape, November to April in e Cape, October to March in Orange Free State, October to November in Transvaal, November to June (mainly December-April) in Zimbabwe. *Nest*: Cup of twigs, grass and roots, untidy outside, but neatly lined inside with fine rootlets, grass and hair; internal diameter 6,2 cm, depth 5,7 cm; on or close to ground in low bush or creeper, often next to rock; sometimes in bushy vegetation up to 10 m above foot of rocky cliff. *Clutch*: (23) 2–2,6–5 eggs (usually 2–3). *Eggs*: White, cream, pale blue or pale green, spotted and blotched with red-brown and some purple and grey concentrated at thick end; measure (62) 20,3 × 15 (17,9–23,2 × 13,6–16,4). *Incubation*: Unrecorded. *Nestling*: Unrecorded; fed by both parents.

---

886 (872)   **Rock Bunting**   **Plate 72**
Klipstreepkoppie
Emberiza tahapisi

'Maborokoane (SS), Mvemvere (Sh), Undenjenje, Undenzeni (X), umDinasibula (Z), [Bergammer, Siebenstreifenammer]

Measurements: Length 14–16 cm; wing (31 ♂) 76–79–83, (23 ♀) 72–75–79; tail (49) 55–66; tarsus (49) 15–18; culmen (49) 9–11. Weight (1 ♂) 13,2 g, (1 ♀) 14,5 g, (44 unsexed) 12–14,8–22 g.

Bare Parts: Iris brown; bill dark horn above, yellow below; legs and feet pinkish brown.

Identification: Size medium to largish (slightly smaller than Cape Bunting). *Male*: Head black; white stripe down

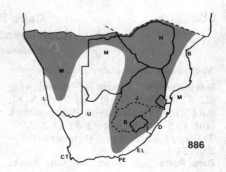

crown, over eye, below eye and on malar region, giving boldly striped head; back rich brown, streaked black; throat speckled black and white (plain white in Cape Bunting); rest of underparts rich cinnamon (diagnostic; Cape Bunting grey below). *Female*: Similar to ♂, but head dark grey, striped off-white. *Immature*: Similar to adult ♀.

Voice: Song repeated shrill *chip chrrEE-rippity-peep*, uttered quickly with pauses between; highly characteristic nasal *pee-PEEwer* callnote; drawn-out *sweee* alarm call.

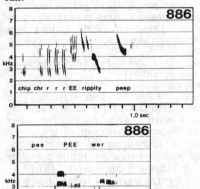

Distribution: S Africa to Eritrea and Nigeria; also s Arabia and Socotra; widespread in e and n parts of s Africa, avoiding dry W, Kalahari basin and most of s and e littoral.

Status: Locally common to uncommon resident; nomadic when not breeding.

Habitat: Rocky outcrops, escarpments, eroding stony slopes and dongas, dry watercourses, abandoned quarries, savanna (especially where overgrazed).

Habits: Usually solitary or in pairs; sometimes in small groups of 3–4 birds; less often in larger flocks when not breeding. Forages on ground, hopping in little shuffling steps; flies to perch on rock when disturbed; flight undulating; on alighting often does about-turn or sideways shuffle. Usually unobtrusive; best located by callnote.

Food: Seeds, insects.

Breeding: *Season*: December to April in Orange Free State, November to February in Natal, October to March (mainly January) in Transvaal, November to June (mainly January-April) in Zimbabwe. *Nest*: Shallow cup of grass in foundation of small sticks, lined with finer grass and rootlets; in shallow scrape on ground at base of grasstuft, rock or clod; when against rock, cup often incomplete at back; inside diameter 5,7 cm, depth 2 cm; on rocky slope, earth bank, crevice in rockface or open rough ground; built by ♀ only in 4–13 days; ♂ accompanies ♀ on collecting trips. *Clutch*: (90) 2–3–4 eggs (usually 3). *Eggs*: Pale green, pale bluish or whitish, heavily spotted and blotched with rust, dark brown and grey; measure (157) 17,9 × 13,3 (16–19,7 × 12,2–14). *Incubation*: 12–14 days by both sexes, mostly by ♀. *Nestling*: 14–16 days; fed by both parents.

Ref. Cumming, S.C. & Steyn, P. 1966. *Ostrich* 37:170–175.
Gartshore, M.E. 1975. *Bull. Nigerian Orn. Soc.* 11:27–33.

887 (871) **Larklike Bunting** **Plate 72**
Vaalstreepkoppie
Emberiza impetuani

[Lerchenammer]

Measurements: Length 12,5–14 cm; wing (18 ♂) 72–75–80, (11 ♀) 70–72–75; tail (14) 52–61; tarsus (14) 16–17,5; culmen (14) 9–10,5. Weight (8 ♂) 13,8–15,1–16,9 g, (7 ♀) 13,3–14,4–17,2 g, (31 unsexed) 13,7–15,1–16,6 g.

Bare Parts: Iris brown; bill dark horn above, pale horn below; legs and feet pinkish brown.

Identification: Size smallish to medium; sexes alike; nondescript brownish, with small conical bill (much heavier in finch-larks); best identified by callnote (*q.v.*);

light buffy brown all over, paler on eyebrow and throat, streaked blackish on upperparts (♀ Greybacked and Chestnutbacked Finchlarks have black in centre of belly, more blotched than streaked above; ♀ Blackeared Finchlark has whitish ring around eye); wing brown, edged dull rufous (diagnostic); bill small, horn-coloured (bill heavier, pale grey in finchlarks). *Immature*: Similar to adult.

Voice: Dull but characteristic single *tip* or *chut* callnote, usually given in flight and on take-off; song monotonously repeated shortish phrase of somewhat canarylike trilled notes, *chiriri chippy-chirpy-chirip*, rather variable individually.

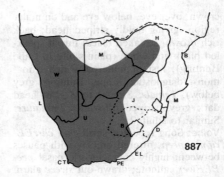

887

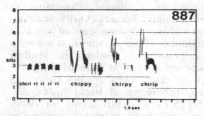

Distribution: Dry w parts of s Africa, to Angola, Zambia and Zaire; irruptive into Zimbabwe and e Transvaal lowveld in drought years and very cold winters.
Status: Common to very common; highly nomadic at all times, appearing and disappearing overnight.
Habitat: Arid savanna, karoo, rocky slopes of koppies and dry watercourses; usually not far from water.
Habits: Gregarious at all times, sometimes in flocks of hundreds, especially at waterholes, often in company with larks. Forages on ground, walking like

lark; also jumps up to get at seeds on standing grass. Flushes reluctantly, usually not flying far; flight jinking and undulating. Sings from top of rock or bush.
Food: Seeds and insects (including small green caterpillars).
Breeding: *Season*: September to November in w Cape, September to May in Karoo, February-March in sw Kalahari; season varies with rainfall in drier areas. *Nest*: Shallow cup of grass and roots in foundation of coarse sticks, lined with fine rootlets; inside diameter (8) 5,3–5,8–6,7 cm, depth (8) 2,4–2,9–3,9 cm; on ground under or at base of rock or stone (84%), or under shrub (16%), usually on SE side; on stony slope, less often on flat sandy or stony ground; built by ♀; ♂ accompanies ♀ on collecting trips. *Clutch*: (50) 2–2,9–4 eggs (usually 3). *Eggs*: White, pale greenish white or pale bluish, spotted and blotched with rust and grey; measure (165) 17,8 × 13,2 (15,5–19,6 × 12,1–15,3). *Incubation*: 13 days. *Nestling*: About 12–13 days.

SPECIES NEW TO THE SOUTHERN AFRICAN AVIFAUNA SINCE 1983

The species of birds in the following accounts have been added since the preparation of the manuscript for the revised (5th) edition of *Roberts' birds of southern Africa* (1985). Those numbered 901–904 were included in the 5th edition. Those numbered 905–920 have been added to the southern African list since then. They include mostly vagrants, but also two pipits, the Mountain Pipit and the Wood Pipit, which have been raised to specific status from formerly subspecific status. This raising of rank has also been proposed for several other southern African birds, formerly included merely as subspecies of the Yellowbilled/Black Kite, Black Korhaan, Cape Parrot, Knysna Lourie, Burchell's Coucal and Spotted Prinia; these proposals are mentioned in the relevant species accounts where the new names are given, but the final decision on them must await wider acceptance (or rejection) before they assume full specific status in this book.

MOTACILLIDAE

901 (–) **Mountain Pipit** **Plate 77**
Bergkoester
Anthus hoeschi

[Hochlandpieper]

Measurements: Length about 18–19 cm; wing (19 ♂) 93–92,5–98 (9 ♀) 88–89,6–92; tail (12 ♂) 63–67,7–71,5, (7 ♀) 61–64,4–66,5; tarsus (4 ♂) 28–28,1,28,5, (1 ♀) 27,5; culmen (9 ♂) 17,5–18,6–19, (6 ♀) 16–17,5–18,5. Weight (4 ♂) 23,5–25,8–28 g, (1 ♀) 26 g, (13 unsexed) 23,5–27–31 g.

Bare Parts: Iris brown; bill dark horn, base yellowish to pinkish; legs and feet brownish pink.

Identification: Size medium (distinctly larger than Grassveld Pipit); very similar to Grassveld and Longbilled Pipits; outer rectrices narrowly edged buff (not white); looks chunkier in field than Grassveld Pipit; above warm brown (darker and more rufous than in Grassveld Pipit) strongly streaked darker on mantle; below white, washed cinnamon on breast and flanks (less buffy than Grassveld Pipit); breast heavily streaked dark brown (usually more boldly than in Grassveld Pipit). *In hand*: Wings and tail longer than those of Grassveld Pipit; wing formula as for Grassveld Pipit.

Voice: Similar to that of Grassveld Pipit, but deeper and slower; *chiri* repeated at intervals during cruising dis-play flight, rapidly repeated *chiri-chiri-chiri* in dive at end of display; song from perch *tuchit tuchit*; alarm call *twit twit twit*.

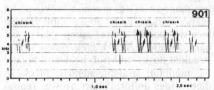

Distribution: Breeds above 2000 m in ne Cape and Lesotho; apparently migrates through n Cape and Namibia to Angola (Lunda and Moxico) after breeding, returning through e Botswana in October.

Status: Rare to abundant breeding intra-African migrant, September to April. Probably Rare (RDB). Formerly considered race of Grassveld Pipit *A. novaeseelandiae lwenarum* (or *A. n. editus*); also called *A. cameroonensis*.

Habitat: Short montane grassland, mainly on e slopes of escarpment.

Habits: Poorly known; mostly similar to those of Grassveld Pipit which occurs in similar habitat in ne Cape. Display flight similar to that of Grassveld Pipit; also sings from perch on rock or fence.

Food: Unrecorded.

Breeding: *Season*: Mainly late November

to early January. *Nest*: Cup of grass, well concealed under grasstuft. *Clutch*: 3–4 eggs. *Eggs*: Similar to those of Richard's Pipit; whitish, spotted with browns and greys forming dense ring around thick end; measure (3) 21,6 × 15,4 (21,4–

21,8 × 15,3–15,4). *Incubation*: Unrecorded. *Nestling*: Unrecorded.

Ref. Clancey, P.A. 1984. *Durban Mus. Novit.* 13:189–194.
Mendelsohn, J. 1984. *Bokmakierie* 36(2):40–44.

SCOLOPACIDAE

902 (–)   **Lesser Yellowlegs**   **Plate 76**
Kleingeelpootruiter
Tringa flavipes

[Kleiner Gelbschenkel]

Measurements: Length 24–28 cm; wing (25 ♂) 149–156,3–168, (27 ♀) 149,5–160–169; tail (15 ♂) 61–62,8–67, (10 ♀) 55–63,2–66; tarsus (15 ♂) 45,5–50–55,5, (10 ♀) 46,5–50,3–52; culmen (15 ♂) 35–36,4–38, (10 ♀) 30–35,5–39.

Bare Parts: Iris dark brown; bill black; legs and feet bright yellow.

Identification: Size medium (somewhat larger and more slender than Wood Sandpiper); proportions rather like those of large Marsh Sandpiper; long bright yellow legs diagnostic (legs greenish in Wood and Marsh Sandpipers); above dull greyish brown, spotted white; rump white; tail barred white and dark grey; below white, streaked dusky on head, neck and breast; bill medium, straight, slender, black; in flight wings uniform sooty brown. *Immature*: Above brown, spotted buff; breast washed greyish.

Voice: Soft whistle of 1–3 notes, *wheu-wheu-wheu*.

Distribution: Breeds Canada and Alaska; migrates to s United States, C an S America; vagrant to Europe and s Africa.

Status: Rare straggler to s Africa, December 1979, Harare (Zimbabwe), Berg River (sw Cape) 1983–1984.

Habitat: Sewage works, mudflats, marshes, flooded grasslands.

Habits: Solitary in s Africa; otherwise in small loose flocks. Bobs head and body frequently. Forages in shallow water, mostly from surface, but also by probing in soft substrate, sometimes with head completely submerged. Flies with rather slow wingbeats.

Food: Insects, crustaceans, small fish, worms, snails.

Breeding: Extralimital.

Ref. Tree, A.J. 1981. *Bokmakierie* 33:44–46.
Ryan, P.G. & Graham, J.M.D. 1984. *Ostrich* 55:222–223.

MOTACILLIDAE

903 (–)   **Redthroated Pipit**   **Plate 77**
Rooikeelkoester
Anthus cervinus

[Rotkehlpieper]

Measurements: Length about 15 cm; wing (6) 75–83,2–91; tail (4) 54–60–70; tarsus (8) 20–23; culmen (8) 10–12,5.

Bare Parts: Iris brown; bill light horn, base yellowish; legs and feet yellowish pink.

Identification: Size medium; similar to Tree Pipit, but rump streaked (not plain); above light olive brown, streaked darker;

below creamy white, broadly streaked black on breast and flanks (in breeding plumage throat and upper breast plain light pinkish rust or cinnamon); outer rectrices white (conspicuous in flight). *In hand*: P2–4 emarginated; P4 markedly shorter than P1–3; hindclaw long (much shorter in Tree Pipit).

Voice: High-pitched metallic *seee* and soft *jeeu*.

Distribution: Breeds n Palaearctic from Scandinavia to Kamchatka; migrates to Africa as far S as Nigeria, Tanzania and probably Zambia, and also to SE Asia; in s Africa recorded once, Umvoti Mouth, Natal, March 1983.
Status: Very rare nonbreeding Palaearctic straggler.
Habitat: Moist grasslands.

Habits: Solitary or in small groups, sometimes in company with Yellow Wagtails. When disturbed flies high and far; flight jerky, accompanied by *seee* call. May perch in tree, but less often than does Tree Pipit.
Food: Insects.
Breeding: Extralimital.

HIRUNDINIDAE

904 (–)   **Redrumped Swallow**   **Plate 77**
Rooinekswael
Hirundo daurica

[Rötelschwalbe]

Measurements: Length about 18 cm; wing (6) 110–121–135; tail (6, outermost rectrices) 85–89,2–125, (19, innermost rectrices) 38–60; tarsus (4) 13–13,8–15; culmen (4) 7–9–11.
Bare Parts: Iris dark brown; bill black; legs and feet dark brown.
Identification: Size medium (between that of Greater and Lesser Striped swallows); crown, back, wings and tail metallic blue-black; no white windows in tail as in other "redrumped" s African swallows (Red-breasted, Mosque, Greater Striped and Lesser Striped); narrow eyebrow, hind-neck, rump and sides of neck chestnut; below cream, buff, tawny or light rufous. *Immature*: Above duller than adult; wings spotted tawny.

Voice: Thin twitter in flight; *keer* alarm call.
Distribution: Breeds s Europe to India and Africa as far S as Senegambia, Nigeria and Malawi; n populations migrate southwards in nonbreeding season; in s Africa recorded only in Zimbabwe.
Status: Rare nonbreeding straggler from tropical Africa, February-March.
Habitat: Woodland, rocky hills, montane grassland.
Habits: Usually in pairs or small groups, sometimes in company with other swallow species. Roosts communally in tall trees along rivers, in W Africa sometimes in flocks of over 50 birds. Attracted to grass fires. Frequents human settlements.
Food: Aerial arthropods.
Breeding: Extralimital.

DIOMEDEIDAE

905 (–)   **Laysan Albatross**   **Plate 74**
Laysan-Malmok
Diomedea immutabilis

[Laysanalbatroß]

Measurements: Length 79–81 cm; wingspan 195–203 cm.
Bare Parts: Iris dark brown; lower eyelid white; bill pale grey, orange or yellowish with darker grey tip and base; legs and feet pink.
Identification: Size medium; back and upperwing blackish grey; tail black; underwing mostly white with dark leading and trailing edges; head, rump and underparts white; face washed with grey, darker on lores; bill pale with dark tip.
Voice: Silent at sea.
Distribution: Northern Pacific Ocean; breeds Hawaiian Archipelago and Bonin Island.
Status: Very rare vagrant to s African waters.

Habitat: Open ocean when not breeding. **Habits:** Glides gracefully in flight; rides high on water. Similar to other smaller albatrosses, but does not follow ships. **Food:** Squid; possibly also fish. **Breeding:** Extralimital.

SCOLOPACIDAE

906 (-)   **Greater Yellowlegs**   **Plate 76**
Grootgeelpootruiter
Tringa melanoleuca

[Großer Gelbschenkel]

Measurements: Length 32,5–37,5 cm; wing (20 ♂) 180–187,8–198,5, (11 ♀) 180–188,9–197; tail (20 ♂) 71–76,9–83, (11 ♀) 71–76,6–83; tarsus (20 ♂) 57–60,7–68, (11 ♀) 55–59,4–62,5; culmen (20 ♂) 52–55,8–61, (11 ♀) 53,5–55,5–58.
Bare Parts: Iris dark brown; bill blackish with paler (greenish, greyish or yellowish) base; legs and feet bright yellow (rarely orange).
Identification: Size medium to large; head, face and breast heavily streaked dark brown and white; eyebrow whitish; rest of upperparts blackish to brownish, heavily spotted and notched with white; underparts white lightly streaked on lower breast with blackish, and lightly barred blackish on flanks; conspicuous white rectangle on rump in flight; wings uniformly dark; similar to Greenshank, but bright yellow legs separate the two; very similar to Lesser Yellowlegs, but size larger and bill paler at base and about one-and-a-half times length of head (bill of Lesser Yellowlegs only slightly longer than head and usually all-dark, without paler base).
Voice: Loud clear *teu-teu-teu*, more less sustained; clearer and more ringing than call of Lesser Yellowlegs.
Distribution: Breeds N America from s Alaska, across central Canada to Atlantic coast; migrates to s United States, Central America, Caribbean and all of S America in nonbreeding season; vagrant to s Africa, Japan, w Europe and Greenland.
Status: Very rare vagrant to s Africa; recorded Noordhoek Pan, Cape Peninsula, S Africa, December 1971.
Habitat: Muddy shorelines of coastal and inland waters.
Habits: Solitary or in small flocks. Forages like Greenshank in shallow or deep water, sometimes wading belly-deep and often darting after small fishes. Rather wary.
Food: Small aquatic animals.
Breeding: Extralimital.

TURDIDAE

907 (-)   **Pied Wheatear**   **Plate 77**
Bontskaapwagter
Oenanthe pleschanka

[Nonnensteinschmätzer]

Measurements: Length about 14,5 cm; wing (20 ♂) 92–94,9–99, (8 ♀) 90–91,6–95; tail (11 ♂) 56–59,4–64, (8 ♀) 54–58,8–62; tarsus (24 ♂) 22,3–23,3–24,3, (12 ♀) 22–23,3–24,1; culmen (41 ♂) 15,8–16,8–18,1, (13 ♀) 15,9–16,9–17,9. Weight (82 ♂) 16–18,3–22 g, (39 ♀) 16–19,2–25 g.
Bare Parts: Iris brown; bill, legs and feet black (sometimes dark brown in ♀).
Identification: Size smallish; build rather light. *Male*: Top of head, nape, upper mantle, lower back and rump white; upper back, wings, face, throat and upper breast black; rest of underparts white, varously tinged buff; tail white with black centre and tip, forming black T on white background; in fresh plumage (September) head and nape brownish, underparts deep buff. *Female*: Head, upper breast, upper back and wings brown, darker on

wings; lower back, rump and tail as in ♂; rest of underparts pale buff to whitish; in fresh plumage (September) dorsal brown feathers edged buff to give scaly appearance. *Immature*: Similar to September ♀.

Voice: Song fluty whistles, often with imitations of other bird species; callnote harsh *zak-zak*.

Distribution: Breeds e Europe to central Asia; migrates to sw Arabia and ne Africa as far south as Tanzania.

Status: Rare vagrant to s Africa; recorded Umvoti Mouth, Natal, S Africa, January 1984.

Habitat: Steppes, stony mountain slopes, desolate stony plains, banks, cliffs, dry cultivation, stock kraals, villages.

Habits: Usually solitary, territorial; sometimes sings from top of tree or on wall, weed or pile of stones; displays with drooped wings and spread tail; forages on ground or by hawking from perch up to 1,5 m high, dropping to ground to catch prey.

Food: Insects; rarely other invertebrates and fruit.

Breeding: Extralimital.

CHARADRIIDAE

908 (–)   **Kentish Plover**   **Plate 76**

Bleekstrandkiewiet

Charadrius alexandrinus

[Seeregenpfeifer]

Measurements: Length 15–17,5 cm; wing (53 ♂) 102–111–115, (26 ♀) 105–112–116; tail (6 ♂) 41–45,3–48, (6 ♀) 39–43,8–48; tarsus (60) 26–28–30; culmen (59) 14–15–17. Weight (22) 27–37–41 g.

Bare Parts: Iris dark brown; bill black; legs and feet dark grey, olive-grey or yellowish grey to black.

Identification: Size small; easily confused with Whitefronted Plover, but separable by black breast patches, rufous crown and pure white underparts (not washed creamy); crown and nape more or less bright rufous or buff; forehead white, separated from crown by black bar in ♂, which is separated from eye by white eyebrow; underparts and collar on hindneck white; line through eye and patches on sides of breast black (diagnostic); rest of upperparts pale brown. *Immature*: Breast patches pale brown; back feathers fringed with pale buff.

Voice: Low *wit, wee-it* and *pu-it*; *kittup* alarm call.

Distribution: Almost worldwide, except high n latitudes and Australasia; in Africa confined to N Africa (except Sahara) as far S as n Kenya.

Status: Very rare vagrant to s Africa.

Habitat: Mostly marine shores; also saline lakes and mudflats, short-grass plains, rivers.

Habits: Similar to those of Whitefronted Plover; singly or in small flocks, sometimes in company with other small waders.

Food: Insects, spiders, small crustaceans, worms, molluscs.

Breeding: Extralimital.

MOTACILLIDAE

909 (–)   **Wood Pipit**   **Plate 77**

Miombokoester

Anthus nyassae

[Miombopieper]

Measurements: Length about 18 cm; wing (18 ♂) 88–93–99, (10 ♀) 84–87,6–90; tail (18 ♂) 60–66,5–70, (10 ♀) 61–63–67; culmen (28) 17–18. Weight (2 ♂) 23,8–25,1 g.

Bare Parts: Iris dark brown; bill horn, base yellowish pink; legs and feet pinkish brown.

Identification: About size of Longbilled Pipit and similar in appearance; bill and tail relatively short (tail usually less than

71 mm long); eyebrow white (buff in Longbilled Pipit); darker above than Longbilled Pipit, less heavily streaked than Grassveld Pipit and more of a woodland bird. Crown and hindneck dark greyish brown, feathers edged paler; back sandy brown, streaked dark brown; below white, well streaked on breast. *In hand*: P2 and P3 longest, P1 = P4, P2–5 emarginate, P5 = 3 mm shorter than P2 and P3. **Voice:** Sparrowlike *teep-tzrrip-reep* similar to song of Longbilled Pipit.

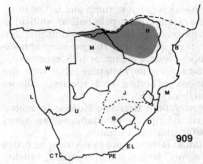

909

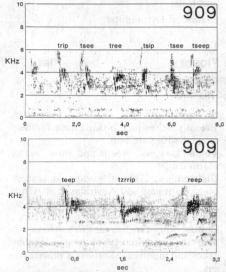

Distribution: Woodlands of Zimbabwean plateau to Caprivi; also Zambia to s Zaire, Angolan plateau, Malawi, n Mozambique and se Tanzania.

Status: Common resident in W of range; elsewhere scarce and local. Formerly considered to be race of Longbilled Pipit.

Habitat: Short grass under canopy of *Brachystegia* woodland, to edges of woodland with scattered trees and bushes, especially on Kalahari sand; also grassland with rocky outcrops in e highlands of Zimbabwe. Absent from *Baikiaea* woodland.

Habits: Very similar to those of Longbilled Pipit, but more frequently arboreal.

Food: Insects.

Breeding: *Season*: July to February; mainly September to November. *Nest*: Similar to that of Longbilled Pipit. *Clutch*: (22) 2–2,2–3 eggs. *Eggs*: White, blotched, spotted and speckled with olive brown and pale lavender, concentrated at thick end; measure (49) 22,1 × 15,6 (20,9–24 × 14,5–17,5). *Incubation*: Unrecorded. *Nestling*: Unrecorded.

Ref. Clancey, P.A. 1988. *Cimbebasia* 10:47–50.

PHAETHONTIDAE

910 (–)   **Redbilled Tropicbird**   **Plate 74**
                       Rooibekpylstert
                       Phaethon aethereus

[Rotschnabel-Tropikvogel]

Measurements: Length (including tail streamers) 76–102 cm; wingspan 99–106 cm; wing (20) 302–311,7–324; tail (20, without streamers) 107–114,3–128; tail streamers (20) 355–480,8–712; tarsus (18) 26–27,8–29; culmen (20) 56–63,2–68. Weight 650–700 g.

Bare Parts: Iris brown; bill crimson to reddish orange; legs and feet dull yellowish, toes tipped black.

Identification: Size large; combination of red bill, black-and-white barred upperparts and white tail streamers diagnostic; rest of plumage white; black line through eye extends to nape; wingtips mostly black. *Immature*: Above more finely and densely barred black-and-white than other immature tropicbirds; broad black eye-stripes meet on nape as black collar (diagnostic); bill yellowish, tip black.

Voice: Loud *prr-tati-tati-hay-hay-hay* near breeding islands; usually silent at sea.

Distribution: Tropical e Pacific, Atlantic and w Indian Oceans; in S Africa recorded at Hout Bay, sw Cape.

Status: Very rare vagrant; one record,

Hout Bay, Cape of Good Hope, November 1984.

Habitat: Open sea; also inshore around breeding islands.

Habits: Flight low over water, with relatively slow purposeful wingbeats; sometimes follows ships. Circles over water and dives to catch fish; may also swoop low and take prey at surface of water. Seldom glides or soars.

Food: Fish, squid.

Breeding: Extralimital.

SYLVIIDAE

911 (–)   Eurasian Blackcap   Plate 54
Swartkroonsanger
Sylvia atricapilla

[Mönchsgrasmücke]

Measurements: Length about 14 cm.

Bare Parts: Iris brown; bill slaty black, paler and greyer below; legs and feet dark slate.

Identification: Size rather large. *Male*: Above brownish olive, greyer on nape and rump, wings and tail browner; crown jet black; below dirty white, washed olive on breast and flanks. *Female*: Buffier below than ♂; crown clear rufous. *Immature*: More rufous above; yellower below; crown rufous (mixed rufous and black in ♂).

Voice: Song rather stumbling at first, later becoming more melodious like song of Garden Warbler, but rhythmic and more structured; harsh *tak-tak* call-

notes; also *churr, sweer* and plaintive *feew*.

Distribution: Europe to w Siberia and nw Africa, Middle East and Iran; also Canary Islands, Madeira, Azores and Cape Verde Islands; migrates to s Europe and Africa as far S as Upper Guinea and Tanzania.

Status: Very rare vagrant to s Africa; recorded Melville Koppies, Transvaal, December 1985.

Habitat: Mature woodland, scrub, gardens and parks.

Habits: Active and lively, but stays well hidden; sings from deep in foliage; flight quick and jerky; wings and tail look long-ish in flight.

Food: Small insects.

Breeding: Extralimital.

CHIONIDIDAE

912 (–)   Snowy Sheathbill   Plate 74
Amerikaanse Peddie
Chionis alba

[Amerikanischer Scheidenschnabel]

Measurements: Length 38–40,5 cm; wing (6 ♂) 246–253,5–260, (12 ♀) 232–240,5–255; tail (6 ♂) 112–122,5–135, (12 ♀) 104–121,5–133; culmen (6 ♂) 30–32,5–34, (12 ♀) 30–30,8–32.

Bare Parts: Iris brown; bill black or brown at tip, base and sheath greenish and yellow, sometimes marked with dull red and

black; strip of bare skin below eye pinkish with yellow papillae; legs and feet greyish or bluish.

Identification: About size of francolin; plump, rather pigeon-like shape; plumage all white; bill and eye dark; bill stout and relatively short with diagnostic horny sheath over nostrils; facial skin pinkish; legs and toes robust, dull bluish grey.

Voice: Harsh throaty *crow* during courtship; usually silent.

Distribution: Breeds on sub-Antarctic islands (South Georgia, South Sandwich), Antarctic Archipelago and Grahamland coast; nonbreeding migrant (and vagrant) to s Chile and Argentina, rarely as far N as Buenos Aires; frequent nonbreeding visitor to Falkland Islands.

Status: Very rare vagrant to s Africa; recorded off Three Anchor Bay, Cape Town, May 1986, and at least 7 sightings since then, w Cape, April to July; birds possibly ship-assisted from sub-Antarctic islands.

Habitat: Marine shores, refuse dumps.

Habits: Solitary or in small groups; wing-beats strong and rapid; flies with tail spread; walks on ground with dovelike head-bobbing; tame and may sometimes be caught by hand.

Food: Carrion, birds' eggs, regurgitated food from penguins, algae and limpets.

Breeding: Extralimital.

HIRUNDINIDAE

913 (–) Whiteheaded Sawwing Swallow   Plate 77
Witkop-saagvlerkswael
Psalidoprogne albiceps

[Weißkopf-Sägeflügelschwalbe]

Measurements: Length about 13 cm; wing 96–102,9–110; tail, longest rectrix (♂) 71–75,4–83, (♀) 60–65,4–68; depth of fork (♂) 22–24–26, (♀) 15–18–20; tarsus 9–9,6–10,1; culmen 6,8–7,7–8,6. Weight 11–12 g.

Bare Parts: Iris black; bill black; legs and feet dark brown.

Identification: Size small; body all brownish black (looks black in the field) with white throat in both sexes and white crown in ♂; tail less deeply forked than in Black Sawwing Swallow.

Voice: Weak twittering; usually silent.

Distribution: East Africa to Angola and northern Malawi; vagrant to Zimbabwe.

Status: Very rare vagrant.

Habitat: Savanna, woodland, scrub and upland forest clearings and glades.

Habits: Usually in small flocks; flight weak and fluttering, rather hesitant; forages low over vegetation; perches often.

Food: Aerial arthropods.

Breeding: Extralimital.

SCOLOPACIDAE

914 (–) Hudsonian Godwit   Plate 76
Amerikaanse Griet
Limosa haemastica

[Amerikanische Uferschnepfe]

Measurements: Length 36–39 cm; wing (14 ♂) 196–206,7–213, (12 ♀) 195–209,4–225; tail (14 ♂) 67–73,5–78, (12 ♀) 67–75–82; tarsus (4 ♂) 54–57,5–62, (4 ♂) 55–58,1–59,5; culmen (14 ♂) 69–75,7–92, (12 ♀) 67–82,3–99.

Bare Parts: Iris brown; bill bright orange to light purplish pink over basal half, shading to blackish toward tip; legs and feet light bluish grey.

Identification: Size large; above dark greyish brown; eyebrow clear white (sharper than in Blacktailed Godwit); below grey on breast, shading to white in centre of belly (more contrasting than in Blacktailed Godwit); in flight rump conspicuously white; tail black; underwing mostly black in front (diagnostic; white in Blacktailed Godwit) with narrow white wingbar behind; upperwing dark with bold white chevron toward tip (Blacktailed Godwit has long white wingbar in upperwing).

Voice: Rather silent; clear high-pitched *wit* or *tuwit*.

Distribution: Breeds Arctic tundra of Canada and Alaska; migrates to coasts

of S America for nonbreeding season; vagrant to Britain, Falkland Islands, New Zealand and some Pacific islands.
Status: Rare vagrant, recorded Swartkops Estuary, Port Elizabeth, March 1987 and Langebaan, w Cape, February 1989.

Habitat: Muddy estuaries, coastal pools, beaches, flooded grasslands.
Habits: Flight fast and strong; wings may be held aloft briefly on landing.
Food: Small aquatic animals.
Breeding: Extralimital.

TURDIDAE

915 (–) **Isabelline Wheatear** **Plate 77**
Vaalskaapwagter
Oenanthe isabellina

[Isabellsteinschmätzer]

Measurements: Length about 16,5 cm; wingspan 27–31 cm; wing (30 ♂) 97–101,7–106, (24 ♀) 93–96,1–100; tail (17 ♂) 54–57,8–62, (19 ♀) 50–53,7–57; tarsus (20 ♂) 31,3–32,4–34,1, (19 ♀) 28,1–29,8–31,8; culmen (26 ♂) 19,4–20,6–21,9, (19 ♀) 18,5–19,5–20,8. Weight (28 ♂) 25–30–34 g, (26 ♀) 22–28,9–38 g.
Bare Parts: Iris dark brown; bill, legs and feet black.
Identification: About size of Capped Wheatear; sexes alike; above sandy brown, suffused silvery; eyebrow whitish; ear coverts tinged rufous; wings brown, feathers edged paler; rump white; tail mostly black with white bases to outer rectrices; below cream to buffy, sometimes paler on belly.
Voice: Song loud, rich and varied, inter-spersing harsh and fluty notes, including imitation of other bird species; callnote loud *weep, weet-it* or *cheep*.
Distribution: Breeds central Asia to e Europe; migrates to nw India, Arabian Peninsula and Sahelian Africa as far S as Tanzania.
Status: Very rare vagrant to s Africa; two birds recorded Chobe Game Reserve, Botswana, December 1972.
Habitat: Short sparse vegetation on open plains in steppe-desert, newly burned grassland, fallow fields, human settlements.
Habits: Usually solitary, territorial; perches on stones and rocky outcrops, seldom on bushes; hawks insects by flying to ground and back to perch.
Food: Mainly insects; also other invertebrates and seeds.
Breeding: Extralimital.

TURDIDAE

916 (–) **Eurasian Redstart** **Plate 77**
Europese Rooistert
Phoenicurus phoenicurus

[Gartenrotschwanz]

Measurements: Length about 14 cm; wing (20 ♂) 77–80,8–84, (11 ♀) 75–78,3–81; tail (18 ♂) 52–55,6–58, (11 ♀) 51–53,9–57; tarsus (64 ♂) 20,5–21,8–23,2, (49 ♀) 20,8–22–23,3; culmen (54 ♂) 13,6–14,7–15,9, (48 ♀) 13,4–14,5–15,8. Weight (460 ♂) 73–79,1–86 g, (456 ♀) 76–81,4–86 g.
Bare Parts: Iris dark brown; bill black to blackish horn; legs and feet black or blackish horn, soles paler.
Identification: About size of Stonechat. *Male:* Crown and back bluegrey; forehead and short eyebrow white; rump and tail bright rufous with black central rectrices; face and throat black; rest of underparts bright rufous-orange, shading to whitish on lower belly. *Female:* Above plain brownish grey; pale eyering; rump and tail as in ♂ (no black tip to tail as in Familiar Chat); below buff to whitish.
Voice: Sweet weak song with sad tone and repeated phrases, with characteristic

squeaky jangle at end; loud plaintive *weet* callnote; liquid popping *twiktwik*.

Distribution: Breeds Europe to central Asia and Iraq; migrates to Sahelian Africa as far S as Uganda and Kenya; rare in Tanzania.

Status: Very rare vagrant to s Africa; recorded Vaal Reefs Township, s Transvaal, May 1988.

Habitat: Woodland, *Acacia* savanna with thickets, edges of cultivated land.

Habits: Solitary; perches freely, but forages from concealed site; sits upright; picks food from ground, branches and tree trunks; flies back to perch; quivers tail constantly up and down.

Food: Largely insects.

Breeding: Extralimital.

MEROPIDAE

917 (–) Whitethroated Bee-eater Plate 77
Witkeelbyvreter

Merops albicollis

[Weißkehlspint]

Measurements: Length about 20 cm; wing (15 ♂) 96–104, (15 ♀) 91–97; tail, not including central streamers (15 ♂) 65–73,6–82 (streamers up to 122 longer), (15 ♀) 64–68,9–74 (streamers up to 85 longer); culmen (15 ♂) 26–30, (15 ♀) 25–28. Weight (7 ♂) 24–25,9–28 g, (48 unsexed) 20,6–24–31,7 g.

Bare Parts: Iris dull crimson to bright red; bill black; legs and feet brown.

Identification: Size medium; body pale green, paler apple green below; head boldly pied; crown, broad eyestripe and throat band black; throat and broad eyebrow white; nape and underwing buff; upper breast, rump and tail blue; central rectrices very long, slender and pointed. *Immature:* More olive green than adult; feathers edged paler to give scaled effect; throat pale yellow.

Voice: Trilled *prrrp-prup* flight call, similar to voice of Eurasian Bee-eater, but higher-pitched.

Distribution: Breeds along s edge of Sahara from W Africa to Saudi Arabia and S to Kenya and Tanzania; migrates in nonbreeding season to forests of equatorial and W Africa.

Status: Very rare vagrant in s Africa; recorded Kalahari Gemsbok National Park, December 1988.

Habitat: Sparsely wooded semi-arid steppes when breeding; otherwise forest clearings, secondary growth, gardens and towns with large trees and lawns.

Habits: Usually highly gregarious, but likely to be solitary beyond normal range. Hawks insects from perch up to 70 m high, catching them in air or by swoop to ground; when not breeding roosts in bamboo thickets or leafy trees; birds greet each other on perch with excited trilling and raised feathers.

Food: Insects; in W Africa also strips of palm-fruit skin discarded by feeding squirrels.

Breeding: Extralimital.

OCEANITIDAE

918 (–) Matsudaira's Stormpetrel Plate 74
Matsudairase Stormswael

Oceanodroma matsudairae

[Matsudaira-Sturmschwalbe]

Measurements: Length 24–25 cm; wing (52 ♂) 178–186,6–194, (44 ♀) 180–187,5–194; tail (5 ♂) 98–99–100; tarsus (52 ♂) 25–27,5–29, (44 ♀) 25–27–29; culmen (5 ♂) 17–17,7–19. Weight (1 ♂) 62 g.

Bare Parts: Iris brown; bill, legs and feet black.

Identification: Size large (larger than Leach's Stormpetrel); uniform dark brown with paler buffy upperwing bar from wrist to trailing edge of wing at body; wings short, narrow, angled; white shafts show at base of primaries when wing fully

spread; tail forked, but no white under tail or on rump as in Leach's Stormpetrel; bill and feet dark.
Voice: Silent at sea.
Distribution: Breeds on North Volcano and Bonin Islands in tropical Pacific, S of Japan; after breeding migrates to tropical Indian Ocean as far W as coast of Somalia and Kenya; also recorded as straggler to British waters.
Status: Very rare vagrant to s African waters; one recorded off Durban, S Africa, July 1988.

Habitat: Open tropical ocean when not breeding.
Habits: Flies slowly with short glides and intermittent darting and twisting low over water; 3–4 flaps followed by bouncing glide, sometimes touching water; lands on water with wings raised to pick up food, occasionally flapping wings; rests on water with folded wings in calm weather; sometimes follows ships at sea.
Food: Zooplankton, scraps from ships' galleys.
Breeding: Extralimital.

COLUMBIDAE

919 (–)   **Eurasian Turtle Dove**   **Plate 75**
Europese Tortelduif
Streptopelia turtur

[Turteltaube]

Measurements: Length 26–28 cm; wingspan 47–53 cm; wing (37 ♂) 174–179–185, (16 ♀) 167–172–177; tail (35 ♂) 110–116–123, (16 ♀) 108–113–118; tarsus (20 ♂) 22,4–23,6–24,9, (14 ♀) 22,1–22,9–23,8; culmen (38 ♂) 15,4–16,8–18,7, (16 ♀) 14,9–16–16,6. Weight (48, April-May) 100–125–156 g, (15, August-September) 120–152–208 g.
Bare Parts: Iris yellowish brown to orange-red; bare skin around eye pinkish to purplish red; bill lead grey, tinged pink at edges and on lower jaw; legs and feet greyish pink.
Identification: Size medium (about size of Cape Turtle Dove); no black ring on hindneck; wings light rufous, heavily spotted black; head and neck grey; patches on sides of neck spotted black-and-white (checkerboard pattern); tail mainly black with white tip (diagnostic); breast pinkish grey; belly and undertail white. *Immature*:

Lacks distinctive colouring of adult, but has black-and-white tail pattern.
Voice: Purring *kurrrr-kurrrr*, usually in 2 syllables.
Distribution: North Africa, Europe and western Asia; migrates to Sahelian regions.
Status: Palaearctic migrant to northern Africa (Senegal to Ethiopia), August to March or early April; very rare vagrant in s Africa; recorded Kalahari Gemsbok National Park June 1988.
Habitat: Farmland, orchards, parks, gardens, dry steppe and savanna.
Habits: Usually singly or in pairs; on migration forms small flocks; forages on ground, but otherwise highly arboreal, flying to trees when disturbed; often perches on power lines and telephone lines; flies strongly, clapping wings on take-off; raises tail slowly on alighting.
Food: Seeds and fruits of weeds and cereals.
Breeding: Extralimital.

CHARADRIIDAE

920 (–)   **Spurwinged Plover**   **Plate 76**
Spoorvlerkkiewiet
Vanellus spinosus

[Spornkiebitz]

Measurements: Length 25–28 cm; wing (18 ♂) 201–209–220, (11 ♀) 193–202–206; wingspur (11 ♂) 8–10,3–12, (7 ♀) 5–7–10; tail (12 ♂) 89–92,8–98, (9 ♀) 86–91,7–98; tarsus (13 ♂) 66–70,7–78, (13 ♀) 66–69,1–72; culmen (13 ♂) 27–28,9–32, (13 ♀) 26–28,3–30. Weight (4 ♂) 142–161–175 g, (2 ♀) 142–177 g, (6 unsexed) 127–148–159 g.

SPURWINGED PLOVER

Bare Parts: Iris crimson to reddish purple; bill, legs and feet black.

Identification: Size medium (about size of Blacksmith Plover); back brown; top of head to just below eyes black; black line joins chin to black breast and upper belly (forms black waistcoat, contrasting with white face and lower belly); rest of head and sides of neck pure white; rest of underparts white; in flight wings have usual black-and-white pattern of *Vanellus* plovers; rump white, contrasting with black tail.

Voice: Loud screeching *did-you-DO-it*, often at night; sharp metallic *tik* alarm call (similar to notes of Blacksmith Plover).

Distribution: Africa from Tanzania to Somalia, across Sahel to Mauretania; also Nile Valley to Israel, Jordan, Syria, Turkey and Greece.

Status: Very rare vagrant to s Africa; recorded July 1989 between Kachikau and Kavimba, edge of Chobe River floodplain, Botswana, July 1989.

Habitat: Shorelines of lakes and rivers, mudflats, short grassland, burnt grassland, cultivated fields; less often on marine shores.

Habits: Solitary or in small flocks, sometimes in company with Blacksmith Plovers; less often in larger flocks of up to 200 birds. Shy and wary; flies up calling loudly when disturbed; at rest stands with head hunched into body; forages mainly at water's edge, stabbing at prey between quick steps.

Food: Insects, crustaceans, molluscs, small lizards; some seeds.

Breeding: Extralimital.

Ref. Aspinwall, D. 1989. *Babbler* 18:34–35.

Indexes

The 13 indexes that follow are respectively to bird names in the following languages: Scientific (genera–species), Scientific (species–genera), English, Afrikaans, Kwangali, North Sotho (Sesotho sa Lebowa), South Sotho (Sesotho sa Lesotho), Shona, Tsonga, Tswana, Xhosa, Zulu and German. Each entry is followed by the bird number (**bold**), the plate number (*italicized*) and the page number (in roman typeface). Where two italicized plate numbers are shown against an entry, that species appears on both plates, one of which shows the bird in flight.

Index to scientific names (Genera—Species)

Index to Scientific names (Species—Genera)

SPECIFIC

Index to English names

Index to Afrikaans names

Index to Kwangali names

Nsense **869** *73* 774
  870 *73* 775
  878 *73* 783
Ntene **541** *47* 468
Nyumbu **89** *7* 70
Poro **368** *34* 316
  369 *34* 317
Rukoko **458** *41* 395
  459 *41* 395
  460 *41* 396
  461 *41* 397
Rumbamba **404** *38* 350
  405 *38* 351
  406 *38* 352
  407 *38* 352
Runkerenkere **255** *26* 226
  258 *26* 229
Ruruworo **508** *45* 439
  515 *45* 445
  516 *45* 446
Samunkoma **62** *5* 45
  67 *5* 49
  70 *6* 52
  Gomugeha **65** *5* 47
  Gomusavagani **69** *6* 51
  Gomuzera **66** *5* 48
Shivo **80** *5* 61
Siguye **847** *71* 755
Sigwali **198** *21* 173
Siimbi **126** *15* *17* 107
  149 *15* *17* 129
Sikambu **447** *41* 385
  448 *41* 386
  449 *41* 386
Sikuta **465** *42* 401
  470 *42* 405
Simbote **344** *30* 294
  345 *30* 295
  346 *30* 296
  347 *30* 297
Simpanda **651** *53* 562
Sipika **210** *22* 186
Sipupa **146** *11* *13* 126
Sisampamema **441** *39* 356
  412 *39* 356
  415 *39* 358
  416 *39* 359
  417 *39* 360
  418 *39* 361

  421 *39* 363
  423 *39* 364
  518 *46* 448
  519 *77* 449
  520 *46* 449
  522 *46* 451
  523 *46* 452
  524 *46* 453
  525 *46* 454
  526 *46* 455
  527 *46* 456
  528 *46* 457
  529 *46* 458
  530 *46* 459
  531 *46* 460
  532 *46* 460
  533 *46* 461
  534 *46* 462
  536 *46* 464
Siswagaragwali **194** *21* 170
Sitembandayi **443** *40* 381
  440 *40* 382
  445 *49* 383
Sitenderenkutji **358** *33* 307
Sitentu **188** *20* 165
Sitjindakarare **189** *20* 166
Siwerewere **560** *49* 486
  561 *49* 487
  562 *49* 488
  564 *49* 489
Siwoyo **104** *9* 85
  106 *9* 87
  107 *9* 88
  108 *9* 89
  112 *9* 92
Suunsu **392** *37* 338
  393 *37* 339
Tepa **599** *51* 520
Tjowe **508** *45* 439
  515 *45* 445
  516 *45* 446
Tuyu **127** *15* *17* 109
  185 *18* *19* 162
Yisimatuli **493** *44* 426
  494 *44* 427
  496 *44* 428
  497 *44* 429
  498 *44* 430
  505 *44* 437

Index to North Sotho names

Index to South Sotho names

Index to Shona names

SHONA

674 *57* 585
677 *57* 588
678 *57* 589
679 *57* 590
681 *56* 592
683 *55* 594
Tsande **771** *62* 679
  772 *63* 678
Tsikidzamutsetse **860** *72* 776
Tsodzo **78** *64* 685
  780 *64* 687
  784 *64* 691
  786 *64* 693
  787 *64* 694

791 *64* 698
792 *65* 699
795 *64* 702
Tsoro **474** *36* 408
vaKondo **81** *7* 62
Zadzasaga **857** *69* 763
Zizi **392** *37* 338
  393 *37* 339
  394 *37* 340
  395 *37* 341
  397 *37* 343
  398 *37* 344
  399 *37* 345
  402 *37* 348

Index to Tsonga names

Index to Tswana names

TSWANA

Mmamarungwane **425** *42* 366
   426 *42* 367
Mmamasiloanokê 81 *7* 62
Mmamolangwane **188** *10 11* 100
Mmamoleane **71** *5* 53
Mmankgôdi **126** *15 17* 107
   165 *15 17* 144
Mmanku **464** *42* 400
Mmapheke **404** *38* 350
   405 *38* 351
   406 *38* 352
   407 *38* 352
   408 *38* 353
Mmatlhapi **428** *40* 369
   429 *40* 370
   430 *40* 371
   431 *40* 372
Modisane **71** *5* 53
Mogale **799** *66* 707
Mogôlôri **208** *24* 184
Mogôrôsi **465** *42* 401
Mohubê **824** *68* 732
Mokagatwê **233** *24* 205
Mokgôrônyane **713** *60* 622
Mokgwarakgwara **347** *30* 297
Mokgwêba **237** *24* 208
Mokôtatsiê **83** *7* 65
   85 *7* 67
Mokuê **373** *34* 320
Molepê **832** *68* 740
Molopê **832** *68* 740
Mongwangwa **297** *25* 258
Mophoê **401** *37* 347
   402 *37* 348
Morôkapula **438** *40* 378
   443 *40* 381
   444 *40* 382
   445 *40* 383
Morubise **401** *37* 350
   402 *37* 348
Morubitshe **392** *37* 338
Motlatlawê **239** *24 75* 210
Motsilodi **735** *61* 642
Mpshe **1** *1* 1
Ntidi **587** *50* 509
Ntšhe **1** *1* 1
Ntsu **131** *12 12* 112
   132 *12 13* 113
   135 *12 14* 116
   137 *12 14* 118
   140 *12 13* 121
   146 *11 13* 126
Ntswi **131** *12 13* 112
   132 *12 13* 113
   135 *12 14* 116
   137 *12 14* 118
   140 *12 13* 121

Pêolwane **411** *39* 356
   412 *39*
   415 *39* 358
   416 *39* 359
   417 *39* 360
   418 *39* 361
   518 *46* 448
   520 *46* 449
   523 *45* 452
   524 *46* 453
   526 *46* 455
   527 *46* 456
   528 *46* 457
   529 *46* 458
   533 *46* 461
   534 *46* 462
Pêtlêkê **146** *11 13* 126
Phakalane **127** *15 17* 109
   154 *15 17* 134
   155 *16 18* 135
   156 *16 18* 136
   161 *16 18* 141
   181 *18 19* 159
   182 *18 19* 160
Phakwê **149** *15 17* 129
   160 *16 18* 140
   165 *15 17* 144
   171 *18 19* 150
   172 *18 19* 151
   173 *18 19* 152
   179 *18 19* 157
Phaphadikôta **481** *43* 415
   483 *43* 416
   486 *43* 418
   487 *43* 419
Phênê **615** *51* 533
Phêtla **411** *39* 360
   412 *39* 356
   415 *39* 358
   416 *39* 359
   417 *39* 360
   418 *39* 361
   518 *46* 448
   520 *46* 449
   523 *46* 452
   524 *46* 453
   526 *46* 455
   527 *46* 456
   528 *46* 457
   529 *46* 458
   533 *46* 461
   534 *46* 462
Pônyane **798** *66* 705
Pupupu **451** *34* 388
Rašêušwanêng **806** *69* 713
Rramatsiababa **425** *42* 366

Rramorutiakolê **567** *48* 492
   568 *48* 493
Rrankundunyane **356** *33* 306
Sebotha **492** *44* 431
   493 *44* 426
   494 *44* 427
   495 *44* 428
   496 *44* 429
   497 *44* 429
   498 *44* 430
Sefalabogôgô **115** *8* 95
Segôdi **126** *15 17* 107
   149 *15 17* 129
Segôôtsane **127** *15 17* 109
   154 *15 17* 134
   155 *16 18* 135
   156 *16 18* 136
   161 *16 18* 141
Segolagola **301** *30* 262
Segelegwele **301** *30* 262
Sehudi **99** *8* 81
   100 *8* 82
   104 *9* 85
   106 *9* 87
   107 *9* 88
   108 *9* 89
   112 *9* 92
   113 *9* 93
Seinôdi **428** *40* 369
   429 *40* 370
   430 *40* 371
   431 *40* 372
Sentsipitsipi **847** *70* 756
Senwabolôpe **779** *64* 686
   787 *63* 694
   791 *64* 698
   792 *65* 699

Sogonokê **196** *21* 172
   199 *21* 174
Talê **814** *66* 724
Talêtalê **779** *64* 686
   787 *63* 694
   791 *64* 698
   792 *65* 699
Thaga **810** *66* 720
   811 *66* 721
   814 *66* 724
   815 *66* 725
   816 *66* 726
   824 *67* 733
Thaga-talê **814** *66* 724
Thulakomê **230** *24* 203
Tilodi **735** *61* 642
Timêlêtsane **55** *4* 38
Tlatlagwê **239** *24* 210
Tlhamê **118** *10 11* 100
Tlhômêdi **732** *61* 732
Tôntôbane **685** *55* 596
Tsêbêru **356** *33* 306
Tshetlho **474** *36* 408
Tshogwi **404** *38* 350
   405 *38* 351
   406 *38* 352
   407 *38* 352
   408 *38* 353
Tshosabannê **200** *20* 175
   201 *20* 201
Tsôkwane **355** *33* 305
Tswangtswang **297** *25* 258
Tswere **801** *65* 710
   802 *65* 711
   803 *65* 712
   804 *65* 713
   805 *65* 714

Index to Xhosa names

Index to Zulu names

ZULU

German Index

INDEX OF FAMILY AND GROUP NAMES